Formal Description of Slavic Languages

Linguistik International

Herausgegeben von

Heinrich Weber
Susanne Beckmann
Abraham P. ten Cate
Wilfried Kürschner
Kazimierz Sroka
Ingo Warnke
Lew Zybatow

Band 20

PETER LANG
Frankfurt am Main · Berlin · Bern · Bruxelles · New York · Oxford · Wien

Gerhild Zybatow/Luka Szucsich
Uwe Junghanns/Roland Meyer
(eds.)

Formal Description of Slavic Languages

The Fifth Conference, Leipzig 2003

PETER LANG
Internationaler Verlag der Wissenschaften

Bibliographic Information published by the Deutsche Nationalbibliothek
The Deutsche Nationalbibliothek lists this publication in the Deutsche Nationalbibliografie; detailed bibliographic data is available in the internet at <http://www.d-nb.de>.

Cover illustration:
Uli Weber

ISSN 1436-6150
ISBN 978-3-631-55160-8

www.peterlang.de

Content

Preface

The present volume contains contributions to the Fifth European Conference on Formal Description of Slavic Languages (FDSL-5) held at the University of Leipzig in November 2003. The FDSL conferences were initiated by Gerhild Zybatow and Uwe Junghanns in Leipzig in 1995 and take place biannually in Leipzig and Potsdam. The aim of the FDSL conference series is to bring together scholars from all over the world presenting their theoretical, computational or experimental linguistic research on Slavic languages. In 2006, a FDSL 'halftime' conference was organized in Nova Gorica by Lanko Marušič and Rok Žaucer. This development attests to the broadening of the community working on Slavic languages within different formal linguistic frameworks. We are confident that this encouraging development will continue in the future.

Many individuals and organizations contributed to the success of FDSL-5. The conference was organized by Gerhild Zybatow, Dorothee Fehrmann, Uwe Junghanns, Roland Meyer and Luka Szucsich. Many students and colleagues volunteered at the conference and helped especially in the conference office. Thanks go to Klaus Abels, Petr Biskup, Matthias Dietz, Ulrike Hoinkis, Ina Mleinek, Nicole Richter, Barbara Sonnenhauser, Olaf Terpitz and Olav Müller-Reichau. We are especially grateful for the support of Uta Schubert with all financial issues in connection with the conference. The editors also want to thank Claudia Hurtig and Marcel Guhl, who took it upon themselves to format most of the papers contained in this volume.

The organizers are greatly indebted to the German Research Foundation (Deutsche Forschungsgemeinschaft) and the Centre for Cognitive Science (Zentrum für Kognitionswissenschaften) at the University of Leipzig for generous financial support.

Last but not least, the organizers would like to thank Lew Zybatow from the editorial board of the Linguistik International series at the Peter Lang Verlag for including this volume into their series.

The Editors

September, 2007

Computational Linguistics

Cvetana Krstev, Duško Vitas & Gordana Pavlović-Lažetić, Belgrade

Resources and methods in the morphosyntactic processing of Serbo-Croatian

1. Introduction

The precise morphosyntactic processing of Serbo-Croatian, taking into account its complex morphology, depends on the availability of annotated electronic lexical resources, in the sense of ISO 1087-2 (2000). At the same time, results of morphosyntactic processing always depend on how precise and detailed the lexical resources are. This paper describes some of the lexical resources for the morphosyntactic processing of Serbo-Croatian that have been developed in association with the RELEX network described in Laporte (2003). These resources mainly constitute a system of a morphological electronic dictionary and local grammars that were implemented using the technique of finite state transducers (FST) in the INTEX programming environment described in Silberztein (1993). The resources developed in this way allow various language experiments and the refinement of results in text analysis.

In Section 2 of this paper we will present lexical resources for the processing of Serbo-Croatian, while in Section 3 we will present methods for morphological and morphosyntactic processing based on these resources and finite state transducers. Various applications using the presented resources and methods are illustrated with several examples.

2. Lexical resources

Following RELEX recommendations, resources for the morphological processing of Serbo-Croatian comprise:

- Morphological dictionaries of simple words DELAS/DELAF
- Morphological dictionaries of compounds DELACS/DELACF
- Morphological grammars - dictionary of lexical transducers DLM
- Local grammars

2.1 Dictionaries of simple words

Simple words are defined as alphabetic strings, or character strings between delimiters, where delimiters are all the characters that do not belong to the alphabet of a language as explained in Vitas (2001). A simple words module consists of three parts:

- Dictionary of lemmas DELAS
- Set of transducers describing the properties of inflectional paradigms
- Dictionary of inflected forms DELAF

All the entries in the DELAS dictionary have the following form:

lemma.Knnn [+*SinSem*]*

where *lemma* is the simple word, in general in the form used in traditional dictionaries, *K* is the part of speech mark, *nnn* is the number denoting the class of lemmas that all share the same inflectional properties described by the appropriate transducer *Knnn*, and +SinSem is the freely attached marker that describes the syntactic, semantic, derivational, or other properties of a lemma (Table 1).

A part of speech code, e.g. N, and an inflectional class code, e.g. 688, uniquely determine the finite state transducer that generates all the forms in a lemma paradigm. A FST, being capable of producing the output, adds to all these forms their possible grammatical categories. A regular expression describing the inflectional paradigm N688 is given in Figure 2. This regular expression applied to a noun of class 688 (for instance, *propoved* 'sermon') generates three different forms of the noun (*propoved*, *propovedi*, *propovedima*) each of which has several possible grammatical realizations. The first of them *propoved*, for instance, represents the inanimate (q) feminine gender (f) form which is in the singular (s), in nominative (1) or accusative case (4) (Table 2).

Category	Tag	applied to	explanation	Example
Syntactic	**+p2**	**prepositions**	**noun phrases in genitive**	**bez,PREP+p2**
	+Ref	**verbs**	**reflexive**	**dičiti,V551+Imperf+It+Ref**
	+MG	**nouns**	**masculine natural gender**	**budala,N601+Hum+MG+FG**
derivational	**+VN**	**nouns**	**verbal noun**	**kiseljenje,N300+VN**
	+Adj	**adverbs**	**derived from adjectives**	**fanatično,ADV+Adj**
	+DerOvaIra	**verbs, nouns, adjectives**	**derivational variety**	**dezinfikovati,V18+...+DerOvaIra**
Semantic	**+Col**	**adjectives**	**colors**	**zelenkastosiv,A6+Col**
	+Hum	**nouns**	**human**	**ljubavnica,N601+Hum**
	+Mat	**adjectives**	**material**	**kožnat,A6+Mat**
Dialectic	**+Ek**	**all**	**ekavien**	**nedelja,N600+Ek**
	+Cr	**all**	**croatism**	**izopćen,A1+PP+Cr**

Table 1. Some markers attached to lemmas in the Serbian DELAS dictionary

```
muslinski,A2+PosQ+Mat
otpozdraviti,V651+Perf+It+Iref
sporije,ADV+Adj+Comp
bogami,PAR
ispod,PREP+p2
desetorica,N623+NumN+MG+Pl
ponešto,PRO13+Indef+ProN
zanovijet,N688+Bot+Ijk
eksportovati,V18+Imperf+Perf+Tr+Iref+DerOvIr
```

Figure 1. An excerpt from the Serbian DELAS dictionary

```
<E>/:fs1q:fs4q +
i/:fs2q:fs3q:fs5q:fs6q:fs7q:fp1q:fp2q:fp4q:fp5q +
ima/:fp3q:fp6q:fp7q
```

Figure 2. The regular expression N688 that describes the inflectional properties of the noun class to which belong *peć* 'stove,' *cev* 'pipe,' *noć* 'night,' etc.

The DELAS dictionary and the set of transducers describing inflectional properties are used to produce the DELAF dictionary of all word forms. All the entries in the DELAF dictionary have the following form:

form,lemma[*:categories*]*

where *form* is a simple word form of a *lemma* that is represented by its DELAS entry form, and *:categories* are the possible grammatical categories of the word *form*, each category represented by the single character code explained in Table 2. The set of grammatical categories that describe the word form depends on the part of speech, and, in some cases, on the form itself. For instance, for verbs, the impersonal forms infinitive, present gerund and past gerund are represented by just one code, W, S, and X respectively, active past participle and passive past participle by codes G and T respectively together with codes representing the gender and number, while other simple tenses are represented by the tense code, number code, and person code. Some Serbian nouns belong to different gender classes depending on the number marking. This is reflected in the set of grammatical codes attached to the inflected forms. For instance, two forms with associated grammatical codes of the noun *sudija* 'judge' are sudija:ms1v:ms5v:fp2v and sudije:ms2v:fp1v:fp4v:fp5v. An excerpt from the Serbian DELAF dictionary is given in Figure 3.

PoS	**Category**	**codes**	**PoS**	**category**	**Codes**
noun – N	Gender	m - masculine	adjective – A	gender	
		f - feminine		case	
		n - neuter		number	
	Case	1 - nominative		animateness	
		2 - genitive		degree	a - positive
		3 - dative			b - comparative
		4 - accusative			c - superlative
		5 - vocative		definiteness	d - definite
		6 - instrumental			k - indefinite
		7 - locative	verb - V	form	W - infinitive
	Number	s - singular			P - present
		p - plural			A - aorist
	animateness	v - animate			I - imperfect
		q - non-animate			Y - imperative
		g - no consequence			G - active PP
preposition - PREP	/	/			T - passive PP
conjunction - CONJ	/	/			F - future
particle - PAR	/	/			S - present gerund
interjection - INT	/	/			X – past gerund
numerals - NUM	Case			person	x – first
	Number				y - second
	Gender				z – third
	Animatness			negation	h - negated clitic
pronouns - PRO	Case				i - positive clitic
	Number			number	
	Gender				
	Animatness				
	Clitic	i - clitic			

Table 2. Partial list of morphological categories and their codes used in Serbian electronic dictionaries

```
ispevati,ispevati.V101+Perf+Ek:W
ispevahu,ispevati.V101+Perf+Ek:Izp
ispevaj,ispevati.V101+Perf+Ek:Yys
ispevavši,ispevati.V101+Perf+Ek:X
ispevaću,ispevati.V101+Perf+Ek:Fxs
ispevala,ispevati.V101+Perf+Ek:Gsf:Gpn
ispevaće,ispevati.V101+Perf+Ek:Fzs:Fzp
ispevana,ispevati.V101+Perf+Ek:Tfs:Tnp
ispeva,ispevati.V101+Perf+Ek:Pzs:Ays:Azs
```

Figure 3. Some forms of the verb *ispevati* 'to compose' in the Serbian DELAF dictionary

Since semantic markers do not form a closed set, they can and are modified and expended during the development of a dictionary. For instance, in the most recent version of the DELAF dictionary some verbs are marked with +Ref as potentially reflexive verbs. Other distinctions, however, are not yet implemented, e.g. distinction between true reflexive verbs such as *smejati se* 'to laugh,' non-true reflexive verbs as *kupati se* 'to bath oneself' and reciprocal verbs as *voleti se* 'to love each other'.

Some of the markers are exclusive, i.e. depending on the respective linguistic context one or the other is realized. For instance, presently one verb can be marked both as transitive +Tr and intransitive +It, e.g. brisati,V21+Imperf+Tr+It+Iref; the transitivity of such verbs depends on the usage. In the sentence *Rekord koji je postigla štafeta brisan je sa liste svetskih rekorda* ('The record accomplished by the relay team has been deleted from the list of world records') the verb *brisati* 'to delete' is transitive, while in the sentence *To telo dahće, cvili, pišti kao stara parnjača, briše, savija, puzi* ('The body gasps, whines, whistles like an old steam locomotive, blows, folds, creeps') it is intransitive.[1] This suggests that in the future and for particular applications such verbs can be treated as two lemmas. An excerpt from the Serbian DELAS dictionary illustrating the usage of +SynSem markers is given in Figure 1.

At present, the Serbian DELAS dictionary consists of approximately 73,000 entries from which more than one million entries in DELAF are generated.

These dictionaries can be applied to an arbitrary text using the Intex programming system, which then enables retrieval of occurrences from the text, using any criteria that can be expressed in terms of dictionary content, such as particular lemmas, particular parts of speech, the realization of specific grammatical categories and word forms with specific syntactic or semantic features, as well as their combinations. The following examples will illustrate some of these possibilities.

Example 1.

Dictionaries and grammars state that nouns belonging to the large class of primarily abstract feminine nouns N704, for instance *aktivnost* 'activity' and *nezavisnost* 'independence,' have two singular forms in the instrumental case, using the inflective ending *–u* or *–i*, respectively: *aktivnošću* and *aktivnosti*, *nezavisnošću* and *nezavisnosti*. The following query

<PREP+p6> <A:fs6>* <N+N704:fs6>

retrieves from the text all the single word form sequences that start with the preposition assigning instrumental case, followed by the optional sequence of adjectives in the singular, feminine gender, and instrumental case, and ending with a feminine noun belonging to the class N704 in the singular instrumental case[2]. An excerpt from the produced concordances is given in Figure 4. The first form of the instrumental case occurred in a number of instances (Figure 4a). All cases that superficially look like the realization of the second form of the instrumental case turn out to be the realization of

---

[1] All the examples in this article have been extracted from the corpus of contemporary newspaper and literary texts and processed with Intex (http://www.korpus.matf.bg.ac.yu/korpus/).

[2] Special markers, such as +N704 are included only in the version of the dictionary for researchers; other versions contain no references to the inflectional classes.

some other case, genitive or accusative, since many prepositions assign more than one case.

```
a) koja je tada bila pod italijanskom vlašću. Došao je u  Beograd, oda
   Leposavić. Time su pred svetskom javnošću  pokazali i svoju nemoć d
   da su oni u suprotnosti sa hrišćanskom savešću  Sveti sinod Grc
   Gotovo u isto vreme sa opasnošću od uranijumske municije suočili su
..............................................................................
b) da izađu na izbore da sa vlasti skinu  ljude kojih se Sombor samo
   avi hodočasnik, a za  slabosti i bolesti našeg društva on je ponudio
```

Figure 4. Sample of concordance lines produced by the query <PREP+p6> <A:fs6>* <N+N704:fs6>. a) Instances of nouns of class N704 in instrumental case using the ending *-u* b) Occurrences of non-instrumental noun forms that coincide with instrumental forms using the ending *–i* with prepositions that potentially assign instrumental case.

Example 2

Agreement with numerals (see Leko (2003)) can be analyzed on the corpus. The complex query

(<NUM> <N+Hum:m> (<V:G> + <V:T>) <jesam>) + (<jesam> (<V:G> + <V:T>) <NUM> <N+Hum:m>)

tries to retrieve from a text certain constructions that illustrate the agreement of the quantified nouns (number <NUM> followed by a noun <N>) of masculine gender denoting humans (<N+Hum:m>) with an auxiliary verb (<jesam>) and active or passive past participle (<V:G> or <V:T> respectively). The produced concordances show that with nouns quantified by numerals equal to or greater than 5 the auxiliary verb exhibits singular marking and the past participle paucal coinciding in form with the neuter singular, while nouns quantified with numerals 2-4 agree with the auxiliary verb in plural and trigger feminine singular markings on the past participle (Figure 5a). However, since the query itself does not take into account the agreement markers, there are a number of false retrievals (Figure 5b). Means to reduce the production of non-relevant concordance lines will be presented in Section 3.1. Furthermore, the query

<N+NumN > <N+Hum:m> <ADV>* <jesam> (<V:T> + <V:G>) +
<N+NumN > <N+Hum:m> (<V:T> + <V:G>) <jesam> <ADV>*

retrieves from a text some instances of numeral nouns (<N+NumN>) that show agreement with auxiliary verbs and past participles. The retrieved occurrences show that these nouns, although used only with the nouns of masculine gender, sometimes agree with the feminine past participle (Figure 5c).

```
a)  28 sekundi pre grupe u kojoj je  bilo deset vozača računajući i Kranje
    Na konferenciji za novinare je predstavljeno osam kandidata sa jedinstven
    zdanja, boje maslačka, u kome je smešteno trinaest  učesnika ovogodiš
    mu oduzete lične stvari, zašto su  pritvorena dva vozača JUL-a i zbog
    TELEFONI I ZRAČENJE Zašto su umrla dva direktora  Korisnici će za šes
    e, dostigao najmanje 107. Dva vojnika ubijena su juče u Severnom Acehu k
    ...........................................................................
b)  "dogodi Sijetl", ova banka je  povukla dva poteza. Tržišno orijentisan
    školu ali je odbijen, jer nije imao šest razreda gimnazije. Ipak,
    ...........................................................................
c)  Ivane Marković na Banjici. Trojica mladića danima su pratili devojku
    pitaja rešavaju putem dijaloga. Dvojica lidera naglasila su zajedničku
```

Figure 5. Some concordance lines illustrating: a) agreement of quantified nouns; b) false produced concordance lines; c) numeral nouns.

2.2 Special dictionaries

Beside the DELAS and DELAF dictionaries, which contain general language lexica, various special dictionaries are also being constructed. Two of the most developed dictionaries at this moment are the dictionary of toponyms and other geographic names DELAS-TOP and the dictionary of Serbian personal names DELAS-PERS as described in Pavlović-Lažetić (2004) and Grass (2002). The entries, both lemmas and forms, have the same format as in general dictionaries — the only difference is in the usage of a different set of semantic markers. The most prominent markers in a DELAS-TOP dictionary are +Top for toponyms, +Hyd for hydronyms, and +Oro for oronyms (see Figure 6a), while in DELAS-PERS +First is used for first names, +Last for surnames, and +Nick for nicknames (see Figure 6b).

```
a) Beograd,N201+NProp+Top+PGgr+IsoYU
   Sava,N623+NProp+Hyd+PRek+IsoYU
   Kozara,N623+NProp+Oro+PPla+IsoBIH

b) Varničić,N28+NProp+Hum+Last
   Zorica,N653+NProp+Hum+First
   Zoka,N623+NProp+Hum+Nick
```

Figure 6. DELAS entries in special dictionaries. a) Toponyms: *Beograd* is a proper name (+NProp), toponym (+Top), a capital city (+PGgr) in Yugoslavia (+IsoYU). b) Personal names: *Varničić* is a proper name (+NProp) for a human (+Hum), surname (+Last).

Some of the syntactical markers assigned to the entries in DELAS special dictionaries are related in a WordNet-like manner, as discussed in Krstev (2004); one marker can signify a concept that is a hypernym of a concept signified by the other marker. For instance, *Sava* is a proper name (+NProp), more precisely a hydronym (+Hyd), and still more precisely a river (+PRek). When retrieving information from a text, different levels of abstraction can be used, depending on the task at hand.

Example 3.

The query (<N+First> <N+Last> + <N+Last> <N+First>) iz <N+Top> retrieves from a text all complete personal names (both first name and surname in an arbitrary order) denoting a person from ('iz') a certain place (<N+Top>). The result of such a query is given in Figure 7. This query is, however, rather naive, since it does not take into consideration the agreement between first name and surname (see Section 3.1).

```
"Orbis" govorili su još Ilija Bakić iz Vršca, Sava Babić  iz Beograda,
uru uručivanjem nagrade Mirku Vukoviću  iz Berana, kao najboljem mladom
so Sovilj iz Prijedora i Novak  Demonjić iz Banjaluke. Likovnu koloniju
  Eustahio iz Rumunije i Miroslav Radonjić iz Jugoslavije. Festivalski sa
```

Figure 7. Retrieved concordance lines with the query (<N+First> <N+Last> + <N+Last> <N+First>) iz <N+Top>. This experiment shows that the order first name followed by surname prevails since not once the other order occurred in a text of 1MW.

2.3 Dictionaries of compounds

Compounds, as defined in Silberztein (1993), are similar to simple words except that they can contain separators, that is non-alphabetic characters, as well. Compounds differ from simple words in that each constituent forming a compound can be inflected, according to particular inflectional rules. They also share properties with simple words since no inserts are allowed between the simple word constituents. Besides, compounds represent distinct, non-decomposable concepts and syntactic and semantic markers can be associated to compounds as a whole (Figure 8).

Recognition of compounds using the appropriate dictionary is important since it can add additional information to morphologically analyzed text that can be useful for syntactic analysis. For instance, the sequence *na vreme* is a prepositional phrase in the sentence *Priprema se muzički program u znak podsećanja na vreme kada je poznati pesnik učiteljevao u tom selu* ('A musical programme is under preparation in remembrance of the time when the famous poet was a teacher in that village'). However, the same sequence is very often the compound adverb, for example in the sentence *Dali smo gol na vreme, ali na kraju nismo iskoristili nekoliko šansi* ('We scored a goal on time, but in the end we missed several chances'). The difference between two usages is that simple word constituents in a compound adverb never change, while the noun *vreme* 'time' can be used also in plural in the prepositional phrase, for instance, *Da li me je već taj pasus podsećao na vremena koja su prošla?* 'Did that paragraph itself already remind me of times that had passed?'

```
u stvari,ADV+C
zbrda-zdola,ADV+C
klin-čorba,N1660+C+NN+Food
vojno lice,N2300+C+AN+Hum
u odnosu na,PREP+C+p4
```

Figure 8. A few entries from the DELACS dictionary of compounds

Although the dividing line between, for instance, compound nouns and syntactically complex nominal groups is not always easy to draw, for many cases the generalization is valid that the compound noun: (a) has its own rules of inflection; (b) does not allow inserts; and (c) represents a concept that differs from the composition of the concepts of its constituents. The compound *Ujedinjene nacije* 'The United Nations' illustrates point (a). Namely, only if used in the plural and with constituents in the given order can it represent the institution (compare to *...za nacije ujedinjene ovim sporazumom* '...for the nations united by this treaty'). The mentioned constraint concerning insertion (point (b)) can be illustrated by cases where an additional adjective is inserted into an adjective + a noun sequence which forms a compound noun. Thus, if the compound *odgovorno lice* 'head, boss' composed of the adjective *odgovoran* 'responsible' and the noun *lice* 'person' is split by an additional adjective the meaning of the compound noun changes, e.g. *Vlada je iz budžeta uplatila 11,5 miliona dinara jednom broju novinskih kuća i odgovornih fizičkih lica* ('The Government has paid 11.5 million diners to a certain number of newspaper houses and responsible physical persons'). In this example, the compound is actually *fizičko lice*, which in administrative language means an individual (as opposed to *pravno lice*, meaning an organization). Finally, the literal meaning of *lice* is 'face,' thus it represents a part of the body, which means that its semantic marker in DELAS could be +BodyPart. However, preceding it with an adjective various compounds are obtained: *odgovorno lice* 'responsible person (boss, head),' *svešteno lice* 'clerical person (clergyman, reverend),' *pravno lice* 'juridical person (firm, house),' *vojno lice* 'military person (military man, serviceman),' all of which would obtain their own semantic markers: for the given examples all could obtain the marker +Hum for human being, except *pravno lice*, which could obtain the marker +Org for organization. A more illustrative example is the compound noun *pokondirena tikva* 'conceited pumpkin (upstart, parvenu),' where simple and compound nouns would be semantically marked as:

```
tikva,N+Bot
pokondirena tikva,N+C+Hum
```

The dictionary of inflected forms of compounds DELACF can be constructed automatically from DELACS in a similar way to the dictionary of inflected simple forms DELAF being constructed from the dictionary of simple lemmas DELAS (Figure 9). However, two types of transducers are needed for this task: the first are transducers used to produce all the inflected forms of simple words (see Figure 2) and the second are transducers that govern the agreement between the constituents in a particular compound. The latter are not implemented in Intex itself, so the production of a Serbian DELACF is for the time being done outside the system. In the future, the formalism for the description of these second transducers, as well as the corresponding format for entries in DELACS, will be developed after the model of Savary (2000).

```
saher-tortama,saher-torta.N1660+C+NN+Food:fp3q:fp6q:fp7q
saher-torte,saher-torta.N1660+C+NN+Food:fs2q:fp1q:fp4q:fp5q
vojnih lica,vojno lice.N2300+C+AN+Hum:np2v
vojnog lica,vojno lice.N2300+C+AN+Hum:ns2v
službenim licem,službeno lice.N2300+C+AN+Hum:ns6v
```

Figure 9. An excerpt from the Serbian dictionary of inflected compound forms DELACF

Example 4

The usage of clitic forms of personal pronouns can be analyzed on the corpus (based on the examples from Milićev (2003)). The query <PREP+p2> <PRO+Prs:2> retrieves all personal (+Prs) pronouns (PRO) in the genitive case (2) that are preceded by a preposition (PREP) which assigns the genitive case (+p2). Both simple (*bez* 'without,' *blizu* 'close to,' *do* 'next to,' *kod* 'at') and compound prepositions (*za razliku od* 'contrary to,' *u okviru* 'in the scope of,' as described in Popović (1966)) are taken into consideration. The produced concordance entries show that the full pronouns follow the preposition (Figure 10a). The query <PREP+p2> <PRO+Prs:2i> produces no relevant concordance lines (i denotes clitic forms). This result confirms the claim that clitics are disallowed with prepositions. Similarly, the query <^> <PRO+Prs:2> retrieves all personal pronouns in the initial position (<^>) in the linguistic unit (usually, a sentence), showing again that only full pronouns can be found in this position (Figure 10b). As before, the query <^> <PRO+Prs:2i> does not yield relevant results. These and similar results can be used to construct disambiguation tools (see Section 3.3).

```
a) čuveni Melanhton priznaje da bez njih ništa ne bi naučio.</seg>
   nuta docnije prođoše sasvim blizu njih da bi izbegli veliku baru koja
   <p><seg><q>Ako vam je stalo do njega, mogli bi vam ga ustupiti jevtino.
   <seg><q type=MI>Novac je kod mene, u mojoj kancelariji.</q> </seg>
   šoj Srbiji,  poručio je on. Za razliku od njih, mi predvođeni zgrade
   Republičkog geodetskog zavoda i u  okviru nje zemljišno-knjižnog
.....................................................................
b) ažljivo pratite ovaj region. Njega ne uništavaju narkomani Zapada, ve
   ospić, u kome je i uhapšen. Njega policija tereti i za više podmetan
   ira  "senzibilitet slikarki". Njih je devet među trinaest učesni
   icali na svedoke ili pobegli. Njih terete za  prikrivanje osumnjičenih
```

Figure 10. Some concordance lines produced by the query a) <PREP+p2> <PRO+Prs:2>; b) <^> <PRO+Prs:2>

3 Finite-state automata and transducers

3.1 Finite state automata and regular expressions

The examples from Section 2 have illustrated how regular expressions can be used to retrieve certain occurrences from texts. However, regular expressions can easily become very complex (see Example 2) and difficult to understand, to correct, and to augment. In such cases it is more appropriate to use finite state automata (FSA), for which an editor is provided in Intex, which provides a convenient way to formulate a query. Moreover, the developed finite state automata can be named and used by that name in other automata.

Example 5

Retrieval precision in Example 2 can be improved if finite state automata are used instead of regular expressions, the former being more suitable for modeling agreement constraints. Figure 11 represents a graph that is an enhancement of the first regular expression from Ex. 2: besides taking care of agreement, it also allows for the insertion of an adverb between the auxiliary verb and past participle. Some produced concordance lines are given in Figure 14a.

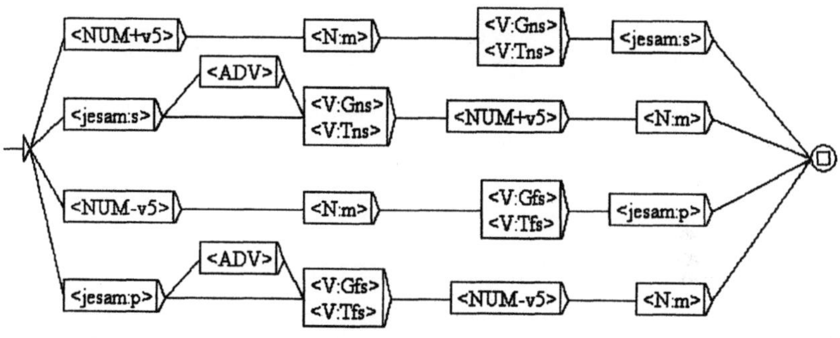

Figure 11. A simple model of grammatical agreement between quantified masculine nouns and corresponding past participles.

In Stanojčić (2000, sect. 492) it is stated that besides grammatical agreement, semantic agreement of quantified nouns with the past participle is also possible; that is the past participle agrees both in number and gender with the quantified noun. A graph of FSA that retrieves from a text agreement of this sort is given in Figure 12. However, in a sample corpus of newspaper and agency texts of more than one million words, no examples of such agreement were found. Nonetheless, if this FSA is augmented to encompass relative clauses as well, as shown in Figure 13, examples of semantic agreement can be extracted (Figure 14b). If the FSA from Figure 11 is augmented in a similar way to cover relative clauses, examples of grammatical agreement of quantified nouns and past participles in relative clause can be also detected (Figure 14c).

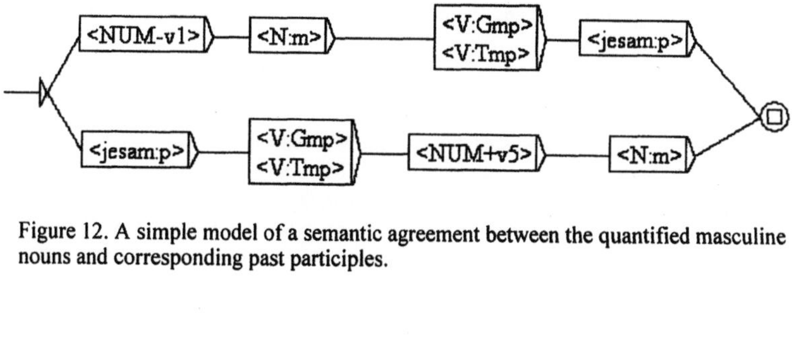

Figure 12. A simple model of a semantic agreement between the quantified masculine nouns and corresponding past participles.

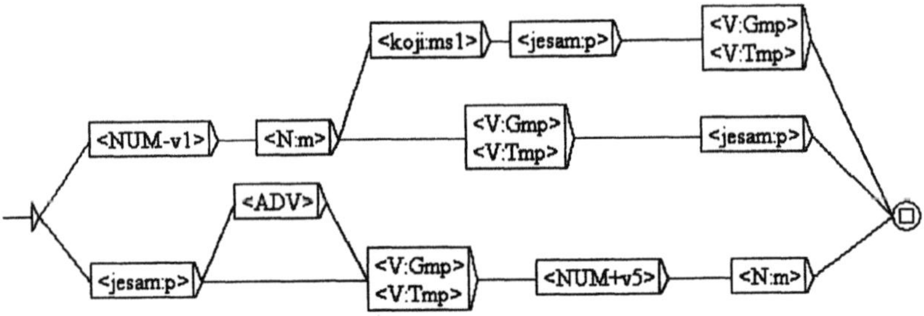

Figure 13. A simple model of semantic agreement between quantified masculine nouns and past participle in relative clause.

```
a) Oko 11.40 časova čak  četiri aviona gađala su ovaj voz pogodivši pri
   fondove. Druga tri kandidata saopštila su da će uložiti žalbu na o
   16-godišnje devojčice. Osam vojnika uhapšeno je u četvrtak zbog otmic

b) razmišljaju o našoj zemlji posle dva turnira koji su okupili toliko mla
   Misija je do sada  finansirala ukupno šest izbora koji su održani u BiH

c) kandidati ne budu prihvaćeni, četiri ministra koja su podnela ostavke r
   tokom vikenda su preminula još dva zatvorenika koja su stupila u štrajk
```

Figure 14. Agreement of quantified nouns with past participles a) grammatical agreement; b) semantic agreement with relative clauses; c) grammatical agreement with relative clauses

3.2 Finite state transducers for text modification and transformation

A local grammar is a finite transducer that, on the basis of lexical resources, enables the extraction of complex structures from a text. The extracted structures can be defined using either some formal criteria (for example, 'identify all the occurrences in the text referring to an inhabitant of Belgrade visiting Greece during the year 2002'), or according to morphosyntactic, syntactic or semantic criteria. One example of such a local grammar is the automaton that recognizes, tags and lemmatizes composite tenses in Serbian, described in Vitas (2003).

Example 6.

A cascade of FSTs Vreme is produced that recognizes a denotation of time periods and points in time in Serbian and encloses them in the XML start and end tags `<period>` and `<datum>`, respectively. The nodes in the main FST in this cascade (Figure 15) represent the use of other FSTs, each of which recognizes a certain class of patterns. One of these subgraphs is given in Figure 16. Such graphs can be used for text preprocessing, namely for automatic XML tagging (Figure 17).

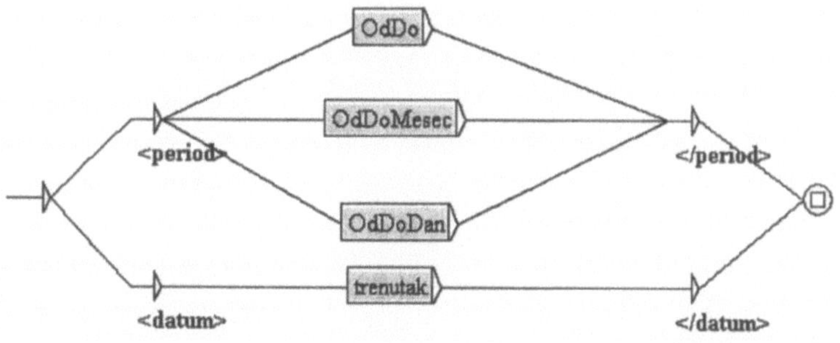

Figure 15. A FST that inserts XML tags for the recognized dates and time periods into a text.

Roughly speaking, finite state transducers are finite state automata that can produce output. In text processing, this output can be used to transform the original text either by replacing the recognized pattern with the defined output or by inserting it in the specified position in text.

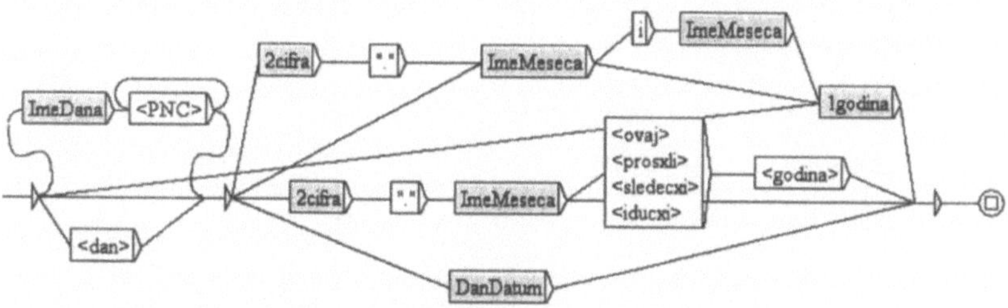

Figure 16. The subgraph trenutak invoked by the FST from Figure 15. It recognizes the points in time representing formal denotation of date (DanDatum) as well as some more informal denotations.

```
Avali kraj Beograda, NATO je <datum>23. aprila 1999. godine</datum> počinio
vrđen i pismom "Trepče" od <datum>6. avgusta prošle  godine</datum> koje je
njene državne teritorije. U <datum>četvrtak, 14. septembra</datum>, Kfor je
xuriti, jer imate vremena do <datum>31. 12. o.g</datum>".. Pare sam uložio u
su saveznici imali sreću. U <datum>septembru 1933. godine</datum>, mađarski
Nj.V. kralja SN br. 38486 od <datum>29. XI 1932. godine</datum> premešten je
lobodilačkih  ratova Srbije <period>1912-1920. godine</period> i Centralni kl
nom polju bila vodeća  sila.<period> Između 1901. i 1932.</period> bila je d
kcije za obnovu zemlje, <period>od 2. avgusta prošle godine do danas</period>
```

Figure 17. A few concordance lines of a text tagged with the FST Vreme.

3.3 Finite state transducers for disambiguation

A simple or compound word form is ambiguous if and only if it has been associated to several different pieces of lexical information after applying one or more lexical resources. The level of ambiguity in Serbian texts is very high since there are a lot of homographs that are not homophones. Roughly speaking, more than two thirds of running words in Serbian text are ambiguous if all the grammatical information is taken into account, and more than one fifth of them have more than one lemma potentially associated to them. Visually, the ambiguity of a text can be represented by a text graph (Figure 18) where through the procedure of lexical recognition separate nodes exist for each running word associated with more than one lemma. An ambiguous text blurs the results of various text analysis tasks and makes the further steps of processing, such as syntactic analysis, difficult, if not impossible. Ambiguity can be automatically resolved using different methods, the aim of which is to introduce no errors in a tagged text:

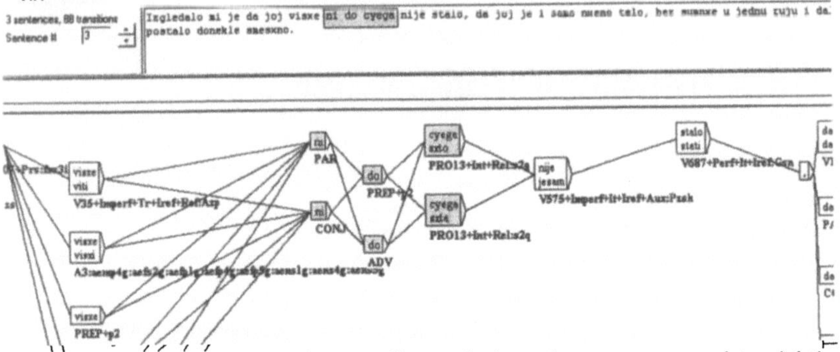

Figure 18. A sample sentence and a part of its graph. A graph represents a non-deterministic FSA due to the different possible interpretations of running words.

- Filter dictionaries. The applied dictionaries can be ranked with respect to priority. The options suggested by higher ranked dictionaries have precedence over the options found in lower ranked dictionaries, and thus resolve the ambiguity. For instance, if an entry `li,.PAR` is put in the dictionary with the highest priority, then it will override the possibility `li,liti.V:Ays:Azs` suggested by some other dictionary: that is, the word form `li` will always be treated as a particle *li*, and the possibility that it is some aorist form of the verb *liti* 'to pour' will be rejected.
- Dictionaries of compounds. Dictionaries of compounds usually increase the ambiguity of a text, since many compounds are homonymous with decomposable complex expressions (see the example *na vreme* from Section 2.3). However, if a compound dictionary gets higher priority, compounds can act as filters themselves. For instance, the entry from the dictionary of compounds of high priority `leptir-mašnom,leptir-mašna.N:fs6q` enforces the following interpretation: if the noun *leptir* 'butterfly' in nominative singular is followed by a hyphen which is followed by a word *mašna* 'bow' in any inflected form, than the whole sequence should be interpreted as a compound *leptir-mašna* 'bow tie' in the same inflected form.
- Disambiguation graphs. Local grammars can be constructed with the aim of eliminating the ambiguity of certain words by specifying some of the contexts in which they appear. These grammars can be formulated in the form of transducers that recognize these particular contexts in order to eliminate the overflow of lexical hypotheses. This can be achieved by associating the lexical constraints to the identified sequences.

Example 7

In Serbian, when prepositions are used with negative pronouns, such as *ništa* 'nothing,' they split negative particle (*ni*) and the pronoun (*šta*), e.g. *ni do čega* instead of **do ničega*. The sentence graph in Figure 18 shows that the word forms *ni* and *do*, among others, are ambiguous: the first can be both a particle ('no') and a conjunction ('neither/nor'), the second a preposition ('to') and an adverb ('only; approximately'). However, in constructions such as this one, the word forms *ni* and *do*, can be unambiguously interpreted. This interpretation is enforced by the FST with the constraints given in Figure 19. The application of this FST to the text yields the modified sentence graph with the ambiguities of word forms *ni* and *do* resolved (Figure 20).

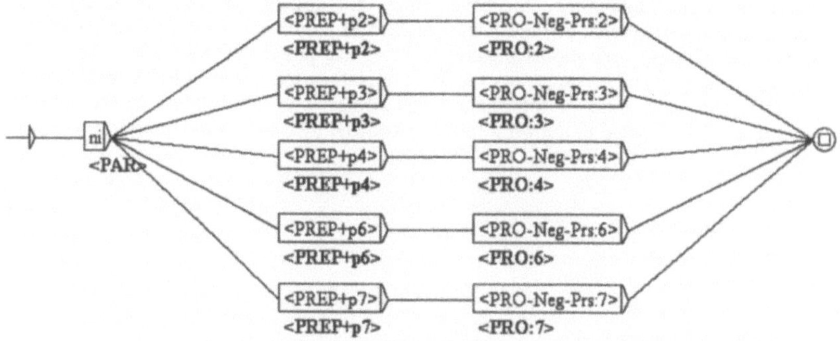

Figure 19. The FST with constraints is interpreted as: if the word form ni is followed by a word form that could be a preposition assigning genitive case (<PREP+p2>), which in turn is followed by a word form that could be a non-personal and non-negative pronoun in the genitive case (<PRO-Neg-Prs:2>), then the word form ni has to be a particle, and other hypotheses are excluded.

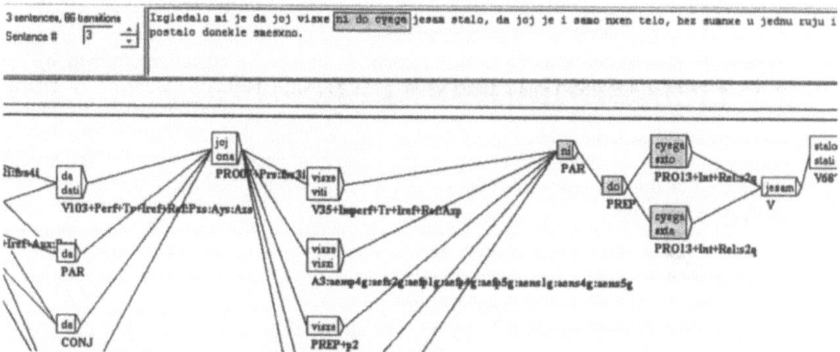

Figure 20. Part of a graph of a sample sentence with some of the ambiguities resolved, which results in a smaller number of paths through the non-deterministic FSA.

3.4 Transducers with lexical constraints

The special transducers with lexical constraints, the so called lexical transducers, allow the expression of morphological rules that govern word formation. The input of lexical transducers is used to recognize word forms, while the output is used to compute the corresponding lemma and other grammatical information. These complex transducers perform the tokenization of word forms into linguistic units that are established on the basis of imposed constraints which are expressed in terms of recognition by e-dictionaries. Furthermore, during the recognition process the values of the recognized linguistic units can be stored in variables, which can later be used for the computation of lemmas and grammatical categories.

Example 8

Many entries in Serbian traditional dictionaries are due to a structural derivation that yields the predictive meaning of a lemma. In a dictionary such entries are recognized by their prototype definitions. Moreover, they are usually derived by using some recognizable derivational pattern. Numerous lexical transducers have been produced that make use of these derivational patterns to recognize possessive adjectives (Figure 21), diminutives, augmentatives, gender motion, prefixation, etc, analyzed in Pavlović-Lažetić (2004). The same kind of information that comes with word forms in the DELAF dictionary is associated to the word forms recognized by these lexical transducers (Figure 22).

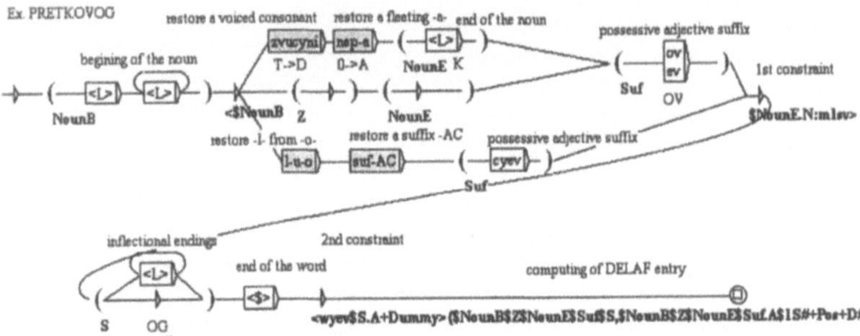

Possessive adjectives of masculine gender nouns with suffixes -ov and -ev

Figure 21. The lexical transducer that recognizes possessive adjectives formed by the suffixes *-ov* and *-in* from masculine nouns that are in a DELAS dictionary of simple nouns. The lexical graph takes into account the morphological transformations fleeting *-a* (*arbitrov*, a possessive adjective of *arbitar* 'arbiter') and the substitution of a voiced consonant with its unvoiced counterpart (*pretkov*, a possessive adjective of *predak* 'ancestor'). A dummy entry w.A1+Dummy is used to recognize the inflectional endings of a possessive adjective.

```
a) čovekovim,čovekov.A+Pos:aems6g:aemp3g:aemp6g:aemp7g:aefp3g:aefp6g:aefp7g…
   Đinđićeve,Đinđićev.A+Pos+NProp:aemp4g:aefs2g:aefp1g:aefp4g:aefp5g
   Firerov,Firerov.A+Pos+NProp:akms1g:aems4q
   javorovog,javorov.A+Pos+Bot:adms2g:adms4v:adns2g

b) adolescentkinja,adolescentkinja.N+Hum:fs1v:fp2v
   bolničarke,bolničarka.N+Hum:fs2v:fp1v:fp4v:fp5v
   bolesnice,bolesnica.N+Hum:fs2q:fs5q:fp1q:fp4q:fp5q

c) antiratnih,antiratni.A2+PosQ:aemp2g:aefp2g:aenp2g
   četrnaestogodišnjaci,četrnaestogodišnjak.N10+Hum:mp1v:mp5v
   dvoipostruki,dvoipostruk.A6:adms1g:adms4q:aems5g:aemp1g:aemp5g

d) dvadesetčetvoro,dvadesetčetvoro.NUM06+Coll:ns

e) ćerčica,ćerčica.N+Dem:fs1v:fp2v
   koferčića,koferčić.N+Dem:ms2q:mp2q
```

Figure 22. Word forms recognized by lexical transducers: a) possessive adjectives; b) feminine gender counterparts of masculine nouns; c) prefixed adjectives and nouns; d) arbitrary collective numbers; e) diminutives.

4 Conclusion

The quality of morphosyntactic processing of Serbo-Croatian written texts highly depends on available electronic lexical resources as well as on methods for morphological and morphosyntactic processing. The electronic lexical resources developed and presented in this paper consist of a system of morphological electronic dictionaries of simple words, compounds and specialized dictionaries of geographic and personal names, as well as of implemented local grammars using the finite state transducers technique in the programming environment INTEX. The processing methods presented include finite state techniques for retrieving occurrences on complex queries, for text modification and transformation, and for disambiguation, as well as lexical transducers for expressing morphological rules that govern word formation of such lexical items as possessive adjectives, prefixed adjectives and nouns, arbitrary collective numbers, diminutives.

Although the described lexical resources must be refined, they already provide useful tools for the morphosyntactic processing of a broad range of phenomena some of which we discussed in this paper.

References

Grass, Th., Maurel, D., Piton, O. (2002): Description of a Multilingual Database of Proper Names. In: Ranchold, E., Mamede, N. (eds.): *Advances in Natural Language Processing, PorTAL 2002*, Springer, Lecture Notes in Artificial Intelligence 2389, pp. 137-140.

ISO 1087-2 (2000): *Terminology work - Vocabulary - Part 2: Computer aplications.*

Laporte, E. (2003): *The RELEX Network.* (http://infolingu.univ-mlv.fr/Relex/Relex.html).

Leko, N. (2003): Syntactic Positions of Numerals in Bosnian. In: Zybatow, G. & al. (2003).

Krstev, C., Vitas, D., Stanković, R., Obradović, I., Pavlović-Lažetić, G. (2004): Combining Heterogeneous Lexical Ressorces. In: Lino, M.T. & al. (eds.): *IV International Conference on Language Resources and Evaluation LREC 2004*, ELRA, Lisboa, pp. 1103-1108.

Milićev, T. (2003): How Strong are Full Pronouns in Serbian. In: Zybatow, G. & al. (2003).

Pavlović-Lažetić, G., Vitas, D., Krstev, C. (2004): Towards Full Lexical Recognition. In Sojka, P., Kopecek, I., Pala, K. (eds.): *Text, Speech and Dialogue*, Springer, Lecture Notes in Artificial Intelligence 3206, pp. 179-186.

Popović, Lj. (1966): Predloški izrazi. *Naš jezik*, XV (3-4). 1966, pp. 195 – 220.

Savary, A. (2000): *Recensement et description des mots composés - méthodes et applications.* Thèse de doctorat en Informatique Fondamentale, Université de Marne-la-Vallée.

Silberztein, M.D. (1993): *Le dictionaire électronique et analyse automatique de textes: Le systeme INTEX*, Paris: Masson.

Silberztein, M.D. (2004): INTEX Manual, v. 4.33. (http://intex.univ-fcomte.fr/downloads/Manual.pdf).

Stanojčić, Ž., Popović, Lj. (2000): *Gramatika srpskoga jezika.* Zavod za udžbenike i nastavna sredstva, Beograd.

Vitas, D., Krstev, C., Pavlović-Lažetić, G. (2001): Flexible Dictionary Entry. In: Zybatow, G., Junghanns, U., Mehlhorn, G., Szucsich, L. (eds.): *Current Issues in Formal Slavic Linguistics*. Peter Lang, pp. 461-468.

Vitas, D.; Krstev, C. (2003): Composite Tense Recognition and Tagging in Serbian. In: Erjavec, T.; Vitas, D. (eds.): *Workshop on Morphological Processing of Slavic languages*, EACL'03, Budapest, pp. 55–62.

Zybatow, G., Fehrmann, D., Junghanns, U., Meyer, R., Szucsich, L. (eds.) (2003): *Formal Description of Slavic Languages*. Abstracts. Institut für Slavistik, University of Leipzig, Leipzig, 26-28 November.

Lucie Kučová and Eva Hajičová, Prague

Coreferential Relations in the Prague Dependency Treebank

1. Introduction

The complex annotation scenario of the Prague Dependency Treebank (henceforth PDT, i.e. a collection of 2000 samples each containing 50 continuous sentences from running Czech texts; the samples are taken at random from the Czech National Corpus), is conceived of as an annotation consisting of three layers, namely the morphemic (POS tagging taking into account the rich inflecting inventory of characteristics of word forms), the analytic (reflecting the surface shape of the sentences) and the tectogrammatical (capturing the underlying syntactic relations). The tree structures on both the analytic and the tectogrammatical level are dependency trees. Attention has been always focused, however, on the tectogrammatical structures (abbreviated henceforth as TGTS), the analytic ones being understood as a kind of an intermediate stage that has no theoretical status, although it might help to formulate automatic procedures for a transition from the surface shape of the sentences to their underlying representations. The specification of the shape of the TGTSs is based on an explicit, formal linguistic framework developed by the Prague team of theoretical and computational linguistics since the late sixties (Functional Generative Description, Sgall et al. 1986); at the same time, the application of the annotation to "real" language helps to discover new subtleties and thus has consequences for the formal description.
The (mostly manual) annotation of the tectogrammatical level proceeds basically in three steps or phases: first, the underlying syntactic tree structures are established (or, more precisely, the input analytic tree structures are manually modified and labeled in order to obtain the tectogrammatical tree structures, including the addition of nodes that are deleted on the shallow structure of the sentences and the mark-up of cases of grammatical coreference relations; for the distinction between grammatical and textual coreference, see below in Sect. 2). These structures are the input for a group of annotators who – in the second phase – add to the labels of the nodes one of the three values of the topic-focus (TFA) attribute (see Hajičová et al. 2003); the trees with this assignment will serve as an input for an automatic procedure of the bipartition of the sentence into topic and focus formulated on the basis of the definition of focus and topic (see Sgall 1979). In the third phase, another group of annotators processes (again with the help of a very useful user-friendly editor) the tectogrammatical tree structures and adds coreferential links to nodes that stand for a (possibly zero) personal or a demonstrative pronoun. For the annotation of grammatical coreference (which has been given a systematic account in the description, see Kučová et al. 2003) a semi-automatic procedure has already been implemented which is giving rather encouraging results (with the success rate for some phenomena concerned reaching almost 97 %).
The present paper is devoted to the annotation of textual coreference links, with some introductory remarks on the two types of coreference in general (Sect. 2). The annotation scheme is described in Sect 3, with some statistics presented and discussed in Sect. 3.3. In Sect. 4 some problematic issues and open questions are being listed illustrated by examples from the PDT.

2. Two types of coreference

In our project, two types of coreference are distinguished: grammatical coreference (typically within a single sentence) and textual coreference (which may, but need not, cross sentence boundaries); the latter type of coreference covers both both endophoric and exophoric links.
Grammatical coreference involves verbs of control, reflexive pronouns, verbal complements, and relative pronouns. In the annotation scheme, the kinds of grammatical coreference are encoded by different lexical values of the node labels; e.g. the "reconstructed" node for the

subject of the embedded infinitival clause with verbs of control, such as *slíbit* (to promise somebody to do something), *přesvědčit* (to convince somebody to do something), *požádat* (to ask somebody to do something), carries a label Cor.
In the present stage of annotation of textual coreference, we restrict ourselves to cases of textual coreference in which a demonstrative or an anaphoric pronoun (also in its zero form) are used (with the demonstrative pronoun, we consider only its use as a noun, not as an adjective). We do not include cases of exophoric coreference rendered by a pronoun of the 1st and 2nd persons (be they expressed explicitly or by a zero form, i.e. deleted in the surface shape of the sentence). For the purpose of the present paper, we also leave out of consideration cataphoric reference such as in (1):

(1)	*„Vidím ho."*	*Velitel:*	*„Oddělej ho."*	*Čečen se hroutí.*
	["I see him."	Commander:	"Kill him."	(The) Chechen falls down.]

For the time being, we also do not cover the so-called bridging anaphor though some preparatory steps in this direction have already been undertaken.

3. Annotation scheme

3.1 In the Prague Dependency Treebank, coreference is understood as an asymmetrical binary relation between nodes of a TGTS (not necessarily the same TGTS), or, as the case may be, as a relation between a node and an entity that has no corresponding counterpart in the TGTS(s). The node from which the coreferential link leads, is called an anaphor, and the node, to which the link leads, is called an antecedent.
The present scenario of the PDT provides three coreferential attributes: *coref*, *cortype* and corlemma. The attribute *coref* contains the identifier of the antecedent; if there are more than a single antecedent of one anaphor, the attribute *coref* includes a sequence of identifiers of the relevant antecedents. The attribute *cortype* includes the information on the type of coreference (the possible values are gram for grammatical and text for textual coreference), or a sequence of the types of coreference, where each element of type corresponds to an element of *coref*. The attribute *corlemma* is used for cases of a coreference between a node and an entity that has no corresponding counterpart in the TGTS(s): for the time being, there are two possible values of this attribute, namely *segm* in case of a coreferential link to a whole segment of the preceding text (not just a sentence) and *exoph* in case of exophoric relation.
In order to facilitate the task of the annotators and to make the resulting structures more transparent and telling, the coreference relations are captured by arrows leading from the anaphor to the antecedent and the types of coreference are distinguished by different colours of the arrows. There are certain notational devices used in cases in which the antecedent is not within the co-text (exophoric coreference), or when the link should lead to a whole segment rather than to a particular node. If the anaphor corefers to more than a single node or to a subtree, the link leads to the closest preceding coreferring node (subtree). If there is a possibility to choose between a link to an antecedent or a postcedent, the link always leads to the antecedent.
In Fig. 1 we present an example of coreference assignment by means of links used by the annotators; sentence (2) is taken from the PDT (the identification number of the sentence is given in brackets). The following abbreviations are used as the labels for the valency relations (functors): PRED(icate) for the main verb, ACT(or), PAT(ient), LOC(ation), R(e)STR(ictive attribute), ORIG(in), T(emporal)WHEN.

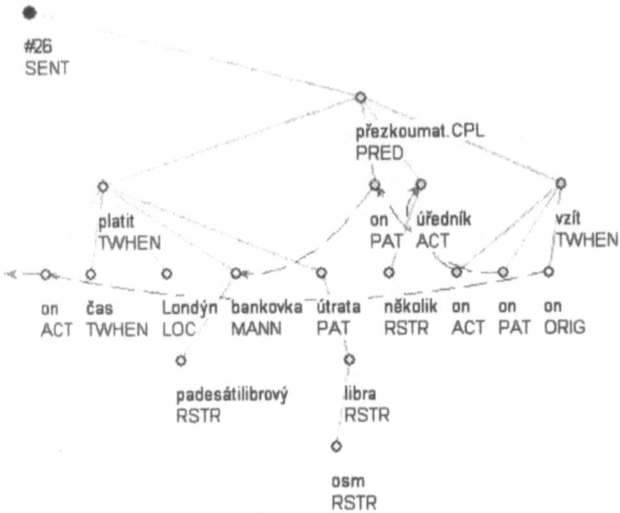

(2) *Když před časem platil v Londýně padesátilibrovou bankovkou útratu osm liber, přezkoumalo ji několik úředníků, než ji od něho vzali.* (lk4#26)
[Lit.: When before time he-paid in London (with) fifty pound banknote amount (of) eight pounds, checked it several clerks(-subj) before it from him they-took.
E.: When he paid a sum of eight pounds with a fifty pound banknote in London some time ago, several clerks checked it before they accepted it from him.]

The manual annotation is made user-friendly by a special tool in the TRED editor used for tree-structure assignment (see Kučová et al. 2003); the values of the attributes of coreference with each node of the tree will be assigned by an automatic procedure.

3.2 To summarize, at the present stage, the following types of textual coreference links are distinguished (some issues related to these types are discussed in Sect. 5 below):

(a) a link to a particular node if this node represents an antecedent of the anaphor;[1]
(b) a link to the governing node of a subtree if the antecedent is represented by this node plus (some of) its dependents;
(c) a specifically marked link (*segm*) denoting that the referent is a whole segment of (previous) text larger than one sentence, or phrase, including also the cases, when the antecedent is understood by inferencing from a broader co-text;
(d) a specifically marked link (*exoph* for exophor) denoting that the referent is "out" of the co-text, it is known only from the situation.

4. Some statistical data

Until now, 289 PDT files of about 50 sentences each have been annotated as for the above types of coreference relations. The total number of nodes that are anaphors relevant for our discussion (i.e. that are rendered by a personal or a demonstrative pronoun, possibly also a zero in the surface shape of the sentence, with the exclusion of the personal pronouns of the

[1] See sentence (2).

1st and 2nd persons) is 5 981; out of this total, 4 816 occurrences belong to the class of personal pronouns and 1 165 to the class of demonstratives.
It may be also interesting to note that in 3 091 cases, the anaphors had an explicit form in the sentences, while in 2 890 cases the anaphors have been deleted in the surface shape of the sentence.
The distribution of the types of links (as specified above in Sect. 3.2) is given in Table:

	a	b	c	d	total
number of links	2971	2996	78	3	6048
% of the total number of links	49,12%	49,54%	1,29%	0,05%	100%

The total number of occurrences of the types of anaphoric links does not equal the total number of the occurrences of the anaphors, because there were cases in which a link has led to more than a single node; this situation can be illustrated by ex. (10), where the (superficially deleted) pronoun *oni* has as its antecedent both *tatínek* and *maminka*.[2]

(3) *Tatínek s maminkou šli do divadla. Vzali [oni] si taxíka.*
[Father and mother went to the theatre. Took (they) a taxi.]

(4) *Tatínek, maminka a obě děti šli do divadla. Vzali [oni] si taxíka.*
[Father, mother and both children went to the theatre. Took (they) a taxi.]

5. Some interesting phenomena and open questions

The first phase of the coreference annotation process has revealed several interesting phenomena concerning anaphoric relations in Czech; in this Section we exemplify some problematic cases of textual coreference as present in real texts of PDT.

(a) The coreferential link (esp. from the neuter pronoun *to* ‚this‘) to a previous/following clause (ex. 5) or a whole previous sentence (ex. 6) is being established; in (5) the link from *toho* (this) points to the root of the tree (*vynesou*, elevate), i.e. to the main verb of the second conjunct, in (6) the link from *tím* ([by] this) points to the governing verb of the whole sentence (*připravuje*, prepares):

(5) *Ale je něco jiného, když je někdo podnikatel a pak jde do politiky, anebo jestli někoho politické změny vynesou na špičku a on toho pak využívá k hospodářské činnosti a zastává vysoké funkce ve velkých firmách.*
[But it is a different thing when someone is an enterpreneur and then goes into politics than when political changes elevate somebody to the top and he then uses this in his economic activities and attains a high position in a big firm.]

(6) *Generál kromě toho připravuje nařízení, podle něhož se na něj budou moci obrátit všichni, kteří se domnívají, že se jim děje bezpráví. Hodlá tím předejít tomu, aby by se redukce armády stala záminkou k vyřizování účtů.*
[The general also prepares an order, according to which all who think that harm is being done to them can turn to him. By this he intends to avoid the reduction of the army being a pretext for paying off old scores.]

[2] A technical remark: this treatment is necessary because in the construction *tatínek s maminkou šli*, *tatínek* stands in the relation of an Actor and *maminka* in the relation of Accompaniment to the verb *šli* rather than a coordination between two Actors; in case of true coordination, as in (4), and in case of apposition, the arrow leads to the node representing coordination [apposition] relation rather than to the members of the relation.

(b) The coreferential link leads to a part of the preceding sentence or clause (it may be an embedded clause or a noun group with or without a preposition, an adjective, etc.); also here the link technically leads to the root of the respective tree or subtree:

(7) *Generální ředitelství má zájem, aby se pracovní vytíženost odsouzených zvýšila alespoň na šedesát procent, jak je to obvyklé v demokratických zemích.*
[The chief management has an interest in raising the working load of the convicted people to at least 60 percent as this is usual in democratic countries.]

(c) The antecedent referred to is a segment of the preceding co-text larger than a sentence, or phrase (ex. (8)), including also the cases, when the antecedent is understood by inferencing from a broader co-text (ex. (9) and (10)):

(8) *Podle Kohla nelze zapomenout na to, že Německo přepadlo 22. června 1941 Sovětský svaz. Němci jménem Německa přivodili ruskému lidu nesmírné utrpení. Stejně tak nelze zapomenout, co Rusové způsobili Němcům. Z* ***toho*** *všeho si chceme vzít společné poučení.*
[According to Kohl it should not be forgotten that on June 22, 1941 Germany attacked the Soviet Union. Germans on behalf of Germany caused the Russians to suffer immensely. It also cannot be forgotten what the Russians did to Germans. From all this we should learn.]

(9) *Potentáti v bance koupí za deset, prodají si za patnáct. Ale povede to k rychlému přerodu. Zmizí výměry kolem 25 ha, přibude vlastníků kolem 500. Odhaduji, že do dvou let budou schopni splatit bance dluh a třetím rokem už budou dělat na sebe. A na práci najmou jen schopné lidi, bude to v jejich zájmu. Kdo to pochopí, má náskok.*
[The big shots buy in a bank for ten and sell for fifteen. But this leads to a rapid transformation. The acrages of about 25 ha disappear, the number of owners raises to 500. I guess that within two years they will be able to pay back the debt to the bank and in the third year they will work for themselves. And they will hire only capable people, it will be in their best interest. Those who understand this, will have an advantage.]

(10) *Jediný důvod k pobytu v Americe jsou pro mě peníze [...]. Každý rok si v Americe najmu dům a po skončení sezony hned spěchám domů. Mám tu přátele, chodíme na ryby, hrát tenis, navštěvujeme se. Často jezdím za rodiči do Martina. Jsem tu prostě doma [...]. V Kanadě je to úplně jiné.*
[The only reason for me to stay in America is money (...). In America, I rent a house every year and at the end of the season I rush home. I have friends here, we go fishing, we play tennis, we visit each other. I often visit my parents in Martin. I am simply at home here (...). In Canada this is totally different.]

(d) Problematic cases with unclear coreferential links: for example cases in which it is not quite clear where are the boundaries of the relevant segment or which concrete events/states in the previous segment are referred to, see ex. (11): by what action the field has been prepared: by the minister's admission or by his opening the possibility?

(11) *Slovenský ministr kultury [...] připustil, že zápůjčky obrazů nemusí být jednosměrné. [...] Otevřel tedy možnost, o které se dosud nemluvilo. Ředitelům obou galerií tím zároveň připravil pole, na němž si mohou vzájemně ustoupit.*
[The Slovak minister of culture (...) admitted that the loans of pictures need not be unidirectional. He thus opened a possibility which has not yet been discussed. By this, he prepared the field for the directors of both galleries so that they can make mutual concessions.]

(e) In complex cases exemplified here by (12), a decision should be made not only on the coreferential links but also on the restoration (and lexical labels, lemmas) of the nodes deleted in the surface shape of the sentence. The Czech verbs *říkat, sdělovat* [tell], *zapomenout* [forget], *ukázat* [show], *zapamatovat* [remember smth], *pochopit* [understand smth] have a semantically obligatory participant [argument] of Patient. This argument is deleted in the surface shape of (12) but it should be reconstructed in the respective TGTS. This reconstructed node receives the lemma *Gen* [it] (present in the outer shape of the sentence), since it can be paraphrased as "everybody concerned" (with no coreferential link) and the lemma *ono* [it] in the second clause of the respective pair because there its reference is not a general one but a link is to be established to the Patient of the first clause:

(12) *Každá kultura má svá rčení, která popisují zkušenosti lidstva s učením. České sděluje: Opakování, matka moudrosti. Čínské praví: Řekni mi [Gen] a já zapomenu [ono]; ukaž mi [Gen] a já si [ono] zapamatuji; nech mne to dělat a já [ono] pochopím.*

[Every culture has its own sayings, which describe the experience of mankind with learning. The Czech says: Repetition is the mother of wisdom. The Chinese say: Say (it) and I will forget (it); show me (it) and I will remember (it); let me do it and I will understand (it).]

(f) A similar example of an unclear coreferential link is (13). Here, it is not clear, who is *oni* [they]: the manager and the leaders of the team? The co-players?

(13) *Hokejista Zdeno Cígler soudí, že by si v klubu zasloužil větší respekt, a chtěl by také pocítit, že ho někdo potřebuje. Před odjezdem řekl generálnímu manažerovi Edmontonu, že chce zvýšit smlouvu, jinak prý zůstane v Trenčíně. Vysmívají se [oni] mi a nevěří tomu.*

[The hockey player Zdeno Cígler believes that he should get more respect from the team and he also would like to feel that somebody needs him. Before his departure he told the general manager of Edmonton that he wants to raise his contract, otherwise he would stay in Trenčín. (They) laughed at me and did not believe it.]

At this moment, we understand such cases as being on the border line between exophora and other types of coreference relations (see below), but there is some support in our data that a new lexeme should be introduced for this kind of textual coreference.

(g) Along with clear cases of exophoric relations (exemplified here by (14)): one should know, at least from the history lessons at school, that the antecedent of the demonstrative pronoun is the Munich Treaty) the corpus provides examples of **boundary case between exophora and other types of coreferential relations.**

(14) *V období vrcholícího léta roku 1939 již málokdo v Evropě mohl uvěřit nadějeplným slovům [...] Chamberlaina, proneseným po návratu z Mnichova: Myslím, že je to mír na celou naši dobu.*

[In the height of the summer of 1939 only a few people could believe the hopeful words (...) Chamberlain uttered after the return from Munich. I think that this is peace for our time.]

For instance, it is difficult to decide between the exophoric coreference, as e.g. in (15) and (16), a coreference to an unspecified element somehow deducible from the preceding context as e.g. in (17), or a co-reference to a segment (perhaps of the "inferential" kind, see ex. (18)):

(15) *Na churáňovských svazích se* <u>*to*</u> *zelená, běžkaři na kvildských pláních masově krouží na posledních zbytcích vlhkého sněhu.*
[On the hills of Churáňov (<u>it</u>) looks green, the cross-country skiers on Kvilda plains make big circles on the last remains of wet snow.]

(16) *Děkuji za sérii povídání o Osvětimi. Jsem rád, že se konečně píše o tom, jak* <u>*to*</u> *skutečně bylo.*
[Thanks for the series of writings about Auschwitz. I am glad that finally one writes about how <u>it</u> really was.]

(17) *Největší tragédie se však stala v Pardubicích. Známý místní rodák Roman M., autor Průvodce pardubickými restauracemi, se upil k smrti po zjištění, že se narodil v Hradci Králové. Tento fakt vydedukoval z kopií žádostí svých rodičů, aby pardubická matrikářka zfalšovala Romanův rodný list. Rození pardubických dětí v Hradci Králové je periodicky se opakující jev. Jednou za dva roky nám je sem* <u>*[oni]*</u> *vozili, sdělila sestra na porodnickém oddělení hradecké fakultní nemocnice.*
[The worst tragedy was in Pardubice. A well-known native of Pardubice, Roman M., (...) had drunk himself to death after he found out that he was born in Hradec Králové. He deduced this fact from a copy of the application of his parents. (...) The birth of children from Pardubice in Hradec Králové periodically happens. Once in every two years (<u>they</u>) brought them here, said the nurse at the obstetric clinic of the Hradec hospital.]

(18) *Smutní lidé píší veselé knížky a veselí lidé smutné. V člověku se* ***to*** *musí nějak vyrovnat.*
[Sad people write bright merry books and merry people write sad (ones). One has to balance **it** somehow.]

6. No referential functions

A form of a demonstrative pronoun can be, of course, used in other than referential functions, as the following examples demonstrate:

(a) a demonstrative pronoun can be used as an <u>intensifying particle</u> *to* (with no coreferential link), see ex. (19):

(19) <u>*To*</u> *ale prší!*
[Boy, is it raining! Lit. (<u>that</u>) but it-rains! = meaning: it rains very much][3]

(b) <u>conceptually "empty"</u> occurrences of a form of the demonstrative pronoun (Šmilauer's "zdánlivý podmět/předmět" ("apparent" subject/object) are illustrated by (19) and (20):

(20) [...] *jak si už dlouho představuju její cestu do ciziny, do Španělska nebo Řecka, kam ji* <u>*to*</u> *táhne.*
[(...) as I have imagined for a long time her trip abroad, to Spain or Greece, where (lit.) <u>it</u> draws her.]

(21) *Všichni slzeli a radovali se tak z toho úspěchu, kam* <u>*to*</u> *dotáhl jeden z nich.*
[All were crying and were glad of the success, where one of them (lit.) worked <u>it</u> (=worked oneself to)]

---

[3] Ex. (20) may be also used (with a different intonation) in a context: „What's happening outside? It is raining.", in which *to* (it) is an exophor, refering out of the text.

(c) If a demonstrative pronoun is used in phrasemes or „frozen" collocations, no coreferential links are established; as a matter of fact, the form *to* (the neuter form for the demontrative *ten*) does not function as a pronoun here, see examples (22) through (24):

(22) *To máte těžké, mladému to beztak obšlápnul táta.*
[Lit. That you-have hard, this young person's father has connections.]

(23) *Nevím, čím to je, ale absolutně se mi tady nedaří.*
[I do not know, what's the matter, but I am absolutely unsuccessful here.]

(24) *Mezitím do Pchanmundžonmu, odkud byli v dubnu vypuzeni pozorovatelé České republiky, přijíždí i mnoho Korejců a hledí nepřítomně do dálky, na sever. Moc toho ovšem v tomto prostoru k vidění není.*
[In the meantime, Pchanmundžonm, from where the Czech observers were expelled in April, is visited by many Koreans and they look absent-mindedly into the distance. There is not much to see in that area.]

7. Open questions

One of the advantages of a corpus-based study of a language phenomenon is the fact that the researchers become aware of subtleties and nuances that are not apparent. It is then desirable to collect a list of open questions which are handeld on the basis of a temporary instruction but which should be studied more intensively and to a greater detail in the future. The result, of course, is an open list, which is complemented during the whole course of the annotation process. The following examples illustrate what kind of problems we have encountered in our work:

(a) a coreferential link leads to the root of the tree but sometimes the antecedent is just a part of the whole sentence rather than the sentence (governed by the given verbal node) as a whole: in (25) the antecedent of *to* [this] is only the main clause *rozklepala se mi nejen kolena, ale i nitro* [not only my knees but also my heart trembled] rather than the whole complex sentence:

(25) *Když mi Jiří Krupička poslal rukopis své Renezance rozumu, která nyní vyšla v Českém spisovateli, a já do ní napoprvé nahlédl, rozklepala se mi nejen kolena, ale i nitro. A to hned z mnoha důvodů.*
[When Jiří Krupička sent me the manuscript of his Renaissance of Reason, which has been published now in the publishing house Český spisovatel, and I looked into it for the first time, not only my knees but also my heart trembled. And this [happened] for several reasons.]

(b) With a coreferential chain, all links (in the backward direction) are established, as in ex. (26); the link would lead from the last (superficially deleted) *on* [they] to the preceding (again superficially deleted) *on* [they], and from there to the preceding *on* [them] (expressed in the surface by the Acc. Pl. *je* and then finally to *protestanti* [protestants]:

(26) *Dohoda pochopitelně nic nevyřešila – pouze prohloubila v protestantech pocit, že je Londýn nechává na holičkách. Dnes tento pocit, že jsou [oni] pro Británii pouze břemenem, s nímž si [oni] neví rady, v ulsterských protestantech pouze zesílil.*
[The agreement of course has not solved anything – it only deepened the feeling in the protestants that London leaves them in the lurch. Today this feeling, that (they) are

only a burden for Great Britain, which (they) do not know how to deal with, has strengthened in Ulster protestants.]

(c) Since the determination of coreferential links is performed after the TGTS's have been built by other annotators, who are instructed not to take coreference into account when deciding on the lemmas with reconstructed nodes, it sometimes happens that the coreference annotators have to change these lemmas, see (27) and (28):

(27) *Kluk odpočívá dlouze, nehnutě na jedné noze. Když přijdu blíž, postaví se na obě nohy a řekne mile: džambo, memsahib, how do you do?*
[The boy rests for a long time, very still on one leg. When I come closer, he stands on both legs and says pleasantly: jumbo, memsahib, how do you do?]

(28) *Tak báseň není pouze jen pytel slov, nespočívá toliko ve věcech, které znamená.* [...] *A ryzí óda, jak tělo překrásné, sluncem i olejem zářící.* [...] *Z výboru Múza přeložil Ivan Slavík.*
[So a poem is not just a sack of words, it is not anchored only in the things it denotes. (...) A true ode as a beautiful body, shining with sun and oil.(...) Ivan Slavík translated from the selection of poems Muza.[4]]

In (27) a (general participant) Addressee is restored (for the verb *řekne* [says]) with the lemma *Gen*, which is during the coreference annotation changed to *on* because the antecedent has been found to be quite specific: *memsahib*. In a similar vein, in (28), a (general) Patient (for the verb *přeložil* [translated]) is restored with the lemma *Gen* and this lemma is then changed to *on* (with a link to *segm*). Tentative criteria have been formulated guiding (and severely restricting) such changes: if it is possible to add some specific referent in place of the deleted node of the surface structure, this means that an arrow can be established pointing to some concrete node (or *segm*, as the case may be) obeying the general guidelines and *Gen* is changed to *on / ten*; else *Gen* is left untouched.

(d) Nodes are reconstructed not only as dependent on a verb but also in cases of productively formed nominalizations if some of their obligatory complementation is deleted in the surface shape of the sentence; the establishment of coreferential links follows the same general guidelines, see (29) and (30):

(29) *[slovo] Má silné citové zabarvení a vyskytuje se zvláště v mluvených projevech mládeže.*
[(It = the word) has a strong emotive colouring and it occurs especially in discourse of young people.]

In the TGTS of (29), two nodes depending on *zabarvení* (colouring, from *zabarvit* [to colour] are restored: both with the lexeme *Gen*, one with the functor Actor and one with Patient. In the course of the coreference annotation, the lemma *Gen* is preserved with the Actor (there is no direct reference, meaning "anybody" colours...), *Gen*.Patient is changed to *on* (with a link to *slovo* [word]).

(30) *Řekl jste, že občan ČR má po pěti letech od listopadu 1989 mnoho důvodů ke znepokojení, poukázal jste zvláště na vysoké daňové zatížení.*
[You said that five years after November 1989 a citizen of the Czech Republic has many reasons to be dissatisfied, you pointed especially to a high tax load.]

[4] Literally: From [...] translated Ivan Slavík.

In the TGTS of (30), again two nodes depending on *znepokojení* [dissatisfaction] are restored, namely *Gen*.Actor and *Gen*.Patient; the same happens with the restoration of two nodes with the deverbative *zatížení* [load]. In the course of the coreference annotation, the lemma *Gen* is preserved with the Actor of *znepokojení* [dissatisfaction] – there is no direct reference, meaning "anybody" dissatisfies – and *Gen*.Patient is changed to *on* (with a link to *občan* [citizen]). In the case of *zatížení* [load] both restored participants are left as "general", no referential link being established.
The annotation process has revealed several other interesting phenomena concerning coreference in Czech, for example the issues of other than referential functions of pronouns (pronouns as intensifying particles) or a wide range of phrasemes and idioms. The study of these issues is open for further investigation.

8. Concluding Remarks

Corpus annotation is a complex task performed in several levels and steps. The annotation of coreference relations is carried out on underlying (tectogrammatical) tree structures assigned to the sentences in the text on independent (and theoretically based) grounds, which makes it possible to systematically include into the annotation the superficially "null" (unrealized) anaphors and other phenomena not realized overtly in the surface shape of the sentences. The use of an original user-friendly software tool results in more accurate and consistent annotations and speeds up the whole process. It also makes it possible to apply annotation on relatively large corpus data (in our case, the procedures described above have already been applied to 14 461 sentences with the aim to assign the links and the values of the coreference attributes to the whole set of 50 000 sentences annotated on the underlying syntactic level). It should be emphasized that the coreference assignment as described here is not done selectively but it is an integral part of a large scale project of dependency-based annotation of underlying sentence structure (along with the annotation of the information structure of sentences) and as such it prepares solid grounds for further linguistic investigations.

9. Acknowledgements

The research reported on in this paper has been supported by the project of the Czech Ministry of Education (MŠMT] LN00A063.

References

Berger, Tilman (1993): Das System der tschechischen Demonstrativpronomina. Habilitationsschrift. Ludwig-Maximilians-Universität, Munich.
Hajičová, Eva (2000): Dependency-based Underlying-structure Tagging of a Very Large Czech Corpus. In: Kahane, Sylvain (ed.): *Les grammairs de dépandance*, 57–78, Paris.
Hajičová, Eva, Jarmila Panevová and Petr Sgall (2000): Coreference in Annotating a Large Corpus. In: *Proceedings of LREC 2000*, volume 1, 497–500, Athens, Greece.
Hajičová, Eva, Petr Sgall and Kateřina Veselá (2003): Information Structure and Contrastive Topic. In: Browne, Wayles et al. (ed.): *Formal Approaches to Slavic Linguistics: The Amherst Meeting 2002*. Ann Arbor, Michigan Slavic Publications, 219–134.
Kolářová, Ivana (2003): Zájmena v textu, jejich funkce deiktická a emocionální [Pronouns in text, their deictic and emotional function]. Poster at the conference "Čeština – univerzália a specifika", Brno.
Kučová, Lucie, Veronika Kolářová, Petr Pajas, Zdeněk Žabokrtský and Oliver Čulo (2003): Anotování koreference v Pražském závislostním korpusu [Annotation of coreference in the Prague Dependency Treebank]. Technical Report of the Center for Computational Linguistics, Charles University, Prague.
Prague Dependency Treebank: http://ckl.mff.cuni.cz

Sgall, Petr (1979): Towards a Definition of Focus and Topic. In: *The Prague Bulletin of Mathematical Linguistics* 31, 3–25; 32, 1980, 24–32; printed in *The Prague Studies in Mathematical Linguistics* 7, 1981, 173–198.

Sgall, Petr, Eva Hajičová and Jarmila Panevová (1986): The Meaning of the Sentence in Its Semantic and Pragmatic Aspects. Dordrecht: Reidel; Prague: Academia.

Šmilauer, Vladimír (1947): Novočeská skladba [Syntax of Modern Czech], Prague.

Štícha, František (1999): K deikticko-anaforickým funkcím lexému *ten*. [On deictico-anaphoric functions of the lexeme ten]. In: *Slovo a slovesnost* 60, 123–135.

Agnieszka Mykowiecka and Małgorzata Marciniak, Warsaw

Phrase structure for an effective Polish HPSG grammar

Introduction

Implementations of formal natural language grammars always face severe efficiency problems. The long response time together with not complete language coverage and overgeneration are the most important reasons why more advanced theories are rarely used in practical applications. In this paper we will try to show that some of these shortcomings can be surmounted by taking efficiency problems into account already at the stage of the theory formulation. We present here problems encountered during the implementation the HPSG (Pollard and Sag 1994) grammar of Polish and formulate some changes of the theory aimed at overcoming efficiency problems while retaining the generality of the theory.

The starting point of this work is the formal HPSG grammar described in Przepiórkowski et al. (2002) – one of a few efforts (i.e. Szpakowicz (1986) and Świdziński (1992)) aimed at creation of a formal and / or computationally tractable grammar of Polish. Our HPSG grammar takes into account a large subset of Polish (agreement, case assignment, binding theory, relative clauses, negation and coordination) and describes it with a single coherent theory.

The first system we used for the grammar implementation was ALE (Carpenter & Penn 2001). The achieved results (Mykowiecka et al. 2001) were not quite satisfactory mainly because of low efficiency. Inspired by the papers published in Flickinger et al. (2000) we took into consideration another system, namely LKB (Copestake 2002), and reimplemented the grammar, introducing, at the same time, some changes into the theory itself. In this paper we discuss the theoretical solutions concerning phrase construction and postulate changes that allow for more efficient implementation.

Phrase structure and argument realisation

In Przepiórkowski et al. (2002) we argued for representing phrases as flat structures, i.e. we postulated for realising the subject, complements and adjuncts on the same level of the parse tree, (1). The main argument for this was free word order phenomena. In Polish, there exists no rule restricting the subject, complements and adjuncts orderings. In (1), only words *w* 'in' and *parku* 'the park' have to be in the given order, all other words can be permuted freely.

(1) Martę Jacek spotkał wczoraj w parku.
Martha Jack met yesterday in the park
Jack met Matha yesterday in the park

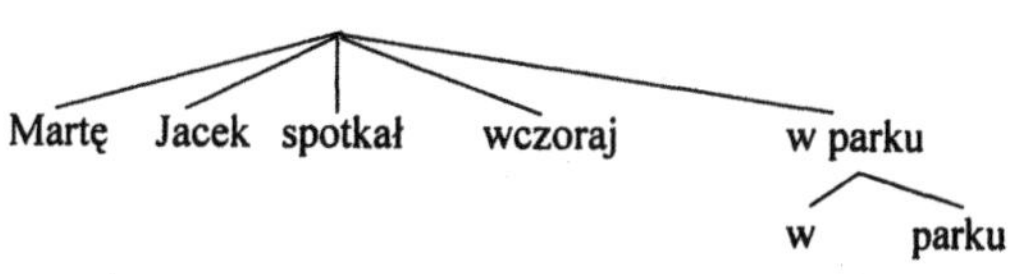

To unify complements and modifiers treatment, we accepted the approach given in Bouma, Mallouf and Sag (2001) and added a list of modifiers to the arguments list of the phrase's head (its ARG-ST|ARGS list). In the ALE implementation of the above idea, adjuncts were added by the *word* rule which built *words* from lexical entries (represented as the *entry* objects).

The first obstacle met while implementing the above solution in ALE was the necessity to declare the maximal number of dependents of each element. While this is not a great problem in the case of complements, it is not clear how many adjuncts have to be allowed. We have to limit it arbitrary, as for every number of adjuncts, a new lexical entry for a word has to be created (and checked during sentence parsing). To realise all dependents in the ALE implementation, a rule trying all possible permutations of all ARG-ST|ARGS list elements has been defined.

Realising all dependents at once leads to a problem of obtaining many parses resulting from permutations differing only in modifiers placement. As a description of an adjunct on the ARGS-ST list has to be general, every given modifier unifies with any adjunct description. The sentence (1) has then two parses – one for *wczoraj* 'yesterday' as the first and *w parku* 'in the park' as the second modifier and the next parse with *wczoraj* 'yesterday' as the second and *w parku* as 'in the park' the first modifier. If we consider a phrase with three modifiers, we obtain 6 parses instead of one.

The solution described above turned out to be very easily implementable, but very slow. Because of low efficiency we allowed only for one adjunct so we did not get additional parses, but many sentences were not analysed at all.

To deal with unspecified number of arguments in the ALE implementation, we only had to determine the maximal number of dependents (we assumed three complements plus one modifier), their realisation was then done by a single rule. In LKB, we cannot realise an unspecified number of arguments as there is no way to implement general permutation relation. We can only manually permute lists' elements, so trying to realise all arguments at one time we have to formulate separate rules for every number of them. This made the problem of many adjuncts representation very hard. We could not accept the same solution as in ALE, because any list with more than four elements become practically untractable. To overcome this obstacle (and at the same time other problems described below), we decided to realise only one argument at a time. We could then resign from adding modifiers to lexical entries and analyse as many modifiers as we encountered (just 'on the fly'). As adjuncts and arguments in Polish can be mixed up, we had to accept the same approach for the subject and complements realisation – they are added one by one. According to this solution the sentence (1) has the structure given in (2).

(2)

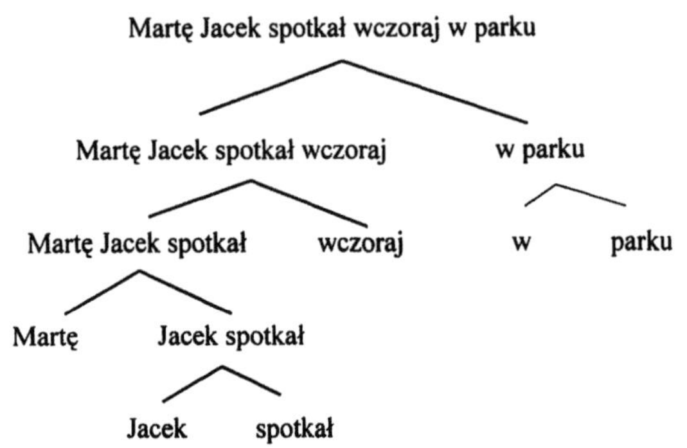

In this approach new kind of redundant parses appear. Extending a phrase, we can choose an argument located to its left or one located to its right. To eliminate those unwanted parses we impose order on argument addition – we attach all left dependents before those occurring to the right. For this purpose two types of phrases: *v-l* and *v-p* are defined. A phrase which is assigned a *v-p* type can not be further extended to the left.

As LKB (just like ALE) does not provide any support for free word order, it had to be manually accounted for, i.e. we have to formulate rules for all arguments orderings. Adopting the idea of realising only one argument at a time and limiting the number of complements to four, we could limit the number of such rules to those realising first, second, third or fourth argument from the ARGST|ARGT list (The ARGT list contains only complements, the subject is placed on the separate ARGST|SUBJ list.) To accept all possible orderings, we introduced two versions of all rules – one accepts an argument before the head, and the second one assumes that an argument is after the head.

Important difference form standard HPSG argument realisation is an introduction of two separate lists: ARGST and ARGST-R. The first one contains only non-realised arguments (originally taken from a lexical entry of a word), while the second one contains every element added to the phrase. Realised complements (and subjects) are removed from the ARGST list.

As Polish is relatively free word order language, it is hard to specify strict word ordering rules. That is why we did not adopt any deliberate word order theory (e.g. Kathol 1995). We have only excluded obviously wrong orderings involving prepositions, question or relative pronouns and subordinate conjunctions. All word types except those just enumerated are assigned to *rl_agrs* type which means that they allow their arguments to occur either to their left or to their right.

Lexicon

As our main goal (both in ALE and LKB) was to implement a syntactic theory, we adopted a simple (non-hierarchical) structure of the lexicon, i.e., a set of lexical entries (of the type *entry*). Words (type *word*) are constructed from lexical entries by rules. In the simplest case, objects of the type *word* share their attributes' values with the corresponding values of the ENTRY attribute which is introduced for *word*s. In both implementations for one lexical entry many word description are created, but in ALE we need more of them than in LKB. In both solutions, for all words which can be modifiers, two descriptions – with empty and non-empty *mod* attribute are created. In ALE, we also need separate versions of word descriptions for any given number of modifiers.

In ALE, transformation from a lexical entry into a word is obtained by one grammar rule, in LKB, the process is made in several steps. The first step is optional and consists in using morphological rules used for inflection and for verb negation. Another transformation concerns those elements which can be modifiers. In the next step – within the definition of the *word* type –most information from lexical entries is copied into a word structure. Then, one of four lexical rules determining information about the subject is used. The last transformation is done by a rule changing every word into one element phrase.

Case Assignment

Following Przepiórkowski (1999) and Przepiórkowski et al. (2002), we split Polish morphological cases into structural and lexical ones. The value of a structural case depends on the context, whereas the value of a lexical case is context-independent and is specified directly in the lexicon.

The case assignment can be divided into two subproblems: the subject and complements case assignment. In general, subjects of personal words are nominative if they are noun phrases but accusative if they are numeral phrases (both cases are structural). Some verbs require the subject in a lexical case and some forms do not allow subject at all. This part of the theory is implemented in LKB by the following lexical rules transforming verb entries:

- for a word without a subject an empty subject list is created,
- for finite verbal forms with nominal subjects in a structural case, number and gender agreement is imposed and the nominative case is required,
- for finite verbal forms with numeral subjects in a structural case, number and gender agreement is imposed and genitive case is required,
- for nonverbal words with nominal subjects (i.e. nouns) the genitive case is required,

- for impersonal verbs no overt subject can occur but semantically it is present, we describe this fact by assigning the null case to the subject.

Case assignment for verbal complements with structural cases is done during the complement realisation. The case is assigned to accusative if the value of NC is *no_t*, and to genitive when this value is *yes_t* (see the section about negation below).

Raising

In our theory and, in consequence also in the ALE grammar implementation, we adopt the idea that some arguments may not be realised locally, but 'raised' higher in the syntactic hierarchy, and realised as they would be the arguments of the higher verb. This mechanism is called optional raising. An example of such a construction is in the sentence below, where arguments of the infinitive *dać* 'to give' can be realised locally or can be raised and realised as arguments of the verb *chciał* 'wanted'.

(3) Janek chciał dać Marysi kwiaty.
John wanted give$_{inf}$ Mary flowers$_{acc}$
John wanted to give Mary flowers.

A motivation for introducing infinitival arguments raising comes form both the genitive of negation phenomena (4) and word order (5). Let us compare the sentences (3) and (4). If the higher verb (i.e. *chciał* 'wanted') is negated, the argument *kwiaty* 'flowers' should occur in genitive not in accusative.[1]

(4) Janek nie chciał dać Marysi kwiatów / * kwiaty.
John NM wanted give$_{inf}$ Marry flowers$_{gen}$ / flowers$_{acc}$
John didn't wanted to give Mary flowers.

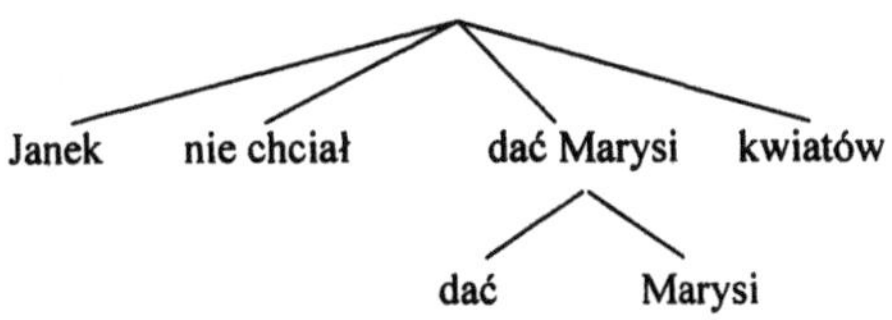

To maintain local case assignment rules we are forced to agree that in (3) *kwiaty* 'flowers' are in some sense the argument of *chciał* 'wanted' not *dać* 'to give'.

The next argument for optional raising is word order. In Polish, it is possible to permute all elements of the sentence (3), so the grammar for Polish should handle the sentence (5), where an argument of the lower verb *dać* 'to give' – *Marysi* 'Marry' occurs between the higher verb *chciał* 'wanted' and its argument *Janek* 'John'.

(5) Janek Marysi chciał dać kwiaty.
John Mary wanted give$_{inf}$ flowers
John wanted to give Mary flowers

The sentence (5) is analysed within the theory because *Marysi* 'Marry' can be realised as an argument of the verb *chciał* 'wanted'. So, the parse tree can look as in (6) or (7). In the case of (6) only *Marysi* 'Mary' is raised and in (7) both arguments of *dać* 'to give' are realised as arguments of *chciał* 'wanted'. Both analyses are equivalent. The number of possible analyses

[1] *Genitive of Negation* phenomenon is sometimes, but very rare, optional in Polish see Przepiórkowski (1999).

increases when the lower verb has more complements or adjuncts. When the number of redundant analyses multiplies, the efficiency of the program reduces. Many parses obtained for different patterns of argument raising was one of the important reasons of unacceptable long processing time of our ALE grammar implementation.

(6)

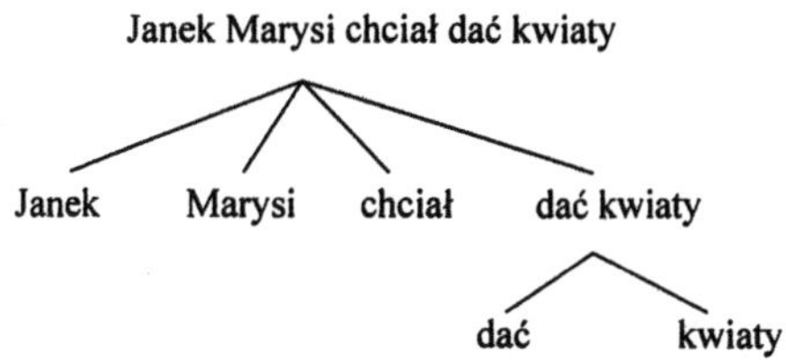

(7)

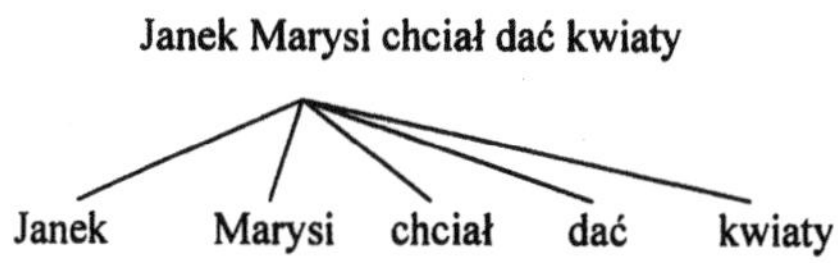

The second element of the optional raising mechanism was the condition for blocking this process at the level of a negated verb. This rule was established to disallow sentences like (8) where *kwiaty* 'flowers' is raised and as the complement of nonnegated verb *chciał* 'wanted' is still in accusative.

(8) * Kwiaty Janek chciał nie dać Marysi.
Folwers$_{acc}$ John wanted NM give$_{inf}$ to Mary
John wanted not to give Mary flowers

But this blocking of raising results in rejecting correct sentences like (9).

(9) Marysi Janek chciał nie dać kwiatów.
Mary John wanted NM give$_{inf}$ flowers
John wanted not to give Mary flowers.

Both words *Marysi* 'Mary' and *kwiatów* 'flowers' are complements of *dać* 'to give'. But the negated verb *nie dać* 'not to give' blocks the possibility of raising its arguments, so *Marysi* 'Mary' can't be raised in (6) and as a result the sentence is not analysed.

In the LKB implementation, we decided to discard the optional raising and replace it with the obligatory raising of all arguments to the highest verb. This allows us to get all possible word orders of a sentence, to keep reasonable time of analysis, and to have one parse for one interpretation of a sentence. In (10), the LKB parse tree of the sentence (3) is presented. Both arguments of the lower verb *dać* 'to give' become arguments of the higher verb *chciał* 'wanted' and are realised one by one, first to the left and then to the right of the verb *chciał* 'wanted'.

(10)

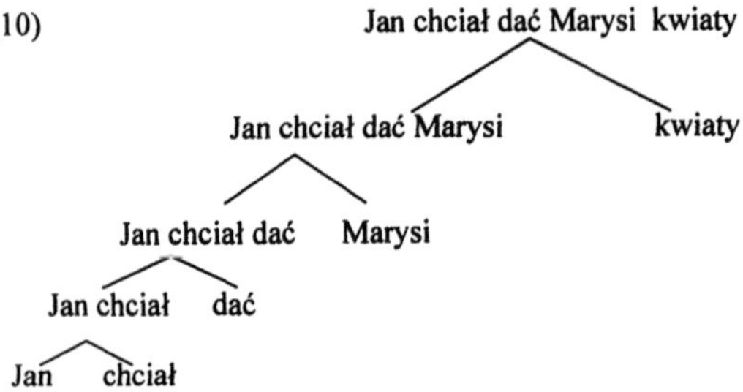

The analysis of the sentence (9) looks in LKB as follows:

(11)

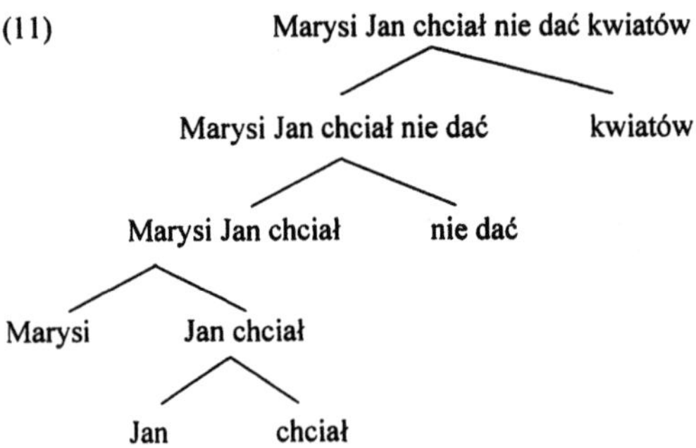

The obligatory raising results in attaching verbal adjuncts always at the highest level of a parse tree, (12). To enable two interpretation of a sentence from (12) (i.e. one in which *szybko* 'quickly' modifies *chce* 'wants' and the other in which it modifies *kupić* 'to buy') we allow verbal modifiers to modify not only the head element of a phrase but also all it infinitival complements.

(12)	Jan	chce	szybko	kupić	kwiaty
	John	wants	quickly	to buy	flowers

Negation

In the theory of Przepiórkowski et al. (2002), we had one mechanism for the two phenomena of word order and negation, but this solution turned out to be not enough. We decided that in LKB we implement obligatory raising to the highest verb to have all possible word orders of a sentence and introduce separate mechanism for negation. Let us present now our changes in the theory of negation. First, we introduced several 'negation' attributes, see (13).

(13)
$$\begin{bmatrix} \textit{synsem} & \\ \text{NONLOCAL} & \begin{bmatrix} \textit{nonlocal} \\ \text{NC} \;\; \textit{bool\_t} \\ \text{NC\_UP} \; \textit{bool\_t} \end{bmatrix} \\ \text{LOCAL|HEAD MORSYN|NEG} \; \textit{bool\_t} & \end{bmatrix}$$

We used the same attribute as in the theory, i.e. NEG, to represent morphological negation of an element. The next two attributes inform us about the negative environment of the element: NC_UP is the negative environment of the upper verb (if it exists) and NC is the negative environment of the element itself. The most important feature of our solution is that it establishes the coindexation of the above attributes on the level of *word* structure. So, for a *word* we require the coindexation of its NC attribute with the NC_UP attribute of *word*'s infinitival complements and with NC attribute of noun phrase complements having structural case. The word *uczył* 'teach' with two complements: noun phrase in accusative (structural case) and infinitival illustrates the above rules, see (14).

(14)
$$\begin{bmatrix} \textit{word} & \\ \text{PHON} \; \langle \text{uczył} \rangle & \\ \text{SS} & \begin{bmatrix} \text{NONLOCAL|NC} \; \#1 & \\ \text{LOC|ARGST|ARGT} & \left\langle \begin{bmatrix} \text{LOC|HEAD|MORSYN} \begin{bmatrix} \textit{nominal} \\ \text{AGR|CASE} \;\; \textit{str\_t} \end{bmatrix} \\ \text{NONLOCAL|NC} \; \#1 \end{bmatrix}, \begin{bmatrix} \text{LOC|HEAD|MORSYN} \;\; \textit{infin} \\ \text{NONLOCAL|NC\_UP} \;\; \#1 \end{bmatrix} \right\rangle \end{bmatrix} \end{bmatrix}$$

Beyond the description of the relation between the negation environment of the head and values of negation attributes of its complements, we have to establish relations among values of the negative attributes within a *word* structure.

- For *word* structures of the verbal but non infinitival type the morphologic negation attribute is coindexed with the negative environment attribute:

$$\begin{bmatrix} \textit{word} \\ \text{SS|LOC|HEAD|MORSYN} \; \textit{noninfin} \end{bmatrix} \rightarrow \begin{bmatrix} \text{NONLOCAL|NC} \; \#1 \\ \text{LOCAL|HEAD|MORSYN|NEG} \; \#1 \end{bmatrix}$$

- For infinitives there are two possibilities. For negated infinitives it is not important what the environment is and NC is assigned *yes_t*:

$$\begin{bmatrix} \textit{word} \\ \text{SS|LOC|HEAD|MORSYN} \begin{bmatrix} \textit{infin} \\ \text{NEG} \quad \textit{yes\_t} \end{bmatrix} \end{bmatrix} \rightarrow \begin{bmatrix} \text{NONLOCAL|NC \#1} \\ \text{LOCAL|HEAD|MORSYN|NEG \#1} \end{bmatrix}$$

- For positive infinitives we have to coindex the value of its NC_UP with NC because negation can come from the upper verb:

$$\begin{bmatrix} \textit{word} \\ \text{SS|LOCL|HEAD|MORSYN} \begin{bmatrix} \textit{infin} \\ \text{NEG} \quad \textit{no\_t} \end{bmatrix} \end{bmatrix} \rightarrow \begin{bmatrix} \text{NC} \quad \#1 \\ \text{NC\_UP} \quad \#1 \end{bmatrix}$$

- For markers (*by, żeby, że*): [NC *no_t*] markers consists a barrier for passing negation but it is important to set on the value of its NC attributes because it can be a head of infinitive complements see (15) and this value is necessary to establish the NC_UP of these complements.

(15) *Jan nie chce żeby kupić kwiaty / * kwiatów.*
John NM wants MARKER buy_{inf} flowers_{acc} / flowers_{gen}
John doesn't want to buy flowers.

Example

Let us analyse a sentence with raising and negation:

(16) Jan chce nie uczyć Marii malować obrazów.
John wanted NM teach_{inf} Mary_{gen} paint_{inf} pictures_{gen}
John wants not to teach Mary to paint pictures.

The same sentence with the positive verb *uczyć* 'teach' is as follows:

(17) Jan chce uczyć Marię malować obrazy
John wanted teach_{inf} Mary_{acc} paint_{inf} pictures_{acc}
John wants to teach Mary to paint pictures.

All elements of the sentences are raised to the highest verb *chce* 'wants' so they are its complements. Both sentences have two different syntactic analyses. The first one (semantically reasonable) where Mary is taught to paint pictures and the second (odd) where pictures are taught to paint Mary. Both parse trees of (17) look as in (18).

(18)

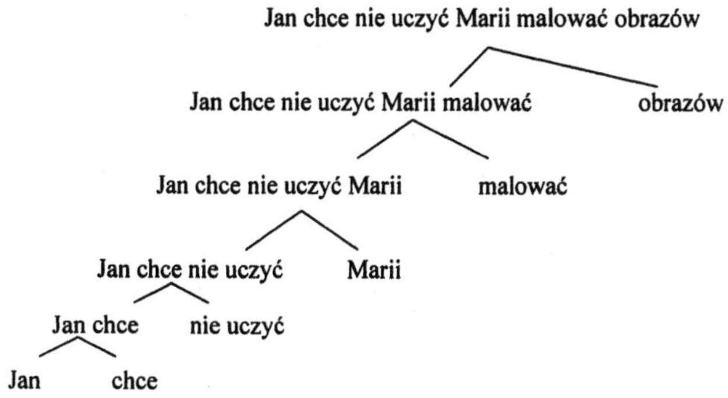

The next figure shows how values of attributes important for negation passing are established for *words* in the sentence (16). The value of a structural case depends on the negative context e.g., the case of *Marii* 'Mary' and *obrazów* 'pictures' is fixed for genitive on the basis of their NC attribute, which shows that the context is negative.

(19) Jan chce nie_uczyć Marii malować obrazów
John wants not to teach Mary to paint pictures

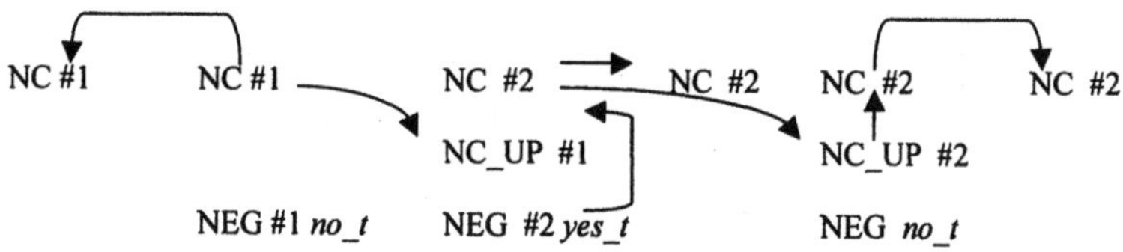

Results

In the table below, we present a comparison made for several simple sentences parsed by both of our grammars. As we did not filter incomplete analyses, correct parses are doubled by the fact that we have two description for the word *kupić* 'to buy' — one with one complement and the other with two complements. In ALE additional solutions with raised arguments appear.

The results show very clear that the LKB grammar is significantly faster. This difference is due to abandoning both optional raising and multiplying word description by adding modifiers to complements list and to better efficiency of the grammar writing environment. To give justice to the ALE grammar, we have to admit that writing grammars in LKB is significantly more difficult, and expressing more complicated constraints is extremely difficult to achieve.

		ALE		LKB	
		nb of parses	time (msec)	nb of parses	time (msec)
1	Jan nie_chce kupić kwiatów *John does not want to buy flowers.*	4	359270	2	270
2	Jan nie_kupił kwiatów *John did not buy flowers$_{gen}$*	2	20710	2	110
3	*Jan nie_kupił kwiaty *John did not buy flowers$_{acc}$*	0	12190	0	17
4	Jan chce kupić kwiaty *John wants to buy flowers*	7	379810	2	220
5	Jan chce szybko kupić kwiaty *John wants quickly to buy flowers*	20	1588280	4	490
6	*Jan nie_chce kupić kwiaty *John wants to buy flowers*	3	250790	0	49
7	Jan nie_chce nie_kupić kwiatów *John doesn't want not to buy flowers*	7	386620	2	220
8	Jan chce nie_kupić kwiatów *John wants not to buy flowers*	7	383980	2	220
9	Kwiatów Jan nie_chce kupić * *Flowers John doesn't want to buy*	14	989370	4	660
10	Jan chce nie_uczyć Marysi malować obrazów *John wants not to teach Mary to paint*	**		2	1320

* In this sentence, the phrase *kwiatów Jan* is interpreted both as consisting of two phrases, or as one phrase in which the noun *kwiatów* is interpreted as a modifier of the word *Jan.*
** Due to very long parsing time for the ALE grammar the test number 10 was not done.
*** Tests were done on IBM PC with Pentium III 750 MHz processor

Conclusion

Research on natural language syntax has its long and gorgeous history. A lot of very important works have been already done and our knowledge about language has widened. But it is only one side of the coin. The other, less splendid one is the fact that there are not many generally available systems using the results of these theoretical efforts. The main reason of this fact is poor effectiveness of formally grounded computers NL grammars. The research presented here is one of the efforts made to make a computer grammar more effective while retaining its generality.

We showed that carefully choosing ways of representing some language phenomena we could lower parse time considerably. We proposed sequential argument realisation and added modifiers 'on the fly' to the syntactic structure. We also showed that choosing separate mechanisms to represent different language phenomena can be better and more general idea than one universal solution. Although LKB as an environment for unification grammar specification is not at all friendly, the results achieved are quite satisfactory, as the difference in parse time was about 1000 times for sentences 5 words long.

Bibliography

Bouma, G., Malouf, R., and Sag, I. A. (2001). Satisfying constraints on extraction and adjunction. *Natural Language and Linguistic Theory*, 19(1), 1-65.

Carpenter, B. and Penn, G. (2001). *The Attribute Logic Engine (Version 3.2.1). User's Guide*. Carnegie Mellon University, Pittsburgh.

Copestake, A. (2002). *Implementing Typed Feature Structure Grammars*, CSLI Publications, Stanford.

Flickinger, D., S. Oepen, H. Uszkoreit and Jun-ichi Tsujii (2000). Journal of Natural Language Engineering. Special Issue on Efficient processing with HPSG:Methods, systems, evaluation", vol 6.

Kathol, A. (1995). *Linearization-Based German Syntax*. Ph.D. dissertation, Ohio State University, Columbus, OH.

Kosta, P., Błaszczak, J., Frasek, J., Geist, L., Żygis, M. (2003). *Investigations into Slavic Linguistics*, Peter Lang GmbH, Frankfurt am Main.

Mykowiecka A, M. Marciniak, A. Przepiórkowski, A. Kupść (2001). An Implementation of a Generative Grammar of Polish. In Kosta et al. 2003.

Pollard, C. and Sag, I. A. (1994). Head-driven Phrase Structure Grammar. Chicago University Press / CSLI Publications, Chicago, IL.

Przepiórkowski, A. (1999). *Case Assignment and the Complement-Adjunct Dichotomy: A Non- Configurational Constraint-Based Approach*. Ph. D. dissertation, Universität Tübingen, Germany. Available from: http://www.ipipan.waw.pl/mmgroup/ap-papers.html.

Przepiórkowski, A., A. Kupść, M. Marciniak and A. Mykowiecka (2002). Formalny opis języka polskiego. Teoria i implementacja. Akademicka Oficyna Wydawnicza RM, Warszawa.

Szpakowicz, S. (1986). *Formalny opis składniowy zdań polskich*. Wydawnictwa Uniwersytetu Warszawskiego, Warszawa.

Świdziński, M. (1992). *Gramatyka formalna języka polskiego*, Wydawnictwa Uniwersytetu Warszawskiego, Warszawa.

Goran Nenadić and Irena Spasić, Manchester

Towards Automatic Terminology Recognition in Serbian

Abstract. In this article we discuss an automatic approach used to facilitate terminological processing of texts in Serbian. The approach combines linguistic knowledge (term formation patterns) with corpus-based statistical measures. Generic morpho-syntactic filters are used to extract individual term candidates. The filters encode information on grammatical agreements used as clues to discover boundaries of term candidates in a free text and to determine their inner structure (nested terms). The extracted candidates are further assorted into sets that unify their inflectional and lexical variants, and are subsequently assigned termhoods (i.e. likelihood to represent actual terms). We present preliminary results of the terminological processing of a textbook corpus in the domains of mathematics and computer science.

1. Introduction

The current growth of electronically available documents has spurred huge interest in natural language processing (NLP) and information technologies, such as information extraction (IE) and information retrieval (IR). These technologies aim at helping humans coping with an overwhelming amount of textual information presented in scientific literature, legal texts, etc. Processing such a huge amount of documents without an automated help (especially when the information content spans across domains) is almost impossible. Therefore, effective tools that can help users to systematically gather and make use of the information and knowledge encoded in text are needed.

The usability of knowledge encoded in texts relies heavily on the identification of relevant domain-specific concepts, which are linguistically represented by *terms* in a given sublanguage (Kittredge and Lehrberger, 1982). A *sublanguage* is a specialised language used in a specific domain (e.g. sublanguages of biomedicine, legislation, mathematics, weather forecast, etc.), and a *term* corresponds to textual representation of a particular concept in the given domain. As indicated by Sager (1990), terms represent the most important notions in a domain. They are the means of scientific and expert communication as they are used to describe the knowledge model of the domain: there is no possibility to understand a scientific article or a legal document without precisely identifying terms and their relationships that are used to communicate the knowledge (Nenadić et al., 2004a).

Terms in a domain are mainly created and used by domain specialists. As the domain evolves, so does its terminology: some terms typically appear in a very short time period, while some of them do not last for long (Jacquemin, 2001). Obsolete terms are being discarded and/or replaced, while, in more dynamic domains, new terms are being introduced in the scientific vocabulary on a daily basis. For example, in the biomedical and pharmaceutical domain, names of genes, proteins, gene products, drugs, chemical compounds, etc. are introduced in almost every new scientific article. A similar situation prevails in technical domains, or in the domain of computer and information sciences. In many cases, there are yet no firm naming conventions, while, even when they exist (e.g. guidelines for some types of biomedical entities) they do not impose restrictions to domain experts who are still by no means obliged to use them.

Given the growing number of terms introduced around the world – it is very difficult to produce up-to-date terminologies that are curated manually, in particular for dynamic domains. Consequently, many terminological units are not included in terminologies (Nenadić et al., 2004b). Furthermore, the existing terminologies have been constructed to facilitate needs of human experts, and not to support automatic processing of documents. Even when present in a controlled terminology, extensive lexical variations can prevent some terms of being identified in a free text. Therefore, automated and dynamic approaches are needed to locate and identify terms in documents.

The automatic identification of terminology has been one of the most challenging research topics in the recent years in NLP. Much of the work has been devoted to automatic term recognition (ATR), which is concerned with the tagging of textual units that are related to domain-specific concepts. Automating this process would enable the large-scale processing of literature by identifying terms across authors and scientific documents.

In this paper we discuss automatic terminology recognition in Serbian, in particular the extraction of multiword terms, which are very frequent in certain domains (e.g. natural sciences, mathematics, etc.). The approach exploits the morpho-syntactic features of term candidates and statistical analysis of their occurrences in text.

The paper is organised as follows: in Section 2 we discuss the role of an ATR system and the related work. In Section 3 we present a term extraction method, called C-value, and we discuss morpho-syntactic filters that are used to select term candidates. Also, an approach to conflation of inflectional and lexical variations is presented. Finally, the experiments and evaluation are described in Section 4.

2. Automatic term recognition

Automatic term recognition (ATR) denotes a set of procedures that are used to systematically recognise pertinent terms in literature, i.e. to highlight lexical units that are related to relevant domain concepts. Its main goal is to differentiate between terminologically relevant (*terms*) and non-relevant units (*non-terms*). Note that we here differentiate between *indexing terms*, which are used in information retrieval (IR) for discrimination between documents, and (domain-specific) *terms* that indicate semantic concepts in specialised sub-languages. Indexing terms are used to facilitate effective retrieval of documents, and are not necessarily terminologically relevant, as a set of indexing terms typically includes a mixture of general language words and domain-specific terms. Their main purpose is to discriminate relevant from non-relevant documents in a collection of texts given a user query. Therefore, not all words are equally suitable as indexing terms: for example, if a word appears in each document of the collection, it is much less useful for the retrieval than a word that appears in just a few documents. However, although not suitable for IR purposes, a frequently occurring word may well indicate the semantic topic of a sub-collection of documents. On the other hand, less frequent words can be useful for IR, but they may not represent semantically relevant concepts. Thus, indexing terms do not necessarily semantically characterise documents, but rather indicate words valuable for discriminating among documents.

In a sublanguage-oriented NLP system, the role of an ATR module is crucial, as it is one of the basic tools (see Figure 1). Many applications depend on term identification as the single most crucial step for accessing information stored in literature. Automatically recognised domain-specific terms can be extremely useful in many NLP applications. They can be used to facilitate IR by combining indexing and domain-specific terms (since domain experts typically look for *terms* when searching documents), and as a basis for semantic document categorisation ("conceptual indexing"). Furthermore, ATR is indispensable for information extraction, where terms are used as a basis for recognition of entities involved in an event, for relation extraction and template filling. Finally, the recognition of terms is useful for knowledge transfer, in particular for computer-aided and machine translation.

Since the vast majority of terms are noun phrases (NPs), the main strategy in many ATR systems is to extract specific NPs (typically referred to as *term candidates*) and then to estimate their *termhoods*, i.e. likelihood of representing domain-specific concepts. Linguistic or rule-based ATR systems mainly rely on internal term characteristics (modelling term formation patterns and naming conventions) in order to locate possible term candidates (cf. (Ananiadou, 1994), (Bourigault et al., 1996), (Hobbs et al., 1997), (Gaizauskas et al., 2000), (Jacquemin, 2001)). They typically target compounds that satisfy a "rather restricted set of syntactic patterns" (Dagan and Church, 1994). Statistical and machine-learning methods, on the other hand, are based on external characteristics and evidences (e.g. statistics such as frequency of occurrence, mutual information and/or surrounding (contextual) information), which are used to filter term candidates (cf. (Smadja, 1991), (Daille et al., 1994), (Collier et al., 2001), (Hatzivassiloglou et al., 2001), (Kazama et al., 2002)). Also, many methods combine different approaches and resources, including acronym, synonym and variation recognition, pre-compiled lists of terms and their components, typical affixes, etc.

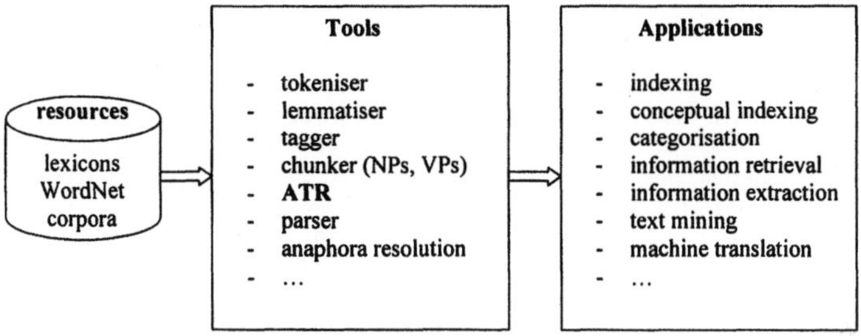

Figure 1: Typical components of an NLP system

Automatic term identification faces many challenges. Apart from distinguishing between terminologically relevant and non-relevant entities, one of the main challenges is to recognise boundaries of terms in text. For example, the word *proizvoljno* 'arbitrary' is part of the term *proizvoljno mala okolina tačke* 'arbitrary small neighbourhood of a point', while *proizvoljna* is not considered as part of the term in [*proizvoljna*] *tačka* 'arbitrary point'. Another problem is identification of nested or embedded terms (e.g. the term *prirodno spajanje* 'natural join' is nested in *operacija prirodnog spajanja* 'natural join operation'), as internal boundaries between nested and maximal terms are often blurred and difficult to recognise. Also, spelling and terminological variation are huge obstacles for automatic identification of terms.

ATR tools have been developed for many languages (e.g. English (Frantzi et al., 2000), French (Jacquemin, 2001), Japanese (Nakagawa and Mori, 1998), etc.). However, few studies have been done for Slavic languages. For example, Vintar (2000) presented two methods for the extraction of terminological collocations in order to assist the translation process in Slovene. The statistical approach was based on the mutual expectation and LocalMax measures, and involved collocation extraction from a raw text. The extracted collocations were filtered with a term list (devised previously by bilingual alignment), and only collocations containing words from the list were accepted as relevant. In another approach, Vintar used regular expression patterns in order to extract term collocations from a morpho-syntactically tagged corpus. However, these patterns were too general, and consequently not all extracted phrases were terminologically relevant.

The performance of ATR systems is typically assessed in terms of accuracy and exhaustivity. Accuracy measures the correctness of lexical units that are suggested as terms, and it is usually calculated as *precision*, i.e. a ratio between the correctly suggested and all suggested term candidates. Exhaustivity denotes the degree to which concepts in a document are recognised, and it is usually measured by *recall*, i.e. a ratio between the correctly recognised and all terms occurring in a given document. Although ATR systems naturally aim at high precision and high recall, there is a trade off between the two measures: high precision can be typically achieved at lower recall points, and vice-versa. The overall performance is commonly measured by a single score called the *F-measure*:

$$F\text{-}measure = 2 * \frac{precision * recall}{precision + recall}$$

Precision and recall are well suited for methods that do not rank their predictions (Jurafsky et al., 2000), but when a ranked list of suggested terms is produced, precision can be considered at fixed rank cut-offs (e.g. cut-offs defined at rank intervals containing the first 50, 100, 150, etc. suggested terms). In this case, precision is calculated as a ratio of correctly recognised terms in a given interval (for example, the percentage of correctly recognised terms in the first 50 suggested term candidates).

3. The C-value method

Our approach to term extraction is based on the C-value method (Frantzi et al., 2000). C-value is a hybrid approach combining linguistic knowledge (term formation patterns) with corpus-based statistical measures. Term formation patterns act as linguistic filters to a part-of-speech (POS) tagged corpus: filtered sequences are considered as potential realisations of domain concepts (*term candidates*). They are subsequently assigned *termhoods* (i.e. likelihood to represent terms) according to a statistical measure, and the method outputs a list of extracted terms ranked according to their termhoods. Termhood is a numeric estimation of the degree to which a given linguistic unit (a multiword compound) is related to a domain-specific concept. The higher the termhood, the stronger the confidence that the given unit is an actual term. However, the values are not normalised in the sense that a multiword, having a termhood value of 10, is ten times more likely to be a term than a term candidate with a termhood value of 1.

The method is implemented as a two-step procedure. In the first step, term candidates are extracted using a set of morpho-syntactic filters which describe general term formation patterns in a given language (see Section 3.1). As a rule, terms form a proper subset of noun phrases, and term candidates are selected as well-formed NPs. In the second step, corpus-based characteristics of a term candidate are calculated. The C-value method aims at enhancing the commonly used baseline method that extracts most frequent term candidates (assuming that termhood directly corresponds to the frequency of occurrence) by making it sensitive to a particular type of terms — nested terms. For each term candidate extracted by a filter in the first step, a set of nested term candidates is generated. The procedure for the generation of nested term candidates is implemented via transformation rules for each morpho-syntactic filter that is used to extract term candidates (see Section 3.2). Then, in order to calculate termhood, the following measures of a candidate term are combined: its frequency of occurrence, its frequency of occurrence as a form nested within other candidate terms, the number of candidate terms inside which it is nested, and the number of words it contains. Formally, the termhood of a term candidate a is estimated as:

(1) $$\text{C-value}(a) = \begin{cases} \log_2 |a| \cdot (f(a) - \frac{1}{|T_a|} \sum_{b \in T_a} f(b)), & a \text{ is nested} \\ \log_2 |a| \cdot f(a), & a \text{ is not nested} \end{cases}$$

where a denotes a term candidate, $f(a)$ corresponds to its frequency, $|a|$ denotes the number of words in a, and T_a is a set of terms that contain candidate term a as a nested term.

The measure assigns termhoods as follows: if a term does not appear as nested (i.e. appears only independently) then its C-value is proportional to its frequency and its length. The idea is that if a longer term appears as frequently as a shorter one, higher value is assigned to the longer term. This positive effect is moderated by the application of the logarithm function. If a term appears as nested, then only candidate terms that appear a significant number of times individually (i.e. not as nested) should be given more credits, as the main indicator that a nested term candidate might be an actual term is that it also appears on its own in a corpus. Therefore, the overall frequency of a nested term is reduced by its frequency as nested, resulting in its independent frequency of occurrence. Further, since a term is more independent if it appears as nested in fewer host terms, its "nested frequency of occurrence" is normalised by the number ($|T_a|$) of term candidates that contain the term candidate in question.

After assigning C-values, term candidates are ranked accordingly. A threshold value is typically used to cut-off the low-scored terms from the extracted list. In the following subsections we describe the approach to the selection of term candidates in Serbian.

3.1 Selection of term candidates

The C-value method uses a POS tagged text as input, and term candidates are filtered out using a set of morpho-syntactic patterns. In our case, we use an initially POS tagged text[1], without further lexical disambiguation of tokens that appear in the text.

As a rule, the vast majority of multiword terms in Serbian match the following general formation pattern:[2]

(2) $(Adj \mid ProAdj \mid Number \mid Noun)^{+}\ Noun$,

which has been used for the recognition of NPs in Serbian (Nenadić and Vitas, 1998a). Similar patterns have been used for English (cf. (Frantzi et al., 2000)). Of course, not all NPs that follow the above pattern are terms or valid term candidates. Moreover, when applied to an initially POS tagged text, this pattern may be too general even for the description of NPs, as not all word sequences in a text that initially match this pattern are valid NPs. For example, in the sequence *naziva relacioni model* 'called the relational model', the word *naziva* can be initially tagged either as a noun (*naziv* 'name') or a verb (*nazivati* 'call'), although, in this sequence, only the latter is correct. Thus, assuming the possible noun tag for the word *naziva*, the string *naziva relacioni model* follows the pattern (2), although it is not a valid NP. This means that classical regular expressions are not sufficient for the representation of such constraints in Serbian, and that more expressive means to model constraints related to the NP structure and agreements of multiword constituents on case, number and gender are needed.

We, therefore, use the notion of *generic patterns* as an extension of regular expressions (Nenadić and Vitas, 1998b). Generic patterns allow the necessary constraints between constituents in a given NP to be explicitly defined. For example, the following generic pattern

(3) $\underline{Adj}.x_1y_1z_1\ \underline{Noun}.x_1y_1z_1\ \underline{Adj}.x_2y_2g\ \underline{Noun}.x_2y_2g$

describes the constraints that have to be fulfilled in NPs following the general NP pattern $Adj_1\ Noun_1\ Adj_2\ Noun_2$, by modelling obligatory agreements: both pairs of adjacent adjective and noun ($Adj_1\ Noun_1$ and $Adj_2\ Noun_2$) must have the same values for certain morphological features (i.e. values for gender, number and case denoted in (3) by x_i, y_i and z_i respectively). These values may differ for each respective pair. In (3), the second adjective and noun pair is "frozen" in the genitive case (g), while the case (z_1) in the first pair is "free". By defining generic patterns one can model the agreements within various structures in a highly inflective language such as Serbian (Nenadić and Vitas, 1998b). As a result, these agreements can be used to detect the boundaries of the structures in questions as well as their inner configuration (see also Section 3.2).

A set of generic patterns was used to model the most frequent term formation patterns in Serbian. Table 1 presents some of them. Note that the first four patterns describe NPs containing a nested NP whose grammatical properties (such as case and/or number) are

---

[1] Initially tagged POS text is a text in which every word occurrence is associated with *all* of its possible lexical and grammatical interpretations. The initial POS tagging is intrinsically ambiguous as each word is analysed separately, without considering neighbouring words (Nenadić et al., 2003). Thus, as a result of initial tagging, possibly highly ambiguous POS sequences are produced (see later).

[2] *Adj*, *ProAdj*, *Number* and *Noun* denote adjectives, possessive adjectives, numbers and nouns respectively.

invariant in all inflected forms of the host NP. As a rule, the frozen part is in genitive. Depending on NP constituents, some agreements are obligatory within the frozen part (see, for example, the third pattern – agreements between an adjective and the corresponding noun) or not (see the fourth pattern – no necessary agreement between the last two nouns in gender, number). The fifth pattern (Table 1) corresponds to NPs that do not have invariant parts.

	generic patterns	examples
1	N_I N_{gen}	*baza podataka* *nejednakost trougla*
2	A_I N_I N_{gen}	*manipulativni aspekt modela* *granična vrednost niza*
3	N_I A_{gen} N_{gen}	*operacija prirodnog spajanja* *niz realnih brojeva*
4	N_I $N_{2;gen}$ N_{gen}	*integritet baze podataka* *kriterijum konvergencije niza*
5	A_I^+ N_I	*prošireni relacioni model* *kompletan metrički prostor*

Table 1: Frequent term formation patterns and examples[3]

Once term candidates have been selected using these patterns, they can be treated separately even when they correspond to the same concept (e.g. inflectional variants of the same term). This would obviously affect the calculation of termhoods, as frequencies of occurrence would be distributed across different surface variants (e.g. inflectional or dialectal) of the same term. Therefore, term candidates need to be additionally "normalised" in order to group different variants. The necessity of taking inflectional term variation into account as part of the ATR process becomes particularly apparent in highly inflective languages. In Serbian, for example, the simplest inflectional variations generally give rise to 14 possible variants of a single term (seven cases and two numbers (singular and plural) – see Table 2). If the C-value method were to be applied without conflating inflectional variants, then termhoods would be distributed across different variants providing separate frequencies of occurrence for individual forms instead of a single frequency of occurrence calculated for a term candidate unifying all of its variants. In addition, the "nesting" factor of the C-value method would cause skewed results, since the case property of nested terms does not have normal distribution. Namely, as indicated previously (Table 1), the majority of nested terms in Serbian are in the genitive case, which means that termhood for a term candidate in the genitive case would differ significantly from its counterparts in other cases. Moreover, this deviation cannot be remedied later by summing up individual termhoods, since C-value is not an additive measure. Hence, in order for the C-value method to be applied correctly in a highly inflective language, term candidates need to be inflectionally normalised *prior* to the calculation of termhoods.

Our approach to inflectional normalisation of term variants is based on the normalisation of individual term constituents. Namely, each word that is a part of a term candidate is mapped onto its lemma (singular, nominative case), and term candidates are treated as sequences of lemmas. This form of a term is referred to as a *normalised* form. At the end of the ATR process, terms are converted into their *canonical* form (singular, nominative case of the whole phrase, possibly with some frozen parts), which is not necessarily identical to the

[3] In order to improve readability of filters, the generic patterns in this table are encoded using the following syntax: *A* and *N* stand for *Adj* and *Noun* respectively, while X_I stands for $X.x_Iy_Iz_I$, X_{gen} stands for $X.xyg$ and $X_{2;gen}$ stands for $X.x_2y_2g$ (for $X \in \{A, N\}$). Also, invariant parts are underlined in the given examples.

normalised form (the sequence of the corresponding single words in singular, nominative case). The normalisation process is illustrated in Table 2.

inflectional term variants	normalised term form
operacija prirodnog spajanja (ns;gp) *operacije* prirodnog spajanja (gs;np;ap;vp) *operaciji* prirodnog spajanja (ds;ls) *operaciju* prirodnog spajanja (as) *operacijo* prirodnog spajanja (vs) *operacijom* prirodnog spajanja (is) *operacijama* prirodnog spajanja (dp;ip;lp)	*operacija* (ns) *prirodno* (nsm) *spajanje* (ns)
Canonical term form: *operacija* prirodnog spajanja (nom. sing. = ns)	

Table 2: Variants and normalisation of term candidates – an example for the term *operacija prirodnog spajanja* 'natural join operation'

At this point, the usage of generic patterns in order to check the agreements on case, number and gender during the phase of filtering of term candidates might seem unnecessary, since all these features are subsequently normalised (conflated) regardless of the internal agreements. However, generic patterns are necessary to extract correct term candidates (by checking the necessary agreements between NP constituents). Once the term candidates have been identified, they can be normalised in order to make the most of the statistical part of the method.

Term variants sharing the same normalised form are grouped together into sets that we denote as *synterms*[4], and the calculation of C-values (i.e. termhoods) is performed for the whole synterm rather than for individual term candidates. Instead of providing separate frequencies of occurrence and obtaining termhoods for individual term candidates, we provide a single joint frequency of occurrence of all candidates from a synterm, and joint termhood is calculated for the synterm as a whole. Consequently, frequencies in formula (1) denote cumulative frequencies of all inflectional term forms, while the number of words in a synterm is defined as the average number of words in its elements. This approach further ensures that all inflectional term variants are naturally dealt with jointly, thus supporting the fact that they denote the same concept. As a consequence, the precision is enhanced by considering joint frequencies of occurrence and termhoods for all variants of candidate terms.

Similar approaches can be utilised to conflate other types of term variation. For example, term candidates containing constituents synonymous on the lexical/word level can be "normalised" by choosing preferred variants from a lexical resource such as the Serbian WordNet database (see Table 3 for examples). Furthermore, synonymous term variants can differ in the structure (e.g. *nejednakost Minkovskog* = *Minkovskijeva nejednakost* 'Minkovsky inequality'; *prostor Hausdorfa* = *Hausdorfov prostor* 'Hausdorf space'), and normalised forms can be obtained by inversions of corresponding constituents. Lexical and structural variations can also be combined (*virus abdomena* = *stomačni virus* 'stomach virus'). An additional term variation phenomenon is the usage of acronyms, which need to be linked to their definitions in order to enhance precision of the method.

[4] Analogously to *synsets* in the WordNet lexical database (Fellbaum, 1998).

term variants (synterm)	normalised term form
elektronski tekst *digitalni tekst*	*elektronski tekst*
računarski virus *komjuterski virus*	*računarski virus*
abdomenalni virus *stomačni virus*	*stomačni virus*
karcinom jetre *rak jetre*	*rak jetra*

Table 3: Neutralising lexical variation of term candidates using entries from the Serbian WordNet

3.2 Generation of nested term candidates

While the patterns given in Table 1 are used to single out term candidates from an initially tagged text, agreements within NPs are used to generate possible nested structures within term candidates. "Nestedness" of an NP in a longer NP in Serbian has to preserve the necessary structure and inner agreements, which are specific for the NP class in question. Therefore, generation of nested term candidates depends on the type of host term candidates (consider examples in Table 4). Nested structures that are not themselves NPs are not considered as term candidates, while "proper" nested term candidates are normalised as described in the previous Subsection.

generic patterns		nested candidates patterns	examples	NP	Term
2	$A_l\ N_l\ N_{gen}$	$A_l\ N_l\ N_{gen}$	*manipulativni aspekt modela*	+	+
		$A_l\ N_l$	*manipulativni aspekt*	+	-
		$N_l\ N_{gen}$	*aspekt model*	+	-
3	$N_l\ A_{gen}\ N_{gen}$	$N_l\ A_{gen}\ N_{gen}$	*operacija prirodnog spajanja*	+	+
		$N_l\ A_{gen}$	*operacija prirodnog*	-	-
		$A_{gen}\ N_{gen}$	*prirodno spajanje*	+	+
4	$N_l\ N_{2;gen}\ N_{gen}$	$N_l\ N_{2;gen}\ N_{gen}$	*integritet baze podataka*	+	+
		$N_l\ N_{2;gen}$	*integritet baza*	+	-
		$N_{2;gen}\ N_{gen}$	*baza podatak*	+	+
5	$A_l^+\ N_l$	$A_l^+\ N_l$	*kompletan metrički prostor*	+	+
		A_l^+	*kompletan metrički*	-	-
		$A_l^+\ N_l$	*metrički prostor*	+	+

Table 4: Generation of nested term candidates

4. Experiments and discussion

The preliminary term recognition experiments were conducted by applying the C-value method on a corpus containing samples from university textbooks in mathematics[5] and computer science[6] (altogether 120.000 words). The corpus was initially POS tagged by a system of electronic dictionaries (e-dictionaries) containing single nominal words for Serbian (Vitas, 1993). E-dictionaries contain an exhaustive description of morpho-syntactic characteristics and they are used for the lexical recognition and initial lemmatisation of words that occur in a text. This process is realised by e-dictionary look-up, which results in an

---

[5] N. Lažetić, *Matematika II/1*, Naučna knjiga, Beograd, 1994

[6] G. Pavlović-Lažetić, *Osnove relacionih baza podataka*, Vesta - Matematički fakultet, Beograd, 1996

initially tagged text: each textual word is associated with its lemma(s) and corresponding morpho-syntactic categories (tags) retrieved from the e-dictionary. In general, e-dictionaries cannot resolve lexical ambiguities that result from the fact that there is no one-to-one correspondence between word forms and their morpho-syntactic features. There are different methods to resolve ambiguities (e.g. cache-dictionaries (Silberztein, 1993) or local grammars (Nenadić and Vitas, 1998b)), but in our experiments no disambiguation techniques were applied.

In order to extract a list of term candidates, the set of morpho-syntactic filters described in 3.1 was applied to the initially tagged corpus. For the conflation of inflectional variants, we used lemmas assigned by e-dictionaries[7], while Serbian WordNet was used to link lexical synonyms. For each term candidate, we generated a canonical form (nominative, singular), a normalised form (a list of normalised words comprising the term candidate) and a list of nested term candidates. In the next step, C-values for term candidates were calculated using statistics based on occurrences of normalised forms, and all term candidates with C-values above an empirically chosen threshold were selected as terms. Tables 5a and 5b give the top ranked suggested terms.

suggested term	C-value
metrički prostor	633.55
topološki prostor	175.13
otvoren skup	93.20
normiran prostor	88.00
Košijev niz	68.11
zatvoren skup	59.20
vektorski prostor	53.13
prirodan broj	44.41
nejednakost trougla	33.98
neprekidnost preslikavanja	28.02
Hausdorfov topološki prostor	19.43

Table 5a: Top ranked terms in the domain of mathematics

suggested term	C-value
funkcionalna zavisnost	156.08
višeznačna zavisnost	129.32
uslov integriteta	40.87
strani ključ	37.00
primarni ključ	35.16
zavisnost spajanja	29.19
referencijalni integritet	27.86
neredundantno pokrivanje	27.51
relacioni model	27.35
skup funkcionalnih zavisnosti	24.29
atribut relacije	24.00

Table 5b: Top ranked terms in the domain of computer science

In order to calculate the precision, we examined precisions separately in sub-corpora of mathematics and computer science. Since the method outputs a ranked list of terms, we calculated interval precisions. Intervals were defined as sets of recognised terms that were placed at certain positions within the list. For example, interval *1-50* contained the top 50 terms, while interval >*150* contained all terms whose positions in the list were above 150.

Suggested terms have been evaluated by the authors, who are Serbian native speakers and have background in both computer science and mathematics. We performed two sets of experiments with respect to the selection of term candidates. In the first experiment, we did not use any word "stop-lists" to discard true negative constituents of term candidates, while in the second experiment a small list of typical true negative examples was used (see Tables 6a and 6b).

In the first experiment, in the top 50 terms for the domain of mathematics, there was only one true negative term candidate (*specijalna klasa neprekidnih preslikavanja* 'special class of continuity mappings'), which contained an "unwanted" adjective *specijalna* 'special'. The reason for the significant drop in the precision in the second and third interval (see Table 6a) is mainly the same: apart from few true negatives[8], the majority of false term candidates

[7] In cases where multiple lemmas were assigned to a single word, we generate multiple normalised forms, which are treated separately.

[8] Such as: *topološka tačka gledišta, kompletnost prostora igra, kod preslikavnja.*

contained common "unwanted" constituents. The results for the computer science sub-corpus were comparably worse since mathematical language seems to be more consistent and restricted.

interval	mathematics	computer science
1 – 50	98%	90%
50 – 100	88%	70%
100 – 150	52%	58%
> 150	69%	68%

Table 6a: Precision of the ATR method (without the usage of a stop-list)

interval	mathematics	computer science
1 – 50	100%	94%
50 – 100	92%	92%
100 – 150	80%	74%
> 150	74%	70%

Table 6b: Precision of the ATR method (with the usage of a stop-list)

In the second experiment, we used a short word stop-list (sampled in Table 7) containing the words detected as frequent "wrong" constituents in the previous experiments. The results (summarised in Table 6b) show that significant improvement can be made by using a simple method to suppress true negative candidates.

prozvoljan	*opšti*	*pojam*
tražen	*dokazan*	*specifičnost*
specijalan	*globalan*	*svojstvo*
važan	*jedinstven*	*slučaj*
odgovarajući	*poznat*	*posledica*
definisan	*veliki*	*gledište*

Table 7: A sample of normalised stop-words

The majority of remaining errors mainly originate from the ambiguous POS tagging (more than 50% of errors, problematic words being *naziv(a)* 'name', *igra* 'play', *kod* 'code' or 'in', etc.). Since no further processing of text has been performed, another source of problems is the detection of boundaries of "frozen parts" in some prepositional phrases. For example, the following true negatives were suggested: [*na*] *osnovu teoreme* 'based on the theorem' or [*u*] *slučaju integriteta baze podataka* 'in case of database integrity', where the prepositional phrases *na osnovu* 'based on' and *u slučaju* 'in case of' have not been "filtered" out correctly. These ambiguities can be resolved by using a set of corresponding local grammars (Nenadić and Vitas, 1998b).

Furthermore, for the computer science domain, some of the false terms were related to a specific application area as the text intensively used examples from a university information system, so term candidates such as *zvanje nastavnika* 'lecturer position', *godina studija* 'year of study', etc. were wrongly suggested as terms in the computer science domain. It is an obvious challenge to discard such candidates in the given domain, as they are valid terms in another domain.

5. Conclusion

In this paper we presented an approach to automatic extraction of terminology in a morphologically rich language, such as Serbian. The approach is hybrid: it combines morpho-syntactic filters for the extraction of term candidates, their inflectional normalisation and statistical analysis that ranks term candidates according to their termhoods.

The extraction of term candidates is based on the recognition of specific subclasses of well-formed NPs. Since describing NPs by means of regular expressions is not sufficient for modelling agreements between NP constituents, we have used generic morpho-syntactic patterns to recognise well-formed NPs and to extract their possible nested sub-terms. In addition, since (candidate) terms appear in texts in many different forms due to their inflectional and lexical variations, the necessity of taking these variations into account becomes particularly apparent. Therefore, we incorporated normalisation of term candidates into the ATR process, which aims at improving the statistical part of the method, as the termhoods are calculated for the whole set that unifies all term variants.

The preliminary experiments in the domains of mathematics and computer science show that for the top ranked terms the precision is well above 90%, and that these terms can be used as semantic indicators for documents. The analysis of errors reveals that the majority of them appear due to POS and lexical ambiguity of the input text. Certainly, if the corpora were POS/lexically disambiguated, we would have better results.

In order to improve the recall of the method, additional morpho-syntactic filters need to be identified. In particular, terms that contain prepositional phrases (e.g. *dovoljni uslov za postojanje lokalnog ekstrema* 'sufficient condition for existence of an extreme') and coordinations (e.g. *model entiteta i odnosa* 'entity-relationship model') are important, as these are common formation patterns in many domains. Further, broader handling of other term variants (e.g. dialectic variants, acronyms, derivational variants) may further improve both precision and recall.

Terms extracted automatically may be used as a basis for a range of classical IR/IE tasks. Furthermore, term variants unification and normalisation provide a broader source for processing documents, as entities and/or queries can be expanded by referring to a class of synonymous terms as opposed to a single term.

Acknowledgements

We would like to thank Dr Sophia Ananiadou for discussions on C-value and terminological management in general, and Dr Duško Vitas for pre-processing the corpus. We also thank Prof. Gordana Pavlović-Lažetić and Prof. Nebojša Lažetić for giving us permission to use their textbooks for the experiments.

References

Ananiadou S. (1994): *Methodology for Automatic Term Recognition*. Proceedings of COLING-94, Kyoto, Japan, pp. 1034-1038.

Bourigault D., Gomzalez-Mullier I. and Gros C. (1996): *LEXTER, a Natural Language Processing Tool for Terminology Extraction*. Proceedings of EURALEX 96, pp. 771-779.

Collier N., Nobata C. and Tsujii J. (2001): *Automatic Acquisition and Classification of Molecular Biology Terminology From a Tagged Corpus*. Terminology, John Benjamins.

Dagan, I. and Church, K. (1994): *Termight: Identifying and Translating Technical Terminology*. Proceedings of Applied NLP (ANLP), 1994, 34-40.

Daille B., Gaussier E. and Lange J. M. (1994): *Towards Automatic Extraction of Monolingual and Bilingual Terminology*. Proceedings of COLING-94, pp. 515-521.

Fellbaum C. (ed.) (1998): WordNet – an Electronic Lexical Database, MIT Press, 1998.

Frantzi K.T., Ananiadou S. and Mima H. (2000): *Automatic Recognition of Multi-word Terms: the C-value/NC-value Method*. Int. J. on Digital Libraries, 3/2, pp. 115-130.

Gaizauskas R., Demetriou G. and Humphreys K. (2000): *Term Recognition and Classification in Biological Science Journal Articles*. Proceedings of the Computational Terminology for Medical and Biological Applications Workshop (NLP-2000), Patras, Greece, pp. 37-44.

Hatzivassiloglou V., Duboue P. and Rzetsky A. (2001): *Disambiguating Proteins, Genes, and RNA in Text: A Machine Learning Approach*. Bioinformatics, 17/1, pp. S97-S106.

Hobbs J., Appelt D., Bear J., Israel D., Kameyama M., Stickel M. and Tyson M. (1997): *FASTUS: A cascaded finite-state transducer for extracting information from natural-language text*. Finite-State Language Processing (E. Roche and Y. Schabes (eds.)), MIT Press, Cambridge, MA, pp. 383-406.

Jacquemin C. (2001): *Spotting and discovering terms through NLP*. MIT Press, Cambridge MA, p.378.

Jurafsky D. and Martin J. (2000): *Speech and Language Processing, An Introduction to Natural Language Processing, Computational Linguistics and Speech Recognition*. Prentice Hall.

Kazama J., Makino T., Ohta Y. and Tsujii J. (2002): *Tuning Support Vector Machines for Biomedical Named Entity Recognition*. Proceedings of the NLP in Biomedicine Workshop, ACL 2002.

Kittredge R. and Lehrberger J. (eds.) (1982): *Sublanguages, Studies of Language in Restricted Semantic Domains*. W. de Gruyter, Berlin – New York.

Nakagawa H. and Mori T. (1998): *Nested Collocation and Compound Noun for Term Recognition*. Proc. of COMPUTERM 98, pp. 64-70.

Nenadić G. and Vitas D. (1998a): *Formal Model of Noun Phrases in Serbo-Croatian*. BULAG 23, Universite Franche-Compte, Besançon, pp. 297-311.

Nenadić G. and Vitas D. (1998b): *Using Local Grammars for Agreement Modelling in Highly Inflective Languages*. Proceedings of TSD 98. Masaryk University, Brno, pp. 91-96.

Nenadić G., Spasić, I. and Ananiadou S. (2003): *Reducing Lexical Ambiguity in Serbo-Croatian by Using Genetic Algorithms*. In: Kosta, P. et al. (eds.): Investigations into Formal Slavic Linguistics, Linguistik International, Peter Lang, Frankfurt, pp. 287-298.

Nenadić G., Spasić I. and Ananiadou S. (2004a): *Automatic Discovery of Term Similarities Using Pattern Mining*. Terminology 10:1 (2004), pp. 55-80.

Nenadić G., Spasić I. and Ananiadou S. (2004b): *Mining Biomedical Abstracts: What's in a Term?* Proceedings of IJCNLP-2004, pp. 247-254.

Sager J. C. (1990): *A Practical Course in Terminology Processing*. Benjamins, Amsterdam, Philadelphia, p. 254.

Silberztein M. (1993): *Dictionnaires electroniques et analyse automatique de textes: le systeme INTEX*. Masson Ed.: Paris, p. 240.

Smadja F. (1991): *From n-grams to Collocations – an Evaluation of Xtract*. Proceedings of Annual Meeting of ACL, pp. 279-284.

Vintar Š. (2000): *Extracting Terms and Terminological Collocations from the ELAN Slovene-English Parallel Corpus*. Proceedings of the 5th EAMT Workshop, Ljubljana, Slovenia

Vitas D. (1993): *Mathematical Model of Serbo-Croatian Morphology (Nominal Inflection)*. PhD thesis. Faculty of Mathematics, Belgrade.

Vladimír Petkevič, Prague

The Structure of the Nominal Group in the Czech National Corpus and its Part-of-Speech and Morphological Disambiguation

0. Introduction

The article consists in the specification of syntactic properties of the nominal group in Czech based on extensive material provided by the corpus of contemporary Czech called *SYN2000* (100 million corpus positions) which is part of the *Czech National Corpus* (CNC) project (cf. Czech National Corpus). As the syntactic structure of nominal groups is quite intricate and cannot be appropriately described on several pages only, my research is limited to the structure of the left part of the nominal group, i.e. to the structure constituted by the governing (head) noun and its left attributive modifiers. The main emphasis is laid on how to identify such structures, on the specification of their syntactic properties and on how to exploit these properties for errorfree rule-based morphological and part-of-speech disambiguation and for shallow parsing.

The paper consists of the following main sections. In the first section, the syntactic structure of the left part of the nominal group in Czech is described. In the following section, a rule-based approach to part-of-speech and morphological disambiguation is presented, and in the third section, it is demonstrated how this approach can be used for the disambiguation of the left part of the nominal group.

1. Structure of the left part of a nominal group in Czech

The study of the structure of nominal groups in Czech is motivated by

- practical reasons: automatic part-of-speech and morphological tagging of Czech corpora and shallow syntactic analysis
- theoretical reasons: to contribute to the development of descriptive grammar of Czech based on corpus material.

As nominal groups are extremely frequent in Czech texts (for instance, each 12th bigram is formed by the simplest nominal group – Adjective-Noun pair – in the SYN2000 corpus!), their disambiguation must be paid special attention and their surface-syntax analysis must be as fine-grained as possible (such an analysis has not been performed yet!). In the sequel, I will present some insights into such analysis.

Syntactic properties of the left part of a nominal group are characterized by the following constitutive factors:

- the presence of the governing (head) noun
- agreement of case-specific elements in *gender, number* and *case*
- specific order of left modifiers.

I am going to study the character of the word forms which modify the head noun from the left and agree with it in *gender, number, case*. Moreover, possible (and impossible) free word order sequences of the modifiers (dependent elements) will be studied.

Let us start with some examples of nominal groups comprising possible sequences of left modifiers of the head noun which agree with it in gender, number and case. In sentence

(1) *Řešil jsem takové*(PronDem[1]) *dva*(NumCard) *spletité*(Adj) *problémy*.
(E. lit: I was solving *such two intricate* problems.
E.: I was solving *such two intricate* problems.)

the sequence (PronDem, NumCard, Adj) is correct as well as the sequence (NumCard, PronDem, Adj) in sentence

(1') *Řešil jsem dva*(NumCard) *takové*(PronDem) *spletité*(Adj) *problémy*.
(E. lit: I was solving *two such intricate* problems.
E.: I was solving *such two intricate* problems.)

As we see, the reversal of PronDem and NumCard is possible here, but e.g. with a negative pronoun and a cardinal numeral the reversal is impossible or at least considerably doubtful, as is shown by the pair of sentences (2) and (2')

(2) *Neřešil jsem žádné*(PronNeg) *dva*(NumCard) *spletité*(Adj) *problémy*.
(E. lit: I was not solving *no two intricate* problems.
E.: I was solving *none of the two intricate* problems.)

(2') ? **Neřešil jsem dva*(NumCard) *žádné*(PronNeg) *spletité*(Adj) *problémy*.
(E. lit: I was not solving *two no intricate* problems.
E.: I was solving *none of the two intricate* problems.)

Thus, not every order of left attributive modifiers is possible. Table 1 shows the most frequent pairs of left modifiers of the head noun occurring in the SYN2000 corpus, the examples of nominal structures corresponding to the given pattern being italicized and glossed.

Table 1

pattern: *tag1* *tag2* *GoverningNoun*

tag1	*tag2*	# of occur.	Example
Adj	Adj	970857	(*špatnému válečnému* filmu; E. lit. *bad war* film)
PronPoss	Adj	122022	(*jeho bílá* tlama; *his white* mouth)
PronDem	Adj	116330	(*té lidské* straně; *that human* side)
NumCard	Adj	81332	(*jednom malém* místě; *one small* place)
Pronsvůj	Adj	78825	(*své přirozené* prostředí; *its natural* environment)
PronIndef	Adj	38048	(*nějaký důvěrný* styk; *some familiar* contact)
Adj	NumCard	33344	(*uplynulých třech* dnech; *last three* days)
PronTot	Adj	30599	(*všem možným* plážím; *all possible* beaches)
NumOrd	Adj	24572	(*první světové* válce; *first world* war)
AdjPoss	Adj	17492	(*Lukasovo mohutné* rámě; *Lukas' powerful* arm)

[1] The interpretation of abbreviations: Adj = Adjective, AdjPoss = Possessive Adjective, Comma = ",", NumCard = Cardinal Numeral, NumOrd = Ordinal Numeral, NumGener = Generic Numeral, PronDem = Demonstrative Pronoun, PronIndef = Indefinite Pronoun, PronNeg = Negative Pronoun, PronPoss = Possessive Pronoun, PronRel = Relative Possessive Pronoun, Pronsvůj = Reflexive Possessive Pronoun *svůj*, PronTot = Total Pronoun.

PronNeg	Adj	14812	(*žádné zatracené* spiknutí; *no damned* conspiration)
Adj	AdjPoss	11259	(*proslulém Gorbačovově* telefonu; *famous Gorbačov's* telephone)
Adj	PronPoss	7849	(*celé naší* republice; *whole our* republic)
PronRel	Adj	7418	(*jehož bledém* obličeji; *whose pale* face)
PronDem	NumCard	7038	(*těch dvou* rovin; *those two* levels)
Adj	NumOrd	5960	(*zmatených šedesátých* let; *confused sixtieth* years)
NumOrd	NumCard	4716	(*prvních třech* stoletích; *first three* centuries)
PronTot	PronDem	4665	(*všech těch* domech; *all those* houses)
PronTot	PronPoss	4333	(*všechny jeho* vrstvy; *all his* layers)
PronTot	NumCard	3304	(*všech čtyřech* křídlech; *all four* wings)
Pronsvůj	NumOrd	2818	(*své první* návštěvě; *her first* visit)
Pronsvůj	NumCard	1684	(*svých dvou* letech; *his two* years)
NumCard	PronDem	1622	(*jednom tom* okně; *one that* window)

The following set of very simple regular expressions concisely summarizes the possible pairs of (types of) tags corresponding to the word order pairs of word forms immediately modifying and preceding their head noun.

Concise summary of possible pairs[2]

(Adj | AdjPoss | PRON | NumCard | NumOrd)	Adj
Adj	(NumCard | NumOrd | PronSvůj | | PronPoss)
(NumCard | NumOrd | PronSvůj | PronDem)	NumCard
PronSvůj	NumOrd
PronTot	(PronDem | PronPoss | PronSvůj | | NumCard)
NumCard	PronDem
PronDem	PronRel

Thus, e.g. the first line can be expanded as follows:

Adj	Adj
AdjPoss	Adj
PRON	Adj
NumCard	Adj
NumOrd	Adj

In addition to Table 1, I also present Table 2 showing the most frequent triples of left modifiers.

[2] Each line describes one pair in which each element of the pair is either simple or it is formed by a disjunction of possible values. PRON denotes any kind of pronoun except for Personal and Reflexive ones.

Table 2

pattern: *tag1 tag2 tag3 GoverningNoun*

tag1	*tag2*	*tag3*	*# of occur.*	Example
Adj	ConjC	Adj	167374	(*němém a zuřivém* zápase; E. lit. *silent and fierce* struggle)
Adj	Adj	Adj	52531	(*velkých nepravidelných přírodních* perel; *big irregular natural* pearls)
Adj	Comma	Adj	29848	(*černém, lesnatém* údolí; *black, woody* valley)
PronDem	Adj	Adj	11314	(*tom velkém starém* domě; [in] *that big old* house)
NumCard	ConjC	NumCard	9845	(*dvou a třech* letech; *two and three* years)
NumCard	Adj	Adj	9424	(*pěti ruských vojenských* lodí; *five Russian military* ships)
PronPoss	Adj	Adj	9401	(*jeho krásné nové* podobě; *his beautiful new* appearance)
Pronsvůj	Adj	Adj	6602	(*své štíhlé vysoké* nohy; *her slim high* legs)
PronIndef	Adj	Adj	4050	(*nějaké důležité úřední* funkci; *some important official* function)
PronDem	ConjC	Adj	3217	(*těchto a podobných* případech; *these and similar* cases)
PronTot	Adj	Adj	3909	(*každá velká byrokratická* organizace; *every big beaurocratic* organization)
Adj	NumCard	Adj	3172	(*zářící dva mladí lidé*; *beaming two young* people)
NumOrd	Adj	Adj	2843	(*první povolená politická* demonstrace; *first authorized political* demonstration)
PronDem	ConjC	PronDem	2658	(*tu a tu* hodinu; *that and that* hour)
NumOrd	ConjC	NumOrd	2269	(*sedmdesátých a osmdesátých* letech; *seventieth and eightieth* years)
Pronsvůj	NumOrd	Adj	1041	(*své první básnické* pokusy; *his first poetic* experiments)

....

The following set of very simple regular expressions summarizes possible triples of (types of) tags corresponding to the word order triples of left modifiers immediately modifying and preceding their head noun and also the triples containing a coordinating conjunction or comma.

Concise summary of possible triples[3]

Adj	(Adj | ConjC | Comma | PronSvůj | NumCard)	Adj
(PronSvůj | NumOrd | NumCard)	Adj	Adj
PronDem	(Adj | ConjC | PronSvůj)	Adj
PronPoss	(Adj | ConjC)	Adj
PronTot	(Adj | PronDem | PronSvůj | NumCard)	Adj
NumOrd	NumCard	Adj
PronSvůj	NumOrd	Adj
(PronIndef | NumCard)	Adj	Adj
Adj	NumCard	NumCard
NumOrd	ConjC	NumOrd
PronDem	ConjC	PronDem
NumCard	(Comma | ConjC)	NumCard
PronSvůj	Adj	NumCard

In Table 3, I also concisely summarize mutual word order of types of pronominal and numeral left modifiers in the form of typical pairs:

Table 3
Most frequent pairs:

PronSvůj	(NumCard | NumOrd)
PronTot	(PronDem | PronPoss | PronSvůj | NumCard | NumOrd)
PronDem	(PronSvůj | PronRel | PronPoss | PronTot | NumCard | NumOrd)
PronPoss	(PronTot | NumOrd | NumCard)
PronIndef	(PronDem | PronPoss | PronSvůj)
PronNeg	(PronDem | PronPoss | PronSvůj)
NumOrd	(NumCard | NumOrd)
NumCard	(PronDem | PronSvůj | PronPoss | NumCard)

For instance, a demonstrative pronoun can immediately precede the reflexive possessive pronoun *svůj* (E. one's own), relative possessive pronoun, possessive pronoun, total pronoun, such as *všechen* (E. all), and cardinal or ordinal numeral.
Below I present some typical examples found in the corpus:

PronSvůj NumCard N
(3) *svůj první úspěch*
(E. lit.: one's own first success
E.: his / her/ their first success)
PronTot NumCard N
(4) *každé dva týdny*
(E. lit.: every two weeks)
E.: every two weeks)
PronNeg PronPoss N
(5) *žádný jeho problém*
(E. lit.: no his problem
E.: no problem of his)

Other pairs are impossible or at least extremely rare – see their list in Table 4.

[3] Each line describes one triple in which each element of the triple is either simple or it is formed by a disjunction of possible values. ConjC denotes Coordinating conjunction.

Table 4

Impossible or very rare/suspicious pairs of (types of) tags:

* PronX	PronX where X = any type of pronoun (except for PronDem)
* PronIndef	(PronNeg | PronTot | NumOrd | NumGen)
* PronDem	PronNeg
* PronNeg	(PronTot | PronIndef)
* PronPoss	(PronTot | PronNeg | PronDem | PronIndef)
* PronTot	(PronNeg | PronIndef)
* NumCard	(PronIndef | PronNeg | PronTot)
* NumOrd	(PronIndef | PronNeg | PronTot)
* NumGener	(PronIndef | PronNeg | PronTot)

So, for instance, a demonstrative pronoun can hardly precede a negative one within an NP:

PronDem PronNeg N
(6) * *takový žádný dělník*
(E. lit.: such no worker
E.: no such worker)

An interesting structure is a combination of an adjective preceding a pronoun. The following pattern characterizes possible word order pairs:

Adj (PronDem | PronPoss | PronSvůj)

Among the adjectives identified with Adj, especially pronominal adjectives[4] appear such as: *jiný* (E. *other*), *druhý* (*the other*), *další* (*next*), *ostatní* (*others*), *celý* (*whole*) etc. This set of „pronominal" adjectives is very small and can be easily enumerated.

The following pair of example structures shows the difference in the word order, the structure (PronPoss, Adj) being at least far more frequent than the reversed one. In the reversed order, i.e. in the (Adj, PronPoss) structure, which is very rare, the adjective modifies the entire remaining structure (*naše dějiny*, E. our history) rather than the noun *dějiny* only; in the (PronPoss, Adj) structure such a distinction can hardly be made:

PronPoss Adj N
(7) *naše pozoruhodné dějiny*
(E. lit.: our remarkable history
E.: our remarkable history)

Adj PronPoss N
(7') ? *pozoruhodné naše dějiny*
(E. lit.: remarkable our history
E.: our remarkable history)

Contrary to this, if Adj is represented by the lemma *celý* (E. whole), for instance, the word order (Adj, PronPoss) is far more plausible (and frequent) than the reversed one:

[4] Pronominal adjectives are those adjectives whose semantic function is close to that of deictic words. They are, however, nominations and they have their own (albeit weakened) semantics.

Adj PronPoss N
(8) *celé naše dějiny*
(E. lit.: whole our history
E.: the whole history of ours)

is at least far more frequent than:

PronPoss Adj N
(8') *?naše celé dějiny*
(E. lit.: our whole history
E.: the whole history of ours))

Thus, I have specified grammatical and ungrammatical word order of types of the congruent left modifiers of the head noun. My goal is not to investigate the reasons for the grammaticality and ungrammaticality of various structures and patterns, I rather ask how this research can be practically exploited for disambiguation and (shallow) syntactic analysis. In the sequel, I shall first briefly describe what I mean by the rule-based approach to part-of-speech and morphological disambiguation.

2. Rule-based part-of-speech and morphological disambiguation
2.1. Disambiguation of Czech

So far Czech corpora, especially SYN2000, have been tagged by stochastic methods (cf. Halič 2004). It turned out that the error rate is approximately 5 % which means that on average every 20th word in Czech texts is incorrectly disambiguated. For any serious research on syntax, this error rate is considered too high, and therefore a group of researchers decided to solve the problem of part-of-speech and morphological disambiguation in a different way (cf. Oliva et al. 2000). The novel approach consists in the development of formally specified (morpho)syntactic rules which capture regularities in the syntactic system of Czech and perform disambiguation. These rules identify correct part-of-speech and morphological interpretation(s) of the word forms based on virtually unlimited context in which these word forms occur.

The input for the disambiguation module is the result of the previous text processing, namely:

- tokenization, i.e. identification of corpus positions
- sentence segmentation
- morphological analysis.

Morphological analysis assigns each word form and punctuation mark its possible part-of-speech and morphological interpretations. As Czech is a language with rich inflexion (maybe the richest and most complicated one within the family of Slavic languages), especially in declension paradigms displaying a lot of case syncretism, the part-of-speech/morphological ambiguity rate is very high (approx. 2,5 interpretations per word on average). In addition to this systemic ambiguity, there are many lexical and casual ambiguities of various types. Thus, correct tagging of Czech corpora constitutes a crucial bottleneck in further processing of Czech corpora, and as statistical methods fail to give satisfactory results, a more linguistically pertinent method for disambiguation has been devised: *rule-based reductive automatic disambiguation method.*

Besides the rivalry with the stochastic disambiguation methods, the motivation of rule-based disambiguation is:

- practical:
  - to improve the tagging of Czech corpora
  - to help to develop a grammar-checker for Czech
  - to constitute a preprocessing phase for (shallow) syntactic analysis of Czech
  - to prepare a solid point of departure for semantic analysis of Czech, esp. word sense disambiguation
- theoretical: to contribute to the preparation of descriptive and formal grammar of Czech.

2.2. Rule-based reductive automatic disambiguation

I shall briefly describe basic features of the rule-based disambiguation method. They can be expressed in the following points:

- disambiguation is based exclusively on (morpho)syntactic rules: the rules are developed on the basis of linguistic intuition and verified on corpus data. Thus, grammatical regularities are inferred from data (esp. by means of *negative bigrams*, cf. Oliva 2001, Květoň / Oliva 2002))
- the rules can use virtually unlimited context but so far the rules operate within the scope of one sentence only
- the rules model the language system of Czech, i.e. they are *language-specific*
- the reduction method initially processes the input provided by morphological analysis. The tags produced by morphological analysis can be characterized by two main parameters:

  recall = 100 % (each word form is assigned a set of tags which comprises the correct one)
  precision = lowest possible (all morphologically plausible tags are assigned to each word form)

  The method is based on

  - the removal of incorrect tags based on negative n-gram (especially for n = 2, i.e. bigram) approach in which *n* (morpho)syntactically incompatible elements form a so-called negative n-gram and this incompatibility results in the removal of a tag being a member of an n-gram with the other tags of the n-gram being fixed
  - the direct identification of the correct tag – a positive approach

- the development of rules is supported by semiautomatic identification of negative bigrams
- the rules are mutually independent and they are applied in a cyclic way, each rule application operating on the results of the previous rule applications
- the rules are written in a special programming language especially suited for the development and maintenance of rules, the language being referred to as LanGr in the sequel (cf. Květoň 2003)
- no syntactic trees or other structures are built
- a special collocation component coping with various non-systemic idiosyncrasies and exceptions from the system is an inherent part of the whole approach and chronologically this component precedes the application of the rules.

The structure of a rule in LanGr can be described as follows

$cont_1\ disamb_1\ cont_2\ disamb_2 \ldots cont_n\ disamb_n\ cont_{n+1}$

where

cont$_i$ describes the context which is only used by the rule being unaffected by it
disamb$_i$ describes a *disambigution place*, where the data is modified.

The *context* must be unambigously specified (formally, the *IsSafe* predicate is used), i.e. each word form in the context *must* have the specified properties. *Disambiguation place* is the place where the data is modified – here the word forms can be ambiguous. Their description is specified by the *Possible* predicate which means that at least one morphological interpretation of the word form(s) being referred to must meet the conditions in the *Possible* directive.

In addition to the static part of each rule, the rules contain also their executive (data modifying) commands:

- *DELETE some (not necessarily all) incorrect interpretations*
- *LEAVE ONLY correct interpretations*
- various functions such as UNIFY which unifies the tag sets assigned to two or more word forms in that it discards those tags which are not in the intersection of values for specified attributes (e.g. the unification of the values of the attributes *number, gender* and *case*, the values being assigned to an adjective and a following noun, respectively)

The whole approach can be demonstrated on the exploitation of a *negative bigram* for the disambiguation. Let *X Y* be a negative bigram, e.g.

(PrepositionNotTakingLocativeCase, NounInLocative)

i.e. this configuration of tags (the order is crucially relevant here!) can never occur in a syntactically correct text. How can this bigram be exploited? From the bigram two following *different* statements can be derived:

1. A preposition not taking the locative case cannot precede a noun in the locative case.
2. A noun in the locative case cannot follow a preposition not taking the locative case.

Thus, two disambiguation rules can be formulated:

Rule 1

X = ITEM IsSafe (Preposition and (not Locative));
/* This statement of LanGr specifies the context: corpus position X is specified as an unambiguous preposition not taking the locative case, i.e. *all tags* assigned to X *are prepositional* tags which differ, e.g., in their case valency, and none of case values equals the locative */
Y = ITEM Possible (Noun and Locative);
/* This statement of LanGr specifies the disambiguation place: corpus position Y is assigned *at least one tag specifying the corpus position as a noun in the locative case* */
DELETE (Noun and Locative) FROM Y;
/* the executive action follows: the properties of X being fixed, Y is not a noun in the locative case, i.e. this interpretation of Y is removed */

The rule successfully applies to the sentence

(9) *Odešel k*(PrepDat) *otci*(NDatSg/~~NLocSg~~/NInstrPl).
(E. lit.: He went to father.
E.: He went away to [meet] the father.)

Here the locative-case interpretation (tag) of the word form *otci* is discarded because the word form with this interpretation cannot occur after a safe preposition taking a case value different from the locative.

Rule 2

X = ITEM Possible (Preposition and (not Locative));
/* Disambiguation place: corpus position X is assigned *at least one tag specifying the position as a preposition taking a case value different from the locative* */

Y = ITEM IsSafe (Noun and Locative);
/* The context: corpus position Y is specified as an unambiguous noun in the locative case, i.e. *all tags* assigned to Y *specify the noun in the locative case* (there can possibly be more such tags, each corresponding to a different lemma) */

DELETE (Preposition and (not Locative)) FROM X;
/* the executive action follows: the properties of Y being fixed, X is not a preposition taking a non-locative case, i.e. all these interpretations (tags) are removed */

This rule successfully applies to the sentences of the following type:

(10) *Záleželo pouze na*(~~PrepAcc~~/PrepLoc) *postojích*(NounLoc) *ke světu.*
E. lit.: It depended only on the approaches to the world.
E.: Only the approaches to the world made a difference.)

Here the accusative valency of the preposition *na* is discarded because the preposition *na* with this valency cannot occur in front of the safe noun in the unambiguously locative case.

After these simple examples demonstrating the exploitation of negative bigrams I shall show how this disambiguation approach can be applied to the identification of intricate relations within a nominal group.

3. Nominal groups and rule-based disambiguation

3.1. Syntactic structure of the left part of nominal groups

Surface syntax analysis of nominal groups in the SYN2000 corpus which was presented in Section 1 can lead to the development of sophisticated disambiguation rules expressed in a special programming language LanGr. These rules are very important because:

- correct disambiguation can crucially help subsequent syntactic analysis by identifying *nominal groups* (chunking);
- correct disambiguation of nominal groups can help to prepare more *disambiguated fixed points*, i.e. the context, for further application of subsequently applied disambiguation rules.

The delimitation of a nominal group NP consists in

- identification of left and right external boundaries of an NP
- identification of internal NP boundaries based on

(1) agreement in *gender*, *number* and *case*
(2) ordering of elements modifying the head noun
(3) head noun itself which is identified with the internal right boundary.

NP delimitation criteria can be specified as follows:

- case-specified elements in NP (arbitrary number of syntactic adjectives in the attributive position) must *agree in case* and also (if there is no coordination within NP, because coordination complicates the situation) *in number and gender*
- if the word order *X Y* is impossible within NP, then X and Y *do not belong* to the same NP
- left external boundary is formed by an element characterized by one of the following types:
    (1) sentence/clause beginning
    (2) case-specified element in a case value or number value or gender value *different* from that of the head noun of NP
    (3) personal pronoun
    (4) preposition
    (5) verb
    (6) subordinating conjunction.
- adverbs, particles (and in a more liberal, but risky approach also: conjunctions and commas) can be part of NP.

Sentences (11) and (12) will illustrate these limitations:

(11) *Včera jsem se díval na*(Prep) *velice*(Adv) *starý*(Adj) *sovětský*(Adj) *film*(N).
(E. lit: Yesterday I was looking at very old Soviet film.
E.: Yesterday I was looking at a very old Soviet film.)

Here the NP is formed by the sequence *velice*(Adv) *starý*(Adj) *sovětský*(Adj) *film*(N), where both adjectives agree with the head noun in case, number and gender; the left external boundary is formed by the preposition *na*.

(12) *Celá lidská existence byla tehdy obklopena*(Verb-pass.part) *jakýmsi*(PronIndef) *neproniknutelným*(Adj) *tajemstvím*(N), *které* ....
(E. lit: Entire human existence was at that time surrounded by an impenetrable mystery which ...)
E.: At that time the entire human existence was surrounded by an impenetrable mystery which ...)

In this sentence the NP is formed by the sequence *jakýmsi*(PronIndef) *neproniknutelným*(Adj) *tajemstvím*(N), where the indefinite pronoun and adjective agree with the head noun in case, number and gender; the left external boundary is formed by the passive participle *obklopena*.

3.2. Two disambiguation rules for nominal groups

In this section I shall present two disambiguation rules performing disambiguation within an NP, the rules are again formulated in the formal language LanGr and commented on.

Rule 3

/* Specification of one type of NP by agreement and an acceptable sequence of its elements */

```
rule AgrInNounGroup {

/* let NP be structured as:

PronSyntAdj (SyntAdj | Adverb | Particle | ConjCoord | Comma)* HeadNoun

where PronSyntAdj is an adjectival pronoun behaving like a syntactic adjective
(SyntAdj), i.e. PronSyntAdj is an adjectival declension paradigm which can function
as a congruent attribute
*/

extrnbound = ITEM IsSafe (SentBeg or Verb or ConjSubord or PronPers or
Preposition);
/* external left boundary – see NP delimitation criteria above; another variant (not
mentioned here) of the rule admits also Adjective here which is not unifiable with the
HeadNoun in case or number or gender */

safepronsyntadj = ITEM IsSafe (PronSyntAdj);
/* internal left boundary – initial element of the nominal group: an adjectival pronoun,
e.g. takový (E. such) */

seqinnp = SEQUENCE OF IsSafe (SyntAdj or Adverb or Particle or ConjCoord or
Comma);
/* material within NP formed by syntactic adjectives, adverbs, particles, coordinating
conjunctions and commas */

headnoun = ITEM IsSafe (Noun);
/* head noun */

REPORT („Elements of NP which begins with " ref.form(safepronsyntadj) „ and ends
with " ref.form(headnoun) „ must agree in gender, number and case; remaining tags
are discarded");
/* if the subsequent unification is actually performed, this message is issued; the
ref.form argument refers to the corresponding word form in the data */

if UNIFIABLE safepronsyntadj seqinnp headnoun IN [number,gender,case]
        then { UNIFY safepronsyntadj seqinnp headnoun IN [number,gender,case]; };
/* if the elements are unifiable in case, number and gender, then unify – this is a
conditional unification. Moreover, unification works as follows: elements not having
the attribute case, number and gender always unify */

}; // end of AgrInNounGroup rule
```

Let us now have a look at the following part of sentence:

(13) ... *této nové a velice často hrané písně* ...
(E. lit.: ... this new and very often played song ...
E.: ... this new and very often played song ...)

where

této (PronDem: *gen.sg.fem.*/dat.sg.fem./loc.sg.fem.)
nové (Adj: *gen.sg.fem.*/dat.sg.fem./loc.sg.fem./nom.sg.neut./acc.sg.neut./voc.sg.neut./ nom.pl.fem./nom.pl.mi/acc.pl.fem./acc.pl.mi/voc.pl.fem./voc.pl.mi)
a ConjC
velice Adv
často Adv
hrané (Adj: *gen.sg.fem.*/dat.sg.fem./loc.sg.fem./nom.sg.neut./acc.sg.neut./voc.sg.neut./ nom.pl.fem./acc.pl.fem./voc.pl.fem.)
písně (Noun: *gen.sg.fem.*/ nom.pl.fem./acc.pl.fem./voc.pl.fem.)

Here, the unification unambiguously yields *gen.sg.fem.* with the relevant word forms.

Similarly, other acceptable word order sequences within an NP can be specified in a rule like this but the rule is too crude – in *seqinnp* all sequences of elements within NP are allowed. Therefore additional rules, especially the word order-related ones, are necessary and here the concept of *negative bigrams* can be used.

This can be illustrated by the negative bigram (Adj PronNeg). As (Adj PronNeg) cannot be a subsequence of elements in any NP, we can infer from the sequence:

Adj1 PronNeg Adj2 Noun

that Adj1 cannot belong to (PronNeg Adj2 Noun)$_{NP}$

This does not always mean that such a subsequence cannot appear in correct Czech sentences:

(14) *Je správné*(Adj1,nom.sg.neut.) *žádné*(PronNeg,acc.pl.fem.) *vdané*(Adj2,acc.pl.fem.) *ženy*(Noun,acc.pl.fem.) *nelíbat*.
(E. lit.: It is appropriate no married women to kiss.
E.: It is appropriate not to kiss any married women.)

but from this sequence we can infer that the adjective *správné* in nominative singular does not belong to the accusative plural NP *žádné vdané ženy*.

In more constrained structures such a sequence is erroneous, e.g. in locative prepositional phrases. For instance, the following sentence part is correct

(15) ... *o*(Prep,Loc) *žádných*(PronNeg,Loc) *vhodných*(Adj,Loc) *efektivních*(Adj,Loc) *opatřeních*(Noun,Loc) ... *jsme nediskutovali*
(E. lit.: about no appropriate effective measures ... we did not discuss)
E.: no appropriate effective measures ... were discussed)

But the sequence

(15') *... *o*(Prep,Loc) *vhodných*(Adj,Loc) *žádných*(PronNeg,Loc) *efektivních*(Adj,Loc) *opatřeních*(Noun,Loc) ... *jsme nediskutovali*
(E. lit.: about appropriate no effective measures ... we did not discuss
E.: no appropriate effective measures ... were discussed)

is syntactically inadmissible: both the locative constraint and the (Adj PronNeg) constraint lead to an error here. The detection of this kind of error can be formulated as disambiguation Rule 4.

Rule 4

```
/* Word order violation in a locative NP is a syntactic error */

rule WordOrderViolationInLocNP {

/* NP within a locative prepositional phrase is structured as:
PrepLoc Adj1  PronNeg  (Adj2 Adv Part)* HeadNounLoc
*/

preploc = ITEM IsSafe (Preposition and Locative);
/* preposition with locative valency – external left boundary of NP */

adj1 = ITEM IsSafe (Adjective);
/* unambiguous adjective */

pronneg = ITEM Possible (PronounNegative);
/* possible negative pronoun */

adjadvpartseq = SEQUENCE OF IsSafe (Adjective or Adverb or Particle);
/* sequence of adjectives and/or adverbs and/or particles and nothing else */

nouninloc = ITEM IsSafe (Noun and Locative);
/* unambiguous noun in the locative case */

REPORT („Negative pronoun “ ref.form(pronneg) „ cannot precede the adjective
pronoun “ ref.form(adj1) „in an NP“);
/* error message is issued */

DELETE PronounNegative FROM pronneg;
/* pronneg element cannot be a negative pronoun – discard it */

}; // end of WordOrderViolationInLocNP
```

4. Conclusion

In the article I studied the structure of the left part of a nominal group in Czech from the viewpoint of surface syntax, automatic disambiguation and shallow parsing. The objective was to show how a rule-based disambiguation approach expressed by formally precise disambiguation rules can help to morphologically disambiguate elements in nominal groups and identify these groups. Two important rules were presented as examples of the approach: it is clear that the whole bunch of sophisticated rules must be elaborated to describe and identify all types of nominal groups in an exhaustive way. The first experiments showed us that the method is very promising, but the demands imposed on the development of the rules which must be as *general* as possible and at the same time as *precise* as possible are very high. However, in my opinion, such a method – unlike too approximative and often erroneous stochastic approach to disambiguation and (shallow) parsing – can lead to far better results, especially in the processing of Slavic languages. I tried to show that if corpora of Slavic languages are to be tagged and parsed much better than it is now the case, *very sophisticated analysis* of many phenomena is inevitable, an NP and its structure being one of the prominent ones. Moreover, comparative analytical studies of the same problem areas (such as the structure of NPs in various Slavic languages) based on *precisely tagged* corpora of Slavic languages or improving to tag such corpora are to be encouraged because they are invaluable for further processing of these corpora on a qualitatively much higher level.

References

Czech National Corpus. Faculty of Arts, Charles University. (http://ucnk.ff.cuni.cz).

Hajič, J. (2004): *Disambiguation of Rich Inflection (Computational Morphology of Czech)*, Vol. 1. Karolinum Charles University Press, Praha.

Květoň, P. (2003): Language for Grammatical Rules. *Technical Report TR-2003-17*. Matematicko-fyzikální fakulta UK, Praha.

Květoň, P., Oliva, K. (2002): (Semi-)Automatic Detection of Errors in PoS-Tagged Corpora. In: Shu Chuan Tseng (ed.): *Proceedings of the 19th International Conference on Computational Linguistics (COLING 2002, Taipei)*. Morgan Kaufmann Publishers, San Francisco, 509–515.

Oliva, K., Hnátková, M., Květoň, P., Petkevič, V. (2000): The Linguistic Basis of a Rule-Based Tagger of Czech. In: Sojka P., Kopeček, I., Pala, K. (eds.): *Proceedings of the Third International Workshop, TSD2000, LNAI 1902*. Springer, Berlin Heidelberg, 3–8.

Oliva, K. (2001): The Possibilities of Automatic Detection / Correction of Errors in Tagged Corpora: A Pilot Study on a German Corpus. In: Matoušek, V., Mautner, P., Mouček, R., Taušer, K. (eds.): *Proceedings of the Third International Workshop, TSD2001, LNAI 2166*. Springer, Berlin Heidelberg, 39–46.

Vladimír Petkevič
Charles University
Faculty of Arts
Institute of Theoretical and Computational Linguistics
Celetná 13
110 00
Czech Republic
e-mail: Vladimir.Petkevic@ff.cuni.cz

Kiril Simov and Petya Osenova, Sofia

A Treatment of Coordination in the Bulgarian HPSG-based Treebank

1 Introduction

In this paper, we present a treatment of coordination on the following basis: HPSG-oriented, induced by Bulgarian data, and correlating systematically with *ellipsis* and *pro-dropness*. We propose an analysis, which is based on the notions of *head's saturation* and *grammatical function* rather than *syntactic category*. The analysis is implemented within the annotation scheme of the HPSG-based Syntactic Treebank for Bulgarian - BulTreeBank. Our motivation for it is twofold. First, we try to present a solution, which is widely applicable to various types of texts. Second, the treatment has to be in accordance with the rest of the annotation scheme for the treebank. It must not violate any of the other principles of the syntactic treatment of the phenomena in the treebank.

In the treatment of coordination on the syntactic level, three main questions play a significant role: (1) what is the category of the coordinated phrase; (2) what are the selectional features of the coordination phrase; and (3) what is its phrase structure. The first two questions determine the behaviour of the coordinated phrase in bigger phrases. The last problem is connected with mechanisms which allow for the construction of coordinated phrases with the relevant categorial and selectional information. In our approach, we assume a flat phrase structure for coordination in which the coordinators and the conjuncts are taken simultaneously. The main problems with coordination arise in cases where the coordinated phrases do not agree in their categories or selectional requirements. In this paper we present our solution to these problems. A hierarchy of possible coordination phrases in the treebank is also presented.

Coordination is one of the most problematic and controversial linguistic phenomena and, consequently, one of the most frequently approached ones by linguists. This fact is due to two main reasons: (1) it is interconnected with other interesting phenomena like *ellipsis, parasitic gaps, free relatives, agreement, pro-dropness* etc., and (2) it is idiosyncratic with respect to both constituency and dependency relations. The proper handling of coordination is very important for the annotation and processing of language resources. At the same time, this phenomenon still remains a 'hard nut' cross-theoretically. Its theoretical unclearness inevitably influences the adequacy/inadequacy of the linguistic decisions in practice. For that reason, when dealing with real dependency-based or dependency-tolerant annotation schemes, one solution is to underspecify the coordinator in some sense or to make decisions, which are positionally-based and not so much linguistically motivated.

Here are some examples from Treebank annotation decisions: In the Prague dependency Treebank (Hajičová et al. 1999), the conjunctions at the tectogrammatical level are not represented by nodes of their own, but they are connected to content words. Constituent coordination is preferred to sentential one, and the missing parts within conjuncts are restored. In the dependency version of TuBa-D (Kübler and Telljohann 2002) the conjunctions within coordinations do not depend on the head of the whole construction and therefore, they are attached to their right conjunct. Only sentence-initial coordinators depend on the head of the sentence. In contrast to NEGRA, in the TIGER treebank (Brants et al. 2002), the shared arguments of the verbs are not attached to the nearest verb, but they are explicitly pointed to by secondary edges. This solution seems to be ideologically closer to Sag's suggestion (Sag 2002).

The structure of the paper is as follows: In section 2, the HPSG language model is discussed. Also, we introduce briefly the BulTreeBank annotation scheme. In section 3, different approaches to coordination are outlined. Section 4 presents some relevant Bulgarian data. In section 5, our proposal for the treatment of coordination is given. Section 6 summarizes our conclusions and outlook.

2 The HPSG language model and the annotation scheme

In this section we first present the general language model, accepted within HPSG, which we use for the creation of our treebank. HPSG is a lexicalist linguistic theory, in which the linguistic objects are represented via feature structures. An HPSG grammar comprises a linguistic ontology (sort hierarchy) and grammar principles (constraints over the sort hierarchy). The sort hierarchy represents the main types of linguistic objects and their basic characteristics. The principles impose restrictions on the objects and thus predict the well-formed phrases. A basic mechanism for ensuring the right sharing of information among the various parts of the linguistic objects is *co-reference*. Within our Treebank, we rely on the standard sort hierarchy of signs: the sort *sign* with subsorts *word* and *phrase*. It is a complex entity that is assigned two features: PHON (string of phonemes) and SYNSEM (syntactic and semantic characteristics). Further within the attribute SYNSEM, there are three important features: CATEGORY (which encodes syntactic information), CONTENT (which encodes semantic information), and CONTEXT (which encodes pragmatic information). The selectional force of signs is represented via three features: ARG(ument)-ST(ructure), VAL(ency), and MOD(ifier). The ARG-ST value is a list of the arguments of a lexical item. The value of the VAL feature is divided into SUBJ(ect), COMP(lement) and SPEC(ifier) features. Each of them has a list value corresponding to the dependents of the respective kind (in our work we do not use specifiers). The values of the valency lists are connected with the ARG-ST list of the lexical head. The valency lists determine the realized arguments of the lexical head. The MOD feature determines the selection of the head by an adjunct. Its value is a synsem object. The constituent structure is encoded for each phrase via the attribute DTRS. Assigning different values to this feature, HPSG theory distinguishes between (at least) the following types of phrases – *headed-phrase* and *non-headed-phrase*. The first kind is additionally divided into *head-complement*, *head-subject*, *head-adjunct* and *head-filler*. The hierarchy of phrases that we assume is the following:

```
sign
     PHON : phonlist
     SYNSEM : phonlist
  word
  phrase
       DTRS : dtrs
     headed-phrase
          head-complement
          head-subject
          head-adjunct
             head-sem-adjunct
             head-pragmatic-adjunct
          head-filler
     non-headed-phrase
```

The distinction between *head-sem-adjunct* and *head-pragmatic-adjunct* is on the basis of whether the given adjunct modifies the semantics of the head or its pragmatic nature only. An example of a pragmatic adjunct are the vocative phrases in Bulgarian – see Osenova and Simov (2002). The *head-filler* phrases account for the cases of unbounded dependency. The *non-headed-phrase* is used for dealing with coordination phrases.

The linearization of the constituents in HPSG is separated from the constituent structure and in this way, the theory allows for different orders of the same constituent structure and discontinuous realization of the constituents. This separation ensures the representation of grammatical relations within the constituent structure. The actual realization of the head dependents is governed by a set of immediate dominance schemata. The realization of the dependents follows the sequence: *complements -> subject -> adjuncts*. The actual number and kind of dependents is determined by lexical elements within each phrase. There are two selectional mechanisms in HPSG: The *valency principle*, which ensures the selection of complements and subjects of the head, and the *modifier principle*, which is responsible for the selection of the head by an adjunct. The two principles work over the constituent structure of the sign. The valency principle ensures that for each phrase of type head-complement, the complement (COMP) valency list of the head daughter is the same as the concatenation of the synsem values of the non-head daughters. Similarly for the head-subject phrase. A sign with empty valency lists is *saturated.* The modifier principle stipulates that for each head-adjunct phrase, the value of the MOD feature of the non-head daughter is the same as the synsem value of the mother. These two principles play a major role in the modeling of coordination. The other important principle that we consider is the Head Feature Principle which says that for each headed phrase, the HEAD value is equal to the HEAD value of the head daughter. In case of coordination (which is a non-headed-phrase) we have to specify similar principles that govern the percolation of the head values of the conjuncts to the coordination phrase.

In order to reflect the above informally stated HPSG theory we designed an annotation scheme which encodes the following information: *constituency* – each sign is represented as a phrasal label corresponding to the *category* of the sign; *head dependent relation* – the labels in the annotation scheme reflect the type of the phrase (head-complement, head-subject etc*);* *linear order* – the original word order is preserved and where necessary discontinuous elements are introduced; *co-referential relations* – each non-inferable co-referential relation is stated explicitly; *unexpressed elements* – unexpressed subject and ellipsis are represented explicitly. Pro-dropness is a characteristic feature of Bulgarian and when necessary, it is represented as a *pro-ss* element. In each headed phrase, the head daughter is represented implicitly and can be inferred automatically. The mechanism of *co-reference* is used for phenomena like pro-dropness, secondary predication, binding etc. Thus in the annotation scheme, the following types of elements have been distinguished:

Syntactico-phrasal elements

VPA(djunct) for verbal head-adjunct phrases, NPC(omplement), etc

Lexical elements

N, V, Prep, etc

Functional elements

Disc(ontinous), E(xtracted)

The phrasal domain in the annotation scheme reflects the standard HPSG hierarchy for the possible head values of signs:

- head
  - substantive(subst)
    - PRD : boolean
    - MOD : mod-synsem none for not adjuncts
      - noun
        - CASE : case
      - verb
        - VFORM : vform
        - AUX : boolean
        - INV : boolean
      - adj
      - prep
        - PFORM : pform

One of the important questions in the treatment of coordination in HPSG is how the head value of the coordination is determined? In the rest of the paper we present our solution to this question with respect to BulTreeBank annotation scheme.

3 Approaching coordination. The 'hard nuts'.

The usual problems connected with coordination can be generalized as follows: (1) asymmetricity/symmetricity in interpretations, and (2) the influence of inner and outer factors on the coordinated phrase. Within coordinated phrases, there are three main types of impact: (a) coordination of unlike categories, (b) differing selectional force of the head, (c) head-dependent relations. Outside the coordinated phrase, subject-verb agreement is considered. Note that problems (1) and (2) interleave. Let us briefly discuss them.

3.1 Unlike categories

One of the issues to be discussed is the so called 'unlike categories' coordination, where the conjuncts have different syntactic categories like NP and PP, or AP and PP etc. Some of these combinations are possible, but some of them are not. Let us recall two examples, taken from (Sag 1985, p. 118):

(1) Pat has become a banker and very conservative. (NP and AP)

(2) * John sang beautifully and a carol. (AdvP and NP)

The suggestions for handling such phenomena are basically two: (1) to assign some common syntactic category for the conjuncts, which is underspecified with respect to compatibility with appropriate free-context grammar rules, or (2) to introduce new sorts reflecting possible combinations of relevant features. The former one means that sometimes the consistent analyses do not need the maximal (most specific) sorts, but rather relies on more general ones in the hierarchy. The latter would make the treatment too complex.

Thus, following the first approach, the grammaticality in the first example is guaranteed by the fact that the auxiliary verb is introduced via the rule VP -> V XP and the XP is a subset of other categories – NP and AP. Similarly, the non-grammaticality of the second example is due to the fact that the verb is introduced via the rule: VP -> V (NP), where there is no such general common category.

3.2 Differing selectional force of the head

Another important case is when the conjuncts have the same syntactic categories, but they differ in their selectional force (Sag 2002):

(3) Er findet(OBJ.ACC) und hilft(OBJ.DAT) Frauen
he finds and helps women
'He finds and helps women.'

In this example, the first verb requires an accusative object and the second verb a dative one. The solution again lies in the underspecification (here – via syncretism) of the accusative and dative cases of the noun form *Frauen* (*findet Frauen* ([CASE acc]) and *hilft Frauen* ([CASE dat])=*findet und hilft* [COMPS <[CASE a&d]>] -> *findet und hilft Frauen* ([CASE a&d]). The rest of the German examples as well as the translation in an analytical language like Bulgarian show that it is better to store the generalization higher, namely at the COMPS list, and thus closer to the grammatical roles than to the syntactic categories. In more general terms, the following is proposed in Sag (2002:5): to keep the notion of totally well-typed feature structures and to abandon the requirement, stated in Pollard and Sag (1994), for sort-resolvedness.

Another related problem when handling the selectional force of the head in coordination is to set a dividing line between the so-called *constituent coordination* and *sentential coordination*. It is especially necessary in structures with shared subjects and/or objects. One of the solutions here is connected with the *across-the-board* movement principle (due to Ross 1967). This principle licenses pre-coordination or *conjunction reduction*, in this case – VP-coordination. However, there is evidence that such an analysis is inadequate with respect to languages like Welsh (Sadler 2003) and Icelandic (Rögnvaldsson 2003). Additionally, there seem to be problems with identity for the deletion operator and the ATB extraction is re-defined as not relying on identical elements, but rather on argument indices (Munn 1998).

3.3 Head-dependent relations

The other problem, as mentioned above, concerns the relation head-dependent within the coordination. It means that there is no one solution to the question what is the head in the coordination phrase, if at all. There are several approaches here: (1) multiheadedness (GPSG), (2) non-headedness or flat structure (Pollard and Sag 1994), and (3) treating conjunctions as weak syntactic heads (Abeille 2003), among others. However, all approaches suffer from problems, and the role of the coordinators remains unclear.

In Sadler (2002), for example, single conjunct agreement with the verb in the sentence is discussed for Welsh and other languages. It is along the lines of LFG, in which two kinds of properties are distinguished: *distributive ones* (they hold of each member of the set) and *non-distributive ones* (they hold of the set as a whole). The possibility of treating the coordination as head-adjunct structure is rejected. In Sadler (2003), sentential coordination is not viewed as *precoordination* of shared elements, but as feature-spreading from the shared element (mostly – subject) of the first conjunct to the second one.

All the considerations listed above lead to two complementary solutions – *un(der)specification of some features and spreading relevant features to the right place*. Here, by the first notion we have in mind *suppressing the linguistic information* to the level which would ensure unproblematic application of the coordinating mechanism. It is up to us to decide what that level is. In our approach the mechanism of spreading features is generalized not only over coordination, but over pre-coordination too.

4 Bulgarian data

Let us now consider some examples from Bulgarian. The data presented here is taken from BulTreeBank. The examples demonstrate different kinds of coordination that we would like to cover in the annotation scheme. The brackets *]* and *[* delimit the coordination phrase. The brackets *}* and *{* delimit each non-conjunction part of the coordination.

4.1 Lexical coordination

Typically, each lexical category in Bulgarian (excepts for participles, interjections, clitics) can be coordinated on lexical level. This means that the coordination is a lexical sign, which has the same values for its VAL and MOD features as the coordinated lexical signs. Here we present an example of verbal lexical coordination:

(4) Tja umeeše da [{prigotvi} i {natâkmi}] vsičko mnogo dobre
she can_{impf} da prepare and adjust everything very well
'She could prepare and adjust everything very well.'

In the above sentence, we have the special *da* construction in Bulgarian, where the verbal particle *da* takes a lexical verb and forms again a lexical sign, which inherits the ARG-ST list of the verb. In this case the two verbs agree in their ARG-ST lists (MOD feature in this case has empty values) and coordination is possible at this level. Thus, the coordination is *prigotvi i natâkmi*.

4.2 Sentential and clausal coordination

Modal and some auxiliary verbs in Bulgarians select for saturated VPs (clauses). Here the coordination is not a problem because the VPs are saturated and their valency lists are empty. Thus they trivially agree in their valency lists. Also they are selected by some of the head features like clausality and the type of the clauses.

(5) Toj$_1$ šteše [{da stoi$_1$ v grada} i {da se obučava$_1$ v strelba}]
he will$_{past}$ da stay in town$_{def}$ and da REFL learn in shooting
'He would stay in the town and learn to shoot.'

In this example, we again have a *da* construction formed from two verbs, but they do not agree on their ARG-ST lists and consequently – on their valency lists. Thus the construction possible in example (4), is not possible here. Because the coordination is selected by the verb *šteše*, it means that the two coordinating phrases have unexpressed subjects and thus they are saturated VPs. The unexpressed subjects are co-referent to the expressed subject of the verb *šteše* (index 1).

(6) [{Deteto$_1$ xvana stareca$_2$ za râka} i {go$_2$ povede$_1$}]
child$_{def}$ takes$_{aor}$ old-man$_{def}$ for hand and him accompanies$_{aor}$
'The child took the old man's hand and accompanied him in his way.'

Here we have a sentence in which the two verbs have identical valency lists, but the first also has an adjunct *za râka* which has to be realized after the realization of the subject. For this reason, it is a coordination of two sentences (clauses, saturated VPs). The second sentence has an unexpressed subject that is co-referential with the subject of the first one – index 1 in the example. Index 2 expresses the co-referential relation between the complement in the first clause and the complement clitic in the second.

4.3 NP internal coordination

NP internal coordination is a coordination of modifiers of the head noun (adjectives, adverbs, relative clauses, and prepositional phrases).

(7) V tišinata se noseše [{ravnijat} i {samoten}] glas na kukuvicata
in silence$_{def}$ REFL come monotonic$_{def}$ and lonely voice of cuckoo$_{def}$
'In the silence there was coming the monotonic and lonely voice of the cuckoo.'

Here the coordination is between two adjectives, which are adjuncts (modifiers) of the head noun. They agree in their MOD feature. There are some cases in which this kind of coordination is not possible, because the values of the MOD features do not agree. For instance:

(8) Dokumentât e podpisan ot [{bâlgarskoto} i {grâckoto}] pravitelstvo.
document$_{def}$ is signed by Bulgarian$_{def}$ and Greek$_{def}$ government
'The Bulgarian and the Greek governments signed the document.'

Here the potential coordination *bâlgarskoto i grâckoto* is not possible, because the referents to which the semantics of the two adjectives is connected cannot be the same object. In cases like this, we use ellipsis to distinguish the two referents. Then the analysis is as follows:

(9) Dokumentât e podpisan ot [{bâlgarskoto EL_1} i {grâckoto $pravitelstvo_1$}].
document$_{def}$ is signed by Bulgarian$_{def}$ EL and Greek$_{def}$ government
'The Bulgarian and the Greek governments signed the document.'

In this case, the coordination is of two NPs, one of which including an ellipsis (EL). The index shows the elliptic element.

4.4 NP-coordination

This is a coordination of two saturated NPs. A crucial problem is the determination of agreement features of the coordination. They are set via principles similar to Head Feature Principle. Here we have coordination between two NPs, which are complements of the preposition.

(10) Izbirateljat ne pravi razlika meždu [{SDS} i {BSP}]
electorate$_{def}$ not make$_{3sg}$ difference between SDS and BSP
'The electorate does not make difference between SDS and BSP.'

4.5 Adjunct coordination

Sentential adjuncts can be coordinated when their MOD features agree in their values. The category of the coordination does not play any role in such constructions and can be underspecified without losing relevant information.

(11) Tja_1 otide doma [{bârzo} i {$razvâlnuvana_1$ kato mlado momiče}]
She go$_{aor}$ home quickly and excited like young girl
'She went home quickly and excited like a young girl.'

In this example, the coordination phrase is an adjunct of the VP phrase. Their MOD features agree in their selection requirements being intersective adjuncts. The index represents the fact that the second conjunct is a secondary predication and is co-referent with the subject *tja*.

These examples demonstrate that coordination cannot connect signs of different degree of saturation and different grammatical roles.

In the sentence below, the two verbs are coordinated and they share the same object. Following the principle of dependents realization: *complements -> subject -> adjuncts*, the subject *toj* separates the verb-complement phrase and for that reason it is marked as *DiscA*, which means that it is realized as a constituent at a higher node:

(12) (VPS nid_1 (VPC(Koj myzh) (DiscA toj_1 [{nameri} i {intervjuira}])))?
which man he found and interviewed
'Which man did he find and interview?'

In all other non-discontinuous cases, we treat subjects at sentential level with a co-reference mechanism to the *pro* in the second clause. In cases of long-distance dependency, the appropriate SLASH feature ensures the right head dependent realization, but we will not discuss these cases here. In (12), brackets mark constituent structure, *nid* stands for the non-immediate dominance relation between the head-subject verbal phrase and the discontinuous phrase.

The selectional preference of the head sometimes can be violated due to some specific properties of wh-words. For example, it concerns the possibility for a coordination of a *subject* and an *adjunct*. In such cases the ATB-like explanation is blocked, and the only reasonable solution would be the ellipsis of the verb in order to keep the dependent realization consistent:

(13) [{Koj} i {koga}] dojde?
who and when came
'Who came and when?'

When an ellipsis of the verb is introduced, the coordination is transferred to the sentential level. Thus, instead of coordinating dependents with two different grammatical roles, we coordinate two clauses:

(14) [{Koj <dojde>$_1$} i {koga dojde$_1$}]?

5 Our proposal

From the presented data and the discussion of the other approaches to coordination it follows that the underlying idea is: conjuncts within a coordination have to agree in their grammatical function in spite of their syntactic category. Such an approach explains the data well. If we reconsider examples (1) and (2) from Section 3, we will see that the first example is grammatical because the verb is copula-like and takes complements. In the second example, however, the verb is meaningful and takes different kinds of dependents – complements, adjuncts, which cannot cross-coordinate. Thus our hypothesis on coordination relies on the following three assumptions:

- The grammatical role of the conjuncts is decisive
- The syntactic categories play a secondary (complementary) role
- The basic factor is the valency of the conjuncts

We assume that coordination has to be treated as a *non-headed phrase* with the following requirements:

- The conjuncts have to agree in their valency potential: *valency lists and MOD feature*
- They can be underspecified with respect to the category: extension of the head value hierarchy

In this respect, we propose not to obligatorily classify each coordination as NP coordination, VP coordination etc., but to classify the coordination as *saturated coordination, adjunct coordination* and *unsaturated coordination.* Saturated coordination has empty valency lists, and the MOD feature has value *none*. Adjunct coordination has empty valency lists, and the MOD feature has a value different from *none*. Unsaturated coordination has at least one non-empty valency list. In most of the cases, the non-conjunction daughters of the coordination may also share the values of their other head features, but in some cases they disagree on them. In order to account for such cases, we changed the sort hierarchy by introducing the distinct sort *coordination*, which is at the same level in the sort hierarchy as *noun*, *verb*, *adj*, and *prep* sorts. In this way we underspecify the head of the coordination. Here is the modified sort hierarchy:

head
substantive(subst)
  PRD : boolean
  MOD : mod-synsem   none for not adjuncts
    coordination
    noun
      CASE : case
    verb
      VFORM : vform
      AUX : boolean
      INV : boolean
    adj
    prep
      PFORM : pform
    ...

This change in the sort hierarchy also has impact on the definition of selectional constraints in the lexicon. One more refined model can include sub-sorts of the sort *coordination,* which reflect the syntactic category of the coordination, if such can be assigned on the basis of the daughters of the coordination phrase. And it will be an underspecified sort for cases in which it is impossible to assign a syntactic category. Such sub-sorts can include sorts like *np-coordination, vp-coordination, ap-coordination, adjunct-coordination* with appropriate features. Having such an extended hierarchy for coordination, we also define specific principles for assigning appropriate head values for each type of coordination. When some of the coordinated signs disagree with the rest in their selectional requirements, ellipses are used in order to satisfy them. We consider pro-dropness as a special case of ellipsis.

Implementing this approach in the annotation scheme has the problem that in some cases, there is more than one analysis with coordination on different levels. For example, in some cases two head-complement VPs require the same type of subject and can be conjoined in a coordination, and then they select the joined subject. But there is also an analysis in which the subject is realized within the first clause and it co-referent with the unexpressed subject within the second clause. For such cases we define preference rules for annotators. For example: *prefer constituent coordination to ellipsis*; prefer *clausal coordination to verbal one*.

6 Conclusion

In this paper we report on a treatment of coordination in an HPSG-based treebank. Coordination appears to be a phenomenon which sharply raises questions about the connection between syntactic categories and grammatical relations. Our main ideas are as follows:

- Coordination is an alternative to the usual POS categories like noun, verb etc.;
- Saturation and grammatical function play a more important role in the coordination treatment than the assignment of the traditional syntactic category;
- The treatment of shared head dependents has to do with the broader context.

This preliminary analysis satisfies the requirements of the construction of the treebank, but needs further development in the direction of the semantic contribution of the coordination, for instance. Also an HPSG theory of ellipses is necessary to be developed. For the moment, it has to be left for future work.

7 References

Abeille, A. 2003. A Lexicon- and Construction-Based Approach to Coordinations. In: Müller, S. (ed.), *Proceedings of the 10th International Conference on Head-Driven Phrase Structure Grammar*. CSLI Publications, Stanford, 5–25.

Brants, S., Dipper, S., Hansen, S., Lezius, W. and G. Smith. 2002. TIGER Treebank. In: Hinrichs, E. and K. Simov (eds.), Proceedings of the Workshop on Treebanks and Linguistic Theories (TLT2002), Sozopol, 24–42.

Hajičová, E., Kruijff-Korbayova, I. and P. Sgall. 1999. Prague Dependency Treebank: Restoration of Deletions. In: Matoušek, V., Mautner, P., Ocelíková, J. and P. Sojka (eds.), *Text, Speech and Dialogue* (= Springer Lecture Notes in Artificial Intelligence 1692), Springer, Berlin, 44-49.

Kuebler S. and H. Telljohann. 2002. Towards a Dependency-Oriented Evaluation for Partial Parsing. In: Carroll, J., Frank, A., Lin, D., Prescher, D. and H. Uszkoreit (eds.), *Beyond PARSEVAL – Towards Improved Evaluation Measures for Parsing Systems (LREC 2002 Workshop)*, Las Palmas, 9–16.

Munn, A. 1998. ATB movement without Identity. In: Austin, J. and A. Lawson (eds.), *Proceedings of ESCOL 97.*

Osenova, P. and K. Simov. 2002. Bulgarian Vocative within HPSG framework. In: Kim, J.-B. and S. Wechsler (eds.), *Proceedings of the 9th International Conference on Head-Driven Phrase Structure Grammar (HPSG)*, Seoul, 233-244.

Pollard, C. and I. A. Sag. 1994. *Head-Driven Phrase Structure Grammar.* University of Chicago Press, Chicago.

Rögnvaldsson, E. 2003. *Coordination, ATB-extractions, and the Identification of pro*. ms., University of Iceland and Harvard University. http://www.hi.is/~eirikur/coord.pdf

Ross, J. R. 1967. *Constraints on variables in syntax.* PhD thesis, MIT, Boston.

Louisa Sadler. 2002. Coordination and Asymmetric Agreement in Welsh. In Butt, M. and T. H. King (eds.), *Nominals: Inside and Out*, CSLI Publications, Stanford, 85-118.

Louisa Sadler. 2003. *Function spreading in Coordinate Structures.* Paper presented at the 4th Celtic Linguistics Conference, Cambridge, September 2003.

Sag I., Gazdar G., Wasow T. and Weisler S. 1985. *Coordination and how to distinguish categories.* In: Natural Language and Linguistic Theory 3, 117-171.

Sag I. 2002. Coordination and Underspecification. In: Kim, J.-B. and S. Wechsler (eds.), *Proceedings of the 9th International Conference on Head-Driven Phrase Structure Grammar (HPSG)*, Seoul, 267–291.

Phonetics and Phonology

Bistra Andreeva and Jacques Koreman, Saarbrücken

The Status of Vowel Devoicing in Bulgarian: Phonetic or Phonological?

Abstract

Vowel devoicing at phrase boundaries is shown to depend on sentence mode (statement, question) and information structure (non-contrastive vs. contrastive and broad vs. narrow focus), which affect the type of nuclear accent and boundary tone. In *li*-questions, considerably less devoicing of the vowels before the phrase boundary is found than in other conditions, because the rising boundary contour prevents devoicing. In all other conditions, mode and information structure only affect the realisation of the vowel in the two syllables before the phrase boundary if the nuclear accent is realised on the last content word of the phrase, just before the boundary. In these positions, the differences in observed vowel devoicing are related to the intonational properties of the utterance, namely to the accent type. In particular, the peak scaling and alignment of the accent explains the presence or absence of voicing, or better the amount of devoicing, since it is clearly a gradient, phonetic phenomenon. In general, the lower and earlier the peak, the greater the tendency towards devoicing.

1. Introduction

In the phonetic typology of Slavic languages Bulgarian is said to be a language with accommodative pronunciation, which is characterised by a large number of contextually conditioned allophones of vowels and consonants, motivated either by the direct segmental context or by their position in the syllable/word or by their distance from the accented syllable. Bulgarian has strong qualitative vowel reduction, depending on accent (Level 2 in the first pre-tonic and in all post-tonic syllables, Level 1 elsewhere) (Tilkov et al. 1982). To our knowledge, no vowel devoicing has been reported in the literature, except in Andreeva et al. (2003).

Vowel devoicing is a well-known phenomenon in a large number of languages (Gordon 1998) and depends on the quality and duration of the vowel, its segmental context, speech rate, level of stress, pitch and morpho-phonological boundaries. It is sometimes also employed for phrase boundary demarcation in addition to boundary tones and F0 resets, final lengthening and voice quality in general (Dauer 1980; Smith 1999). In a recent exploratory analysis of segmental deviation from the canonical phonetic form, intonation-dependent elision and reduction of phrase-final unstressed vowels was observed in a falling (L-L%), but not in a rising (L-H% or H-H%) tonal contour in the spontaneous (Map Task) and read speech recordings of Sofia Bulgarian and of Moscow Russian (Barry & Andreeva 2001). In addition, as we reported in Andreeva et al. (2003), phrase endings can also be marked by vowel devoicing under the same condition.

On closer inspection of the Map Task and read speech data, however, we noticed that there is some variation as to the exact positions and tonal context in which vowel devoicing applies. In order to evaluate factors which cause vowel devoicing and to examine them in some more detail under strictly controlled conditions, a production experiment was conducted. Particularly we investigate whether vowel devoicing is a categorical, phonological or a gradient, phonetic process like other segmental reduction phenomena. In this paper we summarise and extend our earlier analyses (Andreeva et al. 2003). The following three hypotheses regarding the factors regulating the distribution of devoiced vowels are investigated:

- Vowel devoicing depends on mode and information structure (focus and contrast).
- Vowel devoicing is more likely if the nuclear accent occurs earlier in the phrase.
- Vowel devoicing depends on accent type.

2. Material and Method

The subjects for the first experiment were five persons from Sofia (4 female and 1 male, aged 25-45 years). The following 4 test sentences (with the material relevant to phrasal demarcation underlined) where the information structure is controlled for the analysis of the relation between focus structure and intonation were recorded several times in random order in a sound-treated studio. These sentences are a subset of a larger data set.

(1) *'včera 'mama ni po'maga po gra'matika.*
yesterday mama us helped in grammar
'Yesterday mum helped us in grammar.'

(2) *'včera 'mareto po'maga po gra'matika?*
yesterday Mareto helped in grammar
'Yesterday Mareto helped in grammar?'

(3) a. *'včera 'mama li vi po'maga po gra'matika?*
yesterday mama Q[1] you helped in grammar
'Is it mum who helped you in grammar yesterday?'

b. *'včera 'mama vi po'maga po gra'matika li?*
yesterday mama you helped in grammar Q
'Is it grammar that mum helped you with yesterday?'
'Yesterday mum helped you in grammar, didn't she?'

The statements in the material (sentence 1) were embedded in dialogue exchanges as replies to *wh*-queries uttered by the instructor and were produced three times with broad focus or with contrastive[2] and non-contrastive narrow focus on the first or last content word (*'mama'* or *'gramatika'*).

	broad	narrow non-final	narrow final
statements [-contrast]	x	x	x
statements [+contrast]		x	x
checks [-contrast]		x	x
li-questions [-contrast]	x[3]	x	x[3]

Table 1: Realised focus conditions for four sentence modes (black areas indicate missing focus positions)

Besides statements, the material contains both confirmation-seeking yes-no questions (checks), marked only by intonation (sentence 2), and information-seeking yes-no questions with the interrogative particle *'li'*[3] (sentences 3a and b) produced with narrow focus on the same content words as in the statements. Sentence 2 was produced three times as a reaction to a described situational context, which was constructed to induce focus on the first or the last content word

[1] Q = interrogative particle '*li*'
[2] It may be more appropriate to call these foci *corrective* instead of *contrastive* (cf. Gussenhoven 2006).
[3] Typically '*li*' belongs to the focal segment. When it occurs in sentence-final position an ambiguous focus interpretation arises (broad or narrow in final position).

in the sentence. Sentences 3a and 3b were read four times in a random list. The realised focus conditions across sentence mode are given in Table 1.

The recordings were digitised at a sampling frequency of 16 kHz and with an amplitude resolution of 12 bits, using the Advanced Speech Signal Processing Tool[4]. All data were manually labelled on the basis of the synchronised microphone signal and spectrogram. Since we want to investigate devoicing as a cue for phrase demarcation, the material *'-tika(li)'* after the last lexically stressed vowel in the utterance was labelled in great detail (Fig. 1), in particular the vowels, which were divided into devoiced and modally voiced portions. We used a slightly modified SAMPA-notation for Bulgarian by adding the following symbols: <I-h:> and <@-h:> for devoiced (portions of the) vowels, <t> and <k> for closure, <t-r> and <k-r> for release, and <t-h> and <k-h> for aspiration of the voiceless stops. The aspiration phase after the release of the syllable-initial plosive was analysed as part of the following vowel. There are two reasons for this: first, although the aspiration phase is usually considered to be part of the plosive, it cannot be distinguished from a devoiced realisation of the vowel; second, we observed that the aspiration phase is longer in weakening context such as unaccented syllables, so that it is more appropriate to analyse it as part of the vowel than as part of the consonant (the latter would imply that the consonant is strengthened in unaccented positions). For each of the vowels, the duration of the devoiced signal was divided by the total vowel duration *(relative devoiced vowel portions)*.

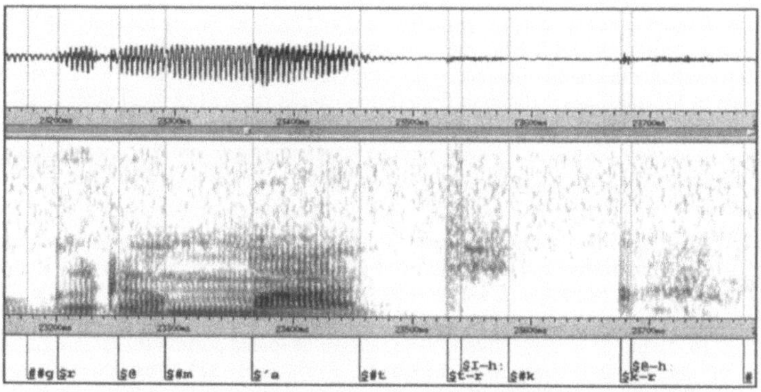

Figure 1: Example of the segmental labelling. The sample material is *'gramatika'*. The labels for the modally-voiced vowels and for the consonants are basically phonemic. For the devoiced (portions of the) vowels there are some phonetic labels, too (<I-h:>, <@-h:>). Special labels are used to refer to sub-phonemic events like closure (<t>, <k>) and release (<t-r>, <k-r>) of voiceless stops.

In addition to the segmental labelling the pitch accents, phrase accents and boundary tones were also labelled, using ToBI (Beckman & Elam 1997), with the peak alignment of the H(igh) tones explicitly specified.

[4] http://www.ipds.uni-kiel.de/forschung/xassp.de.html

3. Results

To analyse the effects on phonatory demarcation, we carried out multivariate analyses of variance, with Scheffé post-hoc tests if appropriate. Significant effects at the 5%-level are reported for the relative devoiced portions of [i] and [a] in the word *'gramatika'*. We shall also report the percentage of *complete* devoicings, which we did not analyse statistically.[5]

3.1. The effect of sentence mode, focus position and boundary tone

To see if there are any phrase-final devoicing effects of mode, focus and focus position, we first compare two sentence modes: statements (with non-contrastive vs. contrastive focus) and questions (checks and *'li'*-questions). They vary with respect to the position of the focus, which either comes on the first or on the last content word. In Andreeva et al. (2001) the focus-associated pitch movements in statements and questions were analysed as follows: Statements and checks with identical morpho-syntactic structure differ only in the nuclear pitch accent and were analysed as L*+H for the checks, as H* with late peak alignment for the contrastive statements and as H* with early peak alignment for non-contrastive statements with broad and narrow focus. The focus-associated accent in *'li'*-questions was analysed as L*+H. In both sentence modes the boundary tones are referred to as L-L%.

3.1.1. Comparison of statements and questions with focus in final position

Although *'li'*-questions are analysed in Andreeva et al. (2001) as having the same nuclear pitch movement as checks (L*+H L-L%), they are not directly comparable. First, when the focus is on the last content word in the utterance, this word is followed by the particle *'li'*. Therefore, the /a/ context in *'li'*-questions is different from that in checks (as well as in all other conditions), since it is followed by /l/ instead of a phrase boundary. This fact is expected to reduce the tendency towards devoicing. Furthermore, a comparison of the penultimate and antepenultimate syllables in *'li'*-questions with the final /ka/ and the penultimate /ti/ in the other conditions is not warranted.

When the focus is on the last content word (final), no complete vowel devoicings occur for checks, while in contrastive and non-contrastive statements 33% and 53% of the /i/'s and 20% and 47% of the /a/'s, respectively, are completely devoiced. On average, /i/ has significantly shorter relative devoiced portions in checks (31%) than in contrastive and non-contrastive statements (65% and 85%, respectively). The relative devoiced portion for /a/ is significantly shorter in checks and contrastive statements (35% and 52% respectively) than in non-contrastive statements (79%). The vowels in non-contrastive vs. contrastive statements never contain modal voicing, while this is only true for /a/ in checks. A large portion of /i/ is modally voiced in checks (69%). In general, a stronger tendency towards vowel devoicing is found in non-contrastive than in contrastive statements, while they are weakest in checks.

We observe that neither /i/ nor /a/ is ever completely devoiced in *'li'*-questions with narrow focus on the last content word (final), although we do sometimes find a short relative devoiced portion (36% for /i/, 28% for /a/). Besides checks with final focus positions, the *'li'*-questions in this condition were the only utterances with modal voicing in /i/ and /a/ (53% and 72%, respectively). Figure 2 shows the distribution of devoicing rate as a function of the sentence mode and focus type in final position.

[5] Wilcoxon tests on the averaged data per subject are possible, but we decided against this because of the small dataset (5 observations per cell).

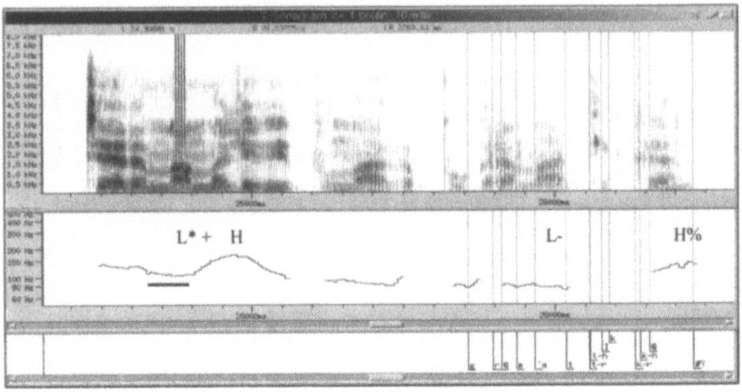

Figure 5: Example of the realisation of L-H% boundary tones in *'li'*-questions (non-final focus)

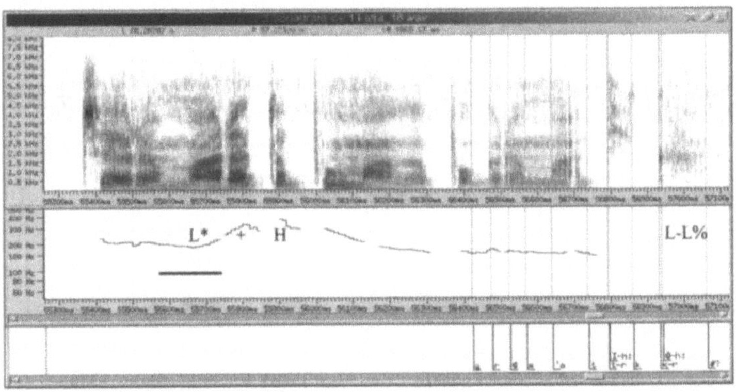

Figure 6: Example of the realisation of L-L% boundary tones in checks (non-final focus)

The finding that the rising boundary contour L-H% prevents devoicing because it requires an increased sub-glottal pressure and a different glottal adjustment compared to the final falling contour [11], fits with the observation in [6] that L-H% also prevents vowel loss and reduction. The fact that we find more devoicing in *'li'*-questions with the non-final accent (cf. Fig. 3) than with a final accent (cf. Fig. 2) is that the syllables under investigation (*'tika'*) are closer to the boundary in the former – since the question particle *'li'* occurs after the nuclear accent early in the phrase in the non-final condition. Additionally, the fact that /a/ occurs in a strong foot position (*'gramatika li'*) and is followed by a sonorant consonant /l/ further reduces devoicing.

3.2. The effect of accent type and position

As expected, differences are only found when there is a focus on the last content word in the phrase and the boundary tone is realised as L-L%. This shows that the vowel realisation in the ultimate and penultimate (post-nuclear) syllables is not dependent on mode per se, but is a consequence of the realisation of the boundary tone as well as the nuclear pitch accent and its position in the utterance. Table 2 summarises the number of pitch accent types used in the different test conditions (numbers given across final and non-final positions). In checks, the pitch accent is *always* realised as L*+H.

Focus x contrast	Accent type				
	H*(early)	!H*(early)	H*(late)	!H*(late)	L*+H
Broad	3	12	0	0	0
Narrow non-contrastive	17	1	12	0	0
Narrow contrastive	2	0	22	8	0
check	0	0	0	0	27

Table 2: Realised accent types for the different test conditions

Broad focus in non-contrastive statements is *always* realised with an early (mostly also downstepped) peak on the last content word in the utterance. The pitch accent signals a complex focus domain in the case of focus projection.

This type of accent was also used in the majority of the narrow non-contrastive foci. When focus is on the last content word the early accent causes ambiguity, since it can be interpreted as a broad focus. Besides an increase in pitch range or emphasis, speakers sometimes use a late peak in an attempt to resolve the ambiguity: we counted 11 early and 4 late peaks in non-contrastive statements with narrow focus in final position.

In contrastive statements, the subjects differ in their realisation of the pitch accent. Like non-contrastive statements, these also have falling nuclear pitch accents, but there is a stronger tendency towards realising late peaks in contrastive statements (2 early and 30 late peaks in final and non-final position).

To test the effect of the particular pitch accent, we shall compare the accents listed in Table 2 in final and non-final position, namely L*+H, with late peak alignment in the post-accentual syllable(s), (!)H*, with late peak alignment at the end of the accented syllable, and (!)H*, with early peak alignment (early in the accented or in the pre-accented syllable). The boundary tones in the test sentences are realised as L-L%. In the non-final conditions there was no significant effect on the devoiced portions in /i/ and /a/: Both vowels showed a strong tendency to devoice, caused by the decrease of sub-glottal pressure and the resulting low volume velocity airflow, which in turns inhibits voicing [3, p. 100]. Therefore we shall report the results for focus *in final position only* (cf. Fig. 7-11).

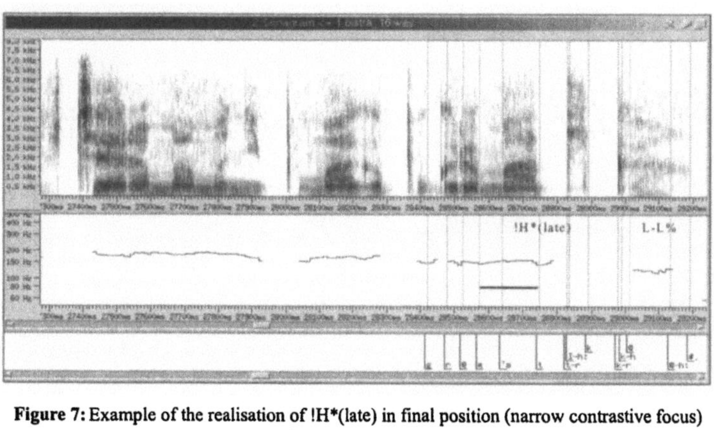

Figure 7: Example of the realisation of !H*(late) in final position (narrow contrastive focus)

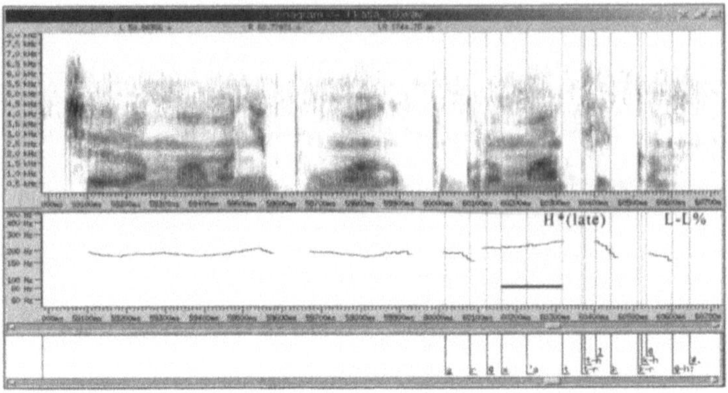

Figure 8: Example of the realisation of H*(late) in final position (narrow contrastive focus)

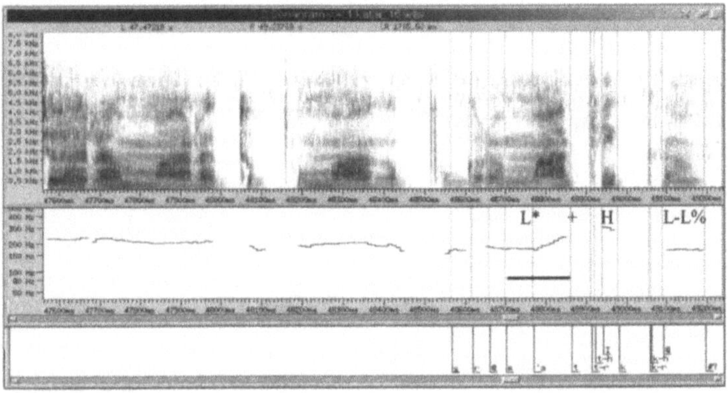

Figure 9: Example of the realisation of L*+H in final position (check)

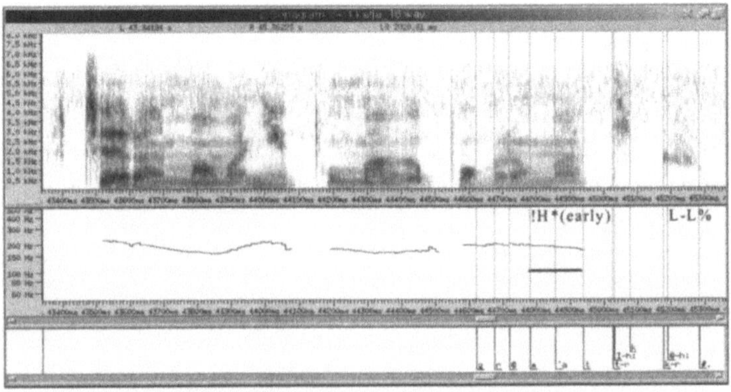

Figure 10: Example of the realisation of !H*(early) in final position (broad focus)

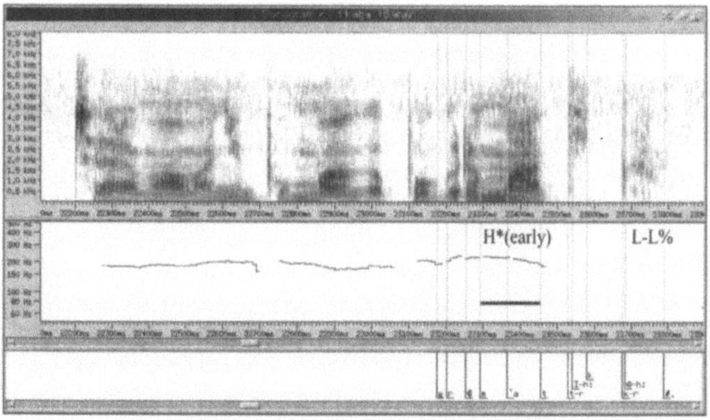

Figure 11: Example of the realisation of H*(early) in final position (narrow non-contrastive focus)

If we reanalyse the utterances with final focus with respect to accent type, we find that the relative devoiced portion of the /i/ and /a/ is dependent on the peak alignment and height of the pitch accent. The relative devoiced portion of /i/ is significantly larger in !H* (early) than in (!)H* (late) than in L*+H conditions. H* (early without downstep) groups together with H* (late) and !H* (early). Therefore, the earlier and lower the peak, the stronger the tendency to devoice the vowel. For /a/ a significant difference was only found between the (!)H* (early) and the other conditions (L*+H and (!)H* (late)). This is probably because the earlier the peak is aligned, the sooner a low pitch is reached, allowing vowel devoicing.

The pooled results for the data discussed in section 3.2 are shown in Figure 12.

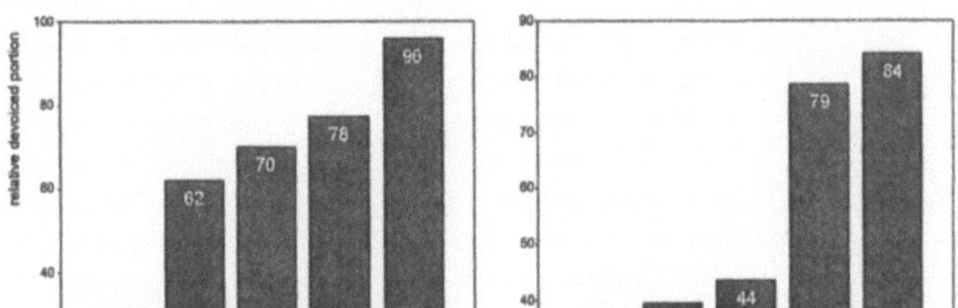

Figure 12: Mean relative devoiced portion for /i/ (left graph) and /a/ (right graphs) for all H* (early), H* (late) and L*+H accents on the last content word, excluding '*li*'-questions

4. Summary

In analogy to the observations for vowel loss and reductions [6], we never observe complete vowel devoicing with final rising intonation contours (*'li'*-questions), while it is quite frequent in falling intonation contours (statements and checks). This is also reflected in the shorter relative devoiced portions in *'li'*-questions as compared to statements and checks. Conversely modal voicing is only found in *'li'*-questions (with focus in final and non-final positions) as well as checks with focus in final position.

For the final falling intonation contours (L-L%), the vowels just before the phrase boundary are (almost) completely devoiced when the nuclear accent comes early in the intonation phrase. When the nuclear pitch accent is realised on the last content word in the phrase, we found that the peak scaling and alignment exert a strong influence on the vowel realisation, since early and downstepped peaks tend to allow for a stronger vowel devoicing than late peaks.

It was also shown that vowel quality determines the strength of the effect, the more closed vowel /i/ being more sensitive to devoicing than /a/.

5. Discussion

The present study, which focuses on Bulgarian, investigates whether vowel devoicing at intonation phrase boundaries is a categorical, functional phenomenon or a gradient, phonetic effect of the implementation of the accent types which signal linguistic functions.

Although vowel devoicing can be phonologically determined (Gordon 1998; Bliese 1976), our results show that it is not in the conditions investigated in the present paper. The choice of the pitch accent is linguistically determined, depending on sentence mode and focus. In turn, the pitch accent influences vowel devoicing. Devoicing occurs when the transglottal pressure is so low that vocal fold vibration can no longer be sustained. The fact that accents early in the phrase do not affect vowel devoicing at the phrase boundary shows that this is not a phonological process. When pitch accents occurs on the last content word in the phrase, the amount of vowel devoicing depends on the scaling and alignment of the accent peak clearly showing a gradient rather than a categorical relationship.

The fact that no devoicing occurs at rising (L-H%) intonation phrase boundaries supports a phonetic analysis. At rising phrase boundaries the transglottal pressure is kept high in order to sustain voicing despite worse phonation conditions caused by stiffening of the vocal folds to reach the high F_0 target, thus preventing devoicing. Further support for the phonetic status of vowel devoicing comes from the observation that there is a stronger tendency towards devoicing for /i/ than for /a/. This coincides with the phonetic argumentation for devoicing, since the drop in transglottal pressure in /i/ is enhanced by the narrower vocal tract compared to /a/.

In conclusion, it was shown that vowel devoicing at the intonation phrase boundary is a gradient, phonetic phenomenon which depends on the phonetic realisation (peak scaling and alignment) of phonological categories (pitch accent type), the choice of which depends on sentence mode and focus type.

References

Andreeva, B., Koreman, J. & Barry, W. J. (2003). "Phonatory demarcations of intonation phrases in Bulgarian." *Proc. of the 15th Int. Congress of Phonetic Sciences (ICPhS 2003)*, Barcelona, pp. 611-614.

Andreeva, B., Avgustinova, T. & Barry, W. J. (2001). "Link-associated and focus-associated accent patterns in Bulgarian." In: Zybatow, G., Junghanns, U., Mehlhorn, G. and Szucsish, L. (eds.) *Current Issues in Formal Slavic Linguistics*, Frankfurt: Peter Lang, pp. 353-364.

Barry, W. J. & Andreeva, B. (2001). "Cross-language similarities and differences in spontaneous speech patterns," *Journal of the International Phonetic Association*, vol. 31/1, pp. 51-66.

Beckman, M. & Elam, G. A. (1997). "Guidelines for ToBI labeling," version 3. Linguistics Department, Ohio State University.

Bliese, L. (1976). „Afar." In: Bender, M. Lionel (ed.). *The Non-Semitic Languages of Ethiopia*. East Lansing, MI: African Studies Center, Michigan State University, pp. 232-277.

Dauer, R. (1980). "The reduction of unstressed high vowels in Modern Greek," *Journal of the International Phonetics Association.* vol. 10, pp. 17-27.

Gordon, M. (1998). "The phonetics and phonology of non-modal vowels: a cross-linguistic perspective," *Berkeley Linguistics Society*, vol. 24, pp. 93-105.

Gussenhoven, C. (2006). "Types of Focus in English." In: Büring, D., Gordon, M. & Lee, C. (eds.). *Topic and* Focus: Cross-linguistic Perspectives on Meaning and Intonation. Dordrecht: Kluwer.

Ladefoged, P. (1967). *Three Areas of Experimental Phonetics.* Oxford University Press, Oxford.

Smith, C. (1999). "Marking the boundary: utterance-final prosody in French questions and statements." *Proc. of the XIVth Int. Congress of Phonetic Sciences (ICPhS 1999)*, San Francisco, pp. 1181-1184.

Tilkov, D., Bojadžiev, T., Georgieva, E., Penčev, J., Stankov, V. (1982). *Gramatika na sâvremennija bâlgarski knižoven ezik (vol. 1): Fonetika,* Sofia: Bâlgarska akademija na naukite.

Ben Hermans, Tilburg

Russian Vowel Reduction with Elements and without Ease of Perception

1. Introduction

Crosswhite (2001) presents an interesting account of vowel reduction in Standard Russian. The main hypothesis defended by Crosswhite is that, cross-linguistically, there are two forces driving vowel reduction: firstly, *ease of perception* requires, among other things, that mid vowels avoid unstressed syllables, and, secondly, *ease of articulation* requires, among other things, that vowels of high sonority avoid unstressed syllables. Crosswhite shows, quite convincingly, that ease of articulation is not sufficient to explain vowel reduction in Russian, because, in certain positions a mid vowel reduces to a vowel of greater sonority. According to Crosswhite, then, Russian is a language where both forces driving reduction are applicable.

Interestingly, ease of perception, as it is applied to Russian vowel reduction by Crosswhite conflicts with some of the conclusions of De Lacey (2002). Crosswhite predicts the existence of systems in which mid vowels attract stress from low vowels, a phenomenon whose existence is vigorously denied by De Lacey.

In this article I try to solve this problem. I propose that there is no family of constraints serving ease of perception. In the analysis of Russian it can be replaced by a family of constraints favoring segments of higher sonority in prominent syllables. As a result of this approach the parallel between vowel reduction and sonority driven stress becomes perfect: all constraint families required to account for vowel reduction are also needed to explain sonority driven stress. This is in accordance with one of the essential hypotheses proposed in De Lacey (2002).

The present proposal is built on two ideas. Firstly, in Russian mid vowels are phonologically RTR (retracted tongue root), which I assume to be phonologically identical to Lax. This corresponds with the fact that they are realized as lower-mid vowels, phonetically. Secondly, it is claimed that RTR-vowels are more sonorous than non-RTR-vowels. The latter claim can be motivated independently with data from Dutch.

At a more formal level the central idea of this paper is that sonority is expressed in terms of A-elements, and the prosodic status of these A-elements in terms of headedness and dependency. Roughly, the idea is that vowels containing an A-element are relatively sonorous, that vowels containing a *head* A-element are more sonorous and that vowels containing a *dependent head* A-element are still more sonorous. The richer the prosodic status of an A-element is the greater its reluctance to occupy a prosodically weak position. This, then, can have two effects in languages: prosodically rich A-elements tend to attract stress (sonority driven stress), or vowels containing these elements in underlying structure lose these elements when they appear in a prosodically weak position (vowel reduction). The final ingredient of the analysis consists of the claim that RTR-vowels have a dependent A-element. As a result, RTR-vowels exhibit the greatest reluctance to occupy unstressed positions. Accordingly, they tend to attract stress (as in Dutch), and they tend to be reduced (as in Russian).

This article is structured in the following way: in the next section I present a sketch of Crosswhite's analysis of vowel reduction in Russian. In the third section I explain why Crosswhite's proposal is problematic. In the fourth section I develop my own analysis.

2. Crosswhite's analysis of vowel reduction in Russian

Russian has two reduction modes: a moderate mode and an extreme mode. Schematically it can be represented as follows:

(1) Moderate reduction (after Crosswhite 2001)

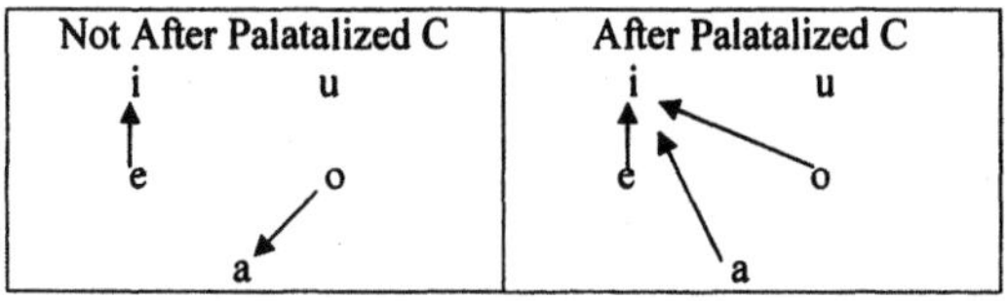

The following data are illustrative:[1]

(2) Not after palatalized C / After palatalized C

/iglá/	[iglá]	'needle'	/pʲilá/	[pʲilá]	'saw, noun'
/ruká/	[ruká]	'hand'	/sʲurtúk/	[sʲurtúk]	'coat'
/etáʒ/	[itáʃ]	'floor'	/rʲeká/	[rʲiká]	'river'
/kotá/	[katá]	'cat, gen.'	/tʲopló/[tʲipló]		'warmly'
/davátʲ/	[davátʲ]	'to give'	/pʲatʲí/	[pʲitʲí/	'five, gen.'

The high vowels do not change. /a/ changes to [i], but only after a palatalized C. /e/ always changes to [i]. /o/ also always changes; it is lowered if not preceded by a palatalized C, otherwise it is raised and fronted.

Moderate reduction applies in syllables that immediately precede stress.[2] Elsewhere extreme reduction applies:

(3) Extreme reduction (after Crosswhite 2001)

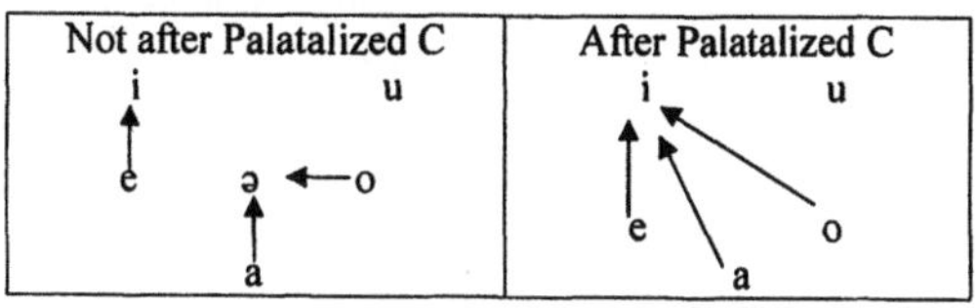

In the following examples extreme reduction applies in the pretonic syllable that is not adjacent to the stressed syllable.

(4) Not after Palatalized C / After Palatalized C

/sinovʲjá/	[sinavʲjá]	'sons' [3]	/mʲilosʲérdnyj/	[mʲilasʲérdnyj]	'merciful'
/kudrʲevátyj/	[kudrʲivátyj]	'ornate'	/lʲudojéd/	[lʲudajéd]	'men eater'
/tsexovój/	[tsixavój/	'shop, A'	/rʲetʃʲovój/	[rʲitʃʲivój]	'speech, adj.'
/gorodók/	[gəradók]	'city,DIM'	/tʲoplotá/	[tʲiplatá/]	'warmth'
/sadovód/	[sədavót]	'gardener'	/pʲatotʃʲók	[pʲitatʃʲók]	'5-kopeck coin'

[1] The Russian data are almost exclusively taken from Crosswhite's work mentioned in the reference list. Particularly important is Crosswhite (2001), which contains a nearly complete overview of the literature on Russian vowel reduction, as well as a detailed analysis of dialectical variation.

[2] The moderate mode also applies to word-initial vowels. Due to lack of space I cannot provide a detailed analysis of this phenomenon. Probably the best approach is in terms of Positional Faithfulness; at the beginning of a word a vowel is relatively faithful to its underlying representation.

[3] Phonetically the high front vowel is retracted after a non-palatalized consonant. I assume that this phenomenon does not belong to phonology proper. I will therefore neglect it.

The difference with moderate reduction is that /o/ and /a/ reduce to schwa if they are not preceded by a palatal consonant.

Crosswhite claims that extreme reduction is driven by *ease of articulation*; this force has the effect of reducing a vowel's sonority in unstressed syllables. Crosswhite also observes that moderate reduction cannot be triggered by ease of articulation, simply because /o/ can be reduced to [a], which is more sonorant than [o].

To explain the change from /o/ to [a] Crosswhite proposes a set of *Licensing* constraints, which facilitate *ease of perception*. These constraints favor peripheral vowels over mid vowels in unstressed position. There are thus two constraint families governing reduction: one favors vowels of low sonority in unstressed syllables (ease of articulation), the other favors peripheral vowels in unstressed syllables (ease of perception).

The distinction between the pretonic syllable that immediately precedes the stress and the remaining unstressed syllables is explained in terms of foot structure. Crosswhite proposes that Russian has an iambic foot and that there is only one foot in a word. The idea, then, is that the unstressed syllable of the foot triggers moderate reduction, whereas the remaining unstressed syllables trigger extreme reduction.

Many aspects of Crosswhite's analysis will play a role in my proposal. I borrow the iamb and also the insight that mid vowels are special with respect to reduction. However, the special character of mid vowels cannot be explained in terms of perceptual ease. That notion creates fundamental problems in the domain of sonority driven stress, as I will show in the next section.

3. Licensing constraints and sonority driven stress

Crosswhite's Licensing constraints are problematic from the point of view of De Lacey (2002). One of De Lacey's central hypotheses is that in a language where stress is sonority driven a vowel of some sonority degree can never attract stress from a more sonorous vowel. This predicts, among other things, that mid vowels can never attract stress from low vowels, because mid vowels are less sonorous than low vowels.

The following two constraint families constitute the core of De Lacey's theory:

(5) (-)DTE-sonority constraints

a) $*\Delta_{(\alpha,\beta)} \leq \text{ə}$, $*\Delta_{(\alpha,\beta)} \leq \{\text{i,u}\}$, $*\Delta_{(\alpha,\beta)} \leq \{\text{e,o}\}$, $*\Delta_{(\alpha,\beta)} \leq \text{a}$

b) $*\text{-}\Delta_{(\alpha,\beta)} \geq \text{a}$, $*\text{-}\Delta_{(\alpha,\beta)} \geq \{\text{e,o}\}$, $*\text{-}\Delta_{(\alpha,\beta)} \geq \{\text{i,u}\}$, $*\text{-}\Delta_{(\alpha,\beta)} \geq \text{ə}$

Δ stands for Designated Terminal Element. For our purposes we can say that DTE is the Head.[4] The rightmost variable specifies the category of the (non-)head; the leftmost variable specifies the head's 'projection'. A few examples might illustrate this formalism: the expression $\Delta_{(\omega,\sigma)}$ denotes the head *syllable* of a prosodic *word* (i.e. the main stressed syllable of the word); $\Delta_{(F,\sigma)}$ denotes the *syllable* head of a *foot*; (i.e. every stressed syllable); $\Delta_{(\omega,F)}$ denotes the *foot* head of a prosodic *word*, etc. In our analysis of moderate reduction we will make use of the last expression. -Δ stands for non-Designated Terminal Element, or, slightly simplifying, non-head. Filling in the variables we get expressions like $\text{-}\Delta_{(\omega,\sigma)}$, which denotes any *syllable* that is not the head of a prosodic *word*. This expression will play an important role in our analysis of reduction in Russian. In the DTE-constraints 'i,u' refers to all high (non-central) vowels, 'e,o' to all mid (non-central) vowels, and 'a' refers to all low vowels.[5] These vowels represent the relevant steps on the notorious sonority scale. Relating the

[4] There are certain differences between DTE and Head. These differences do not concern us here.

[5] In De Lacey's thesis 'ə' represents all mid central vowels. In this article 'ə' literally means 'ə'. I will not discuss central vowels other than schwa. Following Crosswhite I assume that schwa has an empty place node.

sonority scale to expressions of the type just mentioned we derive the (-)DTE-sonority constraints above. Consider the constraint $*\text{-}\Delta_{(\omega,\sigma)}\geq\{e,o\}$. This constraint penalizes any segment that is 1) located in the non-head syllable of a word and 2) has a sonority degree equal to, or higher than the sonority of a mid (non-central) vowel. It thus penalizes mid and low vowels located in a non-head syllable of a word. One final example: $*\Delta_{(\omega,F)}\leq\{e,o\}$ penalizes any vowel which is 1) located in the head foot of a word and which 2) has a sonority degree that is equal to, or smaller than the sonority of a mid vowel.

The (-)DTE-constraints refer to a contiguous range of positions on the sonority scale. The effect of this formulation is that the violation profiles assigned by these constraints are in a relation of proper inclusion. To understand this, consider the violations profiles assigned by the $*\Delta_{(F,\sigma)}$-family.[6]

(6)	$*\Delta\leq a$	$*\Delta\leq\{e,o\}$	$*\Delta\leq\{i,u\}$	$*\Delta\leq ə$
Stressed-a	*			
Stressed-e,o	*	*		
Stressed-i,u	*	*	*	
Stressed-ə	*	*	*	*

The table shows that a stressed syllable containing a vowel of a given sonority harmonically bounds a stressed syllable containing any vowel of lesser sonority, because the violation profile of the former is a proper subset of the profile of the latter. It thus is the case that a stressed low vowel is inherently more harmonic than a stressed mid vowel. This implies that a mid vowel can never attract stress from a low vowel.

This result is undermined by the Licensing constraints proposed by Crosswhite. One instance of this family requires that mid vowels be licensed only in stressed syllables. Let us refer to this constraint as Lic{e,o}. This constraint penalizes any unstressed mid vowel. Consider the following tableau:

(7) What happens if Lic{e,o}is ranked sufficiently high

Ce Ca	Lic{e,o}	$*\Delta\leq\{e,o\}$	$*\Delta\leq a$
Ce Ca (stress on Ca: *)	*!		*
☞ Ce Ca (stress on Ce: *)		*	*

This tableau demonstrates that ranking of Lic{e,o} above $*\Delta_{(F,\sigma)}\leq\{e,o\}$ can derive a system in which mid vowels attract stress from low vowels. Since a system of this type does not exist, this is a highly undesirable result.

If Lic{e,o}would not exist, the non-existing stress system cannot be derived, because the violation profile of a stressed low vowel is a proper subset of a stressed mid vowel's profile. We can conclude, then, that the Licensing constraints of the type proposed by Crosswhite are quite problematic. We should therefore find some other explanation for the fact that in the moderate mode mid vowels are replaced by peripheral vowels. In the next section I will develop a proposal to this effect.

4. An account of Russian vowel reduction based on Elements

In this section I will develop an alternative account of Russian vowel reduction. It consists of two parts. The first part contains the representational part of my proposal. Here, my essential claim is that mid vowels have a more complex structure than the peripheral vowels {i,u,a}.

[6] In the table I have left out the categories F,σ.

Furthermore, I claim that the peculiar behaviour of the Russian mid vowels with regard to stress (in moderate reduction) is not really caused by their mid quality as such, but rather by their *lower*-mid quality. In other words, what really makes them special with respect to stress is their RTR/Lax-character. In terms of elements, RTR is represented as a dependent A-element, that is, an A-element dominated by another element. This greatly adds to complexity. Consequently, RTR-vowels shun unstressed syllables. This claim makes interesting cross-linguistic predictions. It is predicted that not only lower-mid vowels, but in fact the whole class of RTR-vowels tend to avoid unstressed syllables. This again predicts that *all* RTR-vowels (not only lower-mid vowels) tend to reduce to peripheral vowels in unstressed syllables and also tend to attract stress. Both predictions are borne out in Dutch, as I will show. In the second part of this section I work out the constraint ranking that can explain the details of moderate reduction in Russian, and also its relation with extreme reduction.

4.1. The central role of the A-element

In schools of phonology that work with the elements {A,I,U}it has often been claimed that the force driving reduction is elimination of complexity (Harris 1994, and in particular 1997). In this view the peripheral vowels {i,u,a} are simple, because they contain a single element. Mid vowels, on the other hand, are complex, because they consist of a combination of elements. Thus, [e] contains {I,A}, and [o] contains {U,A}. Interesting though this idea might be, it is obvious that it cannot be the whole story. Consider [y]. Quite clearly it is complex, because it contains {I,U}. Yet, it does not reduce more easily than the simple vowels {i,u}. This can readily be explained by the theories proposed in Crosswhite (2001) and De Lacey (2002). In these theories it is explained by the fact that [y] has the same low sonority degree as the vowels {i,u}; since vowels of low sonority are favored in unstressed position, they tend not to undergo reduction. From the point of view of element theories it is obvious, then, that something else, besides complexity triggers vowel reduction.

Building on Anderson (1996) and Scheer (1999, 2003) I propose that the A-element is a relevant factor in vowel reduction, in the sense that it tends to be avoided in unstressed position. At first glance, this does not seem to help us at all. How can /o/ possibly reduce to [a] if reduction is elimination of the A-element! We would expect raising of /o/ to [u], rather than lowering of /o/ to [a]. To solve this problem I propose that in Russian a specific type of A-element tends to be avoided in unstressed syllables, viz. A-elements that are in a dependent position. To explain the notion 'dependent A' I have to explain the notion 'headedness'.

Most linguists working with elements postulate that a segment with feature content must have a head at the feature level. I propose that a vowel's head feature is the 'deepest' feature in the domain of that vowel.[7] Now consider the following representations:

(8) Some examples of headed segments

[i]	[e]	[ɛ]	[u]	[o]	[ɔ]	?	[a]
I	I,A	I,A	U	U,A	U,A	A	A
	│	│		│	│	│	
	I	A		U	A	A	

In the segments {i,e} I is the head. U is the head in the segments {u,o}. In the remaining segments A is the head. I propose that an A-element on top of another element is the equivalent of the traditional feature RTR (retracted tongue root), or Lax. An element dominated by another element I will call 'dependent element'. Dependent-A will play an important role in my analysis of Russian moderate reduction. In the next section I will

[7] Headship is subject to further restrictions, which I have to neglect, due to lack of space.

propose that the Russian mid vowels are RTR/Lax. Phonetically this makes sense, because the Russian mid vowels are clearly relatively low.

Building on De Lacey (2002) I propose that there are two constraint families regulating the interaction between sonority and prominence. One family states that vowels of relatively high sonority avoid non-head positions; the other states that vowels of low sonority avoid head positions. Following primarily Scheer (1999, 2003) I assume that a segment's sonority is determined by its representation, not by its position on some scale, as is traditionally claimed in OT-style analyses. Rather, sonority is read off from a segment's representation by the two families of constraints. I propose the following formulation:

(9) *PRESENCE

$*\text{-}\Delta_{(\alpha,\beta)}F$: Presence of *Feature* is not allowed in Non-Head;
$*\text{-}\Delta_{(\alpha,\beta)}A$: Presence of *A* is not allowed in Non-Head;
$*\text{-}\Delta_{(\alpha,\beta)}A(H)$: Presence of *Head-A* is not allowed in Non-Head;
$*\text{-}\Delta_{(\alpha,\beta)}A(H_{Dep})$: Presence of *Dependent Head-A* is not allowed in Non-Head.

(10) *ABSENCE

$*\Delta_{(\alpha,\beta)}\text{-}F$: Absence of *Feature* is not allowed in Head;
$*\Delta_{(\alpha,\beta)}\text{-}A$: Absence of *A* is not allowed in Head;
$*\Delta_{(\alpha,\beta)}\text{-}A(H)$: Absence of *Head-A* is not allowed in Head;
$*\Delta_{(\alpha,\beta)}\text{-}A(H_{Dep})$: Absence of *Dependent Head-A* is not allowed in Head.

Within each family a given constraint is slightly more complex than the constraint immediately preceding it. As a result, the violation profile assigned by some constraint is a proper subset of the violation profile assigned by the next constraint. To see this consider the following two tables:

(11)	*-ΔF	*-ΔA	*-ΔA(H)	*-ΔA(H_{Dep})
Unstressed-ə				
Unstressed-i,u	*			
Unstressed-e,o	*	*		
Unstressed-a	*	*	*	
Untressed-ɛ,ɔ,ɑ	*	*	*	*

(12)	*Δ-A(H_{Dep})	*Δ-A(H)	*Δ-A	*Δ-F
Stressed-ɛ,ɔ,ɑ				
Stressed-a	*			
Stressed-e,o	*	*		
Stressed-i,u	*	*	*	
Stressed-ə	*	*	*	*

The table in (11) shows that unstressed schwa harmonically bounds any other vowel. In other words, all things being equal, this vowel is the best vowel one can have in unstressed position. High vowels are the next in order. Therefore, if for some reason a schwa is not allowed, high vowels are favored in unstressed position. High vowels harmonically bound mid vowels, which in their turn harmonically bound low vowels, which in their turn harmonically bound RTR/Lax vowels like {ɛ,ɔ,ɑ}. Lax vowels, then, are the worst vowels that can possibly appear in unstressed position. The *ABSENCE-family derives the complementary state of affairs, as is shown in the table in (12). No vowel is worse than a stressed schwa, and no vowel is more harmonic than a RTR/Lax vowel in stressed position.

The two constraint families derive many crucial results obtained in De Lacey's work. Notice in particular that stressed low vowels harmonically bound stressed mid vowels, indicating that the constraint system above cannot derive a system in which mid vowels attract stress from low vowels. We can already tell, then, that an analysis of Russian reduction based on this constraint system will not suffer from the drawbacks of Crosswhite's analysis.

Most members of the families *PRESENCE and *ABSENCE find a parallel in De Lacey's work. We can therefore accept them without further discussion. However, two constraints deserve more attention, because they make rather unusual claims. These are $*\text{-}\Delta_{(\alpha,\beta)}A(H_{Dep})$ and $*\Delta_{(\alpha,\beta)}\text{-}A(H_{Dep})$, the two constraints that specifically evaluate RTR/Lax vowels. According to these constraints Lax vowels avoid unstressed positions with greater rigidity than all remaining vowels, and they also favor stress more forcefully than all other vowels. In short, these constraints predict that RTR/Lax vowels have the highest sonority degree. This should have two effects: firstly, these vowels should undergo reduction in unstressed position more easily than all other vowels; secondly, they should be able to attract stress from all other vowels. Interestingly, it is well know that in many languages RTR/Lax vowels are reduced to their non-Lax (tense) equivalents. In her overview of reduction systems Crosswhite (2001) mentions many languages with this type of reduction. This clearly supports the hypothesis that RTR/Lax vowels indeed have maximal sonority.

As far as stress attraction is concerned, no language has ever been mentioned where RTR/Lax vowels attract stress from other vowels. Yet, there are good reasons to believe that this phenomenon does exist. One of the languages where this phenomenon occurs might actually be Dutch, whose phonology has been extensively studied. It is well known that the default stress of Dutch is on the antepenult syllable if the penult vowel is *tense*. If, however, the vowel in penult position is *RTR/Lax*, the default stress is located on the penult syllable (van der Hulst 1984). Some examples illustrating this pattern are given in (13) and (14).

(13) Tense vowel in penult syllable; stress on antepenult syllable

Can[a]da	'Canada'
mik[a]do	kind of game
reg[i]o	'region'
pag[i]na	'page'
vid[e]o	'video'

(14) RTR/Lax vowel in penult syllable; stress on penult syllable

progr[ɑ]mma	'program'
mad[ɔ]nna	'Madonna'
par[ɔ]chie	'parish'
proc[ɛ]ssie	'procession'
stil[ɛ]tto	'stiletto'

Usually the contrast between (13) and (14) is explained in terms of syllable structure. It is claimed that the penult syllable of the forms in (13) is open, whereas it is closed by a geminate consonant in the forms in (14). In this view the penult syllable is light in (13), whereas it is heavy in (14). The obvious drawback of analyses of this type is that the phonological geminates in forms like those in (14) are phonetically short. This means that the phonetic facts do not support an analysis along these lines. In the constraint system developed here it is not necessary to rely on geminate consonants. In this system default penult stress can be explained in terms of the stress attracting power of RTR/Lax vowels. If correct, this approach lends further credibility to the claim that RTR/Lax vowels indeed have the maximal degree of sonority.

In this section I have developed a theory of vowel reduction and stress attraction based on elements. The essential claim is that RTR/Lax vowels are highly sonorous. Consequently, they shun unstressed positions. For this reason they tend to attract stress (as in Dutch) and they also tend to reduce. This happens in many languages, as has already been shown by Crosswhite. In the next section I will show that Russian reduction can also be explained by a small set of constraints drawn from the two families above. The task of the next section, then, is to determine what these constraints are, and how they are ranked with faithfulness.

4.2. The constraint system

Let us begin with extreme reduction of vowels that are not preceded by a palatalized consonant. The data in (4) have shown that in this mode /o/ and /a/ reduce to schwa, that /e/ is changed to /i/, and that the high vowels do not change at all. The change from /o,a/ to schwa shows that U and A are deleted in unstressed position. Faithfulness to their presence must therefore be lower ranked than the constraint penalizing their presence. I propose that there are three constraint families controlling feature faithfulness:

(15) IDENTITY

a) Corresponding segments have identical *F* (F ∍ {I,A,U}).

b) Corresponding segments have identical *Head-F*.

c) Corresponding segments have identical *Dependent Head-F*

The constraint penalizing presence of U and A in unstressed position must be $*\text{-}\Delta_{(\omega,\sigma)}F$. It requires the elimination of every feature that is not located in a stressed syllable. If $*\text{-}\Delta_{(\omega,\sigma)}F$ is ranked above IDENT-A and IDENT-U, the features U and A are removed from unstressed syllables. This is shown in (16) and (17).

(16) /o/ → schwa; $*\text{-}\Delta_{(\omega,\sigma)}F$ » IDENT-U, IDENT-A

gU,Arodók	$*\text{-}\Delta_{(\omega,\sigma)}F$	IDENT-U	IDENT-A
gU,A (ra dók)	*!*		
gU (ra dók)	*!		*
gA (ra dók)	*!	*	
☞ gə (ra dók)		*	*

(17) /a/ → schwa; $*\text{-}\Delta_{(\omega,\sigma)}F$ » IDENT-U, IDENT-A

sAdovód	$*\text{-}\Delta_{(\omega,\sigma)}F$	IDENT-U	IDENT-A
sA (da vód)	*!		
☞ sə (da vód)			*

The forms under evaluation each have one syllable where extreme reduction applies. This is the unstressed syllable outside the iamb. Only these syllables are considered in the two tableaux.

Obviously, $*\text{-}\Delta_{(\omega,\sigma)}F$ should not lead to the elimination of the element I, because /e/ is not changed to schwa. We can account for this by ranking IDENT-I above $*\text{-}\Delta_{(\omega,\sigma)}F$:

(18) /e/ → [i]; IDENT-I » $*\text{-}\Delta_{(\omega,\sigma)}F$

tsI,Axovój	IDENT-I	$*\text{-}\Delta_{(\omega,\sigma)}F$	IDENT-A
tsI,A (xa vój)		**!	
☞ tsI (xa vój)		*	*
tsA (xa vój)	*!	*	
tsə (xa vój)	*!		*

Since the high front vowel contains just the element I, the ranking in (18) also explains why this vowel does not undergo extreme reduction. However, the behavior of the high back vowel is not so straightforward. The ranking of IDENT-U below $*\text{-}\Delta_{(\omega,\sigma)}F$ incorrectly predicts that it is changed to schwa.

Notice, however, that there is an important difference between the vowels /u/ and /o/. In the former U is the head; in the latter dependent-A is the head. Recall that in our proposal the Russian Lax mid vowels are characterized by a dependent-A. Since this is the deepest element of the segment, it is the head. We can now account for the faithful behavior of /u/ if we rank IDENT-U(H) above $*\text{-}\Delta_{(\omega,\sigma)}F$.

(19) /u/ → [u]; IDENT-U(H) » $*\text{-}\Delta_{(\omega,\sigma)}F$

kU drʲivá tyj	IDENT-U(H)	$*\text{-}\Delta_{(\omega,\sigma)}F$	IDENT-U
☞ kU (drʲi vá) tyj		*	
kə (drʲi vá) tyj	*!		*

The constraint ranking proposed so far explains extreme reduction of vowels that are not preceded by a palatalized C. Let us now turn to the type of extreme reduction that we find after palatalized C.

Recall from (3) and (4) that in this environment /o/ and /a/ reduce to [i], rather than to schwa. I propose that this is a consequence of the spreading of the I-element on the consonant, triggered by I-to-V:

(20) I-to-V
A Vocalic Feature (like I) must be linked to a Vowel.

Spreading is only possible if the vowel does not have any features. This only happens before /o/ and /a/, which lose all their features in extreme reduction, as we have just seen in tableaux (16) and (17). This indicates that I-to-V is dominated by IDENT-U(H), because I-to-V may not eliminate a head-U.[8]

(21) IDENT-U(H) » I-to-V

lʲu dojéd	IDENT-U(H)	I-to-V
☞ lʲu (dajéd)		*
lʲI (dajéd)	*!	
lʲə (dajéd)	*!	*

In its turn I-to-V dominates $*\text{-}\Delta_{(\omega,\sigma)}F$ and also IDENT-I. Otherwise, spreading would be blocked. This is shown in (22) and (23).

[8] We should also evaluate what happens if I spreads and U is maintained. Notice that this creates a place node with two elements. We will see later that three factors conspire to exclude this. Firstly, a complex place node must have a dependent feature; secondly only the A-element can occupy a dependent tier in Russian; thirdly, dependent-A is not allowed in unstressed syllables.

(22) I-to-V » IDENT-I » *-$\Delta_{(\omega,\sigma)}$F

pʲA totʃʲók	I-to-V	IDENT-I	*-$\Delta_{(\omega,\sigma)}$F
pʲA (ta tʃʲók)	*!		*
pʲ?(ta tʃʲók)	*!		
☞ pʲI (ta tʃʲók)		*	*

(23) tʲU,A plota	I-to-V	IDENT-I	*-$\Delta_{(\omega,\sigma)}$F
tʲU,A (platá)	*!		**
tʲə (platá)	*!		
☞ tʲI (platá)		*	*

We now have developed an analysis of extreme reduction. It can be summarized as follows: all elements except I and Head-U are removed from unstressed syllables. Furthermore, the I-element of a palatalized consonant spreads to the right, but spreading is blocked by Head-U. Let us now turn to moderate reduction. First we will look at vowels following a non-palatalized consonant.

Recall from (1) and (2) that in this environment /a/ does not reduce at all, and /o/ reduces not to schwa, but to [a]. This seems to suggest that the A-element cannot easily be eliminated in moderate reduction. In our system this means that *ABSENCE takes effect. The particular instance of this family we need is the following:

(24) *$\Delta_{(\omega,F)}$-A
Absence of A is not allowed in Head-Foot of a word.

This constraint requires the *presence* of an A-element in the domain of the head-foot of a word. I will assume that every vowel located in the head-foot is subject to this constraint.

In the unstressed syllable of the iamb, i.e. the syllable immediately preceding the stressed syllable, *$\Delta_{(\omega,F)}$-A conflicts with *-$\Delta_{(\omega,\sigma)}$F; the former requires presence of A, because this syllable is part of the head-foot of the word; the latter requires absence of A, because the syllable immediately preceding main stress is also unstressed, and therefore a non-head syllable of the word. Since presence of A is favored over its absence in the syllable immediately preceding stress, *$\Delta_{(\omega,F)}$-A must dominate *-$\Delta_{(\omega,\sigma)}$F.

(25) /o/ → [a]; *$\Delta_{(\omega,F)}$-A » *-$\Delta_{(\omega,\sigma)}$F

kU,Atá	*$\Delta_{(\omega,F)}$-A	*-$\Delta_{(\omega,\sigma)}$F	Ident-U
(kU,A tá)		**!	
(kU tá)	*!	*	
☞ (kA tá)		*	*
(kə tá)	*!		*

The tableau above shows that the unstressed syllable of the iamb favors presence of A over its absence. This, then, explains why /o/ reduces to [a], and /a/ is not reduced at all.

The vowel /e/ loses its A-element in moderate reduction. At first sight this seems to contradict our hypothesis that this element tends to be preserved in the syllable immediately preceding stress. How can we solve this paradox? It is here that our definition of headedness becomes important. Recall that a vowel's deepest feature is the head. This means that the presence of two elements in one vowel is only allowed if one of them dominates some other (dependent) feature. Accordingly, mid vowels must have a dependent element. Assuming that in Russian mid vowels are RTR (or Lax), these vowels must have a dependent-A. The constraint requiring that mid vowels be RTR is formulated in the following way:

(26) Mid=Lax (RTR)
Only A can occupy a dependent position.

This constraint conflicts with the *PRESENCE-family. In particular the following constraint is crucial:

(27) $*\text{-}\Delta_{(\omega,\sigma)}A(H_{Dep})$
Presence of Dependent Head-A is not allowed in Non-Head syllable of a prosodic word.

In unstressed syllables these constraints conflict with each other. Mid=Lax requires that mid vowels be RTR/Lax; $*\text{-}\Delta_{(\omega,\sigma)}A(H_{Dep})$ does not allow RTR vowels in unstressed syllables. Together, the two constraints enforce deletion of one of the elements of a mid vowel in unstressed position. Which one will actually be deleted depends on ranking, of course. In the vowel /o/ the U-element is removed, because the relevant faithfulness constraint, IDENT-U, is low in the hierarchy, as we have seen in (16). With respect to /e/, however, faithfulness is ranked in a different way; IDENT-I must be higher ranked than the constraint favoring presence of the A-element in the syllable immediately preceding stress, i.e. $*\Delta_{(\omega,F)}\text{-}A$. Furthermore, Mid=Lax and $*\text{-}\Delta_{(\omega,\sigma)}A(H_{Dep})$ must dominate $*\Delta_{(\omega,F)}\text{-}A$.

(28) Mid=Lax, $*\text{-}\Delta_{(\omega,\sigma)}A(H_{Dep})$, IDENT-I » $*\Delta_{(\omega,F)}\text{-}A$

I,Atáʒ	M=L	$*\text{-}\Delta_{(\omega,\sigma)}A(H_{Dep})$	IDENT-I	$*\Delta_{(\omega,F)}\text{-}A$	$*\text{-}\Delta_{(\omega,\sigma)}F$
(I,A táʃ)	*!				**
(I,AA táʃ)		*!			***
☞ (I táʃ)				*	*
(A táʃ)			*!		*
(ə táʃ)			*!	*	

The tableau above shows that a mid front vowel cannot remain unchanged in the unstressed syllable of an iamb. The reason is that mid vowels must be Lax, but laxness cannot survive in an unstressed syllable. Stated in more formal terms, mid vowels must have a dependent-A, but this element may not occupy a position in an unstressed syllable. Consequently, in the case of /e/ either I or A must go. Since, IDENT-I is highly ranked, A must go, even though A is favored in the syllable immediately preceding stress. In /o/, on the other hand, U must go, since IDENT-U is lowly ranked.

The ranking of IDENT-I above $*\Delta_{(\omega,F)}\text{-}A$ also explains why in a word like /igla/ (cf. (2)) the high vowel is not lowered. Lowering to a mid vowel violates either Mid=Lax if just A is inserted without dependent-A, or it violates $*\text{-}\Delta_{(\omega,\sigma)}A(H_{Dep})$ if A as well as dependent-A is inserted. If it is lowered to [a] it violates IDENT-I. Since these three constraints dominate the constraint $*\Delta_{(\omega,F)}\text{-}A$ nothing happens with a front high vowel in the unstressed syllable of an iamb. Since high back vowels are not lowered either in the unstressed syllable of an iamb, the constraint IDENT-U(H) must also dominate $*\Delta_{(\omega,F)}\text{-}A$.

Of course, the constraint $*\Delta_{(\omega,F)}\text{-}A$ should not be able to change stressed high vowels into (Lax) mid vowels. A word like /igl/ 'needle, gen. pl.', for instance, should remain unaffected. To explain this we cannot rely on $*\text{-}\Delta_{(\omega,\sigma)}A(H_{Dep})$, because this constraint is only relevant in non-head syllables. Neither can we rely on the blocking force of IDENT-A, because this constraint is quite lowly ranked, as I have shown in (16) and (17). The constraint IDENT-A(H) cannot solve the problem either, because it is quite easy to delete a solitary A-element, as I have shown in (17). This means that this constraint must also be lowly ranked. To solve this problem I propose that IDENT-A(H_{Dep}) is highly ranked in Russian. It is only dominated by two constraints: Mid=Lax and $*\text{-}\Delta_{(\omega,\sigma)}A(H_{Dep})$. The former ranking ensures that mid vowels are RTR/Lax, and the latter ensures that mid (= Lax) vowels can only appear in stressed syllables.

We now only have to explain moderate reduction after palatalized consonants. Recall that in this environment /o/ and /a/ are reduced to [i], rather than to [a] (cf. (1) and (2)). This seems to suggest that in the unstressed syllable of an iamb it is more important to spread the I-element, than to preserve the A-element, indicating that I-to-V dominates $*\Delta_{(\omega,F)}$-A. This is shown in the following two tableaux:

(29) I-to-V » $*\Delta_{(\omega,F)}$-A

p'At'í	I-to-V	$*\Delta_{(\omega,F)}$-A
(p'A t'í)	*!	
☞ (p'I t'í)		*

(30) t'U,A pló	I-to-V	$*\Delta_{(\omega,F)}$-A
(t'A pló)	*!	
☞ (t'I pló)		*

This concludes our analysis of moderate vowel reduction in Russian. We have seen that $*\Delta_{(\omega,F)}$-A is a crucial ingredient of our analysis. This constraint favors presence of the A-element, or in more traditional terms, it favors segments of relatively high sonority. At first sight it seems bizarre that a constraint promoting sonority plays a key role in reduction. On closer view, however, it is not strange at all. Recall that the constraint plays a decisive role in the unstressed syllable *of an iamb*. Since this syllable is part of the foot it is part of the foot-head of the word. For this reason it is not strange at all that it attracts segments of relatively high sonority. Of course, the unstressed syllable of an iamb is also a non-head syllable. But in Russian the sonority attracting force of this syllable is stronger than its sonority rejecting force.

The most important rankings I have proposed in this section are given in (31).

(31) Vowel reduction in Russian

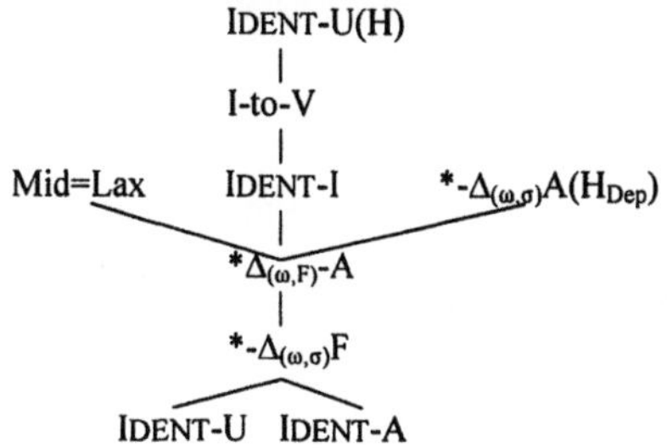

5. Conclusion

I have argued that in Russian vowel reduction two constraint families are active. *PRESENCE is a set of constraints that try to reduce sonority in non-heads. Outside of the foot this set is only restricted by faithfulness, resulting in extreme reduction. Within the domain of the foot, however, it is also mitigated by the opposing force, *ABSENCE, which tries to promote sonority in heads. The mitigating effect of *ABSENCE on *PRESENCE results in moderate reduction in the unstressed syllable of an iamb.

The most dramatic difference between Crosswhite's analysis and the one proposed here is that Crosswhite accounts for moderate reduction in terms of a set of constraints that specifically deal with perceptually difficult vowels, whereas I explain moderate reduction in terms of *ABSENCE. It can easily be shown that the former approach to moderate reduction is incompatible with the theory of sonority driven stress. *ABSENCE does not suffer from this drawback.

The current proposal heavily relies on the hypothesis that RTR/Lax vowels are highly sonorous. This is expressed in terms of representational complexity; Lax vowels are structurally extremely complex, because they contain a dependent A-element. The fact that Russian mid vowels are Lax explains why /o/ is reduced to [a] in moderate reduction (after a non-palatalized consonant); in the unstressed syllable of an iamb *dependent* A cannot be maintained, but A can.

References

Anderson, J. (1996): The representation of vowel reduction: non-specification and reduction in Old English and Bulgarian. In: *Studia Linguistica* 50; 2, 91-105.

Crosswhite, K. M. (2000): The analysis of extreme vowel Reduction. In: A. Albright and T. Cho (eds.): *Papers in Phonology* 4. UCLA Working Papers in Linguistics Vol. IV. Also available on ROA, 582-0203.

Crosswhite, K. M. (2000): Vowel reduction in Russian: a unified account of standard, dialectal, and "dissimilative" patterns. In: Crosswhite, K. M. and J. McDonough (eds.): *University of Rochester Working Papers in the Language Sciences*, Vol. I. Also available on ROA, 583-0203.

Crosswhite, K. M. (2001): *Vowel Reduction in Optimality Theory*. Outstanding Dissertations in Linguistics. Routledge, New York and London.

Crosswhite, K. M. (To Appear): Sonority driven reduction. In: *Berkeley Linguistic Society* 26. Also available on ROA, 591-0403.

De Lacey, P. V. (2002): The Formal Expression of Markedness. Ph. D. Dissertation, University of Massachusetts at Amherst. Also available on ROA, 542-0902.

Harris, J. (1994): *English Sound Structure*. Blackwell, Oxford and Cambridge.

Harris, J. (1997): Licensing inheritance: an integrated theory of neutralisation. *Phonology* 14; 3, 315-70.

Scheer, T. (1999): A theory of consonantal interaction. In: *Folia Linguistica* 32, 201-237.

Scheer, T. (2003): A Syntagmatic Theory of Phonology. Volume I: What is CVCV, and why should it be? Manuscript, Université de Nice.

Van der Hulst. H. (1984): *Syllable Structure and Stress in Dutch*. Dordrecht: Foris.

Roland Meyer & Ina Mleinek, Leipzig

How Prosody Signals Force and Focus – A Study of Rise-Fall Accents in Russian Yes-No Questions

1. Introduction*

Russian shows two fundamental ways of marking a yes-no question (YNQ): First, the particle *li* unambiguously signals a YNQ, as illustrated in (1). *Li* is obligatory in embedded yes-no interrogatives. Second, depending on the prosodic realization, a string as in (2) can be understood as either a YNQ or a declarative.

(1) *Kupila li Maša knigu?*
bought *li* $M._{NOM}$ $book_{ACC}$

(2) *Maša kupila knigu.*
$M._{NOM}$ bought $book_{ACC}$

On the other hand, it has also been known already from traditional descriptive grammars of Russian (Bryzgunova 1977) that intonation serves to mark information-structural distinctions. This paper will only deal with YNQs of the type illustrated in (2) (see Restan 1972 and King 1994 for an analysis of *li*-questions as in (1)). We depart from an important observation discussed in Ladd (1996): Russian YNQs display a pattern of prominence which differs systematically from their declarative counterparts. In an "out of the blue" variant with no special context requirements, the *verb* is the locus of the pitch accent, as shown in (3a).[1] This pattern, which sounds somewhat direct and maybe impolite to English or German ears, is both common and very robust in Russian. It neither conveys rudeness nor an implication that deaccented elements are discourse-old/given. On the other hand, in an "out of the blue" declarative without any special context requirements, the most deeply embedded, sentence-final internal argument is the main locus of prominence (3b). In a YNQ, a pitch accent in the same position would be understood as signalling a contrastive focus on the object.

(3) a. *Maša KUPILA knigu?*
$M._{NOM}$ bought $book_{ACC}$

b. *Maša kupila KNIGU.*
$M._{NOM}$ bought $book_{ACC}$

These facts have a number of interesting consequences: First, a direct comparison of an "unmarked" question tune with an "unmarked" declarative tune (as, e.g., in Bryzgunova 1977; Makarova 2001) seems rather artificial, since the two pitch accents never occur at the same locus in natural sentences. Second, the pitch accent used in YNQs obviously marks both force and focus in an overlapping, intertwined manner. Third, as the pitch accent can never be completely dissociated from the focused constituent, Russian does not fit the pattern of the so-called East European Question Tune (Grice et al. 2000), which – at least in some languages – may signal force exclusively. Fourth, one might think that a language in which intonation

---

* This research project was supported by the German Science Foundation (Research Group "Linguistic Foundations for Cognitive Science", University of Leipzig, Project D2). We wish to thank our speakers and subjects: the audience of the NWCL conference on Prosody & Pragmatics and the audience of FDSL-5, Bistra Andreeva, Robert D. Ladd, Denisa Lenertová and Mark Steedman for helpful advice and discussion; and – last but not least – Carsten Dieckmann who programmed the tool for the perception experiment. All errors are solely our own.

[1] To be precise, the *finite* verb (main verb or auxiliary) carries the pitch accent.

signals YNQ force necessarily lacks seemingly mixed sentence types as, e.g., the English so-called "rising declaratives" (Gunlogson 2001). However, it has to be noted that the *locus* of the pitch accent in Russian YNQs follows the pattern described by Ladd (1996) only in the presence of a syntactic sentence type feature +Q[uestion], whereas the specific *shape* of the pitch accent also applies to declaratives used as YNQ pragmatically (Meyer 2003).
Several background assumptions of our analysis deserve to be mentioned in advance. We distinguish two basic types of focus, namely, neutral (= new-information) and contrastive focus. Neutral focus extends the current context by a proposition, contrastive focus in addition excludes contextually given or accomodated alternatives. Both types of focus can be minimal (i.e., highlighting a minimal constituent) or wide (i.e., encompassing a larger domain). However, we will only deal with three types of focus here – minimal contrastive, minimal neutral, and wide neutral focus. Regarding Russian *declarative* clauses, it has been shown that the accent marking on contrastively focused elements differs from a minimal neutral accent by shape (high rise-fall vs. mid-fall), longer syllable duration, and special prosodic phrasing (Mehlhorn 2002; Zybatow & Mehlhorn 2000; Alter, Mleinek & Richter 2001). The organization of the remainder is the following: Section 2 discusses detailed prosodic measurements based on a reading study in which Russian clauses were embedded into various contexts disambiguating their force and focus marking. Section 3 contains the results of a perception (categorization) experiment. Section 4 sums up the conclusions.

2. A Production (Reading) Study

2.1. Background

In order to disentangle potential force-marking and focus-marking aspects of Russian YNQ prosody, it is essential to compare the right conditions (see also section 1): For contrasts in force marking, minimally and contrastively focused variants of declaratives and YNQs with the same locus of prominence are relevant. For contrasts in focus marking, (i) "out of the blue" YNQs vs. YNQs with a minimally or contrastively focused finite verb and (ii) YNQs with minimally vs. contrastively focused arguments can be compared. Our leading hypothesis – probably too strong, but a useful heuristics – is that both focus and force are marked by distinct prosodic means in a compositional way.

2.2. Reading Study

2.2.1. Materials and Design

We prepared a reading study in which simple artifical subject-verb-object target sentences were presented to participants in various contexts disambiguating their focus-background-structure and their force. The target sentences were matched carefully for the number of syllables and the loci of lexical stress. Due to the need for a controlled task, the examples used are admittedly somewhat artificial. Every subject, verb and object had 3 syllables with the word stress fixed to the second syllable. These sentences were embedded into 10 types of contexts. We distinguished two force conditions (declarative and YNQ) and five information structural conditions: (minimal) contrastive focus on the verb/on the object, minimal (neutral) focus on the verb/on the object, and wide (neutral) focus. The five YNQ conditions are illustrated in (4)-(11) (the contexts are in square brackets):

(4) A: [*Vy včera byli na koncerte?*] *Irina igrala mazurki?*
you yesterday were at concert I.$_{NOM}$ played mazurkas
'A: [Have you been to the concert yesterday?] Did Irina play mazurkas?' (wide focus)

(5) A: [*Kak vam ob"jasnila Irina v tanceval'nom kružke mazurki?*]
how you$_{DAT}$ explained Irina in dancing group mazurkas
Irina igrala mazurki?
I.$_{NOM}$ played mazurkas
'A: [How did Irina explain mazurkas to you in the dancing group?]
Did she play mazurkas?' (minimal focus on V)

(6) [A: *Ja slyšal, čto Irina vo svoëm vystuplenii propustila mazurki.*
I heard that I.$_{NOM}$ in her performance left-out mazurkas
B: *Net.* A: *Čto?*] *Irina igrala mazurki?*
no what I.$_{NOM}$ played mazurkas
'[A: I heard that Irina left out (the) mazurkas in her performance.
B: No, she didn't. A: What?] Irina played (the) mazurkas?' (contrast on V)

(7) A: [*Čto Irina igrala?*] *Irina igrala mazurki?*
what$_{ACC}$ I.$_{NOM}$ played I.$_{NOM}$ played mazurkas
'A: [What did Irina play?] Did Irina play mazurkas?' (minimal focus on O)

(8) [A: *Kakie proizvedenija Šopena Irina ispolnila? Polonezy?*
which works Chopin$_{GEN}$ I.$_{NOM}$ played Polonaises
B: *Net.* A: *Čto?*] *Irina igrala mazurki?*
no what I.$_{NOM}$ played mazurkas
'[A: Which works by Chopin did Irina perform? Polonaises?
B: No. A: What?] Irina performed mazurkas?' (contrast on O)

8 target items per condition were presented together with a set of unrelated fillers in four different pseudo-randomized orders. The conditions are summarized in table 1.

Focus / Force	Wide neutral focus	Contrastive focus on V	Minimal neutral focus on V	Contrastive focus on O	Minimal neutral focus on O
Yes-no-interrogative	maxinter	conVinter	minVinter	conOinter	minOinter
Declarative	maxdecl	conVdecl	minVdecl	conOdecl	minOdecl

Table 1: Conditions used in the reading study

2.2.2. Procedure

All the dialogues (target items embedded in their contexts) were read aloud by 4 female Russian speakers, recorded on DAT-tape, and digitized at 44.1 kHz and a 16 bit sampling rate. The target sentences were extracted from their contexts, marked up for syllable boundaries, and semi-automatically analyzed using the Praat program developed by Paul Boersma and David Weenink. We measured the fundamental frequency and the absolute time at each quarter syllable (i.e., at 37 points per sentence). Additionally, we noted the F0 maxima and minima for every syllable. Altogether, 320 critical items (10 x 8 per subject) were analyzed.

2.2.3. Results

Since an appropriate methodology for the statistic evaluation of F0 and timing data is far from being uncontroversial, we used a relatively conservative and coarse approach and tested for categorial differences using the non-parametric Wilcoxon test. The results thus express a mere *ranking* between values, but not the size of a given contrast. In order to ensure comparability, carefully matched materials and a *relative* time scale were used. Across all the target sentences, the absolute F0 ranges of the four speakers differed (351-434 Hz), but their average F0 values were very similar (arithmetic mean: 223-234 Hz; median: 206-222 Hz), so that a direct comparison of the production data seems justified. As a first step, idealized, average F0 curves over the relative time scale for each condition were constructed. Then, three parameters were evaluated: accent shape, maximal F0 height of the pitch accent, and timing of the accent peak (i.e., its alignment in relation to syllable boundaries). Many, but not all of the apparently clear differences in average pitch patterns turned out to be statistically significant. There are a number of relevant comparisons to be made within the set of conditions: To pin down contrasts related to force, the conditions *conVinter* vs. *conVdecl*, *minVinter* vs. *minVdecl*, *conOinter* vs. *conOdecl*, and *minOinter* vs. *minOdecl* should be taken into account (see table 1 for abbreviations). In order to test for focus-related differences, *maxinter* vs. *minVinter* vs. *conVinter* and *maxdecl* vs. *minOdecl* vs. *conOdecl* are to be contrasted. We would expect the effects established through these comparisons to be consistent with differences found when both focus and force vary, i.e. between *minVdecl* vs. *conVinter*, *conVdecl* vs. *maxinter* etc., although we may not compare the latter directly statistically.

F0 maximum of the pitch accent
The pitch accent in YNQs reaches a higher F0 maximum than in declaratives with equal focus. This holds for both the conditions with a minimal or contrastive focus on the verb and for those with a minimal or contrastive focus on the object. Figure 1 displays the relevant comparisons between YNQ conditions with highest prominence on the verb (*minVinter*, *conVinter*) and the corresponding declaratives with minimal and contrastive focus on the verb (*minVdecl*, *conVdecl*).[2]

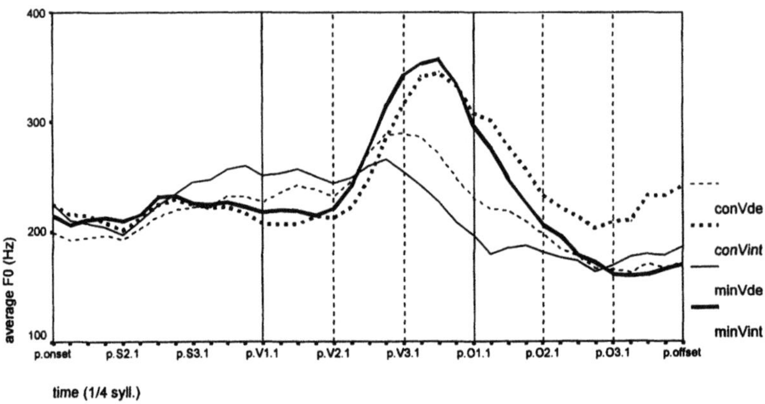

Figure 1: YNQs vs. declaratives - contrastive/minimal focus on V

[2] Figures 1-4 all use an abstract, relative time scale with ¼ syllable as the basic unit. Vertical lines indicate syllable boundaries, p[itch].V1.1 corresponding to the beginning of the first syllable of the verb, p.O1.1 to the beginning of the first syllable of the object etc. The labelling of the single conditions follows table 1, with *decl* shortened to *de* and *inter* shortened to *int* for technical reasons.

The difference between the conditions *minVinter* and *minVdecl* was highly significant ($W = 3$; $N = 27$; $p < .0001$). Unfortunately, a number of realizations of YNQs with contrastive focus on the verb had to be excluded from evaluation for either of two reasons: (i) They contained a strongly rising tone towards the end of the utterance – an alternative prosodic pattern for reactive YNQs in Russian (IK-4 in Bryzgunova's 1977 terminology) –, or (ii) main prominence was wrongly assigned to the object. With this proviso[3], the contrast in the F0 maximum between the conditions *conVinter* and *conVdecl* was also significant ($W = 3$; $N = 14$; $p = .002$).
Figure 2 shows that both YNQ conditions with highest prominence on the object (*minOinter*, *conOinter*) are higher in their F0 maximum compared with the corresponding declaratives with minimal or contrastive foci on the object (*minOdecl*, *conOdecl*). Again, the differences for the relevant comparisons are significant (*minOinter* vs. *minOdecl*: $W = 2$; $N = 16$; $p = .001$; *conOinter* vs. *conOdecl*: $W = 7$; $N = 30$; $p < .0001$).

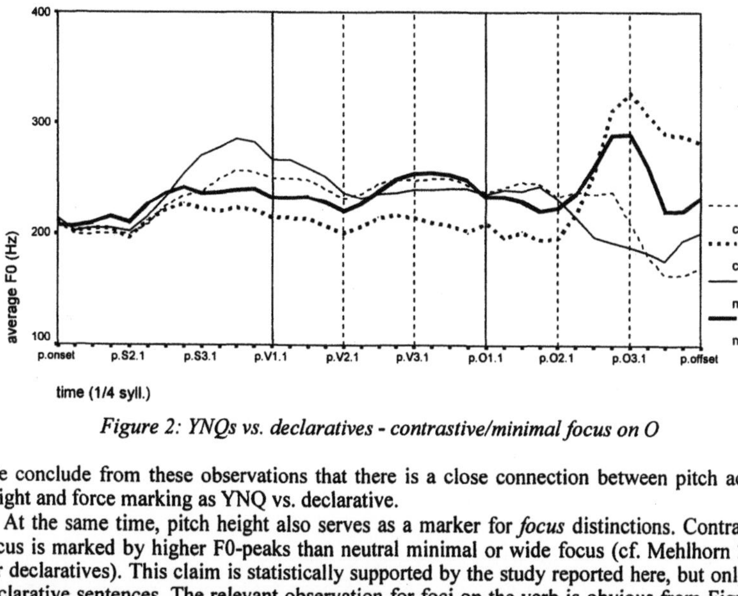

Figure 2: YNQs vs. declaratives - contrastive/minimal focus on O

We conclude from these observations that there is a close connection between pitch accent height and force marking as YNQ vs. declarative.

At the same time, pitch height also serves as a marker for *focus* distinctions. Contrastive focus is marked by higher F0-peaks than neutral minimal or wide focus (cf. Mehlhorn 2001 for declaratives). This claim is statistically supported by the study reported here, but only for declarative sentences. The relevant observation for foci on the verb is obvious from Figure 1 (*conVdecl* vs. *minVdecl*). Among these declaratives, the difference in F0 maximum between the conditions *conVdecl* and *minVdecl* is significant ($W = 83$; $N = 27$; $p < .012$). The declarative conditions with focus on the object showed the same effect: Contrastive focus is marked by a higher F0-peak in the stressed syllable than either minimal or wide focus, as illustrated in Figure 3. The relevant differences are significant (*conOdecl* vs. *minOdecl*: $W = 93$; $N = 28$; $p = .012$; *conOdecl* vs. *maxdecl*: $W = 13$; $N = 18$; $p = .002$).

[3] Note that inclusion of the examples with a final rise would have made it much easier to refute the null hypothesis with respect to *peak alignment* (see below): On average, the peak would misleadingly appear to move to the right in interrogative examples. Exclusion of the non-canonical realizations actually made it harder for us to get a significant effect with respect to peak alignment.

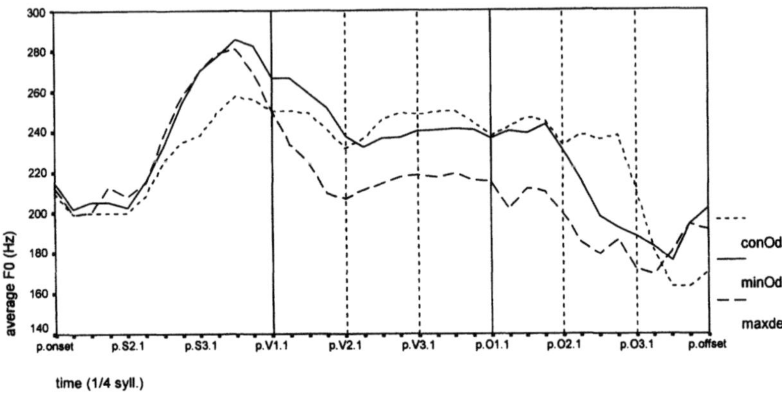

Figure 3: Declaratives with highest prominence on the object

Turning now to YNQs, the average, idealized contours in Figure 1 and 2 suggest that the overall pitch maximum in YNQs with contrastive or minimal focus on the verb was also higher than in "neutral", "out of the blue" contexts. At first sight, the pitch accent in the minimal focus condition seemed to be even slightly higher than in the contrastive condition (see Figure 4).

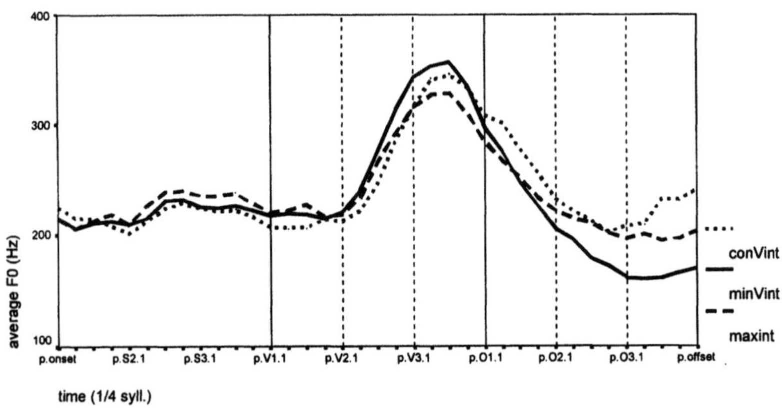

Figure 4: YNQs with highest prominence on the verb

According to statistic evaluation, however, the average F0-tracks betray the eye in this case: There was no difference whatsoever in pitch maximum between the conditions *conVinter* vs. *minVinter* (p = .414) or *conVinter* vs. *maxint* (p = .795). As for the YNQ conditions with highest prominence on the object, it seemed once more that contrastive focus was marked by especially high pitch (cf. Figure 2). But as before, this tendency in the mean contours is deceptive: Statistically, the two F0 maxima did not differ at all (*conOinter* vs. *minOinter*: p = .557). The conclusion we wish to draw from this observation is that in contrast to declaratives, minimal, wide, and contrastive foci in YNQs are not distinguished by means of their F0 maximum.

Accent shape

The general accent shape is a prosodic feature which serves to mark focus distinctions, at least for declaratives, where the pitch accents differ among conditions with the same locus of prominence to a certain extent. While minimal focus on the object is realized prosodically in a way quite similar to maximal focus – both are embedded into sentence declination –, they both clearly differ from contrastive focus, which is realised by a resetting (cf. Figure 3). Concerning minimal focus on the verb in declarative sentences, we observe a difference against contrastive focus on the verb, too (cf. Figure 1). Contrastive focus is realized by a centered rise/fall, while minimal focus starts out at a higher level embedding the pitch accent into a smooth fall.

On the other hand, the pitch accents in all the focus conditions in YNQs have a quite similar shape. In the conditions with highest prominence on the verb, the three accents virtually coincide forming a centered rise-fall (see Figure 4). The shapes of the accents marking contrastive focus and minimal focus on the object do not differ either (cf. Figure 3). Abstracting away from the effect of sentence declination, YNQ focus accents on both the verb and the object may be regarded as having basically the same shape (see Figures 3, 4). It should be borne in mind that a later, lower pitch accent is usually still perceived as equally high – so the four accents represented here are in fact very similar. This supports our above claim that focus distinctions within YNQs are reduced, i.e., prosodically neutralized.

Peak delay

We observed that in YNQs the F0 maximum in the word carrying the pitch accent occurred relatively *later* than in the corresponding declaratives (in terms of quarter syllables). This holds for each of the minimally or contrastively focused conditions. The relevant comparisons for *verbal* prominence (see Figure 1) are statistically significant (*conVinter* vs. *conVdecl*: $W = 7.5$; $N = 18$; $p = .001$; *minVinter* vs. *minVdecl*: $W = 2.5$; $N = 25$; $p < .0001$). Note that YNQs with maximal focus cannot be directly compared to declaratives with maximal focus (both having a different locus of prominence, on the verb vs. on the most deeply embedded constituent). But the YNQs with maximal focus showed the same peak alignment as those with a contrastive or minimal verbal focus (cf. Figure 4). Their F0 maximum occurred even significantly later than the end of the syllable bearing lexical stress, i.e., it was delayed into the postnuclear syllable. Regarding the relative timing of the F0 maximum and of the relevant syllable boundary, we get significant contrasts (*maxinter* vs. boundary: $W = 0$; $N = 23$; $p < .0001$; *minVinter* vs. boundary: $W = 4.5$; $N = 28$; $p < .0001$; *conVinter* vs. boundary: $W = 0$; $N = 16$; $p < .0001$). No such peak delay occurred in any of the declarative conditions. It should be noted that peak delay in YNQ vs. declaratives conditions with prominence on the *object* is less obvious (cf. Figure 2). Since declaratives with a maximal focus or a minimal focus on the object carry a falling pitch accent, it is not fair to compare the timing of the pitch maximum to the one in YNQs, i.e. to a rise-fall. But at least for the case of contrastive object foci, such a comparison makes sense. And as before, the F0 peak occurring in the YNQ condition was delayed significantly here (*conOinter* vs. *conOdecl*: $W = 15$; $N = 28$; $p < .0001$). Obviously then, peak delay is a force-related, distinct feature of Russian YNQs.

2.3. Discussion

How could the three parameters *F0 maximum of the pitch accent*, *accent shape* and *peak delay* compositionally work together to mark the focus and force of a YNQ vs. a declarative in Russian? Turning first to *force* distinctions, if the height of the pitch maximum is a defining feature in this case, then YNQs must have a higher F0 maximum than declaratives with the same locus of prominence. If peak delay is decisive, then it has to be excluded in

declaratives. Both consequences seem to hold: In our reading study, the overall pitch maximum in YNQs with prominence on the verb was higher than in the respective declaratives and occurred relatively later. Disregarding the problematic minimal focus conditions, the same seems true in principle for YNQs with prominence on the object. As concerns *focus* distinctions, only for declaratives could we find a clear difference in the F0 maximum between contrastive and neutral foci; but this was also correlated with a distinction in accent shapes throughout. For YNQs, various foci on the verb and on the object virtually collapse prosodically – at least our results do not support any clear-cut difference. Contrastive and minimal focus accents in all YNQ conditions turned out similar in shape, height and peak alignment. Prosodic marking of focus seems weakened or even completely neutralized in this case. Moreover, peak delay never occurred as a marker for focus distinctions in the above study. We conclude that a distinction in terms of the F0 maximum generally correlates with force as well as with focus distinctions in Russian. Peak delay, however, is sufficient to mark YNQs. The reading study does not answer the question whether peak delay and an especially high F0 maximum can compensate for each other. Gussenhoven (2002) has argued on the basis of YNQ marking in various languages that both higher and later peaks are functionally equivalent manifestations of the so-called *effort code*. According to our findings, higher peaks in Russian are virtually ambiguous – they occur in contrastively (vs. neutrally) focused declarative clauses, but also in connection with YNQ (vs. declarative) force. Three distinct categories in terms of accent shape could be isolated: (i) neutral focus in declaratives, (ii) contrastive focus in declaratives, and (iii) YNQ force (without further focus distinctions). The accents marking (i) vs. (ii) differ at least in shape and height, (i) vs. (iii) differ at least in shape, height and peak alignment, and (ii) vs. (iii) differ at least in peak alignment.
If these generalizations hold, we would expect them to be reflected in the perception mode as well. Specifically, speakers should be able to recognize YNQs with a delayed peak easily, while they should have problems in declaratives with a contrastive focus on the verb or the object. They should distinguish neutrally focused declaratives from YNQs easily, due to their distinct accent shapes. In order to further investigate these points, we undertook a perception experiment on the basis of a selection of the data acquired in the production study.

3. A Perception (Categorization) Study

3.1. Background

The probably easiest way to test the recognition of force distinctions is a categorization task: Speakers listen to target items out of context and have to decide whether they are questions or statements. The zero hypothesis is that speakers can make use of prosodic signals equally well in all conditions. However, according to the generalizations in section 2, we would expect specific difficulties in the conditions marked by high pitch accents with non-delayed peaks, since these occur both in contrastive declaratives and in YNQs. On the other hand, neutrally focused declaratives and, generally, YNQs should be recognized easily and correctly, since these involve unambiguous prosodic signals (a specific accent shape and peak delay, respectively).

3.2. Perception Study

3.2.1. Materials and Design

We tested items from 9 of the 10 conditions used in the production task in a related design, leaving out the neutral wide focus declaratives, which are prosodically maximally dissimilar from YNQs (see above). The sentences recorded during the production study were evaluated for their closeness to the prototypical realizations of each category, and 4 sentences per category were selected in such a way that the prospective comparisons would concern only identical lexical material. We construed questionnaires with 38 critical items intermixed with 24 fillers in four different pseudo-randomized orders. The materials contained 20 YNQs and

18 declaratives (critical items), 14 *wh*-exclamatives and *wh*-questions, 5 *li*-questions and 5 declaratives (fillers), i.e., a total of 62 sentences.

3.2.2. Procedure

The normalized items were presented auditorily one by one and simultaneously displayed on a computer monitor (without punctuation). Speakers were instructed to decide whether a given sentence was (a) a question or (b) an exclamation or statement and mark the respective checkbox in a window on the screen. The presentation was self-paced, and participants could listen to the items as often as they wished. We recorded the timing of responses, correct and erroneous categorizations, and the rate at which each target item was replayed. 20 native Russian speakers (students of the University of Leipzig) took part in the experiment.

3.2.3. Results

All participants achieved overall correctness rates between 50 and 57 (of 62). The fact that the task was such a little demand was unexpected. The participants' ability to recognize the force of the stimuli is represented in the correctness rates across different conditions. As a measure for the certainty upon their decision, we also recorded the rates at which participants chose to replay the target items. The results are presented separately for the five conditions with the main pitch accent on the verb in Figure 5 and 6, and for the four conditions with the main pitch accent on the object in Figure 7, respectively.

Accent on the verb

As for YNQs conditions with the main accent on the verb, categorization errors were generally rare. However, declaratives with a contrastive focus on the verb were categorized correctly only at chance level (see Figure 5).

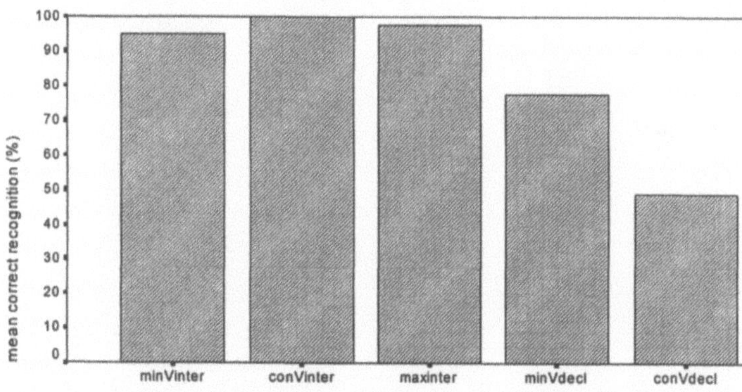

Figure 5: Correct YNQ/declarative recognition (verb prominent; perception study)

A one-way ANOVA revealed a highly significant influence of the original context type in which the item was produced on the amount of correct recognitions ($F(4,16) = 96.837$, $p < .0001$). Pairwise comparisons, using a *t*-test with Bonferroni correction, show that the contrastive declaratives differ from all other conditions significantly ($p = .002$), being recognized worst of all. Minimally focused declaratives take an intermediate position, differing significantly both from the declarative contrastive and from the interrogative conditions ($p = .002$).

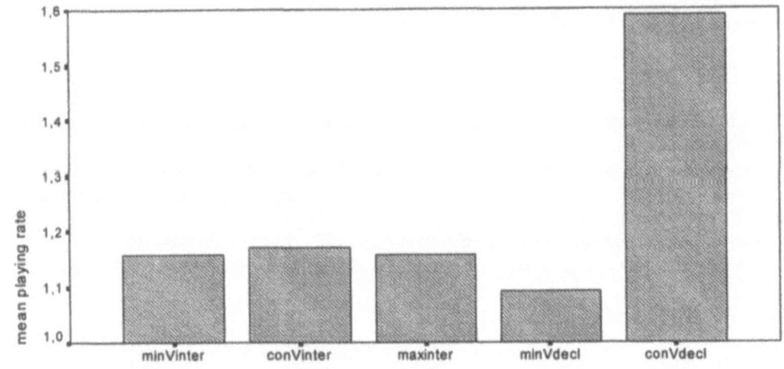

Figure 6: Rate of replaying (verb prominent; perception study)

The rates at which subjects decided to replay the stimuli turned out to be a helpful measure, pointing to the same conclusions as the mere correctness rates. A one-way ANOVA indicates an overall effect of the context of production on the replay rate in the recognition task ($F(4,16) = 6.285$; $p = .003$). Participants chose to listen to the contrastive declaratives more often than to items from any other condition (see Figure 6): The difference in the playing rates between contrastive declaratives and all other conditions was significant across subjects ($p = .003$).

Accent on the object

In the conditions with the main accent on the object, incorrect classifications occurred with extremely low frequency (see Figure 7).

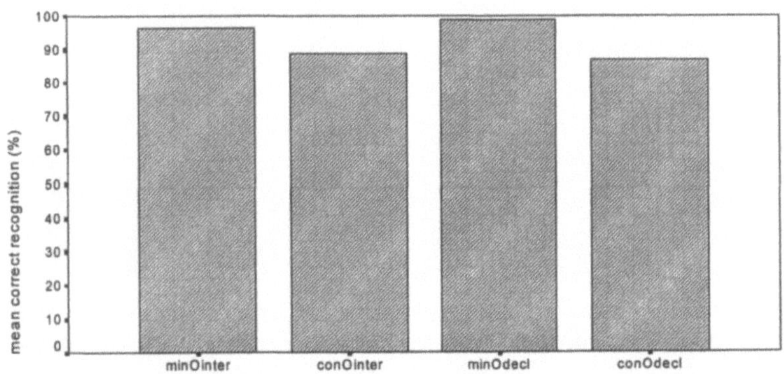

Figure 7: Correct YNQ/declarative recognition (object prominent; perception study)

Replaying rates across all the object conditions did not differ significantly, disallowing further comparisons. As far as the recognition rate is concerned, a one-way ANOVA did reveal a significant overall effect of the original context type ($F(3,16) = 3.484$, $p < .02$). But only the declaratives with minimal focus somewhat stick out by their good recognition rate. The difference between these and the mean of the YNQs was insignificant ($W = 5.5$; $N = 8$; $p = .076$). A clear difference, however, showed up between the minimally and the contrastively focused declaratives ($W = 0$; $N = 12$; $p = .001$). This result supports the idea that the distinct accent shape of neutrally (minimally) focused declaratives can be a useful hint for force recognition. Again, the higher contrastive pitch accent leads to difficulties for categorization. Given that the peak delay in YNQs is necessarily reduced towards the end of the sentence, the lack of a difference between these two conditions and the contrastive declaratives becomes plausible.

3.3. Discussion

The outcome of the perception study shows the following: (i) Neutrally focused declaratives (with minimal or wide focus) are recognized easily and accurately. (ii) Examples involving peak delay (i. e., all YNQs) are recognized easily and accurately. (iii) Items with a high, non-delayed F0-peak (i.e., contrastive declaratives) pose a certain problem for recognition. In the case of a contrast on the verb, they are categorized correctly only at chance level.

All three results fit the production part reported in section 1 very well: Since neutrally focused declaratives are marked by a distinct pitch accent shape (a mid-fall integrated into the declination line) and thus differ maximally from YNQs, (i) is expected. We identified peak delay as a distinctive feature of YNQ pitch accents in section 2. This is supported by result (ii), which also indicates that delayed peaks are not mistaken for very high peaks (as in contrastive declaratives) in Russian. Finally, as we know from the production part, higher pitch is a concomitant feature of YNQ intonation as well as a distinctive feature of contrastive declaratives. This makes the latter good candidates for being misunderstood as a YNQ, as supported by result (iii). Combining our findings in the reading and the perception study, Russian YNQ prosody seem to involve a refinement of Gussenhoven's (2002) *effort code*: While pitch height can in principle substitute for peak delay (leading to difficulties when a sentence's force has to be recognized), the reverse is not true. Peak delay marks YNQs unambiguously.

4. Conclusion

Russian YNQs can be marked by a special pitch accent, a steep rise-fall with peak delay into the postnuclear syllable. This accent marks a sentence as an unambiguous (pragmatic) question act. As the production and perception studies have shown, it does not vary fundamentally with respect to focus distinctions. We may thus plausibly assume that the sentence-type feature [Q] acts similarly as a focus particle, obligatorily binding a focused constituent in its scope (Meyer 2003). Focus on the finite verb could then count as "neutral" in the sense that it imposes the least specific information-structural requirements on the rest of the sentence. Declaratives with a contrastive focus, on the other hand, are marked by a centered, high rise-fall, which is very close in shape to a YNQ accent, but does not show peak delay. We have shown that the similarity between these accents leads to specific perception difficulties: While the delayed YNQ accent is recognized clearly and easily, the contrastive focus declaratives are often falsely analysed as YNQs. Thus, the mutual substitution of peak height and peak delay in question marking (Gussenhoven 2002) seems to work only in one direction in Russian. It would be promising to relate our Russian findings to the cross-linguistic picture of prosodic functions, but also to the rather more structural peak alignment conditions (see also section 1). Further extensions of the research presented here should concern the topic and secondary accents observed in section 1, and the application of our findings to more authentic data.

5. References

Alter, Kai, Mleinek, Ina & Richter, Nicole, 2001. Prosodic Phrasing and Accentuation in Russian. In: G. Zybatow et al., eds., Current Issues in Formal Slavic Linguistics, 317-328. Frankfurt/Main: Lang.

Bryzgunova, Elena Andreevna, 1977. Zvuki i intonacija russkoj reči. Moskva.

Grice, Martine, Ladd, Robert D. & Arvaniti, A. 2000. On the place of phrase accents in intonational phonology. Phonology 17, 143-185.

Gunlogson, Christine, 2001. True to Form. Rising and Falling Declaratives as Questions in English. PhD thesis, UC Santa Cruz.

Gussenhoven, Carlos, 2002. Intonation and interpretation: Phonetics and Phonology. In: B. Bel & I. Marlien, eds., Proceedings of Speech Prosody 2002, Aix-en-Provence, 47-57.

King, Tracy Holloway, 1994. Focus in Russian Yes-No Questions. Journal of Slavic Linguistics 2/1. 92-102.

Ladd, Robert D. 1996. Intonational Phonology. Cambridge: Cambridge University Press.

Makarova, Veronika 2001. Phonetic approaches to issues in Russian intonation. In: G. Zybatow et al., eds., Current Issues in Formal Slavic Linguistics, 49-58. Frankfurt/Main: Lang.

Mehlhorn, Grit, 2002. Kontrastierte Konstituenten im Russischen. Experimentelle Untersuchungen zur Informationsstruktur. Frankfurt/Main: Lang.

Meyer, Roland, 2004. Prosody, Mood, and Focus: A Study of "Intonationally Marked" Yes-No-Questions in Russian. In: Arnaudova, O. et al., eds., Proceedings from the Twelfth Workshop on Formal Approaches to Slavic Linguistics: The Ottawa Meeting 2003, 333-352. Ann Arbor: Michigan Slavic Publications.

Restan, Per, 1972. Sintaksis voprositel'nogo predloženija. Obščij vopros. Oslo: Universitetsforlaget.

Siemund, Peter, 2001. Interrogative Constructions. In: M. Haspelmath et al., eds., Language Typology and Language Universals, 1010-1028. Berlin: de Gruyter.

Wenk, Reinhard, 1992. Intonation und aktuelle Gliederung. Experimentelle Untersuchungen an slavischen Entscheidungs- und Ergänzungsfragen. Frankfurt/Main.

Zybatow, Gerhild & Mehlhorn, Grit, 2000. Experimental Evidence for Focus Structure in Russian. In: T. H. King & I. A. Sekerina, eds., Proceedings from the Eigth Workshop on Formal Approaches to Slavic Linguistics: The Philadelphia Meeting 1999, 414-434. Ann Arbor: Michigan Slavic Publications.

Ina Mleinek, Leipzig

Prosody and Information Structuring in Russian Complex Sentences with *čto*-Object Clauses

1. Introduction

The following article is explicitly dedicated to Russian complex sentences with secondary clauses in object function. I am concentrating on sentences with the complementizer *čto* 'that'.

1.1. Background assumptions

In the literature it has been often stated that secondary clauses don't exhibit their own information structure (IS); on the contrary, secondary clauses should be informationally embedded into the main clause. One explanation for this is, that information-structural distinctions normally are ascribed to whole utterances. So for Mathesius (1975) or Komagata (2001) IS is non-recursive. Another explanation can be seen in the stress behaviour of complex sentences: they normally have only one locus of main stress – therefore they should have only one focus, too. But things are more complicated: if the secondary clause contains a minimally focused constituent, this phonetic focus cannot always be considered the only focus of the whole complex sentence. I take questions or strategies in the sense of Roberts (1996) as an argument to determine the number of foci within complex sentences. The following Russian example is an illustration of this account. Within the context the relevant sentence appears underlined:

Context:
Szadi, iz-za gruzovika, razdalsja vystrel. I Tanja, eščo prižimaja k životu avtomat, pro kotoryj ona ne znala, čto on uže pustoj, sdelala šag vpered, posmotrela napravo i uvidela, čto èto, [...], *streljaet kuda-to v les iz svoej vintovki Xristoforov. Navernoe, vdogonku nemcam, – soobrazila ona. I pošla k nemu.* (Uppsala corpus: Konstantin Simonov / *Poslednee leto*)
'From behind out of the lorry, a shot goes off. And Tanja, still pressing the machine-gun to her stomach knowing that it is already empty made a step forward, looked to the right and saw that there [...] is Christoforov shooting into the wood out of his gun. May-be, behind the Germans, – she thought. And went to him.'

(1)

[$_{CP}$ *I Tanja, ...,*	[$_{VP1}$ *sdelala šag vperED*],				
and Tanja-nom/fem	make-past/sg/fem step-acc forward-adv,				
[$_{VP2}$ *posmotrela naPRAvo*]	*i*	[$_{VP3}$ *uvidela,*	[$_{CP}$ *čto*	*èto, ...,*	
look-past/sg/fem to the right-adv	and	see-past/sg/fem	that-comp	that-pron/dem/neutr	
streljaet	*kuda-to*	*v*	*les*	*iz*	*svoej*
shoot-präs/sg	where-adv/dir/indef	into-präp	wood-acc	out of	his-pron/refl/gen/fem/sg
vintovki	*XristoFOrov.*]]]				
gun-gen/fem	Xristoforov-nom				

Within this complex sentence three VPs are coordinated at main clause level. Each of these VPs has its own focus exponent (FE) the stressed syllable of which is written in capital letters: $_{VP1}$ *vperED;* $_{VP2}$ *naPRAvo;* $_{VP3}$ *XristoFOrov* which is part of the embedded clause. Referring to the before mentioned shooting event the coordinated main clause is answering the question:

Strategy 1: Narration **Answer:**
Super question 1: *What did Tanja do after the shooting?* *Tanja made s step forward, looked to the right and saw x.*

The secondary clause, on the other hand, is answering an own question referring to the same shooting event in the discourse, but bound to it by another discourse relation, namely by elaboration:

Strategy 2: Elaboration		**Answer:**
Super question 2: *What are the properties of the shooting event?*		
Sub question 2.1:	*Who shot?*	*Xristoforov shot.*
Sub question 2.2:	*Where has been shot?*	*Into the wood.*
Sub question 2.3:	*With what has been shot?*	*With his gun.*
Sub question 2.4:	*Whom behind?*	*Probably behind the Germans.*

Probably the most important sub question for the matrix subject (and the speaker too) is sub question 2.1. Therefore the subject of the secondary clause *Xristoforov* has moved out from its base position[1] into sentence final position to mark the FE and the minimal focus of the secondary clause. Although *Xristoforov* is also the FE of the third conjunct within the main clause the main clause focus is not a result of projecting up the embedded minimal focus into the higher clause. Instead, deviating from the default stress position[2] leads to projection abortion of the focus. Obviously then, both the question test and the projection data lead to the consequence that sentence (1) has two foci: one in the coordinated main clause and one in the secondary clause. Therefore complex sentences with *čto*-object clauses should be seen as one instance of so called 'Superman' sentences in the sense of Neeleman & Szendrői (2004). 'Superman' sentences are recursive structures with one focus exponent but more than one focus. But other than Neeleman & Szendrői (2004) I want to claim that independently of the locus of the accent within the secondary clause the secondary clause can have its own focus because a CP intervenes which is the domain for focus placement.
Arguing within the IS-framework of Junghanns & Zybatow (1997) I assume two unrelated dimensions of information structure, namely the Topic-Comment Structure (TCS) and the Focus-Background Structure (FBS). These two dimensions can be recursive in complex sentences in the sense, that both Topic and Focus can contain Focus-Background and Topic-Comment parts; – but this kind of recursivity applies clause-wise and never to a pragmatic Focus or a Topic as it is. The following example will illustrate my account.

(2)	*Ona*	*ponjala,*	*čto*	*ee*	*podrugu*
	she-nom	understand-past/sg/fem	that-comp	her-pron/sg/acc/fem	girlfriend-acc
	pozval	*diREKtor.*			
	call-past/sg/masc	director-nom			

'She understood that the director has called her girlfriend.'

(3)		*Ona*	*ponjala, čto ee podrugu pozval diREKtor.*
	TCD_{MC}:	[Topic]	[-------------------Comment--------------------]
	FBD_{MC}:	[Background]	[----------------------Focus-----------------------]
	TCD_{SC}:		[---Topic---] [---Comment---]
	FBD_{SC}:		[----Background----][- Focus-]

Without contextual information the sentence should be divided into Topic and Focus according to word order variation. Starting with the secondary clause (SC), the direct object moves out of its base position to mark a topic whereas the subject moves to the right periphery of the secondary clause to mark a minimal focus. In a next step the main clause will

[1] The base order of Russian is standardly assumed to be SVO. For economy reasons Junghanns & Zybatow (1997) propose a movement to the right for right peripheral subjects.
[2] Although the right peripheral sentence position is the normal stress position in Russian which should allow for focus projection, projection from the subject is clearly not allowed.

be divided into Topic and Focus, too. The referential subject marks the sentential topic; the rest constitutes the focus[3].

1.2. Goal of the study

It has been often claimed that secondary clauses embedded under factive matrix verbs are backgrounded and serve to identify already given material. Although factive verbs presuppose an embedded sentence only in the sense that they require the truth of it this claim is often sharpened such that the embedded sentence is presupposed as given, thus backgrounded. If we assume that backgrounded material normally does not exhibit the main locus of prominence in a sentence we would conclude that the main accent within complex sentences with factives shifts to the main clause (e.g. to the matrix verb). Accordingly, the embedded clause of factives should be deaccented. Furthermore, a standpoint like this implies that embeddings of non-factive verbs which lack the above mentioned presupposition should convey new information. This then would be prosodically expressed by a main accent in the embedded clause.

Obviously, these simplified assumptions can only serve as a first hypothesis. Clearly one can observe accentuation in embeddings of factive verbs as well, as can be found in Russian spoken corpora. But it has to be shown that accentuation within factive embeddings is a concomitant feature of new information.[4] Therefore I conducted several prosodic experiments which shed some light on interdependencies between accentuation and de-focussing strategies within complex sentences with factive and non-factive matrix verbs.

The article is organized as follows: Section 2 discusses detailed prosodic measurements based on a production study, in which Russian complex sentences with the complementizer *čto* were embedded in various contexts disambiguating their focus types and placement. Section 3 contains the results of a second production study which investigates differences of factive and non-factive embeddings within the Russian sentences in question (see above). Section 4 sums up the conclusions.

2. Production Study 1

2.1. Background

Deaccentuation of the object and accentuation of the main verb in Russian simple *SVO* sentences has been partly studied by Mehlhorn (2002) and Meyer & Mleinek (2005). As there is a syntactic boundary between the V and O part within complex sentences the results within complex sentences can not really be compared to those of simple sentences. They have to be studied carefully before we proceed to the second production study. To ensure backgrounding of the object sentence and accentuation of the matrix verb I used strong triggers as (i) alternative questions (questioning the truth of the event) for neutral focus accentuation and (ii) correction constructions for contrastive focus accentuation. Here the embedded clause would be clearly backgrounded, thus deaccented, with no exception for factive and non-factive embeddings. Condition (i) and (ii) were both contrasted with a neutral condition (iii) – that is neutral focus on the object (e.g. the embedded clause).

2.2. Material

I prepared a reading study in which 8 factive verbs and 8 non-factive verbs were presented in the matrix of subject-verb-(subject-verb-object) sentences (further on named SVO sentences).

[3] Focus is defined as the most important part of the sentence (clause). I distinguish two basic types of focus, namely, neutral (= new information) and contrastive focus. Neutral focus adds a proposition to the current context. Contrastive focus in addition excludes contextually given or accommodated alternatives.

[4] Spenader (2001) however has claimed for English, that factive verbs can be used to introduce new information or (in other terms) information which has to be accommodated instead of being bound by an anaphor as was claimed by Sandt (1992).

To ensure a controlled task every subject, verb and object had 3 syllables, with the word stress fixed to the second syllable. These target sentences were embedded into three types of contexts disambiguating their focus-background-structure. The three conditions (i-iii) defined above are illustrated in (4)-(6) for both factive and non-factive matrix verbs where non-factives are introduced by *$* used as a wildcard:

(i) minimal neutral focus triggered by an alternative question with a factive matrix verb

(4) [A: *Serdilas' ($) li staruška, čto kassirša razbila tarelku?*]
was angry old lady that cashier broke up plate
B: *Staruška serdilas' ($), čto kassirša razbila tarelku.*
'[A: Did the old lady become annoyed that the cashier broke up the plate?]
B: The old lady became annoyed that the cashier broke up the plate.'

(ii) minimal contrastive focus triggered by a correction construction with a factive matrix verb

(5) [A: *Po-moemu, staruška ne serdilas' ($), čto kassirša razbila tarelku.*]
in my opinion old lady not was angry that cashier broke up plate
B: *A kakže. Staruška serdilas' ($), čto kassirša razbila tarelku.*
not at all old lady was angry that cashier broke up plate
'[A: In my opinion, the old lady did not become annoyed that the c. broke up the p.]
B: Not at all. The old lady became annoyed that the cashier broke up the plate.'

Non-factive matrix verb: *($: tverdila* = claimed*)*

(iii) neutral focus on the object (e.g. embedded clause) due to a wh-question

(6) [A: *(Na) čto staruška serdilas' / Čto staruška tverdila?*]
at what old lady was angry / what old lady claimed
B: *Staruška serdilas' / tverdila, čto kassirša razbila tarelku.*
'[A: What was the old lady angry about / what did the old lady claim?]
B: The old lady got annoyed / claimed that the cashier broke up the plate.'

Condition (i) and (ii) were further tested for *OSV* target sentences with fronted embedded clauses. The example below shows the relevant construction:

(7) *Čto kassirša razbila tarelku, staruška serdilas' / tverdila.*
'That the cashier broke up the plate, the old lady was angry at / claimed.'

The conditions are summarized in table 1.

Focus / Word Order / +/-Factivity	Neutral focus on O (O = embedded clause)	Contrastive focus on V	Minimal neutral focus on V
SVO factive / non-factive	SVO_minO	SVO_conV	SVO_minV
OSV factive / non-factive		OSV_conV	OSV_minV

Table 1: Conditions used in production study 1

2.3. Procedure

16 target items per condition (i-iii) were presented together with a set of unrelated fillers in two pseudo-randomized orders. 4 female Russian native speakers were asked to read aloud the contexts, recorded on DAT-tape, and digitized at 44.1 kHz and a 16 bit sampling rate. The target sentences were extracted out of their contexts, then marked up for syllable boundaries, and analyzed semi-automatically within Praat. I measured the fundamental frequency and the absolute time at each quarter syllable for the main clause and at each half syllable for the secondary clause arriving at 46 measure points per sentence. Further, I noted the F0 maxima and minima for every syllable. All in all, 320 experimental items were recorded. By way of a combined introspection of both the auditory signals and the accompanying F0-contours I noticed that there would be no difference for factives and non-factives for the various conditions. That's why I only analyzed 160 of the experimental items, namely the factive sentences.

2.4. Results

Idealized, average F0-contours were drawn for each condition. Two parameters were evaluated: accent shape and maximal F0-height. For the statistic evaluation of F0 and timing data I used the relatively conservative and coarse non-parametric Wilcoxon test. To differentiate between accent shapes (falls and rises, e.g. a nominal scale) I took advantage of the x^2-test. Diagram 1 & 3 use an abstract, relative time scale with ¼ and ½ syllable as the basic unit. Vertical lines indicate syllable boundaries of the matrix verb and of the object within the embedded clause whereby the inner vertical lines identify the syllable with maximal prominence. The relevant contours for SVO sentences are given in diagram 1:

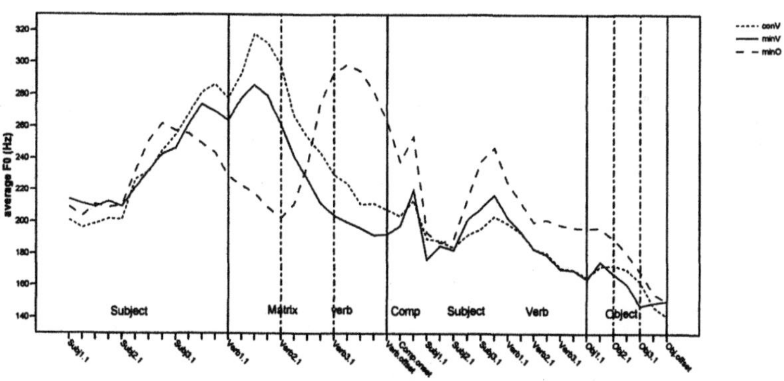

Diagram 1: Condition conV, minV, minO for SVO sentences

I observed that complex *SVO* sentences with minimal or contrastive focus on the matrix verb (conditions *conV, minV* in diagram 1) in fact display the nuclear accent on the matrix verb (with no distinction according to factivity). In both conditions a clear *falling pattern* on the accented syllable of the matrix verb can be attested which can be described as H+L* accent. This is contrary to simple sentences where a minimal neutral or contrastive focus on the verb is marked by an H* or H*+L accent (Meyer & Mleinek 2005). But taking in account that the nuclear accent on the matrix verb within the complex sentence I investigated is followed by a syntactic boundary marking simultaneously a prosodic boundary it can not be surprising that the accent shapes differ.

Both conditions with minimal focus on the matrix verb (*conV, minV*) evoke a straightforward rising up to the F0-maximum of the matrix verb which is reached in the first syllable. But both conditions differ in the F0-maximum on that syllable. This difference in the pitch maxima is significant according to the Wilcoxon test ($W = 108$; $N = 32$; $p = .003$) for the first syllable and carries over to the second ($W = 61$; $N = 32$; $p < .0001$) and third syllables ($W = 84$; $N = 32$; $p = .001$) of the matrix verb. So pitch height serves as a marker for *focus* distinctions within complex sentences as well. As the falling contour takes an almost parallel course for both conditions the degrees of the fall other than the pitch maxima do not differ significantly ($W = 240$; $N = 32$; $p = .645$).
Turning to the condition with neutral focus on the object (*minO*), the nuclear accent sits on the right peripheral argument (object) within the secondary clause. An additional pitch accent can be observed on the matrix verb which surfaces as a *rising pattern* on the second syllable of the matrix verb. The F0-maximum of this rise is reached in the third syllable followed by a fall. The accentual pattern can be described as a L+H* L accent very similar to a yes/no – question pattern in Russian. The rise on the matrix verb indicates the missing closure[5] of the sentence and announces the following new information within the secondary clause marked with a main stress.
Comparing the main clauses of all three conditions we find a clear-cut division between the minimal verb conditions on the one hand and the object condition on the other hand which most apparently is fixed to the second syllable of the matrix verb (e.g. fall and rise). But differences can be ascribed to the main clause subjects already. Within the verb conditions the F0-maximum of the subject which is reached in the third syllable is embedded into the overall rising contour up to the matrix verb. So the contour of the matrix clause is explicitly dedicated to express the fall on the matrix verb. Therefore a prior rise is necessary. Within the object condition on the other hand the subject is followed by a low boundary (L-) marking an intermediate phrase. Comparing the three conditions the F0-maximum of the subject within the object condition is reached significantly earlier than both other conditions, namely within the second syllable. This is borne out by the x^2-test (*conV* vs. *minO*: $P = 23.7$; $N = 64$; $p < .0001$; *minV* vs. *minO*: $P = 21$; $N = 64$; $p < .0001$).
Looking onto the embedded clauses of the various conditions it seems surprising that all conditions are close together and do not vary significantly for their contour. In all three cases a fully effective sentence declination is expressed starting with a reset on the subject. Differences are be found only on the objects of the embedded clause. Here a resetting immediately before the object can be observed within the conditions with minimal (neutral, contrastive) foci on the verb. This observation can well be explained if one assumes that the F0-values at this point in the signal are already too low to allow a further fall on the object. For all experimentees the deepest passages of the signal within these complex sentences are accompanied by a creaky voice. Therefore rendering a further fall makes a prior rise necessary.
But other than the sentence declination the F0-maxima within the contour differ significantly between the minimal verb conditions and the object condition. As a reference point shall serve the F0-maximum on the second syllable of the embedded subject (*minV* vs. *minO*: $W = 101$; $N = 32$; $p = .002$; *conV* vs. *minO*: $W = 47$; $N = 32$; $p < .0001$). As for the minimal verb conditions, they differ significantly in their pitch maxima only within the third syllable of the embedded subject (*conV* vs. *minV*: $W = 84$; $N = 32$; $p = .019$). In both conditions the pitch accent of the embedded clause is perceptually less prominent than the accent on the matrix verb. Acoustically this seems to correlate with the reduced F0-values within the secondary clauses of these conditions. Thus, the secondary clause of the verb conditions can be said to be de-accented.

[5] Looking into the signal of spoken corpora sentences the rising L+H* pitch accent on the verb is mostly followed by a fall and thus cannot be absolutely identified with a *continuation rise* in the British tradition or so called *Progredienz* in German. Contour *minO* in Diagram 1 does not show the full fall. Maybe due to the lack of postaccented material the tune is truncated.

There are no significant timing differences between the minimal verb conditions and the object condition concerning the pause between the offset of the matrix verb and the onset of the complementizer. Only the differences between the conditions *minO* vs. *conV* are reaching almost significance level ($W = 167$; $N = 32$; $p = .07$). But in general, pauses are very short, almost not detectable.

The reset within the embedded clause and the right peripheral pitch accent within both clauses serve as evidence to establish two major phrases (MaP) (e.g. for the main clause and the embedded clause).[6] These are two nuclear accents, with one subordinated to the other. See therefore the following example with a de-accented embedded clause. A single contour of the target sentence in (8) is given in diagram (2):

Context:

Maša s Lidiej vstretilis' na ulice. Oni govorili o novoj inscenirovke p'esy 'Evgenij Onegin'. Maša soobščila Lidii, čto u Mariny uže est' bilety. Možet byt', ona sprosit u nee o biletax. Na sledujusčij den' Maša vstretila Marinu i sprosila ee. No u Mariny uže ne bylo biletov. Maša sožalela, čto Marina vernula bilety.

'Masha and Lidija met each other in the street. They talked together about the new production of the play 'Evgenij Onegin'. Masha told Lidija that Marina already had tickets. Maybe she will ask her for tickets. Next day Masha met Marina and asked her for tickets. But Marina already hadn't any. Masha regretted that Marina had given back the tickets.

(8) *Maša sožaLEla, čto Marina verNUla bilety.*
Masha-nom regret-past/sg/fem that-comp Marina-nom give back-past/sg/fem ticket-acc/pl

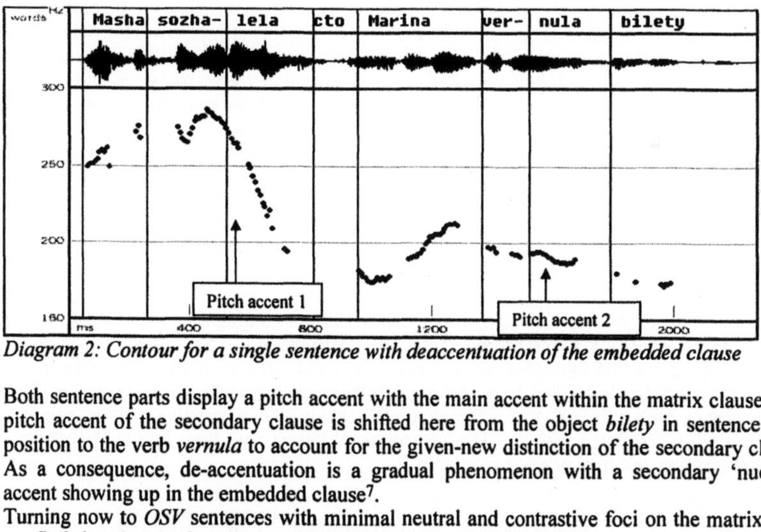

Diagram 2: Contour for a single sentence with deaccentuation of the embedded clause

Both sentence parts display a pitch accent with the main accent within the matrix clause. The pitch accent of the secondary clause is shifted here from the object *bilety* in sentence final position to the verb *vernula* to account for the given-new distinction of the secondary clause. As a consequence, de-accentuation is a gradual phenomenon with a secondary 'nuclear' accent showing up in the embedded clause[7].

Turning now to *OSV* sentences with minimal neutral and contrastive foci on the matrix verb we find that they in fact display the nuclear accent on the matrix verb. I observed a similar

[6] In matrix clauses with the cataphorical argument DP *to*, *to* can almost always attract the rising accent itself, even when it is moved within the matrix clause to another position. I propose that *to* serves as a true focus exponent of the matrix clause.

[7] Interestingly, the option of a secondary 'nuclear' accent within the embedded clause is more or less restricted to cases with focus on the matrix verb. In case the matrix subject is focused, I did not observe a comparable effect (doing away with multiple foci).

falling pattern described as H+L* accent on the matrix verb as for the relevant SVO conditions. This parallelism holds also for the contour of the matrix subject which seems to prepare the fall by being itself embedded into the prior rise. See diagram 3.

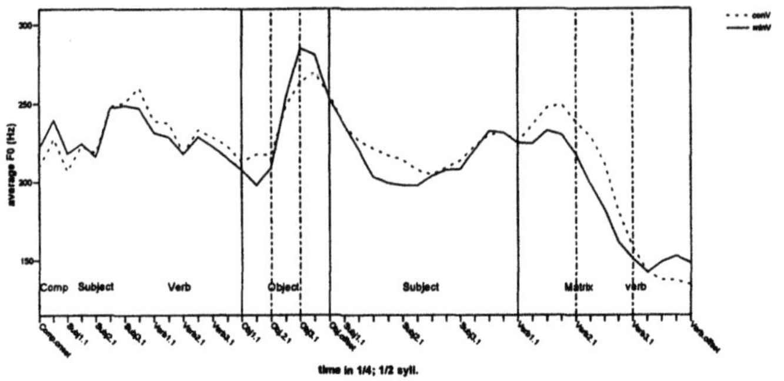

Diagram 3: Condition conV and minV for OSV sentences

As for the pitch maxima of the matrix verb one observes a higher pitch excursion for the contrastive condition. In the second syllable significance was reached ($W = 98$; $N = 32$; $p = .002$). As already pointed out for SVO sentences in OSV sentences too, pitch height serves as a marker for *focus* distinctions.
Looking onto the fronted embedded clause the similarity of the rising tone on the object with that on the matrix verb in the object condition of SVO sentences is apparent. This rising pitch accent interrupts the sentence declination of the secondary clause and clearly signals a continuation of the contour culminating in the nuclear accent on the matrix verb. The reset on the matrix subject is less obvious so that one can say the topicalized embedded clause is more integrated into the whole contour than right peripheral embedded clauses (see above). But interestingly, the rising accent within the topicalized embedded clause is not fixed to the position chosen in this experiment and cannot be seen as a pure rhythmic effect. Instead, it is always confounded to the focus position of the secondary clause and can vary positionally. Additionally, this L+H* L accent marks the topic accent of the whole utterance.

2.5. First conclusions concerning SVO sentences

(i) The positions of the nuclear accent vary systematically according to the constituent which is marked by a focus (e.g. the embedded clause, the matrix verb). (ii) Focus distinctions on the matrix verb are marked by higher pitch in both SVO and OSV sentences. Throughout, the contrastive condition is marked by a higher pitch than the neutral focus condition. (iii) The accent shapes on a minimal focused matrix verb (neutral or contrastive) within complex sentences when compared with simple sentences are different both from foci in intermediate sentence position and final position (see table 2).

Position / Focus Type	Simple Sentence internal	Simple Sentence final	Complex Sentence Internal before clause boundary
Minimal Focus	H*+L	H+L*	H+L*
Contrastive Focus	H*+L	H*+L	H+L*

Table 2: Accent types depending on positions and focus types

As a first approximation there is no simple 1:1 relation between focus types and accent types. They are distinguished within a certain position either by accent shape or by differences in

pitch height. Concerning complex sentences the falling pattern within both focus conditions possibly serves to maximally set apart the accent from the rising accent within the condition with focus on the object. Secondly, it signals the closure of a syntactic and prosodic unit. (iv) As the average contours of the embedded clauses show there is no principled difference between conditions with focus on the object and minimal foci on the matrix verb. And having the nuclear accent within the matrix clause is not concomitant with no stress within the secondary clause. This gives rise to the conclusion that CPs are prosodic units with their own stress. Although one exclusive nuclear accent per complex sentence is both necessary and sufficient the secondary clause is free to mark a separate accent which is admittedly less prominent than the nuclear accent. This secondary accent accounts for the IS of the secondary clause and is not bound to a special position.
Summarizing the facts so far a falling accent signals the closure of a syntactic and prosodic unit. It should be found in all conditions with "de-accented" embedded sentences where the main accent shifts into the matrix clause. Leading over to production study 2, I want to ask whether falling accents within the matrix clause will be used to encode old information concerning the embedded clause.

3. Production Study 2

3.1. Background

After the initial study with strong triggers of backgrounding (using alternative questions questioning the truth of the event or correction constructions) I performed an experiment with neutral contexts which should resemble normal backgrounding strategies for simple sentences. Simplifying the results by Baumann and Grice (in press) who worked explicitly on informational states in German one can assume that old information will be deaccented while new information will be accented. If the deepest embedded argument cannot receive the nuclear stress this implies that the matrix verb will get it. A question which arises is whether these assumptions hold for complex sentences, too. And secondly, I ask in what way do factive embeddings differ from non-factive ones. The null hypothesis then would be that factives and non-factives can both take advantage of the contextual input in the same way. According to the results of the first experiment this would have the following consequence: In case the material of the secondary clause is previously mentioned, I expect a fall on the matrix verb. If on the other hand the secondary clause is new a rising tone will be expected indicating that the main stress will follow in the embedded clause.

3.2. Material

Again, I prepared a reading study in which 10 factive verbs and 8 non-factive verbs were presented in the matrix of subject-verb-(subject-verb-object) sentences. Although a controlled task was desired within this experiment I could not guarantee for reasons of naturalness that in every case the target sentences were matched for the number of syllables and the loci of lexical stress. Within almost natural contexts this demand can simply not be fulfilled. After constructing the target sentences they were embedded into two types of contexts disambiguating their focus-background-structure. The two conditions (old vs. new information) defined above are illustrated in (i/ii) for both factive and non-factive matrix verbs. The targets are underlined, the previously mentioned information is written bold face. In the example below the factive matrix verb *utait' (keep secret)* is opposed to the non-factive verb *zajavit' (declare)* introduced by the $-sign. Pre-information is written in bold face:

i) Conditions with 'old' information:

V magazine po farforovym izdelijam. V magazine byla novaja praktikantka. Uže v pervyj den' ***ona razbila tarelku****. Kassirša vzdoxnula. Večerom ona obsuždala den' s vladel'cem*

magazina. Kassirša utaila ($ zajavila), čto praktikantka razbila tarelku. Devuška etogo ne ožidala.
'In the porcelain shop. There was a trainee in the shop. On the first day already she broke a plate. The cashier sighed. In the evening she gave a report of the day to the shop owner. The cashier kept secret ($ declared), that the trainee broke a plate. The trainee did not expect that.'

ii) Conditions with 'new' information:

V magazine po farforovym izdelijam. Magazin byl zakryt na učet. Kassirša, praktikantka i vladelec magazina vmeste provodili učet. Kassirša utaila ($ zajavila), čto praktikantka razbila tarelku. Devuška etogo ne ožidala.
'In the porcelain shop. The shop was closed for stock-taking. The cashier, the trainee and the shop owner together took stock. The cashier kept secret ($ declared), that the trainee broke a plate. The trainee did not expect that.'

Target sentence:

(9) *Kassirša* *utaila ($ zajavila),* *čto* *praktikantka*
cashier-nom/fem keep secret/declare-past/fem that-comp trainee-nom/fem
razbila *tarelku.*
brake-past/fem plate-acc/sg

The conditions are summarized in table 3.

Factivity \ Information State	Old	New
Factive	F-old	F-new
non-factive	N-old	N-new

Table 3: Conditions used in production study 2

The experiment was divided into two parts: As for the first experiment, in the conditions with old information the target sentence followed the previously mentioned event description immediately. So in a sense, the embedded clause represented truly given material. In the second experiment, I always allowed for a gap of one or two sentences between the pre-information and the target with the potential consequence that the given information was not given any more, but at best accessible.

A further factor comes into play when identifiability of the referent is required to ensure givenness. According to my informants replacement of the embedded clause by the anaphoric demonstrative *eto* is only possible with target sentences immediately following the antecedent or with a target sentence being activated by an anaphoric link chain. As for the contexts in i/ii above *eto* – replacement is impossible, independently of the factivity status of the matrix verb. The target sentence is already too far from the antecedent for being linked to it. But, as Baumann (2005) points out, the identifiability of a referent is not always a necessary pre-requisite for givenness. For givenness it can be sufficient to represent the same textual material, as the contexts above show. But as I said before, the information might be already only accessible, and not given any more. Although both factors – the distance between the target and the antecedent on the one hand and the replacement by *eto* on the other – seem to be somehow correlated, they can predict givenness only in case of a short distance. Should there be a larger distance between target and antecedent the prediction of non-givenness would be too strong. To avoid wrong implications in connection with replacement by *eto* I did not pay much attention to this factor. Instead, the gap between the target and the antecedent was taken as a more neutral measure for givenness.

Factivity
To ensure the (non)factivity of the matrix verbs they were tested for their behaviour under negation. As for the factive matrix verbs, the presupposition of the embedded clause still holds under negation, while for non-factives the presupposition fails. The verbs in table 4 were chosen according to the judgments of my Russian informants.

Verb	Factives	Translation	Nonfactives	Translation
1	*zametit'*	'notice'	*podumat'*	'think'
2	*uvidet'*[8]	'see'	*poverit'*	'believe'
3	*uznat'*	'realize'	*podozrevat'*[9]	'presume'
4	*znat'*	'know'	*polagat'*	'assume'
5	*zabyt'*	'forget'	*zajavit'*	'declare'
6	*utait'*	'keep secret'	*skazat'*	'say'
7	*žalet'*	'regret'	*rešit'*	'decide'
8	*serdit'sja*	'be angry'	*nadejat'sja*	'hope'
9	*gordit'sja*	'be proud'		
10	*udivit'sja*	'be surprised'		

Table 4: Factive and non-factive matrix verbs used in the experiment

3.3. Procedure

In both experiments 10 vs. 8 target items per condition were presented together with a set of unrelated fillers in two pseudo-randomized orders. 8 female Russian native speakers were asked to read aloud the contexts, recorded on DAT-tape, and digitized at 44.1 kHz and a 16 bit sampling rate. 3 out of 8 speakers were not chosen for further acoustic measurements because they did not detect the information status "old" at all resulting in a rise for all conditions. The remaining 5 experimentees were further analyzed in the same manner as in the first production study (see section 2). Some manipulations were indeed necessary to mark up the targets for syllable boundaries resulting in 46 measure points per sentence, and to analyze them semi-automatically within Praat. All in all, 196 experimental items were analyzed. As already in the first production study I used the Wilcoxon test for the statistic evaluation of F0 and timing data. To differentiate between falls and rises the x^2-test was employed.

3.4. Results
3.4.1. The distribution of accent types within different contexts

As I already found out in production study 1 the main difference between the various contours should be seen on the 2nd syllable of the matrix verb (e.g. falls and rises). So the distribution of both contours within all four conditions is of main interest. Although idealized, average F0-contours were drawn for each condition. This is somewhat problematic because different contours could be realized within one condition and would cancel each other out. Therefore I used a different strategy. First, I created a new variable which displays a rising or falling accent by computing a difference between the pitch values of the 1st and the 4th quarter syllables of the 2nd syllable and assigning <0,1> to positive and negative differences. The results for both experiments is given as percentage of falls and rises for all conditions and can be seen in diagrams 4, 5.

[8] According to Karttunen (1970) or Barwise & Perry (1987) perception verbs like *zametit'* or *uvidet'* should count as factive, at least in the affirmative case. When negated they are clearly non-factive.
[9] *Podozrevat'* is only non-factive in an affirmative sentence. In a negative sentence it is factive. According to Karttunen's classification (1972) *podozrevat'* would count as a negative "only-if" verb.

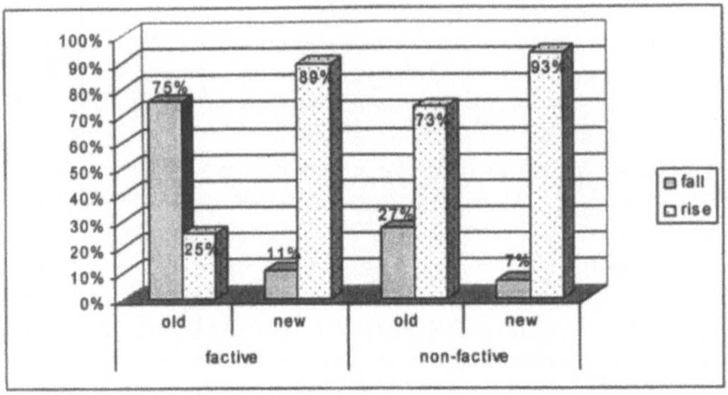

Diagram 4: Falls and rises in all conditions without a gap between pre-information and target sentence

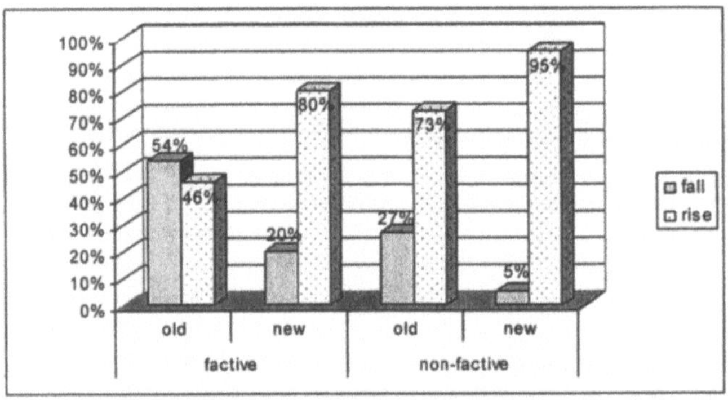

Diagram 5: Falls and rises in all conditions with a gap of one/two sentences between pre-information and target sentence

Concerning both experiments, the variation among the various conditions might be surprising. Falls and rises are not distributed equally across conditions, but seem to be more or less preferred by certain conditions. According to diagrams 4, 5 an influence both of the context (old, new) and of factivity on the number of falls and rises can be asserted.[10] This observation is statistically confirmed by the x^2-test:

Experiment 1:
For factive matrix verbs, the distribution of falls and rises according to the context (old, new) is significant: $P = 47.3$; $N = 112$; $p < .0001$, and for non-factive matrix verbs alike: $P = 7.7$; $N = 112$; $p = .006$. For old information, the distribution of falls and rises according to factivity is significant, too: $P = 26$; $N = 112$; $p < .0001$, but not in the case of new information: $P = 0.44$; $N = 112$; $p = .508$. Concerning new information, no difference can be stated between factive and non-factive embeddings. They perform equally well.

[10] Maybe within condition *F-old* a third accent pattern comes into play hiding among rising tones. One of the speakers used consistently a contrastive rising tone to encode old information. But this observation is only based on auditory introspection and not on an acoustically measurable difference between various rising tones within the F-old condition.

Experiment 2:
For factive matrix verbs, the distribution of falls and rises according to the context (old, new) is significant: $P = 8.2$; $N = 100$; $p = .004$, and for non-factive matrix verbs alike: $P = 7.4$; $N = 80$; $p = .006$. For old information, the distribution of falls and rises according to factivity is significant, too: $P = 6.4$; $N = 90$; $p = .011$, and for new information alike: $P = 7.1$; $N = 90$; $p = .008$. With some deviations this result resembles the percentages reached within the first experiment. The difference in the percentage, especially for condition *F-old*, may be ascribed to the restriction applicable to pre-information which in the first experiment was put right before the target while in the second experiment I always allowed for a gap of one or two sentences between one and the other. It may well be that more material reduces the speaker's ability or the need to detect old information. That the degree of activation is a decisive factor for detecting old information has been stated already for simple sentences by Baumann & Grice (in press). Obviously, that can be confirmed by my experiments for complex sentences, too.

When we turn to the performance of the particular verbs we find that some verbs seem to group together. Especially emotional factives like *žalet'*, *udivit'sja, serdit'sja, gordit'sja* seem to perform well in condition *F-old*. That is, they used the fall as a distinctive feature for old information throughout. As for non-factive verbs, especially speech act verbs like *skazat'* or *zajavit'* have influenced the preference for a rise within condition *F-old* more than for instance believe verbs like *poverit'* or *podozrevat'*. But generally, to say more about the differences between the various verbs and even between semantic classes of verbs would require more than one or two items per verb, but a whole experiment for each verb. Therefore I remain silent about particular verbs in the remainder of the text.

Abstracting away from the particular verbs, the experiment shows that both the information status and the factivity of the verbs are represented in the distribution of the accent shapes. While it is plausible that old information is encoded differently than new information the distinction between factives and non-factives is not. While factives display the division of new and old information non-factives don't. As long as there is no stronger trigger for backgrounding in the main clause or on part of the speaker him / herself, in the tendency the very fact of being old information does not suffice to de-accent the object clause embedded by non-factives. Factives on the other hand embed new information as well as old information. Non-factives more or less embed only new information. They are obviously assertive in the first place. But asking questions pointing to the matrix verb or the truth of the event (as in production study 1), adding a particle or a temporal adverb can shift the accent.

3.4.2. Pitch tracking data – acoustic and prosodic analysis

Turning now to idealized, average F0-contours I only report the data of the second experiment with far antecedents. Here I have to account for the fact that in condition *F-old* falls and rises had almost chance level. The solution then is to single out both contours by way of creating two separate contours (further named *F-old.1* for falls and *F-old.2* for rises). With this proviso condition *F-old* is comparable with condition *F-new* (see diagram 6). Again, the diagrams 6-7 use an abstract, relative time scale with ¼ and ½ syllables as the basic unit. As before vertical lines indicate syllable boundaries of the matrix verb.

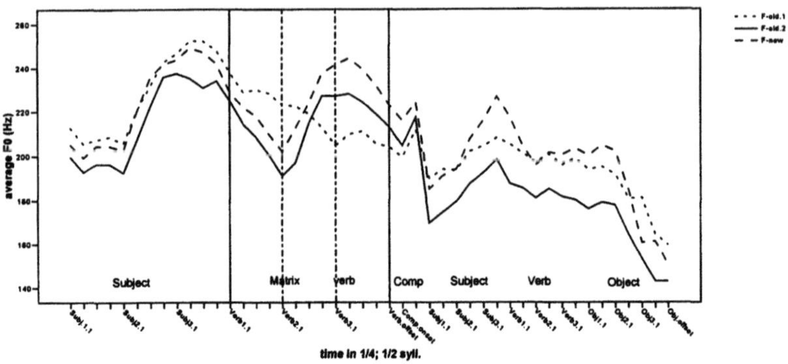

Diagram 6: F0-contours for factive matrix verbs within neutral contexts

As already expected the matrix verbs of condition *F-new* and of condition *F-old.1* would clearly differ in their accent shapes. Interestingly here, and contrary to the minimal verb conditions in the production study 1 the fall on the matrix verb in condition *F-old.1* is embedded into the whole matrix clause declination with the F0-maximum already reached on the subject. This kind of contour resembles a wide focus within simple sentences (see Alter et al. 2001) and can be attributed to the context which presents old information remaining silent about the status of the matrix verb. So the accent shift truly is due to the given-new distinction and is not caused by focus in the first place. Obviously then, in complex sentences too, a non-narrow focus behaves differently than a narrow focus on the matrix verb.
Concerning the second possible contour within condition *F-old* (e.g. *F-old.2*), I did not expect a variation from condition *F-new* at all. As one can read off the contours, the F0-maxima on the second and third syllables of the matrix verb seem to offer some variation. But this observation is not confirmed by the Wilcoxon test ($W = 56$; $N = 19$; $p = .117$ concerning the second syllable) which can be partly explained by the missing test power.
Turning now to the secondary clauses the differences will be more substantial. Here, contour *F-old.2* is truly set apart from condition *F-new* by imitating the contour of *F-new* on a lower level. Taking the differences between the F0-maxima on the subject as a reference point for the differences between both conditions I found a significant variation on the second syllable ($W = 37$; $N = 19$; $p = .02$) and even more on the third syllable ($W = 20$; $N = 19$; $p = .003$). The falling contour within condition *F-old*, on the other hand, takes a mid position between the other contours concerning the F0-values. Looking at the average contours in diagram 6 gives the impression that the embedded subject within that condition does not stick out of the down stepped contour very much. But statistically, the F0-maxima of the embedded subject within that condition did not differ at all from those within condition *F-new*. Neither of the seeming variations within the F0-maxima in each syllable is below $p = .35$. As a consequence, *F-new* differs from *F-old.2*, but not from *F-old.1*.
Switching now to the comparison of condition *N-old* vs. *N-new* the distribution of F0-maxima looks quite similar compared to the rising contours of condition *F-old-2* and *F-new*. The relevant contours are given in diagram 7.

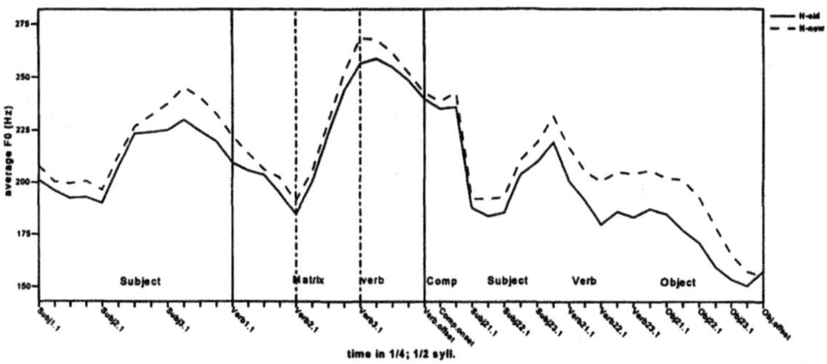

Diagram 7: F0-contours for non-factive matrix verbs within neutral contexts

As for the F0-maxima on the matrix verb no significant variation can be reported between conditions although significance is almost reached within the second syllable ($W = 213$; $N = 36$; $p = .059$). It seems quite unclear if this result may be ascribed to the missing test power here because it is doubled in comparison to the conditions *F-old.2* vs. *F-new*. Again, a clear differentiation is met within the embedded clause. Both contours imitate each other on different F0-levels. As for the F0-maxima of the embedded subject I find significant differences between *N-old* vs. *N-new*, especially on the second syllable ($W = 179$; $N = 36$; $p = .016$).

According to statistics then the rising accents on the matrix verb are the same independently of the condition where they are produced. Still it is in place to ask whether the rises produced in a condition with old information could play the role of a nuclear accent if one assumes the lower pitch within the secondary clause to be evidence for its de-accentuation. Listening carefully to the auditory signal does not lead one to such a conclusion because the nuclear accent lies clearly within the secondary clause. But what could be encoded within the embedded clause by lower F0-values? Although an answer to the question might be rather speculative the acoustic features given here could be ascribed to a reduced effort code on the side of the speaker in the sense of Gussenhoven (2002). He argues that a higher pitch signals newness. Reversing this statement would allow me to say: the lower the pitch, the lower is also the degree of newness of the information encoded. It could well be that a message which has been mentioned before already, cannot be introduced as absolutely new. By lowering the effort to encode the message the speaker might signal the hearer to lower the expectation for receiving new information. Another explanation could be that the specific contour used here unambiguously encodes accessible information avoiding de-accentuation but reducing the F0-values. But these possible explanations have to be supported by more careful studies than this. Obviously, one can conclude from the data that for a de-accentuation of a secondary clause its pitch behaviour is almost not conclusive. I think the prosodic endowment of the main clause is more important here to decide whether a secondary clause is de-accented or not.

3.5. Discussion

The second production study showed that the prosody of Russian complex sentences is sensitive to distinctions concerning the informational state and factivity. But this overall picture can be taken only as a tendency. Old information will be deaccented, but only in case the speaker is willing to do so. There are several reasons to decline deaccentuation. Some are given in Spenader (2001) already. She argues that embeddings which seem to be complete repetitions are not. Speakers tend to repeat material in order to render a new aspect of the already mentioned fact. Oldness in connection with whole CPs is less obvious and not the preferred option. But in principle, the embedded clause can be deaccented in case it will be

detected as old. It will be accented in the default case. A lower pitch within the secondary clause can account for reduced newness or for accessible information.
True de-accentuation of the embedded clause is accompanied by a fall in the matrix clause. The distribution of falls and rises depends on the old-new distinction but also on another factor, namely on the factive – non-factive distinction for matrix verbs which is surprising. Obviously, this semantic distinction is relevant and represented within prosody. Factives tend to obey the old–new distinction whereas non-factives hardly ever do so. It looks like most of the non-factive verbs do not care for the information state of the embedded clause. Maybe some deeper reason can be seen within the different presuppositional possibilities of these verbs (*plugs* vs. *holes*). But to give a coherent semantic explanation goes beyond this text. What I can say so far is that the simplified hypothesis of the introduction that factives will always have a falling accent on the matrix verb for they require given information is proved to be false.

4. Conclusion

This article was dedicated to Russian complex sentences with *čto*-object clauses. Within two experiments I could show that the prosodic realisation of these sentences is sensitive to focus types and placement, and interestingly, to the (non-)factivity of their matrix verbs as well. Two prosodic parameters were investigated: pitch height and accent shape. I leave the durational and boundary behaviour to future research.

Bibliography

Alter, Kai, Mleinek, Ina & Nicole Richter (2001): Prosodic Phrasing and Accentuation in Russian. In: Zybatow, G. et al. (Hrsg.): *Current Issues in Formal Slavic Linguistics*, 317-328. Frankfurt/Main: Lang.

Baumann, S. (submitted): Towards an Integrated Annotation of Prosody and Information Structure. Ms. 2005.

Baumann, S. & M. Grice (in press): Accenting Accessible Information. In: *Speech Prosody* 2004, Nara, Japan.

Barwise, J. & J. Perry (1987): Situationen und Einstellungen. Grundlagen der Situationssemantik. Berlin, New York: de Gruyter.

Chafe, W. (1994): Discourse, Consciousness, and Time. Chicago/London: University of Chicago Press.

Gussenhoven, C. (2002): Intonation and interpretation: Phonetics and Phonology. To appear in: *Proceedings of Speech Prosody* 2002.

Junghanns, U. & G. Zybatow (1997): Syntax and Information Structure of Russian Clauses. In: Browne, E. W. et al. (eds.): *Annual Workshop on Formal Approaches to Slavic Linguistics. The Cornell Meeting 1995.* (= *Michigan Slavic Materials*; 39). Ann Arbor, Michigan: Michigan Slavic Publications, 289-319.

Karttunen, L. (1970): On the semantics of complement clauses. In: *Papers from the 6th Regional Meeting of the Chicago Linguistic Society*, 328-339.

Karttunen, L. (1972): Die Logik der Prädikatskomplementkonstruktionen. In: Abraham, W. & R. J. Binnick (Hrsg.): *Generative Semantik* (= *Linguistische Forschungen*; 11). Frankfurt a. M.: Äthenäum.

Komagata, N. (2001): Entangled Information Structure: Analysis of Complex Sentence Structures. In: *Paper presented at the ESSLLI 2001 Workshop on Information Structure, Discourse Structure and Discourse Semantics.* Edited by I. Kruijff-Korbayová & M. Steedman.

Mathesius, V. (1975): A Functional Analysis of Present Day English on a General Linguistic Basis, edited by Josef Vachek. The Hague: Mouton.

Mehlhorn, G. (2002): Kontrastierte Konstituenten im Russischen. Experimentelle Untersuchungen zur Informationsstruktur. Frankfurt a. M.: Lang.

Meyer, R. & I. Mleinek (2005): How prosody signals force and focus – a study of pitch accents in Russian yes-no questions. To appear in: *Journal of Pragmatics*.

Neeleman, A. & K. Szendrői (2004): Superman Sentences. In: *Lingusitic Inquiry*, Vol. 35, No. 1, 149-157.

Roberts, C. (1996): Information Structure in Discourse: Towards and Integrated Formal Theory of Pragmatics. Ms. semanticsarchive.net

Sandt, R. A. van der (1992): Presupposition Projection as Anaphora Resolution. In: *Journal of Semantics* 9, 333-377.

Spenader, J. (2001): Presupposition or Anaphora: Constraints on Choice of Factive Complements in Spoken Discourse. In: *Proceedings of the ESSLLI (2001) Workshop on Information Structure, Discourse Structure and Discourse Semantics*. Helsinki.

Acknowledgements

This research was supported by the German Science Foundation (Research Group "Linguistic Foundations for Cognitive Science", University of Leipzig, Project D2). I would like to thank my speakers as well as Roland Meyer (University of Regensburg), Denisa Lenertová, Stefan Sudhoff (both University of Leipzig), Bert Remijsen (University of Edinborogh), Stefan Baumann (University of Cologne) and Peter Kosta (University of Potsdam) for helpful comments.

Dominika Oliver and Bistra Andreeva, Saarbrücken

Peak Alignment in Broad and Narrow Focus in Polish and Bulgarian. A Cross-language Study

1. Introduction

Tonal alignment can be defined as the temporal synchronization of tones with some specific segments or prosodic locations (such as syllable onset, syllable offset or rhyme onset) and may be related to phonological and/or phonetic factors. Phonological factors are qualitative and categorical (e.g. align target with syllable X rather then syllable Y) and imply different accent patterns (H+L* vs. H*+L). Phonetic factors are gradient and can often be modelled by means of interacting quantitative parameters (e.g. align target the earlier the closer it is to the next target). These factors additionally "fine-tune" the alignment of tonal targets, determining the differing phonetic realisation of the same phonological tones. Previous studies have suggested that timing of f_0 peaks is a function of: speech tempo, durations of segments in the accented syllable, distance in syllables from the accent to the word boundary and the next stressed syllable, focal structure, as well as sentence mode (Steele 1986, Silverman & Pierrehumbert 1990, Prieto et al. 1995, Rietveld & Gussenhoven 1995, Prieto 2004, Miševa 1991, Ladd 2004, among others). The purpose of this study was to produce a descriptive model of peak placement and to analyse the relationship between peak location and its segmental anchors. Questions posed further pertain to the phonetic realisation of phonologically specified peak alignment in Polish and Bulgarian as a function of the following factors: speech tempo, information structure, and position within utterance.

2. Experimental Design

In this experiment, two tertiary-level educated female speakers of Sofia Bulgarian and two of standard Polish generated read material. The following four sentences were recorded six times per focus condition in a random order at normal and fast speech rate in a sound treated studio at the Inst. of Phonetics (U Saarland). The Bulgarian sentences are a subset of a larger dataset.

Speech material for Bulgarian:

1. *'včera 'mama 'maza 'masata.*
   yesterday mama painted the table
   'Yesterday mum painted the table.'
2. *'včera 'mama po'maga na 'Mareto.*
   yesterday mama helped to Mareto
   'Yesterday mum helped Mareto.'
3. *'včera 'mama ni po'maga po gra'matika.*
   yesterday mama us helped in grammar
   'Yesterday mum helped us in grammar.'
4. *'utre 'mama šte ni po'maga po mate'matika.*
   tomorrow mama will us help in mathematics
   'Tomorrow mum will help us in maths.'

Speech material for Polish:

1. *'mama 'ma te'maty.*
   mother has topics.
   'Mother has topics.'
2. *'mama wy'maga te'matu.*
   mother requires topic.
   'Mother requires a topic.'
3. *a'mator nas na'mawiał do te'matu.*
   amateur us urged to topic.
   'The amateur urged us to accept the topic.'
4. *a'mator nam niedo'magał przy Ka-za'matach*
   amateur us felt unwell in Kazamaty
   'The amateur felt unwell in Kazamaty.'

Since we are primarily interested in the contribution of the intonation, we fixed the word order to reflect the canonical one , i.e., *subject* < *verb* < *direct object* < *indirect object* < *oblique*[1]. Moreover, where possible, we designed the material to make the data easily comparable in the two languages (cf. the four sentences for Bulgarian and Polish above). In the test sentences the distance between metrically strong syllables varies from one to four unaccented syllables. In the Bulgarian material we do not analyse the very first word (*včera* 'yesterday' or *utre* 'tomorrow') but take it as a filling material preceding the stressed syllable in *mama* 'mum' or *Mareto*). The syllables we analyse are always /ma/ so that they have same segmental structure (maximally sonorant) in order to avoid micro-prosodic effects.

We used two methods for eliciting different focus types. In one, the test sentences were embedded in dialogue sequences as replies to wh-queries uttered by the instructor (a) about the entire utterance, resulting in *broad focus*, and (b) directed towards the initial or final word, resulting in a *narrow non-contrastive focus* in the respective position. In the other, *narrow contrastive focus* condition (c), we embedded the test sentences in dialogues consisting of a yes/no-query uttered by the instructor towards the initial, middle or final word, and a correcting reply by the subject. Thus we span broad, narrow and narrow contrastive focus respectively, e.g.:

(a) Co dzisiaj nowego? '*What's new today'?* – [$_F$Mama ma TEMATY]
(b) Co ma mama? '*What has mother got?'* – Mama ma [$_F$TEMATY]
(c) Czy mama ma streszczenia? '*Has mother got summaries?'* –
Nie, mama ma [$_F$TEMATY]

The subjects were not informed about the purpose of the study No explicit instructions were given to them. They only had the test sentences on a sheet of paper and had to read them out in a manner that most suited the instructor's query, i.e., their reaction was elicited by the way the authors presented the material.

In total there were 288 utterances per speaker for Polish and Bulgarian (6 target word per focus[2] x 4 test sentences x 2 tempi x 6 repetitions x 2 speakers).

The recordings were digitised at a sampling frequency of 16 kHz and with an amplitude resolution of 12 bits. All segments in target words in the data were manually labelled on the basis of the synchronised microphone signal and a spectrogram using xassp (Advanced Speech Signal Processor; IPDS 1997) and slightly modified SAMPA transcription (cf. Fig. 1).

In addition to the segmental annotation, the peak position of the L(ow) and H(igh) targets was also identified and marked. To verify the labelling, each of the authors analysed random utterances from both languages and compared each other's analysis.

To sum up, the following points were labelled in each sentence:

- C0 – the beginning of the word initial consonant,
- V0 – the beginning of the word initial vowel,
- C1 – the beginning of the initial consonant of the target syllable,
- V1 – the beginning of the initial vowel of the target syllable,
- C2 – the beginning of the initial consonant of the syllable following the target syllable,
- V2 – the beginning of the initial vowel of the syllable following the target syllable,

[1] Because of difficulties in constructing the stimuli for Polish (fixed stress on the penult) the word order in test sentence 3 and 4 is not the canonical one.
[2] Each focus condition had a different number of target words, i.e., one in broad (object), two in narrow non-contrastive (subject, object) and three in narrow contrastive (subject, verb, object), giving us six target words.

- E – end of target word,
- SA – beginning of target utterance,
- SE – end of target utterance,
- H – point of f_0 maximum in the target word,
- L – point of f_0 minimum in the target word.

In all our utterances C1 = /m/, V1 = /a/, marked with capital letters "M" and "A" (cf. Fig. 1).

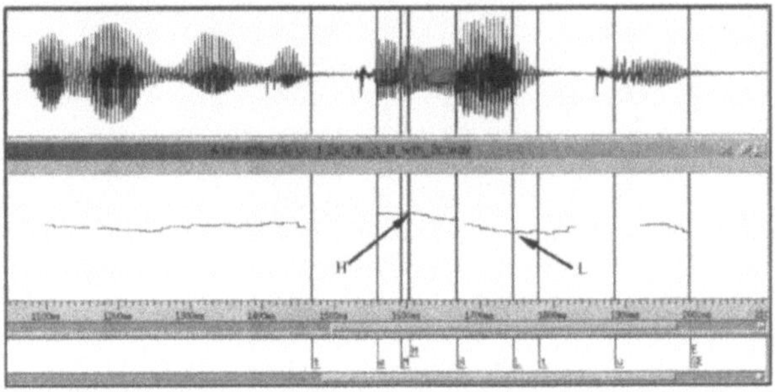

Figure 1. Example of labelled target word *'tematu'* with its waveform and f_0 contour .

3. Measurements

A number of studies have indicated that the following measurements may be significant in terms of segmental anchor points for f0 peak position (Atterer and Ladd 2004, Prieto et al. 1995, Schepman et al. 2006). Thus, we calculated peak delay as a distance measure from the f0 peak to:

- syllable onset
- syllable offset
- rhyme onset

The peak delay was calculated as the absolute distance in time from the f0 peak to syllable onset (H – C1), syllable offset (H – C2) and rhyme onset (H – V1). Due to the possible effect of the varying segmental durations on peak delay, the above absolute measures were also converted to relative, taken as a proportion of syllable (C2 – C1) and rhyme duration (C2 – V1) (cf. Fig. 2). Additionally, the maximum f0 value of the pitch target was measured.

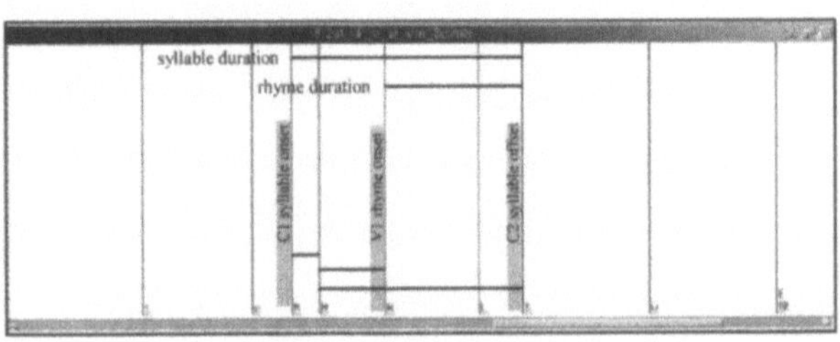

Figure 2. Example of distance measures taken.

4. Results

As reported in Andreeva & Oliver (to appear) the following accent types are used in the examined focus conditions. The Bulgarian speakers use H+!H*/L*, (!)H* and L+H*, and the Polish speakers (!)H+L*, H*+L and L+H*. For both languages, they found different accent types in the same focus condition and the same accent types in different focus conditions.

To analyse the effects on peak alignment, we carried out multivariate analyses of variance, with Scheffé post-hoc tests when appropriate. Since a very large number of the absolute measures and very few of the relative measures showed significant variation, statistical results are reported with reference to absolute measures. However, for better visualisation, we will refer to alignment in text and in Figs. 3, 4, and 7 in terms of the relative peak position, namely the distance in percent of the syllable duration.

The results for both languages will be presented following the focus condition (broad, narrow, narrow-contrastive) and sentence position (initial, medial and final). We compare the data for Polish and Bulgarian with respect to inter- and intra-language differences.

4.1. The effect of speech tempo

4.1.1. Broad focus

In both languages, statements with broad focus were mostly realised as having a falling nuclear pitch movement, i.e. a H(igh) accent followed by a L(ow). In Polish, it is represented only by a fall. Mean peak delays from the onset of accented syllable were -19.1% ((!)H+L*) and 15.7% (H*+L) for speaker WM and 44% for the speaker KA measured as a proportion of the syllable length (cf. Fig. 3). The difference in peak delay between the speakers reflects their choice of accent type: speaker KA uses exclusively H*+L whereas speaker WM prefers (!)H+L* (92% of the cases) and chooses H*+L accent in the remaining cases. Due to the different phonological peak alignment of the two accent types, (in the first case the high target occurs in the accented syllable and in the latter before the syllable onset), KA aligns her peaks much further into the syllable (3.5% into the rhyme onset) than speaker WM.

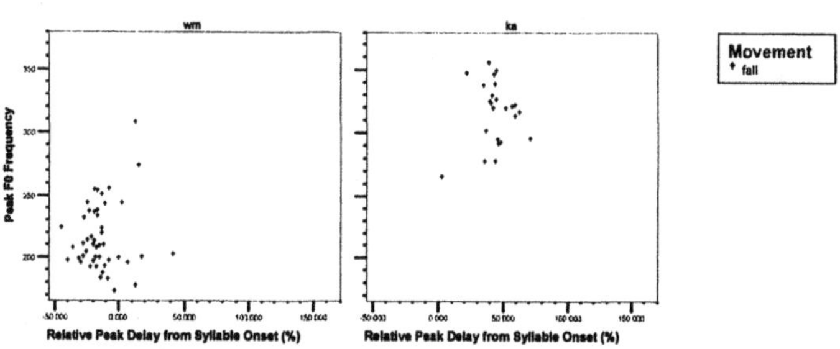

Figure 3. Polish speakers' peak height in broad focus condition

The Bulgarian speaker EK uses a pitch accent which can be analysed as either H+!H* or H+L* (because of the sentence final position and the upcoming low boundary tones L-L%, it is impossible to distinguish between the two accent types). Because it was impossible to mark the position of the peak if any present, we decided to exclude the broad focus data for this speaker. The other Bulgarian speaker, BA, uses predominantly !H* in normal speech rate and only H* in fast speech rate as well as rising pitch in four cases. Therefore, she shows a significant difference in peak alignment in two tempi (normal 3.4%, fast 42.8%). The observed positive correlation between tempo and peak alignment on the one hand, and tempo and f_0 values on the other, results from the two different accent types used in this focus condition (cf. Fig. 4).

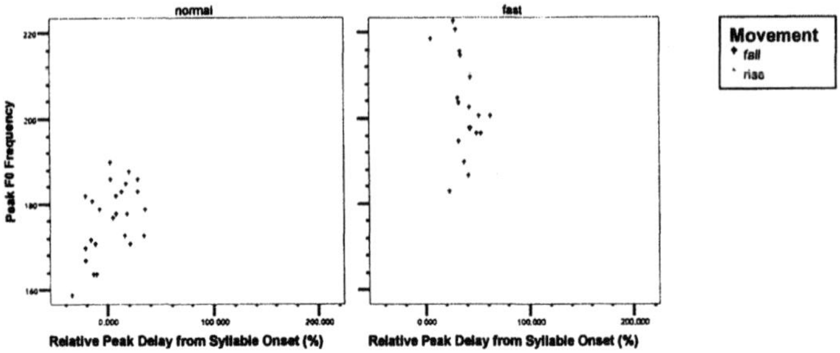

Figure 4. Speaker BA's peak frequency relative to peak position in broad focus condition (Bulgarian)

4.1.2. Narrow Non-contrastive Focus

a) Focus on subject (initial position)

When the first content word (here subject) is in narrow non-contrastive focus, pitch accents across speakers in both languages are realised as falls as well as rises. In Polish, for speaker KA, who uses only rising pitch accents (L+H*) in this condition, there is a main effect of tempo on peak alignment. The mean delay from syllable onset in normal speech rate for this speaker is 75.5% of the syllable duration, whereas in fast speech rate it occurs 26.5% later in the syllable. Additionally we observe significantly higher f_0 values in fast speech tempo for speaker KA (cf. Fig. 6). Speaker WM uses both rises (L+H*) and falls (H*+L) in this condition. The observed tendency in fast speech for this speaker is to align falls 5.5% earlier (58.5% at normal speech rate) and rises 1.7% later (85.6% at normal speech rate) (cf. Fig. 5).

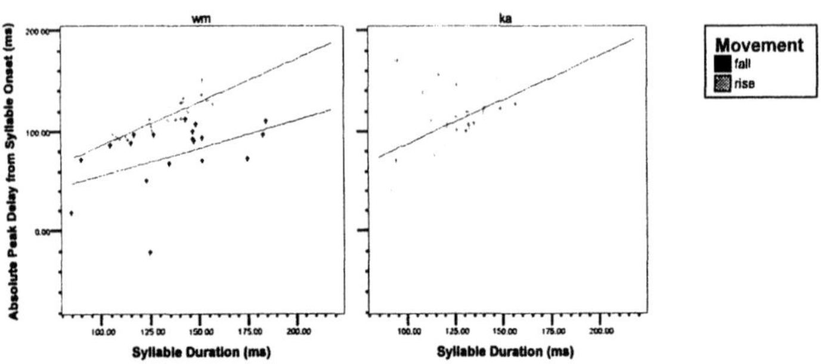

Figure 5. Polish speakers' peak positions in narrow non-contrastive focus condition

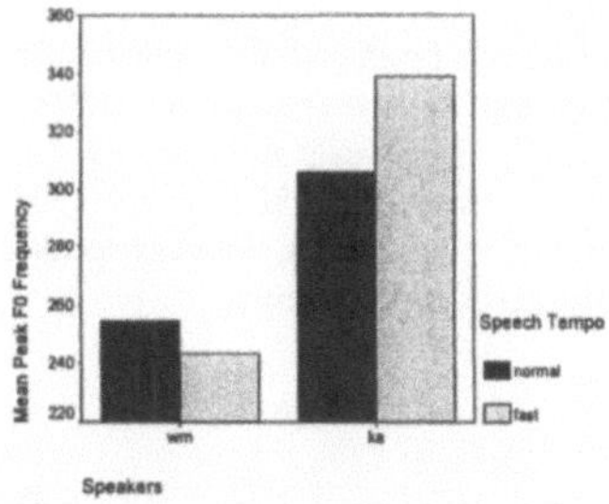

Figure 6. Speaker strategies narrow non-contrastive focus condition (Polish)

In Bulgarian, in this condition, the two speakers behave significantly differently in their alignment of falls and rises. The falling movement (H*) is realised much earlier by speaker EK (-20.6%) than by speaker BA (53.3%). On the other hand, the peak of the rising movement (L+H*) for speaker EK comes later (122.1%) than for speaker BA, who realizes them at 85.8% (cf. Fig. 7).

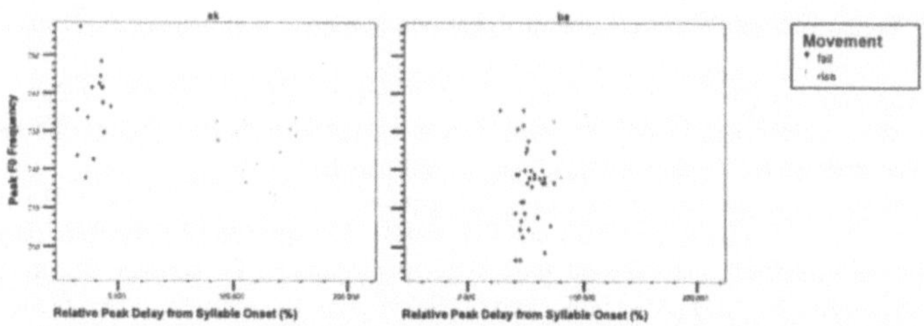

Figure 7. Bulgarian speakers' peak positions relative to pitch height in narrow non-contrastive focus condition

The analysis of the data for speaker BA shows a significant effect of speech tempo and f_0 peak height as well as f_0 peak alignment for both falls and rises in this condition. With the increase in speech tempo the f_0 peak reaches higher f_0 values. At the same time, it is produced earlier with respect to the syllable and rhyme onset for falling and with respect to rhyme onset only for rising contours (cf. Fig. 8).

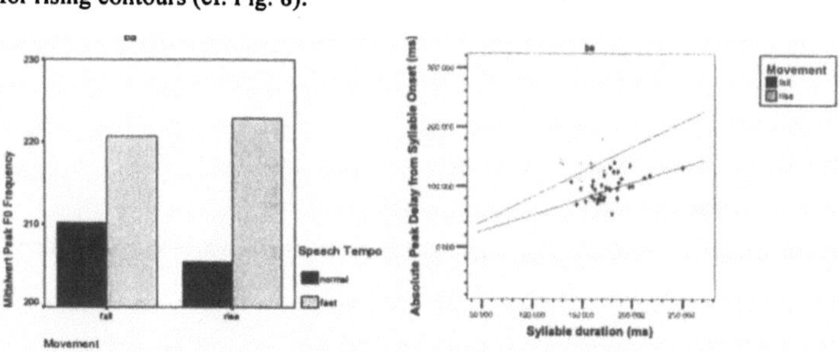

Figure 8. Bulgarian speaker BA's peak height and position in narrow non-contrastive focus

b) Focus on object (final position)
In this condition, both Polish speakers produce falling pitch accents. Speaker WM uses H*+L as well as (!)H+L*, whereas speaker KA uses exclusively H*+L. The analysis of peak alignment for the same accent type (H*+L) reveals significant speaker and tempo differences in that speaker WM puts her peak at 16% and 7.9% from the syllable onset in normal and fast speech tempo respectively (cf. Fig. 9, left panel), whereas speaker KA realises her peaks later (40.9%) without significant difference across tempo.

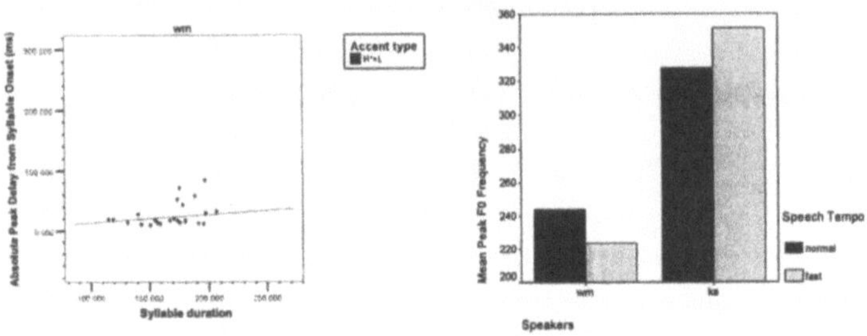

Figure 9. Polish speakers' peak alignment and height in narrow non-contrastive focus cond.

For both speakers we observe a significant effect of speech tempo on f_0 peak values. However, they show contrasting behaviour: with increasing speech tempo, f_0 values decrease for speaker WM and rise for speaker KA (cf. Fig. 9, right panel).

In Bulgarian, while speaker EK uses only rising pitch accents (L+H*), speaker BA prefers H* accents (only four cases of L+H* accents are found). The position of peaks with respect to the syllable onset reflects the different pitch movement choices, for speaker EK at 100.8% (rises), and speaker BA at 33.8% (falls), and at 72.2% (rises). As expected, we found a significant main effect of tempo on peak alignment values for both speakers (cf. Fig. 10), and on f_0 peak height in the case of speaker BA only, i.e. a higher peak in fast speech.

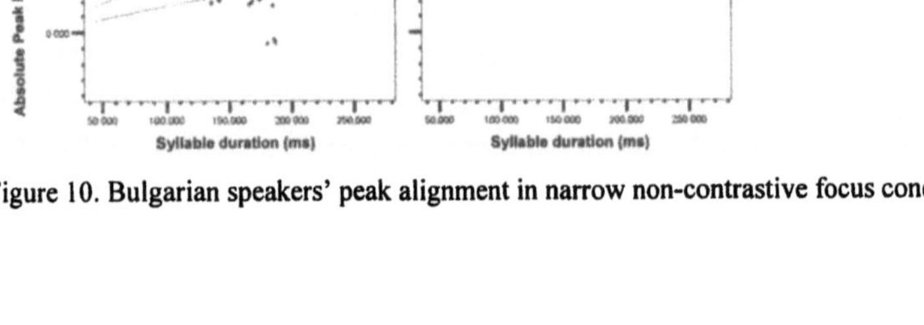

Figure 10. Bulgarian speakers' peak alignment in narrow non-contrastive focus condition

4.1.3. Narrow Contrastive Focus

a) Focus on subject (initial position)

In Polish, in narrow contrastive focus, the accented syllable of the subject is realised with a rising pitch (L+H*) and the peak delay is placed either towards the end of the syllable rhyme or after the syllable offset. In normal speech tempo, speakers WM and KA align the peak at 85.6% and 96.5% of the syllable duration respectively. In fast speech tempo, we observe peak alignment at 81.4% for speaker WM and 105.6% for speaker KA. Speaker WM aligns the peak earlier in fast speech as expected (cf. Fig. 11, right panel). The opposite behaviour found for speaker KA is not significant. Contrasting behaviour for the two speakers was also found with respect to the effect of speech tempo. The effect was significant for both speakers; WM lowered f_0 with increasing tempo, whereas speaker KA showed higher f_0 with increasing speech tempo (cf. Fig 11).

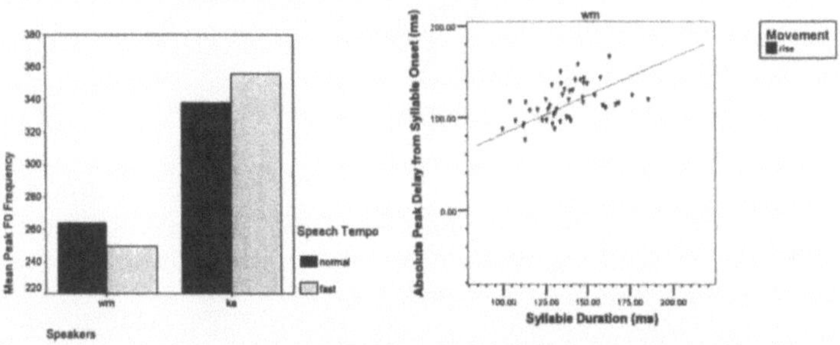

Figure 11. Polish speakers' peak alignment and height in narrow contrastive focus cond.

In Bulgarian, there are main effects of tempo and speaker on peak alignment. As in 4.1.2., speaker EK uses only rising movements (L+H*), whereas speaker BA uses both movement types (L+H* and H*). At a normal speech rate, this speaker uses predominantly L+H*, whereas at a fast speech rate L+H* as well as H* are found. Both speakers align f_0 peak earlier with increasing tempo in rising as well as in falling movements if present (cf. Fig. 12).

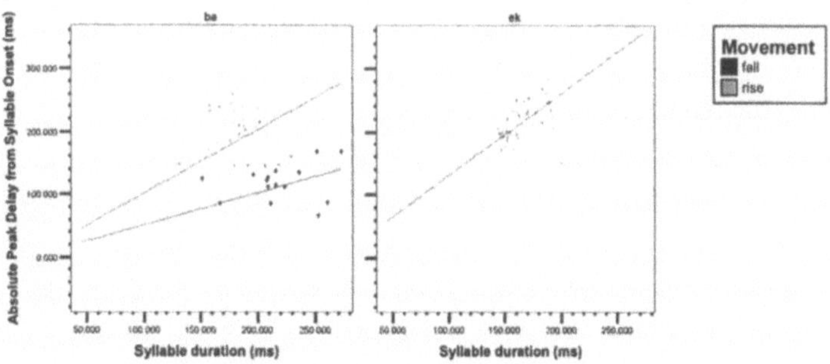

Figure 12. Bulgarian speakers' peak alignment in narrow contrastive focus cond.

There is an opposite tendency between the speakers with respect to f_0 peak height in the rising movement in two tempo conditions. Speaker BA reaches higher f_0 values in fast speech tempo, while speaker EK reduces her f_0 peak values with increasing speech rate. There is no main effect of tempo on peak height in the falling movements of speaker BA (cf. Fig. 13).

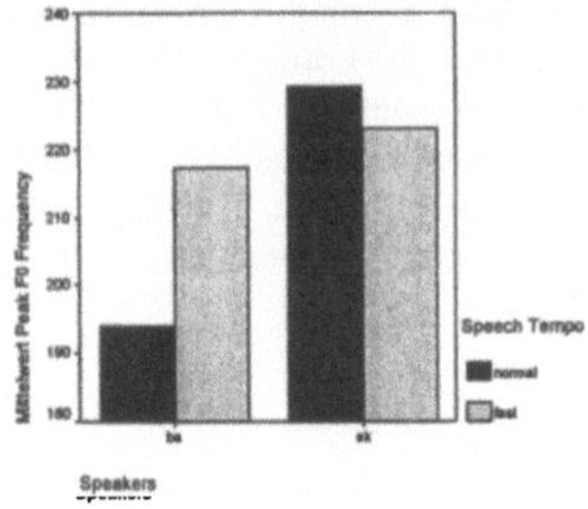

Figure 13. Bulgarian speakers' peak height in narrow contrastive focus cond.

b) Focus on verb (medial position)

In Polish, in medial position, there were significant speaker differences. Speaker KA uses exclusively rises (L+H*), aligning them at 66.4% into the syllable. Speaker WM produces predominantly H*+L (there are only three cases of rising pitch accents). For this speaker, f_0 peak delay is located at half the length of the syllable for falls (51.3%) and at 86.7% for rises. The alignment analysis shows main effect of speech tempo for both speakers, whereby peak occurs earlier in fast speech (cf. Fig. 14).

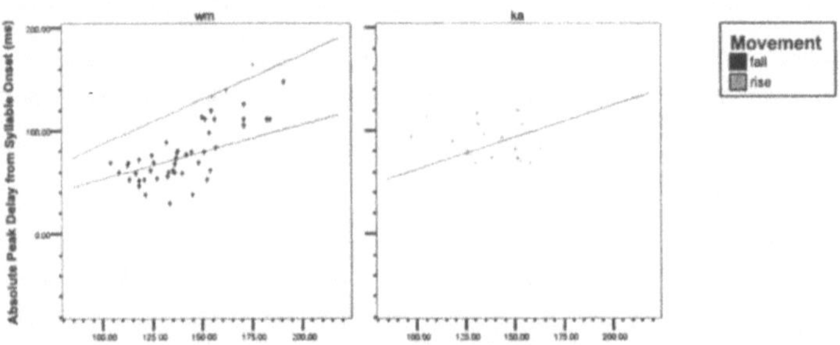

Figure 14. Polish speakers' peak alignment in narrow contrastive focus condition

The falls produced by speaker WM are significantly lower in fast vs. normal speech rate. Again, the opposite is true for rising contours used by speaker KA (cf. Fig. 15).

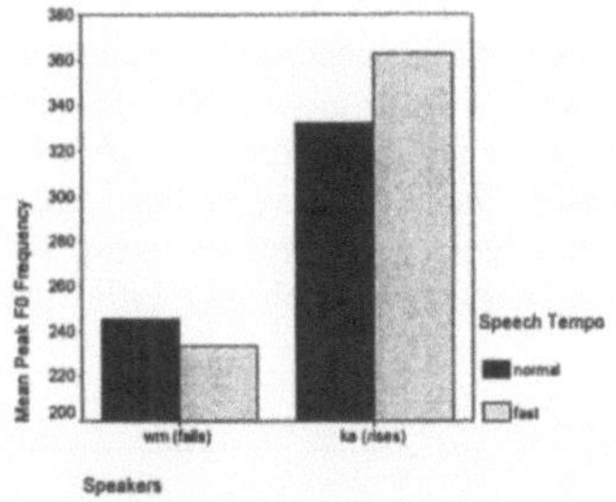

Figure 15. Speaker strategies in narrow contrastive focus condition (Polish)

In the majority of cases in the Bulgarian data, both speakers produce rising pitch accents (L+H*). There is a strong effect of speech tempo on peak location in the rising movements (cf. Fig. 16). The peak f_0 value in the rising movements of the speaker BA increases strongly with speech rate (cf. Fig. 17). The falls (H*) are present in normal speech rate for speaker EK (2 cases) and fast speech rate for speaker BA (7 cases). Speaker EK realises the peak at 64.9% for falls and 124.6% for rises, whereas speaker BA at 95.7% for rises in normal speech rate. In the fast speech condition speaker EK reaches the peak at 107.5% for rising accents and BA at 44.4% for falls and 82.2% for rises.

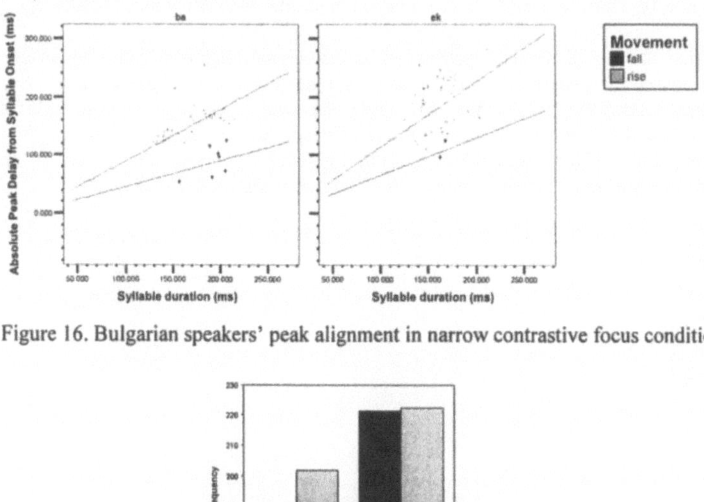

Figure 16. Bulgarian speakers' peak alignment in narrow contrastive focus condition

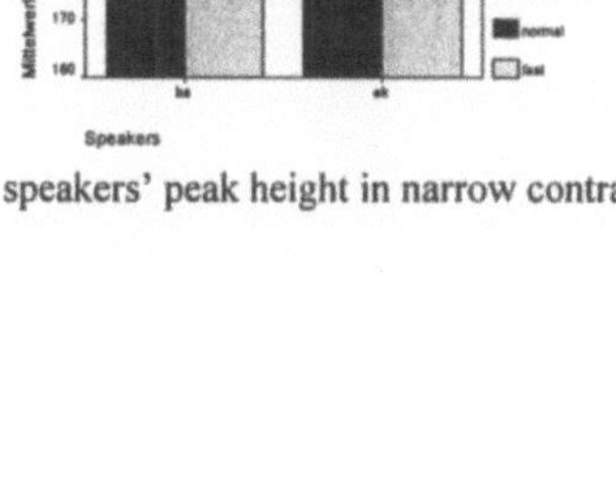

Figure 17. Bulgarian speakers' peak height in narrow contrastive focus condition

c) Focus on object (final position)

In Polish, in terms of peak alignment, this condition is realised exclusively by H*+L by both speaker KA and WM. For speaker WM the mean peak delay values are 16.6% from syllable onset, and the peak is placed before the rhyme onset. Speaker KA, on the other hand, aligns the peak later, at 44.1 % of the syllable duration, and at 4.9% of the rhyme duration. Both speakers show significant peak alignment differences in two tempo conditions as noted for other conditions with falling pitch accents: we observe earlier peak alignment with increased speech rate (cf. Fig. 18).

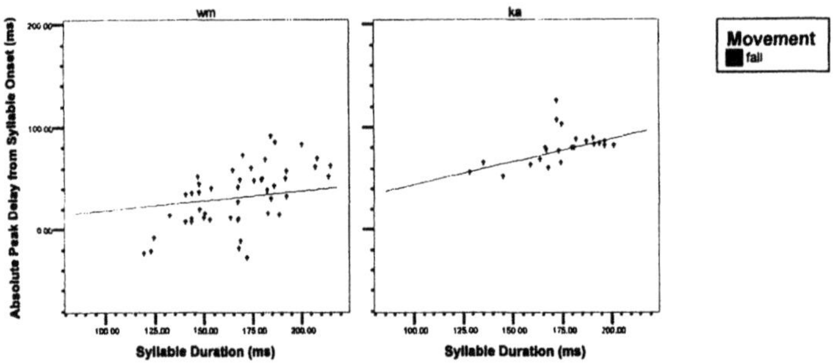

Figure 18. Polish speakers' peak alignment in narrow contrastive focus condition

In Bulgarian, there is an effect of speaker and tempo on peak alignment in this condition. H* is only produced by speaker BA and only at a fast speech rate (peak alignment at 37.3%). In rising pitch accents (L+H*), speaker EK aligns the peak on average later (at 95%) than speaker BA (at 82%). We found a main effect of tempo on peak alignment for this type of movement (cf. Fig. 19). Speaker BA also changes f_0 range with tempo change, i.e. the faster the speech rate the higher f_0 values, which was found to be significant (cf. Fig. 20).

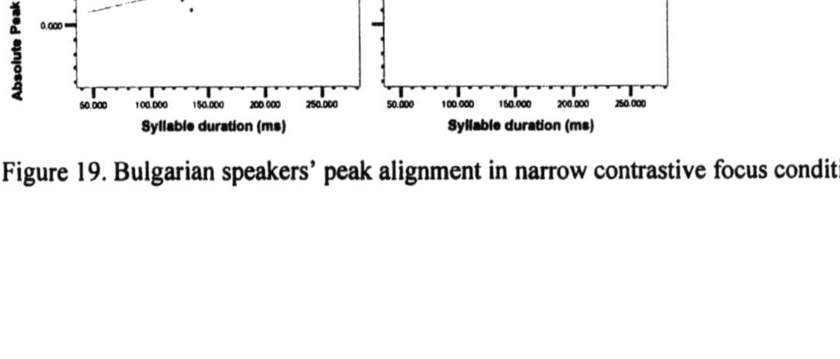

Figure 19. Bulgarian speakers' peak alignment in narrow contrastive focus condition

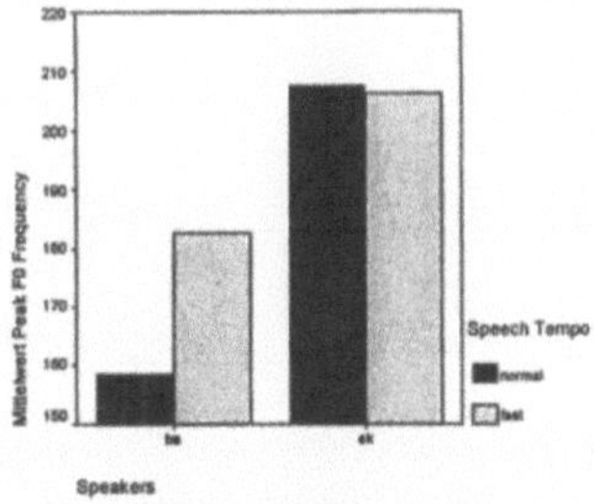

Figure 20. Bulgarian speakers' peak height in narrow contrastive focus condition

4.2. The effect of position in sentence

Another main effect in the analysis is the relationship between the pitch alignment and the structure of the utterance. With respect to the position of the focused item in the utterance, we find the following tendency across focus conditions: the later the focused item occurs in the utterance, the earlier the peak alignment.

4.2.1. Non-contrastive focus

The analysis shows that in the non-contrastive focus condition within the same movement (falling or rising) the f_0 peak is aligned later in sentence initial position than in sentence final. In Polish, in the case of speaker WM, it is linked to different accent types used in the two positions, i.e. in the initial position we observe H*+L, whereas in the final (object) position this speaker additionally uses (!)H+L* and H+L*. The statistical analysis reveals, as expected, a significantly later peak alignment in the initial position (55.6%) than in the final (shown here as a proportion of the syllable length). The alignment measures are not significantly different for the sentence final position between narrow non-contrastive and broad object for this speaker (-15.9% vs. -16.1%, 12.6% vs. 15.7% respectively), which reflects the fact that WM makes use of the same accent types (H*+L and H+L*) in both conditions. As speaker KA chooses to use different movement types in initial and final position (rise vs. fall, respectively), the comparison is limited to the object in final position in the broad and narrow non-contrastive condition. Here, speaker KA uses same accent type (H*+L) and aligns f_0 peaks similarly for object in narrow non-contrastive and broad focus (43.3% vs. 43.9%).

In Bulgarian, the pattern is the same; for speaker BA within falling contours ((!)H*), the f_0 peak in initial position is aligned significantly later than in the final one (53.3%). In final position, the peak for the object in broad focus is situated significantly earlier than for the object in narrow non-contrastive condition in normal tempo (3.4% vs. 27.2%, respectively). That is due to the fact that in the normal speech tempo condition, speaker BA uses !H* in broad and H* in narrow focus. The fact that, in fast tempo, this speaker uses mostly H* accent type explains a non-significantly different peak alignment in this condition. The other Bulgarian speaker (EK), using rising contours (L+H*), aligns her peaks significantly later in initial than in the final position at a fast speech tempo (131.3% vs. 92.8%).

tempo	normal		fast	
Speaker	rise	fall	rise	fall
BA		subj > obj > broad		subj > obj = broad
EK	subj = obj		subj > obj	
WM		subj > obj = broad		subj > obj = broad
KA		obj = broad		obj = broad

Table 1. The effect of position in a sentence on peak alignment across focus and speakers in non-contrastive focus.

4.2.2. Contrastive focus

Within the contrastive focus condition, three sentence positions are compared: initial, medial and final. Polish speaker WM uses a rising accent type (L+H*) in initial and a falling accent type (H*+L) in medial and final positions. With the falling movement, the f_0 peak is aligned significantly later in medial than in the final sentence position (51.3% vs. 16.6% respectively). In the data from speaker KA, we observe a significantly later positioned f_0 peak in initial versus medial position for the accent type L+H* (101% vs. 66.3%).

The Bulgarian speaker BA aligns f_0 peaks of the rising movements significantly later in the initial position than in the medial one (118.6% vs. 95.7%) in normal speech. The f_0 peak on the verb (sentence medial position) is in turn situated at a similar distance from the syllable onset as the peak in the sentence final position (object) in both tempi (e.g. in fast speech 82.2% vs. 81.9% respectively). Both falling and rising accents used by speaker BA have peaks positioned significantly later in the initial than in the final position (e.g. falling movement in fast tempo 53.6% vs. 37%). When the focus is placed in sentence medial position, the f_0 peak can either align at the same place as the subject or the object, e.g. in L+H* in fast speech, the verb aligns at 82.2%, whereas the object at 81.9%.

In the same focus condition, speaker EK, who uses rising contours (L+H*), places the sentence initial f_0 peak either later than in the medial position in fast speech (124.2% vs. 107.5%), or at a non-significantly different position at a normal speech tempo. In comparison with the final position, this speaker aligns the f_0 peak sentence medially significantly later in both tempo conditions (115% vs. 95%) (cf. Table 2).

tempo	normal		fast	
Speaker	rise	fall	rise	fall
BA	subj > verb = obj		(subj = verb) > (verb = obj)	(subj = verb) > (verb = obj)
EK	subj = verb > obj		subj > verb > obj	
WM		verb > obj		verb > obj
KA	subj > verb		subj > verb	

Table 2. The effect of position in a sentence on peak alignment across focus and speakers in-contrastive focus

5. Summary and Conclusion

The goal of this study was to investigate the phonetic details of peak alignment in phonologically specified accent types across different focus conditions (broad and narrow contrastive vs. non-contrastive focus) in Polish and Bulgarian. The relationship between peak location and segmental structure was explored for different speech rates (normal vs. fast) and positions within the utterance (final vs. non-final).

In the production experiment we observed different alignment patterns in Polish and Bulgarian. The statistical analysis of the data showed that apart from accent type itself, speaker, speech tempo, focus type and position in the sentence as well as the interaction between them influence peak alignment at the 5% significance level. Additionally, the peak f_0 frequency was significantly influenced by the following factors: focus, speaker and accent type in both languages, while in Bulgarian, there was also a main effect of speech rate and position in the sentence.

The results showed main speech tempo effects on temporal alignment of f_0 targets and peak f_0 height. The observed correlation between tempo and peak alignment is positive in the two languages. With increasing speech tempo, speakers align their peaks significantly earlier. The f_0 targets are conditioned by the accent type used, and therefore we observe speaker specific strategies: either increasing or lowering f_0 values with tempo changes. The fact that the absolute but not the relative measures for peak alignment differ significantly with changing speech rate clearly lends support to the claim that speakers control the peak alignment in a consistent way relative to the course of the syllable. This confirms the hypothesis about the existence of well-defined targets. However, in our data, they do not appear to be aligned relative to "segmental anchor points" to which the tones would be aligned as defined by Arvaniti et al. (1998), and Atterer and Ladd (2004). The results demonstrate that the target is sensitive to syllable onset, rhyme onset and syllable offset for Bulgarian, and syllable onset and offset for Polish. The alignment pattern found here clearly emerged due to the use of only one syllable type (/ma/) for all conditions. However, further investigations for these two languages need to be carried out with the variety of syllable structures in order to assess the extent to which the target is aligned relative to onset and offset of the syllable or the beginning and end of the sonorant portion.

The following accent types were found to be used by the Bulgarian speakers: H+!H*/L*, !H*, H* and L+H*. Polish speakers use H+L*, !H+L*, H*+L and L+H*. For both languages, we found different accent types in the same focus condition and the same accent types in different focus conditions. This is reflected in the alignment measures where the following patterns are observed.

First, in non-contrastive focus f_0, targets are aligned significantly earlier than in contrastive focus in both languages. This is mainly due to the fact that the speakers tend to use rising accents in contrastive and falling accents in non-contrastive focus conditions. Additionally, alignment of f_0 events in both languages varies with respect to the position of the focused items in an utterance. Within each focus type utterance initial focused items (subject) are aligned significantly later than utterance medial (verb) and utterance final items in focus (object). A possible explanation is the phenomenon of "tonal repulsion". The proximity of the intonation phrase boundary tones leads to temporal readjustments of peak location (Silverman and Pierrehumbert 1990).

Finally, the details of alignment for the H(igh) targets highlight the differences in the phonetic realisation of phonologically specified accent types in the two languages. These findings suggest that Bulgarian speakers align their f_0 peaks later than the Polish speakers and confirm general claims in literature (Arvaniti et al. 2000) that these H target points are language specific in nature. However, the experimental findings demonstrated a cross-language pattern, namely, that in all focus type conditions, speakers controlled the position of the f_0 peak, such that accented items positioned later in the utterance received an earlier f_0 peak alignment than those in sentence medial and initial position. It is not clear to what extent this pattern is a result of what may be a universal tendency, or whether it is partly a reflection of the choice of a different falling accent types used in different sentence positions.

The above study sheds light on the description of temporal alignment of f_0 events in Polish and Bulgarian across focus conditions. Nevertheless, as already stated above, further analysis is needed before the above claims and descriptions can be extended to a more general model of alignment in the two languages studied.

6. Acknowledgements

The first author is funded by the International Post-Graduate College "Language Technology and Cognitive Systems". Both authors would like to thank Prof. William Barry for his invaluable comments and ideas.

7. References

Arvaniti, A, D. R. Ladd and I. Mennen (1998). Stability of tonal alignment: the case of Greek prenuclear accents. *Journal of Phonetics* 26, 2-25.

Arvaniti, A., D. R. Ladd and I. Mennen (2000). "What is a starred tone? Evidence from Greek". In: M. Broe & J. Pierrehumbert (eds.), *Papers in Laboratory Phonology V: Acquisition and the Lexicon.* Cambridge University Press, 119-131.

Atterer, M. and D. R. Ladd (2004). On the phonetics and phonology of "segmental anchoring" of F0: evidence from German. *Journal of Phonetics* 32, 177-197.

IPDS (1997). xassp (Advanced Speech Signal Processor under the X Window System) - . *User's Manual.* Version 1.2.15. AIPUK 32, 31-115.

Ladd, D. R. (2004). "Segmental anchoring of pitch movements: autosegmental phonology or speec production?" In: H. Quen & V. van Heuven (eds.), *On Speech and Language: Essays for Sieb B. Nooteboom.* Utrecht: LOT, 123-131.

Miševa, A. (1991). *Intonacionna sistema na bâlgarskija ezik.* Sofija: BAN

Pierrehumbert, J. (1980). *The Phonology and Phonetics of English Intonation.* PhD thesis, MIT, published 1988 by IULC.

Prieto, P. (2004). "The search for phonological targets in the tonal space: evidence from five-sentence-types in peninsular Spanish". In: T. Face (ed.), *Laboratory Approaches to Spanish Phonology.* The Hague: de Gruyter, 29-59.

Prieto, P., J., van Santen, and J. Hirschberg (1995). Tonal Alignment Patterns in Spanish. *Journal of Phonetics* 23, 429-451

Rietveld, T., and C. Gussenhoven (1995). Aligning pitch targets in speech synthesis: Effects of syllable structure. *Journal of Phonetics* 23, 375-385.

Schepman, A., Lickley, R. and Ladd, D.R. (2006). Effects of vowel length and 'right context' on the alignment of Dutch nuclear accents. *Journal of Phonetics* 34, 1-28.

Silverman, K. and J. Pierrehumbert (1990). "The timing of prenuclear high accents in English". In: J. Kingston & M. E. Beckman (eds.), *Papers in Laboratory Phonology I*, Cambridge: CUP, 72-106

Steele, S. (1986). "Nuclear accent F0 peak location: effect of rate, vowel, and number of syllables." *Journal of the Acoustical Society of America* Supplement 1, 80, s51.

Tobias Scheer, Nice

Syllabic and trapped consonants in (Western) Slavic: different but still the same

1. Phonological hermaphrodites[1]

Syllabic consonants are objects of wonder: they are phonological hermaphrodites. Neogrammarians used to call them "consonants in vocalic function" (Saussure's 1879 laryngeal theory is entirely based on this insight), and this is probably as close as one can get to reality. Indeed, syllabic consonants are consonants physiologically speaking - yet they behave as if they were vowels. As a sound, their body is *only* consonantal - not a bit of vocalicity in sight. As a phonological object, however, they are *only* vocalic - showing no consonantal behaviour at all. In other words, they are males physiologically speaking, but whose behaviour is exclusively female. Except when they are followed by another female (i.e. a vowel), in which case their behaviour patterns with their physiological identity.

Syllabic consonants are the male counterpart of glides, which have opposite distribution of physiological properties and phonological behaviour: glides are female hermaphrodites. They belong to the female vocalic world, but endorse male consonantal function.

On account of this symmetry (among other things, see below), I extend the branching analysis that is commonplace for glides to syllabic consonants: physiological properties determine the syllabic home of all individuals, while spreading defines their function: glides are vowels that have spread onto a consonantal position, while syllabic consonants are consonants which have colonised a vocalic slot.

The way in which syllabic consonants are approached in this article bears a number of peculiarities. For one thing, a catalogue of the specific synchronic and diachronic behaviour that syllabic consonants constantly display in Slavic and Germanic is established. This aims at giving as much, as varied and as detailed flesh as possible to the common-sense statement "syllabic consonants behave like vowels".

The most important piece of evidence, however, comes from the comparison with a closely related relative (both genetically and phonologically speaking): so-called *trapped consonants*. These occur most prominently in Polish,[2] and have been extensively discussed in the literature (foremost in the work by Jerzy Rubach) under the banner of extrasyllabicity. On Rubach's analysis (e.g. Rubach & Booij 1990a, Rubach 1997a), the [r] in Polish words such as *rdza, trwać, Piotr* "rust, to last, Peter" is extrasyllabic.

The ambition of the article, then, is twofold. For one thing, I aim at establishing trapped consonants as an autonomous player in the phonological scene: one that is on a par with, and hence distinct from, other fundamental categories such as syllabic consonants, vowels and non-syllabic consonants. Second, I attempt at crossing the information that is conceded by syllabic and trapped consonants. To all extents and purposes, they show exact opposite behaviour: every time the former act as if they were a vowel, the latter show regular consonantal behaviour. Therefore, any analysis of either category must come up with representations that somehow encode this antagonicity. Building a theory of syllabic consonants without looking at their trapped mates must lead to partial and inaccurate results, just as much as the isolated analysis of trapped consonants does.

---

[1] Comments by Luka Szucsich have greatly improved content and style of this article, which attempts at rendering a chapter of Scheer (2004) (§240). On various occasions, space restrictions do not allow to report on all facets of the data, or to quote all relevant literature.

[2] But also in Czech (see section 3) and Romansch (Montreuil 1999). Another candidate is Georgian (Kartvelian): I strongly suspect the massive clusters that this language is famous for to be created to a large extent by trapped consonants. For example, what is usually called "syllabic" consonants in this language is transparent to voicing (i.e. the voice value of the adjacent consonants must agree, a typical feature betraying trapped consonants, see sections 5 and 11). Relevant material is discussed for example in Butskhrikidze (2002) and Ritter (ms).

2. Syllabic, but not trapped consonants constitute syllabic peaks and can bear stress

Let us first consider Polish. Table (1) below shows trapped consonants in word-internal and word-final position.[3] Relevant Polish words and their Czech cognates are lined up in order to show that the consonants at hand occur in identical contexts in two closely related languages, yet are syllabic only in Czech.

(1) trapped consonants in Polish

a. word-internally

	Common Sl.	Polish	Czech	gloss (Polish)	gloss (Czech)
CrC	trъvati	trwać	trvat	to last	to last
CrzC	grьměti	grzmieć	hřmět	to thunder	to thunder
	brьněti	brzmieć	brnět	to sound	to tickle
	chrьbьtъ	grzbiet	hřbet	back (body)	back (body)
	trьstina	trzcina	trstina	reed (plant)	reed (plant)
ClC	klьn-	klnę	klnout	I curse	to curse
	plьv-	plwocina	arch plvat > plivat	sputum	to spit

b. word-finally

	Common Sl.	Polish	Czech	gloss (Polish)	gloss (Czech)
Cr	bebrъ	bóbr	bobr	beaver	beaver
	větrъ	wiatr	vítr	wind	wind
Crz	pьpьrь	pieprz	pepř	pepper	pepper
	vъnjǫtrь	wewnątrz	vnitř	inside	inner, inside
Cl	myslь	myśl	mysl	thought	sense

Let us compare the behaviour of (Polish) trapped and (Czech) syllabic consonants on two counts: stress and poetry. Following the 19th century characterisation according to which consonants are syllabic when they assume vocalic function, syllabic consonants should be able to bear stress, and they should count in verse.

Czech syllabic consonants such as in *krk, trvat, vlk, slza* "throat, to last, wolf, tear" indeed return a positive answer on both counts. When asked, natives invariably identify two peaks in *trvat* and *slza*, which also count as two units in poetry. In the same way, syllabic consonants are stress-bearing units in Czech: stress being word-initial, it regularly falls on the [r] of *krk, trvat*, and on the [ɫ] of *vlk, slza*.

Further evidence to the end that syllabic consonants count just as much as vowels in Czech comes form a bimoraic constraint that controls infinitives: a well-formed infinitive must either bear a long vowel, e.g. *znát* [znaat] "to know" (vs. *po-znat* [pɔznat] "to recognise"), two short vowels, e.g. *topit* [tɔpɪt] "to heat", or one short vowel and one syllabic consonant, e.g. *trvat* [trvat] "to last" (see Kastler 1995:26, Scheer 2003, Caha & Scheer in press).

By contrast, Polish trapped consonants never count in poetry, and natives recognise only one peak in words such as *trwać, krwi, bóbr, wiatr* "to last, blood GENsg, beaver, wind". Also, trapped consonants are unable to bear stress. Polish has invariable penultimate stress (e.g. *málin* vs. *malína* vs. *malinámi* "raspberry GENpl, NOMsg, INSTpl"). However, words such as *trwáć* "to last" and *krwí* "blood GENsg" are stressed on the vowel, not on the trapped [r]. Were trapped consonants able to bear stress, they surely would in these examples. Also, stress placement ignores trapped consonants: the word *jésiotr* "sturgeon" for example is

[3] Trapped consonants also occur word-initially. However, Rubach & Booij (1990a) have shown that their behaviour in this context is not quite the same as elsewhere (see Scheer 2004:§354s on this issue). Trapped consonants may also be created by vowel-zero alternations, e.g. krew - krwi "blood NOMsg, GENsg" (a near-exhaustive list of these cases appears in Scheer 2004:§244). Finally, note that there are no syllabic consonants in Polish.

stressed on the first vowel. Were the final trapped consonant counted, the <o> would be penultimate and hence tonic.

This picture is confirmed by Czech trapped consonants. In this language, [r] and [l] are trapped if and only if they occur word-initially before another consonant. Thus in words such as *rdít se, rzi, rty, lhát, lžíce* "to go red, rust GENsg, lips NOMpl, to lie, spoon",[4] the initial sonorant is trapped. As in Polish, it is not counted as a syllabic peak by either poetry or natives, and it may not bear stress: despite its being initial, word-initial stress falls on the first vowel.

Finally, there is another category of trapped consonants in Czech: palatalised rhotics <ř> that are flanked by two consonants or occur in word-final position after a consonant. These environments, which make non-palatalised rhotics syllabic (cf. *krk, bratr* "throat, brother" etc.), produce trapped results with <ř>: *hřbitov, křtít, třpytit, hřbet, pepř, vnitř* "cemetery, to baptise, to glance, back (body), pepper, interior". As before in Czech and Polish, <ř> in these words does not count in poetry, natives do not identify it as a syllabic peak (*hřbitov* for example has two peaks), and it is unable to bear stress (stress always falls on the first vowel).

On the bottom line, thus, we can record a consistently opposite behaviour: while syllabic consonants are visible for stress and poetry, trapped consonants are not.

3. Czech syllabic consonants and prefixal vowel-zero alternations

Syllabic consonants also line up with full vowels in regard of another property: in case there is a vowel-zero alternation to their left, zero surfaces.

Relevant evidence comes from Czech consonant-final prefixes (full detail is available in Scheer 1996,2004:§246). Prefixes remain unvocalised if they are followed by CV-initial or C_1C_2V-initial roots. In the latter case, the full cluster C_1C_2 must also be root-initial (as in podø-brad-ek "double chin"). In case C_1 is root-initial, but C_2 root-final, i.e. when the root occurs in zero grade, the prefix is vocalised (e.g. pode-bør-at "to seize from below").

There are various means of identifying the fact that a root occurs in zero grade. One is the existence of another form of the same root where a vowel overtly separates what appears to be the initial cluster on the surface. Such cases are shown under (2)a below.[5]

(2)

	a. root provoking vocalised prefixes				b. root provoking non-vocalised prefixes:
$\sqrt{C_1C_2}$-	zero grade: /$\sqrt{C_1øC_2}$/		full grade: /$\sqrt{C_1VC_2}$/		no occurrence of $\sqrt{C_1VC_2}$
√BR-	pode-brat	pf	pod-bírat	ipf	pod-bradek
√DR-	roze-drat	inf	roz-deru	1sg	roz-drobit
√HR-	přede-hra	noun NOMsg	her	noun GENpl	od-hrabat
√HN-	ode-hnat	pf	od-hánět	ipf	roz-hněvat
√SN-	beze-sný	adj	sen	noun NOMsg	pod-sněžník
√ŠL-	vze-šlý	adj	šel	past act part.	roz-šlapat
√ZD-	pode-zdít	inf	zed'	noun NOMsg	od-zdola

Since the prefixal alternation depends on the vocalisation of the root, we have a handle on syllabic consonants. When occurring in the middle of a root, they indeed have the same effect as a full vowel. That is, the prefix remains unvocalised: roz-drtit "to crush", od-mrštit "to reject", před-krm "starter (dish)" and so forth.

Bearing this fact in mind, let us examine the analogous situation in Polish.

---

4 An exhaustive list of this class of words is available at www.unice.fr/dsl/tobias.htm, section "other stuff to download/ Slavic data". See also Scheer (2007).

5 Glosses, line by line: "to seize from below pf, id. ipf, double chin, to tear up inf, id. 1sg, to crumble, prelude, game, to sweep away, to expel pf, id. ipf, to enrage, to prewash inf, id. 1sg, incentive, sleepless, dream, snowdrop, open adj. (flower), to go past act part., to crush, to underpin, wall, from below, bottomless, day."

4. Vocalisation of Polish prefixes before trapped roots

4.1. Morphology has got a word to say

The Polish situation is more complicated. Prefixal alternations occur as well, but in addition to the phonological rule that governs the Czech picture alone, the vocalisation of Polish prefixes is also subject to morphological restrictions.

The vocalisation of Polish prefixes has been studied in work by, among others, Gussmann (1980a:42s,81s,1980b:148ss), Rubach (1984:186ss), Szpyra (1989,1992:202s), Pawelec (1989) and Rowicka (1999a:267ss,1999b). Regular vowel-zero alternations in prefixes that obey the Czech pattern are found only in related perfective and imperfective (so-called derived imperfectives, "DI") forms of the same verb. This is demonstrated by the following examples.

(3) regular vowel-zero alternations in Polish prefixes

prefix	perfective	imperfective	gloss	prefix	perfective	imperfective	gloss
z(e)-	ze-rwać	z-rywać	to tear off	od(e)-	ode-mknąć	od-mykać	to open
	ze-drzeć	z-dzierać	to tear off		ode-tchnąć	od-dychać	to breathe
	ze-brać	z-bierać	to gather		ode-zwać	od-zywać	to speak
ob(e)-	obe-schnąć	ob-sychać	to dry		ode-przeć	od-pierać	to beat off
w(e)-	we-ssać	w-sysać	to suck in		ode-słać	od-syłać	to send back
	we-trzeć	w-cierać	to rub in	pod(e)-	pode-żreć	pod-żerać	to eat up
roz(e)-	roze-rwać	roz-rywać	to tear apart		pode-słać	pod-syłać	to send

Outside of this specific paradigm, vocalised prefixes hardly ever occur. Some cases in point that I could come by are shown under (4) (Szpyra 1995:132s offers further discussion of exceptional vocalisation in Polish prefixes).

(4) Polish vocalised prefixes outside of the pf - ipf paradigm

vocalised prefix	related forms	gloss
roze-dnieć	dzień, dnia	to grow light, day NOMsg, GENsg
ode-mglać	mgła, mgieł	to de-vaporate, fog NOMsg, GENpl
roze-jm	na-jem, na-jmu	truce, rent (of a flat) NOMsg, GENsg
obe-jm	na-jem, na-jmu	embrace, rent (of a flat) NOMsg, GENsg
beze-cny		infamous
beze-ceństwo		infamy
pode-szwa	szew, szwu	sole, stitch NOMsg, GENsg

The vocalised prefix in the first column is attached to a root whose vowel alternates with zero itself. This may be seen when looking at column two, where the same root appears in vocalised and unvocalised form. The vocalisation of the prefix is expected in these circumstances because alternating vowels are always vocalised when followed by another alternating vowel. This is the basic rule that governs Slavic vowel-zero alternations, known as Lower (e.g. Gussmann 1980a, Rubach 1984).

For the time being, the only thing that needs to be borne in mind is the fact that two alternating vowels in a row are both expected to surface. This holds true regardless of the actual phonetic existence of the rightmost vowel: the <ie> of *pies* "dog NOMsg" is present when the following alternating vowel is expressed as in *pies-ek* "dog dim. NOMsg", but also in case it is absent as in *pies-øk-a* "id. GENsg". Therefore, the vocalisation of prefixes under (4) is regular. However, words such as under (4) represent only a small minority of cases. The unmarked pattern is the one shown under (5), where the non-vocalisation of prefixes is unexpected (as before, the second column allows to control the alternating character of the root vowel).

(5) unexpected non-vocalisation of prefixes in Polish

a. before expressed alternating vowels			b. before unexpressed alternating vowels		
unvocalised prefix	related forms	gloss	unvocalised prefix	related forms	gloss
pod-pieniek	pień, pnia	honey fungus, trunk	od-wszyć	wesz, wszy	to de-louse, louse
pod-szewka	szew, szwu	lining, stitch	od-pchlić	pchła, pcheł	to de-flea, flea
bez-senny	sen, snu	sleepless, dream	bez-cłowy	cło, ceł	duty-free, duty
bez-denny	dno, den	bottom, bottom	nad-dniówka	dzień, dnia	extra day's work, day
od-setek	sto, setka	percentage, hundred	w-śnić się	sen, snu	to start dreaming, dream
przed-dzień	dzień, dnia	the day before, day	roz-łzawić	łza, łez	to draw tears, tears

Traditional descriptions attribute this pattern to the "strong" prefix boundary under (5): prefixes escape the influence of the root because their boundary inhibits communication. Various implementations of this line of thought can be found in the literature. For instance, Rubach (1984:186ss) develops a solution in the spirit of Lexical Phonology: he captures the phonological autonomy of prefixes by feeding them into the derivation on the last cycle, a move that makes them immune against the earlier action of Lower. The autonomy of prefixes has also been analysed along the lines of so-called phonological domains (Kaye 1995, Gussmann 1998,2002:45ss). Domains are used for example by Gussmann & Kaye (1993), Cyran & Gussmann (1998,1999), Rowicka (1999a:267ss) and Szpyra (1989:215ss,1992,1995:132s).

Whatever approach is favoured, however, it should be clear that the recurrently deviating non-vocalisation of prefixes is the result of morphological, rather than phonological action. Put in theory-neutral terms, the prefix and the root "do not see each other" in these cases. But this also means, in turn, that the presence of a prefixal vowel under (3) and (4) is an unerring witness of the fact that the prefix and the root do "see each other" (i.e. form a single domain). In other words, the prefixal behaviour under (3) and (4) is the result of phonological forces alone, while (5) has been produced by joint phonological and morphological rule. Therefore, cases where the prefix is vocalised are phonologically regular: morphology does not interfere. The vocalisation has thus purely phonological reasons.

4.2. How Polish prefixes behave before trapped consonants

We are now in a position to look at the behaviour of prefixes when they are attached to roots that bear a trapped consonant. The total record that I could establish appears under (6) below.

(6) influence of trapped consonants on Polish prefixes

a. vocalised prefix

root	prefix + √trapped	gloss	root	prefix + √trapped	gloss
drg-	roze-drgać (się), roze-drgany	to become vibrating, id. adj	brzm-	ode-brzmieć	to echo back
brn-	roze-brnąć	to flounder (pf)	grzm-	ode-grzmieć	to echo (thunder)

b. unvocalised prefix

root	prefix + √trapped	gloss
trw-	roz-trwonić	to squander (pf)
trw-	roz-trwaniać	to squander (ipf)
trw-	z-trwożyć się, s-trwożyć	to become fearful (pf), id.
brzm-	roz-brzmieć, roz-brzmiewać	start to sound (pf), id. (ipf)
krzt-	od-krztusić, od-krztuszać	to cough up (pf), id. (ipf)
płć-	bez-płciowy	sexless, boring
krew	roz-krwawić, roz-krwawiać, bez-krwawy, bez-krwisty, s-krwawić	to cause to bleed (pf), id. (ipf), bloodless (without casualty), bloodless (e.g. meet), to stain with blood (pf)

We know from the foregoing section that the unvocalised prefixes under (6)b do not reveal any property of the root (hence of trapped consonants): rather, they do not "see" the root for morphological reasons.

By contrast, trapped consonants do betray their phonological identity under (6)a. We are sure that words of this kind constitute a single domain: did they not, the prefix would be mute. Hence, the root "sees" the prefix and therefore determines its vocalisation.

As expected, the result is opposite to what we have seen in Czech: √CRC roots produce vocalised prefixes in Polish, against unvocalised prefixes in Czech. Their sonorant is trapped in Polish, but syllabic in Czech. Again, thus, we may record that trapped consonants, unlike their syllabic cognates, do not behave like vowels.

5. Trapped consonants are transparent to voicing, syllabic consonants are not

The reason why Polish trapped consonants have received attention in the generative literature, foremost in work by Jerzy Rubach (Bethin 1984, Rubach & Booij 1987,1990a,b, Rubach 1996,1997a,b, Gussmann 1992), is their peculiar behaviour with respect to voicing.[6] That is, trapped consonants are transparent for voice assimilation: underlyingly voiced obstruents that precede word-final trapped consonants are devoiced by final devoicing although they are not word-final. Illustration is provided below (T is shorthand for obstruents, R for sonorants).

(7) Polish: trapped consonants are transparent for voice assimilation I
word-final trapped consonants

	...TR#	...TR-V	spelling	gloss
a.	katr	kadr-a	kadr GENpl, NOMsg	staff
	bupr	bɔbr-a	bóbr NOMsg, GENsg	beaver
	ʒupr	ʒubr-a	żubr NOMsg, GENsg	bison
	mukw	mɔgw-a	mógł masc., fem.	could
b.	mɛxaɲism	mɛxaɲizmɨ	mechanizm NOMsg, NOMpl	mechanism
	mjɛlisn	mjɛlizn-a	mielizn GENpl, NOMsg	shallow water

The dental stop of a word like *kadra* "staff NOMsg" under (7)a is underlyingly voiced. This is ascertained by its pronunciation [kadra]. In GENpl where the case marker is zero, however, the stem-final cluster comes to stand in word-final position and is therefore subject to final devoicing, which is a general feature of Polish. As a result, the /d/ appears as [t]. Words like *mielizna* under (7)b demonstrate the same behaviour for fricatives.

The same transparency is found word-internally: obstruents that flank trapped consonants always agree in voicing. That is, the voice contrast in Polish is neutralised altogether in TrT clusters: $T_{[-voice]}$-r-$T_{[+voice]}$ and $T_{[+voice]}$-r-$T_{[-voice]}$ sequences do not exist. Table (8) below shows that beyond this static distributional evidence, there is also active assimilation, which may seep through the liquid in either direction.

(8) Polish: trapped consonants are transparent for voice assimilation II
word-internal trapped consonants

	CRV	CRC	CRVC-C	spelling	gloss
a.		trfat͡ɕ		trwać	to last
b.		plfat͡ɕ		plwać	to spit
c.	krɛf	krf-i	krɛv-nɨ	krew NOMsg, krwi GENsg, krewny	blood, relative
d.	brɛf	brv-i		brew NOMsg, brwi GENsg	eyebrow
e.	jɛndrɛk	jɛntrka		Jędrka NOMsg, Jędrek GENsg	Andy dim.

[6] This is also the phenomenon on which Rubach's Derivational Optimality Theory (DOT) was originally built (e.g. Rubach 1997a,b). His classical extrasyllabic analysis of trapped consonant transparency is discussed below.

The words under (8)a,b are pronounced with an [f] whose underlying identity is probably /v/. Even though morphology does not allow to put them in a position where their voiced character is expressed overtly, spelt <w> and comparative evidence (e.g. Czech *trvat* [trvat] "to last") hint at /v/. Underlying /v/ can be safely demonstrated for (8)c, though: the noun *krew-ny* [krɛvnɨ] "relative" allows to observe /v/ on the surface. In NOMsg of the word "blood" *krew* [krɛf], the [f] can thus be regarded as the result of final devoicing. In GENsg, however, the /v/ is covered by a vowel and should therefore be able to appear as such. Its unexpected devoicing must therefore be ascribed to the presence of the [k] that precedes the trapped [r]. The same holds true for (8)d, except that this time the obstruent preceding the trapped consonant is voiced, which provokes the appearance of [v] in GENsg.

In all cases discussed so far, the assimilation process is progressive. (8)e shows that trapped consonants are also transparent to voice assimilation in case this process is regressive. The TR cluster in *Jędrek* [jɛndrɛk] "Andy diminutive NOMsg" appears as [dr] and therefore must be recorded as underlyingly voiced. In the GENsg *Jędrka* [jɛntrka], however, [tr] is observed. Devoicing must thus be ascribed to the absence of the alternating [ɛ], which puts the TR cluster in contact with the voiceless [k]. The voice value of [k] then rules over the entire TrT cluster.

As before, (Czech) syllabic consonants show opposite behaviour: their flanking consonants are entirely insensitive to the voice value of each other. As in Polish, Czech devoices obstruents in word-final position (e.g. *holub* [hɔlup] vs. *holuba* [hɔluba] "pigeon NOMsg, GENsg"). However, the obstruent of final voiced TR clusters is not subject to this process: the direct cognates of the Polish examples under (7) are *bobr, zubr, mohl* [bɔbr̩, zubr̩, mɔɦl̥] "beaver, bison, he could" where /b,ɦ/ appear unmodified on the surface.[7] Also, syllabic consonants are not transparent word-internally. Again, the direct Czech cognates of the Polish words under (8) are not inclined to produce TrT clusters that agree in voicing: *trvat, krve* [tr̩vat, kr̩vɛ] "to last, blood GENsg".

Hence it must be concluded that the typical Polish transparency of sonorants in C__# and C__C is not just a consequence of the particular position that they come to stand in: their Czech cognates occur in the same environment without being transparent. Rather, transparency is a specific property of trapped consonants that is not shared by their syllabic relatives.

6. Summary syllabic vs. trapped consonants

We thus face a consistent pattern across the board: syllabic consonants in Czech count in poetry, bear stress, provoke unvocalised prefixes and are not transparent to voicing. On the other hand, trapped consonants in Polish cannot be stressed, do not count in verse, trigger vocalised prefixes and are transparent to voicing. Analyses of trapped and syllabic consonants must take this systematic antagonicity into account.

---

[7] Note that the devoiced version of /ɦ/ would be [x], which appears in the word at hand when the final *-l* is left out in colloquial style: *moh* [mɔx] "he could".

7. What kind of animal is a syllabic consonant ?

7.1. The classical view: syllabic consonants sit in Nuclei

The null hypothesis of early generative times is simple. It merely translates the fact that syllabic consonants assume vocalic function: alongside with vowels, they are assigned the feature [+syll]. This feature, replacing earlier [±voc], actually came into being because of the existence of syllabic consonants (see Chomsky & Halle 1968:354).

This approach was carried over to subsequent autosegmental approaches where the feature [±syll] continues to be assigned on the grounds of pure observation: segments are [+syll] if and only if they constitute a sonority peak. The presence of [+syll], then, qualifies the segment in question for occupying a nuclear position (as opposed to segments that are [-syll]). Since it is very common that the same consonant in the same word is syllabic in one form but non-syllabic in another (e.g. English *bottle* [bɒtl̩] vs. *bottling* [bɒtlɪŋ]), the value for its feature [±syll] is manipulated. Rubach (1977:52ss) for example uses syllabicity-imposing and syllabicity-releasing rules. The former make a sonorant [+syll] after an obstruent and before another consonant or a word boundary, while the latter turns [+syll] into [-syll] in the appropriate context. Also, resyllabification must be assumed because the [l] in *bottle* is supposed to be dominated by a Nucleus when it is syllabic, but sits in an Onset or a Coda in case it is non-syllabic.[8]

The classical interpretation of syllabic consonants thus involves the feature [±syll], the existence of consonants in Nuclei and resyllabification. It is expressed by, among many others, Blevins (1995), Bell (1978), Clements (1990:293ss), Hall (2000:215ss), Gussenhoven & Jacobs (1998:28), Kenstowicz (1994:255s) and Carr (1993:55). The representations that result from this approach hardly rest on any phonological evidence (Rubach 1990 is a notable exception). They merely reproduce observation: "whatever constitutes a sonority peak sits in a Nucleus". This is taking into account just one side of the medal: the function of syllabic consonants. Their physiological identity, that is their consonanthood, is left unreflected.

7.2. Why syllabic consonants do not sit in Nuclei

There is good reason to doubt this surface-based analysis. Not only does it neglect one of the two critical properties of hermaphrodite syllabic consonants. It also falls foul of one of the most fundamental autosegmental principles. Multilinear structure allows for interpreting high vowels and glides as one single phonological object, rather than as separate sets of underlyingly contrasting items. That is, the two phonetic objects [j] and [i] are phonologically identical. Their underlying specification defines the high front tongue body position. Whether this object then surfaces as a vowel or as a glide depends on its association with syllabic constituents: a vowel surfaces when it comes to stand in a Nucleus, while a consonant is produced in case it ends up in an Onset or in a Coda. This analysis eliminates [±syll], whose information is encoded structurally. Also, it is generally considered an important achievement of autosegmentalism and by now has become orthodox textbook evidence (Kenstowicz 1994:23, Carr 1993:59,194ss, Hall 2000:106, Hayes 1989, Spencer 1996:96s).

Why should a given melody, then, enjoy contrasting phonetic interpretation according to the syllabic constituent that it belongs to in one case (high vowels vs. glides), but not in the other (syllabic consonants)? No phonetic effect is observed on liquids and nasals when they leave their consonantal home in order to be syllabified into a Nucleus. This is incompatible

[8] All approaches to syllabic consonants along these lines mention the unequal probability for different major classes to occur in Nuclei: in the overwhelming majority of languages, only sonorants (and within this group, preferably nasals) qualify for a nuclear existence; languages that allow for nuclear fricatives or even stops are extremely rare, if not absent from the record altogether (this issue is under debate, see for instance Dell & Elmedlaoui 1985,1988, Bagemihl 1991). In any event, there is an implicational relationship: a language where less sonorous segments occur in Nuclei also admits more sonorous consonants in vocalic function.

with the idea that vowelhood and consonanthood are a matter of syllabic affiliation, rather than of melody.

Fortunately enough, the literature also offers a different take: syllabic consonants sit in a consonantal constituent. The syllabicity effect, then, arises through their spreading onto a neighbouring Nucleus. This is also the reason why syllabic consonants show vocalic behaviour: they participate in the vocalic world because one of their legs belongs to a Nucleus. On this count, the alternation between syllabic and non-syllabic versions of the same consonant is a simple matter of association to an available Nucleus. On this analysis, then, consonants are consonants because they belong to a consonantal constituent. Their eventual syllabicity is a consequence of spreading. No resyllabification at any level is involved.

8. Do syllabic consonants spread to their right or to their left ?

8.1. An argument for left-branchers: the complementary distribution of C̩ and əC

Let us have a closer look at this alternative. It raises the question in which direction syllabic consonants expand. Table (9) below shows both options.

(9) possible representations for syllabic consonants
a. left-branching b. right-branching

Right-branching structures are argued for by, among others, Rowicka (1999a:261ss,2003), Blaho (2001,2004) and Rennison (1999:333ss). The left-branching alternative is advocated for example by Harris (1994:224s), Hall (1992:35s), Wiese (1986,1996), Szigetvári (1999:117ss) and Toft (2002). The frame of an article does not allow to discuss individual proposals and their relationship with the particular theories in which they are couched (Scheer 2004:§256 offers further detail).

A substantial argument in favour of the left-branching option is the complementary distribution of syllabic and non-syllabic versions of the same consonant in the same word. This pattern is recurrent across languages: either the consonant is non-syllabic, in which case it is preceded by a schwa. Or it is syllabic, but then occurs without preceding schwa. This distribution establishes the equivalence "absence of schwa = syllabicity of the consonant". The argument, then, is straightforward: the *preceding*, rather than the following Nucleus is involved in consonantal syllabicity.

The pattern at hand is found for example in English (Toft 2002) and German. In the latter language, syllabic consonants enjoy about the same frequency and distribution as in English: [l] and all nasals, plus [r] in rhotic varieties, may be syllabic. Syllabic consonants typically occur in word-final position after consonants or arise when the vowel of a vowel-initial suffix is dropped. However, this familiar pattern is completed by a peculiar feature of German: syllabic nasals agree in place with the preceding consonant. That is, an underlying /n/ will appear as [m̩,ɱ̩,n̩,ŋ̩,N̩] according to the place of articulation of the preceding consonant. Relevant configurations are created by suffixes that are made of schwa plus an underlying dental nasal. One case in point is the infinitive <-en> /-ən/ (see for example Hall 1992:193ss, Wiese 1996:222s). Consider the behaviour of the nasal under (10).

(10) German infinitive *-en*

schwa present	schwa absent	spelling	gloss
geeb-ən	geeb-m̩	geben	to give
hɛlf-ən	hɛlf-ɱ̍	helfen	to help
vɛt-ən	vɛt-n̩	wetten	to bet
zaag-ən	zaag-ŋ̍	sagen	to say
laχ-ən	laχ-N̩	lachen	to laugh

Each word may be pronounced either with or without schwa. In case schwa is present, the nasal is always dental and non-syllabic. By contrast, it is syllabic and agrees in place with the preceding consonant if schwa is left out. Unlike its English cognate, the German pattern has the advantage of eluding the (phonetic) debate on the eventual presence of a vocalic trace in syncopated forms since the syllabicity of the nasal is independently controlled by its homorganicity. It thus appears that syllabic consonants arise through the syncope of a *preceding* vowel.

8.2. Diachronic situation: syllabic consonants come into being when a *preceding* vowel is lost

Diachronically speaking, the German schwa that alternates with zero today once was a full vowel in unstressed position which engaged on a typical lenition trajectory. The German(ic) situation indeed describes the evolution of a great many languages: syllabic consonants are never diachronically primitive. They come into being because the melodic content of a neighbouring Nucleus fades away.[9] In case the emptied Nucleus occurs before a word-final consonant C__C# or in a closed syllable C__RTV, the consonantal cluster created may be too heavy. One way of resolving this situation is for the emptied Nucleus to acquire new melodic content through spreading from a neighbouring consonant.

If syllabic consonants exist in order to deliver melodic content to an adjacent orphan Nucleus, in principle this could be done by preceding as well as by following consonants. Now the hard observational fact is that syllabic consonants always appear to be born through the syncope of a preceding vowel. The diachronic situation thus replicates the synchronic scenario that was discussed in the preceding section.

Synchronic evidence, however, is not always available. In Slavic for example, the original preceding vowel has been lost definitively and may not even optionally appear on the surface. Only diachronic evidence can establish the correlation between syllabic consonants and the syncope of a preceding vowel. Modern syllabic consonants, which occur only in Czech, Slovak and Serbo-Croatian, continue former vowel-liquid sequences. The vowels at hand are yers, which faded away in late Common Slavic. Yers come in two flavours, one front "ь", the other back "ъ". They continue Indo-European short [i] and [u], respectively. Table (11) provides illustration for the regular correspondences and the origin mentioned: a Common Slavic CyerRC sequence is continued by a syllabic consonant in Czech, Slovak and Serbo-Croatian, while Russian and Polish vocalise the yer (see note 11 on the quality of the vocalic continuator).

[9] Bell (1978:165ss) confirms this statement on the grounds of a cross-linguistic record of 85 languages that bear what he takes to be syllabic consonants, but which actually may well include trapped items (as most authors, Bell does not distinguish syllabic and trapped consonants).

(11) Common Slavic √CьRC-/ √CъRC-
= Czech, Slovak, Serbo-Croatian √CR̩C-
= Polish, Russian √CVRC-

CьRC-	> syllabic			> vocalised		
Common Slavic	Czech	Slovak	Serbo-Croatian	Polish	Russian	gloss
gъrdlo	hrdlo	hrdlo	grlo	gardło	gorlo	throat
mъrk-ъvь	mrkev		mrkva	marchew	morkov'	carrot
sъmьrtь	smrt	smrt'	smrt	śmierć	smert'	death
pьrvъ	prvý	prvý	prvi	pierwszy	pervyi	first
vьlna	vlna	vlna	vuna	wełna	volna	wool
vьlkъ	vlk	vlk	vuk	wilk	volk	wolf

The genesis of syllabic consonants in Slavic is described for example in Stieber (1979:33ss,54ss), Rospond (1979:94ss), Długosz-Kurczabowa & Dubisz (1993:84ss), Nahtigal (1961:111ss), Panzer (1991:296ss), Carlton (1991:151ss), Vondrák (1924:180ss), Vaillant (1950:173ss), Meillet (1934:73ss), Mikkola (1913-50 II:200ss), Mann (1957:54). All authors take up the traditional 19th century description according to which liquids took over the syllabic function from preceding yers as these faded away.

In sum, thus, the argument in favour of the left-branching option is supported by synchronic and diachronic evidence alike: syllabic consonants come into being because a *preceding* vowel has been lost.

9. A theory-internal argument: prefixal vowel-zero alternations again

This section is the only one in the present article where reference is made to the particular theory that I am committed to: Government Phonology (Kaye et al. 1990, Kaye 1990, Harris 1994) in general and so-called CVCV (Lowenstamm 1996, Szigetvári 1999, Cyran 2003, Scheer 1999, 2004) in particular. The core proposal of CVCV is that syllable structure is better represented as a network of lateral relations among segments than in terms of the traditional arborescence. For example, a Coda consonant will enjoy a lateral, rather than an arboreal definition: "Coda consonants occur before a governed empty Nucleus", rather than "Coda consonants belong to a constituent that is the sister of the Nucleus". The overall goal, then, is to achieve the lateralisation of structure and causality. A consequence of this approach is that a number of additional empty constituents are assumed that remain unpronounced (foremost empty Nuclei). Also, no syllabic arborescence is left at all: constituent structure consists of a strict sequence of non-branching Onsets and non-branching Nuclei. The arboreal function is taken over by lateral relations, which identify as Government (spoiling the segmental expression of its target) and Licensing (backing up the segmental expression of its target).

Given the limitations of an article, there is no hope to introduce the theory in any further detail. The only thing that needs to be understood in order to follow the argument is that vowel-zero alternations are supposed to be structure-preserving: the Nucleus where the vowel appears is always present, irrespectively of whether it is actually pronounced or not. It is phonetically absent in case it is governed by the Nucleus to its right, while it is phonetically expressed if it escapes Government. Whether or not the following Nucleus is able to govern depends on its content: contentful Nuclei can, empty Nuclei cannot govern.

On these assumptions, reconsider the fact that Czech syllabic consonants provoke the non-vocalisation of prefixes (cf. section 3).

(12) syllabic consonants in Czech: who governs the prefixal Nucleus?

a. option 1: the Nucleus of a left-branching syllabic consonant

b. option 2: the Nucleus of a right-branching syllabic consonant

Czech rozø-trhat "to tear up" Czech rozø-trhat "to tear up"

(12)a is well-formed provided that the empty Nucleus to the right of the syllabic consonant is governed by the following [a] (all internal empty Nuclei must be governed). Nothing prevents [a] from doing so. By contrast, the structure under (12)b, where syllabic consonants are right-branching, is ill-formed because the empty Nucleus enclosed by the [t] and the [r] remains orphan (see Blaho 2001,2004 and Scheer 2004:§263 for further discussion).

Syllabic consonants thus ought to be left-branching. This result, achieved on the grounds of prefixal vowel-zero alternations in Czech, matches the synchronic and diachronic distributional evidence that has been discussed earlier: syllabic consonants come into being when the *preceding* Nucleus is vacated.

What could then be the identity of (Polish) trapped consonants? Recall from section 4.2 that they provoke the vocalisation of prefixes. Since we now have an idea of how these prefixal alternations work in presence of a following syllabic consonant, the status and identity of their trapped Polish cognates falls out automatically. That is, the presence of the prefixal vowel tells us that its Nucleus is not subject to Government. Consider the relevant representation under (13) below.

(13) trapped consonants in Polish provoke vocalised prefixes

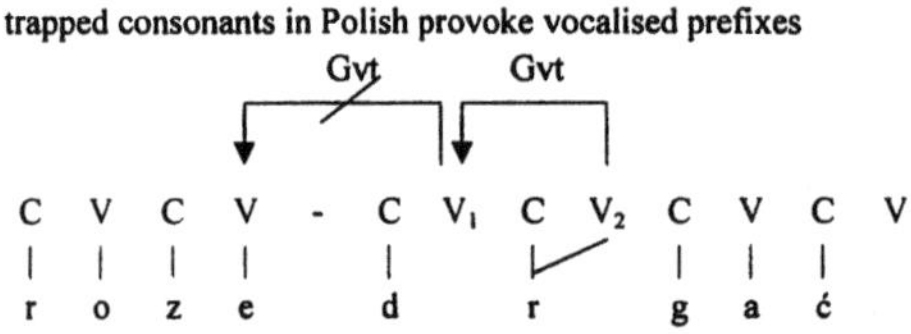

roze-drgać "to set vibrating"

The only reason for the presence of the prefixal vowel can be the fact that the following Nucleus, V_1, does not qualify for lateral actorship: it is unable to govern. This means that it must be struck by Government itself. Continuing this "every other" chain reaction, the Nucleus to its right, V_2, must be the origin of this Government. Therefore, V_2 has to be a sound governor. How could that be? Given what we know about syllabic consonants, the obvious answer is that trapped consonants spread onto the following Nucleus, which acquires full lateral actorship for that reason.

Looking at the prefixal consequences of syllabic and trapped consonants through the prism of CVCV thus puts a name on both candidate structures of (9): left-branching consonants are syllabic, while those that colonise the following Nucleus are trapped.

10. Diachronic confirmation: syllabic consonants are born through the loss of a preceding, trapped consonant through the loss of a following vowel

This representation of syllabic and trapped consonants receives support from their diachronic identity: as a matter of fact, Czech syllabic consonants have been born through the loss of the *preceding* vowel, while Polish trapped consonants have come into being because the *following* vowel has faded away. Here again, full demonstration of the philological detail cannot be offered. Stieber (1979:54ss), Nahtigal (1961:111s), Carlton (1991:151ss,249s), Vaillant (1950:173ss), Panzer (1991:296ss) and Vondrák (1924:181) provide relevant information, of which a digest is available in Scheer (2004:§277).

Given space limitations, the only thing that can be done here is to look at the bare diachronic source of syllabic and trapped consonants. Table (1) actually contains the Common Slavic source of the latter category: it may be seen that Polish trapped consonants were always *followed* by a yer ("ь" and "ъ"). The traditional Slavic literature refers to this pattern as trьt (and trъt, which I leave out for expository reasons). It was already mentioned earlier that yers were lost in late Common Slavic. The analysis, then, is very simple, actually embracing the 19th century common sense statement: the consonant takes over the syllabic function of vowels that die of senility. Modern autosegmental structure explains in greater detail what "taking over" actually means: the adjacent sonorant spreads onto the orphan empty (emptied) Nucleus.

The question now is what happens in tьrt clusters, i.e. when a Common Slavic yer *precedes* a liquid. Relevant data appear under (14) below.[10]

(14) Western Slavic reflexes of CS tьrt
Czech √CR̩C- = Polish √CVRC-

Polish reaction	Common Slavic	Czech	Polish	Czech gloss	Polish gloss
CaRC: 34	gъr-dlo	hrdlo	gardło	throat	throat
	gъrt-tь	hrst	garść	(cupped) hand	(cupped) hand
	dьr-nъ	drn	darń	lawn	lawn
	sьr-na	srna	sarna	roe	roe
CieRC: 16	pьrsi	prsa	pierś	breast	breast
	sьrpъ	srp	sierp	sickle	sickle
CiRC: 4	vьlkъ	vlk	wilk	wolf	wolf
CeRC: 6	vьlna	vlna	wełna	wool	wool
	sьrdь-ce	srdce	serce	heart	heart
	pьlnъ	plný	pełny	full	full

Total: 60

As may be seen, Polish produces pre-vocalised reflexes of CS tьrt items, i.e. simply "vocalises" the yer.[11] On the Czech side, however, syllabic consonants appear. Polish thus has separate continuators for CS tьrt and CS trьt (pre-vocalised vs. trapped consonants), while Czech seems to have merged the two patterns: CS trьt under (1) as well as CS tьrt under (14) produce modern syllabic consonants. Hence there is certainly evidence for a right-branching

[10] (14) is a sample of a 60-item list that I have established on the grounds of various etymological dictionaries and historical grammars. The sources include Havlová & Erhart (1989-2002), Bańkowski (2000), Brückner (1927), Machek (1957), Holub & Kopečný (1952), Rejzek (2001), Rospond (1979:95ss), Stieber (1979:33ss,54ss), Nahtigal (1961:111ss). The philological situation is rather complex and cannot be discussed here. The total number of roots that can be come by probably exceeds 60 a bit (yet not much).

[11] The quality of the vowel depends on the consonantal environment. Its prediction is a classical concern of Polish historical grammar, see for example Stieber (1973:23s,42ss,1979:54ss), Długosz-Kurczabowa & Dubisz (1993:84ss), Rospond (1979:94ss), Nahtigal (1961:111ss), Carlton (1991:249s), Vondrák (1924:183ss), Mikkola (1913-50 II:201s), Wijk (1949-50:44s).

status of trapped consonants, but it seems that nothing allows to decide between a right- and a left-branching identity for Czech syllabic consonants.

This, however, is but the impression when looking at the modern waters, which have been muddied by a secondary evolution. In early Old Czech, CS tьrt and trъt were still distinct: the former pattern was represented by (primary" syllabic consonants, while the latter was identified by trapped consonants (which in subsequent evolution became "secondary" syllabic consonants).[12] The Old Czech opposition syllabic vs. trapped consonants is solidly documented by the fact that the former count in verse, while the latter do not – exactly the modern situation (see section 2). There is even a minimal pair, which led Trubetzkoy (1939:1999) to talk about a "correlation of syllabicity" in Old Czech: syllabic držěti "to hold" (< CS dьržati, pol dzierżyć, ru deržat', mod cz držet) vs. trapped držěti "to tremble, shake" (< CS drъžati, pol drżeć, ru drožat', mod cz extinct). Syllabic dṛžěti "to hold", then, counts for 3 syllables in typical 8-peak Old Czech Alexandrine verse (to jmě drzal takým kmenem, Kat. 24), while trapped držěti "to tremble" weighs only 2 syllables (všecko pohanstvo drzezalo, Kat. 2803) (e.g. Komárek 1962:82, Liewehr 1933:94).

In subsequent evolution, which may be followed progressively in Old Czech script, all trapped consonants then became syllabic.[13] The overall evolution is thus CS trъt > ocz trapped trt > mcz syllabic tṛt.

In sum, thus, it appears that Western Slavic syllabic and trapped consonants owe their existence to the loss of a preceding vs. a following vowel, respectively. I take this to be quite striking a confirmation of the synchronic and diachronic evidence that comes from other languages (section 8). It also matches the conclusion of the theory-internal argument of section 9: syllabic consonants branch on the preceding, trapped consonants on the following empty (emptied) Nucleus.

11. An alternative explanation for the transparency of trapped consonants: they are obstruents

Recall from section 5 that Polish trapped consonants are transparent to voice assimilation. The standard explanation that is proposed in the work of Jerzy Rubach is to identify trapped consonants as extrasyllabic. That is, voice assimilation takes place at a derivational stage where trapped consonants are still unsyllabified: the flanking consonants are in contact at that point of the derivation and therefore regularly agree in voicing.

Word-internal extrasyllabicity, however, is problematic in itself because of the largely consensual Peripherality Condition (e.g. Clements 1990:290,1997 Hayes 1995:57s): only objects at margins can be ignored by phonological structure-building devices, and hence be extrametrical, extraprosodic or extrasyllabic.

Let us thus examine what the solution developed in this article, i.e. a right-branching identity for trapped consonants, has to say with respect to their transparency. In fact, nothing

[12] Relevant literature includes Trávníček (1935:57s,111ss,226ss), Lehr-Spławiński & Stieber (1957:97ss), Komárek (1962:60s, 82, 97ss, 127ss), (Liewehr 1933:93s,162s).

[13] Without context, or almost: the Polish CrzC pattern of table (1) produces CřC on the Czech side, and ř in these clusters is trapped to date (see section 2). Alongside with palatalised ř, word-initial trapped consonants such as in *rdít se*, *lhát* "to go red, to lie" etc. (see section 2) refuse to become syllabic: they are still trapped in the modern language. Palatal ř has good reason for rebelling against syllabicity: demonstrably, it is an obstruent, not a sonorant (for example, it undergoes final devoicing). The ban of syllabic consonants in word-initial position ties in with the fact that Czech is a language with no word-initial restrictions (in contrast to, say, English, where #RT, #TT and #RR do not occur). Assuming CVCV, the latter fact leads to conclude that Czech does not possess the "initial CV" (see Scheer 2004:§§83,402), i.e. an empty CV unit that is the real phonological identity of the diacritic "#" "beginning of the word". In absence of this CV unit and if syllabic consonants are indeed left-branching, it is obvious why word-initial sonorants cannot become syllabic in Czech: they need a preceding empty Nucleus on which they can branch, but no such Nucleus is in sight.

at all: there is no particular reason why right-branching, rather than left-branching consonants should be transparent to voicing.

The transparency of trapped consonants must have an independent reason. The analysis developed in Scheer (2004:§268) builds on the notorious fact that trapped consonants are demoted: for some reason, they lose their status as sonorants. There is no doubt about this fact since trapped consonants, both in Czech and in Polish (<ř> and <rz>, respectively), participate in final devoicing. That is, they have voiced and voiceless allophones, something that is not rendered by spelling. Their underlying identity is voiced since they appear as such in intervocalic and word-initial position (e.g. pol rzeka, cz řeka "river", pol mierzyć, cz měřit "to measure"). In word-final position, however, Polish <rz> and Czech <ř> are voiceless: pol piekarz [pjɛkaʃ], cz pekař [pɛkar̝̊] "baker" (e.g. Palková 1997:213, Scheer 1998:53ss for Czech, Swan 2002:16 for Polish). In the same way, all Polish sources report that r in final Cr# clusters is actually devoiced[14]: Biedrzycki (1978:83s) for example renders this critical phonetic detail: he transcribes *myśl, wiatr* "thought NOMsg, wind NOMsg" as [mɨɕl̥, vjatr̥]. Gussmann (1992) also consistently transcribes devoiced sonorants in this position: *wiatr, Piotrka, mętrka* "wind NOMsg, Peter dim GENsg, wiseacre GENsg" appear as [vjatr̥, pjɔtρ8ka, mɛntρ8ka]. Finally, Montreuil (1999:541ss) provides concomitant evidence from an unrelated Romance language, Romansch, where trapped sonorants are also demoted to obstruents and hence transparent to voicing: they undergo final devoicing themselves and "hand it over" to preceding obstruents.

Since sonorants never participate in final devoicing systems, it is safe to conclude that the trapped consonants at hand are not sonorants. Rather, they *were* sonorants before they became trapped. Trappedness seems to be incompatible with sonorancy: it causes the demotion of sonorants to obstruents. The alternative explanation for the transparency of trapped consonants, then, is simple: CrC and Cr# sequences where r is trapped are made *only* of obstruents; obstruent clusters, as everywhere else in Polish, agree in voicing, and there is nothing more to say.

12. Conclusion

I have tried to do three things in this article. First, to establish trapped consonants as a basic phonological object in its own right: trapped consonants are not some sub-variety of syllabic consonants. Rather, they stand on a par with them. Confusion of both categories is commonplace in the literature. However, taking trapped consonants for some funny variety of syllabic consonants is fatal for the understanding of what is going on: both categories have opposite properties and opposite effects.

Second, I have provided a check-list regarding the behaviour of trapped and syllabic consonants. This catalogue is designed to help dispensing with much previous and current practice where the phonological identity of trapped and syllabic consonants is not determined by their phonological behaviour, but by their mere function as a vowel ("syllabic consonants sit in Nuclei"), or from impressionistic judgements of the analyst (see Bagemihl 1991 on this). My contention, then, is that only the phonological behaviour of a natural linguistic object can betray its identity (this is actually a core claim of Government Phonology). In the particular case at hand, I argue that the examination of the behaviour of either trapped or syllabic consonants in isolation will get us nowhere. It is only when the behaviour of both closely related cluster-building consonant types is run against each other that we can expect to

[14] Even if realisations are somewhat variable. According to Rubach & Booij (1990a:441, note 14), "there is a distinction between liquids and nasals: while liquids devoice, nasals may but do not have to". Elsewhere, Rubach (1997a:558) points out that the predictions made by his analysis produce the most consistently observed voiceless result. The massive prominence of devoiced realisations also coincides with my own observation.

discover who they are. In short, any theory that proposes an identity for syllabic consonants without knowing about, and having integrated, the evidence form trapped consonants (and vice-versa), must fail.

These two goals are theory-neutral. The check-list that I have introduced may be incomplete, but it makes a strong case, empirically speaking, for the absolute antagonicity of syllabic and trapped consonants. It should therefore contribute to a better understanding of these strange phonological hermaphrodites, no matter what the theory.

The study of syllabic consonants has gained some interest recently, especially in Government Phonology (less so, unfortunately, the study of trapped consonants). The perspective that I am arguing for here and at greater length in Scheer (2004:§240) contributes to this movement. The theory-specific part of the article is therefore nothing that should be considered a definite result. Rather, it is a first exploration of the consequences that could be drawn, in the specific environment of CVCV, from the insights of the theory-neutral sections. The conclusion that syllabic consonants branch on the preceding empty (emptied) Nucleus, while trapped consonants have the reverse structure, is certainly perfectible, perhaps simply wrong (foremost on the trapped side).

There is indeed some evidence on which I could not report in the frame of an article, and which does not appear to support the analysis presented. Relevant facts are reviewed in Scheer (2004:§296). We know that trapped consonants, unlike their syllabic peers, are invisible for stress (section 2). This suggests that they do not participate in the vocalic world at all. Their natural representation, then, would be one where they remain unassociated to any Nucleus (see Blaho 2001,2004 on this issue). Also, the right periphery of syllabic consonants begs the question: heavy clusters can appear to the right of syllabic consonants (e.g. in Czech words such as čtvrtek - čtvrtk-u "Thursday NOMsg, GENsg", trpknout "to become bitter"). These enclose additional empty Nuclei that remain orphan in my current understanding.

Be that as it may, it is wise, thus, to consider the present article primarily as a methodological contribution, with a supplement that explores how the insight gained, at an embryotic understanding of what is going on, could be implemented into a particular theory. Further study must uncover the real identity of syllabic and trapped consonants.

References

References followed by "WEB" may be downloaded at www.unice.fr/dsl/tobias.htm.

Bagemihl, Bruce 1991. Syllable Structure in Bella Coola. Linguistic Inquiry **22**, 589-646.

Bańkowski, Andrzej 2000. Etymologiczny Słownik języka polskiego. Vols 1+2. Warszawa: PWN.

Bell, Alan 1978. Syllabic Consonants. Universals of Human Language, Vol 2, edited by Joseph Greenberg, 153-201. Stanford: Stanford University Press.

Bethin, Christina 1984. Voicing assimilation in Polish. International Journal of Slavic Linguistics and Poetics **29**, 17-32.

Biedrzycki, Leszek 1978. Fonologia angielskich i polskich rezonantów. Warszawa: Polskie Wydawnictwo Naukowe.

Blaho, Sylvia 2001. The representation of Slovak syllabic consonants in strict CV. The Odd Yearbook **6**, 3-24.

Blaho, Sylvia 2004. Syllabic consonants in strict CV. MA thesis, Pazmany Peter University.

Blevins, Juliette 1995. The Syllable in Phonological Theory. The Handbook of Phonological Theory, edited by Goldsmith John, 206-244. Oxford, Cambridge, Mass: Blackwell.

Brückner, Aleksander 1927. Słownik etymologiczny języka polskiego. Warszawa: Wiedza Powszechna.

Butskhrikidze, Marika 2002. The Consonant Phonotactics of Georgian. Ph.D dissertation, University of Leiden.

Caha, Pavel & Tobias Scheer in press. The Syntax and Phonology of Czech Templatic Morphology. To appear in the proceedings of FASL 16.

Carlton, Terence 1991. Introduction to the phonological history of the Slavic languages. Columbus, Ohio: Slavica.

Carr, Philip 1993. Phonology. London: Macmillan.

Chomsky, Noam & Morris Halle 1968. The Sound Pattern of English. Cambridge, Mass.: MIT Press.

Clements, George 1990. The role of the sonority cycle in core syllabification. Papers in Laboratory Phonology I, edited by John Kingston & Mary Beckmann, 283-333. Cambridge: Cambridge University Press.

Clements, George 1997. Berber syllabification: derivations or constraints? Derivations and Constraints in Phonology, edited by Iggy Roca, 289-330. Oxford: Clarendon.

Cyran, Eugeniusz 2003. Complexity Scales and Licensing Strength in Phonology. Lublin: KUL.

Cyran, Eugeniusz & Edmund Gussmann 1998. Polish consonantal sequences: a phonological testing ground. Structure and Interpretation, edited by Eugeniusz Cyran, 127-138. Lublin: Pase.

Cyran, Eugeniusz & Edmund Gussmann 1999. Consonant clusters and governing relations: Polish initial consonant sequences. The syllable, Views and Facts, edited by Harry van der Hulst & Nancy Ritter, 219-248. Berlin, New York: de Gruyter.

Dell, François & Mohamed Elmedlaoui 1985. Syllabic consonants and syllabification in Imdlawn Tashlhiyt Berber. Journal of African Languages and Linguistics 7, 105-130.

Dell, François & Mohamed Elmedlaoui 1988. Syllabic consonants in Berber: some new evidence. Journal of African Languages and Linguistics **10**, 1-17.

Długosz-Kurczabowa, Krystyna & Stanisław Dubisz 1993. Gramatyka historyczna języka polskiego. Pochodzenie języka polskiego, Fonetyka, Fonologia. Warszawa: Wydawnictwa Uniwersytetu Warszawskiego.

Gussenhoven, Carlos & Haike Jacobs 1998. Understanding Phonology. London: Arnold.

Gussmann, Edmund 1980a. Studies in Abstract Phonology. Cambridge Mass.: MIT Press.

Gussmann, Edmund 1980b. Introduction to phonological analysis. Warszawa: PWN.

Gussmann, Edmund 1992. Resyllabification and delinking: The case of Polish voicing. Linguistic Inquiry **23**, 29-56.

Gussmann, Edmund 1998. Domains, relations, and the English agma. Structure and Interpretation. Studies in Phonology, edited by Eugeniusz Cyran, 101-126. Lublin: Folium.

Gussmann, Edmund 2002. Phonology: Analysis and Theory. Cambridge: Cambridge University Press.

Gussmann, Edmund & Jonathan Kaye 1993. Polish notes from a Dubrovnik Café: I. The yers. SOAS Working Papers in Linguistics and Phonetics **3**, 427-462.

Hall, Tracy 1992. Syllable Structure and Syllable-Related Processes in German. Tübingen: Niemeyer.

Hall, Tracy 2000. Phonologie. Eine Einführung. Berlin & New York: de Gruyter.

Harris, John 1994. English sound structure. Oxford: Blackwell.

Havlová, Eva & Adolf Erhart (eds) 1989-2002. Etymologický slovník jazyka staroslověnského. 1st – 11th booklet A-poditi. Praha: Nakladatelství Československé Akademie Věd/ Akademie Věd České Republiky.

Hayes, Bruce 1989. The Prosodic Hierarchy in Meter. Rhythm and Meter, edited by Paul Kiparsky & G. Youmans, 201-260. Orlando, Florida: Academic Press.

Hayes, Bruce 1995. Metrical Stress Theory. Principles and Case Studies. Chicago, London: University of Chicago Press.

Holub, Josef & František Kopečný 1952. Etymologický slovník jazyka Českého. Praha: Státní nakladatelství učebnic.

Kastler, Claude 1995. La langue tchèque. Grammaire tchèque pratique et raisonnée. Paris: Ophrys.

Kaye, Jonathan 1990. 'Coda' licensing. Phonology **7**, 301-330.

Kaye, Jonathan 1995. Derivations and Interfaces. Frontiers of Phonology, edited by Jacques Durand & Francis Katamba, 289-332. London & New York: Longman. Also in SOAS Working Papers in Linguistics and Phonetics **3**, 1993, 90-126.

Kaye, Jonathan & Jean Lowenstamm 1984. De la syllabicité. Forme Sonore du Langage, edited by François Dell, Daniel Hirst & Jean-Roger Vergnaud, 123-159. Paris: Hermann.

Kaye, Jonathan, Jean Lowenstamm & Jean-Roger Vergnaud 1990. Constituent structure and government in phonology. Phonology **7**, 193-231.

Kenstowicz, Michael 1994. Phonology in Generative Grammar. Oxford: Blackwell.
Komárek, Miroslav 1962. Historická mluvnice Česká. Volume I: Hláskosloví. Praha: SPN.
Lehr-Spławiński, Tadeusz & Zdzisław Stieber 1957. Gramatyka Historyczna języka czeskiego. Warszawa: PWN.
Liewehr, Ferdinand 1933. Einführung in die historische Grammatik der tschechischen Sprache. 1. Teil: Lautlehre, Erste Lieferung. Brünn: Rohrer.
Lowenstamm, Jean 1996. CV as the only syllable type. Current trends in Phonology. Models and Methods, edited by Jacques Durand & Bernard Laks, 419-441. Salford, Manchester: ESRI. WEB.
Machek, Václav 1957. Etymologický slovník jazyka českého a slovenského. Praha: Nakladatelství Československé Akademie Věd.
Mann, Stuart 1957. Czech historical grammar. Revised edition Hamburg 1977: Buske.
Meillet, Antoine 1934. Le Slave Commun. 2nd edition Paris: Champion.
Mikkola, Jooseppi Julius 1913-50. Urslavische Grammatik. Teil I 1913: Lautlehre, Vokalismus, Betonung. Teil II 1942: Konsonantismus. Teil III 1950: Formenlehre. Heidelberg: Winter.
Montreuil, Jean-Pierre 1999. The Romansch syllable. The syllable, Views and Facts, edited by Harry van der Hulst & Nancy Ritter, 527-550. Berlin, New York: de Gruyter.
Nahtigal, Rajko 1961. Die Slavischen Sprachen. Abriß der vergleichenden Grammatik. Wiesbaden: Harrassowitz.
Palková, Zdena 1997. Fonetika a fonologie češtiny. Praha: Univerzita Karlova.
Panzer, Baldur 1991. Die Slavischen Sprachen in Gegenwart und Geschichte. Sprachstrukturen und Verwandtschaft. Frankfurt am Main: Peter Lang.
Pawelec, Przemysław 1989. Cyclic phonology and the inventory of morpheme-initial consonant clusters in Polish and English. Anglica Wratislaviensia **16**, 35-63.
Rejzek, Jiří 2001. Český etymologický slovník. Voznice: Leda.
Rennison, John 1999. Syllables in Western Koromfe. The syllable, Views and Facts, edited by Harry van der Hulst & Nancy Ritter, 311-347. Berlin, New York: de Gruyter.
Ritter, Nancy ms. Georgian Consonant Clusters: The complexity is in the structure, not in the melody. Ms, University of Connecticut.
Rospond, Stanisław 1979. Gramatyka historyczna języka polskiego. Warszawa: PWN.
Rowicka, Grażyna 1999a. On Ghost vowels. A Strict CV Approach. Ph.D. dissertation, Leiden University.
Rowicka, Grażyna 1999b. Prosodic optimality and prefixation in Polish. The prosody-morphology interface, edited by René Kager, Harry van der Hulst & W. Zonneveld, 367-389. Cambridge: Cambridge University Press.
Rowicka, Grażyna 2003. /r/ syllabicity: Polish *versus* Bulgarian and Serbo-Croatian. Living on the Edge. 28 papers in honour of Jonathan Kaye, edited by Stefan Ploch, 511-526. Berlin, New York: Mouton de Gruyter.
Rubach, Jerzy 1977. Changes of consonants in English and Polish. A generative account. Wrocław, Warszawa, Kraków, Gdańsk: Polska Akademia Nauk.
Rubach, Jerzy 1984. Cyclic and Lexical Phonology: The Structure of Polish. Dordrecht: Foris.
Rubach, Jerzy 1990. Final Devoicing and Cyclic Syllabification in German. Linguistic Inquiry **21**, 79-94.
Rubach, Jerzy 1996. Nonsyllabic Analysis of Voice Assimilation in Polish. Linguistic Inquiry **27**, 69-110.
Rubach, Jerzy 1997a. Extrasyllabic Consonants in Polish: Derivational Optimality Theory. Derivations and Constraints in Phonology, edited by Iggy Roca, 551-581. Oxford: Clarendon.
Rubach, Jerzy 1997b. Polish Voice Assimilation in Optimality Theory. Rivista di Linguistica **9**, 291-342.
Rubach, Jerzy & Geert Booij 1987. Postcyclic versus Postlexical Rules in Lexical Phonology. Linguistic Inquiry **18**, 1-44.
Rubach, Jerzy & Geert Booij 1990a. Edge of constituent effects in Polish. Natural Language and Linguistic Theory **8**, 427-463.
Rubach, Jerzy & Geert Booij 1990b. Syllable structure assignment in Polish. Phonology **7**, 121-158.

Saussure, Ferdinand de 1879. Mémoire sur le système primitif des voyelles dans les langues indo-européennes. Leipzig: Teubner.
Scheer, Tobias 1996. Une théorie de l'interaction directe entre consonnes. Ph.D diss., Université Paris 7. WEB.
Scheer, Tobias 1999. A theory of consonantal interaction. Folia Linguistica **32**, 201-237. WEB.
Scheer, Tobias 2003. The Key to Czech Vowel Length: Templates. Investigations into Formal Slavic Linguistics, edited by Petr Kosta, Joanna Blaszczak, Jens Frasek, Ljudmila Geist & Marzena Żygis, 97-118. Frankfurt am Main: Lang. WEB.
Scheer, Tobias 2004. A Lateral Theory of Phonology. Vol.1: What is CVCV, and why should it be? Mouton de Gruyter, Berlin.
Scheer, Tobias 2007. On the Status of Word-Initial Clusters in Slavic (And Elsewhere). Annual Workshop on Formal Approaches to Slavic Linguistics. The Toronto Meeting 2006, edited by Richard Compton, Magdalena Goledzinowska & Ulyana Savchenko, 346-364. Ann Arbor: Michigan Slavic Publications. WEB.
Scheer, Tobias forth. A Lateral Theory of Phonology. Vol.2: On Locality, Morphology and Phonology in Phonology. Berlin: Mouton de Gruyter.
Spencer, Andrew 1996. Phonology. Oxford: Blackwell.
Stieber, Zdzisław 1973. A Historical Phonology of the Polish Language. Heidelberg: Winter.
Stieber, Zdzisław 1979. Zarys gramatyki porównawczej języków słowiańskich. Warszawa: PWN.
Swan, Oscar 2002. A Grammar of Contemporary Polish. Bloomington: Slavica.
Szigetvári, Péter 1999. VC Phonology: a theory of consonant lenition and phonotactics. Ph.D dissertation. Eötvös Loránd University, Budapest.
Szpyra, Jolanta 1989. The Phonology - Morphology Interface. London & New York: Routledge.
Szpyra, Jolanta 1992. The phonology of Polish prefixation. Phonlogical Investigations, edited by Jacek Fisiak & Stanisław Puppel, 185-218. Amsterdam: Benjamins.
Szpyra, Jolanta 1995. Three Tiers in Polish and English Phonology. Lublin: Wydawnictwo Universytetu Marii Curie-Skłodowskiej.
Toft, Zoë 2002. The phonetics and phonology of some syllabic consonants in Southern British English. ZAS Papers in Linguistics 28.
Trávníček, František 1935. Historická mluvnice Československá. Praha: Melantrich.
Trubetzkoy 1939. Principes de Phonologie. French translation Paris 1986: Klincksieck.
Vaillant, André 1950. Grammaire comparée des langues slaves. Tome 1: Phonétique. Paris & Lyon: Institut d'Etudes Slaves.
Vondrák, Wenzel 1924. Vergleichende Slavische Grammatik. Band I: Lautlehre und Stammbildungslehre. 2. Auflage Göttingen: Vandenhoeck & Ruprecht.
Wiese, Richard 1986. Nichtlineare Phonologie: Eine Fallstudie des Chinesischen. Linguistische Berichte **102**, 93-135.
Wiese, Richard 1996. The Phonology of German. Oxford: Oxford University Press.
Wijk, Nicolaas van 1949-50. Les groupes ъr, ьr, ъl, ьl en slave commun et en russe. Južnoslovenski Filolog **18**, 39-47.

Psycholinguistics

Denisa Bordag, Leipzig, Prague

Psycholinguistic Aspects of Grammatical Gender Production in Second Language Czech

It is a well-known and well-described fact that the acquisition and correct production of grammatical gender cause serious difficulties to second language (L2) learners. Rogers (1987:48) mentions six 'main areas of weakness' in language work, the first of which is 'gender, number, case: of nouns, pronouns, adjectives, articles (or equivalents)'. However, it is not only the L2 learners whose L1 lacks a gender system, who make frequent gender errors despite their proficiency in other parts of their L2 grammar. Both Czech and German have grammatical gender and the number and type of their genders is identical: masculine, feminine and neuter. Yet both Germans learning Czech and Czechs learning German make frequent gender errors in their speech production. The main reason seems to be that despite the aforementioned similarities, the languages differ in how the three genders are assigned to their nouns: Approximately half of their translation equivalents have identical genders; the other half does not. There is also no 1:1 mapping between the genders of Czech and German nouns: It is impossible to say that e.g. most German feminines correspond to Czech neuters or the other way around. Sometimes the gender of Czech nouns can be guessed from their terminations, but this method is not very reliable as there is no ending in the Czech or German language (apart from some derivational suffixes) which would mark e.g. only feminine nouns and not any other.

The purpose of this study is to explore the psycholinguistic mechanisms which might be responsible for the difficulties German learners have when producing Czech gender, particularly whether the difficulties are caused by interlingual interference from German. The theoretical starting point of this study is the modular two-step type of network activation model of lexical production proposed by Levelt (1989), Roelofs (1992) and Levelt, Roelofs and Meyer (1999). Levelt's model is the most thoroughly described model of language production with a wide scope and area of application. It is also the only model which has been applied to bilingual speech production (De Bot 1992).

In this study, it is particularly the lemma stratum of the model which is addressed. Within this stratum, there are abstract grammatical nodes representing e.g. word class, valency or other grammatical categories of a lexical entry. Grammatical gender as an inherent lexical-syntactic property of nouns is also stored on this level. The model assumes (Jescheniak and Levelt 1994, but also Dell 1986 and Caramazza 1997) that all nouns of one gender class (e.g. masculine, feminine and neuter) are linked to a single node, which represents that gender (generic gender representation). The access to a gender marking inflectional ending or article lemma is mediated by the abstract gender node. As soon as a lemma is activated, activation spreads immediately to its gender node. More than one gender node can be activated and compete for selection, but only the most activated one will be selected, before the encoding proceeds to the next stage of phonological encoding.

If we expand this hypothesis to the representation of second language grammatical gender, we might assume that if two languages have the same number and type of grammatical gender, their lemmas are all mapped onto one set of gender nodes. This assumption is supported by theories stressing the fact that the incomplete second language system takes over, or inherits, all it possibly can from the first language (Competition Model by Mac Whinney, 1997), as well as by theories saying that during speech production in L2 both the L1 and L2 systems (or their parts) are activated and searched simultaneously (De Bot 1992, Green 1993, Poulisse and Bongaerts 1994, Hermans et al. 1998, Grosjean 1998).

On the basis of this information it is possible to hypothesize that one of the reasons why acquisition and production of grammatical gender cause so many difficulties for second language speakers at all levels of proficiency is the interference from their first language: If a second language speaker wants to produce a nominal phrase in his or her second language, the

lemmas of the corresponding first language translation equivalents and their grammatical features are also activated and may thus interfere with second language production.
An experiment was constructed in which the following hypothesis was tested: If the gender of a first language noun differs from that of its to-be-selected second language translation equivalent, their lemmas compete for selection and with them their corresponding gender nodes, which they automatically activate. Selection of the second language lemma should thus be delayed and subjects should produce more gender errors compared to the condition where both translation equivalents have congruent genders. We will use the term *gender interference effect* to refer to the negative effect of the first language gender on the selection of the gender of its second language translation equivalent.

Experiment

In the experiment, German subjects had to name pictures in Czech (their L2) in two conditions: Either with a bare noun (short condition) or with an adjective of size (*big* or *small*) and a noun (long condition). Noun phrases with adjective + noun and not solely article + noun were chosen, because Czech as contrasted to German does not have any articles. On the other hand, adjectives in both languages have to agree in gender with their head nouns. Half of the nouns chosen for the experiment had congruent gender in both languages; the other half did not. The assumption was that production of noun phrases (and nouns?) with congruent gender in both languages would be faster than production of those with different gender in German and Czech. To create optimal conditions in which the L1 is most likely (and most strongly) activated (Grosjean 1997), Czech fillers were included in the experiment, so that one third (22) of the pictures was to be named in the subjects' L1 (German) and two thirds (44) in their L2 (Czech) .

Participants

Eighteen learners of Czech as an L2 participated in this experiment, mostly students of West Slavic studies at the University of Leipzig. They were all native German speakers and had neither Czech nor any other language as their second mother tongue. Their knowledge of Czech was from intermediate to low advanced and exceeded the level usually attained by learners after two years of language instruction at a German university. They all started to learn Czech after their 16th year (at 20 years on average) and had been learning Czech for 4.6 years on average. Sixteen of them spent at least one semester in the Czech Republic and all of them had been using Czech regularly during the last year, either for study purposes or as a hobby. All subjects were paid for their participation.

Materials

The target stimuli were 72 line drawings, which had been used in previous experiments. Pictures of forty-four Czech nouns were chosen as experimental items, none of them were close cognates. The gender of half of the nouns was congruent with that of their German translation equivalents (e.g. the noun 'tree', *strom* in Czech and *Baum* in German, is in both languages masculine), the gender of the other half differed from that of their German translation equivalents (e.g. the noun 'picture' in Czech, *obraz,* is masculine, whereas in German, *Bild*, it is neuter). They were all easily depictable concrete nouns with high frequency both in Czech and in German. The majority of the experimental items were monomorphemic and apart from 4 names of animals they were all inanimate. Each set of 22 nouns consisted of 8 masculines, 8 feminines and 6 neuters. Their length ranged between one and three syllables and each set contained the same number of mono-, di- and trisyllabic masculine, feminine and neuter nouns. The sets were also matched for the final letter, because the gender of some Czech nouns can be predicted from word form properties (consonant is a typical masculine ending, -a a typical feminine ending and –o a typical neuter ending, -e is usually either a feminine or a neuter ending). Thus there were the same number of nouns ending with a consonant or one of the above mentioned vowels in each set within each gender group.

In addition to the 44 Czech experimental items, there were also 22 German filler and 14 practice items. They were also very frequent in both languages. Eight of the German fillers were masculines, 6 feminines and 8 neuters. Eight of them were used as Czech practice items, too. German practice items were another 6 pictures of common objects, so that the total number of pictures used in the experiment was 72.

Procedure

The experimental session had three parts and lasted approximately 40 minutes. Participants were tested individually.

In the first part subjects were presented with instructions emphasizing both the speed and accuracy of their responses and with a booklet containing all 72 pictures, which would later appear in the experiment. Under each picture, its Czech name and its German translation equivalent were printed. Subjects were asked to rate on a 7-point scale 1) how well the picture depicted the Czech word, 2) how well it depicted the German word and 3) how familiar they were with the Czech word. The ratings were done to ensure that participants really study the names of the pictures and to obtain data for evaluations of the stimuli materials, of subjects' familiarity with the Czech words and to control whether the words in either the gender congruent or the gender incongruent set were not less familiar or worse depicted than the words in the other set. Later analyses showed that all words were equally well depicted and very well known to all participants (mean total rating of 6.48 on items in gender congruent set and 6.45 in gender incongruent set). Czech words in the gender incongruent set were slightly better rated on familiarity (6.61) than words in the other set (6.41). This, however, should not misleadingly affect results of the experiment, because it is faster reaction times on items from the congruent set which is expected.

In the second part of the experimental session the experiment proper was run. Participants were seated in front of a computer screen at a distance of about 50 cm. Stimulus presentation and recording of the naming latencies were computer controlled. The experimenter monitored the participant's responses through headphones and scored them for correctness.

Before the experiment started, participants were presented with a sheet containing Czech and German examples of noun phrases, which were to be used in the experiment in the long condition. Thus, all possible forms (i.e. Nom.Sg. of all genders) of both adjectives in both languages appeared on the list with exemplatory nouns. Participants were again asked to respond as fast and as accurately as possible and to try not to begin with */vel.../* or */mal.../* (the onsets of Czech words for big and small) or corresponding German equivalents before they knew what they were going to say and to use only the names which they had seen in the booklet. Attention was not explicitly drawn to grammatical gender.

The experimental session started with a block of 14 practice items, which were the same for all subjects. This block was run twice and the subjects received direct feedback on their responses from the experimenter and were allowed to ask questions. After a short break the first half of the experiment was run and after another break also its second half.

Each trial started with a visual fixation point (= * =) presented on a grey background for 600 ms on the right of the screen in the middle of an imaginary square in which the target picture was displayed later. Then, either a yellow or a blue background appeared for 300 ms. The colour of the background defined the language in which the response was required. Half of the subjects had to response in Czech when a picture was displayed on a blue background and in German when a yellow background appeared; the other half of the subjects had the colours reversed. Following this pause, a target picture was presented in the imaginary square on the right of the computer screen and marked with a black arrow pointing at it from the upper right part of the screen. In the long condition, two pictures of the same object appeared simultaneously on the screen: The target picture marked with an arrow in its usual position on the right part of the screen and either a larger or a smaller control picture of the same object on the left. When the left control picture was larger than the target picture, the subjects had to name the target picture with the adjective "small", if the left control picture was smaller than the target picture, subjects had to name the target picture with the adjective "big". Naming latencies were measured from the right or both pictures onset by a voice key. The responses of the subjects were digitally recorded.

The display colour of the arrow was contingent on the participant's response. It turned white as soon as a vocal response was initiated. However, if no response was registered within 5000 ms (time out) the arrow turned red. When the participant was ready for the next trial, he or she pressed the space bar on the keyboard, and after a pause of 300 ms the fixation point of the new trial was displayed.

Subjects were randomly assigned to one of two main randomisation versions. Each item was presented in the long and in the short condition. Half of the subjects saw the items in the long condition first; the other half saw the items in the short condition first. Within each subject, half of the items were long first, the other half were short first. The two main versions of the experiment differed in which items were long first.

Individual randomisations within the two main versions were prepared for each subject with the following restrictions: No more than 3 trials of the same condition (long vs. short), the same size (big vs. small) and the same gender (masculine, feminine, neuter) were allowed to follow each other. The same language of response was allowed in a maximum of 4 successive trials .

In the third part of the experimental session the subjects filled in a questionnaire concerning their knowledge of Czech and their language background.

Apparatus

The experiment was controlled by a computer running the ERTS program. Stimuli were presented to the subjects on a NEC MultisyncXV 17 inch monitor, positioned about 40 cm away from them. Their reactions were registered by a Sony ECM-MS957 microphone, which fed to a custom-built ERTS voice-key device and a DAT recorder. The screen resolution was 640 x 480.

Results and discussion

Observations were discarded from the analyses whenever any of the following conditions held:

a) a picture had been named other than expected;
b) an incorrect adjective had been named;
c) a picture was named in a wrong language (e.g. German instead of Czech);
d) a gender error in the adjective ending occurred;
e) a nonspeech sound preceded the utterance of the picture name or the adjective, triggering the voice key;
f) a disfluency occurred or an utterance was repaired;
g) a speech onset latency exceeded 5000 ms or deviated from the participant's and the length condition by more than two standard deviations.

On the basis of these criteria, a total of 352 observations (14.8%) were marked as incorrect.

Analyses of variance (ANOVAs) were performed on the mean naming latencies per subject (F1) and per item (F2). Overall, naming latencies for pictures with names from the gender incongruent set were slower than naming latencies for pictures with congruent gender in both languages. Both analyses with subjects as a random factor and with items as a random factor showed a significant effect on condition (congruent vs. incongruent), $F1(1, 17) = 10.41$,

$p < 0.01$, MSE = 1048103; F2 (1, 87) = 7.71, $p < 0.01$, MSE = 3184764, showing that reaction times were significantly slower in the incongruent condition. Effect on length (short vs. long) also reached significance in both analyses: F1(1, 17) = 46.37, $p < 0.001$, MSE = 66220598; F2 (1, 87) = 152.10, $p < 0.001$, MSE = 62834201. There was no interaction between condition and length: F1(1, 17) = 0.44, p = 0.517, MSE = 66522; F2(1, 87) = 0.45, p = 0.464, MSE = 191877. This means that the gender interference effect was obtained not only when pictures were named with adjectives, but also with bare noun naming.

Table 1. Overview of the results of the experiment with reaction times (RT) in ms and % of errors in each condition (%e).

Czech exp.	congruent		incongruent		Interf. effect
	RT	%e	RT	%e	
short	1202	1.4	1276	1.3	+ 74
long	1642	3.9	1703	4.1	+ 61

To examine whether the gender interference effect obtained in the RT analysis also showed up in the error analysis, a X^2 test for the given probabilities was performed on the number of gender errors in the gender congruent and gender incongruent conditions. The test was significant: c(52, 22), $X^2 = 12.1622$, df = 1, $p < 0.001$. These findings are in accordance with the results of the RT analyses: Incongruent gender of the L1 translation equivalent induces more gender errors in the adjective + noun condition than when the genders of the translation equivalents are congruent in both languages.

Table 2. Number of gender errors in the experiment.

	number of gender errors	%e (long condition)
congruent condition	22	2.8
incongruent condition	52	6.6

The experiment yielded two important results. First, the response latencies were slower if the gender of a Czech noun differed from that of its German translation equivalent. Second, more gender errors were produced if genders of translation equivalents were incongruent. These two results support the initial hypothesis that there is a gender interference effect from the L1 during L2 production. The same pattern of results was observed also in the replication of this experiment, where the L2 was German and the L1 Czech.

Interestingly, the gender interference effect resembles in some aspects a gender distraction effect obtained in picture-word distractor experiments in some native languages (Schriefers 1993, La Heij et al. 1998, Schriefers and Truel 2000, Van Berkum 1997). In these naming tasks, faster reaction times were obtained when the picture target and the distractor word had the same gender than when their genders differed. This effect is interpreted as reflecting a competition for selection in the gender-incongruent condition: The activated gender feature of the distractor interferes with the name of the picture to be selected. In the gender-congruent condition this is not the case, because the distractor's gender is identical with that of the target noun. The L1 translation equivalents thus seem to affect production in the L2 in the same or a similar way as word distractors affect picture naming: They both slow down reaction latencies and induce gender errors in the incongruent condition.

However, there is an interesting difference between the gender distraction and the gender interference effect: Whereas the former was obtained only with gender marked noun phrase naming (i.e. under conditions where it was necessary to retrieve the gender information for production), the latter was significant also with a bare noun naming (short condition in this experiment). The difference can be interpreted as follows: In picture-word distractor tasks mental representations of the picture and the distractor have nothing in common: They merely appear together in the experimental conditions. On the other hand, L1 and L2 lemmas are semantically closely related. They are often assumed to share the same concepts or semantic features, at least those of concrete nouns ("asymmetry" or Revised Hierarchical Model by Kroll and Steward 1994, Distributed Feature Model by De Groot 1992, De Groot, Dannenburg and Van Hell 1994). The most likely interpretation of the difference between gender distraction and gender interference effects thus holds that when there is a strong relationship between the target noun and its interfering counterpart, e.g. when they share the same concept, their gender representations always compete for selection. However, when the lemmas do not share the same concept, the gender representations compete for selection only when a gender feature is necessary for production. Schriefers and Teruel (2000) provide indirect evidence supporting this interpretation. In their experiments with a picture-word distraction paradigm they also used semantically related distractors in both gender congruent and gender incongruent conditions and observed interaction between semantic relatedness and the gender-distraction effect. The authors claim that "the competition between different gender nodes is strengthened by the semantic relatedness of target and distractor lemma" (Schriefers and Teruel 2000: 1374).

Gender errors analysis

A detailed analysis of gender errors made by subjects in the experiment in the long condition revealed a consistent pattern: Subjects made most gender errors in agreement with nouns which had either an ambiguous or an atypical termination for their gender. In these cases, subjects mostly assigned to these nouns a gender which they „should have had" according to their termination. Figure 1 presents an overview of the average number of agreement errors for items with particular termination.

Figure 1. Average number of errors for particular terminations within each gender in the experiment.

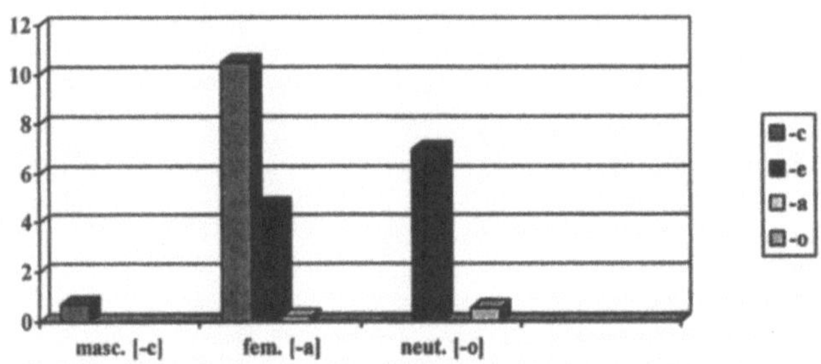

A typical termination for masculine nouns in Czech is a consonant (e.g. *strom* (M) – *tree*), for feminine –a (e.g. *kniha* (F) – *book*) and for neutral –o (e.g. *město* (N) – *town*). Figure 1 shows that if the experimental nouns had a gender predictable from their terminations, subjects made almost no agreement errors. The vowel -e is from this aspect an ambiguous termination in Czech, because nouns ending in -e are usually either feminine or neuter (e.g. *židle* (F) – *chair*

and *slunce* (N) – *sun*). As obvious from the figure, the number of agreement errors with these nouns was higher. Typically, if the participants made a gender error in agreement with a feminine noun ending in -e, it was because they took it for a neuter (e.g. **malé*(N) *židle* – *small chair*), and vice versa (e.g. **malá*(F) *slunce* – *small sun*). Most errors were made in agreement with feminine nouns ending in a consonant (*myš*(F) – *mouse*). As mentioned above, a final consonant is a termination typical for masculine nouns (there are only a few derived Czech masculine nouns which end in a vowel) and though the number of Czech feminine nouns ending in a consonant is quite large, it is still considered an atypical feminine ending. Characteristically, almost all feminine nouns ending in a consonant were considered masculine by the subjects (**malý*(M) *myš* – *small mouse*).

The results of the gender errors analysis shows that intralingual interference affected the gender production in the experiment as well: Subjects clearly overgeneralized the phonological rules for gender assignment in Czech and applied them to nouns with different gender as well. This effect was also replicated in the experiment with German as L2 and Czech as L1. However, the effect was stronger in Czech than in German, because the correlation between grammatical gender and word termination is more straightforward in this language.

Conclusions

Though the experiments reported in this paper were not designed to explore the influence of the phonological form on gender selection, the detailed analysis of the agreement errors clearly suggests that the phonological form (especially a word termination) has an effect on gender selection. Thus there seem to be at least three factors affecting gender production in a second language:

1) The gender of the corresponding first language translation equivalent (interlingual interference/transfer).
2) The phonological form of the to-be-selected second language noun (intralingual interference/transfer).
3) Gender information saved on the second language lemma (otherwise subjects would not be able to produce the correct gender of nouns whose gender differs from that of their first language translation equivalent and/or has an atypical termination).

In the light of these findings it does not seem to be the case that grammatical gender of second language nouns is stored as their inherent property in the same way as it is assumed for native languages. It is more likely that the grammatical gender of second language nouns is computed each time it is needed anew on the basis of stored information, information coming from the first language lemmas and information coming from the phonological form.

The influence of phonological form on gender selection in a second language has important implications for the models of speech production, because it would assume a feedback activation between the level of phonological forms and the lemma level, where gender selection takes place.

The model of Levelt assumes that lexical access is a two-staged, strictly serial and discrete process. During the first stage, one lemma from the cohort of activated lemmas is selected. After the process of selection is completed, the lemma activates a cohort of phonological forms, from which again only one will be selected and articulated. The processes on the phonological level are thus separate from the processes on the higher level of grammatical encoding and cannot influence them.

On the other hand, the Interactive Activation Model of Dell (1986), which has otherwise a very similar architecture to Levelt's model, assumes both top-down and bottom-up processes. The activation can flow in both directions, because links between nodes from different levels are bidirectional. This enables that lexical units from lower levels, e.g. phonological forms, can affect the processes on higher levels, e.g. the selection of a lemma. Furthermore, the activation starts to spread from the level of grammatical encoding to the level of phonological encoding already before the target lemma is selected. The interactive architecture of this model with time overlap between the processes on different levels makes it possible that the selection of a lemma can be affected by its phonological form. Consequently, the Interactive Activation Model of Dell seems to be more compatible with the results of the reported experiments than the strictly serial model of Levelt, unless we assume a different structure for the first and foreign language lexicons, a not very satisfactory solution. Further experiments investigating the relationship between lemmas and phonological forms in both foreign and native languages are necessary to clarify this and other questions.

Bibliography

Bordag, D. (2003): Gramatický rod a řečová produkce v mateřském a cizím jazyce. *Časopis československé psychologie, 2*, 105-122.

Caramazza, A. (1997): How many levels of processing are there in lexical access? *Cognitive Neuropsychology, 14*, 177-208.

De Bot, K. (1992): A bilingual production model: Levelt's speaking model adapted. *Applied Linguistics, 13*, 1-24.

De Groot, A. M. B. (1992): Bilingual lexical representation: A closer look at conceptual representations. In: R. Frost & L. Katz (eds.): *Orthography, Phonology, Morphology, and Meaning*. Amsterdam: Elsevier.

De Groot, A. M. B., Dannenburg, L., & van Hell, J. G. (1994): Forward and backward word translation by bilinguals. *Journal of Memory and Language, 33*, 600-629.

Dell, G. S. (1986): A spreading-activation model of retrieval in sentence production. *Psychological Review, 93*, 231-241.

Green, D. W. (1993): Towards a model of L2 comprehension and production. In: R. Schreuder & B. Weltens (eds.): *The Bilingual Lexicon* (pp. 249-277). Amsterdam: John Benjamins.

Grosjean, F. (1997): Processing mixed language: Issues, findings and models. In: A. De Groot & J. Kroll (eds.): *Tutorials in Bilingualism: Psycholinguistic Perspectives* (pp. 225-254). Mahwah, NJ: Lawrence Erlbaum Associates.

Grosjean, F. (1998): Studying bilinguals: Methodological and conceptual issues. *Bilingualism: Language and Cognition, 1*, 131-149.

Hermans, D., Bongaerts, T., De Bot, K., & Schreuder, R. (1998): Producing words in a foreign language: Can speakers prevent interference from their first language? *Bilingualism: Language and Cognition, 1*, 213-229.

Jescheniak, J. D. & Levelt, W. J. M. (1994): Word frequency effects in speech production: Retrieval of syntactic information and of phonological form. *Journal of Experimental Psychology: Learning, Memory, and Cognition, 20*, 824-843.

Kroll, J. & Steward, E. (1994): Category interference in translation and picture naming: Evidence for asymmetrical connections between bilingual memory representations. *Journal of Memory and Language, 33*, 149-174.

La Heij, W., Mak, P., Sander, J., & Willeboordse, E. (1998): The gender congruency effect in picture-word tasks. *Psychological Research, 61*, 209-219.

Levelt, W. J. M. (1989): *Speaking: From intention to articulation*. Cambridge, MA: MIT Press.

Levelt, W. J. M., Roelofs, A., & Meyer, A. S. (1999): A theory of lexical access in speech production. *Behavioral and Brain Sciences, 22*, 1-75.

MacWhinney, B. (1997): Second language acquisition and the competition model. In: A. M. B. de Groot & J. F. Kroll (eds.): *Tutorials in Bilingualism: Psycholinguistic Perspective* (pp. 113-142). Mahvah, NJ: Lawrence Erlbaum.

Poulisse, N. & Bongaerts, T. (1994): First language use in second language production. *Applied Linguistics, 15*, 36-57.

Roelofs, A. (1992): A spreading-activation theory of lemma retrieval in speaking. *Cognition, 42*, 107-142.
Rogers, M. (1987): Learners' difficulties with grammatical gender in German as a foreign language. *Applied Linguistics, 8*, 48-74.
Schriefers, H. (1993): Syntactic processes in the production of noun phrases. *Journal of Experimental Psychology: Learning, Memory, and Cognition, 19*, 841-850.
Schriefers, H. & Teruel, E. (2000): Grammatical gender in noun phrase production: The gender interference effect in German. *Journal of Experimental Psychology: Learning, Memory, and Cognition, 26*, 1368-1377.
Van Berkum, J. J. A. (1997): Syntactic processes in speech production: The retrieval of grammatical gender. *Cognition, 64*, 115-152.

Irina A. Sekerina, New York

Gender Priming and Mapping of Referential Expressions in Russian*

1. Introduction

The role of grammatical gender in language comprehension has received much attention in the recent psycholinguistic literature (Friederici & Jacobsen, 1999; Schriefers & Jescheniak, 1999). The central question is how and when grammatical gender on a modifier that precedes a noun can influence identification of that noun. This phenomenon is referred to as *gender priming* in literature on word recognition and lexical access. Gender priming has been studied extensively using gender-matching/mismatching paradigm when the preceding modifier, article or adjective, is either congruent or incongruent in gender with the incoming noun. It can manifest itself as two different effects: gender inhibition and gender facilitation. Faster identification of the noun in the gender-matching context in comparison to some gender-neutral baseline is referred to as *gender facilitation* while slower identification is described as *gender inhibition*. Depending on whether both gender inhibition and gender facilitation, or only the former one are found, Friederici and Jacobsen (1999) distinguish between two main approaches in explaining gender priming in language comprehension, *prelexical interactive* and *postlexical checking* models. When both inhibition and facilitation effects are present, such results are taken to support the prelexical interactive model for gender processing (Bates, Devescovi, Hernandez, & Pizzamiglio, 1996 for Italian; Grosjean, Dommergues, Cornu, Guillelmon, & Besson, 1994, for French). These experimental studies employed the gender-matching/mismatching paradigm and the auditory presentation of modifier primes (articles or adjectives) and targets (nouns). The results showed that the congruent gender present on the modifier resulted in faster lexical decisions on the nouns while gender-incongruent modifiers significantly slowed participants' performance in the same task. The postlexical checking model is consistent with experimental findings on gender priming when only a gender inhibition effect is found. According to this model, gender information on the modifier cannot exert its influence immediately since it would have to be maintained longer, until it can be checked against the gender on the noun and, thus, is only detectable for a gender-incongruent situation. Strong and consistent inhibition effects have been reported for most studied languages, such as Serbo-Croatian, Dutch, German, using a variety of tasks in both the visual and auditory modalities (see discussion in *Journal of Psycholinguistic Research,* 1999, 28(5), Special Issue: Processing of Grammatical Gender, Part I).

Gender facilitation effects when found, however, are weak and often inconsistent varying from language to language, task to task, and even from experiment to experiment in the same language employing the same task. Akhutina, Kurgansky, Polinsky, and Bates (1999) reported the results of four gender priming experiments in Russian in the auditory modality using a cue-shadowing task that combines comprehension and production. Experiment 2 examined gender priming of feminine vs. neuter nouns when preceded by a gender-ambiguous adjective and found no evidence for gender facilitation. Experiment 4, on the other hand, compared gender priming for masculine vs. feminine nouns using a different baseline and found a small but reliable gender facilitation effect when both genders were collapsed. However, when analyzed separately, it was significant only for feminine nouns, and not for masculine ones. Since this subtle gender facilitation effect in Russian can be accounted for by an alternative explanation proposed for Italian and French, namely, the phonological transparency between a particular gender and a morphological suffix in the noun, the majority of experimental results so far are more consistent with the postlexical checking model.

* This research was supported by NSF ADVANCE Grant #0137851. Any opinions, findings, and conclusions or recommendations expressed in this article are those of the author and do not necessarily reflect the views of the National Science Foundation.

Note that all of the above-mentioned studies have relied extensively on a gender-matching/mismatching paradigm when half the time the preceding modifier, article or adjective is incongruent in gender with the incoming noun. Participants, thus, have to perform under rather artificial experimental conditions, namely, attending to words that are incongruent in gender. A situation when the preceding adjective is masculine and the subsequent noun is feminine is rare if not impossible in normal language processing. It is also possible that that difficulty in capturing gender facilitation lies in the nature of behavioral tasks. Lexical decision, naming, and cue-shadowing may not necessarily lend themselves to uncover fine-grained and rapid components of gender priming during language comprehension. They are successful only when the component is robust, as is the case with gender inhibition. Lately, with advancement of such experimental techniques as eye movement recording in reading (Deutsch & Bentin, 2001) and ERPs (Gunter, Friederici, & Schriefers, 2000) to examine language comprehension on-line, it has become possible to assess gender priming and its fine-grained temporal course more directly. Introduction of the head-mounted eye-tracking paradigm to study spoken language comprehension (Cooper, 1974; Tanenhaus, Spivey-Knowlton, Eberhard, & Sedivy, 1995) allows us to overcome the artifacts of the behavioral methods and gender-matching/mismatching, capitalize on moment-by-moment sensitiveness of eye movements, and to investigate in detail gender priming in a natural setting of spoken language comprehension in visual context.

Dahan, Swingley, Tanenhaus, and Magnuson (2000) were the first to use the head-mounted eye-tracking methodology to investigate the effects of grammatical gender priming in French spoken word recognition. Specifically, they addressed the question of whether gender priming would tap into lexical access per se or lexical selection, a subtle distinction within the prelexical interactive model. French participants were presented with four pictures on a computer screen and followed spoken instructions to click on one of them. In Experiment 1, when the prime was the plural article not marked for grammatical gender, the participants looked more often at the pictures that shared initial sounds with the target (*les bouteilles* 'the bottles' vs. *les boutons* 'the buttons') than at the two phonologically unrelated distractors (*les chiens* 'the dogs' and *les salières* 'the salt shakers'). This is known as *the cohort effect,* namely, lexical activation of a word candidate that shares the same onset as the target (Allopenna, Magnuson, & Tanenhaus, 1998). Remarkably, in Experiment 2, the cohort effect was eliminated when the plural article was replaced with a gender-marked article, *la* or *le*, demonstrating that the set of lexical candidates considered for recognition of the noun was constrained by the gender-marked article (*la bouteille* 'the bottle-FEM' vs. *le bouton* 'the button-MASC'). However, just mere presence of grammatical gender information on the article preceding phonologically unrelated nouns of different gender did not result in gender priming. The pattern of eye movements revealed that the probability of fixating either the gender-congruent or the gender-incongruent competitor did not differ significantly when the participants were presented with four phonologically unrelated but carefully matched pictures consisting of the gender-matching target (*le zèbre* 'the zebra-MASC') and the competitor (*le balai* 'the broom-MASC'), a gender-incongruent competitor (*la chaussette* 'the sock-FEM'), and a distractor (*la louche* 'the ladle-FEM'). Dahan and colleagues concluded that "gender information carried by the article was not sufficient enough to restrict attention to pictures with gender-matching names, presumably because the pictures did not contain perceptual features onto which gender could be matched." (p. 473).

The present experiment employs the head-mounted eye-tracking methodology to investigate grammatical gender priming in Russian. In contrast to the Dahan *et al.*'s (2000) study, it clearly shows that grammatical gender present on the adjective can induce competition between two referential expressions that are matched in gender. It also provides new evidence from Russian for gender facilitation through more direct and fine-grained measurement of eye movements compared to secondary tasks of lexical decision and cue shadowing of Bates *et al.* (1996) and Akhutina *et al.* (1999). Our results demonstrate that the effects of grammatical gender on the Russian adjectives can be as strong as to prime the gender-matching noun well in advance to noun occurrence in speech.

2. Gender Facilitation: Evidence from an Eye-Tracking Experiment in Russian

Russian has three genders: masculine, feminine, and neuter. Masculine and feminine nouns dominate the Russian lexicon, 46% and 41%, respectively, while neuter gender accounts for about 13% (Akhutina *et al.*, 1999). In addition, Russian nouns are morphologically marked for case and number. All three types of grammatical features -- gender, case, and number -- are morphologically manifested on Russian adjectives through endings: *krasn-yj/-aja/-oe* 'red-MASC/FEM/NEUT-NOM-SG'. For the present research, we selected only masculine and feminine nouns in the Accusative case used to mark direct object and in singular form (thus, we will omit the case and number specifications on the gloss). Since Russian does not have any articles, the experiment presented below was conducted with adjective-noun pairs, in contrast to the Dahan *et al.*'s (2000) article-noun French materials.

2.1. Participants

Sixteen native speakers of Russian, undergraduate students at the Rutgers University. For all of them Russian was their first language. They graduated from a Russian high school, but were advanced L2 speakers of English. The participants were paid to participate in the experiment that took about 40 minutes to complete.

2.2. Design and Materials

Russian participants were presented with a vertical board that consisted of a central fixation (cross placed over digit 5, see Fig. 1) and four flat colored objects.

Figure 1. *Examples of three types of visual contexts.* (Colors are omitted here. The dark gray car and flower are red; the polka dot car is silver; the light gray flower is yellow; the donkey is green).

They were given spoken instructions to move one of the objects to a particular position on the board. The four objects included the target *krasnuju mašinku* 'red-FEM car-FEM', a gender-incongruent color competitor *krasnyj cvetok* 'red-MASC flower-MASC' (Fig. 1B) or a gender-congruent color competitor *krasnuju belku* 'red-FEM squirrel-FEM' (Fig. 1C), a shape distractor (a silver car) and an unrelated distractor (a green donkey). As is typical for the eye-tracking paradigm, the selection of objects was constrained by nouns that referred to concrete picturable objects.

Spoken instructions consisted of adjective-noun pairs and the verb *položite* 'put'. Eight different color adjectives were used repeatedly (red, blue, yellow, green, black, orange, lilac, and silver) combined with 24 unique target nouns, 12 feminine and 12 masculine, both animate and inanimate. Examples of feminine nouns are *košku* 'cat', *devočku* 'girl', *zvezdu* 'star', etc., and of masculine nouns, *domik* 'house', *zajčika* 'rabbit', *zontik* 'umbrella', etc. It is important to note that there were no phonological cohorts among the four objects on the display. All adjectives and nouns were common and highly frequent Russian words, and no special efforts were taken to match them in frequency of occurrence in the language. All the adjectives had grammatical gender unambiguously encoded by their endings: *-yj* (inanimate masculine), *-ogo* (animate masculine), and *-uju* (feminine). Phonologically, these endings are quite distinct (cf. Akhutina *et al.*, 1999) providing listeners with a strong cue with respect to the gender of the upcoming noun.

Two factors were manipulated in the experimental 2 x 2 design, the Visual Context and the Sentence Type. For the Visual Context manipulation, in the gender-incongruent condition, the feminine target *red car* had a color competitor in masculine, *red flower*, and two distractors (Fig. 1B). In the gender-congruent condition, the target *red car* was contrasted with a color competitor in feminine, *red squirrel* (Fig. 1C). Eight items were made unambiguous by color provided the control baseline (Fig. 1A). In these control items, the target was the only red object in the display that also included the shape distractor silver car and two unrelated masculine distractors. For the Sentence Type manipulation, listeners were given spoken instructions in one of the two sentence types:

(1)	Krasnuju	mašinku	položite	v Poziciju 6.
	Red-FEM	car-FEM	put	in Position 6

(2)	Krasnuju	položite	mašinku	v Poziciju 6.
	Red-FEM	put	car-FEM	in Position 6
	'Put the red car in Position 6.'			

In example (1), the instruction starts with the color adjective-noun pair as the direct object of the verb *položite* 'put' moved to the sentence-initial position. This sentence type represents a non-canonical word order variation in Russian. Crucially, the adjective and the noun it modifies are immediately adjacent and were moved as a unit. In contrast, example (2) illustrates a split word order, common in Colloquial Russian, where the adjective is moved to the sentence-initial position while the noun stays in its original post-verbal position (Sekerina, 1997). From the propositional point of view, both sentences mean the same; however, the split construction carries additional contrastive focus interpretation manifested by a prosodic accent on either the adjective or the noun. In the present study, the contrastive accent was always on the adjective. Note that the use of this construction is warranted by the visual context of all three types: the presence of the second member of the color contrastive set of two cars, the red and silver ones, creates a pragmatically acceptable situation. Integration of the adjective and the noun in comprehension proceeds smoothly due to the unambiguous agreement markers on both words. Presence of the split construction allows for a distance manipulation between the adjective and noun not possible in French or English by isolating the gender effect on selection of target noun prior to its appearance in speech.

The spoken instructions presented along with the pictures were recorded by a female native speaker of Russian in a soundproof booth, in a mono mode sampling at 22,050 Hz. The durations of the three critical regions, the adjective, the noun, and the verb were measured. The adjective length varied from two syllables in *krasnyj* 'red-MASC' to five in *serebrjanuju* 'silver-FEM', with mean duration of 600 ms. The nouns were shorter, varying from two syllables in *mišku* 'teddy bear-MASC' to four syllables in *čerepaxu* 'turtle-FEM', with mean duration of 530 ms. The mean duration of the verb *položite* 'put' was 460 ms.

The entire experiment consisted of 16 filler and 24 experimental trials, eight control ones identical for all the participants, eight each for gender-congruent and gender-incongruent conditions. The Visual Context variable was within-subjects, and the Sentence Type was between-subjects resulting in four items in each of the four cells of the 2 x 2 ANOVA design.

2.3. Procedure

Participants were seated at an arm's length from the vertical board. Their eye movements were recorded by the ISCAN ETL-500 head-mounted eye-tracking system (for technical details, see Trueswell, Sekerina, Hill, & Logrip, 1999, pp. 98-99). Eye movements were sampled at a rate of 30 frames per second, and were recorded on a digital SONY DSR-30 video tape-recorder. Auditory stimuli were played to the participant through the speakers on the scene monitor connected to a separate speech-controlling computer and were recorded simultaneously with eye movements. Prior to the experiment, each participant underwent a calibration procedure.

Before each trial the experimenter would position the four flat objects in their designated positions on the board using photographs of the board as a script. During this preparation time, participants were free to scan the display providing them with time to inspect the objects. Each trial consisted of three instructions; all three instructions were recorded as one sound file, with natural pauses of approximately 400 ms between the instructions. First, participants were instructed to look at the cross that was positioned over number 5 on the board (3a). The second experimental instruction asked the participants to put the target object in a particular position on the board (3b) followed by a third distractor instruction to move another object (3c).

(3) a. Posmotrite na krest.
Look at the cross.
'Look at the cross.'

b. Krasnuju mašinku položite v Poziciju 6.
Red-FEM car-FEM put in Position 6
'The red car put in Position 6.'

c. Teper' položite serebrjanuju mašinku v Poziciju 4.
Now put silver car in Position 4
'Now put the silver car in Position 4.'

The initial locations of the target and the competitor as well as their destination locations were randomized across the trials. In the gender-incongruent condition, the color target always differed in gender from the color competitor: the instruction would be to move the feminine target *krasnuju mašinku* 'red car-FEM' in the presence of the masculine competitor *red flower*. In the gender-congruent condition, the color competitor would also be feminine, e.g., *red squirrel*. In half of the items the verb *polozhite* 'put' followed the adjective-noun pair resulting in the nonsplit Sentence Type, and in the other, it was sandwiched between the adjective and noun resulting in the split Sentence Type.

Participants were asked to listen to the instructions and perform the required action as quickly as possible. The task was very easy: the participants' accuracy was almost perfect, with two errors in the entire experiment.

2.4. Data Treatment and Analysis

The data for the Russian experiment were treated in a manner similar to those of Dahan *et al.* (2000). The data were analyzed from the videotape records using the digital SONY DSR-

30 VCR with frame-by-frame control and synchronized video and audio input. The data were coded manually for each trial in 33-ms time resolution from the onset of the word *cross* in the fixation instruction until the participant touched the object to be moved in the experimental instruction. The onsets of the four words were noted, the cross, the adjective, the noun, and the verb *polozhite* 'put'. Determination of fixations for eye movements was performed using the same criteria described in Dahan *et al.* (2000, p. 469). Eight fixation categories were coded: the cross, the target *red car*, the gender-incongruent color competitor *red flower*, the gender-congruent color competitor *red squirrel*, the shape competitor *silver car*, other distractor, looks in between objects, and track loss. The looks at the cross, the shape competitor, other distractor, looks in between objects, and track loss combined accounted for 22.5% of the fixation data, and will not be included in the analyses presented below.

In order to compare the proportions of fixations to the remaining three objects, the target, gender-incongruent and gender-congruent competitors, three time regions were defined. Region 1 was always the adjective region and corresponded to the mean duration of the eight adjectives used in the experiment extending on average from 0 to 600 ms after adjective onset. This region included the average 100 ms duration of the adjective ending *–yj/-ogo*-MASC/*-uju*-FEM that provided the crucial gender information. Region 2 was the noun region in the nonsplit Sentence Type and the verb region in the split Sentence Type (see examples (1)-(2) above). The duration of the noun region corresponded to the average duration of the noun (530 ms) extending from 601 ms to 1130 ms, while the verb region was shorter (460 ms) and ended at 1060 ms. Finally, Region 3 was the reverse of Region 2: the verb region (600-1060 ms) for the nonsplit Sentence Type and the noun region (600-1130 ms) for the split Sentence Type. It should be noted here that in our data analysis, the programming of eye movement estimated at approximately 200 ms before it is launched was included in the region that followed the region where gender information became available. Assuming that the morphological ending of the adjective clearly indicates masculine and feminine gender of the yet-to-come noun, we predicted that it should be able to trigger an anticipatory eye movement to a potential noun approximately 100 ms before the offset of the adjective resulting in noun fixation at approximately 100 ms after the onset of the word (noun or verb) in Region 2. Note also that our Region 2 almost directly coincided with the critical time window from 300 to 700 ms after the onset of the noun of the Dahan *et al.*'s data. ANOVA to assess whether listeners were able to use the grammatical gender on the adjective to restrict their attention to appropriate referential objects on the display were conducted on Regions 2 and 3.

To evaluate the time course of grammatical gender priming, we computed the probabilities of fixation to each of the three objects (the target and the two competitors), for each condition over time and represented them in graphs. These probabilities indicate the proportion of fixations to each object for each participant over all the trials, for each 33-ms video frame. We compared the probability of fixating each of the competitors as a function of their congruency with the gender marking on the adjective preceding the target word. We hypothesized that if listeners were able to use gender marking to restrict their attention to the referential expressions that matched gender, the probability of fixating the gender-congruent competitor should be higher than the probability of fixating the gender-incongruent competitor. We also expected that listeners would identify the target noun faster in the gender-congruent conditions providing evidence for gender facilitation effect captured in real time.

3. Results

For the control items, where the target *red car* was the only red object in the display that contrasted with the shape distractor *silver car* and the two unrelated masculine distractors, *green donkey* and *yellow flower* (Fig. 1A), the results are not surprising. The listeners were able to use the color adjective *red* early on, starting in Region 1, to identify the target *car*. The percentage of fixations on the target grew steadily from 19.0% in Region 1 to 66.4% in

Region 2 to 86.9% in Region 3. The looks to the three distractors combined accounted for only 3.2%, 6.7%, and 3.1% fixations in Regions 1, 2, and 3, respectively.

A very different picture emerged for the target fixation analysis in the experimental items. Table 1 summarizes the proportion of fixations to the target in the three regions of interest, as a factor of the Visual Context (gender-congruent vs. –incongruent) and Sentence Type (nonsplit vs. split word order).

Table 1. *The proportion of fixations to the Target in Regions 1 (the Adjective region), Region 2 (Noun/Verb or Verb/Noun, and Region 3 (Verb/Noun or Noun/Verb),%.*

	Region 1: Adjective 0-600 ms		Region 2: Noun/Verb 600-1100 ms		Region 3: Verb/Noun 1100-1600 ms	
Sentence Type	Gender-incongruent	congruent	Gender-incongruent	congruent	Gender-incongruent	congruent
Nonsplit	17.6	16.9	62.5	41.1	84.6	74.3
Split	20.8	33.2	63.9	36.7	85.7	69.1

For Region 1 (0-600 ms), the Adjective, ANOVAs revealed no significant main effects of either the Visual Context, $F1(1,15)=3.99$, $p=0.0672$ or the Sentence Type, $F1(1,15)=1.51$, $p=0.241$; however, there was a significant interaction of the two factors, $F1(1,15)=6.29$, $p=0.0262$, $F2(2,14)=6.12$, $p=0.268$. The listeners were able to reliably identify the target only in the Gender-Congruent visual context combined with the split word order Sentence Type; their fixations to the target did not differ from each other in the other three conditions. The absence of the main effect of the Visual Context is to be expected: gender information that comes at the end of the adjective is not available until the entire adjective is heard, making it impossible to identify the target by just the beginning of *krasn*... 'red'. In addition, while listening to the adjective (Region 1), it is impossible to decide whether the sentence is of nonsplit or split word order type.

But how could we explain the sudden ability of the participants to decide what the target was in the gender-congruent, split word order condition that is the source of the significant interaction in Region 1? We argue that they could capitalize on another sort of information that was available to them, i.e., the early contrastive stress on the first syllable of the color adjective. Recall that the constraints on the use of split word order in Russian combine an appropriate pragmatic situation and contrastive stress on one of the components of the split adjective-noun phrase. The pragmatic interpretation of the gender-congruent visual context (Fig. 1C) requires taking notice that the target *red car* is contrasted with two other objects, *silver car* and *red squirrel*; however, the red squirrel does not have a color contrastive pair of its own, only the red car does. The participants in the experiment were very sensitive to this pragmatic nuance of the visual display and realized that contrastive stress on the adjective *red* would be appropriate only to distinguish the red car from the silver one.

Region 2 (600-1100 ms), which is the Noun in the nonsplit sentences and the Verb in the split sentences, is the crucial time window to evaluate the effects of gender priming in Russian. During the last 100 ms of Region 1 and the first 100 ms of Region 2, the grammatical gender information encoded on the adjective ending became available to the listeners, and they took full advantage of it. We found a significant main effect of the Visual Context, $F1(1,15)=14.52$, $p=0.002$, $F2(2,14)=9.3$, $p=0.009$. The participants' fixations to the target were reliably higher in the gender-incongruent conditions, 63.3%, than in the gender-congruent conditions, 38.9%. The advantage of fixation to the target when the two red objects are of different gender would be precisely an functional equivalent of the gender inhibition effect: the incongruent gender on the color competitor *krasnyj cvetok* 'flower-MASC' precludes the participants from considering it because the feminine gender marker on the adjective *krasnuju* 'red-FEM' is not compatible with the masculine gender of the competitor referent. What is even more impressive is the absence of a main effect of the Sentence Type, $Fs<1$. Grammatical gender information alone was sufficient for referential identification of the target noun, even before its lexical identity became revealed in Region 3 in the split word order sentence. In addition, the interaction between the Visual Context and Sentence Type that was significant in Region 1 ceased to be significant in Region 2, $Fs<1$: the effect of contrastive prosody, although immediate and effective, turned out to be short-lived and completely disappeared in Region 2.

Finally, in Region 3 (1100-1600 ms), when the target noun appeared in speech and its identity was enforced lexically, the participants were able to complete the referential mapping. The significant main effect of the Visual Context found in Region 2 became even stronger, $F1(1,15)=28.89$, $p<0.001$, $F2(2,14)=10.49$, $p=0.006$, while there still were neither a main effect of the Sentence Type nor interaction between the two factors.

While the analysis of fixations to the target demonstrates an expected gender inhibition effect, i.e., significant advantage of the looks to the target in the gender-incongruent condition, it does not allow us to assess the gender facilitation effect. We suggest that the analysis of fixations to the competitor could do just that. The logic of this argument would be the following. When we put aside the fixations to six objects (cross, distractors, track loss) accounting for 22.5% of the eye movement data, we are left with the fixations to the target and to the competitor that are in complementary distribution. For Region 2 results, we argued that the gender inhibition effect manifested itself in a significant advantage of the looks to the target in the gender-incongruent conditions compared to those in the gender-congruent ones (see Table 1). Then the gender facilitation effect should surface as a mirror-image pattern of eye movements, that is, significantly more fixations to the color competitor in the gender-congruent conditions compared to those in the gender-incongruent ones. Thus, the presence of the color competitor of the same gender as the target noun would result in a robust competition between the two nouns that are both primed by the grammatical gender information on the color adjective. Since the feminine ending on *krasnuju* ... 'red-FEM' is compatible with either the target *mašinku* 'car-FEM' or the competitor *belku* 'squirrel-FEM' both of whom are present in the visual context, the fixations to the color competitor should rise substantially but only in the gender-congruent conditions and only in Region 2. The patterns of fixations to the color competitor presented in Table 2 confirm these predictions.

Table 2. *The proportion of fixations to the Competitor in Regions 1 (the Adjective region), Region 2 (Noun/Verb or Verb/Noun, and Region 3 (Verb/Noun or Noun/Verb),%.*

	Region 1: Adjective 0-600 ms		Region 2: Noun/Verb 600-1100 ms		Region 3: Verb/Noun 1100-1600 ms	
Sentence Type	Gender-incongruent	Gender-congruent	Gender-incongruent	Gender-congruent	Gender-incongruent	Gender-congruent
Nonsplit	0.0	22.8	3.0	36.0	1.4	9.9
Split	0.0	8.8	4.0	33.1	2.0	17.7

Figure 2 displays the probability of fixations to the target over time from 0 to 1600 ms after adjective onset. Just as we saw in the cumulative data analysis in Table 1, moment-by-moment eye movements demonstrated the early target advantage in the gender-congruent (gender-match), split word order condition distributed throughout Region 1. The probabilities of fixating the target for the gender-incongruent (gender-mismatch) conditions merged for both sentence types in Region 2 and showed an immediate and persistent gender inhibition effect starting as early as at approximately 100 ms after noun/verb onset. The difference in the time course of fixating the target between the two gender-congruent (gender-match) conditions that emerged in the second half of Region 2, was the result of the sentence type manipulation. The identity of the target noun became available much earlier for the nonsplit word order than for the split one, because the noun appeared in the speech stream in Region 2 in the former, but only in Region 3 in the latter.

Finally, we can clearly see the time course of the gender facilitation effect if we consider a moment-by-moment analysis of fixations to the color competitor (Figure 3).

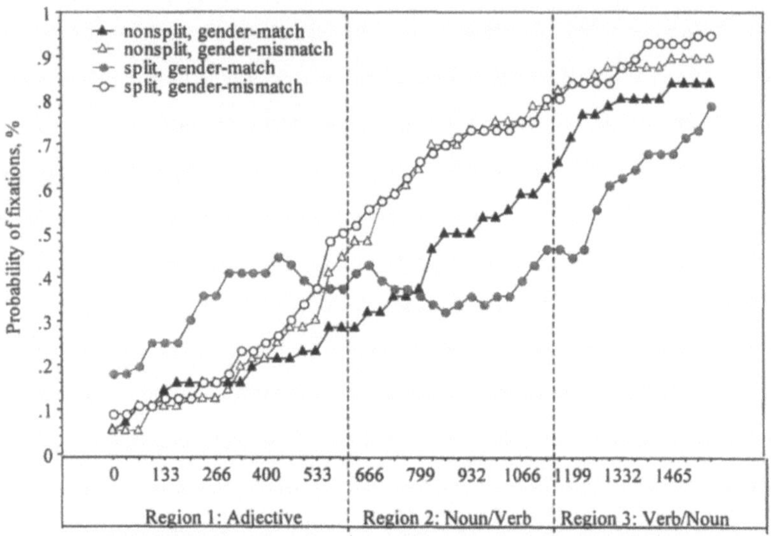

Figure 2. *Probability of fixations to the Target over time, for all regions, %.*

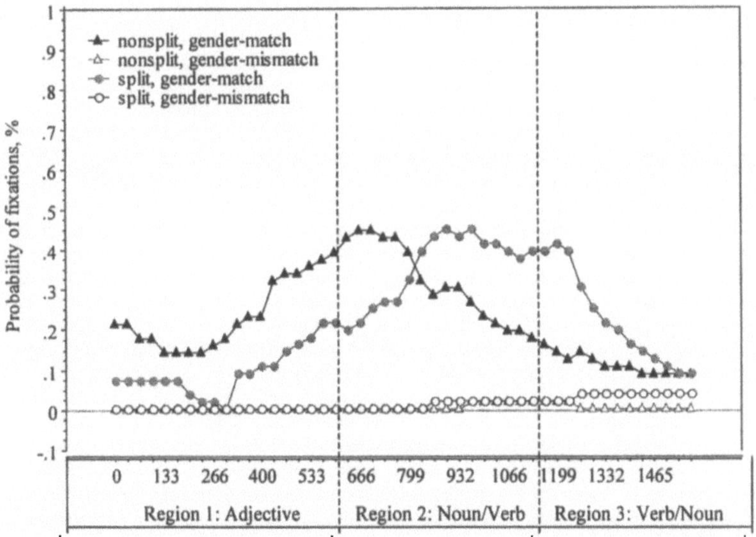

Figure 3. *Probability of fixations to the Competitor over time, for all regions, %.*

Looks to the competitor started to emerge during Region 1 but only in the gender-congruent (gender-match) conditions. They reached their peak at the moment in speech when grammatical gender information appeared on the adjective and subsided faster and earlier, already in Region 2, for the nonsplit sentence type but only after the noun onset in Region 3 for the split sentence type. Thus, the gender facilitation effect rapidly appeared and dynamically changed as the spoken instruction unfolded in the presence of two referents of the same grammatical gender.

4. Discussion

This study explored the use of grammatical gender information in the mapping of referential expressions in Russian. In particular, it focused on the nature and time course of two different components in gender priming. In order to assess gender inhibition and gender facilitation effects, we presented Russian participants with a four-object display and spoken instructions asking the participants to move one of them on the board. Presented with the target noun *krasnuju mašinku* 'red car-FEM' and two unrelated distractors was a color competitor which was either of the same grammatical gender as the target, *krasnuju belku* 'red squirrel-FEM', or of different gender, *krasnyj cvetok* 'red flower-MASC'. Eye movements were measured throughout the duration of spoken instructions, and listeners' fixations to objects were interpreted as evidence for referential mapping in real time of the words that named the objects.

Greater fixation to the target noun in the gender-incongruent visual context (the color competitor was of different gender) than in the gender-congruent visual context indicated a gender inhibition effect in priming. Activation of the competitor noun was inhibited due to gender incongruency between the modifying adjective and the noun resulting in less competition between the target and the competitor and, therefore, significant target advantage in looks. This was a strong and immediate effect that appeared within 200 ms after gender information on the adjective became available and persisted throughout the duration of the entire spoken instruction. Moreover, it was independent of the sentence type, and emerged well before the target noun was encountered in the instructions with split word order. In contrast, greater fixation to the color competitor in the gender-congruent visual context (the target and the competitor were of the same gender) but only while the noun was unfolding and its identity not yet revealed could be taken as evidence for a gender facilitation effect. Gender congruency between the adjective and the target and competitor resulted in priming of the two nouns and greater competition between the two possible referents in the display. This effect was also rapid but short-lived; the looks to the competitor disappeared almost completely within 200 ms after the noun onset. The fact that both gender inhibition and gender facilitation effects were found in the present study provides new evidence in favor of the prelexical interactive approach to gender priming in spoken language comprehension.

Our on-line results establish that priming of referential expressions can be affected by grammatical gender information available in the context preceding such an expression. This finding replicates previous behavioral studies in which gender priming was assessed indirectly through lexical decision and naming tasks. In most studies of gender priming, gender incongruency between the modifier and the noun results in slower identification of the noun. Since the gender inhibition effect is robust and persists until the end of the stimuli, it is not surprising that traditional behavioral methods consistently find it across languages and modalities. The present study has also demonstrated it for Russian in a natural setting of real-time monitoring of eye movements. More importantly, previous behavioral studies are inconclusive with respect to the gender facilitation effect. Gender congruency between the modifier and the noun rarely facilitates identification of the noun, even in the auditory modality and even in languages such as French and Italian with phonologically transparent gender agreement. Our results show that a functionally equivalent gender facilitation effect can be successfully captured when gender priming is evaluated with the eye-tracking method. Since it allows for a more direct assessment of the contribution of various sources of information that dynamically constrain language comprehension in a moment-by-moment fashion, it is more successful than traditional behavioral methods in uncovering such detectable but subtle and short-lived effects as gender facilitation in lexical activation.

References

Akhutina, T., Kurgansky, A., Polinsky, M., & Bates, E. (1999). Processing of grammatical gender in a three-gender system: Experimental evidence from Russian. *Journal of Psycholinguistic Research*, 28(6), 695-713.

Allopenna, P.D., Magnuson, J.S., & Tanenhaus, M.K. (1998). Tracking the time course of spoken word recognition using eye movements: Evidence for continuous mapping models. *Journal of Memory & Language*, 38, 419-439.

Bates, E., Devescovi, A., Hernandez, A., & Pizzamiglio, L. (1996). Gender priming in Italian. *Perception and Psychophysics*, 58(7), 992-1004.

Cooper, R. M. (1974). The control of eye fixation by the meaning of spoken language: A new methodology for the real-time investigation of speech perception, memory, and language processing. *Cognitive Psychology*, 6, 84-107.

Dahan, D., Swingley, D., Tanenhaus, M.K., & Magnuson, J.S. (2000). Linguistic gender and spoken-word recognition in French. *Journal of Memory & Language*, 42, 465-480.

Grosjean, F., Dommergues, J., Cornu, E., Guillelmon, D., & Besson, M. (1994). The gender marking effects in spoken word recognition. *Perception & Psychophysics*, 56, 590-598.

Friederici, A. & Jacobsen, T. (1999). Processing grammatical gender during language comprehension. *Journal of Psycholinguistic Research*, Special Issue: Processing Grammatical Gender, Part I, 28(5), 467-484.

Journal of Psycholinguistic Research (1999), 28(5). Special Issue: Processing of Grammatical Gender, Part I.

Schriefers, H. & Jescheniak, J. (1999). Representation and processing of grammatical gender in language production: A review. *Journal of Psycholinguistic Research*, Special Issue: Processing Grammatical Gender, Part II, 28(6), 575-600.

Sekerina, I.A. (1997). The Scrambling Complexity Hypothesis and processing of split scrambling constructions in Russian. *Journal of Slavic Linguistics*, 7(2), 218-265.

Tanenhaus, M.K., Spivey-Knowlton, M.J., Eberhard, K.M., & Sedivy, J.C. (1995). Integration of visual and linguistic information in spoken language comprehension. *Science*, 268, 1632-1634.

Trueswell, J.C., Sekerina, I.A., Hill, N. and Logrip, M. (1999). The kindergarten-path effect: Studying on-line sentence processing in young children. *Cognition*, 73, 89-134.

Address for correspondence:
Irina Sekerina, Department of Psychology
4S-108, CSI/CUNY, 2800 Victory Boulevard
Staten Island, NY 10314, USA
Email: Sekerina@postbox.csi.cuny.edu

Marina Sherkina Lieber, Toronto

The Cognate Facilitation Effect is a Frequency Effect: Evidence from Russian-English Bilingualism

1. Theoretical Background

The object of this experimental study is the structure of the bilingual lexicon and representation of information that happens to be identical in two languages of a bilingual – that is, the mental representation of cognates. Bilingual lexicon researchers use the term 'cognates' to refer to words that have similar meanings and similar phonological form in two languages (e.g. English *accordion* and Russian *akkordeon* 'accordion'). Usually cognates are not completely identical (especially in languages that are not very closely related, such as Russian and English), but most of their semantic and phonological features coincide.

While most researchers agree that conceptual representations of translation equivalents (including cognates) are shared between languages (Potter, So, Von Eckardt & Feldman 1984, Dufour & Kroll 1995), there is much less consensus about sharing or overlap at the lower levels, such as the lemma level (representing syntactic information, according to Levelt et al. 1999), and the level of phonological form.

However, cognates definitely have a special status in lexical processing. Cognates are easier to learn both in L2 and in bilingual acquisition (Schelletter 2002), and easier to access in bilingual aphasia patients (Roberts & Deslauriers 1999, Stadie et al.1995). In a cross-language priming task, cognates act as repetitions of the same word (Lalor & Kirsner 2001). The Cognate Facilitation Effect has been found for various language combinations (though, to my knowledge, Russian-English bilingualism has not been investigated in this respect). In both word production and in word recognition in various tasks examining lexical access, bilinguals process cognates faster than other words. The magnitude of this effect correlates positively with the degree of semantic and phonological similarity (Wilson 1999), and this effect is larger during processing in a weaker language (Costa et al. 2000, Dijkstra et al. 1999, Dijkstra & Van Hell 2001).

There exists a number of explanations for cognate effects, but there are problems with most of them (see Sherkina 2003, Sherkina Lieber, to appear). The explanation suggested in this paper is based on word frequency. The monolingual Word Frequency Effect (Oldfield & Wingfield 1965, Jescheniak & Levelt 1994, inter alia) has been known for a long time: high-frequency words are produced and recognized faster than low-frequency words, and this effect is attributed to the level of phonological form. Interestingly, findings on the processing of high-frequency words are similar to findings on processing of cognates in bilinguals, such as faster reaction time, and easier access in aphasia (Ellis, Miller & Sin 1983). On the surface, the Word Frequency Effect and the Cognate Facilitation Effect are very similar, and it could well be the case that the latter is a bilingual version of the former. I suggest the Cognate Frequency Hypothesis as an explanation for the Cognate Facilitation Effect.

(1) *The Cognate Frequency Hypothesis:*

1. The representations of two cognates overlap at all levels so that part of a cognate's representation is shared between two languages of a bilingual;
2. Because the shared part is used in both languages, both language-specific frequencies (here, in Russian and in English) contribute to the overall frequency of this part;
3. thus, the Cognate Facilitation Effect is a frequency effect: cognates are processed faster because they have higher frequency for a bilingual, compared to a monolingual.

The hypothesis predicts that cognates must be processed as high-frequency words, and the magnitude of the Cognate Facilitation Effect is expected to be frequency-dependent. The higher the frequency of a cognate in a non-selected language, the larger the effect.

A major argument for the frequency account is the phenomenon which I termed Bilingual Asymmetry: reaction time is slower and cognate effects are larger in a weaker language (Costa et al. 2000). For trilinguals, the same asymmetry exists between L2 and L3 (Dijkstra & Van Hell 2001). Within the frequency account, this phenomenon is explained as follows: words of a stronger language have higher mean frequency than words of a weaker language (since the stronger language is usually used more often), and this is why more facilitation comes from a non-selected language if it is the stronger one.

In order to test the predictions of the Cognate Frequency Hypothesis directly, two experiments with Russian-English bilinguals have been carried out: a subjective frequency rating task and a picture naming task.

2. Experiment 1: Frequency Ratings

The purpose of this experiment was to find out how bilinguals perceive word frequency in both their languages, whether their perception is different from that of monolinguals, and, if so, how[1]. A cognate effect in this task could be manifested as exaggerated frequency ratings for cognates by bilinguals.

2.1. Participants

40 Russian-English bilinguals (20 in each of the two versions) participated in the first experiment. They all were living in Toronto, Canada, at the time of testing. All of them were native speakers of Russian who came to Canada as teenagers or adults. Most of them learned English at school, but started to use it actively only when coming to Canada. They had been working or studying in Toronto in an English-speaking environment for at least 2 years.

For each language, there was a monolingual control group of participants. The English group consisted of 20 monolingual speakers of Canadian English, living in Toronto. The Russian group consisted of 16 monolingual speakers of Russian, living in Samara region, Russia.

2.2. Materials

The materials consisted of 35 cognates and 55 non-cognates for rating in each language (English and Russian), all concrete nouns. The items were pre-selected for Experiment 2 (picture naming): each cognate in each language was matched in language-specific frequency and/or in sum of Russian and English frequencies (taken from frequency dictionaries: Kilgarriff 2002 for English, and Sharoff 2002 for Russian) with a non-cognate.

Both groups of monolinguals rated all items belonging to their language. For bilinguals, two versions were created, each consisting of half English, half Russian items so that each word was present only in one language within a version.

[1] There was also another purpose, that of verification of the frequencies given in frequency dictionaries. For more details on that, see Sherkina Lieber (to appear).

2.3. Procedure

In an unpaced pen-and-paper task, participants were given lists of words and asked to rate how frequently the words are used, on a 1 to 10 scale. Monolingual speakers of Russian were tested via email.

2.4. Results and Discussion

The ratings obtained from bilinguals were compared to the ratings obtained from monolingual speakers of an appropriate language. An analysis of variance with two factors, Language (monolinguals vs. bilinguals) and Word Type (cognates vs non-cognates), was performed on each language data.

The results for English words are summarized in Table 1.

Table 1. Mean frequency ratings for English words

	monolinguals	*bilinguals*
cognates	4.38	4.84
non-cognates	5.83	5.87

A significant interaction was found between Language and Word Type: in the item analysis, $p = 0.015$; in the subject analysis, $p = 0.0039$. Main effect of Language was significant by items ($p = 0.043$), but not by subjects. Main effect of Word Type ($p < 0.001$) was also significant, but this was due to higher number of high-frequency words among non-cognates and is irrelevant to the research question.

Post-hoc tests showed that the difference between ratings obtained from bilinguals and from monolinguals was significant for cognates, but not for non-cognates. For the item analysis, a studentized range test was used (for cognates, $q = 4.61$, $p < 0.01$; for non-cognates, $q = 0.44$, $p > 0.05$); for the subject analysis, a Tukey HSD test (for cognates, $p=0.002$; for non-cognates, $p=0.991$). Bilinguals rated the frequency of cognates in English higher than English monolinguals did, but there was no difference for non-cognates.

The results for Russian words are summarized in Table 2.

Table 2. Mean frequency ratings for Russian words

	monolinguals	*bilinguals*
cognates	4.79	5.05
non-cognates	4.88	5.03

No interaction was found between Language and Word Type (by items, $p = 0.456$, by subjects, $p = 0.479$), and no main effect of Word Type (by items, $p = 0.935$, by subjects, 0.703). Main effect of Language was significant by items ($p = 0.013$), but not by subjects ($p = 0.477$). Thus, unlike in English, no cognate effect was found in Russian frequency ratings.

The data on English words clearly demonstrate the Cognate Frequency Effect in frequency ratings. Bilinguals perceive cognates as having higher frequency, as their subjective ratings show. At the same time, their perception of non-cognates is not different from that of monolingual speakers of English. Therefore, the results support the Cognate Frequency Hypothesis.

Lack of cognate effects on Russian in the presence of those effects in English is somewhat harder to explain. However, it is most likely to be a manifestation of the Bilingual Asymmetry. In previous studies, the Cognate Facilitation Effect in reaction time in on-line tasks was found to be smaller when processing in a dominant language (Costa et al. 2000). It could in principle be so small that it could be detected in some tasks, but not others. In fact, this is not the first case when cognate effects were obtained only in a weaker language: Stadie et al. (1995) found a cognate effect in a trilingual aphasic patient's L2 and L3, but not in his L1.

Another possible reason for lack of effects in the bilinguals' first language is that rating is a more conscious task than, for example, picture naming. The participants once were Russian monolinguals, and they probably could make use of that experience, or tried to recall monolingual usage in the process of Russian words rating. However, given the results of the second experiment, the first explanation appears more relevant.

3. Experiment 2: Picture Naming (Preliminary Results)

The second experiment was designed to test the relationship between the frequency of a cognate in both languages and reaction time in word production. The Cognate Frequency Hypothesis predicts that higher frequency in a non-selected language (Russian, for naming in English, and English, for naming in Russian) should result in larger facilitation. For monolinguals, I expected to replicate the standard Word Frequency Effect as a correlation between reaction time and word frequency in their language. For bilinguals, the Cognate Frequency Effect was expected to surface as a correlation between reaction time and both English and Russian word frequency for naming in any of the two languages (for cognates, but not for non-cognates). The Cognate Facilitation Effect has been previously found for other language pairs, and I expected to replicate the Cognate Facilitation Effect for a new language pair, Russian and English.

3.1. Participants

This analysis was made on the data from 20 Canadian English monolinguals and 22 Russian-English bilinguals (11 in each version). Both groups of participants were drawn from the same populations as the corresponding groups in Experiment 1.

3.2. Materials

Eighty picture names for each language were selected from the set of the items that were used in the first experiment. Thirty-two picture names were cognates, and were present in both languages. The rest of the items were non-cognates: experimental items matched to a cognate in language-specific frequency or fillers. Two versions were created using the same procedure as in the previous experiment. All pictures were black-and-white line drawings of objects.

3.3. Procedure

Participants were tested individually. The task was to name a picture on the computer screen, as quickly as possible, but correctly. For bilinguals, pictures were presented in two blocks, one for naming in Russian and one for naming in English; the order of the blocks was counterbalanced across subjects.

The trial structure was as follows. First, a visual warning signal (an asterisk) appeared on the screen for 500 ms. It was followed by a pause (blank screen) for 500 ms. Then a picture appeared, and the participant named it into a microphone. The picture disappeared after 2000 ms, and the next trial began. Response latencies were measured from the onset of the picture to the beginning of the naming response.

Before naming, the participants looked through a booklet with the pictures used in the experiment, along with their names printed (to reduce the possibility of deviant naming). Five practice trials with filler items were also included before the experiment.

3.4. Results and Discussion

Three t-tests comparing reaction times for cognates and non-cognates were performed: for English monolinguals, for bilinguals naming in English, and for bilinguals naming in Russian[2].

The Cognate Facilitation Effect was replicated in bilinguals' naming in English ($p = 0.025$): bilinguals named cognates in English faster than non-cognates. No difference between cognates and non-cognates was found in English monolinguals' reaction times ($p = 0.463$). Therefore, the effect in bilinguals is not due to differences in picture perception, pictured object frequency, or articulatory differences. However, in bilinguals' naming in Russian, the Cognate Facilitation Effect was not found ($p = 0.94$). These results are consistent with those obtained in the frequency ratings experiment.

Contrary to expectations, there was no significant Word Frequency Effect even in the monolinguals: the correlation between reaction times and frequency in English was negative (that is, in the right direction), but weak and not significant ($r = -0.13$, $p > 0.1$). It is therefore not suprising that no Cognate Frequency Effect was found in bilinguals: it is impossible in the absence of the standard Word Frequency Effect. Failure to detect frequency effects could be due to noise in the experiment (differences in picture processing and in word length could affect reaction times). Also, it might be the case that the sample size was too small.

4. General discussion

The results of both experiments, with the same experimental items and the same population of participants, have the same pattern: cognate effects are obtained in L2, English, but not in L1, Russian. Reaction times for cognates are significantly faster only in that language in which cognates are perceived as having significantly higher frequency. That no difference between cognates and non-cognates was found in the corresponding control group of English monolinguals suggests that the genuine source of the difference in bilinguals is the word type (i.e. whether a word has a cognate in Russian). Given that the results of the two experiments run in parallel, the Cognate Frequency Effect (obtained in frequency ratings) is likely to be what underlies the Cognate Facilitation Effect (obtained in picture naming). The Cognate Frequency Hypothesis is supported by the results of the experiments, though more experimental evidence is needed.

The frequency ratings results can be accounted for only by those models of the bilingual lexicon which allow sharing between language-specific lexicons at the level of the phonological form. Without sharing, cumulative-frequency effects would be impossible. Moreover, partial sharing should be allowed. The exact nature of sharing is complicated by the fact that cognates are not completely identical. The phonological form of cognates used in both experiments described in this paper differs in one or two segments (e.g. English [zibra]/Russian [zebra]) or in one morpheme (English [gitar]/Russian [gitar-a], where [-a] is feminine singular nominative inflection) or in phonetic features (eg. Russian [t] is dental, but the corresponding sound in English is alveolar). The models which allow partial overlap (i.e. distributive representation models, such as in Van Hell & De Groot 1998, Wilson 1999) account for the experimental data better than localist models (De Groot & Nas 1991).

[2] t-tests were chosen rather than ANOVA comparing cognates/non-cognates and bilinguals/monolinguals at the same time because virtually in all studies of non-balanced bilinguals naming in a weaker language takes longer; therefore, direct comparison in ANOVA would not be informative.

In addition, only models with partial overlap can account for previously found correlations between degree of semantic/phonological similarity and the size of a cognate effect.

The question arises: how does the frequency effect work for partial overlap? A possible way of the bilingual lexicon organization is that cognates can be stored similarly to different morphological forms of a word (especially in cases of regular correspondence, e.g. English -*tion* in *revolution, inflation* corresponding to Russian -*tsija* in *revol'utsija, infl'atsija*).

References

Costa, A., Caramazza, A., & Sebastian-Galles, N. (2000): The cognate facilitation effect: implications for models of lexical access. Journal of experimental psychology: Learning, Memory and Cognition, 26 (5), 1283-1296.

De Groot, A.M.B. & Nas, G. (1991): Lexical representation of cognates and non-cognates in compound bilinguals. Journal of Memory and Language, 27, 124-142.

Dijkstra, T., Grainger, J. & Van Heuven, W.J.B. (1999): Recognition of cognates and interlingual homographs: the neglected role of phonology. Journal of Memory and Language, 41 (4), 496-518.

Dijkstra, T. & Van Hell, J. (2001): Testing the language mode hypothesis using trilinguals. Paper presented at the 2nd International Conference on Third Language Acquisition and Trilingualism, Fryske Academy, 13-15 September 2001.

Dufour, R. & Kroll, J.F. (1995): Matching words to concepts in two languages: a test of the concept mediation model of bilingual representation. Memory and Cognition, 23 (2), 166-180.

Ellis, A., Miller, D. & Sin, G. (1983): Wernicke's aphasia and normal language processing: a case study in cognitive neuropsychology. Cognition, 15, 111-144.

Jescheniak, J.D. & Levelt,W.J.M. (1994): Word frequency effects in speech production: retrieval of syntactic information and of phonological form. Journal of Experimental Psychology: Learning, Memory and Cognition, 20, 824-843.

Lalor,E. & Kirsner, K. (2001): The representation of "false cognates" in the bilingual lexicon. Psychonomic Bulletin & Review, 8 (3), 552-559.

Levelt, W. J. M., Roelofs, A., & Meyer, A. (1999): A theory of lexical access in speech production. Behavioral and Brain Sciences, 22, 1-38.

Oldfield, R.C. & Wingfield, A. (1965): Response latencies in naming objects. Quarterly Journal of Experimental Psychology, 17, 273-281.

Potter, M.C., So, K.-F., Von Eckardt, B. & Feldman, L.B. (1984): Lexical and conceptual representation in beginning and more proficient bilinguals. Journal of Verbal Learning and Verbal Behavior, 23, 23-38.

Roberts, P.M. & Deslauriers, L. (1999): Picture naming of cognate and non-cognate nouns in bilingual aphasia. Journal of Communication Disorders, 32, 1-23.

Schelletter, C. (2002): The effect of form similarity on bilingual children's lexical development. Bilingualism: Language and Cognition, 5 (2), 93-107.

Sherkina, M. (2003): The Cognate Facilitation Effect in Bilingual Speech Processing. Toronto Working Papers in Linguistics, 21, 135-151.

Sherkina Lieber, M. (to appear): The Cognate Facilitation Effect in Bilingual Speech Processing: The Case of Russian-English Bilingualism. Cahiers Linguistiques d'Ottawa.

Stadie, N., Springer, L., De Bleser, R. & Burk, F. (1995): Oral and written naming in a multilingual patient. In M.Paradis (ed.), Aspects of Bilingual Aphasia, 85-100. New York: Elsevier Science.

Van Hell, J. & De Groot, A.M.B. (1998): Conceptual representation in bilingual memory: effects of concreteness and of cognate status in word association. Bilingualism: Language and Cognition, 1 (3), 1998, 193-211.

Wilson, H. (1999): The overlapping distributive model for the bilingual lexicon: some evidence from Spanish-English form priming. Ph.D. dissertation, University of New Mexico.

Semantics

Tatjana Heyde-Zybatow, Marko Malink, Leipzig

Russian, Czech, Upper Sorbian *uže / už / hižo* and Aspectual Relations[1]

The aim of the paper is to introduce a two-dimensional formal framework explaining the combinatorial behaviour of the phase particles with respect to the imperfective and perfective aspect in Czech, Upper Sorbian and Russian. It will be shown that ungrammatical combinations yield an incorrect formal representation. This is due to the incompatibilities between different temporal structures built up both from the aspect of the verb and the phase particle.

1. The basic meaning of *uže/už/hižo*

In this paper, we consider the combinatorial behaviour of the phase particles, sometimes called aspectual particles, with respect to the imperfective and perfective aspect in Czech, Upper Sorbian and Russian. We introduce a two-dimensional framework that provides a logical explanation for the important data. For expository reasons we restricted ourselves to the description and analysis of the phase particle *uže/už/hižo* (already), but the introduced framework can be successfully applied to the analysis of the other phase particles *eščë/ještě/hišće* (*still*), *eščë ne/ještě ne/hišće nic* (not yet) and *bol'še ne/už ne/nic wjac* (no longer).[2]
One of the meanings of the phase particles *uže/už/hižo* is illustrated by (1a-c). It is confined to occurrences with a temporal meaning of the phase particle and with wide scope over whole sentences (see Löbner 1989, 1990). The examples in (2) and (3) show that these particles can also have other meanings. For example, in (2a)/(2b) *uže/už* refer to a scale of volume/weight and a local scale, and in (3) *hižo* has narrow scope over the temporal frame adverbial *jutře*.[3]
We follow Löbner (1989, 1990) in assuming that the wide scope use of *uže/už/hižo* in (1a-c) is the basic one. Throughout this paper, we are concerned with the basic use of the phase particles only, unless stated otherwise.

(1) a. *Poezd uže edet.* (Ru)
train already drive$_{impf/pres}$
The train is already moving.

b. *Petr už dosahuje kopce.* (Cz)
Peter already reach$_{impf/pres}$ mountain
Peter is already reaching the mountain.

c. *Pětr hižo jabłuka šćipa.* (USo)
Peter already apples pick$_{impf/pres}$
Peter is already picking apples.

(2) a. *Ėto eščë pis'mo, a ėto už posylka.* (Ru)
This still letter, but this already parcel
This is still a letter, but this is already a parcel.

b. *Varnsdorf už je v České Republice.* (Cz)
Varnsdorf already is in Czech Republic
Varnsdorf is already within the Czech Republic.

[1] We would like to thank Luisa Martí for helpful comments on this paper and Šárka Lešnerová from Prague for information about the Czech data. Of course, all errors are the authors' responsibility.
[2] In Zybatow and Malink (2003), we also show the application of the framework on German data concerning the combination of the phase particles with different verbal classes.
[3] For a more detailed anaylsis of these uses see Löbner (1989, 1990).

(3) *Pětr jabłuka hižo jutře zešćipa*$_{pf/pres}$ *a nic zajutřišim.* (USo)
Peter apples already tomorrow pick-away$_{pf/pres}$ and not the day after tomorrow
Peter will pick the apples already tomorrow, and not the day after tomorrow.

The basic meaning of the phase particles can be divided into an assertion and a presupposition. A sentence like (1a) asserts that the train is moving, and presupposes that the train was not moving at some time in the recent past. More generally, the assertion of *uže/už/hižo* states that the sentence P holds at the time of assertion, i.e. at the reference time t_r of the sentence. The presupposition states that P did not hold at some time before t_r. The assertion and the presupposition give rise to a temporal structure – the phase structure – consisting of a positive and a negative phase of P. During the negative phase P is false, and during the positive one P is true. Therefore, the reference time t_r is part of the positive phase of P. In table (4) the phase structure triggered by *uže/už/hižo* is illustrated graphically and compared to the corresponding phase structures of *eščë/ještě/hišće* (still), *eščë ne/ještě ne/hišće nic* (not yet) and *bol'še ne/už ne/nic wjac (=hižo nic)* (no longer).

(4)
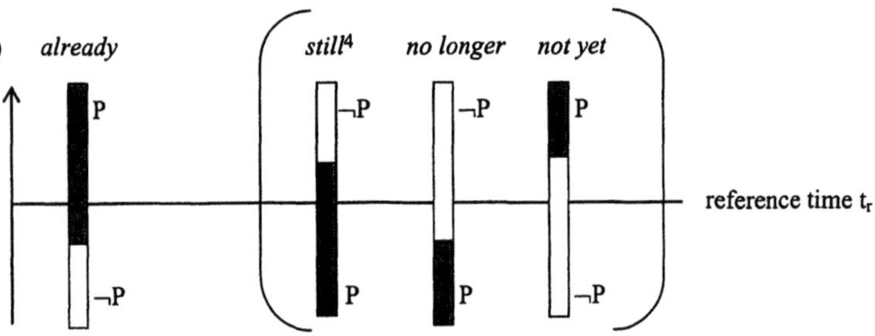

To formalize the basic meaning of the phase particles and their interaction with aspect we will use a many-sorted first order language containing variables of type <time> and <event>[5]. The unary function symbol τ of type <<event> <time>> assigns to every event its event time. The semantic domain of the time variables is an atomic semi-lattice of time points and intervals, ordered by the mereological relation $\subseteq$ (‚improper part of') (see Krifka 1989). 'AT' is an unary predicate denoting the set of atomic times. The precedence relation < is a sharp partial order within this semi-lattice. In (5) there is a set Π of postulates about $\subseteq$ and < we will need, and in the following we only consider interpretations which fulfill these postulates (see 6_{def}). $\pi_{1\text{-}5}$ are well known, only π_6 is rather specific[6] in stating that every time t_1 which has a right boundary has an atomic last point t_2.

(5) set Π of postulates:

π_1 $\forall t_1 \forall t_2 \neg(t_1 < t_2 \wedge t_2 < t_1)$

π_2 $\forall t_1 (AT(t_1) \rightarrow \exists t_2 \exists t_3 (t_2 < t_1 \wedge t_1 < t_3))$

π_3 $\forall t_1 \forall t_2 \forall t_3 (t_1 < t_2 \wedge t_3 \subseteq t_2 \rightarrow t_1 < t_3)$

π_4 $\forall t_1 \forall t_2 \exists t_3 (t_1 \subseteq t_3 \wedge t_2 \subseteq t_3)$

---

[4] If the reference time t_r is the speech time the change from a negative phase to a positive one induced by *still* is after the speech time. In many cases the speaker may not know surely whether the change will actually take place. Nevertheless, she is at least expecting the change to the positive phase which therefore should be considered as belonging to the 'conceptual content' of *still* (see Max and Malink 2001, p. 95-101).

[5] We use the term 'event' in the broad sense here for all kinds of eventualities.

[6] The postulate π_6 could be omitted but the proofs in the last section of this paper would get somewhat more involved in this case.

π_5 $\forall t_1 \forall t_2 \forall t_3 (t_1 \subseteq t_2 \wedge t_2 \subseteq t_3 \rightarrow t_1 \subseteq t_3)$
π_6 $\forall t_1 (\exists t_3 (t_1 < t_3) \rightarrow \exists t_2 (AT(t_2) \wedge \forall t_3 (t_1 < t_3 \leftrightarrow t_2 < t_3)))$

(6_{def}) A classical first order interpretation is said to be a *Π-interpretation* if all the postulates $\pi_{1\text{-}6}$ are true in it. A classical formula is said to be *Π-satisfiable* if there is a Π-interpretation making it true.

Having said that, the phase structure of *uže/už/hižo* and of *eščë ne/ještě ne/hišće nic* can be described by stating the existence of a last atomic time t_x of the negative phase, such that for all times t, P holds at t if t is after t_x and P does not hold at t if t is not after t_x. This can be expressed by the formula $\exists t_x(AT(t_x) \wedge \forall t(t_x < t \leftrightarrow P(t)))$ or shorter $\exists^{AT} t_x \forall t(t_x < t \leftrightarrow P(t))$. By analogy, the phase structure of *eščë/ještě/hišće* and *bol'še ne/už ne/nic wjac* can be described by the formula $\exists^{AT} t_x \forall t(t < t_x \leftrightarrow P(t))$. Thus, both pairs of phase particles share the same presupposition respectively and differ only in asserting or negating $P(t_r)$.
The phase structure triggered by phase particles does not refer to all times but rather to all times within a contextually determined interval. This interval will be much longer in (7) than in (8), where only one change of the traffic lights is considered and all others are neglected.

(7) *Petr už chodí do školy.* (Cz)
Peter already go to school
Peter already goes to school.

(8) *Svetofor uže zelënyj.* (Ru)
Traffic lights already green
The traffic lights are already green.

The reference to a certain contextually determined interval can be captured formally by restricting the quantifiers in $\exists^{AT} t_x \forall t(t_x < t \leftrightarrow P(t))$ to some interval t_i. For the sake of simplicity we do not represent t_i in our formalization and take the whole domain of time to be a constant (unbounded) default interval. To avoid trivial phase structures, t_x must not be an initial or final time of the time domain, which is assured by postulate π_2.
Assertions and presuppositions will be represented by two-dimensional expressions $\begin{bmatrix} \text{A (assertion)} \\ \text{P (presupposition)} \end{bmatrix}$ as suggested e.g. in Karttunen & Peters (1979), Bergmann (1981) or Max (2002). So we will be able to distinguish formally in a simple manner between falseness and incorrectness of sentences containing phase particles.

(9_{def}) Let A and B be classical first order expressions. Then the two-dimensional expression $\begin{bmatrix} A \\ B \end{bmatrix}$ is true in a classical interpretation, if A and B are true in it; it is false in a classical interpretation, if A is false and B true in it; otherwise, i.e. if the presupposition B is false, the two-dimensional expression is incorrect.

The formal definition of *uže/už/hižo* is given in (10a). (10) also contains, for completeness, definitions for the other three phase particles.

(10_{def}) Let P be an unary first order predicate of type <time, t>[7] and t_r an individual variable of type <time>:

[7] In the type notation, 't' is a constant symbol for the type of truth values.

(a) **already** $=_{df}$ $\lambda P \lambda t_r . \begin{bmatrix} P(t_r) \\ \exists^{1T} t_x \forall t (t_x < t \leftrightarrow P(t)) \end{bmatrix}$

(b) **not yet** $=_{df}$ $\lambda P \lambda t_r . \begin{bmatrix} \neg P(t_r) \\ \exists^{1T} t_x \forall t (t_x < t \leftrightarrow P(t)) \end{bmatrix}$

(c) **still** $=_{df}$ $\lambda P \lambda t_r . \begin{bmatrix} P(t_r) \\ \exists^{1T} t_x \forall t (t < t_x \leftrightarrow P(t)) \end{bmatrix}$

(d) **no longer** $=_{df}$ $\lambda P \lambda t_r . \begin{bmatrix} \neg P(t_r) \\ \exists^{1T} t_x \forall t (t < t_x \leftrightarrow P(t)) \end{bmatrix}$

2. Morphological aspect, tense and phase particles in Czech, Upper Sorbian and Russian

The main concern of the present section is the distribution of the phase particles *uže/už/hižo* with respect to morphological aspect and tense. In section four we will show that the combinatorial behaviour of these phase particles can be captured by the two-dimensional formal model of the first section. First we are going to consider perfective and imperfective verbs in the present tense.

2.1. Present Tense:

Along with other Slavic languages Russian, Czech and Upper Sorbian distinguish two morphological aspects – perfective and imperfective. The particle *uže/už/hižo* in its basic meaning can be combined with imperfective verbs in the present tense without any problems or reinterpretations of the verb meanings in all three languages, as the examples (11a-c) show. If the same sentences are used without *uže/už/hižo* as in (11a'-c') then no phase structure is imposed, which means that (11a'-c') do not have a phase presupposition like (11a-c).

(11) a. *Petr už dosahuje kopce.* (Cz)
Peter already reach$_{impf/pres}$ mountain
Peter is already reaching the mountain.

a.' *Petr dosahuje kopce.*
Peter reach$_{impf/pres}$ mountain
Peter is reaching the mountain.

b. *Pětr hižo jabłuka šćipa.* (USo)
Peter already apples pick$_{impf/pres}$
Peter is already picking apples.

b.' *Pětr jabłuka šćipa.*
Peter apples pick$_{impf/pres}$
Peter is picking apples.

c. *Poezd uže edet.* (Ru)
Train already go$_{impf/pres}$
The train is already going.

c.' *Poezd edet.*
Train move$_{impf/pres}$
The train is moving.

The situation is completely different if one considers the combination of *uže/už/hižo* and perfective verbs in the present tense. Firstly, perfective verbs in the present tense normally express simple future. They do not describe ongoing events in the present (see 12a,b).

(12) a. *Petr dosáhne kopce.* (Cz)
Peter reach$_{pf/pres}$ mountain
Peter will reach the mountain.

b. *Pětr jabłuka zešćipa.* (USo)
Peter apples pick$_{pf/pres}$
Peter will pick the apples.

In Czech and Upper Sorbian *už/hižo* cannot be combined with perfective verbs in the present tense, because perfective verbs are incompatible with the phase structure of the phase particles. The reason for this incompatibility is that these kinds of phase structures cannot be imposed on inhomogenous situations as described by perfective verbs in Slavic languages.[8]

(13) a. **Petr už dosáhne kopce.* (Cz)
Peter already reach$_{pf/pres}$ mountain

b. **Pětr hižo jabłuka zešćipa.* (USo)
Peter already apples pick$_{pf/pres}$

c. **Pětr jabłuka hižo zešćipa.* (USo)
Peter apples already pick$_{pf/pres}$

Unlike in Czech and Upper Sorbian, Russian perfective verbs in the present tense can express future perfect as well as simple future. In the future perfect interpretation, a perfect resultant state is introduced which is conceived of as homogenous. This is why the combination of *uže* with perfective verbs is possible in Russian (see 14b). As a matter of fact the combination of a perfective verb and *uže* forces this future perfect interpretation and a simple future interpretation like in (14a) is excluded in (14b) because in (14a) the verb describes an inhomogenous situation.

(14) a. *V vosem' časov, poezd uedet.* (Ru)
At 8 o'clock train depart$_{pf/pres}$
At 8 o'clock the train will depart.

b. *V vosem' časov, poezd uže uedet.* (Ru)
At 8 o'clock train already depart$_{pf/pres}$
At 8 o'clock the train will already have departed.

[8] In Czech there is an emotive secondary use of *už* in the sense of *už konečně* (finally, after all) in which (13a) is an acceptable sentence, expressing that John is expected to reach the mountain eventually after big troubles now. However, this use of *už* as a modal particle lays beyond the basic meaning of the phase particles and will be neglected in the following.

2.2 Past Tenses:

As the combination of imperfective verbs and *uže/už/hižo* is unproblematic in all tenses, we just look at the data with perfective verbs. In Czech and Russian there is only one past tense and perfective verbs are compatible with *už* in this past tense (see 15 and 16). The Sorbian perfect tense allows the combination of a perfective verb with *hižo* as well (17a). But all three sentences need to have a perfect interpretation (reference time = speech time). Simple past interpretations with reference time before speech time like in (17b) are not available in (15), (16) and (17a).

(15) *Petr už dosáhl kopce.* (Cz)
Peter already reach$_{pf/past}$ mountain
Peter has already reached the mountain.

(16) *Pëtr uže vyigral.* (Ru)
Peter already won$_{pf/past}$
Peter has already won.

(17) a. *Pětr je jabłuka hižo zešćipał.* (USo)
Peter has apples already picked$_{pf/perf\text{-}part}$
Peter has already picked (all the) apples.

b. *Jako přińdźech na zahrodu, je Pětr hižo jabłuka šćipał.* (USo)
When came$_{1.sg.aor}$ on garden has Peter already apples picked$_{impf/perf\text{-}part}$
When I came into the garden Peter was already picking apples.

There is another past tense in Upper Sorbian – the synthetic past. This past tense is called 'aorist' for perfective verbs and in some cases it is homonymous with the present tense. When perfective verbs appear in the 'aorist' tense they are incompatible with *hižo* as they are in the present tense.

(18) **Pětr hižo jabłuka zešćipa.* (USo)
Peter already apples pick$_{perf/aorist}$

If the reference time t_r is located before the speech time (i.e. through context) then *uže/už/hižo* force a past perfect interpretation if combined with perfective verbs. Czech and Upper Sorbian have other means to express past perfect[9] (see 19c and 20c) and it cannot be expressed by the perfect or the past tense. Therefore, (19b) and (20b) are ungrammatical. Both sentences are correct without the phase particle *už/hižo* in which case the main clause receives a simple past reading (see 19a and 20a). (19b) and (20b) are grammatical without the preceding subordinate clause and have a present perfect reading in this case. The ungrammaticality of (19b) and (20b) is caused by the subordinate clause, which excludes the perfect reading by shifting the reference time before the speech time.

(19) a. *Jako přińdźe wona do sportoweje hale, je wón dobył.* (USo)
When came$_{Aorist}$ she into gym, is he won$_{perf/pres\ perfect}$
When she came into the gym, he won.

---

[9] Upper Sorbian has a past perfect tense (19c) and Czech can use a possessive resultive construction with the n/t-participle to express past perfect meaning (20c).

b. **Jako přińdźe wona do sportoweje hale, je wón hižo dobył.* (USo)
When came$_{Aorist}$ she into gym, is he already won$_{perf/pres\ perfect}$

c. *Jako přińdźe wona do sportoweje hale, bě wón hižo dobył.* (USo)
When came$_{Aorist}$ she into gym, was he already won$_{perf/past\ perfect}$
When she came into the gym, he had already won.

(20) a. *Když přišla do sportovní haly, vyhrál.* (Cz)
When came$_{Past}$ into gym, won$_{perf\ /past}$
When she came into the gym, he won.

b. **Když přišla do sportovní haly, už vyhrál.* (Cz)
When came$_{Past}$ into gym, already won$_{perf/past}$

c. *Když přišla do sportovní haly, už měl vyhráno.* (Cz)
When came$_{Past}$ into gym, already had won$_{perf\ /passive\ participle\ 3.\ neutr.}$
When she came into the gym, he had already won.

Again the situation is different in Russian. The morphological tense system of Russian is very poor and the past tense can have a past perfect reading when combined with *uže* (21b).

(21) a. *Kogda ona prišla v sportzal, on vyigral.* (Ru)
When she came$_{Past}$ into gym, he won$_{perf/past}$
When she came into the gym, he won.

b. *Kogda ona prišla v sportzal, on uže vyigral.* (Ru)
When she came$_{Past}$ into gym, he already won$_{perf/past}$
When she came into the gym, he had already won.

In summary one can say that, in the basic meaning, *uže/už/hižo* are allowed with imperfective verbs without restrictions. A combination of perfective verbs and *uže/už/hižo* is possible only when a (present, future or past) perfect reading is available.

3. Aspectual Relations

It is well known that one has to distinguish between morphological aspect and semantic aspect or so-called 'aspectual relations'. The task of semantic aspect (aspectual relations) is to introduce the reference time t_r and to determine the relation between the event time $\tau(e)$ and t_r (see Klein 1994; Paslawska and von Stechow 2002). To represent the interplay between the syntax and semantics of aspect and tense, we start from the assumption that the functional aspect category is located between the tenseless VP and the tense phrase TP. For the sake of simplicity, the VP will be represented semantically by an unanalysed event predication F(e). The task of the TP is to determine the relation between the reference time t_r and the speech time.

(22)
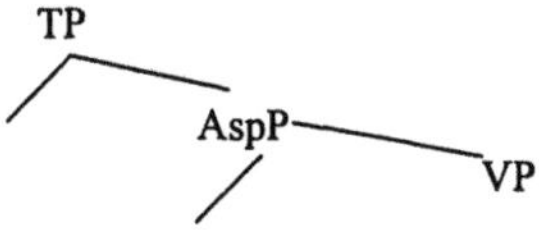

The question now is at which position the phase particles should be located in the semantic composition. Aspectual information determines the (un)grammaticality of phase particles as the above examples have shown. On the other hand, purely temporal information, the relation between the reference time and the speech time, is not relevant for the (un)grammaticality of phase particles. If the combination of the phase particle and a verb is grammatical in the present tense then the combination stays grammatical even if the tense of the verb changes (see e.g. 26). Ungrammatical present tense sentences containing phase particles stay ungrammatical in other morphological tenses as long as aspectual information is not affected by them (19b, 20b). This is why we assume that the phase particle is adjoined to the AspP and therefore beneath the TP-node.

(23)

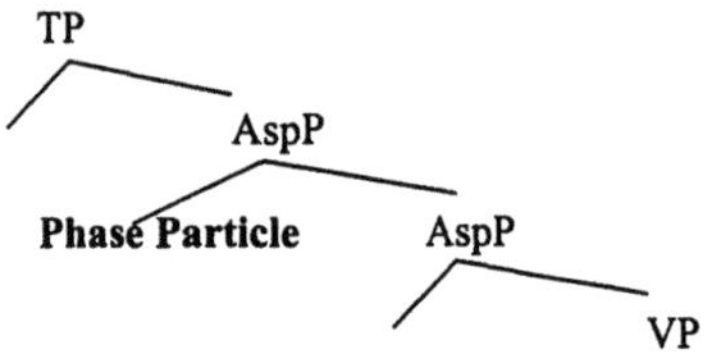

The three most important aspectual relations are defined in more detail in (24) (see Klein 1994; Paslawska and von Stechow 2002).[10]

(24)	PERFECTIVE:	$\lambda F \lambda e \lambda t_r . \tau(e) \subseteq t_r \wedge F(e)$	F of type <event,t>
	IMPERFECTIVE:	$\lambda F \lambda e \lambda t_r . t_r \subseteq \tau(e) \wedge F(e)$	F of type <event,t>
	PERFECT:	$\lambda F \lambda e \lambda t_r . \tau(e) < t_r \wedge F(e)$	F of type <event,t>

The semantic PERFECTIVE aspect states that the event time $\tau(e)$ is included in the reference time. The boundaries of the event lie within the reference time which leads to a bounded interpretation of the event. This corresponds to the intuition that in perfective sentences the event is seen from the outside. On the contrary, the semantic IMPERFECTIVE aspect states that the reference time is included in the event time. The boundaries of the event do not lie within the reference time. This corresponds to the intuition that in imperfective sentences the event is seen from the inside as an unbounded event. The semantic PERFECT aspect simply states that the event time is before the reference time. Due to the transitivity of < the PERFECT aspect can be thought of as expressing an everlasting resultant state (Parsons, 1990: 234f and Kratzer 2000).

(25) *Jurij je hižo klawěr hrał.* (USo)
Jurij has already piano play$_{imperf}$
Jurij has already played the piano.

(26) *Jako wčera do korčmy přińdźech, je Jurij hižo klawěr hrał.* (USo)
When yesterday into pub come$_{aorist}$ has Jurij already piano play$_{imperf}$
When I came into the pub yesterday, Jurij was already playing the piano.

(25) and (26) illustrate the difference between PRESENT PERFECT and PAST IMPEFETIVE interpretations, respectively, of the same morphological tense. (25) has a PERFECT reading with reference time = speech time when uttered by Jurij's father, asking whether he has done his daily stint in playing the piano yet. The same sentence gets a PAST

[10] Note that the definitions in (24) depart from the definitions in Klein (1994) and Paslawska/von Stechow (2002) in that the event variable 'e' is not bound by an existential quantifier. The formal results of this paper can be obtained when 'e' is existentially bound as well. However, the technical details get somewhat more complicated in this case and more postulates are needed than the postulates in (5). For the sake of simplicity we assume that 'e' is bound somewhere above the aspectual node.

IMPERFECTIVE interpretation when the reference time is shifted before the speech time e.g. by a preceding subordinate clause (26).

(27)	Czech		Upper Sorbian.		Russian	
	morph. pf. verb	morph. impf. verb	morph. pf. verb	morph. impf. verb	morph. pf. verb	morph. impf. verb
morph. present tense	PRESENT PERF.TIVE	PRESENT IMPF	PRESENT PERF.TIVE	PRESENT IMPF	PRESENT PERF.TIVE **or** PERFECT	PRESENT IMPF
(perfect) past tense	either PAST + the same aspect like in the morph. present tense **or** PRESENT PERFECT					
simple synth. past	does not exist		PAST PERF.TIVE	PAST IMPF	does not exist	

In order to explain the data of section two we have to assume a relation between morphological and semantic aspect/tense. This is done in table (27) in a straightforward manner. Note that Russian morphological present tense perfective aspect allows for both semantic PERFECTIVE and PERFECT aspect. Russian morphological past tense perfective aspect allows for a PAST PERFECTIVE (21a), PAST PERFECT (21b) and PRESENT PERFECT (16) reading.

What we claim is that phase particles lead to incorrectness in sentences licensing the semantic PERFECTIVE aspect. Table (27) is just a rough guideline to relate this general claim to the concrete morphological categories of the three Slavic languages considered here.[11]

The distributive behaviour of the phase particles with respect to semantic aspect is confirmed by data from non-Slavic languages like German. Even though German has no morphological category of aspect its verbs are distinguishable with respect to verbal lexical classes (like the Vendlerian classes). Without going into detail it can be shown that only process and state verbs – both refering to homogeneous events and licensing the semantic IMPERFECTIVE aspect – can easily combine with the phase particles in all tenses. On the other hand, accomplishments and achievements cannot be combined with phase particles in most cases because these verb classes license the semantic PERFECTIVE aspect (see 27').

(27') a. *Martin arbeitet schon.* (Ger)
Martin work$_{Pres}$ already
Martin is already working.

b. *Hannah schlief schon.* (Ger)
Hannah sleep$_{Past}$ already
Hannah was already asleep.

c. **Peter erreichte schon den Berg.* (Ger)
Peter reach$_{Past}$ already the mountain

d. **Peter isst die Kartoffeln schon auf.* (Ger)
Peter eat$_{Pres}$ the potatoes already up

[11] There are some exceptions of the rules stated in table (27). Particularly in Upper Sorbian the distinction between morphological perfective and imperfective verbs is not as strong as e.g. in Czech. Because of such exceptions we do not insist on the claims about morphological aspect, e.g. that phase particles cannot be combined with morphologically present tense perfective verbs in Upper Sorbian.

4. 'The facts predicted'

In this section we discuss the results of applying the phase particle **already** as defined in (10_{def}) to the three semantic aspects in (24). Thus, we relate the formal apparatus of section one and three to the empirical data of section two. The details of the application of **already** to IMPERFECTIVE are shown in (28)[12] and (29a-c) shows the results of applying **already** to each of the semantic aspects in (24).

(28) **already** (IMPERFECTIVE) =

$$\lambda P \lambda t_r . \begin{bmatrix} P(t_r) \\ \exists^{AT} t_x \forall t (t_x < t \leftrightarrow P(t)) \end{bmatrix} (\lambda F \lambda e \lambda t_r .\ t_r \subseteq \tau(e) \wedge F(e))$$

$$\lambda F \lambda e.\ (\lambda P \lambda t_r . \begin{bmatrix} P(t_r) \\ \exists^{AT} t_x \forall t (t_x < t \leftrightarrow P(t)) \end{bmatrix} (\lambda t_r .\ t_r \subseteq \tau(e) \wedge F(e))) \quad \text{(functional composition)}$$

$$\lambda F \lambda e \lambda t_r . \begin{bmatrix} t_r \subseteq \tau(e) \wedge F(e) \\ \exists^{AT} t_x \forall t (t_x < t \leftrightarrow (t \subseteq \tau(e) \wedge F(e))) \end{bmatrix} \quad \text{(}\lambda\text{-application)}$$

(29a) **already** (IMPERFECTIVE) $= \lambda F \lambda e \lambda t_r . \begin{bmatrix} t_r \subseteq \tau(e) \wedge F(e) \\ \exists^{AT} t_x \forall t (t_x < t \leftrightarrow (t \subseteq \tau(e) \wedge F(e))) \end{bmatrix}$

(29b) **already** (PERFECTIVE) $= \lambda F \lambda e \lambda t_r . \begin{bmatrix} \tau(e) \subseteq t_r \wedge F(e) \\ \exists^{AT} t_x \forall t (t_x < t \leftrightarrow (\tau(e) \subseteq t \wedge F(e))) \end{bmatrix}$

(29c) **already**(PERFECT) $= \lambda F \lambda e \lambda t_r . \begin{bmatrix} \tau(e) < t_r \wedge F(e) \\ \exists^{AT} t_x \forall t (t_x < t \leftrightarrow (\tau(e) < t \wedge F(e))) \end{bmatrix}$

The presuppositions of (29a-c) differ only in the relation between τ(e) and t on the right side of the material equivalence, but this difference has important consequences. The presupposition of (29a) (i.e. $\exists^{AT} t_x \forall t(t_x < t \leftrightarrow (t \subseteq \tau(e) \wedge F(e)))$) behaves like a presupposition should behave: it is Π-satisfiable[13] (see 6_{def}) and it is not trivial in the sense that it follows from the assertion. There are no technical difficulties in applying **already** to IMPERFECTIVE. This corresponds to the unproblematic use of *uže/už/hižo* in imperfective sentences (see 1a-c). The situation changes completely when applying **already** to PERFECTIVE.

CONSEQUENCE 1. **already** (PERFECTIVE) is incorrect in every Π-interpretation, its presupposition is not Π-satisfiable.

[12] For the present purposes it does not matter whether the phase particles are applied directly to the semantic aspect or whether the semantic aspect is applied to a VP-event-predication λe.F(e) first. We have chosen the first option here.

[13] The proof of the Π-satisfiability of $\exists^{AT} t_x \forall t(t_x < t \leftrightarrow (t \subseteq \tau(e) \wedge F(e)))$ is omitted here for brevity.

Proof. If there is a t_x such that $AT(t_x)$ and $\forall t(t_x<t \leftrightarrow (\tau(e) \subseteq t \wedge F(e)))$, there would be a t_1 and a t_2 such that $t_1<t_x \wedge t_x<t_2$ due to postulate π_2. Because of the bivalence $t_x<t_2 \leftrightarrow (\tau(e) \subseteq t_2 \wedge F(e))$ we have $\tau(e) \subseteq t_2 \wedge F(e)$. Postulate π_4 gives us the existence of a t_3 such that $t_1 \sqsubseteq t_3 \wedge t_2 \sqsubseteq t_3$. With $\tau(e) \subseteq t_2 \wedge P(e)$ and postulate π_5 we get $\tau(e) \subseteq t_3 \wedge P(e)$ and by the bivalence $t_x<t_3$. From $t_x<t_3$ and $t_1 \sqsubseteq t_3$ we get $t_x<t_1$ by postulate π_3. But at the same time $t_1<t_x$ does hold, which contradicts π_1.

CONSEQUENCE 1 predicts that *uže/už/hižo* cannot be applied to the PERFECTIVE semantic aspect. Sentences allowing only for a PERFECTIVE reading are therefore incorrect, which explains the incorrectness of the Czech and Upper Sorbian present tense and aorist examples (13a-c, 18), assuming the rules of table (27). In sentences allowing for a PERFECTIVE and a PERFECT reading the PERFECTIVE reading is ruled out by *uže/už/hižo* in the same way. This is what happens in the Russian examples (14b, 21b). In all three languages the PAST PERFECTIVE interpretation of the morphological (perfect) past tense of perfective verbs is ruled out by *uže/už/hižo* and the PRESENT PERFECT reading is forced instead (15-17, 19b, 20b).

CONSEQUENCE 2. The phase particle in **already**(PERFECT) is, so to speak, informationless since the presupposition triggered by it follows logically from the assertion.

Proof. Let the assertion $\tau(e)<t_r \wedge F(e)$ hold in a classical interpretation. Then by $\tau(e)<t_r$ and π_6 there is a t_x such that $AT(t_x) \wedge \forall t(\, t_x<t \leftrightarrow \tau(e)<t)$. Since F(e) is true and the variable t does not occur free in F(e) we get $\forall t(\, t_x<t \leftrightarrow (\tau(e)<t \wedge F(e)))$ and thereby $\exists^{AT} t_x \forall t(t_x<t \leftrightarrow (\tau(e)<t \wedge F(e)))$.

CONSEQUENCE 2 states that applying *uže/už/hižo* to a sentence which licenses the PERFECT semantic aspect does not cause any incorrectness (see the unproblematic sentences 15-17). *Uže/už/hižo* does not add any new information to the sentence at all since the triggered presupposition follows logically from the assertion, which is not affected by the phase particle. Indeed, in (1a-c) *uže/už/hižo* add the phase presupposition that the situation did not hold at some time before the reference time and that the reference time is part of a specific phase structure (see (11a'-c') vs. (11a-c)). In the PERFECT sentences (15-17), on the contrary, the phase particles do not impose a new phase structure since PERFECT sentences already express a phase structure by themselves. The only contribution of *uže/už/hižo* to the meaning of (15-17) is to give rise to the PERFECT reading of the underspecified morphological (perfect) past tense. Once this reading is specified, (15-17) carry exactly the same temporal information as they do without *uže/už/hižo*. Any further contributions of *uže/už/hižo*, e.g. evaluation of the situation as 'early'[14], lie beyond our semantic formalization.
CONSEQUENCE 1 and CONSEQUENCE 2 explain why *uže/už/hižo* is the disambiguator par excellence for sentences allowing for both a PERFECT and a PERFECTIVE reading. It is incompatible with the PERFECTIVE reading and does not change the meaning of the PERFECT reading. Sentences allowing for a (PRESENT) PERFECT and (PAST) IMPERFECTIVE reading stay ambiguous after adding *uže/už/hižo* and have to be disambiguated by other means (see 25 vs. 26).

---

[14] See Löbner (1989), van der Auwera (1993) and again Löbner (1999) for a discussion of the status of such meaning components of the phase particles.

5. Conclusion

The multi-dimensional formalization of phase particles is able to cover a whole range of data concerning the combination of the phase particles *uže/už/hižo* and (im)perfective verbs in Czech, Upper Sorbian and Russian. Examination of the data showed that the only possibility of combining *uže/už/hižo* with a perfective verb, regardless of the morphological tense, is a PERFECT interpretation of the sentence. Russian perfective verbs can have a PERFECT interpretation in the present and the past tense. In Czech and Upper Sorbian only the (perfect) past tense allows for a PERFECT reading. Formally, *uže/už/hižo* gives rise to a contradiction when applied to the aspectual relation PERFECTIVE. In the two other cases (IMPERFECTIVE and PERFECT) the application of *uže/už/hižo* does not lead to a contradiction. Thus, the framework presented above successfully accounts for the data of interest here.

Bibliography

Bergmann, M. (1981): 'Presupposition and Two Dimensional Logic'. *Journal of Philosophical Logic 10*, 27-53.

Karttunen, L. & Peters, S. (1979): 'Conventional Implicature'. In: Choon-Kyu Oh & D. Dineen (ed.): *Syntax and Semantics 11: Presupposition*. Academic Press New York, 1-56

Klein, W. (1994): *Time in Language*. New York, Routledge.

Kratzer, Angelika (2000): *Building Statives*. Berkeley Linguistic Society 26, February 2000; http://semanticsarchive.net/Archive/GI5MmI0M/kratzer.building.statives.pdf

Krifka, M. (1989): *Nominalreferenz und Zeitkonstitution. Zur Semantik von Massentermen, Pluraltermen und Aspektklassen*. Wilhelm Fink Verlag München.

Löbner, S. (1989) 'German *schon – erst – noch*: An Integrated Analysis'. *Linguistics and Philosophy 12*, 167-212.

Löbner, S. (1990): *Wahr neben Falsch. Duale Operatoren als die Quantoren natürlicher Sprache*. Niemeyer, Tübingen.

Löbner, S. (1999): 'Why German *schon* and *noch* still are Duals: A Reply to Van der Auwera'. *Linguistics and Philosophy 22*, 45-106.

Max I. & Malink M. (2001): 'Zur dreidimensionalen Modellierung der Phasenpartikeln um *schon*'. In: J. Dölling & T. Zybatow (ed.): *Ereignisstrukturen*. Linguistische Arbeitsberichte 76, Institut für Linguistik, Universität Leipzig, 89-120.

Max, I. (2002): 'Mehrdimensionale Modellierung von aspektueller Verschiebung und Negation'. In: A. Steube (ed.): *Sprachtheoretische Grundlagen der Kognitionswissenschaft: Sprachliches und nichtsprachliches Wissen*. Linguistische Arbeitsberichte 79, Institut für Linguistik, Universität Leipzig, 79-103.

Paslawska, A. and von Stechow, A. (2002): *Perfect Readings in Russian*. Paper available at http://vivaldi.sfs.nphil.uni-tuebingen.de

Parsons, T. (1990): *Events in the Semantics of English: A Study in Subatomic Semantics*. MIT Press, Cambridge, Massachusetts, London.

van der Auwera, Johan (1993): '„Already" and „still": Beyond Duality'. *Linguistics and Philosophy 16*, 613-653.

Zybatow, T. & Malink, M. (2003): 'Phasenpartikeln und Verbklassen'. In: Weisgerber, M. (ed.): *Proceedings of the Conference sub7 – Sinn und Bedeutung*. Arbeitspapier 114 des FB Sprachwissenschaft der Universität Konstanz, 337-351.

Barbara Sonnenhauser, Leipzig

Imperfective Aspect in Russian: ‘Reference Time’, Semantics and Pragmatics

1. Introduction

Natural language expressions are generally underspecified and require enrichments of different kinds to receive a contextually relevant, truth-conditional interpretation. One instance of this ‘sense-generality’ (Atlas 1989) is aspect in Russian, especially the ipf[1], which allows for a considerable variety of readings. This variety, as well as cross-linguistic differences in aspectual usage raises questions like the following: Are these different readings to be attributed to one invariant meaning of the aspectual marker, or are we confronted with an instance of grammatical polysemy? Are there any regularities involved in the derivation of the contextually relevant readings? If aspect is a cross-linguistic category, what is the common denominator that justifies the subsumption of certain phenomena under the heading of ‘grammatical aspect’, and how should we account for the differences in usage?

An account in purely semantic terms cannot deal with the problems outlined above; what is needed is a more pragmatically oriented approach. Accordingly, this paper combines a ‘selectional theory’ of aspect (Johanson 1971; Bickel 1996) with pragmatic principles interacting with linguistic and non-linguistic context to derive the respective ipf readings.

The paper is organized as follows: Section 2 addresses the basic semantics of the ipf aspect, and section 3 the basic pragmatic assumptions. Section 4 applies the findings to Russian and Turkish, and a short conclusion will be given in section 5.

2. Semantics

2.1. Reference time

Different interpretations of the Reichenbachian notion ‘Reference Time’ (R) have been used in the domain of aspect. Reichenbach himself, however, does not provide an adequate analysis for the aspectual differences between the English simple and progressive forms. What he merely states is that in some tenses an indication is given concerning the time extension of the event, e.g. with the present participle in English (Reichenbach 1947: 290). Thus, as to the relation of R, E and S, there is no difference in his representation of the English simple (1a) and progressive (1b) past:

(1) a. I saw John.

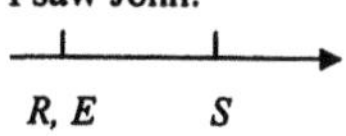

b. I was seeing John.

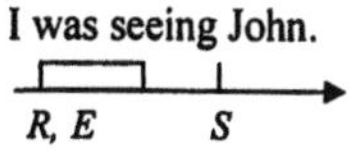

c. I have been seeing John.

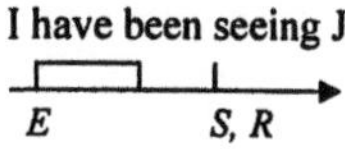

---

[1] ‘ipf’ = (Russian) imperfective aspect; ‘pf’ = (Russian) perfective aspect; this paper is confined to ipf forms in the past tense for two reasons: ipf is more underspecified than pf, and there is an asymmetry in the non-past tenses in that pf forms cannot express semantic present tense and cannot build periphrastic future tense

The only difference between (1a) and (1b) is the additional marking of the 'extension', whereas the relation E-R remains identical. Examples (1b) and (1c) have the same 'extension', but differ in the location of R, i.e. the relation between E and R. It is also left unclear as to what time the extension pertains to – either E includes R, or R includes E. In Russian, an exact representation of this relation is essential in distinguishing aspectual readings, and in Turkish these differences get morphological expression.

Obviously, there is more to aspect than just the relation between R and E. Timberlake (1985: 158) translates Reichenbach's definitions of the simple and the progressive past into statements including intervals – which by itself is not too remarkable – and, what is more interesting, into statements not only in terms of temporal relations but also in terms of inclusion relations. Accordingly, the simple past can be described as $E \subseteq R < S$, and the progressive past as $E \supset R < S$. Implicit in these definitions is the assumption of the "dual character" (Smith 1997: 103) of the reference time. On the one hand, this reference time is part of the system of temporal relations – that is, it is located before, after or at S and E – and on the other hand it gives the temporal standpoint of the sentences, that is the 'aspectual perspective' (Nakhimovsky 1988), which is indicated by the inclusion-relation obtaining between E and R.

But that alone is not enough to distinguish pf and ipf aspect in Russian, as Timberlake (1985: 160ff) illustrates with the durative ipf and the aorist pf:

(2) a. *Uznav* (pf) o bolezni Aleksandra Andreeviča, ja *poechala* (pf) v Moskvu, i *ostalas'* (pf) tam nadolgo.

b. *Uznav* (pf) o bolezni Aleksandra Andreeviča, ja *poechala* (pf) v Moskvu, i *ostavalas'* (ipf) do ego vyzdorovlenija.
'On *learning* about the illness of Alexander Andreevich, I *went* to Moscow and *remained* there until his recovery.'

The decisive units are the verbs *ostalas'* and *ostavalas'*. With the pf *ostalas'* the inception of the state of remaining happens at some time R, that follows the preceding pf events. With the ipf *ostavalas'*, the state of remaining is presented[2] as extending from R of the previous pf event until Aleksandr Andreevič's recovery, that is, it is presented as bounded state.

Accordingly, Timberlake (1985: 161) notes that both have the configuration $E \subseteq R < S$ as illustrated by the following representations:

(3) a. aorist pf: *ostalas'*

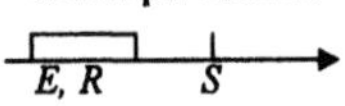

b. durative ipf: *ostavalas'*

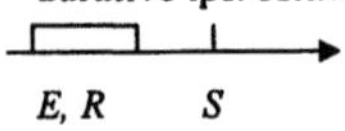

What differentiates them has to do with some internal limit, that is not reached at R with the durative ipf, but is reached at R with the aorist pf. This leads Timberlake (1985: 162) to the introduction of an additional time P that expresses the notion of 'inherent limit' as opposed to the 'actual limit' characterized by the relation between E and R. Clearly, the location of R with respect to an unanalysed E is too crude and misses important distinctions (cf. Moens

[2] It is important to note that the remaining is *presented* as extending to the recovery, as it might well go beyond that if indicated by the context (note, that this defeasibility is due to the pragmatic nature of the specific readings). This does not invalidate Timerlake's claim, contrary to Borik's comment (2002: 162).

1987; Moens&Steedman 1988). As will be argued in more detail below (section 2.2), the difference between the pf aspect and the durative (and the general-factive) reading of the ipf aspect is the part of the event that is selected by the aspect marker.

Padučeva (1996) interprets the Reichenbachian R with the notion of 'točka otsčeta' (henceforth: TO), which she claims to be equivalent to Reichenbach's R and to Glovinskaja's (1982) notion of the position of an observer. Two different types of TO can be distinguished: a retrospective and a synchronous TO. Contrary to Reichenbach's R, however, the localization of TO is oriented towards some relevant part of the event, insofar as it constitutes a validation interval at which (a part of) the event is asserted to hold (see below). This interval may be retrospective to that part or synchronous with it, but of different length, namely 'normal', indicated by phrases like *v ètot moment* ('at this moment') or 'overlong', indicated by phrases like *kogda-to* ('sometime') or *ran'še* ('in former times'; Padučeva 1996: 168).

The different readings of the Russian ipf aspect can be classified according to the TO involved. The group with a synchronous TO is subdivided according to whether TO is normal or overlong. This distinction is of considerable importance in analyzing the aspectual system of Turkish, where it gets morphologically marked.

Another important question is what defines a TO as 'retrospective' and as 'synchronous'. That is, to what part of the event does TO refer in order to establish that relation? To answer this question, another interpretation of R is helpful, namely Klein's (1994; 1995) notion of 'topic time' TT, the time about which an assertion is made. Aspect is defined as the relation of TT and the situation time T-Sit, whereby the part of T-Sit relevant for aspect to operate on – the 'distinguished state' – is different across languages.

For the unmarked Russian ipf aspect (which is rather an 'im-perfective' aspect), there are three possible instantiations of the relation TT – T-Sit:

(4) a. TT my be included in T-Sit

b. TT may include T-Sit

c. TT may be simultaneous with T-Sit

By this definition, aspect picks out a specific part of the situation, thereby asserting it. Assertion and truth-evaluation being different things, this part has to be related to an interval at the time axis where it can be truth-conditionally evaluated. This validation interval corresponds to TO introduced above.

What have we got so far? We have an aspectual reference point TO that indicates the time interval at which a certain part of the event is asserted to hold. What exactly is asserted is determined by the value the aspectual marker gets in the respective context, namely the contextually determined relation of TT and T-Sit (4a-c).

Table 1 summarizes the assumptions made so far[3]:

		TO	Relation	Reading of the ipf Aspect
IPF	I.	synchronous, bounded	TT included in T-Sit	actual-processual
	II.	synchronous, non-bounded	TT simultaneous with T-Sit	habitual, continuous, potential, permanent, atemporal
	III.	retrospective	TT includes T-Sit	general-factual, durative

table 1: classification of the readings of the Russian ipf aspect

TO is in most cases lexically given, predominantly by adverbials specifying the interval at which the focussed part of the event is asserted to hold. It is an important contextual factor

[3] The readings are taken from Padučeva's list (1996: 10), which in turn is based on the work of different authors. By no means does it constitute a complete listing of all postulated readings of the ipf asepct.

contributing to the interpretation of ipf by indicating the group to which the respective reading belongs and thereby constraining the range of possible readings considerably. The 'relation' of *table 1* that indicates which part of the event is selected (more on that below) constitutes the aspectual value. [Although both notions are interpretations of R, TO and the aspectual value have to be kept apart and both have to be taken into account in deriving the contextually relevant reading.] None is sufficient alone to account for the differences between pf and ipf on the one hand, and to capture the differences between the ipf readings on the other hand.

For a distinction between pf and ipf, the position of TO is not enough: for pf it is obligatorily retrospective, for ipf it is one of two possibilities. What distinguishes pf and the general-factual reading of ipf therefore is not the position of TO, but a difference in the relation, i.e. a difference in what part of the event is asserted to hold: pf asserts the boundary, i.e. the 'inherent limit' in Timberlake's terms, whereas the general-factual reading of the ipf is indifferent with respect to that limit. Padučeva claims the difference between the actual-processual reading and the general-factual reading of the ipf to be only a difference in TO: the general-factual reading is derived from the actual-processual one by a shift in TO from synchronous to retrospective. As we will see later, there's also a difference with respect to the selected part of the event. The difference between the readings of *group I* and *II* (*table 1*) is due to an internal difference within TO, which is synchronous in both cases, but bounded with *group I* and unbounded with *group II*. It is important to note that this distinction is not aspectual in the narrow sense; it rather further subdivides the synchronous TO. In Turkish, this difference is morphologically encoded, with the continuous-marker *-iyordu* for the bounded synchronous TO, and the 'Aorist'[4] for the unbounded synchronous TO. This difference is accounted for in terms of 'focality' (Johanson 1971; 1994), a notion that is used to subdivide the different kinds of synchronous TO. Turkish has also means to indicate a retrospective TO, namely the past marker *-di*. *Table 2* shows how the different values ipf may acquire in Russian are morphologically distinguished in Turkish (cf. Sonnenhauser 2003):

		TO	Relation	Reading of the ipf Aspect	Turkish
IPF	I.	synchronous, bounded	TT included in T-Sit	actual-processual	-iyordu
	II.	synchronous, non-bounded	TT simultaneous with T-Sit	habitual, continuous, potential, permanent, atemporal	-irdi ('Aorist')
	III.	retrospective	TT includes T-Sit	general-factual, durative	-di

table 2: comparison with Turkish

The Turkish data thus support the distinction of ipf readings in the three groups listed in *table 1*, and specifically indicate the crucial role of TO in distinguishing these groups.

To summarize so far, what is captured by the notions of R, TO and TT is the following:

(5) a. R accounts for complex tenses.

b. TO indicates a relation of inclusion or exclusion relative to a relevant part of the event; it constitutes the validation interval at which the truth of the selected part is evaluated.

c. TT asserts a certain part of the event and makes it accessible for truth-conditional evaluation by aspectual markers; to be truth-evaluable, that part has to be referred to an interval on the time axis, which is captured by TO.

Accordingly, 'R' is to be confined to indicate tense-temporal relations, mainly by serving in describing complex tenses, whereas 'TO' serves to indicate the position of the validation interval relative to one relevant part of the event that is localized on the time-axis to make it

[4] The term 'Aorist' is somewhat misleading; it is not equivalent with Aorists in the usual sense.

accessible to truth-conditional evaluation. In most cases, TO and R can be subsumed together, provided one does not forget about the difference. In some cases, however, they are distinct, namely in relative past-tenses (Turkish *-mişti*).

Any theory of how to derive and compute aspectual readings has to be aware of these two concepts and has to state them explicitly.

2.2 A selectional theory of aspect

The importance of taking into account the internal structure of events has already been pointed out above. The basic insight here is taken from Moens (1987), who emphasizes the need to study the nature of the entity tense refers to anaphorically. The basic complex entity tense to which refers is the 'Event Nucleus' consisting of a preparation phase, a culmination and a consequent state; the process of temporal reference involves locating the reference time at the appropriate part of the nucleus. This analysis has to be combined with the basic function of aspect as making certain parts of the event truth-evaluable by selecting them.

Within a selectional theory (Johanson 1971; Bickel 1996; 2000) aspectual markers are defined as selectors of phases and/or boundaries which constitute the decisive units for aspectual selection and are located on a separate level of the semantics of the event, the 'temporal tier'. Accordingly, verbs are classified in terms of the phases and/or boundaries they contain[5]. Among phases, one has to distinguish further between dynamic and static phases (Bickel 2000: 4), a claim that is supported by evidence from Turkish, which has aspectual markers for the explicit selection of the dynamic phase *(-mektedi, -iyordu)*, as well as for the explicit selection of the static phase (*-miş*). Aspectual class, that is lexical content, and aspectual operators have to be kept strictly apart. The former functions as the operational basis for aspectual operators, insofar as it provides the selectionable units. Selection is to be understood as making phases and/or boundaries accessible to truth-conditional evaluation at a certain interval of time which corresponds to TO/R.[6]

As Padučeva (1996: 168; see above) notes, the validation interval may also be of different length. This explains the non-actual readings in *group III*: here the interval is overlong, i.e., the time of evaluation is too long to be fixed on one certain moment. The more extended that interval is, the less actual the reference of the denoted event becomes. In Russian, the length of that interval is primarily determined by means of context, but also by inference or by discourse mode (Smith 2003). Turkish, however, is a language that morphologically encodes that interval. There are three aspectual forms for the synchronous TO that differ merely in the length of the evaluation interval ('focality' in Johanson's terms): *-mekte(ydi)*, *-iyor(du)* and *-ir(di)*. The former denotes only situations with actual reference, whereas *-iyor(du)* is mostly used in actual-processual contexts but may also extend to non-actual reference thus reaching into the realm of *-ir(di)*[7].

Presuming a tripartite event structure (Moens 1987; Moens/Steedman 1988) consisting of a preparation phase (dynamic phase φ_{dyn}), a culmination point (boundary τ) and a consequent state (static phase φ_{stat}), there are three possibilities for aspect to select. English and Turkish both have φ_{dyn}-selecting aspectual markers, Turkish also a marker for explicit φ_{stat}-selection; Russian pf explicitly selects τ.

Figure 1 summarizes the claims made in this section[8]:

[5] There are, of course, more possibilities of classifying events, depending on the purpose of classification.

[6] Cf. Smith (1997: 146) who assumes aspect to make visible truth-conditional information about a situation.

[7] The forms *-mekte(ydi)* and *-iyor(du)* are only rarely contrasted, as they are mostly used in different discourse modes.

[8] Note that with this analysis, Klein's notion of 'distinguished state' can be done away with.

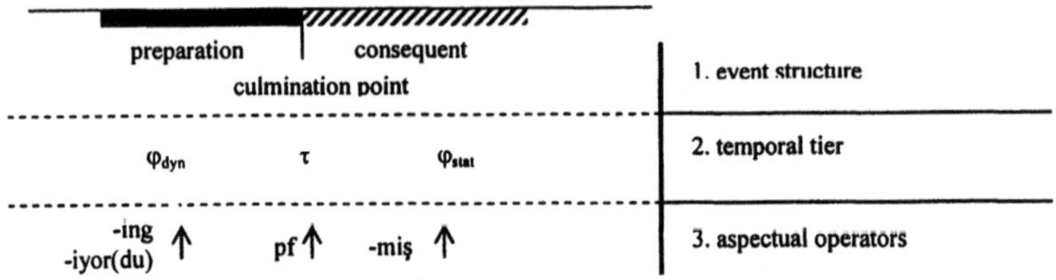

figure 1: a schematic sketch of a selectional theory

The question of with respect to what TO is characterized as being retrospective or synchronous can be answered as follows: it is located with respect to what the aspectual operator used selects. From this it follows that the notion of T-Sit in *table 1* should be replaced by indices showing what part of the event is selected by the respective operator.

		TO	Relation	Reading of the ipf Aspect	Turkish
IPF	I.	synchronous, bounded	TT included φ_{dyn}	actual-processual	-iyordu
	II.	synchronous, non-bounded	TT simultaneous with $]\varphi_{dyn}\ \tau\ \varphi_{stat}[$ [9]	habitual, continuous, potential, permanent, atemporal	-irdi ('Aorist')
	III.	retrospective	TT includes $[\varphi_{dyn}\ \tau\ \varphi_{stat}]$	general-factual, durative	-di

table 3: ipf readings in Russian and Turkish – modified version

Figure 1 shows only the marked members of the aspectual oppositions in English, Russian and Turkish. But the unmarked members are not to be understood as being semantically vacuous (cf. 2.2). Rather they constitute instances of what Atlas (1989) calls 'sense-generality'. The meaning of the unmarked forms is definite, but rather general. It is identical neither to one of the readings it gives rise to, nor to the sum of them and has to be specified in the course of interpretation by linguistic and non-linguistic context (Atlas 1989: 31).

Postulating ambiguity is not appropriate in case of the ipf aspect in Russian as a whole[10], as it can be ascribed one definite meaning: assert anything but the boundary. Rather, one has to assume a highly general, underspecified meaning, that has to be specified in the course of its interpretation in a specific context. This also means that it is not possible to postulate an a priori list of possible readings of one aspectual form as the readings constitute themselves only in the process of interpretation.[11] Sense-general sentences are not interpreted by selecting from readings of an ambiguous sentence, but by constructing a specific content from a general, but definite sense and from collateral information (Atlas 1989: 31).

At this point it becomes obvious that semantics alone is not enough to account for the derivation or even the computation of aspectual readings in Russian. What is needed is a more pragmatically oriented approach as outlined below.

---

[9] The open brackets indicate the unboundedness of TO.

[10] In section 3 it will be argued that there is one level in the derivation of ipf interpretations where ambiguity might be postulated. In fact, deciding on whether an expression is to be classified as ambiguous or sense-general depends on how and on what level one looks at it (Zhang 1998: 29).

[11] This is different for the development of algorithms in applications like text summarization or information retrieval that take certain factors as inputs to compute aspectual readings. In this cases, the possible readings as well as the crucial factors for their computation have to be fixed in advance to make the algorithm suitable for implementation.

3. Pragmatics

Pragmatics here is understood as "taking context into account in a principled way" (Bunt 2000: 25), which raises several questions. First of all, what is context? The notion of context is used in a number of different ways[12], and it seems to be anything but clear what is to be understood by this term. Here, context means linguistc factors on different levels (word level, sentence level and discourse level) as well as conceptual factors pertaining to commonsense knowledge, i.e. context is everything that is not part of the natural language string currently being processed (Perrett 2000: 102). Context is taken into account by algorithms that compute the relevant factors in specific mathematical ways, cf. the 'context-scanning strategy' as implemented by Vazov/Lapalme (2000). And as to the principles involved, these are basically the heuristics proposed by Levinson (2000) which are based on the Gricean Maxims of Conversation. They give rise to default interpretations by evoking certain inferences: Q-inferences are based on the first quantity maxim ('make your statement as informative as possible') and license inference to the negation of a stronger interpretation. M-inferences stem from violations of the manner maxim (esp. 'avoid obscurity of expression' and 'avoid prolixity'), and license the inference from marked expressions to marked interpretations. As to aspectual composition they occur in cases of a mismatch between basis and selector. In such cases, the required phase or boundary has to be induced either semantically by certain adverbs or objects, or pragmatically if there is no lexical hint. Finally, I-inferences are based on the second quantity maxim ('do not say more than necessary') and allow for inference to a stereotype. Contrary to the Gricean view, however, pragmatic inference processes here are assumed to apply on the subpropositional level as well, and can be captured by the relevance theoretical term 'explicature' (Carston 2002).

The inference processes are assumed to operate on the different levels that have to be kept apart in computing aspectual readings (cf. Nakhimovsky 1988: 33). These levels provide the domain of application for the different inferential mechanisms mentioned above: the VP-level or the level of aspectual class, respectively, is the domain of M-inferences, the IP-level or the level of grammatical aspect constitutes the domain of Q-inferences and, finally, the level of aspectual perspective or discourse modes provides the domain for I-inferences.

For dealing with the problem of the meaning of the unmarked aspectual markers[13], Q-inferences are of special importance. They give rise to scalar implicatures[14], 'scales' being understood as ordered sets of semantic concepts, standing in a salient opposition, being lexicalized or grammaticalized to the same degree and having the same degree of currency or prolixity (Bickel 1996: 14). The notion of 'salient opposition' is difficult to capture but what is basically understood by this term here is that the elements of such an opposition are from the same semantic field and that they differ from one another in only one feature parameter. This captures the relations between the Russian aspects: the pf aspect has one feature more, namely the feature of explicit boundary-selection. Thus the scale for the perfectivity field in Russian is <pf, ipf>. If the speaker decides to use the weaker element of the scale, the hearer infers from that the invalidity of the stronger expression. Whereas the use of the pf aspect explicitly marks the selection or a boundary, the use of the semantically weaker ipf aspect does not exclude that selection.

---

[12] For an overview of the concept of context in various fields in AI see Akman/Surav 1996.

[13] 'Marker' is the general term that also subsumes cases of default aspect, where there is no overt morphological marking, as frequently encountered in Russian.

[14] See Hirschberg 1991 for a detailed analysis of scalar implicatures and the difficulty of finding an adequate definition for them, which is partly due to their context-dependency: "People can and do form scales from items that may bear little intrinsic relationship to one another; these scales are hard to predict outside the context in which they are evoked" (114). What all classes of scalar implicatures share are the characteristics of the class of partial ordering relations, so that "a poset condition on scalar implicature appears to capture" all the different instances of that phenomenon (132).

In determining the reading of a certain aspectual form one thus has to look for factors that determine TO. If TO is fixed, then the possible readings are at least restricted to one of the three groups shown in *table 1*. The fixing of TO is achieved mainly by the semantics of temporal adverbials and discourse mode (see Padučeva 1996: 167-181 for a detailed account of their interaction). Different discourse modes are characterized by different deictic centers and introduce different entities into the discourse. Both may contribute to fix TO. That is, in morphologically poor languages like Russian, the discourse modes select the aspectual perspective of the respective sentences and thus strongly constrain the possible readings, whereas in languages with rich aspecto-temporal morphology like Turkish this mechanism basically works the other way round: the use of certain aspecto-temporal forms determines the discourse mode.

Table 1 also shows that several readings of the Russian ipf aspect have the same TO and the same relation. In these cases (cf. 6a-c) one has to resort to the lexical semantics of the verbs and the nominal complements involved (see Glovinskaja 1982). That is, I-inferences have to be drawn that enrich the lexical input by recourse to concepts, whereby frequently encountered concepts are more likely to get activated as their activation requires little effort. This mode of inference poses a certain problem in systematically isolating the factors involved in the derivation and composition of aspectual readings, and is probably best achieved by evaluating and annotating corpora.

(6) a. *Moj otec* *govoril* *po-turecki.*
my father speak:PAST:ipf Turkish
'My father could speak Turkish.'

b. *Perevodčik* *govoril* *po-turecki.*
translator speak:PAST:ipf Turkish
'The translator was speaking Turkish.'

As the potential reading is not relevant with (6b) – translators are supposed to be able to speak a certain language – other interpretations are looked for, here the actual-processual.

c. *Perevodčik* *govoril* *i* *po-turecki.*
translator speak:PAST:ipf also Turkish
'The translator could also speak Turkish.'

The insertion of *i* ('also') creates the appropriate context for the potential reading to be relevant.

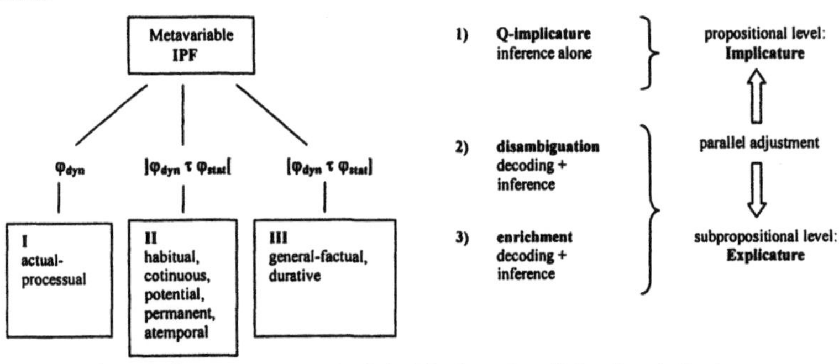

figure 2: the pragmatic reasoning behind the derivation of ipf readings in Russian

To sum up, pf and ipf can be captured by a scale <pf; ipf> and the semantics of the ipf aspect arises due to a scalar Q-inference, stating that the stronger expression is invalid or not possible for the speaker to make. This definite, but sense-general meaning of the ipf aspect can be captured by a metavariable '*IPF*' that comprises the following instances (cf. *table 1*): ipf asserts (I) φ_{dyn}; or (II) the whole event to hold at an unbounded interval ($]\varphi_{dyn}\ \tau\ \varphi_{stat}[$), thereby giving rise to readings of non-actual reference (modal, habitual, future etc. readings); or (III) the event as a whole to hold at a bounded time-interval without actually focussing on the boundary ($[\varphi_{dyn}\ \tau\ \varphi_{stat}]$)[15]. The metavariable gets disambiguated[16] by contextual, discourse-pragmatic or general pragmatic principles and, in a further step, is enriched to yield the contextually relevant reading. *Figure 2* sketches the different processes involved in the derivation of the respective reading, as well as the interaction of pragmatic reasoning on different levels. Note that the lexical content of the verb and aspect strictly have to be kept apart; ipf requires a certain input from the verb, i.e. if a verb is only providing a τ in its semantic representation, the required phase has to be induced – again, by means of context or pragmatic reasoning (7a-b). This may result in an iterative reading, or in 'zooming in' in the (inferred) preparation phase φ_{dyn}.

(7) a. *Ivan vyigral gonku.*
Ivan win:PAST:**pf** race:ACC
'Ivan won the race.'

The pf is applied to a verb *vyigrat'*('win') that provides a boundary in its semantic representation and no interpretational rearrangements are necessary.

b. *Ivan vyigryval gonku (četyre raza).*
Ivan win: PAST:**ipf** race:ACC four times.
'Ivan won the race four times / was winning the race.'

The application of the ipf in (7b) requires a φ_{dyn}; the verb does not provide one, so it has to be induced by iteration, or by inferring the φ_{dyn} and 'zooming in' on it.

This coercion process is to be located at the transition from 1 to 2 (*figure 2*) and may be captured in terms of M-inferences: marked expressions warn 'marked situation'. Again, we are dealing with an interaction of implicature and explicature: 'Marked situation' is the implicature, that gives rise to the explicatures that explain the markedness[17] of the situation in deriving a relevant reading, i.e. steps 2 and 3 are carried out as in the non-coercion case. Note further, that this reasoning process is not carried out step by step, but rather in parallel adjustment, which probably can best be modelled within a game-theoretic framework or within bidirectional optimality theory.

4. Aspectual values in Russian and Turkish

This section applies the findings so far to the aspectual systems of Russian and Turkish. The system established in this paper allows for a systematic comparison of the two languages on a uniform basis that permits a systematic derivation of the respective readings and a principled account of the differences.

What we need in order to describe aspect, is the aspectual value and the interval at which the selected part of the event is asserted to hold. The aspectual value is given by that part of

---

[15] This is what distinguishes the ipf general-factual from the pf aspect, which explicitly selects a boundary.

[16] It is at this level that one might propose ambiguity, but the disambiguated relations are sense-general (cf. fn. 10).

[17] Note that the ipf aspect remains semantically unmarked. The notion of pragmatic markedness has to be distinguished form notions of morphological and semantic markedness.

the event that is asserted, i.e. it is the relation between TT and T-Sit, T-Sit being refined by the exact part(s) that are selected. The interval at which the selected part is asserted to hold is TO, which may be retrospective or synchronous. Reference time R may coincide with TO, but it is important to note that R is used to indicate a tense-temporal relation, not an aspectual one.

The pf aspect in Russian is characterized by a retrospective TO at which the selected boundary is asserted to hold (8a). With certain verbs, however, a perfect (perfektnoe) reading where TO is synchronous to φ_{stat} may arise alongside the event (sobbytijnoe) reading (8b):

(8) a. $(TT \supset \tau) \varnothing TO, R^{18} < S$ event (sobytijnoe) reading

b. $(TT \subset \varphi_{stat}) \supset TO, R \leq S$ perfect (perfektnoe) reading

The ipf aspect as the unmarked member may denote anything but (8), i.e. we have the three possibilities mentioned above:

(9) a. $(TT \subset \varphi_{dyn}) \supset TO, R \leq S$ actual-processual reading, group (I)

b. $(TT = \varphi_{dyn}\ \tau\ \varphi_{stat}) = TO, R < S$ non-actual reading; group (II)

c. $(TT \supset \varphi_{dyn}\ \tau\ \varphi_{stat}) \varnothing TO, R < S$ general-factual reading; group (III)

These relations, or the aspectual value of ipf respectively, are not morphologically fixed, but arise due to contextual or pragmatic specification of the IPF metavariable.

Turkish, however, has morphological means to specify the exact value of the respective intraterminality-marker[19]:

(10) a. $(TT \subset \varphi_{dyn}) \supseteq TO, R \leq S$ -iyor(du) [continuous]

b. $(TT \subset \varphi_{dyn}) \supset TO, R \leq S$ -mektey(di) [progressive]

c. $(TT = \varphi_{dyn}\ \tau\ \varphi_{stat}) = TO, R \leq S$ -ir(di)

What is interesting here is, that Turkish distinguishes between a continuous and a progressive intraterminal form, the continuous form being weaker in that respect, as it may also be used in progressive constructions, wheras *-mekte(ydi)* is confined to progressive constructions and therefore is not possible with stative verbs like *bilmek* ('know').

Furthermore, Turkish has an explicit φ_{stat}-selector that indicates 'postterminality':

(11) a. $(TT \subset \varphi_{stat}) \supset TO, R \leq S$ -miş

b. $(TT \subset \varphi_{stat}) \supset TO < R < S$ -mişti

Finally, the unmarked aspectual form in Turkish is *-di*, which may denote anything but explicit intraterminality and postterminality:

(12) a. $(TT \supset \varphi_{dyn}\ \tau\ \varphi_{stat}) \varnothing TO, R < S$ -di

b. $(TT \supset \tau) \varnothing TO, R < S$ -di

---

[18] Note that 'TO,R' or 'TO < R' shows the interaction of aspect and tense; ∅ allows for retrospective and prospective interpretation.

[19] For the terms 'intraterminality', 'postterminality' and 'adterminality' see Johanson 1971; 1994.

Let's now have a look at some examples to illustrate these claims.

(13) a. *Ja slomal ruku.* [Padučeva 1996: 294]
I break:PAST:**pf** hand:ACC
'I broke my hand.'
$(TT \subset \varphi_{stat}) \supset TO,R \leq S$

Here, we are dealing with the perfect reading of the pf aspect, which indicates the relevance of the consequent state at TO which is synchronous and coincides with R and the speech time (discourse mode: *rečevoj režim* 'dialogue', cf. Padučeva 1996); this sentence is possible only if the breaking happened recently and the consequent state still holds.

b. *Ja lomal ruku.* [ibd.]
I break:PAST:**ipf** hand:ACC
'I broke my hand.'
$(TT \supset \varphi_{dyn}\ \tau\ \varphi_{stat}) \varnothing TO,R \leq S$

Contrary to (13a), this sentence conveys the general-factual reading of the ipf aspect and can be uttered if the breaking happened long ago; what is asserted at TO (retrospective) is the event as such, i.e., the statement of the fact.

c. *V mae 1962 ja priechal v Voronež.* [ibd.]
in May 1962 I arrive:PAST:**pf** in Voronež
'In May 1962 I arrived at Voronež.'
$(TT \supset \tau) \varnothing TO,R < S$

Here, the boundary, i.e. the actual arriving, is asserted to hold at TO 'in May 1962' and the 'perfect' reading is not possible. It is not claimed that the speaker is still at Voronež.

(14) a. *Ben kitab-ı oku-**du**.*
I book:ACC read-**PAST**.
'I was reading / I read the book.'
$(TT \supset \varphi_{dyn}\ \tau\ \varphi_{stat}) \varnothing TO,R < S$ *or* $(TT \supset \tau) \varnothing TO,R < S$

The unmarked *-di* in Turkish covers both the general-factual ipf and the pf aspect of Russian. It cannot assert the consequent state; this is achieved by the postterminality maker *-miş*, where TO is synchronous to φ_{stat}:

b. *Gözlükler-im-i kaybet-**miş**-im.*
glasses.pl.-1sg-ACC lose-**MIŞ**-1sg
'I have lost my glasses.' (= my glasses are lost)
$(TT \subset \varphi_{stat}) \supset TO,R,S$

This sentence asserts the consequent state – that the glasses are gone – without reference to the previous parts of that event; sentences like this easily get an inferential reading.

(15) a. *Moj otec govoril po-turecki.*
My father speak:PAST:**ipf** Turkish
'My father could speak Turkish.'
$(TT = \varphi_{dyn}\ \tau\ \varphi_{stat}) = TO,R < S$

The potential reading is not indicated morphologically; it has to be inferred (I-inference, enrichment of lexical content), whereas Turkish has the morphological means to express it:

b. *Baba-m Rusça konuş-ur-du.*
Father-1sg Russian speak-ir-PAST.3Sg
'My father could speak Russian.' (= he was a Russian-speaker)
$(TT = \varphi_{dyn}\ \tau\ \varphi_{stat}) = TO,R < S$

As becomes obvious from the above mentioned examples from Russian and Turkish, languages vary on where to locate the semantics-pragmatics interface, i.e. differ in the relation between language-particular lexically encoded information and general inferential processes.

5. Conclusion

This paper has argued for a distinction between two concepts of reference time, one dealing with aspectual relations (TO) and one dealing with tense-temporal relations (R). The relation Klein (1994; 1995) ascribes to aspect constitutes the aspectual value that is referred to a certain interval of time, TO, at which that asserted part is truth-conditionally evaluated. The common denominator for aspect is the selection of phases and boundaries. In the case of the ipf aspect, and more generally, in the unmarked members of the aspectual oppositions, we are not dealing with polysemy, but with definite, but sense-general meanings that have to be enriched to be able to get a truth-conditional interpretation. The selection-theoretic and pragmatic assumptions presented in this paper can be claimed to be cross-linguistically valid. Cross-linguistic differences are due to language-specific factors that have to be taken into account to systematically flesh out the semantic and pragmatic skeleton presented here. Languages differ in their respective contribution of semantics and general pragmatic reasoning – which is by no means to be understood in the waste-basket sense.

References

Akman, V., M. Surav (1996): "Steps towards formalizing context". *AI Magazine* 17/3, 55-72
Atlas, J. (1989). *Philosophy without Ambiguity*. Oxford.
Bickel, B. (1996): *Aspect, Mood and Time in Belhare*. Zürich.
Bickel, B. (2000): "Unlogischer Aspekt: zur Bedeutungsstruktur von Aspekt und Aktionsart, besonders im Belharischen". In: Breu, W. (ed), *Probleme der Interaktion von Lexik und Aspekt*. Tübingen, 1-20.
Borik, O. (2002): *Aspect and Reference Time*. Ph.D. dissertation, University of Utrecht.
Bunt, H., B. Black (2000): "The ABC of computational pragmatics". In: Bunt, Harry; Bill Black (eds), *Abduction, Belief and Context in Dialogue*. Amsterdam, Philadelphia, 1-46.
Ceyda Arslan, Z. (2001): *"Perfect" in Turkish: the real puzzle*. ms. Boğaziçi University.
Glovinskaja, M. J. (1982): *Semantičeskije Tipy Vidovych Protivopostavlenij Russkogo Glagola*. Moskva.
Grice, P. (1989): *Studies in the Way of Words*. Cambridge.
Hirschberg, J. (1991): *A Theory of Scalar Implicature*. New York, London.
Johanson, L. (1971): *Aspekt im Türkischen*. Uppsala.
Johanson, L. (1994): "Türkeitürkische Aspektotempora". In: Thieroff, R., *Tense Systems in European Languages*. Tübingen.
Klein, W. (1994): *Time in Language*. London, New York.
Klein, W. (1995): "A time-relational analysis of Russian aspect". *Language* 71/4, 669-695.
Levinson, S. (2000): *Presumptive Meanings*. Cambridge, London 2000.
Moens, M. (1987): *Tense, Aspect and Temporal Reference*. Ph.D. dissertion, University of Edinburgh.
Moens, M., M. Steedman (1988): "Temporal ontology and temporal reference". *Computational Linguistics* 14/2, 15-28.
Nakhimovsky, A. (1988): "Aspect, aspectual class, and the temporal structure of narrative". *Computational Linguistics* 14/2, 29-43.

Padučeva, E. V. (1996): *Semantičeskije Issledovanija*. Moskva.
Perret, D. (2000): *The Dynamics of Tense Construal in Haddiyya*. Ph.D. dissertation, University of London.
Reichenbach, H. (1947): *Elements of Symbolic Logic*. New York.
Smith, C. (1997): *The Parameter of Aspect*. Dordrecht.
Smith, C. (2003): *Modes of Discourse*. Cambridge.
Sonnenhauser, B. (2003): "Aspect and the semantics-pragmatics interface". *Proceedings of RANLP 03*. Borovets.
Timberlake, A. (1985): "Reichenbach and Russian aspect". In: Flier, M. (ed), *The Scope of Slavic Aspect*. Columbus, 153-168.
Zhang, Q. (1998): "Fuzziness – vagueness – generality – ambiguity". *Journal of Pragmatics* 29, 13-31.

Ewa Willim, Kraków

NP-related unboundedness in aspectual composition in Polish*

1. Introduction

It is often held in formal studies on aspectuality in Slavic that bare mass or plural nominal arguments are interpreted as referential definites in perfective structures (cf., among others, Wierzbicka 1967, Filip 1993/99, Slabakova 1997 and 2003, Vekuyl 1999). For example, in (1) and (2) below, the bare nominal arguments *truskawki* 'strawberries' and *mleko* 'milk' are interpreted as 'all the strawberries' and 'all the milk', respectively (cf. Wierzbicka 1967: 2237-8):[1]

(1) On z·jadł^{P} truskawki.
he-Nom PF-eat strawberries-Acc
'He ate all the strawberries.'

(2) On wy·pił^{P} mleko.
he-Nom PF-drink milk-Acc
'He drank (all) the milk.'

In other words, in perfective structures a bare mass or plural noun linked to the direct argument (Incremental Theme) of an incremental verbal predicate includes two crucial components in its semantic representation: specificity and universal quantification. By contrast, when the verb is imperfective, its bare mass or plural nominal predicate is not subject to interpretive constraints. In particular, the bare mass nominal predicate *truskawki* 'strawberries' in (3) can have a specific quantity of strawberries in its denotation (corresponding to *the strawberries* in English), but it can also have some unspecified quantity of individuals that falls under the nominal predicate *truskawki* in its denotation (corresponding to *sm/Ø strawberries* in English):

(3) On jadł^{I} truskawki.
he-Nom eat strawberries-Acc
'He was eating (some/the) strawberries./He ate (some/the) strawberries.'

The presence of specificity and totality entailments in (1) follows on the assumption that the perfective operator takes scope over eventuality predicates and their arguments and quantifies over all the temporal parts of the temporal trace of the eventuality and all the parts of the stuff or individuals denoted by the nominal predicate linked to the Incremental Theme, i.e. the argument whose part-structure is mapped homomorphically onto the part-structure of the event (and vice versa). In this scenario, the perfective operator forces a quantized, definite and totality interpretation of a bare mass or plural direct argument. In contradistinction to bare

* This paper builds on Rozwadowska and Willim (2004). For discussions on the Polish data I am grateful to Bożena Rozwadowska, Ireneusz Bobrowski, Maria Jodłowiec, and Beata Śliwińska. Thanks also go to an anonymous reviewer, whose careful comments have helped me rethink certain aspects of the analysis. All errors are my own responsibility.

[1] The superscripts 'P' and 'I' stand for perfective and imperfective aspect, respectively. Throughout, affixes are glossed in capital letters. 'PF' stands for 'perfective prefix', 'IPF' stands for 'imperfective suffix', 'ADD' stands for 'additive', 'ACM' for 'accumulative', 'DEL' for 'delimitative', and 'ATN' stands for 'attenuative'. 'Nom', 'Gen', 'Dat', Acc', 'Instr' and 'Loc' stand for the nominative, genitive, dative, accusative, instrumental, and locative case-markers, respectively. Affixes are separated from stems with dots, and the verbs are glossed in uninflected forms. Details relating to subject-verb agreement (i.e. person and gender features) are omitted unless agreement is irregular. Unless indicated otherwise, the verbs are in the past tense. 'IMP' is used for 'imperative'.

mass or plural nominal predicates linked to the Incremental Theme, bare count singular nouns as well as Incremental Themes realised as measure expressions, i.e. containing a lexical quantifier, measure noun or a cardinal numeral in their syntactic projection, can have an indefinite interpretation (cf. Wierzbicka 1967: 2244, Filip 1993/99: 243). However, what also seems to matter for the interpretation of a bare mass or plural nominal argument is the perfective prefix which combines with the verbal stem. For example, Wierzbicka (1967: 2238) points out that in the structure illustrated in (4), the mass object has some unspecified amount of water rather than a specific, total object in its denotation:

(4) On na·pił^{P} się wody/*wodę.
he-Nom PF-drink REFL.CL. water-Sg.Gen/water-Sg.Acc
'He drank (some) water.'

In (4), the bare mass noun surfaces in the genitive. Accusative case-marking is not impossible in the contexts of the perfective verb *napić się*, but the nominal predicate linked to the Incremental Theme cannot be interpreted as a referential definite. Instead, accusative case-marking is available when the argument of the verb provides an explicit (vague) measure over the amount of water consumed in the drinking event referred to with *napić się*, such as the measure noun *łyk* 'sip' illustrated in (5) below:

(5) On na·pił^{P} się łyk/*łyka wody.[2]
he-Nom PF-drink REFL.CL. sip-Sg.Acc/sip.Sg.Gen water-Gen
'He drank a sip of water.'

The contrasts in (4) and (5) could be taken to mean that accusative case-morphology marks a quantitatively determinate nominal predicate while genitive case-morphology marks a quantitatively indeterminate predicate. It is well known that verbal prefixes can express vague quantificational notions in Slavic. Filip (1993/99 and 2000) has analysed two such prefixes, the accumulative *na-* and the attenutative *po-* as extensive measure functions, that is, as quantifiers which bind the variable in the nominal predicate linked to the Incremental Theme and determine the size of the quantities of stuff or the number of individuals in the denotation of a bare mass or plural nominal predicate, respectively.[3] For example, the accumulative *na-* in (6) below combines with the bare plural nominal predicate *jabłka* 'apples' and returns a measure corresponding to 'a lot/large number of apples' in English:

(6) Piotr na·jadł^{P} się jabłek/*jabłka.
Peter-Nom PF-eat REFL.CL apples-Gen/*apples-Acc
'Peter ate a lot of apples./Peter ate apples to his heart's content.'

The question that arises in connection with (4) and (5) is whether the prefix *na-* in *napić się* can also be analysed as quantificational. The fact that the argument of the verb *napić się* can include a lexical measure expression could be taken as evidence that the prefix is quantificational in nature: the measure noun would then instantiate agreement between semantic requirements of the prefix and the lexically specified size of the quantity in question (cf. Filip 1993/99: 263). However, while the accumulative *na-* is generally associated with the notion of some considerable or large amount of stuff or number of individuals in the direct argument of the verb, the prefix *na-* illustrated in (4) and (5) does not obviously carry a presupposition condition on the size of the quantity of stuff or individuals. As shown in (5),

[2] Measure nouns, quantifiers like *trochę* ' a little (bit of)', and numerals of the 'five'-type take the complement in the genitive in Polish. Genitive case-marking on the counted noun is restricted to structural case contexts with numerals of the 'five'-type.

[3] Also Piñón (1994) analyses the accumulative *na-* as a measure function.

the size of the amount consumed in the drinking event described by the verbal predicate *napić się* can be insignificant, assuming that in the ordinary circumstances of language use, a sip of water does not count as a considerable amount of water that can be consumed. A web search including 'blogs' and newspaper citations reveals other lexical expressions indicating smallish quantities, including *trochę* 'a little/some' and *nieco* 'a little bit', but among the attested uses of the Incremental Theme argument of the predicate *napić się* one also finds the measure noun phrase *szklankę-Acc wódki-Gen* 'a glassful of vodka', which is arguably not an insignificant amount of the stuff denoted by the predicate 'vodka' that can be drunk in a drinking event.[4] Perhaps the prefix *na-* can still be analysed as quantificational in (4) and (5), but in contrast to the accumulative *na-* and the attentuative *po-* it simply happens to be ambiguous. Then, genitive case-marking on the bare nominal predicate in (4) could be analysed as 'genitive of quantification' and crucially, the genitive-marked object in (4) would not be homogeneous or unbounded in the sense of Kiparsky (1998).[5] If a bare genitive-marked nominal predicate in perfective structures like (4) above is implicitly quantified, it follows that a count singular noun cannot surface in the genitive in such structures, as count singular predicates are inherently bounded. In fact, only a bare mass or plural, but crucially not a bare count singular noun can surface in the genitive when it is linked to an Incremental Theme of a perfective verb of consumption:[6]

---

[4] Śmiech (1986: 50) analyses both *najeść^{P} się* (cf. (6)) and *napić^{P} się* (cf. (4)) as resultative, suggesting that both involve in their semantic structure a change of state in the argument linked to the subject, namely, a transition to the novel state of satiation as a result of eating/drinking'. See Spencer and Zaretskaya (1998) for similar suggestions with respect to Russsian. While this seems to be a natural analysis in the normal course of events, it should be noted that the novel state the subject enters into as a result of an eating/drinking activity can be an undesirable one and may have negative connotations, as is illustrated in (i) below drawn from the web search:

(i) Przez pomyłkę napił^{P} się atramentu-Gen.
'By mistake (he) drank (some) ink.'

Notice, furthermore, that *napić^{P} się* can be used in a context-free utterance without a lexically realised object, in which case the object tends to be interpreted as having an alcoholic substance in its denotation, as in *napić^{P} się z kolegami* 'to drink (alcohol) (to one's heart's content/to some (un)desirable limit) with (one's) friends'. The size of the stuff denoted by a bare, genitive-marked mass noun denoting some alcoholic substance can freely be interpreted as considerable with *napić się^{P}*, as demonstrated in (ii) an example drawn from the web search:

(ii) Jakiś poseł napił^{P} się jabcoka-Gen i pobił do krwi innego posła.
'Some member of Parliament had drunk (some) cheap wine and beat up another member of Parliament.'

[5] In Kiparsky (1998), a predicate is unbounded/atelic iff it is divisive and cumulative. See also Krifka (1998).

[6] Much-discussed examples of count singular nouns marked with genitive case which alternate with accusative-marked objects include objects of inherently resultative verbs like *pożyczyć* 'to lend', *dać* 'to give', *wziąć* 'to take' etc. It is widely held that the genitive on the object serves to encode a vague temporal measure of (relatively) short duration, that is, with predicates like *dać^{P} noża-Gen* 'to give (temporarily) a/the knife', the temporal limitation of the event is encoded via case-marking on the object rather than being provided via a temporal adverbial such as 'for a (short) while' (cf., among others, Zagórska-Brooks 1967, Wierzbicka 1983, Rudzka-Ostyn 2000). That the distinction in the case-marking on the object is orthogonal to the definiteness/indefiniteness distinction is demonstrated with examples like (i) from Zagórska-Brooks (1967: 396), where the noun phrase marked with genitive case refers to some contextually salient, discourse-definite pencil:

(i)	Daj^{P}	mi	tego	czarnego	ołówka	na chwilę.
	give-IMP	me-Dat	this-Gen	black-Gen	pencil-Gen	for moment

'Give me/Let me use this black pencil for a while.'

Examples of this sort offer additional support for Filip's (1993/99 and 2000) analyses of quantification in Slavic as often non-compositional compared with languages in which the dominant mode of quantification is expressed with D-quantifiers. Notice that the genitive-case marking on the object in the examples discussed above is not

(7) Z·jadł[P] kaszy/ ziemniaków/ *kanapki/ *jabłka.[7]
PF-eat porridge-Sg.Gen/ potatoes-Pl.Gen/ *sandwich-Sg.Gen/ *apple-Sg.Gen
'((He) ate (some) porridge/(some) potatoes/(some of) a sandwich/(some of) an apple.'

If a bare mass or plural predicate linked to the Incremental Theme which surfaces in the genitive is implicitly quantified, it is predicted to be interpreted as indefinite, on a par with a quantified noun phrase like *dwie gruszki* 'two pears'. That the bare mass predicate in (4) patterns with the bare mass argument of a verbal predicate derived with the accumulative *na-* illustrated in (6) above, i.e. that both scope with the VP, is shown in (8) and (9) below, respectively.

(8) Każda kobieta na·piła[P] się herbaty.
every woman PF-drink CL. tea-Gen
'Every woman drank (some) tea.'

a. For every woman it is true that she drank (some) tea (not necessarily the same amount).

b. NOT: There is a portion of tea such that each woman drank it.

(9) Piotr nie na·jadł[P] się jabłek.
Peter-Nom not ACM-eat REFL.CL apples-Gen
'Peter did not eat a lot of apples./Peter did not eat a large quantity of apples.'

a. It is not the case that Peter ate a large quantity of apples./It is not the case that Peter ate apples to his heart's content.

b. NOT: There was a large quantity of apples such that Peter did not eat.

At the same time, if a bare mass or plural nominal predicate in the genitive which is linked to the Incremental Theme supplies a variable which can be bound both by an explicit and by an implicit quantifier in the verbal prefix, there should not be any differences in the distribution of the nominal predicates associated with the Incremental Theme. In this paper, I will analyse two classes of verbal predicates which allow accusative/genitive case alternation on a bare mass or plural predicate linked to the direct argument of the verb in Polish. One class includes verbs of consumption illustrated above. The other includes directed motion predicates which typically allow a bare mass (or plural) noun in the object.[8] The former class is generally

---

internal to the syntactic projection of the noun, but rather, seems to be related to the verb(s) allowing their count singular objects/themes to surface in the genitive. Also genitive-marked object/themes in the scope of verbal prefixes endowed with weak quantificational force as in (6) can be realized with mass or count plural nouns, but not on count singular nouns (cf. also Filip (1993/99: 262).

[7] Strictly speaking, a bare count singular noun can surface in the genitive in structures like (7) as long as it can be interpreted as having substance in its denotation, i.e. as having undergone grinding. As (partitive) genitive in Polish can only be marked on (bare) mass and count plural nominal predicates, it seems to be subject to the same condition that determines the distribution of the so-called NP-related partitive in Finnish, where only mass and count plural nominal arguments of a special class of verbs, analysed by Kiparsky (1998) as inherently bounded, e.g. the Finnish counterparts of *get, buy, bring* etc., are marked with partitive case (while count singular nouns surface in the accusative as objects of such verbs). Nevertheless, the parallel is not perfect, because the distribution of both count singular and count plural nouns in (partitive) genitive in Polish is subject to further restrictions discussed in Tabakowska (2001) and Rozwadowska and Willim (2004).

[8] The unmarked case on the direct object in Polish is the accusative, which shifts to genitive under sentential negation, as does the nominative on the argument of existential and presentational sentences with the copula *być* 'to be'. The genitive does not mark the subject of a sentence with a transitive verb and neither is it marked on the

analysed to be derived in the perfective with a perfectivising prefix pure and simple. The prefixes deriving verbs in the latter class, which I will illustrate with *do-* 'in(to)/on(to)', *na-* 'on(to)/in' and *w-* 'in(to)', can be analysed as Aktionsart or lexical prefixes. The purpose of the analysis is to determine if Polish has a ban against bare unbounded (i.e. homogeneous) nominal predicates in perfective structures. The remainder of this paper is structured as follows: in Section 2, I will present some basic facts concerning the classes of verbs allowing accusative/partitive genitive alternation on their direct argument in Polish. Section 3 will deal with verbs of the type illustrated in (1) and (2). In Section 4, goal-oriented verbs of directed motion derived with directional prefixes will be discussed. Conclusions will be presented in Section 5.

2. Accusative/genitive alternation in Polish: some basic facts and observations

According to Tokarski (1973/2001: 72) and Buttler (1976: 122), verbs which systematically allow for the direct argument/theme to surface in the accusative or in the genitive include: 1. verbs of change of possession like *dać*^{P} 'to give' and *kupić*^{P} 'to buy';[9] 2. verbs derived with prefixes expressing weak quantificational measure or cardinality notions including verbs marked with the accumulative *na-* illustrated in (6) above, the attenuative *po-*, and the quantificational *do-*, *przy-*, *od-*, and *u-*, which contribute the sense of increase along the scale of quantity associated with the direct argument in some positive or negative value; 3. verbs of creation/destruction/consumption like *z·jeść*^{P} 'to eat (up)', *wy·pić*^{P} 'to drink (up)', *z·robić*^{P} 'to make', *ze·/u·trzeć*^{P} 'to grate', *z·mielić*^{P} 'to grind', *o·brać*^{P} 'to peel', *u·piec*^{P} 'to bake', *u·gotować*^{P} 'to cook' (but not, among others, *z·budować*^{P} 'to build' and *prze·czytać*^{P} 'to read'); and 4. verbs of directed motion derived with prefixes *na-*, 'in(to)/on(to), *w-* 'in(to)', and arguably also verbs derived with the (additive) prefix *do-* 'in(to)', which select for a Goal phrase. Some examples are provided in (10) below:[10]

(10) a. verbs of change of possession:

kupić^P chleb/ chleba
buy bread-Sg.Acc bread-Sg.Gen
'to buy a/the loaf of bread/to buy (some) bread'

argument of an unergative verb. Some bare nominal subjects of unaccusative verbs can surface in the genitive in the absence of sentential negation. Polish also does not have passives with genitive subjects. There is no special partitive case morphology in Polish, unlike, for example, in Russian and Finnish. Nevertheless, in traditional literature genitive-marked objects alternating with accusative objects are often referred to as partitive (cf. Szober 1921/63, Kempf 1970, Szupryczyńska and Zaremba 1993). Genitive is also lexically selected by a small group of verbs in Polish, which include intensional verbs like *chcieć* 'to desire/want', negative verbs like *zabronić* 'to prohibit' etc. Various regular and idiosyncratic aspects of the choice of accusative or genitive case-marking on direct objects as well as the accusative/genitive alternation are discussed from a descriptive perspective in Buttler (1976) and Szupryczyńska and Zaremba (1993), and from the cognitive grammar perspective in Rudzka-Ostyn (2000) and Tabakowska (2001).

[9] In classifying predicates like *dać* 'to give' as 'verbs of change of possession', I follow Jackendoff (1996: 330), for whom such predicates are inherently telic because they specify in their logical structure two spatial points corresponding, respectively, to the Goal and the Source participants, and what the predicates denote is simply an instantaneous transition between the two points. I will not discuss these verbs here for lack of space.

[10] The examples in (10) are all taken from the studies listed in the references as well as from the Polish Scientific Publisher's (PWN) corpus available at *www.korpus.pwn.pl*.

b. verbs with (weak) quantificational prefixes:

po·pić^{P} łyk wody/ wody
PF-drink sip-Sg.Acc water-Sg.Gen/ water-Sg.Gen
'to take/drink a sip of water/to drink (a little) water'[11]

do·smażyć^{P} słoik-Acc konfitur-Gen/ konfitur-Gen
PF-fry jar-Sg.Acc jam-Pl.Gen/ jam-Pl.Gen
'to make (one) more jar of jam/ to make (some) more jam'

na·łuskać^{P} koszyk orzechów/ orzechów.
PF-shell basket-Acc nuts-Gen/ nuts-Gen
'to shell (a) basket of nuts

U·było^{P} pięć centymetrów wody/ wody w piwnicy.
PF-was five-Nom/Acc cm-Gen water-Gen/ water-Gen in cellar
'The volume of water (has) decreased by 5 cms in the cellar./The volume of water (has) decreased in the cellar.'

c. verbs of creation/destruction/consumption (cf. also (1) and (2)):

z·jeść^{P} pasztet/ pasztetu
PF-eat paté-Sg.Acc/ paté-Sg.Gen
'eat a/the (whole) portion of paté/(some) paté'

d. verbs of directed motion:

na·bić^{P} tytoń do fajki/ tytoniu do fajki
PF-put tobacco-Sg.Acc to pipe/ tobacco-Sg.Gen to pipe
'to put the tobacco in the pipe/to put (some) tobacco in the pipe'

na·lać^{P} wodę do miski/ wody do miski
PF-pour water-Sg.Acc in the bowl/ water-Sg.Gen in the bowl
'to pour the water in the bowl/to pour (some) water in the bowl'

w sypać^{P} cukier do słoika/ cukru do słoika
PF-pour sugar-Sg.Acc in the jar/ sugar-Sg.Gen in the jar
'to pour the sugar in the jar/to pour (some) sugar in the jar'

'do·lać^{P} dziesięć litrów benzyny/ benzyny do zbiornika
PF-pour ten-Acc litres-Gen petrol-Gen/ petrol-Gen to tank
'to pour ten liters of petrol in the tank/to pour (some) petrol in the tank'

---

[11] With verbs of consumption like *pić*^{I} 'to drink' and *jeść*^{I} 'to eat' derived in the perfective with *po-*, the size of the quantity of stuff or individuals supplied by the nominal predicate is determined in the context, i.e. *popić-* can evoke the notion of a relatively small as well as a relatively large measure on the size of a bare mass object in combination, e.g. *po·pić*^{P} *wina-Gen* ' to drink a little/a whole lot of wine'. When the prefix is understood as identifying a large size of the quantity of alcoholic substance, the object is optional, e.g. *po·pić*^{P} 'to drink to one's heart's content, to get drunk'. Used without a lexical object, *po·jeść*^{P} tends to be interpreted as 'to eat to one's heart's content/to satiate oneself by eating'. The polysemy of Slavic prefixes is well known, which both *po-* illustrated in (10b) and *na-* illustrated in (4) and (5) above demonstrate robustly.

As shown above, while the accusative encodes a specific cardinality of the entities in the denotation of the direct argument, genitive is marked on an object whose cardinality is unspecified/vague.[12] In the context of prefixes endowed with (weak) quantificational force, such as the accumulative *na-* illustrated in (6) and (10b), the direct argument in the genitive is interpreted as having in its denotation a considerable, (sufficiently/relatively/exceedingly) large quantity of the entities denoted by the nominal predicate linked to the direct argument, as argued by Filip (1993/99) and Piñón (1994).[13] Filip (1993/99 and 2000) analyses *po-* as attenuative, but as discussed in note 11, *po-* need not range over a small quantity depending both on the semantics of the lexical stem it attaches to and the nominal predicate introducing the variable that it binds. The quantificational *do-* illustrated in (10b), which corresponds to 'more' in English, requires that the size of the entities denoted by a (bare) mass or plural nominal predicate linked to the direct argument should increase (i.e. 'become' more) in the event. The prefix does not seem to impose any requirement on the upper bound on the quantities of stuff or individuals in the denotation of the nominal predicate linked to the direct argument any more than the quantifier 'more' does in English. Rather, it defines a certain threshold value: it is the minimal expectation value that derives from the plurality of the entities in the denotation of a (bare) plural direct argument and a minimal amount of stuff that falls under a mass nominal predicate linked to the direct argument such that it exceeds the pre-existing quantity value determined in a prior event of the same type (e.g. the event of making (some) jam in (10b)), which serves as the comparison standard.[14] By Borer's (2003) reasoning, this suffices for the predicate to become non-homogeneous.[15] Notice that 'to make more jam' is strictly speaking, both divisive and cumulative, hence homogeneous. If the quantificational *do-* should be analysed as an extensive measure function and extensive measure functions serve to delimit situations, the delimitedness of an event described by a

---

[12] According to Wierzbicka (1983:251), the partitive genitive encodes 'uncountable quantity', by which she means that the object marked with partitive genitive is low in individuation. For mass nouns this presumably means that they are substance-denoting rather than unit-of-substance-denoting, i.e. while the accusative on a mass noun indicates the effects of a packaging operation, the genitive lacks this entailment.

[13] Given the scope of this paper, the quantificational *do-* cannot be discussed here in detail. If it should be analysed as introducing an extensive measure function into the logical structure of the predicate it measures, i.e. the nominal predicate *konfitury* 'jam' in (10b), it would yield as a value some undefined amount or number exceeding some contextually determined comparison standard value. Predicates derived with the quantificational *do-* have to meet the condition of additivity and commensurability. Also the quantifier 'more' , which measures the stuff or individuals supplied by the nominal predicate it combines with, is subject to the conditions of additivity and commensurability. Thus *do·smażyć^P dżemu*-Gen '(lit.) MORE-make jam' and *u·smażyć^P więcej dżemu* 'to have made more jam' are interpreted as synonymous.

[14] A count singular noun is possible as the direct argument of a verb marked with *do-*, as illustrated in (i) below. In this case, the entity in the denotation of the direct argument is bought in addition to a distinct, previously bought entity or entities.

(i) Do·kupili^P świecznik-Acc.
'They also bought a candlestick./In addition, they bought a candlestick.'

[15] Borer (2003, Chapter 12) argues against equating resultativity with endpoint telicity. In particular, she points out that (i) below is a resultative, telic construction, in which the floating of the boat need not necessarily end when the boat gets under the bridge, a reading that might be expected if resultativity entailed temporal co-finality. Rather, according to Borer, resultativity (and telicity) arises when a certain threshold point is reached whereby the predicate becomes non-homogeneous, i.e. is decomposable into sub-events. In (ii) this threshold is the point when enough meat is consumed, regardless of whether eating proceeds:

(i) The boat floated under the bridge.

(ii) Kim ate more than enough meat.

verb derived with a quantificational prefix *do-* would have to be assumed to follow from the maximality requirement whereby the eventuality in the scope of the prefix is a discrete, temporally and spatially separable one regardless of the fact that the object measured with the help of an extensive measure function is cumulative or divisive, hence not quantized (cf. Filip 2000). In (11) below, just as in (10b) above, where the upper bound on the amount of stuff in the denotation of the nominal predicate is undefined, the speaker does not expect the addressee to be able to identify the (specific) quantity of individuals in the denotation of the (bare) direct argument of the verb. Rather, (10) would be appropriate in a situation in which a few more books were bought as well as in a situation in which a considerable or large quantity of books was bought: [16]

(11) Do·kupili^{P} książek.
PF-buy books-Gen
'They bought (some) more books.'

Goal-oriented verbs of directed motion illustrated in (10d) are derived from verbs of motion with *na-* and *w-*, and arguably also with *do-*, e.g. *do·sypać*^{P} 'to add (solid stuff) by pouring/to put solid stuff or individuals in the Goal phrase'. The prefixed predicates select for an indirect argument typically realised with a PP. Even if the indirect argument is not expressed, it is strongly implied (and is recoverable). Verbs of directed motion derived with *na-*, *w-*, and *do-* select for a three-dimensional entity in the Goal phrase, as illustrated in (10d) above, but *na-* can also select for a two-dimensional goal, as shown in (12) below:

(12) nasypać^{P} mąkę-Acc/mąki-Gen na stolnicę-Acc[17]
'to put the flour/ (some) flour on the pastry board'

3. Verbs of consumption/creation/destruction with accusative/(partitive) genitive case alternation

According to Szupryczyńska and Zaremba (1993: 13), it is impossible to ascertain any specific cardinality information regarding the entities in the denotation of the genitive marked direct arguments of predicates like (1) and (2) above out of context, but this indeterminacy can be resolved in discourse and indicated with quantity expressions such as *mało* 'little', *odrobinę* 'a tiny bit, *nieco* 'a little bit' as well as *dużo* 'much/a lot', *wiele* ' much/a lot', *górę* 'a heap of' etc.

---

[16] Note that a (bare) mass or plural nominal predicate linked to the direct argument in the scope of the quantificational prefixes *po-* and *do-* is a non-specific indefinite on a par with a direct argument in the scope of the accumulative *na-* in (6):

(i) Nie po·pili^{P} wina-Gen.
1. It is not the case that (they) drank a considerable amount of wine. 2. NOT: There was a considerable amount of wine such that they did not drink.

(ii) Nie do·kupili^{P} książek-Gen.
1. It is not the case that they bought more books. 2. NOT: There was an additional quantity of books such that they did not buy.

[17] The preposition *na* selects for a nominal complement marked with accusative or locative case-morphology, e.g. *na stolnicę*-Acc/*stolnicy*-Loc ' on(to)/on a pastry board'. The former represents the directional variant specifying the goal of movement, while the latter represents the locative variant specifying the location of a (resultant) state or process.

(13) Wy·pił^P herbaty, ale bardzo mało.
PF-drink tea-Gen, but very little
'(She) drank (some) tea, but only very little.'

(14) U·piekła^P ciastek, i to całkiem sporo.
PF-bake cookies-Gen, and it quite a lot.
'She baked (some) cookies, and it was quite a lot.'

As noted by Wierzbicka (1967: 2238), with most of the verbs of consumption/creation/destruction as well as with verbs of change of possession mentioned in section 2 above and illustrated in (10a), the Incremental Theme can surface in the genitive only in the perfective aspect:

(15) a. Piotr z·jadł^P kaszę/ kaszy.
Peter-Nom PF-eat porridge-Acc/ porridge-Gen
'Peter ate a portion of porridge/(some) porridge.'

b. Piotr jadł^I kaszę/ *kaszy.[18]
Peter-Nom eat porridge-Acc/ porridge-Gen
'Peter was eating a portion of porridge/(some) porridge'

There are other asymmetries in the distribution of accusative versus genitive case morphology on direct arguments of verbs of consumption/creation/destruction. For example, a time-span adverbial is licensed in the presence of an accusative-marked direct argument, but not in the presence of a genitive-marked one (cf. also Szupryczyńska and Zaremba 1993: 17):[19]

(16) a. Piotr z·jadł^P kaszę-Acc w pół godziny.
'Peter ate the/a portion of porridge in half an hour.'

b. * Piotr zjadł^P kaszy-Gen w pół godziny.
'Peter ate (some) porridge in half an hour.'

At the same time, regardless the case-marking of the object/theme, a durative adverbial cannot modify the VP-predicate in the perfective:

(17) a. * Piotr zjadł^P kaszę-Acc/kaszy-Gen pół godziny.
'Peter ate the porridge/(some) porridge for half an hour.'

That the genitive-marked direct argument does not encode some vague, grammatically specified but lexically unexpressed measure over the quantity of entities denoted by the nominal predicate that is linked to it is also suggested by the fact that the direct argument in the genitive is incompatible with a modifier highlighting the upper bound in the denotation of

[18] A reviewer has inquired why partitive genitive is impossible with the imperfective of a verb of consumption/creation/destruction in Polish. Following Paducheva (1998), I will assume here that genitive-marked nominal predicates are disallowed in the imperfective interpreted as on-going/progressive, because on this reading the imperfective of a verb of this type is a relation between individuals, hence the thematic arguments of the verbal predicate must be realised with nominal predicates interpreted as presupposed or specific.

[19] As discussed in Ramchand (2004), it is not clear what the distribution of a time-span adverbial in Slavic is diagnostic of, as the compatibility of a time-span adverbial with a perfective predicate could be sensitive to quantizedness of the direct argument or it could be sensitive to the existence of subevents in the decomposition of a verbal predicate such that the time-adverbial could measure the distance between the them.

the nominal predicate. Such a delimiting expression is possible in the presence of an accusative-marked direct argument:

(18) Piotr z·mielił^P kawę-Acc/*kawy-Gen do ostatniego ziarnka.
'Peter ground the (portion of) coffee (beans) to the last grain./Peter ground (some) coffee to the last grain.'

(19) Piotr s·tarł^P ser-Acc/*sera-Gen prawie do końca.
'Peter grated the cheese almost in full./Peter grated (some) cheese almost in full.'

(20) Piotr wy·pił^P wódkę-Acc/*wódki-Gen do dna.
'Peter drank the (portion of) vodka to the last drop/the bottom./Peter drank (some) vodka to the last drop/the bottom.'

The fact that a modifier focussing on the upper bound of the quantity of stuff or the number of individuals in the denotation of the bare mass or plural direct argument is impossible if the direct argument is marked with genitive case-morphology speaks against an analysis on which the syntactic projection of the direct argument realised with a bare mass or plural noun and also its logical structure contain a lexically unexpressed quantifier, measure or cardinality expression. If there were a lexically unexpressed quantifier, measure or cardinality expression in the syntactic and semantic structure of a genitive-marked-object, we would not expect any asymmetries with respect to the distribution of degree modifiers and yet there are such asymmetries. Compare, for example, (19) with (21) below:

(21) Piotr s·tarł^P [kawałek-Acc sera-Gen/całkiem sporo-Acc sera-Gen] prawie do końca.
'Peter grated a piece (of) cheese almost in full./Peter grated quite (a) lot (of) cheese almost in full.'

The asymmetries in (18)-(20) are reminiscent of the contrast between (22a) and (22b) observed by Smollett (2001):

(22) a. Kathleen ate the ice cream to the last spoonful.

b. * Kathleen ate ice cream to the last spoonful.

As shown in (22), in English a modifier specifying the end on the scale of change introduced by the direct argument undergoing incremental changes in its spatial extent is incompatible with a bare mass nominal predicate. Assuming that the function of the delimiting modifiers in (18)-(20) is the same in both languages, it seems well-motivated in the light of the asymmetries in (18)-(20) to conclude that while the accusative marks a quantitatively determinate, i.e. bounded nominal predicate with a linguistically specified upper bound, the genitive marks an unbounded nominal predicate whose upper bound is not specified and cannot be accessed linguistically.

That there is a difference in the semantic status of bare mass and plural nominal predicates linked to the direct argument of a verb of consumption/creation/destruction analysed here which is flagged morphosyntactically with case morphology is further suggested by the contrast in the distribution of distributive modifiers, which are allowed in the context of an accusative-marked direct argument, but which are disallowed in the context of a genitive-marked direct argument:

(23) Z·jadł^P oliwki-Acc/ garść-Acc/część-Acc/trochę-Acc oliwek-Gen jedna za drugą/każdą z osobna.
'He ate the olives one by one/each separately from the others. /He ate a handful of olives/part of the olives/a little olives one by one/each separately from the others.'

(24) * Z·jadł^P oliwek-Gen jedna za drugą/każdą z osobna.
'He ate olives one by one/each separately from the others.'

In (23), the size of the set of individuals in the denotation of the accusative-marked predicates is delimited.[20] The interpretation of the situation described in (23) is that of an eating event in which singular, atomic members of the set of entities which fall under the denotation of the nominal predicate are consumed one by one such that each part of the denotation of the event corresponds to each singular, atomic part in the denotation of the nominal predicate linked to the direct argument and vice versa. In other words, the event progresses in successive stages determined by the part-structure of the object. Thus, the mapping from the event to the object is a homomorphism. Somehow this homomorphism seems to be blocked in (24). This conclusion is supported by the fact that genitive case-marking is disallowed in the presence of a degree modifier which highlights the graduality of the mapping between the event and the object, as is illustrated in (25b) in contrast to (25a):

(25) a. Piotr z·jadł^P kaszę/oliwki-Acc stopniowo.
'Peter ate the/a portion of porridge/olives gradually.'

b. * Piotr z·jadł^P kaszy/oliwek-Gen stopniowo.
'Peter ate porridge/olives gradually.'

Piñón (2000) observes a similar asymmetry as regards the availability of the adverb *gradually* with the English verb *to eat*:

(26) a. I gradually ate a big slice of cheesecake (at the party).

b. * I gradually ate (at the party).

c. * I gradually ate cheese (at the party).

To account for the above asymmetry, Piñón (2000) suggests that gradual predicates lacking a degree argument can nevertheless be accessed by a degree modifier like *gradually* if a degree function can apply to them.[21] Based on the fact that (26a) is well-formed in contrast to both (26b) and (26c), Piñón suggests that the degree function can only apply to a homomorphic predicate satisfying Krifka's Uniqueness of Events and Uniqueness of Object conditions, that is, such that the event it denotes applies to only one (unique) object. An intransitive predicate in (26b) cannot meet this condition and so the degree function cannot apply to it. Neither can (26c) meet this condition on the assumption that the bare mass noun is predicative: a property-denoting nominal is not a unique object and thus cannot measure out the event. Lack of the event-to-object homomorphism in (26c) follows if the verbal predicate is analysed as

---

[20] In fact, predicates like *część oliwek* 'part of the olives' and *porcja oliwek* 'portion of olives' are not, strictly speaking, quantized according to Krifka's (1998) definition, as any part of a portion of olives (down to minimal parts) can be taken to count as a portion of olives. See Zucchi and White (2001) and Rothstein (2004) for discussion. In particular, Rothstein argues that once it is determined in context what counts as 'part of the olives' or 'portion of olives', such predicates are atomic/quantized.

[21] Verbs inherently endowed with a degree argument are Dowty's degree achievement verbs. See also Hay *et al.* (1999).

the incorporating variant of the transitive verb *to eat*. Following van Geenhoven, it can be assumed that such a predicate composes with the predicate of the thematic argument of a transitive verb in the lexicon.

On the assumption that genitive-marked nominal predicates linked to the direct argument of a verb of creation/consumption are quantitatively indeterminate, that is, non-delimited at the grammatical level, an independent delimiter may be expected. to occur with such a predicate. This expectation is confirmed in (27) below from Szupryczyńska and Zaremba (1993: 17):

(27) a. Piotr zjadł^P chleba-Gen do syta.
'Peter ate bread until he was satiated./Piotr satiated himself by eating bread'

b. * Piotr zjadł^P chleb-Acc do syta.
'Peter ate the bread until he was satiated.'

Given the 'one delimiter per event rule' (cf. Tenny 1994), if the modifier *do syta* 'to satiation' can delimit an eventuality, it is expected to be impossible if there is an independent delimiter, i.e. a bounded direct argument, in the structure. Its co-occurrence with a partitive genitive-marked argument of the verb *z·jeść*^{P} suggests that a genitive-marked direct argument is not delimited at the level of syntax. Notice that the presence of a lexical quantifier, measure noun or cardinal numeral in the syntactic projection of the direct argument of a verb of consumption blocks the delimiter *do syta* 'to satiation':

(28) * Piotr zjadł^P trochę/mnóstwo/bochenek-Acc chleba-Gen do syta.[22]
'Peter ate a little/a whole lot/a loaf (of) bread to satiation.'

I thus conclude that with verbs of consumption/creation discussed in this section, the partitive genitive-marked nominal predicate linked to the direct argument is quantitatively indeterminate (i.e. unbounded) on a par with bare mass and plural nouns in English. To account for the lexical restrictions on the type of the verbal predicate and the type of the nominal predicate linked to the Incremental Theme, I will take verbs co-occurring with Incremental Theme arguments in the genitive to be semantically incorporating (variants of the) verbs in the sense of van Geenhoven (1998). If genitive-marked nominal arguments are predicates of the direct argument satisfied (i.e. existentially bound) in the lexicon, they are predicted to be scopeless with respect to other operators.[23] Being quantitatively indeterminate, they block the event-to-object homomorphism. As a result, eventualities described by verbal predicates they combine with cannot be classified as accomplishments, contra Slabakova (2003). As far as their lexical aspectual class is concerned, verbs of consumption can be classified as achievements in that they may be analysed as encoding a change of state, although their direct argument does not undergo a definite change of state by virtue of not providing an explicit scale of change. Rather, it only serves to describe or specify the process in the denotation of the verb. The change of state is a state of satiation or, in some

---

[22] Other verbs of consumption discussed here behave similarly with respect to the distribution of the delimiter *do syta* 'to satiation':

(i) Napili^P się wina-Gen do syta.
'They drank wine to satiation./They satiated themselves by drinking wine.'

(ii) * Napili^P się trochę/dużo/butelkę wina-Gen do syta.
'They drank some/a lot of/a bottle of wine to satiation.'

[23] Both Paducheva (1998) and Topolińska (1976) suggest that Incremental Themes encoded with the partitive genitive are non-referential/predicative.

circumstances, some undesirable mental, physical or emotional state that that the subject enters into by virtue of carrying out the activity described by the verbal predicate, e.g. by drinking wine. Also creation/destruction verbs taking the Incremental Theme in the genitive can be interpreted on a par with achievements. For example, in (18) a transition takes place from one state, there not being any ground coffee in the situation to there being some ground coffee in the situation, but this state does not arise as a result of an activity directed towards the Incremental Theme which undergoes successive changes as the event unfolds. Rather, the event is represented with the focus on the result achieved but as lacking internal structure.

4. Accusative/genitive alternation on the direct argument of directed motion verbs

Among the verbs of directed motion allowing accusative/genitive case alternation on the direct argument are verbs derived with the prefixes *do-*, *na-* and *w-* illustrated in (10d) above. They are included by Grzegorczykowa *et al.* (1984: 480) among directional derivatives to capture the fact that the verbal stems specify manner of movement and the prefixes are dynamic and specify where the entity linked to the direct argument is moving in the event denoted by the prefixed verbal predicate. The Goal phrase must be specified either explicitly or implicitly. If it is implicit, the Goal phrase is recoverable from the larger linguistic or situational context of the utterance. *Do-* is analysed as specifying that the (Holistic) Theme/Locatum comes into direct contact with the entity in the Goal phrase/Location whereby the two may overlap spatially provided the overlap relation is compatible with the semantics of the Locatum and the Location.[24] *W-* specifies that the endpoint on the path of movement is within the space occupied by the entity specified in the Location. *Na-* is also used to express this meaning; however, Grzegorczykowa *et al.* (1984: 481) note that *na-* is used to emphasise that the space occupied by the entity in the Location becomes filled with the moving theme in the event. All three prefixes can combine with the same stem, as illustrated in (29):

(29) a. do·lać^P wina do kieliszka[25]
PF-pour wine-Gen to glass
'to pour (some) wine in the/a glass'

b. na·lać^P wina do kieliszka
PF-pour wine-Gen to glass
'to pour (some) wine in the/a glass'

c. w·lać^P wina do kieliszka
PF-pour wine-Gen to glass
'to pour (some) wine in the/a glass'

Analysed at the level of overt syntax, the examples in (29) have what is known in the literature on the lexical-semantic and lexical-syntactic properties of verb classes in English as the 'theme-on/in-location' syntax (cf., among others, Rappaport and Levin 1998, Dowty 1991, Jackendoff 1996). As is well known, in structures of this particular type, the theme

---

[24] Unlike the directional *na-* and *w-*, *do-* can combine with a one-dimensional Location , e.g. *dobiec do mety* '(lit) DO-run to the finnish line/to reach the finnish line by running.'

[25] (29a) is felicitous both in a situation in which there is some amount of wine in the glass and the activity of pouring is to be carried out to cause an increase in the quantity of wine in the glass by some degree *d*. I will disregard this meaning of *do-*, as it falls together with the quantificational *do-* mentioned earlier. Here, I will focus on the reading of *do-* compatible with a situation in which immediately prior to the activity of pouring, the glass is empty or it does not contain wine. In such a situation, the meaning of a verbal predicate derived with *do-* cannot be analysed as 'add n_1 amount of w to n_2 amount of w'.

(Locatum), which is linked to the direct argument and mapped in the syntax onto the direct object must be quantized for the predicate to be telic (cf. Dowty 1991: 591-2):

(30) a. John sprayed paint onto this wall *in an hour/for an hour.

b. John sprayed this (whole) can of paint onto subway cars in an hour/*for an hour.

For Dowty (1991: 569), with verbs of movement, the homomorphism holds of the relation between the event and the path trace rather than between parts of the event and parts of the moving entity (referred to for this reason as Holistic Theme). Nevertheless, as shown in (30), the event is bounded just in case the Locatum is also bounded.[26] The spatial extent of the Locatum does not matter for telicity just in case the verb of directed motion occurs in the 'location-with-theme' syntax in English and the goal of movement, i.e. the Location argument, is bounded:

(31) John sprayed this wall with paint in an hour/*for an hour.[27]

According to Rappaport and Levin (1998: 27), the (variant of the) verbal predicate appearing in the 'theme-on-location' syntax illustrated in (30) is interpreted as encoding a change of location but not a change of state, while the (variant of the) predicate occurring in the 'location-with-theme' syntax illustrated in (31) encodes a change of state in the goal of movement. Only in the latter case can the theme be unbounded in a telic construction in English, as demonstrated in (31). This conclusion is a stipulation, since on both variants there is a change of state in the Location argument. According to Dowty (1991), telicity can arise only if the extent of change is definite, i.e. if there is an entailment of holistic affectedness. Since (31) has a strong entailment that the wall was completely covered with paint in the event, structures instantiating the 'location-with-theme' syntax are telic. The scale of change associated with the theme/Locatum argument is irrelevant, and the oblique argument is taken to simply be affected in the event. However, Beavers (2004) argues that while telicity and (holistic) affectedness are interconnected, they should nevertheless be dissociated. Alternating verbs of the *load/spray* type do not give semantic prominence to either of the participants: both can be (holistically) affected in the event (cf. also Jackendoff 1996). This is in contrast to predicates of the 'fill'-type, which make the Location participant semantically more prominent in the sense that it has more Proto-Patient entailments which thus qualify it to be linked to the direct object. The question that arises is whether the predicates in (29) are also neutral with respect to the semantic prominence of the Locatum and Location participants.

The authoritative *Słownik języka polskiego* edited by M. Szymczak lists among the equivalents of *do·lać*^{P} illustrated in (29a) a host of verbal derivatives based on the adjective *pełny* 'full', e.g. *do·pełnić*^{P} 'fill (up)', *uzu·pełnić*^{P} 'supplement, replenish', *na·pełnić*^{P} 'fill (up)'. *Na·lać*^{P} as well as *w·lać*^{P} are explained in Szymczak's dictionary as 'getting/bringing liquid stuff into something by pouring'.[28] The PWN-Oxford Polish-English dictionary

---

[26] Jackendoff (1996: 309) also notes that the preposition must introduce a closed-scale spatial path. The relevant data are provided in (i) from Jackendoff (1996: 309) and Rothstein (2004: 31):

(i) a. Bill pushed the cart along the road/toward the house for/*in two minutes.

b. Bill pushed the cart to the store *for hours/in an hour.

c. Bill pushed carts to the store for an hour/*in an hour.

d.

[27] The durative adverbial is compatible with this predicate, but requires the eventuality in its denotation to be interpreted as iterated.

[28] The translation is mine.

paraphrases both *na·lać*^{P} and *w·lać*^{P} with 'to fill with liquid'.[29] According to the latter, the translational equivalent of *na·lać*^{P} *wody*-Gen *do czajnika* '(lit.) to NA-pour water in (the) kettle' is 'to fill the kettle' and the translational equivalent of *na·lać*^{P} *wody*-Gen *do wanny* '(lit.) to NA-pour water in the tub' is 'to fill the bath (up) with water'. Similarly for *do·lać*^{P}. For example, *do·lać*^{P} *bezyny-Gen* is rendered as 'to top up the petrol (tank) or top up with petrol' and *do·lać*^{P} *do pełna wody-Gen do szklanki* as 'to fill up a glass with water', where *do pełna* 'to the brim/full' is a degree modifier corresponding to 'completely' in English. Only *w·lać*^{P} is consistently rendered with 'to pour' used in the 'location-on/in-theme' syntax in all the dictionaries mentioned above. Based on this I propose here that the verbs used in (29), owing to their directional prefixes which act as telic markers give more semantic prominence to the Location argument despite the 'theme-on/in-location syntax'. Thus, the Location serves as the goal for the change of location with respect to the entity linked to the Locatum argument, but it primarily serves to encode a change of state. In other words, the structures in (29) all involve the 'fill water/wine into the glass/bowl' syntax, but their semantics is closer to the 'fill the glass/bowl with water/wine' syntax. Dowty (1991: 593) observes that constructions like *I filled water into the glass*, which are ungrammatical in English, nevertheless cannot be considered ill-formed semantically. The are produced by English-speaking children at a stage in language acquisition. Jackendoff (1996) accounts for the difference between the 'theme-on/in location' syntax and the 'location-with-theme syntax' by postulating that the latter has a bias towards expressing a change-of-state, filling/covering relation while the former is neutral. This would explain why children switch to the 'location-with-theme' syntax once they realise that it is dedicated to encoding a change of state.

In comparison with English, the verbs of directed movement discussed here with respect to Polish do not systematically enter into syntactic alternations. Neither of the verbs in (29) occurs in the 'location-with-theme' syntax, and of the verbs illustrated in (10d), only *na·bić*^{P} has the 'location-with-theme' variant, e.g. *na·bić*^{P} *fajkę*-Acc *tytoniem*-Instr ' to fill the pipe with tobacco'. *Nalać*^{P}, as well as *na·pompować*^{P} 'pump (up)/fill by pumping' and *do·pompować*^{P} 'fill up by pumping' have two syntactic templates, but the variant in which the Locatum argument is lexically expressed is the 'theme-on/in-location' template.[30] The other variant is either possible or best if the theme/Locatum is not expressed at all or if it used with a measure expression. The choice of the syntactic template in part depends on the lexical semantics of the nominal predicate linked to the Location argument and the semantics of the verbal stem:

(32)	a.	na·lać^P	wódki	do kieliszka
		PF-pour	vodka-Gen	to glass
		'to pour (some) vodka in the/a glass/to fill the/a glass with vodka'		
	b.	na·lać^P	kieliszek	wódki
		PF-pour	glass-Acc	vodka-Gen
		'to pour a glass of vodka'		
	c.	na·lać^P	kieliszek	(*wódką)
		PF-pour	glass-Acc	(vodk-Instr)
		'to fill a glass with vodka by pouring'		

[29] The examples that follow have been selected from the 2002 edition of the PWN-Oxford English-Polish Dictionary and the 2004 edition of PWN-Oxford Polish-English Dictionary. Both dictionaries are published by Wydawnictwo Naukowe PWN.

[30] Strictly speaking, *do·pompować*^{P} and *na·pompować*^{P} do not allow genitive/accusative case alternation on the 'theme in/on location' syntax.

(33) a. do·pompować^P powietrza w kołach
PF-pump air-Gen in tyres
'to pump air in the tyres/to pump the tyres up'

b. do·pompować^P koła (*powietrzem)
PF-pump tyres-Acc (air-Instr)
'to pump the tyres up with air'

(34) a. na·pompować^P wody do wiadra
PF-pump water-Gen in bucket
'to pump water into the bucket/to fill the bucket with water by pumping'

b. na·pompować^P wiadro *(wody)
PF-pump bucket-Acc
'to pump up a bucket (of water)'

c. na·pompować^P * wiadro/ materac-acc
PF-pump bucket-Acc/ mattress-Acc
'to pump (up) the bucket/mattress'

d. *na·pompować^P wiadro/ materac wodą
PF-pump bucket-Acc/ mattress water-Instr
'to pump up a bucket/mattress with water'

Given that verbs of directed motion do not enter systematically into syntactic alternations and in some cases have only the 'location-on/in-theme' variant to encode a change of state in the Location argument in Polish (cf., for example, (33b) and (34d)), I conclude that the 'location-on/in-theme' syntax can encode a change of state in the cases analysed here in Polish. I suggest that it is the directional prefix that identifies which is the more prominent semantic argument. This implies that it is not the spatial extent of the moving theme/Locatum but the extent of change of the location argument which provides the dimension on which inner telicity is calculated with such predicates in Polish.[31] In other words, homomorphism is modelled on the relation between the path of the event and the event (and vice versa). The Goal Phrase/Location provides a natural bound on the path trace of the event, which seems to be some assumed or understood limit. The exact upper bound seems to depend on the lexical semantics of the verbal predicate, the semantics of the goal, as well as pragmatic factors. For example, world knowledge tells us that in an event of filling the glass with vodka, vodka hardly ever fills the entire spatial extent provided by the glass. In pumping air into the tyres, there is some assumed bound on the volume of air in the tyre which counts as the relevant threshold bound (even if pumping air can continue) etc. This is why *do·pompować^P* can be found in structures like (35) below:[32]

---

[31] That the verbs of directed motion analysed here are resultatives assertiing a change of state in the (implicit) Location argument is clear in examples like (i) and (ii) below, drawn from the web search:

(i) Bulion powinien przykrywać wszystkie kulki. jeśli jest go za mało, do·lać^P wody-Gen.
'The broth should cover all (meat) balls. If there is not enough of it, add water.'

[32] While both the Locatum and the location carry the entailment of affectedness, neither carries a necessary entailment of holistic affectedness. For example, in (i) below, drawn from a web search, the continuation licenses a reading on which all of the Locatum is exhausted in the event. This entailment is absent in the absence of the continuation. In either case, it is not necessarily the case that the glasses where filled with vodka to an assumed limit to which a glass is typically filled with vodka:

(35) do·pompować^P powietrza w kołach do normalnego ciśnienia
'to pump air in the tyres to the normal pressure level'

If the verbal prefix in verbs of directed movement is responsible for introducing a telos into the semantic structure of such predicates, these predicates are inherently telic despite the 'theme-in/on location' syntax. If the extent of change in the Location argument is understood as not exceeding some assumed, conversationally determined limit, it is not a specific/definite extent of change. Unlike in English, the argument that encodes the relevant change of state, i.e. the Location, does not carry the entailment of holistic affectedness, but the weaker entailment of affectedness. Nevertheless, owing to the prefix, the verbal predicates are resultative. The stuff or individuals in the nominal predicate linked to the Locatum argument simply further specify the change of state, just as unbounded predicates do in the 'location-with-theme' in English (cf. (31)), i.e. a template with a bias towards the filling/covering relation.[33] If the part-structure of the events in the denotation of directed motion predicates is modelled on the part-structure of the path of movement, which is (implicitly or explicitly) bounded, then we can expect that such predicates can be modified by a degree modifier like *gradually* and that they license a time-span adverbial. These expectations are confirmed in (36)- (38) below.

(36) a. Piotr do·sypał cukier-Acc do soku stopniowo.
'Peter added the sugar to the juice gradually.'

b. Piotr do·sypał cukru-Gen do soku stopniowo.
'Peter added (some) sugar to the juice (by pouring) gradually.'

(37) Do·pompował^P powietrza-Gen w kołach stopniowo.
'He pumped air in the tyres gradually./He pumped the tyres (up) gradually.'

(38) Do·pompował^P powietrza-Gen w kołach w 10 minut.
'He pumped air in the tyres in 10 minutes./He pumped the tyres (up) in 10 minutes.'

5. Conclusion

In this paper I have analysed in some detail two classes of verbal predicates allowing for accusative/(partitive) genitive case alternation on the direct argument. I have argued that a genitive-marked (bare) mass or plural nominal predicate linked to the direct argument is interpreted as a weak (existential) indefinite. Following van Geenhoven (1998), I have suggested that (bare) mass or plural predicates linked to the direct argument are predicates of the thematic argument of the verb which are existentially bound in the lexicon. Because they are property-denoting, they do not provide an explicit scale of change and cannot measure out the event. Perfective verbs of consumption/creation/destruction combining with a genitive-marked Incremental Theme can still be analysed as telic if they are interpreted as inherently

---

(i) Na·lał^P ponownie (wódki-Gen) do szklanek. Pustą butelkę chciał wyrzucić do kosza.
'(He) poured vodka in the glasses again. (He) wanted to throw the empty bottle into the dustbin.'

[33] That the Locatum argument is interpreted as a weak (existential) indefinite with directed motion predicates discussed here is shown below:

(i) Każdy pan nalał mi wina-Gen.
'Every gentleman poured me (some) wine.'

1. For every gentleman it is true that he filled my glass with wine (partly or fully).
2. NOT: There is a quantity of wine such that every gentleman poured (it) in my glass.

resultative. Nevertheless, they do not pass standard telicity tests because the only homomorphism suitable with such predicates is the event-to-object homomorphism, which an unbounded nominal predicate linked to the Incremental Theme blocks. Goal-oriented verbs of directed motion have been argued to encode a change of state despite the direct argument's quantitative indeterminacy. I have accounted for the telicity of such predicates by postulating that they select for the path-to-event homomorphism rather than the object-to-event homomorphism. If correct, this analysis provides evidence against the claim that all direct arguments of dynamic verbs (ADD-TO verbs in Verkuyls' 1999 terminology) mapped onto the object in transitive structures and subjects in unaccusative structures are quantitatively determined ([+SQA]) at the grammatical level in Slavic/Polish and that the perfective aspect/prefix always quantises the mass or plural nominal predicate linked to the direct argument of a verbal predicate in its scope.

References

Beaver, J. 2004. Semantic underspecificity in argument/oblique alternations. To appear in: Proceedings of WECOL 2004. University of Southern California, Los Angeles, CA.

Borer, H. 2003. Determining structures. University of Southern California ms.

Buttler, D. 1976. *Innowacje składniowe współczesnej polszczyzny*. Warszawa: PWN.

Carlson, G. 1977. A unified analysis of the English bare plural. *Linguistics and Philosophy* 1: 413-457.

Dowty, D. 1991. Thematic proto-roles and argument selection. *Language* 67: 547-619.

Filip, H. 1993/99. *Aspect, eventuality types and nominal reference*. New York: Garland Publishing.

Filip, H. 2000. The quantization puzzle. In: Tenny, C. and J. Pustejovsky (eds.): *Events as grammatical objects. The converging perspectives of lexical semantics and syntax*, 39-93. Stanford: CSLI Publications.

van Geenhoven, V. 1998. On the argument structure of some Noun Incorporating verbs in West Greenlandic. In: Butt, M. and W. Geuder (eds.): *The projection of arguments and compositional factors*, 225-263. Stanford: CSLI Publications.

Hay, J., C. Kennedy and B. Levin. 1999. Scalar structure underlies telicity in 'degree achievements'. In: Matthews, T. and D. Strolovitch (eds.): *Proceedings of SALT* 9, 127-144. Cornell Linguistic Circle Publications.

Jackendoff, R. 1996. The proper treatment of measuring out, telicity, and perhaps even quantification in English. *Natural Language and Linguistic Theory* 14: 305-354.

Kempf, Z. 1970. Rozwój i zanik polskiego partitivu. *Język Polski* 53: 181-194.

Kiparsky, P. 1998. Partitive case and aspect. In: Butt, M. and W. Geuder (eds.): *The projection of arguments and compositional factors*, 265-306. Stanford: CSLI Publications.

Krifka, M. 1998. The origins of telicity. In: Rothstein, S. (ed.): *Events and Grammar*, 197-235. Dordrecht: Kluwer.

Paducheva, E. 1998. On non-compatibility of partitive and imperfective in Russian. *Theoretical Linguistics* 24.1: 73-82.

Piñón, Ch. 1994. Accumulation and aspectuality in Polish. *NELS* 24/2: 491-506.

Piñón, Ch. 2000. Happening gradually. Universität Düsseldorf ms.

Ramchand, G. 2004. Time and the event: the semantics of Russian prefixes. University of Tromsø unpublished manuscript.

Rappaport, M. and B. Levin. 1988. What to do with *theta*-roles. In: Wilkins, W. (ed.): *Thematic relations. Syntax and Semantics* 21, 7-36. San Diego: Academic Press.

Rothstein, S. 2004. *Structuring events*. Oxford: Blackwell Publishing.

Rozwadowska, B. and E. Willim. 2004. On the accusative/partitive alternation in aspectual composition in Polish. *Papers and Studies in Contrastive Linguistics* 39: 125-142.

Rudzka-Ostyn, B. 2000. *Z rozważań nad kategorią przypadka*. Kraków: Universitas.

Slabakova, R. 1997. Bulgarian preverbs: aspect in phrase structure. *Linguistics* 35: 673-704.

Slabakova, R. 2003. Semantic and morphological reflexes of functional categories: the case of telicity marking in L2 Russian. In: J. Liceras, M. et al. (eds.): *Proceedings of the 6th Generative Approaches to Second Language Acquisition Conference*, 284-297. Sommerville, MA: Cascadilla Proceedings Project.

Smollett, R. 2001. Count nouns don't delimit after all. Poster presented at the Perspectives on Aspect conference. Utrecht, December 12-14, 2001. To appear in: Verkuyl, H. and H. de Swart (eds.): *Perspectives on Aspect*. Dordrecht: Kluwer.

Szupryczyńska, M. and Ch. Zaremba. 1993. Kilka uwag o tzw. dopełniaczu cząstkowym w języku polskim. *Język Polski* 73(1-2): 10-18.

Tabakowska, E. 2001. O motywacji związku rządu derywatów prefiksalnych polskich czasowników z dopełnieniem. In: Kubiński, W. and D. Stanulewicz (eds.): *Językoznawstwo Kognitywne* II, 212-224. Gdańsk: Wydawnictwo Uniwersytetu Gdańskiego.

Tenny, C. 1994. *Aspectual roles and the syntax-semantics interface*. Dordrecht: Kluwer.

Tokarski, J. 1973/2001. *Fleksja polska*. Warszawa: Wydawnictwo Naukowe PWN.

Topolińska, Z. 1976. Wyznaczoność (tj. charakterystyka referencyjna) grupy imiennej w tekście polskim I. *Polonica* 2: 33-72.

Vendler, Z. 1967. *Linguistics in philosophy*. Ithaca: Cornell University Press.

Verkuyl, H.J. 1999. *Aspectual issues. Studies on time and quantity*, Stanford, Ca.: CSLI Publications.

Wierzbicka, A. 1967. On the semantics of verbal aspect in Polish. In: *To Honor Roman Jakobson* (vol. 3), 2231-49. The Hague: Mouton.

Wierzbicka, A. 1983. The semantics of case marking. *Studies in Language* 7: 247-75.

Zagórska-Brooks, M. 1967. The accusative-genitive contrast in some Polish constructions. In: *To Honor Roman Jakobson* (vol. 1), 395-401. The Hague: Mouton.

Zucchi, S. and M. White. 2001. Twigs, sequences and the temporal constitution of predicates. *Linguistics and Philosophy* 24: 223-270.

Syntax/Morphology

Peter Ackema and Amela Čamdžić

Long Verb Movement as LF Complex Predicate Formation

1. Introduction

Long Verb (Head) Movement (LVM) constructions are characterised by the fronting of a verb across one or more verbal head positions. They are found in a variety of languages but in this paper we concentrate on Serbo-Croatian (SC). They are exemplified below in (1). (1a) illustrates the underlying order of the verbs, while (1b) and (1c) are outputs of LVM. In (1b) the participle of *to be* fronts over the tensed auxiliary, while in (1c) it is the participle of the main verb that moves to the sentence initial position over the tensed auxiliary and the participle of *to be*.

(1) a. *Ivan je bio pojeo gljive.*
Ivan-nom is-cl been eaten mushrooms-acc
'Ivan had eaten the mushrooms.'

b. *Bio je pojeo gljive.*
been is-cl eaten mushrooms-acc
'He had eaten the mushrooms.'

c. *Pojeo je bio gljive.*
eaten is-cl been mushrooms
'He had eaten the mushrooms.'

A significant feature of LVM is that the tensed auxiliary (*je* in 1) is a clitic. (Note that SC clitics are second position elements.) In fact, there are instances of LVM across some non-clitic auxiliaries, but we believe there are good reasons to treat them separately. LVM across a nonclitic arguably involves remnant VP-movement (see Čamdžić 2004). We will argue that LVM across clitics involves head-to-head adjunction.[1]

2. Previous analyses

The earliest accounts of (1) involved so-called "long head movement" i.e. head movement that skipped a head position (Rivero 1991, Roberts 1993). Since this violates the Head Movement Constraint (HMC), this locality principle had to be adapted. For example, Roberts (1993) proposed that, like phrasal positions, head positions should be divided into A'- and A-positions, and that A'-head movement could skip A-head-positions. Since LVM, according to this analysis, targets the head position of C, or an A' position, skipping the intermediate A-heads, the movement of the verb does not incur a locality violation. Such modifications to the HMC have, as yet, not found motivation beyond LVM and it remains rather unexpected that we do not found violations of the HMC on a wider scale.

Bošković (1995) proposes that LVM does not involve head movement by substitution, but head movement by adjunction. He argues that the participle adjoins to the auxiliary, just as it does in Verb Raising constructions in the Germanic OV-languages (cf. Evers 1975). We will follow Bošković's basic assumption that head-adjunction is involved in (1). However, if LVM consists of participle-to-auxiliary raising, it has a number of unexpected properties.

First, LVM is blocked by the presence of overt material that is high in the structure, namely by overt non-inverted subjects, sentential adverbs, the question particle *li* and negation (see Rivero 1991 and Bošković 1995). It is not blocked by the presence of lower

[1] Čamdžić (2004) argues that cases like (1c) should be treated on a par with cases of LVM across nonclitics, rather than on a par with cases like (1b); we cannot go into this here, however.

material, such as VP-adverbs. The latter is illustrated in (2). A sentence with an adverbial phrase and auxiliary – participle order is ambiguous: the adverbial can have a VP-modifying reading or a sentence-modifying reading, as illustrated by (2a). But in the participle fronting case in (2b), the adverb can only be a VP-adverb, not a sentential modifier (examples from Bošković 2001).

(2) a. *Ivan je mudro prodao kucu.*
Ivan is wisely sold house
'Ivan sold his house in a wise manner.'
'It was wise of Ivan to sell his house.'

b. *Prodao je mudro kucu.*
sold is wisely house
'He sold his house in a wise manner.'
*'It was wise of him to sell his house.'

Van Riemsdijk (1998) has shown that there is a general condition on head-to-head adjunction, namely that at the moment of application of the rule, the two heads involved must be adjacent (the Head Adjacency Principle, HAP). If any material intervenes between the two heads, the lower one cannot adjoin to the higher one. This means that, if LVM involves participle-to-auxiliary adjunction, we expect that any material in between the source position of the participle and the position of the auxiliary should block it, whereas any material that is higher than the base position of the auxiliary should be compatible with it. The data indicate exactly the reverse, however: the blocking elements (question particle *li*, negation, subjects, sentential adverbs) arguably all occur above T (the base position of the auxiliary), whereas non-blocking VP-adverbs occur in between V and T.

Second, V-to-V adjunction is typical of OV-languages (cf. Bobaljik 2004), so its occurrence in VO Serbo-Croatian is unexpected. Related to this is the question what triggers the process. Verb Raising in the Germanic OV languages is not optional, whereas LVM is. (It is obligatory to have an element in front of the second position clitic, but this need not be the participle).

Finally, if LVM is participle-to-auxiliary raising, the order of the verbs in (1c) can only be derived by having both participles adjoin on opposite sides of the highest verb; this means that the lower participle skips the trace of the intermediate one, instead of adjoining to it, a form of long head movement. Although skipping a trace might not violate the Head Movement Constraint, this option is not attested in the word orders in Germanic verb clusters.We will not go into the pros and cons of the solutions to these problems that Bošković proposes. Instead, we will argue that a shift in perspective on the adjunction process makes the problems disappear.

3. LF complex predicate formation

The previous analyses share one assumption: the participle undergoes some form of raising. Either it substitutes in C (long head movement) or it adjoins to the auxiliary (verb raising). We will argue that a straightforward account of the data is possible if it assumed that the participle is merged directly as the highest head in the structure, above the auxiliary. The auxiliary is merged as the head of the verbal projection containing the arguments and adjoins to the participle at or before LF. The participle does not raise to the auxiliary; rather, it the auxiliary raises to the participle:

(3)

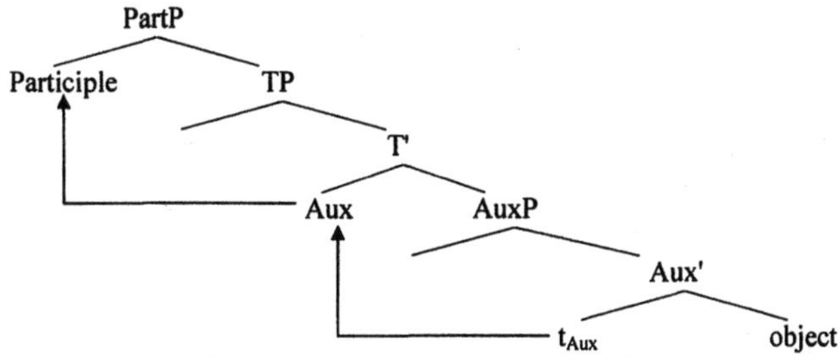

Of course, if the 'classic' view of theta theory is correct, then a structure with inverse merger of main verb and auxiliary as in (3) should be impossible. In GB theory, for example, the dedicated level at which the thematic structure of a predicate is expressed is D-structure, that is, the structure that results from the merger of all elements before any movement applies. The Projection Principle, which holds that the Theta Criterion must be satisfied at all levels of representation, then ensures that movement can never feed or bleed thematic relations (cf. Chomsky 1981).

If the Theta Criterion were indeed to apply to the underlying representation in (3) already, things would obviously go wrong. The auxiliary does not have thematic properties of its own, being a functional rather than a lexical verb. It can therefore not license the arguments in its projection in (3). Neither can the main verb license these, since this would have to involve downward θ-role assignment into the lower phrase, which is impossible. A general restriction on all instances of θ-role assignment is that the argument must c-command the predicate (see Williams 1980 and subsequent work).

However, as Chomsky (1995) observes, the assumption that there is a level like D-structure, the specific role of which is to fully express all thematic relations and nothing else, is superfluous at best. Restrictions on possible syntactic derivations or representations should follow from constraints imposed by the interfaces between syntax and other modules with which it interacts. The interface that is relevant for our concerns is the one between syntax and the conceptual-intentional module, Logical Form (LF). Given that thematic relations must be visible in the conceptual module, it is at this interface level that the Theta Criterion must hold. There is no reason to assume, however, that the Theta Criterion holds throughout the derivation leading to LF. Consequently, it is in principle possible that movement feeds thematic relations. As long as the Theta Criterion is satisfied at LF, the structure will be syntactically well-formed. It has in fact been argued by several authors that a proper account of certain constructions must involve movement that feeds a thematic relation (Neeleman 1997, Bošković & Takahashi 1998, Saito & Hoshi 2000, Fanselow 2002). To illustrate why this is necessary we will discuss two examples, which will turn out to be illustrative for the SC participle fronting case as well.

Consider first PP-complements. The question is how thematic relations are established in phrases containing such a complement, like (4).

(4) *John can always count on his sister.*

The problem is that the θ-role that the complement of the preposition receives is not a θ-role of this preposition. There is no thematic relation between *his sister* and *on* in (29a), as there is in for example *I put the vase on the table*. Rather, the thematic role *his sister* gets appears to be a role of the entire complex *count on*. Nevertheless, the surface structure of examples like these is such that there is a PP-constituent that is independent of the verb. This is indicated by the fact that the PP can, for example, be fronted as a unit:

(5) *On his brother John can never count.*

The problem is very similar to the one posed by (3). The argument is in a phrase headed by an element that does not θ-mark it. But the head of the complex that does θ-mark the argument is too high in the structure, so that cannot θ-mark it (downwards) either.

Neeleman (1997) argues that having the Theta Criterion apply only at LF solves this puzzle. At (or before) LF, the preposition incorporates into the verb, resulting in the two forming a complex predicate. The result of complex predicate formation is that the internal θ-role in the argument structure of the preposition is equated with the internal θ-role in the argument structure of the verb (on a-structure merger in complex predicates, see Grimshaw & Mester 1988, Rosen 1990, and others). Because traces inherit all properties from their antecedents, this means that the trace of P can now assign a θ-role to its complement that is equal to the internal θ-role of the V-P complex predicate.

Another construction that has been argued to involve arguments that are not merged in the immediate projection of the head that thematically licenses them is so-called remnant VP-movement in Germanic languages. The argument is made by Fanselow (2001, 2002). Remnant VP topicalisation involves fronting of the main verb plus one or more parts of its VP, while other elements belonging to this VP are stranded, as in (6).

(6) *Peter gegeben hättest du das Buch nicht dürfen.* (Fanselow 2001:420)
Peter given had you that book not may
'You should not have given the book to Peter.'

Fronting of a nonconstituent is not allowable, but neither is fronting two constituents separately, because this would violate the Verb Second constraint on the finite verb in German main clauses. In order to avoid these undesirable options, it has been proposed that (32) is an instance of ordinary VP-topicalisation, with the stranded constituents being moved out of the VP before it is fronted (Den Besten & Webelhuth 1989, Müller 1998):

(7) *$[_{VP}$ Peter t_i gegeben$]_j$ hättest du $[$das Buch$]_i$ nicht t_j dürfen*

The main problem for this analysis is that the movement that is needed to empty the VP of those elements that are stranded after topicalisation is not independently motivated. Usually it is assumed that the operation of scrambling, which can place objects in pre-VP positions in German, accomplishes this. An object like *das Buch* in (7) can indeed be scrambled across the negator *nicht* in a clause without VP-topicalisation as well. However, in contrast to definite DPs, it is usually infelicitous to scramble nonspecific indefinites. Nevertheless, such objects, too, can be stranded by remnant VP-topicalisation without any problems:

(8) *Peter gegeben hättest du ein Buch nicht dürfen.*
Peter given had you a book not may
'You should not have given Peter a book.'

Fanselow notes that, if the arguments need not be merged in the projection of the main verb but can optionally be merged in a projection higher up, namely in the projection of the auxiliary, a simple account of remnant VP-topicalisation is possible that does not invoke scrambling elements out of VP that cannot be scrambled. This is because 'remnant' VP-topicalisation can then be taken to be full VP-topicalisation: the fronted VP includes all the material that is merged in it and does not contain any internal trace. The arguments (or adverbs) that are stranded are merged outside of VP, in the projection of the auxiliary (fig. 9):

(9)

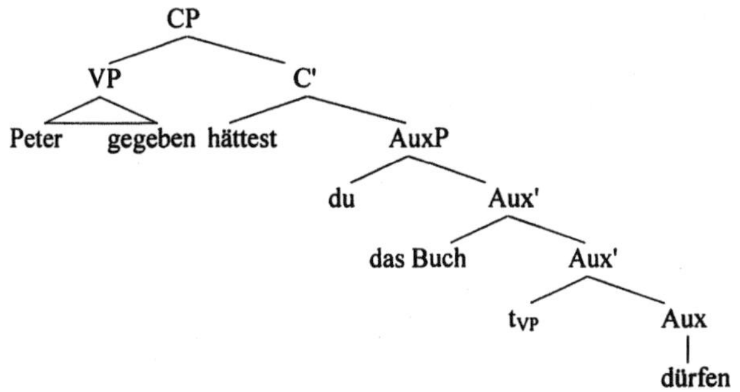

This would be impossible again if the Theta Criterion were to hold throughout a derivation, since the auxiliary does not have the thematic capacities to license arguments on its own. But, as noted by Fanselow, if the Theta Criterion holds at LF only it suffices to form a complex predicate of main verb and auxiliary at or before this level to supply all arguments with their proper θ-role. Complex predicate formation is achieved in this case by the operation of verb raising in Germanic. Fanselow argues that at LF the fronted VP reconstructs to its base position. From this position the participle adjoins to the auxiliary, with the result that the two form a complex predicate, sharing a single argument structure. Any argument in the AuxP projection in (9) can then be assigned a θ-role by this complex predicate. Given that the auxiliary does not have thematic properties of its own, this θ-role will be identical to a θ-role of the participle.

We propose that LVM is another case in which arguments are merged in the projection of the auxiliary rather than in that of the participle, as in Fanselow's analysis. At the same time, because the auxiliary is merged below the participle in this case, it involves another instance in which arguments are merged in a projection below the one of the head that they thematically belong to, as in Neeleman's analysis of PP-complements. Consider the question why a structure is possible with inverse merger of participle and auxiliary, which we claim underlies cases of LVM. This structure can be saved from violating the Theta Criterion by complex predicate formation. At or before LF, the auxiliary adjoins to the participle. As a result of complex predicate formation, the argument structure of the auxiliary is merged with that of the participle. Since the traces of the auxiliary are identical to their antecedent (compare the copy theory of movement), these too will have the relevant thematic properties in the representation in (3) (compare Fanselow's analysis of remnant VP-topicalization, in which it is the participle that raises: both the participle 'upstairs' and its trace 'downstairs' have the same thematic properties – either of them can license arguments). This means that, as a result of complex predicate formation, the arguments in the structure can be thematically licensed at LF by that trace of the auxiliary in the projection of which they appear. Hence, the Theta Criterion, which applies at LF only, is satisfied. We will now show how this analysis of participle fronting in SC provides a good account of the properties of LVM.

4. Deriving the properties of SC participle fronting
4.1 Word order

An analysis as in (3) accounts for the possible and impossible word orders in SC participle fronting cases by straightforward cyclic application of verb raising. No long head movement, not even in the form of skipping traces of intermediate verbs, is necessary. There are two options for verb raising: the lower verb can right-adjoin or left-adjoin to the higher one. Languages show arbitrary variation in this respect. Possible orders inside verb clusters in Germanic vary per dialect, and within a dialect can vary per type of verb, without this being connected to any deeper property of the language (see Wurmbrand 2003). Therefore, let us assume that in principle either option can occur in the SC participle fronting construction.

In case there are only two verbs, the fronted participle and the auxiliary, left-adjunction would lead to a clitic ending up in first position at PF, so that the structure is filtered out there. In this case, therefore, only the right-adjunction option gives a well-formed output. This is different in case there are three verbs, the participle merged on top, and two auxiliaries, the finite clitic auxiliary (Aux1) and the second, participial, auxiliary (Aux2):

(10)

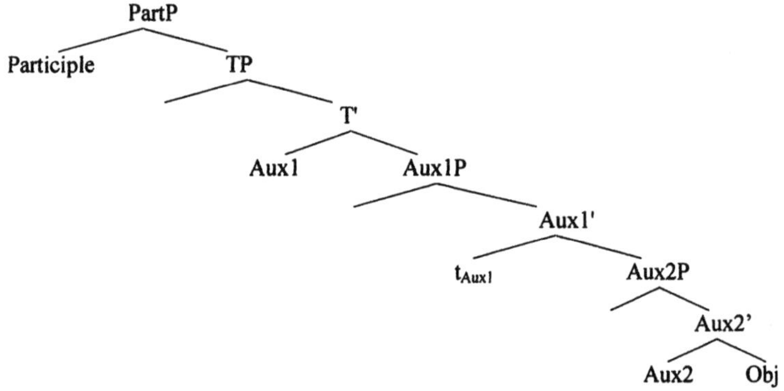

Starting out from (10), verb raising by left-adjunction (left-adjoining Aux2 to Aux1 and then left-adjoining this cluster to Participle) gives the order Aux2-Aux1-Participle, which is instantiated by (1b). Verb raising by right-adjunction gives the order Participle-Aux1-Aux2, which is instantiated by (1c).

Both derivations are strictly cyclic, no separate raising of the lower verb across the position of the intermediate one (whether containing a trace or the intermediate verb itself) is required. Recall that this is a desirable result not only from a conceptual point of view, but also empirically, because the order that would result in Germanic verb clusters from such skipping is one that is not attested. In fact the same holds for SC, at least if the underlying structure is indeed as given in (10). If the two auxiliaries in (10) could move independently and adjoin on opposite sides of the participle in the highest position, we could get orders Aux1-Participle-Aux2 and Aux2-Participle-Aux1, which are impossible:

(11) a. **Je pojeo bio sve gljive.*
is eaten been all mushrooms
'He has eaten all the mushrooms.'

b. **Bio pojeo je sve gljive*
been eaten is all mushrooms

Clearly, (11a) is ruled out anyway because of the second position requirement on the clitic *je*. For (11b), however, this would only be so if the cluster *bio pojeo*, headed by *pojeo*, could not possibly count as first element, which is not clear. We will not go into that here, but we may note that given our analysis this example is ruled out by a general ban against any form of long head movement.

4.2 Intervening elements

As noted in section 2, all head-to-head adjunction is subject to a strict adjacency condition: at the point in the derivation at which head-to-head adjunction is to take place the two heads involved must be strictly linearly adjacent. Any element that intervenes between the two blocks the possibility of adjunction, no matter whether the intervening element is a head or a phrase or whether it is an argument or an adjunct (cf. Van Riemsdijk 1998).

For example, in the case of verb raising in Germanic no PP may intervene between the auxiliary and the verb that raises to it (see Ackema & Neeleman 2002 for discussion). A bare head like a particle may not intervene either (an observation that dates back to Evers 1975). In (12)-(13) a minimal pair is given. If the verb *leren* 'learn' in Dutch takes a verbal complement, then both verb raising of the head of this complement and extrapositon of the entire complement are allowed (see (12a) and (12b) respectively). But in case the matrix verb is the minimally different particle verb *afleren* 'off-learn' (i.e. 'unlearn') only the extraposition option remains (13b), verb raising is impossible now (13a).

(12) a. *dat zij [PRO die liederen t_i] leerde [te zingen]$_i$*
that she those songs learned to sing
'that she learned to sing those songs'

b. *dat zij t_i leerde [PRO die liederen te zingen]$_i$*
that she learned those songs to sing
'idem'

(13) a. **dat zij [PRO die liederen t_i] afleerde te zingen$_i$*
that she those songs off-learned to sing

b. *dat zij t_i afleerde [PRO die liederen te zingen]$_i$*
that she off-learned those songs to sing

It is an interesting question in its own right what causes this adjacency requirement, but not one that is directly relevant for our present concerns. What is relevant here is that verb clustering, as an instance of head-to-head adjunction, is independently known to be constrained by this adjacency condition as well.

Given this, our analysis accounts for why elements that are high in the structure are incompatible with participle fronting, whereas elements that are lower in the structure are not. If the participle raised from its base position to the auxiliary in T, anything in between V and T should block cluster formation, whereas anything above T would not be in the way. But if the participle is merged on top and it is the auxiliary that raises from T to the participle, then anything in between T and the highest head position should block cluster formation, whereas anything below T does not intervene and may be present. As discussed in section 2, the latter prediction is the correct one. Blocking elements include the question particle *li*, negation, sentential adverbs, and (nonfocused) subjects. These arguably occur at or above the TP-level in the left periphery of the clause, that is, in between the participle and the auxiliary. Nonblocking elements include VP-adverbs and, interestingly, focused subjects. Schematically, we can represent this state of affairs as follows:

(14) [$_{\text{PartP}}$ Participle (**li*) [$_{\text{TP}}$ (*Adv) [$_{\text{TP}}$ (*Subject) T-Aux [$_{\text{VP}}$ (√Adv) [$_{\text{VP}}$ ...]] (√Focus)]]]

With respect to the possibility of having a focused subject in cases of participle fronting, the crucial observation is that the adjacency restriction on head-to-head adjunction involves *linear* adjacency. Now, in many languages focused constituents appear in syntactic positions in which their nonfocused counterparts do not appear. Positions at the edge of the clause are particularly popular for focused elements, either at the left edge (in Basque, Hungarian, ...) or at the right edge (in Italian, English, ...). Indeed, SC is another language in which word order correlates with focus structure. Relevant here is that narrowly focused subjects can occur on the right edge of the clause (see Godjevac 2000), so in VOS or OVS orders. No matter how a focused subject ends up there (by moving it rightward into the focus position or by moving everything else leftward out of the focus position), i.e. no matter what its hierarchical position, it is clear that in this right-peripheral position it does not linearly intervene between the auxiliary and participle in the left periphery. Hence, in contrast to nonfocused subjects, it does not block verb clustering.

As a final point, it should be noted again that neither head movement by substitution nor phrasal movement is subject to a linear adjacency requirement between source and goal positions. This means that in the absence of participle fronting, so with Aux ...Participle orders, the auxiliary can substitute into higher heads without problems. No element will block substitution of the auxiliary into C for instance (cf. Bošković 1995), just as no intervening heads or phrases block verb second in a language like Dutch. Note also that the auxiliary and the participle themselves need not be adjacent in Aux...Part orders, since no verb clustering takes place in this case (see section 4.2 below). Indeed, sentential adverbs as well as VP-adverbs can freely intervene in this case:

(15) *Ivan je mudro prodao kucu.*
Ivan is wisely sold house
'Ivan sold his house in a wise manner.'
'It was wise of Ivan to sell his house.'

Similarly, if the participle ends up in the left periphery of the clause because it is taken along under an instance of phrasal movement such as VP-topicalization, no blocking effects are to be expected. Indeed, VP-topicalization differs from participle fronting in being able to cross structurally high elements like negation.

4.3 A trigger for restructuring

Our analysis follows the basic insight of Bošković that SC participle fronting involves verb clustering (V-to-V adjunction) rather than substitution or phrasal movement. However, in section 2 we put forward as a problem for this type of analysis the fact that the trigger for verb raising is unclear. Why should the participle adjoin to the auxiliary? It was noted furthermore that this problem is not just another instance of the question what causes verb clustering in general, but is more serious. This is because verb clustering is not expected to occur in SC at all, given that, as far as the evidence outside SC goes, it appears that verb clustering is restricted to OV-languages and does not occur in VO-languages (cf. Bobaljik 2004).

Indeed, it can be observed that in the regular case there is no verb cluster formation in SC. In Aux...Participle orders, so when there is no participle fronting, material can intervene between the auxiliary and the participle. This can be shown by an example like (16), with an adverb intervening between auxiliary and participle.

(16) Sentential adverb - Aux - VP-adverb - Participle

Mudro bjese brzo prodao kucu.
wisely be-past quickly sold house
'It was wise of him to have sold the house quickly.'

Bošković (1995) does argue that, in cases with three verbs, nothing can intervene between the two lowest ones (the participial ones), which he takes to be an indication that the lowest verb adjoins to the intermediate one. Bošković provides the following paradigm as evidence for this adjacency restriction, hence for verb clustering (his (22) and (23)):

(17) a. *Vas dvoje ste bili čekali Marijinu prijateljicu.*
you two are been waited Marija's friend
'You two had been waiting for Marija's friend'

b. *Vas dvoje ste Marijinu prijateljicu bili čekali.*
you two are Marija's friend been waited

c. * *Vas dvoje ste bili Marijinu prijateljicu čekali.*
you two are been Marija's friend waited

d. * *Marijinu prijateljicu ste bili vas dvoje čekali.*
Marija's friend are been you two waited

However, before it can be concluded that there is a strict adjacency requirement on the two participles, we must first consider what kind of elements we would expect to occur in between them in the first place. In (17b,c) the object that we see in its base position in (17a) is shifted leftward. This is presumably an instance of focus shifting, since the order in (17b) goes together with narrow focus on the object. Taken together, what (17b,c) show then is that the focus fronting must move a constituent to the left edge of the participles' projection. This is not surprising, since it is a general property of focus shifting that it targets particular edges of phrases (cf. Godjevac 2000). In (17d) it is the subject that intervenes between the two participles. What this shows is that a participle cannot be moved into the TP domain, to a position higher than the subject, which is also not really surprising.

What we would expect to possibly occur in between the two participles are modifying adverbials like the VP-adverb that intervenes between auxiliary and participle in (16). As it turns out, there is no problem with having these intervene between the participles:

(18) a. *Ivan je bio brzo prodao kuću.*
Ivan is been quickly sold house
'Ivan has quickly sold the house.'

b. *Ivan je bio loše popravio radio.*
Ivan is been badly repaired the radio
'Ivan has repaired the radio badly.'

Apparently, then, there is a connection between participle fronting and verb clustering in SC: the latter obligatorily occurs if the former occurs, but is absent otherwise.

This is directly accounted for by the analysis put forward above. There is a very clear trigger for clustering if participle fronting consists of merging the participle above the auxiliary, in the form of the Theta Criterion (whatever shape that takes). As explained in section 3, if the auxiliary did not form a complex predicate with the participle (by either adjunction or reanalysis), the arguments in the structure would fail to be thematically licensed. This is not so if the regular order of merger is followed, and consequently clustering is not required in that case, and is not expected to occur then in the VO language SC.

Interestingly, if our analysis is correct SC participle fronting in fact constitutes an OV-niche in an otherwise VO language, at least linearly speaking (not hierarchically). So if the precondition for verb clustering is that the verbs have to start out from a linear OV order (i.e. Participle-Aux order), SC complies with this general condition, even though the trigger for verb raising is different from whatever it is in languages that have verb raising more generally. As it is still an open question what causes the apparent connection between verb raising and OV order, it is also an open question whether purely linear OV order is the proper precondition for clustering.

As a potential problem for invoking the Theta Criterion as the trigger for verb clustering one may point to the fact that participle fronting is possible in clauses without any arguments as well. This potential objection is mostly voided if it is not just the presence of arguments in a projection that is dependent on there being a lexically contentful predicate as head, but the presence of modifiers as well, which seems plausible enough. In other words, the notion of licensing can be generalized from thematic licensing of arguments, used above, to licensing of other dependents of the verb as well (cf. Travis 1988). Hence, in the presence of modifiers, too, the head of the projection must acquire lexical content, which is achieved by raising the auxiliary to the participle and complex predicate formation.

5. Conclusion

We have argued that the properties of LVM constructions in Serbo-Croatian follow in straightforward fashion is the participle is in fact merged as the highest head in the structure, above the auxiliary. Such ' inverse merger' is only allowed if at LF the auxiliary adjoins to the participle, thus forming a complex predicate with it. It is this process of auxiliary-to-participle adjunction that accounted for the observed properties of the construction.

Of course, although complex predicate formation at LF makes inverse merger of main verb and auxiliary technically feasible in principle, it does not explain why it seems to be a rare process, cross-linguistically speaking. Across languages, participle fronting of the Serbo-Croatian type does not appear to occur as freely as 'regular' merger of the auxiliary above the participle. The question why this should be so is discussed in Ackema & Camdzic 2003, which gives a fuller expose of the account proposed above. There, we argue that the occurrence of inverse merger in SC is related to the fact that participles are specified for subject agreement (see also Broekhuis & Migdalski 2003).

References

Ackema, Peter & Amela Čamdžić (2003) LF Complex Predicate Formation: The case of participle fronting in Serbo-Croatian. *UCL Working Papers in Linguistics* 15, 131-175.
Ackema, Peter and Ad Neeleman (2002). Effects of Short-term Storage in Processing Rightward Movement. In: S. Nooteboom, F. Weerman and F. Wijnen (eds.), *Storage and Computation in the Language Faculty*, 219-256. Dordrecht: Kluwer.
Besten, Hans den and Gert Webelhuth (1987). Remnant Topicalisation and the Constituent Structure of VP. *GLOW Newsletter* 1, 15-16.
Bobaljik, Jonathan (2004). Clustering Theories. In: K. É. Kiss and H. van Riemsdijk (eds.), *Verb Clusters: A Study of Hungarian, German and Dutch*, 121-145. Amsterdam: John Benjamins.
Bošković, Željko (1995). Participle Movement and Second Position Cliticization in Serbo-Croatian. *Lingua* 96, 245-266.
Bošković, Željko (2001). *On the Nature of the Syntax-Phonology Interface*. Amsterdam: North-Holland.
Bošković, Željko and Daiko Takahashi (1998). Scrambling and Last Resort. *Linguistic Inquiry* 29, 347-366.
Broekhuis, Hans and Krzysztof Migdalski (2003). Participle Fronting in Bulgarian as XP-Movement. In: L. Cornips and P. Fikkert (eds.), *Linguistics in the Netherlands 2003*, 1-12. Amsterdam: John Benjamins.
Čamdžić, Amela (2004) *On the syntax of Long Verb Movement*. PhD dissertation, UCL.
Chomsky, Noam (1981). *Lectures on Government and Binding*. Dordrecht: Foris.
Chomsky, Noam (1995). *The Minimalist Program*. Cambridge, Mass.: MIT Press.

Evers, Arnold (1975). *The Transformational Cycle in Dutch and German*. Ph.D. dissertation, Utrecht University.
Fanselow, Gisbert (2001). Θ-roles and Free Consituent Order. *Linguistic Inquiry* 32, 405-437.
Fanselow, Gisbert (2002). Against Remnant VP Movement In: A. Alexiadou, E. Anagnostopoulou, S. Barbiers, H.-M. Gärtner (eds.) *Dimensions of Movement*, 91-125. Amsterdam: John Benjamins.
Godjevac, Svetlana (2000). *Intonation, Word Order and Focus Projection in Serbo-Croatian*. Ph.D. dissertation, Ohio State University.
Grimshaw, Jane and Armin Mester (1988). Light Verbs and θ-marking. *Linguistic Inquiry* 19, 205-232.
Müller, Gereon (1998). *Incomplete Category Fronting*. Dordrecht: Kluwer.
Neeleman, Ad (1997). PP-complements. *Natural Language and Linguistic Theory* 15, 89-137.
Riemsdijk, Henk van (1998). Head Movement and Adjacency. *Natural Language and Linguistic Theory* 16, 633-678.
Rivero, Maria-Luisa (1991). Long Head Movement and Negation: Serbo-Croatian vs. Slovak and Czech. *The Linguistic Review* 8, 319-351.
Roberts, Ian (1993). *Verbs and Diachronic Syntax*. Dordrecht: Kluwer.
Rosen, Sara (1990). *Complex Predicates*. New York: Garland.
Saito, Mamoru and Hiroto Hoshi (2000). The Japanese Light Verb Construction and the Minimalist Program. In: R. Martin, D. Michaels and J. Uriagereka (eds.), *Step by Step*, 261-295. Cambridge, Mass.: MIT Press
Travis, Lisa (1988) The Syntax of Adverbs. *McGill Working Papers in Linguistics: Special Issue in Germanic Syntax*, 280-310.
Wurmbrand, Susi (2004). Verb Clusters, Verb Raising and Restructuring. In: M. Everaert and H. van Riemsdijk (eds.), *The Blackwell Companion to Syntax* vol. 5, 227-341. Oxford: Basil Blackwell.

Corresponding author:
Peter Ackema, University of Edinburgh, Department of Linguistics and English Language, 40 George Square (Adam Ferguson Building), Edinburgh EH8 9LL, UK.
packema@ling.ed.ac.uk

Bojan Belić, Columbus (Ohio)

Minor Paucal in Serbian

1. Phenomenon

This analysis deals with the phenomenon of grammatical number[1] in Serbian[2] noun phrases following numerals *dva/dve* 'two.MASCULINE,NEUTER/FEMININE,' *tri* 'three,' *četiri* 'four,' and *oba/obe* 'both.MASCULINE,NEUTER/FEMININE,' [3] as demonstrated in (1) below.

(1) *Noun Phrases after 2, 3, and 4*

a. *Masculine*

Dva/Tri/Četiri	visoka	muškarca	su	bila	na	koncertu.
two/three/four	tall.PA[4]	man.PA	are	were	on	concert

'Two/Three/Four men were at the concert.'

b. *Feminine*

Dve/Tri/Četiri	lepe	žene	su	bile	ovde.
two/three/four	beautiful.PA	woman.PA	are	were	here

'Two/Three/Four beautiful women were here.'

c. *Feminine*

Dve/Tri/Četiri	prave	ljubavi	su	bile	iskrene.
two/three/four	real.PA	love.PA	are	were	honest

'Two/Three/Four real loves were honest.'

d. *Neuter*

Dva/Tri/Četiri	velika	ogledala	su	bila	tu.
two/three/four	big.PA	mirror.PA	are	were	there

'Two/Three/Four big mirrors were there.'

e. *Neuter*

Dva/Tri/Četiri	mala	jajeta	su	bila	zelena.
two/three/four	small.PA	egg.PA	are	were	green

'Two/Three/Four small eggs were green.'

It is proposed that these noun phrases are in neither the singular nor plural, but rather – the paucal. Consequently, it is claimed that, first, the grammatical category of number in the contemporary Serbian language is synchronically composed of *singular*, *plural*, and *paucal*, and, second, that the *paucal* is a *minor number*, therefore different from the *singular* and *plural*.

---

[1] In this analysis, *grammatical number* always refers to nominal number only.

[2] Serbian is here understood as the official language of Serbia and Montenegro; it used to be referred to as the Eastern variant of Serbo-Croatian.

[3] In this analysis, *both* is treated as a numeral, for it displays exactly the same behavior as *two*, with regard to the phenomenon under question. For convenience, therefore, it is not included in the examples.

[4] The following abbreviations are used in the analysis: PA – paucal, SG – singular, PL – plural, SGG – genitive singular, NP – noun phrase.

2. Observation

Serbian grammatical number is clearly expressed in the morphology and syntax of the language. That is to say, all three number values – singular, paucal, and plural – are differentiated one from the other, both morphologically and syntactically. The following two subsections in this analysis focus on the morphological and syntactic expression of the paucal only, for this is the newly proposed number value, and it is its position in the overall system of Serbian grammatical number that is to be demonstrated.

2.1. Morphological Expression of Serbian Paucal

The present analysis claims that the singular, paucal, and plural in Serbian constitute three different values in the system of grammatical number. Indeed, a noun phrase assumes different morphology – in one and the same environment – depending on whether it is in the singular, paucal, or plural. The same five noun phrases from (1a-e) above are now observed in all three different values, but in the same environment – as subjects of sentences.

In (2) below, a masculine noun phrase is given.

(2) *Masculine NP in SG, PA, and PL*

a. Visok muškarac je bio na koncertu.
tall.SG man.SG is was on concert
'A tall man was at the concert.'

b. Dva/Tri/Četiri visoka muškarca su bila na koncertu.
two/three/four tall.PA man.PA are were on concert
'Two/Three/Four tall men were at the concert.'

c. Visoki muškarci su bili na koncertu.
tall.PL man.PL are were on concert
'Tall men were at the concert.'

It is clear that there is no similarity whatsoever among the three different morphological occurrences of the phrase *tall man*.

Now, two different feminine noun phrases are presented:

(3) *Feminine NPs in SG, PA, and PL*

a. Lepa žena je bila ovde.
beautiful.SG woman.SG is was here
'A beautiful woman was here.'

b. Dve/Tri/Četiri lepe žene su bile ovde.
two/three/four beautiful.PA woman.PA are were here
'Two/Three/Four beautiful women were here.'

c. Lepe žene su bile ovde.
beautiful.PL woman.PL are were here
'Beautiful women were here.'

d. Prava ljubav je bila iskrena.
real.SG love.SG is was honest
'A real love was honest.'

e. Dve/Tri/Četiri prave ljubavi su bile iskrene.
two/three/four real.PA love.PA are were honest
'Two/Three/Four real loves were honest.'

f. Prave ljubavi su bile iskrene.
real.PL love.PL are were honest
'Real loves were honest.'

With both a feminine noun phrase with the head noun ending in *a* (3a-c) in the nominative singular, and a feminine noun phrase with the head noun ending in a consonant (3d-f) in the nominative singular, the observation is the same: the morphology of the paucal and the nominative plural is the same; the singular stands apart.

Finally, the neuter noun phrases:

(4) *Neuter NPs in SG, PA, and PL*

a. Veliko ogledalo je bilo tu.
big.SG mirror.SG is was there
'A big mirror was there.'

b. Dva/Tri/Četiri velika ogledala su bila tu.
two/three/four big.PA mirror.PA are were there
'Two/Three/Four big mirrors were there.'

c. Velika ogledala su bila tu.
big.PL mirror.PL are were there
'Big mirrors were there.'

d. Malo jaje je bilo zeleno.
small.SG egg.SG is was green
'A small egg was green.'

e. Dva/Tri/Četiri mala jajeta su bila zelena.
two/three/four small.PA egg.PA are were green
'Two/Three/Four small eggs were green.'

f. Mala jaja su bila zelena.
small.PL egg.PL are were green
'Small eggs were green.'

Clearly, for certain neuter noun phrases (4a-c), both the paucal and the nominative plural are expressed morphologically in the same way; the singular is different. This is the same observation as the one made for feminine noun phrases. On the other hand, for certain other neuter noun phrases (4d-f), all three different number values are differently expressed in the morphology, just as it is the case with masculine noun phrases.

The present analysis also claims that the paucal is morphologically distinct from the genitive singular. Although some earlier accounts (Brabec et al. 1968, and Ivić et al. 1991) of the phenomenon under question, indeed, considered it a curious form, to say the least, they regarded it as the dual (what is here referred to as the paucal). Their explanation, however, essentially read that the dual is the same as the genitive singular. Without going into any discussion about why the term *dual* was used, it has now been demonstrated that, although there might be some apparent morphological similarities between the paucal and the genitive singular, the two forms are quite different. In (5) below, for the same five noun phrases from (1a-e) above, forms of the paucal and the genitive singular are compared.

(5) *PA vs. SGG*

a.	visoka muškarca tall.PA man.PA	visokog muškarca tall.SGG man.SGG
b.	lepe žene beautiful.PA woman.PA	lepe žene beautiful.SGG woman.SGG
c.	prave ljubavi real.PA love.PA	prave ljubavi real.SGG love.SGG
d.	velika ogledala big.PA mirror.PA	velikog ogledala big.SGG mirror.SGG
e.	mala jajeta small.PA egg.PA	malog jajeta small.SGG egg.SGG

It is only in feminine noun phrases (5b and c) that the paucal and the genitive singular are expressed morphologically in the same fashion. For at least feminine noun phrases with the head noun ending in *a* (5b) in the nominative singular, the paucal nominal ending *e* differs from the genitive singular nominal ending *e*, in that the paucal *e* is short, while the genitive singular *e* is long. Therefore, the only place where the morphological sameness between the paucal and the genitive singular actually exists is in feminine noun phrases with the head noun ending in a consonant in the nominative singular.

All of the observations regarding the morphological expression of grammatical number in Serbian made thus far are now summarized in the following chart:

(6) *Chart of Morphological Expression of Number*

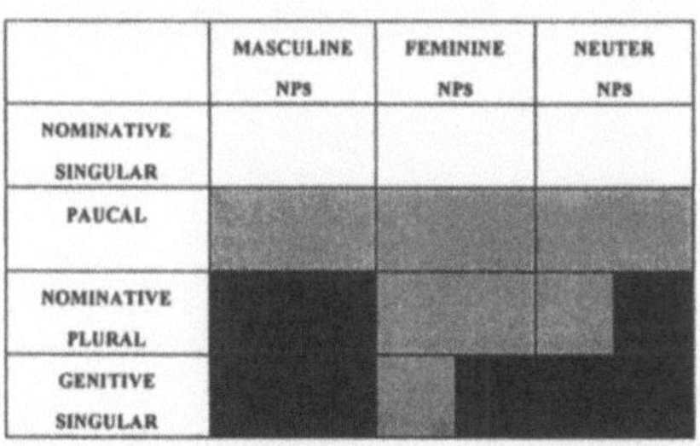

Different shades in the chart represent different morphological expressions of number within a particular gender (that is to say, similarities of shades across all three genders do not imply that the morphological expression is the same across genders, for it, indeed, is not).

Based on the observations and the chart, it is suggested that, when it comes to the morphological expression of grammatical number in Serbian, the differences among the three number values are greater than the similarities among them. It is therefore proposed that, instead of searching for any kind of syncretism between the phenomenon in question, on the one hand, and the nominative plural or genitive singular, on the other, a third number value be adopted, namely the paucal. The paucal is morphologically expressed as follows:

(7) *Morphological Expression of the Serbian Paucal*

Add appropriate suffixes to the singular stem:

a. *-a* to the head and all the constituents agreeing with the head of a masculine noun phrase;

b. *-e* (*-i* for feminine nouns ending in consonants) to the head and all the constituents agreeing with the head of a feminine noun phrase;

c. *-a* to the head and all the constituents agreeing with the head of a neuter noun phrase.

2.2. Syntactic Expression of Serbian Paucal

The paucal in Serbian is distinctly marked in the syntax as well. This is clear from observations made regarding the agreement patterns in sentences containing subject noun phrases in the paucal.

It is generally assumed that a singular subject noun phrase triggers singular predicate agreement, and a plural subject noun phrase triggers plural predicate agreement. A paucal subject noun phrase may trigger either plural or singular predicate agreement. The last statement is exemplified in (8) below in a sample of three noun phrases from (1a, b, and d) above.

(8) *PA NPs Agreement Patterns*

a.

Dva/Tri/Četiri	visoka	muškarca	su	bila	na	koncertu.
two/three/four	tall.PA	man.PA	are.PL	were.PL	on	concert

'Two/Three/Four tall men were at the concert.'

b.

Dva/Tri/Četiri	visoka	muškarca	je	bilo	na	koncertu.
two/three/four	tall.PA	man.PA	is.SG	was.SG	on	concert

'Two/Three/Four tall men were at the concert.'

c.

Dve/Tri/Četiri	lepe	žene	su	bile	ovde.
two/three/four	beautiful.PA	woman.PA	are.PL	were.PL	here

'Two/Three/Four beautiful women were here.

d.

Dve/Tri/Četiri	lepe	žene	je	bilo	ovde.
two/three/four	beautiful.PA	woman.PA	is.SG	was.SG	here

'Two/Three/Four beautiful women were here.

e.

Dva/Tri/Četiri	velika	ogledala	su	bila	tu.
two/three/four	big.PA	mirror.PA	are.PL	were.PL	there

'Two/Three/Four dig mirrors were there.'

f.

Dva/Tri/Četiri	velika	ogledala	je	bilo	tu.
two/three/four	big.PA	mirror.PA	is.SG	was.SG	there

'Two/Three/Four big mirrors were there.'

In order for the syntactic expression of the paucal to be observed, a test with native speakers of Serbian was conducted. There were fifteen native speakers involved in this study. All of them had at least a high school diploma, and were in their late twenties and early thirties. The informants were asked to fill in the blanks with the missing predicates, all of which were forms of the past tense of the verb *biti* 'to be.' All of the sentences were of the type given in (8) above.

Results of the test are given here in the following chart:

(9) *Chart of Agreement Patterns*

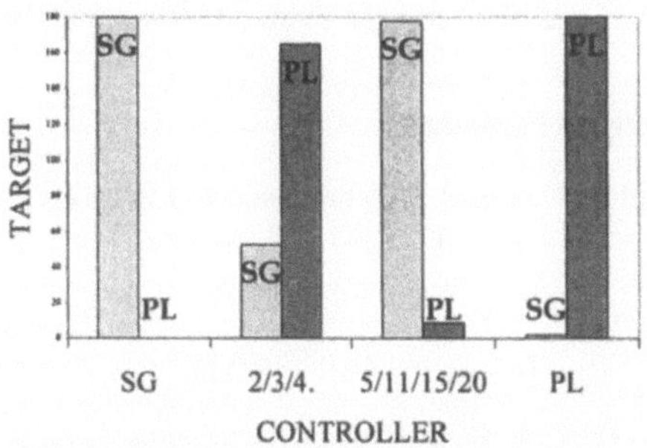

The chart confirms agreement patterns for all three number values in Serbian, while at the same time presenting agreement patterns for subject noun phrases quantified with numerals other than *one*, *two*, *three*, *four*, and *both*, i.e., numerals *five*, *eleven*, *fifteen*, and *twenty*. The most significant observation for the present analysis, however, is that agreement patterns in sentences with paucal subjects sharply differ from agreement patterns in sentences with singular subjects, and clearly are distinct from agreement patterns in sentences with plural subjects[5]. This all leads to the conclusion that the paucal in Serbian is syntactically expressed most frequently by a noun phrase subject in the paucal triggering plural agreement in the predicate, though with the singular as a less preferred possibility. Thus, the paucal is unlike both the singular – where plural agreement is impossible, and the plural – where singular agreement is impossible.

3. Investigation

Corbett (2000:70) arranges all language entities capable of expressing different number values into what he refers to as an *animacy hierarchy*, given here in (10) below.

(10) *Corbett's Animacy Hierarchy*

speaker > addressee > 3rd person > kin > human > animate > inanimate
(1st person pronoun) (2nd person pronoun)

He claims that, "as we move rightwards along the Animacy Hierarchy, the likelihood of number being distinguished will decrease monotonically (that is, with no intervening increase)." This statement implies that there might be cases in which the range of a number value may not involve all the points of the animacy hierarchy, something that Corbett actually demonstrates for languages such as Avar, in which the range of the paucal does not involve

[5] Admittedly, within the predicates chosen semantically for number, i.e., those in the plural, there is yet another – finer – distinction, now based on gender, whereby the choice of the plural gender specific predicate may be made according to syntactic agreement (based on the form of the subject) or semantic agreement (based on the gender of the subject). I do not discuss this question since the present analysis is concerned with number only.

the top segment of the hierarchy, as well as Modern Hebrew and Maltese, in which the range of the dual does not involve the top segment of the hierarchy. The level of involvement of the top segment of the hierarchy is essential in determining the character of the paucal in Serbian as well. More precisely, the question of whether there are separate paucal forms of personal pronouns in Serbian must be addressed in detail.

In the following two subsections of the analysis, first, possible candidates for the paucal forms of personal pronouns are presented and, second, it is demonstrated that those forms cannot be treated as the paucal in the same sense that the forms of other entities of the animacy hierarchy can.

3.1. Personal Pronouns with Respect to the Phenomenon

Serbian personal pronouns are presented in (11) below. Only the nominative forms are given.

(11) *Personal Pronouns in Serbian*

a. *singular*

ja	ti	on	ona	ono
'I'	'you'	'he'	'she'	'it'

b. *plural*

mi	vi	oni	one	ona
'we'	'you'	'they.MASCULINE'	'they.FEMININE'	'they.NEUTER'

Clearly, Serbian personal pronouns distinguish two number values: singular and plural. The possible existence of the paucal number value is never mentioned in connection with this particular part of speech.

As it was demonstrated in the preceding discussion, Serbian paucal is strictly bound in its distribution, namely, it is observed only in noun phrases following numerals *two*, *three*, *four*, and *both*. There is no other environment in which the paucal is found. In order for one to find possible candidates for the paucal of personal pronouns, one must observe them in the same environment in which all other paucal forms are found, as presented in (12) below.

(12) *Personal Pronouns with 2, both, 3, and 4*

a. nas dva~dve/*oba~*obe/tri/četiri
us two.MASCULINE~two.FEMININE/both.MASCULINE~both.FEMININE /three/four
'the two/both/ three/four of us'

b. vas dva~dve/*oba~*obe/tri/četiri
you two.MASCULINE~two.FEMININE/both.MASCULINE~both.FEMININE /three/four
'the two/both/ three/four of you'

c. njih dva~dve/*oba~*obe/tri/četiri
them two.MASCULINE~two.FEMININE/both.MASCULINE~both.FEMININE /three/four
'the two/both/ three/four of them'

The only possible candidates for paucal forms of personal pronouns in Serbian are *nas*, *vas*, and *njih*. Nevertheless, the forms already fail this first test for the paucal. As demonstrated in (12), *nas*, *vas*, and *njih* do not occur in all the paucal environments, namely, they cannot occur in the environment of *both*, unlike the other entities of the animacy hierarchy. The next subsection presents five additional reasons as to why the forms *nas*, *vas*, and *njih* cannot be considered paucal forms of personal pronouns in Serbian.

3.2. Personal Pronouns Have No Paucal

Not only do the forms *nas*, *vas*, and *njih* precede *two*, *three*, and *four*, they also occur in the environment of all other numerals except the numeral *one*.

(13) *Personal Pronouns with Numerals*

nas/vas/njih dva~dve/tri/četiri/pet/šest/sedam/osam/devet/deset
us/you/them two.MASC~two.FEM/three/four/five/six/seven/eight/nine/ten
'the two/three/four/five/six/seven/eight/nine/ten of us/you/them'

In (13) above, numerals *five* through *ten* are used as representatives of all other numerals in Serbian. It is now clear that, unlike other noun phrases, *nas*, *vas*, and *njih* are not strictly bound in distribution because they are not found only in the environment of *two*, *three*, and *four*, which is yet another reason why they are not considered to be paucal.

One other aspect in which *nas*, *vas*, and *njih* are different from other noun phrases after numerals is that they precede rather than follow the numerals. This is apparent in all of the examples in (12) and (13) above. Example (14) demonstrates that *nas*, *vas*, and *njih* cannot be positioned after numerals.

(14) *Personal Pronouns after Numerals*

*dva~dve/tri/četiri/pet/šest/sedam/osam/devet/deset nas/vas/njih
two.MASC~two.FEM/three/four/five/six/seven/eight/nine/ten us/you/them

All of the distributional features cited thus far regarding *nas*, *vas*, and *njih* find parallels in the distributional patterns of Serbian demonstratives *ovaj* 'this.MASCULINE,' *taj* 'that.MASCULINE,' and *onaj* 'that-over-there.MASCULINE:'

(15) *Distribution of Demonstratives*

a. ova/ta/ona dva/tri/četiri muškarca
this/that/that-over-there two/three/four men
'these/those/those-over-there two/three/four men'
*dva/tri/četiri ova/ta/ona muškarca

b. ove/te/one dve/tri/četiri žene
this/that/that-over-there two/three/four women
'these/those/those-over-there two/three/four women'
*dve/tri/četiri ove/te/one žene

c. ova/ta/ona dva/tri/četiri jajeta
this/that/that-over-there two/three/four eggs
'these/those/those-over-there two/three/four eggs'
*dva/tri/četiri ova/ta/ona jajeta

It is clear from (15a-c) above that, just as *nas*, *vas*, and *njih*, demonstratives do not occur with *both*, and they do not follow the numerals, but rather precede them. Moreover, *nas*, *vas*, and *njih*, and demonstratives are mutually incompatible:

(16) *Nas, Vas, and Njih and Demonstratives*

*ova/ta/ona~ove/te/one nas/vas/njih dva~dve/tri/četiri muškarca~žene
*nas/vas/njih ova/ta/ona~ove/te/one dva~dve/tri/četiri muškarca~žene

When it comes to word order in Serbian sentences, *nas*, *vas*, and *njih* again parallel demonstratives – there is no other element (such as *juče* 'yesterday') that can separate them from the numeral that quantifies the phrase (as in 17c, d, g, and h), which shows that they are, indeed, part of that phrase:

(17) *Word Order with Nas, Vas, and Njih and Demonstratives*

a.

Njih	dve	(visoke	žene)	su	pevale	na	koncertu.
them	two	tall	women	are	sang	on	concert

'The two of them (tall women) sang at the concert.'

b.

Ove	dve	(visoke	žene)	su	pevale	na	koncertu.
these	two	tall	women	are	sang	on	concert

'These two (tall women) sang at the concert.'

c.

*Njih	juče	dve	(visoke	žene)	su	pevale
them	yesterday	two	tall	women	are	sang
na	koncertu.					
on	concertu					

'Yesterday, the two of them (tall women) sang at the concert.'

d.

*Ove	juče	dve	(visoke	žene)	su	pevale
these	yesterday	two	tall	women	are	sang
na	koncertu.					
on	concert					

'Yesterday, these two (tall women) sang at the concert.'

e.

Na	koncertu	su	njih	dve	(visoke	žene)	pevale.
on	concert	are	them	two	tall	women	sang

f.

Na	koncertu	su	ove	dve	(visoke	žene)	pevale.
on	concert	are	these	two	tall	women	sang

g.

*Na	koncertu	su	njih	juče	dve	(visoke	žene)	pevale.
on	concert	are	them	yesterday	two	tall	women	sang

h.

*Na	koncertu	su	ove	juče	dve	(visoke	žene)	pevale.
on	concert	are	these	yesterday	two	tall	women	sang

Finally, an encliticization test is applied to *njih* as a representative of the whole class of *nas*, *vas*, and *njih*. Within a sentence, the form is placed in the position (as in 17e and g) in which Serbian personal pronouns always encliticize, unless they are under special emphasis. The results are as follows:

(18) *Encliticization of Njih*

a.

Na	koncertu	su	ih	dve	(visoke	žene)	pevale.
on	concert	are	them.ENCLITIC	two	tall	women	sang

'Out of all people at the concert, two (tall women) sang.'[6]

b.

Na	koncertu	su	ih	juče	dve	(visoke
on	concert	are	them.ENCLITIC	yesterday	two	tall
žene)	pevale.					
women	sang					

'Yesterday, out of all people at the concert, two (tall women) sang.'

Not only does it now appear that *njih*, indeed, behaves as all other Serbian personal pronouns in that it encliticizes to *ih* (18a), but the unacceptable (17g) becomes the acceptable (18b). This is so, however, simply because *ih* in (18a and b) only seems to be the encliticized counterpart of the unencliticized *njih* from (17e and g); it is not a true enclitic of *njih*. This is made absolutely clear after an examination of the sentence in (19) below.

(19) *Enclitic and Non-enclitic*

Na	koncertu	su	ih	njih	dve	(visoke	žene)	pevale.
on	concert	are	them.ENCLITIC	them	two	tall	women	sang

'Yesterday, out of all people at the concert, the two of them (tall women) sang.'[7]

Both the enclitic *ih* and the non-enclitic *njih* occur in (19), a distribution otherwise not permitted, except when the two do not refer to the same entity. This is precisely the case in (19).

This last set of examples (18 and 19) and the encliticization test applied here demonstrate that *njih* (and consequently *nas*, and *vas*) occuring with numerals cannot encliticize when found in the environment in which Serbian personal pronouns regularly encliticize. This is the final reason why these *nas*, *vas*, and *njih* cannot be considered paucal forms of Serbian personal pronouns.

4. Conclusion

In sections 2 and 3, it was respectively demonstrated that there are three grammatical number values in Serbian, and that not all the entities of the animacy hierarchy equally express all three number values. The three values of the grammatical category of number are summarized in (20) below.

(20) *Three Values of Serbian Grammatical Number*

singular paucal plural

The range of each value, however, is not the same. This fact is captured in (21) below.

[6] This was my original reading. Some speakers reported that they do not get this reading whatsoever. Their only reading was 'At the concert, two (tall women) sang them,' where *them* refers to *songs*. Consequently, their reading of (18b) was 'Yesterday at the concert, two (tall women) sang them.' I also get this reading as well. Notice, however, that, whatever the reading, the results that this test presents do not change.

[7] Another possible reading is 'Yesterday at the concert, the two of them (tall women) sang them.' See footnote 6 for explanation.

(21) *Range of Serbian Grammatical Number Values*

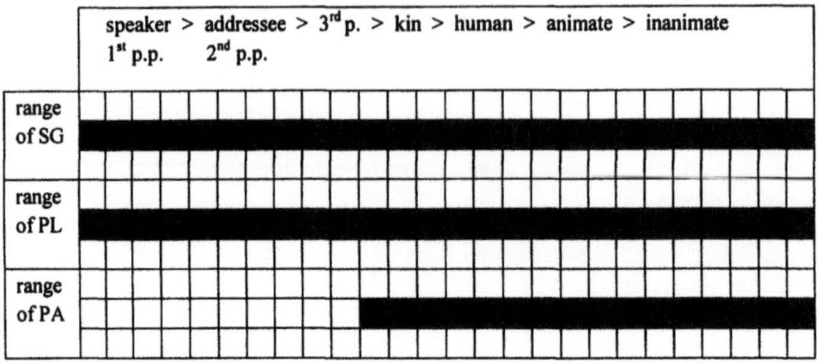

The fact that the range of the paucal does not involve the top segment of the animacy hierarchy, more precisely personal pronouns for the first, second, and third person do not exhibit paucal forms, determines the character of the paucal as clearly distinct from the singular and plural. According to the terminology proposed by Corbett (2000), the paucal in Serbian is a *minor number*[8]. As such, the paucal must be represented in a special manner, different from that in which the singular and plural are represented. Corbett's (2000) theoretical construct, which involves a branching tree of binary choices of number values[9], is adopted here and a representation of the Serbian grammatical number system is formalized:

(22) *Serbian Grammatical Number System*

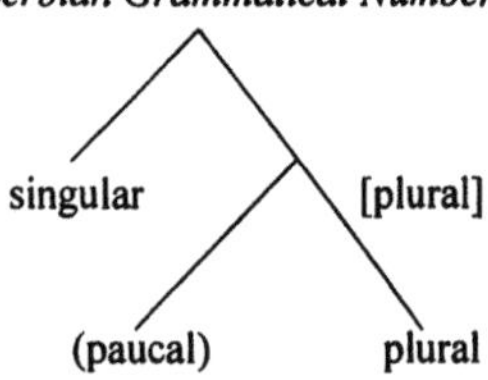

The formalization implies that Serbian grammatical number system differentiates three distinct values, namely *singular*, *plural*, and *paucal*, and at the same time characterizes the paucal as a minor number.

References

Brabec, Ivan, Mate Hraste and Sreten Živković (1968): *Gramatika hrvatskosrpskoga jezika.* Zagreb: Školska knjiga.

Browne, Wayles (1993): "Serbo-Croat". In: Bernard Comrie and Greville G. Corbett (eds.): *The Slavonic languages*. London and New York: Routledge, 306-387.

Corbett, Greville (1983): *Hierarchies, targets and controllers: Agreement patterns in Slavic.* London and Canberra: Croom Helm.

Corbett, Greville (2000): *Number.* Cambridge: Cambridge University Press.

[8] Corbett (2000:95) defines *minor number* as "additional values which involve a relatively small portion of the nominals of a given language."

[9] Corbett (2000:39) explains *branching tree of binary choices of number values* as follows: "[A] language may take any number of the determinate number values ... However, this should be seen as adopting a series of binary choices, and choices in addition to the selection of the plural should be seen as removing a part from the range of the plural and hence dividing the plural."

Corbett, Greville and Richard Hayward (1987): "Gender and number in Bayso". In: *Lingua* 73, 1-28.
Daničić, Đura (1983): *Specimina philologiae Slavicae 50: Mala srpska gramatika*. München: Otto Sagner. (Originally published 1850 as *Oblici srpskoga jezika*).
Ivić, Milka (1989): "Neka zapažanja o broju i rodu u srpskohrvatskom jeziku". In: *Južnoslovenski filolog* 45, 27-44.
Ivić, Pavle, Ivan Klajn, Mitar Pešikan and Branislav Brborić (1991): *Jezički priručnik*. Belgrade: Radio-televizija Beograd, Centar za istraživanje programa i auditorijuma.
Novaković, Stojan (1902): *Srpska gramatika*. Belgrade: Izdanje i štampa državne štamparije.
Sand, Diane Ellen Zubrow (1971): *Agreement of the predicate with quantitative subjects in Serbo-Croatian*. Ph. D. dissertation, University of Pennsylvania.
Stankiewicz, Edward (1983): "The collective and counted plurals of the Slavic nouns". In: Flier, Michael (ed.): *American contributions to the Ninth International Congress of Slavists, Kiev, September 1983*. Columbus: Slavica, 277-293.
Stanojčić, Živojin and Ljubomir Popović (1992): *Gramatika srpskoga jezika*. Belgrade and Novi Sad: Zavod za udžbenike i nastavna sredstva and Zavod za izdavanje udžbenika.
Stevanović, Mihailo (1970): *Savremeni srpskohrvatski jezik: gramatički sistemi i književnojezička norma*, v. 1. Belgrade: Naučna knjiga.

Željko Bošković, Connecticut

A Minimalist Account of Genitive of Quantification[1]

The paper examines one of the thorniest issues of Slavic syntax, namely case and agreement with genitive of quantification (GQ). To account for well-known differences between inherent and structural case in the context of GQ, I will appeal to economy and Θ-theory. Regarding the optionality of agreement with Russian GQ subjects, I will locate its source in the numeral's case properties, which will enable me to keep the categorial status of GQ subjects constant, contrary to the standard analysis, where agreeing and non-agreeing GQ subjects are assumed to differ in their categorial status. I will also explore consequences of the proposed analysis for theories of case and agreement. I first examine case and then turn to agreement.

1. Case

(1)-(2) show what happens when a numeral NP occurs in a structural case context in Russian.

(1) Ivan kupil odnu mašinu.
Ivan bought one(acc) car(acc)

(2) Ivan kupil pjat' mašin.
Ivan bought five cars(gen)

With *one*,both the numeral (Q) and the noun receive case from the verb. However, with higher numerals like *five*, the noun receives genitive, referred to as GQ.[2] This pattern is traditionally interpreted as indicating only higher numerals have the ability to assign GQ. As for inherent case contexts, when a numeral NP occurs as an object of an inherent case assigning V, both the noun and the numeral (*one* as well as higher numerals) bear the inherent case in question.

(3) Ivan vladeet odnoj fabrikoj.
Ivan owns one(instr) factory(instr)

(4) Ivan vladeet pjat'ju fabrikami.
Ivan owns five(instr) factories(instr)

The descriptive generalization is that GQ overrides structural (2), but not inherent case (4). It is well-known that there is a VP/PP parallelism in this respect, accusative assigning Ps patterning with accusative assigning Vs, and non-accusative Ps with non-accusative Vs.

(5) čerez odnu minutu/ pjat' minut
in one(acc) minute(acc)/ five minutes(gen)

(6) o(b) odnoj knige/ pjati knigax
about one(loc) book(loc)/ five(loc) books(loc)

---

[1] I thank S. Franks, S. Stjepanović, and the participants of FDSL 5 and my seminar at the University of Connecticut for helpful comments, L. Grebenyova and A. Stepanov for help with the data, and L. Szucsich for editorial assistance.

[2] *Pjat'* is assumed to be either a syncretic nom/acc or a caseless form, see Franks (1994). For the moment I disregard the issue, returning to it in section 2. Note also that I ignore paucal numerals 2-4, due to the controversy regarding whether they pattern with *one* or *five*. (Compare Babby 1987 and Franks 1994 with Rakhlin 2003. Rakhlin argues that what is standardly analyzed as gen.sg. GQ with 2-4 is actually paucal nom/acc.)

Turning to Serbo-Croatian (SC), SC differs from Russian in an important respect. Numeral NPs in SC pattern with their Russian counterparts in structural case contexts. However, according to Franks (1994), in inherent case contexts, higher numerals still assign GQ in SC, in contrast to Russian. In other words, GQ overrides both structural and inherent case in SC.

(7) Oni kupuju jednu knjigu.
they buy one(acc) book(acc)

(8) Oni kupuju pet knjiga.
they buy five books(gen)

(9) On ide u školu sa jednom knjigom.
he goes to school with one(instr) book(instr)

(10) On ide u školu sa pet knjiga.
he goes to school with five books(gen)

There are many analyses of GQ. For space reasons I will discuss only Franks (1994), which builds on the insights of Babby (1987). Franks takes Slavic morphological case to be a reflex of abstract case. He assumes Chomsky's (1986) theory of the latter, on which structural case is assigned at SS and inherent case at DS, and proposes that GQ is a structural case in Russian and inherent case in SC. In (2), both the V and the Q could assign case to *books* at SS. The Q assigns its case rather than the V because it is closer to *books*.[3] Turning to (4), here the V assigns its inherent instrumental at DS, before the case-assigning ability of the Q is activated. Hence, *factory* bears instrumental. As for SC (10), recall that GQ is an inherent case in SC, i.e. it is assigned at DS. As a result, the Q rather than *sa* assigns case to *books* in (10) (it is closer to *books*). Franks's analysis elegantly captures the above paradigm. However, it faces several theoretical problems. One obvious problem concerns its reliance on DS and SS, given Chomsky's (1995) arguments that these two levels should be eliminated. Another potential problem concerns the assumption that GQ is an inherent case in SC given Chomsky's (1986) position that inherent case is associated with Θ-marking, since the GQ assigning numeral does not Θ-mark the noun. Franks's reliance on the powerful mechanism of case percolation as well as case assignment (see fn. 3) are also problematic in light of the arguments given below for the superiority of case checking over case assignment. On the more empirical side, a serious problem for Franks's analysis is raised by the fact that even in SC, GQ often fails to override inherent case, as shown in (11)-(12), which contain a dative assigning V.

(11) Ivan pomaže jednom čovjeku.
Ivan helps one(dat) man(dat)

(12) * Ivan pomaže pet ljudi.
Ivan helps five people(gen)

In light of these problems I will propose an alternative analysis of GQ. The analysis will still be in line with Franks's position that morphological case reflects abstract Case, which makes Slavic a great tool for studying abstract Case. I will start by presenting the analysis developed in Bošković (UConn class lectures 1996) and then modify one aspect of that analysis.

[3] For details of the analysis, see Franks (1994). Let me just note that assuming case assignment rather than case checking and adopting the concept of case percolation are crucial ingredients of Franks's analysis.

1.1. Economy and Θ-considerations in Russian GQ constructions

It is well-known that *one* in examples like (1) and higher numerals in inherent case contexts like (4) (that is, all non-GQ assigning numerals) are morphologically similar to adjectives, agreeing with the following N in case and ϕ-features (gender and number). To represent this agreement, I adopt one of the traditional analyses of adjectives for such numerals, namely, I assume they are APs located in SpecNP, undergoing spec-head agreement (SHA) with the N.[4]

(13) $[_{NP}$ AP $[_{N'}$ N]]

For GQ assigning numerals, I assume that they project a QP taking NP as their complement, which they case-mark, on a par with case-assigning verbs and prepositions.

(14) $[_{QP}$ $[_{Q'}$ Q NP]]

I furthermore assume that the feature that determines whether a numeral is adjectival or not is not present in the numeration (see Bošković 1997 for an analysis where some elements (more precisely, functional elements) are not present in the numeration).[5] A consequence of the assumption is that since they have the same numeration (and do not cause a truth-conditional difference), structures in (13) and (14) "compete" with respect to economy of derivation. (I appeal here to Chomsky's 1995 assumption that only structures with the same numeration can be evaluated together with respect to economy of derivation.) In my 1996 analysis, I assumed overt movement involves category movement and covert movement feature movement (Move F), following theoretical assumptions of that time. Although I will maintain these assumptions here, it is important to bear in mind that the analysis can be restated in a framework where Agree replaces Move F (see Chomsky 2000). I also adopt Chomsky's (1995) uniqueness of LF hypothesis, which maximizes LF uniformity across languages, as expressed in the following quote from Chomsky (1995:359): "Interpretative operations at the interface should be as similar as possible. The external systems are impoverished so the forms that reach the LF level must be as similar as typological variation permits, unique if at all possible." The hypothesis has an interesting consequence for languages that Chomsky assumes have covert V-to-I movement (i.e. languages that don't have overt V-to-I). Chomsky observes that in a language like Italian, V-to-I movement occurs in overt syntax. The object then undergoes LF Move F to I. He then observes that given the uniqueness of LF hypothesis, languages that have covert V-to-I and LF "object shift"(i.e. accusative case licensing) will first move V to I and then do Move F of the object to I. Consider now consequences of Chomsky's proposal for numeral phrases in structural case contexts, under the assumption that verbs do not move to I in overt syntax in Russian (see Bailyn 1995). Under Chomsky's assumptions, the verb would then move to I covertly in Russian. Applying the uniqueness of LF hypothesis, the object that is to be case licensed by the verb will undergo LF Move F to I after LF verb movement.[6] The non-GQ structure in (13), where the NP is case-licensed by the verb, will then have the derivation in (15) (I will refer to it as the AP derivation). On the other hand, the GQ structure in (14), where the NP is case-licensed by the Q, will have the derivation in (16) (I will refer to it as the QP derivation). Obviously, the case licensing movement of the NP is shorter on the QP derivation than on the AP derivation. I therefore suggest that given economy of derivation, which requires every movement to be as short as possible, the availability of the former blocks

[4] The analysis to be given below can be restated under other analyses of adjectives, including Abney's (1987) A-as-the-head analysis. For a discussion of the structural position of Slavic adjectives, which includes arguments against an Abney-style analysis for Russian and SC, see Bošković (2003).

[5] Call the relevant feature X. The question we are faced with is which element projects when a numeral and a noun are merged. Assuming that only Q numerals have the feature X, the numeral projects iff it bears feature X.

[6] I assume that, as argued in Bošković (1997), even non-finite main verbs undergo head movement at some point, which suffices for the analysis to be presented to be extendable to constructions with non-finite main verbs.

the latter. In other words, the GQ pattern is forced in structural case contexts. (This is also the case if verbs undergo short overt movement in Russian, as in Bailyn 1995. In fact, on this analysis there is no need to appeal to LF V-movement in Russian. Note also that, following Chomsky 1995, I assume that movement cannot target traces.)[7]

(15) $[_{TP}\ V_i + T\ [_{VP}\ t_i\ \ [_{NP}\ AP\ [_{N'}\ N]]$

(16) $[_{QP}\ [_{Q'}\ Q\ NP]]$

The analysis can be extended to GQ within PPs, given that, as Bošković (2004b) and Koopmans (1997) argue, PPs contain additional functional projections, with the P moving to these projections (but see Abels 2003). Case-licensing by a P then requires longer movement than case licensing by a Q, on par with the situation discussed above with respect to V and Q.

Let us now turn to inherent case contexts, where the inherent case "overrides" GQ. Following Chomsky's (1986) approach to inherent case, I assume a verb that assigns inherent case will Θ-mark its object iff it assigns it the inherent case in question. The GQ structure in (14) then cannot converge with inherent case-assigning Vs because the verb will fail to Θ-mark its object. Since economy of derivation compares only convergent derivations (see Chomsky 1995), the fact that the QP derivation requires shorter movement is irrelevant: the only available option is the AP option. This option is therefore forced. The overriding effect of inherent case is thus accounted for.[8] Moreover, this was done without appealing to DS and SS.

1.2. Russian *po*

In this section I discuss the distributor *po*, which will lead me to modify the above analysis. *Po* is a preposition whose complement is distributed over some individuated argument.

(17)	Každyj	učenik	polučil	po	odnomu	rublju.
	each	student	received	distributor	one(dat)	ruble(dat)

Franks argues *po* assigns *structural* dative, which I also assume. With *one*, both the numeral and the N bear dative. As for *five*, both options in (18) are acceptable while (19) is not.[9]

[7] Admittedly, the analysis relies on global economy of derivation (see, however, fn.13). Note also that I assume the choice of case a noun is taking with from the lexicon, accusative or genitive in the case in question (under the checking theory, the noun would enter the computation fully inflected for case, unless we assume Chomsky's 2000 case valuation), does not affect syntactic computation. This is a standardly held assumption, motivated by (i), where Last Resort prevents a pronoun from moving from a case to a case position although the original case position cannot license the case the pronoun is inflected with, and (ii), an instance of superraising where a nominative element is an intervener for accusative Case-licensing movement. (In other words, what matters for syntactic computation is that an NP has case, not which case it has. This is made explicit in Chomsky 2000.)

(i) * He$_i$ seems to t$_i$ Peter is ill.

(ii) * I believed him$_i$ to seem it was told t$_i$ Mary is sleeping.

[8] Note that the strategy pursued here is to enforce Bošković's (1997) inverse case filter for inherent case in an independent way that does not apply to structural case.

[9] *Tysjača* 'thousand' only allows dative in (18) (see Franks 1994). Neidle (1988) notes *tysjača* is ambiguous between a (feminine) N and a *pjat'*-type Q. The Q option is blocked in some cases, as in Corbett's (1979) (i), where the obligatory agreement with *this* suggests the N option is the only possibility. I suggest the same holds for the *po*-construction. (Note that the Q option for *tysjača* is a newer development, see Neidle 1988. It is

(18) po pjat'/pjati rublej
dist. five/five(dat)rubles(gen)

(19) *po pjati rubljam
dist. five(dat) rubles(dat)

On the (somewhat archaic) dative option, *five* gets case from *po*. As for the *pjat'* option, Franks (1994) argues *pjat'* is a caseless form here since no case but dative can be assigned to it in this context. More precisely, being inside a PP, a PP-external case assigner cannot case-license it since outside case licensing relations quite generally cannot penetrate into a PP. On the *pjat'* option, (18) can be analyzed on a par with (2) given that, as discussed above, Ps undergo movement. (Notice also that, according to Heim et al 1991, distributors also move.) The *pjati* option, however, raises an interesting problem. Assuming the same element cannot at the same time assign case and be assigned case, as Stowell (1981) argues,[10] the dative option in (18) provides evidence that the Q does not itself assign GQ. Rather, Franks argues for the structure in (20), where *po* case-marks (in an ECM configuration) *five*, with a null head assigning GQ.

(20) [$_{PoP}$ [$_{Po'}$ Po [$_{QP}$ pjati(dat) [$_{Q'}$ e NP]]]]

Adapting this proposal to the structures adopted in section 1.1. we get the following structures for the AP and the QP option respectively (I refer to the null, GQ assigning head as F for ease of exposition, leaving its precise nature open).

(21) [$_{PoP}$[$_{Po'}$ Po [$_{FP}$ QP [$_{F'}$F NP]]]] QP pattern (i.e. GQ pattern)

(22) [$_{PoP}$ [$_{Po'}$ Po [$_{FP}$ [$_{F'}$ F [$_{NP}$ AP [$_{N'}$ N]]]] AP pattern (i.e. case-agreeing pattern)

On the QP pattern, instantiated by (18), the numeral is located in SpecFP, with F assigning case to the NP. As before, on the AP option, instantiated by (19), the numeral is located in SpecNP, undergoing SHA with the N. For the sake uniformity, I propose FP is always present on both the QP and the AP option.[11] I furthermore propose that, similar to V (V+v for

possible this reanalysis of *tysjača* has not been completed, affecting its availability in the *po*-construction, which is also in flux.)

(i) èta/*èti tysjača soldat
this(fem.sg.)/(pl) thousand soldiers

It is also worth noting that Franks (1995) observes that many speakers disallow the non-agreement, default option, discussed in section 2, with *tysjača* subjects, which, given the discussion in section 2.2., means that for these speakers *tysjača* does not have the caseless Q option from section 2.2. in any context.

[10] In the case-checking approach, such an element would have to be doubly lexically specified for case.

[11] I differ from Franks, who assumes his null Q only for the *po* construction in question. For him, GQ numerals are sometimes specs and sometimes heads. For me, they are uniformly specs (see also Franks and Pereltsvaig in press)

There is another reason (in addition to uniformity) to posit FP not only for all GQ examples, but also for the non-GQ structure in (22). Consider (i), where the predicative NP can be either nominative or instrumental.

(i) Ivan byl durak/durakom.
Ivan was fool(nom)/(instr)
'Ivan was a fool.'

Chomsky 1995), F assigns case to its complement only if it has a specifier. In other words, I am extending the independently needed mechanism responsible for Burzio's generalization to F.[12] The economy account proposed above can be maintained under the structures in (21)-(22). Since case-licensing is more economical on the QP option, the option is preferred in a structural case environment, hence the badness of (19).[13] The option is ruled out in an inherent case environment for Θ-theoretic reasons, as discussed earlier. Note that, as in Franks's analysis, under the current analysis *pjati* is assigned dative by *po*, while *pjat'* is a caseless form in (18). This will become important in section 2, where I argue *pjat'* is ambiguous between a syncretic nom/acc form (which is its standard analysis; note that *pjat'* morphologically fits the paradigm as a nom/acc form) and a caseless form. An important distinction between the current and Franks's analysis in light of the discussion in section 2 is that under the current analysis, the object of *po* has the same categorial status on both the dative and the caseless option in (18). For Franks, the numeral is always in the Spec of a null Q, the QP being dominated by a DP only on the *pjat'* option. Due to the presence of the DP, the numeral is too deeply embedded within the complement of *po* to be Case-licensed by it. On the dative option, the QP is not dominated by a DP, as a result of which the numeral is located in the Spec of the complement of *po*, a familiar ECM configuration. Positing a categorial distinction between the *pjati* and *pjat'* options to account for (18) is actually unnecessary. Franks assumes that *po* only optionally assigns dative, which suffices to account for the two options in (18).

The FP analysis can be readily extended to the VP ((2), (4)) and the PP case ((5)-(6)).[14]

Franks and Pereltsvaig (in press) argue that on the instr. option, the predicate NP is in fact a bare NP, while on the nom. option it contains additional functional structure. Significantly, even the presence of adjectival numerals forces the nom. option, although adjectives are in principle not incompatible with the instr. option. (Higher numerals ending in *one* behave like *one* in that they are adjectival (they also require the following N to be singular). The numeral cannot be naturally used in the context in question. What is important for us is the contrast in (ii)).

(ii) a. Oni byli ?? dvadcat' odin umnyj mal'čik/ * dvadcat' odnim umnym mal'čikom.
they were twenty one(nom) smart(nom.sg) boy(nom.sg)/ twenty one(instr) smart(instr.sg) boy(instr.sg)
'They were twenty-one smart boys.'

b. Oni byli umnye mal'čiki/ umnymi mal'čikami.
they were smart(nom.pl) boys(nom)/ smart(instr.pl) boys(instr)

If Franks and Pereltsvaig's proposal regarding the alternation in (i) is correct, (ii) can be interpreted as indicating that the presence of a numeral forces the presence of a functional projection above NP, which I take to be FP.

[12] We can think of the Fs in (21)-(22) as the active (case-assigning) F (21) and passive/ergative (non-case assigning) F (22) (in work in preparation I extend the FP analysis to adnominal genitive, placing its "assigner" in SpecFP).

[13] We can now eliminate the globality mentioned in fn. 7. If, being a potential case licenser, F always counts as a potential target for movement of the NP, movement to *po* for case licensing would be a dispreferred option even in (22). (No comparison with (21) would be needed. However, failure of proper case licensing/valuation on the shorter derivation in (22) should not take it out of the comparison set).

[14] I assume that an inherent case V has to assign its case to the whole argument, including the N, to be able to Θ-mark it. More precisely, I assume that FP is ignored regarding Θ-role assignment (inherent case as well, given their association) since it is semantically inert. The relevant phrases, then, are those that are immediately dominated by FP (those where the first XP dominating them is FP), i.e. Spec and complement of FP. (This could be instantiated through Θ-feature percolation from these positions to FP.) Note also that assuming Freidin and Babby's (1984) Principle of Lexical Satisfaction, which requires verbs that are lexically specified as assigning inherent case to assign it, instead of Chomsky's (1986) approach to inherent case, which ties together inherent case and Θ-role marking, would not suffice here since under the former (but not under the latter) approach we would incorrectly rule in (i), where the verb assigns instrumental, but not to the whole argument ((ii) is also

Note, however, that adopting the FP analysis makes appealing to V/P movement no longer necessary. Regardless of whether V/P undergo movement, the AP option is less economical than the QP option (i.e. it requires longer movement). The parallelism between *po* constructions and their VP/PP counterparts is in fact complete if we assume that *pjat'* is ambiguous between a caseless form and a syncretic nominative/accusative form. *Pjat'* in (2) and (5) can then be either a caseless form or an accusative form, on a par with the two options in (18).

1.3. Genitive of quantification in Serbo-Croatian

Turning to SC, I suggest that the AP pattern is the only option for *one* (i.e. *one* only has the adjectival form), while the QP option is the only option for higher numerals (i.e. they don't have adjectival forms; in fact, they don't decline, in contrast to As/Ns). The analysis of the structural case context for higher numerals in Russian can be readily extended to SC. As for the inherent case context, there is no acceptable output since the QP option crashes for Θ-theoretic reasons and the AP option is missing in SC. This way, we can easily explain the ungrammaticality of (12).[15] What about prepositions like *sa* 'with', where GQ is assigned? Franks (1994) takes *with* as the basic case, putting aside the *help* case, assuming something special has to be said about it (see Franks in press). My suggestion is to take *help* as the basic case, putting aside the *with* case, assuming something special has to be said about it.[16]

I turn now to a very interesting paradigm concerning *sa*, also discussed in Leko (1986), Franks (1995, in press), and Wechsler and Zlatić (2003), (see Franks's and Wechsler and Zlatić's works for analyses of the paradigm). Consider (23)-(26).

(23) On je ovladao zemljom.
he is conquered country(instr)
'He conquered that country.'

(24) *On je ovladao sa zemljom.
he is conquered with country(instr)

(25) *On je ovladao pet zemalja.
he is conquered five countries(gen)

(26) On je ovladao sa pet zemalja.
he is conquered with five countries(gen)

---

problematic; see also Franks in press).

(i) *Ivan vladeet pjat'ju fabrik.
Ivan owns five(instr) factories(gen)

Note that argumenthood is irrelevant to *po*-constructions like (the dative) (18), since *po* is not a Θ (and inherent case) assigner (see Franks 1994). However, since *po* is not semantically inert it cannot be ignored like FP can (see above). This means that the instrumental case of the V in Babby's (1986) (ii) has to be checked against *po*, which is impossible. (Note that *sa* 'with', discussed in the next section, patterns with *po* in the relevant respect.)

(ii) *Oni vladejut po inostrannym jazykom/ (pjat'ju/pjati) inostrannymi jazykami.
they know dist. foreign(instr) language(instr) five(instr)/five(dat) foreign(instr) languages(instr)

[15] The fact that the relevant input cannot yield an acceptable output may provide an argument against the optimality theory. What we are dealing with here is a case where nothing (i.e. no output of a particular input) is good enough, a situation that raises a potentially serious problem for this theory.

[16] There are several possibilities here (see (28) for one), exploration of which I leave for future research.

Apparently, *sa* can occur in the complement of *conquer* only when the complement contains a higher numeral. Recall now that, being an inherent case assigner, *conquer* must check its instrumental case against its object argument. (25) is ruled out because *conquer* fails to do so. Regarding (24) and (26), I suggest that we are dealing here with last resort *sa*-insertion, which takes place so that *conquer* can check its instrumental case against its object argument. The complement of *conquer* in (26) is a PP, with *conquer* checking its case against the head of its PP complement, namely *sa*. Given that *sa*-insertion is a last resort operation, since there is no need for it in (24) it is not allowed to take place. Alternatively, (24) can be ruled out via case theory: if *conquer* and *sa* check case against each other, the object NP cannot be case-checked. (In other words, the case feature of one of the relevant elements must remain unchecked.) What we have in (26), then, is a situation where a traditional case assigner (a verb) checks case against a traditional case assigner (a preposition). This state of affairs can be easily accommodated under the case checking theory, but not under the case assignment theory.[17] I conclude, therefore, that we have here an argument for the superiority of the case checking theory over the case assignment theory.

Interestingly, Franks (in press) notes *sa*-insertion cannot occur with instrumental adjuncts.

(27) a. Plovio je morem.
sailed is sea(instr)
'He sailed across the sea.'

b. * Plovio je pet mora.
sailed is five seas(gen)

c. *Plovio je sa pet mora.

In work in preparation I argue that we have here evidence that the instrumental in (27a) is not assigned by a null head. If that were the case, (27c) could be analyzed on a par with (26), with *sa* inserted to check the instrumental case of the null head. Rather, I argue that adjunct NPs are not subject to the Case filter, i.e. they are not case-checked like argument NPs (see also Babby 1986). Instead, the function of the instrumental case in (27a), which is not checked/assigned by anything, is to identify the precise semantic role of the adjunct, which *sa* cannot do. On the other hand, due to its semantics, *preko* in (28) can do that. (Its semantics allows *sa* in (10) to perform the same task.)

(28) Plovio je preko pet mora.
sailed is across five seas(gen)

Under this analysis, the inherent case of adjuncts is semantically interpretable, hence not subject to the Case filter: its function is to identify the precise semantic role of the adjunct (different cases identify different semantic roles). SC prepositions can perform the same task. When they function as adjunct semantic role identifiers they are not case checkers; they are essentially interpretable inherent case markers. (I discuss the two usages of SC prepositions in more detail in work in preparation).[18]

[17] Under the former theory, the relationship between the elements involved in a case-licensing relation is inherently symmetrical. The distinction between a case assigner and a case assignee cannot in fact be stated in natural terms without additional stipulations in this theory. On the other hand, in the case assignment theory, the relationship in question is inherently asymmetrical, i.e. unidirectional, with one element (case assigner) essentially transferring its case property to another element (case assignee). Obviously, given the inherent asymmetry in the case assignment process, a case assigner cannot assign case to a case assigner. The problem does not arise in the case checking theory, where there is no distinction between case assigners and case assignees.

[18] Note that paucal numeral constructions show that *mora* in (28) bears GQ, not the regular genitive. (See Franks

To sum up, I have presented an account of GQ which, in contrast to Franks's (1994) analysis, does not require appealing to DS/SS, divorcing inherent case from Θ-role assignment, or adopting case assignment and case percolation. I have also shown that GQ provides empirical evidence for the superiority of case checking over case assignment. Throughout the discussion I have maintained the assumption, also adopted by Franks, that morphological case reflects abstract Case, which makes Slavic, which abounds with case morphology, a perfect tool for exploring Case theory. The fact that we have been able to account for a rather complex paradigm while maintaining the assumption in question provides evidence that the assumption, which also seems inherently more interesting than its alternative (no relation between morphological and abstract case), is on the right track.

2. Agreement

I now turn to agreement in GQ structures, confining myself to contexts where GQ is assigned (the QP option).[19] Franks (1994) notes Russian numeral subjects optionally agree with the verb

(29) Dvadcat' samolëtov pereleteli/pereletelo granicu.
twenty planes(gen) flew-across(pl)/(sg) border

Franks argues that on the singular (sg) option, the subject is a QP and stays in SpecVP, with SpecIP being filled by a null expletive (we are dealing here with a transitive expletive example), while on the plural (pl) option, the subject is a DP and moves to SpecIP.[20] Franks gives a number of arguments for a height distinction between sg and pl subjects (see also Pesetsky 1982 and Neidle 1988). Thus, he shows only pl subjects can bind subject-oriented anaphors (see (31)) and control PRO in constructions like (32)-(33). Furthermore, the Comp-trace effect is operative only with pl subject extraction (34), which follows if the pl subject is extracted from SpecIP and the sg subject from SpecVP (see Koopman and Sportiche 1991).

(30) Pjat' ženščin smotreli/smotrelona Ivana.
five women(gen) looked (pl)/(sg) at Ivan

(31) Pjat' ženščin smotreli/*smotrelo na sebja.
five women(gen) looked (pl)/(sg) at themselves

1994 regarding the distinction. Note that *preko* assigns genitive when it does assign case.)

[19] It is worth noting that Corbett (1979) tried to determine the ϕ-feature status of Russian numerals by considering pronouns referring to numerals. However, his discussion remains inconclusive since he does not rule out the possibility of the pronouns referring to larger phrases containing numerals, e.g.VPs.Thus, this may be a possibility in Corbett's (i), given (ii). (The interfering factor aside, it is actually far from clear what this test shows.)

(i) Ivan s''el vosem' tortov. Èto mnogo.
Ivan ate eight cakes that a-lot

(ii) S''est' vosem' tortov kažetsja mnogo.
to-eat eight cakes seems a-lot

[20] Franks thus assumes only DP subjects move to SpecIP (cf. also Pesetsky 1982). Note that adapting the proposal to the analyses developed here would entail positing a DP above QP in (14) (under the analysis from section 1.1.) or FP in (21) (under the analysis from section 1.2.) only on the agreement/movement to SpecIP option.

(32) PRO vozvraščajas' domoj, pjat' mal'čikov zašli/*zašlo v magazin.
returning home, five boys(gen) dropped-in(pl)/(sg) to store

(33) Pjat' ženščin staralis'/*staralos' PRO kupit' ètu knigu.
five women(gen) tried (pl)/(sg) to-buy this book

(34) Skol'ko čelovek$_i$ Ivan dumaet čto t_i pročitalo/*pročitali ètu knigu?
how-many people(gen) Ivan thinks that read(sg)/(pl) this book

Though most of these tests are not conclusive and/or are based on ill-understood phenomena (the strongest argument seems to be the one involving (34)),[21] there does seem to be an issue to be accounted for here, so I will also assume a height difference between sg and pl subjects.

2.1. Approximative inversion in Russian

Bearing this in mind, I turn now to the Russian approximative inversion construction (AXP), where the NP appears before the GQ assigning numeral and where the sg option is forced.[22]

(35) Studentov pjat' * sdali/sdalo èkzamen.
students five passed(pl)/(sg) exam
'About five students passed the exam.'

To account for (35), Franks (1994) argues AXP involves NP adjunction and stipulates an NP can adjoin to QP, but not to DP. (Recall that for Franks, a sg subject is a QP, and a pl subject a DP, see also fn. 20.) I'd like to propose an alternative analysis that maintains Franks's claim that AXP involves adjunction but eliminates the stipulation in question, allowing AXP adjunction to the maximal projection of a numeral phrase regardless of whether it is a QP or a DP. The account can thus be maintained on the FP analysis from section 1.2., on which all numeral NPs have the same categorial status. It is based on Takahashi's (1994) claim that adjunction to the head of a non-trivial chain is disallowed, since as a result of such adjunction, the head of a chain and copies left by its movement are no longer identical.[23] Takahashi's ban rules out the derivation on which the numeral phrase moves to SpecIP (the agreeing option/ Franks's DP option) and then the NP adjoins to it in (35). The problem doesn't arise on the derivation on which the subject stays in SpecVP (the non-agreeing option/Franks's QP option). What about the derivation on which NP adjoins to the numeral phrase before the latter moves to SpecIP? On this derivation the copies of the subject in SpecVP and SpecIP are identical, so that Takahashi's ban is not violated. However, this derivation is also ruled out if adjunction not only can be acyclic (i.e. late), but in fact must be acyclic, as argued in Stepanov (2001a,b), since AXP adjunction then could not precede movement of its target to SpecIP. The current analysis of agreement in AXP should then be taken as providing additional

[21] The problem with the anaphor test is that we find the same pattern with non-subject oriented anaphors.

(i) Pjat' studentov pomogali/*pomogalo drug drugu.
five students(gen) helped(pl)/(sg) each other

The anaphor in (i) is c-commanded by the matrix subject regardless of whether the latter is located in SpecIP or SpecVP. One way to account for (i) is to adopt Chomsky's (1986) anaphor movement hypothesis, assuming the anaphor undergoes LF movement to the matrix I. As a result, only the pl subject, located in SpecIP, c-commands it. A similar analysis may be applicable to (33) if PRO moves to the matrix I, as argued in Martin (1996).

[22] Franks (1994) notes that, as expected given the discussion in the previous section, AXP subjects cannot bind subject-oriented anaphors and control PRO.

[23] Takahashi demonstrates that the claim has ample empirical motivation. Among other things, he shows that it captures the subject condition effect and, more generally, the impossibility of movement out of moved phrases.

evidence for Stepanov's late adjunction hypothesis.[24] Note also that AXP is possible with objects, which is not surprising given that they need not move.[25]

(36) Ivan kupil knig pjat'.
Ivan bought books(gen) five
'Ivan bought about five books.'

Interestingly, Franks (1995) notes AXP is impossible with inherently case-marked numeral objects and objects containing *one*, which have the AP pattern structure (13)/(22).

(37) a. * Direktor upravljaet fabrikami pjat'ju.
director manages factories(instr)five(instr)
'The director manages about five factories.'

b. * Oni privezli tonnu odnu.
They brought ton(acc) one(acc)
'They brought about one ton.'

I suggest (37) should be related to the fact that AXP is impossible with (non-postposed) adjectives, as Yadroff and Billing's (1998) (38) shows (see this work for relevant discussion).

(38) * knig pjat' starinnyx
books(gen) five old
'about five old books'

Recall that under the current analysis, numerals in case-agreeing examples like (37) are treated like adjectives, i.e. they are located in the same position as prenominal adjectives. It is then not surprising that, like adjectives, they block AXP. (Note that under the proposal that adjectives and adjectival numerals are located in SpecNP, AXP in (37)–(38) cannot involve movement of a maximal projection. For relevant discussion, see also Bošković 2003).

---

[24] One of his arguments for late adjunction concerns (ii). (i) shows adjunction can be late. According to Lebeaux (1988), the condition C violation in (ia) arises before wh-movement. The problem does not arise in (ib) because the clause containing *John* is an adjunct, hence can be inserted acyclically after wh-movement. Stepanov argues that the fact that, in contrast to (iib), condition A is apparently violated in (iia) provides evidence that the adjunct clause must in fact be adjoined after wh-movement (given late adjunction, *the lawyers* cannot bind *each other* at any point of the derivation.) I refer the reader to Stepanov (2001a,b) for an explanation why adjunction must be late, which applies to both base-generated adjunction (as in (iia)) and adjunction via movement (as in (35)).

(i) a. * Which argument that $John_i$ is a genius did he_i believe?

b. Which argument that $John_i$ made did he_i believe?

(ii) a. * What evidence that $other_i$'s friends brought up at court did the $lawyers_i$ refuse to talk about?

b. The $lawyers_i$ refused to talk about the evidence that each $other_i$'s friends brought up at court?

[25] AXP also seems to be possible with scrambled elements, which is expected under base-generation analyses of scrambling such as Bošković and Takahashi (1998) (see Bošković 2004c for its application to Slavic). See also Bošković (2004) for discussion of AXP with adjuncts and PPs from the perspective of the current analysis.

2.2. On the optionality of agreement with Russian numeral subjects

I now return to the optionality of agreement in (29). Recall that on Franks's analysis, the categorial status of the subject differentiates the sg and pl options (more precisely, it is responsible for the height difference between the two kinds of numeral subjects, which is in turn responsible for the agreement difference). I would like to propose that what differentiates the sg and pl options is not the subject's categorial status, but whether or not nominative is assigned, in line with Chomsky's proposal (see George and Kornfilt 1981 for the original suggestion and Wurmbrand and Bobaljik 2003 for a recent discussion) that nominative and subject agreement are correlated. Strong evidence for the correlation is provided by (39)-(40) (see Franks 1994 for relevant discussion).

(39) Pjat' ètix devušek rabotali/rabotalo tam.
five these(gen) girls(gen) worked(pl)/(sg) there

(40) Èti pjat' devušek rabotali/*rabotalo tam.
these(nom) five girls(gen) worked(pl)/(sg) there

In (40), where the nominative case is clearly assigned, the sg option (i.e. non-agreement) is unavailable, which provides strong evidence that assignment of nominative induces agreement (see below for a more detailed analysis of the case options for the demonstrative in (39)-(40)).

What about (39)? Under Franks's QP/DP analysis, on which agreeing subjects are DPs and non-agreeing subjects QPs (see also fn. 20), we can assume that the DP projected by a null D that dominates the numeral phrase bears nominative, which forces the agreement option, given nominative-agreement correlation. However, taking the morphological-case-as-a-reflex-of-abstract-Case hypothesis seriously disfavors positing a hidden nominative (see also Bošković 2003 for arguments against the presence of DP in Russian NPs). Moreover, I will show below that once we take the nominative-agreement correlation seriously, there is no need to posit a categorial distinction between non-agreeing and agreeing numeral subjects.

To that end, I will adopt the FP analysis from section 1.2, on which the categorial status of numeral subjects is kept constant not only in GQ constructions, but also in constructions where GQ is not assigned. I will argue that in (39), the pl (agreeing) option is the only possibility in the presence of a nominative. The sg (non-agreeing) option is the only possibility in the absence of a nominative due to the correlation between nominative case and subject agreement. The analysis is based on the claim that *pjat'* is morphologically ambiguous between a syncretic nominative/accusative form, as standardly assumed (recall that *pjat'* morphologically fits the case paradigm as a nominative/accusative form), and a caseless form, evidence for the latter being provided by (18), where *pjat'* cannot bear nominative or accusative (see section 1.2).[26] In light of the proposal, illustrated in (41), consider (42).

(41) *Pjat'*: a. nominative

b. accusative

c. caseless

(42) Pjat' devušek rabotali/rabotalo tam.
five girls(gen) worked(pl)/(sg) there

---

[26] As discussed in Babby (1987), in Old Russian *pjat'* was a feminine noun. In Modern Russian it has been reanalyzed as a Q. It is possible that the reanalysis has not been fully completed, the case-marked option for *pjat'* being a remnant of the Old Russian nominal *pjat'*. (The reanalysis may have been completed in SC, see section 2.3.)

The proposal is that on the sg option we are dealing with the caseless *pjat'*, and on the pl option with the nominative *pjat'*. In other words, subject-verb agreement is never optional. If *pjat'* bears nominative case it is obligatory, and if it is caseless it is impossible. In constructions like (40), the presence of the nominative then forces the pl option.

Let us spell out the analysis in more detail. Recall that the categorial status of numeral phrases is always FP, with F assigning GQ and the numeral (QP) located in SpecFP. Consider then the abstract structure in (43), which represents the agreement option for (42).

(43) I [$_{FP}$ QP [$_{F'}$ F NP]]
{pl} {nominative, pl}

I agrees with the QP, which is plural, and checks nominative case of the QP. Given that, as argued by Franks (1994), agreeing subjects, like the one in the derivation under consideration, move to SpecIP, while non-agreeing subjects remain in SpecVP, there are now two options, which depend on the status of the EPP in Russian (or the grammar more generally).

a. There is no EPP (or it does not hold in Russian), but nominative requires licensing in Spec IP, as argued in Bošković (2002).[27] The QP, which needs to move to SpecIP, pied-pipes the FP the way the wh-phrase pied-pipes the whole DP in *Whose books did he buy*? (It is possible that F may be an affix on Q(P), just like *'s* is an affix on *who*, which would license pied-piping)

b. The EPP holds (or optionally holds in Russian, see below), and is correlated with agreement in Russian. QP, which agrees with I hence must move to SpecIP, pied-pipes FP (see above).

The non-agreeing option for (42), which involves a caseless Q, is represented in (44).

(44) I [$_{FP}$ QP [$_{F'}$ F NP]]
{sg} {caseless, pl}

Since I does not case-check the QP it cannot agree with it. The numeral phrase does not move to SpecIP. We have the following options to complete the derivation of (44).

a. There is no EPP (or it does not hold in Russian), so SpecIP remains unfilled. I bears the default 3.p.sg. specification.

b. The EPP holds, SpecIP being filled by a null expletive. I either bears the default 3.p.sg specification or agrees with the expletive. (Regarding agreement, on the latter option the expletive would behave like the agreeing French expletive *il* (and bear nominative), rather than English *there.*)

c. The EPP optionally holds in Russian, but it is correlated with agreement. Assuming that I bears the default 3.p.sg. specification, since there is no agreement/nominative case-checking, the EPP would not hold in (44), hence SpecIP can remain empty.

The optionality of agreement in (42) is thus accounted for. The important feature of the analysis is that the category of the subject is kept constant. In contrast to Franks (1994), under the current analysis the numeral phrase has the same category in agreeing and non-agreeing constructions. What differentiates the two is the case of the numeral, a nominative numeral obligatorily leading to the agreement option and a caseless numeral to the non-agreeing option. The crucial ingredient of the analysis is the correlation between agreement and nominative case. We have seen that once the correlation, which has strong independent

---

[27] For arguments against the EPP in general, see Boeckx (2000), Bošković (2002), Grohmann et al (2000), and Epstein and Seely (1999). (Note that, as Stjepanović 1999 argues, under certain conditions nominative NPs that move overtly to SpecIP can be pronounced in a lower position in PF (via lower copy pronunciation), which means PF realization in a lower position does not necessarily rule out the possibility of overt syntax movement to SpecIP.)

justification, is taken seriously there is no need to posit a categorial distinction between agreeing and non-agreeing numeral subjects.[28]

Turning to slightly more complicated examples, consider (45), which contrasts with (39).

(45) * Pjat' èti devušek rabotali tam.
five these(nom) girls(gen) worked there

Why can't a post-numeral *these* bear nominative, in contrast to a pre-numeral *these* (see (40))? I suggest we are dealing here with a defective intervention effect, on a par with English (46).

(46) a. * Students$_i$ seem it was told t$_i$ that Mary knows French.

b. * There seem it was told students that Mary knows French.

To demonstrate that (45) and (46) can be accounted for by the same mechanism, let us first consider Chomsky's (2000) account of (46). The relevant part of (46) is given in (47).

(47) I it students
ϕ-features (uninter.) ϕ-features (interp.) ϕ-features (interp.)
no case case (uninterp.)

It prevents *students* from checking uninterpretable ϕ-features of I.[29] Given Chomsky's activation condition, which requires X to have an uninterpretable feature to be able to undergo movement/feature checking, *it* cannot check ϕ-features of I (its uninterpretable case feature, which would have made it visible for checking, has already been checked off). However, since *it* has ϕ-features and is closer to I than *students*, which could in principle check ϕ-features of I, *it* prevents *students* from entering into a relation with I. This is an example of *defective intervention* (it is defective because the intervener cannot do the job itself; still, it prevents another element from doing it.) (45) can be accounted for in the same way. Consider (48), which gives the relevant part of (45). (During the discussion below the reader should bear in mind that we can prevent I from licensing nominative on *these* by preventing it from agreeing with *these*, given the nominative-agreement correlation. Note that I will discuss only the caseless Q derivation, since if *five* checks I's nominative case there will be no source for the nominative case on *these*, so this derivation is easily blocked.)

---

[28] According to Franks and Pereltsvaig (2004), *bol'šinstvo* 'majority' is problematic for the current analysis. However, as suggested by Steven Franks (p.c.), *bol'šinstvo* can be analyzed as ambiguous between a (neuter) noun and a numeral like *pjat'*, which would be in line with the current account. There is actually evidence that the latter option, if it indeed exists, may need to be blocked in some contexts. This option should always allow pl agreement. However, such agreement is not always possible. The contrast in (i) may suggest that when available, the pl option could in fact be due to semantic agreement (i.e. the source of pl is not *bol'šinstvo*; on semantic agreement, see section 2.3. Note also that pl with *bol'šinstvo* is less frequent than with *pjat'*, see Corbett 1979).

(i) a. Bol'šinstvo naselenija sobralos'/*sobralis'.
majority population(gen) gathered(sg)/(pl)
'The majority of the population gathered.'

b. Bol'šinstvo priglašennyx ne javilos'/javilis'.
majority invited(gen) not appear(sg)/(pl)
'The majority of the invited did not appear.' (Corbett 1979)

[29] Since Agree is a prerequisite for Move (see Chomsky 2000), I disregard below movement of *students* to SpecIP in (46a) (a violation occurs already when I undergoes Agree with *students*, see below), focusing on the agreement relation between matrix I and the NP, which is in fact the only relevant relation in (46b).

(48) I — ϕ-features (uninterp.)
five — ϕ-features (interp.), no case
F
these — ϕ-features (interp.), case (uninterp.)

(48) I	five	F	these
ϕ-features (uninterp.)	ϕ-features (interp.)		ϕ-features (interp.)
	no case		case (uninterp.)

Just like I could not enter into a ϕ-feature checking relation with *students* in (47) due to the intervening *it,* I in (48) cannot enter into a ϕ-feature checking relation with *these* due to the intervening *five,* which asymmetrically c-commands *these*. Like *it* in (47), *five* in (48) itself cannot check ϕ-features of I since being caseless, it is inactive. Still, it prevents *these* from checking ϕ-features of I (the nominative of *these* would be checked as a reflex of ϕ-feature checking) because *five* bears ϕ-features and is closer to I than *these*.[30] (45) and (46) thus receive completely uniform accounts. In particular, we have seen that Chomsky's defective intervention account of (46) readily extends to (45). This point is of some theoretical importance. Defective intervention is not particularly conceptually appealing. It seems that the null hypothesis should be that X blocks Y from entering into a relation with Z only if X itself can do the job in question, which is not the case with defective intervention. As a result, there have been attempts to analyze (46) without employing defective intervention, the hope being that this would enable us to dispense with the mechanism altogether. Particularly interesting is the analysis of (46) from Vukić (2003), which makes no use of defective intervention. In fact, having accounted for (46) without appealing to defective intervention, Vukić argues that the mechanism in question should be dispensed with. However, since in his account of (46) Vukić crucially appeals to the expletive nature of the intervener, his analysis of (46) cannot be extended to (45). (45) thus may provide evidence that defective intervention is indeed needed (see also Chomsky 2000 regarding a somewhat different case from Icelandic).

Note that the intervention problem from (45) does not arise in (40), where *these* also bears nominative but it precedes *five*, which means that *five* is not closer to I than *these*.[31]

Interestingly, as noted by Franks (1994), in contrast to Russian, the demonstrative is marked for genitive in SC even when it precedes a numeral in a GQ configuration.

(49)	Ovih/*ove	pet	djevojaka	radi	tu.
	these(gen)/(nom)	five	girls(gen)	works	here

I speculate the difference should be correlated with another difference between Russian and SC. As shown in (50a), taken slightly modified from Franks (1995), and (50b), inherent case must be preserved under passivization in SC, but not in Russian. (The verb in (50a-b) assigns instrumental case. The reader is referred to Fowler (1987) for relevant discussion of Russian.)

---

[30] Alternatively, we could assume that I is looking for an element to check its case feature, in which case F would function as an intervener, preventing I from establishing a case relation with *these*. (I assume that, being adjectival in nature, *these* is located in SpecNP, as discussed in Bošković 2003. Note that the fact that both I and F are traditional case assigners would not matter under the case checking approach, as discussed in section 1.3.) In fact, it is possible that both the I-as-a-ϕ-feature-checker and the I-as-a-case-checker derivation need to be blocked, in which case (45) may provide further evidence for the superiority of case checking over case assignment, due to the latter derivation. (Note that the latter derivation can also be extended to (21) to explain why *po* (or a V in the same configuration) cannot assign its case to the NP across the intervening case assigner F.)

[31] There are several possibilities for analyzing (40). *These* could be in an additional SpecFP. Another possibility is that FP is dominated by another projection which hosts *these*. Note that the demonstrative still must be part of the subject, i.e. it does not move outside of the subject, since clausal adverbs cannot intervene between the demonstrative and *five*. Furthermore, movement to SpecIP still has to pied-pipe the whole subject.

(i)	* Èti	včera	pjat'	devušek	rabotali	tam.
	these(nom)	yesterday	five	girls(gen)	worked(pl)	there

(50) a. Fabrika/*fabrikoj upravljaet-sja našimi druz'jami.
factory(nom)/(instr) manages-refl. our(instr) friends(instr)
'The factory is managed by our friends.' (Russian)

b. Fabrikom/*fabrika se upravlja od strane naših drugova.
factory(instr)/(nom) refl. manages by our(gen) friends(gen)
'The factory is managed by our friends.' (SC)

We may be dealing here with a situation where two cases are assigned to the same NP, instrumental (before movement) and nominative (after movement). However, for morphological reasons only one can be overtly realized. SC realizes the first case (instrumental) and Russian the second case (nominative). The contrast between (49) and (40) can be accounted for on a par with (50): *these* receives two cases, genitive (in its base position, presumably via SHA with the N) and nominative (after movement in front of the numeral; following Franks, I assume that *these* is generated below the numeral, but can move to its left). As in the case of (50), in SC the first case (genitive) is morphologically realized and in Russian the second case (nominative) (see below for discussion of agreement in SC).

2.3. Agreement in Serbo-Croatian

Like Russian, SC also seems to allow both the agreeing and the non-agreeing option. However, in contrast to Russian, the former is often marked in comparison with the latter.[32]

(51) Pet ljudi je radilo.
five men(gen) is worked(sg)

(52) ? Pet ljudi su radili.
five men(gen) are worked(pl)

Interestingly, Franks (1994) shows that, in contrast to Russian, the numeral phrase passes subject tests even on the sg option in SC, as shown below with respect to control and anaphor binding. (The Comp-trace test cannot be run in SC since SC does not display the effect at all.)

(53) PRO idući kući, pet žena je o tome diskutovalo.
going home five women(gen) is about that discussed(sg)
'Going home, five women discussed it.'

(54) Pet žena je kupilo ovu knjigu za sebe.
five women(gen) is bought(sg) that book for themselves
'Five women bought that book for themselves.'

To account for this, Franks argues the numeral subject moves to SpecIP even on the sg option in SC, but for an independent reason having to do with NP internal ϕ-feature percolation, pl agreement fails. According to him, the pl option is extragrammatical, i.e. due to semantic agreement (because it semantically makes sense), not syntactic agreement (see also fn. 32).

Below I suggest three alternative analyses of the agreement patterns with SC numeral subjects, leaving further exploration and teasing apart of these options for future research.

a. The EPP holds in both SC and Russian but there is a parameter concerning whether the EPP is correlated with agreement (see Hiraiwa 2001). In particular, in contrast to Russian, the EPP is not correlated with agreement in SC. The FP then moves to SpecIP in SC (51), satisfying

[32] See Franks (1994) for further agreement differences between SC and Russian. Among other things, Franks shows that in SC the sg option is possible even with collective verbs like *gather*, in contrast to Russian. This leads him to treat agreement with SC and Russian numeral subjects differently, as discussed below.

the EPP, but since it is not nominative (SC *pet* would be unambiguously caseless) there is no agreement. The pl option (52) is due to semantic agreement, as on Franks's analysis.
b. (Under the following analysis there is no need to posit a difference in the EPP between Russian and SC, in fact there is no need to posit the EPP at all.) *Pet* can be either caseless or nominative. The former corresponds to the sg option, and the latter the pl option. Since the subject moves to SpecIP only on the latter option, some subject tests (namely, those run in (53)-(54)) would have to work differently in SC and Russian. (Recall that the only test we understand, the Comp-trace effect, is irrelevant in SC).
c. *Pet* is caseless and there is no movement of numeral subjects to SpecIP for case/agreement/ EPP reasons. However, they can move independently of these considerations to a higher position in SC, hence they can exhibit higher behavior. (The subject tests could work in the same way in SC and Russian. The agreement option would be due to semantic agreement.)

3. Conclusion

I have presented an account of GQ in Russian and SC that, in contrast to Franks (1994), does not require appealing to DS and SS, dissociating inherent case from ϕ-licensing, adopting case percolation and case assignment instead of case checking, and assuming different categorial status for various numeral subjects. Throughout the paper, I have maintained the hypotheses that Slavic morphological case is a direct reflection of abstract Case and that Slavic morphological agreement is a direct reflection of abstract agree(ment). The fact that we have been able to account for several rather complex case and agreement paradigms while maintaining these hypotheses provides evidence for the hypotheses in question, which, as noted above, seem inherently more interesting than their alternatives (no relation between morphological and abstract case, and morphological agreement and abstract agree(ment)). I have also provided evidence that case checking is empirically superior to case assignment, as well as additional evidence for the obligatory late adjunction hypothesis, the correlation between nominative case and subject agreement, and defective intervention. Finally, I suggested that if there is EPP, we may need to posit a parameter regarding whether it is correlated with agreement.

References

Abels, K. 2003. Successive cyclicity, anti-locality, and adposition stranding. Ph.D. thesis, University of Connecticut.
Abney, S. 1987. The English noun phrase in its sentential aspect. Ph.D. thesis, MIT.
Babby, L. 1986. The locus of case assignment and the direction of percolation: Case theory and Russian. In: *Case in Slavic*, ed. R. Brecht and J. Levine, 170-219. Slavica.
Babby, L. 1987. Case, prequantifiers, and discontinous agreement in Russian. *NLLT* 5:91-138.
Bailyn, J.1995. A configurational approach to Russian "free" word order. Ph.D. thesis, Cornell
Boeckx, C. 2000. EPP eliminated. Ms., University of Connecticut.
Bošković, Ž.1997.*The syntax of nonfinite complementation: An economy approach.* MIT Press.
Bošković, Ž. 2002. A-movement and the EPP. *Syntax* 5:167-218.
Bošković, Ž. 2003. On left branch extraction. *Proceedings of FDSL* 4:543-577.
Bošković, Ž. 2004a. Case and agreement with genitive of quantification in Russian. Ms., University of Connecticut.
Bošković, Ž. 2004b. Be careful where you float your quantifiers. *NLLT* 22:681-742.
Bošković, Ž. 2004c. Topicalization, focalization, lexical insertion, and scrambling. *Linguistic Inquiry* 35:613-638.
Bošković, Ž. and D. Takahashi.1998. Scrambling and last resort. *Linguistic Inquiry* 29:347-366
Burzio, L. 1986. *Italian syntax*. Reidel.
Chomsky, N. 1986. *Knowledge of language: Its nature, origin, and use.* Praeger.

Chomsky, N. 1995. *The minimalist program.* MIT Press.
Chomsky, N. 2000. Minimalist inquiries. In: *Step by step: Essays on minimalism in honor of Howard Lasnik*, ed. R. Martin, D. Michaels, and J. Uriagereka, 89-155. MIT Press.
Corbett, G. 1979. *Predicate agreement in Russian.* University of Birmingham.
Epstein, S., and D. Seely. 1999. Spec(ifying) the GB subject. Ms., University of Michigan and Eastern Michigan University.
Fowler, G.1987.The syntax of the genitive case in Russian. Ph.D. thesis, University of Chicago
Franks, S. 1994. Parametric properties of numeral phrases in Slavic. *NLLT* 12:570-649.
Franks, S. 1995. *Parameters of Slavic morphosyntax.* Oxford University Press.
Franks, S. In press. A Jacobsonian feature based analysis of Slavic numeric quantifier genitive. *Journal of Slavic Linguistics.*
Franks, S., and A. Pereltsvaig. 2004. Functional categories in the nominal domain.
Proceedings of FASL 12:109-128.
Freidin, R. and L. Babby. 1984. On the interaction of lexical and syntactic properties: Case structure in Russian. *Cornell Working Papers in Linguistics* 6:71-104.
George, L. and J. Kornfilt. 1981. Finiteness and boundedness in Turkish. In: *Binding and Filtering*, ed. F. Heny, 105-127. MIT Press.
Grohmann, K, J. Drury,and J. Castillo.2000.No more EPP. *Proceedings of WCCFL*19:139-152.
Heim, I, H. Lasnik, and R. May. 1991. Reciprocity and plurality. *Linguistic Inquiry* 22:63-101
Hiraiwa, K. 2001. EPP and object shift in Scandinavian. Ms., MIT.
Koopman, H. 1997. Prepositions, postpositions, circumpositions and particles. Ms., UCLA.
Koopman, H., and D. Sportiche. 1991. The position of subjects. *Lingua* 85:211-259.
Lebeaux, D. 1988. *Language acquisition and the form of the grammar.* Ph.D. thesis, University of Massachusetts.
Leko, N. 1986. Syntax of noun headed structures in Serbo-Croatian and corresponding phrasal structures in English. Ph.D. thesis, Indiana University.
Martin, R. 1996. A minimalist theory of PRO and control. Ph.D. thesis, University of Connecticut.
Martin, R. 1999. Case, the Extended Projection Principle, and minimalism. In: *Working Minimalism*, ed. S. Epstein and N. Hornstein, 1-25. MIT Press.
Neidle, C. 1988. *The role of Case in Russian syntax.* Reidel.
Pesetsky, D. 1982. Paths and categories. Ph.D. thesis, MIT.
Rakhlin, N. 2003. A case against case conflicts. Presented at FASL 12.
Stepanov, A. 2001a. Cyclic domains in syntactic theory. Ph.D. thesis, University of Connecticticut.
Stepanov, A. 2001b. Late adjunction and minimalist phrase structure. *Syntax* 4:94-125.
Stjepanović, S. 1999. What do second position cliticization, scrambling, and multiple wh-fronting have in common. Ph.D. thesis, University of Connecticut.
Stowell, T. 1981. Origins of phrase structure. Ph.D. thesis, MIT.
Takahashi, D. 1994. Minimality of movement. Ph.D. thesis, University of Connecticut.
Vukić, S. 2003. On features and the Minimal Link Condition. Ph.D. thesis, University of Connecticut.
Wechsler, S., and Larisa Zlatić. 2003. *The many faces of agreement.* CSLI.
Wurmbrand, S. and J. Bobaljik. 2003. Relativized phases. Ms., University of Connecticut.
Yadroff, M. and L. Billings. 1998. The syntax of approximative inversion in Russian (and the general architecture of nominal expressions). *Proceedings of FASL* 6:319-338.

Stefan Dyła and Anna Feldman

On Comitative Constructions in Polish and Russian

1 Introduction

McNally (1993) claims that the NP-with-NP cluster in Polish and Russian comitative coordination like, e.g. (1) and (2), respectively, should be analyzed as a complex NP consisting of a head (NP) and a non-head daughter (PP). In this paper, we will show that there are no empirical grounds for proposing a uniform analysis of comitative coordination in the two languages. More specifically, by applying a number of constituency and coordination tests to Polish and Russian comitative coordination data, we will demonstrate that the two languages behave differently with respect to binding anaphors within the comitatives : Polish allows only zero anaphoric possessive pronominal modifiers within the comitative phrase, whereas Russian, on the contrary, allows only reflexive possessive pronouns to modify comitative conjuncts. We will argue that Polish comitative coordination can be best described in terms of a multi-headed analysis proposed by Dyła (1988), whereas the Russian data call for an asymmetric coordinate structure. In this regard, we will provide additional support for the claim made by Abeillé (2003) that both symmetric [1] and asymmetric [2] coordinate structure are needed for an adequate description of coordination.

(1) Dorota z Mirkiem poszli na plażę.
Dorota-NOM with Mirek-INSTR went-PL.VIRILE to beach-ACC
'Dorota and Mirek went to the beach.'

(2) Daša s Mišej pošli na pljaž.
Dasha-NOM with Misha-INSTR went-PL to beach-ACC
'Dasha and Misha went to the beach.'

We will consider the behavior of the Polish and Russian comitatives with respect to different types of discontinuities such as extraction, the insertion of parenthetical expressions and clitics; number and gender agreement, semantic factors such as the accessibility of the collective and distributive readings and definiteness agreement. Throughout this paper, we will refer to the complex constituent as ' the NP-with-NP cluster' and to the erstwhile comitative PP as 'the with-phrase'.

2 Review of Data

2.1 Constituency Tests

2.1.1 Extraction

Neither Polish nor Russian allows for extraction of either the NP or the with-phrase of the NP-with-NP cluster, as shown by the ungrammaticality of the examples below.

[Polish]

[1] Originally proposed by Gazdar et al. (1985) and modified by Sag et al. (1985).
[2] See Munn (1993) for details.

(3) * Z Mirkiem, Dorota poszli na plażę.
with Mirek-INSTR Dorota-NOM went-3PL.VIRILE to beach-ACC
'With Mirek, Dorota went to the beach.'

(4) * Dorota, sądzę, że z Mirkiem poszli na plażę
Dorota-NOM think-1SG that with Mirek-INSTR went-3PL.VIRILE to beach-ACC
'*Dorota I think that with Mirek (they) went to the beach.'

[Russian]

(5) * S Mišej Daša pošli na pljaž
With Masha Dasha went-PL to beach-ACC
'With Masha Dasha went to the beach.'

(6) * Daša, ya dumaju, pošli na pljaž s Mišej.
Dasha-NOM I think went-PL to beach with Misha
'Dasha, I think, went to the beach with Misha.'

However, extraction out of the subordinate clause is fine when the NP-with-NP cluster is extracted as a constituent.

(7) Dorota z Mirkiem, sądzę, że poszli na plażę.
Dorota-NOM with Mirek-INSTR think-1SG that went-3PL to beach-ACC
'Dorota and Mirek, I think, went to the beach.'

(8) Daša s Mišej , ja dumaju, pošli na pljaž .
Dasha-NOM with Misha-INSTR I think went-3PL to beach-ACC
'Dasha and Misha, I think, went to the beach.'

2.1.2 Adjacency

In order for the NP-with-NP cluster to "trigger"plural agreement with the predicate or attribute, the with-phrase must immediately follow the host NP. Parentheticals cannot be placed between the NP and the with-phrase.

(9) * Dorota, niestety, z Mirkiem poszli na plażę.
Dorota-NOM unfortunately with Mirek-INSTR went-3PL.VIRILE to beach-ACC
'Unfortunately, Dorota and Mirek went to the beach.'

(10) * Daša, k sožaleniju, pošli na pljaž s Mišei.
Dasha-NOM for regret went-PL to beach with Misha.INSTR
'Unfortunately, Dasha and Misha went to the beach.'

Clitics cannot intervene between the NP and the with-phrase either, as can be seen from the ungrammaticality of (11) below.

(11) * Dorota się z Mirkiem spotkali na plaży.
Dorota-NOM CLITIC with Mirek-INSTR met-3PL.VIRILE at beach-LOC
'Dorota and Mirek met at the beach.'

Since parentheticals in Polish tend to occur at major constituent boundaries, as noted by Cichocki (1983), the ungrammaticality of (11) indicates the lack of major constituent boundary between *Dorota* and *z Mirkiem*.

Russian does not seem to exhibit this type of behavior. Russian clitics tend to occur in the so-called second position, i.e. either they follow the first prosodic word or the first constituent of a sentence. Thus, the two cases are grammatical:

(12) Daša že s Mišej pošli na pljaž.
Dasha-NOM with Misha-INSTR went-PL to beach-ACC
'Dasha and Misha went to the beach, afterall'

(13) Daša s Mišej že pošli na pljaž.
Dasha-NOM with Misha-INSTR went-PL to beach-ACC
'Dasha and Misha went to the beach, afterall'

2.1.3 Control of Possessive Reflexives

In both languages, the NP-with-NP cluster acts as a single constituent with respect to reflexivization. The relevant examples are as follows:

(14) Dorota$_i$ z Mirkiem$_j$ wrócili do swego$_{i+j}$
Dorota-NOM with Mirek-INSTR returned-3PL.VIRILE to their-REFL.GEN
mieszkania.
apartment-GEN
'Dorota and Mirek returned to their apartment.'

(15) Daša$_i$ s Mišei$_j$ vernulis' v svoju$_{i+j}$ kvartiru.
Dasha.NOM with Misha.INSTR returned-PL to self's.ACC apartment.ACC
'Dasha and Misha returned to their apartment.'

The NP-with-NP also behaves like a constituent with respect to control of Equi in infinitival complements. the grammaticality of (16) in Polish and of (17) in Russian below indicates that in both languages the NP and the with-phrase that immediately follows it form a constituent.

(16) Kasia z Marcinem chcieli iść na plażę.
Kasia-NOM with Marcin-INSTR wanted-3PL.VIRILE go-INF to beach-ACC
'Kasia and Marcin wanted to go to the beach.'

(17) Katja s Mašej xotjat poiti na pljaž.
Katya-NOM with Masha-INSTR want-PL-3P go-INF to beach-ACC
'Katja and Masha want to go to the beach.'

Another test for constituency that supports the claim that the NP and the with-phrase form a constituent is their ability to jointly control Equi into participial clauses. Consider the following examples:

(18) Przyjechawszy w południe, Kasia z Marcinem zaraz
having-arrived at noon Kasia-NOM with Marcin-INSTR immediately
poszli na plażę.
went-3PL.VIRILE to beach-ACC
'Having arrived at noon, Kasia and Marcin immediately went to the beach.'

(19) Priexav v polden', Katja s Mašej pošli na pljaž .
Having-arrived at noon, Katya-NOM with Masha-INSTR went-PL to beach
'Having arrived at noon, Katya and Masha went to the beach.'

The ability of the NP-with-NP cluster to serve jointly as a controller in (18) and (19), respectively, counts as evidence for the claim that they form a constituent.

2.2 Tests for Coordination

In this section, we will argue that the complex NP evidence for which we presented in the previous section is in fact coordinate. Arguments for coordination take the form of showing that the NP + PP Vpl construction mimics the behavior of ordinary NP coordination.

2.2.1 Number Agreement

In Polish and Russian, a coordination of singular NPs almost always requires plural number agreement on the verb. [3] In Polish, a singular lexical noun subject never triggers plural agreement on its predicate and vice versa, a plural lexical noun subject never triggers singular agreement. Thus, if a phrasal subject NP does trigger plural agreement, it is an indication of its plurality. Since the components of the phrasal NP are not plural themselves, the conclusion follows that the plural verbal forms indicate that the NP-with-NP cluster is an instance of coordination.

2.2.2 Control of Reflexive Possessives Within the With-Phrase

For most speakers of Polish, the first NP in the NP-with-NP cluster cannot serve as an antecedent for a reflexive possessive pronoun within the with-phrase.

(20) * Dorota$_i$ ze swym$_i$ chłopakiem poszli na
Dorota-NOM with her-REFL.INSTR boyfriend-INSTR went-3PL.MASC to
plażę.
beach-ACC
'Dorota and her boyfriend went to the beach.'

In this respect, the Polish comitative coordinate construction mimics the behavior of ordinary NP coordination, as shown in (2.2.2) below.

(21) * Dorota$_i$ i swój$_i$ chłopak poszli na plażę.
Dorota-NOM and her-REFL.NOM boyfriend-NOM went-3PL.MASC to beach-ACC
'Dorota and her boyfriend went to the beach.'

Non-reflexive possessives in the with-phrase cannot be anteceded by the first conjunct either.

(22) * Dorota$_i$ ze jej$_i$ mężem poszli na plażę.
Dorota-NOM with her-INSTR husband-INSTR went-3PL.MASC to beach-ACC
'Dorota and her husband went to the beach.'

Only zero anaphoric possessive in the comitative controlled by the first conjunct seems somewhat acceptable.

[3] The exceptions are rare instances of closest conjunct agreement.

(23) ? Dorota$_i$ z mężem poszli na plażę.
Dorota-NOM with husband-INSTR went-3PL.MASC to beach-ACC
'Dorota and her husband went to the beach.'

Note, however, the non-reflexive possessive pronoun is the best in ordinary coordination. To many speakers, the example with zero possessive sounds odd.

(24) ? Dorota$_i$ i $_i$ mąż poszli na plażę.
Dorota-NOM and zero-poss husband-NOM went-3PL.MASC to beach-ACC
'Dorota and her husband went to the beach.'

(25) Dorota$_i$ i jej$_i$ mąż poszli na plażę.
Dorota-NOM and her-.NOM husband-NOM went-3PL.MASC to beach-ACC
'Dorota and her husband went to the beach.'

Russian, however, exhibits a different pattern:

(26) a. Daša$_i$ i ee$_i$ drug pošli na pljaž.
Dasha and her friend went-PL to beach
'Dasha and her friend went to the beach.'

b. *Daša$_i$ i svoj$_i$ drug pošli na pljaž.
Dasha and her friend went-PL to beach
'Dasha and her friend went to the beach.'

c. Daša$_i$ so svoim$_i$ drugom pošli na pljaž.
Dasha with her friend went-PL to beach
'Dasha and her friend went to the beach.'

d. *Dasha$_i$ s ee$_i$ drugom pošli na pljaž.
Dasha and her friend went-PL to beach
'Dasha and her friend went to the beach.'

There are two types of possessive pronouns in Russian, reflexive and non-reflexive. The former can modify the comitative phrase, whereas the latter can modify the second conjunct in ordinary coordinate constructions. Thus, Russian and Polish comitative coordinate constructions are different in their binding patterns.

2.2.3 Gender Resolution

In ordinary coordinate structures in Polish, virile (masculine human) always overrides non-virile. This happens regardless of whether the gender is inherently specified or assigned by the pragmatic context. Thus, (27) is grammatical only if uttered by a male speaker, (28) is ungrammatical for both male and female speakers since the gender agreement on the verb is non-virile and one of the conjuncts, Marcin, is inherently virile.

(27) Joanna i ja polecieliśmy do Calgary.
Joanna-NOM and I-NOM flew-3PL.VIRILE to Calgary-GEN
' Joanna and I flew to Calgary.'

(28) *Marcin i ja poleciałyśmy do Calgary.
Marcin-NOM and I-NOM flew-3PL.NON-VIRILE to Calgary-GEN
'Marcin and I went to Calgary.'

Note the form of the verb in example (29) is in its third person plural virile form.

(29) Dorota z Mirkiem poszli na plażę.
Dorota-NOM with Mirek-INSTR went-3PL.VIRILE to beach-ACC
'Dorota and Mirek went to the beach.'

The use of the third person plural non-virile form of the verb renders the sentence ungrammatical, as shown in (30) below.

(30) * Dorota z Mirkiem poszły na plażę.
Dorota-NOM with Mirek-INSTR went-3PL.NON-VIRILE to beach-ACC
'Dorota and Mirek went to the beach.'

The grammaticality of (29) taken together with the ill-formedness of (30) indicates that the with-phrase *z Mirkiem* participates in gender resolution. Hence, it must be a conjunct.

Since there is no gender distinction for plural verbs in Russian, this phenomenon is not attested.

2.2.4 Distributive vs. Collective Reading

An *s*-adjunct cannot modify a verb that requires a distributive reading. Thus, for example, verbs such as *believe* or *know* will not have *with*-modifiers. However, *s*-phrases with coordinate meanings are acceptable with these verbs (see (31b)) just as are regular coordinated subjects (31c):

(31) a. * Maša verit s Dašej v boga.
Masha believe-3SG.Pres with Dasha-Instr in God
'*Masha believes in God with Dasha.'

b. Maša s Dašej verjat v boga.
Masha with Dasha-INSTR believe-3PL.Pres in God
'Masha and Dasha believe in God.'

c. Maša i Daša verjat v boga.
Masha and Dasha-Instr believe-3PL.Pres in God
'Masha and Dasha believe in God.'

The ability of a *with*-phrase to occur with verbs like *believe* that only require distributive readings can be considered a diagnostic for (with)-coordination in Russian.

In addition, comitative adjuncts cannot occur with reciprocals:

(32) a. Maša s Dašej ljubjat drug druga.
Masha with Dasha like-3P.PL each other
'Masha and Dasha like each other.'

b. *Maša s Dašej ljubit drug druga.
Masha with Dasha like-3SG each other
'*Masha likes each other with Dasha.'

The NP-with-NP cluster in Polish also occurs as subject with predicates that have exclusively distributive meanings, as can be seen below.

(33) Marcin z Joanną są wysocy.
Marcin-NOM with Joanna-INSTR be-3PL tall-VIRILE
'Marcin and Joanna are tall.'

(34) Marcin z Joanna są zwolennikami postępu w
Marcin-NOM with Joanna-INSTR be-3PL proponent-PL progress-GEN within
granicach zdrowego rozsądku.
boundaries-LOG common-GEN sense-GEN
'Marcin and Joanna are proponents of progress within the boundaries of common sense.'

Additional evidence in favor of the claim that the NP-with-NP cluster is coordinate comes from the following examples:

(35) a. Maša s Dašej zarabotala tri rublja.
Masha with Dasha earned-SG three rubles
'Masha earned three rubles with Dasha.'

b. Maša s Dašej zarabotali tri rublja.
Masha with Dasha earned-PL three rubles
'Masha and Dasha earned three rubles/Masha and Dasha each earned three rubles (6 rubles in total).'

As becomes evident from the translations of the examples provided in this section, the comitative adjuncts do not allow a distributive reading, whereas the comitatives conjuncts allow the object to either distribute over the subject or not, the way ordinary coordinate constructions do.

A closely related piece of evidence for the plurality and the coordinate nature of the phrase in question comes from its co-occurrence with the distributive preposition *po* which subcategorizes for an NP in the accusative case, a test available both in Polish and Russian. Consider the following examples:

(36) Marcin i Tomek zjedli po dwa ciastka.
Marcin-NOM and Tomek-NOM ate-3.PL.VIRILE two-ACC cookies-ACC
'Marcin and Tomek ate two cookies each.'

(37) Miša i Katja s'eli po dva pečenja.
Miša-NOM and Katya-NOM ate-3.PL two-ACC cookies-ACC
'Misha and Katya ate two cookies each.'

The meanings of examples (36) and (37) are identical to that of a coordination of (38) and (40) and of a coordination of (39) and (41), respectively. And so are the meanings of examples (42) and (43), both of which involve the NP-with-NP phrase instead of ordinary coordination.

(38) Marcin zjadł dwa ciastka.
Marcin-NOM ate-3.SG.VIRILE two-ACC cookies-ACC
'Marcin ate two cookies.'

(39) Miša s'el dva pečenja.
Misha-NOM ate-3.SG.MASC two-ACC cookies-ACC
'Misha ate two cookies.'

(40) Tomek zjadł dwa ciastka.
Tomek-NOM ate-3.SG.VIRILE two-ACC cookies-ACC
'Tomek ate two cookies.'

(41) Katja s'ela dva pečenja.
Katya-NOM ate-3.SG.FEM two-ACC cookies-ACC
'Katya ate two cookies.'

(42) Marcin z Tomkiem zjedli po dwa ciastka.
Marcin-NOM with Tomek-INSTR ate-3.PL.VIRILE two-ACC cookies-ACC
'Marcin and Tomek ate two cookies each.'

(43) Miša s Katej s'eli po dva pečenja.
Misha-NOM with Katya-INSTR ate-3.PL two-ACC cookies-ACC
'Misha with Katya ate two cookies each.'

Note that adjunct structures are absolutely impossible with the distributive preposition *po*: [Polish]

(44) * Marcin z Tomkiem zjadł po dwa ciastka.
Marcin-NOM with Tomek-INSTR ate-3SG.VIRILE two-ACC cookies-ACC
'Marcin and Tomek ate two cookies each.'

[Russian]

(45) * Maša s Tanej s'ela po dva pevcenja.
Masha-NOM with Tanya-INSTR ate-3SG.FEM two-ACC cookies-GEN
'Masha and Tanya ate two cookies each'

Basically, this is a test for plurality but it also proves that comitative coordination NP-with-NP can have a distributive reading (unlike adjunct structures) and like ordinary coordination.

2.2.5 Definiteness Agreement

In Polish there is a clear relationship between the features on the nominative NP and the features on the NP within the with-phrase. Compare the following examples:

(46) Mirek z Dorotą poszli na plażę.
Mirek-NOM with Dorota-INSTR went-3PL.VIRILE to beach-ACC
'Mirek and Dorota went to the beach.'

(47) ? Mirek z tą dziewczyną poszli na plażę.
Mirek-NOM with this-INSTR girl-INSTR went-3PL to beach-ACC
'Mirek and this girl went to the beach.'

(48) * Mirek z jakąś dziewczyną poszli na plażę.
Mirek-NOM with some-INSTR.FEM girl-INSTR went-3PL to beach-ACC
'Mirek and some girl went to the beach.'

In (46) where the two NPs are proper nouns, plural agreement with the verb is fine. It becomes more problematic in (47), where one of the NPs is a proper noun and the other a definite description. In (48), where the other NP is indefinite, plural agreement is totally unacceptable. Note, however, that the two NPs agree with respect to definiteness, plural agreement is just fine, (as in (49) and (50)).

(49) Ten chłopak z tą dziewczyną poszli na
this-NOM.MASC boy-NOM with this-INSTR.FEM girl-INSTR went-3PL.VIRILE to
plażę.
beach-ACC
'This boy and this girl went to the beach.'

(50) Jakiś chłopak z jakąś dziewczyną poszli
some-NOM.MASC boy-NOM with some-INSTR.FEM girl-INSTR went-3PL.VIRILE
na plażę.
to beach-ACC
'A boy and a girl went to the beach.'

However, Russian is different in this respect. Native speakers prefer the plural agreement over singular in all the cases regardless whether the comitative phrase is definite or indefinite, as is illustrated by the following examples. The singular agreement is not completely ruled out, but is definitely dispreferred. [4]

(51) Daša s Mišej pošli/pošla na pljaž.
Dasha and Misha went-PL to beach
'Dasha and Misha went to the beach.'

(52) Daša s kakoi-to devočkoj pošli/pošla na pljaž.
Dasha and some girl went-PL/went-SG to beach
'Dasha and some girl went to the beach.'

(53) Daša s toj devočkoj pošli/pošla na pljaž.
Dasha and that girl went-PL/went-SG to beach
'Dasha and some girl went to the beach.'

(54) Etot mal'čik s etoj devočkoj pošli/pošel na pljaž.
This boy with this girl went-PL/went-SG.MASC to beach
'This boy and this girl went to the beach./This boy went to the beach with some girl.'

(55) Kakoj-to mal'čik s kakoj-to devočkoj pošli/pošel na pljaž.
Some boy with some girl went-PL/went-SG.MASC to beach
'Some boy and some girl went to the beach./Some boy went to the beach with some girl.'

[4] To accept a sentence with a singular verb the speakers have the tendency to dislocate the with-phrase farther away from the nominative NP.

2.3 Summary

In a nutshell, the discussion can be summarized as follows. Both Polish and Russian NP-with-NP clusters occur with plural verbs, both can occur with verbs that have exlusively distributive meanings. The NP-with-NP cluster, both in Polish and Russian, can serve an antecedent for reflexive pronominal modifiers of objects. The NP-with-NP is a controller for Equi in infinitival and participal clauses. When the verb is plural, there is a strict linear order (in case the NP-NOM is singular) of the NP-with-NP cluster: the host NP must immediately precede the with-phrase. The host NP can never be an antecedent for a non-reflexive possessive within the comitative phrase; however, in Russian, unlike Polish, it can antecede reflexive possessives within the comitative phrase. Note the differences between Polish and Russian: the host NP and the comitative NP must agree with respect to definiteness in Polish, whereas Russian lacks this requirement; the comitative NP participates in gender resolution in Polish (like ordinary coordination); however, Russian does not have the gender resolution phenomenon.

2.4 Proposed Analyses

For Polish, we propose a slightly modified version of Dyła (1988)'s by incorporating the notion of a 'weak head' proposed by Abeillé et al. (2003). In a nutshell, the NP-with-NP phrase involves is conjunctionless ordinary coordination. The preposition *z* 'with' is a weak head and thus allows the value for GENDER of its complement to contribute to the value for GENDER of its mother.

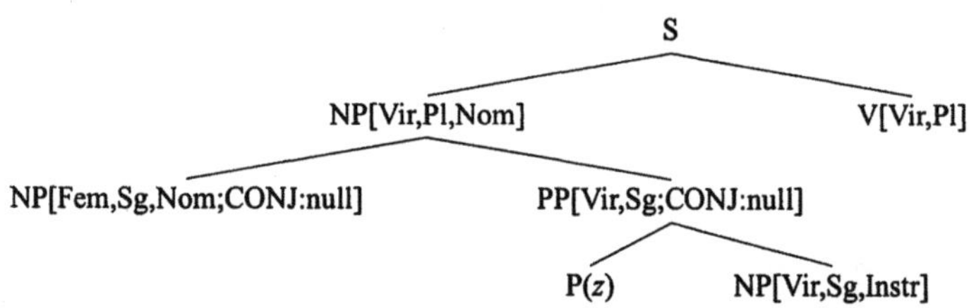

The binding facts in Russian suggest that comitative coordination should be analyzed differently from that of ordinary coordination. The section outlines two possible analyses of Russian comitative coordination.

The first has been proposed in Feldman (2002), who treats *s* as a nominal head that selects two noun (non-pronominal) complements, one of which is instrumental.

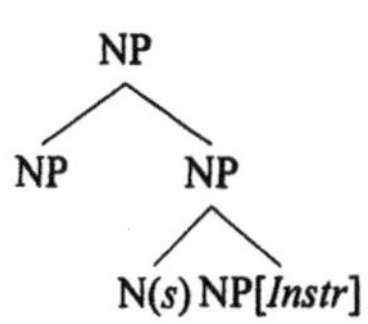

Another analysis is more along the lines of Munn (1993). Under this analysis, the first NP in the NP-with-NP cluster is a head and the with-phrase, the Boolean Phrase (BP) to use Munn's terms, an adjunct. Two options avail themselves with respect to the structure of the with-phrase: One may assume that *s* is a conjunction which heads the BP and takes the second NP as its complement. Note, however, that this hypothesis fails to account for the instrumental case of the second NP which in comitative PPs is assigned by the preposition. An alternative analysis treats the BP as headed by a null conjunction and *s* as a weak head of its NP complement thus allowing the value for NUMBER of the second NP to contribute to the value for NUMBER of the mother.

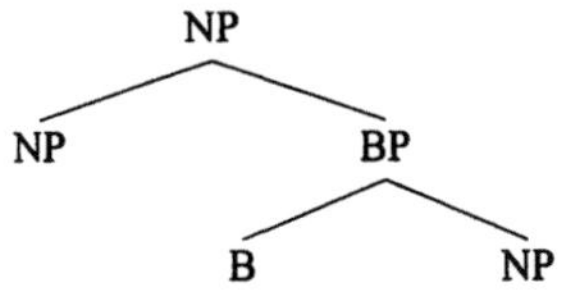

Note that the conjunctionless BP analysis makes the same predictions as the one proposed by Feldman (2002) with respect to (i) the plurality of the mother NP, (ii) the occurrence within the with-phrase of a reflexive possessive pronoun controlled by the first NP, and (iii) the fact that case of the first NP varies in accord with the grammatical relation it bears while the second NP is invariably in instrumental case assigned by the preposition.

3 Conclusions

We have shown in this paper that contrary to McNally's (1993) claim and despite their superficial similarities comitative coordinate constructions in Polish and Russian cannot and should not be analyzed uniformly. The two constructions exhibit different binding patterns, which we account for by proposing that Polish involves symmetric coordination while Russian asymmetric coordination.

References

Abeillé, A. (2003). A Lexicon- and Construction-Based Approach to Coordinations. In S. Müller (Ed.), *Proceedings of the HPSG-2003 Conference, Michigan State University, East Lansing*, Stanford, pp. 5–25. CSLI Publications.

Abeillé, A., O. Bonami, D. Godard, and J. Tseng (2003). The syntax of French á and de: An HPSG analysis. In P. Saint-Dizier (Ed.), *ACL-SIGSEM Workshop on the linguistic dimensions of prepositions and their use in computational linguistics formalisms and applications*, Toulouse, pp. 133–144. IRIT.

Cichocki, W. (1983). Multiple wh-questions in Polish: A Two-comp Analysis. *Toronto Working Papers in Linguistics* (4), 53–71.

Dyła, S. (1988). Quasi-comitative Coordination in Polish. *Linguistics 26*, 383–414.

Feldman, A. (2002). On NP-coordination. In *The UIL OT Yearbook*. Utrecht, the Netherlands.

Gazdar, G., E. Klein, G. K. Pullum, and I. A. Sag (1985). *Generalized Phrase Structure Grammar*. Cambridge, MA: Harvard University Press.

McNally, L. (1993). Comitative Coordination: A Case Study in Group Formation. *Natural Language and Linguistics Theory 11*, 347–379.

Munn, A. B. (1993). *Topics in the Syntax and Semantics of Coordinate Structures*. Ph. D. thesis, The University of Maryland.

Sag, I. A., G. Gazdar, T. Wasow, and S. Weisler (1985). Coordination And How To Distinguish Categories. *Natural Language and Linguistics Theory 3*, 117–171.

Rositsa Panayotova Dekova, Trondheim

Li-Attachment in Multiverb Constructions in Bulgarian

This paper addresses issues concerning *li*-attachment within Bulgarian complex predicates[1]. *Li* is a question marker in Bulgarian and it is considered to be a clitic element together with two other types of clitics (pronominal clitics and the present tense forms of the verb *sâm* 'to be').

Traditionally, it was proposed (e.g. Rivero 1992) that *li* is a bound morpheme generated in C^o, which cannot remain stranded in SS (surface structure). In addition, two options were offered to provide verb support for *li*. The main solution was seen in V^o-raising, incorporating V^o into *li*. In cases where raising was constrained (in negative and future patterns), affix-hopping as *li*-lowering was posited, where *li* was said to lower into the finite complex, right-adjoining to it. Thus, a possible account for sentences like those in (1) was provided.

(1) a. Vidja *li* kâštata? — V^o-raising
saw.2SG li house.DEF
'Did you see the house?'
b. Ne mu go dade *li*? — *li*-lowering
not him it gave.2SG li
'Didn't you give it to him?'
c. Šte govoriš *li*? — *li*-lowering
shall speak.2SG li
'Are you going to speak?'

This treatment, however, left open the question of why sentences like those in (2a) and (2b) are ungrammatical and why (2c) is marginal, if not plainly ungrammatical, while (2d) is grammatical.

(2) a. * Šte *li* govoriš? — *Šte*-raising to C^o or *li*-lowering to *šte* / is constrained
shall li speak-2SG
b. * Ne *li* mu izpratih knigata? — *Neg*-raising to C^o or *li*-lowering to *ne* / is constrained
not li him sent.1SG book.DEF
c. ??/* Ne mu izpratih *li* knigata?
not him sent.1SG li book.DEF
d. Ne mu *li* go dade?
not him li it gave.2SG
'Didn't you give it to him?'

Penchev (1993) argues that *li* is not generated in C^o. Instead, he suggests that the speaker can question any word (phrase) in the sentence by simply attaching *li* to it. Thus, for example, both (3) and (4) will have exactly the same syntactic structure and differ only in the intonation, whereby *li* is assumed to 'search' for the accented word, i.e. the focus of the sentence.

[1] I am most grateful to Mila Dimitrova-Vulchanova for her invaluable advice and suggestions for improvement during many helpful discussions of the data and their significance. Any errors remain, of course, entirely my own. Special thanks to Rurik Greenall and Tsvetana Dimitrova for their help.

(3) Sreštna recenzenta si *li* Ivan?
met.3SG reviewer REFL li Ivan
'Was it his reviewer that Ivan met?'

(4) Srešthna *li* Ivan recenzenta si?
Met.3SG li Ivan reviewer REFL
'Did Ivan meet his reviewer?'

Furthermore, Penchev assumes that movement of *wh*-words in the sentence is generally the same as movement of *li*. The main difference is seen in the possibility of multiple *wh*-elements in questions, while there can be only one *li* in a sentence[2].

A plausible account (Jaeger 2003a) for *wh*-phrase ordering in multiple *wh*-questions is seen in *topicality*. This follows from a definition of *topic* (in the sense of ABOUTNESS, cf. Reinhart 1982, Lambrecht 1994), discussed among others by Jaeger (2003a):

The topic of a sentence is what a sentence primarily provides or requests information about.

Data from sentences with *wh*-phrases (as in (6) to (11)) show that topicality may be a determining factor for *li*-attachment also.

(5) Na kogo e dal knigata Ivan?
to whom is given.3SG book.DEF Ivan
'Whom has Ivan given the book to?'

(6) Na kogo *li* e dal knigata Ivan?
to whom li is given.3SG book.DEF Ivan
'(I wonder...) Who is it that Ivan has given the book to?'

(7) Na kogo *li* kakvo e dal Ivan?
to whom li what is given.3SG Ivan
'(You ask me...) Whom has Ivan given what?'

---

[2] It has been proposed (Krapova & Cinque 2003) that there could be more than one *li* in the sentence:

(i) Kâde *li* kakvo *li* se e slučilo pak?
where li what li REFL has happened again
'(I wonder...) Where and what has happened again?'

This should not, however, be regarded as one sentence. Here, instead, we have two separate questions, asking information about two of the arguments in the act of *happening*. These two sentences have been merged together and the part expressing the situation itself, the identical part, has been expressed overtly only in the second sentence. Thus, we are not restricted to just two *li*-s, but as many as the number of the questions that can be asked about each of the participants (arguments and adjuncts) in the situation. For example, for a sentence verbalizing the act of *giving*, we can have up to seven question words (including *why* which is not reflected in the example below):

(ii) Koj *li* kakvo *li* na kogo *li* kâde *li* koga *li* kak *li* e dal?
who li what li to whom li where li when li how li has given
'(I wonder...) Who has given what to whom and where, when, and how?'

Therefore, for the purposes of this paper, I will assume that there can be only one *li* in a sentence.

(8) Na kogo kakvo *li* e dal Ivan?
to whom what li is given.3SG Ivan
'(I wonder…) What has Ivan given whom?'

(9) */?? Na kogo e dal *li* knigata Ivan?[3]
to whom is given.3SG li book.DEF Ivan

(10) */?? Na kogo e dal knigata *li* Ivan?
to whom is given.3SG book.DEF li Ivan

(11) [Na kogo e dal knigata Ivan] *li*?
to whom is given.3SG book.DEF Ivan li
(You ask me…) 'Whom has Ivan given the book to?'

We can also regard these sentences from the point of view of information structure, where the nature of a question is seen in asking for information about a certain constituent in the sentence. In *wh*-questions, this is the participant denoted by the *wh*-word, whereas the function of *li* in yes/no questions is to question either the predicate or a nominal or adverbial constituent. In the first case *li* usually refers to the entire sentence, and in the second case its scope is limited to the host constituent(s).

Cross-linguistically, *li* and *wh*-words are usually observed in complementary distribution. In Bulgarian, however, we find both occurring one sentence. Therefore, it can be assumed that the *wh*-word and *li* can combine only if *li* attaches to the *wh*-word, as we cannot question two different types of phrases within a sentence. Even then, the interpretation of the sentence is marked in that it can only be interpreted in an embedded structure ('I wonder […]') as in (6).

As noted above, sentences (9) and (10) may be judged to be acceptable by some native speakers. In these cases, we have the strongest accent in the sentence falling on a word other than the *wh*-word, the word preceding *li*. Thus the *wh*-word is no longer the topic of the sentence, i.e. it is not what the *sentence primarily provides or requests information about.* And the sentence itself receives a different reading – it cannot be regarded as *wh*-question anymore, instead the reading is as following

(12) ?? Na kogo e dal *li* knigata Ivan?
to whom is given.3SG li book.DEF Ivan
'You ask me whom was it that Ivan has *given* the book to?'

Where we ask for confirmation about the act of *giving* as opposed to an act of *taking* (for ex.).

(13) ?? Na kogo e dal knigata *li* Ivan?
to whom is given.3SG book.DEF li Ivan
'You ask me whom was it that Ivan has given *the book* to?'

Here we ask for confirmation about the object of the giving act, *the book*, as opposed to *a magazine*, for example. Neither of these sentences asks information about the recipient in the situation (the argument denoted by the *wh*-word). Therefore, we cannot regard these sentences as *wh*-questions. Thus the partial acceptability of (1c) is also explained.

This situation can be further described in terms of presupposition. Presuppositions have been seen as logical preconditions for the sentence to make sense in a given context utterance

[3] Some of the native speakers judge as acceptable (*a bit awkward* or *on the margin*) sentences (9) and (10), as well as sentences (19) and (21) given below. This possibility will be explained later in the paper.

(CoU). Semantic presuppositions originate from the lexemes used, as well as from the structure of the sentence. Selectional restrictions are seen as one sort of presuppositions; when a sentence contains a predicate term, the use of the term in a given CoU requires that the argument fulfil the selectional restrictions.

In a *wh*-question, it is presupposed that the topicalized argument[4], the argument denoted by the *wh*-word, exists; we ask information about it and we expect some input from the answer. In a *li*-question, however, there is no such presupposition — we ask only about the truth value of the clause to which *li* is attached. Therefore sentences where those two types of questioning are syntactically separated will end up with different semantic values (see (12) and (13) compared to (9) and (10) respectively).

Since the empirical data show that any other position of *li* is ungrammatical in such sentences (see (9) and (10) in their original reading), I assume that *li* is attached primarily to the topic of the sentence, which, in case of (6), is the *wh*-phrase, and in case of (12) – the verb.

Note that (9) is also grammatical, but can only be viewed as an echo-question, whereby the whole sentence is regarded as topic.

Within multiverb constructions (clusters of verbal elements (Hinrichs *et al.* 1998), in the present case matrix predicates and control environments), we can observe lowering of *li* from its original position in 'FRONT' of CLargP (as proposed by Dimitrova-Vulchanova and Hellan 1999). Thus independent questioning of a constituent inside the embedded clause is also accounted for, as in sentence (17) in its reading in (a). Yet, there are certain restrictions in the positions *li* can occupy, as we can see in (15) - (21).

(14) Ivan obešta da otide da kupi knigata.
Ivan promised.3SG to go.3SG to buy.3SG book.DEF
'Ivan promised to go and buy the book.'

(15) Ivan *li* obešta da otide da kupi knigata?
Ivan li promised.3SG to go.3SG to buy.3SG book.DEF
'Was it Ivan who promised to go and buy the book?'

(16) Ivan obešta *li* da otide da kupi knigata
Ivan promised.3SG li to go.3SG to buy.3SG book.DEF
'Did Ivan promise to go and buy the book?'

(17) Ivan obešta da otide da kupi knigata *li*?
Ivan promised.3SG to go.3SG to buy.3SG book.DEF li
a. ?'Did Ivan promise to go and buy *this book*?'
b. 'Was it the case that Ivan promised to go and buy this book?

---

[4] Traditionally, it is assumed that *wh*-words are focused and move to Spec-CP or Spec-FocP (cf. Tomić 1996). This does not generally contradict what I propose here, since I follow another definition of topic (namely the one given above), and therefore, I do not account for the standard Focus-Topic distinction.

As we also see in Penchev (1980), the word in front of *li* does not have to convey new information:

(i) (Štom ne iskaš jabâlki), *iskaš li* čereši?
since not want.3SG apples want.3SG li cherries
'Since you don't want apples, do you want cherries?'

where the word preceding *li* is characterised as having the intonation peak of the sentence, and this is also in accordance with what I suggest here.

(18) *Ivan obešta da *li* otide da kupi knigata?
Ivan promised.3SG to li go.3SG to buy.3SG book.DEF

(19) */?? Ivan obešta da otide *li* da kupi knigata?[5]
Ivan promised.3SG to go.3SG li to buy.3SG book. DEF

(20) *Ivan obešta da otide da *li* kupi knigata?
Ivan promised.3SG to go.3SG to li buy.3SG book.DEF

(21) */?? Ivan obešta da otide da kupi *li* knigata?
Ivan promised.3SG to go.3SG to buy.3SG li book.DEF

I choose an approach in which I consider the possible segmentation of the complex predicate and the unification of *li*-semantics with the semantics of the complement over which *li* has scope.

Multiverb constructions in Bulgarian are formed with *da* (cf. Dimitrova-Vulchanova & Hellan 1999). *Da* does not fit into familiar complementizer categories, it differs in that it does not allow a FRONT complex under it (as opposed to *če* - the Bulgarian counterpart of 'that'). *Da* is followed by a T/Agr[p,n]P, i.e. it is finite (as opposed to 'infinitival complementizers' like English 'to'). Some of the complementizer-like characteristics of *da* can be seen in that it functions as a domain for cliticization for Argument clitics and it serves as a barrier to clitic climbing.

Let us now have a look at the syntactic positions *li can* take within multiverb constructions:

(22) [$_{S}$ Ivan obešta [$_{S''}$ da otide [$_{S'}$ da kupi knigata]]].
Ivan promised.3SG to go.3SG to buy.3SG book.DEF
'Ivan promised to go and buy the book.'

(23) [$_{S}$ [$_{ClP}$ Ivan li] obešta [$_{S''}$ da otide [$_{S'}$ da kupi knigata]]]?
Ivan li promised.3SG to go.3SG to buy.3SG book.DEF
'Was it Ivan who promised to go and buy the book?'

(24) [$_{S}$ [$_{ClP}$ Ivan [$_{ClP}$ obešta li]][$_{S''}$ da otide [$_{S'}$ da kupi knigata]]]]?
Ivan promised.3SG li to go.3SG to buy.3SG book.DEF
'Did Ivan promise to go and buy the book?'

(25) a. [$_{S}$ Ivan obešta [$_{S''}$ da otide [$_{S'}$ da kupi [$_{?ClP}$[6] knigata li]]]]?
Ivan promised.3SG to go.3SG to buy.3SG book.DEF li
? 'Did Ivan promise to go and buy the book?'

b. [$_{S=ClP}$ [$_{IP}$ Ivan obešta [$_{S''}$ da otide [$_{S'}$ da kupi knigata]]] li]?
Ivan promised.3SG to go.3SG to buy.3SG book.DEF li
'Was it the case that Ivan promised to go and buy the book?'

---

[5] Sentences (19) and (21) can be viewed as acceptable only if we assume that the phrase preceding *li* (*'da otide'* in (19) and *'da kupi'* in (20)) may be regarded as the topic of the sentence, thus receiving the intonation peak.

[6] According to most of the recent research on *li*-movement, it is still questionable whether *li* can lower so far down in the sentence and form a ClP. As this is not a mater of discussion now, I have left this question open for further research.

(26) a. [S [CIP Knigata li] [IP Ivan obešta [S'' da otide [S' da kupi]]]]?
book.DEF li Ivan promised.3SG to go.3SG to buy.3SG

b. [S [CIP Ivan [CIP knigata li]] obešta [S'' da otide [S' da kupi]]]?
Ivan book.DEF li promise.3SG to go.3SG to buy.3SG

c. [S Ivan obešta [IP [CIP knigata li] [S'' da otide [S' da kupi]]]]]?
Ivan promised.3SG book.DEF li to go.3SG to buy.3SG

d. [S Ivan obešta [S'' da otide [CIP [CIP' knigata li] [S' da kupi]]]]]?
Ivan promised.3SG to go.3SG book.DEF li to buy.3SG

(26a-d) 'Was it the book that Ivan promised to buy?'

A plausible account for the restrictions on the otherwise 'flexible' movement of *li* is seen in the segmentation constraints within multiverb constructions in Bulgarian, as well as some semantic constraints on the conceptual units *li* can take in its scope. The possibility (or rather the impossibility) of those segments to act as topic of the sentence also plays an important role. Therefore, the formal representation of *li*-attachment in multiverb constructions in an HPSG perspective is made with regard to the possible segmentation of the complex predicate and the unification of *li*-semantics with the semantics of the particular unit over which *li* has scope. This is achieved by relying on the MOD feature, basically employing the analysis of adjunction and the Linearization Principle. In addition, a variant of HPSG that contains the notion of order domain (Kathol 1998, cf. Hinrichs *et al.* 1998) is used to license the combination of the potential constituents to be unified within the multiverb construction.

Thus the formal representation of sentence (14) will look like the scheme in (27):

(27)

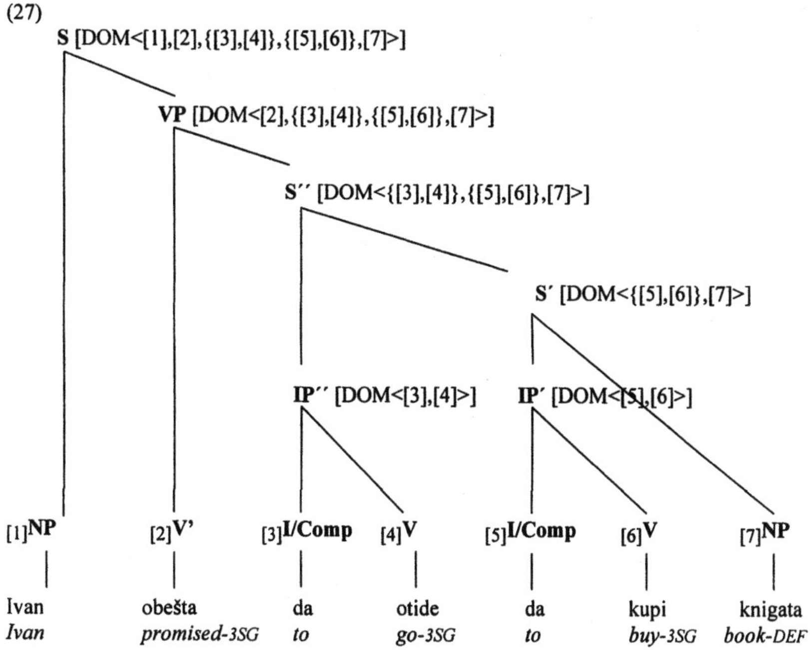

The clitic *li* is presented as shown in (28):

(28)

$$\begin{bmatrix} \text{PHON} & \text{li} \\ \text{CAT} & \begin{bmatrix} \text{HEAD} & \begin{bmatrix} \text{clitic} \\ \text{MOD} \;\; \text{XP} : \begin{bmatrix} \text{INDEX} & [1] \\ \text{RESTRIC} & [2] \end{bmatrix} \end{bmatrix} \\ \text{VAL} & \text{saturated} \end{bmatrix} \\ \text{CONT} & \begin{bmatrix} \text{INDEX} & [1] \\ \text{RESTRIC} & \left\{ \begin{bmatrix} \text{Q - rel} \\ \text{ARG} \;\; [1] \end{bmatrix} \right\} \cup [2] \end{bmatrix} \end{bmatrix}$$

where XP can be any member of the set [NP/AP,AdvP, V', VP, CP] and is marked with the features {+[Topic], +[Question]}.

The formal attachment of *li* basically follows the treatment of adjuncts in HPSG and is governed by the Head-Adjunct Principle as in 29:

(29)

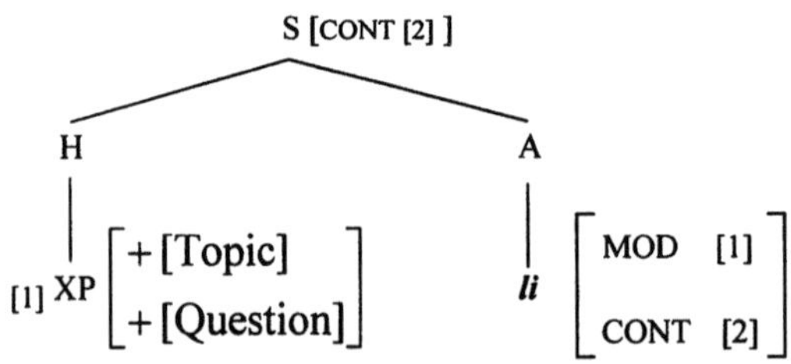

The analysis adopted here explains in an elegant way why sentences like those in (2a) and (2b) are constrained, while (3c) is on the borderline. It also gives explanation for the other cases encountered here, that are not fully acceptable, or acceptable only under special circumstances (different intonation and/or difference in reading). Furthermore, the present approach licences sentences like the one in (30):

(30) 'Ne' *li* mu kaza?
no li to him said.2SG
'Did you say "no" to him?'

It can be felicitously uttered in a situation where the speaker needs a confirmation about a statement like: 'I said "no" to him.'

Conclusions

➢ The distribution of the interrogative clitic *li* in Bulgarian is largely dependent on the topic of the sentence

➢ The attachment of *li* in multiverb constructions depends also on the possible segmentation in the sentence

➢ Syntactically, *li*-attachment is presented as an adjunction of *li* to an XP: [NP/AP/AdvP, V', VP, CP]

➢ Semantically, *li* has a scope over the phrase it modifies and imposes some semantic restrictions upon it {[+T], [+Q]}

Although the analysis presented above is within the HPSG framework, similar analyses can also be presented within LFG and possibly any other formalised grammar.

For future research it would be interesting to have a formal comparison between *li*-attachment in Bulgarian and the other Slavic languages using *li* as an interrogative particle in forming questions.

References

Dimitrova-Vulchanova, M. and L. Hellan. 1999. Clitics and the Bulgarian Clause Structure. In: Van Riemsdijk, H. (ed.), *Clitics in the Languages of Europe,* Berlin: Mouton de Gruyter.

Hinrichs, E. et al. (ed.) 1998. *Syntax and Semantics*, 30. San Diego: Academic Press.

Jaeger, F. 2003a. Topicality and superiority in Bulgarian wh-questions, to appear in: *Proceedings of Formal Approaches to Slavic Linguistics: The Ottawa meeting, 2003*, volume 12. Ann Arbor: Michigan Slavic Publications, 207–228.

Jaeger, F. 2003b. Multiple wh-questions, Superiority and Clitic Doubling in colloquial Bulgarian, A Construction-based HPSG account. Presented at: The 10th International Conference on Head-Driven Phrase Structure Grammar, Michigan State University (July 18-20, 2003).

Krapova, I. and G. Cinque (this volume), *On the Order of wh-Phrases in Bulgarian Multiple wh-Questions.*

Lambrecht, K. 1994. *Information structure and sentence form. Topic, Focus, and the mental representations of discourse referents*. Cambridge: Cambridge University Press.

Penchev, J. 1980. *Osnovni intonacionni konturi v bâlgarskoto izrečenie*. Sofia: BAN.

Penchev, J. 1993. *Bâlgarski sintaksis – upravlenie i svârzvane*. Plovdiv: Plovdivsko univirsitetsko izdatelstvo.

Reinhart, T. 1982. *Pragmatics and linguistics: an analysis of sentence topics.* Distributed by Indiana University Linguistics Club, Bloomington, Indiana.

Rivero, M.-L. 1992. Bulgarian and Serbo-Croatian Yes-No Questions: Vo-Raising vs. Li-Hopping. In: *Linguistic Inquiry* 24, 567-575.

Tomič, O. M. 1996. The Balkan Slavic Clausal Clitics. In: Joan Maling (ed.) *Natural Language & Linguistic Theory* 14 (4), 811-872.

Marija Golden, Ljubljana

2nd Position Clitic Climbing and Restructuring

Clitics continue to be a vibrant area of linguistic research. In this paper, we would like to examine the placement of the so-called Wackernagel or second-position (2P) clitics in Slovenian as well as Czech with respect to two more recent claims: **(i)** Bošković's proposal that in 2P clitic languages clitics do not necessarily cluster together under the same head position in syntax (Bošković 1997; 2000; 2001); **(ii)** Cinque's monoclausal attempt to restrict clitic climbing to verbs which are heads of functional projections (Cinque 2002; cf. also Wurmbrand 2001). Both claims are made in the spirit of the Uniformity Principle (Chomsky 2001: 2) and have a great deal of linguistic appeal. We would like to propose that they do not yet take into account the data presented below. As argued in Golden 2003, the phonological constraints on 2P clitics in the lexicon do not yet account for their placement in clitic climbing contexts, (1). (The clitics are in italics, the climbing clitics are in boldface.)

(1) Sln Janez ***ti*** ***jo*** *je* hotel najprej prepovedati začeti brati že na vlaku.
Janez.Nom to-you.Dat her.Acc is.Aux wanted.Prt at first to-forbid to-start to-read already on train
'At first Janez wanted to forbid you to start reading it on the train.'

Cz Jan ***ti ji*** chtěl nejdříve zabránit začít číst už ve vlaku.

Prosodically, Slovenian and Czech clitics are either enclitic, integrating into the prosodic phrase of the phonological word to their left, or proclitic, cliticizing onto the phonological word to their right (see, among many others, Golden and Milojević Sheppard 2000; Toman 1996; Junghanns 2002). This is exemplified for Slovenian in (2a) and (2b).

(2) a. Janez *jim* *jo* hvali.
Janez to-them.Dat her.Acc praises
'Janez praises her to them.'

b. *Ga* že vidim.
Him.Acc already I-see
'I already see him.'

In Bošković's approach to languages with 2P clitics, the order of clitics with respect to each other is expected to follow from their morphosyntax, whereas their 2P placement derives from the phonological requirements that clitics be initial in their intonation phrase, and on a language-by-language basis enclitic, proclitic or both. In this approach, clitics do not undergo any cluster-forming syntatic movement once they land in their feature-checking positions.

The derivation of sentence (2a), 'Janez praises her to them,' would proceed, simplified, as follows. The clitics *jim* and *jo* are identified as [+ clitic] in the lexicon and merged into the structure in their fully inflected form. The accusative clitic *jo* is merged into the structure as complement of its θ-marking and case-assigning lexical verb 'to praise,' it is its internal object; [$_{V'}$ V° DP]. The dative clitic *jim*, the indirect object, is merged with V' in the specifier position of the verb phrase, [$_{VP}$ [$_{DP}$ *jim*] [$_{V'}$ V° [$_{DP}$ *jo*]]]. As structurally ambiguous X° and XP elements (Chomsky 1995), clitics may undergo X° and XP movement. As overt heads of DPs, their case and agreement features undergo feature-checking by XP substitution into the specifier positions of relevant functional projections. The feature is "checked off" if the feature of the XP attracted into the Spec position of the functional projection agrees with the feature of the verb raised for that purpose into the Head position, ... [$_{TP}$ *Janez* [$_{vP}$ ~~*Janez*~~ [$_{v'}$

$[_{vP}$ *jim* $[_{vP}$ *jo* $[_{VP}$ ~~*jim*~~ $[_{V'}$ *hvali* ~~*jo*~~]]]]]]].[1] In some approaches, 2P clitics now undergo further syntactic movement and form a 2P cluster. This time they raise as heads and end under a single syntactic node, usually high in the tree.[2] Such syntactic accounts of 2P clitics assume that there is a syntactic cluster formation operation, although they have not been successful in suggesting a morphosyntactic feature that would force cluster-forming clitics to raise to a single functional head.

In the approach of Bošković 2001, however, the question of what feature forces the clitics to form a 2P cluster does not arise since the clitics are not seen as undergoing any further syntatic movement once they land in their feature-checking positions. In Bošković 2001, 2P clitics cluster together only as a result of their cliticization in the phonological component. The obligatory nature of clitic clustering in 2P is seen as following from two phonological properties of clitics, both specified in the lexicon. First, as phonologically weak elements, clitics must have a host; much like affixes, they cannot be stranded. The 2P effect in languages with Wackernagel clitics is seen as the result of the phonological requirement that they must be initial in their intonation phrase: (3i) forces the clitics located in the same intonation phrase to form a cluster in PF. Second, the direction of their attachment to the host is language specific: S(erbo)C(roatian) clitics are specified in the lexicon as suffixes, (3ii); Slovenian (and Czech) clitics can be both, suffixes and prefixes, (3iii).

(3) i. "# __"

SC ii. suffix

Sln iii. suffix or prefix

(4) SC a. # *Oni su* $_{Aux}$ *mi* $_{Dat}$ *ga* $_{Acc}$ *predstavili#*
'They introduced him to me.'

Sln b. # *Oni so* $_{Aux}$ *mi* $_{Dat}$ *ga* $_{Acc}$ *predstavili#*

In SC example (4), the auxiliary clitic *su* merges with the preceding phonological word *oni*, satisfying both requirements. The SC verbal clitic is initial in its intonation phrase and a suffix. The dative clitic and the accusative clitic successively encliticize to the phonological word resulting from the phonological merger in the previous step. The Slovenian enclitics in (4b) are described in the same way.

(5) Janez hvali {**jo*, ✓njo }.

Boškovič's approach rules out the unacceptable placement of the accusative clitic *jo* in (5) as a phonological irregularity. Although the accusative case checking places both, the clitic *jo* and its strong pronoun counterpart *njo*, in the Specifier position of the relevant functional

---

[1] The movement of clitics is subject to economy principles. One version of this, the Minimal Link Condition, requires that each instance of movement be the shortest possible, and prevents a category from skipping its closest landing site. The MLC guarantees, for example, that the accusative clitic checks its case before the dative clitic, yielding the acceptable "dative > accusative" clitic order. The unacceptable order of the accusative preceding the dative, as in **Janez jo jim hvali*, is ruled out as a violation of this minimality constraint. In structure "... $[_{TP}$ $[_{AuxP}$ *Janez* $[_{vP}$ *jo* $_{Acc}$ $[_{vP}$ *jim* $_{Dat}$ *hvali*]] ...," the accusative clitic *jo* skipped the dative clitic *jim*, its nearest [Spec, XP] landing site.

[2] In order to state the correspondence between the relative height of clitics prior to clustering and the linear order of clitics within the clitic cluster, Golden & Milojević Sheppard 2000 suggested that Slovenian pronominal clitics right-adjoin by Move α to the C node of their CP domain. For the discussion of the inconsistency of such rightward adjunction with Kayne's 1994 Linear Correspondence Axiom, see Bošković 2002.

phrase, the clitic has to satisfy an additional phonological constraint, namely (3i), which the clitic in (5) does not. The accusative clitic *jo* in (5) satisfies the suffix requirement (3iii), but violates the 2P requirement (3i) that clitics encliticize to the first constituent of their intonation phrase. For Bošković, the accusative clitic in (5) is a stranded affix: it occurs in the syntactically well-formed construction which is filtered out by the 2P constraint ("#__") in the phonological component. We would like to propose that the clitic climbing data presented below show that more is involved in 2P that can be predicted from their assumed morphosyntax and phonology.

For Bošković's analysis of 2P clitic placement, clitic climbing in Slovenian and Czech poses two main problems: (i) the occurrence of clitic climbing, i.e., the fact that clitics seem not to remain in their case-checking positions; (ii) the optionality of clitic climbing.

(6) Sln a. # Jaz *sem* ***ji ga*** moral pošiljati po pošti#
I.Nom am.Aux her.Dat him.Acc must to-send by mail
'I had to send it to her by mail.'

Cz #Musel *jsem* ***jí ho*** posílat poštou#

Sln b. Jaz *sem* moral #pošiljati *ji ga* po pošti#

Cz Musel *jsem* #posílat *jí ho* poštou#

Sln c. #Jaz *sem* moral pošiljati *ji ga* po pošti#

His approach makes the empirically correct prediction that both (6a) and (6b) are well-formed prosodic structures. In the presence of clitic climbing, as in (6a), the approach assumes that the matrix clause and the infinitival complement form one intonation unit, with respect to the phonological constraints the resulting prosodic structure is therefore acceptable. In the absence of clitic climbing, as in (6b), the phonological approach to 2P clitics must assume that the embedded infinitival complement forms its own intonational phrase. In (6b), both phonological requirements of the embedded pronominal clitics can be satisfied within the second intonation phrase, in (6b), they are enclitic. The intended prosodic structure of the syntactically well-formed sentence (6c) is ruled out in the phonological component because the clitics *ji* and *ga* violate the 2P requirement (analogous to ex. (5)).

However, the approach does not address the question why clitic climbing should occur. Since no cluster-formation is assumed to be taking place in syntax, there is no greed-propelled syntactic movement to force the clitics to move overtly out of their case-checking positions. If clitic movement is triggered by the necessity to delete uninterpretable features by the end of the derivation, then it has yet to be explained why clitic climbing takes place.[3] Secondly, the integrating hypothesis of the "economy-driven framework such as minimalism" is that movement is never optional. Clitic climbing seems to be optional, and thus a problem (Bošković 2001: 135, fn. 38).

Clitic climbing is a well researched phenomenon in Romance languages, it is much less so in Slavic languages. Verbs that allow clitic climbing in Romance languages form a semantically and syntactically definable group. Semantically, they are aspectuals, modals, causatives, and verbs of perception; syntactically, they belong to raising, control and ECM verbs. The ability of Romance clitics to escape their base positions in embedded structures has been shown to be highly constrained and open to language variation. Italian, for example, allows clitic climbing with *volere* but disallows it with *desidere*, (7). In Modern French, clitic climbing is not allowed with such subject control verbs as *voulvoir*, (8a); it is available, for instance, in ECM constructions with verb of perception, (8b).

[3] We assume that pronominal clitics in (6) check their features in the domain of the infinitival complement because restructuring is neither sufficient nor necessary for clitic climbing in Slovenian, as we show below.

(7) *Lo*$_i$ voglio fare ec$_i$ (Moore 1994: 337, ex. (7))
'It (I) want to do.'
* *Lo*$_i$ desidero fare ec$_i$
'I desire to do it.'

(8) a. * Jean ***le*** veut faire. (Roberts 1997: 438, ex. (30c))
'Jean wants to do it.'

b. Cette maison, je ***l'***ai vu bâtir. (Martins 1995: 216)
'This house, I saw building it.'

Similarly in Slovenian and Czech, climbing clitics are arguments of the infinitives embedded under raising verbs, (9), and subject control verbs, (10). In (9), the dative *ji* and the accusative *ga*, the underlying indirect and direct objects of the embedded infinitive 'to send,' join the matrix-clause auxiliary clitic *sem*.

(9) Sln Jaz *sem* ***ji ga*** moral pošiljati po pošti.
I.Nom am.Aux her.Dat him.Acc must to-send by mail
'I had to send it to her by mail.'

Cz Musel *jsem* ***jí ho*** posílat poštou.

(10) Sln Janez *se* ***ji ga*** *je* naveličal hvaliti.
Janez.Nom se.refl her.Dat him.Acc is.Aux tired-Prt to-praise
'Janez grew tired of praising him to her.'

Cz Jan ***mu ho*** chtěl představit na recepci.
'Jan wanted to introduce him to him at the reception.'

Clitic climbing in Slovenian and Czech takes place also from infinitives embedded under verbs of perception, as in (11), and from infinitival adverbial clauses of purpose embedded under verbs of motion ("finalen infinitiven"; in (12) the climbing accusative clitic *jo* is argument to the embedded "short" infinitive 'to visit').[4]

(11) Sln Janez *te* ***jo*** *je* videl dati v žep.
Janez.Nom you.Acc her.Acc is.Aux seen.Prt to-put in pocket
'Janez saw you put it in your pocket.'

Cz Jan *tě* ***ji*** viděl dát do kapsy.

(12) Sln Janez ***jo*** *je* šel obiskat (hodil obiskovat) v Ljubljano.
Janez.Nom her.Acc is.Aux gone.Prt. to-visit in Ljubljana
'Janez went to visit (was in the habit of visiting) her in Ljubljana.'

Cz Jan ***jí*** jel navštívit (jezdil navštěvovat) do Ljubljaně.

---

[4] In Romance, clitic-climbing with motion verbs is expected because the structure is taken to be monoclausal: the motion verb is semantically an aspectual verb, with the syntax of a functional (raising) verb. If they turn out to be non-accusatives, they project an internal argument which becomes the external argument for case-theoretic reasons. Slovenian motion verbs do not have the semantics of a light verb: they are not thematically or lexically impoverished, they are morphologically marked for aspect (*iti/ hoditi* 'to go').

However, unlike in Romance, Slovenian and Czech allow clitics to climb out of infinitives of object control verb. In one interpretation of (13), the climbing clitic is the accusative *ga* and it joins the matrix-clause dative clitic *ji*, the controlling NP, and the auxiliary clitic *sem.*

(13) Sln Jaz *sem ji* ***ga*** dovolil poslati po pošti.
I.Nom am.Aux. her.Dat him.Acc allowed-Prt to-send by mail
'I allowed her to send it by mail.'

Cz Dovolil *jsem jí* ***ho*** poslat poštou.

As shown in (14), Slovenian and Czech clitics may also leave right-extraposed subject clauses, when they are infinitival. In (14), the dative and the accusative clitics are arguments of the embedded infinitive 'to send.'

(14) Sln Takrat ***ji ga*** *je* bilo mogoče poslati po pošti.
then her.Dat him.Acc is.Aux been.Prt possible to-send by mail
'Then it was possible to send it to her by mail.'

Cz Tehdy ***jí ho*** bylo možné poslat poštou.

Slovenian and Czech clitics climb also out of infinitival clauses which are complements to nouns, (15), and adjectives, (16). In (15), the pronominal clitics are arguments to the embedded infinitive 'to deliver.' In Slovenian (16), the climbing clitic ***mu*** is dative object of the infinitive 'to apologize;' the reflexive clitic of the matrix verb *čutiti se* 'to feel' licenses the deletion of the phonologically identical reflexive clitic of the embedded infinitive 'to apologize,' *opravičevati se*. It has been suggested that successful cases of clitic climbing are instances of noun or adjective incorporation with the matrix verb. The modification on the "incorporated" noun, however, would seem to speak against the incorporation analysis, note also that adjacency need not obtain, (17).[5]

(15) Sln Ti *si* ***mu ga*** imel priložnost izročiti osebno.
you.Nom are.Aux him.Dat him.Acc had.Prt to-deliver personally
'You had the opportunity to give it to him in person.'

Cz Ty *jsi* ***mu ho*** měl příležitost doručit osobně.

(16) Sln Jaz *se* ***mu*** ne čutim dolžnega opravičevati.
I se.Refl him.Dat not feel obliged.Adj to-apologize
'I do not feel obliged to apologize (for myself).'

(17) Sln Sedaj ***ga*** imaš še zadnjo priložnost osebno pozdraviti, preden odpotuje.
'Now you have the last opportunity to greet him personally, before he departs.'

[5] As observed for Czech in Junghanns 2002, no clitic climbing takes place if a light matrix verb 'to have' in (17) is replaced by a lexically more salient verb 'to find' or 'to feel'.

Sln Nihče ni našel priložnosti izročiti *mu ga* osebno.
'No one found the oportunity to deliver it to him in person.'
* Nihče ***mu ga*** ni našel priložnosti izročiti osebno.

Cz Nikdo nenašel odvahu doručit *mu ho* osobně.
* Nikdo ***mu ho*** nenašel odvahu doručit osobně.

Cz Teď ***ho*** máš ještě poslední možnost osobně pozdravit dříve, než odjedeš.

Slovenian and Czech clitics climb also out of predicative adjective phrases. In (18) the dative clitic is argument to the predicative adjective 'grateful'.

(18) Sln Jaz ***sem ji*** bil vedno (neskončno) hvaležen za vsak nasvet.
I am.Aux her.Dat been.Prt (infinitely) grateful for every piece of advice
'I have always been (infinitely) grateful to her for every piece of advice.'

Cz Já ***jsem jí*** byl vždy (nekonečně) vděčný za každou radu.

In view of this wider distribution of clitic climbing in Slovenian and Czech, we do not think that the analyses proposed for clitic climbing in Romance, be they restructuring, as shown, much simplified, in (10i), or monoclausal, as in (10ii), suffice for a unifying description of clitic climbing.

i. Restructuring biclausal analysis (Aissen and Perlmutter 1983; Rizzi 1978; Kayne 1989; Roberts 1997; Di Sciullo & Williams 1987)

(10) Janez *se* ***ji ga*** *je* [$_{VP}$ naveličal [$_{CP}$ hvaliti]]

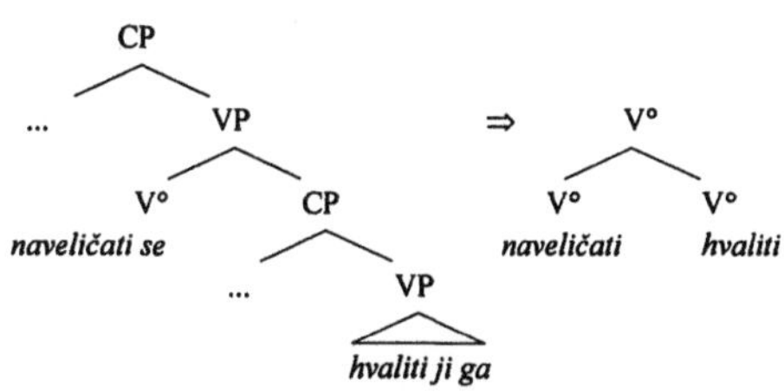

In the analysis of Aissen and Perlmutter 1983 for Spanish, certain matrix verbs trigger clausal union whereby the argument structures of the matrix verb and the embedded infinitive become one. The optional structure-changing transformation of Rizzi 1978 re-analyzes the matrix verb and the embedded infinitive complement as a single verbal complex projected under one V head. Kayne 1989 analyzes restructuring in the *Barriers* framework as raising of the embedded functional head I° to the matrix I°, I°-to-I° raising out of the complement CP is possible when the complement CP is L-marked by the matrix restructuring verb. A similar covert head movement is proposed also by Roberts 1997, only in his approach, as in Rizzi 1978, it is not just the head I° of the infinitival complement that raises to the matrix, restructuring involves also the incorporation of the complement verb into the matrix verb (V°-into-I° incorporation). Di Sciullo and Williams 1987 offer a morphological analysis of restructuring: the restructuring verb and its infinitive form a complex verb by a morphological rule of compounding in the morphological component.

We do not think that a restructuring analysis can provide a general account of clitic climbing contexts. As shown above, clitic climbing in Slovenian and Czech is not restricted to complement clauses of verbs; the adjacency between the "restructuring" predicate (verb, noun, adjective) and the infinitive need not obtain;[6] note also that restructuring can not be postponed to LF because clitic climbing is overt.

[6] Non-adjacency can be explained away by adopting a copy theory of movement, as proposed by Roberts 1997, with restrictions on which intermediate copy of the moved and incorporated head is eventually spelled-out.

These properties of clitic climbing in Slovenian and Czech present problems also for approaches which assume that clitic climbing contexts are monoclausal throughout the derivation.

Monoclausal analyses for Romance clitic climbing are motivated by the fact that most matrix verbs which allow clitic climbing are thematically deficient. It therefore makes linguistic sense to argue that they project in the functional structure of another, thematically complete verb.

ii. Monoclausal analysis (Rosen 1990, Wurmbrand 2001, Cinque 2002)

(10) Janez *se* ***ji ga*** *je* [$_{FP}$ naveličal [$_{VP}$ hvaliti]]

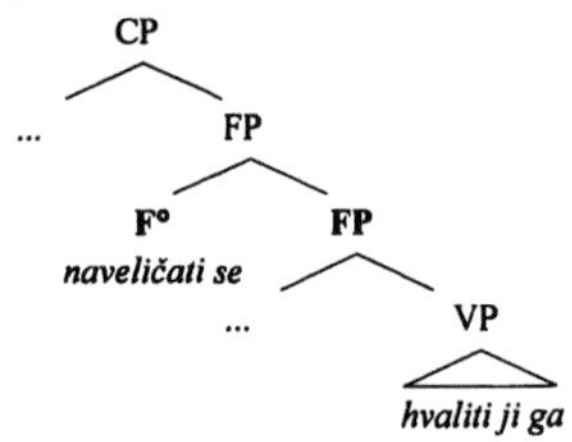

Cinque 2002 starts from two observations. **(i)** Restructuring with clitic climbing as one of its syntactic effects is exhibited by similar sets of verbs cross-linguistically. Romance (as well as Slovenian and Czech) clitics climb into the matrix clause from non-finite complements embedded under a modal or aspectual predicate or a verb of movement. Therefore attempts to deal with restructuring as a lexically governed phenomenon on a language-by-language basis cannot be intuitively satisfying. **(ii)** Verbs that admit restructuring and clitic climbing are similarly ordered relative to each other cross-linguistically. Cinque 2002 proposes to predict both sets of data by treating restructuring verbs, universally, as heads of functional projections, with each restructuring verb lexicalizing the content of a functional head. Not lexical idiosyncracy, but universal hierarchy of functional projections, which is argued for independently of restructuring phenomena, and a subset of which is suggested in (19), determines that verbs denoting epistemic modality precede verbs denoting root modality and both precede aspectual verb like *začeti*.

(19) ... Modality $_{epistemic}$ > ... Modality $_{root}$ ... > ... Aspect ...

Janez ***jih*** $_{Acc}$ *je* $_{Aux}$ utegnil morati začeti reševati sam.
'Janez might have had to start solving them on his own.'

The monoclausal analysis of "restructuring" contexts, simplified in (10ii), does not see "restructuring" verbs as undergoing syntactic simplification. Since "restructuring" verbs are taken to be functional verbs and, much like auxiliaries, transparent to the arguments of the lexical verb in VP, the structure in (10ii) cannot be but monoclausal. The object clitics *ji* and *ga* of the embedded infinitive in (10ii), therefore, do not "climb" across the clause boundary of the embedded infinitival complement. Rather, the clustering of clitics *se ji ga je* should follow from the standard minimalist feature-checking of 2P clause-mate clitics. The proposed monoclausal structure is, of course, more richly articulated by additional functional projections, heads of which are also former raising and control verbs.

Although the monoclausal approach to restructuring and clitic climbing is theoretically appealing because of its universalism with respect to the selection and order among the restructuring verbs, we would like to propose that it cannot take full account of Slovenian or

Czech data on clitic climbing. It fails to account for the fact that Slovenian and Czech clitic climbing is not restricted to infinitival complements of thematically deficient matrix verbs.

The literature on Romance clitics observes that clitic arguments of infinitives embedded under verbs of object control do not climb. The few apparent cases of clitic climbing with Romance object-control verbs can be analyzed as underlyingly causative constructions, as demonstrated in Cinque 2002: 10-12; cf. also Kayne 1989: 248.

(20) * *Me **lo*** invitarono/aiutarono a leggere. (Cinque 2002: 37, n. 35)
'They invited/helped me to read it.'
* *Me **lo*** costrinsero /obbligarono /forzarono a leggere.
'They forced me to read it.'
* *Me **lo*** convinsero /persuasero a leggere.
'They convinced me to read it.'

In the monoclausal approach, the observation that Romance object-control verbs do not allow clitic climbing follows from the defining property of "restructuring" verbs. If "restructuring" verbs are, universally, functional verbs, then the structure projected by the "restructuring" verbs does not provide for any thematic DP arguments. It then also follows that object-control verbs, which do have thematic arguments, cannot be functional verbs and are expected to disallow clitic climbing.

In Slovenian and Czech, object-control verbs allow clitic climbing. Slovenian and Czech equivalents to unacceptable attempts at Italian clitic climbing with object-control verbs in (20) are acceptable. In (21a) the accusative clitic *ga* (*ho*), the direct object of the infinitive 'to read', may join the matrix verbal and the indirect-object clitics; in (22) the accusative clitic *ga* (*ho*), the direct object of the infinitive 'to forge', may join the matrix verbal and direct object clitics.

(21) Sln Janez *mu **ga** je* {dovolil, pustil, branil, naročil, omogočil, prepovedal, svetoval, velel, ukazal} prebrati na samem.
'Janez {allowed, let, prohibited, ordered, enabled, forbade, advised, told} him to read it in private.'

Cz Jan *mu **ho*** dovolil (nechal, zakázal, uložil, znemožnil, radil, přikázal, poručil) přečíst o samotě.

(22) Sln Janez *me **ga** je* {hujskal, opogumljal, naučil, nagovarjal, pregovoril, priganjal, silil, navadil} poneveriti.
'Janez {incited, encouraged, taught, prompted, persuaded, urged, forced, got (me) into the habit (of forging)} me to forge it.'

Cz Jan *mě **ho*** (nabádal, naučil, přemluvil, nutil) zpronevěřit.

For the monoclausal approach to work, these matrix verbs with an internal DP argument, overtly marked either with the dative (21) or the accusative case (22), would have to lend themselves to the kind of analysis proposed for causatives, (23i).

(23) Sln Janez *me **ga** je* prisilil poneveriti.
'Janez forced me to forge it.'

Cz Jan *mě **ho*** nabádal zpronevěřit.
i. ... [$_{vP}$ *Janez* *v°* [$_{VP}$ *prisiliti* [$_{vP}$ *me* poneveriti *ga* ...

In the monoclausal approach, the matrix verb would be taken to be a light verb taking a vP complement. Its internal DP argument would have to be shown to be structural subject of the embedded infinitive. We cannot support this proposal by independent syntactic or semantic evidence.

In (23), the accusative argument *me* is understood as having a dual thematic role: it is goal towards which Janez's action is directed, at the same time it is agent in the embedded event. The infinitival complement can take the form of a finite clause with the same semantics: *Janez je prisilil mene, da sem ga poneveril podpis*, cf. also *Jan přinutil Marii, aby (ona, Marie) ho padělala.* The control approach treated the accusative argument *me* as the internal argument of the matrix verb, controlling the reference of the PRO subject of the embedded infinitive. That two events are involved, is supported also by the fact that each event may be independently modified by a time-when adverbial such that the two adverbials are mutually incompatible as modifiers of a single event, (24).

(24) Zdravnik *nam ga je še* včeraj dovolil jutri zjutraj obiskati.
'The doctor allowed us as recently as yesterday to visit him tomorrow morning.'

If the monoclausal approach treats the internal DP argument of the object-control verb as the structural subject of the embedded infinitive, it cannot predict that such sentences as (25) are ambiguous with respect to the interpretation of the dative argument; note also that this ambiguity is retained with clitic climbing.

(25) Janez *ji jih je* dovolil kupiti.

(i) Janez *ji* ***jih*** *je* dovolil kupiti.
'Janez allowed her to buy them.'

(ii) Janez ***ji jih*** *je* dovolil kupiti.
'Janez allowed (someone) to buy them/it for her/them.'

The fact that object-control verbs have thematic arguments makes it impossible for them to be analysed as functional heads. The observation that in Slovenian and Czech clitic climbing from the infinitival complements of object-control verbs is possible, suggests that clitic climbing is not restricted to monoclausal structure. If it is not restricted to monoclausal structure, then the phonological approach to 2P placement of clause-mate clitics cannot provide an explanation as to why clitics climb.

References

Aissen, J., L., & D. M. Perlmutter (1983): Clause reduction in Spanish. In: D. M. Perlmutter (ed.): *Studies in relational grammar* 1. Chicago: University of Chicago Press, 360–403.

Bošković, Ž. (1997): Second Position Cliticization: Syntax and /or Phonology?. Paper presented at ESSE 4 Debrecen.

Bošković, Ž. (2000): Second position cliticization: syntax and /or phonology. In: Beukema, F. & M. den Dikken (eds.): *Clitic phenomena in European languages*. Amsterdam, Philadelphia: John Benjamins, 71–119.

Bošković, Ž. (2001): *On the nature of the syntax-phonology interface: Cliticization and related phenomena*. Amsterdam: Elsevier Science.

Bošković, Ž. (2002): Clitics as nonbranching elements and the linear correspondence axiom, *Linguistic Inquiry* 2, 329–340.

Chomsky, N. (1995): A Minimalist Program for Linguistic Theory. In: Chomsky, N. (1995): *The minimalist program* (= *Current studies in linguistics*; 28). Cambridge, Mass./London, England: MIT Press, 167–217.

Chomsky, N. (2001): Derivation by Phase. In: Kenstowicz, M. (ed.): *Ken Hale: A Life in Language*. Cambridge, Mass.: MIT Press, 1–52.

Cinque, G. (1999): *Adverbs and functional heads: A cross-linguistic perspective*. Oxford: Oxford University Press.

Cinque, G. (2002): "Restructuring" and functional structure. Ms., University of Venice.

Di Sciullo, A. M. & E. Williams (1987): *On the definition of word*. Cambridge, Mass.: MIT Press.

Franks, S. (1998): Clitics in Slavic. Paper presented at the comparative Slavic morphosyntax workshop, Indiana University, Bloomington; http://www.indiana.edu/~slavconf/linguistics/index.html).

Golden, M. (2003): Clitic placement and clitic climbing. In: *Sprachtypologie und Universalienforschung* 56, 208–233.

Golden, M. & M. Milojević Sheppard (2000): Slovene pronominal clitics. In: Beukema, F. & M. den Dikken (eds): *Clitic phenomena in European languages*. Amsterdam, Philadelphia: John Benjamins; 191–207.

Junghanns, U. (2002): Clitic climbing im Tschechischen. In: Junghanns, U.: *Untersuchungen zur Syntax und Informationsstruktur slavischer Deklarativsätze*. Leipzig: Institut für Linguistik der Universität Leipzig, 57–90.

Kayne, R. S. (1991): Romance clitics, verb movement, and PRO, *Linguistic Inquiry* 22, 647–686.

Kayne, R. S. (1989): Null subjects and clitic climbing. In: Jaeggli, O. & K. Safir (eds.): *The null subject parameter*. Dordrecht: Kluwer, 239–261.

Martins, A. M., (1995): A minimalist approach to clitic climbing. In: *Proceedings of the* 31st *Regional Meeting of the Chicago Linguistic Society*. Chicago: Chicago Linguistic Society 2, 215–233.

Moore, J. (1994): Romance cliticization and relativized minimality, *Linguistic Inquiry* 2, 335–344.

Progovac, L. (1993): Clitics in Serbian/Croatian: Comp as the second position. In: Halpern, A. & A. Zwicky (eds.): *Approaching second: Second position clitics and related phenomena*. Standford: CSLI Publications, 411–428.

Rizzi, L. (1978): A restructuring rule in Italian syntax. In: Keyser, S. J. (ed.): *Recent transformational studies in European languages*. Cambridge, Mass.: MIT Press, 113–158.

Roberts, I. (1991): Excorporation and minimality. In: *Linguistic Inquiry* 22, 209–218.

Roberts, I. (1997): Restructuring, head movement, and locality. In: *Linguistic Inquiry* 3, 423–460.

Rosen, S. T., (1990): Restructuring verbs are light verbs. In: Halpern, A. (ed.): *Proceedings of the* 9th *West Coast Conference on Formal Linguistics*. Standford, CA: CSLI Publications, 477–492.

Stjepanović, S. (1998): On the placement of Serbo-Croatian clitics: Evidence from VP-ellipsis. In: *Linguistic Inquiry* 29, 527–537.

Toman, J. (1996): A note on clitics and prosody. In: Halpern, A. L. & A. M. Zwicky (eds.): *Approaching second: Second position clitics and related phenomena*. Standford: CSLI Publications, 505–510.

Wurmbrand, S., (2001): *Infinitives: Restructuring and clause structure*. In: Studies in Generative Grammar 55. Berlin: Mouton de Gruyter.

Iliyana Krapova and Guglielmo Cinque, Venice

On the Order of *wh*-Phrases in Bulgarian Multiple *wh*-Fronting*

1. Introduction

This paper is more an attempt to enlarge the empirical basis of multiple wh-questions in Bulgarian than to present a new analysis of the quite complex issue of Superiority (only in the last section we briefly discuss some implications which the data seem to point to).
Bulgarian, as opposed to other Slavic languages, is known to display a rather rigid ordering of wh-phrases in (non-echo) multiple wh-fronting, a consequence, it is generally assumed, of Superiority (Rudin 1988; Bošković 1997, 1998a, 2002, Richards 1997/2001, Pesetsky 2000, Grewendorf 2001, among others). See, e.g., (1) and (2):

(1)	a.	Koj	kakvo	pravi?				(Rudin 1988, 481)
		who	what	does				'Who is doing what?'
	b.	*Kakvo	koj	pravi?				(Rudin 1988, 482)
		what	who	does				'What is who doing?'
(2)	a.	Kogo	kak	e	tselunal	Ivan?		(Bošković 1997, 234)
		whom	how	is	kissed	Ivan		'How did Ivan kiss who?'
	b.	*Kak	kogo	e	tselunal	Ivan?		
		how	whom	is	kissed	Ivan		

The literature, nonetheless, reports cases of apparently freely ordered multiple wh-phrases (in fact, with one of the two orders preferred over the other). Cf., e.g., (3)-(7). Moreover some of the possible orders even appear to violate Superiority (see in particular (6b), where a wh-direct object precedes the wh-subject and (7b), where a wh-adjunct precedes the wh-subject):

(3)	a.		Kogo	kâde	ste	videli?	(cf. Bošković 1997, 234)
			whom	where	were-you	seen	'Who have you seen where?
	b.	?(?)	Kâde	kogo	ste	videli?	(cf. Bošković 1997, 234)
			where	whom	were-you	seen	'Where have you seen who?'
(4)	a.	?	Kakvo	kâde	šte	složiš?	
			what	where	will	put-you	'What will you put where?'
	b.		Kâde	kakvo	šte	složiš?	
			where	what	will	put-you	'Where will you put what?'
(5)	a.	?	Kakvo	na kogo	mu	xaresva?	(Billings and Rudin 1996, 40)
			what	to whom	to-him	appeals	'What appeals to whom?'
	b.		Na kogo	kakvo	mu	xaresva?	(Billings and Rudin 1996, 40)
			to whom	what	to-him	appeals	'What appeals to whom?'

* We thank Željko Bošković, Steven Franks, and Luigi Rizzi for their comments on an earlier draft of this paper, as well as the audiences of FDSL-5 and the Geneva workshop on (Multiple) Wh-movement: structures and derivations for their questions and valuable suggestions.

(6) a. ?(?) Kakvo kogo e spoletjalo? (cf. Billings and Rudin 1996, 38)
what whom is stricken 'What struck whom?'

b. Kogo kakvo e spoletjalo? (cf. Billings and Rudin 1996, 38)
whom what is stricken 'What struck whom?'

(7) a. ? Kakvo kâde raste? (Billings and Rudin 1996, 42, and fn. 10)
what where grows 'What grows where?'

b. Kâde kakvo raste? (Billings and Rudin 1996, 42, and fn. 10)
where what grows 'What grows where?'

Despite appearances, we will try to show that the free ordering of wh-phrases is only apparent and that there may be no real Superiority violations. A wh-phrase will turn out to occupy different positions as a consequence of its internal makeup and interpretation, arguably in compliance with (a generalized version of) Superiority (see section 7.).[1]

---

[1] We leave aside cases with more than two wh-phrases, which are said to allow free ordering of all but the first wh-phrase (Bošković 1997, 1999, 2002; Richards 1997, 2001; Pesetsky 2000, among others). The reason we do that is that there are exceptions to this freedom, a fact which clearly requires further investigation. So, for example, while (ia) and (ib) are equally acceptable (cf. Bošković 1997, 239), our informants do not seem to allow free ordering of the second and third wh-phrase in cases like (ii), (iii) and (iv), among others:

(i) a. Koj kogo kak e tselunal?
who whom how is kissed 'Who kissed whom how?'

b. Koj kak kogo e tselunal? (cf. (2)b)

(ii) a. Koj kogo po kakâv način e tselunal?
who whom in what way is kissed 'Who kissed whom in what way?'

b. * Koj po kakâv način kogo e tselunal?
who in what way whom is kissed

(iii) a. Koj kâde kolko e poxarčil?
who where how much is spent 'Who spent how much where?'

b. * Koj kolko kâde e poxarčil?
who how much where is spent

(iv) a. Na kogo koga kak šte pomogneš?
to whom when how will help-you 'To whom will you help when how?'

b. * Na kogo kak koga šte pomogneš?
to whom how when will help-you

We also leave aside embedded contexts, which seem to rescue some of the orderings which are excluded (or dispreferred) in matrix questions. For example, while (19b) in the text below is quite marginal as a matrix question, it improves considerably as an embedded question:

(v) Iskam da mi kažeš koga kogo šte posreštaš utre.
want-I *da* me tell-you when whom will meet-you tomorrow
lit. 'I want you to tell me when whom you will be meeting tomorrow.'

Our first piece of evidence for this conclusion comes from the relative order of wh-adjuncts.

2. The order of wh-adjuncts

As shown by (8) and (9), the order of wh-adjuncts appears to be very strict: *koga* 'when' necessarily precedes *kâde* 'where', and *kâde* 'where' necessarily precedes *kak* 'how'. If transitivity holds, *koga* 'when' should also precede *kak* 'how'. (10) shows that this is precisely the case, which in turn suggests that the overall order of the wh-adjuncts is: *koga* > *kâde* > *kak.*

(8) a. Koga kâde šte xodiš tova ljato?
when where will go-you this summer
'When will you go where, this summer?'

b. * Kâde koga šte xodiš tova ljato?
where when will go-you this summer

(9) a. Kâde kak si se dâržal?
where how are-you refl.cl behaved 'Where did you behave how?'

b. * Kak kâde si se dâržal.
how where are-you refl.cl behaved

(10) a. Koga kak si se dâržal?
when how are-you refl.cl behaved 'When did you behave how?'

b. * Kak koga si se dâržal?
how when are-you refl.cl behaved

3. The order of wh-objects with respect to wh-adjuncts

The rigid ordering of wh-adjuncts proves instrumental in revealing the distribution of wh-arguments. As we will see, a wh-argument bearing a certain grammatical relation (say, direct object), does not occupy one and the same position w.r.t. the wh-adjuncts, but comes to occupy different positions depending on its internal makeup (w.r.t. such features as [human] and [D-linked]).

Consider first prepositional indirect objects (similar facts hold for other prepositional objects). The examples below show that *na kogo* 'to whom' must precede all of the adjuncts, while *na kolko* N 'to how many N' phrases occupy a lower position – they follow *koga* 'when' and *kâde* 'where', but precede *kak* 'how':[2]

The contrast between (v) and (19b) may have to do with the fact that in Bulgarian, a separate contrastive focus position above the interrogative wh-phrase is available in embedded contexts but is quite marginal in root contexts, cf. (vi). (Note that in (v) above, *koga* is pronounced with heavier stress than *kogo*):

(vi) a. ?? UTRE kogo da izpitam?
Tomorrow (focus) whom *da* examine-I 'TOMORROW, who should I examine?'

b. Nikoj ne mi kaza UTRE kogo da izpitam.
nobody not me told tomorrow (focus) whom *da* examine-I
'Nobody told me TOMORROW whom I should examine.'

[2] We come back later to the (quite) marginal, rather than totally ungrammatical, status of (12b)/(13b).

(11) a. Na kogo kak šte prepodadeš tozi urok?
to whom how will teach-you this lesson
'To whom will you teach this lesson how?'

b. * Kak na kogo šte prepodadeš tozi urok?
how to whom will teach-you this lesson

(12) a. Na kogo kâde si daval podarâci?
to whom where are-you given presents
'To whom did you give presents where?'

b. ???Kâde na kogo si daval podarâci?
where to whom are-you given presents

(13) a. Na kogo koga šte se obadiš?
to whom when will call-you 'Who will you call when?'

b. ??Koga na kogo šte se obadiš?
when to whom will call-you

(14) a. Koga / kâde na kolko xora si pomagal?
when / where to how many people are-you helped
'How many people did you help when/where?'

b. *?Na kolko xora koga / kâde si pomagal?
to how many people when/ where are-you helped

(15) a. Na kolko xora kak možeš da pomogneš?
to how many people how can-you Mod.prt help-you
'How many people can you help how?'

b. * Kak na kolko xora možeš da pomogneš?
how to how many people can-you Mod.prt help-you

Putting together the order of the adjuncts with the relative positions of the two types of indirect wh-objects illustrated above, we arrive at the following order:

(16) *na kogo* > *koga* > *kâde* > *na kolko* N > *kak*
'to whom' 'when' 'where' 'to how many' 'how'

We assume that the different distribution of the indirect objects is related to their different feature specification: while *na kogo* is positively specified for the feature [human], *na kolko* N phrases are underspecified for that feature, since their head N can have human, but also non-human reference (e.g., *na kolko studenti* 'to how many students', *na kolko bolnitsi* 'to how many hospitals', etc.).[3]
Multiple questions containing two [+human] wh-objects also show a strict ordering. As noted by Billings and Rudin (1996, 41), and confirmed by our informants,[4] the direct wh-object must always precede the indirect wh-object. Cf. (17):

[3] The relevance of the feature [human], which was first noted in Billings and Rudin (1996), will be shown below to play a role also in the distribution of direct wh-objects, and subjects.
[4] The judgements reported in this article reflect the intuitions of ten native speakers of Bulgarian, in addition to those of the first author.

(17) a. Kogo na kogo šte predstaviš?
whom to whom will introduce-you 'Whom will you introduce to whom?'

b. *Na kogo kogo šte predstaviš?
to whom whom will introduce-you

We expect, then, on the basis of both (16) and (17), that by transitivity *kogo* should precede whatever *na kogo* precedes, i.e. all of the wh-adjuncts, as well as *na kolko* N phrases. That this is correct is shown by the a) examples of (18)-(21). We come back to the more marked (and prima facie unexpected) alternative orders of (18b) and (19b):

(18) a. Kogo kâde šte nastaniš?
whom where will accommodate-you 'Whom will you accommodate where?'

b. ? Kâde kogo šte nastaniš?
where whom will accommodate-you

(19) a. Kogo koga šte posreštaš?
whom when will meet-you 'Whom will you be meeting when?'

b. ??Koga kogo šte posreštaš?
when whom will meet-you

(20) a. Kogo kak šte posrešneš?
whom how will meet-you 'Whom will you meet how?'

b. *Kak kogo šte posrešneš?
how whom will meet-you

(21) a. Kogo na kolko studenti šte predstaviš?
whom to how many students will introduce-you
'Whom will you introduce to how many students?'

b. *Na kolko studenti kogo šte predstaviš?
to how many students whom will introduce-you

(22) summarizes the relative order of the wh-phrases considered so far:

(22) *kogo* > *na kogo* > *koga* > *kâde* > *na kolko* N > *kak*
'whom' 'to whom' 'when' 'where' 'to how many' 'how'

Looking at the distribution of other direct wh-objects, we find that wh-objects which are specified negatively, or are underspecified, for the feature [human] show a distribution which is markedly different from that of the [+human] *kogo* 'whom'. This is shown by the examples below: (23a) and (25a), alongside (4b), feature the [-human] wh-object *kakvo* 'what' [5]; (24a) features the wh-phrase *kolko* (N) 'how much/how many (N)'. Both types of direct wh-objects (similarly to *na kolko* N phrases seen above) ordinarily follow the adjuncts *kâde* and *koga*, and precede *kak*:[6]

[5] *Kakâv / kakva / kakvo / kakvi* N 'what (kind of) N' phrases pattern with *kakvo* and *kolko* (N) phrases in terms of distribution. Like *kolko* (N) phrases, they are also underspecified for the feature [human] (cf. *kakâv student* 'what student', *kakâv stol* 'what chair', etc.).

[6] In fact, *kak* must follow all wh-phrases (cf. (2), (9a), (10a), (11a), and (15a) above), though direct object *kolko* (N) phrases for some (semantic?) reason do not easily combine with *kak*, in any order.

(23) a. Koga / kâde kakvo kupuvaš?
when / where what buy-you 'When are you buying what?'

b. ?(?)Kakvo koga / kâde kupuvaš?
what when/ where buy-you

(24) a. Koga / kâde kolko (pari) si poxarčil?
when / where how much (money) are-you spent
'How much (money) did you spend when/where?'

b. *Kolko (pari) koga / kâde si poxarčil?
how much (money) when/ where are-you spent

(25) a. Kakvo kak šte napraviš?
what how will do-you 'What will you do how?'

b. *Kak kakvo šte napraviš?
how what will do-you

The low position of *kakvo* and *kolko* (N) phrases leads to certain expectations. If a strict hierarchical order is assumed, such phrases should be preceded by whatever wh-material precedes the adjuncts. In other words, we expect that the direct and indirect wh-objects *kogo* and *na kogo* should appear to their left. That this is indeed the case can be seen from the following examples, some well-known from the literature (cf. in particular Bošković 1997):

(26) a. Kogo kakvo e pital Ivan (Bošković 1997 [20])
whom what is asked Ivan 'Who did Ivan ask what?'

b. *Kakvo kogo e pital Ivan
what whom is asked Ivan

(27) Na kogo kakvo e pokazal Ivan?[7]
to whom what is shown Ivan 'What has Ivan shown to whom?'

(28) a. Na kogo kolko pari šte dadeš?
to whom how much money will give-you
'Whom will you give how much money?'

b. *Kolko pari na kogo šte dadeš?
how much money to whom will give-you

Summing up what we have seen so far, the relative orders among object wh-phrases and wh-adjuncts appear to conform to the following generalizations:

1. (Non-D-linked) [+human] wh-objects move to a space above the space to which *koga* 'when' and *kâde* 'where' move to.

---

[7]According to our informants, *kakvo* may more markedly precede the prepositional indirect object (cf. (i) below). Some speakers seem to fully accept such examples (cf. Grewendorf 2001, fn.19) while others seem to fully exclude them (cf. Rudin 1985, 119):

(i) ?(?)Kakvo na kogo e pokazal Ivan
what to whom is shown Ivan 'What did Ivan show to whom'

2. (Non-D-linked) wh-objects which are either negatively specified or underspecified for the feature [human] (namely, wh-phrases like *kakvo* 'what' and (*na*) *kolko* N 'how much/many N') move to a space below *koga* 'when' and *kâde* 'where' and above *kak*.

Table 1 summarizes the orders of the wh-phrases so far reviewed:

kogo 'whom'	*na kogo* 'to whom'	*koga* 'when'	*kâde* 'where'	(*na*) *kolko* N 'to how many N'	*kak* 'how'
				kakvo 'what'	

Table 1.

4. The order of wh-subjects with respect to wh-adjuncts

A comparable situation is found with wh-subjects because they also come to occupy different positions, depending on their internal makeup. As expected, [+human] *koj* 'who' patterns with [+human] *kogo* and *na kogo* in having to precede *kâde*, *koga* ((29)-(30)), and *kak*.

(29) a. Koj kâde šte spi? (Billings and Rudin 1996, 41)
who where will sleeps 'Who will sleep where?'

b. *Kâde koj šte spi?
where who will sleeps

(30) a. Koj koga pristiga?
who when arrives 'Who will arrive when?'

b. *Koga koj pristiga?
when who arrives

On the other hand, subject *kakvo* and *kolko* (N) phrases pattern together with their object counterparts in that they follow *kâde* and *koga*:

(31) a. Koga kakvo te pravi štastliv?
when what you-acc makes happy 'What makes you happy when?'

b. ??Kakvo koga te pravi štastliv?
what when you-acc makes happy

(32) a. Kâde kakvo stava sega po sveta?
where what happens now in world-the
'What is happening where around the world now?'

b. *Kakvo kâde stava sega po sveta?
what where happens now in world-the

(33) a. Kâde/koga kolko se investira v častnija sektor?
where/when how much refl.cl. invests in private-the sector
'Where/when how much is invested in the private business?'

b. *Kolko kâde / koga se investira v častnija sektor?
how much where / when refl.cl. invests in private-the sector

These data are summarized in Table 2:[8]

[+human]					[-human] or underspecified for [human]		
					Subject	(indirect/direct) Object	
koj	*kogo*	*na kogo*	*koga*	*kâde*	*kakvo/kolko* N	*kakvo/* (*na*) *kolko* N	*kak*

Table 2.

Some of the alternative orders in the examples above were seen to vary in marginality. For some speakers *kakvo* (whether object or subject) can (marginally) appear to the left of the following wh-phrases: *kogo* ((6a)), *na kogo* ((i) of fn.6), *kâde* ((4a), (7a), (23b)), and *koga* ((23b), (31b)).
Similarly, for some speakers, *kâde* and *koga* can precede *kogo* (cf. (18b), (19b), Bošković 1997, fn. 7, and Billings and Rudin 1996, 42), as well as *na kogo* (cf. (12b) and (13b)). Such possibilities are thus in apparent violation of the orders in Table 2.
We assume that the problem posed by these marked orders of *kakvo* and *kâde/koga* can be made sense of if they are taken to access (more markedly) a higher position, the one reserved for D-linked phrases (which will be discussed in the next section).
One first piece of evidence comes from the contrast between the impossible (32b), which contains a non easily D-linkable *kakvo*, and (4a) / (7a) above (repeated as (34a-b), which more readily allow for a D-linked interpretation of *kakvo*.

(34) a. = (4a) ? Kakvo kâde šte složiš?
what where will put-you 'What will you put where?'

b. = (7a) ? Kakvo kâde raste?
what where grows 'What grows where'

A second piece of evidence comes from the distribution of *koe* 'which' (the inherently D-linked counterpart of *kakvo*),[9] which obligatorily precedes the wh-adjuncts (and, more generally, all non-D-linked wh-phrases):

[8] Within the same slot wh-subjects appear to precede wh-objects. See, e.g., (ia-b), exemplifying the case of wh-phrases underspecified for the feature [human]:

(i) a. Kakvi grupi xora po kolko pari xarčat na mesets
what groups people each how much money spend-they in month
'What groups of people spend monthly how much money'

b. * Po kolko pari kakvi grupi xora xarčat na mesets
each how much money what groups people spend-they in month

Here, we abstract away from a number of complications, like the apparent ban on combining a *kakvo* subject with a *kakvo* object, as well as with a *kolko* object, regardless of order.
[9] D-linked wh-phrases can show up either as full *which*-phrases or in a reduced (elliptical) form in which the head noun is missing but implicitly understood from previous context. The 'which' paradigm displays the following gender and number forms:

(i) *koj* (*student/stol*) 'which (student/chair) – masculine, singular
koja (*žena/kniga*) 'which (woman/book) – feminine, singular
koe (*momče/spisanie*) 'which (boy/journal) – neuter, singular
koi (*studenti/knigi/spisanija*) 'which students/books/journals) – m/f/n plural

(35) a. Koe (spisanie) kâde si složil?
which journal where are-you put
'Which [one] did you put where?'

b. *Kâde koe (spisanie) si složil?
where which journal are-you put

(36) a. Koe kâde otiva?
which where goes
'Which [one] goes where?

b. *Kâde koe otiva?
where which goes

5. The order of D-linked and non-D-linked wh-phrases

Phrases in which *koj* functions as a specifier, i.e. *koj/koja/koe/koi* (N) ('which' phrases) are inherently D-linked and must precede all non-D-linked wh-phrases. This may lead to the reversal of the canonical order specified in Table 2, as in (37a) (vs. (38a), where both wh-phrases are non-D-linked)[10], and may also lead to apparent violations of Superiority (for previous discussion, see Richards 1997/2001, Grohmann 1998, 2000, and Jaeger 2003, 2004).

(37) a. Koi kartini na kogo za Boga iskaš pak da podarjavaš?
which paintings to whom for God's sake want-you again Mod.prt donate-you
lit. 'Which paintings do you want again to donate to whom on earth'

b. *Na kogo za Boga koi kartini iskaš pak da podarjavaš?
to whom for God's sake which paintings want-you again to donate-you

(38) a. Na kogo za Boga kakvi kartini pak šte davaš?
to whom for God's sake what paintings again will give-you
'What paintings will you again be giving to whom?'

b. *Kakvi kartini na kogo za Boga pak šte davaš?
what paintings to whom for God's sake again will give-you

The only exception to the order D-linked > non-D-linked seems to be the fronting of a D-linked wh-phrase over a *koj*-subject (cf. Krapova 2002b and Jaeger 2004), which is unacceptable under a true question reading in a matrix question (the order becoming more acceptable in an indirect question – cf. fn.1):

(39) a. *?Koja studentka koj šte izpita?
which student who will examine

b. Koj koja studentka šte izpita?
who which student will examine

---

[10] We use *za Boga* 'for God's sake' (one Bulgarian equivalent of "the hell" phrase) to force the non-D-linked reading of *na kogo*.

The ungrammaticality of (39a) may be taken to suggest that *koj* 'who' actually belongs to the same paradigm as *koj* (N) 'which', with the head N left implicit and interpreted necessarily as [+human]. This conclusion appears to be supported by the similar case of the quantifier *vsički* 'all', which also requires a [+human] interpretation when it occurs without the head noun (*Utre šte potârsja vsički* 'Tomorrow I will look for all (=everyone/*all books, etc.)'. If so, the ungrammaticality of (39a) is no longer unexpected as both wh-phrases belong to the same D-linked "space", within which subjects precede objects. (Cf. fn.7, and section 7. below.)

The results so far are summarized in Table 3:[11]

D-linked wh-[12]	**Non-D-linked wh-phrases**						
koj/koja/koe/koi (N) (*kogo*) (*na kogo*) (marked)*kakvo*$_{Sub/Obj}$ (marked) *kâde/koga*	*kogo*	*na kogo*	*koga*	*kâde*	*kakvo*$_{Subj}$ *kolko*$_{Subj}$ N	*kakvo*$_{Obj}$ (*na*)*kolko*$_{Obj}$ N	*kak*

Table 3.

6. The order of clitic resumed and non-clitic resumed wh-phrases[13]

6.1. Clitic resumption with D-linked wh-phrases

Let us now turn to another type of multiple wh-constructions, containing an inherently D-linked phrase resumed by a clitic.

From cases such as (40) it would seem that clitic resumption is optional:

(40) Koja kartina na kogo / na koj prijatel si (ja) posvetil?
which painting to whom / to which friend are-you it dedicated
'Which painting have you dedicated to whom/to which friend?'

This is, however, dubious. For one thing, as (41) shows, clitic resumption is not available for the second of two wh-phrases when the first is not itself resumed by a clitic.

---

[11] Things are actually more complex in that (39a) seems to improve if the wh-phrase refers to a non-human entity:

(i) ?(?) Koja kniga koj e napisal
which book who is written 'Who wrote which book?'

We assume that the contrast between (39)a and (i) is related to the contrast between (iia) and (iib), which suggests that, in Bulgarian, phrases referring to non-human entities are (for some reason) easier to enter a null Operator Topic construction (cf. fn.13 below) than phrases referring to human individuals:

(ii) a. Filma šte gleda Maria
film-the will watch M.
'Maria will watch the film'

b. *? Ivan šte gleda Maria
I. (obj) will watch M. (subj.)
'Maria will look after Ivan'

This in turn suggests that *koja kniga* in (i) is located in higher (operator topic) position, and the Superiority violation is only apparent.

[12] In the D-linked column we have also indicated the possibility of D-linking *kogo* and *na kogo*, although we are not giving evidence for that here.

[13] This section has gained considerably from the extensive discussions Iliyana Krapova had with Željko Bošković during her visit at the University of Connecticut in March, 2002 (sponsored by Research Support Scheme, Project 91/2000 between the University of Bucharest and the University of Plovdiv).

Moreover, as (42) shows, clitic resumption becomes obligatory if the leftmost D-linked wh-phrase is separated by a parenthetical from the second wh-phrase (D-linked or not). (cf. Krapova 2002b):

(41) a. Na kogo koja kartina si (*ja) posvetil?
to whom which painting are-you it dedicated
'Which painting did you dedicate to whom?'

b. Na koj prijatel koja kartina si mu ja posvetil
to which friend which painting are-you him it dedicated
'Which friend did you dedicate which painting to?'

(42) a. Koja kartina, spored tebe, kâde *(ja) e risuval tozi xuždonik?
which painting, according to you, where it is painted this artist
'According to you, which painting did this artist paint where?'

b. Koja kniga, spored tebe, na koj prijatel da (*mu) ja dam?
which book, according to you, to which friend Mod.prt (him) it give-I
'According to you, which book should I give to which friend?'

c. Na koj prijatel, spored tebe, koja kniga da mu (*ja) dam?
to which friend, according to you, which book Mod.prt him (it) give-I
'According to you, to which friend should I give which book?'

What these facts seem to suggest is that material preceding the parenthetical correlates with obligatory presence of a resumptive clitic, while material following the parenthetical correlates with obligatory absence of such a clitic. This in turn means that the apparent optionality in (40) should be interpreted as representing two different structures: one involving a position (call it XP) which can be targeted only by clitic resumed (inherently) D-linked wh-phrases; the other involving a position (call it YP) which can be targeted only by non-clitic resumed (inherently) D-linked wh-phrases. XP and YP occur, respectively, to the left and to the right of the parenthetical. (Cf. Krapova 2002a,b, and Jaeger 2003, 2004 for observations apparently leading in the same direction). This is sketched in (43):

(43) [$_{XP}$*Cl-D-linked wh* [parenthetical [$_{YP}$ *non-Cl-D-linked wh* [$_{ZP}$ *non-D-linked wh* [$_{IP}$ ..cl...

Clear indication that XP and YP are distinct projections comes from the contrast between (44a) and (44b):

(44) a. Koe (meroprijatie), spored tebe, koj trjabva da *(go) provežda?
which (initiative), according-to you, who must Mod.prt it carry out-he
'Which (initiative), according to you, who should carry out?'

b. *Kakvo (ot tezi nešta), spored tebe, koj trjabva da go svârši?
what (from these things), according-to you, who must Mod.prt it finish-he

c. ?Kakvo (ot tezi nešta), spored tebe, na kogo da zanesa?
what (from these things), according to you, to whom Mod.prt bring-I
'What [which] (of these things) should I bring to whom?'

(44b) contains the wh-phrase *kakvo* 'what' (the non-D-linked counterpart of *koe*) which has been forced into a D-linked reading by including it into a partitive phrase. Nevertheless, the question is ungrammatical. As an indefinite quantifier, *kakvo* resists clitic resumption in true questions, although as we mentioned earlier, in the absence of an inherently D-linked phrase, it is in principle possible to D-link it (as also indicated by the possible alternative order *kakvo > na kogo* in (44c) apparently violating their canonical order). The contrast between (44b) and (44c) thus shows that the highest position *kakvo* can target is still lower than the position occupied by *koe* in (44a). Therefore, we can conclude that the pre-parenthetical position cannot be occupied by non-clitic resumed D-linked material.
The parenthetical, in addition to the position it occupies in (44), can also occupy a sentence initial position (cf. (46)), as shown by the examples in (45):

(45) a. Vpročem, koja kartina, spored tebe, koj *(ja) e narisuval?
by-the-way which painting according-to-you who it is painted
'By the way, according to you, who painted which painting?'

b. Vpročem, koja kartina, spored tebe, koj xudožnik *(ja) e narisuval?
by-the-way which painting according-to-you which artist it is painted
'According to you, which painting did which artist paint?'

(46)
parenthetical [XP *Cl-D-linked wh-* parenthetical [YP *D-linked wh-* [ZP *non-D-linked wh-* [IP cl_{XP}

Within a finer-grained CP structure (cf. Rizzi 1997; Benincà and Poletto 2004), XP can be identified with the CLLD Topic position (TopP)[14] (cf. also Krapova 2002b, Jaeger 2003,

[14] Richards (1997, 2001, 95) and Grohmann (1998, 44; 2000, 278) propose that all D-linked wh-phrases target a (Wh-)Topic position (although neither author discusses the issue of clitic resumption). This would need to be qualified in view of the apparent existence of two distinct Topic constructions in Bulgarian: Clitic Left Dislocation topics and topics involving (null) operators, given in (i) and (ii), respectively (see Krapova 2002a, and Lambova 2000, 2001, and Arnaudova 2004 who calls them 'contrastive topics'):

(i) [$_T$Kufara] Ivan NA MARIA li šte *(go) dade?
suitcase-the Ivan to Mary Interr.prt will it(CL) give
'The suitcase, is it to Mary that Ivan will give?'

(ii) [$_T$Kufara] koj šte prenese do garata?
suitcase-the who will carry to railway-station-the

In fact, such apparent Superiority violations as in (iii), and in (iv) below where a D-linked wh-object precedes a D-linked wh-subject, may provide further evidence for distinguishing between the two types of topics:

(iii) Koja kartina koj xudožnik e narisuval?
which painting which artist is painted 'Which painting did which artist paint?'

It can plausibly be argued that in (iii) *koj xudožnik* occupies Spec, YP (i.e. Spec of the D-linked wh-), while *koja kartina* targets the lower of the two Topic positions – the Operator/Contrastive Topic position situated below TopP. This will explain the lack of a resumptive clitic in (iii) vs. the additional availability of (iv), where the fronted wh-object is clitic resumed, as a function of targeting the higher Clitic Left Dislocation Topic:

(iv) Koja kartina koj xudožnik ja e narisuval?
which painting which artist it(CL) is painted

2004, Grohmann 2005); YP with a position specialized for D-linked phrases (D-LP); and ZP with a position specialized for non-D-linked phrases, the traditional CP, we may assume.[15]
In addition to the presence vs. absence of a corresponding clitic, the two D-linked positions can be differentiated on the basis of their quantificational status. While XP, like topical projections in general, is non-quantificational, YP is quantificational, as shown by the systematic contrasts discussed in 6.2 below.

6.2. WCO effects

Lack of WCO effects is one of the properties characterizing CLLD Topic structures in contrast to quantificational structures (cf. Rizzi 1997).
In Bulgarian, all Clitic Left Dislocated (CLLD) material (indefinite affirmative quantifiers with specific interpretation, D-linked universal/distributive quantifiers, partitive phrases, Topics, etc.) do not show WCO effects. The same is true for the clitic resumed wh-phrases illustrated in (47a). On the other hand, WCO effects are present with exactly the same types of elements if the clitic is missing, cf. (47b). We therefore conclude that *na koj student* occupies an operator position in (47b) but not in (47a):

(47) a. Na koj student$_i$ mu e daval pari bašta mu$_i$?
to which student him is given money father his
'Which student did his father give money?'
cf. Na Ivan mu e dal pari bašta mu.
to Ivan him is given money father his
'His father gave money to Ivan.'

b. Na koj student$_i$ e daval pari bašta mu$_{*i/j}$
to which student is given money father his
cf. *Na Ivan e dal pari bašta mu.
to Ivan is given money father his

6.3. Interaction with quantifiers

Another distinction between the two types of positions comes from their interaction with quantifiers (Roumyana Pancheva, p.c.). (48a) shows that while D-linked phrases may have both wide and narrow scope with respect to the (non-D-linked) distributive quantifier *vseki* 'everybody'. Cl-D-linked phrases necessarily have wide scope (cf. (48b)):

(48) a. Koja kniga e pročel vseki? — wide and narrow scope
which book is read everyone
'Which book did everyone read?'

b. Koja kniga ja e pročel vseki? — wide scope only
which book it is read everyone

The evidence that we presented so far shows that Spec,TopP is a non-quantificational position, while Spec,D-LP (the lower position hosting D-linked wh-phrases) is a quantificational position. The results are summarized in Table 4. In the Clitic resumed Topic wh-"space" we have indicated the non-bare inherently D-linked wh-phrases, as well as the D-linkable bare wh-phrases *kogo* and *na kogo*, which can also be clitic-resumed (cf. Dimitrova-Vulchanova & Hellan 1999, Jaeger 2004).

---

[15] We take each "space" (non-D-linked, D-linked, Cl-D-linked) to involve a hierarchy of projections hosting the different wh-phrases, in the fixed order imposed by Superiority (cf. section 7. below).

clitic resumed Topic wh-	D-linked wh-	non-D-linked wh-						
(*na*) *koj/koja/koe/ koi* (N)	(*na*) *koj/koja/koe/ koi* (N)	*kogo*	*na kogo*	*koga*	*kâde*	*kakvo*$_{Subj}$ *kolko*$_{Subj}$ N	*kakvo*$_{Obj}$ (*na*) *kolko*$_{Obj}$ N	*kak*
kogo	(*kogo*)							
na kogo	(*na kogo*)							
*?*kakvo*	*kakvo* (marked)							
	kâde/koga (marked)							

Table 4.

7. Concluding remarks.

The deeper question of what determines the relative order of the various wh-phrases seen above is beyond the scope of this article. We can only hint here at a possible way of approaching it that looks to us promising.
Various clues seem to suggest that such ordering reflects the order of wh-phrases prior to wh-movement (cf. also Bošković 1997, 1998b, 1999).
Consider non-D-linked wh-phrases. The order of the adjuncts (*koga* > *kâde* > *kak*) seems to conform to the UG hierarchy of Merge of these adjuncts, according to which Temporal adjuncts are higher than Locative adjuncts, which are in turn higher than Manner adjuncts (Boisson 1981, Nilsen 2000, Cinque 2002, Schweikert 2005).[16] This appears supported by the fact that in German the corresponding existentially interpreted wh-phrases are ordered within IP in the same way, with Temporal phrases obligatorily preceding (i.e., higher than) Locative phrases:

(49) Hans sollte **wann wo / *wo wann** darüber vortragen (Frey 2000, 113)
Hans should sometimes somewhere about-that talk

Likewise, the surface order of Bulgarian [+human] wh-phrases (*koj, kogo*, and *na kogo*) with respect to the temporal and locative wh-adjuncts (*koga* and *kâde*), and to wh-phrases underspecified (or negatively specified) for the feature [human] (*kakvo* and *kolko/kakâv* N) (cf. Table 4) appears to reflect their relative order prior to wh-movement. This is once again suggested by the relative order in IP of the corresponding German existentially interpreted wh-phrases. As (50)-(53) show, [-human] subject *was*[17] has to follow the temporal and locative adjuncts *wann* and *wo*, while [+human] *wer* has to precede the adjuncts:[18]

(50) Ich weiss nicht ob dort **wann was /*was wann** geschehen ist (Josef Bayer p.c.)
I don't know if there sometime something happened has

[16] As there is reason to assume that they do not move to higher IP-internal licensing positions, their position prior to wh-movement presumably coincides with their Merge position.
[17] The same appears true of object *was*.
[18] This suggests that arguments move from their Merge position to different "spaces" depending on their specification for the feature [human] (cf. the Animacy Hierarchy of the typological tradition). Concerning the relative ordering of elements which bear the same specification for the feature [human], if subjects are merged higher than direct and indirect objects, the pre-wh-movement position of [+human] subject *koj* 'who' will be higher (more to the left) than that of [+human] *kogo* 'whom' and *na kogo* 'to whom' (if not higher, given the discussion following (39)). As to the relative order of *kogo* and *na kogo*, we must assume that direct objects move to a pre-wh-movement position higher than that of indirect objects, since the Merge position of indirect objects is presumably higher than that of direct objects.

(51) Ich glaube dass **wo was / *was wo** geschehen ist (Josef Bayer p.c.)
I believe that somewhere something happened has

(52) Ich weiss nicht ob hier **wer wann / *wann wer** geschlafen hat (Josef Bayer p.c.)
I don't know if here someone sometime slept has

(53) Weil **wer wo / *wo wer** das Buch verloren hat... (Frey 2000, 132)
Because someonc somewhere the book lost has...

It seems to us that this identity of ordering at the IP level in one language and at the CP level in the other can hardly be accidental.[19]

If the order of (non-D-linked) wh-phrases simply reflects their order prior to wh-movement, some principle will have to ensure that this order is preserved under wh-movement. While there have been a number of proposals to capture this (selective) effect (cf. Richards 1997, 2001, Müller 2001, among others) we think that it can be derived in an interesting way by slightly modifying, and extending to A-bar chains, a principle originally proposed in Chomsky (2000, section 6; 2001, (17)) for A-chains. We will phrase such principle in terms of Rizzi's (2001) notion of Relativized Minimality, which is formulated as a condition on chain links ((54)), itself based on the Minimality notion in (55):

(54) $(A_1, \ldots, A_n)$ is a chain iff, for $1 \leq i < n$
(i) $A_i = A_{i+1}$
(ii) A_i c-commands A_{i+1}
(iii) A_{i+1} is in a Minimal Configuration with A_i

In other words "each chain link involves identity (under the copy theory of traces), c-command and Minimality" (Rizzi 2001, 91).

(55) Y is in a Minimal Configuration with X iff
there is no Z such that
(i) Z is of the same structural type as X, and
(ii) Z intervenes between X and Y

In the spirit of Rizzi (2001), we take Z to count as an intervener between a trace Y and a target X if Z c-commands Y without c-commanding X, and if it is specified with the same feature as the target (quantificational; modifier (non-quantificational); etc). Cf. the ill-formedness of (56a-b) vs. the well-formedness of (57a-b):[20]

(56) a. *Combien a-t-il beaucoup consulté de livres?
'How many has he a lot consulted of books?'

*________ a-t-il **beaucoup** consulté **combien** de livres
[+quant] [+quant]

b. * Rapidamente, i tecnici hanno probabilmente risolto il problema

[19] This identity, however, is concealed in many circumstances by the application of additional (focus-related) movements and becomes visible only when such movements are blocked (as happens with wh-phrases interpreted existentially in languages like German, or with interrogative wh-phrases in languages like Bulgarian).

[20] Note that (56a) does not become better if the closest quantifier is attracted (**Beaucoup a-t-il consulté combien de livres*? 'A lot has he consulted how many of books?'). This implies that, unlike Relativized Minimality, Attract Closest cannot relate the violation in (56a-b) to standard Superiority violations like **What did who buy?* or **Who did you persuade who to invite*?, even though the two cases seem to involve similar intervention effects (cf. Rizzi 1990, 2001).

'Rapidly, the technicians have probably solved the problem'

*__________, i tecnici hanno **probabilmente** risolto **rapidamente** il problema
[+modifier] [+modifier]

(57) a. Combien a-t-il attentivement consulté de livres?
'How many has he carefully consulted of books?'

________ a-t-il **attentivement** consulté **combien** de livres
[+quant] [+modifier]

b. RAPIDAMENTE, i tecnici hanno probabilmente risolto il problema (non lentamente)
'Rapidly (focus), the technicians have probably solved the problem (not slowly)'

______, i tecnici hanno **probabilmente** risolto **RAPIDAMENTE** il problema...
[+Focus] [+modifier]

Within a system in which Superiority is subsumed under Relativized Minimality, the preservation of the pre-wh-movement order of the wh-phrases in the case of multiple movements can be ensured through the requirement in (58), which is a modification, as noted, of one of Chomsky's principles:[21]

(58) Only a whole chain, not just a link of a chain, counts as an 'intervener'.

In other words, no (trivial or non trivial) chain can intervene between the trace and the target, if the intervening chain is specified with the same feature as the target.
With (58), contrasts like those in (25a-b) above can now be seen to follow from Relativized Minimality (assuming *kakvo* to move to a Case-related position higher than *kak* prior to wh-movement – cf. Bošković 1997, 239f). The relevant derivations, and the resulting representations are given in (59a-b). (59a) represents the only possible order of the two wh-movements which respects both Relativized Minimality and the Extension Condition. (59b), on the other hand, violates Relativized Minimality whatever the order of the two wh-movements is (and the Extension Condition in one of the two possible derivations).[22]

(59) a. $[_{CP}$ kakvo $[_{CP}$ kak $[_{IP}$ šte napraviš t t
[+wh] [+wh] [+wh]
① ②

b *$[_{CP}$ kak $[_{CP}$ kakvo $[_{IP}$ šte napraviš t t
[+wh] [+wh] [+wh]

[21] Chomsky's condition reads "Only the head of an A-chain (equivalently, the whole chain) blocks matching under the Minimal Link Condition" (Chomsky 2001, (17)). Rizzi reaches a similar conclusion in unpublished work refining his (1990, 2001) notion of Relativized Minimality.
[22] Note that under this account of Superiority, it is crucial that Relativized Minimality applies at the end of the derivation, or on the representation. See Rizzi (2001, especially fn.6) for arguments to this effect. In (59) we abstract away from possible earlier movements leading to the pre-wh-movement configuration.

In (59a) there is only a *link* of a chain (not an entire chain) intervening between the trace of *kak* and the target of *kak*, and similarly only a link of a chain between the trace of *kakvo* and the target of *kakvo*. Not so, in (59b), where the entire (non trivial) chain *kakvo* intervenes between the trace of *kak* and its target. (58) has in fact the quite general consequence of forcing a crossing (rather than a nesting) derivation of wh-phrases.

If D-linked wh-phrases have special features matching corresponding features in their target (say, +D-L wh – but see fn.22), it is understandable why they can reverse the order holding strictly within the "space" of non-D-linked wh-phrases. In the slightly more marked, yet acceptable, (7a) above, even if the whole (non trivial) chain of *kâde* intervenes between the trace of *kakvo* and its target, the feature of the intervener is distinct from that of the target, so that no violation of Relativized Minimality is triggered:[23]

(60) $[_{YP}$ kakvo $[_{CP}$ kâde $[_{IP}$ raste t t]]]
[+D-L wh] [+wh] [+wh]

A comparable case is provided by the apparent violation of Superiority in e.g. (44a), where the target is specified for the feature [Cl-D-L wh] while the intervening chain bears no such feature.

Notice that in order to derive the apparent Superiority violations of (7b) (*Kâde kakvo raste*? 'Where what grows') and similar cases, one has to crucially assume that subject *kakvo* may fail to raise to the preverbal position and may receive Case in situ under Agree with the preverbal position in Spec,IP, much as it happens in normal cases of subject inversion (e.g. *Tuk ne raste treva* lit. Here not grows grass 'Grass does not grow here'). This possibility in turn appears to be relatable to the pro-drop nature of Bulgarian, which allows an expletive empty subject satisfying the EPP feature, along the lines of the original proposal of Rizzi (1982, chapter IV), which relates free subject inversion to the null subject property of the language.

To summarize, the facts discussed here seem to us to provide evidence for two conclusions: 1) that the order of wh-phrases in Bulgarian multiple wh-fronting reflects, up to the finest degree, their pre-wh-movement order, and 2) that all cases which seem to go against preservation of order (leading to seeming violations of Superiority) involve selective movements triggered by a feature that is not present in any of the intervening elements. More tentatively, we also proposed to capture Superiority effects under a version of Rizzi's Relativized Minimality which incorporates Chomsky's insight that links of a chain do not count as interveners.

References

Arnaudova, O. (2005): "Contrastive features, Clitic Doubling and the Left Periphery of the Bulgarian Sentence". In: Franks, S., F. Gladney and M. Tasseva-Kurktchieva (eds.): *Formal Approaches to Slavic Linguistics. The South Carolina Meeting, 2004*, Ann Arbor, Michigan Slavic Publications, 13-26.

Benincà, P. and C. Poletto (2004): "Topic, Focus, and V2: Defining the CP Sublayers". In: Rizzi, L. (ed.): *The Structure of CP and IP. The Cartography of Syntactic Structures*, vol.°2. New York, Oxford University Press, 52-75.

Billings, L. and C. Rudin (1996): "Optimality and Superiority: A new approach to overt multiple-wh ordering". In: Toman, J. (ed.): *Formal Approaches to Slavic Linguistics: the College Park Meeting*, 1994, Ann Arbor, Michigan Slavic Publications, 35-60.

[23] If D-linking is related to Specificity, given that specific indefinites are higher than existentially interpreted ones (cf. Diesing 1992), it could be that in (60) *kakvo* has moved higher than *kâde* prior to wh-movement (which would impose distinctness of features at the IP, rather than at the CP level).

Boisson, C. (1981): "Hiérarchie universelle des spécifications de temps, de lieu, et de manière". In: *Confluents* 7, 69-124.

Bošković, Ž. (1997): "On certain violations of the Superiority Condition, AgroP, and economy of derivation." In: *Journal of Linguistics* 33, 227-254.

Bošković, Ž. (1998a): "Wh-phrases and wh-movement in Slavic". Position paper. *Workshop on Comparative Slavic Morphosyntax,* 5-7 June 1998. Indiana University. Downloadable at http://www.indiana.edu/~slavconf/linguistics/index.html.

Bošković, Ž. (1998b): "Multiple wh-fronting and economy of derivation". In: *Proceedings of the West Coast Conference on Formal Linguistics* 16, 49-63. Stanford: Stanford University.

Bošković, Ž. (1999): "On multiple feature-checking: Multiple wh-fronting and multiple head-movement". In: Epstein, S. D. and N. Hornstein (eds.): *Working Minimalism*. Cambridge, Mass: MIT Press, 159-187.

Bošković, Ž. (2001): *On the nature of the Syntax-Phonology Interface. Cliticization and related phenomena.* Elsevier.

Bošković, Ž. (2002): "On Multiple wh-fronting". In: *Linguistic Inquiry* 34, 351-383.

Chomsky, N. (2000): "Minimalist inquiries: The framework". In: Martin, R., D. Michaels and J. Uriagereka (eds.): *Step by Step. Essays on Minimalist Syntax in Honor of Howard Lasnik*, 89-155. Cambridge, Mass.: MIT Press.

Chomsky, N. (2001): "Derivation by Phase". In: Kenstowicz, M. (ed.): *Ken Hale: A life in language*, 1-52. Cambridge, Mass: MIT Press.

Cinque, G. (2002): "Complement and Adverbial PPs: Implications for Clause Structure". Paper presented at the 25th Glow Colloquium, Amsterdam, April 9-11 [published in 2006 in *Restructuring and Functional Heads. The Cartography of Syntactic Structures,* vol.°4., New York, Oxford University Press, 145-166].

Diesing, M. (1992): *Indefinites*. Cambridge, Mass: MIT Press.

Dimitrova-Vulchanova, M. and L .Hellan (1999): "Clitics and Bulgarian clause structure". In: Riemsdijk H. van (ed.): *Clitics in the European Languages*, 469-514. Berlin: Mouton de Gruyter.

Frey, W. (2000): "Syntactic Requirements on Adjuncts". In: Fabricius-Hansen, C., E. Lang and C. Maienborn (eds.): *Approaching the Grammar of Adjuncts*, 107-134. ZAS Papers in Linguistics, vol. 17.

Grewendorf, G. (2001): "Multiple wh-fronting". In: *Linguistic Inquiry* 32, 87-122.

Grohmann, K. K. (1998): "Syntactic Inquiries into Discourse Restrictions on Multiple Interrogatives". In: *Groninger Arbeiten zur germanistischen Linguistik* 42, 1-60.

Grohmann, K. K. (2000): *Prolific Peripheries: A Radical View from the Left*. Doctoral Dissertation, University of Maryland, College Park.

Grohmann, K. (2005): "Top issues in questions: Topics – Topicalization – Topicalizability". In: Cheng, L. and N. Corver (eds.): *Wh-movement on the move*. Cambridge, Mass: MIT Press.

Jaeger, T. F. (2003): "Topics First! In- and outside of Bulgarian wh-interrogatives". In: Müller, S. (ed.): *The Proceedings of the 10th International Conference on Head-Driven Phrase Structure grammar*, Michigan State University, July 18-20, 2003, 188-202. Standford: CSLI Publications.

Jaeger, T. F. (2004): "Topicality and Superiority in Bulgarian wh-questions". In: Arnaudova, O., W. Browne, M. L. Rivero and D. Stojanović (eds.): *Formal Approaches to Slavic Linguistics: The Ottawa Meeting, 2003*. Ann Arbor, Mich.: Michigan Slavic Publications.

Krapova, I. (2002a): "On the Left Periphery of the Bulgarian sentence". In: *University of Venice Working Papers in Linguistics*, vol. 12, 107-128.

Krapova, I. (2002b): "On D-Linking and Multiple Wh-fronting". Paper presented at FASSBL4, Sofia 2002.

Lambova, M. (2000): "The Typology of Multiple Wh-Fronting in Slavic Revisited". In: *Annual Workshop on Formal Approaches to Slavic Linguistics. The Philadelphia Meeting 1999.*
King, T. H. and I. Sekerina (eds.) (2000): Michigan Slavic Publications, Ann Arbor, 238-258.
Lambova, M. (2001): "On A-bar movements in Bulgarian and their interaction". In: *The Linguistic Review* 18, 327-374.
Müller, G. (2001): "Order Preservation, Parallel Movement and the Emergence of the Unmarked". In: Legendre, G., J. Grimshaw and S. Vikner (eds.): *Optimality-Theoretic Syntax*. Cambridge, Mass., MIT Press, 279-313.
Nilsen, Ø. (2000): *The Syntax of Circumstantial Adverbials*. Oslo, Novus Press.
Pesetsky, D. (1987): "Wh-in-situ: Movement and Unselective Binding". In: Reuland, E. J. and A. G. ter Meulen (eds.): The Representation of (In)definiteness, 98-129. Camrdidge, Mass: MIT Press.
Pesetsky, D. (2000): *Phrasal Movement and its Kin*. MIT Press, Cambridge, Mass.
Richards. N. (1997): *What Moves Where When in Which Language*? Doctoral Dissertation, Massachusetts Institute of Technology, Cambridge.
Richards, N. (2001): *Movement in Language: Interactions and Architectures*. Oxford: Oxford University Press.
Rizzi,L. (1982): *Issues in Italian Syntax*. Dordrecht: Foris.
Rizzi,L. (1990): *Relativized Minimality*. Cambridge, Mass.: MIT Press.
Rizzi, L. (1997): "The Fine Structure of the Left Periphery". In: Haegeman, L. (ed.): *Elements of grammar*, 281-337. Kluwer, Dordrecht.
Rizzi,L. (2001): "Relativized Minimality Effects". In: Baltin, M. and C. Collins (eds.): *The Handbook of Contemporary Syntactic Theory*, 89-110. Oxford, Blackwell.
Rudin, C. (1985): *Aspects of Bulgarian Syntax: Complementizers and wh constructions.* Slavica Publishers, Inc., Columbus, Ohio.
Rudin, C. (1988): "On multiple questions and multiple wh-fronting". In: *Natural Language and Linguistic Theory* 6, 455-501.
Schweikert, W. (2005): *The Order of Prepositional Phrases in the Structure of the Clause.* Ph. D. Dissertation, University of Venice [published in 2005 in the Linguistik Aktuell series of Benjamins].

Mariana Lambova

Multiple Fronting in Bulgarian: Clustering and Separability[*]

In this paper I first review the dialect split evidence from Bulgarian (BG), based on which I motivate a modification of Bošković's (1998a,b; 2002) account of multiple wh-fronting (MWF) as epiphenomenal, and then I present new data from multiple topicalization and multiple negative fronting in support of this modification.

In particular, I take MWF to involve the familiar wh-movement for one wh-phrase and focus fronting for all wh-phrases but, unlike Bošković, I argue that these movements target separate functional projections. The phenomenon of interest is the interaction with topicalization, which blocks the separability of the fronted wh-phrases. I propose an analysis with topic and focus being licensed in a single discourse-related projection ΔP, which C takes as a com-plement. Importantly, it is in SpecΔP that fronted wh-phrases cluster, not in SpecCP as standardly assumed. I also show that multiple topics and negative phrases front to ΔP, and they similarly form a constituent there. I attribute these facts to the properties of the discourse projection. The analysis has consequences for multiple feature checking and clausal architecture.

1. MWF in BG: Constituency and Superiority

BG is a MWF language (1a), and since Rudin 1988 it is generally assumed that all fronted wh-phrases are right-adjoined in SpecCP where they form an inseparable constituent, a *wh-cluster*.

(1) a. **Koj** **kakvo** e kupil?
who what AUX.PRES.3P.SG bought

b.
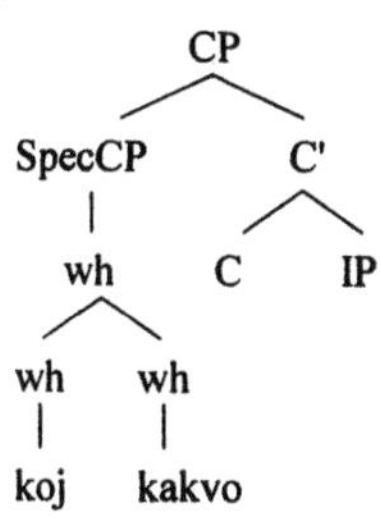

The claim is based on facts such as (2), which is reported as deviant with an item intervening between the first and the second fronted wh-phrase.

(2) * Koj **prâv** kogo e udaril?
who first whom AUX.PRES.3P.SG hit
"Who hit whom first?"

Rudin treats MWF as distinct from both wh-movement and wh-in-situ, essentially a multiple wh-movement. As observed by Toman 1981, in a true multiple movement it is

[*] In addition to FDSL 5, portions of this material have been presented at FASL 11, the discourse workshop at 26th GLOW Colloquium, and 4th GLOW in Asia. I thank the audiences at these forums for their comments and questions. Much is due to my advisors Željko Bošković, Howard Lasnik and Juan Uriagereka for teaching me well, and many others have contributed insights and suggestions. All errors are of course mine.

expected that fronted elements form a constituent. This is clearly not the case in other Slavic languages which also appear to exhibit MWF. There is an interfering factor, though. Fronted wh-phrases in languages such as Serbian/Croatian are typically split by clitics, which appear in second position. BG, whose clitics are verbal, thus seems to be a good test case.

However, the constituency issue hasn't gone unchallenged. Bošković (1998b: 2) acknowledges that some speakers accept (2). I have shown that the variability is robust enough (Lambova 1999, 2001). Besides parentheticals, various particles and adverbs[1] can intervene into the wh-cluster in BG:

(3) a. Koj, **čunkim,** kakvo mi e dal?
who excl.part. what me.CL AUX.PRES.3P.SG given
"Who, for god's sake, has given me what (for free)?"

b. Koj **umelo** kakvo e prikril?
who cleverly what AUX.PRES.3P.SG hidden
"Who has cleverly hidden what?" (sentential reading)
"Who has hidden what cleverly?" (manner reading)

There is another difference among MWF languages that Rudin notes. Fronted wh-phrases in BG can only appear in the order shown in (1) while the order is free in other Slavic languages. The property of having the highest wh-phrase move or surface first is known as Superiority (cf. Chomsky 1973). Here, too, there are more fine-grained empirical facts to account for. Bošković (1998a) shows that in some contexts such as long distance questions Serbian/Croatian shows Superiority effects. On the other hand, he notes that in the presence of a third wh-phrase, the second and the third wh-phrases in BG are freely ordered; he terms that property *selective* Superiority:

(4) a. **Kakvo na kogo** e podaril?
what to whom AUX.PRES.3P.SG given-as-a-present

b. * **Na kogo kakvo** e podaril?
"What did he give to whom as a present?"

(5) a. **Koj kakvo na kogo** e podaril?
who what to whom AUX.PRES.3P.SG given-as-a-present

b. **Koj na kogo kakvo** e podaril?
"Who gave what to whom as a present?"

2. MWF as an Epiphenomenon

Assuming that moving one wh-phrase to satisfy the inadequacy of C should be enough, Bošković suggests that the rest of the wh-phrases move for an independent reason (cf. Toman 1981). Following a long line of research that goes back to DeRijk (1972), he suggests that in MWF languages all wh-phrases undergo focus fronting. The reason is that these languages have overt focus movement, and fronted wh-phrases appear in positions focused elements move to.

Thus contrastively focused phrases in BG are displaced to a preverbal position either at the beginning of the clause or immediately below the subject (6).[2] While in focus fronting

---

[1] Ambiguous adverbs, which presumably have different attachments, preserve both readings.

[2] Contrastively focused elements are given in small capitals.

languages, including BG, multiple contrastive clause-mate foci are not allowed (cf. Kiss 1995), fronted wh-phrases show up in the clause-initial position.[3]

(6) a. NA MARIA **podari** Ivan kartinata.
to Maria (foc) give-PT.3P.SG Ivan painting-the

b. Ivan NA MARIA **podari** kartinata.
Ivan to Maria (foc) give-PT.3P.SG painting-the
"It was to Maria that Ivan gave the painting as a present."

Bošković develops a general theory of MWF as consisting of the familiar *wh-movement* for only one wh-phrase and/or *wh/focus-fronting* for all wh-phrases. Focusing on the order of the fronted wh-phrases, he argues that BG employs both kinds of movement while Serbian/Croatian lacks wh-movement in matrix contexts, thus deriving the differences between the two languages. This is a radically different proposal from Rudin's or other alternative accounts (see Richards 1997).

Bošković (1998b, 2002) shows that MWF languages do not behave uniformly with respect to *wh-movement*: some are like English, i.e. they always have wh-movement (e.g. BG); some are like Chinese, i.e. they never have it (e.g. Russian), and some are like French, i.e. they have it optionally although it is sometimes required (e.g. Serbian/Croatian). Since MWF languages parallel non-MWF languages in the relevant respect, a consequence of the modular approach he advocates, Bošković concludes that MWF must be eliminated from the cross-linguistic typology.

Specifically, following Rudin on the constituency issue, he has all fronted wh-phrases in BG in SpecCP. Bošković proposes that in BG wh-movement and wh/focus-fronting are both licensed by the interrogative complementizer C. The order of the fronted wh-phrases as in (5) is derived through Economy. Since C has a strong [+wh] feature, by Attract Closest the highest wh-phrase moves to SpecCP first. All wh-phrases have a strong [+Foc] feature, which they check against C.[4]

(7) $[_{CP}$ C $[_{IP}$ ... WH WH WH]]
+wh, strong +wh, weak +wh, weak +wh, weak
+Foc, weak +Foc, strong +Foc, strong +Foc, strong
$[_{CP}$ **Koj**$_i$ **kakvo**$_j$ C e kupil $[_{VP}$ ~~**koj**~~$_i$ ~~e kupil~~ ~~**kakvo**~~$_j$]] =(1a)

Importantly, Economy underlies selective Superiority as well: in the configuration z [x y]] where X and Y must move to Z, the order of movement to Z is free, i.e. regardless of whether *x* and *y* move to *z* in a *x*, *y* or *y*, *x* order, the movement is equally economical since the same number of nodes are crossed.

(8) a. $[_{SpecCP}$ [[[**Koj**$_i$] **kakvo**$_j$] **na kogo**$_k$] e podaril [t_i t_j t_k]] = (5a)

b. $[_{SpecCP}$ [[[**Koj**$_i$] **na kogo**$_k$] **kakvo**$_j$] e podaril [t_i t_j t_k]] = (5b)

[3] D-linked wh-phrases behave differently in that only one fronts obligatorily, and echo wh-phrases seem to surface in the lower focused position. I leave these facts out for reasons of space.

[4] The account was originally stated in terms of Attract/Move (Bošković 1998a) but Move is argued to be restatable as Attract-All (Bošković 1998b).

3. The Structural Representation of Topic and Focus

While often appearing to cluster, fronted wh-phrases in BG do not necessarily form a constituent. In fact, based on the penetrability of the wh-cluster, I have motivated a dialect split: *Dialect A* does not allow any lexical material to split the fronted wh-phrases while *Dialect B* does.

Since C licenses both wh-movement and wh/focus-fronting it is possible that the fronted phrases will cluster together. Bošković follows Rudin in suggesting that they right-adjoin in SpecCP but he allows also that they may also land in separate specifiers (cf. Richards 1997). The two representations of the fronted wh-phrases seem to capture the noted dialectal variation: a multiple specifiers structure will allow intervening lexical material.

However, there are restrictions on the separability of the wh-cluster (Lambova 2001). First, intervening lexical material is only possible after the first fronted wh-phrase (9) and never further down in the wh-cluster. Second, in the presence of a topic nothing can split the wh-cluster (10). Both of these facts are problematic for Bošković: multiple specifiers cannot explain the restriction in (9) and a CP-adjoined topic should not affect the constituency in SpecCP.

(9) a. **Koj,** kazvaš, **kâde koga** šte porâča tortata?
who you're-saying where when will order cake-the

b. * **Koj kâde,** kazvaš, **koga** šte porâča tortata?
who where you're-saying when will order cake-the

c. * **Koj koga,** kazvaš, **kâde** šte porâča tortata?
who when you're-saying where will order cake-the
"Who you're saying will have the cake made where and when?"

(10) a. Koj **kazvaš** kâde šte porâča tortata? $\surd wh_1 \ldots wh_2 (wh_3)$
who you're-saying where will order cake-the

b. * *Tortata*[5] koj **kazvaš** kâde šte porâča? *Topic $wh_1 \ldots wh_2 (wh_3)$
cake-the (top) who you're saying where will order

I have proposed a modification of the Economy focus account of MWF to capture these facts. Focus is licensed in ΔP, a complementof C. All wh-phrases first move to SpecΔP to check their focus feature and cluster there. Assuming that moving one wh-phrase should satisfy the inadequacy of C, only the highest one excorporates to SpecCP.[6] Thus I restate Bošković's Attract/ Move analysis as Attract/Move plus excorporation. What this buys me is that I have a single wh-phrase in SpecCP and all the rest in the projection immediately below with space for intervening lexical material between the two projections, and only after the first wh-phrase.

I assume that movement to SpecΔP is subject to Superiority. Therefore, for me, both the target, D, and the moving wh-phrases have a strong [+Foc] feature. Thus the highest wh-phrase ends up first in SpecΔP (11), and it is the one to excorporate. Excorporation is obligatory, enforced by Economy (cf. Watanabe 1993) since carrying less material is more economical.

(11) a. Δ wh-phrase$_1$ wh-phrase$_2$
+Foc, strong +Foc, strong +Foc, strong

[5] Topics are given in italics.
[6] I extend the notion of excorporation (Roberts 1991) from heads to adjunction structures in general.

b. C / +wh, strong — wh-phrase$_1$ / +wh, weak — wh-phrase$_2$ / +wh, weak

C	wh-phrase$_1$	wh-phrase$_2$
+wh, strong	+wh, weak	+wh, weak

(12) [$_{SpecCP}$ koj$_i$ [C [$_{Spec\Delta P}$ t$_i$ [Δ ... [t$_i$ t$_j$]]]]]
+wh, strong (under C); +Foc, strong (under Δ)
t$_i$ = koj$_i$ kakvo$_j$

Note that on my modification, Bošković's Economy account of *selective* Superiority can be fully preserved. That is, after the highest/closest wh-phrase is attracted by Δ, the order of the rest of the wh-phrases is free.

More importantly, I propose that topics are also licensed in ΔP (cf. Koizumi 1994). The idea is that ΔP is a specially dedicated discourse-related projection in the sense of Uriagereka 1995. This avoids the oddness of licensing semantic opposites such as focus and topic in the same projection.

I further argue that, in questions with topics, the highest wh-phrase still excorporates to SpecCP but intonation considerations force the pronunciation of the excorporated wh-phrase below, in SpecΔP. Being now part of the wh-cluster, no intervening material can follow the first wh-phrase.[7]

Let me show how the analysis can be instantiated. I adopt the copy theory of movement so that traces of movement are actually copies. Following Franks 1998, I assume that while it is normally heads of non-trivial chains that are pronounced, lower copies of movement can be pronounced to save a derivation from a PF violation. Thus when there is no topic (13a), we pronounce the head of the wh-movement chain. However, when there is a topic (13b), we pronounce the relevant wh-phrase as part of the wh-cluster in SpecΔP.

(13) a. [$_{CP}$ **koj** C ... [$_{\Delta P}$ [[~~koj~~] **kâde**] e porâčal [$_{VP}$ ~~koj~~ ~~e porâčal~~ tortata ~~kâde~~]]]

b. [$_{CP}$ ~~koj~~ C [$_{Spec\Delta P}$ tortata [$_{Spec\Delta P}$ [[**koj**] **kâde**] e porâčal [$_{VP}$ ~~koj~~ ~~e porâčal~~ ~~tortata~~ ~~kâde~~]]]]

The reason to pronounce a lower copy of the wh-phrase in SpecCP in (13b) is intonation clash, a PF violation, arising when a wh-phrase is immediately followed by a topic. In order to show this, I will have to make a digression on BG intonation facts.

Penchev 1978 is the source of an early and insightful observation that question words in BG attract the high tone. Therefore, wh-phrases as well as phrases followed by the question particle *li* are made more prominent by increasing the pitch range. BG has two intonational contours – a gradual fall and a fall-rise-fall. Specifically, statements and direct questions are pronounced on the same contour but questions require the high gradual fall (14a). While a direct question requires the high gradual fall, an indirect one (as in the equivalent of *John asked who came*) requires the fall-rise-fall (14b). This is so since the question element, which is buried inside the clause, must be associated with a high tone. Finally, topics also require the

---

[7] Supporting evidence comes from embedded topics in BG, which surface below a complementizer (i); importantly, an embedded wh-phrase surfaces below a topic but still licenses an interrogative complementizer (ii):

(i)	Maria	kaza,	če	*tortata*	Ivan	šte	porâča	utre.	
	Maria	say-PT.3P.SG	that	cake-the (top)	Ivan	will	order	tomorrow.	
(ii) a.	Maria	pita	[koj	C$_{+wh}$	šte	porâča	tortata	utre].	
	Maria	ask-PRES.3P.SG	who		will	order	cake-the	tomorrow.	
b.	Maria	pita	[C$_{+wh}$	*tortata*	koj	šte	porâča	utre].	
	Maria	ask-PRES.3P.SG		cake-the (top)	who	will	order	tomorrow.	

fall-rise-fall (14c). That is so because the fall delimits the topic and the comment is pronounced on the rise fall. Significantly, the same is true for topics in questions except that the rise is higher.

(14) a. direct wh-question: high fall 

statement: medium fall 

b. direct wh-question: high fall 

c. indirect wh-question: fall-high rise-fall 

d. topic: medium fall-rise-fall 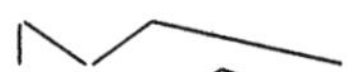

question with a topic: fall-high rise-fall 

Now observe what happens in a question with a topic: the first wh-phrase is in SpecCP and the topic is in SpecΔP. The topic requires a medium fall followed by a rise fall (15a) while the fronted wh-phrase requires a high gradual fall (15b). These two requirements cannot be reconciled without changes as I show in (15c): the high fall on the wh-phrase in SpecCP will not delimit properly the topic which immediately follows it. However, no problem arises on the fall-rise-fall as in (15d); it can accommodate the requirements of both the topic and the fronted wh-phrase provided that all wh-phrases are pronounced below the topic on the rise-fall.

(15) a. 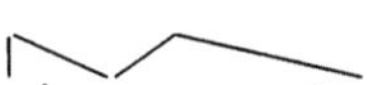 (fall-rise-fall)
topic comment

b.  (gradual fall)
wh$_1$ (wh$_2$)

c. 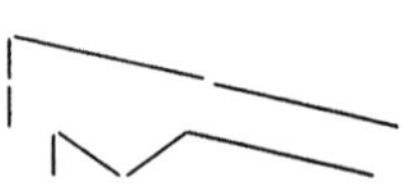 (clash)

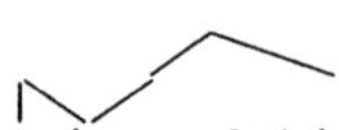
~~wh$_1$~~topic **wh$_1$** (wh$_2$)

I conclude that while topics in BG surface before all fronted wh-phrases they are syntactically below the first one, in fact in the same projection that licenses focus.[8]

Concerning topics, both dialects behave identically. However, if a single wh-phrase excorporates to SpecCP, it is not obvious how to extend the modified Economy focus movement account of MWF to the non-splitting *Dialect A*. In Lambova 2003, I acknowledge a problem for excorporation and offer a solution to the variation problem.

As Jairo Nunes (personal communucation) points out to me, I allow for a segment to excorporate. Assuming that operations cannot target non-constituents, I propose that excorporation is dependent on the adjunction structure. Rudin's (1988) original structure,

[8] A supporting argument for topics and foci being licensed in the same projection comes from the possibility to extract over a topic in BG. It is well-known that this is impossible in English: ***Where** do you think that *the birdseed* Mary is going to put? Putting aside what the correct structure for English topics is, the relevant movement violates Relativized Minimality. Since the issue does not arise in BG, I conclude that topicalization does not block wh-movement in BG, which should be possible only if both are equidistant from the target (see Lambova 2003 for details).

which I also assumed, is an extension of Chomsky's adjunction for multiple elements (16a). In particular, every subsequently moving wh-phrase adjoins to the same host, the first moved wh-phrase. There is an alternative: every subsequently moving wh-phrase may adjoin to a different host, the wh-phrase that moved before it (16b).

(16)
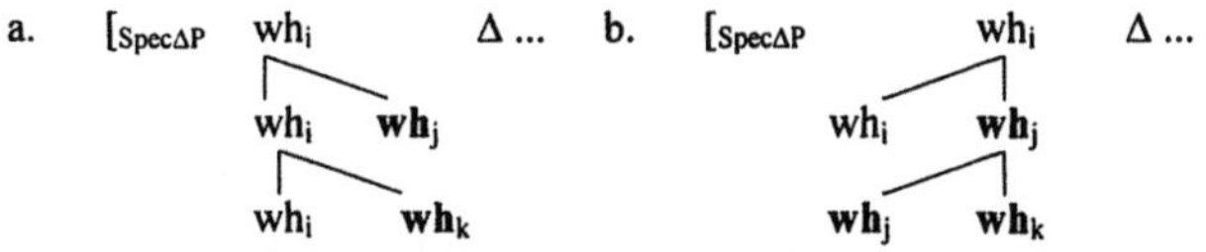

The resulting structures differ with respect to excorporation. Assuming that the operation targets the wh-phrase which has one segment highest, that must be wh_i. Now notice that if the operation applies exhaustively to all segments of the wh-phrase in question, the remaining wh-phrases in (16a) do not form a constituent but those in (16b) do. I suggest that this is a crucial difference between the two structures:

(17) Excorporation out of an adjoined structure must target all segments of a phrase exhaustively and must leave a constituent behind.

When excorporation is blocked, as in the structure in (16a), the whole wh-cluster must move to SpecCP. This essentially derives the assumption of Rudin and Bošković that in the non-splitting dialect *Dialect A* all wh-phrases are in SpecCP:

(18)
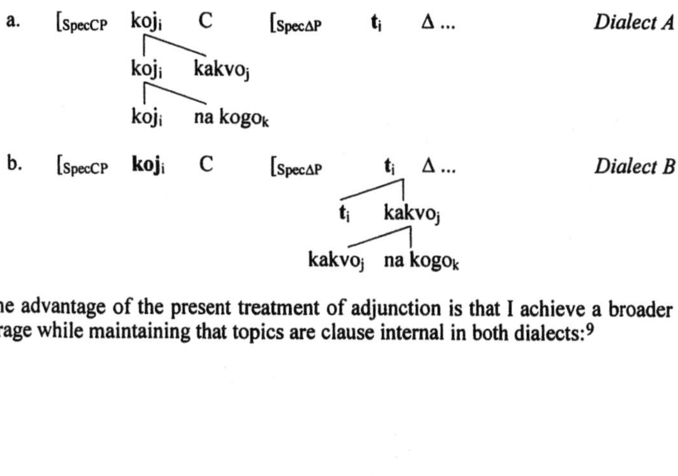

The advantage of the present treatment of adjunction is that I achieve a broader empirical coverage while maintaining that topics are clause internal in both dialects:[9]

---

[9] Further evidence for the proposed analysis comes from variation in sluicing (Fabian Heck, personal communication). Assuming that sluicing involves wh-movement followed by the deletion of the complement of C, it is not surprising that splitters will not allow multiple sluicing since they have a single wh-phrase in SpecCP. In other words, the splitting *Dialect B* is just like English, for which there is no doubt that only one wh-phrase is in SpecCP.

(19)

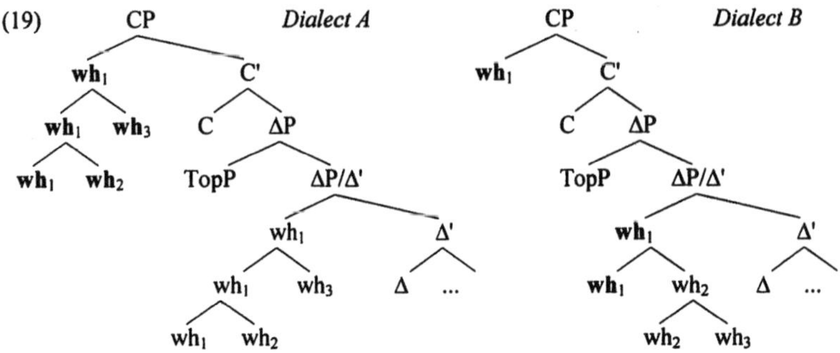

4. Uriagereka's FP

My argument for ΔP as a discourse-related projection is empirical. Uriagereka (1995) provides a conceptual justification. He suggests that information theoretic matters do not carry enough conceptual weight to justify their own level of representation.

Instead, he proposes that discourse is syntactically encoded in what he calls FurtherP, located between IP and CP, suggestive evidence coming from focus fronting languages. "I have not found any conclusive evidence that there are *separate* functional categories to express matters of topic, focus, emphasis, contrast, etc. All of these have an aspect in common: they en-code the *point of view* of a speaker or some other subject....The claim is that all information theoretic operations need to be mediated through a point of view. That is, when emphasis appears in a sentence, someone is responsible for this emphasis. Old or new information is old or new for someone.", writes Uriagereka. He points out that languages with overt focalization can be taken as suggestive evidence.

4.1 The order of the Fronted Phrases

In a wh-question a topic surfaces before the fronted wh-phrases. I argued that although one (or all fronted wh-phrases) are in SpecCP, PF chooses to activate their lower copy in ΔP. By transition, the observed order is determined in the discourse-related projection. The same ordering effects are observed for a topic and a contrastively focused phrase:

(20) a. *Decata* koj/ MAMA šte zavede na cirk?
kids-the (top) who mom (foc) will take to circus

b. * Koj/ MAMA *decata* šte zavede na cirk?
"The kids, who/MOM will take to the circus."

In this latter case the order is not affected by the pronunciation of lower copies. I assume that the contrastively focused phrase moves to ΔP; so the structure is:

(21) [$_{\text{SpecΔP}}$ *decata* [$_{\text{SpecΔP}}$ MAMA šte zavede [$_{\text{VP}}$ ~~MAMA šte zavede decata~~ na cirk]]]

Yet nothing in my analysis ensures that the topic is syntactically higher. Positing adjunction to ΔP for topics while having fronted wh-phrases in SpecDP is a possible technical solution since structural height will be determined in a slightly more principled manner.

However, under bare phrase structure XP adjunction is structurally equivalent to a higher specifier (cf. Koizumi 1994). So I will pursue a different idea instead.

(22)

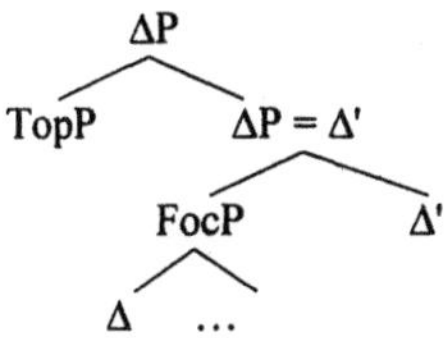

The solution to this problem is found in a seemingly unrelated fact. Fronted wh-phrases as well a contrastively focused phrase require subject verb inversion unlike topics.

(23) a. * Kakvo Ivan podari na Maria?
what Ivan give-as-a-present-PT.3P.SG to Maria
cf. Kakvo **podari Ivan** na Maria?

b. * KARTINATA Ivan podari na Maria.
painting-the (foc) Ivan give-as-a-present-PT.3P.SG to Maria
cf. KARTINATA **podari Ivan** na Maria.

(24) * *Kartinata* podari Ivan na Maria.
painting-the (top) give-as-a-present-PT.3P.SG Ivan to Maria
cf. *Kartinata* **Ivan podari** na Maria.

The verb in BG is not very high in the tree (cf. Izvorski 1993), certainly not in C. Recall that a contrastively focused phrase may also surface lower but still in a preverbal position (6). I propose that BG has a null focal affix responsible for the observed adjacency effect.

This is actually an extension of Bošković's (2001) null C analysis of *li* focalization which I summarize here. In addition to marking yes-no questions (25a), *li* is a focalizer (25b-c): the question in (25a) is neutral while those in (25b-c) are emphatic.

(25) a. Prodade li Ivan novata kola?
sell-PT.3P.SG Q Ivan new-the car
"Did Ivan sell the new car?"

b. [Novata kola] li prodade Ivan?
new-the car Q sell-PT.3P.SG Ivan
"Is it the NEW CAR that Ivan sold?"

c. [Novata] li kola prodade Ivan?
new-the Q car sell-PT.3P.SG Ivan
"Is it the NEW car that Ivan sold?"

The case of interest is (25c). Since left branch violations are not allowed in BG, as (26) shows, Bošković concludes that no syntactic operation can move the modifier alone to SpecCP. Instead, he proposes that *li* is a focal marker and C is null. The focal particle is a phrasal affix, which can be lexically generated on either the noun or the modifier.

(26) a. * Kakva li prodade Ivan kola?
what (kind of) Q sell-PT.3P.SG Ivan car

b. * Čija li prodade Ivan kola?
whose Q sell-PT.3P.SG Ivan car

(27) a. [novata kola-**li**]$_i$ C prodade Ivan t$_i$

b. [novata-**li** kola]$_i$ C prodade Ivan t$_i$

Concerning the subject verb inversion, I propose that there is a null counterpart of focal *li* which is also a verbal affix, i.e. it attaches to phrases undergoing focus fronting and requires adjacency to the verb. Consider the structures for (23):

(28) a. [$_{CP}$ kakvo + ø$_{[+Foc]}$ [C [$_{\Delta P}$ ~~kakvo + ø$_{[+Foc]}$~~ [Δ [$_{IP}$ ~~Ivan~~ [$_I$ podari [$_{vP}$ Ivan ~~podari~~ ~~kakvo+ ø$_{[+Foc]}$~~ na Maria]]]]]] =(23a)

b. [$_{\Delta P}$ KARTINATA + ø$_{[+Foc]}$ [Δ [$_{IP}$ ~~Ivan~~ [$_I$ podari [$_{vP}$ Ivan ~~podari~~ ~~KARTINATA+ ø$_{[+Foc]}$~~ na Maria]]]]] =(23b)

The null focal marker requires adjacency to the verb, and for this reason the subject is pronounced not in SpecTP but in its base generated position. This is yet another instance of activating a lower copy of movement. There is no topic affix.

Returning to the case of topic and focus interaction, as in (29), I suggest that in principle either the topic or the focused phrase can land in the higher specifier, i.e. nothing in syntax rules out the possibilities in (30). However, only (30a) meets the well formedness conditions of PF. In (30b), the intervention effect is due to the topic.[10]

(29) *Kartinata* NA MARIA podari Ivan.
painting-the (top) to-Maria (foc) give-as-a-present-PT.3P.SG Ivan
"As for the painting, Ivan gave it (as a present) TO MARIA."

(30) a. [$_{Spec\Delta P}$ Kartinata$_{[+Top]}$ [$_{Spec\Delta P}$ [NA MARIA]+ ø$_{[+Foc]}$ [Δ [$_{IP}$ ~~Ivan~~[$_I$ podari [$_{vP}$ Ivan ~~podari~~ ~~kartinata$_{[+Top]}$~~ ~~[NA MARIA]+ ø$_{[+Foc]}$~~]]]]]

b. * [$_{Spec\Delta P}$ [NA MARIA]+ ø$_{[+Foc]}$ [$_{Spec\Delta P}$ **kartinata**$_{[+Top]}$ [Δ [$_{IP}$ ~~Ivan~~ [$_I$ **podari** [$_{vP}$ Ivan ~~podari~~ ~~kartinata$_{[+Top]}$~~ ~~[NA MARIA]+ ø$_{[+Foc]}$~~]]]]]

Thus the observed surface order is the result of a morphological requirement. Based on this I suggest that multiple (kinds of) movements targeting the same projection are not ordered in syntax.[11]

---

[10] I assume that topic interpretation is only possible on pronouncing the head of the chain.

[11] Compare Richards (1997) who develops an argument that on the feature based conception of the cycle a subsequent movement to the same projection will not necessarily extend the tree. He actually argues that Shortest Move will enforce "tucking-in". However, he leaves open the case under discussion here, namely when a head has two different features.

4.2 Multiple Topic and Negative Fronting

Multiple fronting can affect elements other than wh-phrases. First, in BG it is possible to have multiple topics, and just like wh-phrases they all front obligatorily (31). I will refer to this phenomenon as *multiple topic fronting* (MTF).

(31) a. *Decata* *na cirk* mama šte vodi utre.
kids-the (top) to-circus (top) mom will take tomorrow

b. * *Decata* mama šte vodi *na cirk* utre. (on the relevant interpretation)
("The kids to the circus, mom will take tomorrow.")

Note that a subject cannot be interpreted as a topic if it is preceded by a topicalized object.

(32) a. * *Decata* *mama* šte vodi na cirk. (on the relevant interpretation)
kids-the (top) mom (top) will take to circus
("As for mom and the kids, she will take them to the circus.")

b. *[Mama]$_1$ [decata]$_2$ t_1 šte vodi t_2 na cirk utre.*
mom (top) kids-the (top) will take to circus tomorrow
("As for mom and the kids, she will take them to the circus tomorrow.")

This is reminiscent of the Superiority Condition as observed with wh-fronting: indeed, the topicalized phrase that surfaces first must be the highest one (cf. Grewendorf 2001: 94, fn.12). Furthermore, multiple topics display selective Superiority effects: the contrast in (33) does not obtain in the presence of a third topic; i.e., a second and a third topicalized phrase can be order-ed freely, just like fronted wh-phrases :

(33) a. ***Decata*** ***na cirk*** mama šte vodi utre.
kids-the (top) to-circus (top) mom will take tomorrow

b. * ***Na cirk*** ***decata*** mama šte vodi utre.
to-circus (top) kids-the (top) mom will take tomorrow
("The kids to the circus, mom will take tomorrow.")

(34) a. ***Mama*** ***decata*** ***na cirk*** šte vodi utre.
mom (top) kids-the (top) to-circus (top) will take tomorrow

b. ***Mama*** ***na cirk*** ***decata*** šte vodi utre.
mom (top) to-circus (top) the kids (top) will take tomorrow
("As for mom, the kids and the circus, she will take them there tomorrow.")

I argued that topics are in ΔP. Further support for a common licensing site of focus and topic comes from the properties MTF and MWF share. Therefore, I extend the Attract/Move analysis of MWF to topicalization in BG. The topic feature on the moved phrases is strong which explains the phenomenon of multiple topicalization.[12] The selective Superiority effects suggest that the target Δ is also the locus of a strong topic feature.

(35) Attract/ Move

Δ	TOP-phrase$_1$	TOP-phrase$_2$
+Top, strong	+Top, strong	+Top, strong

[12] Note that what distinguishes a topic from an XP is precisely the presence of a topic feature.

By attract Closest Δ attracts the closest topicalized phrase, which in (34) is the subject. It moves to SpecΔP satisfying the inadequacy of the target and simultaneously its own strong topic feature. The rest of the topics move in free order due to the Economy of derivation.

Another relevant phenomenon is *multiple negative fronting* (MNF) which, as Izvorski (1995: 66) mentions, obeys Superiority (36). Not surprisingly, selective Superiority effects show here too:

(36) a. **Ništo** **na** **nikogo** ne kaza Ivan.
nothing (foc) to nobody (foc) not say-PT.3P.SG Ivan

b. * **Na** **nikogo** **ništo** ne kaza Ivan.
to nobody (foc) nothing (foc) not say-PT.3P.SG Ivan
"Ivan didn't say anything to anybody."

(37) a. **Nikoj** **ništo** **na** **nikogo** ne kaza.
nobody (foc) nothing (foc) to nobody (foc) not say-PT.3P.SG

b. **Nikoj** **na** **nikogo** **ništo** ne kaza.
nobody (foc) to nobody (foc) nothing (foc) not say-PT.3P.SG
"Nobody said anything to anybody."

What hasn't been noticed before is that similarly to MWF, topicalization can co-occur with MNF, and it should not come as a surprise that topics surface first:

(38) a. *Za kartinata,* **nikoj** **ništo** ne kaza.
for-painting-the (top) nobody (foc) nothing (foc) not say-PT.3P.SG

b. * **Nikoj** **ništo** *za kartinata* ne kaza.
nobody (foc) nothing (foc) for-painting-the (top) not say-PT.3P.SG
"As for the painting, nobody said anything."

In short, MNF parallels MWF. I suggest that focalization underlies MNF as well, i.e. what drives negative fronting is a focus feature on the respective phrase(s). As can be expected, MNF requires subject verb inversion:

(39) * Ništo na nikogo **Ivan** ne kaza. cf. (36a)
nothing (foc) to nobody (foc) Ivan not say-PT.3P.SG

Observe, though, that unlike wh-phrases negative phrases do not have to front obligatorily (40a). Furthermore, only one negative phrase may front (40b) leaving another in situ:

(40) a. Nikoj ne kaza ništo na nikogo.
nobody (foc) not say-PT.3P.SG nothing to nobody

b. Ništo ne kaza Ivan na nikogo.
nothing (foc) not say-PT.3P.SG Ivan to nobody

Apparently, a negative phrase can be optionally drawn from the lexicon with a focus feature,[13] and when it is, it fronts obligatorily. Needless to say, the Attract/ Move analysis extends to this case as well. Finally, all the three types of fronted phrases can co-occur:

---

[13] Just as a topic feature makes an XP undergo topicalization, a focus feature is responsible for the fronting of a negative XP. As for MWF, it is a lexical property of BG wh-phrases that they are inherently focused, i.e. they always have a strong [+Foc] feature.

(41) ***Decata*** **koj nikâde** njama da vodi?
kids-the (top) who nowhere not-will DA take

Thus MWF and MNF reduce to the presence of a strong [+Foc] feature. On the other hand, the obligatory fronting of wh-phrases and topics is due to an inherently present strong feature. Taken together these fronting processes also present an indirect argument that MWF does not involve multiple wh-movement, i.e. wh-fronting is not driven by the [+wh] feature.

The shared properties of MWF, MTF and MNF constitutes strong evidence for a single licensing projection and against Rizzi's (1997) widely accepted articulated CP with several functional projections instead of ΔP.

5. Multiple Feature Checking

Rudin (1988) argued that fronted wh-phrases in BG right-adjoin to one another. Recently, it has been suggested that multiple fronting is instantiated as multiple specifiers (see Koizumi 1994, Bošković 1998, Richards 1997). Constituency can tease apart these two possibilities.[14]

Recall that in the splitting *Dialect B* intervening lexical material is only allowed after the first wh-phrase. I argued this is so because that wh-phrase is in a separate projection. In other words, fronted wh-phrases cluster in SpecΔP. Following Rudin 1988, I assumed they form a syntactic constituent via rightward adjunction.[15]

Now note that adjuncts cannot intervene into topic or negative clusters either.[16] There is no excorporation in these cases, so I assume speakers will stick to the adjunction structure they employ for the fronted wh-phrases (42). Furthermore, multiple fronted phrases of the same type cluster together with Superiority effects holding:

(42) a. * *Decata,* **kazvaš,** na cirk mama šte vodi utre.
kids-the (top) you-are-saying to-circus (top) mom will take tomorrow

b. * Ništo **kazvaš,** na nikogo ne kaza Ivan.
nothing you-are-saying to nobody not say-PT.3P.SG Ivan

(43) a. *Decata*$_2$ *utre*$_4$ koj$_1$ kâde$_3$ **t$_1$** šte vodi **t$_2$ t$_3$ t$_4$**?
kids-the (top) tomorrow (top) who where will take

b. *Decata*$_2$ *utre*$_4$ nikoj$_1$ nikâde$_3$ **t$_1$** njama da vodi **t$_2$ t$_3$ t$_4$**?
kids-the (top) tomorrow (top) nobody (foc) nowhere (foc) not-will DA take

I take these facts as evidence that while multiple movements of the same type are instantiated as adjunction in a single specifier. Multiple specifiers then project only when the head has more than one feature, and thus licenses movements of different types. Accordingly, I modify the structure proposed above (abstracting from dialect variation):

---

[14] See Toman 1981 for an early and illuminating discussion of structure with respect to constituency. In particular, he considered the two possibilities on different theoretical grounds suggesting that a true multiple movement will yield a constituent which will behave as such in long distance contexts (for more details, see Lambova 2003).

[15] The reason is that only rightward adjunction gives the correct surface order.

[16] A parenthetical can follow a topic cluster, which is expected on my suggestion that there is no topic affix:

(i) *Decata* *na cirk,* **kazvaš,** koj/ mama šte vodi utre.
kids-the (top) to-circus (top) you-are-saying who mom will take tomorrow

(44)

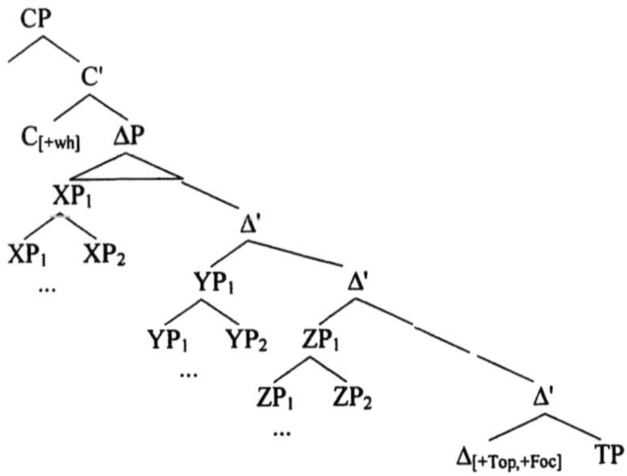

Having reduced MNF and MWF to focus fronting I suggested that Δ has at most two features. It was crucial for me that the relevant features on the target are strong, and therefore must be checked before Spell-Out. Regardless of how strength is interpreted (see Lasnik 1999) this is problematic: obviously, not all sentences contain phrases with topic or focus features.

I suggest that Δ does not have to be obligatorily present in the tree. This is the case of a clause without a topic or a focalized phrase. Also, Δ can be drawn from the lexicon with both or any of the two features. The former will be a case where a topic co-occurs with a focalized phrase and the latter will be a case of a clause with either a topic or a focalized phrase.

Although I draw a parallel between contrastive focalization (which employs focus fronting in BG) and focus fronting as in MWF and MNF with respect to subject verb inversion, these do not seem to be entirely the same.

It is fairly well known, but less understood at present, that focus fronting languages, including BG, disallow multiple contrastive foci (see Kiss 1995):[17]

(45) a. KARTINATA NA MARIA podari Ivan.
painting-the (foc) to Maria (foc) give-PT.3P.SG Ivan

b. Ivan KARTINATA NA MARIA podari.
Ivan painting-the (foc) to Maria (foc) give-PT.3P.SG
"Ivan gave the PAINTING to MARIA as a present.

On the other hand, while nothing prevents the co-occurrence of fronted negative and wh-phrases (46)[18], Rudin (1994) observes that a contrastively focused phrase is not compatible with a fronted wh-phrase in the same clause:

(46) Na kogo ništo ne podari Ivan?
to whom nothing (foc) not give-PT.3P.SG Ivan
"Who didn't Ivan give anything to as a present?"

---

[17] We can only test for clustering contrastive foci in either of two focus positions because of the requirement that they be adjacent to the verb.

[18] Given the Superiority effects for the focus feature, which both objects check, *ništo* "nothing" must be in the higher specifier of ΔP; yet *na kogo* "whom" can still excorporate over it so that the surface order is as (46).

(47) * Na kogo KARTINATA podari Ivan?
to whom painting-the (foc) give-PT.3P.SG Ivan
"Who did Ivan gave the PAINTING to as a present?"

More puzzling is the contrast in (48). The unacceptability of (48a) could be either a Superiority violation or the incompatibility of the fronted negative phrase and the contrastively focused phrase. The latter seems a possibility, given (48b).

(48) a. * Na nikogo KARTINATA ne podari Ivan?
to nobody (foc) painting-the (foc) not give-PT.3P.SG Ivan

b. KARTINATA na nikogo ne podari Ivan?
painting-the (foc) to nobody not give-PT.3P.SG Ivan
"Nobody did Ivan gave the PAINTING to as a present?"

I would like to suggest that MNF is not different from MWF in the relevant respect. Given that there are two focus positions in the language, the two phrases in (48b) might not be in the same projection. It is not easy to test that with an intervening parenthetical, for example, because there is an interfering factor: the parenthetical will have an intervention effect on the adjacency requirement.

I leave these issues for future research.

6. Conclusion

Based on the separability of the fronted wh-phrases in BG, I have modified the Economy/focus movement account of MWF proposing that focus is licensed in DP, a specially dedicated discourse projection. I also presented new evidence for fronting to DP of topics, negative and contrastively focused phrases. Of particular importance is the clustering and separability of the multiple phrases moving to ΔP.

The BG data I discuss here provide a strong empirical argument for Uriagereka's (1995) hypothesis and against Rizzi's (1997) concept of the CP layer. The conclusion is important in view of the recent tendency toward expanding the inventory of functional projections.

References

Bošković, Ž. (1998a): Multiple wh-fronting and Economy of derivation. In: *WCCFL* 16, 49–65.

Bošković, Ž. (1998b): Wh-phrases and wh-movement in Slavic. Position paper, *Workshop on Comparative Slavic Morphosyntax*, 5–7 June 1998, Indiana University. Downloadable at http://www.indiana.edu/~slavconf/linguistics/index.html.

Bošković, Ž. (2001): *On the nature of the syntax-phonology interface: Cliticization and related phenomena.* Amsterdam: Elsevier Science.

Bošković, Ž. (2002): On multiple wh-fronting. In: *LI* 33, 351–383.

Chomsky, N. (1973): Conditions on transformations. In: Anderson, S. & P. Kiparsky (eds.): *A Festschrift for Morris Halle.* New York: Holt, Rinehart and Winston, 232–286.

De Rijk, R. (1972): Studies in Basque syntax. Doctoral Dissertation: MIT.

Franks, S. (1998): Clitics in Slavic. Position paper, *Workshop on Comparative Slavic Morphosyntax*, 5–7 June 1998, Indiana University. Downloadable at http://www.indiana.edu/~slavconf/linguistics/index.html.

Grewendorf, G. (2001): Multiple wh-fronting. In: *LI* 32, 87–122.

Izvorski, R. (1993): On wh-movement and focus movement in Bulgarian. Paper presented at CONSOLE 2, University of Tübingen, December 1993.

Izvorski, R. (1995): Wh-movement and Focus-movement in Bulgarian. In: Eckhardt, R. & V. van Geenhoven (eds.): *ConSole II. Proceedings of the Second Conference of the Student*

Organisation of Linguistics in Europe. The Hague: Holland Academic Graphics, 54–67.
Kiss, K. (ed). (1995): *Discourse-Configurational Languges*, Oxford, UK: OUP.
Koizumi, M. (1994): Layered specifiers. In: *NELS* 24, 255–269.
Lambova, M. (1999): The typology of multiple wh-fronting in Slavic revisited. In: *FASL* 8, 238–258.
Lambova, M. (2001): On A' movements in Bulgarian and their interaction. In: *TLR* 18, 327–374.
Lambova, M. (2002): On the representation of topic and focus in Bulgarian. In: *FASL* 10, 119–142.
Lambova, M. (2003): On information structure and clausal architecture: Evidence from Bulgarian. Ph. D. Dissertation, University of Connecticut.
Lasnik, H. (1999): On feature strength: Three Minimalist approaches to feature movement. In: *LI* 30, 197–217.
Penchev, J. (1978): Osnovni intonacionni konturi v bûlgarskoto izrechenie. In: *Bûlgarski Ezik* 28, 293–302.
Richards, N. (1997): What moves where when in which language? Doctoral Dissertation: MIT.
Rizzi, L. (1997): The fine structure of the left periphery. In: Haegeman, L. (ed.): *Elements of Grammar*, Dordrecht: Kluwer, 281–337.
Roberts, I. (1991): Excorporation and minimality. In: *LI* 22, 209–218.
Rudin, C. (1986): *Aspects of Bulgarian Syntax: Complementizers and Wh-constructions*. Columbus, OH: Slavica.
Rudin, C. (1988): On multiple questions and multiple wh-fronting. In: *NLLT* 6, 445–501.
Rudin, C. (1994): On focus position and focus marking in Bulgarian questions. In: *Papers of the Annual Meeting of the Formal Linguistics Society of MidAmerica* 4, 252–265.
Toman, J. (1981): Aspects of multiple wh-movement. In: May, R. & J. Koster (eds.): *Levels of Syntactic Representation*, Dordrecht: Foris, 293–302.
Uriagereka, J. (1995): An F-position in Western Romance. In: Kiss, K. (ed.): *Discourse-Configurational Languges*, Oxford, UK: OUP, 153–175.
Watanabe, A. (1993): *AGR-based Case theory and its interaction with the A'-system*. Ph.°D. dissertation. MIT, Cambridge, Mass.

Paul Law, Berlin

The Bulgarian clitic *li* in questions*

1. Introduction

The clitic *li* in questions is widely assumed in the literature on Slavic languages to be located in C. Examples like those in (1) are often taken to be the evidence (Progovac 1996:417):

(1) a. Stefan tvrdi [$_{CP}$ da *mu ga je* [[$_{IP}$ Petar poklonio]]] (Serbo-Croatian)
claims that him it is given
'Stefan claims that Peter has given it to him as a present.'

b. [$_{CP}$ da *li je* [[$_{IP}$ Marija stigla]]]?
that Q has arrived
'Has Mary arrived?'

That is, if the complementizer *da* in (1a) is in C and clitics encliticize to it, then the clitic *li* occurring in between *da* and the enclitic *je* in (1b) should also be in C.

The location of the clitic *li* in C has ramifications for other aspects of the grammar. For instance, one may take the occurrence of the (finite) verb to the left of *li* in (2a) to be evidence of a CP structure, and that Travis's (1986) Head Movement Constraint (HMC) can be violated (Lema and Rivero 1989) as the participle apparently moves to C skipping over the auxiliary *si* in (2b) (Rivero 1991, Wilder and Ćavar 1994, Progovac 1996 and Tomic 1996):

(2) a. [$_{CP}$ [izpratix$_i$ *li mu* [$_{IP}$ t_i kniga]]]?
sent.1SG Q him book
'Did I send him a book?'

b. [$_{CP}$ [viždal$_i$ *li* [$_{IP}$ *si go* t_i]]]?
seen Q AUX.2SG him
'Have you seen him?'

Moreover, the impossible occurrence of certain categories to the left of *li* may also be taken to be due to the blocking effects of some intervening categories. Thus, one may take the ungrammatical example in (3), which differs from those in (2) in the presence of the modal *šte* 'will', to be evidence that modals block movement to C (Rivero 1993:572-574):

(3) *[$_{CP}$ [viždaš *li* [$_{IP}$ ... šte *go* t_i ...]]]?
see.2SG Q will him
'Will you see him?'

Similarly, one may argue that the occurrence of the clitic *li* below the modal *šte* 'will' in (4) is the result of *li* lowering to the verb in the VP (Rivero 1993), implying that the option of lowering is in fact available in Universal Grammar (UG), contrary to the widely held view that movement is always to a c-commanding position:

(4) [$_{CP}$ [t_i [$_{IP}$ ... šte *go* viždaš *li*$_i$ ...]]]?
will him see.2SG Q
'Will you see him?'

---

* I wish to thank the audience at the FDSL 5 conference in Leipzig, especially Željko Bošković and Uwe Junghanns for very helpful comments. I am indebted to Koyka Stoyanova, Dora Toneva and Hristo Velkov for lending me their native judgments. All errors and inadequacies are my responsibility. Due to the original sources from which the examples are taken, the transliterations are not uniform.

The facts in (2)-(4) thus have far-reaching consequences for linguistic theory. The syntax of the clitic *li* in questions is therefore of particular theoretical interest, insofar it sheds some light on the general theory of grammar.[1]

I argue here that these various issues posing some difficulties for the view that *li* is independently in C and the concomitant movement to derive the different positions of *li* no longer arise in a base-generation analysis, along the lines Bošković (2001a:239-243) suggests for the focus constructions. More specifically, the clitic *li* is base-generated, right-adjoined to an X° or XP in an independently possible syntactic structure. The clitic *li* can be in C just in case the constituent to which it attaches is in C. I show that *li* is not limited to the position after the first prosodic word (p-word) as is commonly assumed (Izvorski, King and Rudin 1997, Bošković 2001a), but may be located farther to the right and hence lower than C. I suggest a feature-checking account for the distribution of the clitic *li* in Bulgarian questions and its focus property, and exhibit evidence that the modal *šte* 'will' is subject to a verb-adjacency constraint, quite independently of the clitic *li*.

The base-generation account of the clitic *li* offers an empirically more accurate and conceptually satisfying account of its distribution in that the the empirical problems arising from the assumption that modals block movement cease to exist, the HMC can be maintained (cf. also Caink 1999) and movement is generally restricted to a c-commanding position.

2. Some movement analyses

2.1 Lowering of li

Assuming that the clitic *li* is in C, Rivero (1993) argues that the grammatical difference in (5) is due to verb movement to C being blocked when the modal *šte* 'will' intervenes, the Mood Phrase (MP) projected by the modal being a barrier to movement:

(5) a. $[_{CP}$ izpratix$_i$ [*li* $[_{IP}$ *mu* t_i kniga]]]?
sent.1SG Q him book
'Did I send him a book?'

b. *$[_{CP}$ viždaš$_i$ [*li* $[_{MP}$ šte *go* t_i]]]?
see.2SG Q will him
'Will you see him?'

She then claims that although raising is the default case, lowering is also available in UG, as a more costly option:

---

[1] Rivero (1993:572-573) also claims that negation blocks verb-movement and may raise with clitics to C, as the grammatical contrast in (i) illustrates. The example in (ib) is indeed judged ungrammatical by my informants:

(i) a. ne *mu* *li* izpratix kniga?
not him Q sent.1SG book
'Didn't I send him a book?'

b. * izpratix$_i$ *li* ne *mu* t_i kniga?

I am not able to go into the intricate scope and information structure properties of negation here, but like to point out that the example in (ii), comparable to that in (ib), is not impossible (capital letters represent stress):

(ii) ?? kuPUva *li* ne MARko jaBALki, a PEtar doMAti?
buy.3SG Q not apples but tomatoes
'Is it true that MARKO is not buying APPLES, but PETER is buying TOMATOES?'

Lack of appropriate contrastive foci may explain why the example in (ib) is impossible, and the degraded status of that in (ii) may be due to there being too many foci, rather than to negation being a barrier to movement.

(6) [$_{CP}$ [t_i [$_{MP}$ šte *go* viždaš *li*$_i$]]]?
will him see.2SG Q
'Will you see him?'

This is why raising is the only option in (5a), in the absence of the barrier-erecting modal, and lowering is allowed in (6), raising being impossible in the presence of MP.

Rivero's analysis is problematic in several respects. First, if MP is a barrier for head-movement, then it should be a barrier to XP-movement as well, contrary to fact:

(7) [$_{CP}$ Ivan$_i$ [*li* [$_{MP}$ šte [$_{TP}$ viždaš t_i]]]]?
Q will see.2SG
'Will you see Ivan?'

Second, if MP is a barrier for head-raising, it should be a barrier for head-lowering of *li* too.

Third, it is not clear why the clitic *li* should right-adjoin to the thematic V in (6). In (8), *li* is not adjacent and hence not right-adjoined to the thematic V:

(8) a. [$_{CP}$ [t_i [$_{NEGP}$ ne *go* *li*$_i$ *e* viždal]]]?
not him Q AUX.3SG seen
'Did he see him?'
b. [$_{CP}$ [t_i [$_{NEGP}$ ne *mu* *li*$_i$ *go* dadoxte]]]?
not him Q it gave
'Didn't you give it to him?'

Rivero's account is therefore at best incomplete.

Fourth, there are further empirical problems with the claim that MP is a barrier to head-movement. The participle may occur to the left of the modal *šte* 'will', as in (9b) (Izvorski, King and Rudin 1997:191), or even to the left of the clitic *li* preceding the modal, as in (10):

(9) a. šte *e* izpil konjaka.
will AUX.3SG drunk cognac
'He will have drunk the cognac.'
b. izpil$_i$ šte *e* t_i konjaka.

(10) a. viždal$_i$ *li* šte *go* *e* t_i?
seen Q will him AUX.3SG
'Will he have seen him?'
b. viždal$_i$ *li* šte *si* *go* t_i?
seen Q will AUX.2SG him
'Will you have seen him?'

It thus appears that the ungrammaticality of the example in (3) is not due to MP being a barrier to movement, but to something else; therefore, the example in (4) is not necessarily evidence that lowering is an option in UG.

2.2 Prosodic inversion

Izvorski, King and Rudin (1997) argue that the positioning of the clitic *li* is sometimes effected by a PF operation of prosodic inversion (PI) (Halpern 1992). They assume that *li* is in C, and can be hosted by the verbal head complex when it raises to C left-adjoining to it. They suggest that when there is no maximal projection in SpecCP, PI can occur at PF as a last resort mechanism. PI allows a clitic to encliticize to the right-edge of the following p-word if no constituent precedes the clitic (Izvorski, King and Rudin 1997:192). So a p-word ω preceding an enclitic may host it, as in (11a), but a clitic may find itself to the right of a following p-word by PI, if it is not preceded by some phonetically overt material, as in (11b):

(11) a. [XX]$_\omega$ CL [XX]$_\omega$

b. CL [XX]$_\omega$ [XX]$_\omega$

Along these lines, the example in (2a) would be derived as in (12), where PI applies to place *li* after the first p-word:

(12) *li* [izpratix]$_\omega$ – *mu* kniga (=(2a))

In (4), the modal *šte* 'will' and the clitic *go* 'him' bear no stress. Thus, the only p-word in the sentence is the verb plus the modal and the clitic. PI applies to place the clitic *li* to its right:

(13) *li* [šte *go* viždaš]$_\omega$ – ? (=(4))

An important prosodic property of negation is that the constituent appearing after it must bear stress (Izvorski, King and Rudin 1997:188). This is the only syntactic context where clitics can be stressed. In (14), the first p-word is comprised of negation and the stressed clitic pronoun; PI applies to place the clitic *li* after it:

(14) *li* [ne MU]$_\omega$ – *go* dadoxte? (=(8b))

Apart from the question of why PI should apply in (12) and (13) given that the option of raising of the verb to the left of *li* is available and the general conceptual issue of the extent to which PF movement of the sort PI is an instance of is possible (Bošković 2001b), Izvorski, King and Rudin's account is not quite correct empirically. The clitic *li* need not appear after the first p-word of the sentence. As shown in (15), *li* may appear farther to the right:

(15) a. Ivan čete *li* kniga-ta?
read.3SG Q book-the
'Is Ivan reading the book?'
b. Ivan vnimatelno *li* čete knigata (ili nevnimatelno)?
carefully Q read.3SG book-the or carelessly
'Is Ivan reading the book carefully (or carelessly)?'

The examples in (15) also show that the position of the clitic *li* in these cases is not C, as the subject and the verb, or the subject and the adverb do not form one syntactic constituent.

2.3 Pronounce a copy

Franks (1998) assumes the copy theory of movement according to which a moved category leaves a full copy in the position from which it moves. He suggests that the default case of pronunciation is that the higher copy is pronounced, unless pronouncing it would violate some constraint of grammar, schematically as in (16):

(16) ... X ... X ... ⇒
 a. ... X ... ~~X~~ ... (default)
 b. ... ~~X~~ ... X ... (unless other constraints are violated)

If the clitic *li* is in C, then the example in (17a) can be derived by moving the complex consisting of the verb and the clitic to the left of *li*, leaving a full copy behind:

(17) a. **go* vidja *li*?
 him saw Q
 'Did he/she/you see him?'
 b. [$_C$ [*go* vidja]$_i$+*li*] [~~*go* vidja~~]$_i$?

The example in (17a) is the result of pronouncing the upper copy of the verb+clitic complex, and the lower copy is deleted (represented by the strike-through), as in (17b). But this would violate the prosodic constraint barring clitics from appearing in the initial position (cf. The Tobler-Mussafia's Law). According to the principles of pronunciation in (16), the lower copy of the clitic can now be pronounced. On the contrary, the lower copy of the verb cannot be pronounced, as pronouncing the upper copy does not violate any constraint. The upper copy must therefore be pronounced, yielding the grammatical outcome in (18a), with deletion being scattered among the different parts of a chain, as in (18b) (Nunes 2000):

(18) a. vidja *li go*?
 'Did he/she/you see him?'
 b. [$_C$ [~~*go*~~ vidja]$_i$+*li*] [*go* ~~vidja~~]$_i$?

The conceptually appeal of the pronounce-a-copy analysis is that it fits very well in the theory allowing neither optional movement nor rightward adjunction (Kayne 1994).

It also seems to be able to explain some facts regarding adverbs. The sentential reading of the Serbo-Croatian adverb *pravilno* 'correctly', present in (19a) but not in (19b), would be mysterious if the clitic auxiliary verb *je* is located in the same position:

(19) a. Jovan *je* pravilno odgovorio Mileni.
 is correctly answered
 'Jovan did the right thing in anwering Milena.'
 'Jovan gave Milena a correct answer.'
 b. odgovorio *je* pravilno Mileni.
 answered is correctly
 'Jovan gave Milena a correct answer.'
 *'Jovan did the right thing in anwering Milena.'
 c. ... *je* ... sentential adverb ... *je* ... manner adverb ...

Bošković (2001a:132) argues that despite its appearance, the position of the clitic *je* in (19) is not the same. More specifically, it occurs above sentential and manner adverbs in (19a) and below sentential adverbs but above manner adverbs in (19b). This state of affairs may arise as a result of *je* optionally moving from a position below sentential adverbs to one above them, a problem for the theory that allows no optional movement. The pronouce-a-copy approach promises to solve this problem.

Suppose *je* always moves to a high position above sentential adverbs, leaving behind a full copy in a position below them, schematically represented in (19c). On the one hand, the upper copy of *je* must be pronounced according to (16), if the subject appears in a position still higher than it, as in (19a). On the other hand, if the past participle occurs in a position lower than sentential adverbs, as in (19b), and there is nothing to the left of the upper copy of *je*, then pronouncing the upper copy would violate the requirement that *je* be preceded by some phonetically overt material. The lower copy of *je* may now be pronounced.

If the clitic pronoun appearing to the left of the thematic verb, e.g., in (4), is left-adjoined to it, then its occurrence to the right of the thematic verb, e.g., in (18) without *li*, must be due to *li* being right-adjoined to it, impossible if right-adjunction is not an option. As the representation in (18b) shows, the appearance of the clitic pronoun *go* to the right of the verb (and the clitic *li*) need not be an instance of right-adjunction. It is in fact the lower copy of the clitic that has moved leftward. The pronounce-a-copy theory thus seems to be able to accommodate apparent optional movement and right-adjunction is an elegant way.

In spite of the correct results in (17) and (18) as well as the conceptual appeal of the pronounce-a-copy analysis, various empirical and conceptual problems arise. Empirically, it is not immediately clear how the pronounce-a-copy account would explain why the example in (20a) is ungrammatical:

(20) a. *ne GO vidja *li*?
not him saw Q
'Didn't he/she/it see him?'
b. Syntax: [ne GO vidja]$_i$+*li* [ne *go* vidja]$_i$
c. Phonology: [ne GO]$_\omega$ [vidja]$_\omega$ *li* [~~ne~~ ~~*go*~~ ~~vidja~~]$_i$?

If the complex consisting of negation, the clitic and the verb moves to the left of the clitic *li*, leaving a full copy behind, then it is not obvious why the upper copy of the verb cannot be pronounced to yield the outcome in (20a).

Bošković (2001a:208) considers this example, claiming that *li* is a second-position clitic. In particular, it cannot appear in the prosodic environment in (21):[2]

(21) X ... Y ... Z *li*
+stress +stress

That is, the prosodic structure in (20c) is in accord with the principles of pronunciation in (16). As pronouncing the upper copy of the verb, to yield the outcome in (20a), would violate the second-position constraint on *li*. As a result, it is now possible to pronounce the lower copy of the verb, as in (22b), to yield the grammatical outcome in (22a):

---

[2] Bošković (2001a:212-213) claims that the second-position property of *li* is independently motivated, for it accounts for the grammatical contrast in (i) (for some speakers):

(i) a. * koj kakvo *li* kupuva?
who what Q buy
'Who on earth is buying what?'
b. koj *li* kakvo kupuva?

If the clitic *li* is in C and all *wh*-phrases are in COMP (=SpecCP) (Rudin 1986), then there is no reason why *li* cannot follow two *wh*-phrases.

Bošković argues that (ia) is excluded since the pronunciation of the upper copy of the *kakvo* 'what', as in (iia), violates the second-position constraint; as a result, the lower copy may now be pronounced, as in (iib):

(ii) a. * [$_{CP}$ koj kakvo [$_{C'}$ *li* [~~kakvo~~ kupuva]]]
b. [$_{CP}$ koj ~~kakvo~~ [$_{C'}$ *li* [kakvo kupuva]]]

However, as we will see, there is evidence that *li* may occur after two p-words. Cf. also footnote 5.

(22) a. ne GO *li* vidja?
b. [ne GO]$_\omega$ [~~vidja~~]$_\omega$ li [~~ne~~ ~~*go*~~ vidja]$_i$?

Nonetheless, Bošković's analysis does not account for the grammatical contrast in (23):

(23) a. *ne MI *go* *li* dade?
not 1SG.DAT it.ACC Q gave
'Didn't he/she/you give it to me?'
b. ne MI *li* go dade?
c. ne MI *go* DAde *li*?

To appreciate the problem, consider the syntactic structure in (24a) after movement of the verbal complex to the left of *li*, and the prosodic structures in (24b)-(24d) (small caps indicate secondary stress):

(24) a. [ne *mi go* dade]$_i$+*li* [ne *mi go* dade]$_i$
b. [ne MI *go*]$_\omega$ [~~dade~~]$_\omega$+*li* [~~ne~~ ~~*mi go*~~ dade]. (=(23a))
c. [ne MI]$_\omega$ [~~*go* dade~~]$_\omega$+*li* [~~ne~~ ~~*mi*~~ *go* dade]. (=(23b))
d. [ne MI *go*]$_\omega$ [DAde]$_\omega$+*li* [~~ne~~ ~~*mi go*~~ ~~dade~~]. (=(23c))

The clitic pronoun *mi* 'me' occurs immediately after negation, and hence must bear stress. The issue that arises is whether the position of *li* can be correctly accounted for by the second-position constraint requiring it be in second-position.

If *go* 'it' is an enclitic, then it can encliticize to the first p-word that is the complex consisting of negation and the pronominal clitic *mi* 'me', as in (24b). If the upper copy of the verb is pronounced, it would violate the second-position constraint on *li*. As a result, the lower copy can be pronounced. There is then apparently no reason why (23a) is ungrammatical. The grammatical example in (23b) can be derived with the prosodic structure in (24c), where the upper copy of the clitic *go* is part of the second p-word consisting of the verb *dade* 'give'. As pronouncing the second p-word would violate the second-position constraint on *li*, the lower copy of *go* and that of the verb can be pronounced. But the prosodic structure in (24c) is impossible, the clitic *go* not being a proclitic (cf. the ungrammatical example in (17a)). It is therefore unclear how Bošković's account can explain why in (23b) is possible. Moreover, the grammaticality of the example in (23c) is direct counterevidence to the claim that *li* is a second-position clitic. In the prosodic structure in (24d), the clitic *li* is in third-position.

The principles of pronunciation in (16) themselves are not unproblematic. If auxiliary verbs and thematic verbs are Merged initially in some fixed positions, then their surface positions differing from their base-positions must be derived by movement. In this light, examples like those in (25)-(26) are of particular interest, since the thematic verb may occur either to the left or right of the non-clitic auxiliary verb (Rivero 1993:570):

(25) a. pročel beše kniga-ta.
read was book-the
'He had read the book.'
b. beše pročel kniga-ta.

(26) a. zaspal beše Petar.
fallen-asleep was
'Petar had fallen asleep.'
b. beše zaspal Petar.

Suppose the auxiliary verb is initially Merged to the left of the thematic verb, then the order where the auxiliary verb appears to the right of the thematic verb may be derived by leftward movement of the thematic verb, leaving a full copy behind. According to the principles of pronunciation in (16), the pronunciations in (27a) and (28a) are possible, but those in (27b) and (28b) are not:

(27) a. pročel beše ~~pročel~~ kniga-ta.
b. ~~pročel~~ beše pročel kniga-ta.

(28) a. zaspal beše ~~zaspal~~ Petar.
b. ~~zaspal~~ beše zaspal Petar.

The upper copy of the past participle must be pronounced, as pronouncing it does not violate any prosodic constraint. It should therefore be impossible to pronounce the lower copy.

A similar problem arises for the varying position of a non-clitic pronoun. If the clitic pronoun to the right of the verb in (18a) is not the result of right-adjoining the pronoun to the verb, but of it being the lower copy of the moved clitic, then the same should be true of the example in (29a) with a non-clitic pronoun:

(29) a. ~~nego~~ vidja nego.
him saw him
'He/she/you saw him.'
b. nego vidja ~~nego~~.

But it should not be possible to pronounce the lower copy of *nego* 'him' in (29a) because pronouncing the upper copy of the pronoun, as in (29b), violates no prosodic constraint.

One way out of these problems is to claim that the b-sentences in (27)-(29) do not involve movement or right-adjunction, i.e., the past participle or pronoun has not moved from in its base position. However, if this were a possible explanation, then we would have to accept that optional movement is possible. Much of the conceptual appeal of the pronounce-a-copy is lost, as it can no longer be maintained that the apparently optional movement is in fact obligatory and apparent right-adjunction is due to the lower copy being pronounced.

In sum, the pronounce-a-copy account is rather troublesome. Without the second-position constraint on *li*, it cannot account for why the example in (20a) is ungrammatical; with the constraint, it cannot explain why (23a) is ungrammatical or why (23c) is grammatical. Moreover, it cannot adequately explain the different positions of the past participle in (27)-(28) and that of the non-clitic pronoun in (29).

3. The syntactic and prosodic property of the clitic *li* in questions in Bulgarian

As we saw, the various problems in the movement accounts stem from the assumption that the clitic *li* is in C, and the attendant different word-orders are derived by movement. In fact, evidence for the clitic *li* being independently in C in Bulgarian is very tenuous. Quite on the contrary, there is clear evidence that the clitic *li* need not be in C, a state of affairs that is most easily accommodated if *li* is base-generated on a constituent that is part of a larger, independently possible structure.

I will now proceed to argue for this point, and show that the grammatical patterns in (2)-(4) as well as some others are subject to an independent prosodic constraint on the clitic *li* in Bulgarian and a verb-adjacency condition on the modal *šte* 'will'.

3.1. The syntactic positions of da *and* li

Recall that one might argue that in the Serbo-Croatian example in (1) *li* is in C, as it occurs between *da*, a complementizer, and a clitic that encliticizes to *da*. But the Bulgarian *da* is a not complementizer, a point for which Rudin (1986:57-62) argues, despite its appearance in complement clauses like other complementizers like *če* 'that' and *deto* 'that' (Rudin 1986:44):

(30) a. mislja če e izljazŭl.
think.1SG that went-out.3SG
'I think that Ivan went out.'
b. tova e čovekŭt deto e izljazŭl.
that is person that went-out.3SG
'That's the person that went out.'
c. tja predpočita da ostane tuk.
she prefers to stay.3SG here
'She prefers to stay here.'

Positional evidence argues against *da* being on a par with the complementizer *če* 'that'. An embedded subject may follow *če*, but not *da* (Rudin 1986:59, also Rivero 1993:572, fn 52):

(31) a. mislja če Ivan e izljazŭl.
think.1SG that went-out.3SG
'I think that Ivan went out.'
b. *iskam da deca-ta pejat.
want.1SG to children-the sing.3PL
'I want the children to sing.'
c. iskam decata da pejat.

Moreover, *da* can co-occur with other complementizers, like *dali* and *če* (Rudin 1986:60):

(32) a. ne znaja dali da otida.
NEG know.1SG whether to go.1SG
'I don't kow whether to go.'
b. žena-ta sedna aka, če da *me* vižda.
woman-the sat.3SG thus that to me see.3SG
'The woman sat so that she could see me.'

The examples in (30)-(32) clearly show that the Bulgarian *da* is not a complementizer, and that *dali* in (32a) is not composed of *da* and *li*, at least synchronically. We can therefore not conclude that *da* in (32a) is in C.

Rudin (1986:64-65) also argues that the clitic *li* is not in COMP (=C), given its varying positions, especially at the end of a question:

(33) a. (vie) namerihte *li* kušta-ta?
you found.2PL Q house-the
'Did you find the house?'
b. vie *li* namerihte kušta-ta?
you Q found.2PL house-the
'Was it you who found the house?'
c. kušta-ta *li* namerihte (vie) ?
house-the Q found.2PL you
'was it the house that you found?'
d. dnes *li* namerihte (vie) kušta-ta?
today Q found.2PL you house-the
'was it today that you found the house?'

(34) a. da hodim s tramvaj.
to go.1PL with tram
'Let's go by tram.'

b. da hodim s tramvaj *li*?
to go.1PL with tram Q
'Let's go by tram?'

These examples are not unequivocal, however. They are compatible with *li* being in C. In (33b)-(33d) and (34b), what precedes *li* may be in SpecCP, and in (33a) *li* can be adjoined to the verb in C, with the subject *vie* 'you' in its Spec, as in the Germanic main clause.

Nevertheless, there is plenty of clear evidence that the clitic *li* in questions may be in a position other than C. The string preceding *li* may be more than one syntactic constituents:

(35) a. včera Ivana dade *li* na Ivan kniga-ta?
yesterday gave Q to book-the
'Did Ivana give the book to Ivan yesterday?'

b. nikoj ne čete *li* kniga-ta?
no one not read Q book-the
'Is no one reading the book?'

c. Ivan vnimatelno *li* čete kniga-ta (ili nevnimatelno)?
carefully Q read.3SG book-the or carelessly
'Does Ivan read the book carefully (or carelessly)?'

d. Ivan vnimatelno čete *li* kniga-ta (ili ya piše)?
carefully read.3SG Q book-the or it write.3SG
'Is Ivan carefully reading the book (or writing it)?'

e. Ivan často čete vnimatelno *li* knigata (ili nevnimatelno)?
often read.3SG carefully Q book-the or carelessly
'Does Ivan often read the book carefully (or carelessly)?'

The examples in (35) are not expected on the view according to which the clitic *li* is in C and its Spec position can accommodate only one syntactic constituent (cf. also the examples in (15)) as verb-second Germanic main clauses. In fact, they are direct counterexamples to the claim that in Bulgarian only one stress pattern and one position for *li* is possible (Rudin, Kramer, Billings and Baerman 1999:365), or *li* is a second-position clitic.

Moreover, the clitic *li* may also appear in syntactic positions that cannot possibly be C of a yes/no question. In (36a), *li* occurs in a clause embedded under a matrix yes/no question:

(36) a. poznavaš muža, [kojto dade jabalki-te *li* na Ivan] (ili portokali-te)?
know.2SG man who gave apples-the Q to Ivan or oranges-the
'Do you know the man who gave apples (or oranges) to Ivan?'

b. [poznavaš muža, kojto dade jabalkite ~~na Ivan~~]$_i$ *li*
[~~poznavas muža, koito dade jabalkite~~ na Ivan]$_i$?

The derivation in (36b) is conceivable under the copy theory of movement, where the whole clause is fronted to the left of *li* in the matrix clause, with just *na Ivan* of the lower copy pronounced. The problem is, however, that pronouncing the lower copy of *na Ivan* violates the principles of pronunciation in (16), as pronouncing the upper copy violates no constraint.

The example in (36a) cannot be derived by movement (without deletion) as in (37a), since it would involve movement of a VP and a relative clause modifying the object, to the exclusion of the PP that is part of the relative clause. This is not a syntactic constituent:

(37) a. [poznavaš muža, kojto dade jabalkite]$_i$ *li* t_i na Ivan.

b. *li* [poznavaš muža, kojto dade jabalkite t_j] [na Ivan]$_j$ ⇒
[poznavaš muža, kojto dade jabalkite t_j]$_i$ *li* t_i [na Ivan]$_j$

Nor can it be derived by first moving the PP rightward out of the relative clause, and then moving the remnant to the left of *li* (cf. den Besten and Webelhuth 1990), as in (37b), relative clauses being islands for syntactic movement (Ross 1967).

In the same vein, the example in (36a) cannot be derived by successive leftward movement of syntactic constituents, as in (38):

(38) a. jabalkite$_i$ *li* poznavaš muža, kojto dade t_i na Ivan ⇒
b. dade$_j$ jabalkite$_i$ *li* poznavaš muža, kojto t_j t_i na Ivan ⇒
c. kojto$_k$ dade$_j$ jabalkite$_i$ *li* poznavaš muža, t_k t_j t_i na Ivan ⇒
d. muža$_l$ kojto$_k$ dade$_j$ jabalkite$_i$ *li* poznavaš t_l t_k t_j t_i na Ivan ⇒
e. poznavaš$_m$ muža$_l$ kojto$_k$ dade$_j$ jabalkite$_i$ *li* t_m t_l t_k t_j t_i na Ivan

The moves in (38a)-(38d) are either of the head of the relative clause or out of a syntactic island. The examples in (35)-(36) are thus clearly incompatible with the clitic *li* being in C.

3.2 A base-generation account of the clitic li

Bošković (2001a:239-243) suggests a focus inflection analysis for the focus *li* construction in which *li* is a focus particle added to focus elements. More specifically, the *li*-marked element moves to the interrogative SpecCP of a +*wh* C with a +focus feature for feature-checking.

The occurrence of *li* in NP as that in (39a), can now be accounted for without extracting from a left-branch, Bulgarian independently disallowing left-branch extraction:

(39) a. [$_{CP}$ [novata *li* kola]$_i$ C prodade t_i]?
new Q car sold
'Is it the new car that he/she/you sold?'
b. [novata kola]$_i$ prodade t_i
new car sold
'He/she/you sold the new car.'
c. *novata$_i$ prodade [t_i kola]

While Bošković's assumption that the *li*-marked element moves to SpecCP in overt syntax is not warranted, as we will see, I argue that this line of thought is essentially correct. In fact, it extends beyond the fact in (39a) and can explain other cases that are problematic for the account according to which the clitic *li* is base-generated in C.[3]

Suppose the clitic *li* is base-generated, right-adjoined to an X° or XP, and the structure is Merged to form a (larger) syntactic structure in a way that is independently allowed. That is, from the example in (40a) that in (40b) can be derived by base-generating the clitic *li* on the verb as a verbal complex and Merging it in the same position as the verb without *li*:

(40) a. izpratix *mu* kniga.
sent.1SG him book
'I sent him a book.'

---

[3] Bošković (2001a:238) attributes to Steven Franks the idea that the example in (39a) is derived as in (i), by first moving the object *novata kola* 'the new car' to a position just before the verb and then to SpecCP to the left of *li*:

(i) [novata ~~kola~~]$_i$ *li* [~~novata~~ kola]$_i$ prodade t_i?

The upper copy of *kola* 'car' and the lower copy of *novata* 'new-the' are then deleted.

The problem with (i) is that deletion of the lower copy of *novata* violates the principles of pronunciation in (16). It is also unclear why it is not possible to delete the upper copy of *novata* and the lower copy of *kola*.

b. [$_{V°}$ izpratix+*li*] *mu* kniga? (=(2a))
sent.1SG+Q him book
'Did I send him a book?'

If the past participle is the complement of the auxiliary verb, then the order in which it precedes the auxiliary can be derived by leftward movement, as in (41a):

(41) a. viždal$_i$ *si* t_i *go*.
seen AUX.2SG him
'You have seen him.'
b. [$_{V°}$ viždal+*li*]$_i$ *si* t_i *go*? (=(2b))
seen+Q AUX.2SG him
'Have you seen him?'

The example in (41b) is identical to that in (41a), except for the presence of the clitic *li*. If *li* is first Merged with the past participle, then the combination can move leftward, just as the past participle without *li* does in (41a).

Similarly, we can derive the example in (7), repeated in (42), by base-generating the clitic *li* to the right of the object, and moving the two just like moving the object without *li*:

(42) [Ivan+*li*]$_i$ šte viždaš t_i ? (=(7))
Q will see.2SG
'Will you see Ivan?'

As the clitic *li* is right-adjoined to either an X° or XP in an independently possible structure, structures that are independently ungrammatical would remain so with *li* adjoined to any constituent of those structures. The prediction is borne out:[4]

(43) a. *viždaš$_i$ šte *go* t_i.
see.2SG will him
'You will see him.'
b. *[$_{V°}$ viždaš+*li*]$_i$ šte *go* t_i? (=(3))
see.2SG+Q will him
'Will you see him?'

That is, the structure in (43b) is excluded for the same reason as that for the structure in (43a). In Bulgarian, clitics must be adjacent to the finite verb (one that is inflected for person):

(44) a. viždam (*često) *go* (često).
see.1SG often him often
'I often see him.'
b. često *go* viždam.

[4] Both examples in (i) are excluded, as the clitic pronoun *mu* 'him' is not adjacent to the finite verb (cf. the discussion of (44) and (45)):

(i) a. * [$_{V°}$ izpratix+*li*]$_i$ ne *mu* t_i kniga?
sent.1SG+Q not him book
'Didn't I send him a book?'
b. * izpratix ne *mu* t_i kniga.
sent.1SG not him book
'I didn't send him a book.'

(45) a. zaminaval (* často) *e* (často).
leave.IMPF often AUX.3SG often
'He is often leaving.'
b. často *e* zaminaval.

The ungrammaticality of the example in (43) is part of the same pattern in (44a) and (45a). There is thus no reason to suppose that the ungrammaticality of the example in (43b) has anything to do with the clitic *li* being in C, and the verb moving to its left.

In fact, on the account where the clitic *li* is in C, it is not clear why the example in (46a) is possible, the past participle apparently moving to the left of the modal *šte* 'will' just as it does in the ungrammatical example in (43):

(46) a. viždal$_i$ šte *go* *e* t_i.
seen will him AUX.3SG
'He will have seen him.'
b. [$_{V°}$ viždal$_i$+*li*] šte *go* *e* t_i?
seen+Q will him AUX.3SG
'Will he have seen him?'

If the modal erects a barrier for movement in (43), as in Rivero's (1993) account, then it should do the same in (46). The contrast between (43b) and (46b) would then be a mystery. On the base-generation account, the structure in (46b) is essentially the same as that in (46a), with the clitic *li* base-generated on the verb. The combination moves to the left of the modal *šte* 'will' in both cases.

The various problems with the clitic *li* being in C with respect to movement of non-constituents and out of syntactic islands now cease to arise, since there is no movement that is not independently motivated. Since the examples in (47) and (48) without the clitic *li* are independently possible, those in (35) and (36) can be derived by simply adjoining *li* to a X° or XP (we will turn to the interpretive property of the clitic *li* in section 3.4):

(47) a. včera Ivana dade na Ivan kniga-ta.
yesterday gave to book-the
'Ivana gave the book to Ivan yesterday.'
b. nikoj ne čete kniga-ta.
no one not read book-the
'No one is reading the book.'

(48) a. Ivan vnimatelno čete kniga-ta.
carefully read.3SG book-the
'Ivan reads the book carefully.'
b. Ivan često čete vnimatelno knigata.
often read.3SG carefully book-the
'Does Ivan often read the book carefully.'

As there may be other heads and phrases to the left of the X° or XP to which *li* is right-adjoined, it is possible that X°+*li* or XP+*li* does not form a syntactic constituent with them.

If an X° or XP happens to lie in a syntactic island, then X°+*li* or XP+*li* will also be. But this is immaterial, as nothing need to move overtly. In fact, the examples in (49) show that the constituent containing *li* does not move to SpecCP in overt syntax, contra Bošković's claim:

(49) a. Ivan kupuva [skapa *li* kola] (ili evtina)?
buy.3SG expensive Q car or cheap
'Is Ivan buying an expensive or cheap car?'

b. Ivan tiča [mnogo *li* brzo] (ili sredno)?
run.3SG very Q fast or moderately
'Is Ivan running very or moderately fast?'

It is precisely because of the fact that the base-generation account of the clitic *li* does not require movement that the various problems with the movement analyses do not arise. Given that the principles of pronunciation in (16) are not obviously well-motivated, it is all the more desirable that the base-generation analysis does not rely on them.

3.3 A prosodic property of the clitic li

The ungrammaticality of the example in (50a) is surprising at first glance, as the structure without the clitic *li* in (50b) is possible, and there is no obvious reason why *li* cannot be right-adjoined to the clitic pronoun:

(50) a. *včera *go li* dade na Ivan?
yesterday it Q gave to
'Did he/she/you give it to Ivan yesterday?'
b. včera *go* dade na Ivan.
yesterday it gave to
'He/she/you gave it to Ivan yesterday.'

It is not that a clitic pronoun can never occur to the left of the clitic *li*; it can, when negation precedes it, sanctioning stress on the clitic (Izvorski, King and Rudin 1997:188), as in (51a):

(51) a. ne GO li_i *e* viždal? (=(8a))
not him Q AUX.3SG seen
'Did he see him?'
b. ne GO *e* viždal.
not him AUX.3SG seen
'He didn't see him.'

There is a prosodic difference between (50a) and (51a), the clitic before *li* is stressed in (51a), but not in (50a).

It thus appears that the clitic *li* in Bulgarian is subject to the prosodic constraint in (52), accounting for why the example in (50a) is ruled out:

(52) A prosodic constraint on *li*
The constituent preceding *li* must bear an independently sanctioned main stress.

It is crucial that the stress on what immediately precedes the clitic *li* be independently sanctioned. Thus, putting stress on the clitic as in (53a) would not save the structure, as the stress is independently impossible without negation, as shown in (53b):

(53) a. *včera GO *li* dade na Ivan?
b. *včera GO dade na Ivan.

The prosodic constraint in (52) also explains the grammatical contrast in (54). (54a) is grammatical, as expected, since (55a) is. The stress on the pronoun immediately preceding the clitic *li* is independently sanctioned by negation:

(54) a. ne MI *li go* dade. (=(23b))
not me Q it gave
'Didn't he/she/you give it to me?'

b. *ne MI *go li* dade. (=(23a))
c. *ne MI GO *li* dade.

(55) a. ne MI *go* dade.
not me it gave
'He/she/you didn't give it to me.'
b. *ne MI GO dade.

(54b) is excluded, since what immediately precedes *li* is not stressed. The condition in (52) is irrelevant to (55a) as it has no *li*. In (55b), the clitic *go* 'him' does not immediately follow negation, and hence cannot be stressed. Adjoining the clitic *li* to an unsanctioned stressed pronoun as in (54c) is therefore of no use.[5]

3.4 On the interpretive property of questions with the clitic li

Given that structures with the clitic *li* are interpreted as questions, one may naturally wonder how that interpretation arises, especially on the view that *li* may in principle adjoin to any X° or XP. The question is particularly relevant in cases where the (minimal) clause in which *li* appears is not interpreted as questions, e.g. a relative clause (cf. the example in (36a)), and the whole structure is interpreted as a matrix question.

On the one hand, it is clear that the interrogative interpretation may exist independently of the clitic *li*. Constituent and yes/no questions need not contain *li* (Rudin 1986:16, 81) (the example in (56b) is read with rising intonation):

(56) a. kakvo pravi Ivan?
what does
'What is Ivan doing?'
b. Ivan otvori vrata-ta?
opened door-the
'Ivan opened the door?'

On the other hand, *li* obviously can appear only in questions, marking the constituent preceding it as focus. The example in (57a) must be interpreted as a question, and the constituent to which *li* is attached is the focus, as can be seen in the continuation:

(57) a. jabalki *li* kupuva Ivan (, ili domati)?
apples Q buy or tomatoes
'Is it apples that Ivan is buying (, or tomatoes)?'
NOT 'It's apples that Ivan is buying (, or tomatoes).'
b. Ivan čete *li* kniga, ili piše?
read Q book or write
'Is Ivan reading, or writing, a book?'
c. Ivan čete *li* kniga, ili Ivana piše pismo?
read Q book or write letter
'Is Ivan reading a book, or is Ivana writing a letter?'

When the clitic *li* is attached to the verb, the focus is either narrow on the verb, as in (57b), or wide on the whole sentence, as in (57c).

[5] In multiple *wh*-phrase questions without *li*, all *wh*-phrases appear to be in SpecCP (Rudin 1986), with the leftmost *wh*-phrase carrying more stress than the others (cf. the examples in (i) in footnote 2). Since the clitic *li* marks the focus of the sentence, it is more naturally for *li* to appear immediately after the leftmost *wh*-phrase.

Following much work on questions, I take questions to generally have an abstract formal *wh-* (for constituent questions) or Q-feature (for yes/no questions) (cf. Baker's (1970) Q morpheme, also Rudin 1986:75) in C. Suppose *li* also has the formal *wh-* or Q-feature that is uninterpretable on *li*. The clitic *li* raises with the category it is adjoined to not in overt syntax but at LF to SpecCP, as in (58a), to check the formal *wh-* or Q-feature of C, and the IP out of which the focus X raises is interpreted as a predicate, along the lines of von Stechow (1991):

(58) a. LF: $[_{CP}\ [X+li]_i\ [_{C'}\ C\ [_{IP} \dots t_i \dots]]]$
b. $\| X \|^{g}(\lambda b(\| IP \|^{g^{b/x}}))$

In (58b), *g* is a value-assigning function, and the focus X quantifying in the denotation of IP. I assume that focus may spread (Chomsky 1971) to the extended projection (Grimshaw 1990) of the category to which *li* attaches. The wide-focus reading of the V+*li* combination is then the result of spreading the focus from V to its extended projection IP.

It now follows that *li* can only appear in questions, since the formal *wh-* or Q-feature, uninterpretable on *li*, cannot be checked in non-questions, which do not have these formal features in C. Non-questions with *li* crash at LF, on a par with other structures that have unchecked formal features (Chomsky 1995).

3.5 A syntactic constraint on the modal šte

The examples in (59)-(60) apparetntly suggest that the modal *šte* 'will' is subject to the syntactic constraint in (61), although it remains unclear whether it correlates with any other property of the language:[6]

(59) a. (često/ti) šte (*često/*ti) zamineš.
often/you will often/you leave.2SG
'You will (often) leave.'
b. *zamineš šte.

(60) a. (često) šte (*često) *e* zaminal.
often will often AUX.3SG left
'He will often have left.'
b. zaminal šte *e* (često).
c. *zaminal *e* šte.
d. *često *e* šte zaminal.

(61) An adjacency constraint on *šte*
šte must be left-adjacent to the finite verb.

Given the constraint in (61), it is understandable why the example in (43a), repeated in (62a), is impossible, the modal *šte* 'will' being not left-adjacent to the finite verb:

(62) a. *viždaš$_i$ šte *go* t_i. (=(43a))
see.2SG will him
'I will see him'
b. *viždaš$_i$+*li* šte *go* t_i? (=(3))
see.2SG+Q will him
'Will you see him?'

---

[6] If clitic pronouns adjoin to the verb and the resulting category is a verb, then the modal *šte* 'will' in (46) is left-adjacent to the verbal complex *go+e*, observing the constraint in (61).

As the structure in (62a) is already impossible, adjoining the clitic *li* to the verb to derive to example in (3), repeated in (62b), does not result in a grammatical structure.

4 Conclusion

In this paper, I argue for a base-generation account for the clitic *li* in questions in Bulgarian, relating structures with *li* to those without *li*. The facts largely bear out the prediction that structures with *li* are possible only if those without *li* are. The converse fails, however, as the clitic *li* is also prosodically constrained.

Not only does the base-generation analysis avoid the various problems with the assumption that *li* is independently in C and that the different positions of *li* are derived by movement, it also offers an empirically more accurate account of the distribution of *li*. Significantly, it affords an explanation for some apparent exceptions to otherwise quite general principles of grammar, e.g. movement to a c-commanding position and whatever principle deriving the effect of the HMC.

More specifically to Bulgarian, I suggest a feature-checking account for the occurrence of *li* in questions and its focus property. I show that the modal *šte* 'will' is subject to a verb-adjacency constraint, from which follow much of the facts thought to be evidence for the barrierhood of the projection of the modal.

References

Baker, C. L. 1970. Note on the description of English questions: The role of an abstract question morpheme. *Foundation of Language* 6: 179-219.

Bošković, Željko. 2001a. *On the nature of the syntax-phonology interface*. Elsevier.

Bošković, Željko. 2001b. *Li* without PF movement. In Steven Franks, Tracy Holloway King and Michael Yadroff (eds), *Annual workshop on formal approaches to Slavic linguistics: The Bloomington meeting, 2000*, 57-75. Ann Arbor: Michigan Slavic Publications.

Caink, Andrew. 1999. Against 'Long Head Movement'. In Mila Dimitrova-Vulchanova and Lars Hellan (eds), *Topics in South Slavic syntax and semantics*, 91-123. Amsterdam: John Benjamins.

Chomsky, Noam. 1971. Deep structure, surface structure and semantic interpretation. In D. D. Steinberg and L. A. Jakobovits (eds), *Semantics: An interdisciplinary reader in philosophy, linguistics and psychology*, 182-216. New York: Cambridge University Press.

Chomsky, Noam. 1995. *The Minimalist program*. Cambridge, MA: MIT Press.

den Besten, Hans and Gert Webelhuth. 1990. Stranding. In Günther Grewendorf, Wolfgang Steinefeld (eds), *Scrambling and barriers*, 77-92. Amsterdam: John Benjamins Publishing.

Franks, Steven. 1998. Clitics in Slavic. Paper presented at the Comparative Slavic Morphosyntax Workshop. Indiana University, Bloomington. June 1998.

Grimshaw, Jane. 1990. Extended projection. Ms, Rutgers University.

Halpern, Aaron. 1992. Topics in the placement and morphology of clitics. Doctoral dissertation. Stanford University.

Izvorski, Roumyana, Tracy King and Catherine Rudin. 1997. Against *li* lowering in Bulgarian. *Lingua* 102: 187-194.

Kayne, Richard. 1994. *The antisymmetry of syntax*. Cambridge, MA: MIT Press.

Lema, Jose and Maria-Louisa Rivero. 1989. Long head movement: HMC vs ECP. In *Proceedings of NELS 20*, 333-347. GLSA, University of Massachusetts, Amherst.

Nuñes, Jairo. 2000. Linearization of chains and phonetic realization of chain links. In Samuel Epstein and Norbert Hornstein (eds), *Working minimalism*, 217-249. Cambridge: MIT Press.

Progovac, Ljiljana. 1996. Clitics in Serbo-Croatian: Comp as the second position. In Aaron Halpern and Arnold Zwicky (eds.), *Approaching second: second position clitics and related phenomena*, 411-428. Stanford, CA: CSLI Publications.

Rivero, Maria-Louisa. 1991. Long head movement and negation: Serbo-Croatian vs Slavak and Czech. *The Linguistic Review* 8: 319-351.

Rivero, Maria-Louisa. 1993. Bulgarian and Serbo-Croatian yes-no questions: V raising to *li* versus *li* hopping. *Linguistic Inquiry* 24: 567-575.

Ross, John Robert. 1967. Constraints on variables in syntax. Doctoral dissertation, MIT.

Rudin, Catherine. 1986. Aspects of Bulgarian syntax: Complementizers and WH constructions. Columbus: OH: Slavic Publications, Inc.

Rudin, Catherine, Christina Kramer, Loren Billings and Matthew Baerman. 1999. Macedonian and Bulgarian *li* questions: beyond syntax. *Natural Language and Linguistic Theory* 17: 541-586.

Tomić, Olga Mišeska. 1996. The Balkan Slavic clausal clitics. *Natural Language and Linguistic Theory* 14: 811-872.

Travis, Lisa deMena. 1984. Parameters and effects of word order variation. Doctoral dissertation, MIT.

von Stechow, Arnim. 1991. Current issues in the theory of focus. In von Arnim von Stechow and Dieter Wunderlich (eds.), *Semantik: ein internationales Handbuch der zeitgenössischen Forschung*, 804-825, Berlin: de Gruyter.

Wilder, Chris and Damir Ćavar. 1994. Long head movement? Verb movement and cliticization in Croatian. *Lingua* 93: 1-58.

Nedžad Leko, Sarajevo

Syntactic positions of numerals in Bosnian

1. Introduction

Numerals in Bosnian/ Croatian/ Serbian (BCS) show interesting syntactic behavior. Although semantically clearly a single category, syntactically they behave as three distinct categories, namely as quantifiers, nouns and adjectives. Those numerals which behave as quantifiers, and those that behave as nouns are syntactic heads assigning case to their complements, as in (1a), where we find the quantifier *pet* 'five' assigning genitive case to its complement *vojnik* 'soldier', and in (1b), where we find the quantity noun *stotina* 'hundred' also assigning genitive case to its complement. Notice the different agreement forms on the predicate, a default neuter singular form *stiglo* in (1a), and feminine singular form *stigla* in (1b) in agreement with the quantity noun *stotina* 'hundred'. This shows that the semantic head of the subject phrases in (1a) and (1b), namely *vojnik*, is not the syntactic head of these phrases, the syntactic heads being *pet* and *stotina*, respectively. Those numerals that behave as adjectives are noun modifiers agreeing in phi-features and case with the noun head, as in (1c), where we find the adjectival numeral *peti* 'fifth' agreeing in gender, number and case with the head noun *vojnik* 'soldier'. Notice also that the masculine singular form *stigao* in the predicate is in agreement with the head noun *vojnik* 'soldier', indicating that *vojnik* is not only the semantic head, as in (1a,b), but also the syntactic head of the subject phrase in (1c):

(1)	a.	Pet	vojnika	je	stiglo.
		five	soldier-GEN.MASC.PL	AUX-3PS.SG	arrived-NEUT.SG
	b.	Stotina	vojnika	je	stigla.
		hundred-NOM.FEM.SG	soldier-GEN.MASC.PL	AUX-3PS.SG	arrived-FEM.SG
	c.	Peti	vojnik	je	stigao.
		fifth-NOM.MASC.SG	soldier-NOM.MASC.SG	AUX-3PS.SG	arrived-MASC.SG

2. Numerals that behave like Quantity Nouns

I will first elaborate on the class of numerals as in (1b), that is numerals which behave as nouns. They are fully declinable, and, like other nouns, they also assign genitive case to their complement. Two groups of numerals are found in this category:

First, the numerals *desetina* 'ten', *stotina* 'hundred', *hiljada* 'thousand', *milion* 'million', and *milijarda* 'billion'. All of them have full declension as feminine nouns, except *milion*, which declines as a masculine noun. These numerals take a genitive complement and the predicate agrees with them in gender and number, as in (2a), where we find the feminine singular form of the predicate *stigla* in agreement with the feminine singular form *stotina*. This suggests that the syntactic head of the subject phrase in (2a) is the numeral *stotina*, rather than the noun which follows *stotina*. Being fully declinable, these numerals may occur not only in direct case contexts, like nominative in (2a), and accusative in (2b), but also in oblique case contexts, like dative in (2c):

(2)	a.	Stotina	vojnika/	vozila/	balerina	je
		hundred-NOM.FEM.SG	soldiers-GEN/	vehicles-GEN/	dancers-GEN	AUX-3PS.SG
		stigla.				
		arrived-FEM.SG				

b. Vidim stotinu vojnika/ vozila/ balerina.
(I) see hundred-ACC soldiers-GEN/ vehicles-GEN/ dancers-GEN

c. Pišem stotini vojnika/ balerina.
(I) write (to) hundred-DAT soldiers-GEN/ dancers-GEN

Notice that there is also a quantifier denoting ‘hundred’ (and also ‘thousand’ and ‘billion’), in the form with *-u* ending: *stotinu* (and also *hiljadu, tisuću, milijardu*). This form is identical to the accusative form of the noun *stotina*. However, the quantifier form ending in *-u* is used only in direct case contexts, like other numerals that behave as quantifiers, for example *pet* ‘five’. The examples in (3) illustrate that the quantifiers *stotinu, hiljadu,* and *milijardu* indeed behave like the quantifier *pet* ‘five’ in all relevant syntactic respects:

(3) a. Pet/ stotinu/ hiljadu/ milijardu vojnika je stiglo.
five/ hundred/ thousand/ billion soldier-GEN.PL AUX-3PS.SG arrived-NEUT.SG

b. Vidim pet/ stotinu/ hiljadu/ milijardu vojnika.
(I) see five/ hundred/ thousand/ billion soldier-GEN.PL

In (3a) we find neuter singular agreement on the verb, in contrast to (2a) with feminine singular agreement, which clearly indicates that *stotina* behaves as a noun, and *stotinu* as a quantifier.

Numerals that behave like quantity nouns can be modified by a demonstrative or by an adjective that agrees with the numeral for phi-features and case, as in (4a), with nominative forms *ona* ‘that’ and *dobra* ‘good’ in agreement with nominative *stotina* ‘hundred’, and as in (4b), with accusative forms *onu* and *dobru* in agreement with accusative *stotinu*:

(4) a. Ona/ dobra stotina vojnika je stigla.
that/ good-NOM.FEM hundred-NOM soldier-GEN.PL AUX-3PS.SG arrived FEM.SG
‘That/ a good (at least) one hundred men arrived.’

b. Vidim onu/ dobru stotinu vojnika.
(I) see that/ good-ACC.FEM hundred-ACC soldier-GEN.PL

These numerals do not allow for movement of the demonstrative or the pronoun out of their complement, so that (5b) is ungrammatical with the demonstrative *ovih* ‘these’ moved in front of the numeral *stotina* ‘hundred’:

(5) a. Stotina ovih vojnika je stigla.
hundred these-GEN soldier-GEN.PL AUX-3PS.SG arrived-FEM.SG

b. *Ovih stotina vojnika je stigla.

If the numeral quantifier *stotinu* is used in the context of (5b), then the extraction of the demonstrative is possible, as expected. So, although (5b) with the quantity noun *stotina* is unacceptable, the corresponding examples with the quantifiers *sto* and *stotinu* would be perfectly possible, as in (6):

(6) Ovih sto/ stotinu vojnika je stiglo.
these-GEN.PL hundred soldier-GEN.PL AUX-3PS.SG arrived-NEUT.SG

Notice in (6) a default neuter singular agreement in the predicate (*stiglo*), clearly indicating that *sto* and *stotinu* are not quantity nouns, as *stotina*, but rather quantifiers. So, there is a quantity noun *stotina*, with a full nominal declension; *sto*, a numeral quantifier comparable to *pet* 'five'; and also a quantifier form *stotinu*.

The second group of numerals that behave as nouns are numerals ending in *-ica: dvojica, trojica, četvorica,* etc., as in (7). These numerals require a human masculine noun as their complement to which they assign genitive case. They behave like so-called collective nouns such as *djeca* 'children'. These numerals, like collective nouns, have nominal feminine declension, but syntactically they behave as neuter plural nouns, so that the predicate shows up in neuter plural form when the subject phrase contains one of these numerals, as in (7a). They also may occur in any case context, including direct cases, nominative in (7a), accusative in (7b), and oblique cases, like dative in (7c):

(7) a. Dvojica/ trojica/ četvorica/ ... vojnika su stigla.
two-NOM/ three-NOM/ four-NOM soldiers-GEN AUX-3PS.PL arrived-NEUT.PL

b. Vidim dvojicu/ trojicu/ četvoricu/ ... vojnika.
(I) see two-ACC/ three-ACC/ four-ACC soldiers-GEN

c. Pišem dvojici/ trojici/ četvorici/ ... vojnika.
(I) write (to) two-DAT/ three-DAT/ four-DAT soldiers-GEN

The complement of both kinds of numerals that behave as nouns can be a genitive pronoun, like *vas* 'you' in (8).

(8) a. Stotina vas je stigla.
hundred you-GEN.PL AUX-3PS.SG arrived-FEM.SG
'One hundred of you arrived.'

b. Dvojica vas su stigla.
two you-GEN.PL AUX-3PS.PL arrived-NEUT.PL
'Two of you arrived.'

If the form of the predicate in (8) is kept constant and the order of the numeral and the pronoun is reversed, then the resulting string is ungrammatical: the pronoun cannot precede the numeral noun, as in (9):

(9) a. *Vas stotina je stigla.
b. *Vas dvojica su stigla.

However, if the form of the predicate is changed, then the sentence is acceptable as illustrated with the contrast in (10):

(10) a. *Vas dvojica su stigla.
you-GEN.PL two-NOM AUX-3PS.PL arrived-NEUT.PL

b. Vas dvojica ste stigli.
you-GEN/ACC two (males) AUX-2PS.PL arrived-MASC.PL

Notice the distinction in person in the predicate: 3rd person in (10a) vs. 2nd person in (10b). So in (10b) *dvojica* is no longer the head of the subject phrase, at least not the syntactic head. Compare (8b) where the predicate has 3rd person plural neuter agreement, agreeing with the head *dvojica*. Therefore, it means that (10b) is not a result of the movement of *vas* from the complement of *dvojica*. I suspect that here we have an appositive structure: the head is *vas*, and *dvojica* is in apposition to *vas*. The question is why we have the genitive/ accusative form of 2nd person plural pronoun (*vas*), and not the nominative form (*vi*). Namely, the nominative form *vi* appears in appositive structures with common nouns, as in (11a):

(11) a. Vi studenti ste stigli.
you-NOM.2PS.PL student-NOM.PL AUX-2PS.PL arrived-MASC.PL

b. *Vas studenti ste stigli.
you- GEN/ACC student-NOM.PL AUX-2PS.PL arrived-MASC.PL

We don't want to say that a noun is a complement of a pronoun in (11a), but it may be in apposition to a pronoun. But the genitive/ accusative form *vas* is not possible in such contexts, as ungrammatical (11b) illustrates.

However, *vas*, and not *vi*, may appear with all quantified expressions, but crucially, always with the second person plural agreement form in the predicate, which tells us that the predicate agrees with some head in the subject phrase which has second person plural features. A quantifier, or a quantity noun for that matter, cannot have these features, and consequently it is not the head of the subject phrase. Only a pronoun can have these features, and therefore a pronoun must be the head of the subject phrase containing numerals like *dvojica*, or the collective numeral *dvoje*, as in (12a), or the cardinal numeral *dvije*, as in (12c):

(12) a. Vas dvoje ste stigli.
you-GEN/ACC two AUX-2PS.PL arrived-MASC.PL
'You two (where 'two' may be of mixed gender, or only masculine) arrived.'

b. *Vi dvoje ste stigli.

c. Vas dvije ste stigle.
you-GEN/ACC two-FEM AUX-2PS.PL arrived-FEM.PL

d. *Vi dvije ste stigle.

At this point, I don't have a proposal for this mystery - why the genitive/accusative form *vas*, and not the nominative *vi*, with quantified expressions.

In Giusti and Leko (2001), it is proposed that the categorial status of quantity expressions that behave like the numerals discussed in this section is that of a Quantity Noun. They have, in fact, their own functional projection where gender and case are realized. The demonstrative that precedes them agrees with them, and it is therefore in SpecDP in our framework. Furthermore, they do not allow movement of their complement to a higher Spec. The structure is given in (i):

(i)

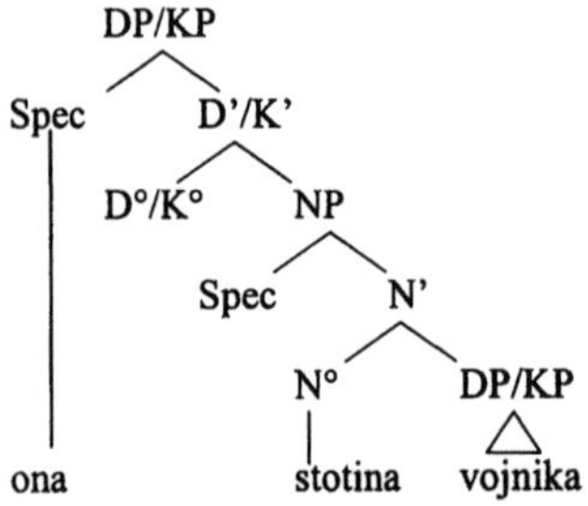

3. Numeral Quantifiers

I will now elaborate on the class of numerals first illustrated in (1a), that is numerals that behave as quantifiers. They are indeclinable and take a genitive complement. Being indeclinable, they may not appear in oblique case contexts.

Numerals which behave as quantifiers contain two classes. First, cardinal numerals from *pet* 'five' onwards, excluding compound numerals which end in 'one', 'two', 'three', and 'four' (namely, numerals like 'twenty-one, 'twenty-two, etc.). So, cardinal numerals like *pet* 'five' are found in direct case contexts, like accusative in (13a), but not in oblique case contexts, like dative in (13b):

(13) a. Vidim pet/ šest/ sedam/ osam/ devet/ deset/ ... vojnika.
(I) see five/ six/ seven/ eight/ nine/ ten/ soldier-GEN.PL

b. *Pišem pet/ šest/ sedam/ osam/ devet/ deset/ ... vojnika.
'I write to five/ six/ seven/ eight/ nine/ ten/ ... soldiers.'

These numerals cannot be modified by an agreeing adjective or demonstrative so that (14) is ungrammatical. They allow a part of the complement noun phrase to move to SpecQP, as in (15b) with a demonstrative/ adjective *ovih* 'these'/ *hrabrih* 'brave' moved in front of the numeral:

(14) *Ovo/ hrabro pet vojnika.
this-NOM.NEUT brave-NOM.NEUT five soldier-GEN.PL

(15) a. Pet ovih/ hrabrih vojnika je stiglo.
five these-GEN brave-GEN soldier-GEN.PL AUX-3PS.SG arrived-NEUT.SG

b. Ovih/ hrabrih pet vojnika je stiglo.
'These/ brave five soldiers arrived.'

Notice that in (15b) *ovih / hrabrih* still modify the complement of the numeral. The structure in (15b) derives from (15a) by movement of *ovih / hrabrih* to the Spec of QP. Therefore, the interpretation of the two examples in (15) is basically the same.

Second, the so-called collective numerals, like *dvoje, troje, četvoro,* etc., also belong to the class of numerals that behave as quantifiers. They require the so-called collective nouns, such as *djeca* 'children', *pilad* 'chicken', *dugmad* 'buttons', etc., as their complement. These numerals also assign genitive to their complement and trigger neuter singular agreement on the predicate, as in (16a), where we find the neuter singular form *stiglo*. They can appear in nominative contexts, as in (16a), accusative, as in (16b), and genitive contexts, as in (16c), as well as in the complement of prepositions, as in (16e), but not in dative contexts, as in (16d), unless there is a preposition assigning dative, or any other oblique case, as in (16e):

(16) a. Dvoje djece je stiglo.
two children-GEN AUX-3PS.SG arrived-NEUT.SG

b. Vidim dvoje djece.
(I) see two children-GEN

c. Bojim se dvoje djece.
(I) am afraid of two children-GEN

d. *Pišem dvoje djece.
'I write to two children.'

e. Pokazujem prema dvoje djece.
(I) point towards two children-GEN

Finally, the numerals that behave as quantifiers also include the cardinal numerals *dva* 'two', *tri* 'three' and *četiri* 'four', but only when used in direct case contexts (the oblique forms of these numerals behave as adjectives). Here we must assume that *dva* has default neuter features, like all quantifiers, but in contrast to other quantifiers which may take complements of any gender, *dva* can combine only with masculine and neuter nouns, as in (17a), whereas another form – *dvije* – is used with feminine nouns, as in (17b):

(17) a. Dva vojnika/ vozila su stigla.
two soldier-GEN.MASC.PAUC/ vehicle-GEN.NEUT.PAUC AUX-3PS.PL arrived NEUT.PL

b. Dvije balerine su stigle.
two dancer-GEN.FEM.PAUC AUX-3PS.PL arrived-FEM.PL

For *tri* and *četiri* we must assume that there are two homophonous forms of these numerals: one which combines with masculine and neuter nouns, as in (18a), and one which combines with feminine nouns, as in (18b):

(18) a. Tri/ četiri vojnika/ vozila su stigla.
three/four soldier-GEN.MASC.PAUC/ vehicle-GEN.NEUT.PAUC AUX-3PS.PL arrived-NEUT.PL

b. Tri/ četiri balerine su stigle.
three/four dancer-GEN.FEM.PAUC AUX-3PS.PL arrived-FEM.PL

Dva, *tri* and *četiri*, which combine with masculine and neuter nouns, behave as quantifiers. They take genitive paucal complements and trigger neuter plural agreement of the predicate, which implies that these numerals are syntactic heads of the subject phrases in (17a) and (18a). Masculine and neuter nouns that follow the numerals *dva*, *tri* and *četiri* have a form ending in *-a*, a genitive singular ending. However, it only appears to be a genitive singular form, because when an adjective is added as a modifier of nouns in (17a) and (18a), it must have a form which is certainly not genitive singular, as obvious from ungrammatical (19b):

(19) a. Ona dva/ tri/ četiri visoka vojnika/ vozila su stigla.
'Those two/ three/ four tall soldiers/ vehicles arrived.'

b. *Ona dva/ tri/ četiri visokog vojnika/ vozila su stigla.
tall-GEN.SG

The sentence with the genitive singular form of the adjective *visokog* in (19b) is unacceptable, and only (19a) with the adjective form *visoka* is possible. The descriptive adjectives have two forms, indefinite and definite: *visok* and *visoki*, respectively. The form *visoka* is the genitive singular of the indefinite form, whereas *visokog* is the genitive singular of the definite form. However, the form *visoka* in (19a) cannot be the indefinite form of the adjective, because the stress pattern is different, and also because the demonstrative is used, and by definition, the demonstrative cannot be followed by an indefinite adjective. Therefore, *visoka* in (19a) cannot be the genitive singular of the indefinite adjective *visok*, but rather the genitive dual/ paucal form of the definite adjective *visoki*. BCS used to have three grammatical numbers – singular, dual and plural. Dual was lost in the development of the language, but the remnants survive in contexts with the numerals *dva*, *tri* and *četiri*.

If *visoka* is genitive paucal, then *vojnika* cannot be genitive singular, although the form is identical to genitive singular, but must be genitive paucal, which happens to have the same form as genitive singular. Therefore, we conclude that the form of masculine and neuter nouns after numerals *dva, tri* and *četiri* cannot be genitive singular, but rather genitive dual/ paucal.

On the other hand, it seems that *dvije*, and *tri* and *četiri* which combine with feminine nouns, do not behave as quantifiers, but rather as adjectives, since the noun following them has the nominative plural form, and the predicate is also feminine plural, as in (17b) and (18b), where we find the form *stigle*. This suggests that the syntactic head of the subject phrase in (17b) and (18b) is the noun *balerine*, rather than the numeral, in contrast to the examples in (17a) and (18a), where the numeral is the head of the subject phrase. But this analysis must be rejected in view of examples like (20), where the phrase containing *dvije* appears after a preposition in the same context as *dva*. The preposition *sa* assigns the instrumental case, but the instrumental plural form cannot follow *dvije* in the same way as it cannot follow *dva*, so that (20b) is unacceptable. Therefore, *dvije* cannot be treated as an adjective. And the same is true for the forms *tri* and *četiri* which combine with feminine nouns:

(20) a. Plešem sa dvije balerine/ dva vojnika.
(I) dance with two dancer-GEN.PAUC/ two soldier-GEN.PAUC

b. *Plešem sa dvije balerinama/ dva vojnicima
(I) dance with two dancer-INST.PL/ two soldier-INST.PL

Therefore, we keep a unified treatment of *dva* and *dvije*, and claim that *dvije* also takes genitive paucal complements which happen to be identical in form with the nominative/ accusative forms. In contrast to *dva*, however, *dvije* has feminine features, and therefore the agreement form of the predicate is feminine.

Like Quantifiers proper, *dva*, *tri* and *četiri* can appear in nominative contexts, as in (17) and (18), accusative, as in (21a), and genitive, as in (21b), but not in dative, or other oblique contexts, as illustrated with the ungrammatical (21c):

(21) a. Vidim dva vojnika
(I) see two soldier-GEN.PAUC

b. Bojim se dva vojnika.
(I) am afraid of two soldier-GEN.PAUC

c. *Pišem dva vojnika.
'I write to two soldiers.'

It is unexpected that (21b) is acceptable, because *dva* is a numeral quantifier which has only direct cases, and therefore it is expected that it may appear only in nominative and accusative contexts. In (21b) it appears in the genitive context. We think that (21b) is acceptable because the morphological genitive is present in the structure, realized on the noun following *dva*, and its presence actually licenses the structure, although the genitive assigned by the verb *bojati se* 'to be afraid (of)' is not realized on *dva*.

The phrase *dva vojnika*, although unacceptable in (21c) after the dative assigning verb *pisati* 'to write', may appear after dative assigning prepositions, as in (22):

(22) Idem prema dva vojnika.
(I) walk towards two soldier-GEN.PAUC

The preposition overtly signals which case is assigned. For example, *dva vojnika* is possible after the preposition *prema* because that preposition not only assigns dative, but also signals which case was assigned: *prema* always assigns dative. On the other hand, the verb *pisati* 'to write' may assign not only dative, but also accusative, and therefore we don't know what the case of the phrase after the verb is, unless the morphological case ending indicates that. Since the numeral quantifier *dva* doesn't have case endings for oblique cases, it cannot be used after this verb. Quantifiers (and *dva* is a quantifier) may appear in oblique case positions only if preceded by a preposition.

The ungrammatical example in (21c) becomes grammatical if instead of the quantifier form *dva*, we use the adjectival form *dvama*, as in (23a), or the nominal form *dvojici*, as in (23b):

(23) a. Pišem dvama vojnicima.
(I) write (to) two-DAT soldier-DAT.MASC.PL

b. Pišem dvojici vojnika.
(I) write (to) two-DAT soldier-GEN.MASC.PL

Numeral quantifiers allow for and actually prefer movement of the modifier of the following noun into the Spec of QP, as in (24b) where the demonstrative *ona* 'those' is moved into the SpecQP. But, differently from the other Quantifiers, they do not allow pronouns like *vas* 'you' in their complement, as in (25), possibly due to the absence of a paucal form of the pronoun *vi* 'you-PL', taking into account that *vi* refers to plurality (notice that *pet vas* is acceptable):

(24) a. ?Vidim dva ona vojnika.
(I) see two those-GEN.PAUC soldier-GEN.PAUC

b. Vidim ona dva muškarca.

(25) a. *Dva vas neka dođe sutra.
two you-GEN let come tomorrow

b. *Vas dva neka dođe sutra.

In Giusti and Leko (2001), the structure given in (ii) is proposed for quantity expressions that behave like this class of numerals:

(ii)

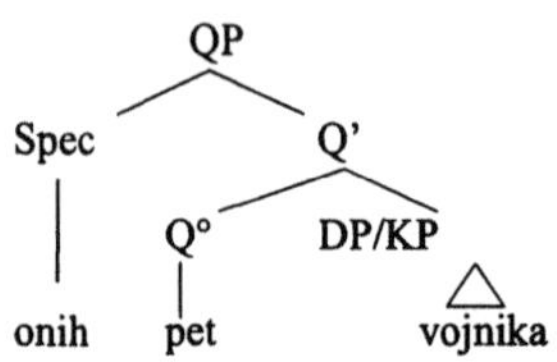

4. Adjectival Numerals

Finally, numerals that behave as adjectives have a full adjectival declension. Three subgroups of adjectival numerals may be distinguished:

1. ordinal numerals, such as *prvi, prva, prvo* 'first-MASC/ FEM/ NEUT'; *drugi, druga, drugo* 'second'; *treći, treća, treće* 'third'; *četvrti, četvrta, četvrto* 'fourth', *peti, peta, peto* 'fifth', etc.
2. plural counterparts of cardinal numerals, such as *jedni, jedne, jedna* 'one- MASC/ FEM/ NEUT'; *dvoji, dvoje, dvoja* 'two'; *troji, troje, troja* 'three'; *četvori, četvore, četvora* 'four', etc.

3. adjectival forms of the cardinal numerals *dva* 'two', *tri* 'three' and *četiri* 'four', which appear only in oblique cases: genitive: *dviju*-FEM, *dvaju*-MASC/ NEUT; *triju, četiriju*; dative/ instrumental/ locative: *dvjema*-FEM, *dvama*-MASC/ NEUT, *trima, četirma*.

Ordinal numerals agree with the noun they modify in gender, number, and case, as in (26), with masculine, feminine, and neuter nominative singular forms of ordinal numerals in agreement with corresponding head nouns:

(26) a. Prvi/ drugi/ treći/ četvrti/ ... vojnik je stigao.
first/ second/ third/ fourth-NOM.MASC.SG soldierNOM.MASC.SG AUX3PS.SG arrived-MASC.SG

b. Prva/ druga/ treća/ četvrta/ ... balerina je stigla.
first/ second/ third/ fourth-NOM.FEM.SG dancer-NOM.FEM.SG AUX-3PS.SG arrived-FEM.SG

c. Prvo/ drugo/ treće/ četvrto/ ... vozilo je stiglo.
first/ second/ third/ fourth-NOM.NEUT.SG vehicle-NOM.NEUT.SG AUX-3PS.SG arrived-NEUT.SG

The declension of ordinal numerals is completely adjectival, so that their endings have the same form as those of definite form adjectives, as in (27a) with nominative forms, (27b) with accusative forms, and (27c) with dative forms:

(27) a. Prvi/ drugi/ treći/ četvrti/ ... hrabri vojnik je stigao.
first/ second/ third/ fourth-NOM brave-NOM soldier-NOM AUX-3PS.SG arrived-MASC.SG

b. Vidim prvog/ drugog/ trećeg/ četvrtog/ ... hrabrog vojnika.
(I) see first/ second/ third/ fourth-ACC brave-ACC soldier-ACC

c. Pišem prvom/ drugom/ trećem/ četvrtom/ ... hrabrom vojniku.
(I) write (to) first/ second/ third/ fourth-DAT brave-DAT soldier-DAT

Ordinal numerals are also adjective-like in the sense that they may occur with singular nouns, as in (28a), and plural nouns, as in (28b):

(28) a. Prva/ druga/ treća/ četvrta/ ... balerina je stigla.
first/ second/ third/ fourth-FEM.SG dancer-FEM.SG AUX-3PS.SG arrived-FEM.SG

b. Prve/ druge/ treće/ četvrte/ ... balerine su stigle.
first/ second/ third/ fourth-FEM.PL dancer-FEM.PL AUX-3PS.PL arrived-FEM.PL

Numerals that behave as nouns are N heads, whereas numerals that behave as quantifiers are Q heads. They both take genitive DPs as their complements. What is the syntactic position of adjectival numerals?

Following Cinque (1994), who argues that adjectival elements are generated in distinct specifier positions, I assume that they are generated in Spec of NP. Adjectival numerals always agree with the noun in gender, number and case. Therefore, they must move from their base generated position in Spec NP to the extended projection of NP, presumably AgrP, in order to check these features. The checking relationship is established by adjectival movement to the specifier position of the Agr head, which doesn't contain any lexical material, but rather gender, number and case features.

Ordinal numerals may check all their agreement features in AgrP. There is no obvious reason for their movement to a higher position, and yet I will show that they indeed occupy some higher position. Ordering restrictions, illustrated in (29), show that this projection must be higher than AgrP, because ordinal numerals, like other adjectival numerals, must precede other adjectives, which also check their phi-features in AgrP:

(29) a. Prvo/ drugo/ treće/ četvro/ ... crveno vozilo je stiglo.
first/ second/ third/ fourth red vehicle AUX-3PS.SG arrived-NEUT.SG

b. *Crveno prvo/ drugo/ treće/ četvrto/ ... vozilo je stiglo.
red first/ second/ third/ fourth vehicle AUX-3PS.SG arrived-NEUT.SG

The second group of adjectival numerals, i.e., the plural counterparts of cardinal numerals, modify only specific kinds of nouns. These are nouns which are plural in form, but singular in meaning, known as *pluralia tantum* nouns, like *svatovi* 'wedding procession', *naočale* 'spectacles, glasses', *kola* 'car, carriage', etc., as in (30):

(30) a. Jedni/ dvoji/ troji/ četvori/ ... svatovi su stigli.
one/ two/ three/ four-NOM.MASC wedding procession-NOM.MASC AUX-3PS.PL arrived-MASC.PL

b. Vidim jedne/ dvoje/ troje/ četvore/ ... svatove.
(I) see one two/ three/ four-ACC.MASC wedding procession-ACC.MASC

Nouns with similar characteristics are those denoting a pair of separate items which are used together and regarded as a unified entity, like *rukavice* '(a pair of) gloves', *cipele* '(a pair of) shoes', *opanci* '(a pair of) peasant shoes', etc. All these nouns may occur in quantified phrases, but only with what is traditionally described as plural forms of collective nouns. These numerals have three forms for three genders: masculine, as in (31a), feminine, as in (31b), and neuter, as (31c):

(31) a. Jedni/ dvoji/ troji/ četvori/ ... svatovi su stigli.
one/ two/ three/four-MASC wedding processions-MASC AUX-3PS.PL arrived-MASC.PL

b. Jedne/ dvoje/ troje/ četvore/ ... naočale su razbijene.
one/ two/ three/ four-FEM glasses-FEM AUX-3PS.PL were broken-FEM.PL

c. Jedna/ dvoja/ troja/ četvora/ ... kola su stigla
one/ two/ three/ four-NEUT carriages-NEUT AUX-3PS.PL arrived-NEUT.PL

The numerals modifying the nouns in (31) are also completely adjectival, agreeing with a noun in gender and case. Therefore, their agreement features would be checked in AgrP. However, the movement to a higher projection would be required in order to check their *pluralia tantum* feature.

The cardinal numeral 'one' should be included in this category, primarily because of its morphosyntactic properties which differentiate it from all other cardinal numerals. It is the only fully declinable cardinal numeral with three forms for three genders (*jedan*- MASC / *jedna*-FEM/ *jedno*-NEUT) and completely adjectival, agreeing with a noun in gender and case. It seems that all its agreement features may be checked in AgrP, and therefore, as in the case of ordinal numerals, there is no obvious reason for a movement to a higher position. But this cardinal numeral, like ordinals, must precede other adjectives, which would imply that it also moves to a higher position.

Finally, the third group of adjectival numerals consists of adjectival forms of the cardinal numerals 'two', 'three', and 'four'. The adjectival forms of these numerals are found only in oblique cases, as illustrated with genitive in (32a), and dative in (32b):

(32) a. Bježim od dvaju/ triju/ četiriju vojnika.
(I) run from two/ three/ four-GEN.MASC soldiers- GEN.MASC

b. Pišem dvama/ trima/ četirma vojnicima.
(I) write (to) two/ three/ four-DAT.MASC soldiers-DAT.MASC

The adjectival 'two' has a separate form for feminine gender, whereas the same form for all three genders is found with 'three' and 'four'. Genitive forms of these adjectival numerals are: *dviju, dvaju, triju, četiriju*, whereas the forms *dvjema, dvama, trima, četirma* are found in dative, instrumental and locative contexts. The endings of these forms, specifically the genitive ending *-ju*, represent the remnants of the old dual declension, and differ from endings in adjectival declension, which suggests that they cannot be checked in AgrP, but that another projection must be postulated for their checking. Ordering restrictions show that this projection must be higher than AgrP, and its head would be responsible for checking specific dual endings on the cardinal numerals 'two', 'three', and 'four'.

The existence of a functional category which contains the number features of the Noun Phrase was postulated for languages like Modern Hebrew (cf. Ritter 1991). It was argued that the head of NumP is the locus of the number specification of NP. I assume that such a projection is available in BCS. In my proposal, the specifier position of NumP is reserved for adjectival numerals.

If we assume that the features of functional heads are binary, then we may propose that the Num head would carry the feature [± Dual]. If the feature is positively specified, dual-like forms of the numerals 'two', 'three', 'four' could be checked in [Spec, NumP]. On the other hand, the [-Dual] feature would neither imply singular nor plural, but rather a specific type of plural, that is *pluralia tantum*, and in such a case, numerals which carry that feature could be checked in [Spec, NumP]. So, only dual and *pluralia tantum* features have to be checked in NumP, whereas singular and plural features would be checked in AgrP.

The syntactic position of adjectival numerals is given in the structure in (iii), as proposed in Giusti and Leko (2001) for quantity expressions that behave as adjectives:

(iii)

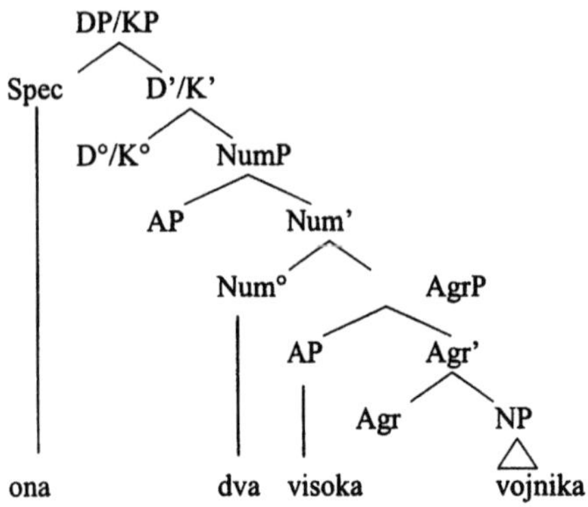

The three proposed categories of numerals are distinguished on the basis of a certain number of diagnostics, and they are summarized in the following table:

Diagnostics in BCS	N	Q	A
1. selection of a genitive complement	+	+	-
2. default (neuter) agreement on the predicate	-	+	-
3. agreement with the following noun phrase	-	-	+
4. co-occurrence with an agreeing demonstrative	+	-	+
5. co-occurrence with a genitive demonstrative	-	+	-
6. rich inflection	+	-	+

References

Babby, L. 1987. "Case, Pre-Quantifiers, and Discontinuous Agreement in Russian". *Natural Language and Linguistic Theory* 5: 91-138.

Cinque, G. 1994. "On the Evidence for Partial N-Movement in the Romance DP". *Paths towards Universal Grammar. Studies in Honor of Richard S. Kayne* ed. by G. Cinque et al. Washington, D.C.: Georgetown University Press, 85-110.

Franks, S. 1994. "Parametric Properties of Numeral Phrases in Slavic". *Natural Language and Linguistic Theory* 12: 597-674.

Franks, S. 1995. *Parameters of Slavic Morphosyntax*. Oxford: Oxford University Press.

Giusti, G. 1991. "The Categorial Status of Quantified Nominals", *Linguistische Berichte* 136: 438-454.

Giusti, G. 1992. *La sintassi dei determinanti*. Padova: Unipress.

Giusti, G. 1994. "Enclitic Article and Double Definiteness. A Comparative Analysis of Nominal Structure in Romance and Germanic". *The Linguistic Review* 11: 241-255.

Giusti, G. 1995a. "A unified structural representation of (Abstract) Case and Article. Evidence from Germanic". In: Haider, H., S. Olsen, S. Vikner (eds.), *Studies in Comparativ Germanic Syntax*. Dordrecht: Kluwer, 77-93.

Giusti, G. 1995b. "Heads and Modifiers among Determiners. Evidence from Rumanian". In: Cinque, G., and Giusti, G., (eds.), *Advances in Rumanian*, 103-125.

Giusti, G. and N. Leko. 1995. "On the syntax of quantity expressions in Bosnian". *University of Venice Working Papers in Linguistics*, vol.5, no.2, 23-47.

Giusti, G. and N. Leko. 1996. "Definite and indefinite quantity expressions in Bosnian". In: R. Benacchio, F. Fici and L. Gebert (eds.), *Determinatezza e indeterminatezza nelle lingue Slave. Atti del Convegno svoltosi a Firenze*, Ottobre 1995. Padova: Unipress, 147-162.

Giusti, G. and N. Leko. 2001. "The Categorial Status of Quantity Expressions". *Current Issues in Formal Slavic Linguistics* ed. by G. Zybatow et al. Frankfurt/Main: Peter Lang, 96-105.

Grimshaw, J. 1991. "Extended Projection", ms., Brandeis University.

Leko, N. 1990. "Case of Noun Phrases in Serbo-Croatian and Case Theory". *Folia Linguistica*, 23/ 1-2, 27-54.

Leko, N. 1995. "Syntactic behaviour of numerals 1,2,3,4,5 in Bosnian and Slovene". *Quaderni del Dipartimento di Linguistica, Università di Firenze* 6, 213-228.

Neidle, C. 1988. *The Role of Case in Russian Syntax*. Dordrecht: Kluwer.

Pesetsky, D. 1982. *Paths and Categories*. Ph.D. dissertation, MIT.

Ritter, Elizabeth. 1991. "Two Functional Categories in Noun Phrase: Evidence from Modern Hebrew". *Syntax and Semantics 25*. ed by Susan Rothstein. New York: Academic Press.

Denisa Lenertová, Leipzig

On the syntax of left peripheral adverbial clauses in Czech

1. Introduction[*]

In Czech, left-peripheral subordinate clauses show a clear contrast with respect to the clitic placement: whereas clitics directly follow fronted subject/object clauses – (1), they need an additional host in case of adverbial clauses (ACs) placed initially – (2). The contrast in (2) has been attributed to the external position of initial adverbial clauses (cf. Junghanns, 2002; Lenertová, 2002/2004): being adjoined to the matrix CP, they are not available as clitic hosts.

(1) Že nikdo neprotestoval, *~ho* nepřekvapilo.[1]
that nobody not-protested$_{SG.MS}$ him not-surprised$_{SG.NT}$
'It didn't surprise him that nobody spoke up against it.' [Fried 1994: 168]

(2) a. Když jsme mluvili, všiml *~jsem si* ...
when aux$_{1PL}$ talked noticed aux$_{1SG}$ refl$_{CL}$
'When we were talking, I noticed ...'

b. *Když jsme mluvili, *~jsem si* všiml...

This paper investigates the syntactic properties of initial ACs to provide further support for their CP-external syntax in sentences like (2). The structure of the paper is as follows. Section 2 presents the evidence from clitic placement in more details. In section 3, 'CP-internal' ACs, which are in the scope of matrix operators like negation and available as clitic hosts, are discussed. The distinction between external and internal ACs is shown to correlate with the syntactic structure of left dislocation and topicalization, respectively. In section 4, a uniform CP-adjunction analysis of dislocated elements is argued for. In section 5, clauses with external ACs are shown to have limited embedding possibilities, being compatible only with the indicative complementizer *že* 'that' but not with the subjunctive complementizer *aby*. Section 6 concludes with an outlook for further research.

2. Evidence from Clitic Placement

Czech 2nd position clitics mark the left-periphery of the clause (forming a fixed sequence auxiliary > reflexive > pronominal if more than one clitic is present). They require a syntactic host to their left, but the direction of their prosodic attachment depends on the prosodic environment. In cases where clitics follow a pause, e.g. (1), they prosodically attach to the right (cf. Fried, 1994, Toman, 1996). Clitic placement[2] in Czech has been argued for to be syntax-driven in the literature (Junghanns, 1999, 2002; Lenertová, 2001, 2002/2004; Toman, 1999; Veselovská, 1995): clitics occupy the highest heads in the extended projection of the verb and their host is placed in [Spec, CP]. The position for elements serving as syntactic

---

[*] I would like to thank Uwe Junghanns and Roland Meyer for helpful discussions at various stages of the paper, as well as the audience of the FDSL-5, Leipzig, November 2003, for comments. Many thanks are also due to the Institute of Czech National Corpus for the opportunity to use the corpus, where the substantial part of the data cited in this paper could be gathered. All errors are mine.

[1] Clitics will be set in bold italics throughout the text, the symbol '~' indicating their syntactic attachment (cf. section 2). Abbreviations: ACC - accusative, aux - past tense auxiliary, aux$_{CD}$ - conditional auxiliary, CL - clitic, DAT - dative, FM - feminine, FUT - future, GEN - genitive, INF - infinitive, LOC - locative, MS – masculine, PL - plural, prt – particle, refl - reflexive, SG - singular, SUBJ- subjunctive.

[2] See Chapter 3 of Franks and King (2000) and citations there for a discussion of the literature on clitic placement in Czech and the characteristic patterns of the phenomenon.

hosts for clitics has a character similar to the German *Vorfeld* 'prefield': it can be occupied by a subject/topicalized element, sentential adverb, particle, WH phrase[3], or by a clausal constituent – a clausal subject or object – (3)-(4), a subject modified by a relative clause – (5), or an adverb modified by an adverbial clause – (6):

(3) a. Jestli to Jana udělá, *~ho* vůbec nezajímalo.
whether it Jana do$_{3FUT}$ him$_{ACC}$ at all not-interested$_{SG.NT}$
'It didn't bother him whether Jana will do it.'

b. * Jestli to Jana udělá, vůbec *~ho* nezajímalo.

(4) a. Jestli ten slovník dostala, *~jsme se* nedozvěděli.
whether the dictionary$_{ACC}$ received$_{SG.FM}$ aux$_{1PL}$ refl$_{CL}$ not-learned$_{PL}$
'We didn't learn whether she received the dictionary.' (ČNK)

b. * Jestli ten slovník dostala, nedozvěděli *~jsme se.*

(5) Ta veverka, kterou krmíte, *~by* *vás* mohla kousnout.
the squirrel$_{NOM}$ which$_{ACC}$ you-feed$_{2PL}$ aux$_{CD3}$ you$_{ACC}$ could$_{SG.FM}$ bite$_{INF}$
'The squirrel you are feeding could bite you.' [Toman, 1996:506]

(6) a. Jednou *~byste* *mu* to měli říct.
once aux$_{CD2PL}$ him$_{DAT}$ it should$_{PL}$ tell$_{INF}$
'You should tell him about it once.'

b. Jednou, až bude větší, *~byste* *mu* to měli říct.
once when is$_{3SG.FUT}$ older aux$_{CD2PL}$ him$_{DAT}$ it should$_{PL}$ tell$_{INF}$
'Once, when he is older, you should tell him about it.'

However, left-peripheral adverbial (temporal, causal, purpose, etc.) clauses seem to be systematically excluded from the group of elements available as clitic hosts:

(7) a. * Až bude větší, *~byste* *mu* to určitě měli říct.
when is$_{3SG.FUT}$ older aux$_{CD2PL}$ him$_{DAT}$ it certainly should$_{PL}$ tell$_{INF}$
'When he is older, you should certainly tell him about it.'

b. Až bude větší, <u>určitě</u> *~byste mu* to měli říct.

As illustrated in (7)-(8), an additional element preceding the clitics is necessary, be it a sentential adverb – (7b), subject (8a), topicalized object – (8b), or verb/participle – (8c):

(8) a. Kdyby to udělala, <u>lidé</u> *~by* *ji* obvinili... (ČNK)
if it did$_{SG.FM}$ people aux$_{CD3}$ her$_{ACC}$ accused$_{PL}$
'If she did it, people would accuse her...'

---

[3] In case of multiple WH movement, only one of the WH phrases targets [Spec,CP] in the default case – (i), however, both WH phrases can exceptionally precede the clitics – (ii), in such case they can only receive a single-pair reading (in contrast to the pair-list reading available in (i)). See Meyer (2003) for an analysis.

(i) <u>Kdo</u> ~by <u>koho</u> pozval?
who aux$_{CD}$ whom$_{ACC}$ invited$_{SG.MS}$
'Who would invite whom?'

(ii) Kdo koho *~si* váží víc?
who whom$_{ACC}$ refl$_{CL}$ respect$_{3SG}$ more
'Who respects whom more?'

b. Až bude větší, <u>čas</u> ~si pro ni pochopitelně najdu.
when $is_{3SG.FUT}$ older, time $refl_{CL}$ for her_{ACC} naturally $find_{1SG.FUT}$
'When she is older, I will find time for her.'

c. Protože přišel pozdě, <u>nedali</u> *~mu* polívku.
because $came_{SG.MS}$ late $not\text{-}gave_{PL}$ him_{DAT} $soup_{ACC}$
'Because he came late, they didn't give him the soup.'

The situation here is parallel to simple matrix clauses: if the subject is *pro*-dropped and no other element is available as a clitic host, the finite verb or the past participle is fronted as a Last Resort. Following Holmberg (2000a,b),[4] I assume that the Last Resort movement is driven by a formal EPP feature attracting the verb/participle as the closest visible accessible category to the C-domain.[5, 6]

3. 'External' vs. 'Internal' left-peripheral Adverbial Clauses

A closer look at the characteristic patterns of ACs in the left periphery reveals that they actually *can* serve as syntactic hosts for clitics, but only in cases when the sentence receives an inverse scope interpretation. It is a well known fact that right-peripheral adverbial clauses interact with matrix quantifiers or operators like negation. For example, the interaction of a *because*-clause with matrix negation can result in two readings, which will be called Negated Head (NH) – (9) and Negated Adjunct (NA) – (10) reading, cf. Johnston (1994):

(9) a. Nevzal si ji, protože měla dluhy. (NH reading)
'He didn't marry her because she had debts.'

b. **because'**(¬ [∃e_2 **[married'** (x, y, e_2)]], ∃e_1 **[had'** (y, debts, e_1)])

(10) a. Nevzal si ji, protože měla vilu. (NA reading)
'He didn't marry her because she had a villa.'

b. ¬ **[because'**(∃e_2 **[married'** (x, y, e_2)], ∃e_1 **[had'** (y, villa, e_1)])

The two readings differ in their presuppositions. The NH-reading in (9) arises when negation has scope over the head clause, as represented in (9b) (the shorthand notation style adopted from Johnston). In this case, the matrix verb is negated and the sentence can be paraphrased 'He didn't marry her and the reason was her having debts'. In (10), on the other hand, the matrix negation takes scope over the (higher order) *because*-relation between the propositions, as represented in (10b). The head-clause is not negated and the sentence can be paraphrased 'He *did* marry her, but not because she had a lot of money'. Although in English, sentences with initial ACs can receive only a NH-reading, Czech allows both readings with initial adjuncts. Crucially, the different readings correlate with the position of clitics, as

[4] But see also Junghanns' (2002) '*pro*-drop topic' account.

[5] Holmberg argues that the movement obeys locality conditions (MLC, cf. fn. 14), but the feature targets only the phonological matrix of the category, thus he avoids problems arising for 'Long-Head-Movement' accounts.

[6] This assumption, also argued for in Lenertová (2002/2004:150-154) differs from Bošković's (2000, a.o.) account of the verb/participle-clitics sequence in Serbian-Croatian (SC). He argues that the structures are smaller than CPs, because SC-participles cannot i) support the interrogative complementizer *–li* and ii) cross sentential adverbs, therefore, they cannot appear as high as C^0. However, (i) and (ii) are available in Czech, thus there is at least no negative evidence against a uniform CP-structure of Czech clauses. On the other hand, the V-movement leading to the sequence verb-clitics is limited to matrix clauses. This strongly suggests that it is blocked in embedded clauses by complementizers, its ultimate target being the CP. The Last Resort character of the verb movement supports the postulation of a formal EPP feature.

illustrated by the contrast between (11) and (12) (an analogous contrast with purposive *aby*-clauses follows in (13)-(14)). The NH-reading with an initial adjunct has the usual structural pattern – the adverbial clause cannot serve as a host for the clitics:

(11) Protože měla dluhy, nevzal ~*si ji*. (NH reading)
because had$_{SG.FM}$ debts not-married$_{SG.MS}$ refl$_{CL}$ her
'Because she had debts, he didn't marry her.'

In case of the inverse scope NA-reading, on the other hand, the initial adjunct serves as a syntactic host for clitics:[7]

(12) Protože měla vilu, ~*si ji* nevzal, (sám měl přece dvě). (NA reading)
because had$_{SG.FM}$ villa$_{ACC}$ refl$_{CL}$ her not-married$_{SG.MS}$
'It's not because she had a villa that he married her.' (he had two villas himself)

Scope interactions of right-peripheral ACs with the matrix clause correlate with different syntactic structures, as can be demonstrated by syntactic tests like ellipsis, VP-preposing, binding, etc. Therefore, various accounts of right-peripheral adverbial clauses argued for their variable attachment sites reflecting the syntax-semantics mapping (cf. e.g., Johnston (1994), Whelpton (1995)). In Czech, syntactic contrasts are also obvious from tests applied to sentences with initial ACs, as can be illustrated by Principle C effects: whereas an R-expression in an initial negated adjunct may not be coindexed with a pronoun in the matrix clause – (13), coindexing is possible in constructions with negated head reading – (14):

(13) Abyste Petra$_{*i}$ uráželi ~*jsem ho*$_i$ nepozvala.
so-that$_{2PL}$ Peter$_{ACC}$ offend$_{PL}$ aux$_{1SG}$ him$_{ACC}$ not-invited$_{SG.FM}$
'I didn't invite Peter so that you offend him.' (= the reason I invited Peter was not that you offend him)

(14) Abyste Petra$_i$ neobtěžovali, radši ~*jsem ho*$_i$ nepozvala.
so-that$_{2PL}$ Petra$_{ACC}$ not-bother$_{PL}$ better aux$_{1SG}$ him$_{ACC}$ not-invited$_{SG.FM}$
'I preferred not inviting Peter, so that you don't bother him.'

A pattern similar to (13) can be found with fronted subject/object clauses: coindexing of the matrix pronoun *mu* with the R-expression in the fronted clause leads to Principle C violation:

(15) Jestli Petr$_{*i}$ vyhraje ~*mu*$_i$ je úplně jedno.
whether Peter wins him$_{DAT}$ is totally equal
'It doesn't matter to Peter whether he wins.'

(16) Že Petra$_{*i}$ někdo hledá ~*jsme mu*$_i$ neřekli.
that Peter$_{ACC}$ somebody looks-for aux$_{1PL}$ him$_{DAT}$ not-told$_{PL}$
'We didn't tell him that somebody is looking for Peter.'

If we assume that the structures (15) and (16) result from fronting/topicalization, the Principle C effect can be explained as a reconstruction effect: the subject/object clause is interpreted in its (VP-) base position, where the R-expression *Petr* is c-commanded by the coindexed matrix pronoun *mu*. Along the same line, if the initial position of the AC in (13) results from movement, the Principle C effect can be attributed to reconstruction of the AC to its base-position in the scope of matrix negation. In (14), on the other hand, no Principle C violation arises. We can thus assume that the AC is base-generated in the initial position. The contrast

[7] The inverse scope constructions like (12)-(13) intonationally differ from the constructions with NH-reading.

suggests there is a structural distinction (movement vs. high base-generation) between the two types of initial adverbial clauses, which correlates with clitic placement in the associated matrix clause.

The structural distinction can also be illustrated by the following contrast concerning the pro-form *tak* 'so'. *Tak* always occupies the first position in the associated clause. Its insertion is complementary to fronting of the verb or any other element:

(17) a. Když to bude nutné, řekneme ~*mu* *to*.
when it's necessary tell$_{1PL.FUT}$ him$_{DAT}$ it
'When it's necessary, we will tell him about it.'

b. Když to bude nutné, tak ~*mu* *to* řekneme.

Crucially, if *tak* is inserted, only the negated head reading is available:

(18) Protože strana výši daně zpochybnila, tak~*jsme ji* samozřejmě nezaplatili.
because party height$_{ACC}$ tax$_{GEN}$ doubted$_{SG.FM}$ so aux$_{1PL}$ it$_{ACC}$ naturally not-paid$_{PL}$
'Because the party casted doubt on the height of the tax, we naturally didn't pay it.'
(ČNK – shortened)

(19) Aby měla záruka nějakýsmysl, tak ~by suma neměla přesáhnout částku ...
so-that$_3$ had guarantee some sense so aux$_{CD}$ sum not-should exceed amount
'The sum shouldn't exceed the amount of ..., so that the guarantee has a sense.' (ČNK)

The negated adjunct reading in sentences like (12) is blocked by insertion of *tak* – (20), as indicated by an asterisk preceding the English paraphrase:

(20) Protože měla vilu, tak ~*si ji* nevzal$_{SG.MS}$
because had$_{SG.FM}$ villa$_{ACC}$ so refl$_{CL}$ her$_{ACC}$ not-married
'*It's not because she had a villa that he married her.'
'ok: Because she had a villa, he didn't marry her.'

The lack of negated adjunct reading in (20) can be accounted for in terms of a positional clash: the connector *tak* occupies the position targeted by the initial negated adjunct – Spec, CP. No such clash arises with the negated head reading, which suggests that the adjunct is external to the matrix CP.

In sum, two types of initial adverbial clauses can be defined according to their attachment site to the matrix CP.[8] The CP-internal ACs occur in 'inverse scope' constructions and pattern with topicalized subject/object clauses, as the shorthand representation illustrates in (21a) and (21b), respectively. On the other hand, the more frequent type of external left-peripheral ACs – (22a), which is compatible with the connector *tak*, seems to be analogous to dislocated

[8] Another systematic distinction made in the literature concerns 'restrictive' (ia) vs. 'non-restrictive' (ib) ACs, cf. Rutherford (1970):

(i) a. He's not coming to class because he's sick.

b. He's not coming to class because he just called from San Diego.

Haegeman (2002, 2003) argues that their distinct semantic/pragmatic contribution is reflected in their external syntax: whereas 'central' ACs like (ia) are more embedded (adjoined to IP), the discourse oriented 'peripheral' ACs are outside the matrix CP. Our distinction between CP-internal and external ACs in Czech concerns the restrictive category only. Note that Czech non-restrictive ACs apparently syntactically pattern with external ACs, cf. (28), but the issue of how the syntax-semantic/pragmatic mapping works in this case has to be left open here.

structures, in which DP- or sentential arguments are associated to/coindexed with a fronted D-pronoun – (22b).

(21) a. [$_{CP}$ [$_{CP}$ *adverbial clause*]$_i$ [$_{TP}$ … [$_{vP}$ … [$_{VP}$ …] t_i]]]

b. [$_{CP}$ [$_{CP}$ *argument clause*]$_i$ [$_{TP}$ … [$_{vP}$ … t_i …]]]

(22) a. [$_{CP}$ [$_{CP}$ *adverbial clause*] [$_{CP}$ XP/verb/participle/*tak*-proform [$_{TP}$ …]]]

b. [$_{CP}$ [$_{CP}$ *clausal/ DP-argument*]$_i$ [$_{CP}$ D-pronoun$_i$ [$_{TP}$ … [$_{vP}$ … t_i …]]]]

At this point, a question arises whether the types of left-dislocation structures in (22) can really be analysed in a uniform way as a base-generated adjunction to CP.

4. Czech Left Dislocation is adjunction to CP

In the recent literature, proposals have been made arguing for a movement analysis of dislocated elements. For clitic left dislocation in Romance (CLLD), Cecchetto & Chierchia (1999) and Cecchetto (2001) argue that argument DPs and their doubling clitics originate in a 'BigDP' base generated in the complement position of the matrix verb – (23b). The Big DP first moves out for case reasons and the DP1 subsequently moves to the Topic position, whereas the clitic undergoes head movement to the verb (23c) (cf. Cecchetto, 2001:110):

(23) a. Maria, Leo la incontra.
Maria Leo her meets

b. [$_{TopP}$ … [$_{IP}$ Leo incontra [$_{XP}$ … [$_{VP}$ … [$_{BIG\ DP}$ Maria la] ...]]]]

c. [$_{TopP}$ [$_{DP1}$ Maria] [$_{IP}$ Leo la$_i$ incontra [$_{XP}$ [$_{BigDP}$ t_{DP1} t_i] … [$_{VP}$ … t_{BigDP}]]]]

Grewendorf (2002) proposes an extension of this account to German:[9] left-dislocated elements are base generated in a spec-head relation with a D-pronoun, the 'BigDP' undergoes movement triggered by an EPP-feature of Fin^0, which is also assumed to be the location of the finite verb in V2-sentences in accounts adopting Rizzi's (1997) Split-CP framework. Due to its additional feature specification, the left-dislocated element subsequently moves to the specifier of a topic phrase (cf. Grewendorf, 2002:46):

(24) a. Den Studenten, den hat Maria geküsst.
the student$_{ACC}$ him$_{ACC}$ has Mary kissed

b. [$_{TopP}$ [Den Studenten]$_i$ Top$_0$ [$_{FinP}$ [$_{BigDP}$ t_i den] [$_{Fin0}$ hat] [$_{IP}$ Maria t_{BigDP} geküsst]]].

The question is whether a movement analysis is plausible for at least some dislocated elements in Czech. Initial adjuncts were shown to be immune to Principle C effects if they are dislocated (cf. the contrast illustrated in (13)-(14)). We take that as sufficient evidence against a movement analysis for these structures. In contrast, DP arguments behave differently with respect to Principle C effects. An R-expression contained in a fronted argument may not be coindexed with a matrix pronoun, regardless whether the DP is dislocated – (25a) or topicalized – (25b):

---

[9] See Frey (2004) for a critical discussion and an alternative proposal in terms of base-generation.

(25) a. [Karlovu•$_i$ knihu]$_k$, tu$_k$ ~*jsme* *mu*$_i$ vrátili t$_k$.
Karel's$_{ACC}$ book$_{ACC}$ that$_{FM.ACC}$ aux$_{1PL}$ him$_{DAT}$ returned$_{PL}$

b. [Karlovu•$_i$ knihu]$_k$ ~*jsme* *mu*$_i$ vrátili t$_k$.
Karel's$_{ACC}$ book$_{ACC}$ aux$_{1PL}$ him$_{DAT}$ returned$_{PL}$

However, other tests fail to confirm this apparent similarity between topicalization and left-dislocation of argument DPs. Left dislocation does not allow variable binding – (26a), in contrast to topicalization – (26b):[10]

(26) a. *Svého$_i$ nejlepšího přítele, toho nikdo$_i$ urazit nechtěl.
his$_{ACC}$ best$_{ACC}$ friend$_{ACC}$ that$_{MS.ACC}$ nobody offend$_{INF}$ not-wanted$_{SG.MS}$
'His$_i$ best friend, nobody$_i$ wanted to offend him.'

b. Svého$_i$ nejlepšího přítele nikdo$_i$ urazit nechtěl.
his$_{ACC}$ best$_{ACC}$ friend$_{ACC}$ nobody offend$_{INF}$ not-wanted$_{SG.MS}$

A similar point can be made with scope interaction. Whereas in topicalization structures, the lower quantifier can have scope over the higher one – (27a), such scope-taking is prevented in left-dislocation structures – (27b):

(27) a. Jednu chybu učitel dovolil každému žákovi. ($\forall\exists$, $\exists\forall$)
one$_{ACC}$ mistake$_{ACC}$ teacher allowed$_{MS}$ every$_{DAT}$ pupil$_{DAT}$
'The teacher allowed one mistake to every pupil.'

b. Jednu chybu, tu učitel dovolil každému žákovi. (*$\forall\exists$, $\exists\forall$)
one$_{ACC}$ mistake$_{ACC}$ that$_{FM.ACC}$ teacher allowed$_{MS}$ every$_{DAT}$ pupil$_{DAT}$

Although they show Principle C effects, left dislocated DPs are not subject to variable binding and scope interactions with the matrix clause. A similar pattern is discussed in Cecchetto & Chierchia (1999) and Cecchetto (2001) for Italian CLLDed PPs. The authors argue for a base-generation analysis of these elements, so that the lack of reconstruction for scope and binding purposes is straightforward, and propose a semantic mechanism of chain binding to account for the Principle C effects in such cases.[11] Analogously, we can argue that left-dislocated arguments in Czech are base-generated. Assuming that the D-pronouns coindexed with the

---

[10] The example (26a) might improve if the binding DP is quantified by *every*. However, universal quantifiers are known to be able to extend their *binding* domain ('telescoping', cf. Roberts (1989)), so even binding into a non-restrictive relative clause – (ia) or into a succeeding independent clause – (ib) becomes possible (the example is taken from Heycock (to appear), fn. 6). Czech equivalents would show the same effect.

(i) a. Every Italian man$_i$ thinks his mother, who has pampered him$_i$ since childhood, is a saint.

b. Every Italian man$_i$ thinks his mother is a saint. After all, she has pampered him$_i$ since childhood.

[11] Thus in sentences like (25a) the R-expression *Karel* is contained in a head of a non regular A-bar CHAIN – (i) which the DP 'Karl's book' forms with a trace of the locally coindexed fronted D-pronoun. Any phrase that c-commands a link of such a CHAIN counts for BT-purposes as if it c-commanded every link of the chain, i.e. the dative pronoun 'him' behaves as if it c-commanded the dislocated DP including the R-expression. This semantic mechanism is a last resort device applied only if the syntactic mechanism does not work. See also Frey (2004) for its application in the account of left dislocation in German.
(i) A-bar CHAIN formation (Cecchetto & Chierchia 1999:139):
A CHAIN $<\beta_1 \dots \beta_n>$ is a sequence of nodes sharing the same θ - role such that for any i, $1 \leq i \geq n$, β_i c-commands and is coindexed with β_{i+1}.

dislocated elements are fronted/topicalized to Spec,CP (thus being available hosts for clitics), the adjunction site for dislocated elements remains CP-external.[12]
Thus the analogy between left-dislocation and external adverbial clauses given in (22) can be kept. The two structures in (22) are most parallel if the proform *tak* is chosen in (22a). However, in contrast to correlative D-pronouns in (22b), *tak* in (22a) is optional. Moreover, it is compatible also with non-restrictive (cf. fn.8) ACs:

(28) a. [Zmizel ve vaší ložnici. 'He disappeared in your bedroom.']
Protože jsem neslyšela cvaknout dveře, tak tam ještě určitě je.
because aux_{1SG} not-$heard_{FM}$ $click_{INF}$ $door_{ACC}$ so there still surely is
'As I didn't hear any door clicking, he must still be there.' (ČNK)

b. Jestli máš žízeň, tak v ledničce je pivo.
If $have_{2SG}$ $thirst_{ACC}$ so in $fridge_{LOC}$ is beer
'If you are thirsty (*then) there's beer in the fridge.'

Therefore, *tak* cannot be a correlative pro-form in a strict sense. However, we can assume that it is a placeholder for various adverbial null correlatives sitting in Spec,CP. As the Spec,CP in Czech has to be overtly filled (cf. section 2), fronting of an element available for the initial position is obligatory if *tak* is not inserted.[13] Still, the presence of null correlates seems to make a crucial difference for the fronting possibilities. In simple matrix clauses, the verb/participle movement to Spec,CP was argued to apply only as a last resort if the subject is dropped – (29), which can be plausibly attributed to the *Minimal Link Condition*[14], restricting the Last Resort attraction to the closest element:

(29) a. Rodiče *~by* *mu* koupili auto
parents aux_{3CD} him_{CDAT} $bought_{PL}$ car_{ACC}
'His parents would buy him a car.'

b. *Koupili *~by mu* rodiče auto.

The situation turns out to be different if (external) adverbial adjuncts precede the matrix clause, as the matrix verb can (though need not) appear initially in spite of the presence of an overt subject:

(30) Protože to měl daleko, koupili *~mu* rodiče auto.
because it had far $bought_{PL}$ him_{DAT} parents car_{ACC}
'Because it was a long way there, his parents bought him a car.'

Thus it seems that the null element in the Spec,CP, which is associated with the adjunct clause and related to the matrix event, licenses the verb movement to the initial position in the matrix clause. At this stage, we cannot go beyond this statement and have to leave this issue for further research. Most importantly, it has been shown that external adverbial clauses can be analysed analogously with other dislocated correlative structures. In the next section, evidence from embedded contexts supporting this conclusion will be discussed.

---

[12] Frey (2004) comes to a similar conclusion for German left dislocation (cf. example (24a)).
[13] On the other hand, if assumed a split CP for the dislocated structure, with the dislocated element sitting in ForceP or TopP and the associated element in FinP, it wouldn't be clear why the dislocated adverbial clauses associated to a null element cannot serve as syntactic hosts for clitics.
[14] K attracts α only if there is no β closer to K, such that K attracts β (Chomsky 1995:310).

5. Evidence from Embedding

If external adverbial clauses pattern like dislocation structures, their embedding possibilities should be restricted. We will discuss a contrast between embedding with two types of complementizer – the indicative 'that' *že* and the subjunctive 'that' *aby*, inflecting for agreement,[15] revealing the predicted embedding restrictions.

In most cases, embedding of ACs under the indicative *že* patterns like matrix contexts. As illustrated in (31), the left-peripheral AC of the embedded sentence is followed by an element serving as a host for clitics:

(31) Věděl, **že** když to bude nutné, Petr ~*se* *ho* zastane.
knew$_{SG.MS}$ that when it will-be necessary Peter refl$_{CL}$ him$_{GEN}$ support$_{FUT}$
'He knew that when it is necessary, Peter will support him.'

However, the complementizer is also compatible with left-dislocation:

(32) … že moje maminka, ta si ještě mohla … (ČNK)
that my mother that$_{FM}$ refl$_{CL}$ still could$_{SG.FM}$
'…that my mother, she could still…'

(33) a. … sdělil nám, že jestli přijede, to sice neví, ale …
told$_{3SG}$ us$_{DAT}$ that whether arrives$_{FUT}$ that$_{NT}$ prt not-knows but
'He told us that he doesn't know whether he will come, but…'

b. Udělal tolik dobrého, 'He has done so much good' (ČNK)
že aby kvůli jednomu výroku odstoupil, to je příliš silné.
that to$_{3SUBJ}$ because-of one$_{DAT}$ statement$_{DAT}$ resigned$_{SG}$ that$_{NT}$ is too hard$_{NT}$
'He has done so much good that to resign because of one statement is too hard.'

Subjunctive *aby*, on the other hand, does not allow left-dislocation – (34), and requires a greater integration of ACs: the ACs directly precede or follow the clitic cluster – (35a) and (35b), respectively (note that these are also positions where parentheticals are inserted), but the matrix pattern for external ACs is out – compare (35c) with (31):

(34) a. *Chtěl, abyste Petra, toho nezvali.
wanted$_{SG.MS}$ that$_{2PL}$ Peter$_{ACC}$ that$_{ACC.MS}$ not-invited$_{PL}$
'He wanted that you do not invite Peter.'

b. *Chtěl, abys jestli přijedeš, to nikomu neříkal.
wanted$_{SG.MS}$ that$_{2SG}$ whether come$_{2SG.FUT}$ that$_{NT}$ nobody$_{DAT}$ not-tell$_{SG.MS}$
'He wanted that you tell nobody whether you arrive.'

---

[15] In case of simple complements, both complementizers can serve as clitic hosts – (i) and both allow topicalization, which targets the position between the complementizer and the clitics (cf. example (36)), suggesting the fronting targets a position below C, e.g., FinP, along the lines of split-CP in Rizzi, 1999:

(i) a. Řekli jsme mu, že ~*jsme* *si* *to* koupili.
told$_{PL}$ aux$_{1PL}$ him$_{DAT}$ that aux$_{1PL}$ refl$_{CL}$ it bought$_{PL}$

b. Řekli jsme mu, aby ~*si* *to* koupil.
told$_{PL}$ aux$_{1PL}$ him$_{DAT}$ to$_{3SUBJ}$ refl$_{CL}$ it bought$_{SG}$

(35) a. Přál bych si, aby až půjde v noci domů, ~*mu* dal
někdo nakládačku.
wish aux$_{1SG}$ that$_{3SG}$ when goes$_{FUT}$ in night home him$_{DAT}$ gave
somebody thrashing
'I wish that when he goes home in the night somebody gave him a thrashing.'
(ČNK)

b. Přál bych si, aby ~*mu*, až půjde v noci domů, dal někdo nakládačku.

c. *aby až půjde v noci domů, dal ~*mu* někdo nakládačku.

Similarly, only *že*-complements are compatible with *tak* – (36) (from 31), in contrast to *aby*-complements – (37):

(36) Věděl, **že** když to bude nutné, **tak** ~*se* *ho* Petr zastane.
knew$_{SG.M}$ that when it is$_{3SG.FUT}$ necessary so refl$_{CL}$ him$_{GEN}$ Peter support$_{3SG.FUT}$

(37) *Požádal nás, **abychom**, až budeme mít čas, <u>tak</u> ~*mu* trochu pomohli.
asked$_{SG.MS}$ us$_{ACC}$ that$_{CD1PL}$ when will$_{3PL.FUT}$ have$_{INF}$ time so him$_{DAT}$ a bit help$_{PL}$
'He asked us to help him a bit when we have time.'

At the same time, subjunctive *aby* allows for clause-internal fronting/topicalization – (38), which is an option available also with indicative *že*:

(38) ... řekl mi, abych jeden ~*si* nechal a ostatní podepsal ... (ČNK)
told$_{SG.MS}$ me$_{DAT}$ that$_{1SG}$ one$_{ACC}$ refl$_{CL}$ kept$_{SG.MS}$ and rest$_{ACC}$ signed$_{SG.MS}$
'...he told me to keep one of them and sign the rest ...'

Consequently, the incompatibility of *aby* with external left-peripheral ACs like, as in (35c), must be due to embedding of structures like (22) which is more complex than clause-internal fronting, as it leads to CP-recursion (cf. Iatridou & Kroch (1992). The complementizer *že* allows CP-recursion, as can be supported by examples like (39) with '*že*-doubling':

(39) ... že když ho neuloví, **tak** <u>že</u> se nic nestane
that if him$_{ACC}$ not-catch so that refl nothing happens$_{3FUT}$
'...that if we don't catch it, nothing will happen.' (ČNK)

Extraction[16] across the external AC is impossible in the CP-recursion structures:

(40) *Koho$_i$ myslíš, že až to bude nutné, <u>mohli</u> ~*bychom* požádat t$_i$?
whom$_{ACC}$ think$_{2SG}$ that when it is$_{3FUT}$ necessary could$_{PL}$ aux$_{CD1PL}$ ask$_{INF}$
'Who do you think that when it's necessary we could ask?'

On the other hand, the ACs do not block extraction out of *že* or *aby* – complements, as they are more deeply integrated or parenthetical:

(41) a. Co$_i$ chceš, abychom, až se vrátí, ~*mu* řekli t$_i$?
what want$_{2SG}$ that$_{CD1PL}$ when refl$_{CL}$ returns$_{3FUT}$ him$_{DAT}$ said$_{PL}$
'What do you want us to tell him when he comes back?'

[16] In contrast the Polish, extraction in Czech is not limited to subjunctive complements, cf. (36).

b.[17] Koho$_i$ myslíš, že až to bude nutné, ~*bychom* mohli požádat t$_i$?
whom$_{ACC}$ think$_{2SG}$ that when it is$_{3FUT}$ necessary aux$_{CD1PL}$ could$_{PL}$ ask$_{INF}$

The contrast concerning the two complementizers can be attributed to their different insertion sites. The subjunctive complementizer *aby* not only expresses mood, but also carries person and number features. Therefore, it also is in an agreement relation with T^0, for which some kind of T-to-C movement (Torrego&Pesetsky 2000) can be assumed. Such an agreement relationship is blocked by a CP-recursion. The indicative *že*, on the other hand, is a pure subordinator inserted in C, therefore, compatible with dislocated structures. A more detailed analysis of the embedded phenomena, including the mechanism of clause-internal frontig with *aby* (cf. (38)) is beyong the scope of this paper. Crucially, embedding of structures like (22) leading to CP-recursion is limited to the indicative *že* 'that', which has a character of a pure subordinating element.

6. Concluding remarks

This paper argued for a syntactic structure of initial adverbial clauses analogous to left-dislocation, as illustrated by the structure in (22). The claim was supported by evidence from clitic placement, embedding and extraction, as well as comparison with other left-peripheral phenomena like topicalization and left-dislocation of arguments and clauses. The CP-external adverbial clauses patterning with left-dislocation structures were contrasted with internal adverbial clauses showing properties of movement. Further research should clarify the distinction between the external and 'peripheral' (cf. fn. 8) adverbial clauses as well as a crosslinguistic parallels. For example in German, all three types of ACs seem to occupy Spec, CP as they are followed by the finite verb. The question is whether this is only a superficial observation and the underlying syntax is analogous to (22), and more generally, how the proposed syntax of left-peripheral ACs in Czech differs from left-peripheral ACs in V2 languages.

Sources

ČNK – Czech National Corpus

Bibliography

Bošković, Ž. (2000): 'Second position cliticization. Syntax and/or phonology?'. In: Beukema, F. & M. den Dikken (eds.), 71-119.
Franks, S. and T. H. King (2000): *A handbook of Slavic clitics*. Oxford: OUP.
Fried, M. (1994): 'Second-position clitics in Czech: Syntactic or phonological?'. *Lingua* 94, 155-175.
Frey, W. (2004): 'Notes on the syntax and the pragmatics of German Left Dislocation'. In: Lohnstein, H. & S. Trissler (eds.): *The Syntax and Semantics of the Left Periphery*. Berlin: Mouton de Gruyter, 203-234.

[17] Embedding of left-peripheral ACs under *že* mostly follows the matrix pattern like in (31) (this also concerns purposive ACs of the type used in the following example (i)). The pattern with the AC directly preceding the clitic cluster, common for *aby* – complements, is less frequent with že, but not impossible:

(i) Vzpomínám si, že abych trochu pozvedl náladu, ~*jsem se* tehdy Romualda zeptal ...
remember$_{1SG}$ refl$_{CL}$ that to$_{1SG}$ little improve$_{SG.MS}$ mood$_{ACC}$ aux$_{1SG}$ refl$_{CL}$ then Romuald$_{ACC}$ asked$_{SG.MS}$
'I remembed that to improve the mood a little I asked then Romuald ...' (ČNK, shortened)

The issue of the more integrated embedded ACs like (i) or (33a,b) touches the area of parenthesis, which we cannot go into here.

Cecchetto, C. (2001): 'Syntactic or Semantic Reconstruction? Evidence from Pseudoclefts and Clitic Left Dislocation'. In: Cecchetto, C., G. Chierchia & M. T. Guasti (eds.): *Semantic Interfaces*, Stanford: CSLI, 90-144.

Cecchetto, C. & G. Chierchia (1999): 'Reconstruction in Dislocation Constructions and the Syntax/Semantic Interface'. In: Blake, S. et al. (eds.): *Proceedings of WCCFL XVII*, Stanford: CSLI, 132-146.

Chomsky, N. (1995): *The Minimalist Program*. Cambridge, Mass.: MIT Press.

Grewendorf, G. (2002): 'Left Dislocation as Movement', ms. University of Frankfurt.

Haegeman, L. (2002): 'Anchoring to speaker, adverbial clauses and the structure of CP'. Ms. Université Charles de Gaulle-Lille III.

Haegeman, L. (2003): 'Conditional Clauses: External and Internal Syntax'. *Mind & Language* 18(4), 317-339.

Holmberg, A. (2000a): 'Scandinavian stylistic fronting: How any category can become expletive'. *Linguistic Inquiry* 31, 445-83.

Holmberg, A. (2000b): 'V2 languages'. Paper presented at the Peripheral Positions conference, University of York, September 2000.

Iatridou, S. & A. Kroch (1994): 'The Licensing of CP-recursion and its Relevance to the Germanic Verb-Second phenomenon'. *Working Papers in Scandinavian Linguistics* 50, 1-25.

Johnston, M. (1994): *The Syntax and Semantics of Adverbial Adjuncts*. PhD thesis, University of California at Santa Cruz.

Junghanns, U. (2002): 'Klitische Elemente im Tschechischen: eine kritische Bestandsaufnahme'. In: Daiber, Th. (ed.): *Linguistische Beiträge zur Slavistik. IX. JungslavistInnen Treffen, Halle/Wittenberg 2000*. München: Sagner, 117-150.

Lenertová, D. (2001): 'On clitic placement, topicalization and CP-structure in Czech'. In: Gerhild Zybatow et al. (eds.): *Current issues in formal Slavic linguistics*. Frankfurt am Main [etc.]: Lang, 294-305.

Lenertová, D. (2002/2004): 'Czech Pronominal Clitics'. *Journal of Slavic Linguistics* 12 (1-2), 139-176.

Meyer, R. (2003): 'On multiple Wh-fronting and Wh-clustering in Czech'. In: Browne, W. et al. (eds.): *Formal Approaches to Slavic Linguistics XI. The Amherst Meeting, 2002*. Ann Arbor: Michigan Slavic Publications, 393-412.

Reis, M. (1997): 'Zum syntaktischen status unselbständiger Verbzweit-Sätze'. In: Dürscheid, C. et al. (eds.): *Sprache im Fokus. Festschrift für H. Vater zum 65. Geburtstag*. Tübingen: Niemeyer, 121-144.

Rizzi, L. (1997): 'The Fine Structure of the Left Periphery'. In: Haegeman, L. (ed.): *Elements of Grammar*, Dordrecht: Kluwer, 281-337.

Roberts, C. (1989): 'Modal subordination and pronominal anaphora in discourse'. *Linguistics and Philosophy* 12, 683-721.

Rutherford, W. (1970): 'Some observations concerning subordinate clauses in English'. *Language* 46, 97-115.

Toman, J. (1996): 'A Note on Clitics and Prosody'. In: Halpern, A & A. M. Zwicky (eds.): *Approaching Second: Second Position Clitics and Related Phenomena*. Stanford, CA, 505-10.

Toman, J. (1999): 'On clitic displacement'. In: Dimitrova-Vulchanova, M. & L. Hellan (eds.): *Topics in South Slavic Syntax and Semantics*. Amsterdam: Benjamins, 205-228.

Torrego, E. & D. Pesetsky (2000): 'T-to-C movement: Causes and Consequences'. In: M. Kenstowicz (ed.): *Ken Hale: a life in language*. Cambridge, Mass.: MIT Press, 355-426.

Veselovská, L. (1995): *Phrasal movement and X^0-morphology: Word order parallels in Czech and English nominal and verbal projections*. Ph.D. dissertation, Univerzita Palackého.

Whelpton, M. (1995): *The Syntax and Semantics of Infinitives of Result in English*. PhD Thesis, University of Oxford.

Šárka Lešnerová, Prague and Marko Malink, Leipzig

Clitic Climbing and Theta-Roles in Upper Sorbian and Czech[1]

This paper examines the position of the reflexive clitic *so/se* in active and passive sentences with an infinitive and the phase verb *přestać/přestat*. It appears that clitic climbing is obligatory for passive sentences, whereas in active structures it can occur, but it need not to. The omission of clitic climbing in passive sentences leads to inappropriate agentive interpretations of the sentence. We sketch three explanations for this: 1. The false agent theta-role of the subject in passive sentences is assigned by a control use of the phase verb *přestać/přestat*. 2. The false agent theta-role is assigned by the infinitive which is misunderstood as an active transitive one. 3. Both principles cooperate.

1. Introduction

In Upper Sorbian as well as in Czech the morpheme *so/se* has several different functions. It serves, for instance, as a reflexive pronoun, a reciprocal pronoun, as a lexical part of deponent verbs (see 1ab) and as a syntactical passive marker in personal (see 1cd) and impersonal passive sentences.

(1) a. *Młynk so wučomnikam wusměwa.* (USo)
miller$_{nom}$ REFL$_{CL}$ apprentice$_{dat/pl}$ laugh at$_{3.sg.act}$
'The miller laughs at the apprentices.'

b. *Otec se věnuje fotbalu.* (Cz)
father$_{nom}$ REFL$_{CL}$ dedicate$_{3.sg.act}$ football$_{dat.sg}$
'The father is engaged in football.'

c. *Kozam so trawa picuje.* (USo)
goat$_{dat.pl}$ REFL$_{CL}$ grass$_{nom}$ feed$_{3.sg.act}$
'The goats are fed with grass.'

d. *Studentům se uděluje odměna.* (Cz)
students$_{dat.pl}$ REF$_{CL}$ award$_{3.sg.act}$ payment$_{nom}$
'Students are awarded a payment.'

According to common assumptions, the position of the morpheme *so/se* does not depend on its morphological or syntactic properties (see e.g. Fasske 1981:210f, implicitly Uhlířová 1987:82-97). However, when embedding sentences containing *so/se*, into a sentence with the phase matrix verb *přestać/přestat* (to stop) there occur important differences in the possible positions of the morpheme *so/se*.
The aim of our paper is to present and compare data about these embeddings in Upper Sorbian and Czech, depending on whether the infinitival contains

a) the free verbal morpheme *so/se* as a lexical part of the verb, which assigns agent theta-role to its subject (agentive reflexive verbs, *so wusměwać*, *věnovat se*, 1ab) or
b) the syntactical passive marker *so/se*, deriving from an active transitive verb a personal passive one, which assigns patient theta role to its nominative subject (reflexive passive, *picować* + *so*, *udělovat* + *se*, 1cd).

In both languages there are considerable differences in word order between these cases.

[1] We would like to thank Anja Nedoluzhko, Uwe Junghanns, Klaus Abels and Jana Vejvodová for comments on this paper. Of course, lack of clarity and errors are the authors' responsibility.

Agentive constructions with neutral information structure:

(2) a. *Po pruwowanju přesta młynk so wučomnikam wusměwać.* (USo)
after exam stop$_{3.sg.aor}$ miller$_{nom.sg}$ REFL$_{CL}$ apprentice$_{dat.pl}$ laugh at$_{inf}$
'After the exam the miller stopped laughing at the apprentices.'

b. *Věnovat se fotbalu přestal otec po válce.* (Cz)
to be engaged$_{inf}$ REFL$_{CL}$ football$_{dat.sg}$ stop$_{3.sg.mask}$ father$_{nom.sg.mask}$ after war
'After the war the father stopped being engaged in football.'

The same word order in a passive construction:

(2) c. # *Wčera přesta trawa so kozam picować.* (USo)
yesterday stop$_{3.sg.aor}$ grass$_{nom.sg}$ REFL$_{CL}$ goat$_{dat.pl}$ feed$_{inf}$

d. # *Udělovat se studentům přestala odměna po vyúčtování.* (Cz)
award$_{inf.}$ REFL$_{CL}$ students$_{dat.pl}$ stop$_{3.sg.fem}$ payment$_{nom.sg.fem}$ after clearance

Passive constructions with neutral information structure:

(3) a. *Wčera přesta so kozam trawa picować.* (USo)
yesterday stop$_{3.sg.aor}$ REFL$_{CL}$ goat$_{dat.pl}$ grass$_{nom.sg}$ feed$_{inf}$
'Yesterday the grass stopped being fed to the goats.'

b. *Po vyúčtování se přestala udělovat studentům odměna.* (Cz)
after clearance REFL$_{CL}$ stop$_{3.sg.fem}$ award$_{inf}$ students$_{dat.pl}$ payment$_{nom.sg.fem}$
'After the clearance the payment stopped being awarded to students.'

The same word order in agentive construction:

(3) c. ?? *Po pruwowanju přesta so wučomnikam młynk wusměwać.* (USo)
after the exam stop$_{3.sg.aor}$ REFL$_{CL}$ apprentice$_{dat/pl}$ miller$_{nom.sg}$ laugh at$_{inf}$

d. ?? *Po válce se přestal věnovat fotbalu otec.* (Cz)
after war REFL$_{CL}$ stop$_{3.sg.mask}$ to be engaged$_{inf}$ football$_{dat.sg}$ father$_{nom.sg.mask}$

(2a) is a grammatical sentence with an unmarked word order for an agentive reflexive infinitival. The same word order with a reflexive passive infinitival (2c) leads to ungrammaticality due to inappropriate theta-marking. (2c) implies that the grass deliberately decided to stop feeding itself to the goats. Intuitively, the grass is conceived of as the agent of the whole sentence (2c), that means as the agent of both the feeding and stopping feeding. However, there are no clear intuitions about which agentivity is caused by the matrix verb or by the infinitive and which is inferred otherwise.
The same difference can be observed in Czech for (2bd). (2d), though having the same word order as the correct agentive sentence (2b), is ungrammatical because it assigns agentive features to the scholarship. Throughout our paper, the double cross # is used to indicate this kind of semantical incorrectness due to inappropriate agentivity of non-animate participants.
On the other hand, (3ab) are grammatical sentences with the unmarked word order for a reflexive passive infinitival. The same word order in a sentence with an agentive reflexive

infinitival leads to a highly marked information structure (3cd). These sentences are acceptable only with an extraordinary corrective focus on the subject *młynk* and *otec* respectively.
In order to investigate the relevant data in more detail, it is necessary to make some remarks on the position of *so/se* as a sentential clitic in Upper Sorbian and Czech.

2. The position of *so/se* in Upper Sorbian and Czech

We assume contra Franks/King (2000:162-186) that in Upper Sorbian there are two default positions of the clitic *so* as a sentential clitic. On the one hand, *so* can occur at the second (Wackernagel) position. In this case the finite verb must occur at the last position (4a). There are only few complements that can (but need not) follow after the finite verb, e.g. infinitivals (4b), subordinated finite clauses or comparative complements (4c) (see Fasske 1981: §275).

(4) a. *Nadźijomnje so Pětrej jutře wulka překwapjenka poradźi.* (USo)
b. *Nadźijomnje so Pětrej jutře poradźi wšitkich překwapić.* (USo)
c. *Nadźijomnje so Pětrej jutře wjetša překwapjenka poradźi hač Janej.* (USo)

On the other hand, the finite verb can occur in the second position. In this case, clitic *so* immediately follows the verb (see 5a), but it must not stand at the end of the whole sentence (5c) (see Fasske 1981: §280). This second option is obligatory if *so* is part of an analytic predicate. Then – like in German – the verbal frame construction demands that the finite part of the predicate occurs in the second position and the infinite in the last position (5b). Of course, there are exceptions from these two rules, mainly in literary language (see e.g. Fasske 1981: §280), but they are stylistically marked and will be neglected in the following.

(5) a. *Pětrej poradźi so jutře nadźijomnje wulka překwapjenka.* (USo)
b. *Pětrej je so wčera wulka překwapjenka poradźiła.* (USo)
c. ** Překwapjenka poradźi so.* (USo)

Within infinitival embeddings *so* commonly occurs as a proclitic at the first (overtly realized) position of the infinitival (6a). Proclitic *so* can occur even at the very beginning of a sentence (see 6b), though the second position in the infinitival is also possible in this case (6c).

(6) a. *Pětr spyta stajnje [so wo wšitko sam starać].* (USo)
b. *[So słabšim wusměwać] je njepřistojne.* (USo)
c. *[Wusměwać so słabšim] je njepřistojne.* (USo)

In Czech, the position of the verb is not so strictly determined (7a-d). There is only one basic position of clitic *se*, the Wackernagel position, which, unlike in Upper Sorbian, must be occupied by the clitic even in an infinitival at the first position in the sentence (8abc).

(7) a. *Po obědě se dal Martin do práce.* (Cz)
b. *Po obědě se Martin dal do práce.* (Cz)
c. *Martin se po obědě do práce nedal.* (Cz)
d. *I dal se Martin po obědě do práce.* (Cz)

(8) a. *[Vysmívat se slabším] je nedůstojné.* (Cz)
b. ** [Se vysmívat slabším] je nedůstojné.* (Cz)
c. ** [Se slabším vysmívat] je nedůstojné.* (Cz)

3. More data

3.1. The free morpheme *so* of agentive reflexive verbs in Upper Sorbian

Among the 6! permutations[2] of the 6 constituents of sentence (2a) there are nine correct sentences with neutral information structure (9a-i). In four of them clitic *so* climbed out of the infinitival and occurs as a sentential clitic in the matrix clause (9a-d), either in the Wackernagel position (9b-d) or in the third position immediately after the finite verb (9a). In five of them clitic *so* occurs as a proclitic within the infinitival construction in the first (overtly realized) position (9e-i).

(9) a. *Po pruwowanju přesta so młynk [wučomnikam wusměwać].*
b. *Po pruwowanju so młynk přesta [wučomnikam wusměwać].*
c. *Po pruwowanju so młynk wučomnikam přesta [wusměwać].*
d. *Po pruwowanju so młynk [wučomnikam wusměwać] přesta.*
e. *Po pruwowanju přesta młynk [so wučomnikam wusměwać].*
f. *Po pruwowanju młynk přesta [so wučomnikam wusměwać].*
g. *Po pruwowanju młynk [so wučomnikam wusměwać] přesta.*
h. *Młynk po pruwowanju přesta [so wučomnikam wusměwać].*
i. *Młynk přesta po pruwowanju [so wučomnikam wusměwać].*

(10) a. *[Wusměwać so WUčomnikam] młynk po pruwowanju PŘEsta.*
b. *[Wučomnikam WUsměwać] přesta so młynk po PRUwowanju.*
c. *Po pruwowanju młynk so wučomnikam přesta [WUsměwać].*

Furthermore, we determined 94 correct permutations with marked information structure (e.g. 10a-c). In 54 of them *so* occurs as a sentential clitic with clitic climbing, in 40 of them *so* remains within the infinitival construction. Of course, it is hard to determine which permutations are still correct and can be uttered in some context. We do not insist on the concrete number of correct sentences. Instead, what is important here is that in the correct sentences with both unmarked and marked information structure we have a quite balanced proportion between sentences with and without clitic climbing. This proportion is not affected by adding or rejecting some correct permutations.
In Upper Sorbian, clitic climbing is not obligatory for the free morpheme *so* of agentive reflexive deponent verbs.

3.2. The free morpheme *se* of agentive reflexive verbs in Czech

Due to stronger restrictions on the position of clitic *se*, there are only 4 correct sentences with unmarked information structure among the 6! permutations (11a-d). In all of them *se* occurs in the Wackernagel position in the matrix clause and, unlike in Upper Sorbian, there is no correct unmarked sentence without clitic climbing.

(11) a. *Po válce se otec přestal[věnovat fotbalu].*
b. *Po válce se přestal otec [věnovat fotbalu].*
c. *Otec se po válce přestal [věnovat fotbalu].*
d. *Otec se přestal po válce [věnovat fotbalu].*

(12) a. *[Věnovat se FOTbalu] otec po válce přestal.*
b. *Po válce se přestal [věnovat fotbalu] OTec.*
c. *[Věnovat fotbalu] se otec po válce PŘEstal.*

---

[2] Prepositional phrases like *po pruwowanju* and *po válce* are treated as a unit in generating the 6! permutations.

However, among the 138 correct sentences with marked information structure there is a more or less balanced proportion between sentences with and without clitic climbing again. In 77 of them clitic climbing occurs (e.g. 12bc), in 63 of them clitic *se* remains within the infinitival (e.g. 12a). The situation is not the same as in Upper Sorbian: there is not a second default position of *se* within the infinitival since lack of clitic climbing leads to a strongly marked information structure in Czech.
In Czech, clitic climbing of the free morpheme *se* of agentive reflexive deponent verbs occurs in all correct sentences with unmarked information structure, but it is not obligatory for sentences with marked information structure.

3.3. The reflexive passive marker *so* in Upper Sorbian

Among the 6! permutations of (3a) there are seven correct sentences with neutral information structure (13a-g) and 41 correct permutations with marked information structure (e.g. 14a-c). The remaining 672 permutations are incorrect, partly because of inappropriate agentive features of the subject *trawa* (e.g. 15a-c), but mainly for other unrelated reasons. In all of the 48 correct permutations *so* occurs in the position of a sentential clitic, either in the Wackernagel position (13c-g, 14a) or in the third position after the finite verb (13ab, 14bc). That the clitic in (13a) in fact climbed out of the infinitival is confirmed by prosodic criteria. In (13a) *so* is enclitic, that means that a prosodic break between the preceding *přestać* and *so* is entirely impossible. However, if *so* does not climb out of the infinitival, it has to be proclitic to the following word like in (9e-i), where prosodic breaks are possible only before, not after *so*.

(13) a. *Wčera přesta so kozam trawa picować.*
b. *Kozam přesta so wčera trawa picować.*
c. *Wčera so kozam přesta trawa picować.*
d. *Kozam so wčera přesta trawa picować.*
e. *Wčera so kozam trawa picować přesta.*
f. *Kozam so wčera trawa picować přesta.*
g. *Wčera so přesta kozam trawa picować.*

(14) a. *Wčera so trawa kozam přesta PICować.*
b. *TRAwa přesta so kozam WČEra picować.*
c. *KOzam picować přesta so trawa WČEra.*

(15) a. # *Trawa wčera přesta [so kozam picować].*
b. # *[Picować so KOzam] trawa wčera PŘEsta.*
c. # *[So KOzam picować] přesta trawa WČEra.*

Lack of clitic climbing leads to inappropriate agentivity of the non-animate subject *trawa* (15a-c). Obviously, there is a connection between clitic climbing and the thematic structure of the sentences under consideration (see section 5.2).
In Upper Sorbian, clitic climbing is obligatory for the reflexive passive marker *so*.

3.4. The reflexive passive marker *se* in Czech

The situation is very similar in Czech. Clitic climbing occurs in both the 5 correct unmarked (16a-e) and the 116 correct marked (e.g. 17a-d) permutations of (3b). It is again prosodic criteria that give evidence for clitic climbing in (17cd). In these sentences a prosodic break is possible only after, not before *se*. Nevertheless, *so/se* in (13a-g, 16a-e) is not generated within the matrix clause as part of a verb *so přestać/přestat se*, but within the infinitival, deriving a reflexive passive infinitive from an active transitive one.[3] In sentences without clitic climbing, like in Upper Sorbian, there appear incorrect agentive and volitional features of the subject *odměna* (18ab).

(16) a. *Po vyúčtování se studentům přestala udělovat odměna.*
b. *Po vyúčtování se přestala studentům udělovat odměna.*
c. *Studentům se po vyúčtování přestala udělovat odměna.*
d. *Studentům se přestala po vyúčtování udělovat odměna.*
e. *Po vyúčtování se přestala udělovat studentům odměna.*

(17) a. *Studentům po vyúčtování se odměna PŘEstala udělovat.*
b. *Studentům se po vyúčtování odměna udělovat PŘEstala.*
c. *Odměna studentům přestala se udělovat PO VYúčtování.*
d. *Po vyúčtování přestala se udělovat studentům ODměna.*

(18) a. # *Po vyúčtování přestala odměna [udělovat se studentům].*
b. # *[Udělovat se studentům] přestala odměna po vyúčtování.*

In Czech, clitic climbing is obligatory for the reflexive passive marker *se*.

3.5. Summary of the data

The following table summarizes the results of the previous sections. Again, the concrete numbers are a matter of discussion and are not of importance to see that clitic climbing is obligatory for the reflexive passive marker *so/se*, whereas it is not obligatory for the free morpheme *so/se* of agentive deponent verbs, though in this case, lack of clitic climbing leads to marked information structure in Czech.

so/se	agentive reflexive verb				reflexive passive			
	Uso		Cz		USo		Cz	
total: 6! = 720	neutr.	mark.	neutr.	mark.	neutr.	mark.	neutr.	mark.
+clitic climb.	4	54	4	77	7	41	5	116
–clitic climb.	5	40	0	63	0	0	0	0

Moreover, the four sets of correct unmarked word orders (9a-i, 11a-d, 13a-g, 16a-e) are mutually disjoint. Within each language, there is no unmarked word order common to the reflexive passive marker *se/so* and the free morpheme of agentive deponent verbs. In Upper Sorbian the sequence *trawa picować* is a good indicator for this. It occurs in (13a-g), but does not occur in (9a-i) as *młynk wusměwać*. Interestingly, *trawa picować* constitutes a close prosodic unit in (13a-g) in which the infinitive *picować* is completely destressed and which is to be considered in the next section.

4. Topicalization of infinitivals and personal vs. impersonal reflexive passive infinitivals

The observed regularities are confirmed by the possible topicalization of infinitivals. In both languages there is topicalization with (10b, 12c) and without (10a, 12a) clitic climbing of the

[3] If *so/se* was generated within the matrix clause as part of a verb *so přestać/přestat se* it could not affect the argument structure of the infinitive *picować/udělovat* at all. The infinitive therefore would remain an active transitive one assigning agent theta role to its external argument. But since raising is possible only from the position of the external argument for active transitive infinitives and the nominative subject *trawa/odměna* obviously is raised in (13a-g, 16a-e), the infinitive would be expected to assign agent theta role to the (trace of) the nominative subject, which clearly is not the case.

free morpheme *so/se* of agentive deponent verbs. On the contrary, for the reflexive passive marker *so/se*, topicalization of the infinitival without clitic climbing is ruled out due to inappropriate agentive features (15bc, 18b).

(10) b. *[Wučomnikam WUsměwać] přesta so młynk po PRUwowanju.* (USo)

(12) c. *[Věnovat fotbalu] se otec po válce PŘEstal.* (Cz)

(10) a. *[Wusměwać so WUčomnikam] młynk po pruwowanju PŘEsta.* (USo)

(12) a. *[Věnovat se FOTbalu] otec po válce přestal.* (Cz)

(15) b. # *[Picować so KOzam] trawa wčera PŘEsta.* (USo)

(15) c. # *[So KOzam picować] přesta trawa WČEra.* (USo)

(18) b. # *[Udělovat se studentům] přestala odměna po vyúčtování.* (Cz)

Topicalizations with clitic climbing of the reflexive passive marker *so/se* are not problematic in Upper Sorbian (14c), whereas they are questionable in Czech and depend on the concrete lexical items (19ab).

(14) c. *[KOzam picować] přesta so trawa WČEra.* (USo)

(19) a. ?? *[Udělovat studentům] se přestala odměna po vyúčtování.* (Cz)

b. ? *[Vytahovat na stožár] se prapory zatím nebudou.* (Cz)
hoist up$_{inf}$ on flagpole REFL$_{CL}$ flags$_{nom/pl}$ at present not-be$_{3.pl.fut}$
'At present the flags will not be hoisted up the flagpole.'

(20) a. * *[Udělovat odměna] se studentům přestala po vyúčtování.* (Cz)

b. *[Udělovat odměnu] se studentům přestalo po vyúčtování.* (Cz)
award$_{inf}$ payment$_{akk.sg}$ REFL$_{CL}$ students$_{dat.pl}$ stop$_{3.sg.neutr.}$ after clearance
'They stopped giving payment to students after the clearance.'

(21) a. *[Trawa picować] přesta so kozam wčera.* (USo)

b. *[Trawu picować] přesta so kozam wčera.* (USo)
grass$_{akk.sg}$ feed$_{inf}$ stop$_{3.sg.aor}$ REFL$_{CL}$ goat$_{dat.pl}$ yesterday
'They stopped feeding grass to the goats yesterday.'

In both languages the personal reflexive passive construction with nominative subject *trawa/ odměna* instead of accusative *trawu/odměnu* is strongly preferred in the correct sentences with unmarked information structure (13a-g, 16a-e). Accusative *odměnu* is prohibited in (16a-e) and *trawu* seems to be possible only in (13g), not in (13a-f).[4]
However, when topicalizing the infinitival together with the argument *odměn-*, the impersonal construction turns obligatory in Czech (20a vs. 20b). In this case the impersonal verb *se přestat* is used and the infinitive remains a transitive active one. Clitic *se* is generated within

[4] In this point further research is necessary. There may be or have been Upper Sorbian dialects which are allowing accusative *trawu* also in (13a-f). This topic is not treated in the volume on syntax of the Upper Sorbian dialectological atlas (Fasske 1996).

the matrix, and consequently, there is no clitic climbing in (20b, 21b) (see Junghanns 2002:62).
On the other hand, in Upper Sorbian, personal (21a) as well as impersonal (21b) topicalization is possible. Even if the impersonal construction (21b) happens to be preferred to the personal (21a), (21a) at the most sounds a bit strange while being perfectly understandable. On the contrary, for the agentive reflexive infinitivals (9a-i, 11a-d), analogous topicalization of *młynk wusměwać* or *otec věnovat* is completely ungrammatical in Upper Sorbian and Czech (22ab).

(22) a. * *{Młynk wusměwać} přesta so wučomnikam po pruwowanju.* (USo)

b. * *{Věnovat otec} se fotbalu přestal po válce.* (Cz)

In the Upper Sorbian personal construction (21a) *trawa picować*, unlike Czech *odměna udělovat* is constituting a close prosodic unit, which can be topicalized as a whole. This kind of prosodic integration or incorporation is typical for indefinite direct objects in Upper Sorbian (23ab) and is preserved when deriving reflexive passive (23cd).

(23) a. *Młynk hižo hodźiny dołho na zahrodźi trawu syče.* (USo)
miller already hours long on garden $\text{grass}_{\text{akk/sg}}$ $\text{mow}_{\text{3.sg.act}}$
'The miller has been mowing the grass in the garden for hours.'

b. ?? *Młynk na zahrodźi trawu hižo hodźiny dołho syče.* (USo)

c. *Na zahrodźi so hižo hodźiny dołho trawa syče.* (USo)
on garden REFL_{CL} already hours long $\text{grass}_{\text{nom/sg}}$ $\text{mow}_{\text{3.sg.}}$
'Grass has been mowed in the garden for hours.'

d. ?? *Na zahrodźi so trawa hižo hodźiny dołho syče.* (USo)

It seems that the sequence of *traw-* and *picować* in (21a), besides prosodic unity, has gained already further properties of nominal compounds. The case ending of the patient internal argument *trawu/trawa* loses importance, the semantic relation between both parts (patient) is no longer expressed formally. That *trawa* in (21a) is not a fullfledged subject due to the strong incorporation or intergration with the infinitive can be seen when using perfect tense instead of the simple past tense (aorist), where the gender of the subject is not encoded. For, in the perfect tense explicite gender agreement in the obligatory verbal frame construction is not possible (24a) and the impersonal construction turns obligatory in Upper Sorbian as well (24b) – as in Czech in the only past tense, the former perfect tense, which still expresses gender agreement (20ab).

(24) a. * *TRAwa picować je so kozam wčera PŘEstała.* (USo)
b. *TRAwu picować je so kozam wčera PŘEstało.* (USo)

5. Inappropriate agentive features

Agentive interpretations instead of required passive ones arise under two conditions. Firstly, as seen, by lack of clitic climbing (15a-c, 18ab). Secondly, by an inappropriate order of the arguments, where the subject occurs too far on the left (25a-d), though the clitic *se/so* climbs out of the infinitival. In this section both cases are discussed separately.

(25) a. # *Trawa přesta so wcěra kozam picować.* (USo)
b. # *Wčera so trawa přesta kozam picować.* (USo)

c. # *Odměna se přestala udělovat studentům po vyúčtování.* (Cz)
d. # *Odměna se po vyúčtování přestala udělovat studentům.* (Cz)

5.1. The order of arguments

In (25a-d) the agentivity is much weaker than in (15a-c, 18ab) and occurs only when interpreting the sentences with neutral information structure. It can be deleted by prosody, e.g. by a focus accent on *trawa/odměna*. Moreover, this kind of agentivity is independent of infinitival constructions and occurs in purely finite clauses as well (26a-d). These differences show that the agentivity in (25a-d) is of entirely different type than in (15a-c, 18ab).

(26) a. *Na zahrodźi so hižo hodźiny dołho trawa syče.* (USo)
on garden $REFL_{CL}$ already hours long $grass_{nom/sg}$ $mow_{3.sg}$
'Grass has been mowed in the garden for hours.'

b. # *Trawa so na zahrodźi hižo hodźiny dołho syče.* (USo)

c. *V sadu se teď češou jablka.* (Cz)
in garden $REFL_{CL}$ now $pick_{pl}$ $apples_{nom.pl}$
'Apples are being picked in the garden now.'

d. #? *Jablka se teď češou v sadu.* (Cz)

The question how the agentive interpretation arises in (25a-d) is connected with the following question. We have seen that every infinitival with the reflexive passive marker *so/se* demands clitic climbing. But the converse does not hold, since not every climbed *so/se* is the reflexive passive marker and the free morpheme of agentive reflexive verbs can climb out of the infinitival (e.g. 9a-d, 11a-d). How can then sentences with climbed reflexive passive marker *so/se* be distinguished from those with climbed free morpheme of agentive reflexive verbs?
Both questions can be accounted for by the order of arguments in sentences with unmarked information structure, the so called 'systémové uspořádání věty' ('Systemic ordering', Sgall et al. 1980:62-78)[5]. According to this theory, non-topical arguments of sentences with unmarked information structure must occur in a certain, quite fixed order: agent, time, place, manner, measure, measurement, instrument, way, addressee, source, patient and so on.
For our sentences, the order *agent – time – addressee – patient* is of importance. In particular, we get the order *agent – time – addressee* for the agentive sentences and the order *time – addressee – patient* for the passive sentences. The free constituent *time* is allowed to interchange the position with *agent* and *addressee* respectively. It can be checked easily that all the neutral active (9a-i, 11a-d) and passive (13a-g, 16a-e) sentences obay this order. It is this order that is the main distinctive feature between the passive sentences (13a-g, 16a-e) on the one hand and the agentive sentences with clitic climbing (9a-d, 11a-d) on the other hand, which, otherwise, follow the same word order patterns within each language.
Now, if the subject (of a sentence with neutral information structure) occurs too far on the left and not after the addressee it tends to be interpreted as agent, provided such an interpretation is syntactically available. This is what happens in (25a-d). Consequently, clitic *so/se* is not interpreted as a reflexive passive marker in (25a-d), but as a direct object of the active infinitive.

[5] Though worked out for Czech this order turns out to be valid for Upper Sorbian as well for the most part.

5.2. Lack of clitic climbing

In (15a-c, 18ab) the strong inappropriate agentive features, caused by lack of clitic climbing, cannot be deleted by prosody. Prima facie, there are three possibilities: the agentive features of the subject in (15a-c, 18ab) can be assigned either by the finite matrix verb, the infinitive or both of them at the same time. In what follows these options are discussed in more detail.

(15) a. # *Trawa wčera přesta [so kozam picować].* (USo)
b. # *[Picować so KOzam] trawa wčera PŘEsta.* (USo)
c. # *[So KOzam picować] přesta trawa WČEra.* (USo)

(18) a. # *Po vyúčtování přestala odměna[udělovat se studentům].* (Cz)
b. # *[Udělovat se studentům] přestala odměna po vyúčtování.* (Cz)

5.2.1. Control vs. raising

If the subject in (15a-c, 18ab) gets an agent theta role from the matrix verb, these sentences must be considered as control constructions and *přestać/přestat* in them as a control verb since only control verbs assign a theta role to their nominative subject. On the other hand, *přestać/přestat* in the correct reflexive passive sentences (13a-g, 16a-e) do not assign any theta role to the subject and must be therefore raising verbs (Schoorlemmer 1995:28, Junghanns 2003). Obviously, the only theta role of the subject *trawa/odměna* in (13a-g, 16a-e) is the patient theta role assigned by the reflexively passivized infinitive. Consequently, a raising verb *přestać/přestat* has to be distinguished from a control verb *přestać/přestat* or, to put it differently, a raising use and a control use of the same verb. Now, the empirical results of the previous sections can be explained by postulating that

A) clitic climbing of *so/se* is obligatory for raising constructions, not for control constructions.

Consequently, also the correct agentive reflexive deponent infinitivals (9e-i, 12ab) without clitic climbing must be interpreted as control constructions. Postulate A immediately explains that clitic climbing is obligatory for subjectless reflexive verbs like *so dešćować* and *stmívat se*, (27a-d), though for personal agentive reflexive verbs there are analogous topicalizations without clitic climbing (see 10a, 12a). For, every construction in which the subjectless of the infinitive carries over to the matrix sentence is a raising construction.

(27) a. *[DEŠćować] přesta so hižo DOpołdnja.* (USo)
to rain stop$_{3.sg.aor}$ REFL$_{CL}$ already in the morning
'It stopped raining already in the morning.'

b. * *[So dešćować] přesta hižo dopołdnja.* (USo)

c. *Stmívat rychleji se začalo už před měsícem.* (Cz)
getting dark faster REFL$_{CL}$ begin$_{3.sg.neutr}$ already before month
'It began getting dark faster already a month ago.'

d. ? *Stmívat se rychleji začalo už před měsícem.* (Cz)

The distinction between a raising and a control use of the same verb is not very typical. In the literature (Zabrocki 1981:138, Schoorlemmer 1995:28, Junghanns 2003) Slavic phase verbs are considered as pure raising verbs – because of sentences of type (13a-g, 16a-e) among other reasons.

(28) a. *Wčera spyta so kózlatkam trawa picować.* (USo)
yesterday $try_{3.sg.aor}$ $REFL_{CL}$ young $goat_{dat.pl}$ $grass_{nom.sg}$ $feed_{inf}$
'Yesterday one tried to feed grass to the young goats.'

b. # *Wčera spyta trawa [so kózlatkam picować].* (USo)

However, in Upper Sorbian e.g. also the verb *spytać* (try), commonly considered as a typical control verb, can be used as a raising verb with clitic climbing (28a). Again, lack of clitic climbing leads to inappropriate agentive features and to the common control use of *spytać* (28b). It is as if the reflexive passive marker *so*, when climbed out of the infinitival, affects the argument structure of the matrix verb and deagentivizes it, i.e. derives a raising verb from a control one. If we – for theoretical reasons – do not want clitic climbing to affect the argument structure of the matrix verb, we have to distinguish between a raising and a control use of *přestać/přestat* already in the lexicon.

5.2.2. Incorrect interpretation of the infinitive

The distinction between a raising and a control use of *přestać/přestat* is dispensable if the agentivity of the subject in (15a-c, 18ab) is assigned by the infinitive and the matrix verb is a raising verb without a thematic role for the subject. Then, to explain the data, one should assume that

B) clitic climbing is obligatory for the syntactical passive marker *so/se*, but it is not obligatory for the free morpheme of agentive reflexive deponent verbs.

In this case, the agentivity of (15a-c, 18ab) is caused by the following mechanism. Due to the lack of clitic climbing, *so/se* in (15a-c, 18ab) cannot be the syntactic passive marker by postulate B. Consequently, the infinitive remains an active transitive one assigning agent theta role to its external argument. But since raising is possible only from the position of the external argument for active transitive infinitives, agent theta role is assigned to the (trace of the) raised subject *trawa/odměna* of (15a-c, 18ab) by the active infinitive *picować/udělovat*. Clitic *so/se* then, like the corresponding long forms *sebje/sebe*, must be interpreted as a reflexive pronoun and as a direct object of a transitive infinitive. Indeed, the incorrectness of (15a-c, 18ab) is the very same as in (29ab).

(29) a. # *Trawa wčera přesta [sebje kozam picować].* (USo)

b. # *Po vyúčtování přestala odměna[udělovat sebe studentům].* (Cz)

The advantage of not having to distinguish a raising verb *přestać/přestat* from a control one is a good reason for prefering the second option with postulate B.

5.2.3. Matrix verb and infinitive cooperating

It remains to have a look at the third possibility that the agentive features in (15a-c, 18ab) are assigned by both the matrix verb and the infinitive, i.e. that postulates A and B hold at the same time. Alternatively, postulates A and B can be connected and strenghtened[6] by R. Růžička's principle:

C) "Controlled clauses are incompatible with reflexive *passive* in Slavic languages […]." (Růžička 1999:134)

Some evidence for the third option is given by personal reflexive non-agentive deponent verbs like *so dlić* 'to last' in Upper Sorbian. *So dlić* has a nominative external argument but

[6] From A and C follows postulate B. For, if lack of clitic climbing forces a control construction by A, and control constructions are incompatible with reflexive passive by C, then clitic climbing is obligatory for the reflexive passive marker *so/se*, i.e. B does hold.

does not assign a volitional agent theta role to it. Nevertheless, *so* is not the syntactic passive marker in *so dlić* since there is no transitive *dlić* (at least synchronically, see Fasske 1981, §260). Lack of clitic climbing leads to inappropriate agentive features of the subject in this case as well (30b), especially when (30b) being read with a slight prosodic break before clitic *so*. Though these agentive features are much weaker than in (15a-c, 18ab) they cannot be deleted by prosody like in (25a-d).

(30) a. *Po interwenciji direktora přesta so twar šule skónčnje dlić.* (USo)
after intervention $director_{gen}$ stop REFL $construction_{nom}$ $school_{gen}$ finally be protracted
'After the intervention of the director the construction of the school finally stopped being protracted.'

b. # *Po interwenciji direktora přesta twar šule skónčnje so dlić.* (USo)

(30b) is a control construction due to postulate A, and the matrix verb *přestać* assigns quite weak[7] agentive features to the subject *twar šule*. Postulate B and the mechanism of the previous section can not be applied to (30b) since *so dlić* is not a reflexive passive and has no agent theta role in its argument structure at all which could be assigned mistakenly to its subject (PRO). Therefore, the nominative subject in (30b) is assigned only a weak agent theta role by the matrix control verb *přestać*. On the contrary, in (15a-c, 18ab), strong volitional agentive features of the active infinitive are assigned to the subject PRO by the controlled infinitive due to postulate B or C (see previous section). Thus, the combination of postulates A and B (or C) explains the agentivity in (30b) and its weakness compared to (15a-c, 18ab).
We have sketched some possible explanations for the complex phenomenon of inappropriate agentive features in (15a-c, 18ab). Further research has to show which of them turns out to be the most adequate.

Bibliography

Dowty, D. R. (1991): *Thematic Proto-Roles and Argument Selection.* In: Language 67, 547–619.

Fasske, H. (1981): *Grammatik der obersorbischen Schriftsprache der Gegenwart. Morphologie*. Bautzen: Domowina Verlag.

Fasske, H. (1996): *Serbski rěčny atlas 15. Syntaksa.* Ed. Serbski institut z. t. Budyšin. Bautzen: Domowina Verlag.

Franks, S. & T. H. King (2000): *A Handbook of Slavic Clitics*. New York, Oxford.

Junghanns, U. (2002): *Clitic Climbing im Tschechischen.* In: Junghanns, U.: Untersuchungen zur Syntax und Informationsstruktur slavischer Deklarativsätze. Linguistische Arbeitsberichte 80, Institut für Linguistik, Universität Leipzig, 57–90.

Junghanns, U. (2003): *Ferne Objekte*. In: Geist, L. & R. Hammel (eds.): Linguistische Beiträge zur Slavistik X. München, 101–123.

Růžička, R. (1999): *Control in Grammar and Pragmatics. A Cross-Linguistic Study*. Amsterdam, Philadelphia.

Schoorlemmer, M. (1995): *Participial Passive and Aspect in Russian.* OTS Dissertation Series. Utrecht.

Uhlířová, Z. (1987): Knížka o slovosledu. Praha: Academia.

Sgall, P., E. Hajičová & E. Buráňová (1980): *Aktuální členění věty v češtině.* Praha.

Zabrocki, T. (1981): Lexical rules of semantic interpretation. Control and NP movement in English and Polish. Poznań.

[7] For a continuum of agentivity instead of a discrete agent theta role see Dowty (1991).

Franc Marušič, New York

CP under control*

1. Observation

Control constructions typically do not have an overt subject, the embedded clause typically does not have a complementizer, and the embedded verb typically does not have any tense morphology.

The standard analysis of control structures from Chomsky and Lasnik (1995) is given in (1), where the embedded clause is a CP with a [-finite] TP as the complement of C. The subject of the control clauses is PRO, receiving null case from the defective T. PRO can be interpreted because it is controlled by an antecedent in the matrix clause.

(1) $[_{CP}[_{TP}$ *John*$_i$ $[_{VP}$ *hopes* $[_{CP}[_{TP}$ PRO$_i$ *to* $[_{VP}$ *get the tickets*$]]]]]]$

Hornstein (1999, 2001) proposes an alternative analysis of control. He divides control structures in two classes: Obligatory control (OC) and Non-obligatory control (NOC), and takes obligatory control structures to be a result of movement parallel to raising constructions. Under this analysis, OC PRO is a trace of the moved argument – the controller in the matrix clause, while the NOC PRO is just a small *pro*. Hornstein's analysis is sketched in (2). The details are suppressed since they are not important at this point.

(2) $[_{IP}$ *John* $[_{VP}$ *hopes* $[_{IP}$ ~~*John*~~ *to* $[_{VP}$ *get the tickets*$]]]]$

Hornstein does not say much about the identity of the phrase with the non-finite clause. He simply takes it to be an IP, but provides no independent evidence for this claim. Under his analysis, it is clear that the embedded clause cannot be a CP/strong phase as it is standardly assumed. Movements over a CP/strong phase are possible only with an intermediate stop in Spec-CP, but Spec-CP is an A'-position and movements out of A' into A-positions are a violation of the Chain Uniformity principle. Movement analysis therefore depends on a non-CP status of control clauses.

The goal of this paper is to open the door for a Hornstein/movement type of analysis of non-finite complementation, by showing that Slovenian non-finite clauses do not have the CP projection[1]. In section 2, I go over six major arguments to support my claim that non-finite clauses are not separated from the matrix clause by a strong phase (Chomsky 2001), that they do not have a CP: scrambling (2.1), clitic climbing (2.2), multiple *wh*-movement (2.3), partial *wh*-movement (2.4). In section 3, I extend the claim and relate it to other proposals in the field. In section 4, I discuss the division of verbs according to their complements. Section 5 is the conclusion.

2. Slovenian non-finite clausal complements

In Slovenian, finite and non-finite clauses differ in a number of ways. The next five subsections go over several syntactic phenomena, which all point to a structural difference

* I am grateful to the FDSL audience for their comments and suggestions, I am also grateful to Dan Finer, Richard Larson, and Francisco Ordóñez for their comments and guidance, but do not want to hold them responsible for the mistakes I made and stupidities I wrote.

[1] The distinction between different classes of non-finite complements taking verbs will be introduced in the 3rd section. Until then I use the most trivial distinction between verbs taking finite and non-finite clauses, but, of course, avoid (for the most part) use of clearly restructuring and/or raising verbs since they have already been shown to exhibit typical monoclausal phenomena (Wurmbrand 2001, Cinque 2002) and thus lack CP.

between finite and non-finite clauses. I will show that they all suggest that non-finite clausal complements do not have the CP projection or the corresponding strong phase.

2.1. Scrambling

The argument presented in this subsection is a version of an argument originally given for Serbo-Croatian by Bošković (1997), this time using Slovenian data. The main point is the observed difference between two types of scrambling with respect to the triggering of weak cross-over (WCO).

Just like Serbo-Croatian, the language used by Bošković, Slovenian allows scrambling from both finite and non-finite clauses. Since finite clauses have a CP, the scrambled embedded DP *Janeza* in (3) has to go over the CP to its landing site in front of the matrix clause. The final landing site of such a long distance scrambling from the finite clause should be an A'-position, since movements from an A' to an A-position are not allowed under the Chain Uniformity principle, and movements over the CP/strong phase are not allowed without the intermediate step through the Spec.CP (Chomsky 2001). The final landing site of scrambling thus corresponds to the landing site of *wh*-movement. The prediction follows that the scrambled DP is subject to WCO. This is also what we see. The scrambled DP in (3a) patterns with *wh*-movement in (3b), *his* cannot co-refer with the fronted XP. But it can if the scrambled constituent does not cross over the pronoun as in (4).

(3)	a.	*Janeza*$_i$	*je*	*njegov*$_{j/*i}$	*oče*	*rekel,*	*da*	*se*	*boji* __ .
		J-GEN$_i$	AUX	his$_{j/*i}$	father	said	COMP	REFL	fear

'John$_i$, his$_i$ father said he fears.'

	b.	*Koga*$_i$	*je*	*njegov*$_{j/*i}$	*oče*	*rekel*	*da*	*se*	*boji* __?
		whom$_i$	AUX	his$_{j/*i}$	father	said	COMP	REFL	fear

'Whom$_i$ did his$_{j/*i}$ father say that he fears?'

(4)	a.	*Janeza*$_i$	*je*	*Peter*	*rekel,*	*da*	*se*	*boji* __	*na*	*njegovem*$_i$	*žuru.*
		J-GEN$_i$	AUX	Peter	said	COMP	REFL	fears	at	his$_i$	party

'Peter said that he fears Janez$_i$ at his$_i$ party.'

	b.	*Koga*$_i$	*je*	*Peter*	*rekel,*	*da*	*se*	*boji* __	*na*	*njegovem*$_i$	*žuru?*
		whom$_i$	AUX	Peter	said	COMP	REFL	fears	at	his$_i$	party

'Whom$_i$ did Peter say that he fears at his$_i$ party?'

Given the pattern observed above, if the control constructions also have an intermediate CP on top of the embedded non-finite clause, we would expect long distance scrambling out of non-finite clauses to show similar kinds of WCO phenomena. As long as there is an intermediate CP, all movements have to go through the Spec.CP position. Every movement through an intermediate A'-position should end in an A'-position. With an intermediate CP projection, we predict scrambling out of non-finite embedded clauses to show the same kind of WCO violations as scrambling out of finite clauses.

This prediction, however, is not born out in the observed Slovenian data. In contrast to scrambling out of finite clauses, scrambling out of non-finite clauses does not induce any WCO as shown in (5). Since scrambling does not trigger WCO, there is no CP node. There is no intermediate A'-projection between the two clauses, so that the DP from the lower clause can move to an A-position inside the matrix clause – the final landing site does not have to be an A'-position and the context for WCO does not arise.

(5) *Janeza$_i$ je njegov$_i$ oče sklenil poslati v semenišče.*
J-ACC$_i$ AUX his$_i$ father decided send$_{INF}$ to theological seminary
'His$_i$ father decided to send John$_i$ to the theological seminary.'

As shown, the non-finite clausal complement behaves as if it does not have the CP.[2]

The lack of WCO is not a direct consequence of non-finiteness of the complement but it is rather the result of the type of scrambling and structure the scrambled element moves over. The landing site of the DP scrambling in (5) is not an A'-position[3], but it is clearly in the clause. The only way over the supposed CP of the embedded non-finite clause is through its A'-specifier position, but movements from A' to A-positions are not licit. The conclusion is that there is no CP in between the two clauses in (5).

2.1.1. A further note on scrambling

Another difference between the two types of clauses that suggests that non-finite clauses have a less complete clausal structure is observed with scrambling. I have nothing to say on the different mechanism involved and responsible for the distinction between A-scrambling (out of non-finite clauses; not triggering WCO) and A'-scrambling (out of finite clauses; triggering WCO). I am simply assuming that whatever theory of scrambling one accepts, the two types of scrambling will have two different landing sites. In this subsection I show this using quantifiers.

As shown in (6a) a universal quantifier inside the embedded finite clause cannot have wide scope interpretation over the existential quantifier in the matrix clause. Scope interpretation does not change when the universal quantifier undergoes scrambling to the beginning of the clause (6b). Since the fronting does not influence the scope interpretation, the scrambled DP apparently has to reconstruct. Radical reconstruction is a sign of A'-scrambling, therefore this scrambling appears to be A'-scrambling and the landing site an A'-position. This is just as expected. The scrambled DP in (6b) moves through the intermediate Spec.CP and thus cannot land in an argument position inside the matrix clause.

(6) a. *Nekdo je rekel, da so vse punce vredne greha.* ∃>∀, *∀>∃
somebody AUX said, COMP AUX all girls worthy sin-GEN
'Somebody said that all girls are worthy of sin.'

b. *Vse punce, je rekel nekdo, da so __ vredne greha.* ∃>∀, *∀>∃
all girls AUX said somebody, COMP AUX worthy sin-GEN

If control constructions have an intermediate CP, than we would expect scrambling out of non-finite clauses to show the same properties as A'-scrambling out of finite clauses. A scrambled universal quantifier should not have scope over the existential quantifier in the matrix clause.

This is not what we find. Example (7a) with the scrambled universal quantifier is ambiguous. This means that the landing site of the scrambled universal quantifier is an A-position from where the DP from the embedded non-finite clause can take scope. Since the final landing site is an A-position, there cannot be any intermediate A'-positions. No intermediate A'-positions means no CP.

---

[2] Note that *wh*-extraction out of non-finite clauses does not trigger WCO in Slovenian. Non-finite clauses again differ from finite clauses, since extraction from finite clauses is subject to WCO. WCO is also not triggered in simple monoclausal questions.

[3] This kind of explanation might not be valid within the current minimalism (e.g. Chomsky 2001), but the facts remain the same. Non-finite clauses are different from finite ones with respect to the presence/lack of WCO.

(7) a. *Vse punce se je nekdo odločil poklicati po telefonu* __ $\exists>\forall$, $\forall>\exists$
all girls REFL AUX someone decided to call$_{INF}$ over phone
'Someone decided to call all girls'

b. *Nekdo se je odločil poklicati po telefonu vse punce* $\exists>\forall$, ?$\forall>\exists$
someone REFL AUX decided to call$_{INF}$ over phone all girls

The interpretation of the non-scrambled sentence (7b) is not entirely clear. For some speakers and with some degree of focus the universal quantifier can have wide scope interpretation, but this is not really important at the present point. In case (7b) is ambiguous, then non-finite clauses show greater transparency than finite clause. They allow embedded quantifiers to have wider QR domain than finite clauses. This would suggest that non-finite clauses lack some structure that prevents universal quantifiers inside embedded finite clauses to take wide scope reading. If on the other hand, (7b) is not ambiguous, then the only way to explain the ambiguity of (7a) is to posit that scrambling is an instance of A-movement. As mentioned before, A-movement means no CP projection.

2.2. Climbing of Pronominal Clitics

The previous section shows that scrambling facts argue for the lack of a CP projection in between the matrix predicate and the embedded non-finite clause. This section makes the same argument with pronominal clitic climbing facts.

As illustrated in (8), clitic climbing is also a long distance movement that does not trigger any WCO, again supporting the claim that non-finite complements lack CP.

(8) *Čist zares* ***ga***$_i$ ***je*** *njegov*$_i$ *oče sklenil poslati v semenišče.*[4]
Seriously him$_i$ AUX his$_i$ father decided send$_{INF}$ to seminary
'Seriously, his father decided to send him to a theological seminary.'

Slovenian clitics are located in the second position in the clause (the Wackernagel position). They follow the first (syntactic) constituent of the sentence. Slovenian second position clitics are analyzed as heads adjoining to the clause initial functional head – C (Golden and Sheppard 2000).

Clitics cannot leave the embedded CP as shown in (9). They must remain in the finite embedded clause. In (9) they follow the complementizer, which can also be seen as the first constituent (element) of the embedded clause, satisfying the requirement of the clitics to be in the second position.

(9) *Res* ***sem se*** (****ji ga***) *naveličal, da* *(***ji ga***) *nonstop hvalim.*
really AUX REFL her him got tired COMP her him constantly praise
'I got really tired of constantly praising him to her.'

It is important to note that the presence of the complementizer is not decisive for the positioning of the clitic inside the embedded clause. The clitics do not have to attach to the overt complementizer as shown in (10) where the clitics follow the *wh*-word in the Spec.CP. A null complementizer in Slovenian finite clauses is allowed only with a *wh*-word in the specifier position, so that clitics either follow the *wh*-word or the complementizer. In both cases they remain inside the CP, adjoined to C.

[4] In this section and in other examples where clitics are relevant, they are written in ***bold***.

(10) *Meta* ***mu*** *je* *povedala* *kaj* *so* *ji* *otroci* *kupili* *za* *razbito* *šipo.*
Meta him AUX told what AUX her kids buy for broke glass
'Meta told him what the kids bought her because of the broken window.'

Given the assumption, the prediction is clear. If the non-finite clauses were to have a CP projection, the clitics should adjoin to its head just like they do in embedded finite clauses.

This is not what we find. Clitics behave differently in non-finite clauses. They climb out to join the clitic cluster of the matrix clause as shown in (11). This is exactly what we expect if non-finite clauses do not have a CP node and therefore do not constitute a phase/phrase for clitics to cluster. Without the CP node for the non-finite clauses, we maintain the generalization that clitics cluster within the first CP phrase/phase available.[5]

(11) *Res* ***sem*** ***ji*** ***ga*** *sklenil* [PRO *opisati* __ __]
really AUX her him decide describe$_{INF}$
'I really decided to try to describe him to her.'

2.2.1. An alternative account of clitic placement

Note that the validity of the preceding argument does not really depend on the kind of clitic placement analysis that is used. Keeping the syntactic approach to clitic positioning, one possibility is to say that clitics actually adjoin to the finite T head rather than C. Climbing out of non-finite clauses would then be a result of the lack of the finite T head rather than lack of the CP projection. This kind of analysis faces the problem that in some cases, clitics can remain inside the non-finite clause.

When the non-finite clause is fronted, clitics remain inside the non-finite clause, (12); therefore if they can adjoin to finite T in this case, they should also adjoin to it in (11). Other examples with a clitic inside non-finite clauses are cases of NOC, discussed in section 5.

(12) [*Reči* ***ji,*** *da* ***sem*** *bolan*], ***mi*** ***je*** *ukazal* *že* *včeraj.*
say$_{INF}$ *her* COMP AUX sick, <u>me</u> AUX ordered already yesterday.
'Already yesterday, he ordered <u>me</u> to tell *her* that I am sick.'

The alternative syntactic approach is thus not supported. We cannot claim that clitics adjoin only to finite T heads and use this to explain why they can climb out of non-finite clauses.

Example (12) represents a problem for the syntactic account presented in the preceding subsection. If clitics indeed adjoin to C head, how do they stay inside the non-finite clause if it has no C head (it cannot have the C head because than, clitics should always adjoin to it)? How could movement of the non-finite clause create the CP projection and allow clitics to adjoin to its head?

In Marušič (in preparation) I argue for a prosodic analysis of Slovenian clitic placement. Following that and similar proposals made for clitic placement in other languages (Anderson 2000, Roberts 1997 for Pashto, Broadwell 2000 for Zapotec, O'Connor 2002 for Serbo-Croatian), I suggest that clitics are positioned in the phonological component of the grammar in the second position of the relevant clausal prosodic phrase. Assuming Chomsky (2001, 2002), phonological phrases can be seen as a prosodic reflex of phases in the syntactic derivation. Since CP is a phase, but not TP, clitics represent a way to test the presence or absence of the CP projection.

Following this proposal, clitics can climb out from non-finite clauses, because there is no strong CP phase between the two clauses that would force the clitics to remain in the lower prosodic phrase. Example (12) represents a case that is not spelled out because of the CP. Rather, it shows a phase created by movement. Following Uriagereka (1999) I assume a

[5] See Golden 2003 for an extended discussion and multitude of clitic climbing data in Slovenian.

moved constituent also represents a phase. The clitics in (13), a case of NOC (see below), remain inside the non-finite clause, because they are closed of with the CP phase and spelled out in that prosodic phrase together with the rest of the embedded clause. Clitics are of course not allowed to jump from one prosodic phrase to another; therefore they have to stay inside the lower non-finite clause.

(13) *Ukazal* ***mi*** ***je*** *[kaj* ***ji*** *reči]*
Ordered me AUX WH *her* say_{INF}
'He ordered me what to say.'

As I have shown, the specific clitic analysis opted for in the previous subsection was not crucial for the argument since even assuming a completely opposing view on clitic movement, i.e. as the prosodic account just offered, the data still argue for the lack of the CP projection.

2.3. Multiple *wh*-movement

Slovenian is a multiple *wh*-movement language. Like Serbo-Croatian and Bulgarian, it fronts all *wh*-words in a sentence. It, however, differs from Bulgarian (Rudin 1988) in that it does not respect any superiority. That is, any *wh*-word can be placed in the first position. Like Serbo-Croatian, Slovenian also allows the *wh*-word cluster to be broken up with clitics. The *wh*-word that follows the two clitics in (14) is thus also taken to be fronted.

(14) a. ***Kdo*** *koga toži?*
who whom sue
'Who is suing whom?'

b. ***Kdo*** *mu je* ***kaj*** *povedal?*
who him is what told
'Who told him what?'

Like Serbo-Croatian (and unlike Bulgarian), Slovenian does not allow multiple long distance *wh*-movements. Only one *wh*-word can move out of an embedded finite clause (15). This restriction is supposedly correlated with the fact that *wh*-words can be separated with clitics, adverbs and parentheticals (Rudin 1988). According to Rudin, only the first *wh*-word is moved to the Spec.CP, which is why only one *wh*-word can move from the embedded CP to the matrix CP.

(15) ***Kaj*** *je* ***(*komu)*** *rekel Janez,* ***(*komu)*** *da je Peter dal* ****(komu)****?*
What is whom said Janez, whom COMP is Peter give whom
'What did Janez say that Peter gave whom?'

If non-finite clauses have a CP projection just like finite clauses, we would predict that they show the same phenomena we observe in (15) – disallow multiple long distance *wh*-movement.

This is not what we find. Multiple *wh*-movement out of non-finite clauses is available in Slovenian. This suggests that non-finite clauses do not have the same structure as the finite clauses do. In particular it shows that non-finite clauses do not have the CP projection, which banned multiple *wh*-movement out of finite clauses. Multiple *wh*-movement is not obligatory in Slovenian, which is why (16) is also good. Although the judgements are actually not as clear for all types of non-finite clauses, sentences like (16) are acceptable while multiple long distance *wh*-movement out of finite clauses is simply out, as shown in (15).

(16) a. ***Komu*** *si* ***kaj*** *pozabil* *dati?*
Whom AUX what forgot give$_{INF}$
'Whom did you forget to give what?'

b. ***Komu*** *si* ***koga*** *sklenil* *predstaviti?*
Whom AUX who decide introduce$_{INF}$
'Who did you decide to introduce to whom?'

From the observation that multiple *wh*-movement out of finite clauses is impossible, but available to some degree in non-finite clauses, it is natural to conclude that non-finite clauses lack the structure that prevents multiple *wh*-movements out of finite clauses. Following Rudin (1988) the relevant structure is the CP projection. The reason why judgements are not always as clear might be related to other factors like the distinction between finite and non-finite T, which I do not address.

Again an immediate question comes to mind: can *wh*-words be in between the matrix and the embedded non-finite clause? If so, in what position could they be? I leave this question aside for now and will return to it in section 5, since embedded sentences with a *wh*-word in front do not involve obligatory control (Hornstein 1999).

2.4. Partial *wh*-movement

Slovenian exhibits the so-called Partial *wh*-movement shown in (17). As extensively discussed by Fanselow (2001), in these constructions the base generated *wh*-word only moves part of the way towards its scope position, while in the specifiers of CPs in between the *wh*-word and the highest CP marked [+Q], the default *wh*-word is added – the *wh*-expletive. In Slovenian this is *kaj* "what". One possible analysis of these constructions says that the *wh*-expletive shows up because of the [+*wh*] feature movement (Cheng 2000). Only the [+*wh*] feature of the *wh*-word moves to the highest CP, while the other features of the *wh*-word, including its phonological features, remain in the Spec of a lower CP. The highest CP with the [+Q] feature ends up with the *wh*-expletive, while the original *wh*-word is realized lower. The complementizer following the *wh*-word is optional in Slovenian.

(17) ***Kaj*** *praviš,* ***kdo*** *(da)* *je* *prišel?*
What say, who COMP AUX came?
'Who do you say came?'

If non-finite clauses do have a CP projection, we would also expect them to allow partial *wh*-movement. This is not observed, though. Partial *wh*-movement is not available with embedded non-finite clauses as shown in (18). This again shows that the lower clause does not have a CP projection where the *wh*-word could be located and from where its [+Q] feature could move out. Only "full" *wh*-movement is possible out of non-finite embedded clauses, (19).

(18) a. ****Kaj*** *ti* *Janez* *ukazuje,* ***koga*** *udariti?*
What you Janez order who hit$_{INF}$
'Who did Janez order you to hit?'

b. ****Kaj*** *je* *Janez* *pozabil,* ***koga*** *pozdraviti?*
What AUX Janez forget, whom salute$_{INF}$
'Whom did Janez forget to say hello to?'

(19) ***Koga*** *ti Janez ukazuje udariti?*
Who you Janez order hit$_{INF}$
'Who did Janez order you to hit?'

Examples (18) are not forbidden because of selectional restrictions on the verb. In Partial movement constructions, the lower CP is not marked [+Q], and both verbs allow also a [+Q] CP complement as shown in (20).

(20) a. *Janez ukazuje,* ***koga*** *moramo udariti?*
Janez order who must hit$_{INF}$
'Janez is ordering whom we have to hit?'

b. *Janez je pozabil,* ***koga*** *je hotel pozdraviti?*
Janez AUX forget, whom AUX want salute$_{INF}$
'Janez forgot whom he wanted to say hello to.'

According to this analysis, (18) is out because OC non-finite clauses do not have a CP projection. An even more illustrative example pointing out to the structural difference between finite and non-finite clauses is observed in examples with multiple embedding, (21). When both, the embedded and the double embedded clause, are finite, the *wh*-expletive shows up in the upper two Spec.CP positions. As shown in (21) the intermediate Spec.CP between the *wh*-word and the CP where it takes scope cannot be empty (cf. Fanselow 2001).

(21) ***Kaj*** *nam je Vid ukazal,* ***kaj*** *moremo reči,* ***koga*** *je Marija poljubila __?*
what us AUX V ordered what must say$_{INF}$ whom AUX M kissed
'Who did Vid order us that we must say that Mary kissed?'

(22) *?****Kaj*** *je Vid mislil, da je Peter rekel,* ***koga*** *da je Marija poljubila __?*
What AUX V thought that AUX P say whom that AUX M kissed
'Who did Vid think that Peter said that Mary kissed?'

In case the first embedded clause is non-finite and the lowest one finite, partial *wh*-movement leaves the *wh*-word in the Spec.CP of the finite clause, but there is no intermediate *wh*-expletive between the matrix and the non-finite clause, (21). Since partial *wh*-movement cannot skip an intermediate Spec.CP, as shown in (23), the lack of the intermediate *wh*-expletive in non-finite clauses again suggests the lack of CP projection.

(23) ***Kaj*** *nam je Vid ukazal (****kaj****) reči,* ***koga*** *da je Marija poljubila __?*
what us AUX V ordered what say$_{INF}$ whom that AUX M kissed
'Who did Vid order us to say that Mary kissed?'

Fanselow observes the same restrictions also in German and Hungarian. His explanation of non-availability of partial *wh*-movement in German relates to the fact, that German does not allow *wh*-headed infinitival clauses, (24). Fanselow (2001, 19) makes the following generalization: "[W7] *A CP related to W*[hat]*P*[hrase] *must be a syntactically legal indirect question.*"

(24) a. ****Was*** *glaubst du [****wen*** *eingeladen zu haben*]?
what believe you who invited to have
'Who do you believe to have invited?'

b. ***Wen*** *glaubst du eingeladen zu haben?*

c. **Ich frage mich* [***wen*** *eingeladen zu müssen*].
I ask myself who invite to must
'I wonder who to invite.'

Wh-phrases have to move to some operator position. Fanselow's [W7] can be violated only if there are intermediate landing sites for *wh*-phrases that are never filled by overt *wh*-phrases in constituent questions. In infinitives such positions do not exist. Non-finite clauses lack a certain structure that finite clauses do not.

The Generalization seems to work for German, but it does not work for Hungarian and Slovenian. Slovenian allows *wh*-headed infinitives as the ones given in (25).

(25) a. *Pozabil sem,* ***kaj*** *reči.*
I forgot what to say.

b. *Odločil sem se,* ***kje*** *zgraditi hišo.*
I decided where to build a house.

I discuss these kind of examples in section 4. Following Hornstein (1999, 2001) I claim these sentences do not involve obligatory control. Only OC constructions are a result of movement for Hornstein and only for them the existence of a CP represents a problem.

The other question is why these non-obligatory control sentences in (25) cannot participate in partial *wh*-movement constructions. I propose that NOC sentences, as in (25), crucially involve an embedded [+Q] CP. When the *wh*-word is moved into its specifier position to check the [+Q] feature, the *wh*-word also gets its [+*wh*] feature checked off. Partial *wh*-movement involves the moving of a single feature to check features on the matrix [+Q] marked CP. Since that feature gets checked in the intermediate CP it cannot move to the matrix CP.

In this section it was shown that OC infinitives do not have the CP. Non-finite clauses in general do not allow partial *wh*-movement. OC constructions cannot exhibit partial *wh*-movement because they do not have the intermediate CP, where the *wh*-word would land and from where the [+wh] would move out. While NOC constructions, which have a CP, crucially involve a [+Q] marked C, which prevents the [+wh] feature to undergo further movement.

3. Consequences and extension

If non-finite clauses do not have a CP node on top, and therefore no boundary for A-movement, a movement analysis of control structures like the one proposed by Hornstein (1999, 2001) becomes available.

The standard analysis of control sentences involves a CP as the verbal complement. The CP has a non-finite TP with a PRO in the subject position. PRO is controlled by the subject/object of the matrix predicate. But it is crucially not governed, which is assured by the CP projection. The standard analysis is given in (26) (from Chomsky and Lasnik 1995).

(26) [$_{TP}$ *John$_i$* [$_{VP}$ *hopes* [$_{CP}$[$_{TP}$ PRO$_i$ *to* [$_{VP}$ *get the tickets*]]]]]

Bošković (1997) claims the notion of government should be dispensed with and offers a Case-theoretic account for the distribution of PRO. He claims that since government by the matrix verb does not need to be blocked, as long as lexical properties of the verb do not require a CP, all control infinitivals without any complementizer lack the CP projection. He extends his claim also to all clauses without any complementizer – null-operator relatives and finite declaratives like *John believes Mary saw Peter.*

His claims seem to be a bit too strong and the class of non-CP infinitives not as precisely defined. In particular, *wh*-initial non-finite clauses (as discussed in section 5) seem to have a

CP projection since none of them passes the tests given in section 2. As mentioned before, they also seem to involve non-obligatory control. All this makes them significantly different from OC, and is potentially a result of the presence of CP. I claim the class of non-CP clauses is much smaller.

Wurmbrand (2001) makes a more detailed proposal. She gives 4 classes of restructuring verbs that take 4 different kinds of clausal complements (*lexical restructuring verbs, functional restructuring verbs, reduced non-restructuring verbs* and *non-restructuring verbs*). The least complete embedded clauses – complements to lexical restructuring predicates – lack in addition to the CP also all functional categories and *v*P. They do not even have their own subject position, since they only consist of the VP projection. This position is again very strong. All non-finite clauses seem to allow at least some adverbs that are usually positioned in between TP and *v*P. If these functional projections do not exist, as claimed by Wurmbrand, these adverbs shouldn't really be possible.

The class of restructuring verbs seems to coincide with Obligatory Control verbs – those that following Hornstein (1999) involve movement. As seen so far, Wurmbrand's approach is compatible with the Slovenian data. According to her, restructuring verbs do not only lack the strong phase/CP, but in some cases also the other strong phase *v*P. But as I said, if restructuring verbs lack all the projections dominating VP, than we would not expect any kind of adverbs in between the restructuring verb and the embedded verb. At first sight this prediction seems to be correct. The adverb in (27a) cannot have the sentential meaning with respect to the lower predicate, although *wisely* can have it as in (27b), here with respect to the matrix predicate. In (27a) *wisely* can only have the lower VP internal manner interpretation.

(27)	a.	*Njegov oče je*	*sklenil*	*pametno*	*poskusiti*	*opisati*	*Petra*	*Meti.*
		His father has	decided	wisely	to try	to describe	Peter	to Meta
	b.	*Njegov oče je*	*pametno*	*sklenil*	*poskusiti*	*opisati*	*Petra*	*Meti.*
		His father has	wisely	decided	to try	to describe	Peter	to Meta

But some other adverbs that are typically positioned in between *v*P and TP are possible. Assuming, following Cinque (1999), that adverbs are placed into the specifier position of strictly ordered functional projections, every such adverb would represent a problem for Wurmbrand's analysis. If these restructuring verbs are biclausal in the sense of having two main verbs, we can imagine the lower clause to be composed of certain but not all functional projections. Such "deficient" sentences lacking certain functional heads could only lack the top most projections, so that all adverbs up to a certain head would be possible, but not others that are located above that particular head.

The example in (28) is constructed so that the position of the adverbs cannot be associated with the upper clause. *Spet* "again" is a fairly low adverb and is used in the upper clause to eliminate confusion as for which clause the second adverb belongs to. I do not give the whole list of sentences, due to the lack of space.

(28)	*frankly*	–	**Peter*	*je*	*spet*	*poskusil*	*iskreno*	*pisati*	*nalogo*
			Peter	AUX	again	begun	frankly	write	assignment
			'Peter again begun ADV to write the assignment.'						
	fortunately	–	**Peter*	*je*	*spet*	*poskusil*	*k sreči*	*pisati*	*nalogo*
	allegedly	–	**Peter*	*je*	*spet*	*poskusil*	*baje*	*pisati*	*nalogo*
	perhaps	–	**Peter*	*je*	*spet*	*poskusil*	*mogoče*	*pisati*	*nalogo*
	necessarily	–	**Peter*	*je*	*spet*	*poskusil*	*gotovo*	*pisati*	*nalogo*
	usually	–	*?? Peter*	*je*	*spet*	*poskusil*	*ponavadi*	*pisati*	*nalogo*
	again	–	*? Peter*	*je*	*spet*	*poskusil*	*znova*	*pisati*	*nalogo*
	often	–	*Peter*	*je*	*spet*	*poskusil*	*pogosto*	*pisati*	*nalogo*
	...								

The prediction was made that if an adverb was unavailable so would be all upper ones and that the division between the two sets of adverbs would be sharp. The results are not as clear as the prediction, although a cut between adverbs is still observed. But this is not really important at the present moment. It seems, therefore, that there are some functional projections present between *v*P and TP. This suggests that a restructuring analysis with a VP complement to *v*P (Wurmbrand 2001) does not seem available for the present set of cases.

Cinque (2002) gives a monoclausal analysis of restructuring verbs – analyzing them as heads of the extended sequence of functional projections (Cinque 1999). According to Cinque verbs can take as their complement only a complete CP clause. All instances of restructuring on the other hand are instances of a restructuring verb in the head of an appropriate functional projection. Such an analysis easily explains the lack of certain adverbs in the complement of restructuring verbs. If all restructuring verbs are functional heads in the extended set of projections, than only adverbs in the specifiers of the lower projections would be allowed in the complement and all adverbs associated with higher projections would be unavailable.

But there seem to be also some problems with Cinque's analysis. Functional heads should not take any internal arguments, therefore no object control verbs should be restructuring. But Slovenian object control constructions do seem to exhibit some transparency phenomena comparable to those of plain restructuring verbs like clitic climbing, (29) (cf. Golden 2003).

(29) a. *Včeraj sem* ***ga*** *Petru ukazal pobrati* __.
yesterday AUX it Peter order pick up
'Yesterday, I ordered Peter to pick it up.'

b. *Mama mi* ***jo*** *je dovolila povabiti* __ *na kosilo.*
mother me her AUX allowed invite on lunch
'Mother allowed me to invite her for lunch.'

Hornstein (1999, 2001) claims that all cases of OC PRO are really only traces of the moved argument. NOC PRO, on the other hand, should be analyzed as little *pro*. A movement analysis of PRO is not compatible with the standard control structure. With a CP projection on top of the embedded clause, movement from the embedded clause to the matrix clause is impossible. Such movement would have to go to the final A-position through Spec.CP, which is an A'-position, thus violating the chain uniformity principle. Because of this, PRO has been postulated to reside in the subject position of the lower clause. Without the CP projection a different theory of control is available.

(30) [$_{TP}$ *John*$_i$ [$_{vP}$ ~~*John*~~ [$_{VP}$ *hopes* [$_{TP}$ ~~*John*~~ *to* [$_{vP}$ ~~*John*~~ [$_{VP}$ *get the tickets*]]]]]]

Barrie and Pittnam (2003) give an extension of Hornstein's theory, they claim all cases of Control involve movement. For them, OC verbs are either restructuring verbs or ECM. All other verbs exhibit partial control, which can also be taken to signal a biclausal structure with a non-movement relation between the two subjects. For them even partial control (NOC) is a result of movement. This is again a very strong position.

The crucial question remained unanswered, what is the actual division of verbs that take non-finite complements. For Cinque they divide into **non-restructuring** taking a CP complement and **restructuring**, which are all monoclausal. For Wurmbrand only **factive** and prepositional verbs take a CP complement, while **others (non factive)** take various non-CP clauses. Hornstein makes the simple distinction between **non-OC** verbs probably taking a CP and **OC** verbs taking an IP. In what follows I will present some further Slovenian data showing that Hornstein's division actually doesn't seem to be in perfect agreement with the structure of Slovenian clausal complements. It seems that all non-*wh*-initial infinitival clauses show transparency and therefore probably also lack CP.

As shown by Landau (1999), non-obligatory or partial control is much more spread than originally thought. For example the English verb *decide* is actually not an obligatory control verb since it allows sentences like (31a). This does not seem to be the case for the Slovenian equivalent of "decide" – *skleniti* – as shown in (31b). *Decide* seems to be an OC verb and as such it was also used in section 2.

(31) a. *John decided to meet at 9*

b. *Črt se je sklenil srečati v parku*
Črt REFL AUX decided hug in the park
'Črt decided to hug in the park.'

A more complicated set of cases is observed with *convince*, a partial control verb that takes an accusative object on top of the clausal complement. As shown in (32) *convince* doesn't allow clitic climbing out of the embedded non-finite clause.[6]

(32) a. **Zvone ji je Micko prepričal dati __ darilo*
Zvone her AUX M$_{ACC}$ convinced give gift
'Zvone convinced Micka to give her a gift.'

b. **Metko sem mu prepričal predstaviti Slavca*
M$_{ACC}$ AUX him$_{DAT}$ convinced introduce Slavc$_{ACC}$
'I convinced Metka to introduce Slavc to him.'

c. **Metko sem ga prepričal predstaviti Petru*
M$_{ACC}$ AUX him$_{ACC}$ convinced introduce Peter$_{DAT}$
'I convinced Metka to introduce him to Peter.'

But otherwise it behaves on a par with other control Vs: it doesn't exhibit WCO, (33), it doesn't allow partial *wh*-movement, (34), and it allows multiple *wh*-movement, (35).

(33) *Slavka$_i$ je Petro njegov$_i$ oče prepričal brcniti __ v piščal*
S$_{ACC}$ AUX P$_{ACC}$ his father convinced kick in fibula
'His father convinced her to kick Slavko in his fibula.'

(34) **Kaj je Jože Zdenko prepričal komu dati fičota?*
What AUX Jože Zdenka convinced whom give Fiat 600
'Whom did Jože convince Zdenka to give Fiat 600.'

(35) *Komu je kaj Marko prepričal Meto dati za rojstni dan?*
whom AUX what Marko convinced M$_{ACC}$ give for birthday
'Whom did Marko convince Meta to give what for birthday?'

Although *decide* and *convince* are no OC verbs, they still exhibit transparency. The claim made in this paper is not rejected but it is weakened with these data. The implication is shown to go only in one way: if we have OC we don't have CP, but lack of CP does not mean anything with respect to the choice between OC and NOC. We can also not make the strong claim in the other direction that actually all non-finite clauses lack CP, because of the *wh*-initial non-finite clauses that I am saving for section 5.

---

[6] For some speakers, clitic climbing out of complements to *convince* type verbs is allowed when the matrix clause argument is also a clitic (cf. Golden and Milojević-Sheppard 2003).

4. WH-initial infinitival clauses

A non-finite clause with a *wh*-word in front, behaves differently from all other non-finite clauses. Non-finite clauses loose all the properties that suggested they lack a CP projection when they have a wh-word in the supposed Spec.CP.

In section 3.2, I showed that clitics front out of non-finite clauses (36a). When the non-finite clause is a constituent question, the clitic cannot climb out of it, (36b,c).

(36)	a.	*Ukazal*	***mi***	***ji***	***je***	[*reči* __,	*da*	*sem*	*bolan*].
		ordered	me	*her*	AUX	say	that	I am	ill

‘He ordered me to tell *her* that I am sick.’

b.	*Ukazal*	***mi***	***je***	[*kaj*	***ji***	*reči*].
	ordered	me	AUX	WH	*her*	to say

c. * *Ukazal* ***mi*** ***ji*** ***je*** [*kaj* __*reči*].[7]

Similar facts hold for other phenomena presented. Scrambling out of *wh*-initial non-finite clauses is impossible. But here the explanation does not have to do only with the presence of a CP projection. Scrambling out of finite clauses is possible in Slovenian (37c), but not out of an embedded question (37b). Therefore (37a) has a CP projection, but the unavailability of scrambling is probably due to the fact that the Spec.CP is already filled with a *wh*-word.

(37) a.	*??	*Janeza se je*	*Peter*	*odločil,*	*kdaj*	*naučiti manir.*
		Janez$_{ACC}$	Peter	decided	when	to teach how to behave
b.	*?	*Janeza se je*	*Peter*	*odločil,*	*kdaj mora*	*naučiti manir.*
		Janez$_{ACC}$	Peter	decided	when has	to teach how to behave
c.		*Janeza se je*	*Peter*	*odločil,*	*da mora*	*naučiti manir.*
		Janez$_{ACC}$	Peter	decided	that has	to teach how to behave

‘Peter decided (that he has) to teach Janez how to behave.’

4.1. Non-Obligatory Control

What do these facts mean for the claim made, that non-finite clauses do not have CP? Firstly I want to say that sentences with the initial *wh*-word all involve non-obligatory Control, (38). If NOC constructions are really just non-finite clauses with a *pro*, we wouldn't necessarily expect them to be structurally deficient – lacking the CP projection.

(38)	*Vid*$_i$	*je*	*svetoval*	*Mariji*$_j$	*kje*	*si*$_{i+j}$	*postaviti*	*šotor*	*za*	*oba.*
	V.NOM	AUX	advised	M.ACC	where	REFL	put$_{INF}$	tent	for	both

‘Vid advised to Marija where to place the tent’

That these cases involve NOC is observed also by Hornstein (1999). Examples with a wh-initial non-finite clause do not involve OC. The subject of the embedded clause does not have to be interpreted as the subject/object of the matrix clause that otherwise controls the PRO.

(39) *He showed me* ***how*** *to fly a plane.*

---

[7] Available readings where the *wh* word is understood as an indefinite pronoun or a wh-in-situ constructions are ignored, since they are not relevant.

The interpretation in (39) is not that I have to fly a plane, since he only showed me how anyone could, or better how flying is to be done. This points out to the second major difference between control constructions and *wh*-initial non-finite clauses. As discussed by Bhatt (2000), all *wh*-initial non-finite clauses involve some form of hidden modality. This modality is not found in simple non-finite complements.

The third major difference is that *wh*-initial non-finite clauses can be complement to verbs, which do not take infinitival clausal complements, as shown in (40). They can be selected by verbs selecting only finite CPs. This suggests that plain non-finite clauses really are different in their lacking of the CP projection. In other words, they cannot be selected by verbs taking a CP complement.

(40)	a.	*Pokazal sem mu* ***kje*** *(mora) pristati.* I showed him where (he must) to land.	vs.	**Pokazal sem mu pristati* *I showed him to land
	b.	*Ugotovil je* ***kje*** *prestopiti* He found out where to change	vs.	**ugotovil sem prestopiti* *He found out to change
	c.	*Vem* ***kaj*** *početi* I know what to do	vs.	**Vem početi.* *I know to do

No true punch-line can be given, but all these differences suggest that we are dealing with a different construction altogether here, and that maybe we don't even want to make it parallel to other non-finite clauses.

5. Conclusion

In this paper I argue for a three way structural distinction between clausal complements:

- **finite clauses** with a complete functional structure and a top CP >
- ***wh*-initial non-finite clauses** (possibly less complete, but with a CP/strong phase) >
- **simple "control" non-finite clauses** (lack at least the CP projection).

Supporting evidence comes from scrambling, clitic climbing, *wh*-movement. With respect to these phenomena, control (in particular OC) constructions behaved differently from finite clauses and *wh*-initial non-finite clauses. Control constructions allow A-movement to the matrix clause, allow AGREE with elements in the matrix clause, and thus seem to involve a single phase for both the embedded and the matrix clause. These results sort of open the door for a movement analysis of control à la Hornstein's (1999, 2001) and Barrie and Pittman (2003). Restructuring on the other hand might probably be best treated in a monoclausal structure following Cinque (2002).

References

Anderson, Stephen. 2000. Toward an Optimal Account of Second-Position Phenomena. In: Dekkers, J., F. van der Leeuw & J. van de Weijer (eds.): *Optimality Theory: Phonology, Syntax, and Acquisition.* Ofxord, OUP, 302-333

Barrie, Michael and Christine M. Pittman. 2003. Partial control and the movement towards movement. to appear in *Toronto Working Papers in Linguistics* 22, University of Toronto.

Bhatt, Rajesh. 2000. Covert Modality in Non-finite Contexts. Ph.D. University of Pennsylvania.

Bošković, Željko. 1997. *The syntax of nonfinite complementation: An economy approach.* Cambridge, Mass.: MIT Press

Broadwell, George Aaron. 2000. On the phonological conditioning of clitic placement in Zapotec. Ms. University at Albany.

Cheng, Lisa. 2000. Moving just the feature. In: Ulrich Lutz, Gereon Müller, & Arnim von Stechow (eds.): *Wh-scope Marking*. Amsterdam: Benjamins, 77 - 99.
Chomsky, Noam. 1995. *The Minimalist Program*. Cambridge, Mass.: MIT Press.
Chomsky, Noam. 2000. Minimalist Inquiries: The framework. In: *Step by step: Essays on minimalism in honor of Howard Lasnik*, ed. Roger Martin, David Michaels, and Juan Uriagereka. Cambridge, Mass.: MIT Press, 89-155.
Chomsky, Noam. 2001. Derivation by phase. In: *Ken Hale: A life in language*, ed. Michael Kenstowicz. Cambridge, Mass.: MIT Press.
Chomsky, Noam and Howard Lasnik. 1995. The Theory of Principles and Parameters. In: Chomsky 1995. Cambridge, Mass.: MIT Press.
Cinque, Guglielmo. 1999. *Adverbs and Functional Heads*. Oxford UP, Oxford.
Cinque, Guglielmo. 2002. "Restructuring" and Functional Structure. ms., University of Venice.
Fanselow, Gisbert. 2001. Partial Movement. Ms University of Potsdam.
Golden, Marija. 2003. Clitic placement and clitic climbing in Slovenian. *Sprachtypologie und Unifersalienforschung* 56.3: 208-233.
Golden, Marija and Milena Sheppard. 2000. Slovene Pronominal Clitics. In: Beukema & den Dikken (eds.): *The Clitic Phenomena in European Languages*. John Benjamins, Amstrdam.
Golden, Marija and Milena Milojević-Sheppard. 2003. 2nd Position Clitic Climbing and Restructuring. Paper presented at FDSL 5, November 2003. Leipzig, Germany.
Hornstein, Norbert. 1999. Movement and Control. *Linguistic Inquiry* 30.1:69-96.
Hornstein, Norbert. 2001. Move! *A minimalist theory of Construal*. Oxford. Blackwell.
Marušič, Franc. In prep. A prosodic account of clitic placement. Ms Stony Brook University.
O'Connor, Rob. 2002. The placement of enclitics in Bosnian, Croatian and Serbian. Ms U of Manchester. [ROA 521-0502].
Van Riemsdijk, Henk. 2002. The unbearable lightness of GOing. *Journal of Comparative Germanic Linguistics* 5:143-196
Roberts, Taylor. 1997. The optimal second position in Pashto. Ms MIT. [ROA 174-0297].
Rudin, Catherine. 1988. On Multiple Questions and Multiple WH Fronting. *Natural Language and Linguistics Theory* 6:445-501
Uriagereka, Juan. 1999. Multiple Spell-Out. In: S. D. Epstein and N. Hornstein (eds): *Working Minimalism*. Cambridge, Mass. MIT Press. pp. 251-282
Wurmbrand, Susi. 1998. Deconstructing restructuring. In: Proceedings of the Troisime Colloque International 'Langues et Grammaire'. Recherches Linguistique de Vincennes.
Wurmbrand, Susanne. 2001. *Infinitives*. Mouton de Gruyter, Berlin.

Franc Marušič, New York
Tatjana Marvin, Ljubljana
Rok Žaucer, Ottawa

Depictive Secondary Predication with no PRO[*]

1. Introduction

In this paper we argue against the standard analysis of depictive secondary predicates – a right-adjoined small clause with a PRO in its subject position – as advocated in Stowell (1981), Koizumi (1994), Bowers (2001), Strigin & Demjjanov (2001), among others (cf. also Rapoport 1999, Baylin 2001, Ardid-Gumiel 2001 and Pylkkänen 2002). Instead we will propose that the host DP and the depictive form a constituent, Dep(ictive)P, which is merged directly in the syntactic position of the host DP. We will provide both empirical and theoretical support for our proposal. In Section 2, we review the standard analysis of depictives and show that its assumption that depictives are restricted to subject- and direct-object hosts is crosslinguistically invalid. We further argue that case-specification identity between the host and the depictive in fact presents a problem for any small-clause analysis with PRO. In Section 3, we present the crucial data and – elaborating on Marušič et al. (2003) – put forth a proposal that makes no use of PRO. In Section 4, we discuss some consequences of our proposal, drawing on several types of data (subject/direct-object vs. indirect-object asymmetry, depictives in embedded clauses, scopal differences with frequency adverbs, multiple depictive predicates), before finally wrapping up the paper with a summary of the results.

2. Depictives in Slovenian: problems for the standard analysis

2.1. Standard analysis and the subject-/direct-object restriction

The bracketed diagram in (1a) below gives the structure standardly proposed for direct object-oriented depictives, the diagram in (1b) gives the structure for subject-oriented depictives. In the former, the small clause is adjoined to V', while in the latter, the small clause is adjoined to VP, thereby avoiding a possible control of PRO by the object.

(1) a. [$_{VP}$ [$_{V'}$ [$_{V}$ *ate*] [$_{NP}$ *meat*]] [$_{SC}$ [$_{DP}$ PRO] [$_{AP}$ *raw*]]]

b. [$_{VP}$ [$_{VP}$ *left the room*] [$_{SC}$ [$_{DP}$ PRO] [$_{AP}$ *angry*]]]

Bowers' implementation of this general idea is given in (2) below, which represents a DO-oriented depictive. The depictive AP is placed inside a small clause, which Bowers calls PrP (Pr for predication), with PRO acting as the subject DP of this secondary PrP. It is usually assumed that the controller of PRO has to be a c-commanding element. This structure is thus built to capture the basic English facts: it allows both subject- and direct object-oriented depictives but cannot derive indirect object-oriented depictives since the indirect object either cannot c-command the PRO from inside a PP or else is embedded too deeply inside the VP. (For a more extensive review of the literature, see Marušič et al. 2003.)

(2) [$_{PrP}$ [$_{DP}$ John][$_{Pr'}$ [$_{Pr}$ Ø][$_{VP}$ [$_{DP}$ coffee][$_{V'}$ [$_{V}$ drink][$_{PrP}$ [$_{DP}$ PRO][$_{Pr'}$ [$_{Pr}$ Ø][$_{AP}$ cold]]]]]]

[*] We thank the audience at FDSL 5 for useful comments.

(2')

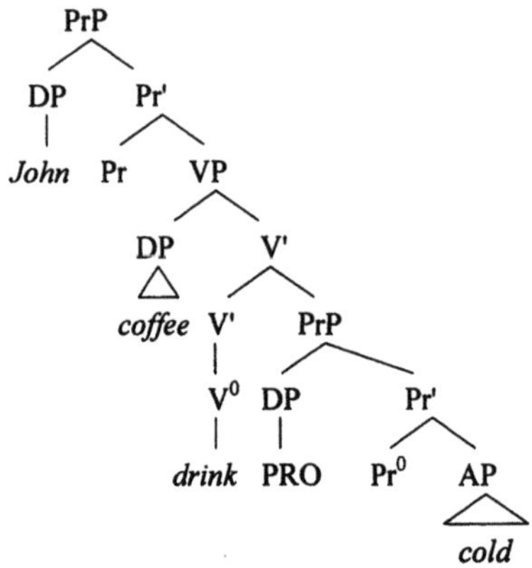

Although such structures nicely account for the basic data in English, they are empirically falsified by the data from several other languages, including Slovenian. In Slovenian, the distribution of depictives is much freer than in English; depictives can be hosted by nearly any kind of arguments or adjuncts, as discussed in Orešnik (1996) and Marušič et al. (2003). Therefore, any proposal that restricts depictive secondary predicates to subject and direct object hosts, such as the structure in (2), is inadequate and needs revision.

In (3) below we give examples of a depictive hosted by a prepositional object, (3a), a locative argument, (3b), and an indirect object, (3c). This is by no means an exhaustive list of the possible depictive-host combinations that escape the standard account (for some further possibilities, see Marušič et al. 2003). There seem to be rather few restrictions on the type of the host, some of which will be discussed below.

(3) a. *Včeraj smo na Vida$_i$ še čisto pijanega$_i$ naleteli na Prešercu*[1]
yesterday AUX onto V$_{ACC}$ still completely drunk$_{ACC}$ ran on Prešeren-square
'Yesterday we ran into Vid$_i$ at Prešeren square, and he$_i$ was still completely drunk$_i$'

b. *Peter je dal knjigo na mizico$_i$ že vso razmajano$_i$*
P$_{NOM}$ AUX gave book$_{ACC}$ on table$_{LOC}$ already all$_{LOC}$ wobbly$_{LOC}$
'Peter put the book on the little table$_i$, and it$_i$ was already completely wobbly$_i$'

c. *Peter je dal Meti$_i$ piškote že vsej polomljeni$_i$*
P$_{NOM}$ AUX gave Meta$_{DAT}$ biscuits$_{ACC}$ already all$_{DAT}$ broken$_{DAT}$
'Peter gave Meta$_i$, some biscuits all broken$_i$ (=back-sore$_i$)'

Similar oblique-hosted depictives are possible at least in Icelandic (Maling 2001), German (Maling 2001), Warlpiri (Schultze-Berndt & Himmelmann 2004), Venda (Pylkkänen 2002) and Russian (Richardson 2003: 460); a Russian example is given in (4a). In fact, Maling provides examples of prepositional argument-oriented depictives even for English, (4b-c).

[1] Note that the judgments of all examples hold under neutral intonation.

(4) a. *Ja dala emu$_i$ den'gi p'janomu$_i$* (Richardson 2003: 460)
I gave him$_{DAT}$ money drunk$_{DAT}$
'I gave him$_i$ money, and he$_i$ was drunk$_i$'

b. *The perverted orderly liked to look at female patients$_i$ nude$_i$* (Maling

c. *The brain surgeon had to operate on the patient$_i$ wide-awake$_i$* 2001: 424)

The absence of the restriction on depictives to subject and direct-object hosts is thus a cross-linguistically fairly widespread phenomenon and cannot be dismissed as a quirk of Slovenian. (Note that restrictions on depictive hosts have also been stated in terms of thematic roles, e.g. Rothstein 1985, but these are likewise empirically incorrect, cf. Rapoport 1999: 655, Marušič et al. 2003: 378, as well as in terms of verb lexical semantics/Vendlerian verb classes, e.g. Rapoport 1999, also empirically incorrect, cf. Marušič et al. 2003: 378-9.) Moreover, besides empirical inadequacy, the standard analysis of depictives also runs into some theoretical problems.

2.2. Phi- and case-specification identity, PRO, and the movement theory of control

The first theoretical problem lies in the fact that Slovenian depictive secondary adjectives obligatorily carry the same gender, number and case specification as their host DP, as in (3a-c) (also Russian (4a)). Since PRO is the subject of the small clause, the matching gender/number/case specification should be transmitted from the host to the depictive via this element. However, if PRO has null case, as argued in Chomsky (1995), case-specification transmission between the host and the depictive should not be allowed over PRO. PRO cannot carry/transmit the nominative, accusative, dative, etc., case from the DP to the depictive.[2]

Secondly, although depictives in English mostly cannot modify indirect objects, (5a) (but cf. (4b-c)) – thus giving some (language-specific) merit to the standard proposal – indirect objects in English otherwise *are* possible controllers, (5b), as pointed out by Koizumi (1994). This discrepancy remains unaccounted for under the standard analysis of depictives.[3]

---

[2] Baylin (2001), in an otherwise fairly standard analysis with a PRO as the subject of a small clause, states for Serbo-Croatian that the accusative on the direct object-oriented depictive is obtained by LF movement of the depictive adjective to the closest structural case-checking position (in this case Spec of *v*P), bypassing PRO, which produces the 'sameness' of case effects and limits them to structural case. Ignoring the details of this mechanism, we just point out that this is designed to work only for subject- and direct object-oriented depictives.

[3] In a recent alternative proposal, Pylkkänen (2002) derives the lack of depictive secondary predication on indirect objects from the distinction between high and low applicative arguments, claiming that depictives are allowed only on high-applicative hosts but not on low-applicative hosts due to semantic-type mismatch. Since English 'indirect objects' are always an instantiation of low applicative arguments, (i), it is expected that they cannot host depictives. On the other hand, 'indirect objects' in languages such as Albanian are said to be merged as high applicatives, and therefore they do allow depictives.

(i) **John baked Mary$_i$ a cake drunk$_i$.*

Such a proposal fails for Slovenian, which has both types of applicative arguments. Contrary to Pylkkänen's prediction, depictives are possible not only on high applicatives, (iia), but also on low applicatives, (iib).

(ii) a. *Jan je Petri odprl vrata že vsej majavi*
J$_{NOM}$ AUX Petra$_{DAT}$ opened door already all wobbly$_{DAT}$
'Jan opened the door to Petra$_i$, and she$_i$ was already all wobbly'

b. *Jan je Petri spekel torto še vsej utrujeni*
J$_{NOM}$ AUX Petra$_{DAT}$ baked cake still all tired$_{DAT}$
'Jan baked a cake for Petra$_i$, and she$_i$ was still all tired'

(5) a. *I$_i$ told her$_j$ the truth drunk$_{i/*j}$.*

b. *I wrote him$_i$ a message to PRO$_i$ show his friend.*

To account for these facts, Marušič et al. (2003) propose a movement analysis of secondary predication, where PRO is replaced by the host DP itself. In taking PRO to be just the trace of the host DP, their proposal comes close in spirit to Hornstein's (1999; 2001) movement analysis of control. For Hornstein, all cases of obligatory control involve movement of the subject of the lower clause to the appropriate θ-position in the matrix clause. To allow such an operation, he considers θ-roles to be simply features checked by the nominals moving into appropriate structural positions. (Some further modifications need to be made but they are not particularly relevant at this point and will thus be ignored.) The sample structures for subject and object control sentences are given in (6a) and (6b), respectively.

(6) a. *John* [$_{VP}$ *hopes* [$_{IP}$ ~~*John*~~ *to* [$_{VP}$ *win the race*]]]

b. *John* [$_{VP}$ *suggested to Mary* [$_{IP}$ ~~*Mary*~~ *to* [$_{VP}$ *wear bigger earrings*]]]

Although Hornstein (1999; 2001) discusses neither depictive small clauses nor secondary predication in general, these phenomena are clearly relevant for such a theory. If there is no place in syntactic theory for an independent control/PRO module, we should dispense with PRO altogether. And since depictive small clauses are typically analyzed as containing a PRO, a movement analysis of depictives is a natural extension of Hornstein's proposal. A similar proposal has been (independently) put forth in Ardid-Gumiel (2001).

3. Proposal

In Section 2, we established that depictives are not restricted to subject and direct-object hosts, and so the standard analysis has to be abandoned. In this section, we present a proposal which is based not on theory-internal motivation but rather on two crucial empirical observations.

First, depictives hosted by prepositional arguments are impossible in Slovenian if the depictive and its host DP are disjoined. As shown in (7a), a depictive can modify the DP inside the locative PP, with which it also exhibits case-specification identity, that is, they both carry the locative case. On the other hand, such modification is ruled out in (7b), where the depictive AP has been moved to the beginning of the clause. Note that the restriction does not come from a more general ban on fronting of depictive APs, since such fronting of the AP is fine when the host DP is in a non-prepositional case, (8).

(7) a. *Kosilo vedno jem* [$_{PP}$ *pri Špeli* [$_{AP}$ *vsej utrujeni od dela*]]
Lunch always eat at Špela$_{LOC}$ all tired$_{LOC}$ from work
'I always eat lunch at Špela's, and she is very tired from work'

b. * [$_{AP}$ *vsej utrujeni od dela*] *vedno jem kosilo* [$_{PP}$ *pri Špeli*]
all tired$_{LOC}$ from work always eat lunch at Špela$_{LOC}$

c. [$_{PP}$ *Pri Špeli* [$_{AP}$ *vsej utrujeni od dela*] *vedno jem kosilo.*
at Špela$_{LOC}$ all tired$_{LOC}$ from work always eat lunch

d. ? * [$_{PP}$ *Pri Špeli*] *vedno jem kosilo* [$_{AP}$ *vsej utrujeni od dela*]
at Špela$_{LOC}$ always eat lunch all tired$_{LOC}$ from work

(8) [*Vsemu utrujenemu od dela*] *sem pomagal Petru pri parkiranju*
all tired$_{DAT}$ from work AUX helped P$_{DAT}$ at parking
'I helped Peter with parking, and he was all tired from work.'

From the set of data in (7) and (8), we can conclude that the depictive and the DP form a constituent, while – crucially – the preposition and the DP on their own, i.e. without the depictive, do not.

The other crucial piece of data is given in (9) below. Since we concluded from the data in (7) that the DP and the depictive form a constituent, we have to establish how intimate this constituenthood is, i.e., how close a constituent the two elements make. The depictive in (9a) is *not* understood as a restriction on the quantifier of the host DP, while this is precisely the interpretation the postnominal adjective in (9b) receives. Another difference lies in that even if the DP and the depictive form some sort of a constituent, it can still be broken up by clitics – in this case the auxiliary clitic *so* – which is not the case for the postnominal adjective in (9b).

(9) a. [*Vse* [*punce*]] *so* <u>*pijane ko mamb*</u> *preganjale fante*
all girls$_{NOM}$ AUX drunk$_{NOM}$ as mambas chased guys
'All the girls were chasing guys, and they were dead drunk'

b. [*Vse* [*punce* <u>*pijane ko mambe*</u>]] *so preganjale fante*
all girls$_{NOM}$ drunk$_{NOM}$ as mambas AUX chased guys
'All the girls who were dead drunk were chasing guys'

In addition, while aspectual adverbials such as *še* 'still' or *že* 'already' are perfectly natural inside depictives, as shown in (10a) below, they are not allowed with postnominal adjectives, (10b). (For some further contrasts between depictives and postnominal adjectives, see Marušič et al. 2003)

(10) a. [*Vse* [*punce*]] *so še čist* <u>*pijane*</u> *osvajale fante*
all girls$_{NOM}$ AUX still completely drunk$_{NOM}$ conquer guys
'All the girls who were still completely drunk were hitting on guys.'

b. ?* [*Vse* [*punce še čist* <u>*pijane*</u>]] *so osvajale fante*
all girls$_{NOM}$ still completely drunk$_{NOM}$ AUX conquer guys
'All the girls who were still completely drunk were hitting on guys.'

Depictives therefore do not lie within the DP, yet they do form a constituent with it. Unlike in post nominal adjectives, the depictive is a small-clause-like constituent with the DP in its specifier and the AP in its complement, which we will call Dep(ictive)P. The several properties that postnominal adjectives and depictives nevertheless have in common arise from a similar underlying structure, namely the noun and the adjective forming a constituent in both cases.

DepP is merged in the position where the host of the depictive would otherwise be merged. If the DP is non-prepositionally case marked, it can move up and leave the predicate behind, as in (3c) above. However, if the host DP is a prepositionally case marked argument/adjunct, such raising is blocked. The DP would have to strand the preposition, and since preposition-stranding is not allowed in Slovenian, the resulting structure is ruled out, as in (7b)/(7d). The pre-movement structure of (7) is given in (11).

(11) [[$_{DP}$ *Vid*]$_i$ *je* [$_{VP}$ t_i [$_{V'}$ *jedel* [$_{VP}$[$_{DP}$ *kosilo*] [$_{V'}$ *e* [$_{PP}$ *pri* [$_{DepP}$[$_{DP}$ *Špeli*] [$_{AP}$ *vsej utrujeni*]]]]]]]]
Vid AUX eat lunch at Špela$_{DAT}$ all tired$_{DAT}$

(11')

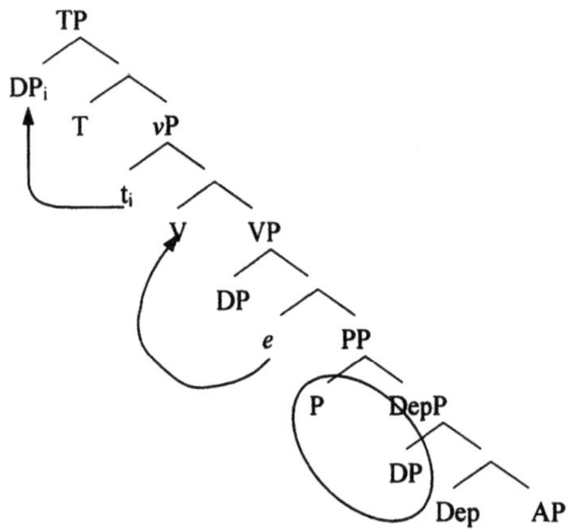

Recall from above that the depictive and its host DP obligatorily match in their number/gender/case specification. Case assignment/checking/valuing on the host DP is implemented with standard procedures, the exact nature of which depends on what structural position the host DP sits in. As for the agreeing case on the depictive, we assume that it is assigned/checked/valued via phi- and case concord/transmission between the host DP and the depictive (cf. Starke 1995: 257, Franks 1995: 225, Richardson 2003: 464-5).

The proposal we have made accounts for all of the empirical facts we mentioned, that is, for depictives not being restricted to a particular type of syntactic argument, for the impossibility of stranding a prepositional host and its depictive, and for the agreement between the depictive and its host. From a theoretical point of view, a first obvious advantage of our proposal is its avoidance of right adjunction, and consequently compliance with the LCA – Antisymmetry (Kayne 1994). The other theoretical advantage is the avoidance of PRO, for which one would have to postulate a number of available cases in order for it to carry the case specification from the host to the depictive. Getting rid of PRO in these structures allows us to preserve the standard view according to which PRO has null case. In addition, it offers a way of accounting for depictive secondary predication if one wants to adopt Hornstein's (1999, 2001) idea of discarding PRO from linguistic theory altogether.

3.1. A recent related proposal

Ardid-Gumiel (2001) makes a similar proposal in that she takes the depictive to form a small clause with the host DP in its subject position. However, her small clause still attaches to the same kind of adjoined positions small clauses attach to in the standard analysis (cf. Section 1), and the host DP is then moved from inside the small clause into the main clause with sidewards movement. Her model thus avoids generating oblique-hosted depictives, but as we have seen, such an outcome is empirically incorrect, making her proposal flawed in the same way as the standard analysis. In the current proposal, on the other hand, DepP is merged directly in the argument position of the host DP, and it can also move to any other position the DP moves to.

4. Consequences
4.1. Subject/direct-object vs. indirect-object asymmetry

Given the nature of our account, the fact that some languages impose restrictions on depictive secondary predication whereby depictives are admissible on subjects and direct objects while they are ungrammatical on indirect objects will have to be treated as resulting from something else rather than from straightforward structural issues, since we have proposed that all depictives share the same structure.

One formal way of going about accounting for crosslinguistic variation in the restrictions on depictives is by reducing the latter to language-particular availability / unavailability of merging the DepP in the specifier position of VP and TP. That is, DepP in English has to be merged in the lowest complement position of the verb, from where the DP moves up. The restriction thus boils down to the unavailability of a licit movement operation from the small clause to the DP position of the indirect object. In Slovenian, on the other hand, DepP can be merged in any argument position, such as Spec of VP, Spec of TP, or complement of PP. Such a solution is clearly stipulative and would at least need to be tied in with other aspects of individual languages. Moreover, even English has been shown to sporadically allow depictives on prepositional arguments (cf. (4b-c) above), and conversely, sometimes even a direct object may not be able to host a depictive (cf. Maling 2001: 421-2, Rapoport 1999: 654-5). At present, however, we do not have a better explanation and thus offer this merely as a hunch for future research. The derivation for an ungrammatical English sentence and its grammatical literal counterpart in Slovenian is thus sketched in (12) (the Slovenian sentence is that from (3b) above).

(12) a. English

[$_{TP}$*Peter*$_i$ [$_{vP}$ t_i [$_{v'}$ *put*$_k$ [$_{VP}$ *the book* [$_{V'}$ e_k [$_{VP}$[$_{PP}$ *on* [$_{DPj}$ *the table*]][$_{V'}$ e_k [$_{DepP}$ t_j [$_{AP}$ *wobbly*]]]]]]]]]

*

b. Slovenian

[$_{TP}$ *Peter*$_i$ [$_{T}$ *je* [$_{vP}$ t_i [$_{v'}$ *dal*$_k$ [$_{VP}$ *knjigo* [$_{V'}$ e_k [$_{PP}$ *na* [$_{DepP}$[$_{DP}$ *mizo*][$_{AP}$ *vso razmajano*]]]]]]]

The only restriction realized in Slovenian, i.e. the unavailability of disjoined depictives hosted by DPs in prepositional cases (cf. (7) above), falls out naturally from this proposal. The host DP and the preposition cannot move up on their own, since the preposition and the DP do not form a constituent (cf. (7b)). On the other hand, the same structure does allow moving out the whole DepP, (cf. (7c)).[4]

4.2. Depictives in embedded clauses

Following our proposal, depictives will always be low in the tree – unless they move up together with the host DP – and inside the clause they are associated with. Given that we have proposed to analyze depictives without recourse to right adjunction (Kayne 1994), it follows from our proposal that when a depictive comes after an embedded clause it will be interpreted as occurring at the same time as the event of the embedded clause. This prediction is borne out, as demonstrated in (13). When a depictive follows an embedded clause, it can only modify the argument of the embedded clause, (13a), but not an argument of the matrix clause, (13b). The depictive can refer to a matrix-clause argument's predicate only when it actually sits inside the matrix clause, (13c).

---

[4] In a recent typological study, Schultze-Berndt & Himmelmann (2004) note that the ability of participants in various thematic roles and syntactic functions to act as depictive hosts remains a matter of further investigation. They tentatively suggest, however, that the potential for functioning as a host may follow the accessibility hierarchy for grammatical relations, as has been suggested by Nichols (1978).

(13) a. *Meta$_i$ mi je razlagala* [*koga* (pro$_i$) *bo volila vsa pametna$_i$*]
M$_{NOM}$ me AUX explain whom AUX vote all clever$_{F,NOM}$
'Meta was telling me who she, all smart, would vote for.'

b. **Meta$_i$ mi je razlagala* [*kdo jo bo občudoval*] *vsa pametna$_i$*
M$_{NOM}$ me AUX explain who her$_{ACC}$ AUX admire all clever$_{F,NOM}$
'Meta, all clever, was telling me who would admire her.'

c. *Meta$_i$ mi je vsa pametna$_i$ razlagala* [*kdo jo bo občudoval*]
M$_{NOM}$ me AUX all clever$_{F,NOM}$ explained who her$_{ACC}$ AUX admire
'Meta, all clever, was explaining to me who will admire her.'

The restriction can be observed in the other direction as well. When the depictive agrees with an argument of the matrix clause that is not present in the embedded clause, it cannot follow the embedded clause, as shown in (14a). Otherwise, there is no such restriction and the agreement pattern is possible, as (14b) shows, when the depictive actually sits in the matrix clause.

(14) a. **Meta$_i$ je Vidu$_j$ razlagala* [*koga* (pro$_i$) *bo volila*] *vsemu pijanemu$_j$*
M$_{NOM}$ AUX V$_{DAT}$ explained whom AUX vote all drunk$_{M,DAT}$
'Meta was explaining to Vid, who was all drunk, who she will vote for.'

b. *Meta$_i$ je Vidu$_j$ vsemu pijanemu$_j$ razlagala,* [*koga* (pro$_i$) *bo volila*]
M$_{NOM}$ AUX V$_{DAT}$ all drunk$_{M,DAT}$ explained whom AUX vote
'Meta was explaining to Vid, who was all drunk, who she will vote for.'

Adopting a right-adjunction analysis, we make the incorrect prediction that a reading should be available where the depictive is associated with the matrix predicate. Even worse, a right adjunction analysis can in fact only derive sentences where the depictive referring to the matrix event is located at the right edge of the clause, but examples like (14b) are perfectly fine.

Contrary to what has just been shown for Slovenian, English does allow sentence-final depictives to modify an argument of the matrix clause and to refer to the time of the matrix-clause event, (15). Following our proposal, this is a result of the English restriction on the position of the merging of the DepP. As suggested above, the English depictive can only merge in the lowest complement position of the verb, from where the argument moves on.[5] In the case of clausal complementation, such a position should still be available, and since it will be lower than the position of the clausal complement, it will also be to the right of the embedded clause, as shown in (16).

(15) *Peter$_i$ explained to Mary* [*where Tom$_k$ lives*] *drunk$_{i/k}$*.

[5] The fact that the other order of the clausal complement and the matrix clause associated depictive is also available, as shown in (i), might be related to a more general version of the heavy NP shift – maybe something like a heavy phrase shift.

(i) *Hank$_i$ told Greg drunk$_i$ how he spent his night in the capital.*

(16)

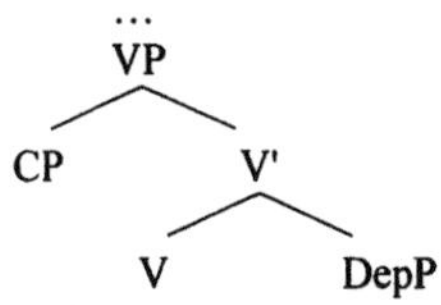

Data from Slovenian embedded finite clauses were shown to clearly favour the analysis proposed here over a right-adjunction analysis. A similar argument using non-finite clausal complementation is given in Marušič et al. (2003).

4.3. Frequency adverbs & scope differences

Frequency adverbs (event quantifiers) can have different scope with respect to the secondary predication. The sentences in (17) and (18) both contain two events, the event of *Švrk*'s going to *Kud*, expressed by the matrix predicate, and the event of *Švrk*'s being drunk, expressed by the subject-oriented depictive predicate. In addition, (17) and (18) both contain the frequency adverb *vedno* 'always'. Nevertheless, the interpretations that (17) and (18) receive are not the same. Casting the scopal differences in neo-Davidsonian representations, (19) captures the interpretation of (17) and (20) captures the interpretation of (18).

(17) *Švrk je pijan vedno šel v Kud.*
Švrk$_{NOM}$ AUX drunk$_{NOM}$ always go to Kud
'Whenever he was drunk, Švrk (always) went to Kud.'

(18) *Švrk je vedno šel v Kud pijan / pijan v Kud.*
Švrk$_{NOM}$ AUX always go to Kud drunk$_{NOM}$ / drunk$_{NOM}$ to Kud
'Whenever Švrk went to Bunker, he was (always) Kud.'

(19) [∀e: drunk(e) & Experiencer(e,š) [∃e': Part-of(e,e') & going(e') & Agent(e',š) & Goal(e',k)]]

(20) [∀e: going(e) & Agent(e,š) & Goal(e,k) [∃e': Part-of(e',e) & drunk(e') & Agent(e',š)]]

From a syntactic perspective, we propose the following scenario. In (17), the depictive has moved to Spec of TP together with the host, thereby escaping the scope of the adverb *always*, which sits below TP (Cinque 1999). (We are assuming a phonologically-driven placement for the second-position clitic.) On the other hand, the sentence in (18) is a case where the depictive has stayed in the original position of the subject, i.e. inside the VP. Consequently, it is interpreted in the scope of the event quantifier *always*, as indicated by (20).

Although the resulting structure for the sentence in (17), given in (21), might not be directly translatable to the corresponding semantic interpretation, we consider the fact that our proposal derives two distinct syntactic structures a welcome result. A right adjunction analysis will predict the sentence in (18) to be ambiguous, since the depictive could be merged either higher or lower than the aspectual adverb, thus falling either inside or outside its scope.

(21)

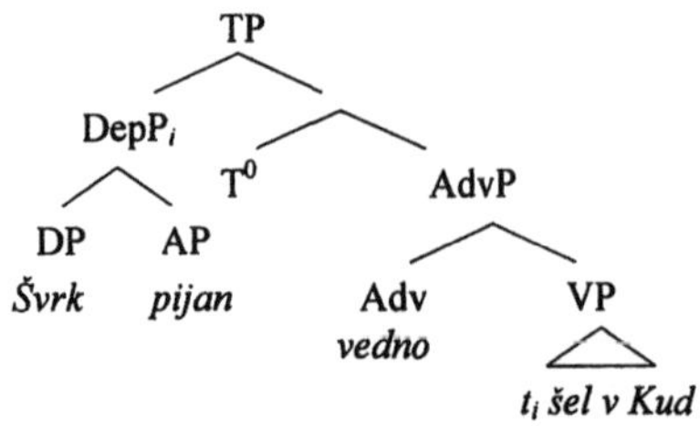

Our proposal, on the other hand, treats (17) and (18) as crucially different. Their different syntactic structures duly reflect the fact that the interpretations of the adverb *always* in the two sentences are not, in fact, simply ambiguous but are rather unambiguously determined as one or the other of the two scope relations, that is, as (19) and (20), respectively. This suggests that the different clausal positions of the two depictives are truly syntactic in nature and cannot be reduced to some scrambling process at PF. If this were the case, (17) and (18) should both be scopally ambiguous, contrary to fact. Note, finally, that the effects we discussed on the example of *always* carry over to other event quantifiers, such as *never*, *frequently*, etc.

Note that in an adjunction analysis, (17) and (18) may yield to an explanation with equal ease – granted that one is not overly restrictive regarding the amount of functional structure in the small clause. The adverb *always* could be seen as coming from the small clause in (17) and from the matrix clause in (18). Given that such an explanation is available also within our account, we give preference to our proposal simply because we have shown that it is superior on independent grounds (cf. Sections 2 and 3).[6]

4.4. Multiple Depictive Predicates

As is widely recognized, a single DP is not limited to hosting just one depictive but can in fact host multiple (stacked) depictives. A Slovenian example is given in (23) (for English see Bowers 2001: 326). Presumably, this has also been a factor leading towards an adjunction

[6] Another thing that needs clarification at this point regards Ardid-Gumiel's (2001) narrower understanding of what a depictive is. For her, only the APs in Spanish counterparts of sentences such as (i), which are said to exhibit a "no restriction reading", qualify as depictives, while she excludes sentences such as (ii) and (iii) as containing "concealed time interval constituents". (ii) and (iii) are said to exhibit a "head-clause restriction reading" and an "adjunct restriction reading", respectively.

(i)	*Micka*	*je*	*spočita*	*brala*	*časopis*	→	"no restriction reading"
	Micka	AUX	rested	read	newspaper		∃ [Micka read the newspaper rested]
(ii)	*Micka*	*je*	*brala*	*časopis*	*spočita*	→	"head-clause restriction reading"
	Micka	AUX	read	newspaper	rested		∃ {Micka read the newspaper} [Micka was rested]
(iii)	*Spočita*	*je*	*Micka*	*brala*	*časopis*	→	"adjunct restriction reading"
	Rested	AUX	Micka	read	newspaper		∃ {Micka was rested} [Micka read the newspaper]

We do not want to dispute the different interpretations of the depictive secondary predicate in (i-iii). However, against the background of the fact that the depictive predicate is temporally dependent on the matrix predicate under a 'part-of' relation (Rothstein 2000), we submit that the different readings simply reflect different scope relations between the two predications and an event quantifier, with the varying scopal relations resulting from syntactic movement. Furthermore, the obligatory agreement between the depictive and its host clearly suggests that we are not dealing with reduced temporal, conditional, etc., clauses but rather with true depictives, but that their interpretation can vary according to its position relative to the position of the main predicate.

analysis. However, adjunction is not the only way of dealing with depictive stacking. On our account, the sentence from (23) would receive the representation in (24), where every DepP can have another DepP in its specifier.

(23) *Že rahlo opitemu$_i$ smo Petru$_i$ obvezovali rane napol golemu$_i$*
already slightly drunk$_{DAT}$ AUX P$_{DAT}$ bandage wounds half naked$_{DAT}$
'We bandaged Peter's wounds when he was half naked and already slightly drunk.'

(24)

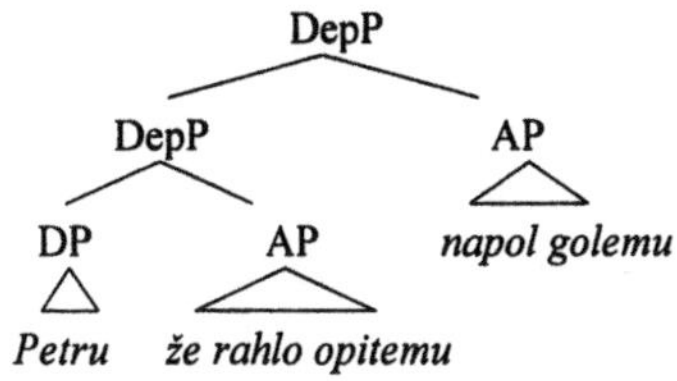

Regarding the issue of stacking, then, our proposal fares no worse than the standard small-clause adjunction analysis. Finally, note that multiple depictives in a clause are of course possible also when each is hosted by a distinct argument (see Marušič et al. 2003: 389 for an example). Such a case likewise does not represent a problem for either analysis. Given that our DepP is merged into the structure in the position where its host would be merged if it appeared alone, the only restriction on the appearance of depictives is the restriction on the arguments of the verb themselves. Therefore, on our account depictives on distinct hosts each come from a separate DepP, while on the standard account they each come from a separate small clause.

5. Conclusion

We argued that the standard analysis of depictive secondary predicates—an adjoined small clause with a PRO subject—is too restrictive in that it rules out oblique-hosts for depictives, a pattern that is crosslinguistically widely attested. In addition, we argued that the analysis is problematic also on theoretical grounds. Expanding on Marušič et al. (2003), we proposed that the host DP and the depictive form a constituent, DepP, which is merged in the position where the DP would otherwise be merged. The host DP can move out of DepP, stranding the depictive. This allowed us to nicely account for an intricate pattern of data from Slovenian, where prepositionally case-marked depictive hosts behave differently from other oblique-object depictive hosts. By accounting for depictive secondary predicates without the use of PRO, we were able to avoid problems that otherwise arise with regard to the transmission of case from the host to the depictive, while the case-specification identity between the host and the depictive can be accounted for by the independently motivated mechanism of concord / case transmission. Finally, we demonstrated how depictive secondary predication can be implemented if one wants to adopt a movement theory of control.

References

Ardid-Gumiel, Ana (2001): The syntax of Depictives, Subjects, Modes of Judgements and I-L/S-L Properties. In: Nina Zhang (ed.): *ZAS Papers in Linguistics* 26. Available, 20/11/03, [http://www.zas.gwz-berlin.de/papers/zaspil/articles/ZASPIL26Ard.pdf]

Baylin, John (2001): The Syntax of Slavic Predicate Case. *ZAS Papers in Linguistics* 22: 1-23.

Bowers, John (2001): Predication. In: M. Baltin & C. Collins (eds): *The Handbook of Contemporary Syntactic Theory*. Cambridge, MA: Blackwell.

Chomsky, Noam (1995): *The Minimalist Program*. Cambridge, Mass.: MIT Press.

Cinque, Guglielmo (1999): *Adverbs and Functional Heads*. Oxford: Oxford University Press.
Hornstein, Norbert (1999): Movement and Control. *Linguistic Inquiry* 30 (1): 69-96.
Hornstein, Norbert (2001): *Move! A minimalist theory of Construal*. Oxford: Blackwell.
Kayne, Richard (1994): *The antisymmetry of Syntax*. Cambridge, Mass: MIT Press.
Koizumi, Masatoshi (1994): Secondary Predicates. *Journal of East Asian Linguistics* 3: 25-79.
Maling, Joan (2001): Dative: the heterogeneity of the mapping among morphological case, grammatical functions, and thematic roles. *Lingua* 111 (4-7): 419-464.
Marušič, Franc, Tatjana Marvin & Rok Žaucer (2003): Secondary Predication in Slovenian. In: W. Browne *et al.* (eds): *FASL 11 (The Amherst Meeting, 2002)*. Ann Arbor: Michigan Slavic Publications.
Nichols, Joanna (1978): Secondary predicates. In: *BLS* 4. Berkeley, CA: Berkeley Linguistics Society, 114-127.
Orešnik, Janez (1996): Nauk novejše slovenistike o povedkovem prilastku [Depictive Secondary Predication in Recent Slovenian Linguistics]. *SAZU Razprave II. razreda - Dissertationes Classis II* XV: 255-267.
Pylkkänen, Liina (2002): *Introducing Arguments*. PhD dissertation, MIT.
Rapoport, Tuva R. (1999): Structure, aspect, and the predicate. *Language* 75/4: 653-677.
Richardson, Kylie (2003): Developing the Case for Meaningful Case: The Link Between Event Structure and Case in Russian. In: W. Browne *et al.* (eds): *FASL 11 (The Amherst Meeting, 2002)*. Ann Arbor: Michigan Slavic Publications.
Rothstein, Susan D. (1985): *The Syntactic Forms of Predication*. Bloomington, Ind.: Indiana University Linguistics Club.
Rothstein, Susan D. (2000): Secondary predication and aspectual structure. *ZAS Papers in Linguistics* 17: 241-264.
Schultze-Berndt, Eva & Nikolaus P. Himmelmann (2004): Depictive Secondary Predicates in Cross-Linguistic Perspective. *Linguistic Typology* 8 (1): 59-131.
Sigurðsson, Halldór (1991): Icelandic case-marked PRO and the licensing of lexical arguments. *Natural Language & Linguistic Theory* 9 (2): 327-363.
Starke, Michal (1995): On the format for small clauses. In: A. Cardinaletti & M. T. Guasti (eds): *Syntax and Semantics 28: Small clauses*. San Diego: Academic Press.
Stowell, Tim (1983): *Origins of Phrase Structure*. PhD dissertation, MIT.
Strigin, Anatoli. & Assinja Demjjanow (2001): Secondary Predication in Russian. *ZAS Papers in Linguistics* 25: 1-79.

Krzysztof Migdalski, Tilburg

The Syntax of the *l*-participle in Bulgarian and Serbo-Croatian[1]

1. Introduction

The paper presents an analysis of the syntax of perfect tenses involving the so-called *l*-participle in two South Slavic languages, Bulgarian and Serbo-Croatian. In both of the languages the *l*-participle always occurs with the auxiliary 'to be', and it always shows agreement with the subject, irrespectively of the fact whether the participle is a transitive or an unaccusative verb. In this way, the compound tenses in South Slavic stand in contrast with the related constructions in Germanic or Romance languages, in which the participle is found with the auxiliary 'to be' and shows agreement with the subject only with unaccusative verbs. In South Slavic the present tense auxiliaries are clitics, with distinct morphophonological requirements in each of the languages. The past tense auxiliaries are non-clitic and pattern like other lexical verbs. In both Bulgarian and Serbo-Croatian the participle may be fronted across the clitic and non-clitic auxiliaries to the clause initial position.

In this paper I will explore the raising of the *l*-participle across the auxiliary in these two languages. I will argue that the participle may move to Spec, IP to check the φ-features in I, and will show that the properties of the movement are contingent on the intrinsic properties of the clitics as well as the selection of the verb 'to be' as the auxiliary.

The paper is organized as follows. First I will briefly discuss the diachrony of the perfect tenses in Slavic, with some emphasis on the semantics of the *l*-participle. Subsequently, I will outline the morphophonological requirements of the auxiliary clitics. Finally, I will compare participle fronting in Bulgarian and Serbo-Croatian, and I will claim that it involves remnant movement of the participle to the subject position.

2. The diachrony of perfect tenses in Slavic and the nature of the *l*-participle

The *l*-participle is a verbal form found in all Slavic languages. According to Damborský (1967), it derives from a group of (Proto)-Indo-European verbal adjectives ending in **-lo*, which signified a likelihood to perform a certain action. In Slavic, Tocharian, and Armenian the adjectives were at some point reanalysed as preterite forms in compound tenses. However, the adjectival forms remained, too. As a result, Slavic languages currently distinguish between *l*-preterite participles and *l*-adjectives (cf. Damborský 1967 for distinguishing criteria). The *l*-preterite forms found in perfect tenses are specified for number and gender, but they are not marked for case. They are not free forms, as they are never found independently. They may occur only in compound tenses, as well as irrealis and conditional constructions.

Given that the perfect tenses with the *l*-participle are largely a Slavic innovation, it is to be expected that their behavior differs from related constructions in Germanic and Romance languages. According to Kowalska (1976), the *l*-participle has always been used in relative tenses. In Proto-Slavic and Old Church Slavonic it was found in the perfect and pluperfect tenses. The perfect tenses co-existed with the simple past tenses, the aorist and the imperfectum. The perfect tense was used rather rarely, and mainly in embedded clauses. Dostál's (1954) analysis of an Old Church Slavonic corpus includes 10,000 uses of the aorist, 2300 of the imperfectum, and approximately 600 of perfect tenses. This means that the perfect tense constituted approximately only 5% of the tense constructions found in the corpus.

As it is well-known, virtually all the verbal forms in Slavic languages are specified for aspect. Furthermore, the old simple past tenses, the aorist and the imperfectum, also rendered aspectual meanings, which usually coincided with those marked by aspectual morphemes. As

---

[1] I am grateful to Hans Broekhuis for extensive discussions of the material presented in the paper. Part of the analysis appears as our joint paper, and is referred to as Broekhuis & Migdalski (2003). I would also like to thank the FDSL-5 participants for comments. The usual disclaimer applies.

a result, verbs in the Old Slavic were frequently doubly-specified for aspect. It is little wonder, then, that due to robust marking of aspectual distinctions, most Slavic languages eventually lost the aorist and the imperfectum. In those languages the present perfect tense took over the temporal meanings expressed by the aorist and was used more often. Due to the increase in usage, the forms of the auxiliary verb 'to be' were simplified, and in many languages they were reduced to clitics, affixes, or they even disappeared completely in East Slavic. The aorist and the imperfectum are still found in Bulgarian, to a much lesser extent in Macedonian, and in some literary variants of Serbo-Croatian. Notably, in these languages the auxiliary 'to be' is still largely homophonous with the copula 'to be'.
Semantics-wise, Whaley (2000: 112) claims that the *l*-participle was used to indicate the result of a (completed) event. It focused on a past, future or present state that results from a previous action. Kowalska (1976: 20) remarks that the *l*-participle has always conveyed the meaning of a 'distance' from the speaker's perspective. The distance could be related to the chronology of events in the case of future or past constructions, or to probability or possibility in the case of modal/conditional constructions. Lunt (1952: 91) points out that the meaning of an event which is 'distanced' in time and reality can be very well traced in the renarrated mood constructions in Bulgarian and Macedonian. The forms are used when the speaker claims that s/he did not witness an event and therefore is not responsible for the accuracy of the statement. They are formed with an *l*-participle form of 'to be' and the *l*-participle form of the main verb.

(1)	Az	sŭm	bil	četjal	knigata.	(Bg)
	I	be$_{1SG.PRES}$	be $_{PART.MASC.SG.}$	read $_{PART.MASC.SG.}$	book-the $_{FEM.SG.}$	

'I am said to have been reading the book.'

Note that in most of the contemporary Slavic languages the *l*-participle is primarily associated with past tense meanings. However, since it is non-finite and since it occurs in a number of different temporal contexts, it cannot be specified for Tense.

3. Properties of clitics in Bulgarian and Serbo-Croatian

The literature on clitics in South Slavic is rather extensive; therefore I will only recapitulate some basic facts in this section. In all South Slavic languages the clitics must cluster and occur in specific sentence positions. In Serbo-Croatian the clitics must always stay in the second position. As Tomić (1996) shows, the first constituent that lends support to the clitics may be the first immediate constituent of the clause (as in 2a), the first phrase of the first immediate clausal constituent (as in 2b), or the first phonological word (as in 2c).

(2)	a.	Veoma	lepu	haljinu	si	mi	kupio.
		very	beautiful$_{ACC}$	dress$_{ACC}$	be$_{2SG.AUX.CL}$	me$_{DAT.CL}$	buy$_{PART.M.SG.}$
	b.	Veoma	lepu	si	mi	haljinu	kupio.
		very	beautiful$_{ACC}$	be$_{2SG.AUX.CL}$	me$_{DAT.CL}$	dress$_{ACC}$	buy$_{PART.M.SG.}$
	c.	Veoma	si	mi	lepu	haljinu	kupio
		very	be$_{2SG.AUX.CL}$	me$_{DAT.CL}$	beautiful$_{ACC}$	dress$_{ACC}$	buy$_{PART.M.SG.}$

'You've bought me a very beautiful dress.'

According to Caink (1999b) and (Franks 1998), in syntactic terms it means that the clitics occupy the highest available head in the extended projection of the verb.
In Bulgarian, the clitics do not have to appear in the second position. However, they are syntactically preverbal (that is, syntactically they are proclitic), but phonologically they are enclitic. In other words, they must appear before the verb if it is at all possible. This means

that they must occur in front of the verb as long as there is another constituent preceding them, so that they are also able to satisfy their enclitic requirements. They may appear after the verb only when the verb is in the clause initial position. Consider the data in (3), taken from Franks & King (2000: 63); the clitics are italicized.

(3) a.

Vera	*mi*	*go*	dade	včera
Vera	me_{DAT}	it_{DAT}	$gave_{3SG}$	yesterday

'Vera gave it to me yesterday.'

b.

Včera	*mi*	*go*	dade	Vera
yesterday	me_{DAT}	it_{DAT}	$gave_{3SG}$	Vera

c.

Včera	Vera	*mi*	*go*	dade
yesterday	Vera	me_{DAT}	it_{DAT}	$gave_{3SG}$

d.

*Vera	*mi*	*go*	včera	dade
Vera	me_{DAT}	it_{DAT}	yesterday	$gave_{3SG}$

e.

**Mi*	*go*	dade	Vera	včera
me_{DAT}	it_{DAT}	$gave_{3SG}$	Vera	yesterday

f.

*Vera	dade	*mi*	*go*	včera
Vera	$gave_{3SG}$	me_{DAT}	it_{DAT}	yesterday

In (3a, b, and c) the clitics precede the finite verb and are preceded by one or more constituents. The string in (3d) is unacceptable, because the clitics are not adjacent to the verb. The example in (3e) is excluded, because the clitic cluster is sentence initial, which is a violation of the phonological requirements. In (3f) the clitics follow the verb, rather than precede it, and as a result the output is ungrammatical.

4. Participle raising in Bulgarian and Serbo-Croatian

Let us move on to the main topic of the paper, which concerns the widely-discussed cases of participle fronting in Bulgarian and Serbo-Croatian. I will first concentrate on Bulgarian, and will point out the way it differs from Serbo-Croatian in sections 4.2 and 6. It will become evident that many of the contrasts are due to the intrinsic properties of the auxiliary clitics in each of the two languages. Next, I will present my analysis of the movement operation, which will be followed by a critique of the previous syntactic accounts.

4.1. Participle raising in Bulgarian

Consider the data in (4) and (5), taken from Lambova (2003).

(4) a.

Decata	sa	gledali	filma
kids-the	$be_{3PL.PRES}$	$watch_{PART.PL.}$	movie-the

b.

Gledali	sa	filma
$watch_{PART.PL.}$	$be_{3PL.PRES}$	movie-the

c.

*Sa	gledali	filma
$be_{3PL.PRES}$	$watch_{PART.PL.}$	movie-the

' (The kids) have watched/WATCHED the movie'

(5) a. Decata bjaxa gledali filma
kids-the be$_{3PL.PAST}$ watch$_{PART.PL.}$ movie-the

b. Gledali bjaxa filma
watch$_{PART.PL.}$ be$_{3PL.PAST}$ movie-the

c. Bjaxa gledali filma
be$_{3PL.PAST}$ watch$_{PART.PL.}$ movie-the
'(The kids) had WATCHED the movie'

Notice that the participle may be preposed across both the present and past tense auxiliaries to the left-most position in the clause. Observe that example (4c) is ungrammatical, because the clitic auxiliary ends up being located in the sentence-initial position. As Lambova (2002, 2003) shows, the participle-auxiliary orderings in Bulgarian are of two kinds. They differ in terms of the movement trigger and the semantic and prosodic results of the operation. As the accompanying translations indicate, the displacement of the participle across the past tense non-clitic auxiliary gives rise to a focused or 'non-neutral' interpretation of the predicate. The fronting of the participle across a clitic auxiliary gives ambiguous results, and the moved element may have a neutral or non-neutral interpretation.
Remarkably, the fronting is also possible in non-root contexts, as the examples below indicate.[2]

(6) a. Decata kazvat, če sa / bjaxa gledali filma
kids-the say that be$_{3PL.PRES}$ / be$_{3PL.PAST}$ watch$_{PART.PL.}$ movie-the
'The kids say that they have/had seen the movie'

b. Decata kazvat, če gledali sa / bjaxa filma
kids-the say that watch$_{PART.PL.}$ be$_{3PL.PRES}$ / be$_{3PL.PAST}$ movie-the
'The kids say that they have/had SEEN the movie'

In embedded clauses, neither the subject nor the participle need to be fronted in order to lend support to the clitic auxiliary, as it is already provided by the complementizer *če*. In fact, as can be seen in the translation of (6b), the movement of the participle always gives rise to a non-neutral reading of the participle. Therefore, a generalization that can be drawn from the data is that the participle fronting is driven by the morpho-phonological requirements of the clitic auxiliaries. When the morpho-phonological requirements of the clitics are satisfied, the movement may take place only for focus reasons.
Let us look closely at a few more properties of the movement. First of all, observe that at first sight it might seem that head movement is at work here, as it is only the participle that can be preposed, and the object must be stranded. As I will argue in section 5, the conclusion cannot be correct.

(7) a. Gledali e / beše filma
watch$_{PART.MASC.SG}$ be$_{3SG.PRES}$ / be$_{3PL.PAST}$ movie-the

b. *Gledali filma e / beše
watch$_{PART.MASC.SG}$ movie-the be$_{3SG.PRES}$ / be$_{3PL.PAST}$
'They have/had watched the movie'

[2] It must be pointed out that not all native speakers accept the participle-auxiliary orders in embedded clauses. It is certain that speaker variation is involved here.

Furthermore, observe that the fronted participle must be rigidly adjacent to the auxiliary, and the only elements that can intervene between the two constituents are clitics, as in (9).

(8) Pročel *(toj/ne/pravilno/kŭde) e / beše knigata (Caink 1999a)
read$_{\text{PART.MASC.SG}}$ he/NEG/correctly/where be$_{\text{3SG.PRES.}}$ / be$_{\text{3SG.PAST}}$ book-the

(9) Dal li mu go e?
give$_{\text{PART.MASC.SG}}$ Q him$_{\text{CL.DAT.}}$ him$_{\text{CL.ACC.}}$ be$_{\text{3SG.PRES}}$
'Has he given it to him?'

I will asssume that is means that the preposed participle lands in the specifier of the projection headed by the auxiliary.
As it has already been pointed out in the literature (c.f., for example, Wilder & Ćavar 1994: 19-20 for Serbo-Croatian and Embick & Izvorski 1995: 111 for Bulgarian), a striking property of the sentences with preposed participles is the fact that they never contain an overt subject in its canonical position. The subject may neither precede nor follow the fronted participle.

(10) a. *Pročel Ivan e / beše knigata (Bg)
read$_{\text{PART.MASC.SG}}$ Ivan be$_{\text{3SG.PRES}}$ / be$_{\text{3PL.PAST}}$ book-the

b. *Ivan pročel e / beše knigata
Ivan read$_{\text{PART.MASC.SG}}$ be$_{\text{3SG.PRES}}$ / be$_{\text{3PL.PAST}}$ book-the
'Ivan has/had read the book'

In fact, it even seems that the moved participle must be normally the left-most constituent in main clauses. The only elements that may ever precede it in main clauses are topics. This is possible when the fronted participle is focused, as Lambova (2003) reports.

(11) Filma gledali bjaxa decata
movie-the$_{\text{TOPIC}}$ watch$_{\text{PART.MASC.SG.FOCUS}}$ be$_{\text{3PL.PAST}}$ kids-the
'As for the movie, the kids have seen it'

On the basis of these observations I would like to propose that the fronted participle competes with the subject for the same position, and that it targets the Spec, IP node. The movement is triggered by a focus feature in the case of non-clitic auxiliaries, or by the requirement of the clitics to be phonologically supported in the case of present tense auxiliaries. Before I present my analysis in detail, I will highlight some differences between Bulgarian and Serbo-Croatian, related to the syntax of the *l*-participle.

4.2. Participle raising in Serbo-Croatian

It appears that the main differences concerning the participle-auxiliary orderings in Bulgarian and Serbo-Croatian follow from distinct properties of clitics. As I have mentioned in Section 3, in Serbo-Croatian the clitics must occur in the Wackernagel position. Franks (1998) and Caink (1999b) take it to mean that the clitics in Serbo-Croatian occupy the highest head projection available. Recall that this requirement does not hold for Bulgarian. One of the results of the second position requirement in Serbo-Croatian is the fact that in embedded clauses the auxiliary must be adjacent to the complementizer, so that the participle may not be fronted across a clitic auxiliary (Wilder & Ćavar 1994: 8).

(12) a. *Ivan kaže da čitala je (Marija) Krležu
Ivan says that read$_{\text{PART.FEM.SG}}$ be$_{\text{3SG.PRES}}$ Marija Krleža

b. Ivan kaže da je (Marija) čitala Krležu
Ivan says that be$_{\text{3SG.PRES}}$ Marija read$_{\text{PART.FEM.SG}}$ Krleža
'Ivan says that Mary has read Krleža'

However, notice in (13a) below that since non-clitic auxiliaries do not have to be adjacent to the complementizer in Serbo-Croatian, the participle may freely raise across them, on a par with Bulgarian. This results in a focused or topicalized reading of the fronted participle. Example (13b) illustrates raising of the participle across a future auxiliary in a Future Perfect construction, taken from Bošković (1995: 251).

(13) a. On tvrdi da istukao bejaše Jovan Petrovog prijatelja.
he claims that beat$_{\text{PART.MASC.SG}}$ be$_{\text{3SG.PAST}}$ Jovan Peter's friend
'He claims that Jovan had BEATEN Peter's friend'

b. Kad istukao budeš Petra, pozovi me
when beat$_{\text{PART.MASC.SG}}$ be$_{\text{AUX.FUT.2SG}}$ Peter call me
'When you BEAT Peter, call me'

Still another important difference concerning the syntax of the *l*-participle in the two languages is related to adjacency requirements. The example in (8) above demonstrated that in Bulgarian the fronted participle must be adjacent to both present and past tense auxiliaries, and the only elements that may ever split the sequence are clitics. In Serbo-Croatian the requirement only holds for present tense auxiliaries, and it can be attributed to the Wackernagel nature of the clitics, which do not tolerate more than one constituent preceding them. As Čamdžić (in prep.) notices, when the participle is fronted across a non-clitic auxiliary in Serbo-Croatian, the two elements may be separated by a subject. Obviously, this is impossible with present tense clitic auxiliaries.

(14) a. Vidjeo Ivan bješe Petra
see$_{\text{PART.MASC.SG}}$ Ivan be$_{\text{3SG.PAST}}$ Peter
'Ivan had SEEN Peter'

b. *Vidjeo Ivan je Petra
see$_{\text{PART.MASC.SG}}$ Ivan be$_{\text{3SG.PRES.}}$ Peter
'Ivan has seen Peter'

Since movement across non-clitic auxiliaries always involves a focused interpretation of the participle, it seems plausible that the participle ends up in a higher position in the phrase structure in (14a) than in (14b).

5. Towards an analysis

Let us recapitulate the observations we have made so far. In both of the languages the participle may be fronted to the sentence initial position across clitic or non-clitic auxiliaries. Movement across non-clitic auxiliaries always gives rise to a focused/topicalized interpretation of the predicate. The fronted participle and the subject apparently compete for the same position, as they may never co-occur. In Bulgarian the fronted participle must be always adjacent to the auxiliary or the clitic cluster containing an auxiliary.

Recall also that the *l*-participle always agrees in φ-features with the subject. In this scenario, I will suggest that the participle may XP-raise to the subject position, that is Spec, IP, in order to check the φ-features of I. Note also that the *l*-participle always co-occurs with the auxiliary 'to be'. I will take it to mean that there is a predicative relationship between the subject and the participle. The two constituents form a Small Clause. As a result of the predicative relationship, *either* the subject *or* the participle may move to Spec, IP and check the agreement features. The agreement is an overt manifestation of the predicative relationship between the two elements. However, on my account the φ-features in I do not trigger the movement operation. They only make it possible. The movement is triggered by the morpho-phonological requirements of clitic auxiliaries that need to be supported by some overt lexical material. Likewise, movement of the participle across a non-clitic auxiliary always triggers a marked interpretation of the predicate, so it takes place for focus or topic reasons. It is also very plausible that then the participle raises to Spec, IP, but that it does not remain there. Rather, it moves still higher, to a focus or topic projection in the functional domain of the verb. This can be observed in the Serbo-Croatian example in (14a), where the fronted participle precedes the subject, which in turn precedes the non-clitic auxiliary. By contrast, in (14b) the participle and the subject are in complimentary distribution, and only one of them may target Spec, IP. Given that the Spec, IP position is never associated with a focused or topicalized interpretation, the sentence does not have a non-neutral reading.

I assume that participle fronting is an instance of predicate inversion, and that it involves A-movement. What is still left to be explained is the fact that it is only the participle alone that may move, and that it may not pied-pipe the object. It seems that this characteristics follows from the auxiliary selection, as well as from the fact that this is an A-movement operation. I would like to follow the insights of Roberts (1987) and Broekhuis & Van Dijk (1995), who argue that the auxiliaries 'to have' and 'to be' differ in their selectional properties. The auxiliary 'to be' is claimed to be unaccusative, whereas the auxiliary 'to have' is transitive. In other words, only the auxiliary 'to have' is able to take an external argument and assign accusative case. When the verb 'to be' is the auxiliary, the subject is generated as the external argument of the participle, rather than the auxiliary. The difference can be illustrated with the following templates.

(15) a. ... [BE [$_{vp}$ DP$_{agent}$ v [$_{VP}$ V$_{PART}$ DP$_{theme}$]]] ('be' as aux)

b. ... [$_{vp}$ DP$_{agent}$ v [$_{VP}$ HAVE [$_{VP}$ V$_{PART}$ DP$_{theme}$]]] ('have' as aux)

I will also assume that (15a) represents a simplified clause structure of Bulgarian and Serbo-Croatian, as in these languages only the verb 'to be' can be used as an auxiliary. The template indicates that when the participle is fronted, the PartP is the largest piece of structure that can be moved. Movement of a larger constituent would mean that the φ-features on the participle were too deeply embedded for checking the φ-features in I. Conversely, movement of the whole PartP would raise the direct object across a position where its case feature must be checked. Therefore the object must be first evacuated for case checking, and as a result, the PartP may only raise via remnant movement into Spec,IP.

There are still a few other properties which suggest that phrasal movement is involved here. As demonstrated in (8) and (9), the fronted participle must immediately precede the clitic auxiliary, with the exception of (other) clitics as the only lexical material that can intervene between the two elements. I conclude that this indicates a rigid specifier-head configuration. Furthermore, (10) and (11) show that the fronted participle must be also the left-most element in IP-clauses. In Serbo-Croatian this fact could be attributed to the requirements of second position clitic placement. However, this cannot be a valid explanation for the Bulgarian data, because the clitics in Bulgarian are not of the Wackernagel type, and can be preceded by more than one constituent, cf. (3c). Rather, it seems that the participle targets the highest specifier available in the clause, that is Spec, IP.

Note that the proposal in (15) also makes the correct predictions concerning participle fronting in the languages that may use the verb 'to have' as an auxiliary. These are the cases of the so-called 'remnant topicalization' in Dutch or German, analyzed by Den Besten & Webelhuth (1987), among others.

(16) a. Jan heeft het boek$_i$ niet [$_{VP}$ t$_i$ gelezen] (Dutch)
Jan has the book not read

b. [$_{VP}$ t$_i$ gelezen] heeft Jan het boek$_i$ niet t$_{VP}$
read has Jan the book not

c. [$_{VP}$ het boek gelezen] heeft niet t$_{VP}$
the book read has not

d. [$_{CP}$[dat boek te snel gelezen]$_i$ [$_{C'}$ heeft hij niet t$_i$]]
that book too quickly read has he not

This is obviously a different type of raising operation, and certainly a larger piece of structure is being moved. Namely, this is A`-movement, triggered by a Focus feature in some focus projection above the IP. Since A`-movement permits reconstruction, the participle does not have to move remnantly. It may pipe-pied its object and the object case can be checked by reconstruction.

6. Some more differences between Bulgarian and Serbo-Croatian

So far we have noticed that Bulgarian and Serbo-Croatian differ with respect to the positions occupied by the clitics. It has been also shown in (12) that the differences relate to the impossibility of raising the *l*-participle across clitic auxiliaries in embedded clauses in Serbo-Croatian. It appears that there is also some variation concerning the highest position in the extended projection of the verb that the participles and the auxiliaries may ever reach in the two languages.

Bošković (1997: 144ff) notices that in Serbo-Croatian the participles may raise across VP adverbs (cf.17), but they cannot ever raise across sentential adverbs (cf. 18). Assuming that sentential adverbs are TP-adjoined, as in Watanabe (1993), he claims that in Serbo-Croatian participles may not raise higher than the TP level.

(17) a. Jovan je juče istukao Petra.
Jovan be$_{3SG.PRES}$ yesterday beat$_{PART.MASC.SG}$ Peter
'Jovan beat Peter yesterday.'

b. Jovan je istukao$_i$ juče t$_i$ Petra

(18) a. Jovan je nesumnjivo istukao Petra.
Jovan be$_{3SG.PRES}$ undoubtedly beat$_{PART.MASC.SG}$ Peter
'Jovan undoubtedly beat Peter.'

b. *Jovan je istukao$_i$ nesumnjivo t$_i$ Petra.

Furthermore, Bošković (1997: 150) shows that the question particle *li*, which is standardly argued to be in C in Serbo-Croatian, cannot be crossed by the *l*-participle, either. Still, as (19a) indicates, finite verbs may move to C in Serbo-Croatian.

(19) a. [$_C$ Ljubi$_i$ *li*] t$_i$ nju
kisses Q her
'Does he kiss her?'

b. *[$_C$ Poljubio$_i$ li] je t$_i$ nju
kiss$_{PART.MASC.SG}$ Q be$_{3SG.PRES}$ her
'Did he kiss her?'

Therefore, Bošković concludes that the participle is head-adjoined to the auxiliary in Aux. The auxiliary clitic may excorporate from this position and move higher, for example in order to satisfy its own second position requirements.
Bulgarian exhibits an interesting contrast. Namely, Krapova (1999) argues that present tense clitic auxiliaries may not move to as high as to C (cf. 20a and b), but the past tense, non-clitic auxiliaries may freely do so (cf. 20c).

(20) a. ?*Kakvo e Ivan pročel?
what be$_{3SG.PRES.}$ Ivan read$_{PART.MASC.SG}$
'What has Ivan read?'

b. *Včera e li Ivana pročela knigata?
yesterday be$_{3SG.PRES.}$ Q Ivana read$_{PART.FEM.SG}$ book-the?

c. Kakvo beše Ivan pročel?
what be$_{3SG.PAST}$ Ivan read$_{PART.MASC.SG}$
'What had Ivan read?'

As far as the position of the participle with respect to sentential adverbs is concerned, the participle and the auxiliary may precede sentential adverbs only on a non neutral reading, as argued by Lambova (2003).

(21) Gledali sa verojatno filma.
watch$_{PART.PL}$ be$_{3PL.PRES}$ probably movie-the
'They have probably SEEN/*seen the movie'

This may indicate that in Bulgarian the participle and auxiliary may move above the IP/TP level only when a focused or topicalized interpretation is involved. The fact that according to Lambova (2003) auxiliary clitics may raise above the IP level is in contrast with Krapova's (1999) findings. This possibly indicates that a speaker variation is involved here.
An analysis of the positions occupied by sentential adverbs allows us to confirm that the syntax of the *l*-participle is contingent on the requirements of clitics in the two languages. In Serbo-Croatian, the participle does not raise higher than the IP/TP level, but the clitic auxiliary may move higher, as it targets the highest head in the extended projection of the verb available. Since the clitics in Bulgarian are verbal, they tend not to raise higher than the IP level.

7. Problems with previous approaches to participle raising

The participle-auxiliary patterns in Slavic have attracted a considerable amount of attention in the generative literature. Here I will briefly discuss previous syntactic accounts, and will point out their shortcomings. Notably, all of the previous approaches assume that the participle moves as a head. The participle-auxiliary structures are argued to be a result of long head movement from V to C, as in Lema & Rivero (1989), or head adjunction of the participle to the auxiliary in C (Wilder and Ćavar 1994), or in Aux (Bošković 1995, 1997). Recently

Lambova (2003) has proposed an analysis for Bulgarian, where she suggests that the participle obligatorily adjoins to the auxiliary in Aux, and may still raise higher as a Part-Aux complex head to a discourse-related projection termed Delta. Still, in spite of the differences, all of the previous approaches face some empirical problems, which I will discuss below.

7.1. Problems with long head movement

The main problem with the long head movement proposal is of a theoretical nature, as it involves a reordering that does not comply with the Head Movement Constraint (Travis 1984). However, it also does not give the correct predictions. For example, the assumption that the participle lands in C predicts that the displacement should be available only in non-root contexts. However, Embick and Izvorski (1995) observe that it is also possible to front the participle in embedded clauses.

(22) Rasbrah če pročel beše knigata (Embick and Izvorski 1995)
understood that read$_{PART.MASC.SG}$ be$_{PAST3SG}$ book-the
'I understood you had read the book.'

Therefore, the participle cannot possibly raise to C. Moreover, as Wilder and Ćavar (1994) note, movement of the participle from V to C leaves open the possibility of merging the subject between the fronted participle and the auxiliary. However, apart from the cases of focus movement of the participle across past tense auxiliaries in Serbo-Croatian mentioned in (14a), this never happens.

(23) *Pročel Ivan e / beše knigata (Bg)
read$_{PART.MASC.SG}$ Ivan be$_{3SG.PRES}$ / be$_{3PL.PAST}$ book-the
'Ivan has/had read the book'

7.2. Problems with Long Head Movement

The adjunction proposals face a number of empirical problems, too. First of all, notice that a head adjunction analysis incorrectly predicts that the fronted participle may be preceded by some overt material in the specifier of the highest projection in the clause. Still, this is never the case, and on a neutral interpretation the participle must be always the left-most constituent, as shown in example (10b), repeated below for convenience.

(24) *Ivan pročel e / beše knigata (Bg)
Ivan read$_{PART.MASC.SG}$ be$_{3SG.PRES}$ / be$_{3PL.PAST}$ book-the
'Ivan has/had read the book'

The fronted participle may only be preceded by topics, but they are clearly phrasal elements, located in a topic projection above the IP (cf.11).

Another problem with the head adjunction accounts concerns the adjacency requirements. Bošković (1997: ch. 5.2.2) analyses past perfect constructions in Serbo-Croatian. They are formed with a finite form of the auxiliary 'to be', the *l*-participle of the verb 'to be', and the *l*-participle of the main verb. He observes that in the base order an object may intervene between the finite auxiliary and the two *l*-participles (Bošković 1997: 157).

(25) Vas dvoje ste čekali bili Marijinu prijateljicu
you two be$_{2AUX.PL}$ wait$_{PART.PL.}$ be$_{PART.PL.}$ Maria's friend
'You two had been waiting for Maria's friend'

He also shows that either of the participles may be fronted across the finite auxiliary to the clause initial position (Bošković 1997: 157).

(26) a. Bili$_i$ ste čekali t_i Marijinu prijateljicu
be$_{PART.PL.}$ be$_{2AUX.PL}$ wait$_{PART.PL.}$ Maria's friend

b. Čekali$_i$ ste bili t_i Marijinu prijateljicu
wait$_{PART.PL.}$ be$_{2AUX.PL}$ be$_{PART.PL.}$ Maria's friend

Importantly, Bošković (1997: 159) claims that in these cases no lexical material can occur between the auxiliary and the participles. He gives objects as examples of intervening phrasal material, and points out that the outputs are ungrammatical.

(27) a. *Bili ste Marijinu prijateljicu čekali
be$_{PART.PL.}$ be$_{2AUX.PL}$ Maria's friend wait$_{PART.PL.}$

b. *Čekali ste Marijinu prijateljicu bili
wait$_{PART.PL.}$ be$_{2AUX.PL}$ Maria's friend be$_{PART.PL.}$

He concludes that the data in (25) and (27) indicate that the participles must be obligatorily left or right adjoined to the auxiliary in the same node. However, his conclusion cannot be correct. As Bašić (2003) notices, when the *l*-participle of the verb 'to be' is moved across the finite auxiliary, it is possible to insert an adverb between the finite auxiliary and the verbal participle (*zaboravio* in (28)). Note that the intervening adverb is clearly phrasal, as it is modified by *skoro* 'almost'.

(28) Bio je skoro potpuno zaboravio na sastanak
be$_{PART.MASC.SG}$ be$_{3SG.PRES}$ almost completely forget$_{PART.MASC.SG}$ about meeting
'He had completely forgotten about the meeting'

Furthermore, recall that Čamdžić (in prep.) observes that when the participle is preposed across a non-clitic past tense auxiliary in Serbo-Croatian, the two constituents may be separated by a subject. The example was given in (14a) and is repeated below for convenience.

(29) Vidjeo Ivan bješe Petra
see$_{PART.MASC.SG}$ Ivan be$_{3SG.PAST}$ Peter
'Ivan had SEEN Peter'

Thus, the examples in (28) and (15) evidence that the *l*-participle cannot possibly be left or right head adjoined to the auxiliary in Serbo-Croatian. Moreover, in view of the data discussed in this section it seems that neither head adjunction nor long head movement can be the appropriate analysis of the *l*-participle raising in Bulgarian or Serbo-Croatian.

8. Conclusions

In this paper I have analyzed instances of participle fronting in two South Slavic languages, Bulgarian and Serbo-Croatian. I have argued that this is an A-movement operation, which is made possible by the presence of φ-features in I. The features can be checked by the participle or the subject, so either of them may XP-raise to Spec,IP. The raising is normally triggered by the morphophonological needs of the auxiliary clitics. In the case of movement across non-clitic auxiliaries, the reordering may take place only for focus reasons. The operation proceeds in a largely uniform fashion in Bulgarian and Serbo-Croatian, and the differences can be attributed to intrinsic properties of auxiliary clitics in each of the languages.

References

Bašić, Monika (2003): "Participle Movement in Serbo-Croatian". Ms. University of Tromsø.

Bošković, Željko (1995): Participle Movement and Second Position Cliticization in Serbo-Croatian. In: *Lingua* 96, 245–266.

Bošković, Željko (1997): *The Syntax of Non-finite Complementation. An Economy Approach.* Cambridge, Mass: The MIT Press.

Broekhuis, Hans and Kees van Dijk (1995): "The Syntactic Function of the Auxiliaries of Time". In: Den Dikken, M. and K. Hengeveld (eds.): *Linguistics in The Netherlands 1995.* Amsterdam, Philadelphia: John Benjamins.

Broekhuis, Hans and Krzysztof Migdalski (2003): "Participle Fronting in Bulgarian". In: Fikkert, P. and L. Cornips (eds.): *Linguistics in the Netherlands 2003.* Amsterdam: Benjamins, 1–12. Available online at: http://fdlwww.kub.nl/~broekhui/publicaties/artikel_TIN_dag.pdf

Caink, Andrew (1999a): "Against 'Long Head Movement': Lexical Insertion and the Bulgarian Auxiliary 'Be'". In: Dimitrova-Vulchanova, M. and L. Hellan (eds): *Topics in South Slavic Syntax and Semantics.* Amsterdam: John Benjamins, 91–123.

Caink, Andrew (1999b): "Serbian/Croatian/Bosnian Clitics at the Lexical Interface". In: Dziwirek, K., H. Coats and C. M. Vakareliyska (eds.): *Formal Approaches to Slavic Linguistics: The Seattle Meeting, 1998.* Ann Arbor: Michigan Slavic Publications, 81–100.

Čamdžić, Amela (in prep.): *On the Syntax of Long Verb Movement.* Ph. D. dissertation. University College London.

Damborský, Jiří (1967): *Participium l-ove ve slovanštině.* Warszawa: Państwowe Wydawnictwo Naukowe.

Den Besten, Hans and Gert Webelhuth (1987): "Remnant topicalization and the constituent structure of VP in the Germanic SOV languages". In: *GLOW Newsletter* 18, 15–16.

Dostál, Antonín (1954): *Studie o vidovém systému v staroslověnštině.* [A Study of the Aspect System in Old Church Slavonic]. Prague: Státní pedagogickě nakladatelství.

Embick, David and Roumyana Izvorski (1995): "On Long Head Movement". In: Fuller, J. M., H. Han and D. Parkinson (eds.): *Proceedings of ESCOL*, 104–115.

Embick, David and Roumyana Izvorski (1997): "Participle-Auxiliary Orders in Slavic". In: Browne, W., E. Dornisch, N. Kondrashova and D. Zec (eds.): *Formal Approaches to Slavic Linguistics: The Cornell Meeting.* Ann Arbor: Michigan Slavic Publications, 210–239.

Franks, Steven (1998): "Clitics in Slavic". Paper presented at the Comparative Slavic Morphosyntax Workshop, Indiana University, Bloomington 1998. Available online at: http://www.indiana.edu/~slavconf/linguistics/index.html

Franks, Steven and Tracy Holloway King (2000): *A Handbook of Slavic Clitics.* New York, Oxford: Oxford University Press.

Kowalska, Alina (1976): *Ewolucja analitycznych form czasownikowych z imiesłowem na -ł w języku polskim.* [The Evolution of Analytical Verbal Forms with the *l*-participle in Polish]. Katowice: Uniwersytet Śląski.

Krapova, Iliyana (1999): "The System of Auxiliaries in Bulgarian". In: Dimitrova-Vulchanova, M. and L. Hellan (eds.): *Topics in South Slavic Syntax and Semantics.* Amsterdam: Benjamins, 162–193.

Lambova, Mariana (2002): "Head Movement is Syntactic: Evidence from Bulgarian. In: *HUMIT* 2001, 89–102.

Lambova, Mariana (2003): *On Information Structure and Clausal Architecture: Evidence from Bulgarian.* Ph. D. dissertation. University of Connecticut.

Lema, José and María-Luisa Rivero (1989): "Long Head Movement: ECP vs. HMC". In: *Proceedings of NELS 20*. GLSA, University of Massachusetts, Amherst, 333–347.
Lunt, Horace G. (1952): *A Grammar of the Macedonian Literary Language*. Skopje: Drzavno knigoizd. na NR Makedonija.
Roberts, Ian (1987): *The Representation of Implicit and Dethematized Subjects*. Dordrecht: Foris.
Tomić, Olga (1996) "The Balkan Slavic Clausal Clitics". In: *Natural Language and Linguistic Theory* 14, 811–872.
Travis, Lisa (1984): *Parameters and Effects of Word Order Variation*. Ph. D. dissertation. MIT, Cambridge, Mass.
Watanabe, Akira (1993): *Agr-based Case Theory and Its Interaction with the A-bar system*. Ph. D. dissertation, MIT, Cambridge Mass.
Whaley, Marika (2000): *The Evolution of the Slavic 'Be(come)'-type Compound Future*. Ph. D. dissertation. The Ohio State University.
Wilder, Chris and Damir Ćavar (1994): "Long Head Movement? Verb Movement and Cliticization in Croatian". In: *Lingua* 93, 1–58.

Tanja Milićev, Novi Sad

How strong are full pronouns in Serbian?[1]

1. Introduction

Personal pronouns in Serbian come in two forms: clitic and "full". When tested against the generalization assumed in most pronominal literature, specifically in Cardinaletti and Starke's (1999a) seminal article on pronoun classes, "full" forms seem to exhibit properties of both strong and deficient pronouns. Instead of discarding the generalizations as non-applicable to Serbian, I will follow Cardinaletti and Starke (1999b) and treat the Serbian "trouble-makers" as categorially different elements, namely, simple demonstratives.

2. Classes of Pronouns

This analysis of the properties of full pronouns in Serbian is based on Cardinaletti and Starke's (1999a) tripartite division of pronominal elements into clitic, weak and strong. The three classes are distinguished on the basis of phonological, morphological, semantic and syntactic properties, given in (1).

(1) Pronominal Classes (Cardinaletti and Starke 1999a)

	morphology	distribution		interpretation	
	+reduced	in FP at SS	*coord.&modif.	no range	-animate
clitic	1	+	+	+	+
weak	2	+	+	+	+
strong	3	-	-	-	-

Deficient elements – clitics and weak pronouns – are mophologically reduced, occur in derived positions, cannot be coordinated and modified, are not restricted by range, do not have a referential index, so they may occur in expletives and impersonals; they are interpreted as referential only through co-reference, in other words, if they are associated with a non-deficient antecedent. Lacking the relevent part of the structure, where the feature [+human] is sitting as a default range-feature, on Cardinaletti and Starke's analysis, a CP-layer, they can have both animate and inanimate referents.

Strong pronouns, on the other hand, remain in their base position, can be coordinated and modified, have a referential index, and are always [+human]. The choice of a certain class is governed by an economy principle – Minimize Structure – which selects the most deficient form compatible with properties of the potential utterance.
The structure of each class is given in (2):

(2) Strong pronouns Weak pronouns Clitic pronouns

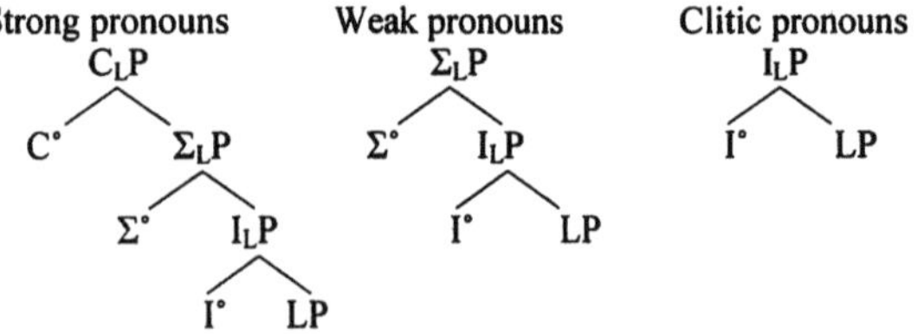

[1] I am grateful to Boban Arsenijević, John F. Bailyn, Jasmina Grković Major, Marijana Marelj, Nataša Milićević, and Olga Tomić for their valuable comments and suggestions, and for language judgements to Lanko Marušič and Rok Žaucer (Slovenian), and Krzysztof Migdalski (Polish).

3. Full Pronouns in Serbian

Only 3rd person object pronouns will be included here. Firstly, in Serbian there are no subject clitics; the full form alternates with *pro*, and is always associated with a range. Apart from the 2nd person pronoun which can be used generically, full pronouns are always referential. Although *pro* qualifies as a deficient element, the properties of full pronouns will be investigated only in comparison with clitics. Secondly, the fact that 3rd person subject pronouns have forms (almost) identical to certain demonstratives (*ona* 3p.f.sg 'she' – *ona* 3 dem.f.sg 'that one') might bias the analysis of their categorial status, and blur the availability of certain tests. 1st and 2nd person pronouns, being intrinsically +human, render the animacy condition on strong pronouns redundant.

The clitic and full 3rd person pronouns are given in (3).

(3)

	m.sg	f.sg	pl
"full"	njega$_{GEN}$	nje$_{GEN}$	njih$_{GEN}$
clitic	ga$_{GEN}$	je$_{GEN}$	ih$_{GEN}$
"full"	njemu$_{DAT}$	njoj$_{DAT}$	njima$_{DAT}$
clitic	mu$_{DAT}$	joj$_{DAT}$	im$_{DAT}$
"full"	njega$_{ACC}$	nju$_{ACC}$	njih$_{ACC}$
clitic	ga$_{ACC}$	ju/je$_{ACC}$	ih$_{ACC}$

Full pronouns in Serbian seem to comply with the Minimize Structure Principle – they are used when the deficient, i.e. clitic is unavailable.[2]

Since clitics in Serbian cannot be complements of prepositions (cf. Abels 2002), a full pronoun is used:

(4) a. *na **ga**
on him$_{ACC.CL}$

b. na **njega**
on him$_{ACC}$

Due to the well-known Second Position requirement, clitics cannot be in clause initial position, so only full pronouns are good as topics, for instance, as illustrated in (5):

(5) ***Ga** /**Njega** znam.
him$_{ACC.CL}$ /him$_{ACC}$ I-know
"Him I know."

Lacking the CP layer, deficient elements cannot be coordinated. As expected, only full pronouns are good as conjuncts:

(6) a. ***je** i **ga**
her$_{ACC.CL}$ and him$_{ACC.CL}$

a' **nju** i **njega**
her$_{ACC}$ and him$_{ACC}$

[2] Cf. Cardinaletti and Starke (1999a) on the (non-) relevance of the prosodic/semantic focus for the choice of pronoun.

b. ***ga** i Roka
him$_{ACC.CL}$ and Rok$_{ACC}$

b' **njega** i Roka
him$_{ACC}$ and Rok$_{ACC}$

Similarly, being dominated by CP, only full pronouns can be modified by c-modifiers:

(7) a. *samo* **njega**
only him.ACC

a' **samo* **ga**
only him$_{ACC.CL}$

NP internal modifiers are impossible with clitics (8a). Generally they are not often found with pronouns, but when they do appear, they follow the pronoun (8b) (cf. Progovac 1998).[3] [4]

(8) a. *ga pametnog
him$_{ACC.CL}$ smart$_{MASC.SG.ACC}$

b. **pametnog* **njega**
smart$_{ACC}$ him$_{ACC}$

b' **njega** *pametnog*
him$_{ACC}$ smart$_{ACC}$

Having no structural deficiency, strong pronouns are allowed to remain in their base position. Instrumental full pronouns, with no corresponding clitic form, are the only full pronoun which are unmarked in their base position.

(9) Rok se izuzetno ponosi **njime.**
Rok se$_{REFL}$ very-much take-pride him$_{INSTR}$
"Rok is very proud of him."

Other pronouns seem to be good either when they are contrastively focused, as in 10a, or when they follow a focused verb, as in 10b.

(10) a. Rok izuzetno poštuje ***nju** /**NJU**.
Rok very-much respects her$_{ACC.CL}$ /her$_{ACC}$
"Rok respects HER very much."

b. Rok izuzetno POŠTUJE nju.

---

[3] The same holds for numerals, except that agreeing numerals are marginally acceptable in the position preceding the pronoun; the numeral in such cases is felt to be contrastively focused:

(i) ?? Dvema njima sam dao propusnice.
two$_{DAT}$ them$_{DAT}$ am$_{AUX}$ given$_{MSC.SG}$ passes
"I gave the passes to TWO of them."

[4] Only quantifiers and depictives can be found with clitics.

(i) a. *Svima* **im** podeli zadatke.
all$_{DAT}$ them$_{DAT.CL}$ assign tasks
"Assign tasks to all of them."

b. Videla sam **ga** *pijanog.*
seen$_{FEM.SG}$ am$_{AUX}$ him$_{ACC.CL}$ drunk$_{ACC}$
"I saw him drunk."

It should be noted, however, that the position in which contrastively focused full pronouns are allowed to appear lower down in the clause does not necessarily equal their base position. The indirect object pronoun, for example, cannot be felicitously focused in the position preceding the direct object.

(11) Rok je poklonio {*?**NJOJ**} buket ruža { **NJOJ**}.
Rok is$_{AUX}$ given$_{MSC.SG}$ her$_{DAT}$ bouquet of-roses her$_{ACC}$
"Rok gave HER a bouquet of roses."

Full pronouns are quite common with no prosodic focus at all, and in these cases they always occupy a derived position:

(12) Rok je **njega** juče video u prodavnici.
Rok is$_{AUX}$ him$_{ACC}$ yesterday seen$_{MSC.SG}$ in shop
"Rok saw him at the shop yesterday."

Since focus is generally not responsible for the occurence of strong pronouns, which clearly is not the case here either, let us see what factors influence the choice of the full pronoun over the clitic.

4. Choice: Some observations

4.1 Specific referent

It is a well-known fact that deficient pronouns are sensitive to their referent. Cross-linguistically, clitics seem to require a specific referent. At first sight, the same seems to hold for Serbian, cf. (13):

(13) a. Pričali su za Roka i *neku Marijanu*. Petar je **njoj/*joj** je navodno poklonio ogroman buket orhideja.
"They spoke about Rok and some Marijana. Peter allegedly gave her$_{DAT}$/*her$_{DAT.CL}$ a huge bouquet of orchids."

b. Pričali su za Roka i Marijanu. Rok **joj** je navodno poklonio ogroman buket orhideja.
"They spoke about Rok and Marijana. Rok allegedly gave her$_{DAT.CL}$ a huge bouqet of orchids."

However, specificity should be understood in its looser sense, as "familiarity" and "being anaphoric on [...] in the discourse" (Uriagereka 1995) or "presuppositionality" (Diesing 1991).[5] A referent can be easily made "specific" through non-linguistics means, as in (14) and (15).

(14) Neki čovek stoji ispred vrata. Neću da **mu** otvorim.
some man stands in-front-of door. I-will-not *da* him$_{DAT}$ open
"A man is standing in front of the door. I won't open it to him."

(15) Tražim dekana. Treba da **mu** uručim poziv za sud.
I-look-for dean I-need *da* him$_{DAT.CL}$ I-give subpoena for court
"I'm looking for the Dean. I need to give him a court subpoena."

[5] For more details on how the notion of specificity relates to deficient pronouns see Cardinaletti and Starke (1999: p.219, fn. 12).

In (15), "the Dean" could be understood both as a particular, unique person or as whoever is the Dean, but the clitic is obviously not sensitive to this difference.

In Serbian, there are contexts, however, which contradict the cross-linguistic generalization that clitics have to refer specifically. They are allowed, for instance, in impersonal (16) and generic sentences (17).

(16) U Amsterdamu su **im** najlepše kuće.
in Amsterdam are them$_{\text{POSS.DAT}}$ most-beautiful houses.
"What is most beautiful in Amsterdam are people's houses."

(17) Holanđani su najsmešniji kad **im** daš malo da popiju.
Dutch are funniest when them$_{\text{DAT.CL}}$ you-give little to drink
"The Dutch are the funniest when you have them a little bit drunk."

In fact, only clitics are allowed as impersonals, due to the fact that they are deficient, i.e. not associated with a range restriction:

(18) *U Amsterdamu su njima najlepše kuće.
in Amsterdam are them$_{\text{POSS.DAT}}$ most-beautiful houses.
"What is most beautiful in Amsterdam are people's houses."

4.2 Referent prominent in the discourse

The full pronoun seems to be preferred when the referent is not "prominent enough". A referent is conceived as not being "prominent" in the discourse after a shift of topic has occurred. Thus, in (19), the full pronoun seems to be better since its referent, *Petar*, is rendered "too far"after the discourse shift from him to the speaker:[6]

(19) (A: **Petar** me jako nervira. Stalno se ponaša bahato. Muka mi je od toga. Prestaću da dolazim na posao.)
("Peter really annoys me. He always behaves rudely. I'm sick of it. I'll stop coming to work.")

B: Ne bih se brinula da sam na tvom mestu. Neko
not would SE$_{\text{REFL}}$ worry if am on your place. Somebody
će **njega** / ??**ga** dovesti u red.
will him$_{\text{ACC}}$ / him$_{\text{ACC.CL}}$ lead in order
"I wouldn't worry if I were you. Somebody will put him in order."

4.3 Contrastive contexts

Full pronouns are also preferred in certain strongly discourse conditioned contexts that have a flavor of "constrastiveness":

(20) a. Vidim da **mu** je svejedno.
I-see that him$_{\text{DAT.CL}}$ is all-the-same
"I see that he doesn't care."

[6] Clearly, discourse conditions at play need a more formal and explicit account. The notions and observations used here are merely for descriptive purposes.

a' Vidim da je **njemu** svejedno.
I-see that is him_{DAT} all-the-same
"I see that he (as opposed to...) doesn't care."

b. Marijana je vodila Roka na koncert, a Rok ***joj** je
Marijana is_{AUX} $\text{taken}_{FEM.SG}$ Rok on concert, and Rok $\text{her}_{DAT.CL}$ is_{AUX}
poklonio buket orhideja.
$\text{given}_{MSC.SG}$ bouquet of-orchids
"Marijana took Rok to a concert, while Rok gave her a bouquet of orchids."

b' Marijana je vodila Roka na koncert, a Rok je **njoj**
Marijana is_{AUX} $\text{taken}_{FEM.SG}$ Rok on concert, and Rok is_{AUX} her_{DAT}
poklonio buket orhideja.
$\text{given}_{MSC.SG}$ bouquet of-orchids
"Marijana took Rok to a concert, while Rok gave her a bouquet of orchids."

That the notion of "contrastiveness" is one of the relevant discourse factors is supported by the fact that coordinators such as *a*, *ali* 'but' almost exclusively go with the full pronoun:

(21) a. (A: **Roka** stalno boli stomak. Skroz je očajan i ne zna šta da radi. Išao je već dvaput kod doktora i niko ne zna da mu kaže šta mu je. Ima osećaj da ga zamajavaju.
"Rok has constant problems with his stomach. He's desperate and doesn't know what to do. He's been to the doctor's twice already but nobody can tell what's wrong with him. He has a feeling he's not been taken seriously.")

B: **A** kad je **njega** to počelo da boli?
and when is_{AUX} him_{ACC} it started *da* hurt
"When did his stomach start to hurt?"

b. (Uzela sam knjige iz biblioteke, stavila ih u kancelariju...)
("I took the books from the library, left them in my office...)

...**ali** kad sam se vratila **njih**$_{ACC}$ više nije/??**ih** više bilo tamo.
...but when am_{AUX} SE_{REFL} come-back, them_{GEN}/$\text{them}_{GEN.CL}$ were-not longer there
"...but when I came back, they're were gone."

There is no doubt that the semantic make-up of full pronouns is responsible for their choice in these contexts, but how their referential index, or range corresponds to the observed discourse factors has yet to be determined. However, it is clear that their displacement is not due to some deficiency (either structural or phonological) imposing either association to a functional case position, as in Cardinaletti and Starke (1999a), or [+FOC] lexical material (Holmberg (1999a)), or attraction by $F^{o}_{[person]}$, as proposed in Sichel (2002). In other words, they do not move because they are weak.

5. Animacy: [-animate] full pronouns

The most striking deviation from the generalization about strong pronouns is that full pronouns in Serbian are not subject to the animacy constraint.

Both animate and inanimate pronouns can be complements of preposition:

(22) Gde su mi naočare? Ništa ne vidim bez **njih**.
where are me$_{DAT}$ glasses nothing not I-see without them$_{GEN}$
"Where are my glasses? I can't see without them."

The only case where inanimate pronouns are felt as not being perfectly felicitous is the accusative masculine:

(23) A: Da li ti smeta vetar u Lajdenu?
"Do you mind the wind in Leiden?"

B: Ne, navikla sam se već na ?**njega**.
no got-used am$_{AUX}$ SE$_{REFL}$ already on him$_{ACC}$
"No, I got used to it."

Also, inanimate full pronouns are perfectly fine outside the PP context, provided again that independent discourse conditions are satisfied:

(24) (Da li sam ti rekla da imam novu haljinu za Novu godinu? Od svile, srednje dužine. Savršena je....
("Did I tell you about my new dress for the New Year's? It's made of silk, medium length. It's perfect...")

... Rok mi je **nju** poklonio za rođendan.
... Rok me$_{DAT.CL}$ is$_{AUX}$ her$_{ACC}$ given$_{MSC.SG}$ for birthday
"... Rok gave it to me for my birthday."

Since there is a large amount of cross-linguistic evidence that animacy is indeed a semantic property distinguishing deficient and strong pronominals, and can hardly be reduced to a tendency, the analysis of Serbian pronouns as strong can no longer be maintained. But notice that inanimate full pronouns in Serbian cannot be analyzed as weak either, since they can be modified (25a) and coordinated (25b), which deficient elements strongly resist.

(25) a. (Neću da nosim puno nakita sa sobom. Gde mi je **lančić** koji mi je Rok poklonio za rođendan?
"I don't want to take too much jewellery with me. Where's the necklace I got from Rok for my birthday?)

Samo njega ću poneti u Lajpcig.
only him$_{ACC}$ I-will take in Leipzig
"I'll take only that one (*lit.*: only it) to Leipzig."

b. **Nju i onu plavu** [=haljinu] sam kupila na rasprodaji.
her$_{ACC}$ and that blue [=dress] am$_{AUX}$ bought$_{FEM.SG}$ on sale
"This one and that blue one I bought on sale."

The possibility of inanimate pronominal conjuncts has been noted for Russian as well (cf. Testelets (2002)):

(26) (Molotok ležit na stole.) Daj mne **ego i gvozdi**.
hammer lies on table give me$_{DAT}$ him$_{ACC}$ and nails
"(The hammer is on the table.) *lit.*:Give it and the nails to me!"

6. Demonstratives

6.1 Simple vs. intensified

Since similar problems have been noted by Diesing (1999) and Holmberg (1999a) in their comments on the tripartite division, Cardinaletti and Starke (1999b) propose that what looks like an inanimate strong pronoun is not a personal pronoun at all, but rather a simple demonstrative.

Demonstratives split into two categorially different groups: simple and intensified. (27) illustrates the opposition for English, German and French.

(27) a. simple: *them* *der* *ça*

b. intensified: *those* *dieser* *cela*

As Cardinaletti and Starke (1999b) point out, the term "simple demonstrative" is a bit unfortunate, since there is very little "demonstrativeness" in these pronouns. Unlike intensified demonstratives, they do not make spatial distinctions of the near/far type; they are only derivatively deictic, and are never ostensive.

What generally distinguishes them from personal pronouns is the presence of a special morphological marker, such as, for instance, *th* in English *them* or *d* in German d-pronouns. This morphological marker is never found in personal pronouns.

6.2 Special morphological marker

If Serbian inanimate full pronouns are simple demonstratives, one of the first things that needs to be established is the presence of the special morphological marker, corresponding to the intensified demonstrative morphology. When compared with the intensified demonstratives *ovaj* 'this'and *onaj* 'that' in Serbian, that latter one stands out as a possible candidite for the shared morphology. However, in order to avoid hasty conclusions based on possible diachronic accident, let us take a closer look at what morphology there is in strong pronouns when compared with clitics.

The most commonly held view of the clitics in Serbian is that they have no internal syntactic structure, they are bare heads, and that this structural deficiency is responsible for their obligatory movement (cf. Franks 1998, Bošković 2001, Abels 2002):

(28) **[nje-[ga]**$_{\text{CL}}$**]**$_{\text{PRONOUN}}$
him$_{\text{ACC}}$

What we are left with when the clitic *–ga* is peeled-off, is *nje-*.

In their account of Slavic pronominal morphology, Cardinaletti & Starke's (1999a) propose that *je-* in Slavic pronouns is in fact a syntactic support morpheme, also found in strong auxiliary forms, e.g. *sam* – ***jesam*** 'am'. Although this semantically empty support morpheme renders the clitic form strong, it does not correspond to the C° layer, i.e. it is not a dummy case marker sometimes found in strong pronouns (overt in Italian ***a*** *loro*$_{\text{STRONG}}$ vs. *loro*$_{\text{WEAK}}$), but rather realizes the Σ layer.

In Progovac (1998) *(n)j(e)-* is identified as definite morphology also found in adjectives and possessives. While the clitic form *–g(a)* corresponds to the agreement morphology, *j/i* morphology corresponds to the definite morphology in adjectives and possessives. Pronominal morphology thus indicates movement through AgrP and DefP. This is illustrated in (29).

g(a) – AgrP, **j**(e) – DefiniteP

(29) a. pametnog Roka
smart$_{ACC}$ Rok$_{ACC}$

b. tvoj kaput
your coat

c. lepi lančić
beautiful$_{DEF}$ necklace

d. nje-ga
him$_{ACC}$

Putting aside the question whether the "definite morphology" on adjectives is definite or specific, we are still faced with the lack of explicit "demonstrative" morphology, which will cancel the [+animate] default range found in strong pronouns. For possible clues, let's extend the search outside the South Slavic group, and take a look at a Slavic language which has different forms for different pronouns. Polish seems to be a good candidate, since it has three types of pronouns: deficient, emphatic and prepositional (30).

(30) Polish:

	3sg.m
deficient (clitic/weak)	**go**
"emphatic" (strong)	**jego**
"prepositional"	**niego**

Emphatic pronouns are strong – they never allow inanimate referents, and there are no discourse conditions which may licence an inanimate emphatic pronoun:

(31) ***Jego** (= samochód) kupiłem w Tilburgu, a **ją** w Amsterdamie.
him$_{ACC}$ (= the car) I-bought in Tilburg, and her$_{ACC}$ in Amsterdam
Lit.: It I bought in Tilburg, and it in Amsterdam.

In (31) both pronouns have been topicalized, the "contrastive" context has been provided as well, yet *jego* and *ją* can only have animate referents.

"Prepositional" pronouns can be both [+/- animate], but they cannot be used in "strong" contexts to refer to inanimate referents, as illustrated in (32) :

(32) ***Niego** (= samochod) kupiłem w Amsterdamie, ne u Tilburgu.
him$_{ACC}$ (= the car) I-bought in Amsterdam, not in Tilburg.
Lit. It I bought in Amsterdam, not in Tilburg.

These facts seem to suggest that Polish n-pronouns are simple demonstratives, whereas j-pronouns are personal. Therefore, the morphology capable of violating the animacy constraint is n-.

6.3 Are all n-pronouns demonstrative?

Since in South Slavic languages all pronouns have n-morphology, let us see if all pronouns are then demonstratives.

In Serbian, for instance, the only case which seems to resist the "demonstrativization" of the personal pronoun is accusative. The diachronic development of the accusative – replacing the old pronoun *nj* with the genitive form *njega* to specially mark the [+animate] category –

supports Cardinaletti and Starke's (1999a) assumption that accusative markers are specified for [+human] feature.[7]

Similar facts can be found in other Slavic languages. In Polish, for instance, the only "prepositional" pronoun that cannot have an inanimate referent is the accusative. Instead, the locative is used:

(33) a. *Postaw go na **niego** (= stół).
put him$_{ACC.CL}$ on him$_{ACC}$ (=table)
Lit.: Put it on it.

b. Postaw go na **nim.**
put him$_{ACC.CL}$ on him$_{LOC}$
Lit.: Put it on it.

Slovenian only marginally allows strong inanimate pronouns; they are usually considered substandard and colloquial. To license them, heavy focus is needed, possibly ostension:

(34) ?**NJIH** (=hlače) bom obleku jutri.
Them (=trousers) I-will put-on tomorrow

Prepositional pronouns in Slovenian are not subject to the animacy constraint, except, of course, the accusative masculine. To override animacy, the unmarked, old *nj*, or a "less" marked (phonologically reduced) *njga* accusative seems to be preferred:

(35) Lej kok je stol usran, pa kaj si to postavu
look how is table dirty on-earth what are$_{AUX}$ that put
?na**nj(o)** / ?na**njga** / *na **njega**?
on-him$_{OLD.ACC}$ / on-him$_{REDUCED.ACC}$ / on him$_{ACC}$
"Look how dirty the table is, what on earth did you put on it?"

Since in Serbian resilient accusatives are judged funny, but are or are becoming possible, it can be said that all 3rd person pronouns in Serbian are simple demonstratives.

7. Demonstratives in Serbian – a preliminary account

Let us see how we can accommodate this "new" type of demonstrative, or rather the intensified-simple distinction into the system of demonstratives in Serbian.

Remember, intensified demonstratives are deictic, showing the near-far opposition. Two demonstrative pronouns fit into this category immediately: *ovaj* 'this' and *onaj* 'that'.
intensified demonstratives:

(36) **ovaj**$_{m}$ **ova**$_{f}$ **ovo**$_{n}$ (near)
onaj$_{m}$ **ona**$_{f}$ **ono**$_{n}$ (far)

However, there is a third demonstrative *taj*, which does not seem to fit in the category of intensified demonstratives since it has nothing to do with deixis, which makes it a good candidate for the simple demonstrative.

(37) **ta**$_{m}$ **ta**$_{f}$ **to**$_{n}$ (where?)

[7] Cardinaletti and Starke (1999a) assume that the case feature in Slavic pronouns is morphologically realized on N°, and "reduplicated" on C°, whereas in Italian it is morphologically realized on C°, as the accusative marker *a*.

Intensified demonstratives significantly differ from simple demonstratives with respect to binding. Whereas intensified demonstratives behave like R-expressions and obey principle C, simple demonstratives pattern with pronouns and obey principle B. The example in (38) is from Holmberg (1999b), showing the opposition for Swedish, while (39) illustrates the intensified-simple distinction in West Flemish subject and object *ze*-pronouns (cf. Haegeman 1993):

(38) Jag köpte inte billen$_i$, för jag gillade varken **den**$_i$ / ***den där**$_i$ eller
I bought not the-car, because I liked neither it / that nor
des ägere
its owner

(39) a. *… dat Marie$_i$ peinst da Jan **ze**$_i$ gezien eet
… that Mary thinks that Jan her seen has

b. … dat Marie$_i$ peinst da **ze**$_i$ Jan gezien eet
… that Marie thinks that she Jan seen has

Serbian t-demonstratives show a dual behavior with respect to allowing antecedents. In (40), only the n-pronoun can refer to 'my new dress', while the t-demonstrative is as bad as the intensified demonstratives.

(40) Ne dopada mu se moja nova haljina$_i$, jer mi je baš
not-likes him$_{DAT}$ SE$_{REFL}$ my new dress, because me is$_{AUX}$ exactly
*ovu$_i$ / *onu$_i$ / ***tu**$_i$ / **nju**$_i$ Rok kupio.
this$_{intens.ACC}$ / that$_{intens.ACC}$ / that$_{T\text{-}dem.ACC}$ / it$_{f.ACC}$ Rok bought$_{MSC.SG}$
"He doesn't like my new new dress because that's the one Rok bought me."

There are cases, however, when a t-demonstrative can have an antecedent:

(41) Sećaš se onog čaja od divlje trešnje$_i$? **Taj**$_i$ / *? **Njega**$_i$
remember SE$_{REFL}$ that tea of wild cherry that$_{T\text{-}dem.ACC}$ / him$_{ACC}$
bih tako rado popila sad.
would so gladly drink now
"Do you remember that wild cherry tea? I really feel like drinking that one now."

In (41) however, the t-pronoun does not refer to the cup of wild cherry tea, but rather the kind of tea. The n- pronoun is out here, since it would refer to the wild cherry tea once made (and most likely consumed).

What n- and t-pronouns seem to have in common is their dependence on the discourse – they both need an antecedent. Unlike intensified demonstratives, they are indeed pronominal. The difference between n- and t-pronouns lies in the fact that they involve distinct kinds of reference. In (42) both the n- and t-pronoun can take "him" as their antecedent. However, coreference by a t-pronoun is tied to the property of "him", either previously mentioned in the discourse or as part of the knowledge shared by the interlocutors. This is absent from the n-pronoun.

(42) a. Ne igraj se s njim$_i$, **tog**$_i$ ne valja provocirati.
not play SE with him$_{INSTR}$ That$_{T\text{-}DEM}$ not good to-provoke
"Don't play with him. That (one) should not be provoked."

b. Ne igraj se s njim$_{i}$, **njega**$_{i}$ ne valja provocirati.
not play SE with him$_{INSTR}$ Him$_{N\text{-}DEM}$ not good to-provoke
"Don't play with him. He should not be provoked."

Roughly speaking, n-pronouns always single out a referent, while t-pronouns pick out the referent and its, possibly defining, property.

Coordination also points to the fact that t-pronouns behave differently from the intensified demonstratives. Whereas n-pronouns can be coordinated with intensified demonstratives, this is impossible with a t-pronoun.[8]

(43) a. Poneću **njih** i **ove** / **one**.
I-will-take them$_{ACC}$ and these / those

b. *Poneću **nju** i **tu**.

At this point it is still unclear how to capture the intuition about the referential capacity of t-pronouns in a formal way. But the idea that they refer to "something more" than n-pronouns, ties in with the fact that they can be used to refer to propositions (44) or events (45) (cf. Progovac 1998).

(44) Rok je duša i **to** je prava istina.
Rok is soul and that$_{T\text{-}DEM.NEUT}$ is real truth
"Rok is an angel and that's the whole truth."

(45) Ko **to** tamo peva?
Who that$_{T\text{-}DEM.NEUT}$ there sings
"Who is that singing over there?"

8. Conclusion

Although 3rd person pronouns in Serbian undergo obligatory movement and are exempted from the animacy restriction, they are not weak pronouns since coordination, modification and the impossibility of non-referential antecedents point to the conclusion that their structure is not deficient. Rather, they are simple demonstratives, whose special morphological marker n- is capable of overriding the animacy constraint. The question of whether n-pronouns are the only members of this category or t-demonstrative pronouns also belong here, I leave for further research.

References

Abels, Klaus (2002): *[P clitic]! – Why?. In: *Procedings of Formal Descriptions of Slavic Languages* 4.

Bošković, Željko (2001): *On the Nature of the Syntax-Phonology Interface: Cliticization in South Slavic.* London: Elsevier North-Holland.

Cardinaletti, Anna and Michal Starke (1996): Deficient Pronouns: A View from Germanic. In: Höskuldur Thránsson, Samuel David Epstein and Steve Peter (eds.): *Studies in Comparative Germanic Syntax*, Volume II. Dordrecht: Kluwer Academic Publishers.

[8] In fact, two t-pronouns can never be coordinated:

(i) *Tu i tog najviše volim
That$_{T\text{-}DEM.FEM.SG.ACC}$ and that$_{T\text{-}DEM.MSC.SG.ACC}$ most love
"I love that (one) and that (one) the most."

Cardinaletti, Anna and Michal Starke (1999a): The Typology of Structural Deficiency. In: Riemsdijk, Henk van (ed.): *Clitics in the Languages of Europe*, 145–234. Berlin and New York: Mouton de Gruyter.

Cardinaletti, Anna and Michal Starke (1999b): Responses and Demonstratives. The Typology of Structural Deficiency. In: Riemsdijk, Henk van (ed.): *Clitics in the Languages of Europe*, 273-290. Berlin and New York: Mouton de Gruyter.

Diesing, Molly (1991): *Indefinites*. Cambridge, Mass.: MIT Press.

Diesing, Molly (1999): Comments on Cardinaletti and Starke: "The typology of structural deficiency". In: Riemsdijk, Henk van (ed.): *Clitics in the Languages of Europe*, 243–247. Berlin and New York: Mouton de Gruyter.

Franks, Steven (1998): Clitics in Slavic. Paper presented at Comparative Slavic Morphosyntax Workshop, Bloomington, Indiana. http://www.cogs.indiana.edu/people/homepages/franks.html. To appear in: *Slavica*.

Haegeman, Liliane (1993): Object Clitics in West Flemish. In: *Geneva Generative Papers* 1, 1–31.

Holmberg, Anders (1999a): Comments on Cardinaletti and Starke: "The typology of structural deficiency". In: Riemsdijk, Henk van (ed.): *Clitics in the Languages of Europe*, 263–266. Berlin and New York: Mouton de Gruyter.

Holmberg, Anders (1999b): Remarks on Holmberg's Generalization. In: *Studia Linguistica* 53, 1–39.

Progovac, Ljiljana (1998a): Even Pronominal To. In: *Journal of Slavic Linguistics* 6, 3–40.

Progovac, Ljiljana (1998b): Determiner phrase in a language without determiners. In: *Journal of Linguistics* 34, 165–179.

Sichel, Ivy (2002): Pronoun Movement and Attraction. In: Falk, Yehuda N. (ed.): *Proceeding of IATL 18*, Bar Ilan University.

Testelets, Yakov (2002): Strong and weak pronouns in Russian: Lexical, Structural, or Pragmatic Difference?. Paper presented at 11th annual meeting of the Workshop on Formal Approaches to Slavic Linguistics, Amherst, May 3–5

Uriagereka, Juan (1995): Aspects of the Syntax of Clitic Placement in Western Romance. In: *Linguistic Inquiry* 26/1, 79–123.

Olga Mišeska Tomić, Novi Sad / Leiden

Mood and Negation in Balkan Slavic

1. Introduction

In this paper, I analyze the structure of negative imperatives in Balkan Slavic. First, I argue that imperative mood is checked in the same node in which the subjunctive complementizer is derived or merged, which is distinct from the node where the future marking modal clitics are derived or merged. Then, I demonstrate that there are two locations for Neg in Balkan Slavic, and argue that shared interpretative and selectional properties lead to the conclusion that the negation operator to the left of the subjunctive complementizer, which operates in subjunctive constructions, also operates in imperatives. The differences in the behaviour of the clitics in different Balkan Slavic languages are argued to follow from distinct cliticization properties of the pronominal clitics, as well as from differences in the strength of Mood and Neg.

2. MoodP

For Rivero (1994) MoodPs are headed by subjunctive mood complementizers, such as the Macedonian and Bulgarian *da*, as well as by invariant future-marking modal clitics, such as the Macedonian *ḱe* or the Bulgarian *šte*. As illustrated in (1), however, the Balkan Slavic modal clitics can cooccur with subjunctive (mood) complementizers, which argues for a ModP distinct from MoodP.

(1) a. *Petar* *će* *da* *dođe.* Serb
Peter will.3Sg.Mod.Cl Subj.Comp come.3Sg.Perf.Pres
'Peter will come.'

b. *Petre* *ḱe* *da* *dojde.* Mac
Petre will.Mod.Cl Subj.Comp come.3Sg.Past
'Petre seems to have come.'

c. *Petăr* *šte* *da* *e* *došăl.* Bulg
Peter will.Mod.Cl Subj.Comp is.Cl come.M.Sg.*l*-Part
'Petar seems to have come.'

In (1a) we have one variant of the Serbo-Croatian future tense, which functions in Serbian, Bosnian and some Croatian dialects.[1] As argued in Tomić (2004), the inflecting Serbo-Croatian modal clitic is derived in AuxP, from where it raises to AgrSP to check its person/number features. The complement of the modal clitic in (1a) is a subjunctive

[1] The other variant, which functions throughout the Serbo-Croatian speaking area, is formed with the infinitive of the verb:

(i) *On* *će* *doći.* SC
he will.3Sg.Mod.Cl come.Inf

(ii) *Doći* *će.* SC
come.Inf will.3Sg.Mod.Cl
'He will come'.

Note that I use the term "Serbo-Croatian" (SC) when speaking of the (common) grammatical structure of the languages into which Serbo-Croatian disintegrated within the past decade, and resort to the term Serbian (Serb) when referring to structures which are specific for this language.

construction introduced by the complementizer *da*, which is homophonous with the indicative complementizer (cf. Ivić 1972).[2] The subjunctive construction in the complement of the modal clitic has a verb that inflects for person and number, but its φ-features are anaphoric – agreeing with and derivable from the features of the modal clitic.[3] Moreover, the verb in the subjunctive construction does not inflect for tense.[4] Thus, the complement introduced by the subjunctive complementizer is a VP rather than a CP.[5] The structure of (1a) is given in (2):

[2] Many authors speak of two different uses of *da* (cf. Bibović 1971; Browne 1981/1986; Vrzić 1996). Nevertheless, what synchronically are referred to as "two different uses of *da*", could diachronically be two different conjunctions. Gołąb (1964: 28) argues that "it is highly possible that Old Slavic *da* represents a homonym: *da* – a modal particle serving to derive an analytic subjunctive mood from the present indicative, and *da* – a paratactic conjunction corresponding to English 'so, thus, also'." Note that the complementizer introducing subjunctive clauses in Serbo-Croatian has the same phonological representation as its counterparts in Macedonian and Bulgarian, where indicative complements are introduced by distinct complementizers – *če* in Bulgarian and *deka* or *oti* in Macedonian.

[3] Sentences in which the φ-features of the verb in the subjunctive complement differ from the φ-features of the modal clitic, such as (i), are not acceptable.

(i)	* *On*	*će*	*da*	*dođem*	*sutra.*	Serb
	he	will.3Sg.Mod.Cl	Subj.Comp	come.1Sg	tomorrow	

purported meaning: 'He wants that I come tomorrow.'

[4] Sentences in which the verb of the subjunctive construction is in the past tense, such as (i) do not occur:

(i)	* *On*	*će*	*da*	*si*	*došao*	*juče.*	Serb
	he	will.3Sg.Mod.Cl	Subj.Comp	be.2Sg	come.F.Sg.*l*-Part	yesterday	

purported meaning: 'He wants for you to have come yesterday.'

[5] Stjepanović (to appear) posits analogous monoclausal structures for configurations in which lexical modal verbs take as complements subjunctive constructions with same φ-features. Thus, for (i) she posits the structure (ii):

(i)	*Petar*	*nije*	*morao*	*da*	*upozna*	*nikoga.*	Serb
	Petar.M.Sg.Nom	not+is	had to.M.Sg.*l*-Part	Comp	get to know.3Sg.Perf.Pres	nobody	

'Peter didn't have to get to know anybody.'

(ii) [*Petar*$_i$ *nije* [$_{FP}$ t$_i$ *morao* [$_{daP}$ *da* [$_{VP}$ t$_i$ *upozna nikoga*] Serb

Stjepanović refers to verbs that take subjunctive complements as "potentially restructuring verbs" since, when the verb of the subjunctive construction has joint reference with the verb of the main clause, clitic-climbing and negative polarity are licensed.

(2) SC

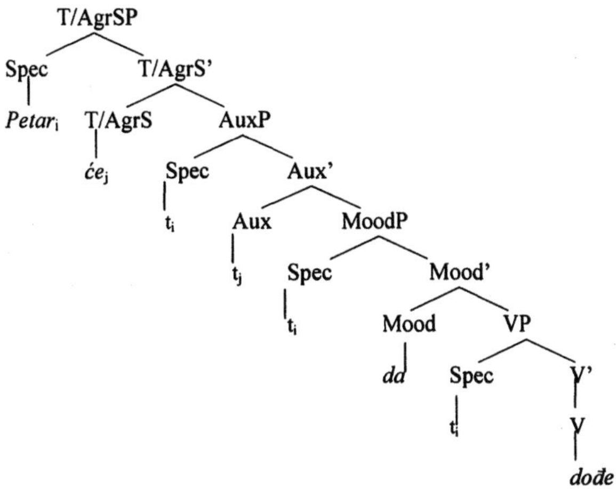

Whereas in Serbo-Croatian the verb of the subjunctive construction to the right of the modal clitic is always in the present tense, in Bulgarian it can also occur in the perfect and in Macedonian it can occur in the present, past or perfect tenses. The Macedonian modal clitic *ḱe* and the Bulgarian modal clitic *šte* do not inflect, however.[6] Accordingly, (1b) and (1c) have monoclausal structures in which both ModP and MoodP are to the left of AgrSP, where the person/number/tense features of the lexical verb or the auxiliary are checked.[7] The structure of the Macedonian sentence (1b) is given in (3):

---

[6] In Bulgarian and the Southeastern Serbian dialects the "will"-modal auxiliaries can also have non-clitic past tense forms, which inflect for person and number.

[7] The Macedonian and Bulgarian sentences in (1) express assumptions. As argued in Tomić (2004), however, a structure such as (3) was an intermediate structure in the diachronic development of the Macedonian and Bulgarian future tenses. The contemporary future tense of the Southeastern Serbian dialects, illustrated in (i), also has this structure:

i)	*Do*	*jutre*	*na*	*pladne*	*mi*	*će*	*da*	*završimo*	*projekat.* S-ESerb
	till	tomorrow	on	noon	we	will.Mod.Cl	Subj.Comp	finish.1Pl.Perf.Pres	project

'Till tomorrow at noon we will have the project finished.'

(3) Mac

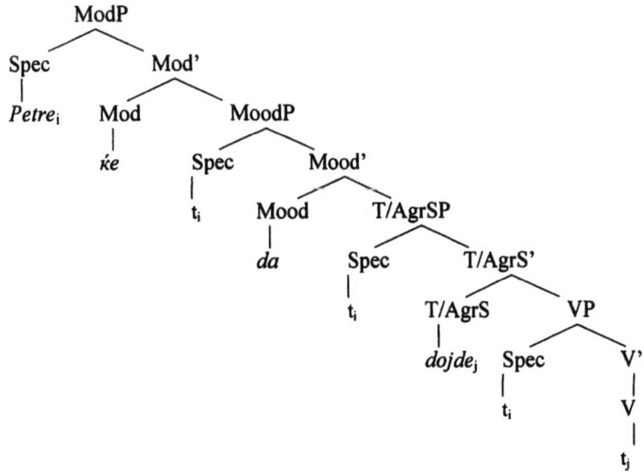

In all the Balkan Slavic languages, bare subjunctive clauses (i.e. subjunctive clauses that occur by themselves and not as complements of main clauses) express orders, as do verbs with imperative morphology:

(4) a. *Dođite* *sutra!* SC
Dojdete *utre!* Mac/Bul
come.2Pl.Imper tomorrow
'Come tomorrow!'

b. *Da* *dođete* *sutra!* SC
Da *dojdete* *utre!* Mac/Bul
Subj.Comp come.2Pl.Perf.Pres tomorrow
'You should come tomorrow!'

Verbs with imperative morphology and bare subjunctive constructions actually share interpretative properties – they both point to "non-veridical" events (cf. Giannakidou 1998) and can be used with imperative force. Arguing for a unified analysis of subjunctives and imperatives, I would check the imperative mood in the same node in which the subjunctive complementizer is derived or merged.[8]

The checking of the imperative mood feature in Macedonian clauses with pronominal clitics may posit a problem. Namely, in Serbo-Croatian and Bulgarian the clitics in imperative clauses behave like the clitics in the indicative clauses of these languages. In Macedonian, however, the pronominal clitics occur to the right of verbs with imperative morphology and to the left of verbs with indicative morphology:

(5) a. *Zemi* *mu* *go!* Mac
take.2Pl.Imper 3Sg.Dat.Cl 3Sg.N.Acc.Cl
'Take it from him!'

[8] In my paper presented at FDSL3, imperative mood was checked in Mod – the node projected by the invariant modal clitics (cf. Tomić 2002a). In that paper, I did not take into account subjunctives, and did not make a distinction between ModP and MoodP.

b. *Mu* *go* *zede.* Mac
3Sg.Dat.Cl 3Sg.N.Acc.Cl take.3Sg.Past
'(S)he took it from him.'

In Tomić (2002b), I accounted for the occurrence of the Macedonian imperative verb to the left of the pronominal clitics by positing a structure such as (6), and argued that the imperative verb moves along with the clitics to AgrSP, and is excorporated due to the strength of Mood.

(6)

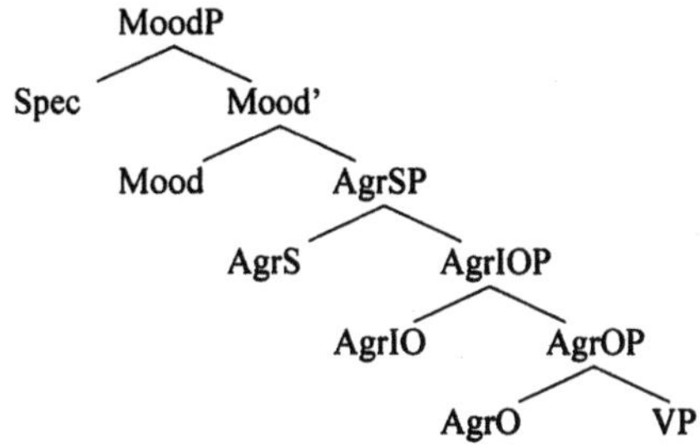

Subsequently, in PF, the negation operator, the verb and the pronominal clitics, in this order, make up a single phonological word with the antepenultimate stress pattern characteristic for the language.

Bošković (2001) offers a PF account for the postverbal position of clitics in Macedonian imperatives. Adopting the copy theory of movement and assuming that a lower copy of a non-trivial chain can be pronounced instead of the head of the chain if this is necessary to satisfy a PF requirement, he argues that the occurrence of the clitics to the right of the Macedonian imperative verb is due to the existence of an underlying PF affix to the left of the verb, with which the verb has to merge. In underlying structure, both indicatives and imperatives have clitic-V order, with a lower copy of the pronominal clitic following the verb. In indicatives, the higher copy of the clitic can be, hence must be pronounced. In imperatives, on the other hand, pronunciation of the higher copy of the clitic leads to a Stranded Affix Filter violation; so, the lower copy of the clitic to the right of the verb, is pronounced. Bošković's analysis, however, does not make provisions for a unified treatment of subjunctives and imperatives and, if extended to cover all the manifestations of negative imperatives, would have to extend the number and nature of PF affixes.

3. Existing Analyses of the Relationship of Negation and Mood

The relationship of negation to imperatives has often been discussed in the literature; in particular, since in some languages imperative morphology can be negated, while in others it cannot. For Zanuttini (1991, 1997), the impossibility to negate imperatives in a number of Romance languages/dialects follows from a subcategorization requirement: The negation operator, which subcategorizes for Tense, does not occur to the left of verbs with imperative morphology. Accordingly, in those languages/dialects in which the negation operator is preverbal, verbs with imperative morphology cannot be negated.

Laka (1994), discussing sentential negation in Spanish, claims that the incompatibility of negation and imperatives in this language is due to the fact that they are elements of the same syntactic category, which she labels Σ. Since, in the presence of negation, imperative morphology is excluded, sentences in which the negation operator immediately precedes verbs with imperative morphology are non-acceptable.

Kallulli (1995) also presupposes a joint mood and negation node, which, following Laka, she labels Σ. Kallulli accounts for the fact that Albanian imperatives are often marked by the occurrence of the verb to the left of the clitics,[9] by assuming that the verb moves overtly to Σ. In negative contexts, however, Σ dominates a modal negation operator *mos*, distinct from the indicative negation operator *nuc*, and there is no verb movement to Σ.

Rivero and Terzi (1995) account for differences in the relationship of negation and imperative morphology through different sites for the mood features. They argue that in Spanish and Modern Greek the imperative mood feature is checked in C – a node to which the verb cannot raise since Neg blocks its path. In Serbo-Croatian and Ancient Greek, however, the mood feature is located in I, which is below Neg, and the verb can raise to it without crossing Neg.

Han (1998) argues that negative imperatives are unavailable in some languages, because they have syntactic configurations in which negation takes syntactic scope over the imperative operator in C, which would lead to semantic incoherence. In languages such as Bulgarian and Serbo-Croatian, where negation is compatible with imperative morphology, the imperative verb is not in C at surface level, but lower in the clause. Having raised overtly to T, to check its T-feature, it attaches to Neg, the two forming a single complex head, which subsequently raises to AgrS for φ-feature checking. The weak imperative feature of the verb is then checked in C at LF.[10]

Isac and Jakab (in press), unifying the syntax of "true" imperatives, i.e. imperatives with imperative morphology, and "surrogate" imperatives, i.e. bare subjunctives expressing orders, propose that imperative morphology is hosted by MoodP,[11] placed to the right of CP but to the left of NegP. They argue that cross-linguistic variation in acceptability of negated imperative morphology follows from the particular properties that clitics and negation operators have across languages. When the negative operator is a syntactic head, it has blocking properties, while when it is a clitic, it can cliticize onto the verb and allow for further movement of the verb past Neg to MoodP. In those cases where pronominal clitics occur between the negation operator and the imperative verb, as in Bulgarian and the Eastern and Northwestern Macedonian dialects (cf. (7)), the Mood feature is checked by the non-clitic Neg, which raises to Mood.

(7)	a.	*Ne*	*MU*	*ja*	*čeTI!*	Bul
		not	3Sg.M.Dat.Cl	3Sg.F.Acc.Cl	read.2Sg.Imp	
	b.	*NE*	*mu*	*ja*	*Čltaj!*	NWMac
		not	3Sg.M.Dat.Cl	3Sg.F.Acc.Cl	read.2Sg.Imp	
		'Don't read it to him!'				

Zanuttini's, Laka's and Kallulli's analyses were designed for Italian, Spanish and Albanian, respectively, and cannot adequately be applied to Balkan Slavic. Rivero and Terzi's analysis did take into consideration Serbo-Croatian – a Balkan language where imperative morphology can be negated. Nevertheless, neither the relative position of the Balkan imperatives with respect to clitics, nor their behaviour with respect to negation, provide a conclusive evidence

[9] Compare the imperative sentence (i) to its indicative counterpart (ii):

(i)	*Hapnie*	*derën!*		Alb
	open.2Pl+3Sg.Acc.Cl	door+the		
	'You (all) open the door!'			
(ii)	*E*	*hapni*	*derën.*	Alb
	3Sg.Acc.Cl	open.2Pl	door+the	
	'You (all) are opening the door.'			

[10] Since morphological/phonological constraints do not apply at LF, the imperative verb can move freely.

[11] Isac and Jakab argue that their MoodP is equivalent to ForceP in Rizzi's 1995 system.

that the illocutionary force of the sentence can be checked at two different places.[12] Moreover, the raising of the Serbo-Croatian negated imperative from I, where it checks its imperative feature, to C, is in need of motivation. Recent research has undermined not only the assumption that constituents can be moved in order to support clitics,[13] but also the assumption that the Wackernagel clitic cluster is always formed in C.[14]

As for Han, she herself admits having problems with the obligatory encliticization in Serbo-Croatian negative clauses and attributes it to some independent constraint of the language. But her theory has a problem with encliticization in Macedonian imperative clauses in general – whether positive or negative. A weak imperative feature predicts that imperative verbs behave like indicative verbs with respect to negation and clitic placement. In Macedonian, however, indicative tensed verbs follow the clitics, whereas imperative verbs precede them – in Standard Macedonian always, in Northwestern Macedonian only in non-negated contexts.

While Zanuttini, Laka, Kallulli, Rivero and Han concentrate on imperatives with imperative morphology, Isac and Jakab offer a unified analysis of verbs with imperative morphology and bare subjunctive constructions, and cover a wide variety of Balkan languages, including Serbo-Croatian, Bulgarian and Macedonian. It poses numerous questions, however. First of all, the path of the movement of the verb with imperative morphology is not discussed. If, as commonly assumed in analyses of South Slavic, VP occurs to the right of agreement nodes projected by pronominal clitics, how do the pronominal clitics end up between the non-clitic negation operator and the imperative verb? Another question: In languages such as Serbo-Croatian and (Standard) Macedonian, in which Neg cliticizes to the verb, how do the clitics end to the right of the verb (cf. (8))?

(8)	a.	*NE*	*čitaj*	*mu*	*je!*	SC
		not	read.2Sg.Imper	3Sg.M.Dat.Cl	3Sg.F.Acc.Cl	
	b.	*Ne*	*čiTAJ*	*mu*	*ja!*	StMac
		not	read.2Sg.Imper	3Sg.M.Dat.Cl	3Sg.F.Acc.Cl	
		'Don't read it to him!'				

Most importantly, the clitic status of the languages discussed by Isac and Jakab (in print) does not follow from independent principles, but is rather determined on the basis of the behaviour of the pronominal clitics in negated imperatives.

In what follows, I will offer an alternative to the existing analyses. Let us first examine evidence that will help us determine the relative position of Mood and Neg.

4. Two NegPs

As illustrated in (9) and (10), in Balkan Slavic, the negation operator can occur to the left of the subjunctive complementizer, as well as to its right.

---

[12] Rivero and Terzi argue that in Serbo-Croatian and Ancient Greek, C cannot be the position associated with imperative force, since in these languages C is reserved as the last-resort landing site for verb movement, in order to rescue Wackernagel (or second-position) clitics from occurring in clause-initial positions.

[13] Among other things, this movement presupposes that syntax can look into phonology.

[14] Franks (1998) contends that Wackernagel clitics move to the highest available site in the extended projection of the verb, head to head, leaving copies at all intermediate sites; at PF the highest clitic copy is pronounced that satisfies the clitic's phonological requirement for encliticization. Bošković (2001) argues that the Wackernagel clitics sit in different positions and the cluster is formed at the first intonation break.

(9) a. *Neće* *da* *dođe.* Serb
not+will.3Sg.Mod.Cl Subj.Comp come.3Sg
'(S)he won't be coming/come.'[15]

(10) a. *Da* *ne* *dolazi!* SC

b. *Da* *ne* *idva!* Bul

c. *Da* *ne* *doaģa!* Mac
Subj.Comp not come.3Sg
'(S)he shouldn't come!'

This leads to the conclusion that the negation operator in the given languages has two distinct sites – a conclusion supported by the existence of clauses such as (11), in which Neg occurs twice:

(11) *Ne* *ḱe* *da* *ne* *dojde.* Mac
not will.Mod.Cl Subj.Comp not come.3Sg.Past
'It is not likely that (s)he has not come.'

In cases such as (11), we would have an underlying structure with two negation operators – one to the left of ModP, and another to the right of MoodP, which itself is to the right of ModP:

(12) $[_{NegP}$ NP/DP$_i$ $[_{Neg}$ *ne* $[_{ModP}$ t_i $[_{Mod}$ ModCl $[_{MoodP}$ t_i $[_{Mood}$ *da* $[_{NegP}$ t_i $[_{Neg}$ *ne* $[_{T/AgrSP}$ t_i $[_{T/AgrS}$ $[_{VP}$ t_i V]]]]]]]]]]]

In cases such as those illustrated in (9) and (10) there are no two negation operators in one single clause. Nevertheless, the site of Neg in clauses such as (9) differs from the site of Neg in clauses such as (10). In cases such as those illustrated in (9) Neg is to the left of the projection where the modal clitic lands or is merged – to the left of AgrSP in Serbo-Croatian (cf. (13)) and to the left of ModP in Macedonian (cf. (14)):

(13) $[_{NegP}$ NP/DP$_i$ $[_{Neg}$ *ne* $[_{T/AgrSP}$ t_i $[_{T/AgrS}$ $[_{AuxP}$ t_i $[_{Aux}$ ModCl $[_{MoodP}$ t_i $[_{Mood}$ *da* $[_{VP}$ t_i V]]]]]]]]]

(14) $[_{NegP}$ NP/DP$_i$ $[_{Neg}$ *ne* $[_{ModP}$ t_i $[_{Mod}$ ModCl $[_{MoodP}$ t_i $[_{Mood}$ *da* $[_{T/AgrSP}$ t_i $[_{T/AgrS}$ $[_{VP}$ t_i V]]]]]]]]]

In cases such as those illustrated in (10), on the other hand, Neg is to the right of the subjunctive complementizer. The structure of such clauses is given in (15):

(15) $[_{MoodP}$ t_i $[_{Mood}$ *da* $[_{NegP}$ t_i $[_{Neg}$ *ne* $[_{T/AgrSP}$ t_i $[_{T/AgrS}$ $[_{VP}$ t_i V]]]]]]]

In the surface structures of imperatives with imperative morphology, which in all Balkan Slavic can be negated, the negation operator is to the left of the verb:

[15] Since the negative counterpart of the lexical verb *hoće* 'will/want' is also *neće*, in addition to this meaning, (9) has also the meaning (i):

(i) 'She doesn't want to come.'

(16) a. *Ne dolazi!* SC

b. *Ne idvaj!* Bul

c. *Ne doaǵaj!* Mac

not come.2Sg.Imper

'Don't come!'

Nevertheless, as pointed out, negated imperatives (with imperative morphology) share interpretative properties with bare subjunctives. They also share selectional properties: As observed by comparing (17) and (18), the negation operator in imperatives and the one in subjunctives always select verbs with imperfective aspect.[16]

(17) a. *Da ne dolazi/*dođe!* SC

b. *Da ne idva/*dojde!* Bul

[16] In Serbo-Croatian, perfective verbs with imperative morphology and subjunctive constructions with perfective verbs can be negated if the context makes it clear that the prohibition does not have immediate effect:

(i) *Ne dođi nikada kasnije nego što ti je rečeno.* SC
not come.2Sg.Perf.Imper never later than what 2Sg.Dat.Cl is said
'Don't ever come later than you are told (to come)!'

(i)' *Da nikada ne dođeš kasnije nego što* SC
Subj.Comp never not come.2Sg.Perf.Pres later than what
ti je rečeno.
2Sg.Dat.Cl is said.
'You should never come later than you are is told (to come).'

(ii) *Ne uzmi ništa, ma koliko nastojali.* SC
not take.2Sg.Perf.Imper nothing no matter how much insist.Pl.*l*-Part
'Don't take anything, no matter how much they insist!'

(ii)' *Da ne uzmeš ništa, ma koliko nastojali.* SC
Subj.Comp not take.2Sg.Perf.Pres nothing no matter how much insist.Pl.*l*-Part
'You shouldn't take anything, no matter how much they insist.'

(iii) *Ne zaboravi da zatvoriš prozor kad* SC
not forget.2Sg.Perf.Imper Subj.Comp close.2Sg.Perf.Pres window when
kreneš na put.
set off.2Sg.Perf.Pres on journey
'Don't forget to close the window when you set off on a journey!'

(iii)' *Da ne zaboraviš da zatvoriš* SC
Subj.Comp not forget.2Sg.Perf.Pres Subj.Comp close.2Sg.Perf.Pres
prozor kad kreneš na put.
window when set off.2Sg.Perf.Pres on journey
'You shouldn't forget to close the window when you set off on a journey!'

In Macedonian and Bulgarian, there is no context in which perfective verbs with imperative morphology can be negated. Note that, when non-negated, the verbs with imperative morphology, as well as the verbs in subjunctive constructions, can be either perfective or imperfective.

c. *Da* *ne* *doaġa/*dojde!* Mac
Subj.Comp not come.3Sg.Imperf.Perf.Pres
'(S)he shouldn't come!'

(18) a. *Ne* *dolazi/??dođi!* SC

b. *Ne* *idvaj/*dojdi!* Bul

c. *Ne* *doaġaj/*dojdi?* Mac
not come.2Sg.Imperf/Perf.Imper
'Don't come!'

Accordingly, the negation operator to the left of the subjunctive complementizer, operating in subjunctive constructions, also operates in imperatives. Thus, in both imperatives and subjunctives Neg follows Mood:

(19) [Mood [Neg

The ordering of Neg to the right of Mood in imperatives and subjunctives accounts for the scopal properties of these operators. A prohibition is interpreted as an order not to do something and not as a lack of order to do something.

5. Imperatives and Pronominal Clitics

The derivation of surface structures in which the negation operator is to the left of the imperative verb, from an underlying structure in which Neg is to the right of Mood, is not a straightforward matter, especially when the imperative clause includes pronominal clitics.

In Serbo-Croatian, the negation operator *ne* is left-adjacent to the verb and forms a phonological unit with it – in both indicative and imperative clauses.[17] Compare (8a), repeated as (20a) with (20b):

(20) a. *NE* *čitaj* *mu* *je!* SC
not read.2Sg.Imper 3Sg.M.Dat.Cl 3Sg.F.Acc.Cl
'Don't read it to him!

b. *Reci* *mu* *da* *mu* SC
tell.2Sg.Imper 3Sg.M.Dat.Cl Subj.Comp 3Sg.M.Dat.Cl
je *ne* *čita!*
3Sg.F.Acc.Cl not read.3Sg.Indic
'Tell him not to read it to him.'

The pronominal clitics follow the negated verb when it is clause-initial or preceded by heavy constituents, and occur to the left of the verb otherwise. In the latter case the negation operator-plus-verb complex is stressed distinctly from the constituent that hosts the clitics.[18]

(21) a. *NE –* *daj* ← *mu* ← *ga!* SC
not give.2Sg.Imper 3Sg.M.Dat.Cl 3Sg.N.Acc.Cl
'Don't give it to him!'

[17] The stressing of the negation operator in Serbo-Croatian follows the rule of stress shift when a prefix is added to a root. (From the point of view of morphology, the negation operator behaves like a prefix.)

[18] The dashes link the constituents of a phonological word; the arrows denote directionality of cliticization.

b.	*TI*	*ako*	*NEćeš*	*NE –*	*daj* ←	SC
	you.2Sg	if	not+want.2Sg	not	give.2Sg.Imper	
	mu ←		*ga!*			
	3Sg.M.Dat.Cl		3Sg.N.Acc.Cl			

'You do not give it to him if you don't want.'

c.	*TI* ←	*mu* ←	*ga*	*NE –*	*daj!*	SC
	you.2Sg	3Sg.M.Dat.Cl	3Sg.N.Acc.Cl	not	give.2Sg.Imper	

'You don't give it to him!'

In Bulgarian negated imperatives –whether occurring in clause-initial position or preceded by other elements – the negation operator forms a phonological word with the pronominal clitics. In this word, the stress always falls on the pronominal clitic to the immediate right of the negation operator. The verb is stressed independently.

(22) a.	*Ne*	*MU*	*go*	*DAvaj!*	Bulg
	not	him.Dat.Cl	3Sg.N.Acc.Cl	give.2Sg.Imper	

'Don't give it to him!'

b.	*Săs*	*TEzi*	*neŠTA*	*ne*	*SE*	*igRAJ!*	Bulg
	with	these	things	not	Acc.Refl.Cl	play.2Sg.Imper	

'Don't play with such things!'

In Standard Macedonian, the negation operator is always to the left of the verb and forms an antepenultimately stressed single phonological word with the verb and any pronominal clitics to the right of the verb. In (23a) the negation operator is followed by a monosyllabic verb and a clitic; the stress falls on the negation operator, which constitutes the antepenultimate syllable of the phonological word made up of the negation operator, the verb and the clitic. In (23b), where the negation operator is followed by a disyllabic verb and a pronominal clitic, the stress falls on the first syllable of the verb, since this is the antepenultimate syllable of the phonological word. In (23c), where the disyllabic verb is followed by two pronominal clitics, the stress falls on the second syllable of the verb, which in this case represents the antepenultimate syllable of the phonological word.

(23) a.	*NE –*	*pij –*	*go!*		Mac
	not	drink.2Sg.Imper	it.N.Acc.Cl		

'Don't drink it!'

b.	*Ne –*	*DAvaj –*	*mu*	*NIšto!*	Mac
	not	give.2Sg.Imper	3Sg.M.Dat.Cl	nothing	

'Don't give him anything!'

c.	*Ne –*	*daVAJ –*	*mu –*	*go!*	Mac
	not	give.2Sg.Imper	3Sg.M.Dat.Cl	it.N.Acc.Cl	

'Don't give it to him!'

In Northwestern Macedonian, which, being the local dialect of the Macedonian capital, has attracted the attention of many researchers, the pronominal clitics occur between the negation operator and the imperative verb; they actually encliticize to the negation operator, which is stressed independently of the head of the clause. The Northwestern Macedonian counterparts of the Standard Macedonian imperative clauses in (23) are given in (24):

(24) a. *NE* ← *go* *PIJ!* NWMac
not 3Sg.M.Acc.Cl drink.2Sg.Imper
'Don't drink it!'

b. *NE* ← *mu* *DAvaj* *NIšto!* NWMac
not 3Sg.M.Dat.Cl give.2Sg.Imp nothing
'Don't give him anything!'

c. *NE* ← *mu* ← *go* *DAvaj!* NWMac
not 3Sg.M.Dat.Cl 3Sg.N.Acc.Cl give.2SG.Imper
'Don't give it to him!'

6. A Proposal

Concentrating exclusively on imperatives, in Tomić (in print) I placed Neg to the left of Mood and argued that these verbs raise first to Mood and then to Neg. But then I did not relate imperatives to subjunctives. The evidence that imperative morphology is checked in the node where the subjunctive complementizer is derived and that the negation operator in imperatives is to the right of Mood demands a re-examination of this scenario.

As argued in Tomić (2000), the Macedonian and Bulgarian pronominal clitics are derived (or merged) in head positions of agreement nodes to the right of AgrS/TP, whereas the Serbo-Croatian pronominal clitic are merged as arguments in VP and possibly "pass" through the agreement nodes on the way to their "second position". Imperatives being tenseless, the underlying structure of imperative clauses would have AgrSP, rather than AgrS/TP.[19] The structure of Balkan Slavic negative imperative clauses with pronominal clitics is given in (25):

[19] AgrSP takes care for the person and number features. Note that in Serbo-Croatian there are distinct forms not only for second person singular and plural, but also for first person plural:

(i) *Pođimo!* SC
start to go.1Pl.Imper
'Let us go!'

(25)

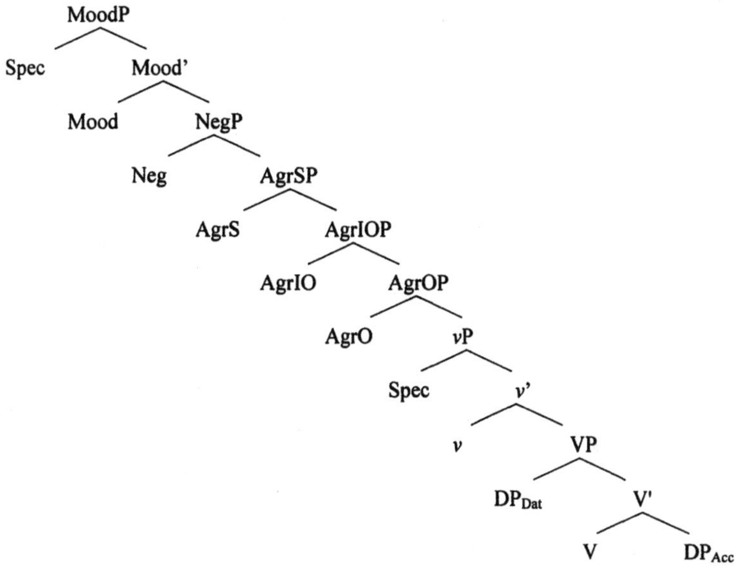

In Serbo-Croatian, the imperative verb raises to AgrSP to check its φ-features, and merges with the week (proclitic) negation operator, while the pronominal clitics, which originate in Spec positions in VP are left behind.[20] Since the behaviour of negated imperative verbs is analogous to that of negated and tensed indicative verbs, we may assume that Mood is weak and the negative imperative verb resulting from that merge, checks its imperative features covertly.

In Macedonian and Bulgarian, the structures of the IP left periphery is the same as in Serbo-Croatian, but the clitics are derived or merged in object agreement nodes.[21] In Bulgarian, as

[20] The Serbo-Croatian pronominal clitics originate in VP and move to second position, either following the verb (as proposed by Franks 1998) or looking for the first intonation boundary (as proposed by Bošković 2001). They appear to the right of the imperative verb if the clause is subjectless and does not have focused constituents and to the left of the verb if the clause has a focused subject, as in (i) or a focused constituent, as in (ii), (iii):

(i)	*TI* ←	*mu* ←	*ga*	*NE-daj!*	SC
	you.Pron	3Sg.M.Dat.Cl	3Sg.N.Acc.Cl	not-give.2Sg.Imper	
	'You don't give it to him!'				
(ii)	*PEri* ←	*ga*	*NE-daj!*		SC
	Pera.Dat	3Sg.N.Acc.Cl	not-give.2Sg.Imper		
	'Don't give it to Pera!'				
(iii)	*Nikad* ←	*mu* ←	*ga*	*NE-daj!*	SC
	never	3Sg.M.Dat.Cl	3Sg.N.Acc.Cl	not-give.2Sg.Imper	
	'Never give it to him!'				

[21] "Traditionally" Macedonian and Bulgarian clitics have been derived as heads of objects agreement nodes, but this involves rightwards adjunction in the movement of the verb and "pushing" rather than trailing. Bošković (2001) argues that the Macedonian and Bulgarian clitics are XP/X^0 elements in specifier positions of AgrIOP and AgrOP with empty heads. His analysis is in line with Kayne's (1994) leftward adjunction system, since each clitic "jumps" and left-adjoins to the verb or verb+clitic complex as soon as they move to the head to its left. But

observed by comparing (22a) with (26), the behaviour of negated imperative verbs is analogous to the behaviour of negated and tensed indicative verbs.

(26) a.	*Ne*	*MU*	*go*	*DAde.*	Bulg
	not	him.Dat.Cl	3Sg.N.Acc.Cl	give.3Sg.Aor	
	'(S)he didn't give it to him!'				

Just as in indicatives the verb raises to AgrS/T to check its φ- and tense features, in imperatives it raises to AgrS to check its φ-features; in both cases, picking up the pronominal clitics from AgrOP and AgrIOP. The clitics + verb complex in AgrS merges with Neg, while imperative morphology is checked covertly.

Since the Bulgarian negation operator can occur clause-initially, it has been treated as an inherently stressed (non-clitic) word (cf. Rudin 1994, 1997; Rudin et al. 1999). In my analysis, however, the Bulgarian negation operator *ne* is clitic. In the spirit of Inkelas (1989), I take it that the non-stressed inherently proclitic *ne* leans upon an inherently enclitic pronominal clitic. At PF, the prosodic subcategorisations "cancel" each other and we have a phonological word in which the stress is placed according to the rules of the language. The fact that in clauses without pronominal clitics – in which the Bulgarian negation operator immediately precedes the imperative verb, the stress falls on the same syllable of the verb on which it falls in non-negated imperatives (compare (27a) with (27b)) – actually argues for its proclitic status.

(27) a.	*RiSUvaj*	*vniMAtelno!*		Bul
	draw.2Sg.Imp	carefully		
	'Draw carefully!'			
b.	*Ne*	*riSUvaj*	*seGA!*	Bul
	not	draw.2Sg.Imp	now	
	'Don't draw now!'			

In Northwestern Macedonian negated imperative clauses, the clitics are between the negation operator and the verb, as in Bulgarian, but their cliticization strategy is different: while in Bulgarian the clitics form a phonological word with the negation operator, in Northwestern Macedonian they encliticize to it. Contrast the stress pattern of the Bulgarian sentence (22a), repeated as (28a), with that of the Northwestern Macedonian sentence (24c), repeated as (28b):

(28) a.	*Ne*	*MU*	*go*	*DAvaj!*	Bulg
	not	him.Dat.Cl	3Sg.N.Acc.Cl	give.2Sg.Imper	
	'Don't give them to him!'				
b.	*NE* ←	*mu* ←	*go*	*DAvaj!*	NWMac
	not	3Sg.M.Dat.Cl	3Sg.N.Acc.Cl	give.2SG.Imper	
	'Don't give it to him!'				

These facts point to a strong Neg in specifier position (cf. Tomić 2001), to which the Northwestern Macedonian clitics + verb complex moves, making possible the encliticization of the

---

if the specifiers of agreement nodes are occupied, there would be serious problems for clitic doubling – a very important feature of Balkan languages and of Macedonian in particular. Moreover, the Macedonian and Bulgarian clitic clusters, which in all current analysis are formed in syntax and include auxiliary clitics and subjunctive and negation operators, in addition to the pronominal clitics, would involve items derived in specifiers as well as items derived in heads. So, the derivation of the Macedonian and Bulgarian pronominal clitics is still open for discussion.

pronominal clitics to the negation operator. The imperative features of the verb are checked covertly, since the strong negation operator "bars" the passage of the verb to Mood, which must be strong since it attracts the verb in positive imperatives.[22]

In Standard Macedonian, in both positive and negative imperative clauses, the negation operator is to the left of the verb and, together with the verb and the clitics to its right, forms an antepenultimately stressed single phonological word. (cf. (29a) and (23a), repeated as (29b)).

(29) a. *Ispij* – *go!* Mac
drink-up.2Sg.Imper it.N.Acc.Cl
'Drink it up!'

b. *NE* – *pij* – *go!* Mac
not drink.2Sg.Imper it.N.Acc.Cl
'Don't drink it!'

In Standard Macedonian negative imperatives, the verb + clitics complex raises as far as AgrSP and then the strong Mood attracts the verb, which excorporates and raises to Mood – along with Neg, with which it merges along the way.[23]

7. Conclusion

Verbs with imperative morphology and bare subjunctive constructions share interpretative properties: they both point to "non-veridical" events and can be used with imperative force. This fact argues for checking the imperative mood in the same node in which the subjunctive complementizer is derived or merged, which is distinct from the node where the future marking modal clitics are derived or merged. Although in the surface structures of Balkan Slavic imperative clauses the negation operator appears to the left of the verb, while in subjunctive constructions it appears to the right of the subjunctive complementizer, shared interpretative and selectional properties argue for analogy in the placement of Neg in subjunctives and imperatives, i.e. leads to the conclusion that the negation operator operating in subjunctive constructions, which obviously is to the left of the subjunctive complementizer, also operates in imperatives.

Differences in the behaviour of the clitics in different Balkan Slavic languages are due not only to the distinct cliticization properties of the clitics, but also to differences in the strength of the Mood and Neg operators. In Serbo-Croatian and Bulgarian, both Mood and Neg are weak and the different positions of the clitics in the two languages follow from features of the pronominal clitics. In Standard Macedonian, Neg is weak, but Mood is strong, and the verb is always attracted by it, so that the pronominal clitics are always to its right. In Northwestern Macedonian, Neg is strong and hosts the pronominal clitics (in imperatives as well as in indicatives). The fact that the behaviour of the pronominal clitics in Northwestern Macedonian negative imperatives differs from its behaviour in positive imperatives, points to a strong Mood. The strong Neg, however, bars the excorporation of the verb and its overt movement to Mood.

---

[22] In positive imperatives the behaviour of the clitics in Northwestern Macedonian is analogous to their behaviour in Standard Macedonian. Note that in Standard Macedonian, where Neg is weak, the verb can "pass" through Neg to Mood.

[23] For a different, PF, movement of the Macedonian imperative verb, involving PF affixes, see Bošković (2001).

References

Bibović Ljiljana (1971): "Some remarks on the factive and non-factive complements in English and Serbo-Croatian." In: Rudolf Filipović (ed.): *The Yugoslav Serbo-Croatian – English Contrastive Project. Studies* 3. Zagreb: Institute of Linguistics, 37–48.

Bošković, Željko (2001): *On the Nature of the Syntax-Phonology Interface: Cliticization and Related Phenomena.* Amsterdam: Elsevier Science.

Browne, Wayles (1981/1986): *Relativna rečenica u hrvatskom ili srpskom jeziku u poređenju s engleskom situacijom.* Ph. D. dissertation, University of Zagreb, 1981. Published as Browne, Wayles: *Relative Clauses in Serbo-Croatian; The Yugoslav Serbo-Croatian – English Contrastive Project; New Studies* 4. [ed. Rudolf Filipović] Zagreb: Institute of Linguistics, 1986. [English translation by the author.]

Franks, Steven (1998): "Clitics in Slavic". Paper presented at the Comparative Slavic Morphosyntax Workshop, Spencer, Indiana.

Giannakidou, A. (1998): *Polarity Sensititivity as (Non)veridical Dependency* [Linguistik Aktuell/Linguistics Today]. Amsterdam: John Benjamins.

Gołąb, Zbignjev (1964): "The problem of verbal moods in Slavic languages". In: *International Journal of Slavic Linguistics and Poetics* 7. The Hage: Mouton, 1–36.

Han, Ch.-H. (1998): "Cross-linguistic variation in the compatibility of negation and imperatives". In: K. Shahin, S. Blake and E.-S. Kim (eds.): *Proceedings of the Seventeenth West Coast Conference on Formal Linguistics.* Stanford, Calif.: CSLI Publications, 1–17.

Inkelas, S. (1989): Prosodic constituency in the lexicon. Ph. D. dissertation, Stanford University.

Isac, Daniela and Edit Jakab (in press): "Mood and force features in the languages of the Balkans". In: O. Mišeska Tomić (ed.): *Balkan Syntax and Semantics* [Linguistik Aktuell]. Amsterdam: Benjamins.

Ivić, Milka (1972): "Problematika srpskohrvatskog infinitiva" [The Serbo-Croatian infinitive], *Zbornik Matice Srpske* XV/2, 115–138.

Kallulli, Dalila (1995): "Optional Verb Movement: Albanian Imperatives". Ms. University of Darham.

Kayne, R. (1994): *The Antisymmetry of Syntax.* Cambridge, Mass.: MIT Press.

Laka, Itziar (1994): *On the Syntax of Negation* [Outstanding Dissertations in Linguistics]. New York and London: A Garland Series.

Rivero, Maria-Luisa (1994): "Clause Structure and V-movement in the Languages of the Balkans", *Natural Language and Linguistic Theory* 12, 63–120.

Rivero, Maria-Luisa and Arhonto Terzi (1995): "Imperatives, V-Movement and logical mood". In: *Journal of Linguistics* 31, 301–332.

Rizzi, Luiggi (1995): "The fine structure of the left periphery". Ms. University of Venice.

Rudin, Catherine (1994): "On Focus Position and Focus Marking in Bulgarian Questions". In: A. Davison et al. (eds.): *Papers from the Fourth Annual Meeting of the Formal Linguistics of MidAmerica,* Iowa City: University of Iowa, 252–265.

Rudin, Catherine (1997): "Kakvo li e *li*: Interrogation and Focusing in Bulgarian". In: *Balkanistika* 10, 335–346.

Rudin, Catherine, Christina Kramer, Loren Billings and Matthew Baerman (1999): "Macedonian and Bulgarian *li* Questions: Beyond Syntax". In: *Natural Language and Linguistic Theory* 17, 541–586.

Stjepanović, Sandra (To appear): "Clitic climbing and restructuring with "finite clause" complements and infinitives". In: *Journal of Slavic Linguistics.*

Tomić, Olga Mišeska (2000): "On clitic sites". In: Beukema, F. and M. den Dikken (eds.): *Clitic Phenomena in European Languages.* Amsterdam: Benjamins, 293–317.

Tomić, Olga Mišeska (2001): "The Macedonian Negation Operator and Cliticization". In: *Natural Language and Linguistic Theory* 19, 647–682.

Tomić, Olga Mišeska (2002a): "Negation and imperatives". In: Zybatow, G., U. Junghanns, G. Mehlhorn, and L. Szuczich (eds.): *Current Issues in Formal Slavic Linguistics.* Frankfurt am Main: Peter Lang, 261–277.

Tomić, Olga Mišeska (2002b): "Modality and mood in Macedonian". In: Barbiers, Sjef, Frits Beukema and Wim van der Wurff (eds.): *Modality and its Interaction with the Verbal System*. Amsterdam: Benjamins, 261–277.

Tomić, Olga Mišeska (2004): "The Balkan Slavic future tenses". In: *Lingua* Vol. 114, Issue 4, 517–545.

Tomić, Olga Mišeska (in press): "Pronominal clitics and imperatives in South Slavic". In: Wurff, Wim van der (ed.): *Imperative Clauses in Generative Grammar*. Amsterdam: John Benjamins.

Vrzić, Zvjezdana (1996): "Categorial status of the Serbo-Croatian 'modal' *da*". In: Toman, Jiři (ed.): *Formal Approaches to Slavic Linguistics: The College Park Meeting 1994*. Ann Arbor: Michigan Slavic Publications, 291–312.

Zanuttini, Rafaela (1991): *Syntactic Properties of Sentential Negation. A Comparative Study of Romance Languages.* Ph. D. dissertation. University of Pennsylvania.

Zanuttini, Rafaela (1997): *Negation and Clausal Structure: A Comparative Study of Romance Languages* [Oxford Studies in Comparative Syntax], New York & Oxford: Oxford University Press.

Adam Przepiórkowski, Warsaw and Alexandr Rosen, Prague

On the Case of Predicative Complements in Czech Infinitival Clauses[1]

1 Introduction

To the ear of a Czech speaker, the examples in (1) sound perfectly acceptable:[2]

(1) a. Pět poslanců se bálo být upřímných. (SC)
five-NOM MPs-GEN feared be-INF frank-GEN
'Five MPs were afraid to be frank.'

b. Donutil jsem ho přijít samotného.
forced AUX-1SG he-ACC come-INF alone-ACC
(OC; Franks 1998 after Toman 1991)
'I forced him to come alone.'

Yet their theoretical account in some more prominent modern syntactic theories, including Principles and Parameters (P&P; Chomsky 1995 and references therein) and Head-driven Phrase Structure Grammar (HPSG; Pollard and Sag 1987, 1994), seems to be problematic.

Both theories assume a clear distinction between raising to subject (SR) and so-called Exceptional Case Marking (ECM; here called raising to object, or OR) constructions, as in (2), on the one hand, and subject control (SC) and object control (OC) constructions, as in (3) and (1) above, on the other hand.

(2) a. John seems to like Mary. (SR)

b. Honza přestal mít rád Marii. (SR)
Honza-NOM stopped have-INF glad Marie-ACC
'Honza stopped liking Maria.'

c. I expect John to help Mary. (OR)

d. Viděl jsem Honzu líbat Marii. (OR)
seen AUX-1SG Honza-ACC kiss-INF Marie-ACC
'I saw Honza kissing Marie.'

(3) a. John tries to help Mary. (SC)

b. Honza zkouší pomáhat Marii. (SC)
Honza-NOM tries help-INF Marie-ACC
'Honza tries to help Marie.'

c. I ordered John to help Mary. (OC)

d. Nařídil jsem Honzovi pomáhat Marii. (OC)
ordered AUX-1SG Honza-DAT help-INF Marie-ACC
'I ordered Honza to help Marie'

[1]The authors would like to thank the audience at FDSL-5 and anonymous reviewers z for helpful comments. The work was partially supported by the Grant Agency of the Czech Republic, grant no. 405/03/0913, and by the governments of Poland and the Czech Republic within the programme KONTAKT (Czech reg. no. 23/2004, Polish no. 25/2004/CZ). See Przepiórkowski and Rosen 2005 for an extended version of this paper, based on parallel Czech and Polish data.

[2]For comments on the quirky (genitive) agreement with the numeral subject in (1a) see §2.1 below, in particular footnote 3.

Two of the most robust cross-linguistic tests distinguishing raising and control involve passivisation (e.g., Pollard and Sag 1994 and, for Czech, Skoumalová 2002) and idiom chunks (e.g., Postal 1974): i) when the lower verb is in the passive, the meaning of the sentence is the same as in the active voice in case of raising constructions, but not in case of control constructions, e.g., (4)–(5), and ii) chunks of sentential idioms can be raised arguments, but they cannot be controllers, e.g., (6)–(7).

(4)	a.	Mary seems to be helped by John.	(SR; ≈(2a))
	b.	I expect Mary to be helped by John.	(OR; ≈(2c))
(5)	a.	Mary tries to be helped by John.	(SC; ≉(3a))
	b.	I ordered Mary to be helped by John.	(OC; ≉(3c))
(6)	a.	The cat seems to be out of the bag.	(SR)
	b.	I expect the cat to be out of the bag.	(OR)
(7)	a.	*The cat tries to be out of the bag.	(SC)
	b.	*I ordered the cat to be out of the bag.	(OC)

In both P&P and HPSG, two systematic differences between raising and control are postulated: i) semantically, raising verbs have one argument fewer than the corresponding control verbs, e.g., *seem* has one semantic argument, while *try* has two; ii) structurally, the raised argument and the subject of the infinitival verb are the same element (so-called structure sharing; henceforth SS), while the controller and the controllee (the subject of the infinitival verb) are two different elements (the latter realised as PRO in P&P). The strong correlation between i) and ii) is ensured by, in one version of P&P, the interaction of Theta criterion (which implies the case filter), Move α and the properties of PRO, and in HPSG, by appropriate lexical entries of raising and control verbs, by the control theory and the Raising Principle.

The reason why the examples in (1) are problematic is that this correlation between semantic and structural properties is missing in control constructions: the controllee's case is shown overtly as the case of the predicative complement, agreeing obligatorily with its subject (the controllee). Thus, the controller seems to share its case value with that of the controllee, contrary to the expectation that the controllee receives its case independently.

In the following, we use Czech data to show that the correlation between semantic and structural properties of raising and control does not hold and, thus, refute the Theta criterion of P&P. In doing this, we follow Hudson 1998, 2003, who postulates a similar dissociation of raising/control and SS on the basis of Icelandic, Ancient Greek, and — in the latter article — Russian, and Przepiórkowski 1999, 2004b, who confirms Hudson's conclusions using Polish data and provides an analysis in HPSG.

The next section, §2, presents the relevant case transmission data from Czech. Section 3 contains an HPSG analysis of the Czech data in terms of dissociating SS from raising. Finally, §4 summarises the main conclusions.

2 The data

2.1 Data on Subject Control/Raising

Consider the case transmission examples (8)–(9) (example (9b) is repeated from (1a)).

(8) a. Petr se zdál být nespokojený. (SR)
Petr-NOM seemed be-INF dissatisfied-NOM
'Petr seemed to be dissatisfied'

b. Pět poslanců se zdálo být nespokojených. (SR)
Five-NOM MPs-GEN seemed be-INF dissatisfied-GEN
9 'Five MPs seemed to be dissatisfied'

(9) a. Petr se bál přijít neohlášený. (SC)
Petr-NOM feared come-INF unannounced-NOM
'Petr was afraid of arriving impromptu.'

b. Pět poslanců se bálo být upřímných. (SC)
five-NOM MPs-GEN feared be-INF frank-GEN
'Five MPs were afraid to be frank.'

Both in SR examples, (8), and in SC examples, (9), the predicative adjective complement of the infinitival copula agrees in case with the matrix subject; the fact that it is agreement and not assignment of the nominative case is confirmed by the quirky (genitive) agreement with numeral subjects in examples (8b) and (9b).[3]

The examples in (8) are expected: the subject of the copula is structure-shared with (raised to) the matrix subject, so they have common case value, and the case on the adjective is the result of the ordinary local case agreement between the subject of the copula and its predicative adjective complement. On the other hand, the examples in (9) are not expected on the standard assumptions of P&P or HPSG: in control constructions, only the content of the controller and the subject of the infinitival is shared, not the case value, so there is no appropriately cased NP/DP (henceforth, NP) with which the predicative adjective could locally agree.

Very similar case transmission data in SR/OR constructions were previously discussed for Polish by Franks 1995 and Przepiórkowski 1999, 2004b, the only significant distinction being the availability of accusative case with numeral subjects (10).[4]

(10) a. Pięć kobiet wydawało się być niespokojnych / niespokojne. (SR)
five-ACC women-GEN seemed be-INF uneasy-GEN uneasy-ACC
'Five women seemed to be uneasy.'

b. Pięć kobiet bało się być niespokojnych / niespokojne. (SC)
five-ACC women-GEN feared be-INF uneasy-GEN uneasy-ACC
'Five women were afraid to be uneasy.'

In order to analyse the Polish data, Franks 1995 argues that PRO must bear case, contrary to P&P assumptions, and sketches a few possible solutions, noting their various drawbacks. Przepiórkowski 1999, 2004b attempts to eliminate those drawbacks and proposes HPSG principles which, in the spirit of Hudson 1998, amount to ensuring that, in Polish, SC involves SS,

[3]This quirky agreement with (a class of) numeral subjects occurs also in simple predicative constructions, e.g., (i) below, and thus requires an independent explanation (Przepiórkowski 2000).

(i) Pět poslanců bylo neklidných.
five-ACC MPs-GEN were uneasy-GEN
'Five MPs were uneasy.'

[4]For the arguments that Polish numeral subjects are in fact accusative, see, e.g., Przepiórkowski 1999, 2004a. For the purpose of this article, we assume that numeral subjects are accusative also in Czech, although for Czech the evidence is less conclusive.

just as SR does, and — hence — case transmission occurs obligatorily. On the other hand, such SS must be forbidden in OC, as there is no case transmission in Polish OC and the predicative adjective occurs in the 'default' instrumental case, so-called 'instrumental of predication'.

Such parochial language-specific behaviour of SS or no SS in control constructions seems to be the rule cross-linguistically, cf., e.g., the fact that in Lithuanian accusative controllers do not allow SS while their genitive of negation counterparts do (Timberlake 1988); cf. also Hudson 1998, 2003 and the work cited therein on Icelandic and Ancient Greek.

2.2 Data on Object Control/Raising

Czech OC constructions provide even more striking evidence for the lack of correlation between raising/control and SS/no SS. In Czech, the non-agreeing case of predicative adjectives is the nominative, with the instrumental acceptable to some extent only with copula, as in (11).

(11) a. Být opilý znamená být hloupý.
be-INF drunk-NOM means be-INF stupid-NOM
'Being drunk means being stupid.'

b. ??Být opilým znamená být hloupým.
be-INF drunk-INS means be-INF stupid-INS

The nominative as the non-agreeing predicative case is present also in Czech OC with dative objects (12) — there is no case transmission.[5]

(12) a. Marie nařídila Honzovi přijít střízlivý / *střízlivému. (OC)
Marie-NOM ordered Honza-DAT come-INF sober-NOM sober-DAT
'Marie ordered Honza to come sober.'

b. Poručil pěti pacientům přijít svlečení / *svlečeným.
ordered-3.SG five-DAT patients-DAT come-INF undressed-NOM undressed-DAT (OC)
'He ordered five patients to come undressed.'

The situation is more complicated in case of OC with accusative objects. When the object is a plain (non-numeral) NP, as in (13), the case of the predicative complement can be either nominative (no case transmission, as in the dative object case) or accusative (case transmission).[6]

(13) a. Marie naučila Honzu chodit domů střízlivý / střízlivého. (OC)
Marie taught Honza-ACC go-INF home sober-NOM sober-ACC
'Marie taught Honza to come home sober.'

b. Donutil jsem ho přijít samotného.
forced AUX-1SG he-ACC come-INF alone-ACC
(OC; Franks 1998 after Toman 1991)
'I forced him to come alone.'

[5]Examples (12) with predicative complements in the dative are acceptable when predicative complements are understood as complementing the higher verb. As in SC constructions, the case of predicative adjectives in OC is rarely instrumental (and if so, only with copula), no matter whether the object is dative or accusative.

[6]Similarly as examples (12) above, examples (13) in the version with the predicative complement in the accusative can have the meaning 'While he was sober, she taught him to come home'. Nevertheless, the glossed reading is the preferred option. Example (13b) is repeated from (1b).

However, when the object is a numeral NP, as in (14), the preferred case of the predicative complement seems to be genitive, i.e., case transmission takes place.

(14) a. Marie přiměla pět pacientů přijít svlečených /
Marie made five-ACC patients-GEN come-INF undressed-GEN
??svlečení / ??svlečené. (OC)
undressed-NOM undressed-ACC
'Marie made five patients come undressed.'

b. Odnaučila mnoho žáků přicházet do školy ??nevyspalí /
untaught-3.SG.FEM many-ACC pupils-GEN come-INF to school sleepy-NOM
??nevyspalé / nevyspalých. (OC)
sleepy-ACC sleepy-GEN
'She taught many pupils to stop coming to school without having proper sleep.'

On the other hand, OR examples including accusative objects, both plain NPs and numeral phrases,[7] seem to behave as expected, i.e., case transmission takes place.

(15) a. Marie viděla Honzu přijít *střízlivý / střízlivého. (OR)
Marie saw Honza-ACC come-INF sober-NOM sober-ACC
'Marie saw Honza come sober.'

b. Marie viděla pět pacientů ležet neošetřených / *neošetření
Marie saw five-ACC patients-GEN lie-INF unattended-GEN unattended-NOM
/ ??neošetřené. (OC)
unattended-ACC
'Marie saw five patients lying unattended.'

As the tentative acceptability ratings of the examples above show, more representative and reliable data are needed, especially for accusative object control verbs. After corpus search, introspective research and judgments of a few speakers had failed to produce conclusive results, we resorted to a web-based survey.[8] Visitors of the site were asked to rate 26 Czech sentences, exemplifying the presence or absence of SS by means of the presence or absence of case transmission from the matrix object to the predicative complement of the embedded infinitive. Table 1 gives the number of sentences in the survey listed according to the type of the matrix verb (control or raising), the case of the *anchor* (the controller or the raised element)[9] and the absence or presence of SS (as shown by the case of the predicative complement).

Two kinds of accusative controllers were tested: plain and numeral NPs, in order to verify the hypothesis that the latter support SS more readily. Dative numeral NPs have not been included — their agreement pattern does not differ from that of plain dative NP. Respondents, whose number reached 699, had to choose one of four options on an acceptability scale (fine, acceptable, strange, impossible).

The judgments may have been influenced by factors other than the control/raising contrast, the form of the matrix object, and the presence or absence of SS. Such factors may include: the linear distance between the matrix object and the predicative complement (the acceptability of the non-sharing option increases with longer distance), lexical setting (e.g., infinitival copula

[7]Only OR verbs with accusative objects have been found.

[8]The second co-author wishes to thank Hana Skoumalová and Johanka Doležalová for gladly provided technical assistance.

[9]We borrow the term *anchor*, as used in this context, from Hudson 2003.

	anchor	no SS	SS
object control	*dative*	1	1
	plain accusative	4	3
	accusative numeral	2	3
object raising	*plain accusative*	2	2
	accusative numeral	2	2

Table 1: Number of sentences in the survey

tends to make non-sharing option more acceptable), idiomatic nature of the embedded predicative, verbal aspect of both verbs, and the often reported difficulty of judgment due to stylistic preference for alternative syntactic structures (finite clauses instead of infinitival clauses, adverbs instead of predicative adjectives).

Table 2 shows the results for sentences with accusative anchors. The third column gives the mean rating value on the four-point scale, while the last column gives the share of respondents for whom the examples were fine or acceptable (i.e., 1 or 2). The intervals reflect the range of acceptability judgments for multiple examples of the same type.

example type	structure sharing	mean	fine or acceptable for
accusative OC	yes	1.8	30–74%
	no	2.8	1–50%
numeral acc. OC	yes	2.4	28–74%
	no	3.4	10–11%
accusative OR	yes	1.6	84–88%
	no	3.6	3–5%
numeral acc. OR	yes	2.2	54–71%
	no	3.2	12–20%

Table 2: The survey results for accusative OC/OR

The results of the survey support the following conclusions:

1. For ordinary accusative NPs as OC objects, SS is slightly preferred, as in (13b).
2. For numeral accusative NPs as OC objects, SS is strongly preferred, cf. (14).
3. In OR, SS is the strongly preferred option, cf. (15).

2.3 Summary of the data

Hudson 2003 provides a summary of sharing (SS) and non-sharing (PRO) options for Russian, Icelandic and Ancient Greek. In Table 3, the summary is extended by Polish and Czech.[10] Czech data are presented in more detail in Table 4 in parallel with comparable Polish data. The comparison shows the striking difference between SC and SR constructions on the one hand, where Czech and Polish behave in a similar way (except for the fact that with numeral subjects Polish allows for two or even three options), and OC and OR constructions on the other

[10] *θ-marked* anchors are controllers, non-*θ-marked* anchors are raised elements.

hand, where OC constructions with the predicative complement in the instrumental are the only possibility in Polish. In current Polish, there are no OR/ECM verbs.

Anchor		Structure (Structure Sharing or PRO)				
θ-marked	function	Russian	Icelandic	A. Greek	Polish	Czech
no	subj	SS	SS	SS	SS	SS
yes	subj	SS	SS (??PRO)	SS	SS	SS
no	obj	–	SS	SS,PRO	–	SS
yes	obj	(SS),PRO	SS,PRO	SS,PRO	PRO	SS,PRO

Table 3: Table I in Hudson 2003, extended with Polish and Czech

Verb	Anchor		Czech pred.			Polish pred.			
	subj	obj	nom	gen	acc	nom	gen	acc	ins
SC	nom		[●] (shaded)			[●] (shaded)			
	№			[●] (shaded)			[●] (shaded)	[●] (shaded)	
SR	nom		[●]			[●]			
	№			[●]			[●]	[●]	
OC		dat	●						
		acc			[●] (shaded)				●
		acc №		[●] (shaded)					
OR		acc			[●]				
		acc №		[●]					

● fine
acceptable
№ numeral phrase
[●] structure sharing
[●] (shaded) unexpected structure sharing

Table 4: Czech and Polish raising/control in detail

3 Analysis in HPSG

The analysis of case transmission in Czech reflects the following observations made on the basis of the data considered above, as well as the data presented in Timberlake 1988 and Hudson 1998, 2003: (i) in many languages (Icelandic, Ancient Greek, Lithuanian, Polish, Russian, Czech...) there are cases of semantic control involving case transmission, i.e., involving SS; and (ii) there are idiosyncratic differences between languages in the specific control environments which allow or force SS. Hence, the analysis should follow as much as possible from general and independently needed principles, but the need for additional parochial principles should not be surprising.

The following subsections present an HPSG account of case transmission in Czech control constructions based on, and extending, the analysis for Polish presented in Przepiórkowski

2004b. We start with various independently needed HPSG assumptions concerning control, raising, and case assignment, §§3.1–3.2, and then we present the additional parochial principles needed to account for Czech case transmission, §3.3. The final subsection, §3.4, contains a discussion of the interaction of the HPSG Raising Principle with the analysis proposed.

3.1 Control and Raising in HPSG

In standard HPSG, raising verbs are assumed to have lexical entries like the one schematically presented in (16).[11]

(16) A Subject Raising verb (e.g., Czech *začít* 'begin')

$$\begin{bmatrix} \textit{word} & \\ \text{ARG-ST} & \begin{bmatrix} \text{SUBJ } \langle \boxed{0} \rangle \text{ COMPS } \langle \text{VP}\begin{bmatrix} \text{DEPS} \mid \text{SUBJ } \langle \boxed{0} \rangle \\ \text{CONT } \boxed{1} \end{bmatrix} \rangle \end{bmatrix} \\ \text{CONT} & \mathbf{P}(\boxed{1}) \end{bmatrix}$$

In (16) the content of the infinitival VP (cf. $\boxed{1}$) is identified with the only semantic argument of the SR verb (cf. **P**($\boxed{1}$), where **P** stands for the semantic predicate expressed by the verb), while the surface subject of the VP ($\boxed{0}$) is structure shared with the deep subject of the SR verb. The boxed numbers (e.g., $\boxed{1}$) are variables whose values are feature structures; multiple occurrences of the same variable in a feature structure denote structure sharing.

In contrast to raising verbs, control verbs have lexical entries like (17).

(17) A Subject Control verb (e.g., Czech *zkusit*, 'try')

$$\begin{bmatrix} \textit{word} & \\ \text{ARG-ST} & \begin{bmatrix} \text{SUBJ } \langle \text{NP}\begin{bmatrix}\text{CONT } \boxed{1}\end{bmatrix} \rangle \\ \text{COMPS } \langle \text{VP}\begin{bmatrix} \text{DEPS} \mid \text{SUBJ } \langle [\text{ CONT } \boxed{1} \text{ }] \rangle \\ \text{CONT } \boxed{2} \end{bmatrix} \rangle \end{bmatrix} \\ \text{CONT} & \mathbf{P}(\boxed{1},\boxed{2}) \end{bmatrix}$$

A SC verb, as in (17), is a (semantically) 2-argument verb: the first semantic argument (i.e., $\boxed{1}$ in **P**($\boxed{1}$,$\boxed{2}$)) is the content of its deep subject ($\boxed{1}$), while the second semantic argument is the content of the infinitival VP (cf. $\boxed{2}$). The lexical entry does not specify full SS between the deep subject of the verb and the surface subject of the VP complement; instead, the two subjects are co-indexed (cf. $\boxed{1}$), i.e., they share their semantics.[12] A related difference between raising and control verbs is that a raising verb does not specify the morphosyntactic makeup of its raised argument, it takes whatever subject is required by its VP complement, while a control verb specifies its controller argument as an NP.

[11]The attributes ARG-ST and DEPS reflect the assumption that there are at least two levels of argument structure: a 'deep' argument structure, constant for all forms of a given lexeme, and a 'surface' argument structure, which depends on the voice of a given word form, the two arguments structures being systematically related via general grammatical principles (cf., e.g., Manning and Sag 1998, 1999, Bouma et al. 2001, Avgustinova 2001). Moreover, DEPS is the locus of syntactic case assignment, as well as — at least in languages such as Czech and Polish — binding.

[12]For the sake of cross-theoretical readability, throughout the paper we present a simplified version of HPSG structures and analyses. In particular, in standard HPSG, only parts of the values of CONT are structure shared in control constructions.

Lexical entries of OR and OC verbs are analogous to the lexical entries of SR and SC verbs above, and they display analogous differences. An entry for OR verbs is shown below.

(18) An Object Raising (ECM) verb (e.g., Czech *vidět*, 'see')

$$\begin{bmatrix} \textit{word} & \\ \text{ARG-ST} & \begin{bmatrix} \text{SUBJ } \langle \text{NP}\begin{bmatrix}\text{CONT } \boxed{1}\end{bmatrix} \rangle \\ \text{COMPS } \langle \boxed{0}, \text{VP}\begin{bmatrix}\text{DEPS}\,|\,\text{SUBJ } \langle\boxed{0}\rangle \\ \text{CONT } \boxed{2}\end{bmatrix}\rangle \end{bmatrix} \\ \text{CONT} & \mathbf{P}(\boxed{1},\boxed{2}) \end{bmatrix}$$

According to (18), the first semantic argument of an OR verb is the content of its deep subject (cf. $\boxed{1}$), while the second semantic argument is the content of the infinitival VP (cf. $\boxed{2}$). The surface subject of the VP complement is structure shared with (raised to) the deep object of the OR verb (cf. $\boxed{0}$).

Finally, OC verbs have three semantic arguments and their objects must be co-indexed with the subjects of their VP complements. In (19), as in (18), the first semantic argument of the OC verb is the content of its deep subject (cf. $\boxed{1}$) and, again as in case of OR verbs, the semantic argument of the OC verb is the content of the infinitival VP (cf. $\boxed{3}$). However, the surface subject of the VP is only co-indexed (cf. $\boxed{2}$) with the deep object of an OC verb and the content of that object (cf. $\boxed{2}$) is the second semantic argument of the OC verb:

(19) An Object Control verb (e.g., Czech *přikázat*, 'order')

$$\begin{bmatrix} \textit{word} & \\ \text{ARG-ST} & \begin{bmatrix} \text{SUBJ } \langle \text{NP}\begin{bmatrix}\text{CONT } \boxed{1}\end{bmatrix} \rangle \\ \text{COMPS } \langle \text{NP}\begin{bmatrix}\text{CONT } \boxed{2}\end{bmatrix}, \text{VP}\begin{bmatrix}\text{DEPS}\,|\,\text{SUBJ } \langle[\text{ CONT } \boxed{2}\ ]\rangle \\ \text{CONT } \boxed{3}\end{bmatrix}\rangle \end{bmatrix} \\ \text{CONT} & \mathbf{P}(\boxed{1},\boxed{2},\boxed{3}) \end{bmatrix}$$

Now, HPSG control theory as formulated in Pollard and Sag 1994 assumes that controlled subjects are really anaphors and that their distribution and reference is accounted for by the binding theory. This does not seem plausible for Czech, where anaphors are strictly bound by subjects, while controlled elements may be controlled by either subjects or complements, so we assume that such a theory is at best a parochial principle for English, corresponding to Czech parochial principles introduced in §3.3.

On the other hand, in case of raising predicates, the correlation between raising as a phenomenon of syntax (SS of arguments) and semantics (no semantic role assigned to the raised argument) has been ensured by the Raising Principle, schematically quoted below.

> In every lexical entry E in which an argument is structure shared with another argument's subject, i.e., in every lexical entry E of the form
>
> $$\begin{bmatrix} \textit{word} & \\ \text{ARG-ST} & \begin{bmatrix} \text{SUBJ} & \langle\boxed{1}\rangle \\ \text{COMPS} & \langle \ldots\ [\ \text{DEPS}\,|\,\text{SUBJ } \boxed{1}\ ]\ \ldots\rangle \end{bmatrix} \end{bmatrix}$$
>
> or

$$\begin{bmatrix} \textit{word} & \\ \text{ARG-ST} & \begin{bmatrix} \text{COMPS} & \langle \ldots \boxed{1} \ldots [\ \text{DEPS} \mid \text{SUBJ} \boxed{1}\ ] \ldots \rangle \end{bmatrix} \end{bmatrix},$$

the element $\boxed{1}$ is assigned no semantic role in E (i.e., the CONT value of $\boxed{1}$ is not a semantic argument of the predicate expressed in the CONT value of E).[13]

Note that the Raising Principle corresponds to the Theta criterion of P&P:[14]

> Each argument bears one and only one theta-role, and each theta-role is assigned to one and only one argument.

We will see in §3.4 that the dissociation of raising/control and structure sharing proposed in §3.3 does not violate the Raising Principle.

3.2 Case Assignment and Case Agreement in HPSG

We follow the general approach of Przepiórkowski 1999 and assume the structural/lexical case dichotomy and the following principles of structural case assignment:[15]

(20) structural case is assigned (checked) at the level of the surface argument structure (DEPS) of words;

(21) in case of raising, when an argument occurs at a number of surface argument structures (DEPS) of different verbs, case is assigned at the highest surface argument structure on which the argument occurs;

(22) assignment of structural case in Czech is guided by the following principles :

a. surface subjects of both finite and non-finite verbs are assigned the nominative;

b. surface complements of verbs are assigned the accusative;

Thus, if an argument occurs on several argument structures, its case is checked only on the highest of these. This way there is no case clash in, e.g., OR, where the lower subject is raised to the higher object position: it is assigned case according to its highest position, i.e., it receives the accusative (cf. (22b)), and no attempt is made to assign the nominative to its lower 'copy' (cf. (21)). On the other hand, in cases of object control, where only the INDEX value is structure-shared, the controller and the controlled unexpressed subject are two different arguments, so they are both assigned case: the object receives the accusative (cf. (22b)), and the controlled subject receives the nominative (cf. (22a)).

Furthermore, we assume that the noun phrase modified by a predicative complement is subcategorized for by the complement as its subject. The modified noun phrase is also an argument of a verb, which serves as the head of the predicative complement. If this verb is non-finite, the argument can be controlled or raised. Then the subject of the predicative complement is overtly realized higher up, possibly in the matrix clause.

A predicative complement may share morphological case with its subject, or may be assigned the nominative, which is captured by the following implicational principle:[16]

[13]In fact, this principle was originally formulated in terms of a single attribute SUBCAT, whose value is the list of all arguments, subjects and complements alike.

[14]This formulation is taken from Haegeman 1991p. 63.

[15]See Przepiórkowski 1999 for formalisation and discussion.

[16]This is a simplified version of the principle, which does not take into consideration quirky (possibly genitive in Polish, obligatorily genitive in Czech) case agreement with numeral phrases; see Przepiórkowski 1999, 2000 for the full version.

(23) $\begin{bmatrix} \text{SUBJ} & \langle \text{XP[CASE } \boxed{1}] \rangle \\ \text{HEAD} & \begin{bmatrix} \text{PRD} & + \\ \text{CASE} & \boxed{2} \end{bmatrix} \end{bmatrix} \rightarrow (\boxed{1} = \boxed{2}) \vee (\boxed{2} = ins)$

According to this principle, for any cased ([CASE $\boxed{2}$]) predicate ([PRD +]) subcategorising for a cased subject ([SUBJ ⟨XP[CASE $\boxed{1}$]⟩]), the case of the subject must agree with the case of the predicate ($\boxed{1} = \boxed{2}$), or else the case of the predicate must be instrumental ($\boxed{2} = ins$). In Czech, the instrumental option seems to be further restricted, but we refrain from any attempt to formalize this restriction here.

3.3 Case Transmission

3.3.1 Subject Raising and Object Raising

Nothing needs to be added to the HPSG assumptions discussed above to account for the case transmission in SR examples such as (8a). In such cases, the subject occurs on three argument structures, i.e., those of the finite raising verb, the infinitive copula and the predicative adjective. Since (21) says that case is assigned on the highest argument structure, the nominative is assigned via (22a). Hence, the subject of the predicative adjective is nominative, and, in order to satisfy (23), the adjective itself must be either nominative or (less likely in Czech) instrumental.

In case of SR examples involving numeral anchors, as in (8b), the reasoning would be essentially the same, although the predicative case marking principle (23) would have to take into account the quirky predicative agreement with numeral phrases; cf. fn. 16.

A similar reasoning can be applied to Czech ECM constructions to explain the agreement between the predicative adjective and the object of the ECM verb.

3.3.2 Subject Control

On the other hand, it seems that the above assumptions lead to blatantly wrong predictions in case of SC, which in Czech (as well as in Polish) involves obligatory SS, cf. (9a). The subject of the infinitive is, again, structure shared with the subject of the predicative adjective, but the subject of the control verb is only co-indexed with the subject of the infinitive (and, hence, with the subject of the predicate). The problem shows up with numeral subjects (cf. (9b)), which should agree with a predicative complement in the genitive. However, the unrealised subject of the non-finite verb in control constructions is assigned the nominative case, cf. (22a). Then, the predicative complement must be in the nominative (or instrumental), contrary to the data.

The matter is not that simple, though. HPSG is a declarative (non-transformational) constraint-based theory, i.e., a structure is grammatical if and only if it satisfies all principles (constraints) of the grammar. That is, structures which are not explicitly forbidden by the grammar are licensed. Now, lexical entries for control verbs require that the controller and the controllee be co-indexed, i.e., that they share (parts of) their semantics, but nothing in the grammar actually forbids full SS of complete controller and controllee.[17]

So, SC verbs, whose structure is repeated in (17), are in principle ambiguous between a non-SS interpretation, in which $\boxed{3} \neq \boxed{4}$, and a SS interpretation, where $\boxed{3} = \boxed{4}$.

(17) A Subject Control verb

[17]The possibility of such analysis of Icelandic data is already suggested in Pollard and Sag 1994p. 140, fn. 40.

$$\begin{bmatrix} \textit{word} & \\ \text{ARG-ST} & \begin{bmatrix} \text{SUBJ} \ \langle \boxed{3}\text{NP}\begin{bmatrix}\text{CONT}\ \boxed{1}\end{bmatrix} \rangle \\ \text{COMPS} \ \langle \text{VP}\begin{bmatrix} \text{DEPS} \mid \text{SUBJ} \ \langle \boxed{4}[\ \text{CONT}\ \boxed{1}\ ] \rangle \\ \text{CONT}\ \boxed{2} \end{bmatrix} \rangle \end{bmatrix} \\ \text{CONT} & \text{P}(\boxed{1},\boxed{2}) \end{bmatrix}$$

The reasoning about case non-transmission in SC constructions assumed the non-identity of the controller and the controllee ($\boxed{3} \neq \boxed{4}$); in case of the identity ($\boxed{3} = \boxed{4}$), the reasoning is the same as for the raising verbs in §3.3.1, i.e., case transmission is predicted. This means that, instead of facing the problem of wrong predictions (nominative or instrumental instead of agreement), we face the problem of overgeneration (nominative or instrumental, as well as agreement). That is, what is needed is a principle *forcing* the SS interpretation of control verbs. Such a principle is presented below (in words and as a formal HPSG principle):

(24) Subject Control with SS

Whenever the deep subject of X is co-indexed with the surface subject of a VP complement of X, the two subjects are the same element.

$$\begin{bmatrix} \textit{word} & \\ \text{ARG-ST} & \begin{bmatrix} \text{SUBJ} & \langle \boxed{1}[\ \text{CONT}\ \boxed{0}\ ] \rangle \\ \text{COMPS} & \langle \text{VP}\begin{bmatrix}\text{DEPS} \mid \text{SUBJ}\ \langle \boxed{2}[\ \text{CONT}\ \boxed{0}\ ] \rangle\end{bmatrix} \rangle \end{bmatrix} \end{bmatrix} \rightarrow \boxed{1} = \boxed{2}$$

3.3.3 Object Control

Czech data concerning OC are considerably more complex than those on SC or SR: case transmission is forbidden with dative controllers, but it is optional with accusative controllers, unless the accusative controller is a numeral phrase, where case transmission is actually obligatory.

For the dative controllers, a Czech-specific principle prohibiting SS must be stipulated:[18]

(25) Dative Object Control without SS

Whenever a dative NP as a deep complement of X is co-indexed with the surface subject of a VP complement of X, the NP and the VP's subject are different elements.

$$\begin{bmatrix} \textit{word} & \\ \text{ARG-ST} \mid \text{COMPS} & \left\langle \begin{array}{l} \boxed{1}\text{NP}\begin{bmatrix}\text{CASE}\ \textit{dat} \\ \text{CONT}\ \boxed{0}\end{bmatrix}, \\ \text{VP}\begin{bmatrix}\text{DEPS} \mid \text{SUBJ}\ \langle \boxed{2}[\ \text{CONT}\ \boxed{0}\ ] \rangle\end{bmatrix} \end{array} \right\rangle \end{bmatrix} \rightarrow \boxed{1} \neq \boxed{2}$$

Similarly, for accusative numeral objects, SS may be enforced as in SC:

(26) Accusative Numeral Object Control with SS

Whenever an accusative numeral NP as a deep complement of X is co-indexed with the surface subject of a VP complement of X, the NP and the VP's subject are the same element.

[18] A similar principle without the restriction to dative NPs covers all OC constructions in Polish.

$$\begin{bmatrix} \textit{word} \\ \text{ARG-ST}\,|\,\text{COMPS} \left\langle \boxed{1}\text{NP}\begin{bmatrix} \textit{numeral} \\ \text{CASE } \textit{acc} \\ \text{INDEX } \boxed{0}\end{bmatrix}, \; \text{VP}\left[\text{DEPS}\,|\,\text{SUBJ} \,\langle \boxed{2}[\,\text{INDEX } \boxed{0}\,]\rangle\right] \right\rangle \end{bmatrix} \rightarrow \boxed{1} = \boxed{2}$$

Finally, in order to account for the optionality of case transmission with other accusative controllers, we need to say... nothing! As discussed in §3.3.2, such SS / no SS ambiguity follows from the independently needed HPSG accounts of control and case marking.

3.3.4 Summary

The parochial principles which had to be added to the general HPSG analyses of control and case assignment in order to account for the distribution of case transmission in Czech constructions are summarised in Table 5. Again, Polish is included for comparison.

verb	controller	Czech	Polish
SC		*force SS* (24)	
OC	**dat**	*disallow SS* (25)	*disallow SS*
	acc		
	acc №	*force SS* (26)	

Table 5: Parochial principles for Czech and Polish

3.4 Raising Principle Revisited

The HPSG Raising Principle quoted in §3.1 seems to be violated by SS in control environments, pivotal for the analysis presented in this paper: the element which occurs simultaneously on the higher ARG-ST and on the lower DEPS|SUBJ does have a semantic role assigned by the higher verb, apparently contrary to the Raising Principle.

However, it should be noted that the Raising Principle, as the only principle of this sort given in Pollard and Sag 1994, is formulated as a constraint on lexical entries (i.e., on descriptions), not on linguistic entities — it constrains the way that words can be described in the lexicon. But it is exactly because of that lexical nature of the Raising Principle that the present account does not violate it: lexical entries for control and raising verbs assumed in this analysis (discussed in §3.1) are the kinds of lexical entries usually given for control and raising verbs, i.e., lexical entries for control verbs do not specify full SS, while lexical entries for raising verbs, which do specify full SS, do not assign a semantic role to the raised argument. To put it succinctly, according to the account proposed here, control verbs receive the SS interpretation outside the realm of the lexicon, i.e., outside the scope of the Raising Principle.

4 Conclusion

Czech turns out to be one of the languages that confirm Hudson's (1998, 2003) claim that it is an empirical issue whether control structures involve SS or not. In Czech, subject control always involves SS, while in various types of OC constructions SS is obligatory, optional or forbidden.

The account presented above is based on the standard HPSG assumptions about the difference between control and raising, and on an earlier HPSG analysis of syntactic case assignment. No modifications of these background assumptions were necessary, with the exception of relegating HPSG's assumption that controllees are anaphors to the status of a parochial principle for English. The analysis of complex case transmission facts in Czech consists in a small number of simple constraints on SS of arguments in control constructions.

This type of analysis is possible because of two crucial traits of HPSG. First, on the linguistic side, raising constructions have the same constituent structure as corresponding control constructions. This is in contrast with the widely different structures of OC and ECM (OR) verbs in P&P. Second, on the formal side, HPSG is a constraint-based formalism, where any structure not explicitly forbidden by a grammatical principle is licensed. Again, this should be contrasted with formalisms in which structures are licensed via explicit structure-building operations. It remains to be seen, to what extent the intuitions embodied in this analysis are valid and, if so, whether they can be accommodated by other syntactic theories.

References

Avgustinova, T. (2001). Arguments, grammatical relations, and diathetic paradigm. In Flickinger, D. and Kathol, A., editors, *Proceedings of the 7th International Conference on Head-Driven Phrase Structure Grammar*, pages 23–42. CSLI Publications, Stanford, CA.

Bouma, G., Malouf, R., and Sag, I. A. (2001). Satisfying constraints on extraction and adjunction. *Natural Language and Linguistic Theory*, 19(1):1–65.

Chomsky, N. (1995). *The Minimalist Program*, volume 28 of *Current Studies in Linguistics*. The MIT Press, Cambridge, MA.

Franks, S. (1995). *Parameters of Slavic Morphosyntax*. Oxford University Press, New York.

Franks, S. (1998). *Parameters of Slavic Morphosyntax* revisited: A minimalist perspective. In Bošković, Ž., Franks, S., and Snyder, W., editors, *Annual Workshop on Formal Approaches to Slavic Linguistics: The Connecticut Meeting 1997*, volume 43 of *Michigan Slavic Materials*, pages 134–165, Ann Arbor. Michigan Slavic Publications.

Haegeman, L. (1991). *Introduction to Government and Binding Theory*. Blackwell Textbooks in Linguistics. Blackwell, Oxford, first edition.

Hudson, R. (1998). Functional control with and without structure-sharing. In Siewierska, A. and Song, J. J., editors, *Case, Typology and Grammar*, volume 38 of *Typological Studies in Language*, pages 151–169. Benjamins, Amsterdam.

Hudson, R. (2003). Case agreement, PRO and structure sharing. *Research in Language*, 1.

Manning, C. D. and Sag, I. A. (1998). Argument structure, valence, and binding. *Nordic Journal of Linguistics*, 21(2):107–144.

Manning, C. D. and Sag, I. A. (1999). Dissociations between argument structure and grammatical relations. In Webelhuth, G., Koenig, J.-P., and Kathol, A., editors, *Lexical and Constructional Aspects of Linguistic Explanation*, pages 63–78. CSLI Publications, Stanford, CA.

Pollard, C. and Sag, I. A. (1987). *Information-Based Syntax and Semantics, Volume 1: Fundamentals*. Number 13 in CSLI Lecture Notes. CSLI Publications, Stanford, CA.

Pollard, C. and Sag, I. A. (1994). *Head-driven Phrase Structure Grammar*. Chicago University Press / CSLI Publications, Chicago, IL.

Postal, P. M. (1974). *On Raising*. Massachusetts Institute of Technology, Cambridge, MA.

Przepiórkowski, A. (1999). *Case Assignment and the Complement-Adjunct Dichotomy: A Non-Configurational Constraint-Based Approach.* Ph. D. dissertation, Universität Tübingen.

Przepiórkowski, A. (2000). Predicative case agreement with Quantifier Phrases in Polish. In Okrent, A. and Boyle, J., editors, *The Proceedings from the Main Session of the Chicago Linguistic Society's Thirty-sixth Meeting*, volume 36-1, pages 343–354. Chicago Linguistic Society, Chicago, IL.

Przepiórkowski, A. (2004a). O wartości przypadka podmiotów liczebnikowych. *Biuletyn Polskiego Towarzystwa Językoznawczego*, LX:133–143.

Przepiórkowski, A. (2004b). On case transmission in Polish control and raising constructions. 39:103–123.

Przepiórkowski, A. and Rosen, A. (2005). Czech and Polish raising/control with or without structure sharing. *Research in Language*, 3:33–66.

Skoumalová, H. (2002). Verb frames extracted from dictionaries. *The Prague Bulletin of Mathematical Linguistics*, 77:19–62.

Timberlake, A. (1988). Case agreement in Lithuanian. In Barlow, M. and Ferguson, C. A., editors, *Agreement in Natural Language: Approaches, Theories, Descriptions*, pages 181–199. CSLI Publications, Stanford, CA.

Toman, J. (1991). Anaphors in binary trees: an analysis of Czech reflexives. In Koster, J. and Reuland, E., editors, *Long-Distance Anaphora*, pages 151–170. Cambridge University Press, Cambridge.

Joanna Rabiega-Wiśniewska, Warsaw

A new classification of Polish derivational affixes

1. Introduction

The need for a formal approach to word formation was recognized by linguists not earlier than in the 1970's (Halle, 1973). Since that time, a number of generative studies have been published, e.g., the fundamental monographs of Aronoff (1976) and Booij (1977). Some observations concerning Polish have also been made by, e.g., Górska (1982), Szymanek (1980). However, for the last 20 years Polish derivational morphology has remained almost untouched by formal linguists. Consequently, we still lack a complete account of Polish word formation in terms of productive derivational rules as expected from the NLP perspective.

The traditional approach to derivation, as that given in Grzegorczykowa *et al.* (1998), is hardly appropriate and sufficient for the purpose. Accounts of that type do not pose the question of pure formal relationships between derivatives and their basis lexemes. On the contrary, they concentrate upon semantic aspects and are limited to that issue. We believe that a formal approach to word formation processes in Polish is not only possible, but also highly recommendable. By combining inflectional and derivational levels, we can get a good foundation.

Our aim in this paper is to introduce main assumptions of a new classification of Polish suffixes and to propose a concept of the formal word formation description. The classification background is partly taken from the computational account by Hoeppner (1980). It should be emphasized that the method of a derivative analysis takes advantage of some principles of generative theory. In order to make our methodological introduction more Polish-based, we start with a sketchy account of the traditional approach to Polish derivation morphology.

Our task is to construct a formal model of word formation in Polish and to design an automatic morphological analyser (synthesizer) capable of recognizing word forms as representing derivatives and of identifying their basis lexemes. Since our aim is to build a computational application, the formalism operates on the grapheme level of text. All morphophonological rules are intended to work on written text.

In Polish, derivational morphemes include prefixes, suffixes, interfixes etc. Since Polish inflectional morphology is located at the end of words, we will only deal with suffixation below.

2. Methodology

If one wants to automatically process texts of highly inflecting languages, a number of formal requirements must be met. In our case, the fulfilment of those requirements gives us the whole formal description in several steps. The most important demand is to design a lexicon of a specific structure that contains roots (or stems). Another independent component of the whole is a set of well-defined formatives. At last, word formation rules can bind an item from the lexicon with a certain formative to obtain the whole word. Note that we do not restrict the application of a given rule in advance. To reach our goal in its empirical aspect, we will try to take advantage of a variety of theoretical approaches to derivation.

2.1 Traditional description

In Polish linguistics, there is a long tradition of the Dokulil-type derivational analysis (cf. Dokulil (1962), adapted for Polish and developed by Grzegorczykowa (1971), Grzegorczykowa and Puzynina (1979), Grzegorczykowa *et al.* (1998)). This account aims at establishing semantic relationship between a derivative and its basis. The description consists of a list of semantic roles that are expressed by different formatives and provides interpretations of lexical items to be found in existing dictionaries. This approach lacks reflection on productivity. Instead, the scholars consider the problem of "frequency" of derivational models, i.e., they distinguish classes of derivatives represented by singular lexical items vs. those represented by a great number thereof. Consequently, word formation and inflection are treated separately, as two distinct branches of morphology.

However, Laskowski (1981) puts emphasis on the fact that the theory of denotation categories has unfortunately too much of an intuitive character. In his opinion, a generative theory gives an appropriate apparatus to pose questions and describe linguistic facts in a more formal and efficient way. Laskowski sketches some points of a well-organized word formation description. He adopts a definition of derivation as a set of rules that define a relationship of motivation between lexical units (WF rules). He points out that there are two kinds of such rules: (a) passive – purely static, which disclose relationships between lexical items in the lexicon; and (b) active – dynamic, which make extension to the lexicon. More empirical facts could also be taken into account in this way as, for instance, cyclic rules, idiosyncrasies, and irregularities of word formation processes.

Let us consider some problems of Polish word formation illustrated by some examples.

(1) bieg-acz(Ø) ← bieg-a-(ć) 'runner' ← 'to run'
otwier-acz(Ø) ← otwier-a-(ć) 'opener' ← 'to open'

The derivatives in (1) are formed by two suffixes with the same grapheme shape. These suffixes also have the same inflectional characteristics and bind the same parts of speech. However, they differ in semantic roles: *nomina agentis* vs. *nomina instrumenti*, respectively. The problem arises, how deep the analysis of a derivative should be: is it worth doing for our purpose to distinguish two textually identical morphemes, even if we cannot predict the semantic meaning of the derivative they found?

(2) krów-k(a) ← krow(a) 'little cow' ← 'cow'
błon-k(a) ← błon(a) 'little membrane' ← 'membrane'
ambon-k(a) ← ambon(a) 'little pulpit ← 'pulpit'

Example (2) shows the vowel alternation in the root of the word *krówka* 'little cow', so typical of Polish. The remaining two derivatives are regularly formed by the same diminutive suffix '-k(a)' but without the alternation. In traditional word formation accounts, the question of why the alternation *o* → *ó* does not occur in the derivative *błonka* 'little membrane' is not asked at all. In the literature (e.g., Grzegorczykowa *et al.* 1998) there is no exhaustive analysis of the phenomenon. On the other hand, the distribution of this alternation is crucial for automatic word analysis purposes if one wants to avoid mere guessing the proper form of a derivative.

(3) racz-ek(Ø) ← rak(Ø) 'little crawfish' ← 'crawfish'
bioloż-k(a) ← biolog(Ø) 'female biologist' ← 'male biologist'
musz-k(a) ← much(a) 'little fly' ← 'fly'

In (3), we can also find many alternations at the root-suffix boundary. Fortunately, most of them follow morphophonologic processes which are well-known as (almost) exceptionless; moreover, they can be formally described by simple rules.

The last set of problems concerns different interpretations of the word formation process. The traditional semantic description (Grzegorczykowa and Puzynina 1979) allows for a given derivative to get two alternative ("simultaneous") interpretations. The question arises what is a real suffix in such a case:

(4)	a.	stolar-ni(a)	← stol-arz(Ø) ← stół(Ų)
		'carpenter's workshop'	←'carpenter' ←'table'
	b.	stol-ar-ni(a)	← stol-arz(Ø)
			← stół(Ų)
		'carpenter's workshop'	←'carpenter'
			←'table'

(5)	a.	bibliotekar-k(a)	← bibliotek-arz(Ø)	← bibliotek(a)
		'female librarian'	← 'male librarian'	← 'library'
	b.	bibliotek-ar-k(a)	← bibliotek-arz(Ø)	
			← bibliotek(a)	
		'female librarian'	← 'male librarian'	
			← 'library'	

If a right-to-left analysis of (4a) or (5a) is performed step by step, two suffixes can be discovered: '-ni(a)'/ '-k(a)' and (palatalised) '-arz(Ø)', respectively. We can also treat such sequences of suffixes as a *complex* suffix: '-arz(Ø)' + '-ni(a)' ⇒ '-arni(a)'. Anyway, as a result of the analysis of that type a chain "basis ⇒ derivative(1) ⇒ ... ⇒ derivative(*n*)" can be obtained.

The multi-motivation analysis allows for derivation of the word from any possible basis, as examples (4b) and (5b) witness. The alternative suffixes of this analysis are: '-arni(a)' or '-ni(a)' (for (4b)) and '-ark(a)' or '-k(a)' (for (5b)). What is overlooked by such an account is, first, the relationship between two possible bases and, second, the complex nature of certain suffixes.

2.2 Generative description

In the late 1970's, word formation issues found their place within the generative theoretical paradigm; the work by Aronoff (1976) played a fundamental role in the development of this area. The following two decades brought different solutions of most important derivational problems, such as the place for word formation in the description of language, the relationship between derivation and inflection, productivity of WF rules, semantics of WF rules, and so on.

For our purpose, the relation between derivation and inflection is crucial. We mention here a hypothesis of Booij (1994, 1996), who argues for two types of inflectional processes, namely *contextual* and *inherent* inflection. The latter is expected to share some properties with derivational processes. The consequence of the co-operation between inflection and derivation is that the morphology does not split into two independent sub-fields. Evidence from Polish will follow.

Cetnarowska (2001) gives evidence from Polish for the phenomenon called *feeding derivation by inflection*. Her research shows that inflectional morphemes in Polish can occur in the word-internal position, "closer" to the root than derivational affixes. She argues that the derivational suffix must have access to extended inflectional verb stems and stem allomorphs. Also, participles and adjectives in comparative and superlative degrees are bases for the process of conversion and derivation. Her work provides Polish data supporting the works of other linguists (Booij 1996, Chapman 1996, Rainer 1996) who have argued that inherent inflection in Germanic and Romance languages can feed derivation. It can also be looked at as evidence against splitting morphology. Since inflectional and derivational processes interact, they should be located in the same grammatical component or module.

Cetnarowska adopts the theory of Booij (1996) who claims that two types of inflectional processes should be distinguished. The former one is *contextual inflection*, where affixes fulfil requirements of sentence structure and have no relevance for the semantic interpretation of a particular word form. Markers of *inherent inflection* can be viewed as "meaning-bearing" in the sense that they add something to the semantic interpretation of a given word form. The difference between *a dog* and *dogs* or between *goes* and *went* is essential for interpretation of sentences or phrases containing those forms.

Let us consider verbal examples. Derivatives (6) - (10) show that particular word forms of verbal lexical items are more accurate bases for derivational analysis than infinitive stems, as traditionally practised. Also, the analysis of Russian complex event verbal nouns examined by Sadler et al. (1997) can be adopted for Polish '-nie' / '-cie' nouns. This could be an instance of the use of extended verb stems as an input to word formation.

(6) mieszał-k(a) 'stirrer' ← mieszał(Ø)$_{3.pers, sg, masc, past}$ vs. miesz-a(ć)$_{inf}$ 'to stirr'

(7) sypial-ni(a) 'sleeping room' ← sypiał(Ų)$_{3.pers, sg, masc, past}$ vs. sypi-a(ć)$_{inf}$ 'to sleep'

(8) grzej-nik(Ø) 'heater' ← grzej(e)$_{3.pers, sg, pres}$ vs. grz-a(ć)$_{inf}$ 'to heat'

(9) pici(e) 'drink' ← pit(y)$_{part}$ vs. p-i(ć)$_{inf}$ 'to drink'

(10) budow-ani(e) 'building' ← budowan(y)$_{part}$ vs. budow-a(ć)$_{inf}$ 'to build'

Substantivals and adjectivals can be analysed in the same way. Consider these examples:

(11) krów-k(a) 'little cow' ← krów(Ø)$_{gen, pl}$ vs. krow(a)$_{nom, sg}$ 'cow'

(12) geści-k(Ø) 'little gesture' ← geści(e)$_{loc, sg}$ vs. gest(Ø)$_{nom, sg}$ 'gesture'

(13) wyższ-ość(Ų) 'superiority' ← wyższ(y)$_{comp}$ vs. wysok(i)$_{pos}$ 'high'

(14) starsz-ak(Ø) 'older child' ← starsz(y)$_{comp}$ vs. star(y)$_{pos}$ 'old'

Examples (11) – (14) show that the root alternation is to be described at the inflectional level of the analysis. In other words, taking a word form of a noun or of an adjective for the derivational basis, instead of operating with a conventional headword of a lexeme, is more accurate from the formal point of view.

Nevertheless, the question of alternation does not disappear. Laskowski (1979) gives some solutions and argues that all alternations divide into two types of markers: (i) markers of category (PoS markers) and (ii) structural markers.

(15) męk(a) – męc(e) 'torture'$_{nom, sg}$ – 'torture'$_{dat, sg}$

(16) biolog(Ø) – biolodz(y) 'biologist'$_{nom, sg}$ – 'biologists'$_{nom, pl}$

For instance, the well-known *k* → *c* (15) and *g* → *dz* (16) alternations are limited to nominal morphemes in Polish. The appearance of this alternation leads to the conclusion that an examined morpheme is nominal (categorial function).

The structural function of the alternation index can be understood as follows: the *o* → *ó* alternation in Polish appears as an index of the zero-ending (no relevance to any category). Let us illustrate the point by these examples:

(17) bóbr(Ø) – bobr(a) 'beaver'$_{nom, sg}$ – 'beaver'$_{gen, sg}$

(18) stój(Ø) – stoj(ę) 'stand'$_{imper}$ – 'stand'$_{1, sg}$

It should be noticed that the *o* → *ó* alternation has a much more complicated distribution. Before the suffix '-(s)tw(o)' the alternation functions as a category marker and reveals syntactic characteristics of the base. This alternation cannot be found in nominal derivation processes:

(19) snob(Ø) → snobstw(o) 'snob' → 'snobbery'

(20) warchoł(Ų) → warcholstw(o) 'brawler' → 'brawling'

The marker indicates a verbal base of the derivative, e.g.

(21) przetworzy(ć) → przetwórstw(o) 'to process' → 'processing industry'

(22) dowodzi(ć) → dowództw(o) 'to command' → 'command'

or, rarely, an adjectival base:

(23) ubog(i) → ubóstw(o) 'poor' → 'poverty'

The influence of inflection on the process of derivation is obvious in conversion cases, where the switch paradigm is the only formative. Consider the examples below:

(24) astronom(Ø) ← astronomi(a) 'astronomer' ← 'astronomy'

(25) korzyść(Ų) ← korzyst-a(ć) 'advantage' ← 'to take advantage'

From the computational perspective, both approaches mentioned above (i.e., Cetnarowska's concept of inflection that feeds derivation and Laskowski's alternation classification) are equally valuable. In particular, taking the inflection stem into account allows one to avoid implementation of numerous alternation rules. The alternation marker can also support a structural analysis. Furthermore, it is possible to find semantic function of formatives that add a new meaning to a given derivative.

2.3 Computational description

From the NLP perspective, there are different requirements for the description of derivatives that have to be fulfilled. First, there must be a clear choice of a basis for a given derivative; in other words, an unequivocal motivation of word formation process must be determined. Second, full inflectional information about the basis and derivative should be available, as well as a complete account of all possible alternations. It is also advisable to gather specific formal premises for semantic description.

Interestingly, computational literature is a good source of accessible solutions. The first work worth mentioning is Koskenniemi's (1983) *two-level morphology* application. Although his monograph deals with phonology and inflection, his concept of a two-level dictionary has appeared profitable for our purpose. To prepare a lexicon of roots, we have taken a grammatical dictionary of the AMOR analyser (Rabiega-Wiśniewska and Rudolf 2003). As a result, a set of entries has been obtained that contains the whole inflectional characteristics and details about internal alternations.

Let us show the lexicon representation of the unit *krowa* 'cow':

(26) lexical entry: krowa 'cow'
lexicon representation:
krOW{O:o(N,G,D,A,B,L,V,n,d,a,b,l,v), **ó**(g); **W:w**(N,G,A,B,V,n,g,d,a,b,l,v), **wi**(D,L)} *k*(a,y,e,ę,ą,e,o,y,0,om,y,ami,ach,y)

The capital letters in **krOW** reveal alternation changes in the root during the process of declension. **O** is represented as **o** or **ó** in appropriate cases (shown in brackets above), **W** – as **w** or **wi**. The last part of the lexicon entry includes set of inflectional suffixes.

The work of Hoeppner (1980) has turned out to be another source of inspiration. He has designed an analyser of German derivatives and defined conditions for a set of suffixes. His classification is based on a number of assumptions:

(a) the list of suffixes should not be too long;

(b) the description should cover both native and foreign suffixes;

(c) in the description, allomorphemes are also included, but

(d) not those taken from special terminology;

(e) non-productive and rare formatives are left out of his account.

By virtue of these assumptions, Hoeppner has collected 27 suffixes represented by 32 textual variants. Developing his approach, he has extended the suffix definition and assumed that each suffix is characterised by seven parameters:

(i) PoS of the derivative;

(ii) morphophonological restrictions (alternations);

(iii) conditions on complex suffix combinations;

(iv) gender of the suffix;

(v) PoS of the base;

(vi) semantic remark;

(vii) the length of the word.

Application of the extended definition of a suffix to his set of formatives has resulted in the list of 90 suffixes.

3. Formal classification of Polish suffixes

Following the authors of the works discussed above, we have developed the basics for the classification of Polish suffixes. We have formulated conditions that allow to establish a set of suffixes:

(a) we assume that each derivative is founded (motivated) only in one way;

(b) suffixes can combine with each other;

(c) a suffix description not only includes its inflectional characteristics, but also that of its basis;

(d) bases and suffixes are bound by linkage rules;

(e) alternations are introduced into rules.

In order to cover a majority of derivatives, we choose formatives with high productivity. The higher frequency helps to find the most probable candidates to formatives.

Following the conditions, we have first analysed a set of native (i.e., not borrowings) suffixes in Grzegorczykowa and Puzynina (1979). The main value of their work is the rich empirical material taken from Doroszewski's Dictionary of Polish (1958-69). The monograph, although openly semantics-based, puts emphasis on formatives, which are of importance for our purpose. The authors do not order their material according to semantic groups ("categories", in Polish derivational terminology); rather, their paper is but a large series of descriptions of particular formatives. Grzegorczykowa and Puzynina's work is the only monograph of that type in Polish literature on derivation.

In the study, 109 native suffixes with 253 variants are listed and thoroughly accounted for. The huge number is probably due to the fact that the authors opt for a multi-motivation description. We have chosen a list of 29 suffixes therefrom (realized by about 50 variants) that have a "lexicon-frequency" between 8000 and 80. The grapheme definition of Hoeppner was then applied to the list. A great number of Grzegorczykowa and Puzynina's variants have been recognized as complex; they have entered our list, since their "suffixal constituents" have done so naturally. After supplementing of a suffix definition by inflectional characteristics, the list of suffixes reaches the number of 45.

NATIVE SUFFIX	"FREQUENCY"
-k(a)	8000
-ość(Ø)	3500
-ik(Ø)	2200
-ek(Ø)	2000
-ec(Ø)	950
-ni(a)	660
-ak(Ø)	630
-acz(Ø)	550
-in(a)	550
-arz(Ø)	550

We have developed the classification of foreign suffixes (borrowings) given by Waszakowa (1994). The author analysed 4300 nouns taken from dictionaries, press, television and radio broadcasts and described 65 suffixes (with 86 variants). Following Grzegorczykowa and

Puzynina, Waszakowa also takes multi-motivation cases into account. This is why we obtain a set of 14 foreign suffixes (with 21 variants). The "lexicon-frequency" of them is significantly lower:

FOREIGN SUFFIX	"FREQUENCY"
-acj(a)	800
-i/yst(a)	600
-i/yzm(Ø)	500
-ator(Ø)	300
-at(Ø)	130
-i/yk(Ø)	100
-i/yzacj(a)	90
-er(Ø)	80
-j(a)	70
-i/yk(a)	50

We would like to introduce a few derivational rules illustrating our approach. The analysis concerns the suffix '-k(a)'. First, we present a piece of Kreja's (1989) research that shows differences between diminutive and feminine nouns derived with this suffix.

suffix	diminutive -k(a)	feminine -k(a)
frequency	1180	913
characteristics	feminine noun	feminine noun
basis POS	feminine noun	masculine-human noun
morph.	11 types of alternations	5 types of alternations
cycle	yes	no

The two suffixes '-k(a)' differ in much more than in meaning. The former suffix combines with feminine nouns and brings numerous alternations. It can be used cyclically, e.g., *krowa* → *krów-ka* → *krów-ecz-ka*. The latter one is founded by masculine-human nouns. Not so many alternations appear during the process of derivation. We should remind here that the distribution of alternations differ.

Let us complete the list of rules for this formative. 'R' stands for morphophonological rule at the border of the stem and the suffix:

(27) $-K(a)_{N,\ nom.sg,\ fem,\ zIII}$

1. $F_{N,\ gen.pl,\ fem} + R + {-k(a)} \rightarrow F_{N,\ nom.sg,\ fem,\ zIII}$

2. $F_{N,\ nom.sg,\ 1} + R + {-k(a)} \rightarrow F_{N,\ nom.sg,\ fem,\ zIII}$

3. $F_{V,\ 3.sg,\ pres} + R + {-k(a)} \rightarrow F_{N,\ nom.sg,\ fem,\ zIII}$

4. $F_{Adj,\ nom.sg} + R + {-k(a)} \rightarrow F_{N,\ nom.sg,\ fem,\ zIII}$

The examples below illustrate the rules in practice:

(28) krów$_{N,\ gen.pl,\ fem}$ + R + –k(a) → krówk(a) 'cow' → 'little cow'

(29) garncarz$_{N,\ nom.sg,\ 1}$ + R + –k(a) → garncark(a) 'potter' → 'female potter'

(30) przesył$_{V, 3p.sg, pres}$ + R + –k(a) → przesyłk(a) 'to mail' → 'a piece of mail'

(31) kiszon$_{Adj, nom.sg}$ + R + –k(a) → kiszonk(a) 'pickled' → 'sth pickled, a silage'

The alternations omitted at the inflectional level of the analysis are described here – by phonetic rules:

(32) *(kwo)***k**$_{N, gen.pl, fem}$ + –k(a) ⇒ *(kwo)***czk**(a) 'hen' → 'little hen'

(33) *(ko)***ść**$_{N, gen.pl, fem}$ + –k(a) ⇒ *(ko)***stk**(a) 'bone' → 'little bone'

(34) *(żagl)***ow**$_{Adj, nom.sg}$ + –k(a) ⇒ *(żagl)***ówk**(a) 'sailing' → 'sailing boat'

(35) *(garnca)***rz**$_{N, nom.sg, 1}$ + –k(a) ⇒ *(garnca)***rk**(a) 'potter' → 'female potter'

4. Residual problems and perspectives

Even the most extensive formal description cannot cope with all morphological problems.

There are at least tree most important troubles for a computational approach. The examples in (36) and (37) illustrate the issue: how should one avoid analysis of words that are not proper derivatives?

(36) matka ≠ matk(a) ← mat(a) 'mother' ≠ 'little mat' ← 'mat'

(37) książka ⇒ książk(a) → księg(a) 'book' → 'large book'/ 'tome'

(38) mistrz(Ø) → mistrz-yn(i) 'master' → 'female master'

The clue of (36) lies in the fact that there is no semantic relationship between 'mother' and 'mat'. The other example is more problematic – diachronically, 'book' is derived from 'a tome', but this link has been lost. Synchronically, the direction of the derivation is inverse. A solution to the former two problems can be as follows: We should keep all words of such a kind in the lexicon of roots as bases.

The last example shows that not each masculine-human noun derives a feminine noun with the suffix –k(a). There are some blockades (mostly phonetic) that should be accounted for by rules.

The formal account should be completed with a collection of productive prefixes, which, as mentioned at the beginning of this paper, are not discussed here:

(39) mini-krow(a), anty-wojenn(y) 'mini-cow', 'anti-war'$_{Adj}$

The rules could also be extended to cover conversion cases:

(40) biel(Ø) ← biał(y) 'whiteness' ← 'white'

Enrichment of the set of rules should of course be still under control. Both accuracy and efficiency of new rules should be confronted with data during experiments.

5. Conclusion

The formal approach to word formation can provide many profits. The main advantage of this description lies in the fact that we base ourselves upon some theoretical knowledge about morphology to solve practical problems that have a reputation of being purely lexical (for example, in text corpora applications).

Each NLP application works on real texts. Obviously, among words to be analysed by such a device, there are word forms of non-derivatives, as well as of derivatives. The device must then be capable of solving inflectional and derivational problems simultaneously. We hope that ours can do both. Moreover, the analyser just sketched is able to properly recognize words that are not included in lexicon; i.e., it is less "lexicon-restricted" than analysers which do not include a "derivational module".

We can get answers to the question of productivity of Polish formatives. Also, we can check the accuracy of various theories of morphology. The derivational module of analysis and synthesis can be helpful in many lexicographical enterprises.

6. Literature

Aronoff, M. 1976. *Word formation in Generative Grammar*. Cambridge, Mass.

Booij, G. E. 1977. *Dutch Morphology - A Study of Word Formation in Generative Grammar*. The Peter de Ridder Press, Lisse.

Booij, G. 1994. Against Split Morphology. *Yearbook of Morphology 1993*, 27-50.

Booij, G. 1996. Inherent versus Contextual Inflection and the Split Morphology Hypothesis. *Yearbook of Morphology 1995*, 1-16.

Cetnarowska, B. 2001. On inherent inflection feeding derivation in Polish. *Yearbook of Morphology 1999*, Kluwer Academic Publishers, 153-183.

Chapman, C. 1996. Perceptual Salience and Affix Order: Noun Plurals as Input to Word Formation. *Yearbook of Morphology 1995*, 175-184.

Dokulil, M. 1962. *Teorie odvozováni slov*. Praha.

Doroszewski, W. (ed.) 1958-69. Słownik Języka Polskiego. vol. 1-11. Warszawa.

Górska E. 1982. Formal and functional restrictions on the productivity of word formation rules WFRs. In: *Folia Linguistica* 16, 149-162.

Grzegorczykowa, R. 1971. *Zarys słowotwórstwa polskiego*. Warszawa.

Grzegorczykowa, R., Puzynina, J. 1979. *Słowotwórstwo współczesnego języka polskiego. Rzeczowniki sufiksalne rodzime*. Warszawa.

Grzegorczykowa, R., Kallas, K., Puzynina, J., Wróbel, H. 1998. Słowotwórstwo. In: Grzegorczykowa, R., Laskowski, R., Wróbel H. (eds.): *Gramatyka współczesnego języka polskiego. Morfologia*. Warszawa.

Halle, M. 1973. Prolegomena to a theory of word formation. *Linguistic Inquiry*, 4(1).

Hoeppner, W. 1980. *Derivative Wortbildung der deutschen Gegenwartssprache und ihre algorithmische Analyse*. Tübingen.

Koskenniemi, K. 1983. *Two-Level Morphology: A General Computational Model for Word-Form Recognition and Production*. Helsinki.

Kreja, B. 1989. *Z morfonologii i morfotaktyki współczesnej polszczyzny*. Wrocław.

Laskowski, R. 1981. Derywacja słowotwórcza. In: Bartmiński, J. (ed.): *Pojęcie derywacji w lingwistyce*. Lublin. 107-126.

Laskowski, R. 1979. Czy alternacje morfologiczne są zbędne? *Slavia Lundensia* 7, 21-33.

Rabiega-Wiśniewska, J., Rudolf, M. 2003. Towards a bi-modular automatic analyzer of large Polish corpora. In: Kosta, R., Błaszczak, J., Frasek, J., Geist, L., Żygis, M. (eds.): *Investigations into Formal Slavic Linguistics. Contributions of the Fourth European Conference on Formal Description of Slavic Languages -- FDSL IV, held at Potsdam University, November 28-30th, 2001*. Peter Lang GmbH, 363-372.

Rainer, F. 1996. Inflection inside Derivation: Evidence from Spanish and Portuguese. *Yearbook of Morphology 1995*, 83-92.

Sadler, L., Spencer, A., Zaretskaya, M. 1997. A Morphic Account of Syncretism in Russian Deverbal Nominalizations. In: *Yearbook of Morphology 1996*, 181-215.

Szymanek, B. 1980. Phonological conditioning of word formation rules. *Folia Linguistica*, XIV/3-4.

Waszakowa, K. 1994. *Słowotwórstwo współczesnego języka polskiego. Rzeczowniki sufiksalne obce*. Wydawnictwa Uniwersytetu Warszawskiego, Warszawa.

Hana Skrabalova, Paris

Coordination: Some Evidence for DP and NumP in Czech

1. Introduction

The aim of this paper is to show that facts about coordination provide an independent piece of evidence for assuming that nominal phrases in Czech (a language without definite articles) contain at least three syntactic projections, as shown in (1). The structure in (1) contains a lexical projection NP, an intermediate functional projection NumP (Ritter 1991), which reflects the syntactic feature of number, and a functional projection DP, which is argumental.

(1)

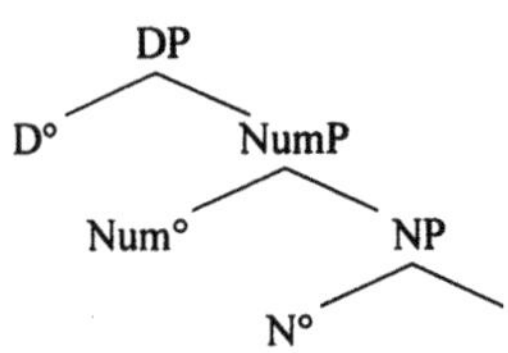

The existence of both NumP and DP levels is semantically supported by the fact that Czech bare noun phrases are always interpreted as either singular or plural (vs. so-called general number), and as argumental or predicative (DPs with null head vs. NPs). But, I would like to concentrate here on coordinate nominals: under the hypothesis that nominal phrases contain three levels, nominal coordination can be considered as three syntactically different coordinations: NP coordination, NumP coordination, and DP coordination.

I will show that distinguishing between these coordinations allows to account for different (semantic) properties of coordinate expressions with the additive conjunctions ***a*** ('and'), ***i*** ('*and*') and ***s*** ('with') on the one hand, and for agreement patterns with preverbal coordinate subjects on the other hand.

My analysis is based on two assumptions:

First, I assume that coordinate nominals are Conjunction Phrases. In particular, I follow Johannessen (1998)'s proposal according to which the first conjunct is the specifier and the second conjunct the complement of the conjunction head, as in (2).

(2)

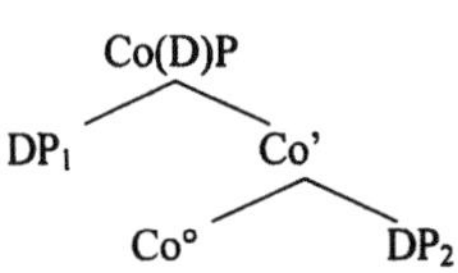

Second, I follow Winter (2000) and Déchaine & Wiltscho (2002), who argue that the intermediate functional projection (D' for Winter, ΦP for D&W) is semantically flexible. That is, I assume that the DP level is rigidly argumental (quantificational), the NP level rigidly predicative, and the NumP level flexible between predicative and argumental reading.

2. Three kinds of nominal coordination in Czech

Czech has three different additive conjunctions: ***a*** ('and'), ***i*** ('and'), ***s*** (preposition 'with' occuring in comitative coordinate-like constructions[1]). These three conjunctions are neither syntactically nor semantically equivalent. Concentrating on binary coordinations in subject

---

[1] See Skrabalova (2003a) for arguments in favor of comitative coordination.

position, we can see they have different possible readings depending on which conjunction we use. The conjunction ***a*** allows both collective and distributive reading, as shown in (3):

(3) *A-coordination*

a. Petr **a** Marie odjeli na prázdniny.
Peter and Mary have-gone on holiday (together / separately)

b. Petr **a** Marie mají modré oči.
Peter and Mary have blue eyes

c. Petr **a** Marie se setkali v osm hodin. / *Petr se setkal.
Peter and Mary met at 8 o'clock / *Peter met

On the contrary, the conjunction ***i*** only allows distributive reading, as shown in (4):

(4) *I-coordination* (distributive coordination)

a. Petr **i** Marie odjeli na prázdniny.
Peter *and* Mary have-gone on holiday (separately)

b. Petr **i** Marie mají modré oči.
Peter *and* Mary have blue eyes

c. * Petr **i** Marie se setkali v osm hodin.
Peter *and* Mary met at 8 o'clock

The conjunction-preposition ***s*** usually only allows collective reading, as shown in (5) (distributive reading in (5b) is acceptable if context makes relevant the group forming of the subject):

(5) *S-coordination* (comitative coordination)

a. Petr **s** Marií odjeli na prázdniny.
Peter and Mary have-gone on holiday (together)

b. ?? Petr **s** Marií mají modré oči.
Peter and Mary have blue eyes

c. Petr **s** Marií se setkali v osm hodin.
Peter and Mary met at 8 o'clock

Furthermore, only the conjunction ***a*** allows the coordination in (6) to refer to either one person or two different people. The conjunction ***i*** in (6b) and the conjunction ***s*** in (6c) only allow the reading involving two people.

(6) a. Poslanec **a** předseda parlamentu mluví[2] několika cizími jazyky.
deputy and chairman (of) parliament speak(s) several foreign languages
(1 or 2 people)

[2] The form "mluví" is ambiguous between singular and plural.

b. Poslanec **i** předseda parlamentu mluví několika cizími jazyky.
deputy *and* chairman (of) parliament speak several foreign languages
(2 people)

c. ?? Poslanec **s** předsedou parlamentu mluví několika cizími jazyky.[3]
deputy with chairman (of) parliament speak several foreign languages
(2 people)

To summarize, examples (3) through (5) show that the conjunction ***a*** is semantically neutral, the conjunction ***i*** is distributive, and the conjunction ***s*** is rather collective. Example (6) shows that only the conjunction ***a*** conjoins both predicates and arguments.

3. Collective vs. distributive coordination

The readings of the coordinations in (3) through (6) could be possibly derived from lexical specifications on each conjunction. However, I'd rather propose that the difference between collective and distributive coordination on the one hand, and between argumental and predicative coordination on the other hand, comes from the type of conjoined nominal projections. Note in particular that the distributive reading of Czech coordinate nominals is forced by the conjunction ***i*** itself, and not by another conjunction-like or quantifier-like marker before a coordination, as in some other Slavic languages, or in Germanic and Romance languages. The conjunction ***i*** can occur before coordinate expressions (contrary to ***a***), see (7a), though it is not a distributive marker here. Rather, it is a focus marker, comparable to 'also' and, as such, it can also introduce non coordinate expressions, as in (7c).

(7) a. * Na prázdniny odjeli **a** Petr **a** Marie.
on holiday have-gone and Peter and Mary

b. Na prázdniny odjeli **i** Petr **a** Marie.
on holiday have-gone *i* (i.e. also) Peter and Mary

c. Na prázdniny odjel **i** Petr.
on holiday has-gone *i* (i.e. also) Peter

Some evidence for my claim that collective (A-)coordination and distributive (I-)coordination are not syntactically equivalent (though both being Conjunction Phrases) comes from coordinate nominals modified by a restrictive relative clause (called *hydras* by Link 1984[4]), as in (8a). In (8a), the coordinate expression *chlapec a dívka* must be interpreted collectively with respect to the predicate of the restrictive relative clause - *to meet in the park*, and distributively with respect to the predicate of the matrix clause - *to have blue eyes.*

(8) a. chlapec **a** dívka kteří se setkali v parku mají modré oči
(the) boy and (the) girl who REFL met in (the) park have blue eyes

b. [$_{CoDP}$ [$_{CoDP}$ chlapec **a** dívka] [$_{CP}$ kteří se setkali v parku]] mají modré oči

There are two facts about these constructions:
First, since the expression *chlapec a dívka* in (8a) functions as an argument, both the conjuncts and the coordination in (8a) seem to be argumental projections, that is DPs. If this is the case, modification by a restrictive relative clause, that is a predicate, should not be

[3] The sentence is more acceptable if they speak to each other.
[4] Link's (1984) *hydra*: (i) the boy and the girl who met => (ii) λz [z=b g ^ met'(z)].

possible, since modification is intersective. For modification to be successful, the coordinate expression *chlapec a dívka* should be a predicate, not an argument. However, the sentence (8a) is quite interpretable.
Second, these constructions are not acceptable with ***i***, which is not surprising if ***i*** is distributive.

(9) a. ***chlapec i dívka kteří se setkali v parku mají modré oči**
(the) boy *and* (the) girl who REFL met in (the) park have blue eyes

b. [$_{\text{CoDP}}$ [$_{\text{CoDP}}$ chlapec **i** dívka] [$_{\text{CP}}$ kteří se setkali v parku]] mají modré oči

It follows from these observations that the coordination in (8a) cannot be a DP coordination, and that the coordinations in (8a) and (9a) cannot be syntactically equivalent.
Assuming that nominal phrases contain a NumP level, I propose the coordination in (8a) not to be a DP, but a NumP coordination, flexible between predicative and argumental interpretation. Which of these two interpretations is activated depends on the syntactic context. Since Czech does not have definite articles, I propose the NumP coordination to be a predicate. This will allow its further modification by a restrictive relative clause attached to the NumP node (cf. Stroik 1994), as shown in (10). In languages with definite articles[5], CoNumP would be interpreted as an expression of type <e> and then shifted into a predicate by the operation IDENT (Partee 1987).

(10)

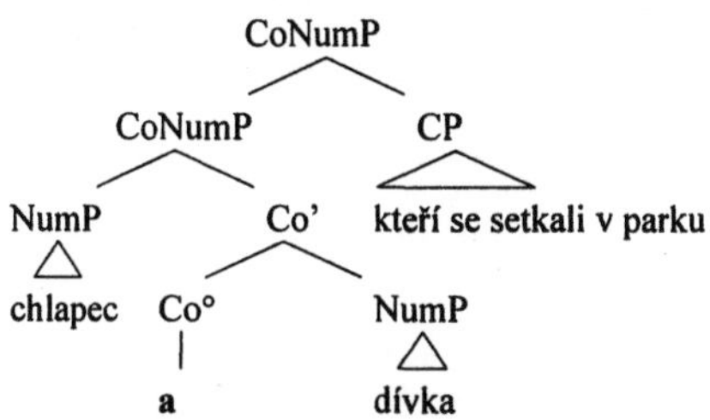

Next, the modified NumP coordination is shifted into an argument, which is a referential expression of type <e>, by the operation IOTA (Partee 1987). This referential expression can combine with another collective predicate, for instance *políbit se* ('to kiss each other'), as in (11).

(11) a. [$_{\text{CoNumP <e,t>}}$ [$_{\text{CoNumP <e,t>}}$ chlapec **a** dívka] [$_{\text{CP <e,t>}}$ kteří se setkali v parku]]

=> b. [$_{\text{CoNumP <e>}}$ [$_{\text{CoNumP}}$ chlapec **a** dívka] [$_{\text{CP}}$ kteří se setkali v parku]] se políbili
(the) boy and (the) girl who met in (the) park kissed each other

But, if this referential expression combines with a distributive predicate, as in (8), how do we get its distributive reading? I propose that the distributive reading comes into play if the

[5] In languages like French, both conjuncts in sentences like (8) must be introduced by a definite article: 'le garçon et la fille qui se sont rencontrés ont les yeux bleus'.
Déchaine & Wiltscho (2002) argue that articles are not in Ds, but rather in Spec-NumPs, since nominal expressions with definite articles are not always referential / definite, but also generic. In their proposal, the difference between definite and generic readings is due to the presence or absence of a null head D:

(i) Jean aime le vin. => Jean aime [$_{\text{NumP}}$ le [$_{\text{NP}}$ vin]] / [$_{\text{DP}}$ ø [$_{\text{NumP}}$ le [$_{\text{NP}}$ vin]]]
'John likes wine / this wine'

whole CoNumP is a complement of a null head D, whose quantificational character (represented by the feature Q in (12)) allows an **independent** quantificational (i.e.distributive) reading of the coordination (in fact the DP) when combining with the distributive predicate of the matrix clause.

(12)

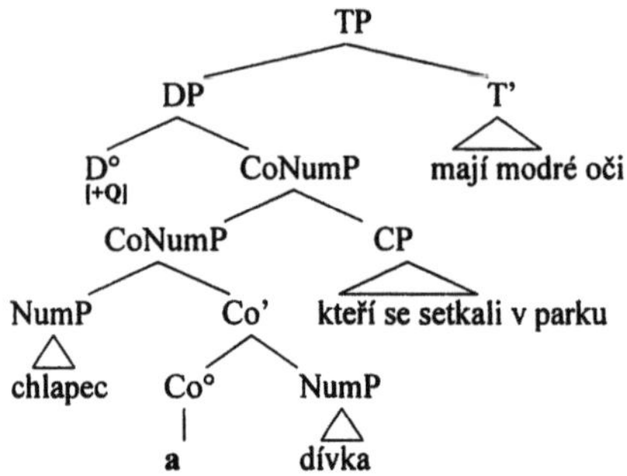

(13) a. [$_{\text{CoNumP} <e,t>}$ [$_{\text{CoNumP} <e,t>}$ chlapec **a** dívka] [$_{\text{CP} <e,t>}$ kteří se setkali v parku]]

=> b. [$_{\text{DP} <<e,t>,t>}$ [$_{\text{CoNumP}}$ [$_{\text{CoNumP}}$ chlapec **a** dívka] [$_{\text{CP}}$ kteří se setkali v parku]] mají modré oči
(the) boy and (the) girl who met in (the) park have blue eyes

Given that the conjunction ***i*** is not acceptable in the sentences (11) and (13), I predict that:
– NumP coordination is always collective. Consequently, I assume that argumental NumPs are only of type <e>, and not of type <<e,t>,t> (= GQ). This corresponds to Link's (1984) proposal that subjects of collective predicates are so-called *individual sums* (i.e. impure atoms).
– distributive reading is linked to the DP level. This is not surprising as DPs are always quantificational (cf. Longobardi 1994). Consequently, I predict that distributive coordination is syntactically either NumP coordination (complement of a head D), or DP coordination. (While the first variant could account for distributive coordination in languages with overt distributive markers, I claim that the second variant accounts for Czech where the conjunction ***i*** will select only quantificational, that is DP conjuncts.)

(14) a. Collective coordination: [CoNumP $_{<e>}$] (cf. *individual sum*: Link 1984)

b. Distributive coordination: (i) [DP $_{<<e,t>t>}$ [CoNumP $_{<e> / <e,t>}$]]
(ii) [CoDP $_{<<e,t>t>}$]

The hypothesis that restrictive relative clauses are adjoined to the NumP level and that NumP is an expression of type <e> also predicts that similar constructions with ***a*** distributive predicate in the relative clause and a collective predicate in the matrix clause are as bad with ***a*** as with ***i***. However, (15a) is not really bad. I think it is nonetheless rather difficult to interpret the relative clause in (15a) as really restrictive. Furthermore, the coordination in (15a) does not interpret strictly "distributively" since the conjunction ***a*** allows to consider *chlapec a dívka* as a group whose relevant property is to have blue eyes (and not green).

(15) a. ? chlapec **a** dívka kteří mají modré oči se setkali v parku
(the) boy and (the) girl who have blue eyes met in (the) park

b. * **chlapec i dívka kteří mají modré oči se setkali v parku**
(the) boy and (the) girl who have blue eyes met in (the) park

4. *A*-coordination vs. *I*-coordination vs. *S*-coordination

In the previous section, I proposed that collective and distributive readings of a coordination are derived from the semantics of its conjuncts. In this section, I generalize this proposition and suggest that, given the possible readings of coordinations with ***a***, ***i*** and ***s***, these conjunctions do (may) not conjoin the same nominal projections.

4.1. *A* conjoins NPs, NumPs and DPs

The conjunction ***a*** is semantically neutral. All readings of *A-coordination* will thus be predicted if ***a*** conjoins the three nominal projections: predicative NPs as in (16), flexible (referential / predicative) NumPs as in (17), and quantificational DPs as in (18).

(16) *NP-coordination* (CoNP = <e,t>, NumP = <e>)

[$_{NumP}$ [$_{CoNP}$ poslanec **a** předseda parlamentu]] mluví několika cizími jazyky
(the) deputy and chairman (of) parliament speaks several foreign languages

(17) *NumP-coordination* (CoNumP1 = <e>, CoNumP2 = <e,t>, DP = <<e,t>,t>)

a. [$_{CoNumP1}$ poslanec **a** předseda parlamentu] se shodli na společném postupu
(the) deputy and (the) chairman of parliament agreed on (a) joint action

b. [$_{CoNumP1}$ [$_{CoNumP2}$ chlapec **a** dívka] [$_{CP}$ kteří se setkali v parku]] se políbili
(the) boy and (the) girl who met in (the) park kissed (each other)

c. [$_{DP}$ [$_{CoNumP2}$ [$_{CoNumP2}$ chlapec a dívka] [$_{CP}$ kteří se setkaliv parku] mají modré oči
(the) boy and (the) girl who met in (the) park have blue eyes

(18) *DP-coordination* (CoDP = <<e,t>,t>)

a. [$_{CoDP}$ poslanec **a** předseda parlamentu] mluví několika cizími jazyky
(the) deputy and (the) parliament chairman speak several foreign languages

b. [$_{CoDP}$ [$_{DP}$ každý chlapec]] **a** [$_{DP}$ každá dívka]]] v této třídě mají modré oči
every boy and every girl in this classroom have blue eyes

c. * [$_{CoDP}$ [$_{DP}$ každý chlapec] **a** [$_{DP}$ každá dívka]] se setkali v parku
every boy and every girl met in (the) park

As for coordination of proper nouns, I follow Winter (2000), who argues that Proper Nouns are NumPs, see (19): the empty definite article in Spec-NP imposes uniqueness so that the *choice function* in NumP chooses the unique element from the noun's denotation. That means that coordinate Proper Nouns are only argumental NumPs and cannot be modified by a restrictive relative clause, as shown in (20b) where CoNumP = <e>.

(19) [$_{NumP}$ Ø$_{cf}$ [Ø$_{the}$ N]].

(20) a. [$_{CoNumP}$ Petr **a** Marie] se setkali v parku
Peter and Mary met in (the) park

b. * [$_{CoNumP}$ [$_{CoNumP}$ Petr **a** Marie] [$_{CP}$ kteří se setkali v parku]]
Peter and Mary who met in (the) park

4.2. *I* conjoins DPs

The conjunction ***i*** is distributive. Assuming that distributive reading is linked to the quantificational DP level, distributive (and argumental) reading of *I-coordination* will be predicted if ***i*** only conjoins DPs[6]:

(21) *NP-coordination* (CoNP = <e,t>, NumP = <e>)

* [$_{NumP}$ [$_{CoNP}$ poslanec **i** předseda parlamentu]] mluví několika cizími jazyky
(the) deputy *and* chairman (of) parliament speaks several foreign languages

(22) *NumP-coordination* (CoNumP1 = <e>, CoNumP2 = <e,t>, DP = <<e,t>,t>)

a. * [$_{CoNumP1}$ poslanec **i** předseda parlamentu] se shodli na společném postupu
(the) deputy *and* (the) chairman (of) parliament agreed on (a) joint action

b. * [$_{CoNumP1}$ [$_{CoNumP2}$ chlapec **i** dívka] [$_{CP}$ kteří se setkali v parku]] se políbili
(the) boy *and* (the) girl who met in (the) park kissed (each other)

c. * [$_{DP}$ [$_{CoNumP2}$ [$_{CoNumP2}$ chlapec **i** dívka] [$_{CP}$ kteří se setkali v parku] mají modré oči
(the) boy *and* (the) girl who met in (the) park have blue eyes

(23) *DP-coordination* (CoDP = <<e,t>,t>)

a. [$_{CoDP}$ poslanec **i** předseda parlamentu] mluví několika cizími jazyky
(the) deputy *and* (the) parliament chairman speak several foreign languages

b. [$_{CoDP}$ [$_{DP}$ každý chlapec]] **i** [$_{DP}$ každá dívka]]] v této třídě mají modré oči
every boy *and* every girl in this classroom have blue eyes

c. * [$_{CoDP}$ [$_{DP}$ každý chlapec] **i** [$_{DP}$ každá dívka]] se setkali v parku
every boy *and* every girl met in (the) park

4.3. *S* conjoins NumPs

Finally, the conjunction ***s*** is (normally) collective. The collective reading of *S-coordination* will thus be predicted if ***s*** only conjoins NumPs.

(24) *NP-coordination* (CoNP = <e,t>, NumP= <e>)

* [$_{NumP}$ [$_{CoNP}$ poslanec **s** předsedou parlamentu]] mluví několika cizími jazyky
(the) deputy with chairman (of) parliament speaks several foreign languages

---

[6] The conjunction i also conjoins PPs and APs. I suppose that the semantics of PPs is determined by the semantics of their nominal complements, and that AP coordination is a nominal coordination with a noun ellipsis in the first conjunct.

(25) *NumP-coordination* (CoNumP1 = <e>, CoNumP2 = <e,t>, DP = <<e,t>,t>)

a. [$_{\text{CoNumP1}}$ poslanec **s** předsedou parlamentu] se shodli na společném postupu
(the) deputy with (the) chairman (of) parliament agreed on (a) joint action

b. [$_{\text{CoNumP1}}$ [$_{\text{CoNumP2}}$ chlapec **s** dívkou] [$_{\text{CP}}$ kteří se setkali v parku]] se políbili
(the) boy with (the) girl who met in (the) park kissed (each other)

c. ?? [$_{\text{DP}}$ [$_{\text{CoNumP2}}$ [$_{\text{CoNumP2}}$ chlapec **s** dívkou] [$_{\text{CP}}$ kteří se setkali v parku] mají modré oči
(the) boy with (the) girl who met in the park have blue eyes

(26) *DP-coordination* (Co DP = <<e,t>,t>)

a. ?? [$_{\text{CoDP}}$ poslanec **s** předsedou parlamentu] mluví několika cizími jazyky
(the) deputy with (the) parliament chairman speak several foreign languages

b. * [$_{\text{CoDP}}$ [$_{\text{DP}}$ každý chlapec]] **s** [$_{\text{DP}}$ každou dívkou]]] v této třídě mají modré oči
every boy with every girl in this classroom have blue eyes

c. * [$_{\text{CoDP}}$ [$_{\text{DP}}$ každý chlapec] **s** [$_{\text{DP}}$ každou dívkou]] se setkali v parku
every boy with every girl met in (the) park

5. Agreement with preverbal coordinate subjects

As I said in the introduction, the existence of three syntactic projections within nominal phrases also allows to explain agreement patterns with preverbal coordinate subjects. Relevant data here are coordinations of two singular nominal expressions (NEs). Most preverbal coordinate NEs only trigger plural agreement on the verb, some NEs only trigger singular agreement, and some trigger either singular or plural agreement[7].
In the previous sections, I claimed that nominal coordinations are predicative, argumental or flexible between these two interpretations. Assuming that predicates cannot be semantically plural while arguments can, I propose that predicates do not trigger (semantically) plural agreement, while arguments do trigger (semantically) plural agreement. Consequently, the coordination of the two nominal predicates in (28) will agree with the verb in singular, while the coordination of the two arguments in (29) will agree in plural:

(27) a. *Predicative coordination* : CoNP / CoNumP => [-PL]
b. *Argumental coordination* : CoNumP / CoDP => [+PL]

(28) a. Můj přítel **a** kolega má / *mají modré oči.
my friend and colleague has / have blue eyes

b. [$_{\text{FP}}$ můj [$_{\text{NumP [-PL]}}$ [$_{\text{CoNP [-PL]}}$ přítel **a** kolega]]] má $_{\text{[-PL]}}$ modré oči

(29) a. Petr **a** Marie mají / *má modré oči
Peter and Mary have / has blue eyes

[7] It has to be noted that coordination of two singular conjuncts in postverbal position can (almost) always trigger singular agreement. However, singular agreement with postverbal coordinate subjects is rather agreement with the first conjunct than agreement with the whole Conjunction Phrase. On the contrary, I assume that agreement with preverbal coordinate subjects is agreement with the whole CoP.

b. [$_{\text{CoDP [+PL]}}$ Petr a Marie] mají $_{\text{[+PL]}}$ modré oči [8]

As for NumP coordination, both singular or plural agreement should be possible, since NumPs are flexible between predicates and arguments. However, not every NumP coordination allows variation in agreement. On the one hand, Proper Nouns, which are always argumental NumPs, must agree in plural, see (30). In general, coordinate NumPs, which must be interpreted as arguments, only trigger plural agreement, see (31).

(30) a. Petr **a** Marie se políbili / *se políbil.
Peter and Mary kissed (each other)-PL / kissed (each other)-SG

b. [$_{\text{CoNumP [+PL]}}$ Petr a Marie] se políbili $_{\text{[+PL]}}$

(31) a. Chlapec **a** dívka se políbili / *se políbil.
(the) boy and (the) girl kissed (each other)-PL / kissed (each other)-SG

b. [$_{\text{CoNumP [+PL]}}$ chlapec a dívka] se políbili $_{\text{[+PL]}}$

On the other hand, some NumPs are interpretable both argumentally and predicatively in the same syntactic position. As a consequence of their variation in interpretation, they will also allow variation in number, as shown in (32) and (33)[9]:

(32) a. Přesnost a srozumitelnost jsou příznačné / je příznačná pro jeho výklady.
preciseness and comprehensibility are characteristic of his explanations

b. [$_{\text{CoNumP [+PL]}}$ přesnost a srozumitelnost] jsou příznačné $_{\text{[+PL]}}$ ...
= 'the preciseness and the comprehensibility are characteristic of ...'

c. [$_{\text{DP [-PL]}}$] [$_{\text{CoNumP [-PL]}}$ přesnost a srozumitelnost]]] je příznačná $_{\text{[-PL]}}$ ...
= 'the property of being precise and comprehensible is characteristic of ...'

(33) a. Uvědomovali si, že stát a společnost se nachází / se nacházejí ve vážné krizi.
they were realizing that state and society are in serious crisis

b. [$_{\text{CoNumP [+PL]}}$ stát a společnost] se nacházejí $_{\text{[+PL]}}$ v krizi
= 'the state and the society are in crisis'

c. [$_{\text{DP [-PL]}}$ [$_{\text{CoNumP [-PL]}}$ stát a společnost]]] se nachází $_{\text{[-PL]}}$ v krizi
= 'the entity which is state and society is in crisis'

The question remains on how to account for the fact that singular agreement seems to be preferred with the quantifier *každý* (every) in every conjunct, as shown in (34a). However, agreement preferences also depend on gender features of the conjuncts, cf. (34b) vs. (34c). To explain agreement patterns in (34), I need to determine the number computation in coordinate and quantified nominals, and also gender resolution. This has been left for further research.

(34) a. Každý chlapec **a** / **i** každá dívka má / ??mají modré oči.
every boy and every girl has / have blue eyes

[8] We can think about a functional projection above CoDP where the plural number of the CoDP would be computed.

[9] The example (31) is from Grepl, M. & P. Karlík (1986), *Skladba češtiny*, Praha: Votobia; and the example (32) from Hroch, M. & V. Kubišová (1998), *Velká francouzská revoluce a Evropa 1789/1790*, Praha: Svoboda.

b. Každý student **a** / **i** každá studentka složili / ???složil / *složila zkoušky.
every student-M and every student-F passed-PL.M /-SG.M /-SG.F exams

c. Každý dobrý student **a** / **i** každý špatný student ??složili / složil zkoušky.
every good student-M and every bad student-M passed-PL.M / -SG.M exams

6. Conclusion

In this paper, I tried to show that the facts regarding nominal coordination provide evidence for the hypothesis of three syntactic projections (NP, NumP, DP) within Czech nominal phrases. Assuming a flexible character of the NumP projection, existence of these projections allows to explain semantic differences between coordinations with the conjunctions ***a***, ***i*** and ***s***: these conjuctions do not conjoin the same projections. Furthermore, the semantic character of each projection also explains agreement patterns with preverbal coordinate subjects: while argumental coordinations trigger plural agreement, predicate coordinations trigger singular agreement. Flexible NumPs allow both plural and singular agreement.

References

Déchaine, R.-M. & Wiltschko, M. (2002): "Decomposing pronouns". *Linguistic Inquiry* 33.3, 409-442.

Johannessen, J.B. (1998): *Coordination*. Oxford: Oxford University Press.

Link, G. (1998 [1984]): "Hydras: On the Logic of Relative Constructions with Multiple Heads". In: Link, G.: *Algebraic Semantics in Language and Philosophy*, chap.1. Stanford: CSLI.

Partee, B. (1987): "Noun Phrase Interpretation and Type Shifting Principles". In: Groenendijk, J. *et al.* (eds.): *Studies in Discourse Representation Theory*. Dordrecht: Foris,115-143.

Ritter, E. (1991): "Two Functional Categories in Noun Phrases: Evidence from Modern Hebrew". In: Rothstein, S. (ed.): *Perspectives in Phrase Structure*. San Diego: Academic Press, 37-62.

Skrabalova, H. (2003a): "Comitative constructions in Czech". In: Kosta, P. *et al.*: *Investigations Into Formal Slavic Linguistics*. Frankufurt am Mein: Peter Lang, 685-696.

Skrabalova, H. (2003b): "Syntaxe de la coordination [Conj DP Conj DP]: comparaison entre le français, le tchèque et l'anglais". Talk given at a *Workshop on Coordination*, University Paris 7 & LLC, 1st March 2003.

Stroik, T. (1994): "Saturation, predication, and the DP hypothesis". *Linguistic Analysis* 24.1/2, 39-61.

Winter, Y. (2000): "DP Structure and Flexible Semantics". *IATL* 7, 191-214.

Anne Sturgeon, Santa Cruz

Topic and Demonstrative Pronouns in Czech*

1. Introduction

Czech linguists have long argued that word order in Czech is primarily determined by discourse factors such as topic and focus (for Topic Focus Articulation (TFA) see Sgall, Hajičová and Benešová 1973; Sgall, Hajičová and Buráňová 1980; Sgall, Hajičová and Panevová 1986). Under traditional Czech analyses, such as TFA, the topic has been defined as 'those nodes that do not belong to the focus' (Hajičová 1983: 271). My goal is to work towards a narrower definition of *topic*.[1] In order to accomplish this goal certain diagnostics are used. Following the discussion of Gundel et al 1993 and Comrie 2000, I suggest that demonstrative pronouns in Czech require that their antecedents be non-topical and argue that elements which are not able to antecede a demonstrative pronoun are topical. A disjunctive definition of *topic*, referencing structural position is proposed for Czech.

2. Syntax of the Left Periphery

Before the distribution of demonstratives can be understood, it is necessary to provide an analysis of the structural position of topical elements in Czech. I follow Lenertová's 2001 proposal for the syntax of the left periphery.

It is first necessary to consider the behavior of second position clitics. Czech clitics generally follow the first XP, with some exceptions (Toman 1981, 1996).[2] In (1) the reflexive clitic follows a sentence-initial DP.

(1) *Celá ta vesnice se těšila na príma večeři.*
whole that village refl-cl looked-forward on nice dinner
'The whole village looked forward to the nice dinner.' (*Mach a Šebestová*: 75)[3]

Lenertová 2001 argues against a prosodic analysis of Czech clitics and proposes that they occur in a fixed syntactic position (see also Veselovská 1995). Evidence for this claim comes from two sources. First, clitics can either pro- or encliticize.

(2) *Pomáhat ~mu, by= dnes stálo mnoho.*
help.inf him.cl would.cl today cost much
'Helping him would cost a lot today.' (Lenertová 2001: (4))[4]

* I thank Judith Aissen, Eva Hajičová and Petr Sgall for helpful discussions of this material. I also thank Věra Kafková, Martina Šímová and Karolina Wencelová for their Czech judgments. All remaining errors are mine.

[1] My use of the term *topic* differs from its traditional use under TFA. What I refer to as *topic* corresponds to their notion of *topic proper*.

[2] Czech has both verbal auxiliary and pronominal clitics. With the exception of nominative and vocative, there are pronominal clitics in all nominal cases. Additionally, there are reflexive clitics; these can be anaphoric to argument positions or used with lexically reflexive verbs. Verbal auxiliary clitics in the past tense mark person and number in the 1st and 2nd person (they are absent in the 3rd person). There are also auxiliary clitics which mark the conditional mood. Clitics are obligatorily ordered: auxiliary-reflexive-dative-accusative.

(i) *Řekla jsem mu to.*
told aux.1sg.cl him.dat.cl it.acc.cl
'I told it to him.'

[3] Abbreviations include: nom (nominative), dat (dative), acc (accusative), gen (genitive), sg (singular), pl (plural), refl (reflexive), cl (clitic), prt (particle), fem (feminine), masc (masculine), neg (negation), inf (infinitive), aux (auxiliary), dim (diminutive).

As there is an intonational break after the preposed IP in (2), the auxiliary clitic procliticizes phonologically to the following material; the pronominal clitic encliticizes. Second, clitics can occur sentence-initially if there is no topic or the topic has been deleted; this is characteristic of casual speech (Fried 1994, Toman 1996, 1999).

(3) *Se mi včera narodil kluk...*
refl.cl me.cl yesterday born boy
'My son was born yesterday...' (Lenertová 2001: (6))

In declarative sentences only one XP can occur in the pre-clitic position. This XP can be interpreted as given, as contrastively topicalized or as focused. Contrastively topicalized and focused XP's are associated with an intonational rise which is indicated by capitalization. In (4), the referent of the pre-clitic DP, *Vítek*, is given and there is no intonational rise associated with it.

(4) *Maminka Vítka zvedla a postavila ho do dveří vagónu. Vítek se těšil...*
mom Vitek raised-up and stood him to doors wagon Vitek refl-cl looked-forward-to
'Mom took Vitek and put him in the door of the wagon. Vitek was looking forward to...' (*Jak jel Vítek do Prahy*: 13)

In (5) *Honzovi* and *Petrovi* are contrastively topicalized; their referents stand in a set relation to the entity denoted by *your sons*. There is a discussion of contrastive topicalization in §3.1.

(5) a. *Co jsi koupila synům k svátku?*
what aux.1sg bought sons.dat towards name-day
'What did you buy your sons for their name days?'

b. *HONZOVI jsem koupila AUTÍČKO a PETROVI KNÍŽKU.*
Honza.dat aux.1sg bought car.dim.acc and Petr.dat book.acc
'Honza I bought a car and Petr a book.'

In (6b) the DP, *a book*, is the narrowly focused answer to a wh-question.

(6) a. *Co jsi dala Honzovi k narozeninám?*
what aux.2sg gave Honza.dat towards birthday
'What did you give Honza for his birthday?'

b. *KNÍŽKU jsem mu dala.*
book.acc aux.1sg him.cl gave
'I gave him a book.'

It is not possible, however, for topics (T) and contrastively topicalized/focused (F) elements to occur together before clitics (see also Lenertová 2001).

(7) **Honzovi*$_T$ *KNIŽKU*$_F$ *jsem dala.*
Honza.dat book.acc aux.1sg.cl gave
'I gave Honza a book.'

---

[4] The symbols '~' and '=' are from Fried 1994 and indicate syntactic and phonological attachment respectively. The appearance of '~' on its own indicates that syntactic and phonological attachments are isomorphic.

(8) **KNIŽKU*$_F$ *Honzovi*$_T$ *jsem* *dala.*
book.acc Honza.dat aux.1sg.cl gave
'I gave Honza a book.'

This suggests that there is one pre-clitic, left edge position which can be associated with both given and contrastive interpretations.

Before determining the structural position of pre-clitic XP's, data from wh-constructions are considered. In contrast to declarative sentences, it is possible for more than one XP to occur before clitics in wh-questions. A contrastively topicalized DP co-occurs with a wh-phrase in (9).

(9) *Také Mirek by vyslovil nesouhlas... Ale tvůj kamarád Josef, tomu by*
also Mirek would pronounce neg-agree but your friend Josef, that would
se to asi líbilo. – A co EMA$_F$ *by na to řekla?*
refl-cl it maybe like and what Ema would on it say
'Mirek would also disagree... but your friend Josef, he would probably like it. – And what would EMA$_F$ say?' (Lenertová 2001: (19))

However, it is not possible for a topicalized DP to occur in this position.

(10) **Kdy to auto*$_T$ *bys teda koupil?*
when that car would.2sg.cl prt bought
'When would you buy the car$_T$?' (Lenertová 2001: (21))

Lenertová 2001 modifies the Rizzi 1997 split-CP proposal to account for Czech. Wh-phrases are found in the highest functional projection, [Spec, ForceP], and topics/contrastive topics/foci are found in a lower position, [Spec, FinP].[5] She posits that clitics are positioned syntactically in Fin^0. Topic, [T], and focus, [F], features in Fin^0 are assumed to motivate movement of topical and contrastive elements into [Spec, FinP].

A tree summarizing this proposal is given in (11).

(11)

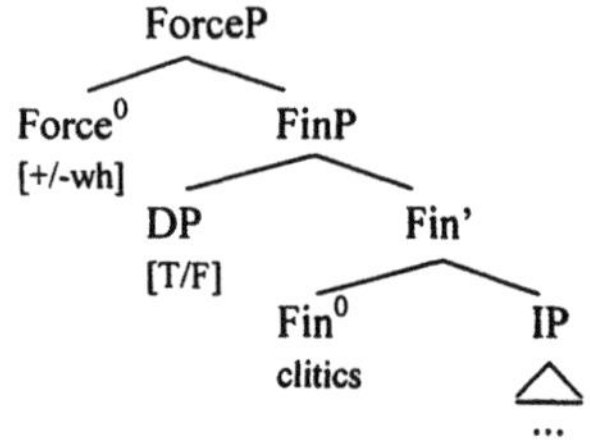

Certain features of the left periphery are predicted by this analysis. Only one XP can occur in the pre-clitic position in declarative sentences because only one pre-clitic specifier position is available, [Spec, FinP]. In wh-questions, however, clitics can occur immediately after the wh-word (if there is no XP in [Spec, FinP]) or following both the wh-word and a fronted contrastively topicalized or focused element.[6] With the syntax of the left periphery in place, now we turn to a discussion of the distribution of demonstrative pronouns and a definition of *topic* in Czech.

---

[5] Czech allows multiple wh-fronting, but I will not consider that here.

[6] Lenertová 2001 accounts for the inability of topicalized elements to co-occur with fronted wh-phrases in a preclitic position by assuming that fronting both a topicalized element and focused a wh-phrase would lead to a feature clash. This issue is a topic for future research.

3. Identifying Topics

Comrie 2000 argues that demonstrative pronouns in Dutch can only be anteceded by non-topical DP's. Similar conclusions are drawn in Gundel et al 1993 for English, Mandarin, Spanish, Japanese and Russian. Kresin 1994 and Koktová 1992 describe the distribution of these pronouns and conclude that antecedents of demonstratives must be less prominent in the overall discourse than other elements. I draw from these approaches and show that demonstrative pronouns require that their antecedent be non-topical. A structural definition of *topic* is given. This analysis correctly accounts for a wide range of data not yet considered in the literature.[7]

Antecedents of demonstrative pronouns in Czech are found in a wide range of contexts.[8] The most common antecedent for a demonstrative is a post-verbal DP in a right edge argument position, a position generally associated with a focus interpretation (both wide and narrow). The first examples I provide show that a nominative DP at the left edge of a clause cannot antecede a demonstrative. In (12) the demonstrative pronoun refers unambiguously to the object of the preposition, *Vítězslav*, though it also shares phi-features with the subject, *soudce* ('the judge').

(12) *Soudce$_1$ se podíval zkoumavě na Vítězslava$_2$ a ten$_{2/*1}$ si požádal...*
judge refl-cl looked searchingly at Vitezslav.acc and that refl-cl requested
'The judge$_1$ looked searchingly at Vítězslav$_2$ and that$_{2/*1}$ requested...'
(Czech National Corpus)

Note that the demonstrative pronoun obligatorily occurs at the left edge of its clause. I assume it sits in [Spec, FinP].

As mentioned above, the most common antecedent of a demonstrative pronoun is a non-nominative DP at the right edge of the preceding clause, as in (12). It is not required, however, that the antecedent of a demonstrative be at the right edge; any post-verbal DP can antecede a demonstrative. In (13) the dative argument, *Vítězslavovi*, antecedes a demonstrative from a position which is not clause final.

(13) *...do lokálu se jako tajfun vřítil chlap$_1$ jako hora a dal$_1$*
to bar refl-cl like typhoon stormed-in man like mountain and gave
hajnému Vítězslavovi$_2$ takovou facku, že ten$_{2/*1}$ skončil i s ruksakem
forester Vítězslav.dat such smack that that ended-up even with backpack
na zádech v rohu místnosti na zemi.
on back in corner room.gen on floor
'...a mountain of a man$_1$ stormed into the bar like a typhoon and gave$_1$ forester Vítězslav$_2$ such a smack in the face that that$_{2/*1}$ ended up, with his backpack still on his back, on the ground in the corner of the room.' (Czech National Corpus)

A DP in the dative case antecedes the demonstrative; co-reference with the (null) subject of the previous clause is not possible.

On the basis of (12-13), one might wonder if a function of the demonstrative is to distinguish between two possible antecedents which share phi-features. However, the demonstrative pronoun is also commonly used when verbal morphology disambiguates between possible antecedents. In (14) the past tense form of the verb in the second clause unambiguously distinguishes between the two possible antecedents from the previous clause

[7] Hajičová et al 1995, within the larger context of pronominal reference in Czech, suggest that demonstrative pronouns generally take elements in the *focus* part of the sentence as antecedents.

[8] Czech has a three way distinction in its demonstrative system: proximal, distal and neutral. The demonstrative pronoun is homophonous with the neutral demonstrative. These pronouns are marked for the gender and number of their antecedent and carry the appropriate case marking for their grammatical function.

(the feminine null subject and the masculine dative object, *strýcovi* ('uncle')), but the demonstrative is still used.

(14) ...*podala ji strýcovi$_1$ a ten$_1$ ji vzal do ruky a šel s*
gave.fem it.fem uncle.dat and that.masc it.fem took.masc to hand and went with
ní okamžitě k oknu...
it.fem at-once to window
'...she gave it to her uncle$_1$ and that$_1$ took it and went immediately to the window...'
(Czech National Corpus)

Examples such as this one suggest that not only can the demonstrative pronoun disambiguate between arguments which share phi-features, but it can also indicate to the addressee that the subject of the current utterance is not continued from the previous one.

In all examples given above the element which is not available as an antecedent for the demonstrative is a left-edge nominative argument. An interesting question then is whether the relevant factor is linear position, grammatical function, or both. These factors are confounded in (12-14) since the disallowed antecedents are both left edge and nominative.

The example in (15) allows us to tease apart the issues of syntactic position and grammatical function. The accusative DP, *Harrison Ford*, is located in the left-edge position, while the nominative DP, *Calista Flockhart*, is found post-verbally. *Calista Flockhart* antecedes a demonstrative pronoun in the following clause, while *Harrison Ford* is unavailable as an antecedent.

(15) *Harrisona Forda$_1$ si po operaci domů odvezla na vozíku jeho*
Harrison Ford.acc refl-cl after operation to-home brought on wheelchair his
*nastávající, seriálová herečka Calista Flockhart$_2$. Ta$_2$ /*Ten$_1$ se nyní*
fiancée serial actress Calista Flockhart.nom that.fem / that.masc refl-cl now
velice těší...
much looks-forward-to
'Harrison Ford$_1$ was taken home in a wheelchair after his operation by his fiancée$_2$, serial actress Calista Flockhart. That$_{2/*1}$ is looking forward to...' (*Dnes*, 9/11/03)

In this example, as opposed to (12-14), a nominative argument at the right edge antecedes the demonstrative: what is relevant to the demonstrative is not grammatical function, but, rather, syntactic position. A generalization about antecedents of the demonstrative pronoun is now possible. Recall that the left edge position is associated with a topic interpretation (in the absence of rising intonation).

(16) The antecedent of a demonstrative cannot refer to a *topic*.

An initial definition of *topic* is provided in (17).

(17) *Topic:* An XP in [Spec, FinP].

In examples (12-15) the antecedent for the demonstrative is in a post-verbal position. If the generalization in (17) is correct, there should be examples in which the antecedent for a demonstrative occurs preverbally, but not at the left edge. In fact, DP's which occur between the clitic and the verb (a position generally associated with an 'old information' interpretation) can also antecede demonstratives.

(18) *Mladá žena se násilníkovi$_1$ bránila, ten$_1$ jí však baťoh*
young woman refl-cl mugger.dat defended that her however backpack

nakonec vyrval z rukou...
at-end took from hand.instr
'The young woman defended herself against the mugger$_l$; that$_l$, however, in the end, took her backpack...' (Czech National Corpus)

In (18) *nasilníkovi* ('the mugger'), located between the clitic and the verb, antecedes a demonstrative pronoun in the following clause. This example shows that it is only the left edge position which is restricted.

Clitic pronouns are also available as antecedents for demonstrative pronouns.

(19) *...chtěli dva anglicky mluvící cizinci po řidiči$_l$ dvě jízdenky*
wanted two English speaking foreigners after driver two tickets
a dali mu$_l$ dvoutisícikorunovou bankovku.
and gave him.cl two-thousand-crown note
„Ten$_l$ jim však nedal jízdenky, ale ani nevrátil peníze," řekl Vlkan.
that them however neg-gave tickets but neither neg-returned money said Vlkan
'...two English speaking foreigners wanted two tickets from the driver and gave him a 2,000 crown note. "That, however, did not give them tickets nor return their money," said Vlkan.' (*Dnes* 3/12/03)

Clitics can, generally, antecede demonstratives, as shown in (19). Assuming that the node dominating the argument position associated with the clitic is not at the left edge, this example provides further support for (16-17).

The generalization presented above makes the correct predictions for the range of data presented in (12-15) and (18-19). However, additional data in the following section suggest that further restrictions on potential antecedents of demonstratives are necessary.

3.1 Contrastive Topics

In (20), a left edge contrastive topic, differentiated from a left edge topic by an intonational rise, antecedes a demonstrative pronoun (see also Lenertová 2001, Hajičová et al. 2002).

(20) *...a paní Moutelíková řekla v krámě Ireně matce, že jsme dobrá rodina a*
and Mrs. Moutelíková said in shop Irena's mother that are.1pl good family and
aby si mě Irena držela, protože jsem takový vážný a rozumný,
so-that refl-cl me.acc Irena held because aux.1sg such serious and good
a ZDEŇKA$_l$ nebral nikdo vážně, poněvadž ten$_l$ byl bůhvíkdo...
and Zdenek.acc neg-take no-one seriously because that was god-only-knows
'...and Mrs. Moutelikova said to Irena's mother in the store that we are a good family and Irena should hold on to me because I am serious and good and Zdeněk$_l$ no one ever took seriously because that$_l$ is a 'God-only knows'...' (Kresin 1994: (37))

The definition in (17) is not fine-grained enough to distinguish a contrastive topic from a topic; both occur in [Spec, FinP]. I argue that contrastive topics differ from topics both in the feature associated with their leftward movement and in their discourse function. The definition of *topic* is modified in (21).

(21) *Topic:* An XP associated with a [T] feature in [Spec, FinP].

This new definition, in conjunction with the generalization in (16), makes the correct predictions for the example in (20). The DP, *Zdeněk*, occupies [Spec, FinP], but is not associated with the feature [T], but rather with a feature attracting DP's which are interpreted contrastively, [F]. Note that reference to structural position (and the associated features) is necessary. Referring solely to linear order would not make the correct predictions since both topics and contrastive topics are located at the left edge.

Contrastively topicalized DP's are associated with a particular discourse function which distinguishes them from left edge topics. Hajičová et al. 2002 argue that contrastive topicalization is felicitous when the entity denoted by the dislocated element stands in an alternative set relation to an entity introduced in the previous discourse (see also Ward and Prince 1991; Prince 1997; Büring 1999; Gregory and Michaelis 2001; Steedman 2002). An example from the Switchboard corpus in (22) illustrates this.

(22) a. Most rap, I don't like.

b. That kind, I kind of enjoy.

The referent of the DP, *that kind*, stands in an alternative set relation to the set containing *most rap*. The previous context for (22a) is not given, so nothing can be said about the topicalization of *most rap*. In (20b) there is an intonational rise associated with the left edge DP, *Zdeněk*, and the entity it refers to stands in an alternative set relation to the set *suitors of Irena*.

Contrastive topics felicitously antecede demonstrative pronouns as predicted by the modified generalization in (21). I have argued that these elements differ both discoursally and syntactically from left edge topics which are disallowed from anteceding demonstrative pronouns. A final restriction on the antecedents of demonstratives is introduced in the next section.

3.2 Bringing in Centering Theory

Data presented in this section show that there is another restriction on antecedents of demonstrative pronouns. In addition to being sensitive to the structural position of their antecedent, demonstrative pronouns are also sensitive to the antecedent's relative prominence in the overall discourse. An adequate characterization of this is the notion of topic associated with *backward looking centers* in Centering Theory (Grosz, Joshi and Weinstein 1983; Grosz, Joshi and Sidner 1986, 1995).

Considered here is an example in which more than one discourse entity has been realized as a pronoun, suggesting that more than one entity is *given* in the discourse. There are two entities in (23): *Petr* and *Jana*. In (23c) the DP's referring to both entities are pronominals; a null pronoun refers to *Jana* and a dative clitic to *Petr*. Can a demonstrative take either of these pronouns as its antecedent? The answer is no.

(23) a. *V sobotu šel Petr$_1$ do krámu.*
in Saturday went Petr to store
'On Saturday Petr$_1$ went to the store.'

b. *Po cestě potkal Janu$_2$.*
along way met Jana.acc
'Along the way he$_1$ met Jana$_2$.'

c. *Řekla$_2$ mu$_1$ o svém novém děťátku.*
told.fem him.dat about self's new child
'She$_2$ told him$_1$ about her new child.'

The infelicity of (23d) can be accounted for by the generalization presented in the previous section.

(23) d. # *Ta*$_2$ *už* *musela* *odejít.*
that.fem already must.fem leave.inf
'She$_2$ had to leave.'

If we assume that the null pronoun referring to *Jana* in (23c) is located in [Spec, FinP], it is unavailable as an antecedent for a demonstrative pronoun.

However, it is also infelicitous to continue the discourse in (23a-c) with a demonstrative pronoun referring to *Petr*, as in (23d').[9]

(23) d' # *Ten*$_1$ *už* *musel* *odejít.*
that.masc already must.masc leave.inf
'He$_1$ had to leave.'

The infelicity of this example is surprising if we assume that the DP associated with the clitic pronoun in (23c) is not at the left edge of the clause. There is nothing in the analysis presented so far that would predict the infelicity in (23d').

Why is it possible for the referent of a dative clitic to antecede a demonstrative in (19c), but not in (23d')? Considering the previous utterances provides clues. In (19) the referent of the demonstrative, *the driver*, is referred to twice in the previous discourse, both times in an oblique case (object of a preposition and in the dative). In contrast, in (23) the referent of the dative clitic, *Petr*, is realized as the subject of both (23a-b).

The Centering Theory notion of backward looking center (Cb) captures this difference in discoursal status between the referents of the dative clitics in (19b) and (23c). Beaver 2003 uses the Centering Theory notion of Cb as the basis for his definition of *topic*:

(24) The *topic* [Cb] of a sentence is the entity referred to in both the current and the previous sentence, such that the relevant referring expression in the previous sentence was minimally oblique. If there is no such entity, the topic is undefined.
(Beaver 2003: (3))

Minimally oblique is defined by Beaver 2003, following standard Centering Theory assumptions, in terms of grammatical function: nominative arguments are the least oblique, followed by objects, then adjuncts. For an entity to be the Cb of a sentence it must be referred to in both the current and previous sentences and be realized in the previous sentence by the DP with the highest grammatical function.

Centering Theory was devised to predict pronoun reference in English. Since Czech differs from English in that word order is determined by discourse factors rather than grammatical function, I propose to change the definition of backward looking center to make reference to structural position. The proposed modification is given in (25).

(25) The *topic* [Cb] of a sentence is the entity referred to in both the current and the previous sentence, such that the relevant referring expression in the previous sentence was maximally structurally salient. If there is no such entity, the topic is undefined.

A structural salience scale in which [Spec, FinP] is maximally salient is proposed: [[Spec, FinP] > [Spec, IP] > [Spec, FP]…].[10] Under this definition of Cb *maximally salient* structural position rather than minimally oblique grammatical function determines the Cb of a sentence.[11] The entity which is realized in both the current and the previous sentence and is

[9] A felicitous continuation in both cases would contain a null pronoun in place of the demonstrative.

[10] I assume that the structural prominence of a clitic is determined by the position of the argument XP with which it is associated.

[11] Rambow 1993 argues for the relevance of linear order in determining discourse saliency in the *Mittelfeld* in German subordinate clauses.

realized by a DP in the maximally salient structural position in the previous sentence is defined as the Cb. Contrastive topics, though they occur in [Spec, FinP], will not realize the Cb of their clause due to their discourse function. The entity denoted by a contrastively topicalized DP has not been mentioned in the previous discourse; it stands in a set relation to a previously mentioned entity.[12]

If the definition of Cb in (25) were incorporated into the definition of *topic*, it would be possible to explain the differences between (19) and (23).

(26) *Topic:* x is a discourse referent, y is an utterance: x is the topic of y if and only if x is the Cb of y or x is realized in [Spec, FinP] and associated with the feature [T] in the sentence corresponding to y.[13]

In (23c) the dative clitic realizes the Cb of its clause and is unavailable as an antecedent for a demonstrative pronoun. The entity referred to by *Petr* is the Cb because it is mentioned in both (23b) and (23c) and the expression referring to it in (23b) occurs in [Spec, FinP]. It is for this reason that the demonstrative pronoun is infelicitous in the discourse (23d'). Example (19) differs from (23) in an important way. The referent of the dative clitic in (19b) is not the Cb of its clause. The entity referred to in both (19a) and (19b) and which is in [Spec, FinP] in (19a) is *the two English speaking foreigners*, not *the driver*. As a result, it is felicitous for the dative clitic to antecede the demonstrative.

Kameyama 1999 has argued for the relevance of two similar Centering Theory notions in predicting pronoun reference. In classic Centering Theory, the Cb is central to determining what patterns of pronominal reference are possible in a given utterance. Kameyama 1999 expands this and argues that reference to Cb alone is not adequate in predicting certain cases of pronominal reference. She argues that pronouns refer to the *maximally salient entity* of the previous utterance and defines *maximally salient entity* disjunctively, referring to two Centering Theory notions: Cb and and the preferred Center (Cp). Under her proposal, the Cb is defined as in (24). The Cp is defined as that entity realized by the minimally oblique expression type; *minimally oblique* is defined in terms of grammatical function. The definition of Cp differs from that of the Cb as it is defined with respect to a single utterance. Within the Centering Theory model, the Cp 'represents a prediction about the Cb of the following utterance' (Walker et al 1998: 3). For Kameyama, these two notions combine to define the *maximally salient entity* in an utterance, and she argues that unstressed pronouns in English are interpreted as referring to this entity. In some examples, the *maximally salient entity* is determinate, but in others it is not.

The entity, *Babar*, is both the Cb and the Cp of (27b). It is the Cb because the entity is referred to in both (27a-b) and is realized by the minimally oblique DP, the subject, in (27a). It is the Cp because it is also referred to by the minimally oblique DP in (27b), the nominative argument. Thus, the *maximally salient entity* in (27b) is determinate. As a result, the referent for the unstressed pronoun in (27c) is unambiguously *Babar*.

(27)	a.	Babar went to a bakery.	Babar(Cp) > Bakery
	b.	He greeted the baker.	Babar(Cp/Cb) > Baker
	c.	He pointed at a blueberry pie.	he:=Babar < Baker

[12] Overt mention is not, strictly speaking, necessary for the Cb. Walker et al 1998 write: 'An utterance U *realizes* a center **c** if **c** is an element of the situation described by U, or **c** is the semantic interpretation of some subpart of U.' I argue that the set relation between the entity denoted by the contrastively topicalized DP and an entity mentioned in the previous discourse is not adequate to satisfy the conditions on the Cb described by Walker et al 1998.

[13] I thank Judith Aissen for help with the formulation of this definition.

In (28b) there is no unique *maximally salient entity* under Kameyama's proposal. The accusative pronoun referring to *Babar* realizes the Cb in (28b) because that entity is referred to in both (28a-b) and is referred to by the minimally oblique DP in (28a). However, the entity referred to by the DP *the baker* is the Cp in (28b) because it is referred to by the minimally oblique DP in (28b), the nominative argument. As a result, there is an indeterminacy in the interpretation of the subject pronoun in (28c).

(28)	a.	Babar went to a bakery.	Babar > Bakery
	b.	The baker greeted him.	Baker(Cp) < > Babar(Cb)
	c.	He pointed at a blueberry pie.	he:= Baker <? Babar

Either *Babar* or *the baker* can be interpreted as anteceding that pronoun.

Under Kameyama's analysis, two concepts are relevant to determining the *maximally salient entity*: the relative prominence of the entity in the discourse context (notion of Cb) and the grammatical function of its realization in the current utterance (notion of Cp).[14] The definition in (26) is conceptually related to Kameyama's proposal. As in her analysis, this definition of *topic* requires reference to both the status of an entity in the discourse (Cb) and the syntactic position of the DP referring to that entity in the current utterance. The example in (23) demonstrates that neither of these notions are by themselves adequate to predict the possible antecedents of demonstrative pronouns (and, by extension, topicality).

The definition of topic in (26) and the generalization in (16) ('The antecedent of a demonstrative cannot refer to a topic') combine to predict the distribution of the antecedents of demonstrative pronouns.

4. Conclusion

It was shown that the distribution of antecedents of demonstrative pronouns correspond negatively to the distribution of topics in Czech: the antecedent of a demonstrative must be non-topical. As such, this distribution was used as a diagnostic to determine a definition of *topic* in Czech. Evidence was provided that a structural definition, rather than one based solely on linear order (Rambow 1993) or grammatical function (Centering Theory) is necessary.

Sources

Czech National Corpus, www.ucnk.ff.cuni.cz
Macourek, Miloš (1984): *Mach a Šebestová*. Prague: Albatros.
Mladá Fronta Dnes. Daily newspaper published in Prague.
Říha, Bohumil (1992): *Jak jel Vítek do Prahy*. Prague: Axioma.
Switchboard Telephone Speech Corpus

References

Beaver, David (2003): The Optimization of Discourse Anaphora. In: *Linguistics and Philosophy* 7 (1), 3–56.

Büring, Daniel (1999): *Topic*. In: Bosch, Peter and Rob van der Sandt (eds): *Focus – Linguistic, Cognitive, and Computational Perspectives*. Cambridge: Cambridge University Press, 142–165.

[14] Gundel 1998 also argues that Centering Theory should allow more than one Cb to be associated with an utterance.

Comrie, Bernard (2000): Pragmatic binding: demonstratives as anaphors in Dutch. In: Juge, Matthew L. and Jeri L. Moxley (eds): *Proceedings of the Twenty-Third Annual Meeting of the Berkeley Linguistics Society*. Berkeley: Berkeley Linguistics Society, 50–61

Fried, Miriam (1994): Second-position clitics in Czech: Syntactic or phonological? In: *Lingua* 94, 155–75.

Gregory, Michelle L. and Laura A. Michaelis (2001): Topicalization and left-dislocation: a functional opposition revisited. In: *Journal of Pragmatics* 33, 1665–1706.

Grosz, Barbara J., Aravind Joshi and Scott Weinstein (1983): Providing a Unified account of definite noun phrases in discourse. In: *Proceeding of the 21st Annual Meeting of the Association for Computational Linguistics*. Cambridge, Mass., 44–50.

Grosz, Barbara J., Aravind Joshi and Candace Sidner (1986): Towards a computational theory of discourse interpretation. Ms.

Grosz, Barbara J., Aravind Joshi and Candace Sidner (1995): Centering: a framework for modeling the local coherence of discourse. In: *Computational Linguistics* 21 (2), 203–25.

Gundel, Jeanette K., Nancy Hedberg and Ron Zacharski (1993): Cognitive status and the form of referring expressions in discourse. In: *Language* 69 (2), 274–307.

Gundel, Jeanette K. (1998): Centering Theory and the Givenness Hierarchy. In: Walker, Marilyn A., Aravind K. Joshi and Ellen Prince (eds.): *Centering Theory in Discourse*. Oxford: Clarendon Press, 183–198.

Hajičová, Eva (1983): Topic and Focus. In: *Theoretical Linguistics* 10, 268–276.

Hajičová, Eva, Tomáš Hoskovec and Petr Sgall (1995): Discourse modeling based on hierarchy of salience. In: *The Prague Bulletin of Mathematical Linguistics* 64, 5–24.

Hajičová, Eva, Petr Sgall and Kateřina Veselá (2002): Information structure and contrastive topic. In: Browne, Wayles, Ji-Yung Kim, Barbara Partee and Robert A. Rothstein (eds): *Formal Approaches to Slavic Linguistics* 11. University of Massachusetts at Amherst.

Kameyama, Megumi (1999): Stressed and unstressed pronouns: Complementary preferences. In: Bosch, Peter and Rob van der Sandt (eds): *Focus, Linguistics, Cognitive and Computational Perspectives*. Cambridge: Cambridge University Press, 306–21.

Koktová, Eva (1992): Anaphoric Expressions Across Clause Boundary in *pro*-drop Languages. In: *Prague Bulletin of Mathematical Linguistics* 58, 39–63.

Kresin, Susan (1994): *Third Person Reference in Russian and Czech*. Doctoral Dissertation. University of California, Berkeley.

Lenertová, Denisa (2001): On clitic placement, topicalization, and CP-Structure in Czech. In: Zybatow, G., U. Junghanns, G. Mehlhorn, and L. Szucsich (eds): *Current Issues in Slavic Linguistics*. Berlin: Peter Lang, 294–305.

Mathesius, Vilém (1915): O pasivu moderní angličtině (On passive in modern English). In: *Sborník filologický* 5, 198–220.

Prince, Ellen (1997): On the functions of left-dislocation in English discourse. In: Kamio, Akio (ed): *Directions in Functional Linguistics*. Philadelphia: John Benjamins, 117–143.

Rambow, Owen (1993): Pragmatic aspects of scrambling and topicalization in German. Presented at the *Workshop on Centering Theory in Naturally-Occurring Discourse*. Institute for Research in Cognitive Science, University of Pennsylvania.

Rizzi, Luigi (1997): The fine structure of the left periphery. In: Haegeman. L. (ed): *Elements of Grammar*. Dordrecht: Kluwer, 281–337.

Sgall, Petr, Eva Hajičová and E. Benešová (1973): *Topic, Focus and Generative Semantics*. Kronberg, Germany: Scripto Verlag GmbH.

Sgall, Petr, Eva Hajičová and E. Buráňová (1980): *Aktuální členění věty v češtině (Functional Sentence Perspective in Czech)*. Prague: Academia.

Sgall, Petr, Eva Hajičová and Jarmila Panevová (1986): *The Meaning of the Sentence in its Semantic and Pragmatic Aspects*. Prague: Reidel, Dordrecht and Academia.

Steedman, M. (2002): The surface grammar of intonation and information structure. Paper delivered at the *Workshop on Contrast and Information Structure*. Leipzig, Germany.

Toman, Jindřich (1981): Aspects of multiple wh-movement in Polish and Czech. In: May, R. and J. Koster (eds): *Levels of Syntactic Representation.* Dordrecht: Foris Publications, 293–302.

Toman, Jindřich (1996): A note on clitics and prosody. In: Halpern, A. and A. M. Zwicky (eds): *Approaching Second: Second position clitics and related phenomena.* Stanford, Ca.: CSLI Publications, 505–510.

Toman, Jindřich (1999): On clitic displacement. In: Dmitrova-Vulchanova, M. and L. Hellan (eds): *Topics in South Slavic Syntax and Semantics.* Amsterdam: Benjamins, 205–228.

Veselovská, Ludmila (1995): *Phrasal Movement and X^0-morphology: word order parallels in Czech and English nominal and verbal projections.* Doctoral Dissertation. Univerzita Palackého, Olomouc, Czech Republic.

Walker, Marilyn A., Aravind K. Joshi and Ellen Prince (1998): Centering in naturally occurring discourse: an introduction. In: Walker, Marilyn A., Aravind K. Joshi and Ellen Prince (eds): *Centering Theory in Discourse.* Oxford: Clarendon Press, 1–30.

Ward, Gregory L. and Ellen F. Prince (1991): On the topicalization of indefinite NP's. *Journal of Pragmatics* 16, 167–77.

Peter Svenonius, Tromsø*

Russian Prefixes are Phrasal

1. Introduction

In a certain view of X-bar theory, an element is 'phrasal' or 'maximal' when it is not dominated by a projection of itself (Muysken 1982, Muysken and van Riemsdijk 1986, Baltin 1989, Chomsky 1995); exceptions are sometimes made for head-adjunction structures, in which an adjoined head, assumed to be nonmaximal, is dominated by a projection of itself only at the root of a head-chain.

In this paper I assume a morphosyntactic decomposition of words and phrases into an X-bar theory of this sort, and so there is a trivial and uninteresting sense in which I am simply assuming without argument that Russian prefixes are phrasal; since they correspond to pieces of syntax, and no piece of syntax projects infinitely, there is some point at which they are phrasal.

The more interesting claim, which is much more difficult to defend, is that Russian prefixes occupy a phrasal position in the surface syntax of Russian; that is, they occupy a specifier position, and are not incorporated into the verb under a nonmaximal projection. This is a highly plausible position for German and Dutch separable prefixes, as I discuss below, but seems on the face of it extremely dubious for Slavic languages in general.

However, I argue here that when the stipulations are weighed against each other, an account that takes the Russian prefixes to be XPs in the specifier of (or adjoined to) an aspectual projection outside VP is superior to an account that takes them to be heads incorporated into the verb. The latter kind of account can surely be made to work, but only by essentially stipulating what it sets out to explain, whereas the purely syntactic XP account promises to be able to derive the properties of Russian prefixes from independently observable facts about morphology, syntax, and semantic scope.

2. Decomposition and Russian prefixes

Russian prefixes are traditionally divided into at least two general types, the lexical and superlexical (or sub-lexical) (setting aside purely perfectivizing prefixes). Generally, lexical prefixes contribute directional or idiosyncratic lexical meanings, as illustrated in (1a–c), much like Germanic particles (cf. e.g. Spencer and Zaretskaya 1998, Svenonius 2004b).

(1) a. *pere-kidat'*
across-throw
'throw across'
b. *pere-kusit'*
across-bite
'bite in half'
c. *pere-bit'*
across-beat
'interfere'

---

*Thanks very much to Eugenia Romanova for extensive discussion and assistance with the Russian data and its interpretation. All data in this paper is Russian and provided by her unless otherwise noted. Thanks also to the participants in the Slavic prefix discussion group in Tromsø in 2003–2004, and to Michal Starke and an anonymous reviewer for comments on a previous draft. Finally, thanks to the organizers and audience at FDSL-5 in Leipzig, where a preliminary version of this material was presented.

Superlexical prefixes, on the other hand, contribute predictable aspectually quantizing meanings as in (2a–c) (cf. Filip 2000).

(2) a. *pere-kidat'*
DISTR-throw
'throw one by one'
b. *pere-kusat'*
DISTR-bite
'bite one by one'
c. *pere-bit'*
DISTR-beat
'beat one by one'

As a convention, I gloss lexical prefixes as prepositions, and superlexical prefixes with abbreviations of their functions (DISTR[ibutive], CUM[ulative], TERM[inative], INCEP[tive], DELIM[itative], and COMPL[etive]).

Lexical prefixes are also generally distinguishable from superlexical ones in that they attach to the directed form of motion verb stems, as in (3).

(3) a. *na-bežat'*
on-run.DIR
'run over'
b. *ot-nesti*
away-carry.DIR
'carry off'
c. *po-past'*
along-fall.DIR
'find oneself somewhere'

Superlexical prefixes attach to the non-directed form as in (4).

(4) a. *na-begat'*
CUM-run.NONDIR
'run (cumulative)'
b. *ot-nosit'*
TERM-carry.NONDIR
'wear to exhaustion'
c. *po-padat'*
DISTR-fall.NONDIR
'fall one after the other'

Lexical prefixes allow the formation of secondary imperfectives, as seen in (5).

(5) a. *iz-brat'/iz-birat'*
out.of-take
'elect' (perfective/imperfective)

b. *za-verit'/za-verjat'*
after-trust
'confirm' (perfective/imperfective)
c. *vo-rvat'=sja/v-ryvat'=sja*
in-tear=RFX
'enter quickly' (perfective/imperfective)

In contrast, the secondary imperfective forms in (6) cannot be interpreted as secondary imperfectives of the superlexically prefixed verbs glossed here (though these secondary imperfective forms are grammatical as imperfectives of lexically prefixed verbs meaning 'play to the limit,' 'bite in half,' and 'walk along').

(6) a. *za-igrat'/*za-igryvat'*
INCEP-play
'start to play' (perfective)
b. *pere-kusat'/*pere-kusyvat'*
DISTR-bite
'bite one after the other' (perfective)
c. *po-guljat'/*po-gulivat'*
DELIM-walk
'walk for a while' (perfective)

Assuming a decompositional approach to morphosyntax, the resultative semantics of the lexical prefixes suggest a low point of attachment. I have argued in Svenonius (2004b) that they originate VP-internally, very much like English particles or German separable prefixes. There, I argue that the VP-internal analysis explains, among other things, the tendency for prefixes to develop highly idiosyncratic meanings, as the VP is a domain for idiom assignment (Marantz 1984).

The same decompositional approach dictates a high point of attachment for superlexical prefixes (cf. Babko-Malaya 1999). This is especially clear when cases of multiple prefixation are examined, as the superlexical prefixes attach outside lexical ones, as illustrated by the Serbian examples in (7) (from Milićević 2004).

(7) a. *pre-trčati — is-pre-trčavati — *pre-is-trčavati*
across-run COMPL-across-run.IMPF across-COMPL-run
'run across' — 'run across each'
b. *na-piti — po-na-pijati — *na-po-pijati*
on-drink DISTR-on-drink.IMPF on-DISTR-drink
'get [sby] drunk' — 'get [people] drunk one by one'
c. *za-pisati — po-za-pisivati — *za-po-pisivati*
down-write DISTR-down-write.IMPF down-DISTR-write
'record, write down' — 'record one by one'

Note, too, that the superlexical prefixes do not carry idiomatic meanings; their meanings are systematically regular and compositional, as expected if they originate outside VP.

Another piece of evidence supporting the relative placement of lexical versus superlexical prefixes is the effect of the secondary imperfective: an unprefixed stem is ordinarily imperfective

(8a), while a prefixed stem is perfective (8b); thus the prefix perfectivizes the stem. A secondary imperfective suffix has the effect of making a lexically-prefixed stem imperfective, as illustrated in (8c) (glossing the theme vowel as *v*, as discussed below).

(8) a. *kold-ova-t'*
magic-*v*-INF
'perform magic' (imperfective)
b. *za-kold-ova-t'*
after-magic-*v*-INF
'cast a spell' (perfective)
c. *za-kold-ov-yva-t'*
after-magic-*v*-IMPF-INF
'cast a spell' (imperfective)

This suggests that the secondary imperfective is structurally higher than the lexical prefix, as illustrated in (9).

(9) *[za-kold-ov]-yva-t'*
after-magic-*v*-IMPF-INF

The impossibility of applying secondary imperfective to a superlexically prefixed stem is explained if the superlexical prefixes attach higher than the secondary imperfective. Note that in the Serbian examples of double prefixation in (7a–c), the lexically prefixed stems are secondarily imperfectivized before the superlexical prefix is attached. The superlexical prefix leads to perfectivization again, proving that it scopes over the secondary imperfective. (7a) is repeated here with a fuller parse.

(10) *is-pre-trč-a-va-ti*
COMPL-across-run-*v*-IMPF-INF

In fact, the superlexical prefix can be more narrowly localized; Russian *zakatal*, for example, means 'started rolling,' not 'starts to have rolled,' suggesting that the superlexical prefix is inside the scope of tense, as illustrated in (11).[1]

(11) *[za-[kat-a]]-l*
INCEP-roll-*v*-PAST

Thus, we can map the Russian verb onto the following hierarchy of projections: AGR[eement], T[ense], SUP[erlexical prefix], ASP[ect], *v* (cf. Hale and Keyser 2002), V, and LEX[ical prefix]. I assume that *v* is represented by the thematic vowel, or is null with certain verbs.

---

[1]Michal Starke has suggested to me that the *-l* in Russian is (still) a participial morpheme, lower than tense proper (as it is in other Slavic languages). However, overt tenses such as the Bulgarian aorist can be demonstrated to be higher than superlexical prefixes. For example, *iz-čet-ja-x-a* 'COMPL-read-IMPF-AOR-3PL' ("[they] read through") shows an aorist suffix on a verb with a prefix, while *b-ja-x-a iz-če-l-i* 'be-IMPF-AOR-3PL COMPL-read-PERF-PL' ("[they] had read through") shows the aorist suffix on an auxiliary, higher than the main verb bearing the prefix (examples from Krapova (1999)).

(12) AGR-T-SUP-ASP-*v*-LEX

I am assuming that the imperfective suffix is one realization of an ASP[ect] projection. I am simplifying the analysis of Tense and Agreement (the *-l* past tense in Russian is at least historically participial, with gender and number (g,n) agreement, while finite tenses take person and number (p,n) agreement; the order of these elements when they cooccur is $Agr_{p,n}$-T_{fin}-$Agr_{g,n}$-T_{part}, as seen e.g. for the Bulgarian examples in note 1; see Svenonius 2004a for more discussion).

3. Head-movement

For those categories realized as suffixes, the actual structure of the verb fits a pattern widely attested cross-linguistically, most directly captured in a head-incorporation approach to morphology (Baker 1988), where e.g. V head-moves to *v*, creating a complex head V-*v* which head-moves to T, etc.

(13) V-*v*-ASP-T-AGR

In fact, even the lexical prefix could be treated this way; since it originates below the verb, the leftward adjunction procedure which is standard for head movement will cause it to surface as a prefix.

(14) LEX-V-*v*-ASP-T-AGR

But the superlexical prefix was included in this line-up in the position between T and Asp, in (12); this seems to wrongly predict it to surface as a suffix between Asp and T. In order to get the superlexical prefix into the structure by head movement, we could assume that prefixes are specially marked in the lexicon as demanding incorporees to right-adjoin, rather than left-adjoin. The right order is now derived, with the right hierarchical structure, as suggested in the partial derivation in (15).

(15) a. ... T ... SUP ... [LEX-V-*v*-ASP]
b. ... T ... [SUP-[LEX-V-*v*-ASP]]
c. ... [[SUP-[LEX-V-*v*-ASP]]-T]

Right adjunction has been argued to be syntactically impossible (Kayne 1994). Below I show that there are other challenges for a head movement analysis of prefixation.

4. Problems for head movement

Phonologically, all prefixes appear to be outside a domain including the root and all its suffixes (Pesetsky 1985, Fowler 1994, Matushansky 2002), suggesting the prosodic structure illustrated by the parentheses in (16).

(16) a. *za-(kold-ov-yva-t')*
after-magic-*v*-IMPF-INF
b. *za-(kat-a-l)*
INCEP-roll-*v*-PAST

This is at odds with the syntactic structure argued for in §2. The two can be resolved if the prefix defines a separate prosodic domain. That is, if the prefix constitutes a separate phonological cycle, then that yields the prosodic boundary between the prefix and the root signified by the left parenthesis in (16). This is illustrated in (17).

(17) a. *[[[[(za)-kold]-ov]-yva]-t']*
after-magic-*v*-IMPF-INF

b. *[[(za)-[kat-a]]-l]*
INCEP-roll-*v*-PAST

The question arises whether this special prosodic status can be made to follow from anything or whether it must simply be stipulated. If prefixes are maximal (extended) projections, then it might follow on independent grounds that they define their own phonological cycles. But if they are heads in the extended projection of V, then the special prosodic status appears to require an additional stipulation, in addition to the one that they require right adjunction by the incorporating verb.

Julien (2002) proposes that many prefixes are actually heads in situ, not actually forming a syntactic constituent with the stem to which they are perceived as being prefixed. If we adopt that solution for Russian superlexical prefixes, then the verb cannot move as high as T in Russian, nor in Slavic in general; but that the Slavic verb remains relatively low is the conclusion drawn by Veselovská (1995) on completely independent grounds.

If the verb remains low, then head movement cannot be the mechanism for combining the verb with T and Agr. Instead, T and Agr must combine with the verb by some other means, for example morphological merger (Halle and Marantz 1993, Embick and Noyer 2001). The idea would be that the verb moves as high as Asp, where it is preceded by the superlexical prefix. Then T attaches to the verb by the postlexical lowering operation, morphological merger. However, morphological merger is assumed to require a kind of adjacency, which would entail that the superlexical prefix is an adjunct, not a head or specifier.

Another alternative to head movement is that proposed by Brody (2000). According to Brody, the phonological realization of a projection line like that in (13) may appear in any specially designated head in that line. But for Brody's system to work for a structure like (12), it is crucial that the superlexical prefix not be a head (at least, not in the same extended projection line as V). Otherwise it would necessarily appear as a suffix, between IMPF and T.

Thus, the fact that the superlexical prefix is a prefix suggests that it has not incorporated, and the fact that higher morphological material can appear suffixally suggests that the superlexical prefix is not a head but a phrase.

The lexical prefix can be assumed to undergo phrasal movement to the preverbal position. This captures the great similarity between lexical and superlexical prefixes: both are perfectivizing operators, binding a variable in Asp, and both have the same prosodic profile. At the same time, it captures the differences; the lexical prefix is a secondary predicate, originating VP-internally, introducing internal arguments, and participating in idioms (as discussed in Svenonius 2004b).

5. Comparison with German separable prefixes

The above proposal suggests that the Russian verb does not form a syntactic constituent with the prefix.[2] This will strike many readers as counterintuitive. It is instructive to compare the case of German. For German, a clearer case can be made that the so-called separable prefix projects a full phrase; Zeller (2001) and Lüdeling (2001) argue at length that separable prefixes occur in a phrasal position to the left of the unmoved verb in German. The arguments are the following.

(18) Arguments that German and Dutch separable prefixes are not morphologically incorporated (see Zeller 2001, Lüdeling 2001 for references and examples)
  a. Stranded by V2 movement
  b. Separated from V by Verb Raising
  c. Separated from V by *zu*
  d. Never change the inflectional class of the verb

In German and Dutch, separable prefixes can be contrasted with inseparable prefixes on each of these points. In Russian, however, there is no V2 movement, and no Verb Raising of the Dutch type, so (18a)–(18b) cannot be demonstrated.[3] There is no preverbal head like *zu* which appears between the prefixes and the verb (though other prefixes may appear between the superlexical prefixes and the verb). Prefixes seem not to change the inflectional class of the verb, which is expected if they are not morphologically part of it, but on the other hand many affixes share this property. Thus, none of the points in (18) can be used to make much of a case for Russian either way.

Zeller and Lüdeling also present arguments that German separable prefixes are specifically XPs.

(19) Arguments that German separable prefixes are XPs (Zeller 2001, Lüdeling 2001)
  a. Can topicalize
  b. Can undergo focus scrambling
  c. Left behind under Gapping
  d. Can be modified

Here Russian seems to contrast with German systematically. Russian prefixes do not topicalize, in contrast to German ones.

(20) a. *An der Haltestelle stiegen hübsche Frauen ein. Aus stiegen nur Männer.*
   at the bus.stop climbed pretty women in out climbed only men
   'At the bus stop, pretty women got on. Only men got off' (German; Zeller 2001: 89)

[2]The prefix appears to form a constituent with the verb in participle fronting, attested in most Slavic languages (e.g. in Slovak *Na-písal som list* 'on-written am letter' "I have written a letter," Rivero 1999). This could be a case of remnant movement or of movement of a prosodic constituent, or else be due to clitic lowering. See Franks and King (2000) for discussion, including arguments against long head-movement analyses.

[3]Slavic languages have participle movement carrying the prefix along, cf. note 2, but when a participle crosses a finite verb, prefixes are carried along even in German: *Ab-getreten is Nixon 1974* 'off-stepped is Nixon 1974' ("Nixon resigned in 1974"), Zeller 2001: 97

b. *V autobus vo-šli krasivyje ženščiny. *Vy toljko mužčiny šli.*
in bus in-climbed pretty women out only men climbed

Nor can Russian prefixes be separated from the verb by scrambling.

(21) a. *Ich weiß, daß die Sonne AUF im Osten und UNTER im Westen geht.*
I know that the sun up in.the East and down in.the West goes
'I know that the sun goes up in the East and down in the West' (German; Lüdeling 2001: 50)
b. **Solnce VOS na Vostoke xodit, a ZA na Zapade xodit.*
sun up on East goes and behind on West goes

In contrast to German, Russian prefixes cannot be stranded by Gapping.

(22) a. *weil Peter ein-steigt und Hans aus-(steigt)*
because Peter in-climbs and Hans out-climbs
'because Peter climbs in and Hans (climbs) out' (German; Zeller 2001: 85)
b. *Ivan vo-shël, a Taras vy-*(shel).*
Ivan in-went and Taras out-went.
'Ivan went in, and Taras went out.'

In German, particles can be modified. At first glance, this appears to be true of Russian, as well.

(23) a. *Peter hat die Tür ganz weit auf-gemacht.*
Peter has the door quite wide up-made
'Peter has opened the door quite wide' (German; Zeller 2001: 100)
b. *On dovoljno široko ot-kryl dver'.*
he rather wide away-covered door
'He opened the door rather wide'

However, the modifier in (23b) might modify the whole verb, rather than just the particle. Zeller shows that the modifier in German is carried along when the particle is topicalized (*Ganz weit auf hat Peter die Tür gemacht*), but as we have just seen topicalization of prefixes is not possible in Russian. However, a modifiers like *prjamo* 'right' which combines freely with PP does not seem to be able to scope over a prefix.

(24) a. *On v-taščil mešok prjamo v komnatu.*
he in-dragged sack right in room
'He dragged the sack right into the room'
b. *On (??prjamo) v-taščil mešok v komnatu.*
he right in-dragged sack in room
'He (??right) dragged the sack into the room'

Thus, the diagnostics in (19) seem to indicate that Russian prefixes are not phrasal.

It should be noted, however, that German and Dutch separable prefixes only topicalize, scramble, strand, and accept modification under very circumscribed circumstances. Generally, it is only the most transparently contentful prefixes which pass these diagnostics. In fact, so many separable prefixes resist them that many of the same diagnostics have been used to argue that German separable prefixes are affixal.

(25) a. **Auf ist er im letzten Moment gesprungen.*
up is he in.the last moment jumped
(German; Stiebels and Wunderlich 1994: 923)
b. **dat Jan het meisje op vaak merkte*
that Jan the girl up often noticed
(Dutch; Neeleman and Weerman 1993: 436)

But the contrast with Russian prefixes appears to be absolute; a few German prefixes can be moved, but no Russian ones can.

6. Prosody

In looking for a reason for the strict adjacency of the Russian prefix and the verb stem, one possibility (which I will reject) is that it has something to do with prosody. The idea would be that the prefix is phonologically weak, and is prosodically a clitic on the verb. When the verb is removed from it, the result is prosodically, not syntactically ill-formed.

There are two problems with this kind of solution. First, it does not explain why the prefix could not prosodically incorporate to some other element; a stipulation has to be made that the prefix specifically seeks the verb.

Second, the prefixes are phonologically indistinguishable from prepositions, but prepositions, under some very limited circumstances, can be stranded by deletion processes like Gapping.

(26) a. *Sullay krasil nad oknom, a Gillian pod.*
Sullay painted above window and Gillian below
'Sullay painted above the window, and Gillian below'
b. *Katja krasil pered oknom, a Kuba za.*
Katja painted in.front.of window and Kuba behind
'Katja painted in front of the window, and Kuba behind it'

Thus, a prosodic account would have to be stipulated, as it cannot be made to follow from any independently ascertainable properties of the prefixes.

7. Scope

Scope-taking elements are often sensitive to movement. For example, the scope of *again* is ambiguous in (27a), but unambiguously wide in (27b).

(27) a. Trina opened the door again.
b. Again, Trina opened the door.

In (27), it appears, a scope-taking element cannot move to a higher position without changing its scope. In other cases, a similar effect is perceived on the domain of the scope. For example, in German a verb like *verdreifachen* 'triple' can be modified by a degree modifier like *mehr als* 'more than,' as shown in (28a); but if it is, then the verb cannot move across it, as illustrated in (28b) (pointed out to me by Hubert Haider).

(28) a. *daß die Erneuerung den Wert des Hauses (mehr als) verdreifachte.*
that the renovation the value of.the house more than tripled
'that the renovation (more than) tripled the value of the house'
b. *Die Erneuerung verdreifachte den Wert des Hauses (*mehr als).*
the renovation tripled the value of.the house more than
'The renovation tripled the value of the house'

This is a striking illustration of a surface requirement because verb movement has so few detectable semantic effects that is sometimes claimed to be purely phonological (e.g. Chomsky 2001).

Of course, other scope-taking elements appear to be able to scope at a distance. Without claiming to understand the difference, I will simply refer to the strictly local kind of scope illustrated in (27)–(28) as local scope.

The absolute immovability of the Slavic prefix could be explained if the Slavic prefix could independently be demonstrated to have local scope over the verb. As it happens, there is a very clear contrast between the role of the Slavic prefix in effecting perfectivity and the role of the Germanic particle. Germanic particles are often claimed to telicize, but they are at best resultative. Slavic prefixes have a much more profound effect on the aspectual character of the predicate.

To indulge in a brief bit of speculation, I suggest that this effect is the result of the binding, by some aspectual operator, of an eventual variable located in the verb (the verb may have moved to the Asp head, thus the relevant variable may in fact be located in Asp). This aspectual operator is apparently not present in ordinary prepositions, with which the prefixes are homophonous. Following this line of reasoning, the operator is a nominal constituent which is the complement of the prefix. It is then this complement that makes the prefix phrasal.[4]

8. Modification

The badness of modification of Slavic prefixes (illustrated above in (24)) is not explained by the local scope hypothesis. However, there is a plausible independent explanation. In Norwegian, certain PPs undergo Particle Shift. These PPs can be phrasal. However, they cannot be modified by adverbial material, as indicated.

(29) a. *Hun kastet kniven (langt) fra seg.*
she threw the.knife (far) from RFX
'She threw the knife (far) away from her'
b. *Hun kastet (*langt) fra seg kniven.*
she threw far from RFX the.knife
'She threw the knife away from her'

[4]This entails that the operator can scope out of the PP projected by the prefix, much as has been observed for constructions like *We spoke [to each woman$_i$] about her$_i$ options.*

(30) a. *Hunden rev hatten (rett) av mannen.*
the.dog tore the.hat right off the.man
'The dog tore the hat (right) off the man'
b. *Hunden rev (*rett) av mannen hatten.*
the.dog tore right off the.man the.hat
'The dog tore the hat off the man'

In these cases, I suggest, the projection of P which undergoes shift to the position between V and DP is smaller than the projection which remains behind; assume, for example, that the complement of V in these cases is *p*P, the head *p* of which takes a PP complement (cf. Zeller 2001, Svenonius 2003). PP undergoes shift, leaving *p* behind, along with the DP in its specifier. If the modifiers are contained in the *p* projection, then they will not be carried along. If they are local modifiers of P, then they cannot be stranded either.

This suggests that there are projections which are too small to contain certain kinds of modifiers. If the Russian prefixes are of this small size, then they will not contain modifiers, even if they are phrasal. Their small size may also explain why they cannot have other complements than the perfective operator.

9. Conclusion

The arguments in favor of a phrasal approach to Russian prefixes must be seen in the context of a theory of morphosyntax. If human language learning admits the postulation of morphological rules which arbitrarily dictate that certain classes of elements must be adjacent to some other class of elements, or must be right-adjoined to their hosts, then a learner faced with Russian data might postulate such rules. If, on the other hand, morphology is minimal, then such rules may not exist. In that case, a learner faced with Russian data must discover a syntactic system that leads to the correct distribution of prefixes. I suggest that the perfectivizing function of prefixes might be a clue to the learner that they take what I called local scope over the verb. In fact, the regular adjacency of prefixes to verbs might also be a clue to which the learner is sensitive (as is often assumed). Possibly, once the existence of a perfectivizing local scope operator is discovered, the extreme adjacency facts follow. There are many details which remain to be worked out, not least how multiple prefixation works. I hope to have at least made the phrasal analysis plausible.

Bibliography

Babko-Malaya, O. (1999). *Zero Morphology: a Study of Aspect, Argument Structure and Case*. PhD thesis, Rutgers, New Brunswick, New Jersey.
Baker, M. C. (1988). *Incorporation: A Theory of Grammatical Function Changing*. University of Chicago Press, Chicago.
Baltin, M. R. (1989). Heads and projections. In Baltin, M. R. and Kroch, A. S., editors, *Alternative Conceptions of Phrase Structure*, pages 1–16. University of Chicago Press, Chicago.
Brody, M. (2000). Mirror theory: Syntactic representation in perfect syntax. *Linguistic Inquiry*, 31(1):29–56.
Chomsky, N. (1995). Bare phrase structure. In Webelhuth, G., editor, *Government and Binding Theory and the Minimalist Program: Principles and Parameters in Syntactic Theory*, pages 383–439. Blackwell, Oxford.
Chomsky, N. (2001). Derivation by phase. In Kenstowicz, M., editor, *Ken Hale: A Life in Language*, pages 1–52. MIT Press, Cambridge, Ma.
Embick, D. and Noyer, R. (2001). Movement operations after syntax. *Linguistic Inquiry*, 32(4):555–595.
Filip, H. (2000). The quantization puzzle. In Tenny, C. and Pustejovsky, J., editors, *Events as*

Grammatical Objects, pages 39–96. CSLI, Stanford, Ca.
Fowler, G. (1994). Verbal prefixes as functional heads. *Studies in Linguistic Sciences*, 24:171–185.
Franks, S. and King, T. H. (2000). *A Handbook of Slavic Clitics*. Oxford University Press, New York.
Hale, K. and Keyser, S. J. (2002). *Prolegomenon to a Theory of Argument Structure*. Number 39 in Linguistic Inquiry Monograph. MIT Press, Cambridge, Ma.
Halle, M. and Marantz, A. (1993). Distributed morphology and the pieces of inflection. In Hale, K. and Keyser, S. J., editors, *The View from Building 20: Essays in Linguistics in Honor of Sylvain Bromberger*, pages 111–176. MIT Press, Cambridge, Ma.
Julien, M. (2002). *Syntactic Heads and Word Formation*. Oxford Studies in Comparative Syntax. Oxford University Press, New York.
Kayne, R. S. (1994). *The Antisymmetry of Syntax*. MIT Press, Cambridge, Ma.
Krapova, I. (1999). The system of auxiliaries in Bulgarian. In Dimitrova-Vulchanova, M. and Hellan, L., editors, *Topics in South Slavic Syntax and Semantics*, number 172 in Current Issues in Linguistic Theory, pages 59–89. John Benjamins.
Lüdeling, A. (2001). *On Particle Verbs and Similar Constructions in German*. CSLI, Stanford, Ca.
Marantz, A. (1984). *On the Nature of Grammatical Relations*, volume 10 of *Linguistic Inquiry Monographs*. MIT Press, Cambridge, Ma.
Matushansky, O. (2002). On formal identity of Russian prefixes and prepositions. In *Phonological Answers (and their corresponding questions)*, volume 42, pages 217–253. MITWPL, Cambridge, Ma.
Milićević, N. (2004). The lexical and superlexical verbal prefix *iz-* and its role in the stacking of prefixes. In Svenonius, P., editor, *Nordlyd 32.2: Special issue on Slavic prefixes*, pages 279–300. University of Tromsø, Tromsø. available at www.ub.uit.no/munin/nordlyd/.
Muysken, P. (1982). Parametrizing the notion 'head'. *Journal of Linguistic Research*, 2(3):57–75.
Muysken, P. and van Riemsdijk, H. (1986). Projecting features and featuring projections. In Muysken, P. and van Riemsdijk, H., editors, *Features and Projections*, pages 1–30. Foris, Dordrecht.
Neeleman, A. and Weerman, F. (1993). The balance between syntax and morphology: Dutch particles and resultatives. *Natural Language and Linguistic Theory*, 11(3):433–475.
Pesetsky, D. (1985). Morphology and lexical form. *Linguistic Inquiry*, 16(2):193–246.
Rivero, M. L. (1999). Verb movement and economy: Last resort. In Dimitrova-Vulchanova, M. and Hellan, L., editors, *Topics in South Slavic Syntax and Semantics*, number 172 in Current Issues in Linguistic Theory, pages 1–23. John Benjamins.
Spencer, A. and Zaretskaya, M. (1998). Verb prefixation in Russian as lexical subordination. *Linguistics*, 36:1–39.
Stiebels, B. and Wunderlich, D. (1994). Morphology feeds syntax: The case of particle verbs. *Linguistics*, 32:913–968.
Svenonius, P. (2003). Limits on P: *filling in holes* vs. *falling in holes*. *Nordlyd. Proceedings of the 19th Scandinavian Conference of Linguistics*, 31(2):431–445.
Svenonius, P. (2004a). Slavic prefixes and morphology: An introduction to the nordlyd volume. In Svenonius, P., editor, *Nordlyd 32.2: Special issue on Slavic prefixes*, pages 177–204. University of Tromsø, Tromsø. available at www.ub.uit.no/munin/nordlyd/.
Svenonius, P. (2004b). Slavic prefixes inside and outside VP. In Svenonius, P., editor, *Nordlyd 32.2: Special issue on Slavic prefixes*, pages 205–253. University of Tromsø, Tromsø. available at www.ub.uit.no/munin/nordlyd/.
Veselovská, L. (1995). *Phrasal Movement and X^0-Morphology: Word Order Parallels in Czech and English Nominal and Verbal Projections*. PhD thesis, Palacký University, Olomouc.
Zeller, J. (2001). *Particle Verbs and Local Domains*. John Benjamins, Amsterdam.

Helen Trugman, Tel-Aviv

What do demonstratives demonstrate?

1. Introduction

The Antisymmetry hypothesis advanced in Kayne (1994) has proclaimed that the linear order of constituents must be fully and non-contradictorily determined by asymmetric c-command relations. Accounts that take up this approach have to resort to multiple functional projections often headed by null heads, in view of the necessary redefinition of c-command. When applied to the relatively free word order attested within the nominal projection, this approach necessitates massive use of reordering operations, and this is what we find in the works of Cinque (1994), Giusti (1995, 1997), Brugé (1996, 2002), Yadroff (1999), among many others.

In the present paper I will focus on the hypothesis put forth in Brugé (1996, 2002) for Spanish and extended to Romance, Slavic, and even some Germanic languages that there exists a universal merging site for demonstrative pronouns. Specifically, Brugé proposes that demonstratives are merged in a separate functional projection FP immediately dominating the lexical projection NP (or a functional projection hosting the possessive satellites of N). Following Cinque's (1994) work, she suggests that this projection is dominated by numerous functional projections accommodating adjectival modifiers (XPs), with the whole hierarchy being topped by the Determiner projection (DP), as shown in (1). The dots indicate that the XP projections can iterate to host multiple adjectival modifiers of the head noun.

(1)

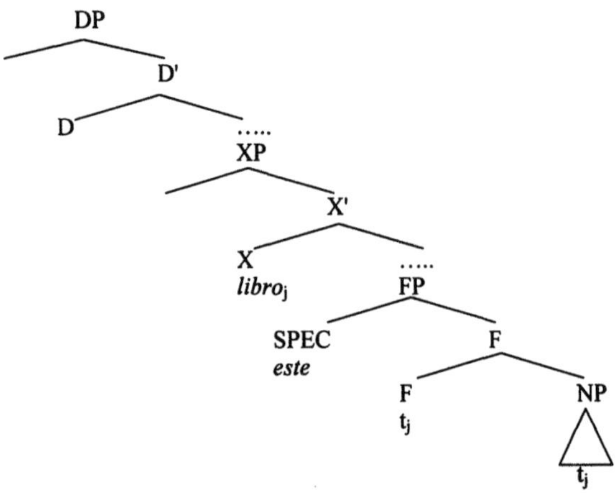

This approach analyzes instances of *postnominal* demonstratives as found in situ (Spec, FP), or in some intermediate Spec, XP, whereas their *prenominal* counterparts are taken to raise to the Spec, DP. Brugé's proposal has been adopted for some Slavic languages, specifically for Russian in Yadroff (1999) and for Polish in Migdalski (2001), though no thorough argumentation has been provided in favor of this analysis. In this paper I challenge the claim that demonstratives in Russian are merged low in the extended nominal projection (in the sense of Grimshaw 1991). In section 2 I will address the empirical and conceptual problems encountered by Brugé's hypothesis. In section 3 I will analyze the properties of Russian demonstratives arguing for their high locus of merge within the nominal projection. Concretely, I will propose that demonstratives are better analyzed as merged directly in the

Spec, DP position. Postnominal occurrences of demonstratives in Russian will be investigated in section 4, and a competing Information Structure-driven account will be suggested there.

2. Problems with Brugé's proposal

The proposal put forth in Brugé (1996, 2002) has a number of conceptual and empirical drawbacks. First, as can be seen from the structure in (1), the adoption of Kayne's (1994) Antisymmetric hypothesis forces Brugé to assume the movement of N to a higher head (X) to ensure the asymmetric c-command configuration and derive the postnominal position of the demonstrative. However, the trigger for this N-to-X movement is not made explicit in her work. In a theory where the dislocation of elements within the syntactic structure is assumed to be driven by strong/uninterpretable features (Chomsky 1995) some feature of N or X should be held responsible for N-to-X movement in Romance DPs. Unfortunately, Brugé does not directly address this issue.[1] We may search for the answer in Cinque (1994), whose original proposal underlies the structure in (1). Cinque does address the issue of what triggers N-to-X movement in Romance versus its lack in Germanic languages. He suggests that this movement can be attributed to *overt* number and gender features that are expressed by Romance noun markers. Specifically, the functional head X that attracts N presumably bears strong uninterpretable features, such as gender and/or number, that require checking before Spell-Out in Romance, but not in Germanic. However, his proposal appears to be invalidated by Russian, a language with rich nominal morphology, yet lacking postnominal adjectival modifiers or demonstratives (see section 4 for exceptions). Therefore Brugé's proposal of the N-to-X movement for many morphologically diverse languages does not seem well motivated, though it may answer the word order needs of Romance DPs.

Another claim, which is conceptually unattractive, concerns the proposed parametrization of demonstrative movement across languages. According to Brugé (ibid.), languages split into three major groups regarding the position of the demonstrative within the DP: (i) those that require obligatory movement of demonstratives within the projection, such as Italian, French, German, and Albanian; (ii) those that require demonstratives to stay in situ until after the Spell-Out, such as Irish and Hebrew; and (iii) those that allow for the optionality in demonstratives' position, such as Spanish, Catalan, Bosnian, Romanian, Russian and others. Brugé proposes to account for this paradigm by the strength or weakness of the feature [+referential] that is inherent to demonstratives. In the first group of languages demonstratives have a strong [+ref] specification that must be checked in the overt syntax. In contrast, in the second group of languages the feature [+ref] is weak and its checking can be postponed till LF. In the last group of languages exhibiting optional movement this feature is claimed to have both weak and strong properties (Brugé 2002: 44).[2] This suggestion lacks explanatory force since it does not reveal a real trigger of the movement but rather reformulates the problem in a different terminology. In addition it leads to wrong empirical predictions in Russian, as will be discussed below.

Brugé (1996:8) also assumes that referentiality implies definiteness, which seems to be too strong. She claims that the presence of the demonstrative in the DP projection is contingent upon the definite specification of the D head. This principle is needed to account for the ungrammaticality of such structures as in (2):

(2)	a.	*un	libro	este	a'.	el	libro	este	*Spanish*
		a	book	this		the	book	this	

[1] Brugé follows Dimitrova-Vulchanova & Giusti (1998) in assuming that a functional projection is instantiated in order to realize some feature φ, which must be visible at all levels of representation, but the nature of φ triggering N-to-X movement is not discussed (Brugé 2002: 19).

[2] As Brugé (2002) acknowledges in footnote 44 it would be better to avoid resorting to such a solution, yet she takes such cases of redundancy in languages to be part of the UG.

b. *băiat acesta frumos
boy.indef this nice

b'. băiatul acesta frumos
boy-the this nice *Romanian*

In the examples (2a'&b'), wherein the demonstrative is found postnominally, the head noun, which presumably has raised into X or D, should be overtly specified as definite. Indefinite noun heads are ungrammatical, as shown in (2a&b). Brugé assumes that the inherent [+ref] specification of the demonstrative is compatible only with the [+definite] feature of D (2002: 19). Specifically, an indefinite D will prevent checking the feature [+ref] of the demonstrative due to the clash of (in)definite features between the head and its specifier after the demonstrative raises to D covertly. However, such strong interdependency between the definite specification of D and the referentiality of the demonstrative is sometimes violated, though no ungrammaticality ensues. It happens in cases of specific indefinite *this* common in colloquial language in Germanic and Romance (see Bernstein 1997, Lyons 1999, Givón 2001 for discussion). Consider the following examples of indefinite *this* in English:[3]

(3) a. There is *this* guy I've been going with for nearly three years. (from Givón, ibid., (52))

b. *This* picture that Bill saw in the gallery sold for $2,000. (from Bernstein, ibid., (44))

c. I was walking to work yesterday morning, when *this* man came up to me and asked me if I was a news announcer. (from Lyons, ibid., (48a))

Colloquial *this* is used in first mentions and is suitable to start a story, a joke or an anecdote (Lyons, ibid: 176). It is stylistically limited and, as argued in Givón (2001, Ch. II, footnote 7), is a recent innovation in a written text, found mostly in the language of young people. The behavior of colloquial *this* in diagnostic environments indicates its indefinite nature. Thus in (3a) *this* is used in a *there*-insertion structure, which allows for indefinite noun phrases exclusively. In (3b) it takes a restrictive relative clause, which is disallowed with deictic definite uses of demonstratives: cf. **This student who is always late to classes is from North Tel-Aviv.*[4] The existence of demonstratives compatible with referential (i.e. specific) indefinites seems to undermine Brugé's contention that the demonstrative cannot be licensed in the presence of the indefinite D in the projection.[5]

[3] I give English examples though similar examples can be constructed in other languages as well (see references above).

[4] This sentence is grammatical with an appositive relative clause, but then commas are needed.

[5] Brugé (2002, footnote 27) discusses some non-standard uses of demonstratives, such as their use as discourse anaphors (i) or as a 'deictic *am phantasma*', (ii). The latter use (ii) can be compared to English indefinite *this* signaling specificity rather than definiteness, as discussed above.

(i) Juan is handsome, intelligent, and likeable. Nevertheless, these qualities do not make him the perfect man.

(ii) "Here I imagine these small Alpine style houses…"

She claims that in such cases demonstratives should be considered as non-referential yet raising to the Spec, DP to check some other feature particular to these specific interpretations. This proposal does not live up to criticism either. In both examples the noun phrases headed by the determiner *does* refer, either to the element(s) previously mentioned in the discourse or to a particular individual that exists in the speaker's mind (see Lyons 1999:170-172 for details). The instances of *this* above and in (3) might be better accounted for by the approach put forth in section 4, though it might need some modification to accommodate Germanic and Romance data. Specifically, the demonstratives in (i), (ii) & (3) might be better analyzed as anaphoric or cataphoric markings of sentential Topics. I will leave this issue for future research.

As mentioned above, Brugé (2002) extends her hypothesis to Russian and classifies it as a language allowing for an optional movement of demonstratives, on a par with Spanish, Bosnian, Romanian and others. This approach makes several predictions for Russian DPs that appear to be empirically falsified. Recall that demonstratives are assumed to be merged in the lowest functional projection FP above the NP, while all adjectival modifiers are merged higher (see (1)). Russian disallows postnominal adjectives or demonstratives under stylistically or/and pragmatically neutral conditions.[6] The unmarked surface word order in a noun phrase is *demonstrative—adjective(s)—noun*, (4a). The word order when the demonstrative is found following adjectival modifiers is ruled out, as shown in (4b):[7]

(4)	a.	*ètot*	krasivyj	bol'šoj	dom
		this	beautiful	big	house
	b.	*krasivyj	bol'šoj	*ètot*	dom
		beautiful	big	this	house

These data run against the predictions of the structure in (1): a demonstrative pronoun merged in the lower FP cannot raise up the projection when the specifiers of the intermediate FPs hosting adjectives are filled. But this is exactly what we find in (4a).[8] At the same time the optionality of *ètot* movement in the overt syntax should allow for (4b), again contrary to the facts.

Nor do we get the correct empirical facts by assuming movement of the head noun to either some intermediate functional head X, (5b), or all the way up to D (5a):

(5) a. *$[_{DP}$ dom$_i$ $[_{XP}$ krasivyj t_i $[_{XP}$ bol'soj t_i $[_{FP}$ *ètot* t_i $[_{NP} t_i]]]]$
house beautiful big this

b. $[_{XP}$ *krasivyj (dom$_i$) $[_{XP}$ bol'soj (dom$_i$) $[_{FP}$ *ètot* t_i $[_{NP} t_i]]]]$
beautiful house big house this

[6] By stylistically and pragmatically neutral conditions I mean the basic word order within a noun phrase or a sentence unaffected by Information Structure (known in traditional grammars as *actual'noe členenie predloženija* 'functional sentence perspective') (see section 4 and Kovtunova 1969, Padučeva 1985, Junghanns & Zybatow 1997, Melhorn 2001, Junghanns 2001 for more details).

[7] In this paper I do not discuss adjectival modifiers used appositively. I assume that such adjectives are adjoined to the DP, thus they are expected to precede the demonstrative merged in the Spec, DP.

(i)	I	byl	sijajuščij	*ètot*	avtobus	soveršenno	pust...
	and	was	glowing	this	bus	absolutely	empty

'And this glowing bus was absolutely empty...'

[8] The same criticism applies to the Bosnian, English and Norwegian data given in (27) in Brugé (2002), where the demonstrative-reinforcer complex moves across the adjective:

(i)	a.	ona	tamo	(nova)	knijiga	*Bosnian*
		that	there	(new)	book	
	b.	this	here	(nice)	book	*English*
	c.	denne	herre	(flotte)	bilen	*Norwegian*
		this	here	(nice)	car-the	

Russian does not allow for the head movement in stylistically neutral contexts, but even on such an assumption we would fail to derive correct empirical data, as illustrated in (5).[9]

In her work, Brugé (1996, 2002) discusses additional evidence for the low merge of demonstratives, namely the locative forms, such as *de aquí* in Spanish, that form a maximal phrase with demonstratives and serve as deictic reinforcers (see also Bernstein 1997). The location of reinforcers within the DP is claimed to help to reveal the initial site of merge of demonstratives. Thus, in Spanish the demonstrative can appear postnominally together with the reinforcer, or the latter may appear postnominally alone, while the demonstrative raises to D. Brugé, hence, concludes that the stranded reinforcer stays in situ and marks the base position of the FP ((6) is originally Brugé's (2002), (25)).

(6)	a.	El	libro	este	*de*	*aquí*	está	mal	hecho.
		the	book	this	of	here	is	badly	made
	b.	Este	libro	*de aquí*	está	mal	hecho.		
		This	book	of here	is	badly	made		

Similarly to Spanish, Russian has deictic reinforcers that may optionally co-occur with demonstrative pronouns, obligatorily agreeing with them in the proximal/distal feature, as shown in (7) below:

(7)	a.	Vot	èta	kniga/	*von	èta	kniga
		here	this	book/	*there	this	book
	b.	von	tot	student/	*vot	tot	student
		there	that	student/	here	that	student

If Russian is taken to exhibit optional movement of demonstratives to the Spec, DP, similarly to Spanish, we may expect to find at least a reinforcer in situ if demonstratives originate there. However, such cases are not attested in Russian either. The examples in (8) demonstrate that Russian does not allow demonstratives together or without their reinforcers to surface in situ, which is quite surprising given the optionality of their movement in overt syntax, as assumed in Brugé (2002).

(8)	a.	*On	kupil	(vot)	vitaminy	(vot)	èti.[10]	*Russian*
		He	bought	(here)	vitamins	(here)	these	
		'He has bought these vitamins.'						

[9] Yadroff (1999), who also assumes the low merge of demonstratives in Russian, following Brugé's work, proposes to amend the wrong word order predicted by the structure in the Morphology component (after the Vocabulary Insertion, in the Distributive Morphology framework of Halle (1994)). Adjectival modifiers are assumed to be linearized there according to the requirements of register and style (Yadroff, ibid.: 184). I find such a solution explanatorily inadequate.

[10] The example in (8a) may have a grammatical reading: 'He bought the vitamins, these ones.' Then the demonstrative phrase has to be separated from the head noun with a comma, and there is a pause in intonation. In such cases the head noun and the postnominal demonstrative phrase do not form one DPs. In addition, the word order in (8a) can be allowed under a contrastive focus: *On kupil vitaminy vot ÈTI, a ne te!* 'He bought THESE vitamins, not those ones!' In such cases the focused demonstrative can be found at the right periphery of the clause, in the default focus domain (Junghanns & Zybatow 1997). Alternatively, the focused demonstrative phrase can surface at the left periphery: *Vot ÈTI on kupil vitaminy.* 'Here THESE he bought vitamins.' I take this word order to be derived via Rightward Backgrounding proposed in Junghanns (2001). Such dislocated uses of demonstratives triggered by the (contrastive) focus will not be discussed in this paper (see also footnote 27).

b. *On kupil èti vitaminy vot.
He bought these vitamins here

c. *băitul acesta (de) aici/ acest băiat (de) aici *Romanian*
boy-the this A here/ this boy A here
(from Brugé (2002: 36))

Russian, thus, seems to pair with Romanian (8c) in lacking any discernible evidence for the original site of merge of demonstratives. For Romanian Brugé assumes that demonstratives in that language *must* raise to an intermediate XP position before Spell-Out, and may continue higher to the DP. The first obligatory step prevents us from seeing them in their base position, the Spec, FP (see (1)).Yet this analysis is inapplicable to Russian for it has no obligatory pre-Spell-Out movement of demonstratives to an intermediate phrase FP, or of N to D, as was shown in (4) and (5). The only logical possibility seems to be that Russian has obligatory movement of demonstratives to the highest specifier of the nominal projection, i.e. the Spec, DP, which may account for their obligatory prenominal position. However, there is another possibility to get similar empirical facts, specifically, by assuming that Russian demonstratives are directly merged in the Spec, DP position. The goal of this paper is to defend this hypothesis for Russian demonstratives. In the following section I will discuss evidence in support of this claim. In section 4, I will address cases of postnominal demonstratives and propose a different account for their non-standard location.

3. Russian demonstratives as merged in the Spec, DP

Demonstratives are often taken to be referential elements across languages (see Longobardi 1994, Giusti 1995, 1997, 1999, Lyons 1999, Brugé 1996, 2002, among many others). The demonstrative-bearing noun helps the listener to identify the referent of the noun by providing the referent in the linguistic or non-linguistic context. In any case the referent can be easily identifiable by both the speaker and the hearer, or by the speaker alone. This property of demonstratives to name an object which is found in the field of the speaker's/hearer's vision is known under the term deixis. Intrinsic referentiality and deixis of demonstratives have been claimed to imply their definiteness in Lyons (1999:21), Brugé (1996, 2002), and others. Bernstein (1997: 95-97), on the other hand, acknowledges the existence of indefinite demonstratives in English, French and Scandinavian languages. [11] As referential and/or definite elements, demonstratives are commonly assumed to be licensed in the DP-layer of the nominal projection, which is achieved by their movement to the Spec, DP in the overt or covert syntax. However, in the Minimalist theory of Chomsky (1998) merging elements in some locus is taken to be less costly than moving them there after a merge at a lower position. Therefore conceptually it is preferable to analyze demonstratives as merged directly in the Spec, DP, provided there is no empirical evidence to the contrary. In addition to being conceptually advantageous, such an assumption avoids empirical problems for Russian discussed in section 2. Specifically, this approach does not run into the problem of the overt movement of demonstratives across prenominal adjectival modifiers seated in Spec, XPs. The direct merge of demonstratives in the Spec, DP will correctly derive the linear word order of prenominal modifiers shown in (4a) (see also footnote 7). Furthermore, this proposal immediately accounts for the lack of stranded reinforcers or demonstratives found in the specifier of the lower FP (see (8)): this site is not their merging locus. On the basis of these conceptual and empirical considerations I assume that demonstratives in Russian are maximal

[11] The claim that demonstratives are always referential and/or definite seems to be too encompassing. On the one hand, we find instances of indefinite specific uses of *this* (as in (3)), wherein the referent is identifiable only by the speaker but not by the listener. On the other hand, the demonstrative can be used in opaque contexts which do not necessarily entail the existence of a referent for the DP: 'Those students who will fail the exam will have to repeat the course.'

phrases merged as the Spec, DP. The support for this claim stemming from syntactic, semantic and morphological properties of demonstratives will be provided below.

3.1. *Phrasal nature of demonstratives in Russian*

Giusti (1995, 1999) argues that demonstratives are maximal phrases cross-linguistically. This claim finds empirical support in those languages that have co-occurring articles and demonstratives (see Lundeby 1965 for a typological overview).[12] Since in Russian there are no overt articles[13] the phrasal nature of demonstratives should be illustrated by other means. For instance, we may take their co-occurrence with various intensifying elements as evidence of their phrasal status. As briefly discussed in section 1, Russian demonstratives can be extended by locative adverbial particles, the so-called deictic reinforcers (Bernstein 1997: 91). In English these are the adverbials *here* and *there*, in Russian their counterparts are *vot* 'here' and *von* 'there'. They exhibit proximal-distal distinction, as shown in (7) above. When used as reinforcers, these deictic particles are contingent on the presence of the demonstrative. This is shown by the optionality of the reinforcers, their ungrammaticality in the absence of demonstratives, (9a); as well as their selection by the latter, (9b).

(9)	a.	Vot	*(ètot)	mal'čik	polomal	moj	velosiped.		
		'Here	(this)	boy	broke	my	bicycle.'		
	b.	*Von	ètot/	vot	tot	mal'čik	polomal	moj	velosiped.
		there	this/	here	that	boy	broke	my	bicycle

As illustrated in (9b), when the selectional properties of a demonstrative are violated the structure is ruled out. Specifically, in (9b) a proximal demonstrative *ètot* 'this' occurs with a distal reinforcer *von* 'there', while the distal demonstrative *tot* 'that' occurs with a proximal reinforcer *vot* 'here', in violation of the selectional requirements.

Moreover, the deictic reinforcers are phonologically dependent elements: they usually lack a sentential stress and seem to form one phonological unit with a stress-bearing demonstrative. This points to their particle-like status in such constructions and their dependence upon demonstratives.[14,15]

---

12 The following examples illustrate this phenomenon (examples (b-d) from Lyons 1999:117&119):

(i)	a.	ha-bait		ha-ze	*Hebrew*
		the-house		the-this	'this house'
	b.	an	leabhar	seo/sin	*Irish*
		the	book	this/that	'this/that book'
	c.	den	här	bil-en	*Swedish*
		the/that	here	car-def	'this car'
	d.	ajt	gdou-n		*Armenian*
		that	cat-def		'that cat'

13 In this paper I assume the validity of the DP-hypothesis for Russian in spite of its lack of overt articles.

14 In contrast, *vot/von* when used as real adverbials, or locatives in existential sentences, can appear alone, are not selected by the predicate, are stressed and are obligatory elements of the clause and cannot be omitted.

(i)	* (Von/	vot)	naš	dom.	'There is our house.'
(ii)	* (Vot)	my	i	prišli.	'Here we came.'

That Russian demonstratives form maximal phrases can also be demonstrated by their co-occurrence with such adverbial intensifiers, as *imenno* 'namely, exactly', *tol'ko* 'only', *daže* 'even', etc.[16]

(10) a. [Imenno èta] zadača trebuet primenenja novoj teoremy.
Namely this task requires application new theorem
'It is this task that requires the application of a new theorem.'

b. [Tol'ko èto] pal'to isčezlo iz razdevalki.
Only this coat disappeared from cloak-room
'Only this coat disappeared from the cloak-room.'

That intensifiers form one phrase with the demonstrative is supported by their behavior under extraction/scrambling, as shown in (11) and (12). Neither a demonstrative nor an intensifier/reinforcer alone can move out of the DP, (12)—they must move together, (11).

(11) [{Tol'ko, vot} èto]$_i$ emu ponravilos' [$_{DP}$ t$_i$ [$_{NP}$ pal'to]]
only here this him.dat was-liked [t [coat]
'He liked {ONLY THIS, THIS (HERE)} coat.'

(12) *{[Tol'ko]$_i$, [èto]$_j$} emu ponravilos' [{[èto t$_i$], [tol'ko t$_j$]} [pal'to]]
only/ this him.dat was-liked this only [coat]]
'* {ONLY, THIS} he liked {THIS, ONLY} coat.'

This ability of demonstratives to be extracted out of the DP together with their dependents argues for their XP-status as well. Demonstratives can easily scramble out of the nominal projection under focus, as shown in (11). Under the assumption that only maximal phrases can move out of DPs demonstratives should be non-heads.[17]

Furthermore, the phrasal make-up of demonstratives is supported by their ability to be used intransitively, i.e. without a complement, as a substantivized element (see Padučeva 1985:125). This behavior of Russian demonstratives makes them similar to adjectives and participles which are standardly analyzed as maximal phrases.[18] In contrast, all functional heads, articles included, disallow such use. This property of functional heads was observed in Abney (1987:64f), who showed that determiners cannot ever surface without their lexical complement, NP. Giusti (1999) also argues that functional heads are always transitive and lack substantive content, in contrast to lexical ones. Compare (13a&b) with (13c&d):

(13) a. Posovetuj Ivanu vzjat' sekretarja$_i$, čtoby *tot*$_i$
advise Ivan.dat take secretary.acc in-order-to that
navel porjadok v ego bumagax.
will-make order in his papers
'Tell Ivan to take a secretary so that he would put his papers in order.'[19]

---

[15] I do not discuss here what element functions as the head of the demonstrtive phrase, yet I am inclined to consider the demonstrative as one, due to the properties of Russian reinforcers discussed above. This conclusion differs from that suggested in Bernstein (1997), who takes the reinforcers to head their own functional projection in whose specifier sits the demonstrative. It also differs from Brugé's (2002: 27) proposal to consider demonstratives and reinforcers as arguments of the preposition *de* dominating a complex predicate structure.

[16] Padučeva (1985:122) considers such particles to be rhematic markers.

[17] This claim is falsified by clitic-movement, which is irrelevant for the discussion here since demonstratives in Russian do not have any clitic properties.

[18] See Spencer (2002) and references cited there for more discussion of substantivization of adjectives.

[19] This example is from Padučeva (1985:126).

b. *Sobravšiesja/* *bol'nye* tolpilis' v koridore.
got-together/ sick crowded in corridor
'Those who got together/ the sick crowded in the corridor.'

c. This/ *the is a fact.

d. We need this/that/*the/*a.

The examples above show that Russian demonstratives seem to have substantive content and should be analyzed as lexical heads. Consequently they can be merged within the extended nominal projection only as maximal phrases, or specifiers. The demonstrative cannot be merged as another head of the extended DP since only one lexical head is allowed per projection.

3.2. Syntactic behavior of Russian demonstratives

In addition to signaling their phrasal nature, the demonstratives' ability to be freely extracted out of the DP also suggests that they are located at the left-hand periphery of the nominal hierarchy, higher than all other prenominal satellites of N. This contention is further reinforced by the blocking effect that Russian demonstratives exhibit in a number of syntactic constructions. For instance, de Wit & Schoorlemmer (1996) discuss focus-scrambling of adjectives out of Russian nominals and notice that while prenominal adjectives can freely scramble out of the nominal, this process is blocked when the nominal is headed by a demonstrative, as in (14):[20]

(14) Klassnye$_i$ ona kupila sebje (**èti*) t$_i$ botinki!
cool$_i$ she bought herself these t$_i$ boots

On the assumption that the movement of demonstratives is optional in Russian and they are merged lower than adjectives, an adjective could in principle move out of the noun phrase unproblematically even in the presence of the demonstrative. The lower merged demonstrative should not interfere in the scrambling process. The ungrammaticality of (14), thus, argues for the higher merge of demonstratives, as proposed here. Similarly, the presence of a demonstrative blocks the extraction of a possessive in (15), which otherwise allows for the violation of the Left-Branch Condition.

(15) Č'ju$_i$ ty čital [$_{DP}$ (**ètu*) [$_{NP}$ t$_i$ poèmu]]?
whose you read this poem
'Whose (*this) poem did you read?'

Such syntactic behavior of demonstratives seems to cogently argue for their Spec, DP-merge.

3.3. Semantic properties of Russian demonstratives

In section 2 I mentioned the existence of specific indefinite *this* in English (Lyons (1999), Givón (2001)) and other languages (Bernstein 1997). In contrast to English and Romance languages, Russian demonstratives seem to disallow a specific indefinite interpretation and are ungrammatical in *there*-insertion constructions or other existential environments, as well as with restrictive relative clauses, as shown in (16). For specific indefinites Russian employs an indefinite pronoun *odin* 'one', similarly to Hebrew (see Givón 2001:156).

[20] This behavior of demonstratives is also attested in Polish, as discussed in Migdalski (2001).

(16) *existential contexts*

a. Est' *èta/ *ta/ odna kniga, kotoruju ty dolžen pročitat'.
is this/ that/ one book which you have to-read

restrictive relative clauses

b. Odna/ # èta kartina, kotoruju Petja videl na vystavke,
one/ this picture which Peter saw on exhibition
prodana za million.[21]
sold for million

This behavior of Russian demonstratives is similar to their German counterparts, which also allow exclusively for definite interpretation (Bernstein (1997:95) citing Dana McDaniel's observation). This is expected under the assumption that Russian demonstratives are directly merged in the Spec, DP position and induce an obligatory definite interpretation on the head noun. If located in the Spec, DP, overt demonstratives will obligatorily govern the null Determiner, thus preventing the existential closure and a possibility of an indefinite reading of the head noun (see Diesing 1992, Longobardi 1994). In contrast, if demonstratives were merged lower in the structure, in a separate functional projection, then their inability to be existentially quantified in Russian would have to be additionally stipulated, for instance, by postulating an obligatory pre-Spell-Out movement of demonstratives to the Spec, DP. Such movement will also preclude existential closure, yet this solution has been shown to be empirically inadequate for Russian.

The Spec, DP locus of demonstratives also accounts for their incompatibility with other inherently definite elements within one DP, such as superlatives, proper names and definite descriptions, which presuppose the uniqueness of the referent. On the assumption that such elements must check their [+def] feature at the DP-layer, the co-occurring demonstrative will compete with them for the locus of licensing and the derivation will crash, as shown in (17):[22]

(17) a. *tot samyj umnyj mal'čik v klasse
that most clever boy in class

b. *ètot ubijca Petra
this murderer Peter.gen

c. *ètot Petin otec
this Peter.poss father

3.4. *Morphological and diachronic evidence for higher merge of demonstratives*

Some indirect evidence for the DP-locus of demonstratives can be drawn from the similarity between the inflection markers borne by the demonstratives and those appearing on the personal pronouns in Russian.

[21] The # notation is used to indicate the ambiguity of the example in (16b), which is grammatical under the definite reading of the demonstrative and the appositive reading of the relative clause. The specific indefinite reading when the listener cannot immediately identify the referent for the noun is, however, ruled out.

[22] When demonstratives co-occur with other definite elements one or the other loses its definite specification. For instance, with proper names demonstratives can be used as emphatic words: *Slavnaj byla devočka, èta Bèla!* 'She was a nice girl, this Bella!' In such cases their use is not semantically motivated, rather serves a pragmatic purpose. Alternatively, the proper name can be used metaphorically, i.e. as a predicate, and the demonstrative is required to allow for its argumental use: *Ètot Don-Žuan mne porjadkom nadoel!* 'I am quite sick and tired of this Don Juan!', where Don Juan stands for some other person. See Padučeva (1985) and Shmelev (1996) for more discussion of such uses of demonstratives. However, such cases in no way falsify the present claim that demonstratives are incompatible with unique expressions.

(18) I videl èt-**ix** studentov/ **ix**.
I saw this.acc.pl student.acc.pl/ them.acc.
'I saw these students/ them.'

The similarity of the declension paradigm of demonstratives and personal pronouns may be revealing. The latter are often analyzed as intransitive Determiners (originally Postal's (1970) insight, lately developed in Ritter (1991)), i.e. occupants of the DP-projection.[23] Hence we might take the similarity of their declension as indicative of the demonstratives' merge as high as DP. If, on the contrary, demonstratives were merged in a lower functional projection such a coincidence in morphological markings would be hard to explain. This hypothesis finds independent support in the diachronic analysis of 3rd person pronouns— the latter are argued to have developed from demonstratives in various languages (see Lyons (1999) for a cross-linguistic overview, Giusti (to appear) for Romance languages, and Spencer (2002) for Russian). Consequently, we may conclude that morphological properties of demonstratives also seem to sustain their analysis as DP-level occupants.

To summarize the discussion in this section, I take the above-mentioned facts as pointing to the high hierarchical position of the demonstratives in the extended nominal projection and to their phrasal nature. Thus the proposal that Russian demonstratives are merged in the Spec, DP seems to be empirically and conceptually justified.

4. Origin of postnominal demonstratives

Now I turn to the infrequent instances of postnominal demonstratives, as those in (19), which are stylistically marked and felicitous only under specific pragmatic conditions. The first observation is that such inverted demonstratives in Russian are attested either in narrative prose or in colloquial language. Both instances of inversion, however, seem to be licensed by the same pragmatic conditions. Specifically, inverted demonstrate ves are found within noun phrases that form part of the Topic, or Background[24,25]. Therefore they are usually, though not necessarily always, attested within the subject of the clause, as shown in (19).[26]

(19) a. Kniga$_i$ [*èta* t$_i$] byla vpervye napečatana v molodežnom žurnale.
Book this was firstly published in youth magazine
'This book was published for the first time in a youth magazine.'

[23] Giusti (1999) argues that personal pronouns are occupants of the Spec, DP rather than intransitive determiners. Irrespective of the status of personal pronouns as determiner heads or specifiers, their similar morphological make-up with the demonstratives argues for the latter's position in the same functional projection.

[24] See Migdalski's (2001:140) similar observation on Polish postnominal demonstratives that they are stylistically marked and used when the noun represents 'old information'. In contrast to the present approach, Migdalski assumes Brugé's hypothesis for Polish and considers postnominal demonstratives as located in situ, in the Spec, FP. However, as discussed above, such an approach would falsely rule out the grammatical *ta ciekawa książka* 'this interesting book' yet rule in the ungrammatical **ciekawa ta książka* 'interesting that book'. The latter example is particularly problematic for Migdalski's and Brugé's hypotheses since the movement of demonstratives to the Spec, DP in Polish is claimed to be optional and the demonstrative should be grammatical in situ.

[25] There are two subtypes of Information Structure: Topic-Comment and Focus-Background. Topic is usually taken to be the starting point of the sentence, what the sentence is about. Russian grammars recognize a third subtype of the IS of Russian clauses: Theme-Rheme subdivision (i.e. old versus new information). I will use the terms rhematic or focused intermittently without committing myself to any theoretical claims about the Theme-Rheme partition. See Kovtunova (1969), Padučeva (1985), J & Z (1997), Melhorn (2001), ao for discussion.

[26] All the examples in this section are cited from modern Russian journals and books, as well as from the Tuebingen Russian Corpora.

b. … [N sobaka$_i$] [DP *èta* [NP černaja t$_i$] uneslas' v kotlovan…
dog this black rushed-away into pit
'and this black dog rushed away into the huge pit'

c. … i [N baton$_i$] [DP *ètot* [NP puxlyj t$_i$] tjagotit…
and baguette this plump is-a-burden
'and this full baguette is a burden'

I propose to analyze the examples in (19) as derived by the syntactic movement of the head noun out of the subject DP into the Topic position at the left periphery of the clause. Such a position was proposed in Junghanns and Zybatow (J & Z henceforth) (1997) for Russian non-thetic clauses, i.e. those that subdivide into Topic and Comment. Thetic sentences lack a topic, comprise only important or new information and predictably will not exhibit such movement. Though J & Z (ibid.: 304) assume that the Topic position is an adjunct to the Agr$_S$P, I propose to amend their claim by postulating an independent Topic Phrase atop the Agr$_S$P in Russian clauses. The need for an independent Topic Phrase (TopP henceforth) seems to be justified by the type of movement illustrated in (19). Since the adjunction of lexical heads to maximal phrases is generally prohibited by the theory, the fronted nouns in (19) cannot be adjoined to the Agr$_S$P. In addition, the stranded adjectives in (19b&c) indicate that the NP stays in situ while the head noun proceeds through D to a higher head. The NP movement, in contrast, will produce a distinct word order in (19b): ??[NP*černaja sobaka*] [DP*èta* t]], and will require an additional escape mechanism for the extracted NP since the presence of the demonstrative in the Spec, DP usually blocks extraction of adjectives and possessives (see section 3).[27] I will further assume that the movement in (19) is triggered by the feature [+topic] residing in the head noun. I assume that the feature [+topic] can trigger two types of movement: the head movement of N-to-Top and the phrasal movement of the whole DP triggered by the [+topic] specification of its head noun. In the latter case the whole noun phrase raises to the Spec, TopP and no stranded demonstratives ensue, as in (20a). Such topic-driven movement could be identified by a topic-particular prosodic pattern (see Alter & Junghanns 2002). In addition, topic demonstratives seem to resist deictic reinforcers, (20a).

In contrast to topics, focused noun phrases are not restricted to a particular structural position within the Russian clause (J & Z 1997). The prenominal demonstratives found in focussed DPs tend to be deictically interpreted, freely co-occur with deictic reinforcers and bear focal stress, (20b).

(20) a. My podxodim k nebol'šomu domu.
we are-approaching to small house.
(**Vot*) *ètot* dom/ dom (**vot*) *èto t* postroen v načale veka.
(here) this house/ house (here) this was-built in beginning century

b. Čto ty delaeš'? Rassmatrivaju (*vot*) *ètu* kartinu.
what you doing investigate (here) this picture.

Therefore we may conclude that Russian noun phrases with prenominal demonstratives are ambiguous with respect to their topic/focus reading. On the other hand, noun phrases with

[27] In a theoretic framework which assumes that all adjectival modifiers are generated in independent XPs (Cinque 1994, ao) the examples in (19) can still be analyzed as instances of NP-movement rather than N-movement, with the stranded APs staying in Spec, XPs. Nevertheless this claim is independently falsified by the fact that there are no cases when N moves together with its complements across a demonstrative. Out of the 922 sentences with *ètot* I examined in the Tuebingen Russian Corpora there was not a single case of an adjective or a complement accompanying the scrambled noun. In addition, such an NP-movement would still need to account for the grammaticality of NP-movement through filled Spec, XPs, which is prohibited in other cases. In view of these problems with the NP-movement approach, I assume that in (19) we have instances of head movement.

postnominal demonstratives are claimed to be unambiguously topical. This generalization, if correct, makes a number of predictions. First, we do not expect to find inverted demonstratives co-occurring with deictic reinforcers, (20a). Next, in thetic clauses, wherein the whole sentence makes up the focus domain (J & Z ibid.: 303), inversion should also be forbidden. This expectation holds, as shown in (21).

(21) a. V čem delo? Menja udaril (*vot*) *ètot* mal'čik/ *mal'čik (*vot*) *ètot*.
in what matter me.acc punched (here) this boy/ *boy here this
'What's the matter?' 'This (here) boy punched me.'

b. Kto tvoj učitel' tancev? (*Vot*) *èta* devuška/ *devuška *(vot)* *èta*.
who your teacher dances (here) this girl/ *girl here this
'Who is your teacher of dances? This (here) girl.'

Likewise we do not expect to find postnominal demonstratives in object DPs associated with contrastive focus (22a), even though such focused objects may be found clause-initially (22b).[28]

(22) a. My opublikovali (vot) *ètu* KNIgu/ *KNIgu (vot) *ètu*, a ne *tot* žurNAL.
we published (here) this book/ book (here) this but not that journal

b. (Vot) ètu KNIgu/ *KNIgu (vot) ètu my opublikovali, a ne *tot* žurNAL.
(here) this book/ book (here) this we published but not that journal

The ungrammaticality of the sentences in (21) & (22) stems from the unmotivated movement of N across the demonstrative: the head noun in rhematic/focused DPs lacks [+topic] specification hence the movement is illegitimate.[29]

Analogously, inverted demonstratives are predicted to be excluded in identity predicate constructions, where the identifying phrase is a referential noun providing new information. In other words, since identity predicates are rhematic (Padučeva 1985: 170) postnominal demonstratives should be ruled out in such constructions, see (23) and (24).[30]

[28] J & Z (1997:311), claim that Contrastive Focus is not bound to a particular position in the clause and is realized by means of a syntactic feature [Fc] with the corresponding phonological and semantic consequences.

[29] If, on the other hand, it is only the demonstrative that comprises the new information then it alone may be found at the right-hand periphery of the clause, a default focus position, while the head noun, which is part of the topic, will appear clause initially as a result of the N-to-Top movement proposed here:

(i) Kakuju knigu vy opublikovali?
What book you published
Knigu my opublikovali vot ÈTU.
Book we published here this
'As for the book, we published THIS one.'

[30] To distinguish identity predicates from regular nominal ones we can use the overt copula *est'* 'be' with an emphatic particle *i* 'and', which are grammatical with the former but not with the latter type of predicate. Consider the two types in (i): while the nominal predicate (ia) disallows the use of the demonstrative due to the latter's inherent referentiality; the identity predicate, (ib), allows or may even require it to mark overtly the definiteness of the noun phrase. See Padučeva (1985: 171) for more discussion of identity predicates.

(i) a. On — (*ètot) professor ximii.
he (is) (*this) professor chemistry.gen
'He is a chemistry professor.'

(23) *On i est' professor *ètot,* o kotorom ja tebe govorju.
he and is professor this about which I you tell

(24) *On-i est' čelovek *tot,* kotoryj ukral tvoju mašinu.
he and is man that which stole your car

To conclude, the data provided in this section seem to confirm our hypothesis that postnominal instances of Russian demonstratives are conditioned by Information Structure, whose relevance for word order in Russian clauses has been independently demonstrated in ample linguistic literature. The clause initial position in Russian in non-thetic sentences is often associated with Topics, consequently the movement to the TopP can be considered obligatory. When the TopP is instantiated via head movement, i.e. only the head noun marked as [+topic] moves to Top°, postnominal demonstratives emerge. When the whole topic DP moves to the Spec, TopP no surface word re-ordering ensues, provided the topic is the subject of the clause. The optionality in the placement of demonstratives within the clause-initial Topics follows from the possibility of licensing the feature [+topic] in two possible ways: either through Spec-Head Agreement between the topic DP in the Spec, TopP and the Topic head, or by substituting N° for Top° through the head-to-head movement.

I propose to consider the feature [+topic] strong in Russian, inducing the rearrangement of clausal elements in the overt syntax (cf. J & Z 1997:300). This proposal finds support from clauses where topic noun phrases are not subjects but objects. Interestingly, such topics require the presence of a demonstrative and tend to appear clause-initially (see Padučeva 1985: 162-163, the examples in (25) are modified after her (21) & (25)).[31] As predicted by the present proposal, such non-subject topics (25b) may leave a demonstrative stranded when only the head noun moves to the TopP for feature licensing.

(25) a. Èto – novyj dom Petrovyx. Dom mne byl ne znakom. *subject*
This new house the-Petrovs house me.dat was not known.
'This is the Petrovs' new house. The house was unfamiliar to me.'

b. *(Ètot) dom ja znaju./ Dom$_i$ ja znaju *(ètot t$_i$). *direct object*
*(this) house I know/ house I know this
'I know this house.'

---

b. On i est' *(ètot) professor ximii, o kotorom ja tebe govorju.
he and is (this) professor chemistry about which I you tell
'He is this chemistry professor about whom I tell you.'

[31] I assume that the demonstrative is needed to mark such topical non-subjects as unambiguously definite. In the absence of an overt definiteness marking the object noun phrase is interpreted as generic or indefinite by default (cf. Padučeva 1985: 162, footnote 1). In contrast, topical subjects, which are by default definite, do not require the presence of the demonstrative. Compare (25) with the following examples adopted from Padučeva (ibid.):

(i) a. Emu podarili bul'doga. Bul'dog (ètot) stal glavnym členom sem'ji.
Him presented bulldog bulldog (this) became main member family
'He got a bulldog for a gift. The bulldog has become the main family member.'

b. My s prijatelem exali na rabotu. Doroga zelenela na vsem protjaženii.
We with friend drove to work. road looked-green on all length
'My friend and I were driving to the summer house. The road was green all its length.'

c. My s prijatelem exali na rabotu. Po *(ètoj) doroge ja nikogda ne *indirect*
We with friend drove to work. On this road I never not *object*
ezdil.
drove
'My friend and I were driving to work. I have never driven this way yet.'

The examples in (25) cogently argue that the topicalized DPs/PPs moves up the clausal projection to the TopP proposed herein. These data as in (25b) and footnote 28(i) seem to run against the hypothesis advanced in Dimitrova-Vulchanova & Giusti (1998) for some Balkan languages that the latter project the Focus Phrase and/or the Topic Phrase within the extended nominal projection. Such an approach, if applied to Russian, would incorrectly allow object Topic DPs to stay in situ and have a postnominal demonstrative within that DP, as in **Ja znaju dom ètot*. 'I know house this.' At the same time it will exclude grammatical *Dom$_i$ ja znaju [ètot t$_i$]*., or will need another mechanism to derive it. Their approach encounters another, conceptual, problem. If the scrambling of the head noun is triggered by the strong feature [+topic] then its raising to the DP-internal TopP will erase this feature and no further movement of the topic N/DP can be motivated by the IS considerations. Consequently, overt movement of topic objects to the clause-initial position, as in (25b&c) should be unattested—the same feature cannot be checked twice by two distinct functional heads, the TopP of the DP and that of the CP. In short, D-V & G's approach does not seem to yield correct word order of topic DPs in Russian sentences. Pending more research on the topic, I will take the proposal that the TopP is part of the extended clausal projection CP and topic-driven scrambling occurs across the DP-boundaries to be better motivated.

5. Conclusion

In the present paper I argued against Brugé's (1996, 2002) claim that Russian demonstratives are merged very low in the extended nominal projection and undergo optional movement to the Spec, DP in the overt syntax. I showed the inadequacy of this approach for Russian and proposed a competing analysis for postnominal occurrences of demonstratives. Specifically, in section 3 I argued that Russian demonstratives should be analyzed as maximal projections merged directly in the Spec, DP, which was supported by a number of tests. In section 4 a different treatment for inverted demonstrative pronouns was suggested. I claimed that such a reordering is triggered by the Information Structure of Russian clauses and is attested in DPs that form part of the Topic. It was further demonstrated that this approach to Russian postnominal demonstratives yields correct empirical results and conceptually is more attractive than other analyses discussed in this paper.

References

Alter, Kai and Uwe Junghanns. (2002): Topic-Related Prosodic Patterns in Russian. In P. Kosta and J. Frasek (eds.): *Current Approaches to Formal Slavic Linguistics*. Frankfurt am Main: Lang, 73-88.

Abney, Steven. (1987): *The English Noun Phrase in Its Sentential Aspect*. Ph.D. dissertation, MIT.

Spencer, Andrew. (2002): Gender as an inflectional category. *JL* 38.2, 279-312.

Bernstein, Judy B. (1997): Demonstratives and reinforcers in Romance and Germanic languages. *Lingua* 102, 87-113.

Brugé, Laura. (1996): Demonstrative Movement in Spanish: A comparative approach. *University of Venice Working Papers in Linguistics* 6.1, 1-53.

Brugé, Laura. (2002): The Positions of Demonstratives in the Extended Nominal Projection. In: G. Cinque (ed.): *Functional structure in DP and IP: the cartography of syntactic structures*. Vol. 1, 15-53. New York: Oxford University Press.

Cinque, Guglielmo. (1994): On the Evidence for Partial N-Movement in the Romance DP. In: G. Cinque,et al (eds.): *Paths towards Universal Grammar*, Washington: Georgetown University Press, 85-110.
Chomsky, Noam. (1995): *A Minimalist Program*. Cambridge, MA: MIT Press.
Chomsky, Noam. (1998): Minimalist Inquiries: the Framework. Ms., MIT.
Diesing, Molly. (1992): *Indefinites*. Cambridge, MA: MIT Press.
Dimitrova-Vulchanova, Mila and Giuliana Giusti. (1998): Fragments of Balkan Nominal Structure. In: Alexiadou, A. and C. Wilder (eds.): *Possessors, Predicates and Movement in the DP*. Amsterdam: John Benjamins, 333-360.
Givón, Talmy. (2001): *Syntax: An Introduction*. Amsterdam: John Benjamins Publications.
Giusti, Giuliana. (1995): A Unified Structural Representation of (abstract) Case and Articles. Evidence from Germanic. In: Haider, H., S. Olsen, S. Vikner (eds.): *Studies in Comparative Germanic Syntax*. Dordrecht: Kluwer, 77-93.
Giusti, Giuliana. (1997): The Categorial Status of Determiners. In: Haegeman, L. (ed.): *The New Comparative Syntax*. London: Addison Wesley Longman, 95-123.
Giusti, Giuliana. (1999): The functional structure of noun phrases: A bare phrase structure approach. *University of Venice Working Papers in Linguistics*, vol. 9, n. 1-2, 1-39.
Giusti, Giuliana. (2001): The birth of a functional category: From Latin ILLE to the Romance article and personal pronoun. In: Cinque, G. and G. Salvi (eds.): *Current Studies in Italian Syntax: Essays offered to Lorenzo Renzi*. Amsterdam: North-Holland.
Grimshaw, Jane. (1991): Extended Projections, ms. Brandeis University.
Halle, Morris. (1994): The Russian Declension: An Illustration of the Theory of Distributed Morphology. In: Cole, J. and C. Kisseberth (eds.): *Perspectives in Phonology*. Stanford, CA: CSLI Publications.
Junghanns, Uwe. (2001): On Rightward Backgrounding. In: Zybatow G. et al. (eds.): *Current Issues in Formal Slavic Linguistics*, Frankfurt am Main: Lang, 329-343.
Junghanns, Uwe and Gerhild Zybatow. (1997): Syntax and Information Structure of Russian Clauses. In: Browne E.W. et al. (eds.): *Annual Workshop on Formal Approaches to Slavic Linguistics*, The Cornell Meeting 1995. Ann Arbor: Michigan Slavic Publications, 289-319.
Kayne, Richard. (1994): *The Antisymmetry of Syntax*. Cambridge, Mass.: MIT Press.
Kovtunova, I. I. (1969): *Porjadok slov v russkom literaturnom jazyke XVIII— pervoj treti XIX veka*. Moskva: Nauka.
Longobardi, Giuseppe. (1994): Reference and Proper Names: A Theory of N-movement in Syntax and Logical form. *Linguistic Inquiry* 25.4: 609-665.
Lundeby, Einar. (1965): *Overbestemt substantive i norsk og de andre nordiske sprog*. Unpublished dissertation, Trondheim.
Lyons, Christopher. (1999): *Definiteness*. Cambridge: Cambridge University Press.
Melhorn, Grit. (2001): Information Structure of Discontinuous Constituents in Russian. In: Zybatow G. et al. (eds.): *Current Issues in Formal Slavic Linguistics*, Frankfurt am Main: Lang, 344-352.
Migdal'ski, Krzysztof. (2001): A Determiner Phrase Approach to the Structure of Polish Nominals. In: Przepiórkowski A. and P. Bański (eds.): *Generative Linguistics in Poland: Syntax and Morphosyntax*. Warszawa: Instytut Podstaw Informatyki Polskiej Akademii Nauk, 135-148.
Padučeva, Elena V. (1985): *Vyskazyvanie i ego sootnesennost' s dejstvitel'nost'ju (referencial'nye askpekty semantiki mestoimenij)*. Moskva: Nauka.
Postal, Paul M. (1970): On so-called pronouns in English. In: Jacobs, R. A. and P. S. Rosenbaum (eds.): *Readings in English Transformational Grammar*. Waltham, Mass.: Ginn.
Ritter, Elizabeth. (1991): Two functional categories in Noun Phrases: Evidence from Modern Hebrew. In: Rothstein, S. (ed.): *Perspectives on Phrase Structure: Heads and Licensing. Syntax and Semantics* 26, 37-62. New York: Academic Press.

Shmelev, Aleksei. (1996): *Referencial'nye mexanizmy russkogo jazyka*. Tampere: University of Tampere.

Wit, de Petra and Maaike Schoorlemmer. (1996): Prenominal arguments in Russian, German and Dutch. *ZAS Papers in Linguistics* 5, 184-202.

Yadroff, Michael. (1999): *Formal Properties of Functional Categories: The Minimalist Syntax of Russian Nominal and Preposition Expressions*. PhD. dissertation, Indiana University.

Ludmila Veselovská, Olomouc

The Extended Verbal Projection in Czech: Three Variants of the verb *be*[1]

1. The Structure of VP

In this paper I assume a minimalist structure of VP based on the analyses of Pollock (1989), Larson (1989), and Chomsky (1995), which divide the verbal projection into several separate heads. There are several reasons to accept this analytic verbal projection for Czech. First, the Czech verbal paradigm is comprised of several **analytic verbal forms** illustrated in the following examples (1) and (2). Notice the distribution of the verbal elements – it is not free and it is impossible to describe the acceptable/ unacceptable word orders without referring to each of the elements in some unique way.

(1) *Já* ***jsem*** */* ***bych*** *včera* ***viděl*** *Marii.*
I am$_{AUX}$ / would$_{AUX}$ yesterday saw Mary
'I saw / would see Mary yesterday.'

(2) (a) Ty **bys** určitě **býval** někoho **viděl.**
you would$_{AUX}$ certainly was$_{AUX}$ somebody saw
'You would certainly have seen somebody.'

(b) *Ty* ***bys*** *určitě* ***býval*** *někoho* ***viděl.***
you **would**$_{AUX}$ certainly **be**$_{PATR}$ somebody **saw**$_{PART}$
'You would certainly have seen somebody.'

word order (i) ***Býval bys*** *asi* ***viděl*** *všechno.*

(ii) * **Viděl bys** asi **býval** všechno.

The second reason for accepting an analytic structure for VP is the **distribution of the verb** with respect to other (adverbial / subject) constituents, as in (3).

(3) (a) **Emil** (??čitelně) **bude** (?čitelně) **psát** dopis (čitelně).
Emil (??legibly) **will**$_{AUX}$ (?legibly) **write** letter (legibly)
'Emil will write the letter legibly.'

(b) ***Bude*** ***Emil*** *psát dopis? (*.)*
will$_{AUX}$ Emil write letter
'Will Emil write a letter?'

Other reasons for the proposed analytic verbal structure can be found in the rich verbal **morphology** (presuming some relation between morphology and structure) and in a theoretical framework which claims a parallel/ universal structure among lexical **categories** and their projections.

The structure of extended verbal projection used in this paper is schematically demonstrated in (4). It is comprised of four heads: two in the predicate (thematic) core of the verbal projection: V and (light) *v**, and two on the level (in the domain) of the finite/ clausal projection: T and C. Chomsky (1995) labels the heads V and T as "lexical" and the heads C and v* as "functional."

---

[1] A preliminary version of this paper was read at the conference Čeština: Univerzália a specifika (Brno, October 2003) and will appear in Czech in the collection of papers of that conference.

(4) The bare sentence structure with a transitive verb

[$_{CP}$ C [$_{TP}$ **T** [$_{vP}$ *v* [$_{VP}$ **V**   *C*-**T** ...... functional/clausal domain
v-**V** ...... predicate/thematic core

The heads of the verbal projection are related to the assignment of structural and lexical (Oblique) Cases according to (5) and (6). The Case reflects an agreement (Agree) between the verbal head carrying the feature <+D> and the nominal element in its domain.

(5) **Structural Case**

(a) NOM is the result of Agree between T_{fin} and +D (in the SPEC(v*))

(b) ACC is the result of Agree between *v** and +D (in the SPEC(V))

(6) **Lexical Case** is the result of Agree between a case assigning verbal head V and/ or P.

2. Distinctions between the positions in the functional vs. thematic domains

Looking at the properties of the Czech verb *be*, it is clear that they can be stated only with respect to each specific usage of this verb. These different usages are important justifications for the categorial distinctions in (4). The most striking distinction can be found contrasting (a) the auxiliary forms of *be* used for the analytic past/ conditional and (b) its other forms (including future auxiliary, passive auxiliary, copula, and existential *be*). I now exemplify these in this section.[2]

The example (7) shows a distinct ability to reduce the 2sg auxiliary *"jsi"* to a bound morpheme *"-s"*. The example (7a) illustrates that the reduction is possible with the past/ conditional auxiliary $AUX_{P/C}$, while (7b) shows it can't occur with the other forms of *be*, i.e. with the passive auxiliary, copula and existential *be*.[3]

(7) (a) (i) *Proč* ***jsi*** *často chválil Petra?*
Why AUX_{2S} often praised $Peter_{ACC}$
'Why did you often praise Peter?'

(ii) Proč(**-s**) často(**-s**) chválil(**-s**) Petra?
Why-AUX_{2S} often-AUX_{2S} praised-AUX_{2S} $Peter_{ACC}$

(b) (i) *Proč* ***jsi*** *často chválen/unavený/studentem/doma?*
Why ACE_{2S} often praised/ tired/ student/ at home
'Why are you often praised/ tired/ a student/ at home?'

(ii) **Proč(-s) často(-s) chválen(-s) / unavený/studentem/doma?*
Why-ACE_{2S} often-ACE_{2S} praised-ACE_{2S} / tired/ student/ at home

The example (8a) demonstrates that the Czech past AUX_{AGR} copula has a distribution of a C2 clitic (for more details see Franks & King (2000), Toman (2000)), while the other forms of

---

[2] The following distinctions were noticed in the studies by Kopečný (1962) and Komárek (1978), and in a generative framework in Toman (1980), Veselovská (1995, Chapter 4), and Veselovská & Karlík (2004, Chapter 3).

[3] To simplify exposition, from now on the past and conditional auxiliaries are represented by the past auxiliary form only (labeled as AUX_{AGR}). The passive Auxiliary, Copula and Existential be will usually be exemplified by the passive auxiliary only (labeled as ACE_{AGR}), which can be expected to be the element minimally distinct from the past auxiliary.

the verb *be* exemplified in (8b) as ACE_{AGR} have the standard distribution of free morphemes in Czech, including initial and final positions.[4]

(8) (a) (i) Chválil/unavil **jsem/bych** Petra
Praised/Exhausted was/would(AUX_{1S}) $Peter_{ACC}$
'I (would) praise(d)/exhaust(ed) Peter.'

(ii) ***Jsem/*Bych*** *chválil/unavil Petra.*

(b) (i) *Chválen/Unavený / Studentem / Doma* ***jsem*** *stále.*
Praised/Tired/ Student / At home ACE_{1S} always
'I am always praised/ tired/a student/ at home.'

(ii) ***Jsem*** *stale chválen/unavený/studentem/doma.*

(iii) *Chválen/unavený/studentem/doma stale* ***nejsem.***

Another distinction between the two contrasted forms concerns negation. (9b) shows that when the verbal complex is negated, the passive auxiliary/ copula/ existential *be* (ACE) carries the negative prefix *ne-*. The contrasting (9a) shows that $AUX_{P/C}$ cannot carry the negative prefix *ne-* and that negation must appear with the participle.

(9) (a) *Já jsem* ***ne-chválil***
I AUX_{1S} not-praised
'I did not praise.'

(a') **Já* ***ne-jsem*** *chválil*
*I not-AUX_{1S} praised

(b) *Já* ***ne-jsem*** *chválen/-unavený/-student/-doma.*
I not-ACE_{1S} praised/-tired/-a student/-at home
'I am not praised/-tired/-a student/-at home

The example in (10) demonstrates that in elliptic contexts the AUX in (a) is not able to represent the whole structure, though ACE in (b) can (in fact must) serve this purpose.

(10) (a) *Chválil jsi Petra?* - **Ano, jsem. / Ano, chválil.*
Praised ACE_{2S} $Peter_{ACC}$? - *Yes, ACE_{1S}. / Yes, $praised_{SM}$.
'Did you praise Peter? - Yes, I did.'

(b) *Jsi chválen často?* - *Ano, jsem. / *Ano, chválen.*
AUX_{2S} praised often? - Yes, AUX_{1S}/ *Yes, $praised_{SM}$.
'Are you praised often? - Yes, I am.'

The following Table (11) demonstrates some specific colloquial (regional) forms written in bold letters in (11). These forms are never used for AUX, while they are rather frequent as the ACE forms of *be*, especially in the Morava region.

The next Table (12) shows the distribution of the initial parenthetic *j-* in the paradigm of the verb *be*, which is distinct for the two contrasted forms. Notice, at the same time, the existence of the zero morpheme used for the AUX_{3sg} and not for the ACE_{3sg}.

Apart from the zero morpheme illustrated in (12c), there exists also a kind of partial complementary distribution between the AUX_{1sg} and an overt pronominal subject. The left column in the table (13) demonstrates that with AUX_{1sg}, the verbal complex requires the presence of either overt AUX_{1sg} or a pronominal 1sg subject (or both). The same choice is not

[4] The verb in final position usually requires some kind of stress which is most salient with negated verbs as in (8b/iii). The same stress is however excluded with AUX in (8a/ii).

available for ACE, where the 1sg pronominal subject cannot license the absence of ACE_{1sg}. The relevant contrast is clear from (13c/c'), while (b) and (b') illustrate the standard dropping of a pronominal subject in Czech.

(11) **Moravian dialectal forms of *být* ('be')**

Past AUX		ACE: passive aux/copula/existential *be*	
(a)	*Já jsem/*(j)su chválil* I AUX_{1S} praised 'I praised'	(a')	*Já (j)su chválen / -zlý / -studentem / -doma* I ACE_{1S} praised /-nasty /-a student /-at home 'I am praised/nasty/a student/at home.'
(b)	*Ty-s chválil* you+AUX_{2S} praised 'You praised'	(b')	**Ty-s chválen/ -zlý / -studentem / -doma* *you+ ACE_{2S} praised/-nasty /-a student /-at home 'You are praised/nasty/a student/at home'
(c)	*Ty jsi/*seš chválil* you AUX_{2S} praised 'You praised'	(c')	*Ty seš chválen / -zlý/ -studentem / -doma* you ACE_{2S} praised /-nasty/-a student /-at home 'You are praised/nasty/a student/at home'

(12) **Standard/primary *j-* and secondary/colloquial *(j-)* / Zero AUX_{3S}**

Past AUX: (j-), $Ø_3$		ACE: passive aux/copula/existential: j-, *$Ø_3$	
(a)	*Já (j)sem chválil.* I AUX_{1S} praised 'I praised.'	(a')	*Já jsem chválen.* I ACE_{1S} praised 'I am praised.'
(b)	*Ty (j)si chválil.* You AUX_{2S} praised 'You praised.'	(b')	*Ty jsi chválen.* You ACE_{2S} praised 'You are praised.'
(c)	*On *je/Ø chválil.* He AUX_{3S} praised 'He praised.'	(c')	*On je/*Ø chválen.* he ACE_{3S} praised 'He is praised.'

(13) **AUX / pronoun complementarity**

Past AUX		ACE: passive aux/copula/existential *be*	
(a)	*Já jsem chválil Petra* I AUX_{1S} praised $Peter_{ACC}$ 'I praised Peter.'	(a')	*Já jsem chválen od Petra* I ACE_{1S} praised by Peter 'I am praised by Peter.'
(b)	*Chválil jsem Petra* praised AUX_{1S} $Peter_{ACC}$	(b')	*Chválen jsem od Petra* praised ACE_{1S} by Peter
(c)	*Já chválil Petra* I praised $Peter_{ACC}$	(c')	**Já chválen od Petra* *I praised by Peter

Another distinction between the two forms of the verb *be* concerns their paradigmatic richness. Table (14) demonstrates the paradigm of the past auxiliary, which is restricted to the unique (present) singular/ plural forms. The contrasting other kinds of *be* (ACE) can appear also in infinitive, imperative and periphrastic future forms.

(14) **Morphological Paradigms**

Past AUX			ACE: passive aux/copula/existential *be*	
IMP	(a)	**Chválil **buď**!* *praised AUX$_{IMP}$	(a')	*Chválen **buď**!* praised ACE$_{IMP}$ 'Be praised!'
INF	(b)	**(Musel) **být** chválil.* *(had to)AUX$_{INF}$ praised	(b')	*(Musel) **být** chválen/-zlý/-studentem* (had to) ACE$_{INF}$ praised /-nasty /-a student 'He had to be praised/nasty/-a student.'
FU T	(c)	**Já **budu** chválil.* *I AUX$_{FUT}$ praised	(c')	*Já **budu** chválen/-zlý/-studentem.* I ACE$_{FUT}$ praised /-nasty /-a student 'I will be praised /-tired /-a student.'

As for the category of aspect, the following example shows in (15b/ii) the possible presence of an aspectual suffix in ACE, which is not possible with AUX. In an analytic past the aspect (iterative) can appear only on the verbal participle in (15a/i), but not on the AUX itself in (15a/ii).

(15) (a) (i) *Já jsem chválil / chválí-**va**-l*
I ACE$_{1S}$ praised / praised$_{ITER}$
'I praised / was repeatedly praising.'

(ii) **Já bý-**vá**-m chválil / chválí-**va**-l*
*I ACE$_{ITER/1S}$ praised / praised$_{ITER}$

(b) (i) *Já jsem chválen / chválí-**vá**-n*
I AUX$_{1S}$ praised / praised$_{ITER}$
'I am praised (repeatedly).'

(ii) *Já bý-**vá**-m chválen / chválí-**vá**-n.*
I AUX$_{ITER/1S}$ praised / praised$_{ITER}$
'I am being praised (repeatedly).'

Referring to the distinctions exemplified in (7)-(15) Veselovská & Karlík (2004, Chapter 3) propose structures for the two forms of the verb *be* as schematically illustrated in (16). The trees show that we proposed to generate the past/conditional AUX in the clausal domain, as the head T (which in Czech at least, most likely correlates with clausal modality).[5]

Assuming the distinct base positions for the AUX and ACE elements, the locations of the verbal features [±NEG/ASP/ITER] as proposed above can explain the distinctions discussed earlier in this section. The base positions also reflect the traditional categorial distinction between 'auxiliary' and 'lexical' verbs *be*.

(16) Veselovská & Karlík (2004)

(a) Past. AUX (b) Passive ACE

[5] Though the head is labeled as T (Tense/Temporal) in (4) I do not assume that this is the position of the [+TENSE] feature in Czech. If Czech has such a feature at all, it is more likely located in the domain of *v**/VP.

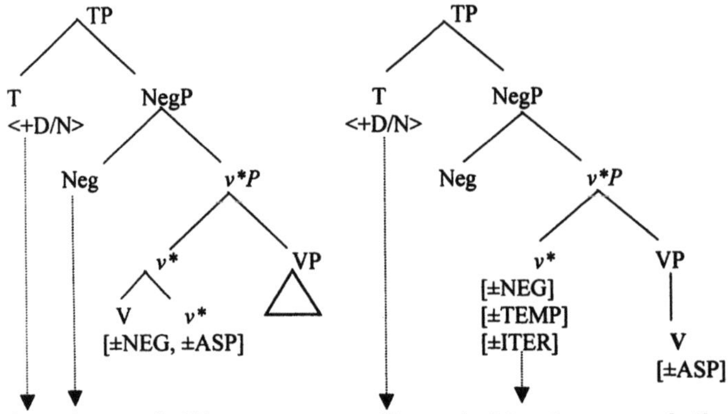

jsem *(ne-)* *chválil* — AUX$_{1sg}$ (not-) praised — 'I (not) praised'

Já -- *(ne-)* ***jsem/su*** *chválena* — I (not-)ACE$_{1sg}$ praised — "I am (not) praised'

3. Two Kinds of Copula *be*

Discussing the properties of the verb *be* in section 2, I was treating the forms of the passive auxiliary, copula, and existential *be* as the same (labelling them ACE), because when contrasted with the past/conditional auxiliary, they do behave in fully comparable fashion. In this section, however, I will demonstrate some distinctions among these elements. I am going to argue that all these distinctions can be best explained in light of the analytic verbal projections proposed in (4).

The distinctions I am going to show in this section will concern the copula *be*, which in Czech (as in many other Slavic languages) can be complemented by nominal predicates in the form of both nominative and instrumental. These options are illustrated in (17).

(17) *Petr je* ***student / studentem*** NP$_{NOM}$ + be + NP$_{NOM}$,/NP$_{INSTR}$
Peter is **student**$_{NOM/INSTR}$
'Peter is a student.'

I will propose that the distinctions between the structures *be* + *NP$_{NOM}$* and *be* + *NP$_{INSTR}$* are the result of (a) distinct structural positions of the verb *být* and (b) distinct characteristics of the nominal complex predicate.

The distinctions between the copulas *be* + *NP$_{NOM}$* and *be* + *NP$_{INSTR}$* are discussed in many studies in part because it is a phenomenon shared by many Slavbic languages. As for such authors working in a generative framework, see e.g. Franks (1995). The Russian example in (18a) is taken from the study by Ludmila Geist (1997), which I will refer to as (GR) in the following text. The (b) Polish example is from Adger and Ramchand (2001).

(18) (a) Rus. Sergej byl **žurnalistom**$_{INSTR}$ (b) Pol. Ewa jest **studentką**$_{INSTR}$
Sergej byl ***žurnalist***$_{NOM}$
Ewa jest ***studentka***$_{NOM}$
'Sergej was journalist'
'Eve is student.'

The above mentioned authors look for distinctions between the *be* + NP_{NOM} (be_{NOM}) and *be* + NP_{INSTR} (be_{INSTR}) structures, and in the following paragraphs I will apply some of their criteria and observations to Czech data.[6]

The example (19) demonstrates a distinct ability of the copulas to be located in the Focus position in the sentence. According to GR (=Geist, 1997, for Russian) the copula be_{NOM} in (a) cannot be focused, while the copula be_{INSTR} in (b) is able to carry the main stress. The Czech equivalents of the GR examples show, however, that the same does not apply in Czech. The informants accept both possibilities.[7]

(19) **Focalisation** A: *Karel asi není učitel.* ('Karel perhaps isn't a teacher')

(a) B: GR*/C? *Ale ne, Karel učitel je.*
Oh no, Karel $teacher_{NOM}$ **is.**
'Oh no, Charles **IS** a teacher.'

(b) B: GR OK/ C? *Ale ne, Karel učitelem je.*
Oh no, Karel $teacher_{INSTR}$ **is.**

The example in (20) illustrates the ability of the two copulas to express some aspectual features, namely an interpretation as a process and repetitive action. It seems that (a) be_{NOM} has a restricted ability to refer to a process or repetitions when compared with (b) be_{INSTR}, which permits this usage. A similar conclusion is also suggested by the contrast in (21), which illustrates a compatibility of the two copulas with phrasal verbs, which additionally in Czech do not tolerate perfective verbal complements. The evaluations in (20) and (21) are again stronger for Russian.

(20) *Karel byl* ***dvakrát/každý den*** *učitelem* / (GR*/C?) *učitel*
Karel was **twice/every day** $teacher_{INSTR}$ / (GR*/C?) $teacher_{NOM}$
'Karel was a teacher twice/every day.'

(21) *Karel* ***přestal*** *být učitelem* / (GR*/C?) *učitel*
Karel **stopped** be $teacher_{INSTR}$ / (GR*/C?) $teacher_{NOM}$
'Karel stopped being a teacher.'

The contrast in process versus stative readings correlates with the ability of the copulas to be related with a locational adverbial. The following example (22) demonstrates that a PP of location in (a), i.e. with be_{NOM}, cannot be interpreted as an adverbial related to the copula but only as a PP attribute. The adverbial interpretation is, however, possible with the be_{INSTR} in (22b). These interpretations are signalled by the position of the PP – the post-verbal position is the position of a PP attribute, while the preverbal PP tends to be interpreted as adverbial.

(22) (a) *Karel byl (GR*/C?* ***v Berlíně****) učitel* ***(v Berlíně)***
Karel was (GR*/C? in Berlin) $teacher_{NOM}$ (in Berlin).
'Karel was a teacher in Berlin.'

[6] I have checked the acceptability of the Czech examples with about 100 non-linguistic university students. Their evaluation was never unambiguous. In the examples below ? signals a dismissal in a substantial number, though not a majority, of cases.

[7] The marking (*GR) in this and the following examples means that the given structure is according to Geist (1997) unacceptable in Russian. The (?C) indicates a Czech acceptability evaluation. The Czech evaluations were clearly influenced by the fact that the NP_{INSTR} form was by all (mostly young) informants perceived as archaic and hyper-correct, and this resulted in their labelling it as ?.

(b) *Karel byl (v **Berlíně**) učitelem (GR/C? v **Berlíně**)*
Karel was (in Berlin) $teacher_{INSTR}$ (GR*/C? in Berlin)
'Karel was a teacher (while) in Berlin.'

On the other hand, we obtain a clearer evaluation for the Czech data in examples like those in (23). As mentioned in traditional descriptive grammars of Czech, the be_{INSTR} is a preferred form when the copula has a participial form. Though these be_{INST} structures are generally perceived as archaic, the contrasting be_{NOM} forms were rejected by most of the informants.

(23) ***Jsa** učitelem / *učitel připojil se Karel ke stávce.*
Being $teacher_{INSTR / *NOM}$ joined REFL Karel to strike
'Being a teacher, Karel joined the strike.'

Surprisingly strong evaluations were also obtained for the examples in (24), which are not illustrated for Russian in Geist (1997) but which are mentioned in Vladimír Šmilauer (1966). Most Czech informants preferred the be_{INSTR} when the copula has an infinitive form.

(24) *Chtěl **být** hrdinou / ?hrdina.*
wanted to-be $hero_{INSTR/?NOM}$
'He wanted to be a hero.'

Even stronger were the preferences in (25), where the subject is expressed by a relative pronoun. As mentioned in Šmilauer (1966), the fully grammatical form with be_{INSTR} contrasts strongly with the low level of acceptability of be_{NOM} in (25).

(25) *výstřel, **který/jež** byl signálem/*signal k útoku*
shot $which_{NOM}$ was $signal_{INSTR/*NOM}$ for attack
'The shot which was the signal for the attack.'

Both Geist (1997) and Adger & Ramchand (2001) discuss in detail the semantic characteristics of the two copulas. Their claims are summarised in (26).[8]

(26) **Semantics:** Geist (1997), Adger & Ramchand (2001)

be_{INSTR} → **S-predicate (stage level predicate)**: assertion of an event of a certain type
be_{NOM} → **I-predicate (individual level pr.)**: atomic property predicated of individual

Based on the above semantic distinction, the authors propose that the two copulas, though phonetically identical, represent two lexical entries and Geist (1997) moreover proposes to generate them in two distinct structures. According to her analysis, the **copula** be_{NOM} occurs in a simple structure containing three verbal heads: T, Neg, Pr(edicate)1; be_{NOM} is generated in T and Pr1 contains an empty category *e* (a small clause structure). The **copula** be_{INSTR} has a more complex structure containing as many as six verbal heads: T, Neg, Pr(edicate)1, Asp, V a Pr(redicate)2. Be_{INSTR} is generated in the position of V (and then raises to Pr1), and the empty category *e* (a small clause head) occurs in the secondary predicate head Pr2.

4. Complex Transitive Predicate

I will not discuss in more detail the analysis proposed in Geist (1997), which is based on the structures already proposed in Franks (1995). The point important for the discussion in this paper is her position for be_{NOM} in the clausal domain, namely in the head T. Recall that in (16)

[8] As for the terminology used here, I refer to the studies cited above.

I claimed that T is the position where the Czech past/conditional AUXs are base generated. The verbal projection of the form (4) does not contain any higher functional head above T with the exception of C. Though C can well be the surface position of the Czech C2 clitics, the agreement shown by the Czech AUXs signals that they must be generated lower than C. Thus, to simply accept the proposal of Geist (1997) for Czech would not allow me to explain the robust distinctions between AUX_{AGR} and (both) copulas as demonstrated in (7)-(15).

To support my analysis for Czech in (16), and not to reject a plausible analysis by Geist (1997), I want to point out some differences between Czech and Russian. One of them is the position of the negative prefix. Recall that in (9) I demonstrated that the AUX_{AGR} cannot carry the negative prefix *ne-*, which must appear rather on the following participle. The same fact is illustrated again in (27a), which also shows that the case marking of the nominal predicate has no influence on the position of the negative prefix. The free negative particle can (marginally) appear in front of the nominal predicate, resulting in a partial (constituent) negation illustrated in (27b).

(27) (a) *Karel* ***nebyl*** *učitel/-em, ale školník/-em*
Karel not-was teacher$_{\text{NOM/INSTR}}$ but schoolkeeper$_{\text{NOM/INSTR}}$
'Karel wasn't a teacher but a schoolkeeper.'

(b) *Karel byl* ***ne*** *učitel/-em, ale školník/-em*
Karel was not teacher$_{\text{NOM/INSTR}}$ but schoolkeeper$_{\text{NOM/INSTR}}$

The example (27) shows that the position of the negative element in Czech is distinct from that of the negative element in Russian, as exemplified in Geist (1997). The Russian *be*$_{NOM}$ copula in (28a) shows in fact the properties of the Czech AUX demonstrated in (27a) in that it cannot carry the negative prefix. In Russian the negative prefix can be attached to the *be*$_{INSTR}$ only, as illustrated in (28b).

(28) (GR) (a) *Sergej* ***(*ne)*** ***byl*** ***(ne)*** *žurnalist a fotograf.*
Sergej **(*not)** **was** (not) journalist$_{\text{NOM}}$ but photographer$_{\text{NOM}}$
'Sergey wasn't a journalist, but a photographer.'

(b) *Sergej* ***(ne)*** ***byl*** ***(ne)*** *žurnalistom a fotografom*
Sergej (not) was (not) journalist$_{\text{INSTR}}$ but photographer$_{\text{INSTR}}$

Another example which treats the Czech AUX and the Russian *be*$_{NOM}$ copula alike concerns the presence of the zero morpheme. The example in (29) shows that the Russian *be*$_{NOM}$ has a zero morpheme for all persons in present tense, while the contrasting Russian *be*$_{INSTR}$ must be overt in the presence of an overt subject.

(29) **θ morpheme** (GR) *Sergej žurnalist / *žurnalistom*
Sergej journalist$_{\text{NOM/*INSTR}}$
'Sergey is a journalist.'

As demonstrated above in (12), in Czech a zero morpheme (with the features 3sg) appears with the past AUX *be* but never with any of the other copulas. The example (12) also demonstrates Czech structures similar to the Russian ones, namely it shows the complementarity of an overt 1sg subject pronoun with $\text{AUX}_{1\text{sg}}$. And again, nothing like this is possible with Czech copulas, regardless of the case marking of the following predicate.

The similarity between one of the Czech auxiliaries and one of the Russian copulas brings to our attention an interesting fact. Though the above cited authors discuss in detail semantic distinctions between the two Russian copulas and relate other (formal) properties to a deep semantic difference, the comparison with the Czech data does not seem to support such a semantic basis. There is no reason to claim any semantic similarity between the Czech past AUX and the Russian be_{NOM} copula in spite of the fact that they share many formal characteristics. On the other hand, the Czech and Russian be_{NOM} copulas are close semantic equivalents, though they do *not* share crucial formal properties. This observation seems to support the hypothesis proposed in the study by Jamal Ouhalla (1991). This author claims that the core of the typological distinctions between languages is the repertory and exclusive properties of the functional elements in a given language (including the feature content of these language specific functional categories).[9]

Referring to Ouhalla's hypothesis I therefore keep the analysis of the Russian copula to Geist (1997), while for Czech I propose to generate both the copulas with predicate nominals in the thematic domain of the sentence. According to (4) this domain is comprised of two heads: *v** and V and thus allows us to express the distinction between the copulas in the terms of their structural positions. The structure proposed is given below in (30). In (30a) the verbal head be_{INSTR} assigns Oblique Instrumental Case to the nominal predicate according to (6). In (30b) the be_{NOM} is a head light verb *v** and the nominal predicate enters an Agree relation (via the *v**) with the subject in SPEC(*v**).[10]

(30) (a) Case assigning **lexical V** (b) Projection of the **light verb** ***v****

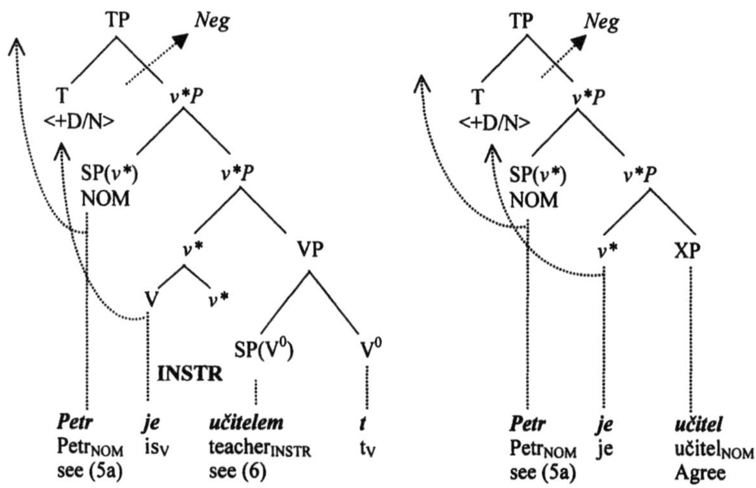

The dotted arrows in (30) show the further movement of the verbal heads to the higher heads, which presumably takes place during the process of derivation towards LF. Notice that the

---

[9] We can see an example of the same phenomenon in Spanish, which encodes the semantic distinction between the Slavic predicate nouns in two phonetically distinct grammatical verbs. The two Czech/ Russian copulas are close semantic equivalents of the Spanish verbs 'ser/ estar' with adjectival/nominal predicates.

The distinction is illustrated below in (a/b).

(a) *Soy 0/un/*el loco.*
I-am a/*the crazy
('I am crazy': permanent property).

(b) *Estoy 0/?un/*el loco*
I-am ?a/*the crazy
('I am crazy': temporary behaviour)

[10] In Veselovská & Karlík (2004) we also propose the same analysis (i.e. a base position in *v**) for the auxiliary be used in the Czech periphrastic passive. The similarity is supported by the same behaviour of the copula(s) and the passive AUX with respect to the criteria illustrated in (7)-(15).

surface realisations of (30a) and (30b) above are identical. A speaker must have a reason to build the more complex structure (30a) in some cases. I propose that the reason for the apparently uneconomical structure with a lexical V is related to the semantic specificity of be_{INSTR}. The position of be_{INSTR} in the lexical head V allows its specific interpretation (indicating a non-permanent, unstable property; see Šmilauer 1966). As a lexical head this copula must be present in a primary Numeration and according to (6) is able to assign an Oblique Case to its SPEC. Its presence in the primary Numeration is at the same time a plausible reason why the copula be_{INSTR} can carry the feature of Focus and can express Aspect (see (19)/(20)/(21)). Moreover, the double projection of *v**-V also provides a position for the VP adverbial in (22).

On the other hand, the Czech data suggest that the 'verbal' interpretation of the be_{INSTR} is not vital for most speakers, and that the complex structure (30a) is in modern Czech being replaced by the more economical (30b). The fact that in spite of the economy factor, there are still some structures with a prevailing usage of the complex (30a) suggests that the reasons for its usage need not be solely semantic. The more complex structure seems to also be required for the realisation of participle and infinitive forms, as demonstrated in (23)-(24).[11]

The structure (30b) with be_{NOM} generated in the position of the light verb *v** results in an interpretation of the predicate nominal as a stable, permanent, inherent property or listing in a larger group of elements (see Šmilauer 1966). This copula is a grammatical element with no idiosyncratic semantic features. This copula cannot assign any Case, but its absence in a primary Numeration allows an Agree relation between SPEC(V) and SPEC(*v**).[12]

In the following section I am going to discuss in more detail the concept of agreement which licenses the structure of the Czech be_{NOM} copula, as represented in (30b).

5. Agree

The concept of Agree is of growing importance in the most recent Minimalist framework. It is departing from its original/ traditional purely morphological interpretation and becoming a term expressing a structural relation (with a possible but not necessary morphological reflection). Without further discussion I will assume the concept of Agree as introduced in Chomsky (1999) and applied and justified in Adger & Ramchand (2001). According to this notion of Agree, the structure in (30a) with the copula be_{INSTR} can be as in (31).

(31)
$[_{TP}$ Pavel **T** $[_{v*P}$ **Pavel** **je** $[_{VP}$ **učitelem ...** t_V

Person [*/3] ←	Person [3]	Case [*/INSTR] ←	Case [INSTR]
Num [*/sg] ←	Num [sg]	See (6)	[*ψ]
Case [NOM] →	Case [*/NOM]		[-EPP]
[+EPP]			

When the verbal head V enters the derivation (on the right of the scheme), it becomes a Probe for its feature content (in the scheme (31) in the right dotted frame) and enters in the relation Agree with the merged nominal complex *učitel* 'teacher'. As a result of this relation

[11] I have no principled explanation at the moment for the strong preference of the be_{INSTR} copula in relative clauses, as in (25). This may be related to the ability/ inability of the nominal predicate to agree with the subject expressed by the relative pronoun.

[12] Using the concept of tripartite levels of insertion of grammatical morphemes as in Emonds (2000), I assume that some kinds of grammatical elements are not part of the primary Numeration though their presence is required (and their features checked) during the process of derivation. If the needed grammatical elements contribute to interpretation, they are inserted during the syntactic derivation, and if not, then at PF.

the nominal complex receives Instrumental. We assume that this Case assignment disallows further Agree with the referential/ nominal features of *učitel* 'teacher' and the features [*ψ] of the head V thus remains unvalued.[13]

The upper dotted arrows show the head movement of the copula to the higher functional projections. When the new head T merges into the structure as a Probe with the feature content listed in the left dotted frame in (31), the copula raises to T and as the head T enters the Agree relation with the merged nominal complex *Pavel*. This Agree results in the Nominative on the latter and at the same time in the setting of the features of Person and Number, which in Czech is a choice within the paradigm of the finite verb.[14]

The following examples in (32) show that in the structures with *be*$_{INSTR}$, the copula always agrees with the feature content (Number and Gender) of the nominative subject.

(32) (a) ***Marie*** ***byla / *byl*** ***učitelem*** *na učilišti* *několik* *let.*
Mary$_{FS.NOM}$ was$_{FS}$/ *was$_{MS}$ teacher$_{MS.INSTR}$ on apprentice school several years.
'Mary was an apprentice school teacher for several years.'

(b) ***Ty knihy*** ***jsou / *je*** ***výsměchem*** *dobrého* *vkusu.*
The books$_{FP.NOM}$ are$_{P}$ / *is$_{S}$ offences$_{S.INSTR}$ of a good taste
'The books offend good taste.'

On the other hand, (33) demonstrates that contrary to *be*$_{INSTR}$, the *be*$_{NOM}$ copula can agree with the nominal predicate as well. As for Number features, (33a/b) show that *be*$_{NOM}$ must agree with either the NOM subject or the NOM predicate depending on their feature content: the one that has a more marked feature content (i.e. is a Plural) determines the agrement.

(33) (a) *Ty knihy* ***jsou / *je*** *vyložený brak.*
the books$_{Pl}$ are / *is a real trash$_{Sg}$
'The books are real trash.'

(b) *Ča* ***jsou / *je*** *peníze.*
Time$_{Sg}$ are / *is money$_{Pl}$
'Time is money.'

The following example (34) shows another specific property of the relation between the agreement and feature content of the subject/ predicate couple. First, if the predicate is expressed by a pronoun, it cannot be related to *be*$_{INSTR}$ (i.e. the predicate must rather be a NOM) as in (34a) and, second, the *be*$_{NOM}$ copula must agree with the pronoun no matter whether it is subject or predicate as in (34b).[15]

(34) (a) *To strašidlo jsem* ***já / *mnou***
the monster am I$_{NOM/*INSTR}$
'The monster is me.'

(b) (i) *To/Pavel* ****je / jsem*** *já.*
it /Pavel *is / am I$_{NOM}$
'This/Paul is me.'

(ii) *Já* ***jsem / *je*** *Pavel.*
I am / *is Pavel$_{NOM}$
'I am Paul.'

My analysis of the agreement relation with the *be*$_{NOM}$ copula is based on the hypothesis that the predicate is a less complex nominal structure than a subject/ object DP. In his detailed

---

[13] For the explanation of the blocking effect of a lexical / Oblique Case see Chomsky (1999) and Adger & Ramchand (2001).

[14] For more details concerning s-v agreement in Czech analytic verbal forms, see also Veselovská 2002.

[15] Copular structures with both subject and predicate pronouns are not common. In those which sound pragmatically acceptable it seems that the first (=subject?) pronoun is preferred for agreement. I leave such structures for some future research.
(i) On je / *jsem já a já jsem / *je on.
He is / *am I and I am / *is he

study of nominal projection Zamparelli (2000) introduces several functional heads dominating the lexical projection of N when the latter serves as an argument. He labels them Strong Determiner, Predicate Determiner, Numeral, Kind Determiner, Numeral, etc. A nominal predicate can plausibly lack some of the high functional projections. Adger & Ramchand (2001) use more abstract terms and divide the nominal projections into those which can satisfy the referential feature [δ] of the verbal Probe (a close equivalent to the feature <+D>) and those, which can satisfy the feature [ψ] (an equivalent of the Phi features of <+N>).[16]

Assuming such a structural deficiency of a NOM predicate, the structures with *be_{NOM}* can be analysed as proposed in (35). The light verb *v** head enters the derivation (on the right on the scheme) with its feature content (in the right dotted frame) and becomes a Probe. Its features are set in the relation Agree with the nominal complex *učitel* 'teacher' merged with *v**, which, however, is deficient. Consequently the referential [δ] feature of the Probe remains unvalued and Case remains unassigned. On the other hand, because Case does not block the feature sharing between the copula and the Goal, the nominal [ψ] features of copula-Probe can be set if the Goal *učitel* 'teacher' has some marked [ψ] features (i.e. Plural or Person).

(35)

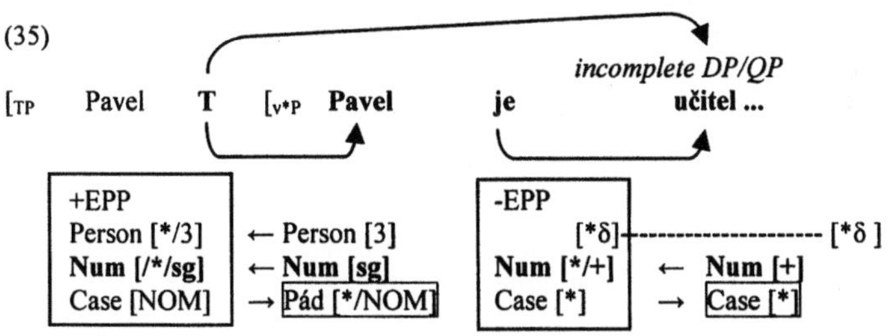

In the next phase of the derivation, after the copula substitutes for the new head T, it becomes a Probe with the feature content listed in the left dotted frame in (35). As the head T it enters the Agree relation with the merged nominal complex *Pavel* in SPEC(v*), which is a full DP. Because the Agree relation satisfies the referential [δ] feature of the Probe, this Agree results in the Nominative marking of the subject. It also results in the setting of the [*ψ] features of Person/ Number on the copula in case they had not been set in the previous phase. The copula in (35) enters the Agree relation with both the nominal predicate and the subject. I therefore conclude that the NOM Case is transferred to the predicate via the copula.

This multi-level setting of the Probe feature content seems to be supported by structures with the expletive subject *to* ('it$_{3SN}$'), which never allow *be$_{INSTR}$* as demonstrated in (34a/b), with the copula agreement always reflecting the nominal predicate features. These structures prove that the lower domain in v*-V remains open for feature setting if the referential feature [*δ] is valued by an expletive lacking Phi [ψ] features.

6. Conclusion

The purpose of this paper was to illustrate and account for a number of differences between three kinds of the Czech verb *be*. First I contrasted the properties typical of the past/ conditional AUX (clitic) with those of the other auxiliaries, the copulas and existential *be*. I concluded that the whole range of contrasts can be explained by referring to the distinct positions in which the forms of the verb *be* are generated. I proposed that the past/ conditional

[16] For Czech nominal structures see similar discussions in e.g. Veselovská (2002). For present purposes it is important that Czech nominal complexes show clear signs of being composed of several projections, even though the feature content of these separate functional heads is clearly not fully comparable to e.g. the English system.

AUX (clitic) is generated in the clausal domain, in the head T, while the other forms of the verb *be* are generated lower, in the thematic domain v*-V.

In the second part of the paper I compared some semantic and formal properties of two Czech copulas: the be_{NOM} copula which is followed by a nominal predicate is in the Nominative Case and a phonetically identical be_{INSTR} copula whose nominal predicate in the Instrumental Case. Comparing the Czech structures with some Russian data I proposed that the distinctions between the copulas can also be expressed in structural terms, namely as the distinction between the positions in V and in v*.

The following (36) summarises the proposed analysis of the three kinds of the Czech verb *be,* with a brief list of the characteristics discussed in sections 2 and 3-4.

(36) **(a) $\mathbf{be_{INSTR}}$ copula : V, [$\mathbf{D_{INSTR}}$]**

(i) temporary /limited interpretation, non-substantive property (Šmilauer 1966)
(ii) present in the primary Numeration: (a) assigns INSTR, (b) can be focused,
(c) has Aspect, (d) can host a VP adjunct
(iii) has a full verbal paradigm, including participle and infinitive forms,
(iv) is being replaced by be_{NOM} in current speech.

(b) $\mathbf{be_{NOM}}$ copula : *v**

(i) permanent, substantive property, situating within a set (Šmilauer 1966)
(ii) grammatical element with conceptual features only (no theta role)
(iii) not present in the primary Numeration
(iv) the structure allows/ requires Agree to license a predicate

(c) $\mathbf{be_{PRET/COND}}$ AUX : T

(i) grammatical element with no interpretive LF features of its own
(ii) post-syntactic/PF insertion as a 'flection'

In section 5, I demonstrated the process of the Agree relation applying in copular structures. I showed that the be_{INSTR} copula acts as a verbal head assigning a lexical Case, while the be_{NOM} copula relates structures whose predicates have deficient feature content. The lack of a referential feature [*δ] on the predicate nominal results in the multilevel setting of the features of the Probe which enters several Agree relations with several Goals. This process is summarised below in (37)

(37) **Multi-level Agree**

(a) (Local) Agree inside v*P: Probe v*, Goal: [ψ] of the predicate nominal

(b) (Local) Agree inside TP: Probe T, Goal DP [+δ] in SPEC(v*) → [NOM]
If the FF of T remain still incomplete (the Goal is an expletive)

(c) (Non-local) Agree: probe T, goal: closest [ψ]
i.e. v*/predicate NP (the domain is still open)

Many problems and data remained unexplained, e.g. a more principled formal motivation for the position of the elements in the structure, some obligatory paradigms, or copular structures with expletives and many others. The discussion nonetheless clearly shows that a range of detailed Czech data provides highly promising material for analysis in a developed theoretical framework and thus deserves to be carefully investigated in future research.

Bibliography

Adger, David & Ramchand, Gillian (2001): *Prediation and Equation*. University of York.
Chomsky, Noam (1995): *The Minimalist Program*. Cambridge, MA: MIT Press.
Chomsky, Noam (1999): *Derivation by Phase*. MITOPL 18.
Emonds, Joseph E. (2000): *Lexicon & Grammar: the English Syntacticon*. The Mouton de Gruyter, Berlin.
Franks, Steven (1995): *Parameters of Slavic Morphosyntax*. Oxford University Press, New York Oxford.
Franks, Steven & King Tracy Holloway (2000): *A Handbook of Slavic Clitics*. Oxford University Press.
Geist, Ludmila (1997): 'Russisch *byt*: zwei Kopulae, zwei Kasus, ein integrierter Ansatz'. In: Kosta & Frasek (eds): *Current Approaches to Formal Slavic Linguistics*. Peter Lang, Frankfurt am Main 2002, 169-178.
Komárek, Miroslav (1978): *Příspěvky k české morfologii*. Praha, SPN.
Kopečný, František (1962): *Základy české skladby*. Praha, SPN.

Kosta, Petr (2001): Negace a větná struktura v češtině. In: Hladká, Z. & Karlík, P. (eds.): *Čeština-univerzália specifika*, 3, Brno: Masarykova univerzita, 117-138.
Larson, R. K. (1988): On the Double Object Construction. In: *Linguistic Inquiry* 19.3, 335-391.
Larson, R. K. (1989): Light predicate raising. In: *Lexicon Project Working Paper* #27. Department of Linguistics & Philosophy. MIT.
Ouhalla, Jamal (1991): *Functional Categories and Parametric Variation*. Routledge, London.
Pollock, Jean-Yves (1989): Verb Movement, Universal Grammar, and the Structure of IP. *Linguistic Inquiry* 20, 365-424.
Šmilauer, Vladimír (1966): *Novočeská skladba*. Státní pedagogické nakladatelství, Praha.
Toman, Jindřich (1980): 'Weak and Strong: Notes on *be* in Czech'. In: Brettschneider, G. & Lehmann, Ch. (eds.): *Wege zur Universalien Forschung*. Gynter Narr Verlag Tübingen.
Toman, Jindřich (2000): 'Prosodické spekulace o klitikách v nekanonickch pozicích'. In: Hladká, Zdeňka & Karlík, Petr (eds.): *Čeština – univerzália a specifika* 2. Brno.
Veselovská, Ludmila (1995): *Phrasal Movement and X-Morphology: Word Order Parallels in Czech and English Nominal and Verbal Projections*. Ph. D diss. Palacký University, Olomouc.
Veselovská, Ludmila (2002): 'Struktura subjekt-predikátové shody'. In: Hladká & Karlík (eds): *Čeština-univerzália specifika* 4, Masarykova univerzita, Brno, 199-212.
Veselovská, Ludmila & Karlík, Petr (2004): 'Analytic Passive in Czech'. In: *RsF* 2/3, 2004.
Zamparelli, Roberto (2000): *Layers in the Determiner Phrase*. New York, Garland.

Ludmila Veselovská
Katedra anglistiky a amerikanistiky
Filozofická fakulta UP
Křížkovského 10
771 80 Olomouc
lidave@aix.upol.cz

Valja Werkmann, Leipzig

Clitic Doubling, Specificity and Focus in Bulgarian

1 Introduction

The purpose of this article is to present the facts of clitic doubling in Bulgarian with special reference to the conditions under which doubling is licensed, required or forbidden. With clitic doubling (henceforth CD) I refer to the overt doubling of an argument-DP by a phonologically weak clitic pronoun, which agrees with the DP in case, person, number and gender. In this paper I am interested only in structures with direct object CD in which the doubled argument-DP appears post-verbally as in (1).[1]

(1) Vidjax go Ivo.
saw-1Sg him.Cl Ivo
'I saw Ivo.'

The article presents an analysis of the function of this construction which accounts for its distribution and explains its special discourse function. It shows that CD is not optional but interacts in a systematic way with the semantic notion of specificity and the information structural notion of focus. The presence or the absence of the doubling clitics leads to different interpretations of the sentence. The non-clitic doubled DP can be neutral focus, contrastive focus or background, whereas the clitic doubled DP can only be background. Thus, doubling clitics in Bulgarian have interpretative import, since they indisputably mark the DPs they double as [-focus]. Under this view, CD can be considered as a defocusing strategy whose function is to exclude the doubled argument-DP from the focus domain.

The paper is organized as follows: Section 2 discuss the formal characteristics of Bulgarian CD which distinguishes it from the same phenomenon in Romanian and Spanish. In section 3, I show that CD is different from clitic right dislocation. Sections 4, 5 and 6 discuss the interaction of CD with nominal expressions of different semantic type. In section 7, I illustrate how CD effects the information structural interpretation of the sentence and close with a summary in section 8.

2 Properties of clitic doubling

CD is attested not only in Bulgarian but also in other languages like Romanian or Spanish[2]. However, there are two major differences between CD in Bulgarian and CD in Romanian and Spanish. The first one is the fact that Bulgarian CD violates Kayne's Generalization.

[1] I am not concerned with clitic doubling of accusative quirky subjects, as in (i):

(i) Ivan *(go) boli glavata.
Ivan.Acc him.Cl.Acc hurts the head.NOM
'Ivan has a headache.'

[2] One of the main difficulties that the analyse of CD constructions in Spanish has faced has arisen from the fact that in certain dialects of Spanish such as Porteño Spanish (Suñer 1988) or Limeño Spanish (Sanchez 2003) CD appears to be optional with direct object arguments. The only doubling of direct objects sanctioned in Normative Spanish (the idealized Spanish described by traditional grammarians) is the doubling with personal pronouns, as in (i).

(i) *La recordamos a elle con gran cariño.*
Her we-remember her with great love
'We remember her fondly.'

According to Kayne's generalization CD is possible whenever a nominal expression can receive case by means of some non-verbal device which has case-assigning properties, namely a preposition. In CD constructions in Romanian and Spanish the clitics absorb Case, requiring the presence of another Case assigner. The result is that in these languages the doubled direct objects must be accompanied by the prepositions *a* and *pe* (cf. (2b) and (2a) respectively), in order for doubling to be licit.[3]

(2) a. L_i-am văzut *(pe) Ion.[4] Ro
Him.Cl-have-I seen pe Ion[5]
'I have seen Ion.'
(Dobrovie-Sorin 1990:355, ex. (6a))

b. La_i vi *(a) $Maria_i$. Sp
Her.Cl saw-I a Maria
'I saw Maria.'
(Sanchez 2003: 5; ex. (3))

c. Vidjax go_i Ivo_i. Bg
Saw-I him.Cl Ivo
'I saw Ivo.'

In Bulgarian argument-DPs appear in the same form whether or not they are doubled by a clitic. As the Bulgarian example (2c) shows, the idea that dummy prepositions, such as *a* (in Spanish) or *pe* (in Romanian) constitute a necessary and sufficient syntactic condition for CD is not correct.

The second difference is the fact that Bulgarian CD is not subject to the semantic constraints characteristic for this construction in Romanian and Spanish. In Romanian CD is sensitive to the feature [±human], cf. Dobrovie-Sorin (1990), Gierling (1997), Popescu (1997), whereas in Spanish it is sensitive to the feature [±animate], cf. Jaeggli (1986), Borer (1984), Suñer (1988), Sanchez (2003). Semantic features of these types do not pose restrictions on Bulgarian doubling. As example (3c) illustrates, doubling of inanimates is fully acceptable in Bulgarian contrary to Romanian and Spanish where it leads to ungrammaticality.

(3) a. (*L-)am asteptat pe tren. Ro
him.Cl-have-I waited pe train
'I've waited for the train (to come).'
(Gierling 1998: 8, ex. (46))

b. (*La) compramos (a) esa novela. Sp
it.Cl.Fem bought-we that novel
'We bought that novel.'
(Suñer 1988: 396, ex. (8))

---

[3] According to Jaeggli (1986) the verb gives away the accusative Case absorbed by the clitic and, simultaneously, to the preposition-like element *a* resp. *pe*, which transmits it to the nominal.

[4] In Romanian the dummy preposition *pe* appears in all constructions in which the clitic doubles a post-verbal argument-DP. On the other hand, topicalized clitic doubled arguments can appear without *pe* (cf. Gierling 1997).

[5] I use the following glosses: Cl – clitic, Def – definite suffix, Fem – feminine, Masc – masculine, Neutr – neuter, Sg – singular, Pl – plural, Refl – reflexive pronoun, Prt – participle, Part – particle.

c. Pročetox ja$_i$ statijata$_i$ ošte včera. Bg
read-I it.Cl.Fem article.Def.Sg.Fem still yesterday
'I read the article still yesterday.'

To summarize, in this section I have demonstrated that Bulgarian direct object CD differs from Romanian and Spanish with respect to two properties: (a) violation of Kayne's Generalization and (b) insensitivity to the feature [±animate].

In the next section I will show that CD in Bulgarian is formally distinct from clitic right dislocation.

3 Against the Right Dislocation Hypothesis

In this section I will present a number of arguments which convincingly show that the construction observed in Bulgarian is different from clitic right dislocation. The term 'right-dislocation' is used to refer to the coexistence of a clitic pronoun and a lexical DP associated with it, where the corresponding DP appears at the right periphery of the sentence and there is a perceptible intonational break between the DP and the rest of the sentence.
It is standardly assumed that all Romance languages freely allow right dislocation but only some of them allow doubling. French and Italian are the languages, which do not permit CD. Simultaneously they are the typical examples for right dislocation structures. In these languages clitics and lexical DPs are in complementary distribution. If the sentence is pronounced with main accent on the right-most constituent, as in (4c), the co-occurrence of clitic and lexical DP causes ungrammaticality. The coexistence of clitic and lexical DP is only possible, if the sentence is uttered with a special intonation contour, as the example (4d) indicates.[6]

(4) a. Marie connaît Louis.
Marie knows Louis

b. Marie le connaît. Fr
Marie him knows

c. *Marie le connaît Louis.
Marie him knows Louis

d. Marie le connaît, Louis.
Marie him knows, Louis

The outstanding characteristic of these constructions consists in the fact that right-dislocated constituents are completely stress-less, or more accurately, their degree of stress contrasts sharply with the immediately preceding intonation peak, which falls on the last clause-internal element (cf. Lambrecht 1981: 86).[7, 8] The right-dislocated constituents always occur after the

[6] Following the more or less established convention, I use a comma to separate the right-dislocated constituent from the clause. This comma is not meant to indicate a pause (cf. Lambrecht 1981: 76).

[7] The fact that right dislocation by definition follows an immediately preceding intonation peak may explain why it is often said that right-dislocated constituents are uttered after a more or less salient pause (cf. Lambrecht 1981: 86).

[8] Right dislocation can also be found in languages without object clitics, as the English examples in (i) and the German examples in (ii) illustrate.

(i) a. I don't like them$_i$ at all, the cops$_i$.
b. He$_i$ is a nice guy, your brother$_i$.

(ii) a. Er hat sie$_i$ geschält, die Kartoffeln$_i$.
He has them peeled, the potatoes
'He has peeled them, the potatoes.'

b. Sie$_i$ wohnen im dritten Stock, die Müllers$_i$.
'They live on the third floor, the Müllers.'

normal clause boundary. This clause boundary is marked in French by stress on the last constituent of the clause, which is the verb in (4d). It is important to notice that right-dislocated constituents can never occur before stressed constituents belonging to the same clause (Lambrecht 1981: 80).[9] This leads to the assumption that in French or Italian sentences which contain an object clitic and a co-referential DP, this DP does not appear in one argument-position. According to the right dislocation hypothesis the clitic is merged as argument of the verb, whereas the DP is inserted in a peripheral position and plays a role other than that of an argument since that is already satisfied by the clitic. The hypothesis is that the co-referential DP in (4d) occupies an A-bar-position, so that it would be an adjunct.[10]

Unlike Italian or French, in Bulgarian the co-referential DP may appear not only in a right-peripheral position (5a) but also within the clause (5b), cf. Werkmann (2003, in press). The sentences (5a) and (5b) are congruent answers to the question 'What did Ivo to the chocolate?'.

(5) a. Ivo go$_i$ isjade ošte včera, šokolada$_i$. Bg
Ivo it.Cl ate still yesterday the chocolate
'Ivo ate the chocolate still yesterday.'

b. Ivo go$_i$ isjade šokolada$_i$ ošte včera.
Ivo it.Cl ate the chocolate still yesterday
'Ivo ate the chocolate still yesterday.'

In both sentences the adverbial is the carrier of main prominence, whereas the co-referential DP is de-accented. These sentences show that in Bulgarian the DP may not only appear after the focus of the sentence as in French, but also before the focused constituent belonging to the same clause; an option which is excluded for French. We thus have one piece of evidence that the construction in (5b) is not right dislocation. An additional argument has to do with the observation that in Bulgarian, structures like (5b) are fully productive without the right-dislocation intonation. The conclusion is that the phenomenon observed in Bulgarian is clitic doubling.

The most important argument against the view that constructions as in (5b) represent clitic right dislocation comes from the fact that clitic doubled constituents may occur in positions, which are typically associated with theta-marking and case-marking, i.e. in A-positions such as subjects of small clauses. The argument holds for both definite and indefinite DPs, as (6a) and (6b) illustrate.

(6) a. Marija ne bi go$_i$ narekla Ivan$_i$ krasiv.
Maria not would him called John pretty
'Maria wouldn't call John pretty.'

[9] In (ia) the right-dislocated *Jean* is marked as post-focal with respect to the clause-final stressed element *à Pierre*. The same example is ungrammatical if *Jean* is placed before the focused constituent *à Pierre*, as in (ib).

(i) a. Il$_i$ a envoyé une lettre à PiÉRre, Jean$_i$.
He has sent a letter to Pierre, Jean

b. * Il$_i$ a envoyé une lettre, Jean$_i$, a PiÉRre.
He has sent a letter, Jean, to Pierre

[10] Clitic right dislocation is often viewed as (base-generated) right adjunction of the dislocated DP to the VP, IP or CP area (cf. Jaeggli 1986, Zubizarreta 1996). But see also Kayne (1994) and Cecchetto (1999) for a different syntactic account of these structures.

b. Ivan ne bi go$_i$ smetnal [edno takova momiče]$_i$ za inteligentno.
Ivan not would her.Cl.Neutr consider-Prt one such girl.Neutr Prep intelligent
'John would not consider such a girl intelligent.'

Subjects of small clauses are unlikely to occupy an A-bar-position. The occurrence of CD in such structures constitutes conclusive evidence against the adjunct status of the doubled element. These data can be considered as the crucial argument against doubling as right-dislocation.

In fact, there is additional evidence in favour of this analysis. It is impossible for a right-dislocated direct object to occur between the verb and the post-verbal focused indirect object, the reason being that the post-verbal focused indirect object occupies a VP-internal position. For instance, if the doubled argument-DP in Bulgarian were indeed right-dislocated, a focused constituent to the right of a right-dislocated DP would be precluded. This prediction is borne out, however, as the example in (7) illustrates.

(7) a. Ivo ja$_i$ dade knigata$_i$ na Marija.
Ivo it.Cl gave the book to Marija
'Ivo gave the book to Maria.' 'It was Maria that Ivo gave the book to.'

The facts presented so far strongly suggest that Bulgarian CD is different from right-dislocation and that this difference is well supported by prosodic, syntactic and interpretative evidence.

In the next four sections CD constructions in Bulgarian will be discussed, with special reference to the conditions under which doubling is licensed, required or forbidden.

4 Clitic doubling and bare expressions

The generative literature on CD considers specificity as the major factor for CD cross-linguistically (cf. Suñer 1988, Dobrovie-Sorin 1990, Uriagereka 1995, Sportiche 1996, Corver/Delfitto 1999; for Bulgarian: Guentchéva 1994, Alexandrova 1995, Avgustinova 1997, Schick 2000, Arnaudova 2002, Werkmann 2003). Unfortunately the term 'specificity' is used quite loosely, often not distinguished from 'referentiality', 'familiarity', 'presuppositionality', 'strong reading', 'discourse-linking' or 'a DP having wide scope over an operator'. In what follows I will show that CD in Bulgarian is acceptable with specific DPs, regardless of whether we define specificity in terms of scope, partitivity or with the indefinite's picking out a particular individual.
Doubling of non-specific nominal expressions is not allowed in Bulgarian, as example (8) illustrates.

(8) a. Ana iskaše da si (*ja) kupi roklja.
Ann wanted Part it.Cl buy dress

b. Ana iskaše da si (*gi) kupi kartini.
Ann wanted Part them.Cl buy pictures

Examples (8a) and (8b) are ungrammatical when a bare singular respective a bare plural object is clitic doubled in spite of the fact that the clitic and the direct object agree in phi-features (that is, in number, person, gender and structural case). I assume that the impossibility of doubling bare singulars and bare plurals is due to feature mismatch between the clitic and the direct object with respect to specificity. Object clitics are inherently specific, cf. Werkmann 2003, whereas bare singulars as well as bare plurals represent non-specific entities. It is argued that the locus of specificity is the D-position, cf. Abney (1987). The phonologically realized article can be associated with specific or non-specific reference, while a phonologically empty D is a diagnostic for non-specificity, cf. Longobardi (1994), Schick (2000). The clitic and the doubled phrase must always match in features under CD. Thus, in (8) ungrammaticality ensues if there is no agreement between the clitic and the doubled DP in terms of the D-feature [+specific].

5 Clitic doubling and indefinites

While doubling of nominal expressions with zero articles is not allowed, CD of nominal expressions with an indefinite article is permitted. We must explain the conditions under which doubling is licensed or required.
It is now a well-established view in the semantic literature that indefinites can have either a specific/referential reading or they can have a non-specific/existential reading. The classical reconstruction of the contrast between specific and non-specific indefinite DPs is formulated in terms of a scope interaction between the indefinite DP and other operators, cf. Fodor/Sag (1982). An indefinite is interpreted either as a referential term and receives wide scope, or as an existential quantifier, which has to obey scope islands. In this view the two readings of (9)

(9) Ana iskaše da si kupi edna roklja.
Ann wanted Part Refl buy a dress
'Ann wanted to buy a dress.'

are paraphrased as (10a) where the existential quantifier has scope over *wanted*, yielding the specific reading; and as (10b) with narrow scope for the existential quantifier yielding the non-specific reading.

(10) a. There is a dress and Ann wanted to buy it.

b. Ann wanted that there is a dress such that she could buy it.

Importantly, certain inferences, which follow on a specific reading, are invalid on a non-specific reading. In the specific reading (10a), the existence of the item referred to by the indefinite expression is presuppositional. No existence claims follow from the non-specific reading in (10b). However, if the indefinite object is clitic doubled, as in (11), it must be interpreted as specific/referential.

(11) Ana iskaše da si ja_i kupi edna $roklja_i$.
Ann wanted Part Refl it.Cl buy a dress

Thus, while example (9) is ambiguous with respect to specificity, CD, as in (11), offers the possibility of unambiguously marking the indefinite DP as specific. The contrast between (9) and (11) illustrates the fact that the co-occurrence of a clitic and an indefinite DP in Bulgarian has certain effects in the interpretation of the latter. In this way, the clitic not only guarantees that the argument-DP will not be interpreted existentially, but also abolishes the ambiguity between the existential and presuppositional reading that non-clitic doubled indefinite DP would otherwise have.

Diesing (1992) distinguishes two types of indefinites, presuppositional and non-presuppositional.[11] Presuppositional indefinites presuppose the existence of the entity/entities

[11] She proposes that the interpretation of an indefinite DP is determined by the structural position of that indefinite at LF. Roughly put, with respect to the interpretation of indefinite DPs, Diesing's analysis makes two specific claims:

(i) An indefinite outside the VP (at LF) will be interpreted as generic or presuppositional.
(ii) An indefinite within the VP (at LF) will be interpreted as non-generic or non-presuppositional.

they are applied to, whereas non-presuppositional indefinites assert the existence of this entity/these entities. The examples in (12) illustrate the presuppositional reading of an indefinite DP for Bulgarian.

(12) a. Vidjax edin student da izliza ot cafeto.
saw-I a student Part walks-he out of café.Def
'I saw a student leaving the café.'

b. Vidjax go$_i$ [edin student]$_i$ da izliza ot cafeto.
saw-I him.Cl a student Part walks-he out of café.Def
'I saw a student leaving the café.'

In (12b) the indefinite *edin student* 'a student' is specific in sense of 'the speaker has a specific referent in mind.' The internal argument *edin student* in (12b) can only be a student whose face the speaker has previously seen but cannot associate with a name; however, never anyone who happens to look like a student, the reading, which example (12a) can have. When an object clitic co-occurs with an indefinite DP, as in (12b), only the presuppositional/specific reading of the DP is allowed. In such cases, the use of the pronominal clitic acts as a disambiguating device, because it explicitly marks uniquely and existentially presupposed individuals.

Enç (1991:10) claims that lexical partitives are always specific because they represent an element in a defined set. Indefinite partitives such as *two of the roses* in (13) refer to groups that are a subgroup of the referent of the definite DP contained in the partitive, in this case *the roses*. Therefore, partitives are necessarily specific. We predict that object clitics can double Bulgarian partitives in the object position. This is in fact the case, as example (13) shows.

(13) Podarixa gi$_i$ [dve ot rozite]$_i$ na Marija.
Gave-they them.Cl two of roses.Def to Marija
'They gave two of the roses to Mary as a gift.'

It is quite common that the expression of specificity may interact with modality in relative clauses. In sentences like (14a) in which the use of the subjunctive is an indicator of a non-specific interpretation, the argument-DP cannot be doubled. In example (14b) the use of the indicative in the relative clause makes possible the interpretation of the internal argument as specific and it can be clitic doubled. The examples in (14) show that Bulgarian allows CD of specific indefinites whereas CD of non-specific indefinites leads to ungrammaticality.

(14) a. Târsja (*go) edin advokat, kojto da si razbira dobre ot rabotata.
Looking for-I him a lawyer that Part Refl knows-he well Prep job.Def
'I am looking for a lawyer such that he knows his work well.'

b. Târsja go$_i$ [edin advokat]$_i$, kojto trjabva da mi objasni njakoi podrobnosti po
Looking for-I him a lawyer who must Part to-me clear-up some details about
deloto.
court-procedure.Def
'I am looking for a lawyer who shall clear up some details on the court procedure for me.'

As the data illustrate the exclusion of specificity correlates with the exclusion of doubling clitics. By CD the only possible reading of the doubled DP is the specific/presuppositional one. In the light of these facts, it may be plausible to assume that specificity in the sense of partitivity (cf. Enç 1991) as in (13) or specificity in the sense of presuppositionality (cf.

Diesing 1992), as in (12), seems to be the accurate requirement for the direct object to be doubled by a clitic in Bulgarian.
However, all sentences with indefinite DPs presented above are grammatical also without doubling. More exactly said the doubling clitic is unacceptable if the internal argument bears main prominence. This means that CD in Bulgarian falls not only under specificity but requires an additional condition. To prove this I will discuss briefly how CD interacts with definiteness and information structure of the sentence.

6 Clitic doubling and definites

Bulgarian allows CD of definite expressions, as in (15b).

(15) a. Ivan prodade kolata.
Ivan sold car.Def
'Ivan sold the car.'

b. Ivan ja_i prodade $kolata_i$.
Ivan it.Fem sold car.Def
'Ivan sold the car.'

The fact that definite DPs in Bulgarian may be doubled does not mean that they always can be. The examples in (16) and (17) show that not every definite expression may be clitic doubled.
As already mentioned, the referential status (specific reference) is a crucial condition for the appearance of doubling clitics.[12] This is illustrated in idiomatic expressions. Idioms even if they include definite expressions disallow doubling. This is evident from a comparison of the well-formedness of (16a) with the ill-formedness of (16b). In (16) the definite DP *života* 'the life' does not receive any theta-role from the verb and thus, has non-argumental status. In (16b) the clitic cannot establish identity, as it is dependent on its associate for descriptive content. Because in (16b) the argument-DP has a non-specific referent, CD is excluded. If the DP is doubled, the clitic suppresses the metaphorical in favour of the literal, strictly referential reading, which causes the ungrammaticality of the sentence.

(16) a. Te í otrovixa života.
They her poisoned life.Def
'They made her life {hell/a misery}.'

b. *Te í go_i otrovixa $života_i$.
They it her poisoned life.Def

The example in (17) delivers further evidence for the fact that definite expressions can not be doubled invariably. The definite object *rejsa* 'the bus' in (17) does not get a referential reading but forms part of an activity, i.e., it functions as part of the predicate. If part of the predicate interpretation of the direct object is available, CD is not allowed.

(17) Do you walk to school or do you take the bus?

Njama da vârvja peša, šte (*go) vzema rejsa.
Not walk with feet it.CL take bus.Def
'I don't walk, I take the bus (to school).'

[12] For more details see Werkmannn (in press).

The fact that the definite DP in (17) cannot be doubled is problematic for the specificity/presuppositionality approaches to doubling, if we assume with Enç (1991) and Diesing (1992) that all definites are specific and/or presuppositional. This would mean that all definite expressions must be clitic doubled because all of them are specific. As indicated by example (15), there are indisputably specific/presuppositional definites (and indefinites) in Bulgarian that need not and/or cannot be doubled. It is so far clear that CD of direct objects in Bulgarian cannot be adequately described only in terms of specificity. There is another relevant factor, which must be taken into consideration. In what follows I will show that CD in Bulgarian interacts in a systematic way with information structure marking the doubled argument-DP as [-focus].

7 Clitic doubling and Information Structure

In defining the feature [-focus], I will proceed indirectly by defining the notion focus first. Informally speaking, focus is viewed as that part of the sentence that the speaker wants to emphasize as important information in a given context. Consequently, background is that part of the sentence that is not emphasized and, therefore, marked as less important information in a given context, cf. Junghanns/Zybatow (1997). Following a long-established tradition in generative grammar, I assume that focus is a syntactic feature on phrases interpretable at both the LF and the PF interfaces as [+focus], cf. Jackendoff (1972), Brody (1990), Rosengren (1993), Junghanns/Zybatow (1997).

It is important to notice that focus is not defined as new information and the complement of focus, the background, is not necessarily old/familiar information. This can be clearly seen in examples like (18). Phrases denoting old/familiar referents – pronouns – can be either [+focus] as in (18a), or [-focus], as in (18b):[13]

(18) a. I like [$_F$ him].
b. Him [$_F$ I like].

Since every utterance has an informative segment and thus always has a focus it is plausible to assume that the [+focus] feature is the unmarked value in a markedness theory for natural language and that [-focus] is the marked one. The derivational syntax then makes this feature relevant. I claim that CD is one of the means by which this feature is licensed.

The next three sub-sections are devoted to a brief review of some recent ideas on the syntactic encoding of focus and to how focus interacts with CD of direct objects in Bulgarian.

7.1 Focus, wh-element and clitic doubling

Accent placement appears as one of the most important factors in the realization of the background-focus structure as it is both obligatory and unambiguously associated with (at least part of the) focus. On the one hand in broad focus the nuclear accent has to fall on the right-most constituent. On the other hand, accent on the right-most constituent gives rise to a broad focus interpretation. As a possible method for the establishment of the focus domain of isolated sentences one can use the embedding of the sentences into question-answer contexts. It is a well-known characteristic of *wh*-questions that they require an answer whose focus is the constituent corresponding to the *wh*-phrase. This insight is clearly reflected in sentences such as (19), which are felicitous in the context of the questions in (20).

[13] There are, of course, a number of correlations between cognitive status and information structure. Novel referents, for instance, are generally introduced in the discourse by appearing in the focal segment of a sentence rather than as part of the background, and background and/or topics must denote familiar referents of one kind or other.

(19) a. Ana pročete knigata.
Ana read book.Def
'Ann read the book

b. Ana pročete edna kniga.
Ana read a book
'Ann read a book.'

(20) a. What happened here?
b. What did Ana do?
c. What did Ana read?

The examples in (19) can realize an all focus structure or allow an intermediate or a narrow focus interpretation. Focus ambiguity is demonstrated in (21), where the square brackets indicate the size of the focus domain. In all three cases the nuclear accent falls on the direct object *a/the book*, since this is the most deeply embedded (or right-most) constituent in the VP.

(21) a. [$_F$ Ana [$_F$ pročete [$_F$ knigata]]]. b. [$_F$ Ana [$_F$ pročete [$_F$ edna kniga]]].

Additionally, the examples in (19) are appropriate in the context of the questions in (22).

(22) a. Who read the book?
b. What did Ana do with the book?

This is demonstrated in (23). Although (23) has the same constituent order SVO as (19), it correlates with a different intonational structure. The examples in (23) are a congruent answer to the question (22a) when the subject bears the main accent.

(23) a. [$_F$ Ana] pročete knigata.
Ann read the book
'ANN read the book.'

b. [$_F$ Ana] pročete edna kniga.
Ann read a book
'ANN read a book.'

The sentences in (24) are a felicitous answer to the question (22b) only with narrow focus reading on the verb.

(24) a. Anna [$_F$ pročete] knigata.
Ana read book.Def
'Ann READ the book.'

b. Anna [$_F$ pročete] edna kniga.
Ana read a book
'Ann READ a book.'

Doubling constructions as in (25a,b) are inappropriate as answers to object *wh*-question, as in (20c), as answer to questions, which are used to identify VP-focus, as in (20b), or even as answer to question of the type "what happened" (presentational context), as indicated by the examples (25c) and (25d).

(25) a. Ana ja$_i$ pročete knigata$_i$.
Ana it.Cl read book.Def
'Ann read the book.'

b. Ana ja$_i$ pročete [edna kniga]$_i$.
Ana it.Cl read a book
'Ann read a book.'

c. *[$_F$ Ana [$_F$ ja pročete [$_F$ knigata]]]. d. *[$_F$ Ana [$_F$ ja pročete [$_F$ edna kniga]]].

If the object is focused or belongs to the focus domain, doubling is not licensed. In fact, sentences with focus accent on a clitic doubled object are unacceptable, irrespective of the context they appear in.
However, (25a,b), the doubled version of (19), is possible as an answer to question like (22a) with narrow focus on the subject and to question like (22b) with narrow focus on the verb, as the examples in (26) and (27) show.

(26) [F Ana] ja pročete knigata.
Ann it.Cl read the book
'ANN read the book.'

(27) Anna ja [F pročete] knigata.
Ana it.Cl read the book
'Ann READ the book.'

The contrast between (19) and (25) is explained by the feature specification of the direct object: those in (19) are interpreted as [+focus] while those in (25) receive an interpretation as [-focus]. The examples above illustrate the fact that the distribution of doubled and non-doubled DPs differs in discourse. A sentence with a non-doubled argument-DP can be uttered out-of-the-blue, while the clitic doubled DP requires a specific context. Thus, the two constructions correspond to two different types of Information Structure. A non-doubled DP can be neutral focus, contrastive focus or background, while the clitic doubled one receives only the interpretation as background.[14]

The fact that indefinite as well as definite DPs in Bulgarian cannot be doubled, if they are narrowly focused or belong to the focus domain can be taken as evidence that CD in Bulgarian does not depend on its specification as [±definite]. The data show that in Bulgarian constructions involving doubled indefinites are fully grammatical if (and only if) the direct object is interpreted to be outside the focus domain.

All this points to the conclusion that CD in Bulgarian is not optional.[15] Argument-DPs, which represent narrow focus or are contained in the focus domain, cannot undergo doubling. By CD the argument-DPs form part of the background. Under this view, CD is an instance of excluding of an internal argument from the focus domain.

The following section shows that a similar conclusion can be drawn with respect to the interaction between CD and focus particles.

7.2 Focus particles and clitic doubling

Focus is most clearly brought out in association with so-called focus particles, such as *even* and *only*. In this section, I investigate the effects of their interaction with direct object CD.
In example (28a) the direct object *Plovdiv* appears in the scope of the focusing adverb und thus is marked as [+focus]. The same holds for the indefinite DP *edno selo* 'a village' in (28b). We expect that focused constituents cannot undergo doubling. That this is true is illustrated by the examples in (28).

(28) a. Papata (*go) poseti daže i Plovdiv (ne samo Sofia).
Pope.Def it.Cl visited even Plovdiv (not only Sofia)

b. Papata (*go) poseti daže i edno selo do Plovdiv.
Pope.Def it.Cl visited even a village near Plovdid

The general unacceptability of accented doubled objects in Bulgarian is due to the conflicting information conveyed by the information structural realization of these objects. Accent marks the object as focus, while doubling marks it as background.
The data with focus operators show that focused DPs can never be clitic doubled. In the next section, I will present some additional evidence that lends further support to this analysis.

[14] For the topic-comment dimension of information structure and the possibility of clitic doubled DP to be topic in Bulgarian see Werkmann (2003, in press).
[15] According to Rudin (1991, fn. 10), „clitic doubling ... is generally optional". Franks/King (2000: 251) state that "in Bulgarian, most clitic doubling is, at least superficially, optional."

7.3 Contrastive Focus and its interaction with clitic doubling

Contrastive focus differs from non-contrastive focus with respect to its communicative weight. Contrastive focus exactly like neutral focus expresses important information. But additionally it has emphatic meaning indicating the contrast with a contextually restricted set of alternatives. By contrastive focus the referential set of potential alternatives is closed (often restricted to two entities), whereby by neutral focus the corresponding set is open. In (29) the explicitly mentioned closed set contains two elements: {*John, Peter*}.

As Junghanns/Zybatow (1997) have argued for Russian, and Werkmann (2003) for Bulgarian, a contrastive focus feature can be assigned to any constituent in situ or after movement. Consequently, a contrastively focused constituent can appear in different positions in the clause. Examples (29a) and (29b) represent sentences with sentence-initial and sentence-final contrastive focus.[16]

(29) Who did Elena fire; Ivan or Petâr?

a. Elena (*go) uvolni [$_{Fc}$ Ivan]. Bg
Elena him.Cl fired-she [$_{Fc}$ Ivan].
'Elena fired Ivan.'

b. [$_{Fc}$ Ivan] (*go) uvolni Elena.
[$_{Fc}$ Ivan] him.Cl fired-she Elena
'Elena fired Ivan.'

In Bulgarian CD of contrastively focused argument-DPs is ruled out. Contrastive focus is characterized by prosodic prominence at PF, whereas the object clitics due to their weak phonological nature cannot be stressed. Thus, the ungrammaticality in (29) ensues if there is no agreement between the clitic and the doubled DP in terms of the information structural feature [±focus] which correlates with the prosodic feature [±stress].

The data thus systematically reveal that CD in Bulgarian has information structural consequences: the clitic doubled arguments are unambiguously interpreted as [-focus].

In this respect, direct object CD in Bulgarian differs from CD in Romanian and Spanish, which does not necessitate a [-focus] reading. As examples (30) and (31) indicate, clitic doubled direct object can be narrow focus, an option which is excluded for Bulgarian.

(30) Who are you looking for?

Il$_i$ caut pe [$_F$ ION]$_i$. Ro
Him.Cl look-for-I pe Ion
'I'm looking for Ion.'
(Gierling 1997:63, ex (6))

(31) Who did they nominate?

La$_i$ nombraron a [$_F$ Maria]$_i$. Sp
her nominated- they a Maria
'They nominated Maria.'
(Suñer 1988: 419, ex. (63))

On the other hand, the fact that a doubling clitic in Bulgarian identifies the doubled object as [-focus] is strongly reminiscent of so-called clitic right dislocation structures in French (32)

[16] If a sentence contains a contrastively focused constituent, realization of neutral focus is excluded.

and Italian (33), which are incompatible with [+focus]-reading of the right dislocated phrases (cf. Antinucci/Cinque 1977, Lambrecht 1981, Ashby 1988, Benincà 1988, Cinque 1990, Zubizarreta 1996, Rizzi 1997, Cecchetto 1999). In examples (32) and (33) the DP appears in a right-peripheral position with an intonational break obligatorily separating it from the rest of the sentence. In addition, the element immediately preceding it – *à midi* 'at lunch' in (32) and *domani* 'tomorrow' in (33) – bears main prominence (cf. Zubizarreta 1996), and thus functions as focus. The right-dislocated constituents *the cakes* in (32) and *il giornale* in (33) appear after the focus and represent post-focal material. In the Information Structure they are marked as [-focus] and are prosodically de-accented.[17]

(32) Je les$_i$ ai mangés à midi, les gâteaux$_i$. Fr
I them.Cl ate at lunch the cakes
'I ate the cakes at lunch.'

(33) Lo$_i$ porto domani, il giornale$_i$. It
It bring-I tomorrow, the newspaper.
'I will bring the newspaper tomorrow.'

This supports the view that the right-dislocated constituents in (32) and (33) are adjuncts rather than part of the core clause. The fact that in CD constructions in Bulgarian the doubled DPs may occur in clause-internal positions (cf. examples (5b) and (7)) and in positions where adjuncts are simply not tolerated, as was shown in Section 3, ex. (6), ultimately rules out a right dislocation approach to these constructions.

8 Summary

We have looked at Bulgarian direct object doubling constructions, focusing on the conditions on CD. It has been shown that CD in Bulgarian is not optional. The presence or absence of the doubling clitics affects the semantics and leads to different interpretations of the sentence. Thus, Bulgarian clitics have interpretative import, since they indisputably mark the argument-DPs they double as [-focus] in the information structure. This suggests that defocusing is, at least in part, encoded in the syntax for this language. The evidence discussed in this paper supports the view that Bulgarian CD is subject not only to specificity but also to a defocusing condition. It has turned out that under this condition the various grammatical and ungrammatical instances of CD can be successfully derived.[18]

References

Abney, Steven (1987): *The English noun phrase and its sentential aspect.* Doctoral Dissertation. MIT, Cambridge, Mass.

Alexandrova, Galia (1995): Pronominal Clitics as G(eneralized) F(amiliarity)-Licensing Agr°. In: *Formal Approaches to Slavic Linguistics.* 4, The Cornell Meeting, 1995, Michigan, Slavic Publications, Ann Arbor, 1997, 1-32.

Anagnostopoulou, Elena (1999): Conditions on CD in Greek. In: Riemsdijk, H. van (ed.): *Clitics in the Languages of Europe,* Mouton de Gruyter, Berlin/New York, 761-798.

Antinucci, Francesco and Cinque, Guglielmo (1977): Sull'ordine delle parole in italiano: l'emarginazione. In: *Studi di Grammatica Generativa* 6, 121-146.

[17] As has been noted by Ladd (1996: 178-179), the right-dislocated constituent is always pronounced as an intonational tag, which implies low pitch in ordinary statement intonation. Right-dislocation is a strategy for "achieving de-accenting".

[18] For the syntactic analysis of clitic doubling in Bulgarian see Janewa (2002) and Werkmann (2003, in press).

Arnaudova, Olga (2002): Clitic Left Dislocation and Argument Structure in Bulgarian. In: *Annual Meeting on Formal Approaches to Slavic Linguistics 10: The Philadelphia Meeting 2002*. Ann Arbor: Michigan Slavic Publications, 23-46.

Ashby; W. J. (1988): The syntax, pragmatics, and sociolinguistics of left- and right-dislocations in French. In: *Lingua* 75, 203-229.

Avgustinova, Tania (1997): *Word order and Clitics in Bulgarian*. Unpublished Ph. D. Dissertation, Saarbrücken, Germany.

Benincà, Paola (1988): L'ordine degli elementi della frase e le costruzioni marcate. In: Renzi, L. and Salvi, G. (Eds.): *Grande grammatica italiana di consultazione*. Il Mulino, Bologna, 115-119.

Borer, Hagit (1984): Parametric Syntax: Case studies in Semantic and Romance languages, Foris, Dordrecht.

Borer, Hagit (ed.) (1986): The Syntax of Pronominal Clitics, Syntax and Semantics 19, Academic Press.

Bródy, Michael (1990): Some remarks on the focus field in Hungarian. UCL Working Papers in Linguistics 2, 201-225.

Bródy, Michael (1995): Focus and Checking Theory. In: Kenese, István (ed.): *Levels and Structures, Approaches to Hungarian 5*. JATE, Szeged, 31-43.

Cardinaletti, Anna (2002): Against optional and zero clitics. Right Dislocation vs. Marginalization. In: *Studia Linguistica* 56;1, 29-57.

Cecchetto, Carlo (1999): A comparative analysis of left and right dislocation in Romance. In: *Studia Linguistica* 53;1, 40-67.

Cecchetto, Carlo (2000): Doubling structures and Reconstruction. In: *Probus* 12;1, 1-34.

Cinque, Guglielmo (1990): *Types of A' dependences*. Cambridge, MA: MIT Press.

Corver, Norbert and Delfitto, Denis (1999): On the nature of pronoun movement. In: Riemsdijk, H. van (ed.): *Clitics in the Languages of Europe*. Mouton de Gruyter, Berlin/New York, 799-861.

Diesing, Molly (1992): Indefinites. Cambridge, Mass.: MIT Press.

Dobrovie-Sorin, Carmen (1990): CD, Wh-movement and quantification in Romanian. In: *Linguistic Inquiry* 21, 351-397.

Drubig, Bernhard (2003): Toward a typology of focus and focus constructions. In: *Linguistics* 41;1, 1-50.

Enç, Murvet (1991): The semantics of specificity. In: *Linguistic Inquiry* 22,1-25.

Fodor, Janet and Sag, Ivan (1982): Referential and Quantificational Indefinites. In: *Linguistics and Philosophy* 5, 355-398.

Franks, Steven and King, Tracy Holloway (2000): *A Handbook of Slavic Clitics*. Oxford Studies in Comparative Syntax. New York, Oxford.

Gierling, Diana (1997): Clitic doubling, Specificity and Focus in Romanian. In: Black, J. R. and V. Motapanyane (eds.): Clitics, Pronouns and Movement. John Benjamins publishing company, 63-85.

Guentchéva, Zlatka (1994): *Thématisation de l'objet en bulgare*. Bern; Berlin; Frankfurt/M.; Paris; Wien. Peter Lang.

Heim, Irene (1982): The Semantics of Definite and Indefinite Noun Phrases. Doctoral dissertation, University of Massachusetts.

Jackendoff, Ray (1972): Semantic Interpretation in Generative Grammar. MIT Press, Cambridge MA.

Jacobs (1994): The syntax of focus and adverbials in German. In: Abraham, W. and S. de Meij (eds.): Topic, Focus and Configurationality. Amsterdam: John Benjamins, 103-127.

Jaeger, Florian and Gerassimova, Veronica (2002): Bulgarian word order and the role of the direct object clitic in LFG. In: Butt, M. and King, T.H. (eds.): *Proceedings of the LFG02 Conference*, downloadable at: http://www.stanford.edu/~tiflo/papers.html.

Jaeggli, Osvaldo (1986): Three issues in the theory of clitics: case, doubled NPs, and extraction. In: Borer, H. (ed.): *The Syntax of Pronominal Clitics*. Orlando: Academic Press, 15-42.

Janewa, Valja (= Werkmann, Valja) (2002): Object clitics and Information Structure. In: Mila Dimitrova-Vulchanova, Donald L. Dyer, Iliyana Krapova and Catherine Rudin (eds.): *Balkanistica Volume* 15, *2002. Papers from the Third Conference on Formal Approaches to South Slavic and Balkan Languages-3, Proceedings 1999*, Published for The South East European Studies Association, 271-293.

Junghanns, Uwe and Zybatow, Gerhild (1997): Syntax and Information Structure of Russian Clauses. In: Browne, E. W. et al. (eds.): *Annual Workshop on Formal Approaches to Slavic Linguistics. The Cornell Meeting 1995 (= Michigan Slavic Materials; 39)*. Ann Arbor, Michigan: Michigan Slavic Publications, 289-319.

Kayne; Richard (1994): *The Antisymmetry of Syntax*. The MIT Press Cambridge, Massachusetts London, England.

Ladd, D. Robert (1996): *Intonational Phonology*. Cambridge university Press, Cambridge.

Lambrecht, Knud (1981): *Topic, anti-topic and verb agreement in non-standard French* (Pragmatics and Beyond, II, 6). Amsterdam. Benjamins.

Lambrecht, Knud (1994): *Information Structure and Sentence Form*. Cambridge University Press, Cambridge.

Leafgren, John Robert (1992): Object Reduplication and Topicality in Bulgarian. Ph. D. Dissertation, University of Virginia.

Longobardi, Guiseppe (1994): Reference and proper names: A theory of N-movement in syntax and logical form. In: *Linguistic Inquiry* 26, 609-665.

Popescu, Alexandra (1997): Objektklitika und Argumentlinking im Rumänischen. Magisterarbeit. Heinrich-Heine-Universität Düsseldorf.

Rizzi, Luiggi (1997): The fine structure of the left periphery. In: Haegeman, L. (ed.): *Elements of Grammar*. Dordrecht, Kluwer, 281-337.

Rosengren, Inger (1993): Wahlfreiheit mit Konsequenzen – Scrambling, Topikalisierung und FHG im Dienste der Informationsstrukturierung. In: Marga Reis (Hrsg.): *Wortstellung und Informationsstruktur*. (= *Linguistische Arbeiten*, 306), Tübingen, Niemeyer, 251-312.

Rudin, Cathrin (1991): Topic and Focus in Bulgarian. In: *Acta Linguistica Hungarica* 40, 429-447.

Rudin, Cathrin (1997): Agro and Bulgarian pronominal clitics. In: Lindseth, M. and Franks, S. (eds.): *Formal Approaches to Slavic Linguistics: The Indiana Meeting 1996*, Ann Arbor: Michigan Slavic Publications. 224-252.

Sanchez, Liliana (2003): Clitic-doubling and the checking of Focus. Downloadable at: http://www.rci.rutgers.edu/~lsanchez/researchprojects/Focus_doubling.pdf

Schick, Ivanka (2000): Clitic doubling constructions in Balkan-Slavic Languages. In: Beukema, Frits and Marcel den Dikken (eds.): *Clitic Phenomena in European Languages*. Amsterdam/Philadelphia: Benjamins, 259-292.

Sportiche, Dominique (1996): Clitic Constructions. In: Rooryck, J. and L. Zaring (eds.): *Phrase Structure and the Lexicon*. Dordrecht: Kluver Academic Publishers, 213-277.

Suñer, Margarita (1988): The Role of Agreement in clitic-doubled constructions. In: *Natural Language and Linguistic Theorie* 6, 391-434.

Uriagereka, Juan (1995): Some aspects of the Syntax of Clitic Placement in Western Romance. In: *Linguistic Inquiry* 26, 79-123.

Werkmann, Valja (2003): *Objektklitika im Bulgarischen*. (= *studia grammatica 57*). Berlin: Akademie Verlag.

Werkmann, Valja (in press): Clitic doubling constructions in Bulgarian. To appear in: Steube, Anita (ed.): *Information Structure: „Theoretical and Empirical Aspects"* (= *Language, Context and Cognition*, Vol. I), Berlin/New York: de Gruyter (2003), 30 pp.

Zubizarreta, Maria Luisa (1996): *Word order, Prosody and Focus*. Manuscript, USC.

Zybatow, Gerhild and Junghanns, Uwe (1998): *Topiks im Russischen.* (= *Sprache und Pragmatik*, 47). Lund.

Jacek Witkoś, Poznań

Phases, Agree and Genitive of Negation in Polish

1. Introduction.

This paper is inspired by an observation made in Błaszczak (2001) that, on the basis of examples such as (7) below, Long Distance Genetive of Negation (GoN) in Polish is essentially entirely incompatible with Chomsky's (1998, 1999, 2001) hypothesis concerning derivations proceeding in phases.

As an introduction, we first present the basic tenets of the single cycle syntax approach, the empirical domain of the Genitive of Negation in Polish and, ultimately, the reason for the incompatibility of the two. In subsequent sections we present some conditions which a system based on single cycle syntax should meet to account for GoN.

2. Probes, goals and phases.

Chomsky proposes that the process of computation proceeds in stages comprising a minimum number of Lexical Items (a subarray) consisting of a lexical category and a functional category (CFC).[1] The number of LIs in a subarray is sufficient to build vP, the verbal predicate phrase licensing all the arguments, and CP, the clause, augmenting the argument structure with the tense, thematic prominence (subject-topic) and force specifications. Once the process of construction of a phase is completed, or at the latest by the time the next higher phase is completed, the phase undergoes operation Transfer, feeding PF and LF. Thus the memory load of the computation itself is lessened and once a given phase is built, the computational machinery begins to construct another phase. Technically, once a given phase is completed, any access to it from the outside is severely limited. This property is known as the Phase Impenetrability Condition (PIC):[2]

(1) Phase Impenetrability Condition (Chomsky 1999:10):
The domain of H is not accessible to operations at ZP, but only H and its edge.
Where: ZP is the least strong phase and the edge consists of specifiers.

Feature checking is said to rely on the relation of case-agreement, based on c-command, between a functional head, whose label acts as probe, and a substantial category, whose label is goal. Features are checked if they match, if the probe and the goal are active, that is they

---

[1] Chomsky considers only the so-called Core Functional Categories (CFCs) such as the Complementizer (Comp) and the light verb (v). He does not rule out the possibility that there should be other functional categories such as Determiner (D) or elements from the articulated left periphery of the clause in the sense of Rizzi (1997) or Cinque (1999). If such functional categories are admitted, one should wonder as to what phase status they should have.

[2] The description of the subarray that feeds the construction of a phase is as follows (Chomsky (1998:20): The next step is to characterize the subarrays LA_i that can be selected for active memory. LA_i should determine a natural syntactic object SO, an object that is relatively independent in terms of interface properties. On the "meaning side", perhaps the simplest and most principled choice is to take SO to be the closest syntactic counterpart to a proposition: either a verb phrase in which all theta roles are assigned or a full clause including tense and force. Call these objects "propositional". Considerations on the "sound side" support the choice, given properties of the kind mentioned earlier distinguishing CP from TP, which extend to vP (fronting, extraposition, pseudoclefting, response fragments, etc.). [...] Take a phase of a derivation to be a syntactic object SO derived in this way by choice of LA_i. A phase is CP or vP, but not TP or a verbal phrase headed by H lacking φ–features and therefore not entering into Case/agreement checking: neither finite TP nor unaccusative/passive verbal phrase is a phase.

both still have unchecked uninterpretable features and if the goal is the minimal search space (D(P)) of the probe, practically within its sister constituent:

(2) Matching and Agree (Chomsky 1998:38):

a. Matching is feature identity

b. D (P) is the sister of P

c. Locality reduces to 'closest c-command'

(3) Matching and Agree (Chomsky 1999:4):

a. Probe and goal must both be active for Agree to apply;

b. α must have a complete set of [+φ] features (it must be φ complete) to delete uninterpretable features of the paired matching element β.

Case licensing, for example Accusative, is performed in situ by agreement between the probe v and DP_{OB}:

(4) $[_{vP}\ v_{[+\varphi]}\ [_{VP}\ V\ DP_{OB[+\varphi,\ +case]}]]$

A transitive v is said to have a full set of [+φ] features, so the feature [+case] in the DP is deleted and the case is valued as Accusative. Any displacement of the object DP to the edge of vP is not attributed to the case-agreement relation as such but rather to the (parametrically determined) presence or absence of the [+EPP] feature on v (or a functional head in general). So the [+EPP] feature and the spec/head relation is now dissociated from the case-agreement relation, yet the [+EPP] feature can be satisfied only by constituents, which are visible to the head (probe) with the [+EPP] feature. Because visible means still active, i.e. carrying an unchecked uninterpretable feature, the same head (probe) is involved in both case agreement and forcing external merge.

3. Empirical Domain of the Genitive of Negation.

For readers unfamiliar with the phenomenon of the Genitive of Negation in Polish, here are some rudimentary facts.[3] In simple clauses it is obligatory whenever the verb is negated and the nominal object would otherwise appear in Accusative in an affirmative sentence:

(5) a. Maria pije kawę.
Maria drinks coffee-ACC
'Maria drinks coffee.'

b. Maria nie pije kawy.
Maria not drinks coffee-GEN/*ACC.
'Maria does not drink coffee.'

Negation in the main clause causes GoN in the embedded infinitive, as long as the infinitive is not introduced by any complementizer or Wh-phrase. If there is any CP-related material at the

[3] This is only a very sketchy, yet at this point sufficient presentation of the data. For a more careful review of the data see further parts of this paper and Witkoś (1999) and Przepiórkowski (1999).

head of the infinitive (6c-d), Long GoN is cancelled and the embedded nominal object appears in Accusative:

(6) a. Maria nie mogła wypić kawy.
Maria not could drink coffee-GEN/*ACC
'Maria could not drink coffee.'

b. Maria nie pozwoliła Janowi pić kawy.
Maria not let John drink coffee-GEN/*ACC
'Maria did not let John drink coffee.'

c. Maria nie pozwoliła [$_{CP}$ żeby Jan pił kawę].
Maria not let so that John should drink coffee-ACC/*GEN
'Maria did not allow for the fact that John should drink coffee.'

d. Maria nie wie [$_{CP}$ kiedy Jan wypije kawę].
Maria not knows when John will drink coffee-ACC/*GEN
'Maria does not know when John will drink coffee.'

From the point of view of our analysis, a very relevant aspect of the Long Distance Genitive of Negation is the fact that it does not distinguish between the infinitives in the control and raising contexts. In example (6a), it affects the object embedded in the infinitive selected by a raising verb (epistemic modal) and in (6b) it affects the object embedded under an object control verb.[4]

4. Long Distance GoN and phases: the problem.

Following this brief introduction, consider a classic case of Long Distance GoN: negation on the control verb forces Genitive on the embedded DP object:

(7) a. Maria nie chce wypić kawy.
Maria not wants drink coffee-GEN/*ACC
'Maria doesn't want to drink coffee.'

b. ... [$_{NegP}$ Neg-P [$_{VP}$ ... [$_{CP}$ [$_{TP}$ PRO$_{[+\varphi]}$ [$_{vP}$ t$_{PRO}$ ... DP$_{OB}$-G$_{[+\varphi]}$]]]]]]

Błaszczak (2001) follows the following plausible assumption, based on previous analyses in Willim (1990), Dziwirek (1997) and Witkoś (1998): if Chomsky's recent hypotheses are correct, Genitive on the object should be caused by some case-agreement relation involving the object as the Goal (DP$_{OB}$-G) and matrix negation as the Probe (Neg-P). She observes that this is, however, exactly the type of relation prohibited by the Phase Impenetrability Condition (PIC). As example (7b) shows, the goal DP$_{OB}$ is not at the edge of the strong phase vP, so it ceases to be accessible to any probing past the point at which embedded CP has been constructed. Even if Neg were assumed to be a part of the matrix vP phase, it is separated from its purported goal by the CP phase and the embedded vP phase. Błaszczak concludes, to

[4] Note that example (6c), where the Long GoN cannot appear, illustrates the fact that GoN cannot be regarded as A'- type dependency, as Wh-movement can take place across the boundary of the subjunctive clause in Polish:

Co chcesz [$_{CP}$ żeby studenci przeczytali t na jutro]?
what (you) want so that students read for tomorrow
'What do you want the students to read for tomorrow?'

our mind correctly, that phase-based minimalism is unable to account for the phenomenon of Long Distance GoN.[5]

It must be said that there is another conceptual problem for GoN in an approach based on the single cycle; that is an approach discarding the separation of the overt and covert cycles in the derivation.[6] Even if we lump the whole example (7) into a single phase, so that PIC is rendered inoperative, there is the issue of the Defective Intervention Constraint (DIC), also exemplified in (7b); an interference in the case-agreement relation between Neg-P and DP_{OB}-G could come from PRO, whose [+φ] features are interpretable, hence visible to the Probe, yet its uninterpretable case feature is checked, which makes it an invalid goal, though a valid intervener (β) in the case-agreement relation between α and γ, (Chomsky 1998:38-39):[7]

(8) $*\alpha > \beta > \gamma$

It appears that the status of PRO is equally relevant for any case agreement relation taking place across it, as the status of intervening projections (phases).

5. Probes, Goals and GoN: a proposal.

We now present an outline of our proposal, based on two key ideas, the first that derivational phases correspond to the constituent level of CP and the other that the properties of the relations involving Agree, Match, Probe and Goal may be more complex than originally assumed.

5.1. Match, check, delete and resurrect.

Chomsky (1998, 1999, 2001) suggests that there are no case features per se on the functional head that checks them, rather the case feature of a DP is checked and deleted when valued by a set of full agreement features on a c-commanding probe. We propose to keep the [+case] feature on functional heads and try to capitalize on two aspects of the probe-goal relation: the proposal that only a full set of agreement features checks case and that there is a phase internal process of resurrection of checked features.[8]

Narrow syntax is driven by the need to eliminate uninterpretable features, so once the case feature of the goal is valued (eliminated) the DP is frozen in place and inaccessible to further case-agreement relations.

(9) Features involved in object case checking under agreement:

a. Probe: v {uninterpretable [+φ] features}

b. Goal: DP_{OB} {interpretable [+φ] features; uninterpretable case feature}

---

[5] Note that the problem of Long Distance GoN remains even if it is assumed that the object is moved to the edge of vP in overt syntax (if Polish has Object Shift), as the edge of the embedded vP phase is visible only up to the CP level and for the object to be visible to the matrix Neg, it would have to be at the edge of the CP phase, an empirically untenable position.

[6] Chomsky's is not the first single cycle system of minimalist grammar. Earlier proposals to this effect were made in Brody (1995, 1996) and Groat and O'Neil (1996).

[7] Chomsky (1998:38) comments on the Defective Intervention Constraint: "We therefore have the possibility of a defective intervention constraint [in structure (8), J.W.], where > is c-command, β and γ match the probe α, but β is inactive, so that the effects of matching are blocked."

[8] So we implicitly reject the following assumption, Chomsky (1999:4): "Structural case is not the feature of the probes (T, v) but it deletes under agreement if the probe is appropriate – φ complete. Case itself is not matched but deletes under matching of [+φ] features."

As for the timing of the case-agreement relation, valuing and elimination of uninterpretable features is supposed to take place as soon as a valid probe-goal configuration arises. In a sense then, feature checking is subject to Pesetsky's (1989) Earliness Principle rather than Chomsky's (1995) Procrastinate; as soon as features match, they should be maximally checked and deleted, subject to the following principle (Chomsky 2000:12):

(10) Maximize matching effects.

This principle seems an obvious and natural consequence of the cycle and the Extension condition on structure building but leads to intriguing consequences with defective probes.

Let us consider Chomsky's view of heads that are defective probes and do not have a full set of agreement features. Chomsky (1999:14) discusses the following example in great detail:

(11) [$_{\beta}$ There seem to have been [$_{\alpha}$ caught several fish]].

The derivation involves two cycles, corresponding to the particpial phrase (α) and the matrix TP (β). On the first cycle the participle and the object become involved in the probe-goal relation, manifested in many languages through morphological agreement, sometimes including agreement for case. The participle has an incomplete set of [+φ] features: {number, gender and case}, but not [+person]. Although the participle c-commands the object, a valuing of the feature [+case] on both the participle and DP_{OB} cannot take place, as the participial probe is incomplete. On the other hand though, DP_{OB} has a full set of (interpretable) [+φ] features, so the incomplete [+φ] features of the participle are matched, valued and deleted. By the end of cycle α DP_{OB} is still an active goal, as its case feature has not been valued and deleted. Technically speaking, the participle should be inactive, although its [+case] feature has not been valued. Why? Because only unchecked uninterpretable [+φ] features render probes active.[9] At stage β, a complete probe T with a full set of [+φ] features engages in two case-agreement relations: with DP_{OB} and the participle. The former relation is fully legitimate: the probe and the goal are within the same strong phase, the probe c-commands the goal, the probe is complete and the goal is still active. How is the probe-goal relation between T and the participle possible? Chomsky claims that although valued and deleted, [+φ] features of the participle are eliminated from the computation only at the strong phase level (matrix CP), as part of operation Transfer to PF. So at stage β they are still visible to the T probe and render the participle active as a goal of the case-agreement relation.[10] The most significant aspect of the analysis of (11) is that a syntactic object with its [+φ] features valued and deleted in one case-agreement relation can be resurrected and still active in the derivation as long as the second case-agreement relation takes place within the same strong phase.

Any non-local relation of case agreement raises the issue of intervention effects. In the concrete example at hand, does the participle (an incomplete probe) screen the DP object from T (a complete probe)? The answer is no, as the intervention effect is induced only by complete probes and complete goals, the incomplete ones do not value case and allow for maximal matching effects. One illustration of this phenomenon is given in (11) above and another is provided by the expletive construction below:

(12) we expect [there to arrive a man].

---

[9] Chomsky (1999:4): "For the case-agreement systems, the uninterpretable features are [+φ] features for the probe (verbal elements, including participles, J.W.) and structural case of the goal N. [+φ] features of N are interpretable; hence N is active only when it has structural case."

[10] It seems that Chomsky implicitly uses the notion of features checked and 'marked for deletion' proposed in Pesetsky and Torrego (2000).

In (12) the DP argument of the embedded unaccusative verb is said to be assigned Accusative case by matrix v. The expletive *there* is assumed to have only the feature [+person], so it does not value the set of complete [+φ] features of matrix v and they are able to probe over the (chain of the) expletive within the same phase and match and value the case feature of the object.

5.2. The Genitive of Negation: a proposal.

We try to capitalize on the idea that features marked for deletion are still accessible within the strong phase and propose an account based on slightly different premises. Chomsky's classification of probes into complete and defective ones is too coarse grained. We propose that there are thee types of probes:

(13) a. complete: $T_{[+\varphi,\ case]}$, $v_{[+\varphi,\ case]}$

b. near complete: $v_{[+\varphi]}$

c. incomplete: $T_{[+person]}$, $Neg_{[+case]}$

d. a successful case-agreement relation resulting in valuing case involves an active goal and a simple or 'split' probe equipped with complete [+φ] features and the [+case] feature, related to each other within ZP, a strong phase (ZP = CP):

i) $[_{ZP}\ldots T/v_{[+\varphi,\ case]} \ldots DP_{[+case]}]$

ii) $[_{ZP}\ldots Neg_{[+case]} \ldots v_{[+\varphi]} \ldots DP_{[+case]}]$

iii) $*[_{ZP}\ldots T_{[+person]} \ldots PRT_{[-\varphi]} \ldots DP_{[+case]}]$

Crucially, the difference between (13dii) and (13diii) is that the combined 'split' probe consisting of a defective T and the participle in the latter case is still short of feature [+case] and is thus still incomplete.[11]

The rationale behind our move is that Polish seems to differ from English in that the task of case licensing, performed in English by a single head is spread onto two heads: the verb and Polarity/Negation. Chomsky (1995, 1998, 1999) claims that relevant features are introduced into the computational procedure via lexical items that carry them. Consider the

---

[11] An empirical motivation for introducing an additional feature in the case-agreement relation, here called [+case], rather than lumping two defective probes into a complete one, comes from examples like the one below:

(i) John is believed $[_{TP}$ t $T_{[+pers]}$ to have been mugged$_{[-\varphi]}$ t].

Here, the combination of two defective probes: the participle with number and gender features and the embedded Tense with the person feature may not result in a successful case-agreement relation. The case of the embedded object is valued by the matrix complete probe T.

The feature composition suggested above also prevents licensing of GoN in a passive construction:

(ii) Jan nie został pobity t_{Jan}
John-NOM not was beaten up

(iii) $[_{TP}\ T_{[+case,\ +\varphi]}\ [_{NegP}\ Neg_{[+case]}[_{VP}\ V/Prt_{[+number,\ +gender]}\ DP_{[+case,\ +\varphi]}]]]$

The combination of two incomplete probes: Neg equipped with feature [+case] and the participle Prt with an incomplete set of [+φ] features does not produce a legitimate full 'split' probe able to value the case of the object in its base position.

following assumption: the probe can value case on the goal DP only if it carries four features, instead of three usually regarded as the complete [+φ] set: person, number gender and [+x]. There is a parametric option according to which either all relevant features are assigned to one head or more than one head, English shows it in (14a) and Polish in (14b):[12]

(14) a. $[\ldots P_{[+pers,+num,+gen,+x]} \ldots DP_{[+case]} \ldots]$

b. $[\ldots P^{1}_{[+x]} \ldots P^{2}_{[+pers,+num,+gen]} \ldots DP_{[+case]} \ldots]$

As a consequence, the unitary probe can value case on the DP in (14a) and the split probe can achieve the same goal in (14b): first the features of P^2 (inexhaustively) match those of the goal and get checked on the probe, in accordance with the Maximize Checking Principle in (10). The case feature on the goal DP is not checked, as P^2 is still incomplete. The features on P^2 are checked but disappear only at the level of the strong phase. Hence they are still visible when P^1 has been merged and together with the feature [+x] on P^2 they can still affect the goal. Note that we are following the idea implicit in the analysis of example (11) above, namely, that checked formal features are still live and accessible until the point of Transfer at the end of the strong phase. Naturally, we predict that P^1 and P^2 can constitute a split probe only if they are both placed within the same derivational phase. Because feature [+x] is necessary for case-agreement we call it simply the [+case] feature, though we could as well have pleased ourselves just with [+x].

In sum, the checking of the case of the object in Polish involves an amalgamated probe consisting of two heads that complement each other, separately they are unable to check any case but jointly they can valuate the case of the object.

In concrete terms we propose the following representation of the Polish vP area:

(15) $[_{FP}\ F_{[+case]}\ [_{vP}\ v_{[+\varphi]}\ [_{VP}\ V\ DP_{[+case,\ +\varphi]}]]]$

In order to make our picture empirically adequate, we introduce a non CFC (Core Functional Category) F as the head of the Polarity Phrase (Positive or Negative). The idea is that Polish transitive verbs are defective and do not show a full set of features relevant for valuing of case. We assume for concreteness that v has a full set of [+φ] features, in contrast to the passive participle, but the [+case] feature is missing from it.[13] However, the head of the

[12] Optional GoN in Russian can be treated as a case of instantiating both (14a) and (14b) in one system of grammar as options. We must leave this issue for further analysis.

[13] The idea that there could be 'split' Probes or 'half' Probes is not new and was explicitly considered at the previous stage of the minimalist enterprise. Chomsky (1995) observed that unaccusatives and participles showed agreement features and, judging from the fact that they were supposed to include a 'bare' V rather than the combination of v-V (VB), he suggested that V could be the locus of agreement features, while v could be the locus of the case feature. According to this suggestion, a transitive verb would be a combination of the following heads and feature labels:

(i) $[_{vP}\ v_{[+case]}\ [_{VP}\ V_{\ [+\varphi]}\ ]]$

Our view of Polish transitive verbs and Polarity Phrases as involving 'split' Probes is related to this idea. The notion of a 'split' probe is also inherent in Agr-based minimalism. For example think of the feature checking of the subject with Agr and T in place but in the context of case-agreement under c-command rather than Attract F:

(ii) $[_{AgrP}\ Agr_{[+\varphi]}\ [_{TP}\ T_{[+case]}\ [\ DP_{Sub[+case,\ +\varphi]} \ldots]]]$

Agr and T act jointly as a 'split' probe. It seems then that 'split' probes were known in minimalism, though the name was not.

Polarity Phrase F is equipped with a missing [+case] feature: when F is set to the positive value, the case on the object comes out as Accusative, when F is Neg, it values the case as Genitive. The near-complete probe v has all its [+φ] features matched by the DP object and these features can delete without valuing the case of the object, in line with the maximization principle in (10). Importantly, the object is still active in the process of computation. Once F is merged into the syntactic object, it acts as a complementary probe and becomes involved in the probe-goal relation with the (still active) object. In a way v intervenes and provides the necessary (deleted but still visible phase internally) features.[14]

Let us point out general features of the system we have proposed so far:

(16) a. Probes can be either uniform (say T), or 'split' F/Neg-v, subject to a parametric option for a given language.

b. F/Neg-v is a 'split' Probe;

c. A 'split' probe can be involved in relation Agree only with a Goal that is c-commanded by both 'half' probes.

d. 'Split' probing is operational only if the 'half' probes are placed within the same derivational phase.

Our assumption in (16d) ultimately aims at accounting for Long Distance GoN.

We should now present the outline of the GoN within the single cycle and next we consider possible problems, mainly in form of two cornerstone assumptions of Chomsky's recent work: the PIC and the DIC.

5.3. Long GoN and single cycle syntax.

Witkoś (1998) and Błaszczak (2001) classify long GoN cases into two categories: raising constructions and control constructions. Let us start with the less problematic case of a raising construction:

5.3.1. GoN and epistemic Modals:

(17) a. Jan nie może teraz pić kawy.
John not may now drink coffee-GEN
'John may not be drinking coffee now.'

b. [$_{CP}$ [$_{TP}$ Jan [$_{NegP}$ nie [$_{VP}$ może [$_{TP}$ t teraz [$_{vP}$ t pić kawy]]]]]].

c. [$_{CP}$ [$_{TP}$ Jan T $_{[+\varphi, case]}$ [$_{NegP}$ Neg $_{[+case]}$ [$_{VP}$ [$_{TP}$ t$_{Jan}$ T [$_{vP}$ t$_{Jan}$ v$_{[+\varphi]}$ kawy]]]]]]

As example (17c) shows the CP constituent, to be treated as a simple phase, includes the following set of relevant probes and goals: the near complete 'half' probe v of the embedded verb, the defective Probe T of the embedded clause, the other 'half' Probe Neg of the main clause and the full Probe T of the main clause. We also indicate copies of the subject in its thematic and intermediate positions.

A sort of 'split' probing is implicit in the following quote from Chomsky (2001:13): "T functions in the case-agreement system only if it is selected by C, in which case it is also complete. [...] Hence T enters feature checking only in the C-T configuration and [...] the two phase heads C and v are the operative elements."

[14] Intervention effects, if relevant phase internally, are induced by complete probes and goals. As probe v is technically speaking, still incomplete, it does not induce negative intervention effects.

We assume that the modal construction in (17) above involves two clauses.[15] Descriptively speaking, negation in the subordinating clause forces Genitive on the nominal object of the embedded verb. How does the licensing of case take place? The Genitive is licensed in the relation of case-agreement by the 'split' Probe Neg/v. The transitive verb is defective in that it does not have a [+case], though it has a full set of [+φ] features. The missing feature [+case] is provided by the Neg head in the subordinating clause. Both 'half' Probes c-command the Goal, the object DP. As both Probes are in the same phase, the cycle is not violated.

Two points of our analysis are worth emphasizing: it contravenes Chomsky's proposals in two aspects; we assume 'split' probes while his system does not and reject the claim that vP is a strong phase. If vP is not taken to be a strong phase, its interior is accessible to external probing to the next strong phase (root CP).[16] There are two relevant maximal projections between T and Neg on the one hand and embedded vP on the other, neither of them a strong phase: matrix VP headed by a raising verb, so defective, and the TP infinitive, also defective. Hence the matrix T Probe can access the subject in its thematic position and Neg can access the object.

With PIC out of the way, we ask whether either copy of *Jan* interfere with the 'split' Probe/Goal relation. As Chomsky (1995) claims only complete A-chains act as interveners and cause DIC effects and NP traces do not. Consequently, neither trace of *Jan* causes problems for the Neg/v probing.[17]

Consider an example of the same type, also involving subject raising, to illustrate a complication that must be presented before we move on to control constructions.

(18) a. Jan może teraz nie pić kawy.
John may now not drink coffee-GEN
'John may not be drinking coffee now.'

b. $[_{CP}$ $[_{TP}$ Jan $[_{VP}$ może $[_{TP}$ teraz $[_{TP}$ t_{Jan} $[_{NegP}$ nie $[_{vP}$ t_{Jan} pić kawy]]]]]]].

c. $[_{CP}$ $[_{TP}$ Jan $T_{[+\varphi]}$ $[_{VP}$ $[_{TP}$ t_{Jan} T $[_{NegP}$ $Neg_{[+pers]}$ $[_{vP}$ t_{Jan} $v_{[+\varphi]}$ kawy]]]]]]

The relevant probe/goal relations in (18) involve the object DP as a goal of the 'split' Neg/v probe and the subject as the goal of the complete matrix T probe. Both components of the 'split' probe c-command the object and they are very close to each other, as close as in a regular simple tensed clause. Thus the licensing of Genitive case is much more local than in example (17); specifically, neither the positive or negative content of the head F in the subordinating clause has any impact on the case valuation of the embedded object. At this point the following technical question emerges: if embedded negation in (18) forces Genitive, how to prevent embedded Accusative licensing if the content of F is positive? In other words example (17) could have the following representation:

(19) $[_{CP}$ $[_{TP}$ Jan $T_{[+\varphi]}$ $[_{NegP}$ $Neg_{[+case]}$ $[_{VP}$ $[_{TP}$ t_{Jan} T $[_{FP}$ $Pos_{[+case]}$ $[_{vP}$ t_{Jan} $v_{[+\varphi]}$ kawy]]]]]]

Observe that the technical, but potentially lethal, problem is that the presence of the positive F 'half' Probe equipped with the [+case] feature in the embedded clause would mean completion of the F/v 'split' Probe and accusative case valuing for the object DP irrespective of the presence of negation in the matrix clause, contrary to fact.

We acknowledge this problem and propose the following postulate:

---

[15] See Błaszczak (2001) and Witkoś (1998) for a justification of this view.

[16] Alternatively, as suggested by a reviewer, vP could be treated as a strong phase only when complemented by the F probe.

[17] A reviewer points out that the idea that incomplete chains constitute non-interveners carries a non-derivational flavor. We acknowledge this fact and admit that our system, just like Chomsky's, combines traits of both the derivational and the representational approach.

(20) As a default option, embedded bare infinitives in Polish do not have [+Positive] content of the F Probe.

We realize that we should do better but our assumption in (20) effectively excludes (19) as a possible representation of (17) and helps us avoid unwanted complexities in the derivation.[18] Effectively, principle (20) forces either absence of F or presence of F/Neg in the embedded infinitive clause.[19]

5.3.2. Control Constructions

We propose to solve the problem of the Defective Intervention Effects caused by PRO in configurations of obligatory control through the adoption of the control-as-movement hypothesis of Hornstein (1999, 2000, 2001).

We also submit that vP should not be treated as a strong phase and that only CPs successfully meet all the criteria for phases. We cannot present any justification for these claims here for lack of space but see Witkoś (forthcoming) for a detailed analysis. As a preview, consider two facts.

First, consider the derivation below:

(21) a. Which book do you think Susan lost?

b. $[_{CP}$ [which book]$_i$ … $[_{vP}$ t_3 … $v_{[+EPP]}$ … $[_{CP}$ t_2 … $[_{vP}$ t_1 … v … t_i]]]]

Śmiecińska (2003: 63-64) challenges the minimalist rationale for such derivations, asking why the matrix v should have the [+EPP] feature. For instance, there is no indication of reconstruction into the position marked t_3 and thus no independent evidence for it.

Second, Chomsky (1998:22) finds support for the vP as the phase in reconstruction facts. In example (22) the restriction on the Wh operator can only be interpreted in the position marked with t at the edge of vP:

(22) [which of the papers {that he_1 wrote for Ms. $Brown_2$}] did every $student_1$ t get her_2 t* to grade e*?

---

[18] This assumption helps to avoid the problem of look-ahead or backtracking in the derivation and case re-checking, presented in Witkoś (1998).

[19] Przepiórkowski (1999:6-10) provides examples of optional Long GoN:

(i) Nie mógłbyś przestać studiować algebry/?algebrę?
not could (you)give up studying algebra-Gen/?Acc
'Could you not give up studying algebra?'

(ii) Nie sposób sprawdzić im biletów/?bilety.
No way (to)check their tickets-Gen/?Acc
'There is no way to check their ticket.'

All the cases can be accounted for by the assumption that Polish infinitive clauses may, optionally, be equipped with the head F/Pos constituting a part of a 'split' probe valuing the case of the object as Accusative. Thus, we can modify our postulate in (20).

(iii) $[_{TP}$ $T_{[+\varphi]}$ $[_{FP}$ F:Pos/$Neg_{[+case]}$ $[_{vP}$ DP_{SU} $v_{[+\varphi]}$ $[_{TP}$ $T_{[+\varphi]}$ $[_{FP}$ F(Pos)$Neg_{[+case]}$ $[_{vP}$ DP_{SU} $v_{[+\varphi]}$ $[_{VP}$ V DP_{OB}]]]]

When F/Pos appears in the structure of the infinitive, the case of DP_{OB} is valued as Accusative; when there is no F/Pos in the infinitive c-commanding Neg takes over as the missing part of the 'split' probe and Genitive is licensed.

The presence of t is motivated by the PIC and the vP strong phase status. Yet, Chomsky himself hints at a different possibility in several places. He repeatedly claims (inspired by Reinhardt 1995 and Fox 1999, 2000) that optional features are present in the derivation if they make an interpretative difference. Thus an optional EPP feature on v can facilitate a bleeding of Principle C, instrumental for receiving a particular interpretation at the LF interface independently of the strong phase status of vP.

5.3.3. DIC and subject control contexts.

Chomsky's comments pertaining to the DIC effects and their cancellation by traces are of direct relevance to our discussion of Long GoN.[20]

Adoption of Hornstein's control-as-movement hypothesis brings a twofold bonus: cancellation of minimality problems in subject control configurations and identical treatment of raising and control infinitives as only TPs. Here is how example (7) can be handled:

(23) $[_{TP}$ Maria T $[_{NegP}$ $Neg_{[+case]}$ $[_{VP}$ t_{Maria} chce $[_{TP}$ t_{Maria} T $[_{vP}$ t_{Maria} $v_{[+\varphi]}$ $DP_{OB[+case]}]]]]]]$.

With (23) treated as a case of A-movement, there is no PRO, or to be more precise, there is no argument chain of PRO separating probe Neg from v and DP_{OB}. The intervening element is now only an incomplete A-chain, a series of traces (copies) of the subject. We assume that the embedded T, though defective, has the [+EPP] feature. This fact forces the presence of one link of the subject chain in the embedded subject position. Now, as argued above, copies do not cause defective intervention effects (only complete A-chains do) and they do not disrupt relations of case-agreement and Move.

5.3.4. DIC and object control contexts.

Now the only real problem left is the issue of the defective Intervention Effect in cases previously analyzed as object control. Here the full A-chain of the indirect object intervenes between Neg and the embedded v and DP_{OB}:

(24) a. Maria nie kazała Janowi czytać książek.
Maria not told Jan (to)read books
'Maria did not tell Jan to read books.'

b. $[_{CP}$ $[_{TP}$ Maria $[_{NegP}$ Neg $_{[+case]}$ …$Janowi_{DAT}$ $[_{TP}$ t_{Janowi} T $[_{vP}$ t_{Janowi} $[v_{[+\varphi]}$ $książek_{GEN}]]]]]]$

Our solution is based on the idea that inherently case-marked DPs are not defective interveners. We have been assuming that there is a parametric difference between languages with quirky case-marked DPs that still require licensing of structural case and the ones whose inherent case-marked DPs do not participate in structural case licensing.

The idea that Polish belongs to the latter group seems corroborated by some facts in passive constructions with double object verbs. According to the distinction drawn in McGinnis (1998), Polish shows the so-called long passive, while English shows the short passive:

(25) a. John was sent five apples.

b. ? * Five apples were sent John.

[20] DIC Effects (Chomsky 1999:13):
Only the head of the A-chain (equivalently the whole chain) blocks matching under the Minimal Link Condition. Traces do not interfere with matching of other probes and goals.

(26) a. * Jan został przesłany dwa jabłka.
John was sent two apples

b. Dwa jabłka zostały przesłane Janowi.
two apples were sent John-DAT
'Two apples were sent to John.'

(27) $[_{TP}\ \alpha\ T_{[+EPP,+\varphi]}\ [_{vP}\ DP_{IO[+\varphi]}\ [_{v'}\ V\ DP_{DO[+\varphi,\ +case]}]]]$

In the configuration shown in (27) the direct object moves over the indirect object in Polish, while in English such movement is disallowed. How is it at all possible that probe T should access goal DP_{OB} if the indirect object is between them and its interpretable [+φ] feature acts as an intervener? A plausible answer is that inherently case-marked DPs are not visible to the probe-goal relation at all, possibly subject to language variation. Hence in example (24) the trace of *Janowi* is not an intervener and the inherently case marked head of the chain is not an intervener either.

5.3.5. The case of *nauczyć/teach* and Multiple Agree.

The relation of feature checking, based on relation agree involving a probe and a goal identified in the minimal search space, solves the problem of the *nauczyć* 'teach' case. Consider the following example:

(28) a. Jan nie nauczył Marii stroić harfy.
John not taught Maria-GEN/*ACC tune harp-GEN/*ACC
'John did not teach Mary to tune the harp.'

b. Jan nauczył Marię nie siorbać zupy przy gościach.
John taught Mary-ACC/*GEN not slurp soup around guest
'John taught Mary not to slurp soup in the company of guests.'

If case-agreement, based on c-command, is the relevant checking configuration, the problem with (28b) disappears in the following fashion: Neg forces the nominal object it c-commands to appear in Genitive. In (28a) both objects are in the c-command of Neg, so both appear in Genitive; in (28b) one object is in the c-command of Neg and appears in Genitive, while the other is not and appears in Accusative.

Let us now turn to (28a), apparently more problematic in the framework based on Agree:

(29) a. $[_{CP}\ [_{TP}$ Jan $[_{NegP}$ nie $[_{vP}$ nauczył Marii $[_{TP}$ PRO $[_{vP}$ stroić harfy]]]]]]

b. $[_{CP}\ [_{TP}$ Jan T $[_{NegP}$ $Neg_{[+pers]}$ $[_{vP}$ $v_{[+\varphi]}$ Marii $[_{TP}$ PRO T $[_{vP}$ $v_{[+\varphi]}$ harfy]]]]]]

Here is a pressing concern; both verbs are only near-complete probes and must be complemented by F (Neg/Pos). There is, however, only one F (Neg) in the structure and it should be used up in one case-agreement relation. Agreement features of probes are uninterpretable and deleted upon participation in an Agree relation (or marked for deletion at the point of Transfer). It seems that we need to look at this case as multiple case-agreement, where one probe (here: Neg) can value more than one case. Cases like (29) are discussed in the literature and we can simply rely on one such account.

Hiraiwa (2001) observes that Chomsky's account of the Defective Intervention Constraint coupled with abandonment of the principle of Equidistance, leads to complications in empirical cases dealt with in previous stages of minimalism through multiple specifiers, multiple satisfaction of the [+EPP] feature and multiple feature attraction:

(30) a. DIC: $*\alpha > \beta > \gamma$

(*Agree (α,γ), α is a probe and β is a matching goal, and β is inactive due to a prior Agree with some other probe)

b. Multiple Feature Checking:
$\alpha > \beta > \gamma$

(Agree (α,β) and Agree (α,γ), where α is a probe and both β and γ are matching goals for α.)

Defective Intervention Constraint (DIC) and Multiple Agree both occur in practically the same configuration and it is not so obvious that they could be distinguished.[21]

This is a very unwelcome result and leaves many cases of Multiple Agree unaccounted for. Hiraiwa (2001:69) proposes that, parametrically determined, Multiple Agree option becomes licit if the following principle is introduced:

(31) Multiple Agree/Move:
Multiple Agree (multiple feature checking) with a single probe is a single simultaneous syntactic operation; Agree applies to all the matched goals at the same derivational point derivationally simultaneously. Multiple Move (movement of multiple goals into multiple specifiers of the same probe H) is also a single simultaneous syntactic operation that applies to all the Agreed goals.

(32) Multiple Agree as a single simultaneous operation:
$\alpha > \beta > \gamma$

(Agree (α, β, γ), where α is a probe and both β and γ are matching goals for α)

We can incorporate Hiraiwa's account of Multiple Agree into our account of GoN and propose further refinements. For the case of the construction with *nauczyć/teach* above, we propose that the F (Neg/P) part of the 'split' probe can be [+multiple] in Polish. At the point of its merger into the phrase marker it searches through the structure for both near-complete probes and DP goals:

(33) [$_{NegP}$ Neg$_{[+case]}$ [$_{vP}$ v$_{[+\varphi]}$ Marii-GEN [$_{TP}$ (PRO T) [$_{vP}$ v$_{[+\varphi]}$ harfy-GEN]]]]]

Neg matches the two DPs in the matrix and in the embedded clause, it also complements both near-complete probes (the verbs). Then, as a part of two 'split' probes it simultaneously engages in two case-agreement relations. Consequently, the DP_{OB} in the matrix is still an active goal when the DP_{OB} in the embedded clause is accessed. One more remark is in order;

[21] The system of case-agreement proposed by Chomsky assumes single Agree relations; probe α accesses goal β, they match in features and the case feature of β is valued, checked and deleted (or marked for deletion). Even if the [$+\varphi$] features of the probe do not check and delete and the probe is [+multiple], it cannot access goal γ, c-commanded by β, as the interpretable [$+\varphi$] features of β are visible and block access to any goal lower in the structure.

as we argue below, both the embedded and the matrix clause constitute one derivational phase, so the phase unity condition on Multiple Agree is met.[22]

6. Conclusion.

This paper is an attempt at providing an account of Long GoN within the system of minimalism based on case-agreement and single cycle syntax, closely related to the system developed in Chomsky (1998, 1999, 2000). In order to account for example (7) and similar cases, we made several novel assumptions and tested them empirically.

(7) a. Maria nie chce wypić kawy.
Maria not wants drink coffee-GEN/*ACC
'Maria doesn't want to drink coffee.'

b. ... $[_{NegP}$ Neg-P $[_{VP}$ ... $[_{CP}$ $[_{TP}$ $PRO_{[+\varphi]}$ $[_{vP}$ t_{PRO} ... DP_{OB}-$G_{[+\varphi]}]]]]]]

First, we propose that a successful relation of case-agreement can be established not only between full probes and complete goals but also between 'split' probes and complete goals. We define a 'split' probe as a (predefined) pair of heads that complement each other and jointly have features [+case, +φ]. In the concrete case of GoN and Long GoN, the two heads involved are F/Neg [+case] and v [+φ].

Second, the distance holding between the two half probes in the cases of Long GoN and the punitive power of the PIC, force us to revise certain assumptions concerning the status of phases in the derivation. We propose that for a successful case-agreement relation both the 'split' probe and the goal must be placed within the same derivational phase. We therefore submit that neither the vP nor the infinitive embedded under control verbs constitute strong phases.

In order to deal with infinitives embedded under control verbs, we reject the idea that they are CPs and propose instead that they are best treated as bare TPs, following Hornstein (1999, 2000, 2001). This hypothesis, based on movement into thematic positions and treatment of OC PRO as an NP trace, has the advantage of explaining lack of defective intervention effects that a PRO, with its interpretable [+φ] features visible to the probe, is otherwise expected to cause.

References:

Błaszczak, J. (2001): Covert movement and the genitive of negation in Polish. *Linguistics in Potsdam* 15.
Brody, M. (1995): *Lexico-Logical Form*. Cambridge, Massachusetts: MIT Press.
Brody, M. (1996): Towards Perfect Syntax. *Working Papers in the Theory of Grammar* 2/4. Budapest: Research Institute for Linguistics, Hungarian Academy of Sciences.
Chomsky, N. (1995): *The Minimalist Program*. Cambridge, Massachusetts: MIT Press.
Chomsky, N. (1998/2000): Minimalist inquiries. In: Martin, R., D. Michaels and J. Uriagereka (eds.): *Step by step: Essays in honour of Howard Lasnik*. Cambridge, Massachusetts: MIT Press, 89-156.

[22] An analogous mechanism of Multiple Agree is predicted for the positive counterpart to (25a):

Jan nauczył Marię stroić harfę.
John taught Maria-ACC (to)tune harp-ACC
'John taught Maria to tune the harp.'

Here the matrix probe F (Pos) complements both near-complete probes and is involved in double Accusative valuation.

Chomsky, N. (1999): Derivation by Phase. *MIT Occasional Papers in Linguistics* 18.
Chomsky, N. (2001): Beyond explanatory adequacy. Ms. MIT, Cambridge, Massachusetts.
Cinque, G. (1999): *Adverbs and functional heads: A crosslinguistic perspective*. Oxford: Oxford University Press.
Dziwirek, K. (1998): Reduced constructions in Universal Grammar: evidence from the Polish object control construction. *Natural Language and Linguistic Theory* 16: 53-99.
Fox, D. (1999): Reconstruction, Binding Theory and the Interpretation of Chains. *Linguistic Inquiry* 30: 157-196.
Fox, D. (2000): *Economy and Semantic Interpretation.* Cambridge, Massachusetts: MIT Press.
Groat, E. and O'Neil (1996): Spell-out at the LF interface. In: Abraham, W. (ed.): *Minimal Ideas.* Amsterdam, John Benjamins, 113-139.
Hiraiwa (2001): Multiple Agree and the Defective Intervention Constraint in Japanese. *MIT Working Papres in Linguistics* 40: 67-80.
Hornstein, N. (1999): Movement and control. *Linguistic Inquiry* 30: 69-96.
Hornstein, N. (2000): *Move! A minimalist theory of construal.* Cambridge, Massachusetts: Blackwell.
Hornstein, N. (2001): On control. Ms. University of Maryland.
McGinnis, M. (1998): *Locality in A-movement.* Doctoral dissertation MIT, Cambridge Mas. MITWPiL.
Pesetsky, D. (1989): Earliness. Manuscript, MIT, Cambridge, Massachusetts.
Pesetsky, D. and E. Torrego (2002): T-to_C Movement: causes and Consequences. In: Kenstowicz, Michael (ed.): *Ken Hale: a Life in Language*. MIT Press.
Przepiórkowski, A. (1999): Long distance Genitive of Negation in Polish. *Journal of Slavic Linguistics* xx: xx.
Reinhart, T. (1995): Interface strategies. *OTS Utrecht University Working Papers*, 1-109.
Rizzi, L. (1997): The fine structure of the left periphery. In: Haegeman, L. (ed.): *Elements of Grammar: Handbook of Generative Syntax*. Kluwer, Dordrecht, 281-337.
Śmiecińska, J. (2003): Bridge requirements and island conditions on Wh-movement in English: An evaluation of successive cyclic derivation of Wh questions. Doctoral dissertation, Adam Mickiewicz University, Poznań.
Willim, E. (1990): On case marking in Polish. *Papers and Studies in Contrastive Linguistics* 25: 204-220.
Witkoś, J. (1998): *The syntax of clitics: Steps toward a minimalist account*. Poznań: Motivex.
Witkoś, J. (1999): Clause Union and non-local Genitive of Negation. Ms. University of Poznań.
Witkoś, J. (2003): Reviewing phases: On some concepts and consequences of phase-based minimalism. *Poznań Studies in Contemporary Linguistics* 39: 197-251.

Linguistik International

Herausgegeben von Heinrich Weber, Susanne Beckmann,
Abraham P. ten Cate, Wilfried Kürschner, Kazimierz Sroka, Ingo Warnke und Lew Zybatow

Band 1 Hans Otto Spillmann / Ingo Warnke (Hrsg.): Internationale Tendenzen der Syntaktik, Semantik und Pragmatik. Akten des 32. Linguistischen Kolloquiums in Kassel 1997. 1999.

Band 2 Cäcilia Klaus: Grammatik der Präpositionen. Studien zur Grammatikographie. Mit einer thematischen Bibliographie. 1999.

Band 3 Käthi Dorfmüller-Karpusa / Ekaterini Vretta-Panidou (Hrsg.): Thessaloniker Interkulturelle Analysen. Akten des 33. Linguistischen Kolloquiums in Thessaloniki 1998. 2000.

Band 4 Lew N. Zybatow (Hrsg.): Sprachwandel in der Slavia. Die slavischen Sprachen an der Schwelle zum 21. Jahrhundert. Teil 1 und 2. 2000.

Band 5 Gerhild Zybatow / Uwe Junghanns / Grit Mehlhorn / Luka Szucsich (eds.): Current Issues in Formal Slavic Linguistics. 2001.

Band 6 Christoph Küper (ed.): Meter, Rhythm and Performance – Metrum, Rhythmus, Performanz. Proceedings of the International Conference on Meter, Rhythm and Performance, held in May 1999 at Vechta. 2002.

Band 7 Reinhard Rapp (Hrsg.): Sprachwissenschaft auf dem Weg in das dritte Jahrtausend. Akten des 34. Linguistischen Kolloquiums in Germersheim 1999. Teil I: Text, Bedeutung, Kommunikation. Linguistics on the Way into the Third Millennium. Proceedings of the 34th Linguistics Colloquium, Germersheim 1999. Part I: Text, Meaning, and Communication. 2002.

Band 8 Reinhard Rapp (Hrsg.): Sprachwissenschaft auf dem Weg in das dritte Jahrtausend. Akten des 34. Linguistischen Kolloquiums in Germersheim 1999. Teil II: Sprache, Computer, Gesellschaft. Linguistics on the Way into the Third Millennium. Proceedings of the 34th Linguistics Colloquium, Germersheim 1999. Part II: Language, Computer, and Society. 2002.

Band 9 Peter Kosta / Jens Frasek (eds.): Current Approaches to Formal Slavic Linguistics. Contributions of the Second European Conference on Formal Description of Slavic Languages. FDSL II held at Potsdam University, November 20-22, 1997. 2002.

Band 10 Peter Kosta / Joanna Blaszczak / Jens Frasek / Ljudmila Geist / Marzena Xygis (eds.): Investigations into Formal Slavic Linguistics. Contributions of the Fourth European Conference on Formal Description of Slavic Languages - FDSL IV. Held at Potdsam University, November 28-30, 2001, Part I and Part II. 2003.

Band 11 Lew N. Zybatow (Hrsg.): Europa der Sprachen: Sprachkompetenz - Mehrsprachigkeit - Translation. Akten des 35. Linguistischen Kolloquiums in Innsbruck 2000. Teil I: Sprache und Gesellschaft. 2003.

Band 12 Lew N. Zybatow (Hrsg.): Europa der Sprachen: Sprachkompetenz - Mehrsprachigkeit - Translation. Akten des 35. Linguistischen Kolloquiums in Innsbruck 2000. Teil II: Sprache und Kognition. 2003.

Band 13 Stojan Bračič / Darko Čuden / Saša Podgoršek / Vladimir Pogačnik (Hrsg./eds.): Linguistische Studien im Europäischen Jahr der Sprachen / Linguistic Studies in the European Year of Languages. Akten des 36. Linguistischen Kolloquiums in Ljubljana 2001. Proceedings of the 36th Linguistic Colloquium, Ljubljana 2001. 2004.

Band 14 Rolf Herwig (Hrsg./ed.): Sprache und die modernen Medien. Language and the Modern Media. Akten des 37. Linguistischen Kolloquiums in Jena 2002. Proceedings of the 37th Linguistic Colloquium, Jena 2002. 2004.

Band 15 Paweł Karnowski / Imre Szigeti (Hrsg.): Sprache und Sprachverarbeitung / Language and Language-processing. Akten des 38. Linguistischen Kolloquiums in Piliscsaba 2003 / Proceedings of the 38th Linguistics Colloquium, Piliscsaba 2003. 2006.

Band 16 Maurice Vliegen (Hrsg.): Variation in Sprachtheorie und Spracherwerb. Akten des 39. Linguistischen Kolloquiums in Amsterdam 2004. 2006.

Band 17 Tania Avgustinova: Language Family Oriented Perspective in Multilingual Grammar Design. 2007.

Band 18 Sabine Kupper: Anglizismen in deutschen Werbeanzeigen. Eine empirische Studie zur stilistischen und ökonomischen Motivation von Anglizismen. 2007.

Band 19 Franc Marušič / Rok Žaucer (eds.): Studies in Formal Slavic Linguistics. Contributions from Formal Description of Slavic Languages 6.5. Held at the University of Nova Gorica, December 1-3, 2006. 2008.

Band 20 Gerhild Zybatow / Luka Szucsich / Uwe Junghanns / Roland Meyer (eds.): Formal Description of Slavic Languages: The Fifth Conference, Leipzig 2003. 2008.

www.peterlang.de